American
Jewish
Year Book

The American Jewish Committee acknowledges with appreciation the foresight and wisdom of the founders of the Jewish Publication Society (of America) in the creation of the AMERICAN JEWISH YEAR BOOK in 1899, a work committed to providing a continuous record of developments in the U.S. and world Jewish communities. For over a century JPS has occupied a special place in American Jewish life, publishing and disseminating important, enduring works of scholarship and general interest on Jewish subjects.

The American Jewish Committee assumed responsibility for the compilation and editing of the YEAR BOOK in 1908. The Society served as its publisher until 1949; from 1950 through 1993, the Committee and the Society were co-publishers. In 1994 the Committee became the sole publisher of the YEAR BOOK.

American

Jewish

Year Book 2007

VOLUME 107

Editors
DAVID SINGER
LAWRENCE GROSSMAN

AMERICAN JEWISH COMMITTEE
NEW YORK

COPYRIGHT © 2007 BY THE AMERICAN JEWISH COMMITTEE

All rights reserved. No part of this book may be reproduced in any form without permission in writing from the publisher, except by a reviewer who may quote brief passages in a review to be printed in a magazine or newspaper.

ISBN 978-0-87495-142-4

Library of Congress Catalogue Number: 99-4040

PRINTED IN THE UNITED STATES OF AMERICA
BY MAPLE-VAIL BOOK MANUFACTURING GROUP, BINGHAMTON, N.Y.

Preface

To mark the culmination of the American Jewish Committee centennial, the 2007 AMERICAN JEWISH YEAR BOOK features two special articles on the history of the organization: "AJC and Intermarriage: The Complexities of Jewish Continuity, 1960–2006," by Marianne R. Sanua, author of the new history of AJC, *Let Us Prove Strong: The American Jewish Committee, 1945–2006,* and "A Century of Involvement: AJC and Russian Jewry," by AJC Executive Director David A. Harris.

In its regular articles, the volume covers the events of 2006. The YEAR BOOK's coverage of American Jewish life includes treatments of national affairs, anti-Semitism, Jewish communal affairs, and American Jewish population trends. The article on Israel and those about other Jewish communities around the world chronicle important events and trends. Updated demographic data are provided in the article on world Jewish population. Carefully compiled directories of national Jewish organizations, periodicals, and federations and welfare funds, as well as religious calendars and obituaries, round out the volume.

We gratefully acknowledge the assistance of our colleagues, Cyma M. Horowitz and Michele Anish, of the American Jewish Committee's Blaustein Library, and the contribution of Rachel Kaufman, our assistant, in preparing the index.

The American Jewish community suffered a profound loss on August 20, 2007, with the passing of Morris Fine at the age of 93. In the course of an extraordinarily long and fruitful career at AJC that began in 1937, Morris served as editor of the AMERICAN JEWISH YEAR BOOK for volumes 48 through 79 (1947–1979). Even after retiring from AJC in 1979 he maintained an abiding interest in the YEAR BOOK, and, until very shortly before his death, continued to provide sage advice and kind encouragement. We miss him deeply, and dedicate this volume to his memory.

THE EDITORS

Contributors

TOBY AXELROD: Correspondent, Jewish Telegraphic Agency and *Jewish Chronicle* (London); Berlin, Germany.

STEEN CADAN: International freelance journalist; Copenhagen, Denmark.

JEROME A. CHANES: Faculty scholar, Brandeis University; adjunct professor, sociology and Jewish communal issues, Yeshiva University; former national affairs director, National Jewish Community Relations Advisory Council.

ARNOLD DASHEFSKY: Professor of sociology and director, Center for Judaic Studies and Contemporary Jewish Life and Mandell L. Berman Institute-North American Jewish Data Bank, University of Connecticut.

SERGIO DELLAPERGOLA: Professor and head, Division of Jewish Demography and Statistics, Avraham Harman Institute of Contemporary Jewry, Hebrew University of Jerusalem, Israel; senior fellow, The Jewish People Policy Planning Institute.

BERNARD EDINGER: Former longtime international correspondent for Reuters; Paris, France.

ETHAN FELSON: Assistant director, Jewish Council for Public Affairs (JCPA); New York.

ELISE FRIEDMANN: Editor in chief, *Nieuw Israelitische Weekblad;* Amsterdam, Holland.

PAULINA GAMUS: Former minister of culture, senator, member of Congress, Venezuela; former vice president, Union of Jewish Associations in Venezuela; attorney, newspaper columnist; Caracas, Venezuela.

LAWRENCE GROSSMAN: Editor, AMERICAN JEWISH YEAR BOOK; associate director of research, American Jewish Committee.

RUTH ELLEN GRUBER: European-based American journalist and author, specialist in contemporary Jewish affairs; Morre, Italy.

GEORGE E. GRUEN: Adjunct professor, international affairs, Middle East Institute and School of International and Public Affairs, Columbia University.

DAVID A. HARRIS: Executive director, American Jewish Committee.

MIRIAM L. KOCHAN: Freelance journalist and translator; Oxford, England.

LEV KRICHEVSKY: Bureau chief, Jewish Telegraphic Agency; Moscow, Russia.

JEFFREY LESSER: Winship distinguished research professor, director, Tam Institute for Jewish Studies, Emory University.

REBECCA NEUWIRTH: Director, special projects, American Jewish Committee; executive director, Thanks to Scandinavia, an AJC institute.

COLIN L. RUBENSTEIN: Executive director, Australia/Israel and Jewish Affairs Council; honorary associate, Monash University; Melbourne, Australia.

MARIANNE R. SANUA: Associate professor, history and Jewish studies, Florida Atlantic University.

GEORGES SCHNEK: President, Jewish Museum of Belgium; former president, Jewish Central Consistory of Belgium; emeritus professor of biochemistry, Free University of Brussels, Belgium.

MILTON SHAIN: Professor, Hebrew and Jewish studies, and director, Kaplan Centre for Jewish Studies and Research, University of Cape Town, South Africa.

HANAN SHER: Senior editor, *The Jerusalem Report;* Jerusalem, Israel.

IRA M. SHESKIN: Associate professor, geography, and director, Jewish Demography Project of the Sue and Leonard Miller Center for Contemporary Judaic Studies, University of Miami.

MURRAY GORDON SILBERMAN: Adjunct professor, Austrian Diplomatic Academy, Vienna, Austria.

BRIGITTE SION: Former secretary general, CICAD, the Committee against anti-Semitism and Defamation; Geneva, Switzerland.

HAROLD M. WALLER: Professor, political science, McGill University; director, Canadian Centre for Jewish Community Studies; Montreal, Canada.

Contents

OTHER COUNTRIES

DIRECTORIES, LISTS, AND OBITUARIES

Special
Articles

AJC and Intermarriage: The Complexities of Jewish Continuity, 1960–2006

By Marianne R. Sanua

The American Jewish Committee was founded as a "defense" organization, not to make Jews more Jewish. Its purpose, as stated in its first constitution adopted November 11, 1906, was "to prevent the infringement of the civil and religious rights of Jews, and to alleviate the consequences of persecution." After the founding generation, which included some Jewish scholars of note, membership was drawn mainly from the philanthropic upper classes. These people were deeply integrated into the mainstream of American legal and political life and not known for their piety or adherence to Jewish tradition. "Assimilationist" was the epithet most often hurled at AJC from other sectors of the American Jewish community, a stereotype strengthened by the organization's coolness toward Zionism before 1948.

Beginning in the early 1960s, however, a striking evolution took place as AJC intensified its Jewish consciousness and soon became a major source of surveys, studies, and policy recommendations on Jewish identity in the modern world. Ironically, this allegedly least Jewish of Jewish organizations began addressing such controversial issues as intermarriage and Jewish continuity years before they came onto the American Jewish agenda, and its pioneering work laid the foundation for subsequent communal strategies.

The 1963 Image Study and AJC's Jewish Identity

AJC's first serious attempt to enhance its Jewish profile came in the wake of problems faced in raising funds for the new organizational headquarters on the corner of 56th Street and Third Avenue, which opened in 1960. A.M. Sonnabend, who became president of the organization in 1962, discovered over the two years he spent fund-raising for the building a need for "improvement of the image of AJC in the community." The problem, he felt, was "the way we present ourselves to the Jewish public." A

3

specially commissioned "Image Study" was conducted in which 300 Jewish leaders across the country not associated with AJC were interviewed in depth about their attitudes toward the agency. The results were presented to the AJC Executive Committee in 1963.[1]

They confirmed that others saw AJC as a group of wealthy, socially exclusive, self-sufficient, upper-class German Jews—a kind of "Jewish four hundred"—that drew its membership from the ranks of Reform Judaism. Its leaders were viewed as "confirmed assimilationists," interested more in associating with non-Jews than in concerning themselves with Judaism and the perpetuation of Jewish tradition.[2]

In the wake of the Image Study, AJC launched a campaign to change both outsiders' perceptions and its own reality. The Public Relations Department worked to get the word out about AJC's work in the Jewish community; a new membership drive sought out Conservative and Orthodox Jews as well as Reform; more attention was given to the Jewish Communal Affairs Department, inaugurated in 1958, with programs planned on Jewish identity and Jewish education; and chapters in Milwaukee and St. Louis sponsored chairs in Jewish studies at local universities, both to show new respect for this field as an academic discipline and as a way of reaching out to Jewish college students who, by all accounts, were becoming alienated from their heritage. The agency drew physically closer to Israel than ever before, pouring resources into its office there and arranging trips to Israel for AJC members and their children.[3]

AJC leaders also began to reconsider their vaunted organizational independence and distrust of Jewish umbrella organizations, rejoining the National Community Relations Advisory Council (NCRAC) in 1966. An original member of that body, AJC had left in 1952 when changes were proposed that appeared likely to limit the autonomy of the individual agencies. Announc-

---

[1]"The Image, Role and Potential of the AJC," report by Social Research, Inc., May 1963, in AJC Executive Committee Minutes, November 1–3, 1963, Blaustein Library, American Jewish Committee.

[2]On the Image Study and its ramifications see Marianne Sanua, *Let Us Prove Strong: The American Jewish Committee, 1945–2006* (Waltham, Mass., 2006), pp. 103–05.

[3]American Jewish Committee, *The AJC and Israel* (New York, 1998), p. 6. AJC produced this pamphlet to mark Israel's 50th anniversary.

ing the return to NCRAC, John Slawson, AJC's executive vice president, said, "We are getting back into the fold."[4]

But there was much further to go. Throughout most of his career at AJC, Slawson himself had been interested above all else in "American-centeredness," the successful integration of Jews into the American landscape. All the social science research and programming on Jewish identity that AJC had done up to the early 1960s was designed to further that end. Rabbis, to be sure, delivered the invocation and said the blessing over bread at AJC official dinners, but otherwise Jewish tradition and observance were absent. The renowned rabbi and theologian Abraham Joshua Heschel, addressing several hundred members at a plenary session of the AJC annual meeting in 1960, gently criticized the organization when he reminded them of the famous George Bernard Shaw quip: "Youth is a wonderful thing. It's a shame that it's wasted on the young," and then said to his audience, "Judaism is a wonderful faith . . . " and let the sentence hang.[5]

A Crisis of Jewish Continuity

It was during the early 1960s that doubts emerged about AJC's single-minded focus on the integration of Jews into all avenues of American life. For one thing, society was becoming more accepting of cultural pluralism and no longer demanded the total absorption of its minority groups. And for another, the AJC thrust had become perhaps too successful, especially when it came to the creation of families. Decrying the rising tide of marriage to non-Jews among the young people of his community, AJC member Max Stocks of Syracuse said in 1963, "We encourage our children to have friends who are not Jews . . . . However, there is an extraordinary tendency among young people to marry people they know and not people they don't know." [6] Dr. Irving Greenberg,

---

[4]John Slawson, "AJC at Seventy: A View from the Sixtieth," AJC Annual Meeting Proceedings, May 12–15, 1966, p. 22, Blaustein Library; Sanua, *Let Us Prove Strong,* p. 105.

[5] Abraham Joshua Heschel, "The Moral Challenge to America," AJC Annual Meeting Proceedings, April 22–24, 1960, p. 95, Blaustein Library. Caroline K. Simon, who was then chair of the Jewish Communal Affairs Committee, reacted by saying, "We want to plan so that Judaism will not be wasted on us, but will be strengthened by us." See also Sanua, *Let Us Prove Strong,* pp. 114–16.

[6]Discussion following speech by Dr. Marshall Sklare, AJC Annual Meeting transcript, May 17–19, 1963, p. 14, Blaustein Library.

then a professor at Yeshiva University, addressing an AJC audience in 1966, said, "I think one reason why the first generation had less intermarriage was because the kids knew the parents would drop dead, literally. Whereas in the second generation, they know that given the ideology of the parents is pluralism and brotherhood, it won't be quite as disastrous."[7]

Paralleling the perception of accelerating intermarriage was Jewish concern about low birthrates. Both issues, presaging a decline in the size of the American Jewish community, became subjects of intense examination. The first blip on the screen came with the publication of an article, "Jewish Fertility in the United States," by Erich Rosenthal, then an associate professor of anthropology and sociology at Queens College, in the 1961 *American Jewish Year Book*. Rosenthal found that the Jewish fertility rate—25 percent below that of Catholics and 20 percent below that of Protestants—was not sufficient to replace the parent generation. The article ended on a hopeful note, however. Rosenthal theorized that as American Jews moved to the suburbs and achieved a more secure position in society, the number of children might rise.[8]

There was no optimistic scenario in a second article by Rosenthal that appeared in the 1963 *Year Book*. "Studies of Jewish Intermarriage in the United States" revealed that rates of marriage to non-Jews rose sharply with each succeeding generation of American Jews.[9] It was this study that brought the term "Jewish continuity" into the American Jewish lexicon and signaled what might be called the first Jewish continuity "crisis." AJC librarians reported receiving more requests for reprints of this Rosenthal article than anything else the AJC had ever published before.

In New York City, a conference of 50 rabbis and social workers convened in December 1964 to discuss strategies for synagogues and Jewish social agencies "to preserve the continuance of the American Jewish community against threats of assimilation through intermarriage." Among its recommendations were the es-

[7]Irving Greenberg, AJC Annual Meeting transcript, May 12–16, 1966, p. 130, Blaustein Library.

[8]Erich Rosenthal, "Jewish Fertility in the United States," *American Jewish Year Book* (hereafter AJYB) 62 (New York and Philadelphia, 1961), pp. 4, 24, 26.

[9]Erich Rosenthal, "Studies of Jewish Intermarriage in the United States," AJYB 64 (1963), pp. 3–53.

tablishment of counseling centers and institutes devoted to the problem, and a suggestion that Jewish social workers point out to clients contemplating intermarriage the consequences of such a step and inform them of the "growing evidence" that mixed marriage had less likelihood of success than inmarriage. Similarly, a conference of rabbis from Canada and Minnesota urged parents "to take a firm stand" against all interfaith dating and to encourage their children to date only other Jews. They, too, claimed not only that the children of mixed marriages were usually lost to Judaism, but also warned that there was a greater frequency of broken homes among intermarried couples than among those of common religious background.[10]

John Slawson, executing a complete about-face from his concern that American Jews were not integrating into their surroundings well or quickly enough, was seized with virtual terror when he examined the new data on Jewish families. Introducing Marshall Sklare, AJC's resident social scientist, to a meeting in 1963, Slawson declared that he had been reading the latest Rosenthal study and woke up one Saturday morning with a start. "Does this mean extinction?" he asked himself. "I called up Dr. Sklare and woke him from his Sabbath slumber, and from what I could hear among the noises, about a half dozen babies were there, and I found out that there is some hope . . . . We should be concerned about Jewish population policy, which has not occurred to anyone in the Jewish group up to this time." Sklare, for his part, confessed that it had only *sounded* as if he had a dozen babies, and noted that large-scale conversion of non-Jews might be a good thing for the American Jewish population. "Once you show Jews that the *goyim* like it," he said, "they will undoubtedly be prepared to buy the product themselves." The remark was greeted with loud applause.[11]

Look magazine, picking up on Rosenthal's research, published a cover story entitled "The Vanishing American Jew." At the AJC

---

[10]"New York Rabbis, Social Workers Offer Program to Check Intermarriage," "Canadian Rabbis Urge Study on Intermarriage in Small Communities," "Minnesota Rabbis Urge Parents to be Firm against Interfaith Dating," clippings from the Jewish Telegraphic Agency in Jewish Communal Affairs Department (hereafter JCAD), December 14, 1964, box 5, folder: "Interoffice Memos from Manheim Shapiro, 1960–64," AJC Archives.
[11]Discussion following speech by Dr. Marshall Sklare, AJC Annual Meeting transcript, May 17–19, 1963, p. 10, Blaustein Library.

annual meeting of 1964, copies of the *Look* article were distributed to all those attending the plenary session on "What Future for American Jews? A View of the Evidence Pro and Con for the Survival of the American Jews." At that annual meeting, six of the 13 roundtable sessions were devoted to Jewish continuity. The *American Jewish Year Book* reported that in 1964 the "vanishing American Jew" was "the major preoccupation of American Jewry." The next year it noted that the problem remained "a focus for national attention," with "prognostications, repeated widely, that the forces of assimilation, secularization, and intermarriage presented a real threat to American Judaism."[12]

The sense of alarm spread to the world of Zionism. David Ben-Gurion, Israel's prime minister, had warned for years that American Jews were doomed to assimilation and disappearance if they did not come to Israel, but no one in the Zionist movement had realized the apparent urgency of the problem before. The World Zionist Organization (WZO) now called for stepped-up aliyah from Western countries; it said that emphasis had previously been given to bringing Jews from lands of oppression, but now the countries of the Free World needed to become a top priority. At its convention in October 1964, the Zionist Organization of America passed a resolution urging the aliyah of middle-class American Jews, and proposed that Israel build large housing projects and even new cities to house and employ them.[13]

A key step in AJC's move toward enhanced Jewishness was the retirement of John Slawson and the choice of Bertram H. Gold to succeed him. Gold—a product of Yiddish schools in his native Toronto and a former director of all the Jewish community centers in Los Angeles—took over on August 1, 1967, immediately after the Six-Day War, with the specific goal of bringing AJC nearer to Israel and to the American Jewish mainstream. Under his leadership the phrase "Jewish peoplehood," a term shunned by earlier AJC leaders because it seemed to separate Jews from other Americans, began to make its way into the organization's public pronouncements.

---

[12]Louis Shub, "Zionism," AJYB 66 (1965), p. 311; Sefton D. Temkin, "Religion," AJYB 67 (1966), p. 92.

[13]Shub, "Zionism," pp. 311–12; Sanua, *Let Us Prove Strong*, p. 116.

Another change that gave further indication of a shift in organizational direction was the appointment of Yehuda Rosenman as director of a reinvigorated Jewish Communal Affairs Department. Born in Poland after World War I, Rosenman had grown up in a traditionally Jewish, Zionist, and Hebrew-speaking home. One week before the outbreak of World War II he left Poland to visit relatives in the U.S.; with the exception of one sister, who had immigrated to Israel two years earlier, Rosenman lost his entire family in the Holocaust. Obtaining a degree in social work, he served for many years as executive director of Pittsburgh's Jewish community centers. He was just finishing a two-year stint working for the American Jewish Joint Distribution Committee in Geneva and Paris when he was recommended for the Jewish Communal Affairs position at AJC, while Slawson was still at the helm.

Rosenman said years later that the greatest contribution he made to AJC was not changing his first name. In an early interview with Slawson, he offered to anglicize the name "Yehuda," feeling self-conscious about his European birth and accented English, and fearing that "Yehuda" might not be appropriate in the halls of the American Jewish Committee. There was no need, Slawson answered him, explaining that AJC had changed a great deal and needed to change more. "John Slawson became very Jewish in the last years of his stewardship of the AJC," Rosenman recalled. "After I came here I used to kibbitz with John and say, why the hell didn't you do it 20 years ago? You remind me of the man who before he dies, suddenly comes back to his religion."[14]

AJC Tackles the Intermarriage Issue

It was during Rosenman's tenure at the head of the Jewish Communal Affairs Department that AJC transcended its earlier history as simply a "defense" organization that favored the integration of Jews into American life and became one of the Jewish community's major centers for the study of intermarriage and analysis of its implications. Through its surveys, interpretation and publication of data, conferences and consultations, and policy statements, AJC

---

[14]Yehuda Rosenman Interview, December 2, 1980, p. 20, AJC Oral History Collection, New York Public Library.

took an issue that cut to the heart of personal identity and Jewish survival and made it its own.

Much of the apprehension that greeted Rosenthal's 1963 article and the *Look* cover story was rooted in shock. Available surveys showed that up to 1940, the proportion of Jews intermarrying was 2–3 percent, rising to about 7 percent between World War II and 1960.[15] According to Halakhah, Jewish law, a marriage ceremony between a Jew and a non-Jew was invalid, and therefore the Orthodox and Conservative movements forbade their rabbis from officiating. Even Reform Judaism, which did not accept the binding authority of Halakhah and supported the autonomy of the individual rabbi, strongly disapproved of intermarriage.[16] Traditional parents were known to disown children who married out of the faith and even to mourn them as if they had died. Most secular Jews were deterred by strong social taboos against marrying non-Jews. And surveys indicated that Gentiles, for the most part, were distinctly disinclined to accept Jews as sons- and daughters-in-law.

But the situation was changing quickly. Among Jews marrying between 1961 and 1965, 17 percent intermarried, and for those marrying between 1966 and 1972 the rate was over 30 percent.[17] Moreover, conditions seemed to favor a continuing rise in mixed marriages. The vast majority of Jewish young people — perhaps as high as 85 percent — attended colleges and universities, settings where deep and intimate relationships between people of different religious and ethnic backgrounds were highly likely to occur. Social barriers had fallen; Jews and non-Jews often worked as colleagues, and not, as had generally been the case in the past, in a merchant-customer relationship.[18] Americanization and upward mobility had made Jewish men desirable mates, and fewer Gentile parents would object if their daughters married them. At the same time, observers speculated that Jewish men felt somehow drawn to marry non-Jewish women, and developed sociological,

---

[15] Fred Massaryk and Alvin Chenkin, "United States National Jewish Population Survey: A First Report," AJYB 74 (1973), p. 296; Sanua, *Let Us Prove Strong,* pp. 273–80.

[16] Norman Mirsky, "Mixed Marriage and the Reform Rabbinate," *Midstream* 16, January 1970, pp. 40–46.

[17] Massaryk and Chenkin, "National Jewish Population Survey," p. 292.

[18] Arnold Schwartz, "Intermarriage in the United States," AJYB 71 (1970), p. 116.

economic, and psychological theories seeking to explain the phenomenon.[19] Individual rabbis found themselves unprepared to deal with large-scale intermarriage and its accompanying complexities. Hillel Foundation rabbis on campuses across the country could not comply with the requests of frantic parents who called up begging the rabbis to break up relationships or impending marriages. Other parents, intent on securing rabbinic officiation, threatened that the upcoming wedding would take place in a church if their rabbi did not agree to preside. In 1970, one Reform rabbi, David Max Eichhorn, circulated a list of 89 of his fellow rabbis (about 10 percent of the Reform rabbinate at the time) who were ready to state publicly that they would officiate at intermarriages without requiring the conversion of the non-Jewish partner. In an accompanying letter Eichhorn wrote, "It is clear that the unrestricted availability of this list will help to combat the defection of many of our people who are being lost to Judaism because of the spiritual insensibility of so many of our colleagues."[20] Some of his peers praised his honesty and inclusiveness, while others criticized him for countenancing and encouraging intermarriage.

CBS aired a popular situation comedy during the 1972–73 television season called "Bridget Loves Bernie." It portrayed a marriage between Bernie Steinberg, a Jewish aspiring writer working as a cabdriver (an unacceptable vocation in most American Jewish families), and Bridget Fitzgerald, a teacher from a wealthy Catholic family. The pair lived in an apartment above the delicatessen owned by Bernie's parents. Most of the plotlines had to do with the two families' divergent social, cultural, and ethnic backgrounds, and their attempts to get along for the sake of the young couple.

Catholic organizations protested, but the response from the Jews was far stronger: a Jewish community already worried about demographic erosion was outraged that national TV would present

---

[19]See, for example, Louis A. Berman, *Jews and Intermarriage: A Study in Personality and Culture* (New York, 1968), p. 341; Edwin H. Friedman, "The Myth of the Shiksa," in Monica McGoldrick, John K. Pearce, and Joseph Giordano, eds., *Ethnicity and Family Therapy* (New York, 1982), pp. 499–526; and an AJC publication, Rela Geffen Monson, *Jewish Campus Life: A Survey of Student Attitudes Toward Marriage and Family* (New York, 1984), pp. 28–29, 37.
[20]Schwartz, "Intermarriage in the United States," p. 120.

intermarriage in a positive, lighthearted way. As AJC legal director Samuel Rabinove noted, Jewish organizations reacted this way even though they traditionally espoused freedom of speech and expression, and opposed censorship of any kind. The Synagogue Council of America, comprised of rabbis from all three major denominations, led a successful campaign to have the show canceled. The New York Board of Rabbis, which also had members from the different denominations, adopted a resolution strongly condemning any of their number who performed mixed marriages or who referred couples to rabbis who did.[21]

It was against this background that AJC's Jewish Communal Affairs Department, in February 1975, initiated a series of rabbinic "consultations" on intermarriage and conversion. AJC headquarters provided neutral ground where rabbis of the different denominations could talk to one another. A verbatim transcript was kept, indicating the meetings' importance in AJC eyes. Among the participating rabbis were Norman Lamm, Emanuel Rackman, Sol Roth, and Steven (Shlomo) Riskin (Orthodox); Max Routtenberg and Judah Nadich (Conservative); Harold Saperstein (Reform); and Ludwig Nadelman (Reconstructionist).[22]

By this time large-scale intermarriage was already a reality and discussion focused on the feasibility of developing a procedure for conversion to Judaism that would be acceptable to all segments of the Jewish community. Maximizing the number of universally recognized conversions would ensure that more children of such marriages would be raised in unambiguously Jewish homes. According to Halakhah, conversions had to be supervised by a bet din (Jewish religious court), and posed three requirements: commitment to live an observant Jewish life; ritual immersion in a *mikveh* (pool of water); and, for men, ritual circumcision. Persons born to a Jewish mother were deemed Jewish regardless of the background of the father, whereas a person born to a Jewish father but a non-Jewish mother was held, in the absence of conversion, to be a non-

---

[21]Samuel Rabinove, "Intergroup Relations and Tensions in the Unitd States," AJYB 75 (1974–75), pp. 130–32; Sanua, *Let Us Prove Strong,* p. 275.

[22]"Consultation on Intermarriage and Conversion: Summary Report, Jewish Communal Affairs Department," February 27, 1975, Bertram H. Gold Collection (hereafter BHG), box 136, folder: "Intermarriage and Conversion 1975–77"; and JCAD, box 13, folder: "Intermarriage: General Materials and Correspondence 1973–76," AJC Archives.

Jew. Orthodox authorities did not acknowledge conversions that did not meet their standards.

The rabbis at the consultation struggled to find common ground. One idea that came up was the creation of a "super bet din," a rabbinical tribunal recognized by all groups that would arrange conversions, but the proposal met with several objections. Rabbi Saperstein pointed out that Reform was already accepting, de facto, children of Jewish fathers as fully Jewish if they underwent a bar mitzvah or confirmation, which counted as a public profession of Jewish commitment (in 1983 Reform would adopt this position officially). While Reform rabbis might be convinced to require ritual immersion and circumcision, he said, their feeling was that "we are saving these children for Judaism rather than closing the door to them," and there was no chance that the movement would give any outside body veto power over its conversions.

Rabbi Rackman discouraged the proposal on practical grounds, saying it would be "almost futile in the present climate, especially in the Orthodox group," which did not recognize the validity of the other movements. He suggested a more modest goal, seeking to ensure that children of intermarriage who had Jewish mothers— and who thus were indisputably Jewish— would be raised as Jews. He said, "Their children are not 50 percent but 100 percent Jewish. There may be 50,000 or 100,000 children of such marriages who are Jewish, and we ought to do everything in our power to claim them. We don't know how these children are being raised." Rackman also believed that "all the social workers in New York City ought to be sensitized to these problems. When a mixed couple comes to Jewish Family Service, the social worker should know enough to steer them to a sympathetic, understanding rabbi who may reclaim the family for the Jewish community."

Rabbi Riskin, also Orthodox, suggested bypassing the rabbinate entirely and establishing a bet din of three committed and observant laymen, one from each of the major movements. They would be taught the relevant rules and rituals as well as the basics of the Sabbath and the dietary laws, which they would teach the converts and require them to accept. Again, Rackman disagreed. "Let us not get into an area now which is as difficult as splitting the Red Sea," he countered. "Let us strike out in the one area in which we can function — reclaiming those Jews whom we have the power to bring back into the fold."

Riskin, for his part, argued that Rackman's plan for raising children of non-Jewish fathers as Jews would not work because most Orthodox synagogues would not accept into membership anyone in a mixed marriage, even if the wife was Jewish. "I repeat, therefore, that nothing is going to happen within the three establishment organizations," Riskin declared. "We shall have to proceed on an individual basis. Let me make it clear that personally I am very stringent with conversions and I do not relax any of the Halakhic standards. At the same time, I believe we need desperately in America a kind of bet din that will require only minimum Halakhic standards, and I am willing to go on line saying that."[23]

The next year AJC cosponsored an event that brought together virtually every synagogue body and rabbinical association, as well the major American Jewish civic organizations. What was billed as the First National Conference on Mixed Marriage convened in December 1976, in New Jersey. Attendees participated in workshops and open discussions on how to combat intermarriage and "enhance Jewish survival." Yehuda Rosenman contributed by giving a talk on the demography, statistics, and sociology of the issue. After the conference, Rabbi Robert Gordis suggested the creation of a national institute to deal with intermarriage.[24]

Still, neither consultations nor conferences brought agreement on a course of action, and debates about intermarriage were still going on with undiminished force into the twenty-first century. Sharp differences of opinion arose. Some argued that intermarriage was actually a good thing for the Jewish community since, if handled properly, it could bring a net gain of Jews; therefore, the argument went, Jewish outreach to such couples was a wise use of communal resources. Others believed that this approach would only serve to lower whatever religious, cultural, and social barri-

---

[23]Minutes, Informal Rabbinic Consultation on Intermarriage and Conversion, November 3, 1975, section of verbatim transcript, JCAD, box 15, folder: "Intermarriage/ Rabbinic Consultations/ Max Routtenberg 1975–76," AJC Archives; Sanua, *Let Us Prove Strong*, p. 277.
[24]"Program, National Conference on Mixed Marriage, December 14–15, 1976, Long Branch, N.J.," JCAD, box 13, folder: "Jews, Judaism and Jewish Community: Intermarriage and Conversion 1976"; "Suggestions of National Institute on Intermarriage," letter from Yehuda Rosenman to Rabbi Steven C. Lerner, February 10, 1977, JCAD, box 14, folder: "Intermarriage General 1975–77," AJC Archives.

ers to intermarriage still existed, leading to more such marriages and, ultimately, the loss of far more Jews than could ever be gained back through outreach efforts. Also, these critics alleged, outreach programs expending valuable and limited communal resources on the periphery of the community that might be more wisely and effectively spent on shoring up the strength of two-parent Jewish families.

Data and Interpretations

Yehuda Rosenman took the position that AJC could best facilitate the communal debate by research: finding out and publicizing what could be known about just how many Jews were being won or lost. "We cannot determine what, if anything, should be done," he declared, "until we have the objective data which tells us what the problems are and what the plus-minus effect for Jewish continuity is, stemming from increased interfaith marriages."

Pointing out that AJC was well-known for its "objective research and fact-finding," he announced that the Jewish Communal Affairs Department was embarking on the first nationwide study of marriages between Jews and non-Jews. It would begin with six communities: New York, two of its suburbs—Westchester and Nassau-Suffolk (Long Island)—Philadelphia, Cleveland, and San Francisco. Egon Mayer, at the time assistant professor of sociology at Brooklyn College, was designated to direct the research.[25] He had been one of several social scientists invited to AJC for a "brainstorming" session about intermarriage, and both Rosenman and Milton Himmelfarb, AJC's director of research, had been impressed by him. Data would be gathered via questionnaires and interviews administered by AJC volunteers under the direction of Mayer, and the results of the study would form the basis for an AJC policy statement on the subject.

The most challenging part of AJC's first foray into intermarriage research was identifying the sample and convincing people to fill out the questionnaire, a process that revealed almost as much about the phenomenon of intermarriage in the 1970s as the data

---

[25]AJC press release, February 7, 1976, JCAD, box 13, folder: "Intermarriage, Study of Effects of, Publicity, Articles, etc. 1976," AJC Archives.

gleaned from it.[26] Volunteers and local project directors in each of the six communities were first asked to get names of intermarried Jews from relatives, friends, and acquaintances. Then, Mayer suggested they contact Jewish and non-Jewish clergymen, "especially rabbis who officiate at mixed marriages, Unitarian ministers, etc.," and ask them to provide lists of names, addresses, and telephone numbers from their records or from people they knew. A letter to one minister, he assured them, had yielded several hundred names. Another technique was to ask local Jewish organizations to sponsor lectures with titles like "Intermarriage and Intergroup Relations" or "A Look at Mixed-Married Life," which, advertised in newspapers, would presumably attract intermarried couples. A representative of the project would give the lecture, and use the opportunity to describe the study and encourage members of the audience to participate. Those agreeing to do so would be asked, in turn, to submit more names, addresses, and telephone numbers.[27]

A master list of thousands of names was thus compiled, and each got a questionnaire, along with a letter from Egon Mayer announcing:

> We are embarking on a nationwide study on the effects of Jewish intermarriage so as to shed some light, rather than heat, on this issue. For the purpose of this study I need to develop a large and representative sample of families with mixed religious backgrounds .... You can help me accomplish this difficult but important goal by filling out the enclosed questionnaire. You may be assured that our survey will be conducted with complete scientific objectivity and the right of privacy of all concerned will be faithfully honored by us.

The response rate was very low, and the final sample consisted of only 446 couples from all six communities combined. Presumably, people who felt the least bit ambivalent or uncomfortable about their marriages chose not to answer. Some recipients of the

---

[26]The study later received criticism for what was described as the ad hoc nature of the sample gathering and the lack of a control group of endogamous Jewish couples. See Sidney Goldstein, "Jews in the United States: Perspectives from Demography," AJYB 81 (1981), pp. 25–26.

[27]Memo: "Project on the Effects of Intermarriage—Instructions for the Conduct of Telephone Interviews"; Instructions for Interviewers, April 27, 1976; form letter from Egon Mayer sent to 275 people, April 6, 1976; Memo: Study on the Impact of Intermarriage: Supplementary Techniques for Obtaining Names," JCAD box 13, folder: "Intermarriage Study, Correspondence 1976–77," AJC Archives.

letter were enraged, as was one man from Philadelphia who made an incoherent phone call to his local AJC office, and then wrote and sent the following missive:

According to the letter from Dr. Egon Mayer on AJC stationery, my wife and I were selected from a "comprehensive" list of 1,000 people in and around Philadelphia. I want to know first, how this was acquired and second, who has access to this list. As I told you before you banged down the receiver, rabbis have told me it is a sin to bring up conversion to a converted Jew. I don't care if AJC members believe in sin. But if the rabbis are correct, it is horrendous on this one point alone that the AJC should do this. But more to the point as far as I'm concerned as an individual is that this has been a tremendous invasion of the privacy of my wife, my children and myself, with potential repercussions beyond what you know and which I only hope I can prevent.[28]

In March 1978, Mayer submitted a draft of his final report, entitled "Mixed Blessings under the Canopy," to Rosenman and the rabbinical advisory board of the Jewish Communal Affairs Commission (AJC "commissions" were the lay counterparts to the staff departments). The report found that in only one-third of the intermarriages surveyed did the couple state an intention to raise the children as Jews. Nevertheless, in interpreting the data Mayer took an optimistic, almost enthusiastic, stance toward intermarriage, asserting that the old negative attitude was obsolete. He wrote that rising intermarriage rates demonstrated a climate of growing acceptance of Jews, and that the increasing numbers of Gentiles who had Jewish relatives because of intermarriage would, in turn, lead to even more acceptance.[29]

Mayer claimed—as the words "mixed blessings" in his title implied—that intermarriage represented a significant opportunity for American Jews to increase their numbers; that there was no evidence that it hurt family relations in any way; and that rabbinic officiation at such weddings enhanced the likelihood that the

---

[28]Letter from Seymour Schubin to Dr. Murray Friedman, July 1, 1977, JCAD, box 13, folder: "Intermarriage, Study on Effects of, Correspondence 1976–77," AJC Archives.

[29]Egon Mayer, Confidential: "Mixed Blessings Under the Canopy, summary of study and findings of survey on the impact of marriage between Jews and non-Jews on individuals, families, and the Jewish community"; "Reactions to Study," memo from Yehuda Rosenman, March 2, 1978, BHG, box 135, folder: "Jews, Judaism and Jewish Community, Intermarriage and Conversion 1978," AJC Archives.

couple would identify with Judaism. He recommended that inter-married couples and their children be welcomed into the Jewish community, noting that "there appears to be an urgent need for programs and materials which would help Jewish families integrate non-Jewish members in such a way as to make the Jewish way of life an attractive alternative to the new couple."[30]

When the consulting rabbis met to discuss the draft, some urged that it not be published, or at least that certain parts be omitted. Noting the "delicacy of the topic," they feared that the study might be misused, misinterpreted, or taken out of context. Some said that while most American Jews saw intermarriage as a familial and sociological issue, for them it was a matter of Halakhah, and, in the words of one, "any sociological report which seems to say that we can increase our numbers through intermarriage will be used as a tool" against the position of Jewish law on the matter. The claim that rabbinic officiation led to positive Jewish outcomes was also controversial. A rabbi warned that this assertion could weaken the resolve of rabbis who were "holding the fort" and refusing to solemnize such marriages. If rabbis agreed to officiate without conversion, he continued, there was little motivation for the non-Jew to convert. In the end, the consensus of the rabbis was that intermarriage threatened Jewish identity, it should not be viewed as an opportunity to increase Jewish numbers, and "no statement issued by AJC should be construed as indicating resignation to, or approval of, intermarriage."[31]

Yehuda Rosenman refused to remove the claim about the possible beneficial impact of rabbinic officiation, but on everything else he and the Jewish Communal Affairs Commission, chaired by E. Robert Goodkind, agreed with the rabbis. Mayer's interpretation of the data, in the words of another staff member of the department, "was not one which we felt that the American Jewish Committee should associate itself with."[32] A final compromise was to issue two versions of the report. One, written by a program spe-

---

[30]Ibid.
[31]Jewish Communal Affairs Commission Minutes, January 18, 1979, JCAD, box 16, folder: "Jewish Communal Affairs Commission Minutes 1979," AJC Archives.
[32]Memo, Confidential: "To Yehuda Rosenman from Carl Sheingold: Subject: Authorship of the Intermarriage Pamphlet," November 30, 1978, BHG, box 135, folder: "Jews, Judaism and Jewish Community Intermarriage and Conversion 1978," AJC Archives.

cialist in the department, Dr. Carl Sheingold, presenting Mayer's data but without his controversial assertions, was published in 1979 as a pamphlet with AJC's imprimatur under the title *Intermarriage and the Jewish Future.* Mayer's original, more detailed report was available in mimeograph form for anyone who requested it. Mayer was also free to publish it elsewhere, which he did.[33]

Controversy of a different sort occurred when the Jewish Communal Affairs Commission then sought to have a statement on intermarriage passed by the AJC Board of Governors, the organization's highest policy-making body. The original proposed statement opened with these words:

> Mixed marriage is a threat to Jewish continuity. Most children in mixed marriages are exposed to little of the Jewish cultural or religious tradition, receive no formal Jewish education, and have parents who lack the knowledge to impart such an education on their own. If this pattern continues, mixed marriage at its current rate or higher will almost certainly lead to an erosion of the size, strength, and vitality of the Jewish community.[34]

Commission chairman Goodkind, who would go on to become president of AJC in 2004, presented the statement for debate. One board member objected to the characterization of intermarriage as a "threat," claiming that the actual threat was "what could flow from a mixed marriage." Several other members requested the insertion of a statement supporting rabbinic officiation at mixed marriages. This was a politically explosive issue, Goodkind explained, and had therefore been left out of the statement. One prominent board member who had been active in AJC for decades and headed several important committees had a Christian wife who regularly attended and participated in AJC events. He too objected to calling intermarriage a "threat," and joined others in requesting language that would call for a change in communal attitudes toward mixed-married couples. The initial sentence was

---

[33]One summary of Egon Mayer's own interpretations was "Intermarriage Among American Jews—Consequences, Prospects and Policies," published by the National Jewish Resource Center (CLAL) in its series *Policy Studies,* February 15, 1979, BHG, box 135, folder: "Jews, Judaism and Jewish Community Intermarriage and Conversion 1978," AJC Archives.

[34]Discussion on Proposed AJC Statement on Intermarriage, Minutes, AJC Board of Governors Meeting, March 21, 1979, JCAD, box 17, folder: "Intermarriage Study 1979," AJC Archives.

eventually changed to: "Mixed marriage currently poses serious problems for Jewish continuity." With this and several other amendments, the statement was approved.

NJPS 1990 and the Second Jewish Continuity Crisis

No previous demographic study of American Jewry matched the complexity and scientific rigor of the National Jewish Population Survey (NJPS) of 1990, sponsored by the Council of Jewish Federations, and none of its findings were more explosive than the data on intermarriage, which circulated through word of mouth well before the report was published.

Of all married born-Jews surveyed, 31 percent had non-Jewish spouses. This in itself was hardly news to informed members of the Jewish community.[35] Far more shocking was the generational breakdown: of those Jews who had married over the previous five years, 1985–1990, only 48 percent had married other Jews, so that the intermarriage rate among these younger Jews was 52 percent. Furthermore, only 28 percent of intermarried couples said that they were trying to raise their children only as Jews. Of the others, 41 percent said that the children were being raised at least partly in another religion, and 31 percent reported raising their children in no religion at all.[36] People who had been born Jewish but now considered themselves members of other religions numbered 625,000, and many of these were the parents of some 700,000 individuals under the age of 18 who were of Jewish descent but were being raised in other religions.[37] And only 14 percent of American Jewish households fit the traditional definition of a Jewish family—mother and father, both Jewish, married for the first time, with children.

The 1990 NJPS raised once again the fears about "Jewish con-

---

[35]Author's interview with Steven Bayme, May 25, 2006; Sanua, *Let Us Prove Strong*, pp. 369–73.

[36]The CJF released the study in the spring of 1991. The complete study is available on line from the North American Jewish Data Bank—a collaborative project between United Jewish Communities (the successor to CJF) and the University of Connecticut's Center for Judaic Studies and Contemporary Jewish Life and Roper Center for Public Opinion Research—at www.jewishdatabank.org/NJPS1990.asp. See also Barry Kosmin and Jeffrey Scheckner, "Jewish Population in the United States," AJYB 91 (1991), p. 206, and Sidney Goldstein, "Profile of American Jewry: Highlights from the 1990 National Jewish Population Survey," AJYB 92 (1992), pp. 126–27.

[37]Lawrence Grossman, "Jewish Communal Affairs," AJYB 93 (1993), p. 178.

tinuity" that had previously surfaced in the early 1960s. While subsequent recalculation would show that the most spectacular NJPS
claim, the 52-percent intermarriage rate for young Jews, was exaggerated,[38] the fearsome "news" that more than half of American Jews were intermarrying made headlines. The *New York Times,*
Wall Street Journal, and *Newsweek* ran long, prominently placed
features about Jewish continuity and intermarriage, and Brown
University sociologist Sidney Goldstein referred to the situation
revealed by the study as a "silent Holocaust."[39] Jewish institutions
and organizations feared that potential donors, members, and
clients were literally passing out of existence before their eyes.
Federations began to question their large allocations to Israel,
since a large investment of funds would likely be necessary to but-
tress Jewish identity in the U.S. Indeed, some argued, such a real-
location would help Israel in the long run, since an American
community with atrophied Jewish connections could hardly be of
much help to the Jewish state.

The NJPS decisively reversed the optimistic spirit that had captured the American Jewish community in the late 1980s, best expressed by Charles E. Silberman in his 1985 book *A Certain People:*
American Jews and Their Lives Today.[40] Silberman's picture of a
thriving American Jewry, proud and sure-footed in its Jewishness
and expanding numerically through the addition of spouses and
children gained through intermarriage, fell by the wayside as more
pessimistic portrayals, some using the NJPS data, appeared.[41]

Philanthropists and communal leaders sought new approaches
to stave off demographic erosion. To energize Jewish life among
college students, Hillel, the campus organization previously administered by B'nai B'rith, was revitalized and reorganized in 1994
as an independent nonprofit organization.[42] Among the philan-

---

[38]The 2000–01 National Jewish Population Survey found a 47-percent rate. It can be ac-
cessed at www.jewishdatabank.org/NJPS2000.asp.

[39]Goldstein, "Profile of American Jewry," p. 77.

[40]Charles E. Silberman, *A Certain People: American Jews and Their Lives Today* (New
York, 1985).

[41]Among these were Arthur Hertzberg, *The Jews in America: Four Centuries of an Uneasy Encounter* (New York, 1989) and Samuel C. Heilman, *Portrait of American Jews: The
Last Half of the Twentieth Century* (Seattle, 1995).

[42]For a brief history of Hillel, see Jeff Rubin, "The Road to Renaissance, 1923–2003:
Hillel," at www.Hillel.org.

thropists who stepped up to spearhead new programs for Jewish youth were Charles Bronfman and Michael Steinhardt, who, along with several other wealthy associates, established Birthright Israel in late 1998 (known as *Taglit* in Hebrew), which provided free, ten-day educational trips to Israel for young Jewish adults who had never been to Israel before. By 2006 Birthright would log its 100,000th participant, with thousands more on waiting lists.[43]

AJC on Intermarriage in the 1990 s

AJC, which had entered the debate over Jewish continuity in the 1960s, sought to confront this new reality. It first worked to update its 1977 statement on intermarriage in light of the NJPS findings and the results of its own new research studies. AJC position statements were understood as setting agency guidelines for policy and programming, and would also undoubtedly influence other Jewish organizations and institutions.

Both the AJC Board of Governors and local AJC chapters were deeply divided on the issue. In light of the proliferation of intermarriage, how far could they go in decrying the trend and advocating conversion for non-Jewish spouses without alienating members of their own families? Another weighty question, as it developed within the ranks of AJC and elsewhere, was the proper allocation of communal resources. Should limited funds be spent on "outreach" to the periphery—to those who had already chosen to intermarry—or on "inreach," the term then coming into use to denote supporting and shoring up the ranks of those already moderately affiliated, in the hope that they would lead more intensive Jewish lives?[44] A third matter of controversy, already surfacing in some congregations, was what role, if any, should non-Jewish spouses and relatives play in their Jewish children's synagogue life-cycle events, for example, at a bar/bat mitzvah or a wedding.[45]

Charlotte Holstein, who chaired the Jewish Communal Affairs

---

[43]See www.birthrightisrael.com.

[44]For a treatment of this debate suggesting that by the late 1990s the proponents of "outreach" appeared to be winning, see Lawrence Grossman, "Jewish Communal Affairs," AJYB 99 (1999), p. 191. For an overview of AJC's approach, see Steven Bayme, "Intermarriage and Jewish Leadership in the United States," *Jerusalem Center for Public Affairs,* April 16, 2006, at www.jcpa.org.

[45]Sanua *Let Use Prove Strong,* pp. 379–80.

Commission in 1991, wrote movingly of her divided feelings as both a Jewish communal leader and the parent of a soon-to-be-intermarried child: as the commission was working to update the statement on intermarriage, her own daughter was planning her marriage to a longtime boyfriend, a born Catholic. "I love and respect my daughter and I would do anything to protect her happiness and future," she wrote.[46] As the statement was being drafted, she went on, "I felt that many aspects of it were directed at me personally." Reading that intermarriage ought to be prevented, that in such families it was difficult to impart Jewish knowledge and tradition to children, and that current rates of intermarriage would lead to "an erosion of the size, strength and vitality of the Jewish community," Holstein reflected that her own family was contributing to the problem.[47]

Even so, she recognized that she had to "draw the distinction between what I felt emotionally and what rationally was good for the survival of the Jewish community as a whole." She was not alone in her dilemma; many other AJC leaders had intermarriage in their families or were intermarried themselves, and thus there prevailed among them "a more accepting attitude toward intermarriage" than was the case in more traditional segments of the community, elements that AJC could not ignore if it wanted to assert leadership and act to preserve Jewish unity.[48]

The adoption of the 1991 Statement on Intermarriage was as lengthy and complex a process as ever took place within AJC. The organization had long since ceased to be a "committee" and was now a highly complex organization, with numerous lay subcommittees, many separate departments, and dozens of chapters and regional offices. While the president, officers, and executive vice president were empowered to act swiftly when there was an immediate danger to Jews, other decisions had to go through procedural channels that could take a great deal of time.

The first draft of the new intermarriage statement was composed by staff and then submitted to the commission members,

---

[46]Charlotte Holstein, "When Commitments Clash: One Leader's Personal Dilemma," in *The Intermarriage Crisis* (New York, 1991), pp. 36–37; Elliott Abrams, *Faith or Fear: How Jews Can Survive in a Christian America* (New York, 1997), pp. 106–07.

[47]Holstein, "When Commitments Clash," p. 35.

[48]Ibid.

who came from different parts of the country and belonged to a variety of Jewish denominations. Revisions were suggested and approved, and then the draft was submitted to the board of governors, which decided on additional changes and sent the text off to the local chapters for their input. Twenty chapters responded: 17 of them approved; Minneapolis and St. Louis disapproved, and Cleveland abstained.[49] Chapters made their feelings known via letters, phone calls, and, in one instance, a video presentation. This chapter input led to a few additional changes. The amended statement came before the national board a second time where it was debated again, leading to another addition. Only then did it pass and become official AJC policy.

The final version was strongly anti-intermarriage in tone, saying, "AJC studies as well as other studies show that the rapidly rising number of intermarriages represents a serious risk to the vitality of the Jewish community, Jewish continuity, and identity. Clearly the Jewish community prefers that Jews marry other Jews." Yet while clearly stating that endogamy was preferable, it also held out conversion of the non-Jewish spouse as the best outcome of intermarriage, and added that in the absence of conversion the children should still be raised exclusively as Jews. The statement, then, assumed that it was possible to do "inreach" and "outreach" simultaneously. "The challenge for the Jewish community," according to the AJC in 1991, was "to offer positive communal and personal connection to the intermarried while at the same time to develop and encourage programs that lead to Jews marrying other Jews."[50]

Similarly controversial was the 1996 "Statement on the Jewish Future." It was not, strictly speaking, an AJC document, but was received as if it were. Its origins lay in an article published in *Commentary* that year on "How to Save American Jews."[51] AJC's Jewish Communal Affairs Commission, in consultation with leading academics, rabbis, and communal professionals affiliated with all the major Jewish movements, developed a programmatic state-

[49]Minutes, AJC Board of Governors Meeting, May 2, 1991, AJC Archives.
[50]AJC Statement on Intermarriage 1991, at www.ajc.org, under "Jewish living—Jewish continuity and intermarriage."
[51]Jack Wertheimer, Charles S. Liebman, and Steven M. Cohen, "How to Save American Jews," *Commentary* 101, January 1996, pp. 47–51.

ment out of it, to which 30 prominent Jewish leaders appended their names. Although it did not represent official AJC policy, the *Statement on the Jewish Future* was published by the agency along with 13 essays responding to it—seven written by signatories and the other six by individuals who refused to sign.[52]

The statement began by noting the rising tide of intermarriage and the community's attempts since 1990 to foster Jewish continuity. "Certain initiatives, however, seem to us more likely to undermine North American Judaism than to strengthen it," the statement declared. "In a well-intentioned effort at inclusiveness, some in the Jewish community seem all too willing to sacrifice distinctive Jewish values and teachings. In response, we call upon American Jews to declare the following five values fundamental to any program of Jewish continuity in North America." The five were given Hebrew names: (1) "Torah," Jewish learning; (2) *"Am Yisrael,"* Jewish peoplehood; (3) *"Klal Yisrael,"* the community of Israel, denoting pluralism and mutual respect; (4) *"Brit,"* covenant; and (5) *"Keruv,"* outreach.

The last two had significant implications, according to the signers. *Brit* "serves to differentiate Jews from non-Jews and insure that the Jews remain a people apart." Thus there should be "strong, visible boundaries" between Jews and those not party to the "covenant," non-Jewish relatives. Only Jews should take leadership roles within the Jewish community and in Jewish religious life. And in terms of allocating communal priorities, the principle of *Keruv* was formulated as follows: "The moderately affiliated are the most promising candidates for outreach and—given scarce resources—outreach programs are most productively directed toward them." While noting that "outreach directed toward those who have moved furthest from Judaism and toward the non-Jewish marriage partners of Jews may also be valuable and should remain on the Jewish communal agenda," the statement cautioned:

> Outreach to mixed-marrieds should never encourage religious syncretism or ideological neutrality to mixed marriage itself. We part company both with those who believe that any kind of Jewish involvement, no matter how superficial, promotes Jewish continuity,

---

[52]American Jewish Committee, *Statement on the Jewish Future: Texts and Responses* (New York, 1996), also at www.ajc.org.

and with those who look upon outreach as a panacea and seek to dilute Judaism to make it more attractive to potential converts. Both of these efforts, while well-meaning, are doomed to fail; they promote not continuity but radical discontinuity and are at variance with our tradition.[53]

The statement concluded by reiterating its rejection of the communal consensus favoring unlimited outreach. It defended the need to make hard choices, saying, "There is no effective route to Jewish continuity that will not prove offensive . . . . Some losses are inevitable, and many of these will be personally painful to the leadership of the American Jewish community."[54]

The appended essays in support of the statement cited both strategic and principled arguments in its favor. Steven M. Cohen, professor of sociology at Hebrew University, wrote that "the moderately affiliated (even if they're intermarried) are much easier to reach than the unaffiliated (especially if they're intermarried)," and therefore "the same effort, the same dollars, the same rabbis and educators can have a more profound impact on families and individuals who are visible and are already somewhat committed to conventional Jewish life than they can on a population that is remote, uninterested, and invisible."[55]

Jack Wertheimer, a history professor and provost at the Jewish Theological Seminary, pointed out that Jewish schools and summer camps were already starved for adequate funds, and recalled some parents who had told him with "tears in their eyes" that they were removing their children from a day school because they could not afford the tuition. "Our present course seems hell-bent on harming that more engaged population," he claimed. Wertheimer concluded:

> The more we try to make intermarried families feel comfortable in Jewish settings, the further we demolish barriers to intermarriage. Why should young people oppose intermarriage if they see interfaith families treated as equals in the synagogue? How can our youth develop a resistance to interdating and intermarriage when the Jewish community is becoming ever more reluctant to stigmatize intermarriage—and on the contrary, is creating a vast population of lobby-

---

[53]Ibid, p. 7.
[54]Ibid, p. 8.
[55]Ibid, pp. 14–15.

ists who favor the elimination of barriers to intermarriage because they themselves are intermarried?[56]

The statement's six opponents were equally vehement, and some were downright offended. Rabbi Jeffrey K. Salkin, who chaired the Reform movement's Outreach Commission, called the document unrealistic. "It is far too late in American Jewish history to turn back the clock," he wrote,

> The authors know that only a time-machine-induced trip back to the thirteenth century has any hope of completely ameliorating the threat of mixed marriage. Time and circumstances being what they are, what should the community do? To *not* invest money in interfaith families and their unique needs is tantamount to abandonment.[57]

John Ruskay, a top official at UJA-Federation of New York, believed that the federation system was already reaching out to the moderately affiliated, and added that the statement's critique of outreach to intermarried families smacked of an unfair Conservative-Orthodox attempt to cast Reform outreach "beyond the pale."[58] Jonathan Woocher, director of JESNA (Jewish Education Service of North Africa) said he did not sign the statement in part because it was "needlessly strident and confrontational."[59]

Rabbi Eric H. Yoffie, president of the Union of American Hebrew Congregations, the Reform synagogue organization, charged that the aim of the statement seemed to be to "attack the outreach work initiated in the late 1970s by the Reform movement and subsequently emulated by many others in the Jewish community." He accused the authors of engaging in "Jewish Darwinism . . . the belief that only the fittest Jews will survive, and that therefore only they are deserving of our support and attention."[60] The notion that Jews on the periphery of the community should be left unattended was, he felt, "theologically offensive, sociologically blind, and practically disastrous." He believed that the community was capable

---

[56]Ibid, p. 41. For more on Wertheimer's views on outreach see his "Surrendering to Intermarriage," *Commentary* 111, March 2001, pp. 25–32.

[57]*Statement on the Jewish Future,* p. 34.

[58]Ibid, pp. 31–32.

[59]Ibid, p. 42

[60]Ibid, p. 45. The "Jewish Darwinism" formulation was first made by Chief Rabbi Jonathan Sacks of Great Britain.

both of outreach to the intermarried and programs directed at those already engaged in Jewish life.

Deborah Dash Moore, then a professor at Vassar College, was also intensely critical of the statement. "Why should we trust these self-appointed gatekeepers with their penchant for drawing boundaries?" she asked. "They would plan to leverage the future by laying guilt over the survival of the people at the feet of every American Jew and Jewish organization." Moore, a historian, argued that in the U.S. the Jewish "periphery" had always been larger than the "center," and "vigorously" objected to adopting what she called an Orthodox agenda. The writers of the statement, she charged, were "obsessed with excluding Jews, with building ever higher barriers to participation."[61]

Inreach, Outreach, or Both?

These disagreements were by no means resolved by the AJC Board of Governors when it met in 1997 to issue a new policy statement and action plan on Jewish continuity. Again, the AJC consultative process ensured that months would go by before an acceptable text was approved. This statement, like its predecessor of 1991, affirmed a preference for endogamy; where intermarriage did occur, conversion; and raising the children as Jewish. However, unlike the 1996 Statement on the Jewish Future, it affirmed the value of both inreach and outreach. The board resolved: "The Jewish community must develop a multi-track approach to strengthen Jewish identity and positive Jewish experience in both in-marriages and mixed-marriages . . . . We must reach in and reach out."[62]

This policy statement reflected a new social reality. As the population of mixed-married couples and their children grew, old Jewish intermarriage taboos had all but collapsed. Rabbis reported fearing that their contracts would not be renewed if they spoke out against intermarriage, and in the Reform rabbinate, candidates for pulpits found that congregational search committees were increasingly seeking to hire rabbis willing to perform such marriages. In AJC's annual survey of American Jewish public opinion

---

[61]Ibid, pp. 24–27.

[62]"Jewish Continuity: Policy Statement and Action Plan," adopted by the AJC Board of Governors, December 8, 1997, at www.ajc.org.

conducted in the fall of 2001, well over half the sample—56 percent—disagreed with the statement, "It would pain me if my child married a Gentile," and were either positive or neutral toward such a prospect. Only 39 percent agreed that "it would pain me," and 5 percent were not sure. Seventy-nine percent of the respondents thought rabbis should officiate at mixed marriages and 50 percent said they should do so even if Gentile clergy was also involved. In reaction to the statement, "The best response to intermarriage is to encourage the Gentile to convert," 68 percent disagreed, 25 percent agreed, and 7 percent were not sure. Most telling was the response to the statement, "It is racist to oppose intermarriage." Exactly half the sample agreed.[63]

The boundaries that had separated Jewish from Christian religious practice were also eroding. A study that Brandeis University sociologist Sylvia Barack Fishman did in 2001 for AJC, *Jewish and Something Else: A Study of Mixed Married Families,* compared mixed-religion families with endogamous Jewish families and those in which an originally non-Jewish spouse converted to Judaism. Fishman found that in the mixed-religion households, even in cases where the parents had agreed to raise the children as Jews, Christian practices tended to creep in over the years, especially if it was the mother who was Christian.[64]

In the sample of respondents studied by Fishman, more than 80 percent of mixed-married families reported Christian activities of some sort, Christmas and Easter celebrations being most common. Two-thirds of the families celebrated Christmas at home and 16 percent went to church as well. Over half celebrated Easter at home, 12 percent also attending church on that holiday.[65] In a finding that seemed to contradict the regnant assumption that nothing could be done to minimize the incidence of intermarriage, the study found that parental attitudes made a difference. Among the Jewish mixed-marrieds, 62 percent claimed their parents had said nothing to them about the importance of marrying a Jew; in contrast, 62 percent of the Jews married to Jews and 48 percent of those whose originally non-Jewish partner had converted indi-

---

[63]"Widespread Acceptance of Intermarriage," *AJC Journal,* December 2000, p. 10.

[64]Sylvia Barack Fishman, *Jewish and Something Else: A Study of Mixed Married Families* (New York, 2001), and at www.ajc.org. On the role of gender in the dynamics of mixed-married households see pp. 2 and 31–33.

[65]Ibid, pp. 6–7.

cated that their parents had discouraged mixed marriage. Furthermore, Fishman reported, there was little "backlash effect, of negative reactions to discouragement of mixed marriage . . . ." [66]

In February 2001, as *Jewish and Something Else* was going to press and in the wake of the annual AJC opinion survey showing that half of American Jews considered it racist to oppose intermarriage, AJC's Contemporary Jewish Life Department (the new name for the old Jewish Communal Affairs Department) followed a strategy similar to what it had done in 1996, when it produced the *Statement on the Jewish Future.* It convened a coalition of some 25 communal leaders, rabbis, and Judaic scholars—including Professor Fishman—determined to "work together to restore the ideals of in-marriage" and to encourage Jewish leadership to take on the responsibility of promoting it as a norm. "In the face of an American culture that has declared interfaith marriage to be as American as apple pie," asserted Steven Bayme, director of the department, "only Jews themselves can articulate the importance of Jewish in-marriage. The question is whether the Jewish leaders have the will do so." [67] In cases where intermarriage did take place, the group—which soon adopted the name Jewish In-Marriage Initiative—pledged to advocate forcefully in favor of conversion. [68]

Sharp criticism came quickly. Egon Mayer, whose research on intermarriage had begun under the sponsorship of AJC and who was now founding director of the Jewish Outreach Institute, called the new endeavor "ludicrous" and "comical," since fighting intermarriage was like "arguing against the weather." "They're going to make speeches to people who in every other aspect are integrated into American life, and expect those people to listen?" he asked. [69] Edgar Bronfman, businessman, philanthropist, and chairman of the World Jewish Congress, told a London newspaper that opposing intermarriage was "racist and begins to sound a little like Nazism." For him, the choice was between "an attempt to double

---

[66]Ibid, pp. 7–8.
[67]Steven Bayme's foreword, ibid, p. vi.
[68]AJC press release, "AJC Convenes Communal Leaders, Rabbis, Judaic Scholars to Explore Strategies to Address Intermarriage," February 27, 2001, at www.ajc.org.
[69]Debra Nussbaum, "Coalition to Fight Intermarriage," Jewish Telegraphic Agency News Bulletin, March 9, 2001.

the amount of Jews that there are" through outreach to the inter-married, or, alternatively, "we can irritate everybody who's inter-married and lose them all."[70]

Although several important AJC lay and professional leaders were part of the In-Marriage Initiative, the AJC Executive Com-mittee, a small body that met in between meetings of the board of governors, voted not to grant it official endorsement. The coali-tion disbanded and reconvened outside the boundaries of AJC.

A few years later, yet another AJC study— *Young Jewish Adults in the United States Today: Harbingers of the American Jewish Community of Tomorrow?*—suggested that the concomitant prob-lems of prolonged singlehood and childlessness might soon surpass intermarriage as the major threat to Jewish continuity. Completed in 2006 by Ukeles Associates, Inc., the report showed that more than half of all American Jews under the age of 40 were not yet married, and that 56 percent of American Jewry consisted of non-Orthodox singles and married couples without children. The Or-thodox community, which was far less affected by the trend and therefore had many more children, was likely to grow in size and as a percentage of the total Jewish population as time went on. An-other implication of this research was, outside Orthodox circles, the further weakening of parental resistance to intermarriage. As Jewish children grew older without marrying, parents were more likely to accept a son- or daughter-in-law of any faith, so long as they would be assured of grandchildren.[71]

The debates over intermarriage and Jewish continuity that were heard in AJC corridors and meeting rooms as it celebrated its cen-tennial in 2006 might have surprised earlier generations of lead-ers, for whom the problem of anti-Semitism was the paramount reason for creating AJC and ensuring acceptance into the Ameri-can mainstream was the overriding priority. But the very promi-nence of concerns about continuity 100 years later provided clear evidence of AJC's ability to anticipate and adapt to changing com-munal priorities.

In its work on intermarriage, AJC proved its worth both as a re-

---

[70]Lawrence Grossman, "Jewish Communal Affairs," AJYB 105 (2005), p. 207.

[71]Jacob Ukeles, Ron Miller, and Pearl Beck, *Young Jewish Adults in the United States Today* (New York, 2006). The results of the study were presented to the centennial annual meeting of AJC in May 2006 before publication.

search institution and as a Jewish body able to bring to the table all sides of the debate on one of the community's most explosive issues. Contrary to its former image as the least "Jewish" of Jewish organizations, it had come down decisively on the side of Jewish tradition by affirming endogamy and conversion at a time when both were slighted in many sectors of American Jewry. While there was no way to predict AJC's influence on the broader community, and diverse views about intermarriage and the inreach-outreach question still characterized much of the AJC membership, the organization's prominent involvement in the issue assured it a place where its leaders since the 1960s had wished it to be—in the mainstream of Jewish communal life.

A Century of Involvement: AJC and Russian Jewry

By David A. Harris

ONE IMPERATIVE runs consistently through the hundred-year history of the American Jewish Committee: action on behalf of the Jews of Russia. The issue was present at the creation and remains central today. AJC was formed in 1906 in direct response to deadly attacks against Russian Jews; a century later, in 2006, the situation of Jews in the former Soviet Union and the welfare of the Russian Jewish community in the U.S. were AJC priorities.

The Plight of Russian Jews and the Founding of AJC

Conditions for the Jews of Russia became especially bad after the assassination of Czar Alexander II in 1881, as Jews were alleged to have been among the assassins. Anti-Jewish legislation followed, pogroms broke out in many communities, and Konstantin Pobedonostsev, a top adviser to the next czar, Alexander III, reportedly suggested a plan for one-third of Russia's Jews to emigrate, one-third to convert to Russian Orthodoxy, and the other third to starve to death.

The particularly bloody pogrom in Kishinev in 1903 aroused indignation around the world, and a new wave of anti-Jewish violence in the wake of the unsuccessful Russian revolution of 1905 made it abundantly clear that Jewish communities in Russia were in no position to defend themselves, and could expect no help from the authorities. The Jews' only hope for protection would have to come from outside the region.

A group of American Jews formed AJC for that express purpose. On January 8, 1906, Louis Marshall, Samuel Greenbaum, Nathan Bijur, Cyrus L. Sulzberger, and Joseph Jacobs cosigned a letter to 57 prominent Jews inviting them to attend a meeting in New York the following month. It read, in part:

> The horrors attending the recent Russian massacres, and the necessity of extending to our brethren a helping hand in a manner most

conducive to the accomplishment of a permanent improvement of their unfortunate condition have, with remarkable spontaneity, induced thoughtful Jews in all parts of the United States, to suggest the advisability of the formation of a General Committee to deal with the serious problems thus presented, which are likely to recur, even in their acute phases, so long as the objects of our solicitude are subjected to disabilities and persecution, owing to their religious belief.

Ten months later, on November 11, 1906, the American Jewish Committee was created. Strikingly, one of its very first steps was the creation of a press bureau. The rationale—which could as easily have been written in the mid-1960s, when the worldwide Soviet Jewry campaign began in earnest—was set forth in a resolution adopted by AJC's executive committee on January 27, 1907:

For the prevention of massacres of Jews in Russia, no means can be considered so effective as the enlightenment of the people of the western world concerning real conditions in Russia, which have hitherto been systematically concealed or distorted by the power of the Russian Government; that to this end a Press Bureau should be established to gather and disseminate correct news of affairs in Russia . . . .

It was not at all clear to the embryonic organization if the American government could be persuaded to act decisively to assist persecuted Jews overseas. AJC's leaders, therefore, came up with an ingenious approach to send an unmistakable message of disapproval to Russia.

The provisions of the Treaty of Commerce and Navigation, signed in 1832 by Russia and the United States, served as the principal bilateral agreement between the two countries. It stated that "the inhabitants of their respective States shall mutually have liberty to enter the ports, places and rivers of the territories of each party, wherever foreign commerce is permitted," and yet American Jews, beginning in the 1890s, were routinely denied entry visas by Russian consular officials. The U.S. State Department, in 1907, appeared to sanction this objectionable policy, announcing that it would refuse to issue passports "to Jews who intend going to Russian territory, unless it has the assurance that the Russian Government will consent to their admission."

Although the State Department subsequently reversed itself, AJC became convinced that the appropriate response to Russia's discriminatory policy against some (i.e., Jewish) Americans was to press for outright abrogation of the 1832 treaty. It took five years for the AJC leadership, collaborating with key congressional leaders while facing resistance from the White House and the State Department, to achieve that goal.

Particularly noteworthy in reviewing this campaign is its similarity, in several striking ways, to the effort that led to the adoption of the Jackson-Vanik Amendment 65 years later. That measure, named for its principal sponsors, Senator Henry Jackson (D., Wash.) and Congressman Charles Vanik (D., Ohio), linked the granting of most-favored-nation trade status to the right of emigration from non-market countries — i.e., the communist bloc, and in particular, the Soviet Union.

One similarity was the same division between American Jewish communal leadership and a majority of the U.S. Congress, on the one hand, and the executive branch on the other. On both occasions, each side invoked diametrically opposed arguments about whether punitive measures would, at the end of the day, achieve the desired objectives.

Second, in the early twentieth century no European country joined with the U.S. in applying a "stick" to protest Russia's discriminatory policy, thus weakening the American effort. The same European resistance occurred in the wake of the adoption of Jackson-Vanik: not a single West European country went beyond rhetorical opposition to Soviet policy on emigration, or such admittedly important symbolic acts as sending diplomats to the Moscow synagogue or to trials of activist Jews.[1] Neither diplomatic sanctions nor economic measures were ever seriously considered by any Western nation other than the United States.

And third, once the 1832 treaty was, in fact, abrogated, each side sought vindication for its position. The White House argued not only that American businesses were negatively affected, but also that the position of Jews in Russia deteriorated further because of

---

[1] At the same time it should be noted, with appreciation, that the Netherlands undertook the task of representing Israel in Moscow after the Kremlin severed diplomatic ties with the Jewish state in 1967; that Austria, despite unrelenting Arab pressure, served as the country of first arrival for hundreds of thousands of Soviet Jews able to secure exit visas; and that Italy provided a temporary home for those many Soviet Jews obliged to wait months for the processing of their applications to resettle permanently in the U.S., Canada, Australia, and New Zealand.

the belligerent American approach. Proponents of abrogation, meanwhile, hailed the move as a victory for high-minded principle in American foreign policy. Again, this split was a forerunner of the conflicting and self-justifying views expressed by the two contending sides in the months and years following Jackson-Vanik's enactment in 1975—and which continue to this day, without concession by either party.

AJC's Jacob Schiff dramatically stated the case of the winning side in the battle over the 1832 treaty:

> We have just passed through an episode which, in my opinion, is of greater importance than anything that has happened since civil rights were granted Jews under the first Napoleon, or since English Jews were admitted to Parliament. . . . For the first time, Russia, that great Colossus, has received a slap in the face from a great nation, which act, I cannot help thinking, must be of the greatest consequence in the history of civilization.[2]

The difficulties for Jews in Czarist Russia, however, continued. In 1911, Mendel Beilis, a manual laborer, was arrested in Kiev and, without any evidence, charged with the ritual murder of a 13-year-old Ukrainian boy—a classic case of blood libel. The trial began in September 1913. (Bernard Malamud produced a fictionalized account of the case in his acclaimed book *The Fixer*.) In what came to be the signature style of AJC, the organization sought, beyond its own advocacy efforts, the support of prominent non-Jews to demonstrate to the Russian government the breadth of concern about the trumped-up charges. As a result, distinguished Protestant and Catholic clergymen signed a letter, dated October 31, 1913, addressed to "His Imperial Majesty, Nicholas II, The Czar of All the Russias," in which they declared:

> We are convinced that the blood accusation against the Jews, which has been made sporadically, is as unfounded as was the same accusation which, as history shows, was frequently directed against the early Christians. It has been subjected to the most careful investigation for centuries, and no evidence warranting the slightest credence has ever been discovered, and it has been rejected as unworthy of serious consideration both by Church and by State.

Beilis was exonerated and immediately left the country.

Less than 60 years later, as will be noted below, AJC would es-

---

[2] Quoted in Naomi W. Cohen, "The Abrogation of the Russo-American Treaty of 1832," *Jewish Social Studies* 25, January 1963, p. 40.

tablish the National Interreligious Task Force on Soviet Jewry, once again calling upon Christians of good will to join in the international campaign to address the hardships suffered by Jews, this time under communist rather than czarist rule.

AJC and Soviet Jewry in the Cold War Years

There is scant evidence of AJC or other Jewish organizational involvement with regard to the condition of Jews during the early years of Bolshevik rule, when restrictions on religious life were introduced. Little information was available to the outside world at the time, as possibilities for emigration came to an end and the Soviet Union sought to project itself as a new society based on equality of nationalities and devoid of anti-Semitism. It was not until after the Second World War—in which Soviet Jews fought valiantly in the ultimately victorious Red Army, while the Jewish civilian population in the western part of the nation suffered untold losses at the hands of the invading Nazi forces and those who collaborated with them—that Stalin's pathological and paranoiac anti-Semitism became unmistakably visible, especially after Moscow's early support for Israel's statehood dissipated.

Consistent with its traditional emphasis on research and analysis, AJC sponsored the first book-length study about the effect of Soviet rule on the life of Jewish communities. The book, *The Jews in the Soviet Union* by Solomon M. Schwarz, was published in 1951 by Syracuse University Press. Three years later, a companion volume, *The Jews in the Soviet Satellites* by Peter Meyer, was issued by the same publishing house. AJC also produced pamphlets about Soviet Jewry throughout the 1950s, and articles on the subject appeared as well in *Commentary* and the *American Jewish Year Book*, both sponsored by AJC.

In 1954, AJC president Irving Engel was called to testify before the House Select Committee on Communist Aggression against the Jews in the Soviet Union and Eastern Europe, as part of hearings that resulted in a special congressional report entitled *Treatment of Jews by the Soviet*. Engel pulled no punches in describing the perilous situation of "the Jews caught behind the Iron Curtain, both in the Soviet Union proper, and in the countries the Soviet Union has either annexed or transformed into puppet states through ruthless imperialist aggression." He denounced the show trials, the "anti-cosmopolitan" campaigns, the targeting of Jewish intellectuals, the denial of religious rights, the infamous 1953 Doctors' Plot, and other examples of incitement and hatred.

On January 15, 1959, an AJC delegation met with Anastas Mikoyan, the Soviet first deputy prime minister, in New York City. This was the first high-level meeting between a Soviet official and American Jewish leaders to discuss the status of Soviet Jews since the USSR was established in 1917. Among the concerns expressed by AJC were reports that the Kremlin was seriously considering the wholesale deportation of Jews to Birobidzhan, the Soviet-established so-called Jewish Autonomous District in the Far East; the paucity of rabbis, numbering no more than 60, to serve nearly three million Jews; the failure to build a single synagogue since World War II, leaving hundreds of sizable Jewish communities without any house of worship in the wake of the destruction wrought by the Nazis; and the mounting barriers to Jews' advancement in Soviet society.

The landmark meeting resulted in a front-page story in the *New York Times* the following day, January 16, under the headline "Mikoyan Denies Exiling of Jews. Talk of Soviet Plan to Send Them to Siberia Is Untrue, He Tells A.J.C. Unit Here." At the meeting, Mikoyan, pressed by the AJC delegation, had declared that "the reported plans for the recreation of a Jewish state in Birobidzhan and the transfer of the Jewish population in Russia to that area are without foundation." Following the session, AJC sent Mikoyan a lengthy letter further documenting instances of cultural, religious, and other discrimination against Soviet Jews. The *Christian Science Monitor* reported, on February 24, 1959, that the Soviets, in response to the harsh attack Mikoyan had encountered in his U.S. visit, would permit the publication of some books in Yiddish, including selected works of the noted author Sholom Aleichem.

In August of that year, AJC issued yet another report on the condition of Jews behind the Iron Curtain, *The Plight of the Jews in Eastern Europe.* In addition to focusing on the internal threats and difficulties encountered by Jews, the report noted that "the Soviet Union has steadfastly opposed any emigration from that country" and called "for the right of Jews to emigrate freely to places of their choice, with all their possessions." It received widespread media coverage across the nation, including in the *New York Times, New York Herald Tribune, Boston Globe, Christian Science Monitor, Catholic News,* and scores of other papers.

International attention once again focused on Soviet anti-Semitism when Morris Abram, AJC's president at the time, held a press conference in New York in 1964 to denounce *Judaism Without Embellishment,* an anti-Semitic polemic containing Nazi-like caricatures, written by T.K. Kichko and published by the Ukrainian Academy of Sciences. Abram noted that the booklet "reflected in a most primitive and vulgar fashion the Soviet government's official anti-Semitic campaign in which some three million Russian Jews are being used as scapegoats for internal economic problems. The situation of Soviet Jews continues to worsen as the Soviet government regresses to the crudest forms of anti-Semitism."

The resulting international furor, it should be noted, extended to Western communist parties, which did not want to be associated with blatant Jew-hatred. Indeed, as reported in *Midstream* (June 1964), "There was literally not one major communist party or leader or organ in the Western world that did not protest, either timidly or vehemently." The uproar convinced the Kremlin to disavow the book and its author, though this was far from the last such publication to appear. Three years later, AJC publicized and denounced another piece by Kichko, "Zionism: A Tool of Imperialism," published in a prominent Soviet newspaper. Many more such anti-Semitic screeds were to follow, both by Kichko and a host of other Soviet pseudo-scholars and polemicists.

Launching the Soviet Jewry Movement

In 1964, AJC was one of four original sponsors — together with the Synagogue Council of America, the Conference of Presidents of Major American Jewish Organizations, and the National Community Relations Advisory Council (NCRAC) — of the American Conference on Soviet Jewry. Seven years later, AJC became a founding member of the successor organization, the National Conference on Soviet Jewry (NCSJ), which coordinated and led organized American Jewry's efforts on behalf of Jews in the USSR. In fact, the first president of the NCSJ, Richard Maass, and the first executive director, Jerry Goodman, came from the lay and professional ranks, respectively, of AJC.

On December 3, 1966, Soviet premier Alexei Kosygin, speaking at a Paris press conference, stunned the Jewish world when he declared that those Soviet citizens wishing to be reunited with their families abroad would be allowed to do so. While he made no specific reference to Jews, this declaration gave new impetus to those seeking to leave.

The following year, Israel's lightning victory in what came to be known as the Six-Day War had an electrifying effect on many Soviet Jews. Not only had Israel achieved one of the greatest military victories in history, but also its principal adversaries, Egypt and Syria, were close allies of the Kremlin and had relied heavily on Soviet-made weapons. With Kosygin's Paris declaration ringing in their ears and Israel's success awakening a long-dormant pride, some Soviet Jews, despite the risks, began the search for a positive self-identity, denied them by the authorities, and wondered whether there might be a chance to begin new lives outside what had for decades been the hermetically sealed borders of the Soviet Union.

The issue came dramatically to the world's attention when, on June 15, 1970, a group of Soviet Jews, joined by two non-Jews, sought to hijack an airplane at the Leningrad airport and divert it to Israel. The plan was foiled by the authorities, and the perpetrators were arrested together with their alleged accomplices. At their first trial, two of the defendants were sentenced to death and the others to lengthy prison sentences. AJC sprang into action.

In the Cause of Soviet Jewry, an AJC pamphlet issued in 1971, summarized the organization's response to the startling turn of events:

> The AJC issued an appeal to some 100 influential individuals—industrialists, clergymen, academicians and authors—and in almost every case these people made their voices heard among government officials and opinion molders, national and international. AJC Executive Council Chairman Max M. Fisher helped arrange meetings between Jewish leaders and Secretary of State Rogers, and subsequently with President Nixon. The President's expression of sympathy and concern for the Russian Jews was flashed around the world. Conferences with other White House and State Department officials enlisted further powerful support for the Jewish victims . . . .
> The Committee also helped organize a national emergency meeting of Jewish leaders in Washington, with major figures from the arts, sciences and public affairs in attendance.

The international outcry led Moscow to reconsider the death penalty for the hijackers, and, in a second trial, sentence the plotters to long prison terms in harsh conditions.

That same year, 1971, AJC utilized its extensive contacts with other American religious groups to establish the National Interreligious Task Force on Soviet Jewry, whose first honorary chair was R. Sargent Shriver, and quietly provided the new entity with financial support. Drawing on the leadership of the Protestant, Roman Catholic, Greek Orthodox, and Jewish communities, the task force would add an important, broad-based ecumenical voice to the Soviet Jewry campaign over the next two decades.

Among the many highlights of its activities was the testimony of Sister Margaret Ellen Traxler, on behalf of the task force, before the Senate Finance Committee on April 10, 1974, in support of the proposed Jackson-Vanik Amendment. When she concluded her remarks, according to an internal AJC memorandum from Gerald Strober to Rabbi Marc Tanenbaum, Senator Bob Packwood (R., Oreg.) stated:

> I have sat here day after day listening to trade association after trade association tell the Committee of our need to trade with Russia and how such trade would have little effect upon the Soviet Jews. I want to thank you for being the first to bring a moral word to this Committee. You are to be commended for your testimony, which greatly points out how the Jackson Amendment can alleviate the plight of the Soviet Jews.

Turning Up the Pressure

During the height of the Soviet Jewry campaign, from 1971 to 1991, as Soviet policy on Jewish emigration zigzagged dramatically, AJC was deeply involved in all phases of the effort, both individually and in collaboration with other interested agencies. AJC activity was especially notable in the political and diplomatic arenas in Washington, through AJC's offices, at the time, in Paris, Buenos Aires, and Mexico City, and in other capitals throughout Europe and Latin America.

The kickoff for this period of activism was the landmark World Conference of Jewish Communities for Soviet Jewry, held in Brussels in February 1971. It was planned with the assistance of AJC leaders, particularly Abraham Karlikow of the Paris office and Sergio Nudelstejer of the Mexico City office. A sizable AJC contingent, including President Philip E. Hoffman, participated. The conference's impact was felt worldwide.

> From thirty-eight countries on five continents came more than fifteen hundred delegates, including scores of prominent public offi-

cials, civil rights activists, scholars, poets, writers, financiers, union leaders and philosophers . . . . To the astonishment of the secretariat, the Soviet media on the eve of the conference launched a propaganda attack that captured the attention of the world media. Nearly three hundred journalists from every part of the world covered the Brussels event . . . . From the World Conference came the demand for Soviet authorities "to recognize the right of Jews who so desire to return to their historic homeland in Israel." This demand went beyond the American campaign's demand that had focused on family reunion. It mirrored the demands of the Jewish movement in the Soviet Union.[3]

AJC lay and staff leaders, as well as representatives of the National Interreligious Task Force on Soviet Jewry, attended the periodic review conferences of the Helsinki Final Act, the 1975 document signed by the Soviet Union and 34 other countries that, among other things, established human rights standards by which signatory countries could be judged. This attendance took two forms—as public members of official U.S. delegations and as representatives from the nongovernmental organization (NGO) sector. Moreover, AJC sent delegates to advocate in the corridors of the U.S.-Soviet summits and at times on the streets nearby, including the critically important 1986 Reykjavik encounter between President Ronald Reagan and Chairman Mikhail Gorbachev. It was AJC's contacts in Iceland that gained permission for ten representatives of American Jewish agencies to travel to the island nation—when, for security reasons, admission was severely restricted—enabling their voices to be heard by Soviet officials and the hundreds of media representatives covering the summit.

Other noteworthy AJC efforts included involvement in and financial support for the Association of Jewish Book Publishers, which, beginning in 1977, participated in the biennial Moscow International Book Fair. The fair, a commercial enterprise, provided a unique opportunity—under the constant gaze of the KGB, to be sure—not only for direct contact with the local community but also for distribution of books and other materials to information-starved Soviet Jews. There were also many visits to "refuseniks"—those thousands of Jews denied exit visas by OVIR, the responsible So-

---

[3] Albert D. Chernin, "Making Soviet Jews an Issue," in Murray Friedman and Albert D. Chernin, eds., *A Second Exodus: The American Movement to Free Soviet Jews* (Hanover, N.H., 1999), pp. 60–61.

viet agency, for one reason or another—and to synagogues in major Soviet cities, demonstrating solidarity and sending a message to Soviet authorities that their Jewish citizens had a lifeline to the West. AJC, through its Paris and New York offices, was also involved in preparing Russian-language material on Jewish themes that made its way into the hands of Jews in the Soviet Union eager for information otherwise denied them. And AJC focused on yet another way to get news to Jews in the Soviet Union—convincing the Voice of America, the overseas broadcasting arm of the U.S. government, to expand its Russian-language programming to the Soviet Union, aimed specifically at Jewish listeners.

One major distinguishing feature of AJC's approach was support for the broader Soviet human-rights movement. Most other Jewish organizations refrained from participation, fearing it could further complicate advocacy efforts on behalf of Soviet Jewry by persuading the Kremlin—which needed little convincing—that the larger Jewish aim was not simply "repatriation to the Jewish homeland," as the Soviet Jewry movement insisted, but, in fact, the overthrow of communism.

While never breaking with the consensus of the Soviet Jewry movement, AJC, consistent with its longstanding commitment to human rights and democratic values, managed to demonstrate solidarity with Soviet dissidents through its semiautonomous Jacob Blaustein Institute for the Advancement of Human Rights, led by its founding director and self-effacing visionary, Sidney Liskofsky. The institute regularly published material on and by Soviet human-rights activists, sponsored seminars and symposia, and awarded grants to NGOs that addressed broad Soviet human-rights issues, including, it should be noted, cases related to the right to practice one's religion and to speak one's language, i.e., Hebrew, consistent with relevant international covenants.

In addressing the contributions of the Jacob Blaustein Institute, Elena Bonner, the legendary human rights activist and widow of Nobel laureate Andrei Sakharov, said in 1997:

> In the early 1970s, the Jacob Blaustein Institute was one of the very few, if not the only one, among Jewish organizations concerned with the general state of human rights in the Soviet Union. The Institute did not limit itself to issues of Jewish emigration, understanding that an injustice anywhere on the face of this earth is a threat to justice everywhere.

The Blaustein Institute also, in 1972, joined with the International Institute of Human Rights and the Faculty of Law at Uppsala University (Sweden) to convene the landmark Uppsala Conference, as it came to be called, on the right to leave and to return. Attended by legal scholars from a number of Western countries, the conference focused on the fundamental rights enshrined in the Universal Declaration of Human Rights, the International Covenant on Civil and Political Rights, and the International Convention on the Elimination of All Forms of Racism, as they pertained to those Soviet Jews—and others—demanding the right to emigrate. The gathering thus gave an important international legal imprimatur to the still fledgling Soviet Jewry movement. Its proceedings were published as a book by the American Jewish Committee in 1976 under the title *The Right to Leave and to Return*.

Freedom Sunday

In October 1987, when Chairman Gorbachev was scheduled to make his first visit to Washington for meetings with President Reagan, the organized American Jewish community, led by the National Conference on Soviet Jewry and the Council of Jewish Federations, asked me, as the director of the American Jewish Committee's Washington office, to coordinate the organization of a mass demonstration. Morton Yarmon, AJC's director of public education and information, was charged with overseeing the public relations dimension of the rally.

There was, however, widespread concern in the organized Jewish community about the prospect of such a rally since, unlike New York, Washington had never successfully mounted a major Jewish demonstration. Therefore, in connection with Gorbachev's expected visit, some suggested simply to rent a hall and fill it with hundreds of Jewish leaders, who would claim to speak for the larger community, and be joined by political personalities from the nation's capital. But Natan Sharansky, recently released from the Soviet Gulag, refused to settle for such a truncated demonstration, and instead urged a mass mobilization. He prevailed and, with his tireless assistance in going from campus to campus, community to community, in the run-up to the December 6 date, he helped achieve the ambitious vision.

In the 37 days from confirmation of Gorbachev's arrival date in

Washington to his actual visit, American Jewry mobilized as never before, leading to the largest single gathering of American Jews in the nation's history. Two-hundred-and-fifty-thousand people, including a sizable number of non-Jews, came to the nation's Mall on December 6, 1987, to participate in Freedom Sunday for Soviet Jewry. They expressed support for the right of Soviet Jews to emigrate ("Let my people go" was the principal slogan), called particular attention to the plight of the Prisoners of Conscience (or Prisoners of Zion, as they were sometimes called) and the thousands of long-term refuseniks, and demanded an end to restrictions on the study of Hebrew and the practice of Judaism. Vice President George H.W. Bush, leaders of the Senate and House of Representatives, Catholic and Protestant clergy, governors and mayors, union officials and civil rights activists, and Natan Sharansky—along with other recently released Prisoners of Conscience Ida Nudel, Yuli Edelshtein, and Vladimir Slepak—were among the many prominent speakers at the daylong event, which took place on the eve of Gorbachev's first meeting with Reagan in the White House.

That evening, AJC, which had brought its entire board of governors and hundreds of other members to Washington for the rally, organized a dinner at which it presented its highest award, the American Liberties Medallion, to Sharansky. He used the occasion to express appreciation to AJC for its steadfast efforts on his behalf and its support for his wife's advocacy efforts while he was in the Soviet Gulag.

Among the reasons for the rally's success, as I wrote in the *Washington Jewish Week* (December 10, 1987), were:

First and foremost, the post-Holocaust legacy played a central role. People again and again indicated that they wanted to demonstrate their understanding of the lessons of history. They wanted to be counted among those who acted, not among those who stood by . . . . Many felt a special kinship with Jews from that great wellspring of Jewish life, Russia . . . . Virtually every Jewish institution and leader sent out a clear and constant call. Freedom Sunday was the Jewish obligation of the year, perhaps of the decade . . . . People also participated because they felt that there truly might be a chance to affect events in this period of improving Soviet-American relations . . . . The Washington area Jewish community, the key to a successful event, responded magnificently to the mobilization, forever putting to rest the notion that ours is an impossible community to move.

According to later reports by then government officials, President Reagan referred to the demonstration in his meeting with Chairman Gorbachev the next morning, indicating that it expressed the sentiment of the American people and needed to be taken into account by the Soviet leader if he wished to pursue improved ties with the United States. Whether the demonstration was the straw that broke the camel's back may never be known. Nonetheless, those who participated in the rally felt it to be a watershed—a gathering of American Jews as never before, with widespread support from politicians, religious and ethnic leaders, and average Americans, that also generated extensive front-page media coverage.

Conflicts and Quandaries

In fact, it was not long after the rally that the Soviet floodgates opened and Jews streamed out by the hundreds of thousands, primarily to Israel. By the 1990s, there were over one million Jews from the now former Soviet Union living in Israel, comprising approximately 20 percent of the nation's Jewish population. The stream to the United States, however, slowed during this period, as Washington narrowed the criteria for entry in what some observers believed was a tacit agreement with the Israeli government. What was perhaps most striking during the 1990s was the surge in Soviet Jewish migration to Germany, making it the fastest-growing Jewish community in the world. The number of Jews formally registered with the German Jewish community has nearly quadrupled since the late 1980s to well over 100,000, while the unofficial number is at least twice as high.

The 1987 rally evoked an unprecedented display of unity in the Soviet Jewry movement, temporarily hiding longstanding fissures. Both before and after, however, the divisions were real.

The principal one, which first emerged in the mid-1970s, had to do with the issue of country of destination for those Soviet Jews able to leave the USSR. With few exceptions, their legal basis for departure was a *vyzov,* or invitation, from relatives in Israel, on the basis of which they could begin the protracted emigration, or repatriation, process. But upon arrival in Vienna, the first processing center in the West, an increasing number of Soviet Jews, in the wake of the 1973 Yom Kippur War, insisted on exercising their right to freedom of choice. They refused to be dealt with by the

Jewish Agency for Israel (in Hebrew, the *Sochnut*) for transfer to Israel, and turned instead to the Hebrew Immigrant Aid Society (HIAS) and the American Jewish Joint Distribution Committee (JDC) for assistance in visa processing, principally to the U.S., Canada, and Australia, and for financial aid during the time they were in transit in Rome, Italy.

This caused a furor. Israel insisted that all Soviet Jews leaving the USSR with documents for Israel were obligated to go there. Anyone who wanted to emigrate to the United States or elsewhere, Israeli leaders argued, should seek exit visas for those countries in Moscow through the appropriate diplomatic legations. Israel had two main concerns. First, it viewed the millions of Soviet Jews as the greatest potential reservoir for new immigrants to the Jewish state. They would affirm the vitality of Zionism and bolster the Jewish state in every way imaginable, while sending a message to Israel's adversaries that, given the steady influx, time was not necessarily on their side. Second, it feared that if Soviet Jews went elsewhere, the Kremlin might pull the plug on the entire process. After all, the USSR recognized the right of emigration only in rare cases, fearing that if some could leave many more would try to follow. Instead, it justified the Jewish exodus as repatriation to the Jewish homeland.

For organizations like AJC, this controversy was inescapable, as it was impossible to be involved in the Soviet Jewry movement and circumvent it. In the face of competing pressures, AJC took the position that, though it sympathized with Israel's desire to maximize aliyah, it could not in good conscience take any action that would curtail the freedom of the individual to choose where to resettle, consistent with entry laws in the various Western countries.

AJC's position—which resembled those taken by most major American Jewish organizations—was summed up in a statement adopted by its board of governors on March 23, 1987:

> We believe that the overriding goal of the Soviet Jewry movement must remain to secure the release of the maximum number of Jews seeking to leave the USSR, and to permit them to establish new lives as free human beings and as Jews. While we would hope that the greatest number of Jews would choose to live in Israel and avail themselves of the extensive resettlement opportunities offered by the Israeli Government, we oppose any step that would serve to limit the right of Soviet Jews to select the final destination of their choice . . . .
> Even as we continue to seek ways of encouraging more Soviet Jews to consider resettlement in Israel, we affirm the position taken

by the [AJC] National Executive Council in 1976 that " . . . every Jew who manages to get out of the Soviet Union should be helped to go to the destination of his choice and receive resettlement assistance." In that statement AJC went on record as "warmly supporting all proposals whose aim is to assure that Jews coming out of the USSR be as fully informed as possible before making their choice of destination."

There were other areas of disagreement within the Soviet Jewry movement. One was between the so-called establishment and nonestablishment advocacy organizations. The former were grouped around the National Conference on Soviet Jewry, of which, as previously noted, AJC was one of the four founders. The nonestablishment activists, in contrast, looked to the Union of Councils for Soviet Jews, formally established in 1970 and describing itself as a community-based, grassroots organization, and the Student Struggle for Soviet Jewry, founded in 1964. In retrospect, the differences seem inconsequential, but, at the time, there was little cooperation between the two clusters and considerable mutual suspicion. The establishment, as befits its name, was accused of timidity and bureaucratic inertia, whereas the nonestablishment was considered by its critics to be too confrontational and its actions, consequently, counterproductive.

The Iron Curtain Falls

With the collapse of communism, first, in the Soviet satellite states of Eastern Europe and, within two years, in the USSR itself, AJC saw an unprecedented opportunity for the United States, Israel, world Jewry, and, not least, the people of the region. A four-pronged agenda emerged, which remains to this day the overall blueprint for AJC programming in the entire region.

1. *Assisting local communities.* Jewish communities in the former Soviet Union needed to achieve full protection under the law and equal status with other citizens. Only then would these communities—now mere shadows of what they had been before the double toll of Nazi occupation and communist domination—be able to reconstitute themselves.

Eager to maintain an appropriate division of labor, AJC enthusiastically applauded, but did not seek to duplicate, the estimable efforts of the Jewish Agency for Israel, the American Jewish Joint

Distribution Committee, the Memorial Foundation for Jewish Culture, the Ronald S. Lauder Foundation, the religious movements, and other groups to strengthen Jewish life through the rebuilding of synagogues, founding of Jewish day schools and summer camps, provision of essential social services, sponsorship of communal leadership-training programs, introduction of Israeli cultural and Hebrew-language programs, and publication of books and periodicals on a multitude of Jewish themes. Instead, as mentioned, AJC sought to help ensure the place of Jews and Jewish communities in the emerging postcommunist societies.

2. *Addressing Holocaust-related issues.* Such issues, applicable to Central and Eastern Europe as well as the FSU, included pensions for survivors; identification, preservation, and protection of sites of tragedy; restitution of communal property; national acceptance, where appropriate, of historical and moral accountability; and introduction of nationally tailored curricula on Holocaust education and local Jewish history.

3. *Strengthening relations with Israel.* Bilateral ties between Israel and the nations of Central and Eastern Europe, as well as the 15 successor states of the USSR, had to be broadened and deepened. It was clear early on that, as the new governments sought to reorient their foreign policies, Israel could become one of the principal beneficiaries of communism's collapse. Traditional East European support for anti-Zionism, anti-Israel terrorist groups, and the most hard-line Arab states gave way, in most cases, to pro-Western policies that included favorable attitudes toward Israel. The reasons for the change ranged from desire for access to Israeli technology and investment, to the view that close ties with the Jewish state could advance a nation's standing in the U.S., to a more generalized belief, however exaggerated, in international Jewish political and economic power, to a genuine desire to repair and rebuild frayed relations with the Jewish people and Israel.

Many of the postcommunist societies came to believe that their attitudes toward Jews were regarded in the West (and often by democrats within these societies themselves) as the best possible litmus test of the sincerity and effectiveness with which they pursued their new reformist policies. Thus, the opportunities available to Jewish agencies such as AJC throughout the region seemed almost limitless. This entirely new geopolitical situation—and the enhanced role it afforded world Jewry—also permitted AJC to assist Israel not only by encouraging closer bilateral ties, but also by pressing the postcommunist states to end their supply of weapons, know-how, and personnel to nations in the Middle East posing a threat to Israel, including Iran, Iraq, Libya, and Syria.

4. *Building democracy.* Consistent with AJC's longstanding philosophy, the agency recognized the importance of participating in the formation of robust democratic institutions, the rule of law, civil society, human- and civil-rights protections, and tolerance-building programs for ethnically diverse, sometimes stratified, societies. In the final analysis, the best protection for minority communities living within majority cultures, be they Jews or others, is safeguarding the rights of all by fostering respect for democracy and pluralism. Furthermore, in this case it was not simply a matter of trying to protect Jewish communities, important though this obviously was, but extending the reach of freedom and ending, once and for all, the East-West conflict.

This explains why AJC was the first Jewish group to call on the U.S. government to recognize the independence of the three Baltic states and Ukraine, at a time when the administration hesitated to offend Moscow. Later, AJC sought to help anchor these and other post-Soviet states in the European and transatlantic architecture. Partial success came with the accession to NATO of the Baltic states in 2004, but more work remains.

Tangible Results

PENSIONS FOR HOLOCAUST SURVIVORS

In the early 1990s, shortly after the break-up of the Soviet bloc, AJC began developing close working ties with the emerging leaders of the remnant Jewish communities in the region. Understandably, the first priorities of these communities were to reconstitute themselves, begin to find fellow Jews—many of whom had hidden their identities or were even unaware of them because their parents had never revealed the truth—organize basic communal services, deepen links with world Jewry, and ensure their rightful place within the newly independent societies.

As they assessed their needs, these leaders quickly recognized the importance of providing some modicum of support for the rapidly aging and often indigent Holocaust survivors in their midst. Unlike their counterparts in the West who had undergone identical wartime experiences, these survivors were denied pensions from the German government. Bonn's reasoning was that even in the unlikely case that agreement with the communist countries could be reached, their regimes could not be trusted to live up to such accords. Hence these Jews, ravaged by the Holocaust and unable to secure compensation because of their residence behind the iron curtain, were "double victims," in the words of Stuart Eizenstat, then serving as U.S. under secretary of state.

Once communism collapsed, Bonn offered other rationales for refusing to provide monthly payments: it feared a flood of new claimants from Russia, Belarus, Ukraine, and elsewhere, well beyond the limited number of Jews still alive; its economy was battered, its budget already stretched, its unemployment rolls growing; it preferred to consider, instead of pensions, modest one-time payments made through national foundations provided with German funds. In fact, a billion deutsche marks (DM) had been transferred to Moscow for precisely this purpose just before the USSR imploded. These funds were then distributed among rather poorly administered and inadequately audited foundations established in Russia, Ukraine, and Belarus—400 million, 400 million, and 200 million, respectively. In Ukraine, for example, well over 90 percent of the recipients were non-Jews, and the average one-time payment for Jewish and non-Jewish survivors of Nazi persecution was a paltry 600 DM, or about $350.

In 1996, AJC discovered that while Holocaust survivors in, for instance, Latvia were deemed ineligible for German pensions, disabled veterans of the Third Reich were eligible. Consequently, a Latvian Waffen SS veteran injured during the war received a monthly check from Bonn, while a Latvian Jewish survivor received nothing.

To summarize a long and complex story that then unfolded, AJC's talks with the German government—first in private, but later, after achieving no progress, coupled with public pressure generated by the White House, Congress, and the media—resulted in a German decision, announced January 12, 1998, to allocate 200 million DM (approximately $120 million). The funds were intended specifically for the estimated 20,000 Jewish Holocaust survivors who had spent at least six months in a Nazi concentration camp or 18 months in a ghetto or hiding. Two days after the announcement, a *Washington Post* editorial commented:

> Germany overall has set a positive model for the world, one that few other nations have matched, in facing up to the evils of its history and paying about $60 billion in reparations for admittedly unrightable wrongs. But in the case of the Eastern Europeans, it stalled for nearly half a decade, offering varying untenable excuses. Only when the American Jewish Committee went public with its tenacious campaign, beginning last spring, did it begin to make progress. Recent State Department pressure and a Senate resolution endorsed by 82 Senators may also have helped.

The Senate resolution, introduced by Senators Chris Dodd (D., Conn.) and Kay Bailey Hutchison (R., Tex.), was drafted in close cooperation with AJC.

RESEARCH AND PUBLICATIONS

AJC, known for its frequent polling of attitudes toward Jews around the world, conducted several pioneering surveys.

In the fall of 1990, the Soviet Center for Public Opinion and Market Research, at the request of AJC, carried out the first — and the last — survey to be conducted in the Soviet Union that systematically examined, on a national level, attitudes toward Jews, Israel, and a broad range of other Jewish concerns. The results, extensively reported in the *New York Times,* were published in 1992 by AJC in Lev Gudkov and Alex Levinson, *Attitudes Towards Jews in the Soviet Union: Public Opinion in Ten Republics.*

In the first post-Soviet survey, undertaken in 1992 by the Moscow-based Russian Center for Public Opinion and Market Research on AJC's behalf, 3,965 respondents were interviewed face to face in their homes in ten of the fifteen successor states (Russia, Ukraine, Belarus, Moldova, Azerbaijan, Kazakhstan, Uzbekistan, Estonia, Latvia, and Lithuania). The 144 questions dealt with a wide range of topics, including views of Jews and of a broad array of nationalities, political and economic opinions, civic values, and feelings about ethnicity.

Among the key findings were a wide variation in attitudes toward Jews from one state to another; overall unfavorable views about Jews when compared with earlier available studies; and the importance of placing attitudes toward Jews in the context of attitudes toward other groups, many of which, especially those from the Caucasus region, were viewed even more negatively than Jews. The full results and interpretive data were published in 1994 by AJC in Lev Gudkov and Alex Levinson, *Attitudes Toward Jews in the Commonwealth of Independent States.*

A second post-Soviet AJC survey, conducted in 1996 by ROMIR, a public-opinion and market-research company in Moscow, was geographically narrower in focus, limiting itself to the Russian Federation. Published by AJC under the title *Current Russian Attitudes Towards Jews and the Holocaust: A Public-Opinion Survey,* it used a number of the questions regarding attitudes toward Jews that had been asked previously, allowing a degree of longitudinal analysis. And several questions focusing on the Holocaust were identical to those asked by AJC in eight other countries at more or less the same time (United States, England, France, Germany, Austria, Poland, Slovakia, and Australia), permitting a comparative perspective.

The striking findings included a decidedly pessimistic view about the overall situation in Russia, especially among older and relatively less educated respondents; a plurality of support for the Communist Party; a rather low level of hostility toward Jews, although, given the large percentage of "don't know" responses to a number of questions dealing with Jews, the potential for an increase in such hostility; greater negative attitudes toward some other groups, among them Chechens, Azerbaijanis, Armenians, and Gypsies (Roma); and the absence of basic factual knowledge about the Holocaust coexisting with a widespread recognition of the importance of keeping the memory of the Holocaust alive.

Mention should also be made of a pioneering three-day conference, "Jews of the Former Soviet Union: Yesterday, Today and Tomorrow," held in St. Petersburg in June 1996, that was sponsored by AJC and the London-based Institute for Jewish Policy Research, and cosponsored by the Moses Mendelssohn Zentrum of Potsdam University (Germany), the European Council of Jewish Communities, the National Conference on Soviet Jewry, and Petersburg Jewish University. The conference brought together 150 Jewish leaders from across the FSU, Europe, Israel, and the United States to discuss the political, cultural, religious, and educational challenges facing Jews in the FSU and appropriate strategies for responding to them. One of the speakers was Galina Starovoitova, the courageous activist for democracy and human rights who would be fatally shot in St. Petersburg two years later. Regrettably, I was unable to attend the conference. A Russian entry visa was denied me on the grounds of my "past political history," which, though never explicitly defined, presumably referred to my years of involvement in the Soviet Jewry struggle and two detentions by authorities in Moscow, in 1974 and 1981. State Department and congressional efforts, including a letter to Russian president Boris Yeltsin urging him to reverse the visa denial signed by more than 40 members of Congress, proved unsuccessful. (A year later, after a meeting with Foreign Minister Yevgeny Primakov, I was issued an entry visa to participate in an AJC delegation visiting Moscow for meetings with political officials and leaders of the Jewish community.)

In addition to a summary report of the 1996 conference, a publication including the texts of the three principal addresses — by Professor Shlomo Avineri of the Hebrew University, Dr. Michael Chlenov, president of the Russian Va'ad, and Professor Zvi Gitelman of the University of Michigan — was issued by AJC in 1997.

POLITICAL CONTACTS

Traditionally known as the "American Jewish State Department," AJC sought to establish links with high-level political officials in the FSU in pursuit of the four-pronged agenda enumerated above, adapted to the specific conditions of each individual country.

AJC delegations have traveled frequently to Russia, Ukraine, Belarus, Estonia, Latvia, Lithuania, Armenia, Azerbaijan, Georgia, and Moldova for meetings with government officials and representatives of the Jewish communities. Moreover, AJC has met regularly with the foreign ministers of most of the FSU countries each fall during their visits to New York for the opening of the UN General Assembly sessions. In a 14-month span during 2006–7, for example, AJC held five private meetings with Sergei Lavrov, the foreign minister of the Russian Federation, three in New York and two in Moscow.

It is difficult to evaluate the results of such meetings, for there is seldom a cause-and-effect relationship between a single meeting, or even a series of them, and a policy decision. Yet it is clear from the fact that these leaders carve out substantial blocks of time from very busy schedules to meet with AJC delegations—and do so repeatedly—that they understand the importance of the Jewish community on the American scene, especially in the international-affairs arena.

Other than, possibly, segments of the business world, a narrow band of scholars, and Americans with ethnic roots in one of these nations, Jews are most likely to take an interest in what goes in Russia, Ukraine, Belarus, the Central Asian countries, and the Baltic states, and the decision-makers there know it. After all, there are Jewish communities, big or small, within each of these countries to be considered, ties with Israel and the U.S. to be cultivated, potential links with Israel's foes to be monitored, and a long history of a Jewish presence that invites study and commemoration. Moreover, many of these countries, lacking any significant or well-organized diaspora community in the U.S., believe they can entice American Jewry to play that representational role or, in the case of Ukraine, to supplement the efforts of Ukrainian Americans. In the process, they also have come to understand the AJC agenda.

Our FSU interlocutors know that we want our fellow Jews to live in an atmosphere of equality that is free of anti-Semitism, above all from mainstream sources; that the state of their bilateral relations with the U.S. and Israel is vitally important to us; that concern for Iran's quest to acquire weapons of mass destruction ranks at the top of our priorities; and that we care deeply about the health of democracy and respect for human rights. Moreover, with the encouragement of the relevant Jewish communities, we often raise matters of local concern, such as the restitution of communal property, return of Jewish libraries and ritual objects, or cemetery desecrations and other instances of anti-Semitism.

LEADERSHIP TRAINING

A number of Jewish agencies have done laudable work in training Jewish leaders in the FSU for communal service. AJC's particular aim has been to identify those Jewish leaders who interact with the general community in their countries and to help them develop their skills in working in the political arena, fostering interreligious and interethnic dialogue, strengthening understanding of pluralism and tolerance, countering hate groups, and developing research programs. A key element of this initiative has been AJC's International Jewish Leadership Conference, held each May since 1994, in Washington, D.C., immediately following the AJC annual meeting. By design, nearly half of the 150 overseas delegates who spend a week attending both events come from the countries of the FSU. The aim is to help develop their skills in the areas cited above.

To be sure, the American Jewish model is not readily exportable to these countries, but specific knowledge and materials can be utilized. In addition, these annual gatherings permit the participants to exchange information and experiences with each other, as well as to create a network linked by e-mail and other means of communication that minimizes the sense of isolation of the smaller communities and at the same time bolsters their self-confidence.

PROJECT UKRAINE

Largely as a result of AJC's longstanding connections with an important segment of the Ukrainian American community and with the generous financial support of AJC benefactors, AJC launched Project Ukraine in 1993. In initiating the undertaking, AJC assumed—correctly, as it turned out—that the bulk of attention in the post-Soviet world would go to Russia. Therefore, given Ukraine's considerable size and large Jewish community, we would be well served devoting resources to the second most populous FSU state.

The aims of the project were twofold: to assist Ukraine in navigating the transition to a multiethnic, democratic nation by strengthening selected institutions of civil society that could mediate between the state and the citizen, acting as a watchdog for democracy and pluralism in the country; and working directly with Ukrainian Jewish leaders in enhancing their civic, political, community-relations, and defense skills so that they themselves could help ensure the protection of their own rights.

The program began with the first annual American Seminar for Ukrainian Leaders, held in December 1993. Government officials, educators, journalists, and representatives of Ukrainian Jewry and other national minorities participated in a ten-day program in the U.S. during which they learned about the role of civil society in American democracy, relations among American ethnic and religious minorities, and how Ukraine was viewed by American leaders.

Evaluations from this first initiative were very positive, especially about the value of the skills, knowledge, and training received. Other seminars followed. In addition, AJC professionals traveled to Ukraine to provide skills-training workshops. In 1994, for instance, AJC's legal director, Sam Rabinove, visited to discuss concepts of civil liberties, and, in 1995, AJC specialists in interreligious and interethnic relations were invited to Ukraine to share their extensive experiences on "intervention models that protect vulnerable groups" with the Jewish community and with representatives of Ukrainian civil society.

Regrettably, outside funding for Project Ukraine ended a decade ago, compelling AJC to curtail these particular programs even as it stepped up contact with Ukrainian government officials, continued to pay frequent visits to Kiev, attended events commemorating the Nazi massacres at Babi Yar, developed close ties with Jewish community leaders, focused attention on the anti-Semitic activities of leaders of MAUP, Ukraine's largest private university, and worked with the U.S. Congress to "graduate" Ukraine from the Jackson-Vanik Amendment, for which Ukrainian political leaders, including President Viktor Yushchenko, gave AJC special credit.

RUSSIAN JEWISH LEADERSHIP PROGRAM IN THE U.S.

In 1996, two Russian Jews living in the U.S., Peyrets Goldmacher and Sam Kliger, visited AJC with an idea. They sought to build bridges between the sizable Russian-speaking Jewish community, especially in New York, and the established Jewish organizations. At their previous meetings with other Jewish agencies, the two recounted, they had been politely but firmly rebuffed. Would AJC take up the challenge? The answer was a resounding yes. The result has been a unique partnership that began the following year and recently marked its first decade of successful activity.

The centerpiece has been an annual Russian Jewish Leadership Program. Between 20 and 30 Russian-speaking Jews are selected to participate in a ten-week program at AJC headquarters, where they are exposed to the panoply of internal and external challenges faced by American and world Jewry and encouraged to join existing institutions or establish their own. In fact, both have resulted from this program.

In 2003, AJC hired Dr. Kliger, who at the time was with the New York Association for New Americans, as full-time director of a new division, Russian Jewish Community Affairs. The division has become a central address for research and programming related to Russian-speaking Jews in the U.S. and around the world—including in Germany, home to the world's fastest-growing Jewish community because of the heavy influx of Jews from the FSU. In May 2006, a pathbreaking conference on Russian-speaking Jews in the U.S., estimated to comprise 10 percent of the total American Jewish population, was held in conjunction with AJC's centennial anniversary in Washington. Titled "From Immigration and Resettlement to Integration and Engagement," it brought together 75 leaders from across the country to discuss strategies for strengthening the Jewish identity and commitment of Russian-speaking Jews and for bridging the gap that still separates them from the rest of the Jewish community.

An Enduring Commitment for a New Century

The well-being of Jews hailing from what was once Czarist Russia, later the Soviet Union, and now its 15 successor states remains of paramount importance to the agency's agenda today.

A great deal has changed since AJC was founded in response to the deadly attacks against the Jews of Kishinev. Millions of Jews emigrated until the Bolshevik regime closed the nation's borders. Other Jews welcomed the end of the Romanov dynasty, which had marked them with second-class status, restricted their residence to the Pale of Settlement, and stood by as the Black Hundreds and other anti-Semitic groups carried out periodic assaults on defenseless Jews. For some, communism, with its promise of equality and brotherhood, seemed like salvation. But it soon became abundantly clear that any hope of achieving equality and brotherhood would come, at a minimum, at the price of suppression of a distinctive Jewish religious and cultural identity.

And once Nazi Germany attacked the Soviet Union on June 22, 1941, Soviet Jews from all of the western territories, including the Baltic states, Belarus, Ukraine, Russia, and Moldova, became prime targets of the Nazi "Final Solution," in some cases abetted by local collaborators. Other Jewish civilians were fortunate to be evacuated to Central Asian republics and thus survived the war. Meanwhile, Jews in heavy numbers fought in the Red Army, and many received the nation's highest military decorations.

Once the war was over and Stalin was no longer impelled to rally the entire nation, including the Jews, to defeat the Nazi aggressor, and had no further need for American assistance, he began to turn on the Jews. In this instance, Jews were vilified not as individuals, but as a collectivity. From the "anti-cosmopolitan" campaign, to the plans for deportation of all Jews to the Soviet Far East, to the so-called Doctors' Plot on the eve of his death in 1953, Stalin made clear his deep distrust of Jews and his determination to target them.

A new era opened in the mid-1960s, beginning with Premier Kosygin's remark in Paris supporting family reunification, followed by the indescribable infusion of pride among Soviet Jews in response to Israel's stunning victory in the 1967 war. Largely deprived for decades of any Jewish education or religious upbringing, some Soviet Jews hungrily sought information about their identity—and about Israel, which had been pilloried in the Soviet media after the short-lived diplomatic infatuation with the new state in 1948 gave way to a markedly pro-Arab, anti-Israel stance, climaxed by Moscow breaking diplomatic relations after the Six-Day War.

From that point until the implosion of the Soviet Union in 1991, an increasing number of Jews attempted to assert their identity, and demanded repatriation to Israel and family reunification. At the same time, a broader dissident movement arose that focused on human-rights violations, and the Kremlin countered with a variety of responses, including harsh punitive measures.

Who could have predicted at the onset of these dramatic events that more than 1.5 million Jews would eventually succeed in leaving the Soviet Union, resettling primarily in Israel but also in the U.S., Germany, Canada, Australia, and, in tiny numbers, even New Zealand? Against all the odds, this became one of the most ambitious and successful human-rights campaigns in history. Who could have foreseen the ascension to power of Mikhail Gorbachev, with his policies of *glasnost* and *perestroika,* which led directly to the collapse of the world's most powerful tyranny? Who could have imagined that on former Soviet space Jewish life in its multitudinous forms—synagogues of various kinds, community centers, study groups, cultural organizations—would reemerge decades after a deliberate Soviet effort to extinguish every last vestige of Jewish identity and pride? Who could have conceived that Israeli embassies would be established in these post-Soviet states, with bilateral relations flourishing, in many cases, today, as representatives of Israeli institutions are permitted to open offices and educate Jews about the true nature of Zionism and contemporary Israeli life? And who could have pictured Jews—who fled the USSR on one-way tickets to the West—now traveling back and forth to their former homes, for purposes of business, tourism, or even extended stays to reconnect with their places of origin?

Throughout this tumultuous history, AJC has sought, whenever possible, to play a constructive role, whether focusing the spotlight on the travails of Jews in that part of the world, defending their right to leave and resettle elsewhere, demanding that the religious and cultural rights of Jews be protected, encouraging ties with Israel, or enhancing the links between resettled Soviet Jews in the U.S. and the larger American Jewish community.

Varying with the circumstances, these AJC efforts have taken place through diplomatic back channels, demonstrations in the streets, skillful navigation of regional and international organizations, outreach to longstanding non-Jewish partners, prodigious research and publications, constant travel for advocacy purposes, and direct links with local Jewish communities and their frontline leaders. This pattern of activism reveals an agency driven by courage, commitment, conviction, and compassion.

In light of the entirely unforeseeable events of the twentieth century that affected the millions of Jews from Eastern Europe, it would be foolhardy indeed to anticipate likely scenarios for the next century. But it is clear that as long as there are Jews in that part of the world—and undoubtedly there will be—active engagement with them, their governments, key institutions in civic society, and other interested countries, especially the U.S. and Israel, will be necessary. AJC's century-long record of steadfast commitment and its current active and forward-looking agenda give every reason to believe that the organization will continue its record of unparalleled dedication.

Review
of
the
Year

UNITED STATES

United States

National Affairs

AMERICANS, ISRAELIS, and Palestinians held elections during 2006, leaving a dramatically different cast of leaders by year's end. When all the ballots were counted in the U.S., a record number of Jews were among the winners.

The Israeli-Palestinian conflict influenced all aspects of the American Jewish public-affairs agenda. Internationally, it impacted Jewish attitudes toward the war in Iraq, the prospect of a nuclear Iran, and even Jewish advocacy to end the genocide in Darfur. Domestically, ad hominem attacks on "the Israel lobby" had the ring of anti-Jewish conspiracy charges, and much of the Jewish interfaith encounter revolved around the positions of evangelical and mainline Protestants on Israel.

THE POLITICAL ARENA

Midterm Elections

On Election Day 2006, Democrats swept into power in both houses of Congress, returning to full control after 12 years in political exile. In the House, Democrats gained 30 seats, sending 22 incumbent Republicans down to defeat. They would have a 17-vote majority in the 110th Congress. In the Senate, Democrats defeated six incumbent Republicans, increasing their own strength from 44 to 49. With the benefit of two independents opting to caucus with the Democrats, they would hold a 51-49 Senate majority.

Polls showed that the war in Iraq and the condition of the economy topped the list of issues motivating voters, displacing appeals to "values" that had spelled success for Republican candidates in recent elections. Amendments and referenda restricting marriage to heterosexual couples were on the ballot in several states, but the issue seemed to be losing steam, going down to defeat in one state and passing in others by closer margins than in previous years. Pundits also suggested that swing voters and even part of the Republican base were turned off by an unpopular war and a series of scandals involving administration officials, congressional leaders, well-placed lobbyists, and an outspoken evangelical leader (see below).

Every Jewish member of Congress who sought reelection was successful. In all, 43 Jews were elected to the new Congress, all Democrats with the exception of the two independents in the Senate and three Republicans, one in the House and two in the Senate. A record 13 senators would be Jewish, including two newcomers, Ben Cardin (D., Md.) and Bernard Sanders (I., Vt.). Two incumbent senators, Dianne Feinstein (D., Calif.) and Herb Kohl (D., Wis.), were handily reelected.

In the House, newly elected Jews came not just from areas with high Jewish populations but also from states with few Jews, including Tennessee, Kentucky, and New Hampshire. Another Jew, Gary Trauner, narrowly lost his bid to replace Barbara Cubin (R., Wyo.) for Wyoming's at-large seat. The six new Jewish House members were Steve Cohen (D., Tenn.), Gabrielle Giffords (D., Ariz.), Paul Hodes (D., N.H.), Steve Kagen (D., Wis.), Ron Klein (D., Fla.), and John Yarmuth (D., Ky.).

Two Jewish Democrats were widely credited with doing much to aid their party's return to power. Charles Schumer (D., N.Y.) and Rahm Emanuel (D., Ill.) chaired, respectively, the Senate and House Democratic campaign committees. Meanwhile, the ranks of Jewish governors grew to three with Elliott Spitzer (D., N.Y.) joining the reelected Linda Lingle (R., Hawaii) and Ed Rendell (D., Pa.).

The new Congress included the first Muslim and the first two Buddhists. It would also witness the highest political rank ever achieved by a Mormon and a woman, with Harry Reid expected to become Senate majority leader and Nancy Pelosi speaker of the House. And for the first time, Congress would include more Jews than Episcopalians. Jews, just 2 percent of the population, would hold 7 percent of House seats and 13 percent of Senate seats.

To be sure, Episcopalians, Methodists, and Presbyterians together continued to hold a larger share of seats in Congress than pews in America. Albert Menendez, a researcher and writer who biennially tracked the religions of members of Congress, noted that those mainline Protestant denominations would account for 20 percent of the new Congress, four times their share of the general population—but down from the 43-percent share the three denominations represented in the 1972 Congress. Among religious groups, the most notable electoral shift, according to John Green of the Pew Center for Religion and Public Life, was that Democrats garnered a majority of Catholic voters for the first time in many years.

The Jewish electorate remained unresponsive to a concerted campaign to get it to vote Republican, giving as much as 87 percent of Jewish votes to Democratic candidates. The 12 percent of Jews voting for Republicans was half the level of support given to President Bush in 2004, and a rebuke to the Republican Jewish Coalition, which had taken out numerous ads painting the Democratic Party as anti-Israel, weak on terrorism, and beholden to critics of Israel such as Jimmy Carter and antiwar activist Cindy Sheehan.

The largest segment of Jews to vote against a Democratic candidate lived in Connecticut, where Joseph Lieberman garnered just 60 percent of the Jewish vote in winning reelection. The three-term senator ran successfully as an Independent, having lost the Democratic primary to antiwar candidate Ned Lamont.

Pro-Israel campaign contributions bolstered several successful incumbent candidates including Lieberman, and aided challengers such as Sheldon Whitehouse (D., R.I.), who ousted Republican Lincoln Chaffee, considered cool towards Israel. However, significant pro-Israel campaign dollars did not stave off defeat for four Republican senators: Rick Santorum of Pennsylvania, Mike DeWine of Ohio, Conrad Burns of Montana, and James Talent of Missouri. In the House, one race that was closely watched and later celebrated by friends of Israel was in southwest Indiana, where six-term incumbent John Hostettler, a Republican, went down to a crushing 20-point defeat at the hands of a local sheriff, Democrat Brad Ellsworth.

On Election Day, the residents of Somerville, Massachusetts, handily defeated a hard-fought, multiyear, pro-Palestinian effort to pass two nonbinding resolutions. The first, affirming the so-called Palestinian "right of return," was defeated by 55 to 45 percent. The second, calling for divestment from Israel, failed by 70 to 30 percent. A broad coalition led by the Boston Jewish Community Relations Council and the Jewish Labor Committee was instrumental in defeating the measures. Speaking out in various forums against them and in support of Israel were Congressman Mike Capuano, Massachusetts governor-elect Deval Patrick, Lieutenant Governor Kerry Healey, and Somerville mayor Joe Curtatone, as well as the *Boston Globe* and the *Boston Herald*.

Election Controversies

Republicans in Congress seemed unable to recover from a series of political scandals during the year. On January 3, lobbyist Jack Abramoff entered a guilty plea on felony counts of conspiracy, fraud, and tax evasion related to his lobbying work for Native American tribes. He also agreed to pay a $1.7-million fine to the Internal Revenue Service. Still unproven was the accusation made in 2005 that the pro-Israel Abramoff had diverted money from an urban charity to Israeli settlers. The Abramoff scandal was but one of a chain that had brought down such powerful figures as House Majority Leader Tom DeLay (R., Tex.), who ended his re-election bid after being indicted on campaign-finance charges. His former colleague Randy "Duke" Cunningham (R., Calif.) was sentenced on March 3 to more than eight years in prison and fined $1.8 million for bribery, fraud, and tax evasion.

Two of the most salacious scandals of the year, each with broader electoral implications, involved ironic twists on an issue that had helped Republicans in recent years, opposition to homosexuality. Mark Foley (R., Fla.), a six-term congressman known for his initiatives to protect children from exploitation, resigned on September 29 after it was revealed that he had sent sexually suggestive telephone "instant messages" to teenage boys who were serving as Congressional pages.

Conservative candidates who wished the Foley scandal would disappear from the headlines were hardly happy when it was replaced by revelations that Ted Haggard, a giant in the evangelical Christian world, was implicated in a sex-for-hire scandal with a male prostitute, from whom he had allegedly purchased the drug methamphetamine. Haggard, head of the National Association of Evangelicals (NAE), at first denied the charges, but his accuser produced voicemail recordings. On November 3—just four days before the midterm elections—Haggard resigned his NAE post. Jewish leaders, who remembered Haggard's veiled threat that Jewish criticism of Mel Gibson's film *The Passion of the Christ* could jeopardize evangelical support for Israel, had little sympathy.

Former Florida secretary of state Kathleen Harris's unsuccessful campaign for a Senate seat from that state was not helped by her prayer, uttered on a conference call, that God would "bring the hearts and minds of our Jewish brothers and sisters into alignment." When confronted about it, Harris said the prayer was intended to request that Jews become Republicans, not Christians, but many doubted her sincerity, as she had made similar comments in the past.

Conservative columnist Dennis Prager, who was Jewish, set off a firestorm with a scathing piece he wrote assailing the patriotism of Minnesota's Keith Ellison, the first Muslim elected to Congress, who had announced that he would take the oath of office on a Qur'an, the Islamic holy book. Prager charged that Ellison's oath would do "more damage to the unity of America and to the value system that has formed this country than the terrorists of 9/11." Prager's column was rife with errors, perhaps the most significant being that in fact, members were sworn in en masse, and could opt, as Ellison did, for private ceremonies later. Rep. Virgil Goode (R., Va.) echoed Prager and wrote a letter to his constituents asserting that swearing an oath on the Qur'an posed a threat to "the values and beliefs traditional to the United States of America." The major Jewish organizations strongly defended Ellison.

Judicial Appointments

With the confirmation of Judge Samuel Alito Jr. to fill the seat of Associate Justice Sandra Day O'Connor, who had announced her retirement, President Bush succeeded in placing a second justice on the Supreme Court. Alito was actually Bush's third choice for the seat. He withdrew his first choice, White House counsel Harriet Miers, and then, upon the death of Chief Justice William Rehnquist, nominated his second choice, John Roberts, to succeed him as chief justice. Alito's 58-42 Senate confirmation marked the first time that a majority on the Supreme Court would be Catholic.

There was no consensus in the Jewish community about Alito. A letter from the Union of Orthodox Jewish Congregations of America (OU) to the Senate Judiciary Committee expressed the agency's policy not to weigh in on judicial nominations, but offered praise for Judge Alito's record on religious liberties. The National Council of Jewish Women (NCJW) opposed the nomination, calling Alito an "ideologue with a demonstrated commitment to pulling the court to the far right." The Union for Reform Judaism (URJ) agreed, asserting that adding Alito to the court "would threaten protection of the most fundamental rights."

The American Jewish Committee maintained its traditional policy of neither supporting nor opposing judicial nominees. Instead, AJC sent a letter to the Judiciary Committee urging it to examine closely the nominee's record and judicial philosophy, focusing in particular on issues related to religious liberty and the separation of church and state, civil rights and civil liberties, and separation of powers. The Anti-Defamation

League (ADL) sent a similar letter raising such concerns. More than two dozen religious groups signed a letter to the Judiciary Committee that posed a range of Establishment Clause questions for Alito. Among the signatories were the NCJW, Jewish Council for Public Affairs (JCPA), URJ, and United Synagogue of Conservative Judaism.

The midterm elections, by placing the Senate under Democratic control, would apparently diminish the influence of the so-called "gang of 14" senators, which had played a key role in confirming judges during 2005. The seven Republicans in the group had agreed to take off the table the "nuclear option" of revoking, for judicial nominations, the requirement of 60 votes to end a filibuster; the group's seven Democrats, in exchange, agreed to filibuster nominations only in "extraordinary circumstances." Together, the 14 had allowed the confirmation of three controversial nominees to the federal bench in 2005 and blocked two others (see AJYB 2006, pp. 34–35).

The Jewish defense agencies closely watched the actions of the three confirmed judges during 2006 because their previous positions and statements raised concerns. They were William Haynes, who faced criticism for his approval of interrogation methods at Guantánamo Bay, Cuba, while he was the Pentagon's general counsel; William G. Myers, whose record on environmental issues aroused controversy; and Terrence W. Boyle, who was opposed by civil rights groups. In keeping with Senate rules, several of the unconfirmed nominations were returned to the White House before the August recess. They were renominated in September, only to have the clock run out on them before the midterm elections.

THE INTERNATIONAL POLICY ARENA

U.S.-Israel Relations

A NEW ISRAELI GOVERNMENT

The year started with great uncertainty in the U.S.-Israel relationship. Late in 2005, Israeli prime minister Ariel Sharon dissolved the Knesset and called for new elections. Sharon also announced his intention to run at the head of a new centrist party, Kadima, on a platform that included continuing the policy of unilateral territorial withdrawal that had resulted in Israel leaving Gaza and several settlements in the northern West

Bank. Sharon suffered a mild stroke in mid-December 2005, but returned to work soon after. Four days into the New Year he was felled by a massive and debilitating stroke. Doctors announced that he was in a coma from which he was not likely to emerge.

Statements of support and concern for the ailing prime minister poured in from many quarters, a remarkable turn of events considering how unpopular he had been among "dovish" groups prior to his disengagement plan. Television evangelist Pat Robertson, however, took a different approach on his 700 Club cable broadcast, suggesting that the stroke might be divine retribution. "He was dividing God's land, and I would say, 'Woe unto any prime minister of Israel who takes a similar course to appease the [European Union], United Nations, or the United States of America,'" Robertson said, adding, "God says, this land belongs to me, and you better leave it alone."

These comments evoked a stinging reaction from liberals and conservatives alike, revealing a telling faultline within the evangelical Christian world. The public policy director of the Southern Baptist Convention, Rev. Richard Land, scored the televangelist who had often upstaged him and other more mainstream evangelical powerhouses, saying he was "appalled" by Robertson's "spiritual ignorance and . . . arrogance."

Sharon's deputy, Ehud Olmert, assumed the post of acting prime minister. Kadima finished first in the March 28 election with 29 of 120 Knesset seats, most of them at the expense of Likud, which had been home to both Sharon and Olmert. Less than two months later, Olmert paid his first visit to Washington as prime minister, meeting with President Bush and addressing the U.S. Congress. Warm welcomes and rounds of applause masked divisions over the prime minister's plan to move unilaterally, something the administration supported only in the absence of a Palestinian partner. The president stressed, and Jerusalem seemed to agree, that the eventual permanent borders between Israel and a Palestinian state would need to come from a negotiated settlement.

THE PALESTINIAN ELECTIONS

Palestinian elections were scheduled for January 25, 2006. Wary of the potential for a strong Hamas showing, the U.S. and the EU threatened not to recognize a Palestinian government led by a party whose charter called for the destruction of Israel. In this they went a significant step further than their partners in the "Quartet," Russia and the UN, which had called on Palestinian groups participating in the election to renounce violence, recognize Israel's right to exist, and disarm immediately, but did not raise the possibly of withholding recognition.

Even so, as Palestinians headed to the polls, researchers said that Fatah, the party of the late Yasir Arafat and his successor, Mahmoud Abbas, continued to lead, with more than 40 percent of the vote; Hamas was expected to win around 25 percent. The actual result was far different: Hamas drew 60 percent, setting off a flurry of surprised reactions.

Congressional leaders and the Bush administration quickly lined up to oppose U.S. financial aid to a Hamas-led Palestinian Authority, in the hope of driving the Palestinians back to Fatah and other less overtly violent factions. Secretary of State Condoleezza Rice said, "The United States is not prepared to fund an organization that advocates the destruction of Israel, that advocates violence and that refuses its obligations . . . ." The EU followed, boycotting all non-humanitarian assistance to the PA.

With unemployment skyrocketing and household income plummeting, a crisis loomed in the Palestinian areas. American Jewish leaders wrestled with whether a "starve the beast" approach, as the boycott idea was called, was the best way to advance Israeli-Palestinian peace. In the end, even the URJ, a group that had been outspoken about Palestinian suffering, supported a Senate resolution that "no United States assistance should be provided directly to the Palestinian Authority if any representative political party holding a majority of parliamentary seats within the Palestinian Authority maintains a position calling for the destruction of Israel." The director of the URJ Religious Action Center (RAC), Rabbi David Saperstein, wrote: "While we support the democratic process carried out by the Palestinians, we cannot ignore the fact that Hamas has for many years been at the forefront of terror attacks against Israel, designed to thwart the peace process and harm innocent Israelis."

Support for a boycott was not universal, though. Arthur Waskow, head of the dovish Shalom Center, emphasized that much of the electoral support for Hamas was due to its charitable activities. Waskow declared: "Insisting that the Palestinian government recognize Israel's legitimacy is a just and praiseworthy goal, but this is a perverse and unjust way of getting there. It is far likelier to cause even more intense misery for the Palestinians, throwing them even deeper into the arms of a party that has shown great humanitarian success and was elected not for its hostility to Israel but for that humanitarian success." He went on to liken the proposed boycott to Allied punishment of Germans after World War I, which, he said, "produced a demonic Germany."

World leaders sought, and found, ways to get aid to Palestinians while bypassing Hamas. According to the UN Office for the Coordination of Humanitarian Affairs, aid to the PA totaled $900 million in 2006, up from $349 million a year earlier. Total aid to Palestinians, including that distributed through nongovernmental organizations such as the World Food Program, increased to more than $300 per capita, and rose overall by more than 20 percent to $1.2 billion, the UN and the International Monetary Fund reported.

A CONTROVERSIAL WAR

Israel's unilateral withdrawal from Gaza in 2005 was met with an increasing barrage of rocket fire into Israel, and Israel returned fire into the newly evacuated territory. As the summer of 2006 approached, tensions escalated. In June, Hamas, now the governing party in the PA, was among the militant groups claiming responsibility for kidnapping an Israeli soldier at a Gaza crossing. The Iranian-sponsored Hezballah (Party of God) fired rockets from Lebanon into northern Israel, and kidnapped two more Israeli soldiers. After a failed rescue attempt, Israel responded with artillery and airstrikes, destroying Hezballah rocket caches along with significant parts of the southern Lebanon civilian infrastructure — including roads, bridges, and broadcast stations — which Hezballah used to support its operations.

President Bush attended a mid-July meeting of the leaders of the G8 industrialized nations in St. Petersburg. The group issued a statement attributing the origins of the conflict to the actions of Hamas and Hezballah. It called for an end to attacks on Israel and the release of the captured Israelis, to be followed by a withdrawal of Israeli forces from Gaza and the release of detained Palestinian legislators belonging to Hamas. The statement, while critical of the scope and impact of Israel's response, did not call for a cease-fire. American leaders expressed the view that Israel had a right to defend itself, but the president admonished the Jewish state to be "mindful of the consequences."

American Jewish groups quickly organized large pro-Israel rallies in several cities, including Boston, Chicago, Denver, New York, Philadelphia, San Francisco, and Washington, D.C. In New York, Senator Hillary Clinton said, "We will stand with Israel because Israel is standing for American values as well as Israeli ones." Jewish organizations also launched fund-raising campaigns to help Israelis — Jewish, Christian, and Muslim — affected by the rocket attacks. The families of the kidnapped soldiers became symbols of the grief of all Israelis, and made frequent appearances pleading for the safe return of their loved ones, Gilad Shalit, Ehud Goldwasser, and Eldad Regev. American opinion about the war was mixed. Some groups were highly critical of Israel. A July 14 statement from the National Council of Churches USA and Church World Service, for example, started the timeline of the current conflict with the Israeli "occupation" and "Israel's missile strike on Gaza and the death of innocent Palestinians." According to the statement, the Palestinian rocket fire and the kidnapping of an Israeli soldier was "retributive." There were also voices of support for Israel. The American Federation of Teachers (AFT) passed a resolution condemning Hezballah and Hamas for precipitating the crisis with their bombings, killings, and kidnappings, and recognizing Israel's responsibility to defend its borders and citizens from attack. The union defeated a competing resolution that called for an immediate cease-fire and placed blame on both sides.

U.S. diplomats tried to mediate a solution to the crisis but held firm in opposing any Israeli withdrawal from southern Lebanon without guarantees of security on the northern border. A compromise was reached on August 11, when the UN adopted a resolution that specified a larger UN peacekeeping force as well as Lebanese troops patrolling that nation's southern region.

Darfur

The crisis in Darfur, Sudan, entered its fourth year as government-backed Arab militias and rebel groups continued to wreck havoc on villagers in the troubled region. Estimates of the number of dead through violence and disease ranged from 200,000 to 450,000.

The American Jewish community added its voice to the chorus calling for an end to the genocide. On the local level, Jewish groups were instrumental in organizing rallies in Austin; Boulder; Chicago; New York City; Portland, Oregon; Rutland, Vermont; Somerville, New Jersey; Seattle; St. Paul; San Francisco, South Palm Beach; and Tucson.

Nationally, three dozen Jewish agencies were among the 150 organizations in the SaveDarfur coalition. That group launched a campaign, "Million Voices for Darfur," to have one million handwritten and electronic postcards delivered to the White House calling for a stronger multinational force to intervene and protect Darfuris. By April 30, more than 760,000 postcards had been collected, and they were delivered to President Bush in Washington while tens of thousands held a national rally there for an end to the genocide. Speakers included representatives of the three Jewish agencies serving among the 15 organizations that comprised the SaveDarfur executive committee: American Jewish World Service president Ruth Messinger; JCPA executive director Rabbi Steve Gutow; and Rabbi David Saperstein, director of Reform Judaism's RAC. In addition, Elie Wiesel was among the celebrities who spoke. The coalition reached its goal of a million postcards during the summer.

A peace agreement for Darfur was signed May 5 by the Sudanese government and the Sudan Liberation Movement, the region's largest rebel group. It ostensibly required the government to disarm and demobilize the Janjaweed militia and restrict movements of other militant forces. When the UN General Assembly opened in New York on September 19, Sudanese president Omar Hassan al-Bashir said that Jewish organizations were the source of media "fictions" regarding the atrocities in Darfur. Eighty-eight members of the House of Representatives sent a letter to al-Bashir condemning the remarks and praising the American Jewish community for its efforts to bring an end to the killings.

On October 13, President Bush signed the Darfur Peace and Accountability Act. The law bolstered the African Union Mission in Sudan (AMIS); directed the U.S. government to assist efforts by the International Criminal Court to bring to justice those guilty of war crimes; and called on the president to freeze the assets of, and impose a travel ban on, those committing atrocities in Darfur. The act also urged a greater NATO role in support of the AMIS and called for the administration to impose other sanctions, including denying entry to U.S. ports, on ships containing Sudanese oil. The bill had passed the House on April 12, and the Senate, by unanimous consent, on September 21. The same day the president signed the bill he also issued an executive order "blocking property of and prohibiting transactions with the government of Sudan."

At year's end, several more Darfur-related bills were pending, including one sponsored by Sen. Harry Reid (D., Nev.) requiring the Department of Defense to report to Congress on ways the U.S. could assist the AMIS, and another sponsored by Sen. Joseph Biden (D., Del.) calling for the creation of a "no-fly zone" in Darfur.

Iraq

The Jewish community continued its delicate dance around the issue of the war in Iraq. Polls, including the annual survey of Jewish opinion conducted by the American Jewish Committee, indicated that Jews opposed the war by a three-to-one margin. And yet the URJ and the Reconstructionist Rabbinical Association stood virtually alone among major Jewish organizations in voicing this dissent. Most Jewish groups avoided issuing statements about the war. One, the Republican Jewish Coalition, took strong exception to Jewish criticism of the war efforts. RJC executive director Matt Brooks told the Jewish Telegraphic Agency, "This is a time for people who should know what's at risk and what's at stake and not give in to the prevailing political winds. It sends the wrong message to men in uniform. It sends a white flag to our friends and allies around the world."

The long-awaited report of the Iraq Study Group—a bipartisan panel charged with researching and proposing policy for Iraq, led by former secretary of state James Baker and former House leader Lee Hamilton—included 79 recommendations to President Bush. The report, in fact, went well beyond the immediate Iraq war, endorsing a comprehensive review of U.S. policy in the Middle East. This included a controversial call for a more robust American role in mediating the Israeli-Palestinian conflict. The Baker-Hamilton report's call for consideration of the Palestinians' "right of return" was not appreciated by many in the pro-Israel community, nor was its suggestion that Israel return the Golan Heights in return for peace with Syria.

Refugees from Arab Countries

An "International Rights and Redress Campaign" was spearheaded by the World Organization of Jews from Arab Countries; its American arm, Justice for Jews from Arab Countries; and local groups, such as the San Francisco-based Jews Indigenous to the Middle East and North Africa.

Resolutions were introduced in both houses of Congress on May 23 to instruct American representatives at international forums to match any reference to Palestinian refugees with mention of Jewish and other refugees from the Middle East, North Africa, and the Persian Gulf. Proponents of the measure said the plight of Jews who were expelled or forced to flee their Middle East and North African homelands had been overshadowed in the debate about Israeli-Palestinian peace. Greater attention to their narrative, they felt, would counterbalance the "right of return" that Palestinian groups sought for refugees from the 1948 and 1967 wars.

Among the points they wished to stress was that Israel resettled those

Jews who were forced out of countries like Syria, Lebanon, Iraq, Iran, Morocco, and Libya, while Palestinian refugees, under instructions from the Arab League, were not integrated, but rather kept in refugee camps. The bill was sponsored in the House by Tom Lantos (D., Calif.), along with Jerrold Nadler (D., N.Y.), Ileana Ros-Lehtinen (R., Fla.), and Michael Ferguson (R., N.J.). A companion bill was introduced in the Senate by Rick Santorum (R., Pa.), Norman Coleman (R., Minn.), Richard Durbin (D., Ill.), and Frank Lautenberg (D., N.J.).

Iran

Iranian president Mahmoud Ahmadinejad, who had already shocked world leaders in 2005 by calling for Israel to be "wiped off the map" and supporting Holocaust denial, started off 2006 by welcoming Ariel Sharon's ill health and hoping for his death. More statements proposing the elimination of Israel and questioning the historicity of the Holocaust continued throughout the year. In addition, Iran held a contest for best Holocaust caricatures, in retaliation for cartoons published in Denmark that allegedly depicted the Muslim prophet Mohammed in a negative light (see below, p. 000).

Iranian threats against Israel were gravely exacerbated by Tehran's continuing nuclear program, which posed an existential threat to Israel and to others. But the debacle over the apparently nonexistent weapons of mass destruction in neighboring Iraq cast a long shadow over the response to Iran's nuclear quest, making it seem like "boy cries wolf." It was only when the International Atomic Energy Agency (IAEA) announced that its inspections were unable to remove lingering doubts about Iran's program that the charges gained international credibility. The American Jewish community found itself in an all-too-familiar position, worrying about Israel's security but assiduously avoiding public expression of these concerns lest it be seen as a warmonger. Such anxieties were quelled neither by a UN Security Council resolution on July 31 demanding that Iran abandon its nuclear ambition nor by a December 23 resolution imposing sanctions.

Both houses of Congress unanimously adopted the Iran Freedom Support Act (IFSA), "to hold the current regime in Iran accountable for its threatening behavior and to support a transition to democracy in Iran." The IFSA codified sanctions preventing U.S. companies from conducting business with or in Iran that had previously been barred under executive order. The act urged support for democratic forces in Iran, endorsed

American divestment from foreign companies that invested in Iran's petroleum sector, and extended parts of the Iran-Libya Sanctions Act. The Senate bill was sponsored by Rick Santorum (R., Pa.), Bill Frist (R., Tenn.), John Cornyn (R., Tex.), and Bill Nelson (D., Fla.), and the House version was proposed by Ileana Ros-Lehtinen (R., Fla.), joined by Henry Hyde (R., Ill.), Tom Lantos (D., Calif.), and Gary Ackerman (D., N.Y.). House action, followed by a same-day presidential signature, came on September 30.

Tehran hosted a Holocaust-denial conference in December. Among the participants were several anti-Zionist Orthodox Jews—including some from the U.S.—as well as other Americans and Europeans who disputed the facts of the Nazi era, among them former Ku Klux Klan leader and would-be politician David Duke. Ahmadinejad said at the conference, "Just as the Soviet Union was wiped out and today does not exist, so will the Zionist regime soon be wiped out." President Bush called the gathering "an affront to the entire civilized world." The House of Representatives unanimously approved a resolution, sponsored by Rep. Alcee Hastings (D., Fla.), condemning the conference.

The "Israel Lobby," Imagined and Real

WALT-MEARSHEIMER

Alarms went off in the Jewish community with the publication of an ostensibly academic article, "The Israel Lobby and U.S. Foreign Policy," by Stephen M. Walt of the John F. Kennedy School of Government at Harvard and John J. Mearsheimer of the University of Chicago. Touching on themes of great sensitivity for Jews, the paper suggested conspiracy and dual loyalty—perhaps even disloyalty. Its target was the pro-Israel community, a "Lobby" that allegedly harmed American interests by manipulating U.S. foreign policy in favor of Israel. Among the results of such manipulation, charged the authors, was the war in Iraq. What they meant by the term "Israel Lobby" was those arms of the Jewish and evangelical Christian communities that advocated for Israel, as well as political neoconservatives, a term that many considered code language for influential Jews.

The authors were both well-regarded academics, and their article was posted on the Web site of Harvard's Kennedy School. Shortly after its publication, however, the school distanced itself from the piece by removing its logo from the cover and adding a disclaimer indicating that the opinions expressed were those of the authors, not necessarily those of Harvard or the University of Chicago. The paper presented the Jewish community with a Catch-22. Since part of the authors' indictment was that the "Israel Lobby" silenced those who differed with it, criticism would feed into that very charge. Such criticism was voiced in Jewish quarters nonetheless. It pointed out historical inaccuracies—such as giving short shrift to Israeli offers of territorial compromise—noted a double standard that seemed to justify Arab terrorism, and pointed to the fallacy of attributing all Middle Eastern problems to the Israeli-Palestinian conflict. The ADL concluded that the paper "has elements of classic anti-Jewish conspiracy theories." Ironically, even MIT professor Noam Chomsky, one of Israel's most vocal critics, charged that the article exaggerated the role of the "Israel Lobby" and overlooked the role of special interests such as oil companies and the arms industry in devising American policy in the area.

JIMMY CARTER

Adding fuel to the fire was former president Jimmy Carter. Never considered a close friend of the Jewish state, Carter launched a missile of his own at Israel with a controversial book, *Palestine: Peace Not Apartheid.* The Nobel laureate and one-term president inflamed passions, first, with the title's analogy to the old South African system of racial separation and discrimination. The content of the book did little to assuage the worst fears of the pro-Israel community. Carter accused Israel of the "colonization of Palestinian land" and placed blame for the conflict foursquare in Israel's court. The book's lack of balance and significant factual errors led to the resignation of 15 board members from the Carter Center, led by Professor Kenneth Stein of Emory University.

Carter responded to the criticism through a "Letter to Jewish Citizens of America" in which he explained that his use of the term "apartheid" related only to conditions in the Palestinian territories, not within Israel itself. The issue was not racism, he wrote, but the "desire of a minority of Israelis for Palestinian land." He condemned terrorism and said he did not claim that Jews controlled the American media. Rather, he objected to the pro-Israel sentiments of fellow evangelical Christians, who, he said, had been raised to support "God's chosen people." As for the charge that the book contained errors, the president said it had been fact-checked by experts. This letter did not mollify the book's critics.

AIPAC'S WOES

With accusations flying about the putative "Israel lobby," the actual Israel lobby was dealing with a crisis of its own. Steven Rosen and Keith Weissman, former staffers at the American Israel Public Affairs Committee (AIPAC), were awaiting trial. The two had been indicted under the Espionage Act of 1917 for giving "national security information" (presumably about Iran) to parties who were "not entitled to receive it" (presumably the Israeli government). Early in the year, Larry Franklin, the Defense Department analyst who shared the classified information with them, was sentenced to almost 13 years in prison and fined $10,000. In August, Judge T.S. Ellis III upheld the constitutionality of the law under which the prosecution was proceeding, but ruled that to win its case the government would have to show it had suffered harm as a result of the unauthorized sharing of information.

AIPAC's angst was surely increased by talk of a new and well-funded Jewish "pro-peace" lobby. Supporters of the idea, including Rabbi David Saperstein, the head of the Reform movement's RAC, denied that the effort was intended to provide an alternative to AIPAC, the venerable and unflinching pro-Israel lobby, which more dovish Jewish groups believed hewed too closely to the positions of the Israeli right wing. Powerhouse philanthropists involved in talks about the new initiative included George Soros and Charles Bronfman. As the year ended the project remained little more than a trial balloon.

THE DOMESTIC POLICY ARENA

Homeland Security

Critical provisions of the USA PATRIOT Act, the antiterrorism law passed in the aftermath of the attacks on America of September 11, 2001, were to expire at the end of 2005. Supporters of the law sought to make its law-enforcement tools permanent, while civil rights groups and many of the Jewish organizations pressed for enhanced individual protections and judicial oversight. In 2005, Congress temporarily extended the homeland security measure while it sought to work out an agreement. A Senate reauthorization measure included several safeguards for civil liberties, but the House version was similar to the original legislation. The conference committee that reconciled the two removed many of the new protections, and President Bush signed the bill into law on March 9.

The administration suffered two setbacks in its attempts to apprehend and try alleged terrorists. On July 29, the Supreme Court ruled in *Hamdan v. Rumsfeld* that the executive order setting up military commissions to try terror suspects on Guantánamo Bay violated both the Uniform Code of Military Justice and the Geneva Conventions. Then, on August 17, a federal judge in Michigan ordered the National Security Agency to stop its Terrorist Surveillance Program. The court held unconstitutional the program's practice of eavesdropping on conversations without getting warrants from the special courts designated to hear classified matters under the Foreign Intelligence Surveillance Act (FISA).

Congress had already been conducting hearings about the once-secret program. On March 12, Senator Russell Feingold (D., Wis.) went so far as to introduce a resolution censuring the president for initiating the plan, which, the senator argued, was in violation of the FISA's requirement of court approval for wiretaps of U.S. citizens. Feingold, who was being mentioned as a possible presidential contender, was joined by Senators Barbara Boxer (D., Calif.), Tom Harkin (D., Iowa), and John Kerry (D , Mass.). Sen. Patrick Leahy (D., Vt.) also expressed support for the censure.

In the aftermath of the *Hamdan* case, Congress passed the Military Commissions Act to establish a structure for trying "enemy combatants." The law was adopted over the objections of many in the civil rights community and signed on October 17. RAC director Rabbi David Saperstein noted that the legislation's broad definition of "enemy combatant" could allow indefinite detention of individuals who posed no threat to the nation, risked exposing those in U.S. custody to mistreatment, lacked appropriate judicial oversight, and "would put our nation on a collision course with the generally accepted, longstanding interpretation of the Geneva Conventions' prohibition on cruel and inhuman treatment of prisoners." Those conventions, he noted, were adopted in their present form in response to World War II-era atrocities.

Congress acted to improve security at nonprofit institutions that were at high risk for international terrorism. United Jewish Communities (UJC), the umbrella organization for the Jewish federation system, secured $25 million in federal grants to help such institutions. A House-Senate agreement reached in September, eagerly sought by Jewish communal organizations, set the conditions for release of the funds. The move came just two months after Pam Waechter, an employee of the Seattle Jewish Federation, was killed and five others injured after a man who claimed to be "angry at Israel" forced his way through the building's security door by holding a handgun to a teenage girl's head. The suspect, Naveed Afzal Haq, was arrested and his bail set at $50 million.

Immigration

Experts estimated that between 200,000 and a million undocumented migrants illegally crossed the U.S.-Mexican border in 2006. The total population of illegal aliens, placed at 8–12 million in 2003 by Tom Ridge, who was then secretary of homeland security, had grown to as many as 20 million by the end of 2006. CNN anchor Lou Dobbs made the situation the mantra of his nightly newscast, becoming a part of the story himself while drawing attention to an immigration system that, most agreed, was in need of repair. Suggested solutions ranged from amnesty for those already in the U.S. and temporary worker programs to allow American businesses—especially agricultural—to benefit from the cheaper labor supply, to increased border security and the construction of a fence stretching all across the 2,000-mile length of the border.

The issue was a priority for several American Jewish groups, especially HIAS, AJC, JCPA, and Reform Judaism's RAC, all of which devoted resources on their Web sites to the complicated issue. Although far from unchallenged, the consensus in Washington and among the Jewish groups favored "comprehensive" immigration reform. Elements of such an approach included "earned" legal status, enhanced border security and enforcement, cross-border cooperation, increased worker protections, penalties for employers knowingly hiring undocumented workers, and expediting the backlog of family-reunification cases. Even President Bush broke ranks with hardliners in his own party by supporting an ostensible path to citizenship for those in the country illegally.

In the end, though, hopes for a comprehensive solution were dashed. Congress, fearful of facing voters without doing anything about immigration, settled on a fix that was heavy on law enforcement and measures such as the fence, and weak on those provisions endorsed by pro-immigrant groups. Congress passed and the president signed the Secure Fence Act, authorizing construction of up to 700 miles of fencing across the southern border. The project could cost as much as $9 billion.

The immigration debate also took other forms. On July 1, a new rule went into effect requiring American citizens applying for or receiving Medicaid to show proof of citizenship. Critics said the regulation could harm eligible beneficiaries who, for various reasons, might be unable to produce the necessary documentation. Also, several states tightened procedures at polling stations to prevent those who were not citizens from voting. Liberal groups decried these moves as voter intimidation.

The Environment

The House passed the U.S.-Israel Energy Cooperation Act. Championed by the American Jewish Congress, this bill would create a grant program to foster joint research between U.S. and Israeli scientists to develop renewable and sustainable sources of energy. The grants would total $140 million dollars over the next seven years.

The Coalition on the Environment and Jewish Life (COEJL) launched a nationwide campaign to address the global warming crisis. The campaign, called "A Light among the Nations," combined education, awareness, advocacy, and action to conserve energy and reduce greenhouse gas emissions. The centerpiece of the program was to get Jews to install energy-efficient, cost-effective, compact fluorescent light (CFL) bulbs during Hanukkah 2006. COEJL noted that if every U.S. household replaced one bulb with a CFL, it would have the same impact as removing 1.3 million cars from the road.

CIVIL RIGHTS AND INDIVIDUAL LIBERTIES

Voting Rights

The Jewish community enthusiastically supported extension of the Voting Rights Act, the 1965 law that removed many obstacles to the franchise, such as literacy tests, and required federal approval (pre-clearance) to change voting rules in certain jurisdictions. Congress rejected amendments to the bill that would have weakened its provisions, such as the requirement that translators or multilingual ballots be provided for non-English-speaking voters. On July 27, President Bush signed a 25-year extension of the act.

Claims of voter fraud, often unsubstantiated, were a rallying cry behind a handful of state legislative efforts to enact more stringent requirements for voting. In Georgia, a bill requiring photographic identification for voting in person was challenged on the grounds that it could infringe on the rights of citizens lacking such identification. More than two dozen civil rights groups sent a letter urging the Department of Justice to block the law. Among those signing were the Atlanta chapters of AJC, ADL, and NCJW, as well as the Atlanta Black-Jewish Coalition and the JCPA. In Arizona, a federal court removed an injunction and allowed enforcement of an identification law for voting that had been approved in a referendum.

The U.S. House of Representatives considered a similar measure for federal elections. The proposed bill would force states to enact proof-of-citizenship requirements for voter registration. Critics said the measure would disenfranchise American citizens, particularly poor, elderly, disabled, minority, and rural voters.

The Supreme Court upheld the controversial 2003 redistricting of several congressional districts in Texas, permitting former U.S. House majority leader Tom DeLay's unusual move to redraw district lines a second time within the same ten-year census period. The court held that one of the districts, however, had to be reconfigured because its new composition constituted racial gerrymandering. The DeLay plan had shifted six seats to the Republican column in 2004, ousting longtime Jewish congressman Martin Frost. In the 2006 election, two of the seats Republicans gained then moved back into Democratic hands.

Church-State Issues

FREE-EXERCISE AND ESTABLISHMENT MATTERS

The U.S. Supreme Court upheld a portion of the 1993 Religious Freedom Restoration Act (RFRA), ruling in *Gonzales v. O Centro* that Congress had the constitutional authority to require that if actions of the federal government burdened free exercise of religion they were only permissible if they served a compelling government interest. The case involved a church's use of a tea containing a substance barred under federal law. In 1990, in a case involving ritual use of peyote, another controlled substance, the Supreme Court had struck down the "compelling interest" test. In response, Congress passed RFRA in 1993 to prevent federal o-state governments from enacting laws placing substantial burdens on individual religious practice unless the laws served a compelling government interest and were drawn in the least restrictive manner possible. The Supreme Court struck down the part of RFRA that applied to the states in 1997, but had left until this year the question of whether the law still applied to federal legislation.

In September, the House approved by a vote of 244-172 the Veterans' Memorials, Boy Scouts, Public Seals, and Other Public Expressions of Religion Protection Act of 2006. The bill would prevent plaintiffs in Establishment Clause cases from recouping attorneys' fees. The Senate, however, did not consider the proposal before the recess. The legislation was part the "American Values Agenda," a Republican package of legislation dealing with a number of matters, including the Pledge of Allegiance, same-sex marriage, and similar issues designed to energize the party's conservative base.

The two largest Jewish defense agencies, ADL and AJC, filed briefs in a closely watched case that might become a pivotal test of so-called "faith-based initiatives." Ostensibly to reduce recidivism, Iowa funded Prison Fellowship Ministries to conduct a Christian program in which prisoners were granted special benefits for participating, including the chance for early parole. This evangelical Christian program was founded by former Nixon White House counsel Charles Colson, who had served seven months in prison himself for obstruction of justice during Watergate. A federal district court found that the Iowa program violated the Establishment Clause, a position in line with the arguments of the Jewish organizations. At year's end an appeal was pending.

STEM-CELL RESEARCH

Therapeutic stem-cell research was one of the rare items of domestic policy that united Jewish agencies, including both the Reform and Orthodox streams. Jewish groups lined up to support research into whether embryonic stem cells — derived from the inner cell mass of developing embryos — might hold the key to treating a wide range of life-threatening conditions, due to their potential to develop into healthy organ tissue. There seemed to be a similar consensus in the country as a whole, as both houses of Congress, by comfortable margins, voted to negate President Bush's executive order of August 9, 2001, that limited federal funding to stem-cell lines derived before that date. Those margins, though, were not enough to override the president's first use of his veto power, which occurred on July 19, one day after the Senate approved the legislation 63-37, just four votes short of the two-thirds threshold needed to override the veto.

PROSELYTIZATION IN THE MILITARY

Early in the year, Mikey Weinstein, an alumnus of the U.S. Air Force Academy, announced the formation of the Military Religious Freedom Foundation to draw attention to the pervasive proselytization that he said had transformed the academy into an institution where religious minorities were harassed and intimidated (see AJYB 2006, pp. 61–63). A lawsuit filed by Weinstein against the academy for violating the rights of religious minorities was dismissed by a federal court in October 2006 on a technicality.

With elements of the religious right complaining that guidelines adopted in August 2005 prevented chaplains from invoking the name of Jesus in their prayers, the Air Force issued new "interim guidelines" in February 2006 on the place of religion in the military. The new rules reasserted the need for religious neutrality and the right of free religious expression, but also affirmed that superior officers could discuss their faith with subordinates and that chaplains could not be coerced into reciting prayers that went against their conscience (i.e., nonsectarian prayers). Jewish groups were divided over the guidelines, some praising them and others characterizing them as marking a retreat from previous efforts to restrain proselytization. After receiving a request from the Air Force in June for their input, four Jewish organizations—AJC, ADL, American Jewish Congress, and Reform Judaism's RAC—jointly presented recommendations for implementing the guidelines.

The issue was also debated in the House of Representatives. An amendment to the 2007 Defense Appropriation Act stated that "each chaplain shall have the prerogative to pray according to the dictates of the chaplain's own conscience." Rep. Steve Israel (D., N.Y.), a member of the House Armed Services Committee, argued that such language virtually guaranteed the use of prayers for proselytization, and therefore proposed adding that chaplains should "demonstrate sensitivity, respect and tolerance for all faiths present" at the prayer service. On May 4, the committee voted his suggestion down, leaving intact the original amendment. The Senate bill did not contain this language, and the discrepancy between the two versions delayed passage of the appropriations bill until late September, when a conference committee reached a compromise: th-amendment in the House version would be removed; the guidelines issued in February would not be implemented; and the matter would be reviewed in 2007.

INTERRELIGIOUS RELATIONS

Catholics and Jews

Jewish groups downplayed their disappointment that Pope Benedict XVI did not clearly condemn anti-Semitism when he visited the site of the Auschwitz-Birkenau camp in June (see below, p. 000). Jewish leaders instead emphasized positive statements from the pontiff, including that the death camp was "particularly difficult and troubling for a Christian, for a pope from Germany." He also said that the Nazis, by seeking to eliminate the Jews, "ultimately wanted to tear up the taproot of the Christian faith . . . ."

Another matter that strained relations was Vatican reaction to Israel's war against Hezballah in southern Lebanon a month later. Vatican secretary of state Angelo Cardinal Sodano issued a statement saying: "A state's right to self-defense does not exempt it from respecting the norms of international law, especially as regards the protection of civilian populations. In particular, the Holy See deplores the attack on Lebanon, a free and sovereign nation, and gives assurances of its closeness to those people who have suffered so much in the defense of their own independence." Even though Pope Benedict said that "terrorist acts or reprisals, especially when they have such tragic consequences on the civilian population, cannot be justified," American Jewish leaders believed that the Church's response was, in the words of ADL national director Abraham Foxman, "terribly one-sided and shortsighted."

Mainline Protestants and Jews

Tensions between the mainline Protestant churches and the Jewish community had been exacerbated in recent years over Middle East policies, as considerable support emerged in some church groups for divestment from Israel and companies that did business with it. These tensions continued in 2006, although there were also glimpses of reconciliation and improved understanding.

In April, leaders of the Episcopal Church, Presbyterian Church (USA), and United Church of Christ (UCC) issued statements condemning a terrorist attack outside a Tel Aviv restaurant. Clifton Kirkpatrick, the stated clerk of the Presbyterians, also called on Hamas leaders in the Palestinian government to "renounce tactics of terrorism." The UCC statement, however, sought to balance the condemnation with criticism of Israel as well, stating: "The killing or wounding of innocent people, whether they are Israelis or Palestinians can never be called legitimate . . . . As we pray for those who grieve the loss of loved ones from this recent attack, we also pray for all who suffer from the impact of the occupation and the separation barrier . . . ."

In June, a two-year drama reached its climax as the commissioners of the Presbyterian Church (USA) gathered in Birmingham, Alabama, for the organization's General Assembly. Over the preceding year, Presbyterians and Jews had met in more than 100 communities to discuss actions taken by the Presbyterians in 2004 deemed harmful to Jews: continued support for conversionary activities aimed at Jews; a call for removal of Israel's security barrier; a verbal attack on Christian Zionism; and an initiation of "phased, selective divestment" from "companies operating in Israel." The divestment resolution had laid all the blame on Israel, noting that the occupation of Palestinian territory is "at the root of evil acts committed against innocent people on both sides of the conflict." Since 2004, more than two dozen resolutions on the matter had been adopted by local Presbyterian groups, most calling for rescission or significant modification of the divestment action and for greater balance in the Presbyterian approach to Middle East peacemaking.

A broad coalition of national Jewish agencies wrote to the Presbyterian General Assembly saying, in part: "Our collective voices can play an instrumental role, working with the American government and others, to help Israeli, Palestinian, and other Middle Eastern leaders to pave a path toward the cessation of violence and a resumption of negotiations . . . . Divestment is a stumbling-block to all we envision collectively. Our prayer is that you permanently remove this obstacle to peace." Signing the letter were leaders from AJC, American Jewish Congress, ADL, B'nai B'rith International, Hadassah, JCPA, Jewish Labor Committee, Jewish Reconstructionist Federation, Jewish War Veterans, NCJW, OU, URJ, and United Synagogue of Conservative Judaism.

The General Assembly, by an overwhelming 483-28 vote, "replaced" the divestment language adopted in 2004. Instead, there was a new resolution stating that church holdings in the region would be subject only to "customary" practices of corporate engagement. While those practices did not rule out the sale of stock, the resolution directed that policy be implemented with an eye toward "practical realities," a "commitment to positive outcomes," and an awareness of the potential impact of strategies on "both the Israeli and Palestinian economies." The General Assembly also recognized Israel's right to defend its pre-1967 boundaries with a security barrier and lamented the pain caused by the 2004 statement. A separate resolution called suicide bombings a "crime against humanity."

Immediately after the General Assembly, however, a new crisis developed. A "Frequently Asked Questions" (FAQ) sheet was distributed regarding the divestment vote that contained several inaccurate statements seeming to suggest that the vote had not really reversed the 2004 pro-Palestinian position. When this was pointed out, yet another FAQ was produced without the objectionable language, and those present were told that either document could be used, presumably depending on the audience. The General Assembly did officially retract two statements originally included in another just-released document, "Assembly in Brief." One was a section on the divestment action that had been removed from the resolution by the drafting committee because it implied that divestment was a likely scenario, and the other was an assertion that the final vote had been taken to calm "volatile relations with the Jewish community," ignoring the strong internal opposition that had developed to the 2004 divestment action.

Controversy continued about the way the organization described its actions. Although the General Assembly had voted to "replace" the earlier divestment resolution, the Presbyterian body later said it had only "reframed" its previous position, implying that divestment had not been entirely rejected, and subsequently claimed that church policy had merely been "clarified." Even later, the Presbyterian News Service announced that the vote had been "to continue its efforts to 'engage' those multinational corporations whose business in Israel/Palestine, the church believes, promotes violence." Another element that surprised the Jewish community throughout the process was the Presbyterian insistence on meeting only with Jewish denominational bodies, excluding the defense and other agencies that had been actively involved in direct dialogue with Presbyterian leaders around the country.

Evangelicals and Jews

One result of cooling relations between Jewish and mainline Protestant groups was the lowering of barriers that had previously kept Jewish agencies from exploring closer ties with Christian evangelicals. One evangelical leader who called himself a Christian Zionist, Rev. John Hagee, announced in February the creation of a national origination, Christians United for Israel (CUFI), which would network and mobilize pro-Israel churches and their members by, among other activities, sponsoring "A Night to Honor Israel" events in American cities and an annual national lobbying conference. David Brog, former chief of staff to Senator Arlen Specter (R., Pa.), was chosen to head the group.

Whereas in years past the formation of such an organization would have elicited considerable distrust in the Jewish community, the reaction now was generally positive. Lee Wunsch, director of the Houston Jewish Federation, offered strong praise for Hagee, who was based in Houston. Wunsch noted that the minister strictly prohibited proselytizing Jews, and had raised large sums of money for Jewish causes in America as well as many millions for humanitarian aid to Israel. In some communities, top Jewish leaders attended the pro-Israel events run by CUFI, in others they stayed away. In all, CUFI programs run in 40 cities raised more than $10 million. One event alone, in San Antonio, made more than $7 million in one night.

A national consultation hosted by JCPA in New York on Jewish relations with evangelicals brought together AJC, American Jewish Congress, ADL, the Israeli embassy and consulate, the New York Jewish Community Relations Council, URJ, OU, and United Synagogue of Conservative Judaism. The participants reviewed empirical data, examined the theological and political positions of the American evangelical community, and discussed the major points of cooperation and divergence between evangelicals and Jews.

Muslims and Jews

Judea Pearl, father of murdered journalist Daniel Pearl, used the foundation he had created in his son's memory to promote dialogue and understanding between Muslims and Jews. Such programs notwithstanding, American Jewish groups continued to take a very cautious approach to relations with Muslims. Counterterrorism experts, including Daniel Pipes and Steven Emerson, delivered a continuing stream of warnings, underlining the ties between American Muslim groups and leaders with those responsible for violence against Israelis. In their search for moderate voices with which to dialogue and forge coalitions, American Jews avoided such national Muslim groups as the Council on American Islamic Relations (CAIR).

A controversy erupted in Chicago after Nation of Islam (NOI) leader Louis Farrakhan, in his Saviors' Day Speech, condemned Israel and wove conspiracy theories about alleged Jewish control of America. Jewish groups put pressure on Governor Rod Blagojevich to dismiss Claudette Marie Johnson—not only a NOI activist but also Farrakhan's director of protocol—from her position on the Illinois Commission on Discrimination and Hate Crimes when she refused to condemn Farakhan's remarks. When the governor did not dismiss her, four Jewish members of the commission resigned rather than sit alongside Johnson: local ADL director Lonnie Nasatir; Illinois Holocaust Museum director Richard Hirschhaut; Jewish federation and JCRC leader Howard Kaplan; and Lou Lang, a Democratic member of the state legislature representing Skokie.

ETHAN FELSON

Anti-Semitism

In 2006 THE SECURITY of Jews in the U.S. remained strong and anti-Semitism continued to be a marginal phenomenon. Nevertheless, there was increased anti-Zionist and anti-Israel activity and visibility in a number of disparate quarters; indeed, much anti-Semitic expression was related to the Arab-Israeli conflict, underlining once again the question of "threshold"—at what point does criticism of the policies of the State of Israel, or questioning the legitimacy of the state, cross the line into anti-Semitism?

Assessing Anti-Semitism

The Jewish community in the U.S.—the largest concentration of Jews in the world outside Israel—experienced remarkably low levels of anti-Semitic expression, both behavioral and attitudinal, in 2006. This followed a 50-year pattern that reflected the strengths of a pluralistic society, even as intergroup tensions in general continued to concern political leaders and social analysts.

There are a number of criteria for assessing anti-Semitism—actions and statements on the part of public officials and religious communities, political developments, attitudinal surveys, and so on. In 2006 there were no new data from attitudinal surveys; the Anti-Defamation League (ADL), long a generator of such data, announced that it was planning a new round of surveys in 2007 and 2008.

According to the ADL's annual *Audit of Anti-Semitic Incidents,* there was a decline in such incidents in the U.S. for the second consecutive year in 2006. The overall total of 1,554 was down 12 percent from the 1,757 reported in 2005. (The average annual total during the ten-year period 1996–2005 was 1,618.) While social scientists had long questioned the significance of an audit that reports on relatively few incidents in a population approaching 300 million—and the nature of the reporting itself—the *Audit* remained a useful indicator.

To be sure, the year was marked by some violent attacks, most notably the shooting spree that occurred at the Greater Seattle Jewish Federation on July 28, when Naveed Afzal Haq, a 30-year-old U.S. citizen of Pakistani descent, killed staffer Pamela Waechter and seriously wounded five others. Haq, who allegedly forced his way through a security door

90

by holding a gun to a 13-year-old girl's head, began shooting after telling staff members that he was "a Muslim American" who was "angry at Israel." He surrendered shortly afterwards. That attack and others underscored a continuing threat to Jewish community institutions, particularly at a time of heightened conflict in the Middle East.

In 2006, cases of harassment against Jews decreased by 22 percent, with 885 incidents reported as compared to 1,140 in 2005. Acts of vandalism increased by 8 percent to 669, up from 617 incidents reported in 2005 and 644 in 2004. Examples ranged from synagogue desecration to swastikas and other anti-Jewish graffiti painted on schools, private homes, and public buildings. Vandalism accounted for 43 percent of the total of incidents reported in the ADL *Audit,* as compared to 35 percent in 2005, while harassment of individuals—less violent but more direct and personal —constituted 57 percent, as compared to 65 percent in 2005. (Incidents of harassment have predominated since 1991; before that, more instances of vandalism were reported.)

As in previous years, the states with the highest numbers of incidents were New York (284, down from 381 in 2005); New Jersey (244, down from 266); California (204, down from 247); Florida (179, down from 199); Massachusetts (96, up from 93); Pennsylvania (94, down from 95); and Connecticut (77, up from 57).

In 2006, a total of 77 incidents related to racist and/or ultra-right-wing activity were recorded, a decline from 112 in 2005, a drop possibly related to the factional infighting within these groups (see below).

There were 193 incidents of anti-Semitic harassment and vandalism reported at middle schools and high schools. In the eight states with the highest overall totals of anti-Semitic acts in 2006, 15 percent of all incidents were school based, compared to 13 percent in 2005. These included swastikas painted or scratched on desks, walls, and other school property, as well as name-calling, slurs, mockery, and bullying.

On college campuses there were 88 anti-Semitic incidents reported in 2006, a decrease of 10 percent from the 98 reported in 2005 but still more than the 2004 total of 74. Besides vandalism of property belonging to Jewish student organizations, some actions were included in this category that escalated from antiwar and anti-Israel rallies and demonstrations to harassment of Jewish students and other anti-Semitic phenomena, placing them beyond the category of mere political expression.

The Federal Hate Crime Statistics Act (HCSA) required the Justice Department to gather data on crimes that manifested prejudice based on race, religion, sexual orientation, disability or ethnicity from law enforcement agencies across the country, and to publish an annual summary of its findings. According to FBI statistics for 2005 (the most recent available), 7,163 criminal incidents involving 8,380 offenses were reported that resulted from such bias. Of these, 17.1 percent (1,227) were motivated by religious prejudice. In that category, 68.5 percent were anti-Jewish and 11.1 percent anti-Islamic. These numbers were down marginally from those reported in 2004. According to the ADL, two of the largest American cities — New York and Phoenix — did not submit hate-crime data in time to be included in the report, and thousands of smaller police agencies did not participate in the FBI data-collection effort.

Another way of looking at anti-Semitism is to measure how Jews themselves perceive it. According the *2006 Annual Survey of American Jewish Opinion,* conducted for the American Jewish Committee (AJC) by Market Facts, Inc., 26 percent of American Jews said that anti-Semitism was a "very serious problem" and 65 percent that it was a "somewhat serious problem." These data were virtually identical to those found in 2005. Thirty-two percent of those surveyed said that "most" Muslims were anti-Semitic and 27 percent placed "many" Muslims in that category, deeming Muslims far more prone to anti-Semitism than any other American religious or ethnic group.

Intergroup Relations and Anti-Semitism

MAINLINE PROTESTANTS AND DIVESTMENT

The Presbyterian Church (U.S.A.) had been in the forefront of the movement for "divestment," the withdrawal of funds invested in Israel, Israeli companies, or companies doing business with Israel (see AJYB 2005, p. 164; 2006, p. 67). On June 15, 2006, the group's General Assembly met to reconsider its position. While many observers expected this body to send the matter back to the churches for further study, it instead voted to replace its 2004 position advocating "phased selective divestment" from Israel with a new, more balanced resolution. The church would now hold companies working in Israel to the same standards demanded of recipients of its other investments. There was also a change in the Presbyterian stance on Israel's security barrier, no longer calling for its removal but instead focusing on problems with its location. The 2006 resolution also acknowledged the "pain and misunderstanding" to "Jewish friends" caused by the 2004 statement. Even though it became evident after the resolution's passage that certain Presbyterian elements were eager to minimize its significance (see above, p. 87), the Jewish community saw it as a significant step forward.

EVANGELICALS, JEWS, AND THE AIR FORCE ACADEMY

In the aftermath of the 2005 flare-up over evangelical-sponsored activities at the U.S. Air Force Academy in Colorado Springs (see AJYB 2006, pp. 61–63), the Air Force, in February 2006, issued revised guidelines that marked something of a compromise: while barring chaplains from invoking the name of Jesus during official ceremonies, they also stated that "nothing in this guidance should be understood to limit the discussion of voluntary discussion of religion, or the exercise of free speech, where it is reasonably free of the potential for coercion." On the floor of the House of Representatives opposition was voiced by some Republican members, who viewed the guidelines as too restrictive, but also, for the opposite reason, from some Democrats like Rep. Gary Ackerman (D., N.Y.), who asked, "'Reasonably free'? What does that mean? You're talking about the military, about a guy who has a lot of stripes on his arm."

Jewish leaders and groups were split over the new guidelines. The ADL opposed them. AJC, the American Jewish Congress, and the Religion Action Center of Reform Judaism issued a joint statement commending the Air Force for issuing the guidelines, which, it said, "go far in addressing the unfortunate situation which prevailed at the Air Force Academy." Richard Foltin, the AJC legislative director, said, "It is important that steps be taken to ensure these guidelines be implemented in the spirit in which they were intended, which was to provide clear lines that ought not be crossed" (see above, pp. 84–85).

CATHOLICS AND JEWS

Pope Benedict XVI, now in the second full year of his papacy, had an unusual opportunity to address the subject of anti-Semitism when he visited the Auschwitz-Birkenau death camp complex in Poland on May 28. Although the pope's words were moving, he failed to speak directly about the Jewish victims of the Holocaust or to mention that the day before, Polish chief rabbi Michael Schudrich had been attacked on a Warsaw street by a man yelling, "Poland is for Poles," suggesting that the Jew-hatred that fueled the Holocaust was hardly extinct (see below, pp. 495–96).

Jewish officials, used to the more effusive and publicly sympathetic Pope John Paul II, generally kept their disappointment to themselves and praised the pope's decision to go to Auschwitz. But Father John Pawlikowski, a Chicago-based theologian and a leader in American Catholic-Jewish relations, noted with regret the "omission of any strong statement on anti-Semitism past and present and the Church's own role in propagating it, including among affiliated Catholic groups in Poland today."

Two days after the pope's Auschwitz visit, Edward Cardinal Egan, archbishop of New York, spoke in that city's Jewish Center, a large Orthodox synagogue, where he stressed the need for Jews and Catholics to work together on issues of common concern. Observers of Catholic-Jewish relations viewed his presentation as symptomatic of the warm ties between the two religions in the U.S., which contrasted with the sometimes rocky relations between Jews and the Vatican.

One matter on which many Jews had strong feelings was the ongoing Vatican process that seemed likely to lead to the canonization of Pope Pius XII, the wartime pontiff who had been criticized in many quarters for allegedly failing to speak out against the Nazi regime. To be sure, fault lines emerged within the Jewish community on this matter. ADL national director Abraham H. Foxman suggested, in December, a linkage with another issue, saying, "If the Vatican rushes to judgment on sainthood without allowing open access to the files of the Holocaust years, that would seriously damage the [Catholic-Jewish] relationship." But Rabbi David Rosen, AJC's director of international interreligious relations and president of the International Jewish Committee on Interreligious Consultations (IJCIC), said that while canonizing the wartime pope would create unhappiness among Jews, it would not rupture Catholic-Jewish relations. Rosen characterized Foxman's position as "apocalyptic," and stated: "It is a fallacy to suggest that opening the archives would resolve the debate over Pius, since the difference between the two sides is substantive in nature. Catholics look at the evidence and say, 'Pius did everything he could to save the Jews.' We see it differently and no amount of new evidence will change that."

Mel Gibson, the actor and director whose 2004 film, *The Passion of the Christ,* raised fears of anti-Semitism (see AJYB 2005, pp. 160–63), was back in the news in 2006 for his anti-Jewish venom. Following an arrest for drunk driving in Malibu, California, on July 28, he blurted out a barrage of vulgar anti-Semitic remarks to the arresting officer, who he believed was Jewish. Gibson subsequently apologized profusely, saying, "I am asking the Jewish community, whom I have personally offended, to help me on my journey to recovery," and "Please know from my heart that I am not an anti-Semite." In January, an important book was published that provided the broad historical context for Gibson's 2004 film. Its title was *Christ Killers: The Jews and the Passion from the Bible to the Big Screen.* The author, Jeremy Cohen, was professor of history at Tel Aviv University.

Blacks and Jews

In his annual Saviours' Day Address delivered in Chicago in February, Minister Louis Farrakhan, the Nation of Islam (NOI) leader with a long anti-Semitic record, blamed Jews and Israel for the war in Iraq, claimed that Jews controlled Hollywood, and charged them with promoting "immorality." By September, weakened by illness, Farrakhan relinquished the leadership role he had held for nearly 30 years. Some observers suggested that the NOI would fold without Farrakhan, but others expected a battle for succession, with Ishmael Muhammad, Farrakhan's assistant minister at Mosque Maryam in Chicago (and son of former NOI leader Elijah Muhammad), considered the strongest contender.

The New Black Panther Party (NBPP), the largest anti-white (and anti-Semitic) black militant group in the country, continued to capitalize on media interest in racially charged issues by organizing protests—often threatening violence—under the guise of championing black empowerment and civil rights. Cloaking a conspiracy-oriented worldview in religious and democratic rhetoric, NBPP figures managed to achieve frequent appearances on national television during the year. In an interview on "The O'Reilly Factor," for example, NBPP leader Malik Zulu Shabazz blamed Jews for creating negative images of blacks, and Zionists for terrorist attacks against them. Shabazz sought to strengthen the organization's influence by solidifying relationships with street gangs and developing close ties with the NOI, joining Farrakhan at the Saviours' Day convention. There was some speculation that some NOI members might switch their allegiance to the NBPP once Farrakhan was out of the picture.

The Campuses

After the turmoil of the previous two years, 2006 was relatively quiet on the nation's campuses. There were, however, a number of incidents. Brandeis University—a secular, nonsectarian institution even though

it was Jewish-sponsored and had a majority Jewish student body—
encountered some opposition from donors over the appointment to the
faculty of Khalil Shikaki, a political scientist who, according to the Zionist Organization of America, had once had ties to the Palestinian terrorist group Islamic Jihad. Shikaki was made a senior fellow at the
university's Crown Center for Middle East Studies (see below, p. 118).

Another controversial university appointment came up at Yale regarding Juan Cole, one of the country's top Middle East scholars. In June,
Yale's tenure committee voted down his appointment after he had been
approved by the history and sociology departments. Cole was known for
his pro-Palestinian views, and a number of Jewish donors to Yale made
their disapproval known. In December, the university opened the Yale Initiative for the Interdisciplinary Study of Anti-Semitism, reportedly the
first such university-based program in America.

At the University of California at Irvine, where tensions between
Muslim and Jewish students had simmered for some time, Chancellor
Michael V. Drake drew severe criticism for not publicly deploring anti-
Israel activities surrounding a series of lectures and symposia, "Holocaust
in the Holy Land," held at an annual weeklong event in May. Drake de-
fended what happened by citing the right to free speech on campus.

An important contribution to the debate over how Zionism was treated
on many college campuses appeared in the spring issue of *Jewish Political Studies Review,* "The Columbia University Report on its Middle Eastern Department's Problems: A Paradigm Obscuring Structural Flaws,"
by Noah Liben.

The "New" Anti-Semitism

Debate continued during 2006 over whether criticism of Israel and
Zionism had become the "new anti-Semitism." For those who thought it
had, a prime example appeared in the March 26 issue of the *London Review of Books,* "The Israel Lobby and U.S. Foreign Policy," by John
Mearsheimer, an international-relations theorist at the University of
Chicago, and Stephen Walt, the academic dean at Harvard's John F.
Kennedy School of Government (their essay appeared in longer form on
the Kennedy School Web site). These scholars depicted "the Israel
Lobby" as a "loose coalition" of politicians, media outlets, research institutions, Jewish groups, and evangelical Christians that steered—indeed, had a stranglehold on—American Middle East policy, which it
directed towards Israel's benefit even if such a course harmed American

interests. To many observers, this argument seemed reminiscent of the classic anti-Semitic charges that Jews exercise undue influence over key institutions in society and that their attachments to parochial Jewish interests override loyalty to the state.

Specifically, the report revived the claim that Jewish and pro-Israel groups played a major role in pressing for the Iraq war in 2003. "The charge isn't new," observed Martin Raffel, associate director of the Jewish Council for Public Affairs (JCPA). "But this is Harvard and the University of Chicago we're talking about; it's the credibility of the writers." Initially, Jewish groups were torn between a reluctance to engage in frontal debate with the two scholars, on the one hand, and a strong desire to discredit their arguments, on the other. "The key," said Malcolm Hoenlein, executive vice president of the Conference of Presidents of Major American Jewish Organizations, "is not to have them say that they are being silenced." Instead, Jewish groups hoped for rebuttals to emerge from the academic community. Analytical treatment of the Walt-Mearsheimer essay varied widely, from outright dismissal on the grounds of anti-Semitism to overall agreement with the thesis, even if some of the details were wrong. Walt and Mearsheimer, meanwhile, were at work on a book-length version, scheduled for 2007 publication by Farrar, Straus & Giroux.

The controversy was replayed in late September when the *London Review of Books* staged a lively debate in New York featuring Mearsheimer, Tony Judt—the New York University professor who had argued in the *New York Review of Books* in 2004 against the legitimacy of the State of Israel—Columbia University's Rashid Khalidi, former Israeli foreign minister Shlomo Ben-Ami, and U.S. Middle East specialists Martin Indyk and Dennis Ross.

Judt, meanwhile—who had argued in a *New York Times* op-ed on April 19 that the charge of anti-Semitism against Walt and Mearsheimer amounted to censorship of their legitimate charges against Israel's supporters—became, he believed, another victim of the same tactic several months later. On October 3, less than three hours before he was to give a talk at the Polish consulate about the "Lobby," Poland's consul general, Krzysztof Kasprzyk, abruptly canceled the event after being contacted by some organizations. ADL director Foxman acknowledged that his agency had talked with Kasprzyk, but denied urging cancellation of the speech. Judt commented in an e-mail, "This is, or used to be, the United States of America."

The imputation of censorship aroused considerable concern. A strong protest letter signed by 113 intellectuals and academics, published in the *New York Review of Books,* asserted: "What does surprise and disturb us is that an organization dedicated to promoting civil rights and public education [the ADL] should threaten and exert pressure to cancel a public lecture by an important scholar." Foxman responded by denying any exertion of pressure on the consul general and complaining that the authors of the letter "did not seek me out to get the perspective of the ADL." A number of observers hostile to the Walt-Mearsheimer position noted that diverting the discussion to the issue of censorship served to make the two men into martyrs in the cause of free expression and minimize attention to the weakness of their case.

That same month, an award-winning anti-Israel play about the Gaza occupation, *I Am Rachel Corrie,* opened at the New York Theatre Workshop. It had originally been scheduled to open in May, but was cancelled—according to the workshop's artistic director—due to pressure from "Jewish leaders."

And if all of this were not enough, former president Jimmy Carter's book, *Palestine: Peace Not Apartheid,* was released on November 14. In it, Carter characterized Israeli activities in the West Bank as being "even worse" than the apartheid policies of the old white supremacist government in South Africa, and, like Walt and Mearsheimer, accused pro-Israel groups of stifling legitimate debate on U.S. Middle East policy. Response from Jewish leaders was immediate. The ADL's Abraham Foxman charged that Carter was "engaging in anti-Semitism," and AJC executive director David Harris, noting that the Carter affair followed hard on the heels of Walt-Mearsheimer, suggested that "what's particularly worrisome is the accretion factor." Analysts, noting that the South Africa analogy—which, by its racial nature, also conjured up Nazi policies— was deeply offensive to most American Jews, recalled that the former president had always had a troubled relationship with Israel. Those interested in the political fallout wondered if the book might harm traditional Jewish support for Democratic candidates, and major figures in the party dissociated themselves from Carter's views on the subject.

A key publication that sharpened and informed the controversy over the blurry boundary between anti-Semitism and hostility to Israel was Alvin H. Rosenfeld's *"Progressive" Jewish Thought and the New Anti-Semitism,* published by AJC in December. Rosenfeld argued that a number of Jews, primarily academics of the liberal/left persuasion (he named names and provided quotations), were feeding a rise in anti-Semitism by questioning Israel's right to exist or, in more euphemistic terms, urging a "one-state solution" that would inevitably bring the Jewish state to an end. The publication evoked great hostility, as Rosenfeld was charged with seeking to intimidate Jewish critics of Israeli policies by conflating them with anti-Semites, and making unwarranted generalizations about "progressives." But he had his defenders. Brandeis University sociologist Shulamit Reinharz, for example, told the *Boston Jewish Advocate* that "in a world in which there is only one Jewish state, to oppose it vehemently is to endanger Jews." Acknowledging that the publication "deals with matters of great sensitivity," AJC research director David Singer said, "[The essay] is an act of courage on the part of AJC and the author."

Arts, Letters, and Anti-Semitism

Playwright David Mamet took a controversial position on anti-Semitism in his 2006 book, *The Wicked Son: Anti-Semitism, Self-Hatred, and the Jews.* Many reviewers suggested that he seriously overstated the extent of anti-Semitism in the U.S., apparently harking back to a period when American Jews, for good reason, were profoundly insecure. Another provocative work dealing with anti-Semitism was Princeton sociologist Jan Gross's *Fear: Anti-Semitism in Poland After Auschwitz.* Sparing no detail in illuminating the full extent of Polish malevolence toward Jews in the aftermath of the Nazi defeat, Gross encountered criticism from those who thought he missed the highly nuanced, centuries-old relationship between Poles and Jews. A third book that touched on anti-Semitism was *Shylock Is Shakespeare,* by Kenneth Gross, which theorized that Shylock, like his creator, was a product of profound artistic and personal isolation whose success came at great personal costs. Finally, AJC issued Kenneth S. Stern's *Anti-Semitism Today: How It Is the Same, How It Is Different, and How to Fight It,* which summarized much of the data about recent expressions of anti-Semitism worldwide.

A serious crisis emanating from works of art began with the publication of cartoons in the mass-circulation Danish daily *Jylands-Posten* in September, 2005, which depicted the Prophet Mohammed. While Muslim anger led to riots and boycotts in many parts of the world, American Jewish communal leaders pointed out that the same Muslim governments that condemned the cartoons routinely allowed the publication of anti-Semitic cartoons. "It's the pot calling the kettle black," said David Harris, AJC's executive director. Muslim groups, for their part, accused Western organizations and governments of censoring views offensive to Jews while defending attacks on Muslims under the guise of free speech.

The opening, in November, of comedian Sacha Baron Cohen's spoof film *Borat: Cultural Learnings of America for Make Benefit Glorious Nation of Kazakhstan,* provided an opportunity for both comic relief and serious discussion of anti-Semitism in the arts. The central character, played by Cohen, was casually anti-Semitic, and viewers differed over whether the satirical nature of the movie encouraged anti-Semitism or made it a butt of ridicule.

The United States Holocaust Memorial Museum hosted an exhibition in April, "A Dangerous Lie," on the history and contemporary significance of the old anti-Semitic libel, the *Protocols of the Learned Elders of Zion.* It focused particularly but not exclusively on the use made of the *Protocols* in Muslim and Arab lands.

Anti-Semitism and the Political Arena

There were only a few, minor expressions of anti-Semitism in politics during 2006. Perhaps the most significant was language in the biennial platform of the Texas Republican party, issued in June, that America was a "Christian nation," and describing separation of church and state as a "myth." Jewish members of the state party criticized these planks of the platform, while leaders of the organized Jewish community there acknowledged that they had expended most of their energy in opposing pro-Palestinian planks.

On June 14, Rep Steven King (R., Iowa) wrote a letter to the ADL demanding that it apologize for defaming him by claiming that he compared illegal immigrants to Nazis. The congressman, who was strongly opposed to illegal immigration, said in a speech on May 22 that "We have a slow-motion holocaust on our hands," referring to Americans killed by illegal immigrants. King explained to the ADL, "I never capitalized the word 'Holocaust.'"

The question of the cynical use of anti-Semitism for political purposes was addressed in September by Sam Gejdenson, a former Democratic congressman from Connecticut. In an op-ed article in the *Forward* (Sept. 26), Gejdenson objected to repeated Republican allegations that Democrats were insufficiently supportive of Israel. Gejdenson pointed to the use by conservative commentators of anti-Semitic posts on progressive on-line sites to argue that the entire political left—and, by implication, the Democratic Party—was anti-Semitic. Said Gejdenson, "The use of anti-Semitism for blatant political purposes should have no place in the American political dialogue."

On the local level, New York City, in September, approved tax-exempt bond financing for a not-for-profit arts group that was founded by Lenora Fulani, a leader of the Independence Party and an activist in a bizarre political cult. She had, over the years, run for virtually every city office, in the course of which she had made numerous anti-Semitic remarks. The lone voice in opposition to the financing plan was that of New York State comptroller Alan Hevesi, who said, "Providing financial assistance to a misogynistic and anti-Semitic cult is tantamount to providing public validation of and support for these ideas."

AIPAC's legal problems, which began back in 2004, continued in 2006, and some believed that the drawn-out saga could have anti-Semitic implications. In January, Pentagon analyst Larry Franklin, who had passed classified information to two AIPAC staffers, was sentenced to a harsh prison sentence, perhaps boding ill for Steven Rosen and Keith Weissman, the men who received this material and allegedly passed it on to Israel. In March, Judge T.S. Ellis, the federal judge assigned to hear the case against Rosen and Weissman, suggested that the Espionage Act under which they were being prosecuted was vague, and might be unconstitutional. A *Time* magazine report in October claimed that the FBI investigation of AIPAC had been expanded to include possible meddling in the affairs of the House Intelligence Committee. There were claims that Rep. Jane Harman (D., Calif.) had entered into a deal with AIPAC whereby the latter would support Harman's bid to become the next chair of the House Intelligence Committee if Harman would press the government to drop the charges against Rosen and Weissman. Both sides denied the report. At year's end, Rosen and Weissman were reported to be considering suing AIPAC for having stopped payment of their legal fees.

Jewish groups not only speculated about possible anti-Semitic motives behind the government's pursuit of the case, but also worried over potential anti-Semitic fallout, particularly involving the "dual loyalty" issue: the charges against the former AIPAC people could well be linked in the public mind with the "Israel Lobby" and its alleged clout in the determination of American foreign policy.

Extremist Groups and Activities

While the main focus of American Jewish concern was anti-Semitic stereotyping and anti-Israel propaganda, there were still extremist organizations, mostly racist and/or neo-Nazi, that sometimes engaged in threats, vandalism, and violence. In 2006, according to the ADL *Audit,* there were 77 incidents ascribed to extremists as compared to 112 in 2005, a significant decline possibly related to factional infighting within these groups. In addition, the national discussion over illegal immigration, with rallies and protests that drew much attention, presumably diverted extremist energies away from some of their usual targets and toward Hispanics. The anti-Jewish activity that did take place generally took the form of leafleting, rallies, and distribution of hate propaganda, often via the Internet.

Racist organizations in the U.S. underwent a number of important developments in 2006. As the year began, the National Socialist Movement (NSM), a Minneapolis-based organization descended from the 1960s-era American Nazi Party, was the largest neo-Nazi group in the country. Its members, who wore Nazi uniforms at rallies, called for a "Greater America" that would deny citizenship to Jews, nonwhites, and homosexuals. By summer, however, internal strife led to the ouster or resignation of several high-profile leaders, including the media liaison, Bill White, and the chairman, Cliff Herrington. Each man proceeded to start his own new organization, White establishing the American National Socialist Workers Party (ANSWP) and Herrington the National Socialist Freedom Movement, which existed primarily on the Internet.

The National Alliance (NA) in 2006 had a small, largely inactive membership. In June, federal authorities arrested Shaun Walker, its leader, in his West Virginia compound after a federal grand jury in Salt Lake City indicted him on conspiracy to interfere with civil rights and with a federally protected activity. Two other NA members, Travis Massey and Eric Egbert, were arrested in Utah on the same charges. According to the indictment, between December 2002 and March 2003, the three conspired to threaten, provoke, and fight with minorities in order to deter them from living in and around Salt Lake City.

The National Vanguard, led by former NA activist Kevin Strom, had been created out of an organizational split within the NA in April 2005. By March 2006, however, the Tampa and Denver Vanguard units, two of the largest and most active, split off to form yet another organization, the Nationalist Coalition.

By 2006, Volksfront, based in Portland, Oregon, had become one of the most active white-supremacist groups on the West Coast. One of its primary goals was to establish an autonomous "whites only" living space in the Pacific Northwest, and to this end the group claimed to have purchased several acres of property in Oregon. Many members of Volksfront had records of conviction for violent hate crimes. In August, for example, two brothers, Jacob and Gabriel Laskey, pleaded guilty in a federal court in Portland, Oregon, to throwing swastika-etched rocks at Temple Beth Israel in Eugene during a religious service in 2002.

On the Klan front, the Ku Klux Klan (KKK), with more than 40 active groups—most with multiple chapters, or "klaverns," around the country—increased its activities in 2006. The KKK's central issue remained immigration, a mainstream concern that Klan leaders believed would gain new adherents for the movement. The Tennessee-based Brotherhood of Klans (BOK) organized a series of events in 2006 that included "unity" gatherings for white supremacists. The BOK also established new chapters in many parts of the country. Among the newer Klan groups, the Empire Knights of the Ku Klux Klan, based in Florida and founded largely by former members of the Southern White Knights of the Ku Klux Klan, expanded to 18 states. In the Midwest, the Michigan-based United Northern and Southern Knights of the Ku Klux Klan, created in 2005 as a splinter group that seceded from another Klan, expanded to nine states in 2006. Also, new Klan groups formed in areas where the Klan had previously been weak, such as Iowa, where Douglas Sadler established the Fraternal White Knights of the Ku Klux Klan, and in the Middle Atlantic region.

The Christian Identity movement promoted a racist and anti-Semitic agenda through the manipulation of religious themes, maintaining that people of white European ancestry descended from the Lost Tribes of Israel, and thus whites were the "chosen people" of the Bible. Identity groups in the U.S. included America's Promise Ministries of Sandpoint, Idaho; Dan Gayman's Church of Israel in Schell City, Missouri; Scriptures for America Worldwide, led by Pete Peters in Laporte, Colorado; and Kingdom Identity Ministries in Harrison, Arkansas.

Aryan Nations, a paramilitary neo-Nazi group formed in the mid-1970s that subscribed to Identity ideology, continued the decline that had begun following the death of its founder and leader, Richard Butler, in 2004. By 2006 Aryan Nations consisted of only two small factions. In May, Morris Lynn Gulett, a former high-ranking member of Aryan Nations and leader of the Church of the Sons of Yahweh, one of the group's factions, and Charles Scott Thornton of Piedmont, Alabama, were sentenced, respectively, to 72 and 60 months in prison following convictions on several charges, including conspiracy to commit armed robbery.

Since 2002 the skinhead movement in the U.S. had enjoyed a resurgence as both the number of groups and of independent skinheads increased. One of the most active skinhead groups to emerge in 2006 was the Vinlanders Social Club. Originating in Knightstown, Indiana, the Vinlanders began as a loose association of skinhead gangs from Indiana, Ohio, and Michigan. Within a short period of time the Vinlanders grew to over 100 members and close associates, and began to develop rivalries with other racist groups.

The criminal activity committed by extremist groups included murders and attempted murders of African Americans, Hispanics, multiracial couples or families, Asians, gays and lesbians, homeless people, and Jews. There were also instances of kidnapping, assault, drug trading, identity theft, and counterfeiting. A number of high-profile trials involved the Aryan Brotherhood, especially in California. One trial, in Santa Ana, resulted in the convictions of four Aryan Brotherhood leaders: Barry "The Baron" Mills, Tyler "The Hulk" Bingham, Edgar "The Snail" Hevle, and Christopher Gibson. In Texas and Oklahoma, Brotherhood members Brandon James Horne and Michael Sean Rose were charged with first-degree murder in October 2006 for the alleged killing of a prison inmate who was a sex offender.

On November 28, a federal court in Jackson, Tennessee, sentenced white supremacist Demetrius "Van" Crocker to 30 years in prison, plus lifetime supervised release, for trying to obtain ingredients for Sarin nerve gas and C-4 explosives from an undercover agent. During his trial, a jury heard hours of taped conversations between Crocker and the undercover agent during which Crocker talked about exploding a bomb and releasing Sarin gas outside a courthouse, making batches of poisoned marijuana to kill black residents of Jackson, and spraying African American neighborhoods with mustard gas from a helicopter. Crocker also told the agent that he hated Jews and admired Adolf Hitler.

Many regional racist gangs caused problems in 2006. Michael David Cottler, a member of the Nazi Low Riders (NLR), was arrested in August for allegedly conspiring with another man in prison to murder a California Highway Patrol officer who was going to testify against one of them in court. In Maricopa County, Arizona, federal and local authorities arrested 42 members of a racist skinhead gang known as the AZ 88 Boot Boys ("88" is neo-Nazi code for "Heil Hitler"), including leader Todd Streich, on weapons and drug charges. Most were from Phoenix and Glendale. These arrests, which took place in May, resulted from a 14-month, multi-agency investigation.

Anti-government militia groups continued to conduct paramilitary training in relative secrecy. The revived Internet militia discussion board, "A Well Regulated Militia," as well as individual militia Web sites and lists, were used to stimulate recruitment. War veterans, especially targeted because of their training, were viewed as potential leaders. Popular topics of discussion were immigration, skepticism about the government's "war on terrorism," and rumors about a future North American Union that would unite the U.S., Canada, and Mexico. Racist and anti-Semitic themes were not uncommon.

Following his release from prison in May 2004, former Ku Klux Klan leader David Duke continued promoting his anti-Semitic theories both in the U.S. and abroad (see AJYB 2006, p. 84). In March 2006, Duke praised Mearsheimer and Walt's "The Israel Lobby and U.S. Foreign Policy," which claimed that an "Israel Lobby" controlled American foreign policy (see above, pp. 96–98). Duke claimed that their work "validated" his own assertions over the years, and he made a rare appearance on mainstream television on March 21, when he was interviewed by Joe Scarborough on the MSNBC program "Scarborough Country." In October he addressed an audience at the MAUP (Interregional Academy of Personnel Management) in Ukraine — which had awarded him a doctorate in history in 2005 — on the topic of Zionist influence (see below, p. 000). December found Duke in Tehran for President Ahmadinejad's Holocaust-denial conference, where he publicly reiterated his view that Zionists control and manipulate governments. He condemned the war in Iraq "being fought on behalf of Israel" and the imprisonment in Europe of Holocaust deniers, whom he referred to as "scholars and researchers."

Hal Turner, an independent New Jersey-based white supremacist who previously belonged to the National Alliance, hosted an Internet radio show that spewed hardcore anti-Semitism, and his Hal Turner Radio Network provided air time to other white supremacists. During the year Turner repeatedly encouraged listeners to attack and to kill Jews, Hispanics, and federal officials.

The Left and the Lebanon War

Antiwar rallies organized throughout the country during the summer in response to Israel's war in Lebanon and military strikes in the Gaza Strip — both precipitated by the kidnapping of Israeli soldiers — often included support for terrorist groups, calls for the destruction of Israel, the equation of Zionism with Nazism, and outright anti-Semitism.

Indeed, many on the far left conflated these hostilities with the war in

Iraq, so that Israel's conflict with Hezballah in Lebanon validated the notion that the fundamentalist Shi'ite movement, Iraqi insurgents, and Palestinian terror organizations constituted an important ideological partner of progressive movements in the West.

One typical sign at the largest anti-Israel rally, in Washington, D.C., featured a Star of David with the caption: "The Nazis are back." One protester at a rally in San Francisco on August 12 held a sign that proclaimed: "Nazi kikes out of Lebanon." At several of the rallies, crowds called on Hezballah to bomb Israeli cities. A common chant in Arabic, with variations, was: "Nasrallah, dear: bomb Tel Aviv . . . bomb Kiryat Shmona." (At the time, Hezballah was bombing northern Israel and threatening to hit Tel Aviv). Speakers at the rallies denounced U.S. support for Israel, which many blamed on Israel's alleged stranglehold on American policy. At a demonstration in Dearborn, Michigan, in July, one speaker said, "We know that the president is being bought by the Zionist lobby. We know that the Congress is being bought by the Zionist lobby."

Anti-Semitism on the Internet and the Web

The Internet continued to play a substantial role in the dissemination of anti-Semitism, with hate literature being transmitted through hundreds of sites on the Web and through bulletin boards, chat rooms and, e-mail messages. Hate groups actively contributed to the continued Internet circulation of anti-Jewish conspiracy charges related to the events of September 11, 2001, while also promoting theories of Jewish control of government, finance, and the media.

The expansion of the extremist presence on the Internet during 2006 suggested that these groups were becoming more technologically adept. Thousands of Web sites spread racism, anti-Semitic and anti-Israel views, and Holocaust denial through the use of the latest technology, such as streaming audio, video, and e-commerce sections, as well as sophisticated flash videos and background music, along with original artwork and cartoons. Many extremist groups based overseas utilized servers located within the U.S. to circumvent laws in their home countries prohibiting racist, extremist, bigoted, and anti-Semitic content.

Virtually every major U.S.-based extremist group had some form of Internet presence, and many individuals with such ideologies created their own personal sites, pages, or blogs. Conspiracy theorists maintained Web sites and e-mail lists linking current world events to Jews and Israel, and neo-Nazi sites promoted not only their own theories but advertised merchandise and magazines as well. Information about Iran's Holocaust cartoon contest and its Holocaust-denial conference was posted on-line by U.S.-based sites such as Stormfront, David Duke, Institute for Historical Review, and Vanguard News Network. International terrorists that targeted the U.S. and Israel, such as Hamas, Hezballah, and Al Qaeda-affiliated groups, were finding that U.S. Internet providers were less willing to host their materials than they had been in the past. Nevertheless, these groups managed to find ways to post and distribute their propaganda, urging audiences to participate in the "Internet jihad." Pronouncements by Al Qaeda leaders, including Osama bin Laden and Ayman al-Zawahiri, against "the Crusaders" and "the Jews" were posted in videos on-line using file-sharing services in countries around the world, including the U.S.

It was now illegal in the U.S. to have business dealings with Hezballah Web sites such as al-Manar or al-Nour radio. In 2006 the government filed a case against a person in New York for rebroadcasting al-Manar programs over cable systems and the Internet.

Responses to Anti-Semitism

Jewish groups continued to expend significant resources on programs aimed at prejudice reduction. Amongst the most visible, the ADL's "A World of Difference" (AWOD) was the subject of two evaluative-research studies. In 2006, the Yale University Evaluation Study of AWOD's Peer Training Program—a pioneering effort in high schools around the country—studied 500 students in ten schools who were involved in the program, and found that the training had "important effect on reducing bias in schools." An earlier study, conducted by the Cantor-Fitzgerald Center for Research on Diversity in Education in June, 2000, but not posted on the ADL Web site until 2006, studied AWOD pilot programs in three public-school districts in New York, Missouri, and New Jersey. It affirmed the efficacy of the programs.

Left-wing activists concerned about anti-Semitism in their own ranks gathered in New Jersey in April for a conference, "Facing the Challenge Within," which examined anti-Semitic expression in organizations of the progressive "left." It included workshops on the history and ideology of progressive Zionism and on methods of coping with anti-Zionism on campus, where left-liberal views tended to predominate. Mainstream Jewish groups applauded the event, seeing it as the possible beginning of a broader effort to influence a range of groups on the left.

On the international front, UN Watch, a Geneva-based monitoring group affiliated with AJC, launched a petition aimed at calling for the Security Council to expel Iran from the UN. This followed a similar call by Israel in the spring, after Ahmadinejad spoke publicly about wiping Israel off the map.

In September, the World Jewish Congress, notwithstanding its internal problems, convened a mission to Israel for Jewish leaders from around the world to discuss the bias attacks that followed the summer's Lebanon conflict. While the WJC meetings were inconclusive, they did reenergize the debate about whether threats to the security of Diaspora communities ought to play a role in forging Israeli policy. Along the same lines, the Jewish People Policy Planning Institute (JPPPI), a Jerusalem think tank affiliated with the quasi-governmental Jewish Agency, launched a Crisis Management Project to help leaders in Israel and Diaspora communities deal with crises involving Jews. Not all Diaspora leaders welcomed the JPPPI recommendation for Israel to consult with and aid Diaspora communities on such matters; American Jewish leaders were of the view that Israel should have a say only in regard to Israeli politics and policies, but that the security problems of Diaspora communities ought be dealt with by authorities in their respective countries.

Legislation/Law Enforcement

As of the end of 2006, 46 states and the District of Columbia had hate-crimes laws that provided for enhanced penalties.

The Hate Crimes Prevention Act/Local Law Enforcement Enhancement Act (LLEEA), S.1145 in the Senate and H.R.2662 in the House, were introduced in 2005, both with numerous cosponsors, but still awaited passage at the end of 2006. The measures, which enjoyed broad support from Jewish groups, sought to increase cooperation between local, state, and federal authorities in bringing hate-crimes offenders to justice, especially in states without special statutes. They also added gender, disability, and sexual orientation to the federally protected categories of race, color, religion, and national origin. The House bill explicitly encompassed transgendered persons as well, and provided additional First Amendment protection by stating that it did not seek to punish bias, speech, or association. On September 14, 2005, the House passed its version as an amendment to the Children's Safety Act of 2005 (H.R.3132), but in March 2006 the amendment was stripped when the Senate included the Children's Safety Act in an omnibus crime package, H.R.4472, which was signed into law July 27.

Under the provisions of the Global Anti-Semitism Awareness/Review Act of 2004, the U.S. Department of State was mandated to report on the condition of anti-Semitism throughout the world. The first report was issued in 2004 (see AJYB 2005, p. 182). The legislation had not mandated further reports.

There were a number of court decisions that bore implications for the treatment of suspected terrorists. The U.S. Supreme Court ruled on June 11 in *Hamdan v. Rumsfeld* that the military commissions established by the president to try terror suspects detained at Guantánamo Bay, Cuba, lacked "power to proceed" because their "structure and procedures" went against both the Uniform Code of Military Justice and the Geneva Conventions, the international agreements covering treatment of prisoners of war. The president could now either ask Congress for authority to proceed, or else try the detainees under the rules of traditional military courts-martial. In response to *Hamdan,* the president asked for, and Congress passed, a new Military Commissions Act that stripped detainees of their right to seek review of their detentions in federal courts. Another relevant legal case, *Boumediene v. Bush,* was pending before the Court of Appeals for the District of Columbia as the year ended. It dealt with the question of whether federal courts had jurisdiction over the habeas petitions of aliens deemed enemy combatants.

A case with important implications for hate-crimes laws around the country was *Cunningham v. California,* which was argued before the U.S. Supreme Court in October. At issue was the constitutionality of a California sentencing law that allowed judges to impose a heightened sentence based on facts found by the judge rather than the jury. In an earlier case, *Apprendi v. New Jersey,* the court had ruled that facts pertaining to hate-crime sentence enhancement must be found by juries, not judges. *Cunningham* was not yet decided at year's end.

On April 17, a federal judge approved an agreement that prosecutors made with Sami Al-Arian, a Palestinian born in Kuwait, whereby he would plead guilty to a charge of conspiring to "make or receive contributions of funds, goods or services" to, or for the benefit of, a terrorist organization, and be deported from the U.S., according to an attorney involved in the negotiations. Al-Arian and three codefendants were arrested in 2003 and charged with providing money and support to the Palestinian Islamic Jihad (see AJYB 2006, p. 90).

On July 21, the Federal District Court in Manhattan sentenced Uzair Paracha to 30 years in prison for attempting to help Majid Khan, a Pakistani member of Al Qaeda, obtain documents to travel from Pakistan to the U.S. in 2003. Paracha was convicted on all charges of a five-count federal indictment, which included conspiracy to provide and supply material support to Al Qaeda, conspiracy to provide and supply funds, goods or services to that organization, and identification-document fraud committed to facilitate an act of international terrorism.

On June 23, seven men were arrested for allegedly plotting to attack the Sears Tower in Chicago, the FBI headquarters in Miami, and other buildings. The suspects, described as "homegrown terrorists" by Attorney General Alberto Gonzales, allegedly sought to obtain funding and support for their plot from a government informant posing as a member of Al Qaeda. Five of the arrested men were U.S. citizens, one a legal permanent resident, and the other a Haitian national who was an illegal alien.

JEROME A. CHANES

Jewish Communal Affairs

American Jews and the Middle East

IN LATE JANUARY, the Hamas victory in the Palestinian Authority elections came as a shock to the organized American Jewish community, as it did to everyone else. Voicing the mainstream consensus, American Jewish Committee executive director David A. Harris told the *New York Jewish Week* (Feb. 3) that despite the clear Western insistence on no recognition of Hamas unless it renounced violence and recognized Israel, contacts on a pragmatic level were "unavoidable." It was the responsibility of the Jewish community, he said, to make sure that such contacts did not turn into tacit recognition.

AIPAC (American Israel Public Affairs Committee), the key pro-Israel lobby, threw its support behind proposed legislation setting strict limits on aid to the PA so long as the ruling Hamas maintained its support for terrorism and refused to recognize Israel. Symptomatic of how single-mindedly AIPAC pressed its case was the reaction of one generally pro-Israel member of Congress, Betty McCollum (D., Minn.), who refused to meet with AIPAC again unless it apologized for a remark she said an AIPAC representative made, that her opposition to the bill made her a supporter of terrorism.

Left-leaning Jewish groups, however, tended to agree with McCollum that the policy espoused by AIPAC would mean a cutoff of food and humanitarian assistance to innocent Palestinians. Americans for Peace Now, the Israel Policy Forum, and the Religious Action Center (RAC) of Reform Judaism urged amendments to the legislation that would allow such assistance. And Brit Tzedek V'Shalom published a letter to the president, signed by hundreds of rabbis, urging him "to preserve the prospects for peace through constructive engagement of moderate Palestinians and continued humanitarian aid."

It was at this crucial juncture that the ongoing legal case against two former AIPAC staffers entered a new stage, raising questions about the lobby's ability to argue Israel's case. In 2004, the two—Steven Rosen and Keith Weissman—had been accused of passing classified information to people not entitled to receive it, that is, Israeli agents. In late January 2006, the man who had passed them the information, former Pentagon analyst

Larry Franklin, was given a prison sentence of more than 12 years, subject to reduction should he cooperate with the government in its case against Rosen and Weissman. The judge's remarks at the sentencing, applying the Espionage Act to individuals who did not work for the government, did not bode well for the two men. Fears were voiced in the Jewish community that the case might not only "neuter" AIPAC, but also deter other Jewish organizations from pursuing aggressive pro-Israel advocacy.

Judging by the turnout at AIPAC's annual policy conference in early March, one would not have known that the organization was having any problems. Vice President Dick Cheney was the major speaker, and many of those mentioned as potential presidential candidates in 2008 were prominent participants. Divisive issues, such as how strictly to monitor the ban on contact with the PA, or whether pro-Israel forces should say anything about the situation in Iraq, were played down. The issue arousing the most interest was the threat Iran posed to Israel and the West: officeholders and politicians vied with each other to assure the AIPAC audience that they considered the Tehran regime evil and dangerous.

The AIPAC event took place when many Orthodox Jews were still seething over the Israeli government's evacuation of Amona, a small outpost on the West Bank, in February, in which more than 200 people were injured (see below, p. 261). The Union of Orthodox Jewish Congregations of America (OU), which saw this as a continuation of an anti-settler policy initiated by the 2005 evacuation of settlements in Gaza and the northern West Bank, sent a letter to Prime Minister Olmert expressing deep dismay at the demonstration of "brutality and palpable hate . . . where Israeli citizens are trampled by horses of their own police force." In June, the OU publicly pleaded with the prime minister to reach out to Orthodox Jews and get their input before proceeding with further territorial withdrawals. Criticized by many of its own members for not speaking out unequivocally against the destruction and abandonment of settlements in 2005, the OU, in December, would pass a formal resolution giving its leadership the authority, for the first time, to take public stands on "Israeli domestic policies and territorial integrity."

In March, meanwhile, Olmert's victory in the Israeli elections and the certainty that his party, Kadima, would anchor the new government coalition induced mainstream American Jewish organizations to pledge support for his stated policy of unilaterally evacuating areas of the West Bank, even as groups on the right and the left expressed their doubts. Olmert's May visit to Washington, where he addressed a joint session of

Congress and met with President Bush and other leaders, brought the fissures in the American Jewish community into bold relief.

The prime minister's eloquent statement before Congress of the case for withdrawal from a significant amount of territory—preferably through negotiations with the Palestinians, but unilaterally if necessary—evoked the wrath of right-of-center Jewish groups such as the Zionist Organization of America (ZOA) and Americans for a Safe Israel, as well as their evangelical Christian allies, and they placed ads in the media denouncing the policy as a concession to terror. On the other side of the Jewish political spectrum, the more dovish organizations, Americans for Peace Now, the Israel Policy Forum, and others, sharply criticized the unilateral thrust of the Olmert plan and urged a greater emphasis on negotiations instead.

These debates became academic, at least temporarily, in July, with the outbreak of Israel's war against Hezballah in Lebanon. Pro-Israel rallies took place across the country. American Jewish philanthropies immediately launched fund-raising campaigns to aid residents of northern Israel affected by the fighting: United Jewish Communities (UJC), the umbrella organization of the federations, announced a $300-million campaign, New York UJA-Federation set a goal of $60 million, American Friends of Magen David Adom raised hundreds of thousands of dollars for medical supplies, and many other groups initiated their own emergency drives.

The Jewish community also found itself in a battle for the hearts and minds of the American people and its government. "As Mideast Churns, U.S. Jews and Arabs Alike Swing Into Action," was the headline of a *New York Times* article on the subject (July 28). It noted that American Jewish groups were "sending lobbyists to Washington, solidarity delegations to Jerusalem and millions of dollars for ambulances and trauma counseling" as they had in previous wars, but this time Arab and Muslim organizations were doing the same. The Jews were prevailing, the article noted, as Congress and U.S. policymakers, with scarcely any dissent, took Israel's side and resisted Arab calls for an imposed cease-fire. Equally remarkable, in the reporter's eyes, was the virtual unanimity of the American Jewish community in backing Israel. David Besser, writing in the *New York Jewish Week* (July 28), found that some American Jews were disturbed by Israel's actions, but "there was a deep fear of moving too far outside the consensus views."

Even the July 30 attack on the Lebanese village of Qana, which killed dozens of civilians and aroused criticism both internationally and within

Israel, did not shake American Jewish backing for the war. Martin Raffel, associate executive director of the Jewish Council for Public Affairs (JCPA), told the *Forward* (Aug. 4), "I see 100 percent support and not one iota of decrease in support in the Jewish community for Israel's conduct in Lebanon."

Thus it came as a shock when Adrian Shanker, a college student working as a summer intern at the Religious Action Center (RAC) of Reform Judaism in Washington, collected almost 50 names of other young Jews on a petition urging the Union of Reform Judaism (URJ), which had condemned Arab attacks on Israeli civilians, also to condemn "the Israeli Defense Force's killing of unarmed Lebanese and Palestinian civilians." Shanker explained that Reform Jews sharing his views felt ignored by the movement.

The war was made more personal for Jews in the U.S. with reports that two young Americans were among the Israeli dead. Michael Levin of Bucks County, Pennsylvania, moved to Israel at age 18 and joined the army. He was killed in fighting against Hezballah in southern Lebanon. David Lelchook, a Boston-born resident of Kibbutz Sa'ar, four miles from the Lebanese border, died in a rocket attack as he was riding his bicycle to a bomb shelter.

The war's inconclusive end left American Jews with mixed feelings. The Rabbinical Council of America (RCA), the organization of Modern Orthodox rabbis, issued a statement in late August arguing that Israel had been too solicitous of the lives of Lebanese civilians. Gary Rosenblatt, editor of the *New York Jewish Week,* admitted, in a September 1 editorial, to "Thinking the Unthinkable," the possibility that Israel might cease to exist. The mainstream Jewish organizations, meanwhile, sought to create a linkage between Israel's recent war and another, even more ominous threat. Turning their attention to the pending visit of Iranian president Mahmoud Ahmadinejad to the UN General Assembly session in New York, they organized a rally at the UN on September 20 in support of Israel, in opposition to "global terrorism," and for the freeing of Israeli hostages held by Hamas and Hezballah.

AIPAC came under considerable scrutiny again in October. *Time* magazine carried a report on it Web site that the FBI was looking into charges that AIPAC offered to use its influence to have Rep. Jane Harman (D., Calif.) named chair of the House Intelligence Committee if the Democrats won control of the House in the November elections, in return for government leniency toward Rosen and Weissman, the two former AIPAC staffers being prosecuted for passing classified information to Israel. While certain wealthy Jewish activists were indeed promoting Harmon for the post, all those involved denied any AIPAC offer of a deal.

Potentially more damaging to AIPAC in the long run was the news that billionaire George Soros was considering getting involved in the creation of an alternative pro-Israel lobby that would advocate more dovish policies. The Jewish Telegraphic Agency reported on a meeting in late September between Soros associate Morton Halperin and leaders of Americans for Peace Now, the Israel Policy Forum, Brit Tzedek V'Shalom, the RAC of Reform Judaism, and others, where discussions were held about the possibility of joining forces to create a counterbalance to AIPAC's influence. A second meeting, on October 25, was attended by Soros himself and focused on fund-raising. Several of those involved told reporters that the proposed new body should not be seen as an AIPAC competitor, but rather as a collaborator that would have a somewhat different policy focus.

AJC's *Annual Survey of American Jewish Opinion* for 2006, which appeared in mid-October, indicated widespread anti-administration sentiment in the Jewish community. For example, only 29 percent of the sample believed that American military action in Iraq had been the "right thing" to do, while 65 percent felt the U.S. should have "stayed out"— 11 points more than those opposing the war in the general population, according to a *Newsweek* poll. When it came to Iran, 54 percent of Jews expressed opposition to a U.S. military strike to prevent that country from developing nuclear weapons—roughly the same as in the population as a whole—but a majority of Jews approved of Israel conducting such a strike.

It was hardly a surprise, then, that Prime Minister Olmert raised the hackles of many American Jews when, visiting the White House in mid-November, just after the midterm elections that the president's party had lost, he praised the Bush administration for its Iraq policies. Olmert said, "We are very much impressed and encouraged by the stability which the great operation of America in Iraq brought to the Middle East" and expressed hope for its "full success." Pro-Israel Democrats were especially appalled, but even those who did not see the matter in partisan terms worried that Olmert's remark might provide ammunition to those who argued that the Iraq war was fought for Israel's benefit. Leaders of mainstream Jewish organizations sought to minimize the significance of the Olmert statement, suggesting that it was said out of courtesy to a proven friend who came out strongly against the existential threat Iran posed to Israel.

Iran, in fact, was the central theme at Olmert's other important stop on his American visit, the annual General Assembly (GA) of the UJC, held this year in Los Angeles. While the prime minister did discuss the recent war in Lebanon and profusely thanked American Jewry for their outpouring of help, the potential nuclear capability of Iran was his primary focus. In this Olmert was joined by Knesset opposition leader Benjamin Netanyahu, the head of Likud, who phrased the issue in words that would be quoted often afterward: "It's 1938. Iran is Germany, and racing to acquire nuclear arms."

Iran's Holocaust-denial conference in December further blackened that regime's reputation in American and Jewish circles. The White House and Congress condemned the event, and on December 21 the Conference of Presidents of Major American Jewish Organizations hosted a public meeting where well-known diplomats and jurists denounced the Tehran gathering and called for the UN International Court of Justice to try President Ahmadinejad for incitement to genocide. But Duvid Feldman, an Orthodox resident of Monsey, New York, who attended the conference as part of a delegation from the anti-Zionist Neturei Karta group, said that opposition to Zionism, not Holocaust denial, was the focus of the presentations, and complained to the *New York Jewish Week* (Dec. 22) that even before he returned home from Iran his ten children were being harassed in their ultra-Orthodox school for their father's presence at the conference.

THE BATTLE FOR PUBLIC OPINION

Advocates of Israel's cause in the American public square confronted a highly publicized, double-barreled assault in 2006. In March came "The Israel Lobby and U.S. Foreign Policy," a report by Stephen Walt and John Mearsheimer, two academicians, charging that pro-Israel forces exercised undue influence on American Middle East policy and effectively silenced all opposition, and in October there was a book by former president Jimmy Carter, *Palestine: Peace Not Apartheid,* which suggested a parallel between Israel's treatment of the Palestinians and South Africa's old policy of racial separation.

The Walt-Mearsheimer essay took on something of an authoritative aura by virtue of one author's association with Harvard, the other's with the University of Chicago, and its placement on the Web site of Harvard's Kennedy School of Government, after an initial appearance in the *London Review of Books.* (The Kennedy School subsequently announced that it did not necessarily endorse views presented on its site.) Jewish leaders avoided any public battle with the authors so as not to give them more publicity. When questioned by the media, Jewish organizations pointed out that the idea of an overly powerful pro-Israel lobby was an old and discredited one. They worried that the charge could feed into current disillusionment with the situation in Iraq by suggesting that U.S. actions there were undertaken in Israel's interest, and also focus unwarranted public attention on statements already made by President Bush that in part justified possible action against Iran on the grounds of its threat to Israel.

The argument that the Israel lobby silenced anyone daring to challenge it reappeared in early October. On two separate occasions, critics of Israel charged, invitations to speakers were withdrawn under pressure from pro-Israel forces. The Polish consulate in New York canceled a lecture it was scheduled to host—not sponsor—on October 3 by Prof. Tony Judt of New York University, after Jewish leaders informed Polish officials that Judt was on record in favor of replacing Israel with a binational Jewish-Arab state. And a week later the French embassy canceled an event marking the publication of a new book on Vichy France when it discovered that in a postscript to the volume the author condemned Israeli treatment of the Palestinians.

The Carter book added to the claim of a powerful pro-Israel lobby the incendiary charge of Israeli racism. Appearing less than three weeks before the midterm elections, *Peace Not Apartheid* immediately became a political weapon in the hands of Republicans, who urged Jewish voters to abandon Carter's Democratic Party. But that argument had little effect, as Democratic leaders and candidates disavowed the former president and denied that his views on the Middle East were shared by the party. Several scholars associated with the Carter Center in Atlanta disassociated themselves from the institution to protest not only the book's thesis but also outright misstatements and possible cases of plagiarism they found in it.

Carter himself seemed surprised at the wave of anger the book evoked in Jewish circles and took steps to assuage it. But his meetings with rabbis and other Jewish leaders did little to bridge the gap since he continued to insist that the situation of the Palestinians in the territories was akin to South African apartheid. As his book rose on the best-seller list—it reached number seven on the *New York Times* list in early December—Jewish anxiety grew. AJC executive director David Harris told the *New York Jewish Week* (Dec. 15) that the Jewish community found itself in a bind, eager to defend Israel against the former president but reluctant to lend credence to the canard that it sought to silence debate. Abraham Foxman, national director of the Anti-Defamation League (ADL), bluntly called Carter's charges anti-Semitic.

THE MIDDLE EAST ON CAMPUS

Complaints over the years about anti-Israel bias in American academia finally received scholarly attention in 2006 with the publication of *The Uncivil University: Politics and Propaganda in American Education,* by Gary Tobin of the Institute for Jewish and Community Research. His key finding was that prejudice against Israel was part of a much broader leftist ideological tilt epitomized by the finding that 63 percent of faculty members said they believed their colleagues were sometimes reluctant to express their opinions against dominant views on campus. Tobin warned that unless the academic community came to see "that ideological uniformity of any kind is dangerous," taxpayers and donors would ultimately withdraw support.

The debate about the treatment of the Middle East conflict on American college campuses took a surprising turn in 2006, focusing on Jewish-sponsored Brandeis University in Waltham, Massachusetts. Brandeis, which despite its Jewish affiliation was nonsectarian, had long struggled with how to balance Jewish and universal concerns. On April 4, 2006, for example, an opinion piece in the student newspaper argued that the university was "too Jewish for its own good" in that its pronounced Jewish identification discouraged qualified non-Jews from applying—a charge the administration vehemently denied.

Brandeis took great pride in teaching the Middle East in a balanced manner. For several years it had conducted a summer program to equip college teachers to develop objective, scholarly courses about Zionism and modern Israel on their own campuses. And its team-taught seminar on the Middle East led by three scholars—an Israeli, a Palestinian, and an Egyptian—received laudatory front-page coverage in the January 6 issue of the *New York Jewish Week*. Almost immediately after that article appeared, however, the Zionist Organization of America (ZOA) called on donors to stop giving to Brandeis because the Palestinian professor involved in the seminar, political scientist and pollster Khalil Shikaki, had past ties to Islamic Jihad, and had allegedly passed money to it. In response, Brandeis president Jehuda Reinharz issued a statement saying: "We live in a country where people are presumed innocent until proven guilty."

The ZOA once again attacked Brandeis in the spring, when Pulitzer Prize-winning playwright Tony Kushner was awarded an honorary degree. Kushner was a harsh critic of Israel, a fact of which the university committee that decided on honorary degrees had been unaware, Reinharz explained, but he refused to buckle under to the ZOA and rescind Kushner's degree.

YEHOSHUA ON ISRAEL-DIASPORA RELATIONS

AJC marked its centennial meeting in Washington, D.C., in early May with a series of symposia on the Jewish future, featuring major intellectuals and literary figures. One participant, Israeli writer A.B. Yehoshua, used the occasion to declare the irrelevance of Diaspora Jewish life. As an Israeli, Yehoshua said, he had no interest in discussions of Jewish identity, saying, "It's your problem, not mine," and refused to back down from his dismissive stance even when challenged by other panel members and the audience. His presentation generated considerable media attention in Israel, where the classic Zionist doctrine of "negation of the Diaspora" that he espoused had long since been replaced, in much of the population, by ignorance of other Jewish communities.

Communal Issues

INTERMARRIAGE

The debate over whether to encourage the conversion of non-Jewish spouses in mixed-married families continued unabated. In a *New York Jewish Week* opinion column (Jan. 13), Steven Bayme and Jack Wertheimer, founding members of the Jewish In-Marriage Initiative, lauded statements made by some Conservative and Reform leaders in 2005 favoring the promotion of such conversions (see AJYB 2006, pp. 102, 105), and stressed that the transformation of intermarried families into wholly Jewish ones was likely to enhance the Jewish identification of the children and thereby strengthen the Jewish community in the next generation.

Their views received scholarly support from Prof. Sylvia Barack Fishman of Brandeis University, who completed a three-year study of the subject for the American Jewish Committee. Her report, *Choosing Jewish: Conversations About Conversion,* was based on interviews with Jews and non-Jews involved in intermarriages, as well as with some who had converted to Judaism. She was surprised to find that many of those who ultimately converted had been "waiting to be asked," which suggested to Fishman that rabbis, community leaders, and Jewish spouses should shed inhibitions about advocating conversion and recast programs for the intermarried to make conversion the explicit goal.

The pro-conversion message aroused great controversy. At a panel discussion hosted by the *New York Jewish Week* in late February, Bayme was attacked by Paul Golin, associate executive director of the Jewish Outreach Institute, and Bethamie Horowitz, research director at the Mandel Foundation, who argued that intermarriage could not be combated in an open society and that the Jewish community had no choice but to put significant resources into programs for mixed-married families without pushing conversion. Editor Gary Rosenblatt, the moderator, came away with the clear sense that most of the audience agreed with their approach.

In November, release of data from the 2005 study of the Boston Jewish community, commissioned by the Combined Jewish Philanthropies and carried out by a team of Brandeis scholars led by Leonard Saxe, appeared to corroborate the view that outreach to the intermarried could work in the absence of conversion. It found that about 60 percent of intermarried families in the city were raising their children as Jews, which was a possible explanation for the Boston Jewish population rising even with an intermarriage rate approaching 40 percent. As in the past, almost all such families in which the mother was Jewish were raising Jewish children; what was new was an increase in the propensity of families where the father was Jewish to raise the children as Jews.

Optimists declared that other Jewish communities might get similar results if they allocated money to replicate Boston's programs for the intermarried. Some went even further, suggesting that the Boston survey, by showing that intermarriage could generate a net increase in Jewish numbers, should bring to an end the widespread pessimism about the future of American Jewish life. Sociologist Steven M. Cohen, however, expressed skepticism, pointing out that the survey's criterion for children being raised "Jewish" was rather amorphous and could encompass those raised with no religion, or with Judaism as well as another religion.

JEWISH CONTINUITY

The centrality of Jewish education for the perpetuation of American Jewry received significant attention from private foundations in 2006. In

February, the San Francisco-based Jim Joseph Foundation, with more than $500 million in assets, announced that it would direct all of its giving to Jewish schools, meaning that it would spend at least $25 million annually on Jewish education, an enormous sum. And in March, the Avi Chai Foundation announced that its "Match" initiative, cosponsored by the Jewish Funders Network and the Partnership for Excellence in Jewish Education, had raised nearly $26 million for 159 day schools by matching gifts made by donors to the schools of their choice.

Jewish education was also the subject of scholarly interest. *Linking the Silos: How to Accelerate the Momentum in Jewish Education Today,* a report that appeared in February, noted significant improvement in educational opportunities in recent years. It cautioned, however, that local turf battles and lack of communication unnecessarily fragmented the educational system, leading to breakdowns in coordination and insufficient planning. The report summarized results of a study of seven communities by a team headed by Prof. Jack Wertheimer, and was funded by Avi Chai.

Another institution promoting Jewish identity that attracted both money and scholarly attention was the Jewish summer camp. In early March, the Foundation for Jewish Camping held the first North American Camping Leaders Assembly, which drew a surprising 400 professionals, lay leaders, and funders. The *Forward* (May 19) reported that the Reform movement's camps had boosted their annual philanthropic income from $30,000–$50,000 to $1.5 million by a coordinated, aggressive campaign aimed at alumni, campers' families, and foundations. Of the latter, the Grinspoon Institute for Jewish Philanthropy was by far the most involved. And in December, *A Place of Our Own: The Rise of Reform Jewish Camping* was published, edited by Michael Lorge and Gary Zola. It contained scholarly essays on the evolution and impact of Reform summer camps.

Birthright Israel, the program that, beginning in 1999, provided young American Jews with free ten-day trips to Israel, was widely viewed as a potent means of awakening Jewish consciousness. On December 11, at the annual Birthright Israel gala dinner, a donation of $5 million was announced from a new foundation started by Sheldon and Miriam Adelson, part of the astounding sum of $200 million that the foundation was planning to give annually to Jewish causes. Earlier in the year, a team of scholars at Brandeis University measured the impact of Birthright Israel by comparing the attitudes of participants with those of individuals who applied but did not go. The report of the findings, entitled *Birthright Is-*

rael: Impact on Jewish Identity, Peoplehood, and Connection to Israel, indeed found that the experience made a significant positive difference in terms of Jewish identity, but also noted that despite their stay in Israel, participants had a surprisingly weak understanding of the country's democratic nature and its role as a refuge for persecuted Jews.

How synagogues might improve their effectiveness as agents of Jewish continuity was the focus of "Synergy," a two-day conference in New York sponsored by the city's UJA-Federation in January. The perception of some of the rabbis present that very few Jews viewed the synagogue as a major focus of their lives was affirmed by Prof. Amy Sales of Brandeis University, whose research found that only a small core of activists even cared very much about what went on the synagogue. An entirely different—and apparently more successful—synagogue model was featured in the *New York Times* (April 4), which reported on congregations that "refashion their synagogues into religious multiplexes on the Sabbath, featuring programs like 'Shabbat yoga' and comedy alongside traditional worship." The reporter ascribed the new approach to Jewish fears of "shrinking numbers," and compared these synagogues to the evangelical Christian mega-churches.

Despite the closing of the Elat Chayyim retreat center in Accord, New York, due to lack of funds, the vogue of Jewish mystical spirituality that it represented showed no sign of abating. "Kabbalah: The Newest Denomination?" was the headline of a front-page article in the *New York Jewish Week* (Dec. 29) about a conference in San Diego on "Kabbalah for the Masses" that attracted about 100 people. The speakers—students and teachers of Jewish mysticism—agreed that Kabbalistic teachings would continue to be popular and should be spread. Differences developed, however, over whether it should be taught to non-Jews or outside the framework of normative Judaism; especially controversial were the aggressive advertising and marketing practices of the Los Angeles-based Kabbalah Centre.

There were two clear examples during the year of Jewish "spirituality" crossing over into the general American culture. One was the success of Rabbi Irwin Kula's PBS television series on "The Hidden Wisdom of Our Yearnings." Kula was the president of CLAL–The National Jewish Center for Learning and Leadership. The other was the emergence of the bearded, black-coated, Chabad-oriented singer Matisyahu as, in the words of the *New York Times* (Mar. 8), "America's most popular reggae singer."

Perhaps the most heartening Jewish cultural event during 2006 was the second annual Limmud conference, held in January in New York. Over the course of four days, some 750 Jews spanning a broad spectrum of beliefs and practices attended more than 200 sessions on topics of Jewish interest, ranging from religion to politics to economics. The entire program was organized by volunteers, with financial support from New York UJA-Federation. Limmud was modeled on a similar annual conference in England that had been functioning for 25 years.

WJC WOES

The drawn-out controversies regarding the World Jewish Congress (see AJYB 2005, p. 205; 2006, pp. 110–11) accelerated in 2006. As the year began the organization faced a lawsuit in Israel and an investigation by New York State, both about allegations of financial impropriety, and was seeking to block publication in Switzerland of a series of articles in the newsmagazine *Weltwoche* that contained allegedly damaging information. Seeking to retrieve its reputation, the WJC steering committee, at a meeting on January 19, approved the creation of an audit committee and a policy council; both would include people with international reputations from outside the WJC.

This was too little and too late. The 35-page report from the New York Attorney General's Office, released January 31 in the form of an agreement between the office and the WJC, said that the organization "lacked appropriate financial controls to safeguard charitable assets." Israel Singer, for years the major force within the organization, was barred from any "financial management or oversight" role and would have to pay back $132,000 to the WJC within 90 days (he had already returned more than $100,000); others who had worked for the group also came in for criticism.

The WJC reacted to the report by focusing attention on the finding that no criminal conduct had been discovered and on the words of praise for managerial reforms that had been put in place in recent months. It filed a $6-million lawsuit for defamation against Isi Leibler, an Australian-born former WJC leader now living in Israel, who had initiated the charges against the organization, claiming that his allegations had cost it that amount of money in donations. Leibler responded that the attorney general's report proved his charges of financial impropriety correct and that it was the revelation of Singer's actions that had brought the drop in contributions. In August, under considerable pressure from its affiliates around the world, the WJC dropped its suit against Leibler.

Denominational Life

ORTHODOX JUDAISM

Recent trends in American Orthodoxy received considerable scholarly attention in 2006. In November, the Los Angeles-based organization Synagogue 3000 issued a report by Steven M. Cohen indicating that although the Orthodox constituted roughly 10 percent of the American Jewish community, 37 percent of all children affiliated with synagogues were Orthodox, far more than any of the other streams. "Non-Orthodox Jews ought to think about their relation to the Orthodox," Cohen told the *Forward* (Oct. 27). "The growing number of Orthodox Jews means they will play a much more central role in defining American Jewry in the years to come." Sociologist Samuel Heilman, a noted authority on American Jewish life, published *Sliding to the Right: The Contest for the Future of American Jewish Orthodoxy,* which traced what he believed was a sharp decline of the modernistic elements in the Orthodox community. Yet in June, the University of Scranton hosted an international conference on the history of Modern Orthodoxy—apparently the first such formal meeting on the topic ever held in the U.S.—a seeming indication of modernism's ongoing vitality.

Perhaps subconsciously reflecting trepidation about the swelling Orthodox numbers, Jews were fascinated during the year by stories of Orthodox dropouts. Hella Winston's well-received book, *Unchosen: The Hidden Lives of Hasidic Rebels,* presented sympathetic profiles of several such individuals, even attracting the interest of the *New York Times,* which published an op-ed by Winston (Apr. 23) about a Passover seder for formerly Orthodox Jews. Other rebels who were not yet ready for an open break with their families told their stories under pseudonyms on Internet blogs. And Adam Vardy's film *Mendy: A Question of Faith,* which opened in May, depicted the experiences of a Williamsburg Hasid who enters the world of modernity.

American Orthodoxy in 2006 was beset by controversy. As the year opened, the New York City Health Department and some Orthodox groups remained locked in combat over *metzitzah b'peh,* a controversial procedure immediately after circumcision in which the *mohel* sucks blood from the wound. Talmudic law mandated the practice on health grounds, to draw blood away from the place of incision, but many rabbinic authorities—mostly outside the Hasidic community—ruled that the suction did not have to be done orally. In 2005, the Health Department announced that three babies circumcised by the same *mohel*—who had done *metzitzah b'peh*—had contracted herpes, and one had died. Calls to ban the practice were met by adamant claims, mostly from the Satmar Hasidic group, that it was an integral part of the circumcision ritual and therefore a matter of freedom of religion. That December, the Health Department nonetheless issued an advisory noting that oral suction could spread neonatal herpes and should be avoided (see AJYB 2006, pp. 107–08).

Supporters of the practice saw this as an attempt to go over the heads of the rabbis, and Satmar leaders met with Mayor Michael Bloomberg on January 5, 2006, to get the advisory rescinded. Not receiving satisfaction, they launched an ad campaign in the Orthodox press warning that the authorities were gearing up for an outright ban, and urging parents to call a 24-hour hotline to report any conversations in which doctors or other caregivers criticized *metzitzah b'peh*. An agreement was reached in June between the (Satmar) Central Rabbinical Congress and the New York State health commissioner on practical guidelines for *mohalim* that were expected to reduce the risk to the babies, even as medical experts expressed skepticism.

Another controversial issue for the Orthodox community had to do with conditions in a major kosher slaughterhouse. In March, People for the Ethical Treatment of Animals (PETA) obtained, under the Freedom of Information Act, a 2005 report prepared by the inspector general of the Department of Agriculture about AgriProcessors, the country's largest producer of "glatt kosher" meat—the highest standard of kashrut—located in Postville, Iowa. Both the report and a video of activities in the plant taken surreptitiously by a PETA operative seemed to indicate inhumane treatment of the animals, unsanitary practices, and dereliction of duty on the part of federal inspectors. Subsequent investigations raised claims that workers at the plant, many of them illegal immigrants, were mistreated. The management denied all the allegations. The Union of Orthodox Jewish Congregations (OU), the country's largest kosher certification agency, said it was studying the charges, and the Conservative movement created a task force to address the issue.

On June 7, Temple Grandin, perhaps the nation's leading expert on humane treatment of animals, visited AgriProcessors and afterward reported that conditions for the animals had improved greatly. But later in the month more problems emerged as a federal grand jury served subpoenas on AgriProcessors and several other kosher slaughterhouses on suspicion of antitrust violations.

Not all the disputes roiling American Orthodoxy involved friction with outside forces. Of the internal squabbles that emerged during 2006 the most bitter was over succession to the leadership of Satmar, the large, insular, and militantly anti-Zionist Hasidic group that was estimated to have about 100,000 adherents around the world. The incumbent *rebbe,* 91-year-old Rabbi Moshe Teitelbaum, based in Williamsburg, Brooklyn, died in April (see below, p. 705), immediately setting off a factional fight between the followers of two of his sons, Aaron and Zalman Leib. At stake was not only spiritual leadership of the movement but also some $500 million in assets. Even while the father was still alive lawsuits and physical violence had poisoned the atmosphere between the two sides. The deceased leader's will declared the younger son, Zalman Leib, his heir, but Aaron and his followers refused to accept the decision. As the parties voiced their respective arguments through public-relations firms, speculation grew about a possible Satmar schism.

For Modern Orthodox rabbis, the big story in 2006 was an unprecedented challenge to their legitimacy from the Israeli chief rabbinate. In its May 5 issue, the *New York Jewish Week* reported that conversions to Judaism supervised by American Orthodox rabbis were no longer being recognized in Israel unless the rabbis' names appeared on a list of about 50 "approved" rabbis, some of whom were no longer alive. Previously, any conversion performed by a member of the (Modern Orthodox) Rabbinical Council of America (RCA) was automatically accepted. In a letter to the *New York Jewish Week* (May 12), the RCA denied that it was being targeted and suggested that the chief rabbinate was merely tightening up standards across the board. Sephardi chief rabbi Shlomo Amar, meanwhile, suggested that rabbis outside Israel could have their conversions accepted if they first came to Israel and passed an examination on the laws of conversion.

Hoping to resolve the problem, an RCA delegation traveled to Jerusalem in June for meetings with officials of the chief rabbinate. Afterwards, the RCA issued a statement announcing "reciprocal understandings and agreements" whereby a joint commission would examine conversion standards "to achieve clarity and consistency whenever possible." Rabbi Basil Herring, the RCA executive vice president, said he had been given assurances that all RCA conversions would be approved. Subsequent reports from Israel indicated a significant drop in the number of RCA "problem" conversions. At year's end the organization said that discussions with the Israeli chief rabbinate were "ongoing."

This episode, symptomatic of growing pressure from traditionalist forces upon Modern Orthodoxy to conform to stricter standards, necessarily impacted on the behavior of the latter group toward those slightly to the left of it. As if determined to prove their own Orthodox bona fides, elements within the RCA and the rabbinical school of Yeshiva University (YU) sought to block the professional advancement of alumni of Yeshivat Chovevei Torah. Founded in 1999 by Rabbi Avi Weiss in reaction to a perceived rightward tilt at YU, Chovevei Torah espoused what it called "open Orthodoxy," and generally took more liberal positions than were taught at the older school. There had been some reluctance on the part of YU-oriented synagogues to hire Chovevei Torah students as interns and assistants, and now that the new institution had graduated three classes of rabbis, the RCA—made up overwhelmingly of YU-trained rabbis—was called upon to rule on their applications for membership. No decision was reached in 2006.

Edah, another institution founded to fight Orthodoxy's movement to the right, announced in June that it was closing. Created a decade earlier by Rabbi Saul Berman to encourage greater Orthodox involvement in social issues and to enhance the participation of women in Jewish life, Edah could not raise the funds to continue its work, although its highly regarded Internet journal would continue under the aegis of Chovevei Torah. Berman sought to put the best possible face on Edah's demise, suggesting it had succeeded in influencing the climate of Orthodox opinion.

Just two months later there was at least one vivid proof that the climate had indeed changed. In August, Congregation Orach Eliezer on Manhattan's West Side hired a woman, Dina Najman-Licht, as *rosh kehillah* (communal leader). While she was not given the title rabbi and would not perform roles that Halakhah (Jewish law) denied to women, and the synagogue—whose membership was mostly Orthodox—did not formally affiliate with Orthodoxy, her appointment was hailed by Orthodox feminists as a major step forward.

Yeshiva University, meanwhile, seeking to maintain its balance amid the treacherous rightward and leftward Orthodox currents, enjoyed a major financial triumph. In September, President Richard Joel announced that Chairman of the Board Ronald P. Stanton, who had made his money in the transportation of petrochemicals and chemical fertilizers, was donating $100 million to the university. This was believed to be the single largest gift ever made to a Jewish educational institution. Stanton said he hoped to spur other Jewish philanthropists who gave the bulk of their donations to non-Jewish causes to shift their priorities to the Jewish community.

Allegations surfaced several times during the year about the sexual abuse of children and adolescents in the Orthodox community; in the case of one of the accused, a yeshiva teacher, the abuse was said to have occurred decades earlier. While the charges were often accompanied by assertions that Orthodox authorities covered up for the guilty, spokesmen for Orthodox organizations claimed that the problem was no worse among the Orthodox than elsewhere, and that there was a concerted effort in some quarters to discredit Orthodoxy through such claims.

CONSERVATIVE JUDAISM

The winter 2006 issue of *Judaism* magazine was devoted to a symposium on "The Situation of Conservative Judaism Today." The 17 contributors, all relatively young rabbis, were asked to identify "the distinguishing features of Conservative Judaism today, the nature of its religious message, the extent of its fidelity to Halakhah, and its animating commitments." Symposium organizer Jack Wertheimer, provost of the Jewish Theological Seminary (JTS), could barely suppress his disappointment at the submissions. They were filled, he said, with meaningless "buzzwords," and pervaded with the assumptions that religion was a consumer good and that contemporary Jews could only be brought into the synagogue "through inducements" that facilitated their "personal journeys."

The central institutions of Conservative Judaism, meanwhile, prepared for a final decision on the religious status of gays and lesbians in the movement, a contentious matter that had been on their agenda for several years. Two issues were under consideration: the ordination of openly gay clergy, and the performance of same-sex commitment ceremonies. The underlying questions were, on the one hand, whether these practices could be condoned without severing the movement's commitment to Halakhah, and on the other, whether failure to keep up with the changing sexual mores of American society might alienate younger people. Orthodox Judaism still retained the Biblical and rabbinic ban on homosexuality, while the Reform and Reconstructionist branches, which made no pretense to be bound by Halakhah, had already eliminated them.

The movement's Committee on Jewish Law and Standards (CJLS) met behind closed doors for two days in early March at an undisclosed Maryland location to discuss four position papers that had been submitted to it the year before, which covered the spectrum from maintaining the traditional position to repudiating it outright—the latter view being given the status of *takkanah,* that is an outright change in the law, rather than a reinterpretation of it. A final decision would be made at the next CJLS meeting scheduled for December.

On March 19, Ismar Schorsch, who was retiring from his post as chancellor of JTS — the major training school for Conservative rabbis — after 20 years, delivered a scathing critique of those seeking to change the status quo on homosexuality. At the annual convention of the movement's Rabbinical Assembly (RA), held in Mexico City, he declared that without adherence to Halakhah the movement was doomed, and charged that "internally, we have already become Reform." Three days later, the convention delivered Schorsch an implicit vote of no confidence by lowering the threshold required for the 25-member CJLS to pass a *takkanah* and revise, rather than just reinterpret, existing law, from 20 votes to 13, making it far easier to overturn current policy on homosexuality. (A reinterpretation, *teshuvah,* required only six votes.)

On April 4, the search committee designated to choose a replacement for Schorsch as JTS chancellor chose an unconventional candidate, 54-year-old Arnold Eisen, who would become chancellor-designate upon Schorsch's impending retirement, and chancellor a year later, on July 1, 2007. Six days later the JTS board approved the decision. A non-rabbi and a highly regarded professor of Jewish culture and religion at Stanford University, Eisen had very little experience in raising funds, and since his academic position had kept him aloof from the movement's rabbinic battles, Eisen's views on the divisive issues were unknown. A number of Conservative rabbis expressed disappointment that one of their own had not been chosen for the post. In response to questions from journalists, Eisen said he respected the integrity of the Halakhic process, wanted the JTS faculty to play a major role in decision-making, and personally favored the ordination of gays and lesbians. His rabbinic role model was the late Rabbi Abraham Joshua Heschel.

Chancellor Schorsch delivered his final JTS commencement address on May 18, blasting students for rejecting "the dense and demanding discourse of scholarship" in favor of "instant gratification . . . . The primitiveness of rap and the consumerism of the mall . . . ." Alluding to the inevitable changes on the horizon, he lamented, "Our forebears embraced history to enlarge and enrich Jewish observance; we wield it, if at all, to shrink it."

In August, the movement's congregational organization, the United Synagogue of Conservative Judaism, held meetings in New York and Toronto to familiarize the lay leadership with the various positions advanced on the issue of gay rights and to prepare the congregations for what was widely believed to be an inevitable CJLS decision in December to liberalize the movement's stance. The possibility that such a ruling might splinter Conservative Judaism was very much on the mind of Eisen, who spoke at a number of Conservative synagogues in an effort to ease anxieties.

On December 6, the CJLS approved two opinions, one reaffirming the traditional view and the other allowing ordination and commitment ceremonies for gays and lesbians. To the chagrin of many, however, the latter retained the ban on anal intercourse, even though this restriction was hardly enforceable. According to the rules of the movement, both of the mutually contradictory opinions were acceptable; individual Conservative seminaries and congregations might choose between them. Four traditionalist members immediately resigned from the committee in protest. Rabbi Jerome Epstein, executive vice president of the United Synagogue, hailed the result as an exemplary model of Jewish pluralism. The Ziegler School, the Conservative seminary in Los Angeles, was expected to begin admitting openly gay students in the fall of 2007. Conservative congregations in Canada were believed to be opposed to having their rabbis perform homosexual commitment ceremonies, and the movement's seminaries outside the U.S. were unlikely to ordain gays and lesbians. As for JTS, Eisen announced that a decision would be made only after intensive discussions with faculty members and students, and the tabulation of results of a poll by sociologist Steven M. Cohen, who was commissioned to survey the views of thousands of Conservative leaders around the country.

The movement's focus on the issue of homosexuality somewhat obscured the next challenge on the Conservative horizon, the status of children of intermarried Jews. Unlike Reform, which, through its patrilineal descent decision, had accepted as Jewish anyone having at least one Jewish parent and who identified as a Jew, Conservative Judaism retained the traditional principle that only children of Jewish mothers (and converts) were Jews.

In 2006, some 30 Conservative synagogues around the country were participating in the movement's Keruv Initiative whereby rabbis and lay leaders developed programs to make the congregations more welcoming to intermarried families. In addition, a new program called Edud encouraged intermarried families in which the mother was not Jewish to send their children — non-Jews, accorded to the movement's standards — to Conservative synagogue schools until the age of 13, at which point they could only continue if they converted. In March, Chancellor Schorsch suggested this approach for the Conservative summer camps as well. In December, Rabbi Epstein of the United Synagogue recommended the same policy for the movement's Solomon Schechter day schools. In all three cases the Conservative institutions would clearly have to tailor elements of their programs and curricula to the needs of such children.

REFORM JUDAISM

The status of mixed-religion families was high on the agenda of Reform Judaism as well. Even though the movement, through its acceptance of patrilineal Jews, did not confront questions about the Jewish status of offspring of intermarriages, quite often families belonging to Reform temples included non-Jewish spouses, and many of their children were being raised in two religions. In November 2005, Rabbi Eric Yoffie, president of the URJ, urged the group's biennial conference to do more to encourage such spouses to convert, and thus make the families unambiguously Jewish (see AJYB 2006, p. 102).

There was considerable uneasiness among many Reform Jews about the idea, due both to the widespread notion that Judaism was not a missionary religion and to a distaste for anything smacking of coercion, which seemed to contradict the principle of individual autonomy that was central to Reform. The *New York Times* ran a front-page article on the issue under the heading, "Reform Jews Hope to Unmix Mixed Marriages" (Feb. 12). It described the programs that some congregations had developed to expose non-Jewish spouses to Jewish life without actually pressing for their conversion. One vice president for membership of a New Jersey temple told the reporter, "With conversion you don't want to be too aggressive. That's a personal decision that I would never push on anyone. We're trying to find less in-your-face ways to make people aware that it's an option." In April, the URJ's 90 New York synagogues held a seminar to discuss morally acceptable ways of encouraging conversion.

Another initiative taken at the URJ biennial in November 2005 was passage of a resolution condemning the war in Iraq and calling for "a clear exit strategy" and "specific goals for troop withdrawal." The URJ thus became the first large Jewish organization to repudiate the war, a position in line with the views of a majority of American Jews (see AJYB 2006, p. 102). But the movement's antiwar voice was considerably muted during 2006. While it did initiate and participate in a panel discussion on the war at the annual plenum of the Jewish Council for Public Affairs

(JCPA) in February, it refrained from proposing any resolution to the plenum on the matter. There was some grumbling on the part of Reform antiwar activists in subsequent months, but sources within the movement suggested that a combination of factors had made Reform reluctant to speak out: the perceived priority of the humanitarian crisis in Darfur; concern over the implications for Israel of a precipitate withdrawal from Iraq; and the absence, as yet, of any concrete alternative for Iraq that would not risk chaos and civil war.

Reform's longstanding complaint that Israel, with its Orthodox religious establishment, did not recognize the legitimacy of Reform as a valid expression of Judaism was underlined in June, when Rabbi Yoffie turned down an invitation to a Jerusalem reception hosted by Israeli president Moshe Katzav. Yoffie explained that he made this decision to protest the fact that at previous meetings between the two men Katzav pointedly refrained from calling the URJ president "rabbi." Several dozen Israelis demonstrated outside Katzav's residence in support of Yoffie. The URJ president told the *New York Jewish Week* (June 23) that the insult was "an ongoing incident in a long story." Katzav, who was Sephardi, said he had been brought up to call only "traditional . . . authentic" rabbis by that title. A Katzav spokesman later said that the president was willing to call Yoffie a "Reform rabbi," and complained that the matter should have been handled privately, not through the media.

LAWRENCE GROSSMAN

Jewish Population in the United States, 2007

"CONSIDERABLE CONTROVERSY EXISTS about the size and character of the Jewish population of the United States. Available sources of data about American Jewry are based on complex surveys that have become increasingly difficult to conduct."[1] So begins an assessment, entitled *Reconsidering the Size and Characteristics of the American Jewish Population,* based on a meta-analysis of 34 national surveys with a combined total of nearly 84,000 interviews. Its conclusion, that the American Jewish population totals between 6.0 and 6.4 million individuals — a range close to the sum reported in Table 1 of this article — is substantially higher than the estimate provided by the National Jewish Population Survey (NJPS) of 2000–01. The contentious nature of U.S. Jewish demographic data was also illustrated by the debate aroused by our article in AJYB 2006 (pp. 133–93), which was widely reported in the press, from the *Forward,* to *Ha'aretz,* to the *Times of India,* and on numerous Web sites. Why are there differences in the estimates?

First, American Jews are a "rare population," demographically speaking. As hard as it is to grasp for Jews living in New York, Los Angeles, or South Florida, the Jewish share of the total American population has declined by almost half, from 3.7 percent in the 1930s to about 2 percent in the first decade of the twenty-first century. A rare population is difficult to locate and interview. Second, response rates in surveys vary widely, and evidence suggests that lower response rates lead to lower estimates of the Jewish population. Third, the wording of national and local survey questions seeking to identify Jews also varies; a prime example is the difference in criteria for inclusion used in the three recent National Jewish Population Surveys, those for 1971, 1990, and 2000–01.[2] In addition to these issues, there are variations in sampling techniques, the order of questions, and the culture of the institution sponsoring the research.

Since there is no consensus on the most effective and efficient strategy

---

[1]Leonard Saxe, Elizabeth Tighe, Benjamin Phillips, and Charles Kadushin, *Reconsidering the Size and Characteristics of the American Jewish Population: New Estimates of a Larger and More Diverse Community* (Waltham, Mass., 2007), p. 5.

[2]Compare http://www.Jewishdatabank.orgNJPS1971.asp, http://www.Jewishdatabank.org/Archive/NJPS1990-Study_Highlights_Part_1.pdf, and http://www.ujc.org/page.html?ArticleID=46185

to study the Jewish population of the U.S., estimates of the number of Jews vary between about 5.2 million (NJPS 2000–01) and about 6.4 million, the figure reported below in Table 1.[3]

Methodology

Based upon a summation of local Jewish community studies (Table 3), the estimated size of the American Jewish community in 2007 is 6,443,805 (Table 1), as compared to an estimated 6,452,750 in 2006. As mentioned above, the 6.4 million is about 1.2 million more than the Jewish population identified in NJPS 2000-01.[4]

The methodology used to develop our estimate is similar to that used for 2006. Local communities were contacted via the Internet. For those communities that did not reply, estimates from previous years have been maintained.

The estimates derive from two sources:

Scientific Estimates: These are based upon the results of some type of scientific study of a community, which, in almost all cases, involved the use of random-digit-dialing (RDD) telephone surveys, the currently accepted best practice for making Jewish population estimates.

Informant Estimates: For communities where no scientific study has been completed, local informants were contacted. They generally have access to information on the number of households on the local Jewish federation's mailing list and the number of people who belong to local Jewish organizations and synagogues.

More than 80 percent of the total of more than 6.4 million Jews estimated by this article was located through scientific studies, and only 20 percent based upon the less reliable informant procedure—although the analysis presented below strongly suggests that informant estimates are more reliable than previously thought. Also, less than 0.1 percent of the

---

[3]The authors thank Dr. Laurence Kotler-Berkowitz and Dr. Jonathon Ament, current staff members of the Research Department of United Jewish Communities (UJC), for their advice in the development of this article, and former staff members Dr. Jim Schwartz, Jeffrey Scheckner, and Dr. Barry Kosmin, who authored the article on U.S. Jewish population in previous years. Many of the estimates in this article are based upon their efforts. We also thank Dinur Blum, graduate assistant, and Lorri Lafontaine, program assistant, both at the Mandell L. Berman Institute-North American Jewish Data Bank at the University of Connecticut, for their assistance.

[4]See Ira M. Sheskin and Arnold Dashefsky, "Jewish Population in the United States, 2006," AJYB 2006, pp. 134–38; and Sheskin, "Four Questions about American Jewish Demography," *Jewish Political Studies Review,* forthcoming, 2008.

total derives from communities where the informant estimate is more than ten years old.

All estimates are for Jews, living both in households and institutions, and do not include non-Jews living in households with Jews. The estimates of Jewish population include both Jews who are affiliated with the Jewish community and Jews who are not affiliated.

Population estimation is not an exact science, and therefore readers should not assume that because a number changed from last year's AJYB figure that the change occurred in the past year. Rather, it most likely occurred over a longer period of time, but has only recently been substantiated.

We have endeavored to provide the most reliable estimates available, utilizing statistics derived, whenever possible, from scientifically based studies in the archive of the Mandell L. Berman Institute-North American Jewish Data Bank at the University of Connecticut. Readers are invited to offer suggestions for improving the accuracy of the estimates and the portrayal of the data. Please send all correspondence to Ira M. Sheskin at isheskin@miami.edu.

Features in the Local Population Estimates

Table 3 provides estimates for almost 1,000 Jewish communities and parts of communities. In some cases, the geographic areas in Table 3 coincide with Jewish federation service areas. In other cases, where data are available, we have disaggregated those service areas into smaller geographic units. Thus separate estimates are provided for such places as Boulder, Colorado, and Boynton Beach, Florida.

Included as well is information for each community as to whether the estimate is based on a scientific study or an informant estimate. Estimates for communities in boldface type are based on a scientific study. The boldface date is the year the field work for the study was conducted.

Estimates for communities that are not boldfaced are based on the informant methodology. Because detailed records are not available for many communities as to the date of the last such contact, only a range of years (pre-1997 or 1997–2001) is available for many of them. And where the date in the "Date of Informant Confirmation or Latest Study" column of Table 3 is more recent than the date of the latest study shown in boldface, the study estimate has been either confirmed or changed by a local informant some time after the scientific study.

Finally, the number of Jews who live in part-year households (living there for from three to seven months of the year) is presented for communities for which such information is available as part of Table 3. Jews in these households constitute an essential part of some Florida Jewish communities, joining local synagogues and making donations to Jewish charities. Thus our methodology allows the reader to gain a better perspective on the size of certain Jewish communities without double-counting the persons in these households in the totals produced in Tables 1–2. Note that Jews in part-year households are reported with respect to the community that constitutes their "second home."

Three improvements are introduced this year in Table 3. First, Jewish population estimates for more than 230 sub-areas of Jewish federation service areas are shown for the first time. While in previous years sub-area information was presented only for the largest Jewish communities such as New York and Boston, it is now provided for all communities that have completed scientific studies since 1988. Thus readers can now discern the Jewish population of, for example, Squirrel Hill (in Pittsburgh) and Brighton (in Rochester). In some cases, such as the sub-area "Northwest" in Las Vegas, interested readers will need to consult the reports for the Las Vegas Jewish community, available at www.jewishdatabank.org, for a detailed definition of that geographic area.

To be sure, the shelf life of population estimates of sub-areas may be shorter than those for estimates of "whole" Jewish communities. For example, while the Jewish population of Rochester as a whole has probably not changed significantly since the 2000 Jewish community study, it is rather more likely that the Jewish population of the sub-area Brighton, already decreasing in 2000, continued to decrease as Jews moved from this traditional core area of Jewish settlement to other neighborhoods.

A second change is that the column showing the number of counties covered by some of the population estimates has been removed from Table 3. Instead, the counties covered in a given estimate are named in parentheses within the "Geographic Area" column. And third, the information that had been included in the "Notes" section of Table 3 has now been incorporated into the table itself.

Informant Estimates and Scientific Study Estimates

As mentioned above, the estimates in Table 3 derive from two sources: informant estimates and scientific study estimates. While the latter are clearly superior, to what extent do informant estimates reflect "reality" as found by scientific studies? Table 4 shows the results of 78 scientific community studies that have been completed since 1981, as well as the

AJYB estimate for each of those communities in the year just prior to the completion of a scientific study. (Note that some Jewish communities have completed two or more scientific studies within this time frame; in such cases the informant estimates just prior to the second or third studies were themselves informed by an earlier scientific study, albeit one that was six or more years old.)

Two examples will illustrate the importance of Table 4. The first scientific study for Jacksonville, Florida, was completed in 2002. Until that time the AJYB estimate for Jacksonville was 7,300, a number provided by a local Jewish federation informant. The study found 12,900 Jews in the city, a difference of 5,600, or 43 percent. In this case, the local federation executive had long suspected that the 7,300 was too low an estimate, but had simply never updated the estimate with the AJYB authors. In Chicago, with some guidance from a 1981 scientific study, the AJYB estimate for 1989 was 248,000. A scientific study the next year put the number of Chicago Jews at 261,000, a figure that remained in the AJYB until a 2000 scientific study revised it to 270,500.

Some of the greatest absolute overestimates by the AJYB occurred in older and more established communities such as New York, Philadelphia, and Detroit. The AJYB published estimates from old scientific studies even though local informants no doubt suspected decreasing Jewish populations in these communities, since there was no methodology to document such losses.[5] When the decrease, for example, in the New York Jewish population was offset by immigration, and the Jewish population of New York leveled off, the 2002 New York study showed only 38,000 fewer Jews than reported in the AJYB, out of a total of 1.4 million.

Conversely, some of the greatest absolute underestimates by the AJYB occurred in newer and especially Sunbelt communities, such as San Francisco, Washington, D.C., Atlanta, and West Palm Beach. These were also caused by publishing estimates from old scientific studies. While local informants no doubt suspected an increasing Jewish population, there was no methodology to document such gains, and the results of the last local Jewish community study continued to be published.

It must also be noted that in many cases there was a rather close correspondence between the number of Jews found by the scientific study and the number estimated by informants. Thus the 1999 Baltimore study found 91,400 Jews compared to the informant estimate of 94,500. The

---

[5]This is one reason the current authors, starting with AJYB 2006, began publishing, in Table 3, the year of the last scientific estimate, allowing the reader to judge the accuracy of each estimate.

corresponding numbers for Minneapolis were 29,300 and 31,500; for San Antonio, 10,200 and 11,000; for Pittsburgh, 42,200 and 40,000; and for Tucson, 22,400 and 20,000. Most important, the 78 studies totaled 9,047,175 Jews. The informant estimates totaled 8,756,500 Jews, a difference of only 290,675, about 3 percent. Thus, while informant estimates may sometimes be far off the mark when looked at community by community, *on average,* they pretty much correlate with reality as the underestimates and overestimates seem largely to offset one another for the country as a whole. This is one more reason to have confidence that the current AJYB estimate of 6.4 million is closer to the truth than is the NJPS estimate of 5.2 million.

Yet another finding of interest in this table is that 51 communities had estimates that were "off" by 10 percent or more. Of these, 44 were underestimates and seven were overestimates. This wide disparity casts grave doubt on the conventional wisdom that informants tend to exaggerate population numbers in order to make their communities look "better," and should, like the point made in the previous paragraph, give pause to those who assume that informant estimates are generally inflated.

Local Population Changes

NEW SCIENTIFIC STUDIES

In the past year, nine new local Jewish community studies or "small update studies" were completed in the U.S. Population estimates for three of them (Atlanta, Detroit, and Las Vegas) were reported in AJYB 2006. Based on a new study in San Antonio, the estimate for that community listed in Table 3 decreased by 800, from 11,000 to 10,200. This same study produced a first-ever estimate for seven counties surrounding San Antonio—Atascosa, Bandera, Comal, Guadalupe, Kendall, Medina, and Wilson—of 1,000.

A new study in Boston apparently lowered the estimate of Jewish population by 16,800, from 227,300 to 210,500. As its authors revealed that the previous estimate had included non-Jews in Jewish households, and the new estimate, like all others in Table 3, excludes such non-Jews, the figures do not really imply a decrease in Jewish population, just a correction of a previous "error." In reality, the number of Jews in Boston increased from about 179,000 in 1995 to the current 210,500.

Based on a new study in Denver, the estimate for that community in Table 3 increased by 9,100, from 72,400 (a 2006 informant estimate based on assuming a certain rate of increase in the 63,300 estimate from a 1997 scientific study) to 81,500.

A scientific study of Southern Maine and neighboring New Hampshire has led us to change the previous informant estimate of 6,000 for Cumberland and York counties (Maine) by an estimate of 8,350. This study also produced a new estimate for Androscoggin County, Maine, where an informant estimate of 500 was replaced by a scientific estimate of 600, a first-ever estimate for Oxford County, Maine, of 750, a first-ever estimate for Sagadahoc County, Maine, of 400, and the replacement of an informant estimate of 600 for Strafford County (Dover and Rochester, New Hampshire) by a scientific estimate of 700.

A small update study in Tucson confirmed the population estimates in AJYB 2006. A small update study in Delaware confirmed the 2006 estimate for Newark and Wilmington, but increased the estimate for Kent and Sussex counties from 1,600 to 3,200.

New Informant Estimates

Based on new informant estimates, significant increases are reported for Volusia and Flagler counties (Daytona Beach), Florida (+1,500); Durham-Chapel Hill, North Carolina (+1,400); Greenwich, Connecticut (+1,000); and Poughkeepsie-Dutchess County, New York (+600). Significant decreases were reported for North Louisiana, that is, Shreveport and Monroe (−215), and Springfield, Illinois (−290).

Due mostly to Hurricane Katrina in 2005, the estimate for New Orleans was decreased from 13,000 to 7,000, although the New Orleans informant suggests that the number of Jews there had already decreased to 10,000 before Katrina, and thus the estimated loss to that Jewish community from the hurricane is 3,000. The devastation caused by Katrina affected not only New Orleans but also many other Gulf Coast communities in Alabama, Mississippi, and Louisiana, scattering much of their Jewish populations to other locales. Thus the estimates for Alexandria, Baton Rouge, Lake Charles, and Lafayette, Louisiana; for Biloxi/Gulfport, Diamondhead, Hattiesburg, and Jackson, Mississippi; and for Mobile, Alabama, shown in Table 3 should be treated with caution because, unlike the New Orleans estimate, they do not yet reflect changes that may have occurred following Katrina.

State and Regional Totals

Tables 1 and 2 show the total Jewish populations of each state, census region, and census division. Overall, about 2.2 percent of Americans are

Jewish, but the percentage is 4 percent or higher in New York (8.4 percent), New Jersey (5.5 percent), Washington, D.C. (4.8 percent), Maryland (4.2 percent), and Massachusetts (4.0 percent). Eight states have a Jewish population of 200,000 or more: New York (1,618,000); California (1,194,000); Florida (655,000); New Jersey (479,000); Pennsylvania (285,000); Illinois (279,000); Massachusetts (258,000); and Maryland (235,000). The four states with the largest Jewish populations account for more than 60 percent of the more than 6.4 million American Jews.

Note that, in addition to the state totals shown in Table 1, Florida has 81,000 Jews who reside in the state for three to seven months of the year.

Table 2 shows that, on a regional basis, the Jewish population is distributed very differently from the American population as a whole. While only 18 percent of Americans live in the Northeast, 43 percent of Jews live there. While 22 percent of Americans live in the Midwest, 11 percent of Jews do. While 36 percent of Americans live in the South, 22 percent of Jews do. Approximately equal percentages of all Americans (23 percent) and Jews (24 percent) live in the West.[6]

Vignettes of Recently Completed Local Studies

Five local demographic studies have been completed for Jewish federations since the last article on Jewish population that appeared in AJYB 2006: Atlanta, Boston, Detroit, Las Vegas, and San Antonio. In addition, small update studies were completed for Delaware and Tucson. Since local studies produce much information about a Jewish community beyond its size, this section presents a few of the major findings of each study.

In reading them it is important to bear in mind the difference between the number of Jews in a community and the number of persons in Jewish households, which also include non-Jewish spouses and children not being raised Jewish. Also, in these vignettes, when a community is compared to other Jewish communities, the comparison is to communities that have completed scientific studies during the past 13 years. Full reports of the results of these studies are available from the North American Jewish Data Bank at www.jewishdatabank.org. Finally, while

---

[6]See Ira M. Sheskin *Geographic Differences among American Jews*, United Jewish Communities Series on the National Jewish Population Survey 2000–01, Report Number 8 (2005), for an analysis of changes in the geographic distribution of Jews over time, also available at http://www.ujc.org/local_includes/downloads/6760.pdf.

random digit dialing (RDD) produces the most truly random sample, most studies, for economic and other reasons, combine it with the use of Distinctive Jewish Name (DJN) sampling or sampling from mailing lists, known as List sampling. In all surveys that employ either DJN or List sampling, weighting factors are used in combining the samples so as to remove much of the bias introduced by their use.

The authors are aware of several new studies that will soon be completed: Cincinnati; Denver; Lehigh Valley, Pa.; and Southern Maine (Portland). Vignettes on these communities will appear in AJYB 2008. The new population estimates for Denver and Southern Maine are included in Table 3.

ATLANTA

This 2006 study covers Greater Atlanta. Jack Ukeles and Ron Miller of Ukeles Associates were the principal investigators for this study that was based upon 1,007 telephone interviews, of which 322 were completed using RDD sampling and 685 using List sampling. The survey was conducted by International Communications Research (ICR, the firm that conducted NJPS 1990). This is the first survey of Atlanta's Jewish population since 1996.

A total of 156,900 persons live in 61,300 Jewish households. Of those persons, 119,800 (76 percent) are Jewish. Jewish households comprise about 4.3 percent of households in the study area, compared to 4.4 percent in 1996, implying that Atlanta's Jewish population has been increasing at a rate comparable to that of the general population of the area. Atlanta is now the 11th largest Jewish community in the U.S., up from 17th in 1996.

The study shows the Jewish population of Atlanta to have increased by almost 60 percent since 1996. The current number of Jewish households, 61,300, has risen significantly from the 38,000 estimated in 1996; so has the number of Jews, from 77,000 in 1996 to 119,800 in 2006. Thirty-one percent of Jewish households moved to Atlanta in that decade while 46 percent have lived there for at least 20 years, meaning that Atlanta, while growing, now has a significant proportion of its community that should feel "rooted" in the area. That 46 percent is about average among some 40 comparison Jewish communities. Nineteen percent of Jewish survey respondents were born in Georgia, and 30 percent in New York.

Atlanta is a relatively young Jewish community, with children age 0–17 comprising 25 percent of Jewish persons and the elderly comprising only 12 percent. While the 25 percent is about average among about 45 comparison Jewish communities, the 12 percent is the sixth lowest among the comparison communities.

In regard to income, 14 percent of Jewish households earn less than $35,000 and 20 percent earn $150,000 or more. About 30 percent of households say they are, at best, "just managing." About 4 percent of Jewish households live below 150 percent of the federal poverty guidelines. About 10 percent of respondents report that someone in their household had sought assistance in finding a job or choosing an occupation, and of those, about 11 percent used a Jewish agency.

Since 1996, the percentage of respondents who identify as Orthodox increased from 3 to 9 percent, seventh highest of about 45 comparison Jewish communities. The percentage who identify as Conservative decreased from 30 to 26 percent, a figure about average among comparison Jewish communities. The percentage who identify as Reform increased from 34 to 46 percent, sixth highest of the comparison Jewish communities. The percentage identifying as "Just Jewish" decreased from 33 percent to 18 percent, seventh lowest of the comparison Jewish communities.

In findings that did not change since 1996, 56 percent of Jewish respondents indicated that being Jewish is very important to them, with only 9 percent saying that being Jewish is not at all important. Also remaining the same since 1996 was the percentage of people who always or usually light Hanukkah candles, 74 percent, about average among about 45 comparison Jewish communities. Always or usually attending a Passover Seder decreased from 76 percent in 1996 to 62 percent, fourth lowest of comparison Jewish communities. The percentage of households keeping a kosher home increased from 9 percent in 1996 to 13 percent in 2006, about average among comparison Jewish communities.

The percentage of households belonging to synagogues decreased slightly from 37 percent in 1996 to 33 percent in 2006. Ten percent of households report membership in the Marcus Jewish Community Center, and 46 percent contain a member who attended a Jewish cultural event or museum in the past year, with synagogue members being twice as likely to report such attendance.

The 50 percent of married couples that are intermarried in Atlanta (not the rate of individual Jews who are intermarried) is the third highest of about 50 comparison Jewish communities, and has increased from 37 percent since 1996. Sixty-seven percent of couples that married since 1990 are intermarried, compared to just over one-third of couples who married in the 1970s and 1980s, and 25 percent of couples who married prior to 1970. In intermarried households, 39 percent of children are being raised Jewish, 15 percent in two faiths, 28 percent in a different religion, 14 percent are "undecided," and 4 percent are being raised in no religion. In other findings, 48 percent of households contributed to a Jewish charity in the past year and 25 percent to the Jewish Federation of Greater Atlanta. Forty percent of Jewish respondents have visited Israel, and the same percentage report that they are very emotionally attached to Israel. About 91 percent of Jewish respondents agree that Jews have a special responsibility to take care of other Jews in need around the world, as compared to 71 percent of respondents in the NJPS 2000–01.

BOSTON

This 2005 study covered Greater Boston, including Brighton, Brookline, Newton, Central Boston, Cambridge, Greater Framingham, the Northwestern Suburbs, Greater Sharon, and other towns in the Boston area. Leonard Saxe, Benjamin Phillips, and Charles Kadushin, all of the Steinhardt Social Research Institute at Brandeis University, were the investigators for this study, which was based upon 1,766 telephone interviews, of which 401 were completed using RDD sampling and 1,365 using List sampling. The survey field work was conducted by Schulman, Ronca & Bucuvalas, Inc. This is the first survey of Boston's Jewish population since 1995.

A total of 265,500 persons live in 105,500 Jewish households. Of these persons, 208,500 (79 percent) are Jewish. An additional 2,000 Jews live in institutions, for a grand total of 210,500 Jews. Jews comprise about 7.2 percent of the population of the Boston area.

The study shows the Jewish population of Boston to be increasing. Over the 1995–2005 period, the number of Jewish households increased from 86,000 to 105,500 and the number of Jews in Jewish households from 177,000 to 208,500. The study authors attribute at least part of this increase to the fact that 60 percent of children in intermarried households are being raised Jewish.

The Jewish population of Boston continues to be geographically dispersed. However, the geographic distribution did not change significantly since 1995, after years of a consistent movement of the Jewish population westward. Newton and Brookline continue as the core areas of the Jewish community.

The age distribution of Jews suggests that there may be a need to increase social and health services for older adults in the future. Nineteen percent of Jews are age 50–59, 10 percent age 60–69, 8 percent age 70–79, 5 percent age 80–89, and 1 percent age 90 and over. About 91 percent of Jews age 25 and over have a college degree. While 6 percent of households earn less than $15,000, 43 percent earn $100,000 and over, including 12 percent earning $200,000 and over. Two percent of households describe themselves as poor; 1 percent as nearly poor; 10 percent as just getting along; 53 percent as living reasonably comfortably; 28 percent as living very comfortably; and 6 percent as prosperous. Five percent of respondents report that they were unable to purchase needed medication in the past year.

The 46 percent of married couples that are intermarried is the seventh highest of about 50 comparison Jewish communities. Most important, as noted above, 60 percent of children in intermarried households are being raised Jewish, the sixth highest percentage of about 50 comparison Jewish communities. The 72 percent of households that always or usually participate in a Passover Seder is about average among about 45 comparison Jewish communities, the 79 percent of households that always or usually light Hanukkah candles is the sixth highest of comparison communities, and the 26 percent of households that always or usually light Sabbath candles is about average among such communities.

About 49 percent of Jewish adults are synagogue members, 19 percent belong to Jewish community centers (JCCs), and 21 percent to Jewish organizations. Sixty percent of Jewish adults belong to a synagogue and/or a JCC and/or a Jewish organization. Fifty-four percent of Jewish adults volunteered to work for some type of organization in the past year, including 5 percent who volunteered only for Jewish organizations, 21 percent who volunteered for both Jewish and non-Jewish organizations, and 28 percent who volunteered for non-Jewish organizations only. About 46 percent of Jewish adults have visited Israel, including 7 percent who visited within the past five years.

About 3 percent of respondents give all their charitable donations to Jewish causes; 17 percent give mostly to Jewish causes; 38 percent donate about equally to Jewish and non-Jewish causes, 26 percent donate mostly to non-Jewish causes, and 10 percent donate only to non-Jewish causes.

DELAWARE

This small 2006 update study involved no new telephone interviewing but did include counts of Distinctive Jewish Names by zip code throughout the state and in adjoining areas of southern Pennsylvania, as well as information on membership and enrollment collected from synagogues, the JCC, and the Jewish day school. Ira Sheskin of the University of Miami was the principal investigator.

New population estimates were derived by calculating a ratio between the RDD estimate of Jews from the 1995 Delaware Jewish community study and the number of households with a DJN in the 1995 telephone directory, and applying this ratio to the DJN count from the 2006 telephone directory.

The study showed that the Jewish population of New Castle County (Wilmington and Newark) has not changed significantly since 2000. A total of 15,100 persons live in New Castle County in 5,700 Jewish households. Of those persons, 11,900 (79 percent) are Jewish. Small increases in Jewish population were shown for Kent County and a significant increase for Sussex County, although many homes in Sussex are beach homes and the Jewish population resides there only in the summer and sometimes only on weekends. Overall, the Jewish population of Kent and Sussex counties doubled from 1995 to 2006. Thus a total of 5,000 persons live in Kent and Sussex, in 2,200 Jewish households. Of those persons, 3,200 (64 percent) are Jewish. Consistent with this increase in Jewish population was a doubling of the membership of the one synagogue located in Sussex County.

Because Jews in southern Pennsylvania have begun to avail themselves of the facilities of the Delaware Jewish community, this study examined the growth of the Jewish community in Pennsylvania zip codes contiguous to the Delaware/Pennsylvania border and in the Route 202 corridor. These areas are technically within the service area of the Jewish Federation of Greater Philadelphia. The number of Jewish households in this area was shown to have increased from about 3,800 households in 1995 to about 8,800 (with 25,500 persons) in 2006.

A survey of Delaware synagogues showed a significant decrease in household membership from 2,004 in 1985, to 1,927 in 1995, and 1,559 in 2000. (These counts include only households residing in Delaware.) Consistent with the Jewish population of New Castle County remaining the same from 2000 to 2006, the number of synagogue member households rose only slightly, from 1,559 households in 2000 to 1,580 in 2006. The number of member households in Delaware synagogues who reside in Pennsylvania increased from 123 in 2000 to 171 in 2006.

Information provided by the JCC and the Jewish day school shows significant increases in involvement from southern Pennsylvania. From 2000 to 2006, the number of such Jewish JCC member households increased from 80 (10 percent of total membership) to 226 (22 percent of total membership). Likewise, the number of Jewish children in the JCC preschool from Pennsylvania increased from 10 in 2000 to 28 in 2006, and the number of Jewish children in the JCC day camp from Pennsylvania increased from 110 to 178 over that same period. About 16 percent of children in synagogue Hebrew schools now come from Pennsylvania, as do 10 percent of teenage youth-group participants.

Finally, the average donation per household to the Jewish Federation of Delaware increased from $54 per household in 1995 to $72 per household in 2005, adjusted for inflation.

DETROIT

This 2005 study covered Macomb, Oakland, and Wayne counties, Michigan. Ira Sheskin of the University of Miami was the principal investigator for this study, which was based upon 1,274 telephone interviews, of which 403 were completed using RDD sampling and 871 using DJN sampling. The survey was conducted by International Communications Research (ICR). This is the first survey of Detroit's Jewish population since 1989.

A total of 78,000 persons live in 30,000 Jewish households. Of these persons, 71,500 (92 percent) are Jewish. An additional 500 Jews live in institutions, for a grand total of 72,000 Jews. Jews comprise about 1.8 percent of the population in the three-county area.

The study shows the Jewish population of Detroit to be decreasing. The current number of Jewish households, 30,000 is far less than the 42,500 estimated by the 1989 study. Based upon counts of households with Distinctive Jewish Names, the number of Jewish households decreased by 2,500, or 8 percent, from 1999 through 2005. Data on migration of Jews into and out of Detroit suggest that the latter exceeds the former. The number of donors to the Jewish Federation of Metropolitan Detroit annual campaign decreased from 16,609 in 1995 to 10,474 ten years later. Only half of adult children remain in the locality after leaving their parents' homes and an increasing proportion of young adults are attending college outside the area. The age distribution also strongly suggests an aging population with a decreasing number of children.

The geographic distribution of Jewish households in Detroit has changed. During 1999–2005, the percentage of Detroit Jewish households in the Core Area (including Bloomfield Hills, Farmington Hills,

Oak Park, Southfield, and West Bloomfield and adjacent areas of southern Oakland County) decreased from 77 percent to 73 percent. Despite the decrease in Jewish population and the small decrease in its geographic concentration, the Detroit Jewish community is, in many ways, one of the strongest Jewish communities in the country. Among about 35–50 comparison Jewish communities, Detroit has the second highest percentage of respondents who keep kosher in and out of the home (14 percent) and who refrain from using electricity on Shabbat (10 percent). It has the sixth highest percentage of households that always or usually participate in a Passover Seder (82 percent) and keep a kosher home (22 percent). It has the seventh highest percentage of households with a mezuzah on the front door (77 percent). It has an above average percentage of households that always or usually light Sabbath candles (29 percent) and an average percentage of households that always or usually light Hanukkah candles (77 percent). Also, all Orthodox Jewish children and 95 percent of non-Orthodox Jewish children receive some formal Jewish education. Households under age 35 have stronger Jewish identities than is true in most comparison Jewish communities.

The 16 percent of married couples that are intermarried is the fourth lowest of about 55 comparison Jewish communities. However, as is true in all the comparison Jewish communities, the trend in Detroit is for higher intermarriage rates among younger couples: the rate is just under 20 percent in households under age 65 and 10 percent in households age 65 and over.

The 50 percent of Jewish households reporting current synagogue membership is about average among some 55 comparison Jewish communities, a surprising result given the overall level of Jewish connectedness and the fact that 88 percent of the households have been in Detroit for at least 20 years, the highest percentage among 40 comparison Jewish communities. The 71-percent rate of current synagogue membership for households with children is the highest of about 40 comparison Jewish communities, and the 57-percent rate for households under age 35 and the 64-percent rate for those 35–49 are the highest of about 35 comparison Jewish communities. Clearly, the reason for an only average percentage of overall synagogue membership is the fact that only 39 percent of households age 65 and over are synagogue members. This may suggest that income is a significant factor in whether a household joins.

The organized Jewish community is relatively well known and well regarded among the Jews of Detroit. As a result, the federation had the most successful campaign, on a per-household basis, of 55 Jewish federations, with about $35,000,000 being raised from approximately 30,000 households. The 37 percent of respondents saying they are very familiar with the local federation is the third highest of about 35 comparison Jewish communities, while the 35 percent who perceive the Federation as "excellent" is the fourth highest of about 30 comparison Jewish communities. Fifty percent of Jewish respondents used the Internet for Jewish-related information in the past year, including 30 percent who used it for information about the Detroit Jewish community. Younger respondents were more likely to use the Internet for Jewish-related information than were older respondents, and, similarly, were much more likely to obtain information about the local Jewish community from the Internet than from the *Detroit Jewish News*—which is one of the most successful Jewish newspapers in the country.

LAS VEGAS

This 2005 study covered all of Clark County, Nevada. Ira Sheskin of the University of Miami was the principal investigator for this study, which was based upon 1,197 telephone interviews, of which 398 were completed using RDD sampling and 799 using DJN sampling. The survey was conducted by International Communications Research (ICR). This is the first survey of the Las Vegas Jewish population since 1995.

A total of 89,000 persons live in 42,000 Jewish households. Of those persons, 67,500 (76 percent) are Jewish. From 1995 to 2005, the number of Jewish households increased by 44 percent, from 29,100 to 42,000, while the number of persons in Jewish households increased by 33 percent, from 66,900 to 89,000, and the number of Jews in Jewish households increased by 21 percent, from 55,600 to 67,500. Las Vegas is one of the fastest-growing Jewish communities in the U.S., but the rate of growth was found to be significantly slower than had been earlier touted by community officials.

The Jewish population of Las Vegas is geographically dispersed and has shifted location over the past decade. The percentage of Jewish households who live in the Northwest increased from 24 percent to 31 percent; that in the Southeast increased from 19 percent to 25 percent; and that in the Northeast increased from 7 percent to 11 percent. In contrast, the percentage of households in the Southwest decreased from 30 percent to 23 percent, and the percentage in the Central area decreased from 20 percent to 10 percent.

Las Vegas is not "home" for many Jewish households. Only 1 percent of adults in Jewish households were born in Southern Nevada, and only

21 percent of Jewish households have lived in the area for 20 years or more. Five percent of Jewish households say they will definitely move out within the next three years, the fifth highest percentage of about 30 comparison Jewish communities. These factors lead to a high level of attachment to other Jewish communities, as shown by the 8 percent of charitable dollars donated by Jewish households in the past year to Jewish federations other than the Jewish Federation of Las Vegas. Also, 69 percent of Jewish respondents reported that they feel "not very much" or "not at all" a part of the local Jewish community.

Large percentages of children in Jewish households live in nontraditional households. Eleven percent of children age 0–17 in Jewish households live with only one parent, the fourth highest of about 35 comparison Jewish communities. Forty-seven percent of children that age in Jewish households live with an adult who is or has been divorced, the second highest of about 30 comparison Jewish communities. The divorce rate, 164 divorced adults in Jewish households per 1,000 married adults, is the third highest of about 35 comparison Jewish communities.

The study points to a clear need for singles programs, as 39 percent (16,000) of Jewish adults age 18–64 are single and 28 percent (3,900) of households with single Jewish adults age 18–64 were interested in singles programs in the past year. Included in the 28 percent are 14 percent of households with Jewish singles who attended Jewish programs, 1 percent who attended non-Jewish programs, and 13 percent who did not attend singles programs in the past year. As in all Jewish communities for which this measure is available, there is a strong tendency for Jewish singles who attended singles programs to attend Jewish programs. Thus while the intermarriage rate in this community is significant (48 percent of married couples), single persons are attempting to find Jewish mates.

Membership levels are low in Las Vegas. The 14 percent of Jewish households reporting current synagogue membership either in the vicinity or elsewhere is the lowest of about 55 comparison Jewish communities. The 16-percent rate of current synagogue membership of households with children is the lowest of about 40 comparison Jewish communities. Among about 35 comparison Jewish communities, Las Vegas has the third lowest percentage of synagogue membership for households under age 35 (14 percent) and the lowest percentages for households age 35–49 (10 percent), age 50–64 (12 percent), and age 65 and over (19 percent). Perhaps the very low 1 percent of adults born in the area contributes to the low levels of membership in synagogues and other local Jewish institutions.

Only 45 percent of Jewish children age 5–12 in Las Vegas currently receive formal Jewish education, the second lowest of about 30 comparison Jewish communities. For those who are age 13–17 the figure is only 11 percent, which is also the second lowest of the comparison Jewish communities.

Almost all Jewish communities the size of Las Vegas—and many that are significantly smaller—have Jewish campuses that often house the Jewish federation, a JCC, and other Jewish institutions. Las Vegas currently has its federation, JCC, and Jewish Family Service Agency operating from office buildings.

SAN ANTONIO

This 2007 study covered Bexar County, Texas. Ira Sheskin of the University of Miami was the principal investigator for this study, which was based upon 675 telephone interviews, of which 290 were completed using RDD sampling and 385 using DJN sampling. This is the first scientific survey of San Antonio's Jewish population.

About 11,200 persons live in 4,500 Jewish households in San Antonio. Of these persons, 9,100 (81 percent) are Jewish. An additional 70 Jewish persons live in institutions, making a total of 9,170. Jews comprise about 0.6 percent of the population of Bexar County. An additional 1,000 are estimated to live in the seven counties surrounding Bexar.

The study shows the Jewish population of San Antonio to be relatively stable. Based upon counts of households with Distinctive Jewish Names, the number of Jewish households decreased by 300, or 6 percent, from 2000 through 2007. Survey results suggest that migration into San Antonio is about equal to migration out. The number of donors to the federation annual campaign decreased from 1,501 to 1,437 in that period. Only about one-third of adult children remain in San Antonio after leaving their parents' homes. The age distribution also suggests an aging population with a decreasing number of children. Thus, while evidence suggests current stability, the future will have to be carefully monitored.

The geographic distribution of Jewish households has changed in recent years. During 2000–2007, the percentage of area Jewish households inside Loop 410 decreased from 31 percent of all Jewish households to 25 percent; the percentage of Jewish households between Loop 410 and Loop 1604 remained about the same; and the percentage outside Loop 1604 increased from 10 percent to 17 percent. Thus while the Jewish population has moved significantly further from the downtown area, the core area (between Loop 410 and Loop 1604) has remained strong.

The study finds that San Antonio is a relatively strong Jewish community in several ways. Measures of Jewish religiosity are average among about 35–50 comparison Jewish communities. This is true for households having a mezuzah on the front door (68 percent), always or usually lighting Hanukkah candles (70 percent), always or usually lighting Shabbat candles (20 percent), keeping a kosher home (10 percent), keeping kosher in and out of the home (5 percent), and refraining from using electricity on Shabbat (2 percent). It has a below average percentage of households who always or usually participate in a Passover Seder (69 percent). The 25 percent of respondents who say they never attend services is about average among about 40 comparison Jewish communities, and the 25 percent of respondents who say they attend services at least once a month is also about average among about 45 comparison Jewish communities.

The 37 percent of married couples that are intermarried in San Antonio is about average among about 55 comparison Jewish communities. But unlike many of the comparison Jewish communities, the trend in San Antonio is for high intermarriage rates among all age groups: 35 percent of married couples in households age 35–49, 43 percent in households age 50–64, 36 percent in households age 65–74, and 26 percent in households age 75 and over.

San Antonio shows particular strength in Jewish community participation. Current synagogue membership (52 percent) is above average among about 40 comparison Jewish communities, the percentage of households who were members of a synagogue at some time during their adult lives (83 percent) is the fourth highest of about 30 comparison Jewish communities. JCC membership (29 percent) is the fourth highest of about 45 comparison JCCs, the 52 percent of households who participated in a JCC program over the past year is the third highest of about 45 comparison JCCs, and the JCC's 52-percent market share of the fitness facility and health club market among Jewish households is the fifth highest of about 25 comparison JCCs. The percentage of households who are associated with the Jewish community (anyone in the household is a member of a synagogue, the JCC, or a Jewish organization) is above average among about 40 comparison Jewish communities. The percentage of Jewish children age 0–5 in a preschool/childcare program who attend a Jewish program in 92 percent, the highest Jewish market share among about 30 comparison communities. The Jewish day camp market share for Jewish children age 3–17 attending a day camp the summer prior to the survey was 78 percent, fourth highest of about 30 comparison Jewish communities.

The *Jewish Journal of San Antonio* is always or usually read by 49 percent of respondents, the second highest of about 20 comparison Jewish communities. The 53 percent of households that reported donating to the Jewish federation in the past year is the fifth highest of about 50 comparison Jewish communities, and the average donation per household of $476 is about average among about 45 comparison Jewish communities. The 68 percent of households that donated to some Jewish charity in the past year is the fourth highest of about 40 comparison Jewish communities.

TUCSON

This small 2006 update study involved no new telephone interviewing, but did include counts of DJN households by zip code. New population estimates were derived from calculating a ratio between the RDD estimate of Jews from the 2002 Jewish community study of Southern Arizona and the number of households with a DJN in the 2002 telephone directory, and applying this ratio to the DJN count from the 2006 directory. Ira Sheskin of the University of Miami was the principal investigator.

The study suggests that a small decrease in the Jewish population occurred over the past four years, much of it due to a decline in the number of DJN households in zip code 85719, which contains the University of Arizona. The cause was a shift in American campus culture: the percentage of students with land lines in 2002 was considerably higher than is the case in 2006, as many now use cell phones only. Thus the Jewish population probably did not change significantly.

The study also showed no significant change in the size of the Jewish population in the West/Northwest from 2002 to 2006, an area that had seen a significant increase in Jewish population from 1994 through 2002.

Comparisons among Local Jewish Communities

Since 1993, more than 50 American Jewish communities have completed one or more scientific demographic studies. Starting with this AJYB volume, we are introducing a new feature in the article on U.S. Jewish population consisting of comparison tables. This year, the tables illustrate length of residence in the local community (Table 5); Jewish identification (Table 6); intermarriage (Table 7); and the percentage of children being raised Jewish in intermarried households (Table 8). In cases of communities where more than one study was completed since

1993, only the latest is used. The Jewish communities shown in Tables 6–8 have a combined Jewish population that comprises about 75 percent of the total U.S. Jewish population estimated in Table 1. Comparison tables with the results of 18 Jewish community studies completed between 1982 and 1995 that are not included in the tables in this section are available elsewhere.[7] These comparisons of Jewish communities should be treated with caution for three major reasons. First, the studies used were completed over a 14-year period, and thus differences between communities may be due, at least in part, to temporal factors. Second, even though only studies that used some RDD sampling are included, the individual studies used varying amounts of DJN and List sampling as well, and so differences in sampling techniques may lead to different results. And third, the questionnaires used were not uniform, and the literature on survey research indicates that even small changes in question wording or in the sequence of questions asked in a telephone survey can have a significant impact upon the results.[8]

To compensate somewhat for these factors, at least a five-percentage-point difference is required in these tables for the difference to be considered significant.

LENGTH OF RESIDENCE

Table 5 compares length of residence of respondents in 41 Jewish communities. The two most important columns show the percentages of respondents in residence for 0–4 years (new residents) and those in residence for 20 or more years (long-term residents). Length of residence is important for understanding levels of attachment to the local Jewish community and its Jewish institutions, as many studies show that it tends to correlate with membership and participation in Jewish institutions and activities. Communities with many long-term resident households thus have an advantage over those with fewer such households. As noted in the table, the percentage of long-term households varies from 11 per-

---

[7]See Ira M. Sheskin, *How Jewish Communities Differ: Variations in the Findings of Local Jewish Demographic Studies* (New York, 2001), published by the North American Jewish Data Bank and the City University of New York, for 124 comparison tables containing older data, also available at www.jewishdatabank.org

[8]For a more complete discussion of the difficulties in comparing study results see Ira M. Sheskin, "Comparisons between Local Jewish Community Studies and the 2000–01 National Jewish Population Survey," *Contemporary Jewry* 25 (2005), pp. 158–92.

cent in Martin-St. Lucie, Florida, to 88 percent in Detroit, with the median value at 52 percent. It should be noted that in-migration is only one demographic component of population change, the others being out-migration, births, and deaths.

Low percentages of new residents are found in mostly older, northern communities such as Hartford, Pittsburgh, Minneapolis, Philadelphia, St. Louis, Baltimore, Rochester, and Detroit. In contrast, high percentages of new residents are found in growing, mostly Sunbelt communities as Martin-St. Lucie, Orlando, Charlotte, Las Vegas, Denver, West Palm Beach, Seattle, and Harrisburg.[9] Even so, two of the largest Sunbelt communities, Los Angeles and Miami, have very low percentages of new residents. The percentage of new residents varies from 3 percent in Detroit to 32 percent in Orlando and Martin-St. Lucie. The median value is 14 percent.

It is also useful to examine the absolute numbers, which can be derived by multiplying the percentage of new residents by the number of households in the community. For example, although only 7 percent of Los Angeles Jewish households are new to the city, as compared with 31 percent in Charlotte, the absolute number in Los Angeles is about 17,000 households, compared to 1,200 in Charlotte.

Since there are now eight large Jewish communities that completed scientific community studies both before and since 2000, it is possible to gauge the rate of growth of communities. Atlanta is the fastest growing Jewish community in the country (4,800 Jews per year), followed by West Palm Beach (4,700), San Francisco (4,500), Washington, D.C. (3,100), South Palm Beach (2,400), Phoenix (2,000), Las Vegas (1,200), and New York (800). While there may be other Jewish communities that are growing rapidly, that growth cannot be documented.

JEWISH IDENTIFICATION

Table 6 shows Jewish identification for 48 Jewish communities. Respondents were generally asked whether they consider themselves Orthodox, Conservative, Reconstructionist, Reform, or Just Jewish. Thus Jewish identification is based on self-definition and not necessarily on synagogue membership, ideology, or religious practice. In fact, discrep-

---

[9]The high percentage of new residents in Harrisburg can be explained by the small Jewish population as well as the city's role as a state capital, where changes in administrations lead to migration in and out of the city.

ancies between identification and practice are evident. For example, respondents may identify as Orthodox or Conservative, but report that they do not keep kosher. Respondents may identify as Reform, but report that they never attend synagogue services. Conversely, some respondents identifying as Just Jewish are synagogue members.[10] Note that by calling a *household,* say, Orthodox because the respondent is Orthodox, we can project the number of Orthodox households in a community. The comparisons here are somewhat affected by the wording of the question. While the most common wording is the one provided in the previous paragraph, alternative have sometimes been used, such as "Do you consider yourself Orthodox, Conservative, Reconstructionist, Reform, or something else?" The extent to which alternative wordings produce different responses to this question is unknown.

The percentage of respondents who consider themselves Orthodox varies from 1 percent in Atlantic County, N.J, Martin-St. Lucie, Fla., and York, Pa., to more than 10 percent in Detroit (11 percent); Bergen County, N.J. (12 percent); Baltimore (17 percent); and New York (19 percent). The median Orthodox value is 4 percent. But since size of Orthodox households is almost always higher than Jewish household size of non-Orthodox households, the percentage of *Jews* who are Orthodox is higher than the percentage of Orthodox *households.* In addition, because Orthodox Jews tend to join synagogues at higher rates than others, Orthodox Jews comprise a much higher percentage of synagogue members. In Miami, for example, 9 percent of households are Orthodox, 12 percent of Jews are Orthodox, and 26 percent of synagogue-member households are Orthodox. Thus the overall influence of Orthodox Jews in a community often exceeds the influence implied by the percentages shown in Table 6.

The percentage of respondents who identify as Conservative varies from 15 percent in Denver to 39 percent in Tidewater (Norfolk-Virginia Beach). The median value is 28 percent. Four of the six communities with the lowest percentages are in the West: Denver (15 percent), San Francisco (17 percent), Seattle (19 percent), and Tucson (21 percent). Note that ten of the 13 communities with the highest percentages are in the South, including four Florida retirement communities. Such Florida communities tend to have high percentages of second-generation American Jews

---

[10]See also Bernard Lazerwitz, J. Alan Winter, Arnold Dashefsky, and Ephraim Tabory, *Jewish Choices: American Jewish Denominationalism* (Albany, N.Y., 1998).

(born in the U.S. of foreign-born parents), and these tend to identify as Conservative. The percentage of respondents who identify as Reform varies from 22 percent in Harrisburg to 60 percent in St. Louis. The median value is 37 percent. In this case, it is hard to identify any geographic patterns. The percentage of respondents who identify as Just Jewish varies from 11 percent in Cleveland to 47 percent in Las Vegas. The median value is 30 percent. The percentage identifying with this category is roughly indicative of the size of the Jewish population that does not feel connected to the Jewish community or their Jewish heritage. Nevertheless, the Just Jewish are not a monolithic group, and large numbers are involved in some type of Jewish activity—86 percent of such households in South Palm Beach, for example. And there are wide differences among them by community. In Detroit, for example, 59 percent always or usually participate in a Passover Seder, compared to 32 percent in Las Vegas, and 29 percent contributed to the Jewish federation in the past year in Detroit, compared to 12 percent in Las Vegas.

INTERMARRIAGE

Table 7 shows intermarriage rates for 50 Jewish communities. Intermarriage, which has reached significant proportions, has become one of the most important issues for the Jewish community. Although some intermarried couples are contributing significantly to the Jewish community, it is clear from comparisons of in-married and intermarried couples that the phenomenon of intermarriage has a negative affect on measures of Jewishness, and therefore on Jewish continuity. In Detroit, for example, 70 percent of in-married couples are synagogue members as compared to 17 percent of intermarried couples.[11]

The local Jewish community studies usually distinguish between three types of marriage. An in-marriage is between spouses who were born or raised Jewish and currently consider themselves Jewish. A conversionary in-marriage is between one spouse who was born or raised Jewish and currently considers himself/herself Jewish, and the other who, while not born or raised Jewish, currently considers himself/herself Jewish, whether or not there was a formal conversion. An intermarriage is between one

---

[11]See, in particular, Steven M. Cohen, *A Tale of Two Jewries: The Inconvenient Truth for American Jews* (New York, 2006).

spouse who was born or raised Jewish and currently considers himself/herself Jewish and the other who was not born or raised Jewish and does not currently consider himself/herself Jewish.

While Halakhah (Jewish law) does not differentiate between in-marriages and conversionary in-marriages, social scientists make this distinction in order to study several aspects of marital choice and their influence on Jewish behaviors.

Intermarriage rates may be reported based on *married couples* or *individuals*. As an illustration, imagine two weddings. In the first, Moshe (a Jew) marries Rachel (also a Jew). In the second, Abraham (a Jew) marries Christine (a non-Jew). Thus there are two married couples, one of which is intermarried, and so the *couples* intermarriage rate is 50 percent. However another method of calculating the rate is to note that there are three Jews (Moshe, Rachel, and Abraham), one of whom (Abraham) is married to a non-Jew (Christine), and the *individual* intermarriage rate is 33 percent. Each rate can be useful for different purposes. The local community studies generally cite the *couples* rate.

Two more points should be noted. The intermarriage rates reported in local Jewish community studies are for persons who currently consider themselves Jewish, and do not normally include those who have converted to another religion or attend services of another faith on a regular basis. Also, the rates reported in Table 7 are for all existing married couples, not just for marriages that have occurred recently (in the past five years, for example), as are often reported for both the 1990 and 2000–01 NJPS.

Table 7 shows that the *couples* intermarriage rate varies from 9 percent in South Palm Beach to 55 percent in Seattle and San Francisco. The median value is 33 percent. Note that six of the ten communities with the lowest rates (20 percent or lower) are retirement communities, mostly in Florida. Four of the nine Jewish communities with rates in excess of 45 percent are western, including the top two, Seattle and San Francisco.

Many American Jewish institutions today are developing policies, even if only informally, concerning intermarriage. They address such questions as: To what extent should intermarried couples be encouraged to affiliate? In religious institutions, will non-Jews be allowed to participate in religious services? How does the community welcome the children of intermarried couples while at the same time encouraging Jews to marry other Jews? While the answers entail a number of ideological and practical considerations, communities with relatively low intermarriage rates might well select different strategies than communities with high rates.

CHILDREN BEING RAISED JEWISH IN INTERMARRIED HOUSEHOLDS

Table 8 shows the percentage of children being raised Jewish in 49 Jewish communities, a figure that varies from a low of 18 percent in Martin-St. Lucie to 75 percent in South Palm Beach. The median value is 42 percent.

Three factors complicate these comparisons, and therefore only relatively large differences between two percentages (15–20 points) are given credence. First, the sample sizes are often small, and so the standard errors of these percentages are relatively high. Second, the question has often been asked in varying ways, making the basis for comparison somewhat suspect. Third, respondents often do not give clear answers, and non-Jewish interviewers sometimes interpret responses differently than Jewish interviewers might.

Four of the five communities with the smallest percentages are in the West: Palm Springs (19 percent), San Diego (21 percent), Seattle (23 percent), and Phoenix (26 percent). Detroit, which is otherwise one of the more Jewishly-connected communities, has a relatively low percentage of children in intermarried households, 31 percent, being raised Jewish. One possible explanation is that Detroit has a very low overall intermarriage rate, 16 percent, and only 4 percent of married couples who are members of Detroit synagogues are intermarried, compared to 35 percent of married couples who are non-members. Perhaps intermarried couples investigating a synagogue in Detroit do not find too many other intermarried couples there, and may feel uncomfortable joining for that reason alone.

The data indicate that some communities have been more successful than others in convincing intermarried Jews to raise their children Jewish, and/or in attracting such couples into the community.

IRA M. SHESKIN
ARNOLD DASHEFSKY

TABLE 1:   JEWISH POPULATION IN THE UNITED STATES, 2007

State	Estimated Jewish Population	Total Population*	Estimated Jewish Percent of Total
Alabama	9,000	4,559,030	0.2
Alaska	3,425	670,053	0.5
Arizona	106,100	6,166,318	1.7
Arkansas	1,675	2,810,872	0.1
California	1,194,190	36,457,549	3.3
Colorado	87,720	4,753,377	1.8
Connecticut	112,830	3,504,809	3.2
Delaware	15,100	853,476	1.8
Washington, D.C.	28,000	581,530	4.8
Florida	654,935	18,089,888	3.6
Georgia	127,245	9,363,941	1.4
Hawaii	6,990	1,285,498	0.5
Idaho	1,100	1,466,465	0.1
Illinois	278,520	12,831,970	2.2
Indiana	17,420	6,313,520	0.3
Iowa	6,140	2,982,085	0.2
Kansas	18,225	2,764,075	0.7
Kentucky	11,450	4,206,074	0.3
Louisiana	9,975	4,287,768	0.2
Maine	13,915	1,321,574	1.1
Maryland	234,550	5,615,727	4.2
Massachusetts	258,230	6,437,193	4.0
Michigan	87,270	10,095,643	0.9
Minnesota	46,685	5,167,101	0.9
Mississippi	1,500	2,910,540	0.1
Missouri	59,165	5,842,713	1.0
Montana	850	944,632	0.1
Nebraska	6,850	1,768,331	0.4
Nevada	69,600	2,495,529	2.8
New Hampshire	10,070	1,314,895	0.8
New Jersey	479,200	8,724,560	5.5
New Mexico	11,250	1,954,599	0.6
New York	1,617,720	19,306,183	8.4
North Carolina	27,745	8,856,505	0.3
North Dakota	430	635,867	0.1
Ohio	144,955	11,478,006	1.3
Oklahoma	5,050	3,579,212	0.1
Oregon	31,850	3,700,758	0.9

TABLE 1:   JEWISH POPULATION IN THE UNITED STATES, 2007 (CONTINUED)

State	Estimated Jewish Population	Total Population	Estimated Jewish Percent of Total
Pennsylvania	284,850	12,440,621	2.3
Rhode Island	18,750	1,067,610	1.8
South Carolina	11,335	4,321,249	0.3
South Dakota	295	781,919	0.0
Tennessee	19,300	6,038,803	0.3
Texas	130,170	23,507,783	0.6
Utah	4,400	2,550,063	0.2
Vermont	5,510	623,908	0.9
Virginia	98,040	7,642,884	1.3
Washington	43,135	6,395,798	0.7
West Virginia	2,335	1,818,470	0.1
Wisconsin	28,330	5,556,506	0.5
Wyoming	430	515,004	0.1
TOTAL	6,443,805	299,398,484	2.2

*July 1, 2006 http://factfinder.census.gov

TABLE 2:   DISTRIBUTION OF U.S. JEWISH POPULATION BY REGIONS, 2007

	Total Population	Percent Distribution	Jewish Population	Percent Distribution
Northeast	54,741,353	18.3%	2,801,075	43.5
Middle Atlantic	40,471,364	13.5%	2,381,770	37.0
New England	14,269,989	4.8%	419,305	6.5
Midwest	66,217,736	22.1%	694,285	10.8
East North Central	46,275,645	15.5%	556,495	8.6
West North Central	19,942,091	6.7%	137,790	2.1
South	109,083,752	36.4%	1,387,405	21.5
East South Central	17,754,447	5.9%	41,250	0.6
South Atlantic	57,143,670	19.1%	1,199,285	18.6
West South Central	34,185,635	11.4%	146,870	2.2
West	69,355,643	23.2%	1,561,040	24.2
Mountain	20,845,987	7.0%	281,450	4.4
Pacific	48,509,656	16.2%	1,279,590	19.9
TOTAL	299,398,484	100.0%	6,443,805	100.0

State	Date of Informant Confirmation or Latest Study	Geographic Area*	Jewish Population	Regional Totals	Part-Year Jewish Population**
ALABAMA					
	1997-2001	Birmingham (Jefferson County)	5,300		
	1997-2001	Dothan	100		
	1997-2001	Huntsville	750		
	1997-2001	Mobile (Baldwin and Mobile Counties)	1,100		
	1997-2001	Montgomery	1,200		
	1997-2001	Tuscaloosa	300		
	1997-2001	Other Places	250		
		Total Alabama	9,000		
ALASKA					
	1997-2001	Anchorage (Anchorage Borough)	2,300		
	1997-2001	Fairbanks (Fairbanks and North Star Borough)	540		
	1997-2001	Juneau	285		
	1997-2001	Kenai Peninsula	200		
	1997-2001	Other Places	100		
		Total Alaska	3,425		
ARIZONA					
	2002	**Cochise County (2002)**	450		
	1997-2001	Flagstaff (Coconino County)	500		
	1997-2001	Lake Havasu City	200		
	2002	**Northwest Valley (Glendale-Peoria-Sun City) (2002)**	10,900		
	2002	Phoenix (2002)	23,600		
	2002	Northeast Valley (Scottsdale) (2002)	34,500		
	2002	Tri Cities Valley (Ahwatukee-Chandler-Gilbert-Mesa-Tempe) (2002)	13,900		
	2002	**Phoenix Total (2002)**		82,900	
	1997-2001	Prescott	300		

*Estimates for communities with boldface type are from a scientific study in the year shown. **Part-year population shown only for where such information is available.

State	Date of Informant Confirmation or Latest Study	Geographic Area*	Jewish Population	Regional Totals	Part-Year Jewish Population**
	2005	West-Northwest (2002)	3,450		
	2005	Northeast (2002)	7,850		
	2005	Central (2002)	7,150		
	2005	Southeast (2002)	2,500		
	2005	Green Valley (2002)	450		
	2005	Tucson (Pima County) Total (2002)		21,400	1,000
	1997-2001	Yuma	150		
	2002	Santa Cruz County (2002)	100		
	1997-2001	Other Places	100		
		Total Arizona	106,100		1,000
ARKANSAS	1997-2001	Fayetteville	175		
	1997-2001	Hot Springs	150		
	1997-2001	Little Rock	1,100		
	1997-2001	Other Places	250		
		Total	1,675		
CALIFORNIA	1997-2001	Antelope Valley-Lancaster-Palmdale	3,000		
	1997-2001	Bakersfield (Kern County)	1,600		
	1997-2001	Chico-Oroville-Paradise (Butte County)	750		
	1997-2001	Eureka (Humboldt County)	1,000		
	1997-2001	Fairfield	800		
	1997-2001	Fresno (Fresno County)	2,300		
	1997-2001	Long Beach (in Los Angeles County: Cerritos-Hawaiian Gardens-Lakewood-Rossmoor-Signal Hill and, in Orange County: Cypress-Huntington Harbor-Los Alamitos-Seal Beach	18,000		

Year	Location	Population
1997	Malibu-Palisades (1997)	27,190
1997	Santa Monica-Venice (1997)	23,140
1997	Airport Marina (1997)	22,140
1997	Fairfax (1997)	54,850
1997	Beverly Hills (1997)	20,500
1997	Cheviot-Beverlywood (1997)	29,310
1997	Westwood (1997)	20,670
1997	Central City (1997)	4,710
1997	Hollywood (1997)	10,390
1997	Culver City (1997)	9,110
1997	Central Valley (1997)	27,740
1997	Burbank-Glendale (1997)	19,840
1997	Encino-Tarzana (1997)	50,290
1997	Southeast Valley (1997)	28,150
1997	Simi-Conejo (1997)	38,470
1997	High Desert (1997)	10,920
1997	North Valley (1997)	36,760
1997	West Valley (1997)	40,160
1997	Beach Cities (1997)	17,270
1997	Central (1997)	11,600
1997	Palos Verdes Peninsula (1997)	6,780
1997	San Pedro (1997)	5,310
1997	Eastern Belt (1997)	3,900
1997	Los Angeles-Pasadena-Santa Monica (1997)	519,200
1997-2001	Mendocino County (Redwood Valley-Ukiah)	600
1997-2001	Merced County	190
1997-2001	Modesto	500
1997-2001	Monterey Peninsula	2,300
1997-2001	Murrieta Hot Springs	550
1997-2001	Napa County	1,000
1997-2001	Orange County (most of Orange County-excluding parts included in Long Beach)	60,000

State	Date of Informant Confirmation or Latest Study	Geographic Area*	Jewish Population	Regional Totals	Part-Year Jewish Population**
	1998-2002	Palm Springs (1998)	4,400		
	1998-2002	Cathedral City-Rancho Mirage (1998)	3,100		
	1998-2002	Palm Desert-Sun City (1998)	2,500		
	1998-2002	East Valley (Bermuda-Dunes-Indian Wells-Indio-La Quinta) (1998)	1,300		
	1998-2002	North Valley (Desert Hot Springs-North Palm Springs-Thousand Palms) (1998)	700		
	1998-2002	Palm Springs Total (1998)		12,000	5,000
	1997-2001	Redding (Shasta County)	150		
	1997-2001	Riverside-Corona-Moreno Valley	2,000		
	1997-2001	Sacramento (El Dorado, Placer, Sacremento, and Yolo Counties)	21,300		
	1997-2001	Salinas	1,000		
	1997-2001	San Bernardino-Fontana area	3,000		
	2003	North County Coastal (2003)	24,000		
	2003	North County Inland (2003)	18,100		
	2003	Greater East San Diego (2003)	18,900		
	2003	La Jolla-Mid-Coastal (2003)	14,400		
	2003	Central San Diego (2003)	12,200		
	2003	South County (2003)	1,400		
	2003	San Diego (San Diego County) Total (2003)		89,000	
	2006	Alameda County (Oakland) (1986)	40,000		
	2006	Contra Costa County (1986)	60,000		
	2006	East Bay Total (1986)		100,000	
	2007	Marin County (2004)	26,100		
	2007	North Peninsula (2004)	40,300		
	2007	San Francisco County (2004)	65,800		

Year	Place			
2007	**Sonoma County (Petaluma-Santa Rosa) (2004)**	23,100		
2007	**South Peninsula (Palo Alto) (2004)**	72,500		
2007	**San Francisco Total (2004)**		227,800	
2006	**San Jose (Silicon Valley) (1986)**	63,000		
	San Francisco Bay Area		390,800	
1997-2001	San Gabriel and Pomona Valleys-Ontario (Alta Loma-Chiro-Calremon-Cucamonga-La Verne-Montclair-Ontario-Pomona-San Dimas-Upland	30,000		
1997-2001	San Luis Obispo-Paso Robles (San Luis Obispo County)	2,000		
1997-2001	Santa Barbara (Santa Barbara County)	7,000		
1997-2001	Santa Cruz-Aptos (Santa Cruz County)	6,000		
1997-2001	Santa Maria	500		
1997-2001	South Lake Tahoe (El Dorado County)	150		
1997-2001	Stockton	850		
1997-2001	Sun City	200		
1997-2001	Tulare and Kings counties (Visalia)	350		
1997-2001	Vallejo area	900		
1997-2001	Ventura County	15,000		
1997-2001	Other Places	200		
1997-2001	Total California	1,194,190		
COLORADO				
1997-2001	Aspen	750		5,000
1997-2001	Colorado Springs	1,500		
2007	**Denver (2007)**	25,800		
2007	**South Metro (2007)**	19,600		
2007	**Boulder (2007)**	12,600		
2007	North and West Metro (2007)	11,200		
2007	Aurora (2007)	6,700		
2007	North and East Metro (2007)	5,600		
2007	**Greater Denver (Adams, Arapahoe, Boulder, Broomfield, Denver, and Jeffersron Counties) Total (2007)**		81,500	

State	Date of Informant Confirmation or Latest Study	Geographic Area*	Jewish Population	Regional Totals	Part-Year Jewish Population**
	1997-2001	Fort Collins-Greeley-Loveland	2,000		
	1997-2001	Grand Junction (Mesa County)	320		
	1997-2001	Pueblo-Lamar-Trinidad	425		
	1997-2001	Steamboat Springs	250		
	pre-1997	Telluride	125		
	1997-2001	Vail-Breckenridge-Eagle (Eagle and Summit Counties)	650		
	1997-2001	Other Places	200		
	1997-2001	Total Colorado	87,720		
CONNECTICUT	1997-2001	Bridgeport-Shelton (Easton-Fairfield-Monroe-Shelton-Stratford-Trumbull)	13,000		
	1999-2001	Danbury-Newtown (Bethel-Brookfield-Danbury-New Fairfield-Redding-Ridgefield-Sherman)	3,200		
	2007	Greenwich	7,000		
	1997-2001	Stamford-Darien-New Canaan	9,200		
	2001	Westport (2001)	5,000		
	2001	Weston (2001)	1,850		
	2001	Wilton (2001)	1,550		
	2001	Norwalk (2001)	3,050		
	2001	Westport-Weston-Wilton-Norwalk Total (2001)		11,450	
		Fairfield County Total		43,850	
	2000	Bloomfield-Hartford-West Hartford (2000)	15,800		
	2000	East Hartford-Glastonbury-Manchester-South Windsor (and adjacent Tolland County) (2000)	4,800		
	2000	Farmington Valley (and adjacent Litchfield County) (2000)	6,400		
	2000	Bristol-New Britain-Middletown (adjacent Middlesex County)-Meriden-Wallingford (adjacent New Haven County)-Plymouth-Terryville (adjacent Litchfield County) (2000)	5,000		
			800		

Date	Place		
2000	**Hartford County Total (including northern Middlesex County, western Tolland County, eastern Litchfield County, northern New Haven County) (2000)**		32,800
	Other Places in Litchfield County	50	
	Litchfield County Total (excluding towns in adjacent Hartford County)		630
1997-2001	Lower Middlesex County (Branford-Clinton-Durham-Guilford-Killingworth-Madison	1,600	
	Old Saybrook-Old Lyme-Westbrook)		
	Middlesex County Total (excluding towns in adjacent Hartford County)		1,600
1987	**New Haven (Ansonia-Bethany-Branford-Derby-East Haven-Guilford-Hamden**	24,300	
	Madison-Meriden-Milford-North Haven-Orange-Quinnipiac-Seymour-Wallingford		
	West Haven-Woodbridge) (1987)		
1997-2001	Waterbury-Cheshire (Bethlehem-Litchfield-Middlebury-Morris-Naugatuck-Oakville-Oxford-Plymouth-Prospect-Roxbury-Southbury-Southington-Thomaston-Torrington-Washington-Waterbury-Watertown-Wolcott-Woodbury-and other parts of Litchfield County and northern New Haven County	4,500	
	New Haven County Total (excluding towns in adjacent Hartford County)		28,800
pre-1997	Colchester-Lebanon; Hebron (adjacent Tolland County)	300	
1997-2001	New London-Norwich (central and southern New London County and parts of Middlesex and Windham Counties)	3,850	
	New London County Total (including adjacent Tolland County)		4,150
2006	Storrs-Columbia	400	
2006	Other Places in Tolland County	100	
	Tolland County Total (excluding towns in adjacent Hartford and New London Counties)		500

State	Date of Informant Confirmation or Latest Study	Geographic Area*	Jewish Population	Regional Totals	Part-Year Jewish Population**
	pre-1997	Danielson	100		
	2006	Willimantic	300		
	2006	Other Places in Windham County	100		
		Windham County Total		500	
		Total Connecticut	112,830		
DELAWARE					
	2005	**Kent and Sussex Counties (Dover) (2005)**	3,200		
	2005	**Newark area (2005)**	4,300		
	2005	**Wilmington area (2005)**	7,600		
		Total Delaware	15,100		
DISTRICT OF COLUMBIA					
	2003	**District of Columbia (2003)**	28,000		
	2003	**Lower Montgomery County (2003)**	88,600		
	2003	**Upper Montgomery County (2003)**	24,400		
	2003	**Prince Georges County (2003)**	7,200		
	2003	**Arlington-Alexandria-Falls Church (2003)**	27,900		
	2003	**South Fairfax-Prince William County (2003)**	25,000		
	2003	**West Fairfax-Loudoun County (2003)**	14,500		
	2003	**Greater Washington Total (2003)**		215,600	
FLORIDA					
	1997-2001	Brevard County	5,000		
	pre-1997	Crystal River	100		
	1997-2001	Fort Myers-Arcadia-Port Charlotte-Punta Gorda (Charlotte, De Soto, and Lee Counties)	8,000		
	1997-2001	Fort Pierce	1,060		
	1997-2001	Gainesville	2,200		

Year	Location			
2002	Jacksonville Core Area (2002)	8,800		
2002	The Beaches (Atlantic Beach, Neptune Beach,	1,900		
2002	Jacksonville Beach, Ponte Verde Beach) (2002)			
2002	Remainder of Duval, Nassau, Clay, and			
	St. Johns Counties (including St. Augustine) (2002)	2,200		
2002	Jacksonville Total (2002)		12,900	200
1997-2001	Key West	650		
pre-1997	Lakeland	1,000		
1997-2001	Naples (Collier County)	4,200		
1997-2001	Ocala (Marion County)	500		
1997-2001	North Orlando (Seminole County and southern			
	Volusia Counties) (1993)	7,800		
1997-2001	Central Orlando (Maitland-Orlando-Winter Park) (1993)	7,700		
1997-2001	South Orlando (Orlando and northern Osecola			
	Counties) (1993)	5,200		
1997-2001	Orlando Total (1993)		20,700	400
1997-2001	Pasco County (New Port Richey)	1,000		
1997-2001	Pensacola (Escambia and Santa Rosa Counties)	975		
1997-2001	North Pinellas (Clearwater) (1994)	9,850		
1997-2001	Central Pinellas (Largo) (1994)	4,050		
1997-2001	South Pinellas (St. Petersburg) (1994)	10,300		
1997-2001	St. Petersburg (Pinellas County) Total (1994)		24,200	1,500
2001	Sarasota (2001)	8,600		
2001	Longboat Key (2001)	1,000		
2001	Bradenton (Manatee County) (2001)	1,750		
2001	Venice (2001)	850		
2001	Sarasota Total (2001)		12,200	3,300
2005	East Boca (2005)	8,900		
2005	Central Boca (2005)	33,800		
2005	West Boca (2005)	17,000		
2005	Boca Raton Subtotal (2005)		59,700	13,000

State Date of Informant Confirmation or Latest Study	Geographic Area*	Jewish Population	Regional Totals	Part-Year Jewish Population**
2005	Delray Beach (2005)	47,800	107,500	10,800
2005	South Palm Beach Subtotal (2005)			23,800
2005	Boynton Beach (2005)	45,600		10,700
2004	Lake Worth (2005)	21,600		3,300
2005	Town of Palm Beach (2005)	2,000		2,000
2005	West Palm Beach (2005)	8,300		2,000
2005	Wellington-Royal Palm Beach (2005)	9,900		1,400
2005	North Palm Beach-Palm Beach Gardens-Jupiter (2005)	13,950		3,500
2005	West Palm Beach Subtotal (2005)		101,350	22,900
2005	Palm Beach County Total (2005)		208,850	46,700
2004	North Dade Core East (Aventura-Golden Beach-part of North Miami Beach) (2004)	34,000		
2004	North Dade Core West (Ojus and parts of North Miami Beach) (2004)	13,100		
2004	Other North Dade (north of Flagler Street) (2004)	3,800		
2004	North Dade Subtotal (2004)		50,900	4,500
2004	West Kendall (2004)	13,750		
2004	East Kendall (parts of Coral Gables-Pinecrest-South Miami) (2004)	15,650		
2004	Northeast South Dade (Key Biscayne-parts of City of Miami) (2004)	8,300		
2004	South Dade (2004)		37,700	800
2004	North Beach (Bal Harbour-Bay Harbor Islands-Indian Creek Village-Surfside) (2004)	3,700		
2004	Middle Beach (parts of City of Miami Beach) (2004)	10,300		
2004	South Beach (parts of City of Miami Beach) (2004)	3,700		
2004	The Beaches (2004)		17,700	1,700
2004	Miami-Dade County Total (2004)		106,300	7,000

1999	Hollywood-Hallandale (1999)	32,900		3,400
1999	Pembroke Pines-Cooper City-Davie-Weston (1999)	44,200		1,900
1999	Plantation-North Lauderdale-Tamarac-Lauderdale Lakes-Sunrise (1999)	65,600		5,700
1999	Coral Springs-Parkland (1999)	28,000		0
1999	Margate-Coconut Creek-Wynmoor-Palm Aire-Century Village (1999)	30,300		7,400
1999	Fort Lauderdale (1999)	11,300		2,400
1999	Broward County Total (1999)		212,300	20,800
	Southeast Florida (Miami-Dade, Broward, Palm Beach Counties)		527,450	74,500
2005	Stuart (Martin County) (2005)	2,900		
2005	Southern St. Lucie County (Port St. Lucie) (2005)	2,900		
2005	Stuart-Port St. Lucie Total (2005)		5,800	900
1997-2001	Tallahassee	2,200		
1997-2001	Tampa (Hillsborough County)	20,000		
1997-2001	Vero Beach (Indian River County)	400		
2007	Volusia and Flagler Counties (Daytona Beach)	4,000		
pre-1997	Winter Haven	300		
1997-2001	Other Places	100		
1997-2001	Total Florida	654,935		80,800
	GEORGIA			
1997-2001	Albany Area	200		
1997-2001	Athens	600		
2005	Intown (2005)	28,900		
2005	North Metro Atlanta (2005)	28,300		
2005	East Cobb Expanded (2005)	18,400		
2005	Sandy Springs-Dunwoody (2005)	15,700		
2005	Gwinnett-East Perimeter (2005)	14,000		
2005	North and West Perimeter (2005)	9,000		
2005	South (2005)	5,500		
2005	Atlanta Total (2005)		119,800	

State	Date of Informant Confirmation or Latest Study	Geographic Area*	Jewish Population	Regional Totals	Part-Year Jewish Population**
	1997-2001	Augusta (Burke, Columbia, and Richmond Counties)	1,300		
	1997-2001	Brunswick	120		
	1997-2001	Columbus	750		
	1997-2001	Dalton	125		
	1997-2001	Macon	1,000		
	1997-2001	Savannah (Chatham County)	3,000		
	1997-2001	Valdosta	100		
	1997-2001	Other Places	250		
		Total Georgia	127,245		
HAWAII	1997-2001	Hilo	280		
	1997-2001	Oahu (Honolulu)	6,400		
	1997-2001	Kauai	100		
	1997-2001	Maui	210		
		Total Hawaii	6,990		
IDAHO	1997-2001	Boise (Ada and Boise Counties)	800		
	1997-2001	Ketchum	100		
	1997-2001	Moscow-Lewiston	100		
	1997-2001	Other Places	100		
		Total Idaho	1,100		
ILLINOIS	1997-2001	Aurora area	750		
	1997-2001	Bloomington-Normal	500		
	2007	Champaign-Urbana (Champaign County)	1,400		
	2000	**Chicago (Cook and DuPage Counties and parts of Lake County) (2000)**	270,500		

1997-2001	Decatur (Macon County)		130
1997-2001	DeKalb		180
1997-2001	Elgin (northern Kane County and southern McHenry County)		500
1997-2001	Joliet (Will County)		210
1997-2001	Kankakee		100
1997-2001	Peoria		800
1997-2001	Quad Cities-Illinois portion (Moline-Rock Island)		400
1997-2001	Quad Cities-Iowa portion (Davenport) (Scott County)		500
1997-2001	Quad Cities Total	900	
1997-2001	Quincy		100
1997-2001	Rockford-Freeport (Boone, Winnebago, and Stephenson Counties)		1,100
1997-2001	Southern Illinois (Carbondale-East St. Louis) (all of Illinois south of Carlinville)		500
2007	Springfield (Morgan and Sangamon Counties)		800
1997-2001	Waukegan		300
1997-2001	Other Places		250
1997-2001	Total Illinois		278,520
INDIANA			
1997-2001	Bloomington		1,000
1997-2001	Evansville		400
1997-2001	Fort Wayne		900
1997-2001	Gary-Northwest Indiana (Lake and Porter Counties)		2,000
2006	Indianapolis		10,000
1997-2001	Lafayette		550
1997-2001	Michigan City (La Porte County)		300
1997-2001	Muncie		120
1997-2001	South Bend-Elkhart (St.Joseph and Elkhart Counties)		1,850
1997-2001	Terre Haute (Vigo County)		100
1997-2001	Other Places		200
	Total Indiana		17,420

State	Date of Informant Confirmation or Latest Study	Geographic Area*	Jewish Population	Regional Totals	Part-Year Jewish Population**
IOWA					
	1997-2001	Cedar Rapids	420		
	1997-2001	Council Bluffs	150		
	1997-2001	Des Moines-Ames	2,800		
	1997-2001	Iowa City (Johnson County)	1,300		
	1997-2001	Postville	150		
	1997-2001	Quad Cities-Illinois portion (Moline-Rock Island)	400		
	1997-2001	Quad Cities-Iowa portion (Davenport) (Scott County)	500		
	1997-2001	Sioux City (Plymouth and Woodbury Counties)	400		
	1997-2001	Waterloo (Black Hawk County)	170		
	1997-2001	Other Places	250		
		Total Iowa	6,140		
KANSAS					
	2006	**Kansas City area-Kansas portion (1985) (Johnson and Wyandotte Counties)**	16,000		
	2006	**Kansas City area-Missouri portion (1985)**	4,000		
		Kansas City Total		16,000	
	1997-2001	Lawrence	200		
	pre-1997	Manhattan	425		
	1997-2001	Topeka (Shawnee County)	400		
	1997-2001	Wichita (Sedgwick County and Salina-Dodge City-Great Bend-Liberal-Russell-Hays)	1,100		
	1997-2001	Other Places	100		
		Total Kansas	18,225		
KENTUCKY					
	1997-2001	Covington-Newport area	500		
	1997-2001	Lexington (Bourbon, Clark, Fayette, Jessamine, Madison, Pulaski, Scott, and Woodford Counties)	2,000		
			8,700		

1997-2001		Other Places		100
1997-2001		Total Kentucky		11,450
	LOUISIANA			
1997-2001		Alexandria (Allen, Grant, Rapides, and Vernon Parishes)		175
1997-2001		Baton Rouge (Ascension, East Baton Rouge, Iberville, Livingston, Pointe Coupee, St. Landry, and West Baton Rouge Parishes)		1,600
1997-2001		Lake Charles area		200
2007		New Orleans (Orleans and Jefferson Parishes)		7,000
12007		Shreveport-Bossier area		450
2007		Monroe-Ruston area		150
2007		North Louisiana (Caddo and Bossier Parishes) Total	600	
pre-1997		South Central La. (Abbeville-Crowley-Franklin-Hourma-Lafayette-Morgan City-New Iberia-Opelousas-Thibodaux)		250
1997-2001		Other places		150
		Total Louisiana		9,975
	MAINE			
pre-1997		Augusta		140
1997-2001		Bangor		3,000
2007		Androscoggin County (Lewiston–Auburn) (2007)		600
2007		Oxford County (2007)		750
pre-1997		Rockland area		300
2007		**Sagadahoc County (2007)**		400
2007		**Portland Area (2007)**		4,425
2007		**Other Cumberland County (2007)**		2,350
2007		**York County (2007)**		1,575
2007		**Southern Maine Total (2007)**	8,350	
pre-1997		Waterville		225
1997-2001		Other places		150
		Total Maine		13,915

State	Date of Informant Confirmation or Latest Study	Geographic Area*	Jewish Population	Regional Totals	Part-Year Jewish Population**
MARYLAND					
	1997-2001	Annapolis area	3,000		
	1999	**Owings Mills–Reisterstown (1999)**	22,300		
	1999	**Pikesville–Mt. Washington (1999)**	34,100		
	1999	**Park Heights (1999)**	8,680		
	1999	**Randallstown–Liberty Road (1999)**	3,840		
	1999	**Central Baltimore (1999)**	9,230		
	1999	**Towson–Lutherville–Timonium Corridor (1999)**	6,580		
	1999	**Carroll County (1999)**	2,650		
	1999	**Other Places (1999)**	4,020		
	1999	**Baltimore Total (1999)**		91,400	
	1997-2001	Cumberland	275		
	1997-2001	Easton (Talbot County)	100		
	1997-2001	Frederick (Frederick County)	1,200		
	1997-2001	Hagerstown (Washington County)	325		
	1997-2001	Harford County	1,200		
	1999-2001	Howard County (Columbia) (1999)	16,000		
	2003	**Lower Montgomery County (2003)**	88,600		
	2003	**Upper Montgomery County (2003)**	24,400		
	2003	**Prince Georges County (2003)**	7,200		
	2003	**Greater Washington Total in Maryland (2003)**		120,200	
	1997-2001	Ocean City	200		
	1997-2001	Salisbury	400		
	1997-2001	Other places	250		
		Total Maryland	234,550		
MASSACHUSETTS					
	1997-2001	Amherst area	1,300		
	1997-2001	Andover-Lawrence (Boxford-Dracut-Methuen-North			

2002	Attleboro area (2002)	800
2005	Brighton-Brookline-Newton and Contiguous Areas (2005)	61,500
2005	Central Boston-Cambridge and Contiguous Areas (2005)	43,400
2005	Greater Framingham (2005)	18,700
2005	Northwestern Suburbs (2005)	24,600
2005	Greater Sharon (2005)	21,000
2005	Other Towns (2005)	41,300
2005	Boston Region Total (2005)	210,500
1997-2001	Cape Cod-Barnstable County	3,250
1997-2001	Fall River area	1,100
1997-2001	Greenfield (Franklin County)	1,100
1997-2001	Haverhill	800
1997-2001	Holyoke	600
1997-2001	Lowell area	2,000
1997-2001	Martha's Vineyard (Dukes County)	300
1997-2001	New Bedford (Dartmouth-Fairhaven-Mattapoisett)	2,600
1997-2001	Newburyport	280
1997-2001	North Adams (northern Berkshire County)	400
1997-2001	North Worcester County (Fitchburg-Gardener-Leominster)	1,500
1997-2001	Northampton	1,200
1997-2001	Pittsfield (Central and Southern Berkshire County)	4,000
1997-2001	Plymouth area	1,000
1997-2001	South Worcester County (Southbridge-Webster)	500
1997-2001	Springfield (Agawam-East Longmeadow-Hampden-Longmeadow-West Springfiled Wilbraham)	10,000
1997-2001	Taunton area	1,000
1997-2001	Worcester (central Worcester County) (1986)	11,000
1997-2001	Other places	150
	Total Massachusetts	258,230
	MICHIGAN	
1997-2001	Ann Arbor (Washtenaw County)	7,000
2006	Bay City	150

State	Date of Informant Confirmation or Latest Study	Geographic Area*	Jewish Population	Regional Totals	Part-Year Jewish Population**
	2007	Benton Harbor-St. Joseph	150		
	2007	**West Bloomfield (2005)**	19,500		
	2007	**Bloomfield Hills-Birmingham (2005)**	5,200		
	2007	**Farmington (2005)**	12,500		
	2007	**Oak Park-Huntington Woods (2005)**	12,600		
	2007	**Southfield (2005)**	8,100		
	2007	**East Oakland County (2005)**	1,900		
	2007	**North Oakland County (2005)**	3,500		
	2007	**West Oakland County (2005)**	2,400		
	2007	**Wayne County (2005)**	5,700		
	2007	**Macomb County (2005)**	600		
	2007	**Total Detroit (2005)**		72,000	
	2007	Flint (Genesee County)	1,300		
	2007	Grand Rapids (Kent County)	2,000		
	2007	Jackson	200		
	1997-2001	Kalamazoo (Kalamazoo County)	1,500		
	2007	Lansing area	2,100		
	2007	Midland	120		
	2007	Mt. Pleasant (Isabella, Mecosta, Gladwin, and Gratiot Counties)	75		
	2007	Muskegon (Muskegon County)	210		
	2007	Saginaw (Saginaw County)	115		
	2007	Traverse City	200		
	2007	Other places	350		
		Total Michigan	87,270		

MINNESOTA

Year	Place		
1997-2001	Duluth (Carlton and St. Louis Counties)	485	
1997-2001	Rochester	550	
2004	City of Minneapolis (2004)	5,200	
2004	Inner Ring (2004)	16,100	
2004	Outer Ring (2004)	8,000	
2004	Minneapolis Subtotal (2004)		29,300
2004	City of St. Paul (2004)	4,300	
2004	Southern Suburbs (2004)	5,900	
2004	Northern Suburbs (2004)	700	
2004	St. Paul Subtotal (2004)		10,900
2004	Twin Cities Sorrounding Counties (Anoka, Carver, Goodhue, Rice, Scott, Shelburne, Washington, and Wright Counties) (2004)	5,300	
2004	Twin Cities Total (2004)		40,200
1997-2001	Other places	150	
	Total Minnesota	46,685	

MISSISSIPPI

Year	Place		
1997-2001	Biloxi-Gulfport	250	
1997-2001	Greenville	120	
1997-2001	Hattiesburg (Forrest and Lamar Counties)	130	
1997-2001	Jackson (Hinds and Rankin Counties)	550	
1997-2001	Other places	450	
	Total Mississippi	1,500	

MISSOURI

Year	Place		
1997-2001	Columbia	400	
1997-2001	Joplin	100	
2006	Kansas City area-Kansas portion (1985)	16,000	
2006	Kansas City area-Missouri portion (1985)	4,000	
2006	Kansas City Total (1985)		20,000
1997-2001	St. Joseph (Buchanan County)	265	

State	Date of Informant Confirmation or Latest Study	Geographic Area*	Jewish Population	Regional Totals	Part-Year Jewish Population**
	2006	**St. Louis City (1995)**	2,400		
	2006	**Chesterfield-Ballwin (1995)**	9,900		
	2006	**North of Olive (1995)**	12,000		
	2006	**Ladue-Creve Coeur (1995)**	10,000		
	2006	**Clayton-University Cities (1995)**	7,300		
	2006	**Other Parts of St. Louis and St. Charles Counties (1995)**	12,400		
	2006	**St. Louis Total (1995)**		54,000	
	1997-2001	Springfield	300		
	1997-2001	Other Places	100		
	1997-2001	Total Missouri	59,165		
MONTANA	1997-2001	Billings (Yellowstone County)	300		
	1997-2001	Butte-Helena	100		
	1997-2001	Kalispell (Flathead County)	150		
	1997-2001	Missoula	200		
	1997-2001	Other places	100		
		Total Montana	850		
NEBRASKA	1997-2001	Lincoln-Grand Island-Hastings	700		
	1997-2001	Omaha	6,100		
	1997-2001	Other places	50		
		Total Nebraska	6,850		
NEVADA	2005	**Northwest (2005)**	22,000		
	2005	**Southwest (2005)**	16,000		
	2005	**Central (2005)**	6,300		

2005	**Southeast (2005)**	16,400		
2005	**Northeast (2005)**	6,800		
2005	**Las Vegas Total (2005)**		67,500	
1997-2001	Reno-Carson City (Carson City and Washoe Counties)	2,100		
	Total Nevada	69,600		
NEW HAMPSHIRE				
1997-2001	Concord	500		
1997-2001	Conway-Franklin-Laconia-Meredith-Plymouth	270		
pre-1997	Hanover-Lebanon	600		
pre-1997	Keene	300		
1997-2001	Littleton area	200		
1997-2001	**Manchester area (1983)**	4,000		
1997-2001	Nashua area	2,000		
1997-2001	Portsmouth-Exeter	1,250		
1997-2001	Salem	150		
2007	**Strafford (Dover-Rochester) (2007)**	700		
1997-2001	Other places	100		
1997-2001	Total New Hampshire	10,070		
NEW JERSEY				
2004	**Atlantic County (2004)**	11,700		7,300
2004	**Cape May County-Wildwood (2004)**	500		900
2004	**Atlantic and Cape May Counties Total (2004)**		12,200	8,200
2001	**Pascack-Northern Valley (2001)**	11,900		
2001	**North Palisades (2001)**	16,100		
2001	**Central Bergen (2001)**	17,200		
2001	**West Bergen (2001)**	14,300		
2001	**South Bergen (2001)**	1,000		
1997-2001	Other Bergen	23,200		
2001	**Bergen County (Total) (2001)**		83,700	
1997-2001	Bridgeton	110		

State	Date of Informant Confirmation or Latest Study	Geographic Area*	Jewish Population	Regional Totals	Part-Year Jewish Population**
	2006	**Cherry Hill-Southern N.J. (Camden, Burlington, and Gloucester Counties) (1991)**	49,000		
	2006	**East Essex (1998)**	10,800		
	2006	**Livingston (1998)**	12,600		
	2006	**North Essex (1998)**	15,600		
	2006	**South Essex (1998)**	20,300		
	2006	**West Orange-Orange (1998)**	16,900		
	2006	**Essex County (Newark) Total (1998)**		76,200	
	1997-2001	Flemington (Hunterdon County)	1,500		
	2001	**North Hudson County (2001)**	2,000		
	1997-2001	Bayonne	1,600		
	2006	Hoboken	1,800		
	1997-2001	Jersey City	6,000		
	2001	Hudson County Total		11,400	
	2006	Middlesex County (Edison-New Brunswick) (in Somerset County: Kendall Park, Somerset, Franklin; and in Mercer County: Hightstown; and Middlesex County)	45,000		
	2006	**Western Monmouth (Marlboro-Freehold-Manalapan-Howell) (1997)**	37,800		
	2006	**Eastern Monmouth (Deal-Asbury Park-Long Branch) (1997)**	17,300		
	2006	**Northern Monmouth (Highlands-Middletown-Hazlet-Union Beach) (1997)**	8,900		
	2006	**Monmouth County Total (1997)**		64,000	6,000
	2006	**Morris County (1998)**	33,500		
	1997-2001	Ocean County (Lakewood)	29,000		
	1997-2001	Passaic County	17,000		

1997-2001	Princeton area	3,000	
1997-2001	Somerset County (Bridgewater-Somerville) (most of Somerset County (excluding parts included in Middlesex County and parts of Hunterdon County)	11,000	
1997-2001	Sussex County	4,100	
1997-2001	Trenton (most of Mercer County excluding parts included in Middlesex County)	6,000	
2006	Union County (Elizabeth) (Union County (except Springfield) and adjacent areas of Somerset and Middlesex counties)	30,000	
1997-2001	Vineland (most of Cumberland County and parts of Salem and Camden counties)	1,890	
1997-2001	Warren County	400	
1997-2001	Other Places	200	
	Total New Jersey	479,200	14,200
NEW MEXICO			
1997-2001	Albuquerque (Bernalillo)	7,500	
1997-2001	Las Cruces	600	
pre-1997	Los Alamos	250	
1997-2001	Santa Fe-Las Vegas	2,500	
pre-1997	Taos	300	
1997-2001	Other Places	100	
	Total New Mexico	11,250	
NEW YORK			
1997-2001	Albany (Albany County)	12,000	
1997-2001	Amsterdam	100	
1997-2001	Auburn (Cayuga County)	115	
1997-2001	Binghamton (Broome County)	2,400	
2006	**Buffalo (Erie County) (1995)**	18,500	
1997-2001	Canandaigua-Geneva-Newark-Seneca Falls	300	
1997-2001	Catskill	200	

State	Date of Informant Confirmation or Latest Study	Geographic Area*	Jewish Population	Regional Totals	Part-Year Jewish Population**
	1997-2001	Cortland (Cortland County)	150		
	1997-2001	Ellenville	1,600		
	1997-2001	Elmira-Corning (Chemung, Schuyler, and Tioga Counties)	950		
	1997-2001	Fleischmanns	100		
	1997-2001	Glens Falls-Lake George (Warren, Washington, southern Essex, and northern Saratoga Counties)	800		
	1997-2001	Gloversville (Fulton County)	300		
	1997-2001	Herkimer (Herkimer County)	130		
	1997-2001	Hudson (Columbia County)	500		
	1997-2001	Ithaca (Tompkins County)	2,000		
	1997-2001	Jamestown	100		
	1997-2001	Kingston-New Paltz-Woodstock (eastern Ulster County)	4,300		
	2002	**Kingsbridge-Riverdale (2002)**	21,500		
	2002	**Northeast Bronx (2002)**	13,900		
	2002	**Other Bronx (2002)**	9,600		
	2002	**Bronx Subtotal (2002)**		45,000	
	2002	**Bensonhurst-Gravesend (2002)**	40,000		
	2002	**Borough Park (2002)**	76,600		
	2002	**Coney Island- Brighton-Sheepshead Bay (2002)**	49,700		
	2002	**Flatbush-Midwood-Kensington (2002)**	101,100		
	2002	**Kingsbay-Madison (2002)**	33,700		
	2002	**Williamsburg (2002)**	52,700		
	2002	**Crown Heights-Prospect-Lefferts Gardens (2002)**	15,700		
	2002	**Brooklyn Heights-Park Slope (2002)**	23,000		
	2002	**Canarsie-Flatlands (2002)**	33,100		
	2002	**Other Brooklyn (2002)**	30,400		

Year	Location	Subtotal	Detail
2002	Brooklyn Subtotal (2002)	456,000	
2002	Gramercy Park-Murray Hill (2002)		32,500
2002	Lower Manhattan (2002)		41,100
2002	Upper East Side (2002)		64,700
2002	Upper West Side (2002)		59,400
2002	Chelsea-Clinton (2002)		24,600
2002	Washington Heights (2002)		8,800
2002	Other Manhattan (2002)		11,900
2002	Manhattan Subtotal (2002)	243,000	
2002	Fresh Meadows-Kew Garden Hills-Hillside (2002)		28,200
2002	Northeast Queens (2002)		24,100
2002	Rego Park-Forrest Hills (2002)		39,100
2002	The Rockaways (2002)		10,700
2002	Other Queens (2002)		83,900
2002	Queens Subtotal (2002)	186,000	
2002	Mid-Staten Island (2002)		29,500
2002	Other Staten Island (2002)		12,500
2002	Staten Island Subtotal (2002)	42,000	
2002	East Meadow-Bellmore (2002)		30,100
2002	Five Towns-Atlantic Beach (2002)		41,400
2002	Great Neck (2002)		47,900
2002	Northeast Nassau (2002)		37,500
2002	South Shore (2002)		25,200
2002	Other Nassau (2002)		38,900
2002	Nassau County Subtotal (2002)	221,000	
2002	Western Suffolk (2002)		36,500
2002	Central Suffolk (2002)		34,200
2002	Eastern Suffolk (2002)		13,400
2002	Other Suffolk (2002)		5,900
2002	Suffolk County Subtotal (2002)	90,000	
2002	Southeastern Westchester (2002)		21,900

State	Date of Informant Confirmation or Latest Study	Geographic Area*	Jewish Population	Regional Totals	Part-Year Jewish Population**
	2002	**Central-Southeastern Westchester (2002)**	56,800		
	2002	**Northern Westchester (2002)**	45,000		
	2002	**Other Westchester (2002)**	5,300		
	2002	**Westchester County Subtotal (2002)**		129,000	
	2002	**New York City Total (2002)**		972,000	
	2002	**New York (New York and Nassau, Suffolk, and Westchester Counties) Total (2002)**		1,412,000	
	1997-2001	Niagara Falls	150		
	1997-2001	Olean	100		
	1997-2001	Oneonta (Delaware and Otsego Counties)	300		
	1997-2001	Orange County (Middletown-Monroe-Newburgh-Port Jervis)	19,000		
	1997-2001	Plattsburgh	250		
	1997-2001	Potsdam	200		
	2007	Poughkeepsie (Dutchess County)	4,200		
	1997-2001	Putnam County	1,000		
	2007	**Brighton (1999)**	10,700		
	2007	**Pittsford (1999)**	3,100		
	2007	**Other areas of Monroe County and Victor in Ontario County (1999)**	7,250		
	2007	**Rochester Total (1999)**		21,050	
	1997-2001	Rockland County	90,000		
	1997-2001	Rome	100		
	1997-2001	Saratoga Springs	600		
	1997-2001	Schenectady	5,200		
	pre-1997	Sullivan County (Liberty-Monticello)	7,425		
	1997-2001	Syracuse (Onondaga County, western Madison County, and most of Oswego County)	9,000		

1997-2001	Troy area	800
2007	Utica (southeastern Oneida County)	1,100
1997-2001	Watertown	100
1997-2001	Other places	600
1997-2001	Total New York	1,617,720
	NORTH CAROLINA	
1997-2001	Asheville (Buncombe, Haywood, and Madison Counties)	1,300
1997-2001	**Charlotte (Mecklenburg County) (1997)**	8,500
2007	Durham-Chapel Hill (Durham and Orange Counties)	6,000
1997-2001	Fayetteville (Cumberland County)	300
1997-2001	Gastonia	210
1997-2001	Greensboro-High Point (Guilford County)	2,500
1997-2001	Greenville	240
1997-2001	Hendersonville (Henderson County)	250
1997-2001	Hickory	260
1997-2001	Raleigh (Wake County)	6,000
1997-2001	Southeastern North Carolina (Elizabethtown-Jacksonville-Whiteville-Wilmington)	1,200
1997-2001	Winston-Salem	485
1997-2001	Other places	500
	Total North Carolina	27,745
	NORTH DAKOTA	
1997-2001	Fargo	200
1997-2001	Grand Forks	130
1997-2001	Other places	100
	Total North Dakota	430
	OHIO	
2006	**Akron-Kent (1999) (Portage and Summit Counties)**	3,500
pre-1997	Athens	100
2006	**Canton-New Philadelphia (Stark and Tuscarawas Counties) (1955)**	1,000

State	Date of Informant Confirmation or Latest Study	Geographic Area*	Jewish Population	Regional Totals	Part-Year Jewish Population**
	1997-2001	Cincinnati (Butler and southern Hamilton Counties)	22,500		
		(new estimate due in 2008)			
	2006	Inner Core (1996)	24,200		
	2006	Outer Core (1996)	17,100		
	2006	Northern Heights (1996)	17,000		
	2006	Northeast (1996)	5,600		
	2006	Southeast (1996)	4,600		
	2006	Cleveland Cuyahoga (1996)	13,000		
	2006	Cleveland (Cuyahoga and parts of Lake, Geauga, Portage, and Summit Counties) Total (1996)		81,500	
	2001	Perimeter North (2001)	5,450		
	2001	Bexley area (2001)	6,800		
	2001	East-Southeast (2001)	3,550		
	2001	North-Other areas (2001)	6,200		
	2001	Columbus Total (2001)		22,000	
	1997-2001	Dayton (Greene and Montgomery Counties)	5,000		
	1997-2001	Elyria-Oberlin	155		
	1997-2001	Hamilton-Middletown-Oxford	900		
	1997-2001	Lima (Allen County)	180		
	pre-1997	Lorain	600		
	1997-2001	Mansfield	150		
	1997-2001	Marion	125		
	1997-2001	Sandusky-Freemont-Norwalk (Huron and Sandusky Counties)	105		
	1997-2001	Springfield	200		
	1997-2001	Steubenville (Jefferson County)	115		
	2006	Toledo-Bowling Green (Fulton, Lucas, and Wood Counties) (1994)	3,900		

Date	Place	Number
1997-2001	Wooster	175
1997-2001	**Youngstown-Warren (Mahoning and Trumbull Counties) (2002)**	2,300
1997-2001	Zanesville (Muskingum County)	100
1997-2001	Other Places	350
1997-2001	Total Ohio	144,955
	OKLAHOMA	
1997-2001	Oklahoma City-Norman (Oklahoma and Cleveland Counties)	2,300
1997-2001	Tulsa	2,650
1997-2001	Other places	100
1997-2001	Total Oklahoma	5,050
	OREGON	
1997-2001	Bend	500
1997-2001	Corvallis	500
1997-2001	Eugene	3,250
1997-2001	Medford-Ashland-Grants Pass (Jackson and Josephine Counties)	1,000
2007	Portland	25,500
1997-2001	Salem (Marion and Polk Counties)	1,000
1997-2001	Other places	100
1997-2001	Total Oregon	31,850
	PENNSYLVANIA	
2007	Altoona (Blair County)	550
1997-2001	Butler (Butler County)	250
1997-2001	Chambersburg	150
1997-2001	Erie (Erie County)	850
1997-2001	**East Shore (1994)**	5,300
1997-2001	**West Shore (1994)**	1,800
1997-2001	**Harrisburg Total (1994)**	7,100
1997-2001	Beaver Falls (northern Beaver County)	180

State	Date of Informant Confirmation or Latest Study	Geographic Area*	Jewish Population	Regional Totals	Part-Year Jewish Population**
	1997-2001	Hazelton-Tamaqua	300		
	1997-2001	Johnstown (Cambria and Somerset Counties)	275		
	1997-2001	Lancaster area	3,000		
	1997-2001	Lebanon (Lebanon County)	350		
	1997-2001	Lehigh Valley (Allentown-Bethlehem-Easton)	8,500		
		(New estimate due in 2008)			
	1997-2001	New Castle	200		
	1997-2001	Oil City	100		
	2006	**Bucks County (1997)**	34,800		
	2006	**Chester County (Oxford-Kennett Square-Phoenixville-West Chester) (1997)**			
	2006	**Delaware County (Chester-Coatesville) (1997)**	10,100		
	2006	**Montgomery County (Norristown) (1997)**	15,700		
	2006	**Philadelphia (1997)**	58,900		
	2006	**Philadelphia Total (1997)**	86,600	206,100	
	pre-1997	Pike County	300		
	2002	**Squirrel Hill (2002)**	13,900		
	2002	**Squirrel Hill Adjacent Neighborhoods (2002)**	5,700		
	2002	**South Hills (2002)**	6,400		
	2002	**East Suburbs (2002)**	5,500		
	2002	**Fox Chapel-North Hills (2002)**	5,000		
	2002	**Western Suburbs (2002)**	1,600		
	2002	**East End (2002)**	1,700		
	2002	**Mon Valley (2002)**	800		
	2002	**Other Areas of Greater Pittsburgh (2002)**	1,600		
	2002	**Pittsburgh (Allegheny and parts of Washington, Westmoreland, and Beaver Counties) Total (2002)**		42,200	

1997-2001	Pottstown	650
1997-2001	Pottsville	120
1997-2001	Reading (Berks County)	2,200
1997-2001	Scranton (Lackawanna County)	3,100
1997-2001	Sharon-Farrell	300
1997-2001	State College	700
1997-2001	Stroudsburg	600
1997-2001	Sunbury-Lewisburg-Milton-Selinsgrove-Shamokin	200
1997-2001	Uniontown area	150
pre-1997	Wayne County (Honesdale)	500
1997-2001	Wilkes-Barre (Luzerne County, except Hazelton-Tamaqua)	3,000
1997-2001	Williamsport-Lock Haven (Clinton and Lycoming Counties)	225
1999-2001	**York (1999)**	1,800
1997-2001	Other places	900
	Total Pennsylvania	284,850

RHODE ISLAND

2007	**Providence-Pawtucket (2002)**	7,500
2007	**West Bay (2002)**	6,350
2007	**East Bay (2002)**	1,100
2007	**South County (Washington County) (2002)**	1,800
2007	**Northern Rhode Island (2002)**	1,000
2007	**Newport County (2002)**	1,000
	Total Rhode Island	18,750

SOUTH CAROLINA

1997-2001	Charleston	5,500
1997-2001	Columbia (Lexington and Richland Counties)	2,750
1997-2001	Florence area	220
1997-2001	Greenville	1,200
1997-2001	Myrtle Beach-Georgetown (Georgetown and Horry Counties)	475
1997-2001	Rock Hill-York	100
1997-2001	Spartanburg (Spartanburg County)	500

State	Date of Informant Confirmation or Latest Study	Geographic Area*	Jewish Population	Regional Totals	Part-Year Jewish Population**
	1997-2001	Sumter-Kingstree (Clarendon, Lee, Sumter, and Williamsburg Counties)		140	
	1997-2001	Other places	450		
		Total South Carolina	11,335		
SOUTH DAKOTA					
	1997-2001	Sioux Falls	195		
	1997-2001	Other places	100		
		Total South Dakota	295		
TENNESSEE					
	1997-2001	Chattanooga	1,450		
	1997-2001	Knoxville	1,800		
	2006	Memphis	7,800		
	2002	Nashville (2002)	7,800		
	1997-2001	Oak Ridge	250		
	1997-2001	Other places	200		
		Total Tennessee	19,300		
TEXAS					
	1997-2001	Amarillo (Carson, Childress, Deaf Smith, Gray, Hall, Hutchinson, Moore, Potter, and Randall Counties)	200		
	1997-2001	Austin (Travis County)	13,500		
	pre-1997	Baytown	300		
	1997-2001	Beaumont	500		
	1997-2001	Brownsville-Harlingen-South Padre Island (Cameron County)	450		
	pre-1997	College Station-Bryan	400		
	1997-2001	Corpus Christi (Nueces County)	1,400		
	2006	Near North Dallas (1988)	12,300		
	2006	Far North Dallas-Richardson (1988)	9,900		

Year	Location	Population	Total
2006	East and Northeast Dallas-West Garland (1988)	5,700	
2006	Plano-Carrollton (1988)	6,900	
2006	Other areas of Dallas (1988)	10,200	
2006	**Dallas (1988)**		45,000
1997-2001	El Paso	5,000	
1997-2001	Fort Worth (Tarrant County)	5,000	
1997-2001	Galveston	400	
2007	Braeswood (1986)	16,000	
2007	Bellaire-Southwest (1986)	5,100	
2007	West Memorial (1986)	5,000	
2007	Memorial Villages (1986)	2,500	
2007	Rice-West University (1986)	3,300	
2007	University Park-South Main (1986)	450	
2007	Near Northwest (1986)	2,700	
2007	Northwest-Cypress Creek (1986)	3,000	
2007	Addicks-West Houston (1986)	2,100	
2007	Clear Lake (1986)	1,350	
2007	Other areas of Harris County (1986)	3,500	
2007	**Houston (Harris, Montgomery, Fort Bend Counties and parts of Brazoria and Galveston Counties) Total (1986)**		45,000
1997-2001	Laredo	130	
1997-2001	Longview	100	
1997-2001	Lubbock (Lubbock County)	230	
1997-2001	McAllen (Hidalgo and Starr Counties)	500	
1997-2001	Midland-Odessa	200	
1997-2001	Port Arthur	100	
2007	**Inside Loop 410 (2007)**	2,000	
2007	**Between the Loops (2007)**	5,600	
2007	**Outside Loop 1604 (2007)**	1,600	
2007	San Antonio Sorrounding Counties (Atascosa, Bandera, Comal, Guadalupe, Kendall, Medina, and Wilson Counties) (2007)	1,000	
2007	**San Antonio Total (2007)**		10,200

State	Date of Informant Confirmation or Latest Study	Geographic Area*	Jewish Population	Regional Totals	Part-Year Jewish Population**
	1997-2001	Tyler	400		
	1997-2001	Waco (Bell, Coryell, Falls, Hamilton, Hill, and McLennan Counties)	300		
	1997-2001	Wichita Falls	260		
	1997-2001	Other places	600		
		Total Texas	130,170		
UTAH	1997-2001	Ogden	150		
	1997-2001	Salt Lake City (Salt Lake County)	4,200		
	1997-2001	Other places	50		
		Total Utah	4,400		
VERMONT	1997-2001	Bennington area	500		
	pre-1997	Brattleboro	350		
	1997-2001	Burlington	2,500		
	1997-2001	Manchester area	325		
	1997-2001	Montpelier-Barre	550		
	1997-2001	Rutland	625		
	1997-2001	St. Johnsbury-Newport (Caledonia and Orleans County)	140		
	1997-2001	Stowe	150		
	pre-1997	Woodstock	270		
	1997-2001	Other places	100		
		Total Vermont	5,510		
VIRGINIA	1997-2001	Blacksburg-Radford	175		
	1997-2001	Charlottesville	1,500		

Year	Place		
1997-2001	Danville area	100	
1997-2001	Fredericksburg (parts of Spotsylvania, Stafford, King George, and Orange Counties)	500	
1997-2001	Lynchburg area	275	
1997-2001	Martinsville	100	
1997-2001	Newport News-Hampton-Williamsburg-James City-York County, and Poquoson City	2,400	
2007	Norfolk (2001)	3,550	
2007	Virginia Beach (2001)	6,000	
2007	Chesepeake-Portsmouth-Suffolk (2001)	1,400	
2007	Norfolk-Virginia Beach Total (2001)		10,950
2003	Arlington-Alexandria-Falls Church (2003)	28,000	
2003	South Fairfax-Prince William County (2003)	25,000	
2003	West Fairfax-Loudoun County (2003)	14,500	
2003	Greater Washington Total in Northern Virginia (2003)		67,500
1997-2001	Petersburg-Colonial Heights	350	
2006	Central (1994)	2,200	
2006	West End (1994)	2,400	
2006	Far West End (1994)	4,800	
2006	Northeast (1994)	1,200	
2006	Southside (1994)	1,900	
2006	Richmond (Henrico and Chesterfield Counties) Total (1994)		12,500
1997-2001	Roanoke	900	
1997-2001	Staunton-Lexington (Augusta, Bath, Highland, Page, Rockingham, and Shenandoah Counties)	370	
1997-2001	Winchester (Clarke, Frederick, Warren, and Winchester Counties)	270	
1997-2001	Other places	150	
	Total Virginia	98,040	
WASHINGTON			
1997-2001	Bellingham	525	
1997-2001	Kennewick-Pasco-Richland	300	

State	Date of Informant Confirmation or Latest Study	Geographic Area*	Jewish Population	Regional Totals	Part-Year Jewish Population**
	1997-2001	Olympia (Thurston County)	560		
	pre-1997	Port Angeles	100		
	2000	**Eastside (2000)**	11,200		
	2000	**Seattle-Ship Canal South (2000)**	10,400		
	2000	**North End-North Suburbs (2000)**	12,600		
	2000	**Other Areas of Seattle (2000)**	3,000		
	2000	**Seattle (Kings County and parts of Snohomish and Kitsap Counties) Total (2000)**		37,200	
	1997-2001	Spokane	1,500		
	1997-2001	Tacoma (Pierce County)	2,000		
	1997-2001	Vancouver-Longview-Kelso	600		
	1997-2001	Yakima-Ellensburg (Kititas and Yakima Counties)	150		
	1997-2001	Other places	200		
	1997-2001	Total Washington	43,135		
WEST VIRGINIA	pre-1997	Bluefield-Princeton	200		
	2007	Charleston (Kanawha County)	975		
	1997-2001	Clarksburg	110		
	1997-2001	Huntington	250		
	1997-2001	Morgantown	200		
	pre-1997	Parkersburg	110		
	1997-2001	Wheeling	290		
	1997-2001	Other places	200		
		Total West Virginia	2,335		
WISCONSIN	1997-2001	Appleton area	100		
	1997-2001	Beloit-Janesville	120		

1997-2001	Green Bay	500
1997-2001	Kenosha (Kenosha County)	300
1997-2001	La Crosse	100
2007	Madison (Dane County)	5,000
2006	**City of Milwaukee (1996)**	3,100
2006	**North Shore (1996)**	11,000
2006	**Mequon (1996)**	2,300
2006	**Metropolitan Ring (1996)**	4,700
2006	**Milwaukee (Milwaukee, eastern Waukesha, and southern Ozaukee Counties) Total (1996)**	21,100
1997-2001	Oshkosh-Fond du Lac	170
1997-2001	Racine (Racine County)	200
1997-2001	Sheboygan	140
1997-2001	Wausau-Antigo-Marshfield-Stevers Point	300
1997-2001	Other places	300
	Total Wisconsin	28,330

WYOMING

1997-2001	Casper	150
1997-2001	Cheyenne-Laramie	230
1997-2001	Other places	50
	Total Wyoming	430

TABLE 4: COMPARISON OF INFORMANT ESTIMATES TO SCIENTIFIC STUDY ESTIMATES

Community	Year of Study	Informant Estimate of Number of Jews in AJYB Prior to Study	Number of Jews Found by Scientific Study	Over or (Under) Estimate by Informant	Percentage Over or (Under) Estimate by Informant
Atlanta	1996	70,000	76,800	(6,800)	-8.9
Atlanta	2006	85,900	119,800	(33,900)	-28.3
Atlantic County	1984	12,000	14,700	(2,700)	-18.4
Atlantic County	2004	15,800	20,226	(4,426)	-21.9
Baltimore	1985	92,000	87,000	5,000	5.7
Baltimore	1999	94,500	91,400	3,100	3.4
Bergen	2001	83,700	83,700	0	0.0
Boston	1995	228,000	233,000	(5,000)	-2.1
Boston	2005	227,300	210,500	16,800	8.0
Broward	1997	237,000	219,600	17,400	7.9
Buffalo	1995	17,000	26,400	(9,400)	-35.6
Charlotte	1997	6,000	7,800	(1,800)	-23.1
Chicago	1990	248,000	261,000	(13,000)	-5.0
Chicago	2000	261,000	270,500	(9,500)	-3.5
Cleveland	1987	70,000	80,500	(10,500)	-13.0
Cleveland	1996	65,000	81,500	(16,500)	-20.2
Columbus	1990	15,000	15,600	(600)	-3.8
Columbus	2001	15,600	22,000	(6,400)	-29.1
Delaware	1995	10,150	15,100	(4,950)	-32.8
Denver	1981	30,000	38,600	(8,600)	-22.3
Denver	1997	46,000	63,300	(17,300)	-27.3
Denver	2007	72,400	81,500	(9,100)	-11.2
Detroit	1989	70,000	96,000	(26,000)	-27.1
Detroit	2005	94,000	72,000	22,000	30.6
Harrisburg	1994	6,500	7,100	(600)	-8.5
Hartford	1981	23,500	25,111	(1,611)	-6.4
Hartford	2000	25,200	32,800	(7,600)	-23.2
Howard County	1999	10,000	16,000	(6,000)	-37.5
Jacksonville	2002	7,300	12,900	(5,600)	-43.4
Las Vegas	1995	20,000	55,600	(35,600)	-64.0
Las Vegas	2005	75,000	67,500	7,500	11.1
Los Angeles	1979	455,000	503,000	(48,000)	-9.5
Los Angeles	1997	490,000	519,200	(29,200)	-5.6
Martin-St. Lucie	1999	3,000	6,650	(3,650)	-54.9
Miami	1994	145,000	153,600	(8,600)	-5.6
Miami	2004	118,000	113,300	4,700	4.1
Milwaukee	1983	23,900	30,000	(6,100)	-20.3
Milwaukee	1996	28,000	21,100	6,900	32.7
Minneapolis	2004	31,500	29,300	2,200	7.5

TABLE 4: CONTINUED

Community	Year of Study	Informant Estimate of Number of Jews in AJYB Prior to Study	Number of Jews Found by Scientific Study	Over or (Under) Estimate by Informant	Percentage Over or (Under) Estimate by Informant
Monmouth	1997	33,600	65,700	(32,100)	-48.9
New York	1991	1,671,000	1,420,000	251,000	17.7
New York	2002	1,450,000	1,412,000	38,000	2.7
Orlando	1993	18,000	19,200	(1,200)	-6.3
Palm Springs	1998	9,850	13,850	(4,000)	-28.9
Philadelphia	1984	295,000	252,364	42,636	16.9
Philadelphia	1997	250,000	206,100	43,900	21.3
Phoenix	1983	30,000	45,000	(15,000)	-33.3
Phoenix	2002	60,000	82,900	(22,900)	-27.6
Pittsburgh	2002	40,000	42,200	(2,200)	-5.2
Rhode Island	1987	17,500	16,000	1,500	9.4
Rhode Island	2002	16,000	18,750	(2,750)	-14.7
Richmond	1994	8,000	12,150	(4,150)	-34.2
Rochester	1986	19,600	25,800	(6,200)	-24.0
Rochester	1999	22,500	21,000	1,500	7.1
San Antonio	2007	11,000	10,200	800	7.8
San Diego	2003	70,000	89,000	(19,000)	-21.3
San Francisco	1986	80,000	119,000	(39,000)	-32.8
San Francisco	2004	122,500	208,600	(86,100)	-41.3
Sarasota	1992	10,000	12,200	(2,200)	-18.0
Sarasota	2001	17,500	15,500	2,000	12.9
Seattle	1990	19,500	29,300	(9,800)	-33.4
Seattle	2000	29,300	37,200	(7,900)	-21.2
South Palm Beach	1995	83,500	110,800	(27,300)	-24.6
South Palm Beach	2005	93,000	107,600	(14,600)	-13.6
Southern Maine	2007	6,000	8,350	(2,350)	-28.1
St. Louis	1995	53,500	54,000	(500)	-0.9
St. Paul	2004	9,200	10,940	(1,740)	-15.9
St. Petersburg	1994	9,500	25,700	(16,200)	-63.0
Tidewater	1988	15,000	18,850	(3,850)	-20.4
Tidewater	2001	11,000	10,950	50	0.5
Tucson	2002	20,000	22,400	(2,400)	-10.7
Washington (D.C.)	1983	160,000	157,334	2,666	1.7
Washington (D.C.)	2003	165,100	215,600	(50,500)	-23.4
West Palm Beach	1987	50,000	60,400	(10,400)	-17.2
West Palm Beach	1999	67,000	73,900	(6,900)	-9.3
West Palm Beach	2005	74,000	101,400	(27,400)	-27.0
Westport	2000	9,100	11,450	(2,350)	-20.5
York	1999	1,500	1,800	(300)	-16.7
Total		8,756,500	9,047,175	(290,675)	-3.2

TABLE 5: LENGTH OF RESIDENCE IN THE LOCAL METROPOLITAN AREA
COMMUNITY COMPARISONS, PERCENTAGES

Community	Base: Respondents			Years in Residence	
	Year	0-4	5-9	10-19	20+
Martin-St. Lucie	1999	32	28	29	11
Orlando	1993	32	20	30	18
Charlotte	1997	31	21	20	29
Las Vegas	2005	29	21	30	21
Denver	1997	23	14	19	44
West Palm Beach	2005	21	23	33	23
Seattle	2000	21	16	22	40
Harrisburg	1994	21	11	19	50
Phoenix	2002	19	23	19	39
St. Petersburg	1994	19	20	35	26
South Palm Beach	2005	19	19	39	23
San Diego	2003	19	13	24	45
Sarasota	2001	18	24	33	26
Tucson	2002	18	20	21	41
Westport	2000	17	20	20	44
Washington	2003	17	11	20	54
Wilmington	1995	17	11	14	58
Broward	1997	16	17	37	31
Atlanta	2006	15	16	23	46
Richmond	1994	15	13	21	51
Jacksonville	2002	14	9	24	53
San Antonio	2007	13	7	18	62
Monmouth	1997	13	15	26	46
Bergen	2001	13	12	20	56
St. Paul	2004	13	6	21	60
Atlantic County	2004	12	15	23	50
Miami	2004	12	9	17	62
York	1999	11	17	25	47
Tidewater	2001	10	11	19	59
Milwaukee	1996	10	10	13	68
Rhode Island	2002	10	8	13	69
Hartford	2000	9	7	16	69
Pittsburgh	2002	9	7	11	73
Minneapolis	2004	9	5	18	68
Philadelphia	1997	8	8	10	75
St. Louis	1995	7	11	9	73
Los Angeles	1997	7	8	20	65
Baltimore	1999	7	8	11	74
Rochester	1999	6	9	15	70
Detroit	2005	3	2	7	88

TABLE 6: JEWISH IDENTIFICATION COMMUNITY COMPARISONS, PERCENTAGES

Community	Year	Base: Jewish Respondents Orthodox	Conservative	Reconstructionist	Reform	Just Jewish
Las Vegas	2005	3	23	1	26	47
Tucson	2002	2	21	2	32	44
San Francisco	2004	3	17	2	38	40
Howard County	1999	2	17	1	40	40
St. Paul	2004	2	32	1	28	37
Sarasota	2001	2	22	1	38	37
Jacksonville	2002	2	38	1	24	36
St. Petersburg	1994	3	23	0	39	36
Minneapolis	2004	2	31	0	32	35
Rhode Island	2002	6	30	1	28	35
Seattle	2000	5	19	NA	41	35
Westport	2000	2	22	0	41	35
Orlando	1993	2	33	0	30	35
Washington	2003	2	30	3	31	34
Columbus	2001	5	22	1	39	34
Hartford	2000	4	31	0	31	34
Broward	1997	4	37	1	24	34
Milwaukee	1996	3	24	1	39	34
Wilmington	1995	6	28	4	29	33
San Diego	2003	3	22	3	40	32
Charlotte	1997	2	26	0	40	32
Harrisburg	1994	10	33	4	22	32
Miami	2004	9	32	1	27	31
San Antonio	2007	4	25	2	39	30
Bergen	2001	12	31	1	25	30
Denver [1]	1997	3	15	5	37	30
Richmond	1994	4	37	0	29	30
West Palm Beach	2005	2	32	1	37	29
Atlantic County	2004	1	32	1	37	29
Rochester	1999	6	24	0	41	29
Phoenix	2002	3	24	0	44	28
Tidewater	2001	3	39	1	29	28
Monmouth	1997	9	37	NA	26	28
South Palm Beach	2005	4	35	1	34	26
Martin-St. Lucie	1999	1	22	0	51	26
Los Angeles	1997	4	28	2	40	26
New York	2002	19	26	1	29	25
York	1999	1	24	1	49	25
Buffalo	1995	6	31	5	35	23
Philadelphia [2]	1997	4	38	4	28	22
Essex-Morris	1998	3	27	NA	51	20
Atlanta	2006	9	26	0	46	18

TABLE 6: CONTINUED

Community	Year	Base: Jewish Respondents				
		Orthodox	Conservative	Reconstruc-tionist	Reform	Just Jewish
Detroit [3]	2005	11	28	3	36	18
Pittsburgh	2002	7	32	2	41	18
St. Louis	1995	3	21	1	60	15
Baltimore	1999	17	33	NA	36	14
Palm Springs [4]	1998	6	31	NA	42	14
Cleveland	1996	10	29	1	49	11

[1] 10% of respondents reported that they identify as Traditional.

[2] 5% of respondents reported that they identify as Traditional.

[3] 3% of respondents reported that they identify as Jewish Humanist and 1%, Jewish Renewal.

[4] 7% of respondents reported that they identify as Traditional.

TABLE 7: INTERMARRIAGE COMMUNITY COMPARISONS

Community	Year	Individual Rate: Percentage of Married Jews Who Are Married to Non-Jews	Couples Rate: Percentage of Married Couples Who Are:		
			Inter-married	In-married 2 Born/Raised Jews	Conver-sionary
Seattle	2000	36	55	35	10
San Francisco	2004	38	55	40	5
Atlanta	2006	33	50	50	
Essex-Morris	1998	33	50	50	
Las Vegas	2005	32	48	46	6
Charlotte	1997	30	47	44	10
York	1999	29	46	41	14
Tucson	2002	30	46	46	8
Boston	2005	30	46	54	
Howard County	1999	31	45	47	8
Columbus	2001	29	45	55	
San Diego	2003	28	44	45	11
Jacksonville	2002	28	44	45	11
Tidewater	2001	28	43	45	12
Washington	2003	26	41	52	6
Phoenix	2002	27	40	51	9

TABLE 7: CONTINUED

Community	Year	Individual Rate: Percentage of Married Jews Who Are Married to Non-Jews	Couples Rate: Percentage of Married Couples Who Are: Inter- married	In-married 2 Born/ Raised Jews	Conver- sionary
Denver	1997	26	39	48	14
St. Paul	2004	25	39	49	12
San Antonio	2007	23	37	50	13
Pittsburgh	2002	24	36	51	13
Richmond	1994	21	34	56	10
Rhode Island	2002	21	34	59	7
Harrisburg	1994	20	33	56	11
Minneapolis	2004	20	33	59	8
Wilmington	1995	19	33	60	7
Westport	2000	20	33	61	6
Orlando	1993	19	32	59	9
Rochester	1999	17	30	62	8
Chicago	2000	18	30	70	
St. Petersburg	1994	17	29	58	14
Milwaukee	1996	16	28	68	4
Martin-St. Lucie	1999	15	27	62	12
Atlantic County	2004	15	26	68	6
Buffalo	1995	15	26	71	3
St. Louis	1995	15	25	64	11
Hartford	2000	13	23	69	8
Los Angeles	1997	13	23	71	6
Cleveland	1996	13	23	74	3
New York	2002	13	22	72	7
Philadelphia	1997	13	22	73	5
Sarasota	2001	11	20	76	4
Palm Springs	1998	10	19	81	
Broward	1997	10	18	78	4
Baltimore	1999	10	17	75	8
Bergen	2001	10	17	78	5
Monmouth	1997	9	17	81	3
Miami	2004	9	16	75	9
Detroit	2005	9	16	76	8
West Palm Beach	2005	9	16	79	5
South Palm Beach	2005	5	9	88	3

TABLE 8: CHILDREN BEING RAISED JEWISH IN INTERMARRIED HOUSEHOLDS
COMMUNITY COMPARISONS

Community	Year	Base: Children Age 0-17 in Intermarried Households Percentage
South Palm Beach	2005	75
Sarasota	2001	74
Cleveland	1996	66
St. Louis	1995	65
Baltimore	1999	62
Boston	2005	60
Atlantic County	2004	60
Hartford	2000	59
Bergen	2001	59
Harrisburg	1994	57
Westport	2000	56
Essex-Morris	1998	50
Jacksonville	2002	49
Howard County	1999	48
Philadelphia	1997	47
Tucson	2002	45
Washington	2003	45
Tidewater	2001	45
Broward	1997	43
York	1999	43
Los Angeles	1997	43
Miami	2004	42
Denver	1997	42
Las Vegas	2005	42
Columbus	2001	40
San Antonio	2007	39
Atlanta	2006	39
Orlando	1993	39
San Francisco	2004	38
Chicago	2000	38
St. Paul	2004	37
Pittsburgh	2002	36
Milwaukee	1996	36
Wilmington	1995	36
Richmond	1994	36
Rhode Island	2002	35
West Palm Beach	2005	34
Charlotte	1997	34
Rochester	1999	32
Monmouth	1997	31
Detroit	2005	31
Minneapolis	2004	30

TABLE 8: CONTINUED

New York	2002	30
St. Petersburg	1994	29
Phoenix	2002	26
Seattle	2000	23
San Diego	2003	21
Palm Springs	1998	19
Martin-St. Lucie	1999	18

Review
of
the
Year

OTHER COUNTRIES

Israel and the Middle East

Israel

THE YEAR WAS full of surprises for the people of Israel. Prime Minister Ariel Sharon, who had created the new centrist party Kadima and removed Israeli settlers from Gaza and the northern West Bank in 2005, seemed poised to continue a policy of unilateral withdrawal from the territories, but was felled by a stroke. His successor, Ehud Olmert, won the Knesset elections in the spring. His plans to carry on Sharon's program, however, could not be implemented as the Palestinian Authority, which came under Hamas control in elections held in January, refused even to recognize Israel, Qassam rockets began falling on the western Negev with some regularity, and an Israeli soldier was kidnapped in June.

The kidnapping of two more Israeli soldiers on July 12, this time near the northern border with Lebanon, precipitated a bloody war against the Iranian-backed Hezballah, which controlled southern Lebanon. The 34-day conflict cost both sides dearly, and in the end, while an international force would be stationed in southern Lebanon and thus remove, at least temporarily, the immediate threat to northern Israel, the Israelis did not achieve their goals — return of the hostages and the infliction of a debilitating defeat on Hezballah.

There were other surprises as well. While Israel had, over the years, become used to charges of misdeeds directed against high officials, what happened in 2006 — the prospect of the president of the nation being tried for sexual misdeeds — came as a shock. One pleasant surprise was the resilience of the Israeli economy, which continued to grow despite the effects of the war.

POLITICAL DEVELOPMENTS

Sharon Leaves the Scene

Prime Minister Ariel Sharon briefly lost consciousness on December 18, 2005, when he suffered a form of stroke called paradoxical embolism caused by a small hole in his heart. On January 4, 2006, one day before he was due to undergo a catheterization procedure to correct that birth defect, Sharon complained of weakness and chest pains, and was rushed to Hadassah Medical Center in Ein Kerem, Jerusalem, by car from his ranch in the northern Negev. Apparently unconscious by the time he reached the hospital, Sharon was diagnosed as having suffered a massive cerebral hemorrhage. Bleeding in his brain was brought under control in two separate operations, and he was placed on a respirator. Doctors induced a coma to ease his treatment, and Sharon's duties were assumed by Vice Prime Minister Ehud Olmert, who took on the role of acting prime minister.

The doctors at first expressed optimism. On January 7, the neurosurgeon who had performed the operations deemed that the patient's chances of survival very high, and said: "He will not continue as prime minister, but maybe he will be able to understand and speak." But when the precautionary sedation was eased and then stopped a few days later, Sharon showed no sign of improvement. On January 25, *Ha'aretz* quoted expert opinion that Sharon's state was vegetative, and that while it was still possible that he might wake up, it might take weeks or months. The prime minister had another emergency operation for serious damage to the digestive system caused by a small blood clot. Fifty centimeters (about 20 inches) of intestine were removed.

On April 11, more than three months after the stroke, the cabinet formally declared Sharon incapacitated. Three days later Sharon's term as prime minister was officially terminated and Olmert's status changed from "acting" to "interim" prime minister. The fact that previously scheduled elections had already taken placed on March 28 (see below) and that Olmert, as head of the leading party, was negotiating to form the new government, obviated the need for the formation of an interim cabinet.

Hadassah Medical Center strongly denied an April 21 report on Channel 2 TV that doctors had admitted they made a major mistake when they gave Sharon large doses of blood thinners after the first, mild stroke in December. Hadassah claimed that the doctors, when debriefed, said "the elements leading to the decisions and treatment were correct, and they would repeat them if needed." In late May, Sharon was moved to Sheba Medical Center at Tel Hashomer, near Tel Aviv. Doctors said they hoped at least to wean the former prime minister off his respirator so that he could eventually be taken to his Negev ranch. At Sheba, he was temporarily moved into the intensive care unit when he contracted double pneumonia, but then returned to the respiratory ward, where he remained through the rest of the year.

Palestinian Elections

On January 25, three months before Israelis went to the polls, elections were held for the Palestinian parliament, the Legislative Council. These had originally been scheduled for July 2005, but Palestinian Authority president Mahmoud Abbas, the head of the governing Fatah party, postponed them for "technical reasons." Nine days before the election, the Israeli cabinet decided to allow Palestinian residents of East Jerusalem and 27 surrounding localities—areas considered part of Israel—to vote. Although Change and Reform, the Hamas electoral list, had five candidates running, members of Hamas and other terrorist groups were not allowed to enter Jerusalem to campaign. Quoting government sources, *Ha'aretz* said that wanted Hamas members who showed up in East Jerusalem on election day would be arrested.

Acting prime minister Olmert had originally insisted that East Jerusalem Palestinians vote outside the municipal borders of the city. But the PA responded that it would not submit to such a restriction, and threatened to postpone the elections once again. The U.S., eager for the elections to take place, exerted pressure on Olmert to allow voting in East Jerusalem. Aware of the political damage that could follow should Israel be blamed for another postponement, Olmert acquiesced.

President Abbas, speaking to reporters in Nablus on January 18, said he would resign if the new parliament blocked his efforts to make peace with Israel. However he said he would not mind if Hamas won some representation in the Legislative Council. "I won't say if Hamas joins I will withdraw. There is a political program . . . and if I feel I can't implement it, then staying in my chair is not the ultimate goal," he said. Abbas raised the possibility that Hamas might moderate its views. "Maybe it will change its policy, no one knows," he said. "Maybe it will say it will accept negotiations."

The next day, 20 people were wounded—miraculously, none were killed—in a suicide-bomb attack at the Rosh Ha'ir schwarma stand near

Tel Aviv's Old Central Bus Station. Defense Minister Shaul Mofaz said there was "clear evidence" of Iranian and Syrian involvement in the attack, and that Israel would tighten security around Nablus, hometown of the Islamic Jihad attacker, Sami Abdel Hafez Antar. Abbas, speaking in Nablus, said the attack had been an attempt to sabotage the elections and undermine Palestinian security, but Ra'anan Gissin, a senior spokesman for incapacitated Ariel Sharon, blamed inaction by Abbas's own PA security forces, charging that militant groups had "moved into the void."

Hamas won a great victory on election day, capturing 76 seats in the 132-member Palestinian parliament. Fatah, which had dominated PA politics since its founding in 1994, gained only 43 seats, with independents winning the remainder. The sweep gave Hamas an absolute majority in parliament and the consequent ability to form a new cabinet on its own. As information about the size of the Hamas victory circulated in the PA, Prime Minister Ahmed Qurei of Fatah resigned. "It is the choice of the people," he said, and "should be respected."

But any new cabinet and prime minister heading it would have to cooperate with PA president Abbas, who had been elected in 2005, shortly after the death of Yasir Arafat, for a four-year term. Abbas retained broad power to create national policy and control the security services, although he would need parliamentary approval for his budget and legislative proposals. And as head of the Palestine Liberation Organization, which did not include Hamas, he would also be in charge of negotiations with Israel.

Shortly after the ballots were counted, international donors expressed reservations about dealing with or providing financial aid to a Hamas government that embraced the use of terror and refused to accept Israel's right to exist. Speaking on January 26, U.S. president George W. Bush called the returns "a wake-up call." Later, after a meeting of his cabinet, Bush said that so long as Hamas did not recognize Israel, "we will not support a Palestinian government made up of Hamas." Bush said Hamas would have to get rid of its arms and disavow terrorism. "I don't see how you can be a partner in peace if you advocate the destruction of a country as part of your platform. And I know you can't be a partner in peace if you have a — if your party has got an armed wing," he said. Bush made the same point in an Oval Office interview with the *Wall Street Journal.* "A political party, in order to be viable, is one that professes peace, in my judgment, in order that it will keep the peace," he said.

In Brussels, European Union foreign ministers jointly urged Hamas to recognize the State of Israel, renounce violence, and accept previous PA agreements with Israel, and threatened to cut off financial assistance if the demands were ignored. UN secretary general Kofi Annan also said that future aid for the PA would depend on the willingness of the Hamas-led government to renounce violence and recognize Israel.

There were predictions that though Western and Arab states would not let the Palestinians starve, international aid to the new PA government would fall far below previous levels. "Money is going to be the weapon and a very effective one," analyst Mustafa Allani of the Gulf Strategic Studies Center told AP. "If Hamas wants to deliver basic requirements for the Palestinians, basic services, they're going to need money, and this is going to be the point of pressure. I think Hamas is going to have to consider a major shift in political ideology." Ephraim Kam, deputy director of Tel Aviv University's Jaffee Center for Strategic Studies, said Iran could provide several million dollars in extra aid if the West turned off the taps, a development that would only increase Iran's popularity in the region. But at the start of the year the PA needed much more: two-thirds of its $1.6-billion operating budget came from international donors, including Western governments and aid agencies. There was a dilemma, Kam said: "The West doesn't want to give money to Hamas, but it doesn't want the PA to collapse either," because of "the deepened human misery that would bring."

Violence rose in the PA in the aftermath of the Hamas victory. With many of the Fatah-linked police fearful of losing their jobs, firefights broke out between members of Hamas and police in Khan Younis in the southern Gaza Strip. Ismail Haniyeh, the Hamas leader expected to become prime minister, tried to assuage fears and assert control. Weapons, he said, "should be turned only against Israel. Our battle is not against our own people."

The battle was indeed directed across the border. A seven-month-old Israeli infant suffered a serious head wound and three other family members were moderately injured when a Qassam rocket hit a mobile home in Kibbutz Karmia, a few kilometers north of the Gaza Strip, on February 3. The baby's grandfather, a Magen David Adom paramedic summoned to the site of the attack, said the Palestinian rocket "landed in the mobile home's bedroom and blew the husband, the baby and the mother in the air." Two days later, a Palestinian terrorist carrying a knife killed one woman and wounded five others during a stabbing spree on a minibus traveling from Petah Tikva to Tel Aviv. Eyewitnesses said an angry crowd beat the man before police arrived.

Acting prime minister Olmert said on February 13 that Israel had broad international support for its policy of not talking to Hamas, although he added that Israel was not "closing off diplomatic avenues, if those exist." The *New York Times* reported the next day that Washington and Jerusalem were considering a campaign to starve the PA of cash so Palestinians would grow disillusioned with their incoming militant Hamas rulers and return ousted Fatah moderates to power, perhaps through new elections. On February 19—the same day U.S. secretary of state Condoleeezza Rice was meeting in Cairo with the Egyptian foreign minister about economically isolating the Hamas government—Israel's cabinet decided to cut off the transfer of about $50 million a month in taxes and customs duties that it collected for the PA.

Palestinian prime-minister-designate Haniyeh gave off moderate signals. He said Hamas would establish a "peace in stages" if Israel were to withdraw to the 1967 borders. Asked to elaborate in a late-February interview with the *Washington Post,* Hanieyeh said that while he did not see "peace" in the immediate future, an end to the Israeli-Palestinian conflict could take the form of a long-term truce. Hamas, he added, did not wish "to throw them [Jews] into the sea. All we seek is to be given our land back, not to harm anybody." Pressed on whether Hamas recognized Israel's right to exist, Haniyeh countered, "Which Israel should we recognize? The Israel of 1917; the Israel of 1936; the Israel of 1948; the Israel of 1956; or the Israel of 1967? Which borders and which Israel? Israel has to recognize first the Palestinian state and its borders, and then we will know what we are talking about." And he concluded, "If Israel declares that it will give the Palestinian people a state and give them back all their rights, then we are ready to recognize them."

But Mahmoud al-Zahar, a Hamas Palestinian legislator slated to be the new government's foreign minister, maintained a hard line. Israeli-Palestinian negotiations were a "failed experiment that would not be repeated," he told the AP on February 27. Zahar considered his movement's election victory as confirmation of its tough stand against recognizing Israel. "We don't consider the Israeli enemy a partner. By winning the elections, we defeated Israel," he said. Speaking to security officials in Tel Aviv the next day, Olmert said Israel was not frightened of Hamas and would not deal with it, but even so would keep up peace efforts.

Abbas and Haniyeh—who had just been officially given five weeks in which to form a government—found common ground on February 24, when they both denounced an Israeli sweep through the Balata refugee camp in Nablus in which five Palestinians were killed. The Balata action was Israel's largest in the northern West Bank since the disengagement from Gaza and small areas of the northern West Bank the previous August. According to an AP report, one of the five terrorists killed in the action, said to be responsible for the deaths of five Israelis, had boasted he would never be caught.

Hamas's diplomatic isolation was broken on March 3, when a delegation led by Khaled Mashaal, the Damascus-based Hamas chief, arrived in Moscow for three days of talks at the invitation of Russian president Vladimir Putin. Russia's Middle East envoy, Alexander Kalugin, explained that the invitation was by no means intended to subvert the West's policy of nonrecognition. Rather, he said, Russia hoped to persuade Hamas to moderate its position. Experts doubted that this was possible. "Hamas won't listen to Russia because Moscow has no real levers of influence over them," said Fyodor Lukyanov, editor of the magazine *Russia in Global Affairs*. "This is not the time of the Soviet Union, when we had real clout in the region."

On his arrival in the Russian capital, Mashaal said Hamas had no intention of recognizing Israel, and dismissed recognition as "a decided issue." That remained true even after the three days of meetings, although, according to the Russians, Hamas did agree to extend the *tardiyeh,* cessation of hostilities, agreed to in March 2005. Russian foreign minister Sergei Lavrov said Hamas needed "to transform itself into a political party" and make its military wing "a legitimate part of the Palestinian security structures." He urged the West to have patience since "we don't expect that Hamas will do all this and change itself overnight."

The Americans took a positive view of the meetings. Adam Ereli, deputy spokesman for the State Department, said the Moscow talks "served the purpose to deliver the message. We think it's important that Hamas get the message loud and clear. We have a common front and a united purpose to make clear to Hamas that it has before it a clear and unambiguous choice."

Israeli Elections

On January 2, with elections scheduled for March 28, Likud ministers authorized party leader Benjamin Netanyahu to pull out of the government, something Netanyahu had planned to do since his election as Likud leader in December. The ministers—even Foreign Minister Silvan Shalom and Education Minister Limor Livnat, who had advocated staying in the cabinet until the elections—resigned the following day, less than 48 hours before Sharon's massive stroke.

Presiding at his first cabinet meeting four days after Sharon was incapacitated, Olmert promised to "carry out the wishes" of Sharon in leading the country. He said that if Sharon were able to speak, the prime minister would tell the nation to get back to dealing with pressing social, economic, and security issues. "This we will continue to do," he declared. Netanyahu, who had anticipated challenging Sharon in the upcoming elections, also praised the fallen prime minister. "History will judge him as the great leader that he is," said Netanyahu, who had resigned as Sharon's finance minister the previous summer in what he said was a protest against the Gaza disengagement. "I don't think time will judge Sharon harshly in the larger perspective of his contributions to Israel's security."

As Sharon showed no signs of emerging from his coma, the centrist party he had created, Kadima, began to close ranks behind Olmert. Shimon Peres, the former Labor leader who had joined Kadima in 2005, said on January 8 that he would support Olmert for party's top spot, adding that he would probably join the party's list for the Knesset. Olmert met with Peres and Tzipi Livni, the former justice minister who now took over the Foreign Ministry, on January 12, and an agreement was reached whereby Peres would have the second position on the Kadima list and Livni would be third. Since Kadima still did not exist as a grass-roots political party, the rest of its slate of candidates was chosen by the leadership, not through a primary election.

Likud held its party primary on January 12, and taking the second spot, after Netanyahu, was the relative unknown Moshe Kahlon, a backbench Knesset member. He was followed by two other relatively young backbenchers, Gilad Erdan and Gideon Sa'ar, and only then by older, veteran MKs.

Labor's list, chosen in primaries on January 18, included a number of new faces such as Avishay Braverman, the former president of Ben-Gurion University in Beersheba and, before that, a top-level economist at the World Bank; Ami Ayalon, who had headed both the Shin Bet security service and the Israeli Navy; and Sheli Yechimowitz, a sharp-tongued journalist on Channel 2 TV. Five ex-generals, including former party leader Binyamin (Fuad) Ben-Eliezer and former chief of Army Intelligence and cabinet minister Ephraim Sneh, were among the top 15 candidates.

Olmert's first press conference as acting prime minister, on January 18, was also the opening gun in Kadima's election campaign. Olmert, assuming that Fatah would win the upcoming Palestinian elections, said he hoped to begin negotiations with PA president Abbas about "a permanent peace agreement between us and the Palestinians." These talks, he continued, should be based on the internationally backed "road map" peace plan, which called for the creation of a Palestinian state and outlined steps, so far unrealized, for the two sides to abandon the conflict.

On January 25, the day of the Palestinian elections, Olmert once again spoke of his plans in a major policy address at the Herzliya Conference on Security, an annual event at which Sharon had presented his disengagement plan two years earlier. Olmert said, "The choice between allowing Jews to live in all parts of the land of Israel and living in a state with a Jewish majority mandates giving up parts of the Land of Israel." Olmert declared that Israel "will keep security zones, main settlement blocs, and places important to the Jewish people, first of all, Jerusalem, united under Israeli control. There can be no Jewish state without Jerusalem under Israeli sovereignty." He called implementation of his program "a turning point for the State of Israel."

After the surprising Hamas victory, at ceremonies honoring the anniversary of the Knesset's founding on February 13, Olmert elaborated. Should negotiations with the PA fail, he said, there would be further unilateral withdrawal from some parts of the West Bank. The next Knesset, he said, would "be faced with a series of historic missions," the first of which was "the determination of the final borders of the State of Israel." Three weeks later, speaking in Tel Aviv, Olmert favored reducing spending on settlements in the West Bank and diverting the funds to underdeveloped areas in Israel itself. Billions of dollars would be spent on three regions—Jerusalem, the Negev, and the Galilee. And on March 6, speaking via satellite link to the annual conference of AIPAC (American Israel Public Affairs Committee), the main pro-Israel lobbying group in the U.S., Olmert repeated that Israel "will take the initiative if we find out that the Palestinians are not ready, are not prepared or are not mature enough to be able to take the necessary adjustments within themselves," and decide its own borders.

In subsequent newspaper interviews, Olmert made his intentions even clearer. Setting a four-year horizon for securing permanent borders either through negotiation or unilateral action, he sketched an outline of the projected map. Ma'ale Adumim, the "Jerusalem satellite city," would be part of the Jewish state, as would Gush Etzion and Ariel on the West Bank. Residents of isolated settlements would be evacuated and moved into these major blocs. Jerusalem and its environs as well as the Jordan Valley on the frontier with Jordan would fall within Israel. PA president Abbas seemed willing to go along, telling the Italian paper *Corriere della*

Sera: "We'll respect the will of the Israeli people . . . . I hope Olmert wins. I know him well. I believe that with him we could work in a productive way."

Shortly before Sharon's stroke polls had shown his party, Kadima, winning 42 of the 120 Knesset seats in a general election, compared to Labor's 19 and Likud's 14. In the immediate aftermath of Olmert's assumption of power, the surveys continued to show strong support for Kadima. But the party began to slip in the polls as time went on. Five days before the election, a Dahaf poll for *Yediot Aharonot* had Kadima winning 36 seats and a *Ma'ariv* survey had it at 37. Unfazed, Olmert told *Yediot* that he would include in his government only parties willing to support his "consolidation" program. "I presented a political plan at the center of which is determining Israel's final borders during my term in office. In the framework of the plan, settlements in Judea and Samaria will be consolidated into settlement blocs," Olmert said.

The big surprise of the preelection polls was the performance of Yisrael Beitenu, the rightist party led by Avigdor Lieberman, who came from the part of the former Soviet Union that was now the independent country of Moldova. Lieberman, 48, served as director general of Likud during Netanyahu's successful 1996 race for prime minister and later as director general of the Prime Minister's Office before breaking with Likud to form his own party. Supported largely by Russian immigrants, it had only two seats in the outgoing Knesset, but was expected to do much better in 2006. He hoped to win votes outside the immigrant community by adding several native Israelis to his list.

When final returns were tabulated, Kadima won a disappointing 29 Knesset seats, but remained the largest party. It was followed by Labor, with 19. Likud and Shas, the Sephardi Orthodox party, each had 12; Yisrael Beitenu 11; the National Union-National Religious Party alliance 9; the Pensioner's Party 7; the ultra-Orthodox United Torah Judaism 6; the left-wing Meretz 5; and Ra'am-Ta'al, Hadash, and Balad, the three Arab parties, a combined total of 10. Shinui, the anticlerical party that had come in a surprising third with 15 seats in the previous election but then splintered into factions, won none in 2006.

While Yisrael Beitenu's exceptional performance had been foreseen by the pollsters, the strong showing of the Pensioners Party had not. In the last few days before the election it went from being a marginal party that might just barely win the minimum percentage necessary to win Knesset representation, to being a major force, winning seven seats. Paradoxically, the party was led by oldsters and represented the interests of senior citizens, but its support came largely from younger voters; instead of voicing their protest against "the system" by supporting the pro-marijuana Green Leaf party, which many of them were expected to do, or not voting at all, they cast ballots for the Pensioners. "It's like voting for your grandparents," said one student at Tel Aviv University.

After the results were in, Western leaders voiced support for Olmert. President Bush had a brief congratulatory phone conversation with him. EU external relations commissioner Benita Ferrero-Waldner said her 25-nation group looked forward to working with the Israeli leadership and hoped that both new governments, the one in Israel and the other in the PA, could move together to bring peace to the region.

Olmert, in a victory speech, reiterated his plans for the future: "In the coming period, we will move to set the final borders of the State of Israel, a Jewish state with a Jewish majority. We will try to achieve this in an agreement with the Palestinians." Addressing Palestinian leader Abbas, Olmert said: "We are prepared to compromise, give up parts of our beloved land of Israel, remove, painfully, Jews who live there, to allow you the conditions to achieve your hopes and to live in a state in peace and quiet." He went on, "The time has come for the Palestinians . . . to relate to the existence of the State of Israel, to accept only part of their dream, to stop terror, to accept democracy and accept compromise and peace with us. We are prepared for this. We want this." But Olmert would not wait indefinitely. "It is time for the Palestinians to change their ethos, to accept compromise as soon as possible. If they manage to do this soon, we will sit and work out a plan. If not, Israel will take control of its own fate, and in consensus among our people and with the agreement of the world and U.S. president George Bush, we will act. The time has come to act."

The New Israeli Government

President Moshe Katzav formally asked Olmert to form a government on April 7. Olmert responded that he hoped to put together a coalition and cabinet "which will have the broadest possible support, as quickly as possible." He soon indicated that a coalition with Labor was his first choice. The two parties basically agreed on the major foreign-policy issue, seeking a peace deal without recognition of the Hamas-led PA, although Labor tended to be more insistent on enabling international humanitarian aid to get through to the Palestinians. The key stumbling block to a coalition was the desire of Labor leader Amir Peretz to hold the Finance

Ministry, seeing it as a springboard for realizing the party's social agenda. Though he recognized that Labor had to be given a senior portfolio, Olmert felt obliged to give Foreign Affairs to Tzipi Livni, who had taken over that portfolio after the Likud ministers resigned in January, and Finance to Avraham Hirschson, a longtime close associate. That left only Defense, where the other leading candidate was Shaul Mofaz, the incumbent, who had come over to Kadima from Likud in 2005.

There were indications that Shas and the Pensioners would also joint the new coalition. Indeed, Peretz and MK Eli Yishai, the Shas leader, met in early April to agree on a "social package" to present to Olmert during coalition negotiations. It focused on three primary points: legislation ensuring pensions for every citizen; increases in the size of old-age pensions; and a rise in the minimum wage. When the meeting at Labor headquarters in Tel Aviv's Hatikva Quarter ended, Yishai told reporters, "We have much in common with the Labor Party, as well as between us and the Pensioners. The people of Israel spoke its part regarding social issues. We were invited for a meeting and we came to hear Labor's positions."

On April 4, Olmert and Peretz appeared at a joint press conference, amid smiles and embraces, to announce their impending partnership. Peretz would become defense minister, the first civilian to hold the post in decades. Meanwhile, rumor had it that Peretz had secretly tried, after the election, to form his own coalition out of an odd mix of leftist, religious, and right-wing parties. Sources close to Peretz described this as a sincere effort to bring together disparate movements that agreed on social issues, while postponing diplomatic progress with the Palestinians for two years. Critics called the exercise a clumsy, naked power grab that would thwart the plain will of the voters and betray the interests of Peretz's own dovish electoral base.

Labor officially rejected Kadima's idea of bringing Yisrael Beitenu into the government as a third major element of the coalition. But sources in Yisrael Beteinu said they did not believe this was "the end of the story." Ha'aretz quoted a senior figure in the party as saying that "Peretz said many things recently that he took back . . . . We have no reason to think this time he will be consistent. From our point of view, nothing is final yet."

Olmert completed his coalition on May 1 by adding Shas with its 12 seats after the party's rabbinical council approved the deal. Kadima pledged to increase child allowances—a key issue for Shas's supporters, many of whom were poor and had many children. And as a gesture towards the hawkish Shas electorate, the party did not have to obligate itself to back a unilateral pullback in the West Bank: according to the coalition agreement, once an evacuation plan was placed on the government's agenda Shas could decide whether or not to support it. (Earlier, during the campaign, Olmert had insisted that his coalition partners would have to accept the plan.) The government now encompassed 67 seats—29 from Kadima, 19 from Labor, 12 from Shas, and seven from the Pensioners.

On May 4, Olmert's new cabinet was approved by the Knesset:
Tzipi Livni (Kadima): Vice Prime Minister, Minister of Foreign Affairs
Shimon Peres (Kadima): Vice Prime Minister, Minister for the Development of the Negev and Galilee
Amir Peretz (Labor): Deputy Prime Minister, Minister of Defense
Eli Yishai (Shas): Deputy Prime Minister, Minister of Industry, Trade and Labor
Shaul Mofaz (Kadima): Deputy Prime Minister, Minister of Transportation and Road Safety
Avraham Hirschson (Kadima): Minister of Finance
Ariel Attias (Shas): Minister of Communications
Avi Dichter (Kadima): Minister of Public Security
Ronnie Bar On (Kadima): Minister of Interior
Yuli Tamir (Labor): Minister of Education
Haim Ramon (Kadima): Minister of Justice
Isaac Herzog (Labor): Minister of Tourism
Yacov Ben Yizri (Pensioners): Minister of Health
Benjamin Ben-Eliezer (Labor): Minister of National Infrastructure
Ze'ev Boim (Kadima): Minister of Immigrant Absorption
Rafi Eitan (Pensioners): Minister of Pensioner Affairs
Gideon Ezra (Kadima): Minister of Environmental Protection
Meir Sheetrit (Kadima): Minister of Housing
Shalom Simhon (Labor): Minister of Agriculture
Yitzhak Cohen (Shas): Minister without portfolio responsible for the religious councils
Eitan Cabel (Labor): Minister without portfolio responsible for the Israel Broadcasting Authority
Ya'akov Edri (Kadima): Minister without portfolio responsible for Knesset liaison and Jerusalem affairs
Meshulam Nahari (Shas): Minister in the Finance Ministry

Bush acted quickly to show his support for the new government, inviting Olmert to visit Washington in late May. On May 23, Olmert became one of fewer than a dozen foreign leaders ever to address a joint session of Congress.

Speaking to an audience that also included Jewish leaders and the family of Weston, Florida, teenager Daniel Woltz, who had died of injuries suffered in a Tel Aviv terror attack, Olmert recalled his long relationship with the U.S., expressed admiration for the country's bipartisan support for the State of Israel, stressed the values that the two nations shared, declared that Israel and the U.S. were allies in fighting international terrorism, and invoked the memory of Ariel Sharon. Olmert made it clear that the "realignment" policy (a new term replacing "consolidation") was still very much on his agenda. "We have to relinquish part of our dream to leave room for the dreams of others, so that all of us can enjoy a better future," he told the packed chamber of the House of Representatives. Noting that he preferred a negotiated arrangement with the Palestinians, he warned once again, "We cannot wait forever."

He received an enthusiastic reception from Congress, but this, Israeli sources reported, was only the icing on the cake. Olmert's greater achievement, according to the *Jerusalem Post,* was the warm reception Bush gave him. In a joint press conference at the end of their White House meeting, the president pledged that the U.S. would defend Israel against any Iranian attack. Olmert said he was "very, very pleased from the content of the talks I had with the president."

The Katzav Affair

For years, the presidency of the State of Israel was a largely ceremonial office. The only substantive power possessed by the head of state was that of pardoning convicted criminals. But in July 2006, a heavy cloud settled over the office and over Beit Hanassi, the official residence of the president, on Jabotinsky Street in Jerusalem's Talbieh neighborhood. The threat of criminal charges, including rape, hung over President Moshe Katzav.

The affair came to light after the president himself called in Attorney General Menahem Mazuz to report that a former employee in his office, later to be identified only by her initial, Aleph, had sought to extort large sums of money from him in exchange for her silence on alleged offenses he had committed, including sexual assault on her and accepting payments from "pardon contractors" to "fix" presidential pardons. On July 11, Mazuz ordered a preliminary investigation both of Katzav's charges of extortion and Aleph's reports of sexual impropriety.

Katzav consistently denied the charges and said he would neither suspend himself from office nor resign. "I am glad that the attorney general decided to investigate this issue. I believe that the investigation will clear away the fog and bring the true picture to light," he said. But as police began their investigation, several other women came forward with stories of how Katzav had sexually harassed them and coerced them to have sex with him, either during his more than six years as president, or previously, when he served as a government minister. *Ha'aretz* reported it had testimony from five different women formerly employed by the president who described the difficulties they had working with him as well as various inappropriate comments he made to them. And *Yediot Aharonot* described how Aleph, before she left the Beit Hanassi staff, had spent an hour in Katzav's office with him each afternoon, with the door locked. There were also published reports of how, after leaving Katzav's staff, Aleph had sent him sexually explicit letters from New York.

On August 22, a day before Katzav was to be interrogated by police for the first time—at Beit Hanassi rather than at police headquarters—officers swooped down on the presidential residence and seized documents and computers. After the interrogation, which lasted five hours, Katzav attorney Tzion Amir said that the president "never broke any law and didn't sexually harass anyone."

Given the delicacy of dealing with possible criminal charges against the head of state, it was clear even in the early stages that the Katzav investigation would take a long time, possibly until the end of his term in July 2007. Indeed, there was speculation that his attorneys would attempt to drag the probe out in the hope that, if Katzav were no longer president, the embarrassing matter would be allowed to "disappear" rather than end up in a criminal trial.

Katzav's legal team demanded that the police give the media access to a tape the president had made of his conversation with Aleph in which she allegedly sought to extort money, saying it would prove that the extortion attempt had nothing to do with sexual harassment. The lawyers also wanted Attorney General Mazuz to investigate "the source of the numerous and tendentious leaks from the police investigation," and objected to the description of the police visit to Beit Hanassi as a "raid."

On September 7, police said they had an evidentiary basis for an indictment. A week later, after first refusing to do so, Katzav relented to demands that he not officiate at the swearing-in of Justice Dorit Beinisch as the new president of the Supreme Court, and the president absented himself from the state ceremony.

In a September 18 television interview, Mazuz said that the president had "a long line of women who complained against him, and therefore the chances that he has been made a victim of a libel against him are slim." A few days later there were reports that yet another woman had come forward to say Katzav had sexually molested her while he was a government minister. Lawyer Amir called it "a shocking story bordering on fantasy," adding: "The evidence that we have in our hands completely disproves this woman's testimony . . . she was fired from her job and swore to seek revenge." By the end of the investigation, ten women had filed complaints against Katzav.

The police issued their recommendation on October 15—that rape and sexual harassment charges by five of the women against Katzav should be pursued in an indictment. The complaints by the other five could not be followed up due to the statute of limitations. Police also said they had evidence of illegal wiretapping at Beit Hanassi, as well as witness tampering. Yohanan Danino, head of the police's Investigation and Intelligence Department, and Brig.-Gen. Yoav Segalovitch, head of the investigation team, met with Mazuz and State Attorney Eran Shendar, and recommended that the president be put on trial.

Under Israeli law, the president is immune from criminal prosecution while in office unless he voluntarily waives his immunity or it is lifted by the Knesset. In late October, Katzav turned down advice from Mazuz that he step down and suspend himself from office for as long as his indictment was under consideration. Mazuz had not yet decided what course to take as the year ended. It remained possible that the attorney general might offer Katzav the possibility of a hearing on the evidence, called *shimua* in Hebrew, before formally issuing an indictment.

SECURITY AND DIPLOMACY

Israel and the Palestinians

SECURITY CONCERNS

On March 14, after a daylong siege of the Jericho prison in which they were being held, Popular Front for the Liberation of Palestine head Ahmed Saadat and four other PFLP members surrendered to Israeli troops. They were being held for the October 2001 murder of then tourism minister Rechavam Zeevy in Jerusalem's Hyatt Regency Hotel (see AJYB 2002, p. 554). Also in that jail was Fuad Shubeiki, a long-time Palestinian financial operative and Arafat confidant who had been responsible for financing the purchase of 50 tons of arms captured on the *Karine A* weapons ship in 2002 (see AJYB 2003, p. 184). All six were transferred to an Israeli prison. The Israeli action was prompted by PA president Abbas's statement a week earlier that he was prepared to free Saadat, who had been taken to the jail and kept under foreign custody in a compromise deal reached after Israeli troops besieged him in Yasser Arafat's Muqa'ata complex in Ramallah.

Police foiled an attempted suicide bombing on March 22, apprehending the would-be perpetrator with his 7-kg (15 lb.) bomb after a highspeed chase along one of Israel's busiest highways in mid-afternoon. Nine of the van's ten passengers were Palestinians working illegally in Israel, which was the reason the driver had fled police. The tenth, an Islamic Jihad member, was carrying the bomb.

In an interview published on Ynet, the Web site of the *Yediot Aharonot* news organization, Defense Minister Shaul Mofaz charged that Iran had given the Islamic Jihad group $1.8 million to kill Israelis. The Iranian-born former chief of staff said that Hezballah also sent money and messages to Islamic Jihad in Gaza via Iran.

Israel opened the Kerem Shalom crossing into the Gaza Strip on March 22 to allow emergency food shipments from Egypt to enter the impoverished Palestinian area. Egypt sent 7,000 tons of supplies, mostly wheat, rice and sugar, through Kerem Shalom. Earlier, Israel had temporarily opened the Karni crossing in northern Gaza for the same purpose. The shipments offered only a brief respite from the growing food crisis in Gaza, as entry points from Israel into the Strip had been closed off most of the time since the start of the year. On April 11, John Ging, director of Gaza Operations for the UN Relief and Works Agency (UNRWA), on which 765,000 refugees depended for basic items, said: "The clock is now ticking and distribution will have to be shut down entirely for the second time in less than a month if the crossing does not open immediately." He noted that UNRWA faced a bill of almost $900,000 in penalties for port and other charges arising from the Karni closure.

An Israeli Bedouin and his son were killed near the Gaza Strip on March 28, when they attempted to salvage an unexploded Qassam rocket for scrap metal. And three days later, four Israelis — a married couple and two hitchhikers — were killed when a terrorist disguised as an ultra-Orthodox Jewish hitchhiker blew himself up in the couple's car near the settlement of Kedumim, in the West Bank not far from Nablus. The bomber was a 24-year-old man from a village near Hebron. This was the first suicide attack since February 2005 that was not perpetrated by Islamic Jihad.

Early April saw Israeli warplanes and helicopters striking targets in Gaza, in an attempt to stop the Qassam attacks on Sderot and other Israeli communities adjacent to the Gaza Strip. On April 4, three missiles were fired into the Ansar 2 compound, a largely unused PA base about 100 meters from Abbas's office. At the time, the PA leader was in the West Bank. His spokesman said, "This escalation will lead the area to more violence and instability." On April 7, five Palestinians, including a Hamas bomb maker and his five-year-old son, were killed by a rocket strike on the car in which they were riding in Rafiah, at the southern end of the Strip. Nine more were killed in an airborne attack on a terrorist training camp the next day.

Eleven people were killed (nine died immediately and two later on) in an April 17 suicide bombing in the Rosh Ha'ir shwarma stand in the area of Tel Aviv's Old Central Bus Station, the same place where 20 people had been injured in a similar bombing on January 19 (see above, pp. 211–12). The next day Israeli troops raided the village of Arakeh, near Jenin in the northern West Bank, and arrested the father of the bomber, 21-year-old Samer Hamad. According to his mother, Samer had been working as a waiter. "I thought he really went to work," she said, asserting that she only found out about her son's involvement in the bombing, and with Islamic Jihad, through the media.

Attempting to ward off a food crisis in Gaza that appeared imminent in light of the world's cutoff of aid to the Hamas government, PA president Abbas demanded on April 23 that Hamas recognize Israel. If it did not, he told CNN, "The constitution gives me clear and definite authority to remove a government from power." Hamas immediately rejected the demand and threatened to end the 15-month informal cease-fire that had greatly lowered the level of violence after five years of bloodshed.

Five Palestinian security officers were injured in a firefight on April 26 with Palestinian terrorists, who tried to ram a car filled with explosives into the Karni checkpoint, a main crossing between Israel and northern Gaza. After the incident, which took place on the Palestinian side of the crossing, Israel closed the Karni facility.

At its April 30 session, the Israeli cabinet modified the route of the still incomplete 760-km security fence. The change would put 30,000 Palestinians who lived in the area around the settlement city of Ariel, in the northern West Bank, on the Palestinian side of the enclosure instead of on the Israeli side, as envisioned in the original plan. In addition, it voted to put up temporary fencing in areas of Jerusalem where the barrier was not yet built. Olmert said the decision "will allow us to complete the construction of the fence very quickly in critical areas, and therefore improve our ability to thwart attempted [terror] attacks." Palestinian geographer Khalil Tafakji, interviewed by the AP, took a different view, charging that the Jerusalem fencing plan was a way of "keeping Palestinians outside the city in an effort to create facts on the ground and preempt a final agreement between the sides."

On May 1, a 41-year-old Palestinian woman, Etaf Zalat, was killed during the siege of a house near Tul Karm, in the West Bank, where an Islamic Jihad terrorist had taken refuge. Her two daughters were wounded. The army opened an investigation. According to an AP report that quoted army sources, Israeli troops had spent more than an hour trying to convince the wanted man to surrender before a bulldozer was brought in to level the structure. During the demolition, troops fired into the house, apparently hitting Zalat and her daughters.

James Wolfensohn, the former World Bank head, announced that he was resigning as the Quartet's special envoy for Israeli-Palestinian mediation on May 3. U.S. secretary of state Rice said he would not be replaced.

GAZA: ROCKETS AND A KIDNAPPING

The persistent rocket fire from Gaza, which Israel had evacuated the year before, prompted debate within the Israeli security establishment over what steps to take. Maj.-Gen. Yoav Galant, head of the army's Southern Command, told *Ma'ariv* on April 21: "If the price we have to pay becomes unreasonable as a result of increased attacks, then we shall have to take all steps, including occupying the Gaza Strip. It could be anything from a partial occupation . . . to a full occupation." Asked by *Ha'aretz* at the beginning of May what he thought, Chief of Staff Dan Halutz disagreed, saying, "I am not pushing for the occupation of Gaza. I am pushing in the opposite direction . . . . I can't recall that in all the years of fighting when we were there that we succeeded in reducing the firing of Qassams to zero." Public Security Minister Avi Dichter, a former chief of the Shin Bet security services, advocated escalating Israeli pressure against the area in the northern Strip from which the Palestinian-made rockets were fired. "Beit Hanoun should be turned into a ghost town," he said.

On May 9, Israel announced that a few days earlier its navy had thwarted an attempt to smuggle arms into Gaza by sea, intercepting

Egyptian and Palestinian boats in the act of transferring about half a ton of military-grade explosives along the Gaza Strip's maritime border with Egypt. Once aware that the Israeli patrol boats had spotted them, the would-be smugglers dumped the bags of explosives into the sea and tried to flee. The Egyptians escaped, but five Palestinians were detained. Israeli divers retrieved 11 bags from the sea floor at a depth of 30 meters. The source and the exact destination of the explosives were not known.

Several Katyusha rockets fired from Lebanon by the Popular Front for the Liberation of Palestine-General Command terror group hit northern Israel on May 28, lightly wounding one soldier. In response, Israel sent warplanes to rocket and bomb PFLP-GC targets, including a base at Sultan Yacoub, in eastern Lebanon not far from the Syrian border, and on bases in the hills 20 km south of Beirut.

Eight Palestinian civilians were killed in a June 9 blast on the crowded beach at Beit Lahiya in the northern Gaza. Among the dead were three children; their sister, who was swimming, survived. Television footage showed a woman and a child dead on the sand, and another child screaming in agony while a lifeless man was carried away by an ambulance crew. Abbas called the killings "a bloody massacre against our civilians, without discrimination," but an Israeli inquiry found that all shells fired that day hit their intended targets, and so Israel could not have been responsible. Olmert expressed confidence in the inquiry and dismissed calls for an international probe. But Marc Garlasco, a former U.S. battle-damage assessment officer with experience in Bosnia and Iraq, studied the shrapnel and the wounds of the victims and concluded, "this was from an Israeli shell." Garlasco was in Gaza at the time, working for Human Rights Watch.

June 10, the day after the explosion on the beach, Hamas announced it was ending the 16-month official cease-fire—which had not, in any case, prevented the firing of some Qassam rockets into Israel during that period. Shortly after Hamas fired its first rocket barrage on targets just across the Israeli border, PA prime minister Haniyeh rejected a call by President Abbas for a referendum on the establishment of a Palestinian state alongside Israel. The idea for a referendum had come from the so-called "Prisoners' Document" formulated by jailed Fatah leader Marwan Barghouti and other security prisoners in Israeli jails as a way to end Israeli pressure against the Palestinians, which had mounted since the election of Hamas in January.

Tzachi Hanegbi, chairman of the Knesset Foreign Affairs and Defense Committee and a confidant of Prime Minister Olmert, told Israel

Radio on June 12 that Prime Minister Haniyeh was himself a possible target for assassination. If Haniyeh planned attacks against Israel, Hanegbi said, he could face the same fate as Hamas spiritual leader Sheikh Ahmed Yassin and his successor, Dr. Abdel Aziz Rantisi, both killed in targeted missile strikes in 2004. Earlier, Defense Minister Peretz spoke in a similar vein, saying that no one involved in attacks on Israel could claim immunity from retaliatory action.

On June 14, Israel expressed regret after eight civilians were killed in a Gaza air strike that also netted two terrorists, one of them Hamad Wadiye, a top Islamic Jihad rocket expert. Israel said it had fired two missiles at terrorists transporting a Grad or Katyusha long-range rocket towards a launch site. The first hit the van containing the terrorists and the second hit shortly thereafter, as civilians, including two children who were killed, crowded around the burning vehicle.

Hamas and Popular Resistance Committee terrorists used a previously dug tunnel under the border fence near the Kerem Shalom crossing in the southern Gaza Strip to attack Israeli units stationed there on June 25. Two soldiers and two terrorists were killed, and IDF Cpl. Gilad Shalit was captured and taken into Gaza. Though Hamas claimed the attack was in response to the killings on the Beit Lahiya beach two weeks earlier, Israeli experts said that digging the tunnel must have taken between three and six months. Shalit's captors, including Hamas's Izz al-Din al-Qassam military wing, issued a series of statements demanding the release of all female Palestinian prisoners and all prisoners under the age of 18.

Egypt immediately deployed an additional 2,500 troops along its border with Gaza to prevent the smuggling of captive Shalit into its territory. Palestinian forces, meanwhile, blockaded roads into Gaza in preparation for a major Israeli thrust. Egyptian security czar Omar Suleiman phoned Hamas leader Khaled Mashaal, who was living in Damascus, to ask for his help in obtaining Shalit's release.

Operation Summer Rain began on June 28, when Israeli forces searching for Shalit entered the southern Gaza town of Khan Younis, and four Israeli jets buzzed the summer home of Syrian president Bashar al-Assad near Latakiya, a move reflecting Syria's sponsorship of terrorism and the fact that it allowed Mashaal to reside and maintain a headquarters in Damascus. Israeli forces also hit a power station supplying electricity to about two-thirds of Gaza's population, attacked Hamas training and administrative sites, and took over the Gaza International Airport at Dahaniya, in the southern part of the Strip. At day's end, after massing troops on Gaza's borders, Israel said it would put a hold on ground operations there to give Shalit's captors a chance to free him.

Prime Minister Olmert emphasized that the objective of the thrust was to gain Shalit's freedom. "We do not intend to reoccupy Gaza. We do not intend to stay there. We have one objective, and that is to bring Gilad home," he said. But Osama Hamdan, a close associate of Mashaal, told AP that if Israel did not negotiate for Shalit's release, his organization would conclude that it should "kill soldiers even if they have the opportunity to capture them." In Jordan, the Muslim Brotherhood said Israel had launched its offensive into Gaza "for the sake of one soldier, while Arabs, Muslims and the free world remain silent on the arrest of 10,000 Palestinians, including women and children." And Abdel-Bari Atwan, editor in chief of the London-based *Al-Quds Al-Arabi* newspaper, called the Israeli incursion an "unprecedented blackmailing threat." Noting that thousands of Gazans were left without electricity after the power plant was hit, he asked in an editorial, "Is the life of the captive soldier worth the suffering of all of those people?"

In sweeps across the West Bank on June 29, Israel arrested 64 Hamas officials, including Finance Minister Abed Razak; Labor Minister Muhammad Garghouti; Muhammad Abu Tier, a parliament member who was number two on the Hamas electoral list in the January election; and Religious Affairs Minister Naef Rajoub, brother of Jibril Rajoub, former chief of Fatah's West Bank preventive security forces. At least a third of the PA cabinet was arrested and other important Hamas figures went into hiding. Israel said the anti-Hamas operation had been planned for several weeks.

Foreign ministers from the major industrialized nations, meeting in Moscow in advance of the G-8 summit scheduled for July, called on Israel and the Palestinians to do everything possible to calm the crisis. "With restraint, perhaps we can get back to a place where there can be hope for a peaceful resolution," commented U.S. secretary of state Rice, adding that "reasonable Palestinians" were involved in efforts to gain Shalit's freedom.

Meanwhile, Israel's offensive continued. When its planes bombed the office of the Palestinian prime minister in Gaza on July 2, a statement allegedly coming from Shalit's captors announced that Israel had less than 24 hours to free 1,500 Palestinian prisoners "or bear the consequences." Israel ignored it. Egypt's *Al-Hayat* newspaper reported on July 4 that Egyptian officials had visited with the captured Shalit and that he was being treated by a Palestinian doctor for three bullet wounds, but this was not confirmed by other Cairo sources. Efforts to obtain the release of Shalit, often coupled with rumors about the possible creation of a Palestinian unity government involving both Hamas and Fatah, continued throughout the year. On several occasions it seemed that a deal was about to be struck involving a prisoner exchange, but nothing happened by year's end. And despite periodic reports that Shalit was alive and well, nothing about his condition could be verified.

As humanitarian distress in Gaza mounted, Israel, which had closed the Gaza border crossings for security reasons and to prevent Shalit from being smuggled out of the Strip, opened the Karni cargo terminal at the northern end of the Strip on July 2 to allow the entry of 50 trucks with food, medical supplies, and fuel into Gaza. Other trucks entered via the Nahal Oz checkpoint. But Israel abruptly stopped cross-border traffic for what it said were security reasons. With the Strip hermetically shut off, Palestinians blew a hole in the wall on the Egyptian border about two weeks later, allowing hundreds to cross the frontier in both directions. Karni was partially reopened on July 24, and the Rafiah crossing at the southern end of the Strip was allowed to open for one day on August 25.

Israel's security cabinet approved a deepening of the military incursion into the Gaza Strip on July 5, after the southern Israeli city of Ashkelon suffered its first Qassam hit, which Olmert called "a major escalation." The rocket, fired from Gaza, struck a schoolyard in the city about seven miles north of the frontier. No one was injured. Ze'ev Schiff, the influential and well-connected commentator for *Ha'aretz*, called the hit on Ashkelon "an unequivocal invitation to war." Extensive ground and air operations continued in the ensuing days, and Qassam rocket fire fell intermittently on Sderot and other areas adjacent to the Gaza border.

The U.S. vetoed a Qatar-sponsored UN Security Council resolution on July 13 that demanded an end to the Israeli offensive in Gaza, along with the release of Shalit and the Palestinian leaders that Israel took into custody after his abduction. Ten nations voted for the proposal and four abstained. John Bolton, the American ambassador to the UN, explained his country's veto by saying that "in light of the fluid events on the ground," his government felt the resolution would have only inflamed regional passions. According to the Al Jazeera TV and Internet news network, the Arab League's secretary general, Amr Musa, said he was "surprised and disappointed" by the veto, which, he said "can be used to protect Israeli actions against civilians."

Five Palestinians, including a terrorist, a mother, and two children, were killed when the house of Hamas activist Muhammad Harara was hit by an IDF tank shell on July 21. The army said that two gunmen tried to fire an antitank weapon from the home's balcony. Five days later, Israeli forces began a two-day sweep of northern Gaza in which they killed 29 Palestinians. According to Palestinian sources, the dead included a 75-year-old woman and a 12-year-old boy who was shot as he stood on a roof in Gaza's Jebalya refugee camp.

The burned body of Dr. Daniel Yaacobi, 60, reported missing from his home in Yakir in the northern West Bank, was discovered stuffed in the trunk of a car near the Palestinian village of Haja east of Qalqilya on July 28. He was last seen on the way to a car repair shop in a Palestinian village near his home. That evening, three officers were wounded when a terrorist, who was killed in the exchange of fire, shot at Border Police at the Israeli Armon Hanatziv checkpoint in southern Jerusalem.

Two Palestinians were killed and four more wounded when an Israeli air strike completely destroyed a house in Khan Younis, in the southern Gaza Strip, on August 15. The army said the house, which belonged to local Al-Aqsa Martyrs Brigades leader Hassan Shaath, was used as a weapons storehouse.

On August 20, Israeli soldiers burst into the home of Palestinian deputy prime minister Nasser Shaer in Ramallah. Four days later, Younis Abu Daka, a local Hamas leader and a lecturer at Islamic University in Gaza City, was taken prisoner in the Gaza Strip in an operation in which Abu Daka's brother, Yousef, was killed.

AP reported on August 30 that Israeli troops engaged in antiterror actions in Gaza, and particularly in Gaza City's Shijaiyeh neighborhood, had killed 15 Palestinians, including several terrorists and a four-year-old boy. The next day, Fadi Khafisha, reputedly the chief "engineer" for Fatah's Al-Aqsa Martyrs Brigades who had been involved in preparing suicide bombings, was shot dead in fighting in Nablus.

According to an AP report, Hussam Jaradat, the West Bank leader of Islamic Jihad's militant wing, died in Jordan on August 30 of wounds suffered on August 23, when, according to Palestinian sources, he was shot in the head by undercover Israeli soldiers in the Jenin refugee camp. Islamic Jihad said that Jaradat, 43, had been hunted by Israel for two years and had survived five attempts on his life. The IDF, however, said it did not know of any troops operating in the Jenin area at the time Jaradat was shot.

On September 5, Palestinian security officers demanding back pay from the cash-strapped Hamas-led government attacked the parliament building in Gaza City. In the West Bank, meanwhile, a work stoppage by teachers and civil servants escalated into a full-scale general strike as shop owners closed their stores. In one town, gunmen from the opposition Fatah shot weapons in the air after some businesses tried to open.

Israel continued its offensive against terror suspects. On September 6, Israeli aircraft struck three times in southern Gaza, killing five militants. Eighteen bystanders were wounded in the attacks, which the army said were aimed at Hamas. In exchanges of fire near the Kissufim crossing into Gaza, an Israeli soldier was killed on September 12.

Israeli air strikes on the house of a weapons dealer in the southern Gaza Strip town of Rafah early on September 27 reportedly killed a 14-year-old girl and wounded ten others. The building was leveled in a first strike, but there were no casualties because Israel had warned that the attack was coming. A few minutes later, however, children who had gathered to look at the rubble were hit in a second strike. Two members of the Al-Aqsa Martyrs Brigades were killed and three bystanders, including a six-year-old boy, were wounded in a missile attack in the southern Gaza Strip on October 1. It came not long after one Israeli was wounded by a Qassam in Sderot.

DIPLOMATIC EFFORTS

Meanwhile, diplomatic activity continued. Meeting in Washington on September 15, Livni and Rice agreed that both their countries would maintain contact with PA president Abbas. The move was attributed to a growing American conviction that in order to maintain a solid coalition against international terrorism and Iranian nuclear ambitions, progress would have to be shown on the Israeli-Palestinian peace track. In this spirit, President Bush, speaking before the UN General Assembly, said that creating "a Palestinian state that has territorial integrity" was "one of the great objectives" of his presidency, and that Rice would "lead a diplomatic effort to engage moderate leaders across the region" to help Abbas and Olmert "in their efforts to come together to resolve their differences."

When Rice visited the area again and scheduled a meeting with Abbas for October 5, a group calling itself Al Qaeda in Palestine posted a five-minute Web video. It contained previously aired clips of Osama bin Laden and slain Iraqi Al Qaeda leader Abu Musab al-Zarqawi, as well as footage of a masked man sitting alongside an automatic weapon and a rocket-propelled grenade launcher. "My speech is directed against . . . those who announce blasphemy against Islam and who are allied with enemies of God and religion, and work in the service of the Jews and the Christians," the masked man said. That same day IDF soldiers killed three Islamic Jihad militants—one while he was trying to break through the Gaza perimeter fence into Israel, and the two others in an air strike.

On October 11, Israeli troops killed a terrorist carrying an explosive belt who had just made his way into Israel south of the Karni crossing between Israel and the northern Gaza Strip. According to a report in *Ma'ariv,* Palestinians had begun calling the Gaza perimeter fence "the wall of death" because of the large number of militants killed while trying to infiltrate through it into Israel.

Israeli soldiers killed an additional seven Palestinian gunmen in air strikes in the Gaza Strip on October 14. And at dawn that day, IDF troops and tanks took over a swath of the Gaza-Egypt border, including the Rafah terminal. Troops carried out house-to-house searches and bulldozers leveled agricultural land near the border. An IDF spokesman said the continuing operation was aimed at uncovering tunnels used by Palestinian militants to smuggle weapons into Gaza from Egypt.

When Prime Minister Olmert arrived in Moscow on October 19 for talks with Russian officials, the Israeli-Palestinian situation was high on the agenda. Russian foreign minister Sergei Lavrov told Olmert that Russia's contacts with Hamas did not mean that Moscow agreed with the policies of the Islamic fundamentalist movement. According to the *Jerusalem Post,* Lavrov told Olmert that since the visit of Khaled Mashaal and a Hamas delegation in March (see above, p. 215) the two sides had remained in touch, but had held no high-level talks. The Russian said he felt that these contacts could be used to press Hamas to renounce terror, recognize Israel, and accept previous agreements of the PA government, the three stipulations that the West required before recognizing the new PA regime.

More than 40,000 people crowded into Gaza City's Yarmouk sports stadium on October 23 to hear Prime Minister Haniyeh mark the start of the Id al-Fitr feast ending the holy month of Ramadan by imploring patience from Palestinians hard-pressed to make ends meet. Referring to the fact that the international financial boycott since the election of the Hamas government in January had meant that about 165,000 civil servants had not been paid their salaries, he said: "I know there are many homes living in pain, and some people shed tears last night because they had no money to give in charity, and could not find food for their children's mouths." And he added, ""If any other people had faced the siege, hardship and destruction you faced, they would have raised the white flag."

On November 6–7, Israeli troops moved out of Beit Hanoun after a six-day operation dubbed Autumn Clouds. Britain's *Guardian* newspaper reported that one Israeli soldier and at least 50 Palestinians, including two women civilians, had been killed, and nine Qassam-firing cells had been hit by the Israelis. But on November 18, Israeli artillery shells aimed at a Qassam launching site instead hit a house, killing 18 Palestinian civilians, including 13 members of one family. The EU expressed "profound shock," and Defense Minister Peretz ordered an investigation. PA prime minister Haniyeh called the incident "an awful massacre" and said talks on forming a Palestinian unity government would be suspended. The PA announced three days of national mourning.

Tens of thousands of Palestinians converged on Yasir Arafat's gravesite on November 11 to commemorate the second anniversary of his death. The occasion also appeared aimed at reinvigorating Fatah, his faltering party. Fatah bused in Palestinians from across the West Bank for the event, dropping many of them in the center of Ramallah, the Palestinians' de facto capital. They then marched through the city carrying Palestinian flags, Fatah banners, and pictures of Arafat to the Muqa'ata compound in the city center, which had served as Arafat's headquarters.

Two Hamas legislators crossed into Gaza from Egypt on November 15 carrying $4.2 million in their luggage for the cash-strapped Hamas-run government. PA Legislative Council member Mushir al-Masri said the $2 million he carried in would be registered with the Palestinian Finance Ministry. Ahmed Bahr, deputy speaker of the Assembly, brought in $2.2 million.

Despite Israeli pressure against the Qassam crews, Fatima Slutsker, 57, was killed, and one of the bodyguards of Defense Minister Peretz lost both legs in a November 15 Qassam hit on Sderot. With Qassams continuing to fall, parents of the Sderot and Shaar Hanegev school districts kept their children out of school as a form of protest against the lack of fortified rooms in the school buildings.

Internal Security Minister Avi Dichter reportedly angered Prime Minister Olmert at the November 19 cabinet meeting with severe criticism of the way the Quassam threat was being handled. Dichter later told *Yediot Aharonot,* "It's time to tell ourselves the truth: we need to stop the Qassams today, because I don't suggest waiting for a time when the Palestinians have better rockets. As a government, we can do much more. We can't allow ourselves to be dragged into a war of attrition . . . ." On the same day, Israel called off an air strike on the home of a Popular Resistance Committee rocket-unit commander in Gaza because a large crowd of Palestinian civilians had gathered around the home, forming a human shield.

A Qassam rocket landed in a chicken-processing factory in the Sderot industrial zone on November 22, killing Ya'akov Yaakobov, 43, a forklift operator at the plant who had immigrated from the Caucasus area of the former Soviet Union 12 years earlier. Also that day, the Red Cross suspended its activities in the Gaza Strip after Palestinian gunmen kidnapped two of its workers, capping a wave of abductions of foreigners. The two, both Italians, were released the next day.

The Israeli-Palestinian conflict recorded a first on November 24: Fatma Najar, 57, became the first grandmother to play the role of suicide bomber. Najar blew herself up near IDF soldiers operating in the Jabalya area in north Gaza, wounding three of the troops. Her family said she had nine children and nearly 30 grandchildren. "I am very proud of what she did," one of her sons told Reuters.

Israeli and Palestinian leaders reached an agreement to end the five months of fighting in Gaza on November 26. The deal ostensibly pledged an end to rocket fire from the Strip into Israel in exchange for a withdrawal of Israeli troops, but by the following morning nine more Palestinian-made Qassams had been launched into southern Israel, even as IDF soldiers were pulling out of Gaza.

AP reported on November 28 that Israel had agreed in principle to let Jordanian-based Palestine Liberation Organization forces loyal to Abbas enter the Gaza Strip to help shore up the two-day-old truce. The next day, in a meeting with EU ambassadors, Olmert said Israel was "a little disappointed by the continued Qassam firings in the south by the Palestinians." Quoting sources in the Prime Minister's Office, the *Yediot* news organization reported that Israel would continue its policy of restraint in the hope that the PA "will contain the terrorists who are attempting to sabotage the cease-fire."

On December 7, Prime Minister Olmert rejected the report of the Iraq Study Group, released the day before in Washington. Chaired by former secretary of state James Baker and former U.S. representative Lee Hamilton, the group concluded that a concerted effort to resolve Israel's conflict with its neighbors would help stabilize the situation in Iraq. The report therefore called for direct talks between Israel and Syria, Lebanon, and the Palestinians. Olmert, while asserting that Israelis wanted "with all our might" to resume peace talks with the Palestinians, denied that there was any connection between Israel's situation and the war in Iraq. He added that "to the best of my knowledge, President Bush, throughout the recent years, also had a different view on this," and noted that on his recent visit to Washington he had received no indication that Bush would push Israel to start talks with Syria. White House officials said that Bush would study the Hamilton-Baker document. Palestinian negotiator Saeb Erekat, however, said he hoped the U.S. "will translate it into deeds. The region needs peace, the region needs dialogue, and we have always stuck to dialogue toward a comprehensive peace."

Intra-Palestinian tensions mounted after the funerals of three children of Baha Ballousheh, a senior Fatah security official, who were murdered on December 11. As security men protested at main Gaza intersections, calling for vengeance and firing shots in the air, PA prime minister Haniyeh said "the government will do whatever it takes to locate the children's murderers and prosecute them." Fatah security officers said that "there cannot be a situation in which children are murdered and no one is held accountable."

Haniyeh's car was fired on and his son, Abed, was injured in an apparent assassination attempt on December 15, after Israel stopped Haniyeh from bringing $35 million in cash from Egypt to aid the financially strapped PA. The shooting came as Hamas gunmen seized control of the Gaza Strip's border crossing with Egypt in a ferocious gun battle with Fatah-allied border guards. PA president Abbas expressed regret for the shooting.

On December 27, after two 14-year-old Sderot boys were wounded by one Qassam and a "strategic facility" in Ashkelon was hit but not severely damaged by another, the Prime Minister's Office issued a statement saying that Israel would respond to Qassams with limited, pin-point attacks, but still "continue to preserve the cease-fire." Ten Qassams landed harmlessly in Israel on December 29, bringing to about 70 the number of Palestinian-made rockets launched at Israel in the month since the informal cease-fire was declared.

At year's end, Olmert spokeswoman Miri Eisen declined to comment on a *Yediot Aharonot* report that Olmert was prepared to hold backchannel negotiations with Abbas on the final borders of a Palestinian state, the status of Jerusalem, and the Palestinian refugee problem. Abbas said he had proposed such talks.

War in Lebanon

The 34-day summer war in Lebanon took a heavy toll on all those involved. It also triggered a political and moral crisis in Israel, and arguably altered the balance of power between Israel and its enemies.

KIDNAPPINGS, ROCKETS, BOMBS

The war started at about 9 a.m. on July 12, when—under cover of diversionary rocket attacks along Israel's northern border—Hezballah ground forces crossed into Israel near Zar'it, in the east, where they ambushed an Israeli patrol, killing three and kidnapping two Israeli soldiers, Eldad Regev and Ehud Goldwasser, both reservists. Five more Israeli soldiers were killed in unsuccessful attempts to rescue them.

Prime Minister Olmert called the kidnap raid an act of war and said that Lebanon would "bear the consequences of its action," since the raid was carried out from its territory by its citizens. The Lebanese cabinet, convened in emergency session by Prime Minister Fouad Siniora, condemned the attack and denied any knowledge of or involvement in its planning.

Sheikh Hassan Nasrallah, the Hezballah leader who masterminded the action, claimed it as "our natural, only and logical right," and said that Goldwasser and Regev had been taken "far, far away," to be held until Israel released three Lebanese it was holding, including Samir Kuntar, the perpetrator of a 1979 seaborne terror attack on the Israeli coastal city of Nahariya in which three members of the Haran family were killed. Gideon Meir, a spokesman in the Israeli Foreign Ministry, ruled out talks, saying Israel wanted the soldiers back "immediately without any precondition." If the prisoners were not returned, CNN quoted Chief of Staff Dan Halutz as saying, "we will turn Lebanon's clock back 20 years."

In the hours after the attack, Israel launched more than 100 air strikes against key Hezballah installations and facilities, such as roads and bridges, which the Shi'ite terrorists might use to transport the captive soldiers. In addition, it would later emerge that during those first hours of the war, Israel Air Force planes struck the launchers of long-range Syrian- and Iranian-made Fajr and Raad missiles in the Hezballah arsenal, severely limiting Nasrallah's ability to launch rocket strikes deep into Israel, while leaving over 10,000 shorter-range, less deadly 122mm Katyusha rockets virtually intact. Hezballah proceeded to fire about 120

Katyushas into Israel that day, mostly on targets near the border with Lebanon.

On July 13 Israel broadened its attacks, hitting civilian and infrastructure targets inside Lebanon, including the main Damascus-Beirut highway, the route over which Hezballah-bound shipments of materiel moved into Lebanon. Israel also struck the runways of Beirut International Airport, closing the facility and causing diversion of flights to Cyprus. Hezballah responded with barrages of Katyushas, hitting Nahariya, just south of the Lebanese border, the mountain town of Safed, and Kiryat Shmona. Two Israelis were killed, one in Nahariya and one in Safed, and 29 were wounded.

Israel imposed an air and sea blockade on Lebanon with the express purpose of preventing the massive resupply of Hezballah arms stores. And on July 14, responding to massive Katyusha rocket fire on northern Israel, Israeli air and seaborne attacks hit a-Dahiya, the fortified south Beirut neighborhood that had become Hezballah's stronghold; a major fuel installation at the Jiyheh power station south of Beirut; and bridges and roads.

That night, Hezballah gunners firing a C-802 Iranian-made Chinese-developed Silkworm-type missile hit the *Ahi-Hanit*, an Israeli Saar-5 class missile-firing corvette, killing four crewmen. The crippled ship, which had suffered damage to its steering section, was towed back to Haifa port in plain view of the Lebanese shoreline. A later inquiry disclosed that missile-detecting systems had been turned off on the mistaken assumption that there was no danger from shore-to-sea missiles, an assumption based on ignorance of the fact that Hezballah possessed Silkworm missiles. A second C-802 hit and sank an Egyptian civilian vessel sailing off the Lebanese coast.

Nasrallah magnified the attack on the Israeli ship for propaganda purposes. Speaking from hiding on the Hezballah al-Manar TV station, he boasted: "Look at the warship that has attacked Beirut, while it burns and sinks before your very eyes." Nasrallah also threatened Israel, saying, "You wanted open war and we are ready for an open war." He predicted that Haifa would come under attack, "and believe me, even beyond Haifa . . . . Our homes will not be the only ones to be destroyed, our children will not be the only ones to die." Indeed, that weekend Hezballah rockets slammed into Haifa, killing two Israelis.

One of the heaviest hits on Haifa took place on Sunday morning, July 16: eight workers were killed when a Fajr rocket went through the flimsy sheet-metal roof of an Israel Railways maintenance workshop not far from the port. The rocket, more powerful than the conventional 120-mm Katyusha, was part of a barrage of ten heavy weapons fired on the city. Civil defense officials warned Israelis in the north of the country to stay close to home or near a place where they could take shelter. At about the same time, the Home Front Command told residents of areas farther south to be on the alert for a possible attack.

Prime Minister Olmert declared that Israel would not give in to Nasrallah's threats. "Our enemies are trying to disturb daily life. They will fail," he said. Israel warned noncombatant residents of south Lebanon of possible danger. "We recommend that they leave their villages and homes and go to the north of the country," Maj.-Gen. Udi Adam, head of Israel's Northern Command, said at a news conference, explaining that IAF planes had dropped leaflets on south Lebanon warning of an attack.

There were also international efforts to end hostilities. At a meeting of the UN Security Council, Israeli ambassador Dan Gillerman declared that by capturing two Israeli soldiers, Hezballah had "taken the whole of Lebanon hostage." Saying that Israel's goal was a free, prosperous, and democratic Lebanon, Gillerman pointed across the room at Lebanon's UN envoy and said, "You know we are doing the right thing, and if we succeed, Lebanon will be the beneficiary."

Javier Solana, the European Union's foreign policy chief, traveled to Beirut for talks. Lebanese Prime Minister Siniora called for a UN-backed cease-fire so that his government might reestablish its authority in the country's south. Israeli transport minister Shaul Mofaz, a former defense minister and chief of staff, told reporters: "I understand Siniora will put his army in the south. Nobody is blocking his way. He should do so and without conditions." Siniora asked the White House to pressure Israel to stop fighting. Spokesman Tony Snow responded, "The president is not going to make military decisions for Israel," but noted that President Bush had urged Israel to limit civilian casualties. Secretary of State Rice told a television interviewer that she was ready to travel to the region to encourage negotiations "when I believe that I can make a difference," but "simply going in and shuttling back and forth, if you don't know where you're trying to go, is not going to help."

With Katyushas still falling on the northern part of the country, Israel continued its air attacks on July 17, hitting a Lebanese army barracks in Tripoli; Hezballah bases in Baalbeck, in the Bek'a valley of eastern Lebanon; and the Beirut area. Missiles fired from the sea killed nine Lebanese in the southern city of Tyre, according to the *New York Times*.

The next day Israeli planes bombed four civilian trucks believed to be carrying rockets on the Damascus-Beirut highway, and over 150 Hezballah rockets fell on Israel's north. Much of the rocket fire came from civilian areas, according to a senior intelligence officer quoted by *Ha'aretz,* who noted that "the firing was from built-up areas, from towns and the outskirts of villages."

On July 19 about 120 rockets were fired into Israel, hitting Haifa, Kiryat Shmona, Karmiel, and Tiberias. Two Israeli Arab brothers, aged three and nine, were killed as they played outside their home in Nazareth. "A Katyusha that is fired does not discriminate," local Arab leader Shawki al-Khatib told an Israeli TV news reporter, while complaining that the town did not have air-raid sirens like those in most Jewish communities. The following day, Nasrallah, in an interview with Al-Jazeera, apologized for killing the boys and called them "martyrs for Palestine." The Hezballah chief also denied an Israeli estimate that its air attacks — including the dropping of 23 tons of bombs on a bunker housing senior Hezballah operatives in Beirut's a-Dahiya neighborhood—had destroyed half of Hezballah's military assets. "They are unable, up until this moment, to do anything to harm us, and I assure you of that," he said.

THE GROUND WAR

Reserve units called up by Israel began massing along the Lebanese border in what seemed to be preparation for a major ground offensive. Actions along the thin border strip, where Hezballah had established a line of fortified positions, intensified on July 20: three Israeli soldiers were killed in clashes just inside Lebanon north of the Israeli village of Avivim, and two more killed opposite Zar'it, in the west. The day was marked by a sharp decrease in the number of Katyusha hits on Israel, only 40, leading to brief hopes that the air campaign against rocket launchers was showing its effectiveness. But heavy fire resumed in ensuing days, including a massive barrage of about 50 rockets aimed at the Haifa area. Secretary of State Rice announced plans to travel to the region on July 23, but said she would not push for an early halt to the fighting since "an immediate cease-fire without political conditions does not make sense."

The first major ground engagement of the war occurred at Maroun al-Ras, opposite the eastern edge of the central sector. After soldiers of the elite Maglan unit tried to clear the village and destroy rocket-launching positions, the army began pouring in forces from other infantry units and tanks. Fighting in the town, according to a report in the *Jerusalem Post,* was "fierce, often at very short-range, with the soldiers advancing from bunker to bunker." Some fortifications were blown up "with the Hezballah men inside them." In four days of fighting, Israel claimed to have destroyed an underground complex of bunkers at the cost of seven soldiers killed.

The press reported criticism inside the army of what was seen as a too-hasty entry into the village during daylight that exposed troops and tanks to missiles and buried bombs. And the claim, reported July 22 by Maj.-Gen. Benny Ganz, head of the IDF's Ground Forces Command, that control of the Maroun al-Ras area had "more or less" been completed turned out to be untrue. On July 26 the IDF encountered additional resistance from dug-in Hezballah fighters who had remained hidden in underground bunkers after the Israeli withdrawal. A similar situation persisted in another fortified town, Ait al-Shaab, which Israeli forces thought they controlled on July 23. As soon as the Israelis left, Hezballah fighters, many of whom were concealed in underground bunkers all along, reemerged. Intermittent fighting persisted there until the mid-August cease-fire.

With the fighting accelerating and threatening to move farther north, hundreds of thousands of people who lived in south Lebanon fled. More than 200,000 found their way across the border into Syria, some 35,000 crammed into the seaside town of Sidon near the Litani River, and those who could afford it or who had foreign passports—including 7,500 Lebanese Americans—headed abroad.

On July 24 the main battlefield moved to the outskirts of Bint Jbail, a large Shi'ite town north of Maroun al-Ras and about two miles from the Israeli border. Soldiers from the Golani Brigade entered the town early the next morning and almost immediately encountered Hezballah forces stationed on the upper floors of buildings, with a commanding view of the battlefield. In the ensuing firefight, the Israelis suffered heavy casualties, with almost 50 percent of the force hit. Only hours later, under heavy fire, did Israel manage to land Blackhawk helicopters to evacuate the wounded; the bodies of the dead were taken out by other Golani soldiers under cover of darkness.

The attempt to capture Bint Jbali, initially planned to take 48–72 hours, dragged on much longer, and it was not until July 29 that Israel troops pulled out—only temporarily, as it turned out—claiming that heavy casualties had been inflicted on Hezballah and confirming that ten of their own soldiers were dead. Miri Eisen, a government spokesperson, said Israel would not fall into a trap set by Hezballah. "Israel is going to do it at our own pace, at our own time, to make sure that when we go in we go in carefully, and that we don't walk into their booby traps," Eisen said. "They have booby-trapped the entire area."

In his fourth speech since the outbreak of fighting 18 days earlier, Nasrallah took a different view, telling viewers on Al-Manar TV (and simultaneously on Israel's Channel 2, which broadcast a translation in real time) that Israel had suffered a "serious defeat" at Bint Jbail. He went on to say that his fighters were actually winning, and that Israel had not registered a "single military accomplishment" in its Lebanon offensive. Fighting began again in Bint Jbail on August 6, continuing until the cease-fire. Journalists who visited the town afterward said that "Hezballah's fighters were as elusive . . . as they were deadly," and that there was now "no sign" of them.

The heavy toll of Israeli casualties in Bint Jbail prompted Justice Minister Ramon to suggest the use of heavier firepower to minimize losses. Before Israeli troops moved in, he suggested, villages should be almost flattened by the air force. But some human rights organizations were already charging that Israeli attacks on roads in order to prevent the transport of weapons to Hezballah had hit civilian convoys, some of which were flying white flags. In a report covering 20 Israeli air attacks released on August 3, Human Rights Watch concluded that "in many cases, Israeli forces struck an area with no apparent military target. In some instances, Israeli forces appear to have deliberately targeted civilians"—a claim tantamount to a war-crimes accusation.

Foreign ministers and other senior officials from 15 European nations and the U.S., as well as UN secretary general Annan, met in Rome on July 26 to seek ways of resolving the conflict. The Europeans generally pushed for an immediate cease-fire, while the U.S. wanted to give Israel more time to deal with Hezballah. There was a broad consensus, however, on the need for a multinational force to keep the peace once the shooting stopped, and for major relief efforts in Lebanon.

A July 30 Israeli air strike on a residential building in the Lebanese town of Qana, under which a Hezballah rocket-launching team spotted from the air had apparently taken refuge, triggered an international uproar when the building collapsed. According to initial reports, 60 bodies were pulled from the rubble, 37 of them those of children. A subsequent official Lebanese report said that 54 people had been killed. A Human Rights Watch report, however, released August 3, lowered the number to 28 confirmed dead, including 16 children, and provided their names and ages. Another 13 people were missing, possibly still buried under the rubble. Human Rights Watch said that its researchers, who visited Qana on

July 31, did not find destroyed military equipment in or near the site, nor did rescue workers recover any "bodies of apparent Hezballah fighters from inside or near the building."

Convened in emergency session shortly after the incident, the UN Security Council unanimously adopted a statement condemning the attack, and asked Secretary General Annan to report within a week "on the circumstances of this tragic incident." Annan had originally wanted a call for "an immediate cessation of hostilities" in the resolution, but after U.S. objections the language was softened to requesting an end to the conflict and warning that continued fighting could have "grave consequences for the humanitarian situation." Israel insisted that Hezballah was to blame because its rocket teams were taking shelter among civilians and effectively using them as human shields against Israeli efforts to root them out. Nevertheless, in the wake of the international uproar, Israel agreed to a 48-hour halt in its air campaign, while reserving the right to take immediate action against targets preparing to attack it.

Secretary of State Rice—who was in the region as part of an eight-day effort at shuttle diplomacy—canceled a planned visit to the Beirut area, but continued work on a draft document that would establish an international peacekeeping force in south Lebanon. Speaking to reporters in Israel before departing for Washington, she said she would push for a cease-fire and a lasting settlement. "I am convinced that only by achieving both will the Lebanese people be able to control their country and their future, and the people of Israel finally be able to live free of attack from terrorist groups in Lebanon," she said. A few days later, speaking on the "Larry King Live" TV program, Rice appeared to be moving toward the European position favoring an immediate cease-fire. "We need to end the hostilities in a way that points forward a direction for a sustainable peace," Rice said.

Hezballah fired more than 200 Katyushas into Israel on August 2, the heaviest barrage so far. As ground fighting continued in and around fortified Hezballah villages along the border, an Israeli elite unit launched a commando raid on Baalbek, a Hezballah stronghold in the Bek'a Valley of eastern Lebanon, the deepest penetration of Israeli ground troops into Lebanon since the 1994 kidnapping of Hezballah leader Mustafa Dirani. The main target now was the Dar al-Hikma Hospital, a Hezballah-run facility believed to be sheltering senior commanders of the group. According to *Ha'aretz,* only a few low-ranking operatives were captured.

Israel severed the last road link between Lebanon and the outside world on August 4. Then, at about 9 p.m. that night, rockets hit near

Hadera, south of Haifa, the deepest penetration of rockets so far. There were no injuries and little panic. Loud blasts were reported over a wide area; Hezballah later that night identified the missiles as Khaibar-1, which carried large explosive charges and made a lot of noise. A version of the Iranian Fajr-13 and Fajr-5 rocket, the Khaibar-1 carried an explosive charge of about 100 kg and had a range of 75 km. It had previously been fired on Afula, in the Jezreel Valley.

Hezballah said it had fired three rockets at Hadera in response to what it called the "vicious crime" of an IAF bombing in the Bek'a Valley that allegedly killed 28 noncombatant farm workers. Home Front Command reminded Israelis living south of Haifa that while they did not need to stay in shelters or fortified rooms, they should know where to locate them, and take into account that a warning siren would give residents about one minute to seek shelter.

Fadia Jamaa, 60, and her two daughters, Samira, 33, and Sultana, 31, were immediately killed on August 5 when a Katyusha hit the yard of their home in the Israeli Bedouin village of Arab al-Aramshe, near the northern town of Shlomi and only a few kilometers from the Lebanese border. The women were sitting in the yard, which was located next to a fortified structure. The village was too close to the Lebanese border for residents to be warned in time of incoming rockets. The next day, 12 Israeli reservists in a staging area at the entrance to the Kfar Giladi kibbutz in the Upper Galilee were killed by a direct Katyusha hit.

A FINAL PUSH AND A CEASE-FIRE

Since early in the war Prime Minister Olmert had resisted calls to have the army push northward to the Litani River line—in some places 20 miles north of the border—in order to prevent the firing of short-range missiles from there into Israel. On August 7, however, Olmert hinted that he was reconsidering. On a tour of the northern border area with Amir Peretz and senior army commanders a day after 160 rockets were fired into Israel, he said he had given an order "that if within the coming days the diplomatic process does not reach a conclusion, Israeli forces will carry out the operations necessary to take control of rocket-launching sites wherever they are."

With more of their troops massing on the border, Israeli forces moved into the key south Lebanese town of Al-Khiam for the first time on August 10. Also, leaflets dropped on Shi'ite neighborhoods in southern Beirut told residents to leave their homes. The next day Olmert and Peretz authorized a major ground offensive into southern Lebanon, and infantry and armored forces, kept on hold for days, surged north. The decision to authorize the offensive—which would later come under harsh criticism for gaining nothing and piling up heavy Israeli casualties—was made after compromises on the wording of a draft Security Council resolution appeared unacceptable to Israel. But there were reports of ongoing diplomatic efforts at the UN to satisfy Israel's requirements on the mandate and powers of an international force; indeed, as intensive negotiations among key Security Council members continued, Olmert was quoted as saying a new proposal being drafted "has positive significance that may bring the war to an end." Thus the authorization of the offensive might have been little more than a negotiating tactic.

Later that day the Security Council adopted Resolution 1701, to take effect on the morning of August 14. It called for the "full cessation" of fighting, including Israeli offensive operations and Hezballah attacks; expanding UNIFIL, the existing UN Interim Force in Lebanon, from 2,000 to as many as 15,000 troops to help coordinate the deployment of 15,000 Lebanese troops and the withdrawal of Israeli forces; mandating a series of steps toward a permanent cease-fire and lasting political solution, including disarmament of all armed groups in Lebanon and respect by both parties for the "Blue Line," the UN-demarcated border separating Israel and Lebanon; supporting the principle that Lebanon's government should be the only armed force in the country, thus barring Hezballah militias from retaining weapons; requesting the international community to extend immediate financial and humanitarian assistance to the Lebanese people, including funds needed to help the tens of thousands of displaced Lebanese to return; and making all parties responsible for ensuring that no action would be taken that would endanger humanitarian efforts, including safe passage for convoys to distribute food and medical supplies.

In a televised speech on August 12, Sheikh Nasrallah said Hezballah would "not be an obstacle" to a Lebanese government decision accepting the UN cease-fire resolution, but he added, "our ministers will express reservations about articles that we consider unjust and unfair," and rocket strikes on northern Israel would end only when Israel stopped its air strikes and other attacks on Lebanese civilians. CNN reported that two Hezballah ministers in the Lebanese cabinet expressed reservations about the resolution's demand for their organization to disarm in the south.

On August 13, Israeli forces pushed forward to positions near the

Litani River, while Hezballah fired about 250 rockets into northern Israel and launched two pilotless aircraft that were shot down by Israeli planes. That same day, the Israeli cabinet conducted a stormy debate about the conduct of the war—Culture and Sports Minister Ophir Pines-Paz of Labor, for example, criticized the decision to launch the ground offensive when a cease-fire appeared imminent. Nevertheless, the cabinet voted 24-0 to accept the cease-fire. There was one abstention—Transport Minister Shaul Mofaz, a former chief of staff and defense minister. Prime Minister Olmert told Army Radio that as a result of the decision, "Hezballah won't continue to exist as a state within a state . . . . The Lebanese government is our address for every problem or violation of the agreement."

The next day, as the shaky cease-fire took hold in south Lebanon, Olmert addressed the Knesset. Urging Israelis not to bicker about "blame and guilt" for the war, the prime minister said the military campaign had "hurt the murderous organization [Hezballah] to a degree that is not yet known to the public," and taunted Nasrallah and the rest of the Shi'ite leadership for fleeing into hiding places as soon as fighting began. "We will hunt them down at every time and in every place, and we won't ask permission from anyone," he pledged.

Lebanese troops begin deploying south of the Litani River on August 17, and, in coordination with UN forces, gradually began taking over territory from which Israeli forces withdrew. "The process of transferring authority has begun," an IDF statement said, adding that an agreement had been reached after a three-way meeting between Israeli and Lebanese officers and a representative of UNIFIL. UN secretary general Annan demanded on August 29 that Israel lift its air and sea blockade of Lebanon, but Israel said it would do so only when it was assured that forces deployed on Lebanon's borders could stop new weapons shipments to Hezballah. The blockade was lifted on September 9.

THE BALANCE-SHEET AND SOME SECOND THOUGHTS

On the Israeli side, 119 soldiers were killed and hundreds more wounded, in addition to 43 civilians killed and about 1,350 wounded. The number of Lebanese dead due to the war was estimated at 1,100–1,200, with almost 4,500 wounded. Hezballah at first claimed that only 70 of its fighters were killed, but later raised the figure to 250. Other estimates were at least double that, AP claiming 565 and the IDF 600–700.

All of northern Israel was paralyzed for more than a month, as a million citizens lived under threat of attack from thousands of Kaytusha and other rockets. Israeli losses were estimated at several billion dollars, including hundreds of millions of dollars in property damage, the near total shut-down of the multibillion-dollar tourism industry, and significant business and commercial losses. The conflict left much of Lebanon's civilian infrastructure in ruins; experts believed that it would take at least a decade to recover. According to a UN survey, about 35,000 homes and businesses in Lebanon were destroyed in the conflict, and a quarter of the country's road, bridges, and overpasses were damaged. The total cost to Lebanon was at least $15 billion.

In separate reports, two nongovernmental organizations (NGOs), Amnesty International and Human Rights Watch, criticized both sides for attacking civilian targets. Amnesty condemned Israel's use of white phosphorus and suggested that the harm done to the civilian infrastructure of Lebanon was not just collateral damage, but part of a deliberate strategy. It called for "the immediate establishment of a comprehensive, independent and impartial inquiry into violations of international humanitarian law" by Israel and Hezballah. Human Rights Watch said that Israel's systematic failure to distinguish between combatants and noncombatants might constitute a war crime. It raised the possibility that Hezballah had also committed war crimes by directing rockets at civilian population centers in Israel and by packing the warheads of its rockets with ball-bearings and other small bits of metal, which suggested "a desire to maximize harm to civilians."

The Association for Civil Rights in Israel (ACRI) charged Israel with putting Lebanese civilians in harm's way by preventing them from leaving the war zone during its attacks on Lebanese infrastructure. The IDF, however, maintained that Hezballah had blocked the exits to villages and used civilian houses as firing posts, and that Israel had, whenever possible, tried to distinguish between protected persons and combatants.

There was no consensus either inside Israel or in the international community on who had won the war and who had lost. Israeli chief of staff Dan Halutz said that although Israel had not landed a knockout blow, it won "on points." Undeniably, Israel's efforts had broken Hezballah's hold on south Lebanon and secured its replacement by UNIFIL. Others, however, noted that the failure to score a decisive victory severely damaged Israel's military deterrent against possible future attacks from Hezballah and Iran, for which it had acted as a proxy, and possibly Syria—which had, at the very least, allowed itself to be used as a conduit, and perhaps even directly supplied arms for use against Israeli forces.

Some foreign observers both in the Arab world and the West gave considerable credit to Sheikh Nasrallah and his Hezballah fighters. By surviving an asymmetrical conflict with Israel, the argument went, Hezballah had emerged as the military and political victor. Israel had been forced to end the fighting without achieving its two main objectives, the release of kidnapped soldiers Goldwasser and Regev, and the destruction of Hezballah as a fighting force. Hezballah also seemed to be making political gains after the war: with money presumably suppied by Iran, it distributed cash in Lebanon for the repair of homes and businesses damaged in the conflict.

On August 27, Nasrallah stated publicly that he had not intended to start a war. Apologizing to the Lebanese people, he said: "Had we known that the kidnapping of the soldiers would have led to this, we would definitely not have done it." Nevertheless, speaking to close to a million supporters at a "victory" rally in Beirut on September 22, Nasrallah said his organization was celebrating a "divine and strategic victory."

Most Israelis were highly critical of the outcome, and as the days passed, criticism of those who had managed the war mounted. There were calls for the removal of both the political and military leadership, the latter gaining special impetus from the revelation that Dan Halutz, the chief of staff, had ordered his bank to sell his entire portfolio of stocks on the morning the fighting began. On August 21, demobilized reservists claiming 2,000 supporters set up a protest tent near the Knesset and the Prime Minister's Office in the Givat Ram complex in Jerusalem. The Movement for Quality Government, a voluntary watchdog group that had existed for years, joined in the protest movement, as did families of soldiers killed and wounded and displaced residents of northern Israel. By August 25, 63 percent of the participants in one survey thought Prime Minister Olmert should resign. Complaints about management of the war soon expanded into a broader critique of the lack of accountability in Israeli society.

Olmert continued to balk at one of the protesters' key demands, the establishment of a formal state commission of inquiry headed by a retired Supreme Court justice. Instead, he announced on August 28 that there would be two internal inquiries, one to investigate the performance of the political echelon and the other to examine that of the IDF. He also raised the possibility of a third commission to look into the management of the home front. Since these would have more limited mandates than a state commission of inquiry, they were denounced by the critics as providing the recipe for a whitewash. The makeup of the first of the internal panels, that probing the political leadership, was announced in

September. Its chairman was retired judge Eliyahu Winograd, and the other members were two professors—Yehezkel Dror, a political scientist, and Ruth Gavison, a legal scholar—and two retired generals, Menahem Eilon and Haim Nadel.

Backbiting among army officers grew especially intense. In early October, after Maj.-Gen. Yiftah Ron-Tal, a former commander of the ground forces who had earlier attacked the 2005 disengagement from the Gaza Strip, called for Halutz and Olmert to resign over their conduct of the war, Halutz dismissed him from the army. In a letter to Ron-Tal, Halutz said he was terminating the general's stay in the military because "Israeli soldiers are forbidden to deal with political subjects and make public comments on political and diplomatic issues, and all the more so, it is forbidden for soldiers to publicly criticize the government."

Another top officer who left the army was Brig.-Gen. Gal Hirsch, commander of the Galilee Division during the war. Hirsch resigned on November 12, shortly before a report by former general Doron Almog into the July 12 incident in which Eldad Regev and Ehud Goldwasser were kidnapped and eight soldiers killed. The Almog report pointed out inadequacies in the conduct of the soldiers in the field and also drew personal conclusions against the commander himself, Hirsch. In his letter of resignation, Hirsch charged that he had received no backing from the very beginning of the war, and had been subjected to a constant barrage of unjustified criticism.

The Syrian Conundrum

Syria's shadowy role in aiding Hezballah during the Lebanese conflict could easily have escalated the war into a regional conflict, and Israel took steps to minimize that possibility. Though Israel maintained that Syrian-made equipment was being used by the Hezballah fighters and that Syria was resupplying its allies with rockets and other weapons, Prime Minister Olmert reportedly vetoed plans to deploy reserve forces on the Golan Heights after intelligence reports claimed that Damascus had placed its troops on high alert.

But Israel did use air power to attack convoys from Syria, which Damascus insisted were carrying civilian aid rather than military materiel. In late July, for example, the official Syrian news agency termed "totally baseless and unfounded" Israeli allegations that a convoy of trucks hit by Israel was of a military nature. In fact, the Syrians asserted, the vehicles carried medical aid donated by the United Arab Emirates to

Lebanese war victims, and were accompanied by ambulances. The UAE Red Crescent—the Arab equivalent of the Red Cross—subsequently condemned the air raid, saying it violated "all international charters, the Geneva Conventions, and international humanitarian laws."

In mid-August, Israel appeared interested in renewed talks with Syria. Shortly after the cease-fire in Lebanon went into effect, Defense Minister Peretz said that "every war creates opportunities for an extensive diplomatic process," and that it was necessary to "lay the groundwork for negotiations with Syria." Foreign Minister Livni also expressed the hope that the cease-fire would pave the way for a better Middle East, specifically referring to Syria and the "change it has to make in order to be accepted by the international community and play a more positive role."

But Israel changed its tune after Syrian president Bashar Assad's speech on August 15 to the Syrian Journalists Association, in which he claimed credit for what he termed Hezballah's "victory" in the just-ended Lebanon war, supported "resistance" to Israel, and called for the removal of the incumbent Lebanese government. Praising Hezballah's actions, the Syrian president spoke of "turning the military victory into a political victory." He also deemed Security Council Resolution 1701, which brought about the cease-fire, unacceptable, because it held Hezballah accountable for starting the war. Assad did not lay all the responsibility on Israel. He said the conflict was "an Israeli aggression in tools, but an American aggression in decision." And, hinting at the possibility of going to war, Assad warned that a peace deal with Israel was not the only way to achieve Syrian goals, meaning the return of the Golan Heights.

Israel's interpretation of the Syrian leader's statements was that Damascus had opted to align itself with extremist Islam and could not be considered a partner for peace. An official communiqué issued after the August 20 meeting of the Israeli cabinet said, "Syria, as can be seen from Bashar Assad's speech praising Hezballah, has come out clearly, in word and in action, on the side of the axis of opposition to Israel."

At the same time, Olmert warned that constant talk of a war with Syria might be misunderstood in Damascus. "People do not have to warn us of the Syrian war threat on a daily basis, and on the other hand, to immediately leap forth to negotiate with the country," he commented during the cabinet meeting, according to the *Jerusalem Post*. "Every comment of this nature brings forth a feeling that the other side doesn't necessarily understand us in the way we would strive to be understood. We must be more cautious during this time, despite the fact that we are prepared for anything."

Yet such mixed signals were delivered the very next day, when Internal Security Minister Dichter said that Israel should resume negotiations with Syria toward a deal in which the Golan Heights, captured in the 1967 Six-Day War, would be exchanged for peace. "What we did with Egypt and Jordan is also legitimate in this case," Dichter said. Vice Prime Minister Shimon Peres, however, also speaking that day, said the time was not right to resume negotiations with Damascus, since Israel was still preoccupied with Lebanon and the Palestinians.

Olmert, visiting northern Israel the following day, August 22, declined to criticize Dichter, a close political associate. But according to Ronny Sofer of *Yediot Aharonot,* he did express severe reservations about any Syrian initiative. "I have heard voices speaking about our neighbors to the north and the need to speak to them," Olmert said. "Let's remember that a few days ago missiles from that country to our north were killing Israeli civilians. All terror organizations have headquarters in Damascus and enjoy full support from Syria. The kidnappers of Gilad Shalit, too, received their instructions from Damascus . . . . Let's not get sucked in by false hopes, or create illusions that tomorrow we'll blink our eyes and all of a sudden they will be negotiating partners."

Olmert reiterated this view in September, after Assad, in an interview with the German magazine *Der Spiegel,* said, "We want to make peace— peace with Israel." Olmert told Israel Radio on September 28, "It [Syria] was and remains the main supporter of the Palestinian terror groups who daily try to carry out terrorism against the State of Israel. In my opinion, this is not a foundation on which it is possible to hold peace negotiations." This position was aligned with that of the U.S., which considered Syria part of the network of international terror.

Tensions between Israel and Syria increased in October. After repeated statements from Damascus that it was readying for war, including a claim by Assad that preparations had begun to ward off an impending Israeli attack, Israel visibly beefed up its military presence in the Golan Heights and placed its army on high alert. But Assad sent a contradictory signal on October 21. In an interview with the Spanish newspaper *El Pais,* Assad repeated his desire for peace negotiations with Israel and expressed the belief that the achievement of an "encompassing and just" agreement would solve the area's recurring problems.

The idea of Syrian-Israeli talks surfaced again in December, when President Assad, in an interview with the Italian newspaper *La Repubblica,* said his country was ready to hold peace negotiations with Israel, but was also preparing for the possibility of a war. "I say to Olmert: make an attempt. Call our bluff," he declared.

Speaking to *Yediot Aharonot* a few days later, Ami Ayalon, the former chief of Israel's navy and the Shin Bet security services—who was, at the time, running for the leadership of the Labor Party—said Israel could not reject what seemed to be a Syrian initiative out of hand. Even so, he continued, there should be preconditions for such talks—Syria would have to dissociate itself from terror, distance itself from Iran, and make it clear that an Israeli withdrawal from the Golan Heights need not be immediate, but gradual. He concluded, "Whoever wants to talk needs to be talked to, but in coordination with the Americans."

Another Israeli view, held by a minority, held that the government should enter into immediate negotiations with Syria. The celebrated Israeli writer Amos Oz, for example, said: "Israel is demanding, as a precondition, that Syria give all that it has to give—even before sitting down at the negotiating table. That is a ludicrous demand."

But Olmert was not about to make any overtures to Syria in contravention of American wishes. He asked, "At a time when the president of the United States, Israel's most important ally, with whom we have a network of strategic relations—when he is fighting in every arena, both at home in America, in Iraq and in other places in the world, against all the elements that want to weaken him—is this the time for us to say the opposite?"

The Iranian Threat

Tensions between Israel and Iran increased sharply over the course of 2006, spurred on by President Mahmoud Ahmadinejad's continued predictions that the Jewish state would be "wiped off the map"; Iranian support for and supply of weapons and training to its client, Hezballah, in Lebanon; and the rising threat of a nuclear Iran.

At a press conference in Tehran on April 24, the Iranian president said Israel could not "continue its existence," adding that the Middle East conflict could only be settled with a just peace plan. And in an interview with *Der Spiegel*, the German newsmagazine, in May, Ahmadinejad said there were "two opinions" about the Holocaust. In response to a question on whether the Holocaust was a myth, he said: "I will only accept something as truth if I am actually convinced of it," adding that if it turned out that there had been no Holocaust, "the Jews have to go back to where they came from." In an obvious riposte to uncomplimentary caricatures of the Prophet Muhammed in a Danish newspaper (see below, pp. 433–35), the Iranian government sponsored an international contest for Holocaust cartoons. There were 204 entries. More vitriolic rhetoric came with the outbreak of war in Lebanon. Ahmadinejad said on July 15 that just as Hitler had sought pretexts to conquer other European nations, "the Zionist regime found baseless pretexts to invade Islamic countries, and right now it is justifying its attacks with groundless excuses." In early August, while calling for an immediate cease-fire in Lebanon, the Iranian president said that "the main solution is for the elimination of the Zionist regime," which was "illegitimate" and had "no legal basis for existence."

Speaking shortly after he became acting prime minister in January, Olmert said that "under no circumstances can Israel allow someone with hostile intentions against us to have control over weapons of mass destruction that can endanger our existence." In April, responding to threatening statements by Ahmadinejad, Olmert said that "the Jewish people and the very existence of Israel" were Iran's targets. Israel, he went on, did not take the threat lightly, and "we are powerful and able to defend ourselves." And at a gathering at the Yad Vashem Holocaust memorial in October, the prime minister wondered out loud how Iran could continue to be "a legitimate member of the United Nations."

Throughout the war in Lebanon, Israel insisted that Iran was the source of weapons that flowed through Syria to Hezballah. In early August, Defense Minister Peretz made clear Israel's view of the Iranian role. "Hezballah," he said, "is Iran's advance commando unit. In effect, it is the Iranian vanguard." Writing in the December issue of *Foreign Affairs,* Ze'ev Schiff, the eminent military analyst for *Ha'aretz,* stated: "The Iranians may not have been physically present on the front lines in Lebanon, but they were active there nonetheless," and cited specific instances of Iranian involvement discovered by Israeli intelligence. Schiff wrote that Israel was lucky that Iran did not yet have nuclear weapons. "From Iran's perspective," he went on, "the conflict started too soon."

Over the course of the year, Iran stonewalled UN efforts to get it to suspend its uranium-enrichment and reprocessing-related activities and to implement full transparency measures. Ali Larijani, Tehran's chief nuclear negotiator, responded to UN pressure in July by insisting that Iran would expand, not suspend, uranium enrichment. Israel, which understood that it was the primary target of the potential Iranian nuclear threat, warned the world repeatedly of the danger.

Speaking to newspaper editors, Prime Minister Olmert said Israel "cannot remain indifferent to . . . serious attempts to develop a capability with which they will be able to advance toward the production of a nonconventional bomb. We will work with our friends, first and foremost with the U.S., in order to prevent this." He seemed to prefer efforts to reach a political solution before using other means. "The way to deal with it, first and foremost, is to see to it that Iran will not have the ability to develop nuclear weapons. This is the goal. The ways are various and manifold. I hope that it will be possible to achieve this via negotiations, as I have said more than once, including through compromise," Olmert said.

The threat to Israel from Iran became increasingly palpable over the course of the year. In January, Iran tested a missile that may have had a range of nearly 2,500 miles, capable of reaching Israel and American forces in the Middle East. During war games in November, Iranian TV carried pictures of missile firings, and reported that Shihab-2 and Shihab-3 missiles with ranges from 300 to 2,000 miles had been used. According to one report, some had been modified to carry cluster warheads capable of delivering over 1,000 individual warheads.

There were signs that Iran was getting close to nuclear bomb-making capacity. In May, UN inspectors found traces of highly enriched uranium near an Iranian military research center, and the uranium, they said, was close to but not quite at the level needed to make nuclear warheads. Israel had its own assessments of the Iranian nuclear timetable. Ha'aretz reported that Gen. Amos Yadlin, head of military intelligence, told the Knesset Foreign Affairs Committee that Iran would have nuclear weapons by 2010, and a similar prediction, quoting unnamed sources in the Israeli defense establishment, was published in the Jerusalem Post. There were reports during the year, all denied, of Israeli plans to hit Iranian nuclear facilities before bomb-making capability became irreversible. In December, after the Security Council passed Resolution 1737 threatening sanctions against Iran, the Israeli cabinet issued an official communiqué saying that the UN decision "makes it clear that there are many more options for action that — correctly used and enforced by the international community — will enable the attainment of better results in blocking Iran's nuclear option."

Ahmadinejad opened a two-day Holocaust-denial conference in Tehran in early December. Rasoul Mousavi, head of the Iranian Foreign Ministry's Institute for Political and International Studies, said it was an opportunity for scholars to discuss the subject "away from Western taboos and the restriction imposed on them in Europe." According to the New

York Times, citing Iranian reports, 67 researchers from 30 countries took part, including former Ku Klux Klan leader David Duke. Also in attendance were seven members of the Neturei Karta anti-Zionist ultra-Orthodox sect. At the same time, Iranian leaders indignantly denied that they were anti-Semitic.

A Nuclear Israel?

On December 10, at the start of an offical visit to Germany, Prime Minister Olmert gave an interview to the German N24 news channel in which he appeared to confirm the widespread suspicion that Israel had nuclear weapons. He said: "We have never threatened any nation with annihilation. Iran, openly, explicitly, and publicly threatens to wipe Israel off the map. Can you say that this is the same level, when they are aspiring to have nuclear weapons, as America, France, Israel, Russia?"

His statement might have been a slip of the tongue or, alternatively, a considered comment in reponse to the growing Iranian nuclear threat. Whatever his intentions, Olmert immediately found himself in political hot water for breaking with the long-standing Israeli policy of "nuclear ambiguity," whereby Israel said only that it would not be the first country to introduce nuclear weapons into the region.

The Prime Minister's Office hastened to say that Olmert was only putting Israel "among the list of responsible nations, and not the list of nations that have nuclear weapons." But Likud MK (and former chairman of the Knesset Foreign Affairs and Defense Committee) Yuval Steinitz said the prime minister should resign. "The terrible statement made in Germany undermines 50 years of Israel's policy of ambiguity . . . . A prime minister who is unable to control his statements on sensitive matters of security must quit," said Steinitz, a close ally of Likud leader Benjamin Netanyahu. A similarly strong condemnation came from the left side of the political spectrum. Meretz leader Yossi Beilin said that "the fantastic statement of the prime minister on the nuclear issue . . . raises serious doubts whether this is a person worthy of serving as prime minister."

Meanwhile, Abdul Rahman al-Attiya, secretary general of the Gulf Cooperation Council, urged the U.S. to take steps against a nuclear Israel. Washington, he argued, "should not apply double standards." Having called for sanctions against Iran, which had no plans to use nuclear power for war, the Americans should certainly clamp down on Israel, whose prime minister had admitted possessing nuclear weapons, he said.

DOMESTIC DEVELOPMENTS

The Economy

GROWTH DESPITE WAR

The performance of the Israeli economy in 2006 made it seem as though the war never happened. The country's Gross Domestic Product (GDP), the standard measure of production and thus the key indicator of economic performance, grew by 5.1 percent for the year, lagging behind the super-fast growth of Far Eastern economies like those of China and India, but still 70 percent higher than the 2.9 average growth rate for all 30 developed countries of the Organization for Economic Development (OECD). Beyond that, Israel ranked a respectable 28th in the world in per-capita GDP, at a little more than $18,000 for each Israeli. This was a remarkable figure given the relatively low Israeli rate of participation in the work force, a situation created by the large numbers of ultra-Orthodox men and Arab women who, for reasons of religion and tradition, did not work.

According to revised figures published by the Bank of Israel in March 2007, when most of the relevant statistics were in, GDP rose at a whopping annualized rate of 11 percent in the fourth quarter of 2006, after declining by 1.8 percent in the previous quarter because of the war. Indeed, there was great pessimism about the economy in August and September due to the 34 days of combat. The high cost of the war, the need to rearm the military, and the hundreds of millions of dollars needed to repair war damage raised fears of an economic slowdown. But the economy bounced back instead.

"On a macroeconomic level, the effect of the war was only temporary," Bank Leumi economist Hanoch Frankovits told the *Jerusalem Report* magazine. Frankovits said that economic damage was minimal because the war was relatively short. Despite stories of ripe fruit rotting on the trees of northern kibbutzim and moshavim, he observed, even damage to agriculture was not as great as anticipated. True enough, farmers in the north suffered losses, but the overall statistics were hardly affected. According to Frankovits, agricultural exports in August and September averaged 70–80 million shekels a month, about what they would have been in a "normal" year.

Equally important, the economy was able to snap back because it had been in good shape during the first half of the year, when annualized growth was a very high 6.6 percent. Had the conflict taken place in 2003, during the recession that coincided with the intifada, the situation would have been much worse and the recovery much slower, most Israeli economists agreed.

Another reason the economy was able to absorb the shock of the war was its diversification. Israel no longer depended almost entirely on high-tech exports, mostly in information technology, electronics, and software. While high-tech still played a key role, other sectors had emerged in recent years and picked up a greater share of the load, such as chemicals for agriculture. Alternative sources of energy had become more widespread, and the domestic market had grown. In 2003 and 2004, as the domestic economy contracted under the influence of the second intifada and the continuing effects of recession, expansion of exports was the main force driving the economy forward. But since then, Central Bureau of Statistics (CBS) figures showed that the domestic economy's share of GDP expansion, 2.9 percent each year, accounted for more than half of the over-5-percent growth rate.

One final element helping explain the economic resiliency was suggested by Roby Nathanson, director general of the Macro Institute of Political Economics, a Tel Aviv think tank. He said, "We are not the Swiss, we are accustomed to war. So when there is a war, it's a shock all right, but we do not collapse. We have been having wars here for almost 100 years, not like any regular country."

The only sector that really suffered from the war was tourism, which displayed its usual high degree of sensitivity to security problems and political events. For the year, 1.8 million tourists visited Israel, a drop of only 5 percent from 2005 but way below the 2.4 million who had been expected in a year people thought would be the best since the start of the second intifada in 2000. According to industry statistics, revenues from tourism and related services were only $3.4 billion in 2006, far short of the $4.4 billion that had been anticipated.

To be sure, the war had other costs as well. Activists like Shlomo Swirski of the Adva Center, a Tel Aviv-based social-policy think tank, pointed out that in order to pay the war's costs, estimated at several billion dollars, monies had been diverted that would otherwise have gone to social programs, infrastructure projects, and cutting university tuitions—which, low by Western standards, was still more than many young Israelis and their families could afford. Two major programs planned to begin in 2007—the so-called War on Poverty, which was to have gotten allocations of 14 billion shekels (about $3.3 billion) over five years, and Negev 2015, which envisioned spending 17 billion shekels on the development of the long-neglected south of the country over a ten-year span—had to be sidelined.

ECONOMIC BALANCE SHEET

Israel's fiscal deficit for the year was 6.1 billion shekels ($1.45 billion), amounting to 0.9 percent of GDP. What kept it that low was a $3-billion rise in tax revenues, which helped offset the negative effects of the war. Israel's external debt declined by $16 billion, reaching $14 billion, the lowest figure in the country's history, according to figures published by the Bank of Israel. The central bank said that the value of Israeli assets abroad in December 2006 was about $156 billion, while foreign liabilities totaled slightly less than $171 billion. The value of foreign assets rose sharply to $156 billion from only $122 billion at the end of 2005. The bank also noted that Israel had a balance-of-payments surplus amounting to $6.8 billion in 2006, up from $4.6 billion in 2005. Foreign investment was calculated at a record $22.7 billion, including $14.1 billion in direct investment and $8.6 billion in Israeli securities. At the same time, Israelis deposited $9.3 billion in foreign banks, mostly by the business sector for the financing of its activities and acquisitions.

Israel's public, or governmental, debt fell by 8.9 percent in 2006 to 545 billion shekels (about $128 billion), 88 percent of GDP, its lowest level in four years, according to the Ministry of Finance. For the period 2003–06, the public debt fell by 14 percentage points, or $15.5 billion. Israel's public debt was now far below its 1986 peak of 159.8 percent of GDP, but the 88-percent figure was still substantially above the average of 60 percent in the developed countries of the OECD.

According to Bank of Israel figures, the shekel appreciated by 8.2 percent against the dollar over the course of 2006, and by 5.2 percent against the basket of currencies. The country's foreign-currency reserves stood at $29.028 billion at the end of 2006, compared to $27.858 billion a year before.

Merger-and-acquisition activity reached an all-time high in 2006, with more than $10.6 billion in 76 separate transactions. A list published by the *Globes* business daily of high-tech companies—which did not include the $4-billion purchase of 80 percent of the Iscar cutting-tools firm by U.S. investor Warren Buffett's Berkshire Hathaway—was topped by HP's $4.5-billion purchase of Mercury Interactive; the $1.55-billion sale of flash-memory maker M-Systems to Sandisk; Verifone's acquisition of Lipman Engineering for $793 million; PMC-Sierra's $300 million buy of chipmaker Passave; and the $245-million cash-and-shares deal for Power Dsine made by Microsemi. In addition, according to *Ha'aretz,* Israeli companies paid about $3 billion for foreign companies in 51 transactions, the largest of which was the December purchase of Sweden's Protect Data by CheckPoint software for $625 million.

At year's end, the unemployment rate stood at 7.7 percent, the lowest figure in a decade, the CBS reported. Average unemployment for all of 2006 was 8.4 percent, as compared to 9 percent in 2005. Analysts pointed out that the economy's performance on the job front was even more impressive taking into account a growth in the population of about 1.8 percent and new rules that tightened requirements for unemployment compensation, pushing more Israelis into the workforce.

According to a report by Dr. Rafi Melnik of the Herzliya Interdisciplinary Center, 74,000 new business-sector jobs were created during 2006, an increase of 4.2 percent, to reach a record of 1.85 million. Most of those jobs—about 52,000—were added before the outbreak of the war on July 12, and the others after its conclusion. Still, economist Roby Nathanson claimed that the drop in unemployment was no cause for celebration. "We should be doing much better," he said, pointing out that in the OECD developed countries unemployment stood at an average of 6 percent. And he added that Israel was not going to close the gap between rich and poor—the second widest in the West (the U.S. had the widest)—by creating more low-paying jobs.

Poverty indeed remained a problem, although the year 2006 did see some small improvement. The Bank of Israel's annual poverty index showed a drop of three-tenths of a percentage point to 24.4 percent, after rising in the three previous years and reaching 24.7 percent in 2005. The Arab and Haredi populations, both characterized by large families and a low level of participation in the workforce, accounted for 60 percent of Israel's poor. Poverty was most widespread, however, among Israel's Bedouin population, where the rate was 66.4 percent.

The official Bank of Israel report said that cutbacks in social welfare payments—such as child allowances for large families and pensions for the disabled and the elderly—were responsible for much of the increase in poverty over the last several years. These policies were instituted in 2002 under then-finance minister Benjamin Netanyahu, who maintained—and still maintained at the end of 2006, as opposition leader—that radical governmental budget-cutting was necessary to save the economy from collapse.

Territorial Issues

A study by the independent Israel Research Institute for Economic and Social Affairs issued in February disclosed that $14 billion had been spent on West Bank settlements, not including military expenses, over the previous four decades.

At a Jerusalem press conference in late November called by Peace Now and billed as "The Great Land Robbery," it was reported that 40 percent of the roughly 130 West Bank settlements were fully or partly built on private Palestinian lands, and were therefore illegal. "We are talking about an institutional land grab," said Peace Now settlement expert Dror Etkes. In demanding that Attorney General Mazuz launch a criminal investigation, Yariv Oppenhcimcr, Peace Now's secretary general, called the revelation "a very severe indictment, which says that contrary to the Supreme Court's ruling and legal decisions, Israel stole private Palestinian lands and built settlements on them."

However the Council of Settlements in Judea and Samaria (known in Hebrew as the Yesha Council) dismissed the complaint as untrue. "There is nothing new in Peace Now's claims," it said in a statement. "As usual in the struggle against Jewish settlement all means are valid. The State of Israel has not built communities on private lands since 1979," when the Supreme Court ruled that it could not.

On February 1, about 10,000 police and soldiers evacuated the tiny Amona outpost in the West Bank and demolished the nine homes there. In doing so they faced an estimated 4,000 protesters, some 3,000 in the surrounding area and 1,000 inside and around the houses, included youths from nearby settlements and schools who had fortified themselves inside the homes and on the roofs in an effort to block the order from being carried out. Demonstrators claimed to have been beaten repeatedly on the skull and in the testicles with metal riot clubs, and trampled by riot-trained horses. About 300 protestors and police were injured, among them three right-wing Knesset members. There were also complaints from girls of sexual abuse, both verbal and physical, by police.

The Knesset voted 37-32 on February 9 to launch an inquiry, and the decision was considered a major victory for the rightist opposition. Likud leader Benjamin Netanyahu told *Yediot Aharonot* that the probe should focus on political responsibility for the events. The committee conducting the hearings found that the police had employed excessive brutality. It expressed criticism of Internal Security Minister Gideon Ezra for preventing police commanders from testifying, and said it found contradictions between the testimonies of Ezra and Chief of Staff

Dan Halutz. No action was taken as a result of the Knesset investigation.

In a report released March 8, State Comptroller Micha Lindenstrauss blasted the Sela Disengagement Authority, the Prime Minister's Office, and the Finance Ministry for their poor performance in handling the evacuation and resettlement of 1,750 families from the Gaza Strip and the northern West Bank in the disengagement of August 2005. The report found that a cumbersome government bureaucracy prevented efficient preparation for the pullout; that the authorities did not treat the evacuees appropriately; and that government ministries ignored the needs of the local authorities that took them in.

Lindenstrauss noted the government's severe underestimate of how much temporary housing would be necessary. Until a short time before the evacuation, only 1,800 rooms were booked for the evacuees, and an additional 1,000 rooms had to be found when the operation was already under way. The displaced people ended up dispersed in 31 hotels, yeshivas, and seminaries across the country, making it difficult for workers from the Disengagement Administration to reach them. In addition, the Prime Minister's Office had assumed that the evacuees would not stay in the temporary housing for longer than 14 days. As it turned out, some 40 percent of the evacuated families were still living in hotels three months after the pullout.

In April, three Jewish families moved into an abandoned home in Hebron, near the settler enclave of Avraham Avinu. They presented documents allegedly showing that they had rented the property from its Palestinian owner. Israeli authorities determined that these documents were forged. On May 7, police used a buzz saw to break down a metal door, and, in riot gear, stormed the building, forcibly evicting the families and dozens of their supporters. The Supreme Court had originally ordered the squatters removed by May 5, but then postponed the eviction because of Shabbat. About 500 Jewish settlers live in heavily guarded compounds in Hebron, which was home to some 170,000 Palestinians.

In early December, Education Minister Yuli Tamir ordered that maps in Israeli text books should include the Green Line designating the boundary between pre-1967 Israel and the territories captured in the Six-Day War. This drew an enraged reaction from some advocates of holding on to the territories. Tamir said that rabbis warned she would suffer the fate of Ariel Sharon. *Yediot Aharonot* quoted Rabbi David Drukman, chief rabbi of Kiryat Motzkin, as calling for a boycott of the books that included the Green Line "Whosoever rips out parts of Israel, his fate is as one who rips the Torah of Israel," he said. But Prime Minister Olmert supported Tamir's decision. "There is no reason not to mark the Green Line and where the borders of the country were in 1967," he said. "However, there is a duty to present the fact that the government's stance and the consensus in the country rule out returning to the 1967 borders."

Religion, State, and Society

The Supreme Court on May 11 rejected four petitions against the so-called Tal Law, under which yeshiva students could delay army service even if they were no longer continuing their studies. The law, recommended by a special panel seeking ways to bring ultra-Orthodox men into the job market, was approved by the Knesset in July 2002. It allowed draft-eligible students who left yeshiva a year's grace period, after which the individual could return to his yeshiva studies or else be inducted into the army or be taken for a year's national civilian service. The Movement for Quality Government in Israel had submitted a petition signed by 24,000 citizens claiming that the special privileges enjoyed by the ultra-Orthodox men exempted from the army because of their yeshiva studies discriminated against the "body, assets, ability to earn, and honor of those who do serve in the army and carry the security burden on their shoulders."

While the court's decision upheld the statute for the time being, it warned that it "could become unconstitutional," depending on how it was implemented. *Ha'aretz* later quoted an army spokesman to the effect that the number of yeshiva students getting deferments under the Tal Law had reached 50,000 by the end of 2006, rising from 30,000 in 2000 and 46,000 in 2005.

A conference scheduled in Jerusalem for November 7–8 to tackle the vexed issue of *agunot*—women whose husbands refused to grant them Jewish divorces—was canceled at the last moment. The conference, organized by the International Council of Jewish Women and Sephardi chief rabbi Shlomo Amar, would have brought together, behind closed doors, rabbis and religious judges from around the world who dealt with the issue. A few days before the expected opening of the proceedings—with some of the would-be participants already in Israel—Rabbi Amar's office sent out faxes saying that the event had been canceled. While there was no official word on why the conference was sidetracked, those interested in ameliorating the plight of *agunot* saw it as another example of the intransigence of the Israeli Orthodox establishment.

Jerusalem's gay pride parade, scheduled for November 10, did not take place, after a compromise was reached allowing a rally for gays and their supporters at the Hebrew University stadium in the capital. In the days leading up to the parade date there were incidents of stone-throwing, burning cars, and destruction of traffic lights in the Haredi Meah She'arim neighborhood protesting the impending event, which many Orthodox Jews viewed as a desecration of the holy city. A number of non-Orthodox public figures also opposed the parade as an unnecessary provocation. According to *Yediot Aharonot,* the deal to use the stadium followed deliberations by top Haredi figures, including Rabbi Shalom Elyashiv, leader of the "Lithuanian," non-Hasidic community, and Shas spiritual leader Rabbi Ovadia Yosef.

About 3,000 police were deployed to protect the rally in the stadium, which drew about an equal number of participants and proceeded without major incident. Speakers declared that the principles of individual rights and freedom of expression were at stake, and criticized government officials for not standing up to the forces of religious coercion.

In late November, an El Al flight from Miami to Israel flew on Shabbat, creating a sensation among many Orthodox Israelis. The airline, which had been privatized in 2004, had not flown on Shabbat for a quarter century, at an estimated cost to the company of $40 million a year in lost flight time. Once the news of the Shabbat flight got out there was a rash of cancellations of reservations by Orthodox Jews, well-known rabbis were quoted as calling for a boycott, and negotiations began between Orthodox leaders and Israir, El Al's major competitor, about taking over as the airline of choice for the community. El Al said that the questionable flight was an exception made necessary by the fact that its passengers had been stranded in Miami due to an airport strike in Israel, and that its Sabbath rest policy remained in effect.

In mid-December, Labor MK Ophir Pines-Paz introduced a bill in the Knesset making it illegal to seek to change the religious beliefs of anyone below the age of 14. While the language of the measure encompassed all religions, and also included coaxing youngsters to give up religion in favor of secularism, it was clearly aimed at Orthodox, and especially Chabad, outreach activities. Pines-Paz admitted as much. He also noted that he fully realized that the proposal had no chance of passage, but felt it important to make a statement against a phenomenon that he said was creating "unbearable strain" on families.

Legal Matters

On May 14 the Supreme Court upheld a controversial 2002 law placing restrictions on Palestinians married to Israeli Arabs from living inside the Green Line. According to the law, only Palestinian women over age 25 and Palestinian men over age 35 were permitted to live in Israel with their Israeli spouses. The State Attorney's Office said that the state had granted 6,000 of 22,000 requests for family reunification to such Israeli-Palestinian families since the Oslo Agreements of 1993; the rest had been rejected for security reasons.

A panel of 11 judged voted 6-5 against a petition to strike down the law. Since each of the justices wrote a separate opinion, the ruling took up 265 pages. The petitioner, Murad al-Sana, an Israeli attorney married to a Palestinian woman from Bethlehem, called the decision "a black day" for his family and for the State of Israel. "The government is preventing people from conducting a normal family life just because of their nationality," he told Israel Radio. Attorney Orna Kohn of Adalah, a civil rights group, was strongly critical of the decision, saying, "The bottom line is that the Supreme Court of Israel refused to intervene against a law that is racist."

In another landmark case, the Supreme Court ordered the government to recognize same-sex marriages performed abroad. The November 21 decision, by a vote of 6-1, was celebrated by Israel's gay community and by human rights groups, but infuriated the ultra-Orthodox, MK Moshe Gafni of United Torah Judaism commenting, "We don't have a Jewish state here. We have Sodom and Gomorrah here." The court's decision, however, was largely symbolic, as gay couples in Israel already had many of the rights of heterosexual partnerships. Under the new ruling they would also get the same tax breaks as married couples and be able to adopt children.

The route of the security fence in the Bir Naballah area north of Jerusalem was legal, the Supreme Court ruled on November 26. In doing so, a special nine-justice panel rejected five petitions that opposed the fence route because it left 1,500 Palestinians, many of them with the blue ID cards indicating Israeli residency, outside Israel. Chief Justice Aharon Barak wrote that the court accepted "the state's position that there is a need to build a separation wall to advance the security objectives of protecting Jerusalem, nearby communities and roads leading to it, from terror activities."

Some targeted killings of Palestinian militants were legal under international law, the Supreme Court ruled on December 14, refusing to issue a blanket ban against the killings. Two human rights groups, the Public Committee Against Torture in Israel and the Palestinian Society for the Protection of Human Rights and the Environment, had petitioned the court to ban the policy in 2002, but the court repeatedly delayed issuing a decision until now. The ruling gave legal legitimacy to a practice Israeli forces had routinely used against militants since the outbreak of the second intifada in late 2000. The Israeli human rights organization B'tselem estimated that 339 Palestinians had been killed in these targeted operations. The three-judge panel unanimously ruled that "it cannot be determined in advance that every targeted killing is prohibited according to customary international law," while also noting that the tactic was not necessarily legal in every case.

Attorney General Menahem Mazuz said on April 27 that Ahmad Saadat, head of the radical Popular Front for the Liberation of Palestine, could not be tried for masterminding the October 2001 assassination of former tourism minister and right-wing leader Rechavam (Gandhi) Zeevy. Even though Israel had said for years that Saadat had masterminded the killing, Mazuz said the evidence was insufficient. Four other PFLP men would go on trial for the crime. In March, Israeli forces had taken Saadat and the others from a prison in Jericho where they had been held under international supervision (see above, p. 224). Mazuz said Saadat would be tried in military court on other terror-related charges.

The Jerusalem District Court ruled on September 11 that Asher Weisgan, of the West Bank settlement of Shvut Rachel, was guilty of the August 2005 murder of four Palestinian laborers and the attempted murder of another (see AJYB 2006, p. 212). A driver who transported Palestinian laborers, Weisgan grabbed a gun from a security guard and then opened fire at the workers in his car at close range. Weisgan subsequently claimed that he acted to thwart the disengagement plan.

In a plea-bargain deal, the Nazareth District Court on September 14 found Violet and Haim Habibi guilty of conspiracy, arson, rioting, and disorderly conduct for disturbing the city's Church of the Anunciation in early March. Police had rescued them from the church after they detonated fireworks during a prayer service. Ensuing riots lightly injured 13 police officers and 13 civilians. Four cars were set on fire, including two police vehicles. *Ha'aretz,* quoting a Channel 10 TV news report, said Haim Habibi had a history of mental illness and had previously attempted attacks on a number of churches.

In November, at the Nazareth District Court, the government reached a compensation agreement with some of the families of the 13 Israeli Arabs killed by security forces during rioting in October 2000 (see AJYB 2001, pp. 504–05). The state did not accept responsibility for the deaths, and the amount of the compensation was not disclosed. Some of the families refused to sign the agreement, and there were reports of disputes within families over whether to accept the money.

While determining that campaign donations received by Shimon Peres during the campaign for the 17th Knesset were "improper," State Comptroller Micha Lindenstrauss on November 6 declined to recommend initiation of a criminal investigation against the vice prime minister. Lindenstrauss said "it would be appropriate for Peres to either return the funds or transfer them to the country's ownership." In the same report, Lindenstrauss ordered Likud leader Benjamin Netanyahu to return 84,000 shekels (slightly less than $20,000) contributed to his campaign.

At year's end, government authorities were looking into several cases of possible corruption involving Prime Minister Ehud Olmert: suspicions that while serving as finance minister in 2005 he had interfered to create conditions that would promote the candidacy of two of his friends in the privatization sale of Bank Leumi; questions about the low $75,000 price for which Olmert purchased a house on Cremieux Street in Jerusalem from the Alumot real estate company when he was trade and industry minister, possibly in exchange for accelerating an Alumot building project; suggestions that, as trade minister, he gave unwarranted benefits to clients of Uri Messer, his former law partner; and allegations that he had made illegal political appointments to the Small Business Authority. Earlier in the year, it was determined that no offense had been involved in Olmert's sale of his house in Jerusalem's prime Talbiyeh neighborhood for $2.69 million to an overseas supporter, who then rented it back to Olmert at a below-market price.

A formal indictment was filed against former cabinet minister Tzachi Hanegbi on September 25 charging fraud, bribery, and perjury in connection with political appointments he made to Likud associates when he was environment minister in 2001–03. Hanegbi, chairman of the Knesset's Foreign Affairs and Defense Committee, was a close Olmert associate who almost certainly would have been given a ministerial post were it not for these criminal charges hanging over him. Denying the charges, Hangebi rejected suggestions that he give up his committee chairmanship until his case was resolved.

Justice Minister Haim Ramon resigned from his post on August 21 to face criminal charges for kissing a 21-year-old female soldier against her will at the Prime Minister's Office in Tel Aviv on July 12. Ramon admitted kissing the soldier during a farewell party for her, but said she had flirted with him and initiated the kiss.

Omri Sharon, the oldest son of incapacitated Prime Minister Ariel Sharon, was sentenced in February to nine months in prison for illegal fund-raising during his father's successful 1999 primary campaign for the Likud leadership. The previous November he had entered into a plea bargain in which he admitted falsifying corporate documents, committing perjury, and violating campaign-funding laws. Implementation of the sentence was delayed because of his father's condition.

Yigal Amir, the convicted assassin of former prime minister Yitzhak Rabin, spent ten hours in a conjugal visit with Larissa Trimbobler on October 23. This took place in a special cell in Ramle's Ayalon prison, where he was serving a life sentence. This was the first conjugal visit for the couple, who married by proxy in 2004. The Prison Service only allowed the visit after Shin Bet security service head Yuval Diskin told a Tel Aviv court that Amir no longer presented a risk to Israeli society. Yuval Rabin, son of the slain prime minister, expressed outrage, telling *Yediot Aharonot,* "It started with a conjugal visit, from there it will move on to the *brit* for the child and his bar mitzvah and his wedding, and more children . . . and this is how this vile man's road to freedom will be paved."

Aliyah

Aliyah, immigration to Israel, dipped 9 percent to 19,264 in 2006, the lowest number since 1988, before the major wave of aliyah precipitated by the collapse of the Soviet Union. Nearly three million people had immigrated to Israel since the country's founding in 1948, roughly one third of them during the 1990s. The wave of former Soviet immigration abated in 2002, and since then there had been a steady drop in aliyah. In late December Nefesh B'Nefesh, a U.S.-based organization that helped North Americans move to Israel, reported its 10,000th immigrant since it launched operations in 2001.

Transportation

Tel Aviv, Israel's major metropolitan area, had long lacked a light-rail system. In December, MTS won the contract to build the Red Line, which was to be the first stage of the planned system. Work was not expected to start before 2008, and the first Red Line trains would leave in 2013.

The MTS group was headed by diamond merchant Lev Leviev's Africa Israel firm and also included Siemens of Germany, Israel's Egged bus cooperative, infrastructure firms CCECC of China and Da Costa Soares of Portugal, and HTM, a top Dutch transportation firm. The MTS bid for the largest private construction contract in Israel's history was 7.1 billion shekels ($1.7 billion), just 400 million shekels less than that of Metrorail, a group headed by Shari Arison, the owner of Bank Hapoalim and heiress of her late father Ted Arison's Carnival Cruise Lines fortune.

Personalia

HONORS AND AWARDS

The Israel Prizes for 2006 were awarded on Israel Independence Day eve in Jerusalem. The laureates: Jewish Thought—Prof. Ya'akov Blidstein; Education—Profs. Haim Adler and Mirian Ben-Peretz; Law—Profs. Ruth Lapidoth and Amnon Rubinstein; Agriculture—Prof. Nahum Kedar; Chemistry—Prof. Tzvi Rappaport; Sports—Ya'akov Chodorov and Ralph Klein; Music—Profs. Pninah Saltzman and Mendi Rodin; Lifetime Achievement—Dvora Omer; Contribution to the State—Al Schwimmer, and the Andalucia Orchestra.

Other awards: Hesse Peace Prize—pianist-conductor Daniel Barenboim; Tel Aviv University's Hugo Ramniceanu Prize for Economics—entrepreneur and high-tech guru Yossi Vardi, developer of the ICQ Internet instant messaging program; TAU's Dan David Prizes—Profs. John Mendelshon of the University of Texas and Joseph Schlessinger of Yale for cancer research, Magdi Allam of Rome's *Corriere della Serra,* Chilean investigative reporter Monica Gonzalez, Polish journalist-activist Adam Michnik, and Goenawan Mohamad, a spokesman for moderate Islam, for print-media journalism, and cellist Yo-Yo Ma; EMET Prize for Physics—Prof. Yosef Imry, Weizmann Institute; Yakir Keren Hayesod Award—Alexander Maskevitch, Russian billionaire with extensive holdings and contacts in Central Asia, and chairman of the Euro-Asian Jewish Congress; Israel Venture Association's Israel Hi-Tech Awards—Vice Prime Minister Shimon Peres, New York State Comptroller Alan Hevesi, Dr. Shimon Eckhouse, chairman of the board of Syneron Medical, and Yadin Kaufmann, founding partner of the Veritas venture capital fund and chairman of Tmura; Rothschild Prizes—Profs. Gideon Dagan, Tel

Aviv University, for his seminal work in groundwater hydrology, Asher Koriat, Haifa University, a cognitive psychologist, Ada Yonath, Weizmann Institute, for work in x-ray crystallography, and Benjamin Weiss, a Hebrew University of Jerusalem mathematician; Guber Justice Prize — retiring Supreme Court president Aharon Barak.

DEATHS

Andrea (Andy) Bronfman, 60, wife of businessman-philanthropist Charles Bronfman and a full partner with her husband in philanthropic and educational activities in Israel and the U.S., and who lived about half the year at their home in Jerusalem, after being hit by a taxi in New York's Central Park, on January 23; Rabbi Yitzhak Kadourie, thought to be 106, revered Jerusalem kabbalist and a major force among ultra-Orthodox Sephardi Jews, on January 28; Shoshana Damari, 83, Yemen-born first lady of Israeli popular song in the early days of the state, on February 15; Prof. Yuval Ne'eman, 81, world-class nuclear physicist, founder and longtime chairman of the Israel Space Agency and member of the Atomic Energy Commission, winner of the Israel Prize and Einstein Medal, and former minister and leader of the Tehiya right-wing political party, on April 26; Yitzhak Ben-Aharon, 99, a founding father of the kibbutz movement, secretary general of the Histadrut trade-union federation, two-term Knesset member, and transportation minister, on May 19; Prof. Haim Barkai, 80, eminent Hebrew University economist, on May 26; novelist S. Yizhar, 89, born Yizhar Smilansky, winner of the 1958 Israel Prize for Literature, on August 21; Uri Dan, 71, journalist and close confidant of Ariel Sharon, on December 25; Gershon Shaked, 77, influential literary critic and winner of the Bialik Prize and the Israel Prize, on December 29.

HANAN SHER

Turkey

National Affairs

T HE TERM OF President Ahmet Necdet Sezer was due to end in July 2007, and speculation about his successor heightened tension between the secularist traditions of modern Turkey and the rising popularity of political Islam. The leading candidate was Foreign Minister Abdullah Gül, whose extensive experience, both in domestic politics and foreign affairs, qualified him for the post. But all previous presidents, including Sezer, had been staunch secularists, whereas Gül was a founding member of the ruling Adalet ve Kalkinma (Justice and Development) Party, known by its initials as AKP, which had come to power in the 2002 elections.

Militant secularists in Turkey as well as a good number of European leaders thought the AKP harbored a hidden Islamist agenda, a suspicion strengthened by the fact that Gül's wife wore a headscarf. They feared that the AKP planned ultimately to consolidate its power not only by gaining control of the presidency, but also by taking over the country's educational and administrative bureaucracy and imposing sharia, Islamic law, on Turkey. It was indeed true that Prime Minister Recep Tayyip Erdoğan, the AKP leader, had, as mayor of Istanbul in the 1990s, sought certain Islamist objectives, but he had been careful not to do so since assuming national power, knowing full well that the Turkish military leadership—which saw itself as a defender of the republic's secular values—had removed governments or forced changes in them four times since 1960.

AKP spokesmen insisted that their party was a progressive but socially conservative mainstream group that was no more Islamist than the Christian Democratic parties of Western Europe were fundamentalist Christian bodies. The AKP had spearheaded Turkey's efforts to join the European Union, adopting a wide variety of reform measures to satisfy the EU's entry requirements, but so far to no avail. The objections to an AKP president, the party claimed, were one more indication—along with the persistent European resistance to Turkey's entry into the EU— that European leaders considered Christianity an essential component of the continent's civilization, and that Turkey, no matter what it did, would never be accepted into the "club."

On April 12, 2006, President Sezer issued a public warning about what he considered the Islamist threat, saying: "Religious fundamentalism has reached alarming proportions. Turkey's only guarantee against this threat is its secular order." This statement was followed by massive public demonstrations in the major cities, including Istanbul, Izmir, and Ankara. Hundreds of thousands of people—more than a million, according to some estimates—turned out, carrying Turkish flags with the star and crescent, together with large photos of Mustafa Kemal Atatürk, the founder of the secular state, and large banners carrying messages like "No imam in Çankaya [site of the presidential palace]!" Significantly, many demonstrators carried signs saying, "No to sharia and no to a [military] coup," in other words rejecting both religious and secular extremes.

Turkish secularists in fact faced a dilemma. They certainly did not want to see the country turn into another Islamic state, and yet a coup by the generals to prevent such an eventuality would suggest that Turkey lacked the democratic safeguards to assure the supremacy of civilian authorities over the military, and was therefore not ready to join the EU.

To a great extent, secularists were victims of the Turkish electoral system. Under present law, only parties receiving at least 10 percent of the total vote could enter the Grand National Assembly, the country's parliament, and the ballots of those voting for parties that did not achieve that threshold were disregarded. As a result of the plethora of small parties that could not garner 10 percent, the AKP's share of parliamentary seats far exceeded its percentage of the popular vote. Indeed, with the exception of a score of seats won by individuals running as independents, the only party other than the AKP in parliament was the staunchly secularist Republican People's Party (CHP), which had been founded by Atatürk himself. Efforts were ongoing to merge small parties, or at least to forge a combined electoral list from among the secular parties. Fierce personal and ideological rivalries had so far prevented this.

Israel and the Middle East

Some observers considered Turkey's relations with Israel as a litmus test of the AKP's ability to follow a pragmatic foreign policy not clouded by Islamic religious sentiment. Turkish-Israeli ties, underpinned by growing trade and defense cooperation, were among the oldest and strongest in the region. Upon assuming office in 2003, however, Prime Minister Erdoğan spurned invitations to come to Israel, saying he was too busy. In 2004, reacting to Israel's killing of Hamas leader Sheikh Ahmad

Yassin, Erdoğan publicly accused Israel of perpetrating state terrorism against the Palestinians. This remark was not necessarily an expression of Islamist fervor, as it differed little from the reaction of his secularist predecessor, Bülent Ecevit, in 2002, after Israeli military action in the Palestinian city of Jenin (see AJYB 2003, p. 289).

Erdoğan, accompanied by some 200 businessmen, journalists, and advisors, finally paid an official visit to Israel (and the Palestinian Territories) in early May 2005. *Ha'aretz* headlined its editorial about the visit "A *New* Friendship." While in Israel, the Turkish leader declared that anti-Semitism was "a crime against humanity" and that Iran's nuclear ambitions were a threat not just to Israel but to "the entire world." Officials both in Turkey and Israel denied reports in the international media that Erdoğan's visit was aimed at mending ties with the Jewish state, claiming that there had never been a lapse in good relations. Erdoğan himself told the *Turkish Daily News,* on the eve of his trip, that a "solid and time-honored bond" existed between the two countries. "Our strong relationship with Israel does not preclude us from making frank criticisms. Turkey has always condemned terrorist attacks against Israeli civilians as well as any excessive and indiscriminate use of force by the Israeli side," the prime minister said.

Erdoğan offered his services as a mediator between Israel and the Palestinians. Clearly, his initiative was aimed at furthering Turkey's desire to play a major role in the region. Turkey, with an annual $2 billion in bilateral Turkish-Israeli trade, around $3 billion in arms purchases from Israel over the past three years, and a historic record of friendly relations with both Israel and the Palestinians, was indeed well situated to facilitate negotiations. Israeli prime minister Ariel Sharon, for his part, praised Turkish efforts to promote regional peace.

It was also widely assumed that the Erdoğan visit was connected with Turkish attempts, at the time, to improve bilateral relations with the U.S., which had been hurt on March 1, 2003, when the Turkish parliament turned down an American request to use the country as a staging ground for the Iraq war, and again in April 2005, when President Sezer paid an ill-advised visit to Damascus just as the Syrians were being pressured to leave Lebanon. Turkish public opinion had turned strongly anti-American since the accession to power of the AKP; a Pew Center survey in July 2006 showed that only 12 percent of Turks viewed America "positively," a significant decline from the more than 50 percent who had felt that way in the 1990s.

Turkish leaders had always appreciated—and in fact often exaggerated—

the political clout of the pro-Israel or "Jewish" lobby in the U.S., and had sought help from the organized American Jewish community in counteracting the pro-Greek and pro-Armenian lobbies, which had sometimes sought to restrict American aid to Turkey. American Jewish leaders and Israeli officials had also been active behind the scenes in supporting Turkey's earlier efforts to be admitted to the European Economic Community and, now, to join the EU. Erdoğan's well-publicized trip to Israel would go over well in American pro-Israel circles.

Even so, Turkey's Middle East policy remained ambiguous. On January 4, 2006, during a visit to Israel and Palestine, Foreign Minister Gül stopped in Ramallah to meet with Palestinian prime minister Ahmed Qurei. He told Qurei that to help the Palestinians "stand on their own two feet economically" Ankara would donate $5 million toward the rehabilitation and reopening of the Erez Industrial Zone in the Gaza Strip, along the border with Israel. An estimated 10,000 jobs would be created by the Turkish companies that were planning to invest there, in the town of Beit Hanun. Palestinian-Israeli clashes over the previous five years had resulted in frequent closings of the industrial zone. Soon after, however, Prime Minister Erdoğan hosted Khaled Meshaal, a Hamas leader based in Damascus. Despite criticism from the West and from pro-Western Turks, the AKP defended the visit and maintained contact with Meshaal. The government also opposed Western efforts to isolate Hamas.

In the summer of 2006, violence erupted on the Lebanese-Israeli frontier. Israeli civilian settlements were shelled and Hezballah forces killed eight Israelis and kidnapped an Israeli soldier, taking him across the border into Lebanon. Israel then launched heavy bombardments against buildings in Beirut and southern Lebanon believed to be harboring Palestinian fighters and Shi'ite Lebanese militants. It was widely believed that Syria was encouraging the renewed hostilities.

The Turkish media prominently displayed images of dead and wounded Arab women and children provided by Arab television stations. Islamic groups organized an anti-Israel rally in Istanbul in the early days of the war that drew almost 100,000 people. Prime Minister Erdoğan and other officials issued statements harshly condemning the Israeli actions as excessive and indiscriminate violence, the prime minister going so far as to accuse Israel of seeking to "wipe out the Palestinians" in Lebanon. Some observers viewed this Turkish reaction as another sign that the government—for all its protestations of maintaining good relations with the Jewish state—considered solidarity with the Muslim world more important than ties with Israel.

A cease-fire in southern Lebanon was declared on August 14. Two days later, Foreign Minister Gül embarked on a fact-finding mission to the region. After a few days of talks in Beirut he went on to Israel and the Palestinian Territories, where he met with Foreign Minister Tzipi Livni, Prime Minister Ehud Olmert, and Defense Minister Amir Peretz of Israel, and with PA chairman Mahmoud Abbas and foreign policy advisor Saeb Erekat. Gül emphasized to both sides that Ankara's objective was to establish a permanent and lasting peace. He then traveled to Damascus where, on August 22, he had a 90-minute meeting with President Bashar Assad and his advisors. Gül reportedly told the Syrians that Turkey expected them to stop the flow of arms to Hezballah and to pressure it to comply fully with the cease-fire.

There was considerable discussion, both within the country and in foreign capitals, about whether Turkey should contribute troops to the proposed UN multinational peacekeeping force in southern Lebanon. Beginning with the Korean War, Turkey had participated in many such operations, and since 2001 had deployed some 1,700 soldiers in Afghanistan as part of the International Security Assistance Force (ISAF). Many argued that as a Muslim yet Western-oriented nation, Turkey was well positioned to act as a buffer between Israel and Hezballah. Israel expressed opposition to participation by Muslim countries that did not recognize it, such as Malaysia and Bangladesh, but would welcome Turkey.

The plan aroused much criticism. Devlet Bahçeli, chairman of the right-wing Nationalist Movement Party (MHP), opposed participation, stating that Turkish forces should instead be used to suppress Kurdish separatist forces. He charged that sending troops to southern Lebanon would "launch Turkey into a dangerous adventure which will drag it into the Middle East maelstrom." Also opposed was the Deniz Baykal, leader of the secularist Republican People's Party (CHP). He asserted that a total of 731 Turkish troops had already lost their lives in such missions, and that "no one can guarantee that Turkish soldiers will not face clashes" this time. Even President Sezer, whose post was largely ceremonial, spoke out strongly against the idea on the grounds that it was not Turkey's responsibility "to protect the interests of other countries."

The government, however, was under considerable pressure from the U.S. and the EU to contribute men to the international force, and hoped that by cooperating it might enhance the country's international stature and strengthen the case for Turkish accession to the EU. Foreign Minister Gül answered the parliamentary critics by emphasizing that the Turkish soldiers would open fire only if attacked, and that they would not be expected to disarm Hezballah. After a lengthy and stormy debate, the Grand National Assembly, on September 5, approved by 340 to 192 a motion to send troops to southern Lebanon to help monitor the tense ceasefire. The number of troops was not specified in the motion, but the foreign minister said it was unlikely to exceed 1,000. While the parliament deliberated, thousands protested outside, carrying banners and placards against the move.

The Turkish contribution to the UN mission in Lebanon was expected to include a naval task force patrolling the eastern Mediterranean to prevent arms smuggling, as well as officers to train Lebanese troops. According to the resolution that was passed, Turkey would also provide sea and air transport in support of other national contingents in the UN force.

In the end, Turkey was not the sole predominantly Muslim state to participate. The small Persian Gulf country of Qatar, which had maintained limited contacts with Israel since 1991, pledged 200–300 troops on September 3. And after Israel dropped its objections, the very large and populous state of Indonesia, which had no relations with Israel, said it would send up to 1,000 troops.

On August 30, a ship pulled into Beirut harbor transporting a Turkish humanitarian relief convoy of 50 fully loaded trucks containing 575 tons of food, cleaning materials, baby food, and emergency aid materials, which were handed over to Lebanese authorities the following morning. The aid convoy had been organized by the Istanbul-based Humanitarian Aid Foundation (IHH in Turkish). Speaking at its arrival, Turkey's ambassador to Lebanon, Irfan Acar, said that the IHH had been sending aid to Lebanon since shortly after hostilities began. He claimed that Turkey had been one of the countries sending the most help: $1 million directly from the government; $4 million from the Red Crescent Society; and $6–$7 million from a variety of nongovernmental organizations. The IHH immediately began work on the reconstruction of schools and hospitals damaged or destroyed during the fighting.

Economic ties between Turkey and Israel continued to flourish. In April, there were reports, subsequently confirmed, of negotiations between the two countries for the construction if a multimillion-dollar energy-and-water project. It would transport from Turkey water, electricity, natural gas, and oil via four underwater pipelines to Israel, from where the oil would to be transferred by tankers to the Far East. The scope of this project would greatly exceed previous plans for Turkey to export 50 million cubic meters of water annually to Israel using large tankers, which had been canceled in 2005 because it was prohibitively expensive. "The whole premise is based on the assumption that Turkey is becoming a major hub for energy in the region," said Gabby Levy, director of international relations at Israel's National Infrastructure Ministry. The water would be earmarked for Israel, the Palestinian territories, and Jordan, all of which suffered from chronic shortages. The project, which needed foreign economic backing, was undergoing a feasibility study sponsored by the Luxembourg-based European Investment Bank.

Over the previous decade and a half, nearly 100 smaller bilateral agreements had been signed between Israel and Turkey, many of them in the fields of arms, tourism, and agriculture. Turkey had also become a top vacation spot for Israelis, 380,000 of them visiting the country during 2005. So well-known had the Israeli penchant for vacationing there become that terrorists were drawn there as well. In the summer of 2005, a Syrian linked to Al Qaeda was caught off the Turkish coast with 750 kilograms of explosives. He explained to his captors that he had planned to pack speedboats with the explosives and ram them into Israeli cruise ships "without harming Turkish civilians." In early 2006 a Turkish television station reported that Taliban leader Mullah Omar had put up $50,000 to pay for the aborted attack.

Another Middle East hot spot of great concern to Turkey was neighboring Iraq, where elections held after the overthrow of Saddam Hussein's dictatorial regime produced a government whose president, Jalal Talabani, and foreign minister, Hoshyar Zebari, were both Kurds. Turkish authorities and military leaders watched with growing anxiety the resurgence of popular support for the PKK, the Kurdish separatist group, both in northern Iraq and southeastern Turkey. In Istanbul, Foreign Minister Gül signed a declaration together with Iraqi representatives on May 1, 2005, pledging to support a federal structure for Iraq "if that is what the Iraqi people decide." Nevertheless, military circles in Turkey were increasingly calling for a major cross-border action to eliminate PKK bases in northern Iraq.

Anti-Semitism

While there had always been anti-Semitic articles and cartoons in the publications of fringe groups—the ultranationalist and fundamentalist Islamic right—observers noted an alarming infiltration of anti-Jewish motifs in the mainstream media in the wake of the war in southern

Lebanon. This was the case even in some of the more liberal and secular papers, such as *Milliyet*.

Another indication of anti-Semitism (and anti-Americanism) was the immense popularity of the film *Kurtlar Vadisi—Irak* (Valley of the Wolves—Iraq). Set in northern Iraq, it portrayed U.S, troops in an extremely negative light, and depicted an American Jewish army doctor surgically removing organs from Iraqi prisoners so they could be sold for profit by U.S. troops. The movie also did well in other countries with significant Turkish-speaking minorities, such as Germany (see below, pp. 464–65).

JEWISH COMMUNITY

The Turkish Jewish community was estimated to number between 20,000 and 25,000 people. Precise figures were not available since official Turkish statistics no longer included data on religion or ethnic identity. By far the largest organized Jewish community was in Istanbul and its suburbs, and the second largest was in Izmir. Smaller communities, with fewer than 100 Jews in each, were in Ankara, Adana, Bursa, and Antakia, the Turkish name for the ancient city of Antioch.

The leadership of the Jewish community was vested in its president, currently Sylvio Ovadya, and a lay council. There was also a smaller religious council, which assisted *Hahambaşi* (Chief Rabbi) Isak Haleva. In early January 2006, Rabbi Haleva went to Jerusalem to participate in the Sixth General Assembly of Orthodox Jewish Leadership. In his address, the rabbi said that the Jewish community's international contacts could be helpful in Turkey's efforts to become a member of the EU.

In April 2005, the small but impressive new Turkish Jewish Museum finally opened in the heart of downtown Istanbul. With bilingual signs in Turkish and English, the museum chronicled the Jewish community's long history and wide range of accomplishments in the Ottoman Empire and the Turkish Republic. The museum board was chaired by Naim Güleryüz, who had played a leading role in organizing the activities of the Quincentennial Foundation, created in 1992 to mark the 500th anniversary of the welcome given by Sultan Beyazit II to the Jews fleeing the Inquisition and expulsion from Spain in 1492. Another recent development was the complete renovation of the Or-Ahayim Jewish Hospital in Balat, transforming it into a modern geriatric center.

On the educational front, enrollment in the modern Jewish day school in Istanbul was over 600, and there were several new Jewish kindergartens. A network of youth centers and sports clubs continued to serve the community. *Şalom*, the Jewish weekly published in the Turkish language, now also included a section in Ladino (Judeo-Espagnol). Many of the articles in the Ladino section were written for younger readers as part of the community's effort to preserve and transmit the Sephardi heritage to the next generation.

In November 2005, Ankara University for the first time hosted an international conference on a Jewish theme, a three-day event titled "Sephardi Culture and History." Participating were some 60 prominent scholarly experts from Turkish and foreign universities. Among the sponsors were the Ibero-American Friendship and Culture Society, the Spanish embassy, the Cervantes Institute, and the host institution, Ankara University. Such events were extremely important for the Jewish community, reassuring it that whatever political and ideological tensions roiled Turkey, the Jewish cultural and religious heritage was respected in the country.

GEORGE E. GRUEN

The Americas

Canada

National Affairs

THE ECONOMY moved ahead during the year at a modest pace with continuing low inflation. After making substantial gains in recent years, the currency declined against the U.S. dollar, largely due to declining commodity prices.

The Liberal Party, which had governed continuously since 1993, lost power in the January general election, and Paul Martin's tenure as prime minister ended after less than two years. Stephen Harper's Conservative Party won the most seats and formed the government, but failed to gain a majority and had to depend on support from other parties. At year's end Harper was clearly in control, but faced the prospect of another election in 2007 or 2008, depending in part on the whims of the smaller parties.

The Conservative caucus had no Jewish MP's while the Liberals had four: Irwin Cotler, Raymonde Falco, Anita Neville, and Susan Kadis, all of whom were named as opposition critics in the new Parliament. Two Jewish parliamentarians from Quebec, Jacques Saada and Richard Marceau, were defeated, the former facing opposition from some Muslims in his constituency because of his Zionist background and support for Israel.

In an election advertisement the Liberals highlighted improvements in their record on Israel since Martin took over, and, in the end, retained most of their vote among Jews. Harper, for his part, told Jewish leaders during the campaign that the Jewish community "has a good friend in the Conservative Party," condemned anti-Semitism, and promised to shift Canada's voting pattern in the UN in a more pro-Israel direction.

Martin resigned as party leader after his defeat, and the Liberals held a convention in Montreal in December to choose a successor. Stephane

Dion, a former minister, won a surprising victory. Dion, during the Israel-Hezballah war, had criticized the government for favoring Israel and called for a more even-handed approach. In response to questions posed to the candidates prior to the convention by the *Canadian Jewish News* (CJN), Dion affirmed that "our friend Israel has the full right to exist and defend itself," and that Hamas and Hezballah were terrorist groups. But he reiterated his criticism of Israeli strikes against Hezballah, stressing their ineffectiveness, and recalled calling for an immediate ceasefire when hostilities began. Most of the other candidates for leadership of the party were supportive of Israel, some with various degrees of qualification.

The Liberal contest was marred by attacks on Bob Rae, a former Ontario premier, who was running for the top job. A flyer distributed at the convention labeled Rae a supporter of "Israeli Apartheid" and pointed to his Jewish wife's role in the Canadian Jewish Congress (CJC). Evidence pointed to the Canadian Arab Federation (CAF) as the disseminator of the flyer. The CAF, in any case, endorsed its message and criticized Rae for addressing a Jewish National Fund meeting, on the grounds that the JNF was "complicit in war crimes and ethnic cleansing."

The new Conservative government recalled the controversial Yvon Charbonneau from his post as ambassador to UNESCO in August, midway through his four-year term. Charbonneau had gained notoriety for his sharp attacks on Zionism and Israel, first as a union leader and then as a Liberal MP from 1997 through 2004.

Canadian Jews were active in efforts to draw attention to the genocide in Darfur. Many participated in rallies and other events held in several cities to support the victims, and Jewish groups were prominent among the organizers of a demonstration in Toronto that drew thousands in September. Rabbi Chaim Steinmetz of Montreal led a group of high school students to meet MPs in Ottawa in June to discuss the issue. The students had participated in the March of the Living, which included visits to extermination camps in Poland, and were outspoken about preventing further genocide. The rabbi averred that his group was responding to the biblical injunction to love the stranger, and insisted that after the Holocaust every Jew was obligated to stand up for human rights.

National Post columnist Barbara Kay created a stir with a column that appeared in August on "The Rise of Quebecistan." It was triggered by a rally in Montreal attended by several leading politicians. Although ostensibly an antiwar gathering, Kay claimed that it had a decidedly pro-Hezballah and anti-Israel tone. She pointed to the historical identification of leftist Quebec intellectuals with French-speaking Arab countries, and charged that such sentiments "joined with reflexive anti-Americanism and a fat streak of anti-Semitism" to make "Quebec the most anti-Israel of the provinces . . . ."

TERRORISM AND RADICAL ISLAM

Stewart Bell, the country's leading journalistic authority on terrorism, warned Canadians to take the threat of an Al Qaeda attack seriously. Addressing a January conference of the Canadian Federation of Jewish Students, Bell claimed that the terrorist group was already making plans and identifying targets, that it was raising funds inside Canada, and that neither the government nor private citizens were prepared, a situation that he blamed, in part, on the prevalence of moral relativism. Similar views were expressed by David Harris, national security senior fellow at the Canadian Coalition for Democracies, in a talk on "Confronting Terrorism at our Doorstep" delivered in July. Harris argued that Canada's immigration system was too lax, allowing potential terrorists to enter the country. As a result he claimed, Canada had become a terrorist haven, and what he called excessive political correctness weakened the authorities' ability to identify the danger.

Daniel Pipes, the American Middle East expert, pointed specifically at Quebec in remarks to a Montreal audience in April. Pipes asserted that the province seemed oblivious to the danger of radical Islamists entering its territory and that it was, "by far, the worst of any area in North America" in its openness to extremists.

A rally under the name United Against Terrorism took place in June in Toronto, sponsored by a number of Jewish and non-Jewish groups. The main speaker was Stockwell Day, minister of public safety, who promised increased international cooperation against terrorism, challenged the hatred that he said emanated from "twisted religious notions," and defended the country's participation in the NATO operation in Afghanistan. Tarek Fatah, founder of the Muslim Canadian Congress (MCC), denounced Islamic radicals. Claiming that "our faith has been hijacked," Fatah said, "We will do what we can to take back our faith from these murderers." Prime Minister Harper sent a message of support.

The significance of these warnings was driven home in June, when 17 alleged Islamic terrorists were arrested in the Toronto area. Investigation revealed plans for bomb attacks on sites in southern Ontario; there were no indications that any Jewish institutions had been targeted. Prime Minister Harper said that the thwarted plot showed that "Canada is not immune to the threat of terrorism." That same month, in response to calls from several religious groups, the government barred British imam Sheik Riyadh ul-Haq from entering Canada for a lecture tour. He had been accused of vilifying Jews, Hindus, and moderate Muslims. At year's end, however the *National Post* revealed that government intelligence assessments showed Hezballah continuing to operate in Canada, raising funds and stockpiling equipment.

In view of the reports of danger within Canada, Liberal Parliamentarians for Israel called upon the government to help defray the security costs of targeted communities, such as the Jews, and Public Security Minister Day promised to consider the request. Spokespeople for the Jewish community stressed the high costs that had already been incurred to protect people and institutions. In Toronto, for example, the federation estimated that it would have to spend $11–12 million over the coming three years.

A Montreal man, Naji Antoine Abi Khalil, was convicted in a U.S. federal court of planning to export military equipment to Hezballah. A judge in New York City sentenced him to five years in prison for attempted material support to terrorists, attempted contribution to terrorism, conspiracy to export banned material, and money laundering.

Two deportation cases made news during the year. Mahmoud Mohammad Issa Mohammad, a Palestinian who had been living in Ontario for years while fighting a deportation order because of his part in the 1968 hijacking of an Israeli airliner in Athens, claimed that he was now too sick to be deported. A one-time member of the Popular Front for the Liberation of Palestine, he had initially been ordered deported in 1988 but had managed to forestall any action through a series of legal maneuvers. And the long-running case of Issam Al-Yamani, also a former PFLP member, neared its conclusion as the Federal Court decided in December against his claim that membership in the group was a form of protected expression. The judges ruled that there was no right to belong to a terrorist organization.

Israel and the Middle East

In January, after Hamas won the Palestinian Authority election, Stephen Harper, not yet officially installed as prime minister, declared that his government would not recognize Hamas so long as it refused to renounce terrorism. Indeed, as soon as the Hamas-led government took office in April, Canada severed diplomatic ties and suspended all direct monetary aid to the PA; money channeled through UNRWA continued to flow. The Israeli ambassador and mainstream Jewish organizations praised the government, while Canadian Friends of Peace Now and the Canadian Islamic Congress were critical, the latter terming the action "a resounding slap in the face to Canadian values."

In Israel's summer war with Hezballah, the government supported Israel solidly and unequivocally, a stance that supporters of Israel considered a great improvement over past Canadian attempts to play the neutral honest broker. Prime Minister Harper bluntly rejected any hint of ambivalence, saying: "What we refuse to do is to be drawn into a moral equivalence between a pyromaniac and a fireman." In a CJN interview, Harper asserted that Canada would respond similarly to provocation against itself. Criticized by interim Liberal leader Bill Graham for abandoning Canada's traditional position, Harper defended his policy as "principled and in the best interests of this country. We're not concerned with opinion polls. We take what we feel is the right position."

Louise Arbour, a Canadian who was the UN High Commissioner for Human Rights, set off a storm in the early days of the conflict by suggesting that senior Israeli military and political leaders possibly bore "personal criminal responsibility" for alleged war crimes. Her words provoked outrage from supporters of Israel. MP Irwin Cotler, a former justice minister, described her statement as "simplistic" and "misleading," and wrote that if Israel were prohibited from defending its northern border, the entire country would become a sitting duck. CJC president Ed Morgan, like Cotler a law professor, compared Israel's actions in Lebanon to the NATO campaign against Serbia. B'nai Brith Canada's (BBC) senior honorary counsel, David Matas, accused Arbour of appealing to the "anti-Zionist states who tyrannize the UN human rights institutions" and of feeding the terrorist groups' propaganda machines.

In August several prominent Quebec politicians joined a Montreal rally billed as a protest against the war, but which many perceived as directed against Israel. Among the 15,000 marchers were Gilles Duceppe, leader of the Bloc Quebecois, André Boisclair, leader of the Parti Quebecois, and former federal Liberal cabinet minister Denis Coderre. In a statement issued before the rally, the sponsoring organizations denounced Canada's alignment with the policies of the Bush administration and Israel's "murderous offensive," and called Lebanon a "martyr country."

Some observers spotted a number of Hezballah flags and T-shirts in the crowd. Israeli ambassador Alan Baker sharply criticized the presence of the politicians, remarking, "We're seeing the leaders of opposition parties marching in Montreal under Hezballah flags—Hezballah, which is a terrorist organization that's been outlawed by Canadian law." But in an interview with the CJN, Duceppe said he had no regrets about his participation, arguing that his party did not support Hezballah and that neither did the rally, whatever some "radicals" might have done there. One MP from Duceppe's party, Maria Mourani, told Montreal's *Le Devoir* that "it's clear to me . . . that there were war crimes in Lebanon" committed by the Israelis. The next day she backtracked, saying that such a judgment could only be made by duly mandated authorities, and added that both Israel and Hezballah may have committed war crimes.

The issue of war crimes was raised again by Michael Ignatieff, an aspirant to the Liberal leadership. In an October interview on a French television show, he was asked to clarify an earlier statement asserting that Israeli actions at Qana (see above, pp. 243–44) did not constitute a war crime. This time he proclaimed, "I was a professor of human rights. I am also a professor of rights in war. What happened in Qana was a war crime. I should have said that." MP Susan Kadis immediately resigned as Toronto cochair of his leadership campaign. MP Irwin Cotler, who backed Bob Rae for the leadership post, defended Ignatieff as a supporter of Israel in general terms, but said he questioned "Michael's judgment in the matter of Qana." Ignatieff, meanwhile, tried to make amends by stressing his lifelong friendship with Israel.

The Liberal foreign affairs critic, MP Borys Wrzesnewskyj, was forced to resign in August because of the outcry over his remarks on a trip to Lebanon, where he reportedly labeled Israel a terrorist state and urged that Hezballah be removed from Canada's terrorist list. Liberal leader Graham not only replaced Wrzesnewskyj but also reaffirmed Hezballah's terrorist status. In September the New Democratic Party's biennial convention accused Israel of a "drastically disproportionate" response in Lebanon, termed Hezballah a "recognized political party," and called for the restoration of balance in Canadian foreign policy. Canada-Israel Committee (CIC) chair Marc Gold termed the resolutions "biased and one-sided."

In an October speech to a B'nai Brith gathering, Prime Minister Harper declared that "when it comes to dealing with a war between Israel and a terrorist organization, this country and this government cannot and will never be neutral." He went on to say, "those who attacked Israel, and those who sponsored such attacks, don't seek merely to gain some leverage, to alter some boundary or to right some wrong. They seek what they and those like them have always sought: the destruction of Israel and the destruction of the Jewish people. Those who seek to destroy the Jews, who seek to destroy Israel, will for the same reason ultimately seek to destroy us all, and that my friends, is why Canada's new government has reacted with speed and spoken with clarity on recent events in the Middle East."

The potential Iranian nuclear threat to Israel was an issue throughout the year. In April, Prime Minister Harper condemned the call by Iranian president Mahmoud Ahmadinejad for the destruction of Israel as well as his denial of the Holocaust. In December, both he and Opposition Leader Dion expressed concern about Iran's Holocaust-denial conference. Harper, speaking for the government, condemned "in the strongest terms this latest example of anti-Israeli and racist statements from the president of Iran," and called it an "offense to all Canadians." Dion expressed "shock and indignation" about a conference "solely designed to inflame anti-Israeli rhetoric and spread hate and racism throughout the world." MP Cotler, meanwhile, urged the international community to enforce the genocide convention against Iran and to prosecute the country's leaders in the International Criminal Court.

Under the Conservative government there was a noticeable change in Canada's voting pattern at the UN on matters involving Israel. Canada opposed three resolutions in the Human Rights Council condemning Israel's retaliation against rocket attacks from Gaza and its settlement policies in the territories. In the General Assembly, however, where some 20 anti-Israel resolutions are presented annually, Canada's record was inconsistent. It voted for several of the resolutions, abstained on some, and voted against several others, with no discernable pattern. Even so, this was a marked improvement over past years, when Canada supported most such resolutions, abstained on a few, and rarely opposed any.

In April, the government released data showing that nearly 500 applications for refugee status from Israeli citizens were processed in 2005. Of these, 151 convinced examiners that they had a well-founded fear of persecution if they returned to Israel, 269 had their claims rejected, and the others withdrew their applications. The "success" rate, 31 percent, was the highest since 1994. The notion that Canada would recognize Israelis as people requiring refuge had long been a sensitive bilateral issue.

The Federal Court, in May, refused a request from a Canadian teenager born in Jerusalem to have his passport show his country of birth as Israel. Canada's policy, based on its view of the disputed status of Israel's capital, was to use only the city designation, with no country name, for someone born in Jerusalem.

During the summer, El Al Israel Airlines reduced its weekly flights between Toronto and Tel Aviv from eight to five because of exceptionally high landing fees at Toronto's Pearson International Airport. In the fall, there was a further reduction to three flights per week. Jon Allen was appointed Canada's ambassador to Israel in September, the third Jew to serve in that post.

PUBLIC OPINION, DIVESTMENT ISSUES, AND THE CAMPUSES

A public opinion poll conducted in August for the Association for Canadian Studies found that 31 percent of Canadians believed that the 9/11 attacks in the U.S. were at least partly due to Israel's actions in the Middle East. The proportion was higher (38 percent) in Quebec and lower (27 percent) in the rest of the country. In response to another question, about half of the respondents believed that Canada should pay more attention to the concerns of terrorist groups.

Of the organized efforts to boycott Israel that developed during the year, the one that attracted the most attention was launched by the Canadian Union of Public Employees (CUPE), one of the largest and most powerful unions in the country. Delegates of its Ontario division, representing some 200,000 workers, voted unanimously at their May convention to support "the international campaign of boycott, divestment and sanctions" against Israel because of its treatment of the Palestinians, and to apply leverage until Israel recognized the Palestinian right to self-determination. They also condemned Israel's "apartheid wall." Katherine Nastovski, who chaired CUPE's Ontario International Solidarity Committee, declared that "we believe the same strategy [that worked in South Africa] will work to enforce the rights of Palestinian people, including the rights of refugees to return to their homes and properties."

CJC regional director Steven Shulman denounced the resolution as a "propaganda statement" that was "based on falsehoods." The vote was controversial within the union itself: both Jewish and non-Jewish members picketed headquarters after the result was announced. Members of CUPE Local 2063 who worked in various Jewish community agencies were "absolutely outraged at this ridiculous anti-Israel initiative," according to the local's president. In June, Local 265, which also represented community workers, withdrew from the Ontario union in protest. Carolyn Roberts, president of another local affiliated with national CUPE, attacked Ontario CUPE president Sid Ryan for becoming "an embarrassment to the dignity, equality, respect and goodwill associated with the CUPE name." She also pointed out that the vote was held on a Saturday, thereby depriving observant Jewish delegates of the opportunity to participate.

At Toronto's Labor Day parade, the union's float featured a banner that read "End Israeli Apartheid," provided by the Coalition Against Israeli Apartheid. By November, however, dissident views began to prevail. Local 3902, representing lecturers at the University of Toronto, explicitly rejected the resolution, while Local 79, representing Toronto municipal workers, refused to participate in an educational campaign to support it. And in December, when a motion to endorse the CUPE resolution was made at a council meeting of the Ontario high-school teachers union, opposition was so great that the proposal was withdrawn.

Some church groups also dealt with boycott efforts. In April, Archbishop Andrew Hutchinson, primate of the Anglican Church of Canada, told an interfaith dinner about reported attempts within the world Anglican communion to promote divestment from Israel, and dissociated the Canadian church from such efforts. Later, in August, the United Church of Canada, at its General Council meeting, rejected its Toronto chapter's position in support of the CUPE resolution, instead voting to support investments that fostered the security and economic vitality of both Israel and a future Palestinian state, and to discourage investment that promoted Israel's occupation of the West Bank or the refusal of Israel's neighbors to recognize its right to exist as a Jewish state.

Jewish community organizations considered the university campus a crucial battleground for combating anti-Israel attitudes and activities. Susan Davis, executive vice president of National Jewish Campus Life (NJCL), spoke about this at the General Assembly of the United Jewish Communities (UJC) that took place in Los Angeles in November. She argued that the summer war in Lebanon had become an excuse for renewed anti-Israel agitation. The vast majority of Canadian Jewish students, Davis said, had no strong opinions about the Arab-Israeli struggle. Furthermore, although idealistic and generally academically gifted, they often had only a tenuous relationship to Jewish tradition and little detailed Jewish knowledge. Her organization, which coordinated the activities of individual campus Hillel groups, developed a Web site, Road to Peace, specifically geared to college students.

The Arab Students' Collective at the University of Toronto held an Israeli Apartheid Week in February, as the university turned down Hillel's request to compel the sponsors to drop the word "apartheid" from the title. Among the events held during that week were lectures on the alleged

Israel-South Africa connection, ethnic cleansing, the Palestinian right of return, and "myths" of Israeli democracy. Betar-Tagar, a Zionist group, responded with its own Know Radical Islam conference. The featured speaker was Nonie Darwish, an Arab writer who lived in the U.S., who, referring to militant Islam, declared that "there are powerful forces in our culture working against peace."

York University in Toronto was a major hotbed of anti-Israel sentiment. After Darwish expressed support for Israel and criticized radical manifestations of her own religion in a speech at York in March, Muslim groups claimed she had defamed Islam. Hillel, which sponsored her visit, was condemned by the York Federation of Students for condoning her "racist remarks." Hillel responded by publicly rejecting Islamophobia, but did not apologize for inviting Darwish and defended her freedom of expression. Various pro-Arab groups at York organized a demonstration calling for the resignations of university president Lorna Marsden and York University Foundation director Julia Koschitzky, and for the university to sever its ties to Israeli corporations and universities.

In November, York students, organized by a number of Arab and leftwing groups, demonstrated against Israel's security fence. This came a short time after the offices of a pro-Israel group at the student center were vandalized. York's Hillel president, Adam Hummel, lamented the negative atmosphere. "There is a lot of hostility, much more than last year . . . . It's reaching some sort of climax." Despite the large Jewish enrollment, he added, it was becoming increasingly uncomfortable to be a Jew on the York campus. Hummel contributed an article to the CJN in December in which he blamed "campus politics, the student government and the lack of action on behalf of the administration" for allowing the situation to fester.

York history professor David Noble, who is Jewish, sued 13 Jewish individuals and organizations for allegedly defaming him when they responded in 2004 to a flyer that he had distributed attacking alleged ties between the York University Foundation and supporters of Israel (see AJYB 2005, p. 296). He also filed a complaint with the Ontario Human Rights Commission demanding that York no longer cancel classes on the Jewish High Holy Days. A York spokesman said that the university would defend its policy.

Daniel Freeman-Maloy, suspended by Marsden in 2005 for his role in anti-Israel campus protests, had his suspension reversed in court. He then sued York for libel, misfeasance, and breach of academic freedom.

The university fought the suit on technical grounds, but in September the nation's Supreme Court ruled against York, so that the case would now proceed on the merits.

In 2005, B'nai Brith Canada had filed a complaint with the Quebec Human Rights Commission against Concordia University because it had refused to invite former Israeli prime minister Ehud Barak to speak. The complaint also alleged that a "poisoned atmosphere" for Jewish students had existed there since 2001. The complaint was withdrawn in April 2006 because the campus atmosphere had improved under its new president. One positive sign was the victory achieved by a moderate slate in the annual student elections in March.

George Galloway, the anti-Israel British MP, addressed a Concordia audience in November. He was quoted in a student newspaper as calling Israel a "terrorist state," and asserting Prime Minister Harper had committed "an act of war" by stopping Canadian aid to the Palestinian Authority.

The Hillel House at the University of British Columbia in Vancouver was vandalized in November, for the third time in as many years.

Anti-Semitism and Racism

B'nai Brith Canada's annual audit of anti-Semitic activity for 2006 showed 935 reported incidents, 13 percent more than in 2005 and the highest number in 25 years. Almost two-thirds of the total was categorized as harassment, one-third as vandalism, and about 3 percent as acts of violence. While incidents were reported in almost every region of the country, close to half occurred in Toronto—where nearly half of Canada's Jews lived—and roughly 25 percent in Montreal. Reporting the findings, Frank Diament, BBC's executive vice president, said, "The acts of harassment and violence are increasing. It's going beyond ordinary vandalism. That means that more individuals are feeling personally threatened, and that's a frightening experience." The problem was underlined in a Toronto police hate-crimes report for 2005, which noted that whereas the number of such offenses declined 19 percent from 2004, Jews were the victims of 84 percent of all hate crimes motivated by religious animus.

B'nai Brith Canada warned the community to watch out for anti-Semitic actions and possibly terrorist attacks as well during the summer, when the Israel-Hezballah war got underway. Indeed, the BBC audit later found a sharp rise in incidents during that period, including a bomb threat in July against a Montreal synagogue and subsequent throwing of stones at some of the worshippers when they exited the building. The authors of the audit suggested that the war functioned as a "global trigger phenomenon" for anti-Semitic acts. For the year, people of Arab and/or Muslim background were involved in the commission of 56 incidents, and thus constituted the largest single group of identified perpetrators.

Among the most serious anti-Semitic incidents were the desecration, within a few days in March, of two Montreal synagogues and the Jewish community center. All three buildings were located in the same neighborhood. Vandals smashed windows and did physical damage to a synagogue building in Winnipeg in May, and in that same city considerable damage was done to cemetery headstones in September.

One of the highest-profile attacks involved the throwing of Molotov cocktails into a Jewish school building in the Montreal suburb of Outremont, home to several Hasidic groups. The resulting fire caused considerable damage to the Skver boys' school. Numerous political leaders condemned the firebombing, and although the police were reluctant to describe the incident as a hate crime, a number of Jewish leaders called it exactly that. Another incident in Montreal occurred toward the end of December, when two large swastikas and anti-Semitic slogans were spray-painted on three buildings that were part of the city's Jewish Community Campus—including the structure housing Federation CJA—as well as on a nearby synagogue.

Dissemination of anti-Semitism over the Internet was a growing problem. The Canadian Friends of the Simon Wiesenthal Center became aware of a Farsi-language Web site that recruited suicide bombers and provided a link to a Hamas Web site. After Canadian Friends contacted the Montreal-based Internet service provider (ISP) in May and made it aware that the site violated not only Canadian law but also the service's own code of conduct, the site was removed.

Richard Warman, an Ottawa attorney who represented the CJC, asked the Canadian Radio and Telecommunications Commission in August to allow ISPs to block two U.S.-based neo-Nazi Web sites that were threatening Warman's life, but the request was denied on technical grounds. Warman had been active for years in combating racial hatred on the Web, initiating 16 cases. CJC president Ed Morgan expressed disappointment at the CRTC's failure to act.

Several court cases involving hate content on Web sites were underway. Two Toronto white supremacists were found to have violated the Internet hate laws and were ordered to pay fines, in a decision announced in

March by the Canadian Human Rights Tribunal. In June, Jean-Sebastien Presseault pleaded guilty in a Quebec court to willfully promoting hatred through his site. Tomasz Winnicki, a London skinhead, was sentenced to nine months in jail in July for defying a court order to stop posting racist messages, including Holocaust denial, on the Internet. Reni Santana-Ries of Edmonton was sentenced to 16 months in prison in September, after having been convicted in 2005 for using a U.S. Web site to promote hatred of Jews. The sentence was the longest ever imposed in Canada for such a crime, and the judge commented on the appalling level of hatred in his Web postings. And in a case initiated by Richard Warman, another Edmonton man, Glenn Bahr, was fined $5,000 by the Canadian Human Rights Commission in December for operating a site that promoted hatred against Jews and others.

Bank of Montreal CEO Tony Comper and his wife, Elizabeth, continued to lead a coalition of non-Jewish business and community leaders united under the name Fighting Anti-Semitism Together. Among its projects was a curriculum for students in grades six through eight. Tony Comper himself, in a speech delivered in September in Montreal, cautioned critics of Israeli policies to avoid crossing the line and espousing anti-Semitism.

Three cases of anti-Semitism from previous years remained in the news. David Ahenakew, a former Native American leader, had been convicted in 2005 for willfully promoting hatred against Jews through various public statements (see AJYB 2006, p. 296). But in June 2006, Judge C.J. Laing of Saskatchewan's Court of Queen's Bench overturned the conviction on appeal and ordered a new trial. The Crown said it would appeal the ruling. The firebombing of the United Talmud Torahs school in Montreal in 2004 (see AJYB 2005, pp. 299–300) was not forgotten. Rouba Fahd Elmerhebi, the mother of the convicted bomber, had been out on bail since her arrest in 2004. In 2006, she was charged with being an accessory after the fact, and a trial date was set for 2007. And Yves Michaud, censured by the National Assembly in 2000 for anti-Jewish remarks (see AJYB 2001, p. 288), had his attempt to void the censure turned down by the Quebec Court of Appeal in June 2006.

Holocaust-Related Matters

In the 20 years since the Deschenes Commission cleared the way for war-crimes prosecutions, results were meager despite constant pressure for government action from the Jewish community. Since 1995, when the program was overhauled, the government managed to bring only 21 cases to court: three of the accused left the country either voluntarily or through deportation, eight had their citizenship lifted for making false statements upon entering Canada, four cases awaited action by the cabinet, and the other accused individuals died in the course of legal proceedings. Efraim Zuroff of the Simon Wiesenthal Center came to Canada in June to draw attention to Operation Last Chance, a final effort to get governments to act. A rally was held on Parliament Hill in Ottawa to publicize the initiative. A recent report by the Wiesenthal Center gave Canada a grade of "C" for its record in dealing with suspected war criminals, but Zuroff termed this "overly generous."

Two alleged Nazi war criminals, both over 80, went on trial in St. Catharines in June. Josef Furman and Jura Skomatchuk were accused of lying about their World War II activities, and faced loss of citizenship and deportation. Furman allegedly participated in the liquidation of the Warsaw and Bialystok ghettos, and then served as a concentration camp guard at Flossenburg. Skomatchuk was charged with serving as a guard at the notorious Trawniki SS training camp and at several concentration camps. In August, Judge Judith Snider of Federal Court found that both had indeed misrepresented themselves when they entered the country and in filling out their citizenship applications, thus proving the government's allegations.

Prime Minister Harper spoke at Canadian Holocaust Memorial Day observances in April on Parliament Hill. He linked contemporary threats against Israel with the Nazi Holocaust and vowed not to ignore the announced positions of Hamas and President Ahmadinejad of Iran. Harper said, "Words are not enough. It is only in our vigilance and in our actions that we will honor those who died in places like Dachau and Auschwitz."

Twice during the year artworks that Nazis had looted from Jewish owners and were later purchased by legitimate buyers were returned to the families of the owners. In August the National Gallery of Canada returned a painting by Edouard Vuillard to the descendants of the original Parisian Jewish owner; CJC played a significant role in persuading the gallery to act. In October, the estate of the late Max Stern, a German Jewish art dealer who eventually settled in Montreal, recovered the first of perhaps 400 paintings that the Nazis had forced Stern to relinquish. The recovery of Stern's collection was expected to help two Montreal universities and the Hebrew University in Jerusalem, all of which were the beneficiaries of his estate.

JEWISH COMMUNITY

Demography

The Jewish People Policy Planning Institute, based in Israel, published comparative demographic data for Jewish communities around the world, and found that Canada, Germany, and Australia were the only Diaspora countries with substantial Jewish population growth between 1970 and 2005. Canada, which grew from 286,000 to 372,000 in that time span, was also one of the very few countries where further growth was anticipated. The JPPPI report noted that the Canadian community was also notable for its high level of day-school attendance and visits to Israel, and for relatively low intermarriage.

Others were not as sanguine. A study issued by Statistics Canada revealed that the percentage of Jews married to someone of another religion jumped from 9 percent in 1981 to 17 percent in 2001. Another study, by Charles Shahar, showed substantially higher intermarriage rates in smaller communities than in the two major ones: 41 percent in Vancouver, 34 in Calgary, 32 in Ottawa, and 23 in Winnipeg, as compared to 13 percent in Montreal and 16 percent in Toronto. Nationally, the rate among younger Jews was much higher than among older Jews.

The *Canadian Jewish News* carried an important piece in January by Prof. Leo Davids about the demography of Canadian Jewry. Davids emphasized the community's low rates of birth and marriage—which mirrored those of the broader society—as well as the relatively high average age of Jews and the growth of intermarriage. Whatever modest growth the community had experienced, he noted, came from immigration, which, if not sustained, would lead to population decline. Davids lamented the lack of action by the community, "despite the dire outlook for the future of Canadian Jewry." He called for a substantial increase in financial support for matchmaking, aiding young parents, and fostering Jewish education.

Toronto's UJA Federation sponsored a survey of Jews in its area that also provided comparisons with other communities. About 37 percent of Toronto Jews were Conservative, 14 percent Orthodox (the third highest Orthodox concentration on the continent), and 19 percent Reform. About half the respondents reported synagogue membership and about 13 percent attended services at least weekly. Levels of religious observance were higher and intermarriage rates lower than in the rest of North America, only 11 percent reporting a non-Jewish spouse. Nearly 75 percent had visited Israel at least once, and 47 percent felt "very close" to Israel. Over a third of respondents were sending their children to Jewish day schools, a much higher rate than in the U.S.

A unit of Toronto's Israeli consulate sponsored a study, *The Israeli Community in the Greater Toronto Area,* which was released in March. It showed that between 1946 and 2004 nearly 65,000 Israelis immigrated to Canada, most settling in the Toronto area. David Gidron, who wrote the report, estimated that about 50,000 Israelis currently resided in and around Toronto, making up about 25 percent of the Jewish population.

Communal Affairs

A number of capital improvements to community facilities were completed or announced during the year. UJA Federation of Greater Toronto decided to build a new facility, to be called the Prosserman Family Jewish Community Center, as a component of the community's "central square." It would replace the Bathurst Jewish Community Center. The other three elements composing the square were to be a new Koffler Center for the Arts, a Latner Family Center for Jewish Knowledge and Heritage, and a renovated and expanded Lipa Green Building to house the federation's offices. The project was slated for completion in 2009. In addition, recognizing the explosive growth of the Jewish community in the far northern suburban area of Vaughan, the federation began construction of the Wolf Lebovic Jewish Community Campus.

In one of the largest charitable gifts ever made to a Canadian Jewish community foundation, Larry and Judy Tanenbaum donated $50 million to the Jewish Foundation of Greater Toronto.

Montreal's community was also expanding into the suburbs, and Federation CJA opened a new center in the West Island city of Dollard des Ormeaux. In Winnipeg, the Asper Jewish Community Campus's interior space was scheduled for redesign and remodeling.

In a June column in *CJN,* Gerald Gall lamented the decline in the Canadian Jewish Congress's social-advocacy role. He contended that the organization's social-justice agenda "seems to have been placed on the back burner," apparently because of budgetary constraints. Gall felt that the CJC could deal with Jewish issues while at the same time reclaiming its role as "one of the leading voices promoting Canada as a fair, just and equitable society."

Israel's summer war against Hezballah was a major community concern, eliciting special fund-raising drives, public demonstrations, and political activity. Major rallies were held in late July in Montreal's Dominion Square and Toronto's Center for the Arts, attracting about 2,000 and 8,000 participants respectively. At the Toronto event numerous politicians from all levels of government attended. At the Montreal rally, Rabbi Reuben Poupko praised Prime Minister Harper for his "clarity and honesty," and MP Irwin Cotler blamed the conflict on the Arabs' "unwillingness to accept the legitimacy of a Jewish state." Pro-Israel demonstrations were also held in smaller communities.

Some 376 Canadians immigrated to Israel in 2005, a significant rise from 2003 and 2004, and nearly two-thirds of them were Orthodox. The number of Israelis living in Canada, however, was a sore point for Israel. Minister of Absorption Ze'ev Boim came to Canada in October, together with several colleagues from his department, to try to persuade Israelis to return home. Boim explained to the *CJN* that "we make great efforts in aliyah. Why not reach out to Israelis abroad?"

Based on the findings of recent market research, the Canadian Council for Israel and Jewish Advocacy (CIJA), which was part of UIA Federations Canada, stressed the theme of "shared values," that is, commonalities between Canada and Israel, in its work on college campuses and elsewhere. One consequence of adopting this positive approach was an abandonment of arguments that denigrated Israel's foes.

The Canadian Jewish Political Affairs Committee (CJPAC) was formed just weeks before the federal election in January. CJPAC, a nonpartisan, independent body supported by non-tax-deductible contributions from its members, was an innovative attempt to advance the political objectives of Canada's Jews. After the election, executive director Josh Cooper termed its first foray into politics a success.

Prof. Alan Dershowitz of Harvard University was the featured speaker at a community rally in December at a Toronto synagogue aimed at drawing attention to the dangers posed by Iran. He told the crowd that he and MP Cotler were drafting an indictment against Iranian president Mahmoud Ahmadinejad for incitement to genocide, based on his threats against Israel and the Jewish people. Dershowitz described Iran's leader as "this Hitler of the twenty-first century." Other speakers included representatives of the federal and provincial governments.

Members of the Neturei Karta ultra-Orthodox group who participated in the Holocaust-denial conference that took place in December in Tehran were roundly condemned by several rabbis. Thus Rabbi Dovid Schochet, president of the Vaad Harabonim (Rabbinical Council) of Toronto, likened their actions to "embracing Hitler after he killed the

Jews, and saying we're your friend," and Rabbi David Lowy, head of Agudath Israel in Toronto, termed their actions a "chilul HaShem [desecration of God's name], disgusting, repulsive."

Some 100 people, styling themselves the Alliance of Concerned Jewish Canadians, published an open letter to the Jews of Canada explaining why they were distancing themselves from Israeli government policies. In November the group ran an ad in the *CJN* expressing "profound dissatisfaction with the direction in which the leaders of our community have taken us," and claiming that its request to be included as an affiliated organization of CJC had encountered resistance.

In cooperation with Montreal's Federation CJA, seven Israeli universities joined together in January to present the first Israel Universities Fair. Hundreds of students attended, attracted by the opportunity to speak directly with representatives of the various Israeli institutions about educational opportunities.

Religion

In December, the Rabbinical Assembly's Committee on Jewish Law and Standards issued an opinion that the ordination of gays and lesbians and commitment ceremonies for gay and lesbian couples were acceptable under Jewish law, while also approving another opinion upholding the traditional ban on both (see above, p. 130). This created a stir in Canada, where the Conservative movement tended to be less accepting of such innovations than was the case in the U.S. To be sure, differences between Conservative opinion in the two countries were already noticeable before this decision. Many Conservative synagogues in Canada, for example, had not adopted gender egalitarianism with regard to participation in services. Nevertheless, the decision on gays and lesbians exacerbated tensions.

It was expected that most Canadian Conservative congregations would not accept the permissive ruling. Thus Rabbi Steven Saltzman of Toronto described the responsum that accepted homosexuality as "a social, political, dogmatic, philosophic statement, but it does not come up to Halakhic standards of any sort," and Montreal's Rabbi Lionel Moses said that the ruling "unquestionably" contravened Halakhah. Clearly, the new ruling portended a serious division between the Canadian and American parts of the movement.

Orthodoxy, especially in Toronto, had for some time been moving to the religious right, and questions were raised over whether the influence of "yeshiva world" leaders in the city, especially Rabbi Shlomo Miller, head of Kollel Avreichim, was pulling the community in an extremist direction. Among the issues that arose during the year were denunciations of a visiting speaker, Rabbi Natan Slifkin, for his allegedly heretical views about creation (see AJYB 2006, p. 107), a decision by a supervisory charity board to stop certifying female charity collectors, and an attempt by the Vaad Harabonim (rabbinical council) to challenge the validity of the city's longstanding *eruv,* which enabled observant Jews to carry items out of doors on Shabbat. Another controversial issue was a tightening of standards for certification of food products as kosher. In defense of the stringencies, Rabbi Mordechai Levin, executive director of the Kashruth Council of Canada, said that the reduction in the use of pesticides meant that more bugs were being found in raw fruits and vegetables.

Rabbi Reuven Tradburks, secretary of the Vaad Harabonim, defended the increased emphasis on strict observance as a positive development, reflecting the desire of many Jews to comply more fully with the requirements of Jewish law. He contended that the higher quality of Jewish education had led more Orthodox Jews to demand more stringent levels of observance for themselves and others. "This is not a shift to the right," he declared, "it is a shift to the correct."

In an embarrassing situation, the Toronto Board of Rabbis, whose members were overwhelmingly Conservative and Reform rabbis, announced in April that it would not participate in the community's Yom Hashoah commemoration because only the boys from a youth choir were invited to sing. The girls, who made up about two-thirds of the choir, had reportedly been barred from participation in deference to the Vaad Harabonim, which, as a strictly Orthodox body, followed the tradition of not listening to women sing.

Prof. Martin Lockshin of York University, an Orthodox rabbi, published "A Modern Orthodox Manifesto" in the *CJN* in October. Although not labeled as such, it was clearly a contribution to the debate over the influence of right-wing rabbis that had been going on for several months. Lockshin presented a vigorous case for Modern Orthodoxy in terms of observance, commitment to Israel as a religious value, affirmation of the value of secular knowledge, participation in public life, involvement in universal moral causes, and maximum equality for women within the limits of Jewish law, and expressed optimism that his brand of Orthodoxy could flourish in Toronto.

At year's end, the Toronto bet din (religious court) decided to suspend all conversions to Judaism pending resolution of a dispute between the

Israeli rabbinate and Diaspora communities over conversion standards, specifically, what level of religious observance should be demanded of parents who wish to convert an adopted child. Rabbi Saul Emanuel, executive director of Montreal's Vaad Ha'ir, expressed support for a stringent position, indicating that it was already the norm in his city. However other rabbis called for openness to converting adopted children for families that were not yet fully Orthodox, in the expectation of religious growth over time.

Winnipeg's community encountered serious problems when its only kosher butcher lost his kosher certification in a dispute over standards only weeks after the city's only kosher market, which included a delicatessen, closed. The market eventually reopened with kosher certification, but since there was no kosher butcher in town, meat had to be brought in from larger cities like Toronto.

Montreal's Vaad Ha'ir announced in October that it was elevating its standards for kosher certification in the light of a scandal that occurred in Monsey, New York, where unkosher meat was found in a kosher store. New rules required closer supervision at all stages of the process, from slaughterhouse to consumer, and as a result, the Vaad had to look for several new recruits for supervisory positions.

Ontario's Bill 27, an amendment to the Arbitration Act motivated by a desire to prevent the operation of Islamic courts based on sharia, had the effect of weakening the long established bet din system in the Jewish community. Attorney John Syrtash, representing several Orthodox groups, expressed strenuous opposition to the bill, suggesting that it might be unconstitutional and terming it "blatantly unfair." The legislation, passed in February, took no notice of Jewish community objections and prohibited all forms of binding arbitration in family matters that were not carried out in accordance with Canadian law. CJC Ontario's honorary legal counsel Mark Freiman said that the law inaccurately "presumes that faith-based arbitration is innately exploitative and coercive," and Syrtash announced he would challenge it in court.

Education

Toronto's CJA Federation task force on Jewish education released its report in September, focusing on the rising financial challenges faced by the day schools and families that patronized them, especially in light of the province's refusal to provide any funding. Among the many recommendations were a $100-million educational endowment fund, a loan program to help parents with tuition, and the transformation of the Board of Jewish Education into a Center for Jewish Education with increased responsibilities, including marketing. The report also urged the maintenance of tuition subsidies at least at current levels. Objections were raised to the proposed loan program on the grounds that it would merely defer the problem faced by the families, not alleviate it. Earlier in the year, provincial opposition leader John Tory expressed his support for public funding, arguing that it was not fair that only Catholic schools, among the various religious institutions, received government support.

Despite the financial crunch, a study conducted for the Board of Jewish Education and released early in the year showed that the percentage of Jewish children enrolled in day or supplementary schools in the Toronto area had increased to 61 percent of children aged 6–13 and 33 percent of those aged 14–17. Moreover, 78 percent of children who started first grade in a Jewish school later went on to a Jewish high school, as compared to about 50 percent 20 years earlier.

In Montreal, where Jewish day schools did benefit from government funding, questions were raised about whether several Hasidic schools adhered to the prescribed official curriculum. After newspaper reports that the Skver Hasidim were not teaching secular subjects at all in their high schools and only part of the required material in their elementary schools, further investigation indicated that at least five other schools were similarly remiss. When it was also revealed that the high schools of Skver, Belz, and Lubavitch did not have the required permits, the Quebec government ordered an investigation. Speaking for Federation CJA, vice president Marc Gold stressed that "it goes without saying that all Quebecers are bound by the laws of society," and urged the regularization of the status of schools that were not currently complying with the law. Alex Werzberger, a Satmar leader who headed the Coalition of Outremont Hasidic Organizations, acknowledged that Satmar schools did not comply with the law and that the same was true for other Hasidic high schools for boys.

In December, the matter was raised in the National Assembly. Responding, Jean-Marc Fournier, the minister of education, said that he could not close down the Skver high school for boys because it provided only religious training, and was therefore, legally speaking, a religious center and not a school. The situation of the high school for girls, however, which clearly was a "school," was referred to the justice minister.

Community and Intergroup Relations

Amid the tension over the David Ahenakew affair (see above, p. 292), more than 20 Jewish and aboriginal leaders went on a joint mission to Israel in February, under the auspices of the Assembly of First Nations and CJC. They toured the country and met with governmental leaders, diplomats, and scholars, focusing on agriculture and the preservation of minority languages, both topics of intense interest for the aboriginal group. Afterwards, AFN national chief Phil Fontaine said he had "always believed that the struggle of the Jewish people in so many ways mirrors our own struggle."

During the international flap over the publication of the Danish cartoons offensive to Muslims (see below, pp. 433–35), the *Jewish Free Press,* a newspaper in Calgary, reprinted three of them. Publisher Richard Bronstein said he wanted people to see what the controversy was all about. The Canadian Islamic Congress warned about possible damage to Jewish-Muslim relations and asked for an apology. Bronstein instead offered a Muslim leader the opportunity to write a piece for the *Jewish Free Press.* The Calgary Jewish Community Council dissociated itself from the paper.

A new children's book, *Three Wishes: Palestinian and Israeli Children Speak,* by Deborah Ellis, was the center of considerable controversy in Ontario through much of the year. Critics asserted that it cast Israel in a negative light and featured young Palestinians who aspired to be suicide bombers and kill Jews. The York Region District School Board agreed, and, in January, removed it from a special reading program for older elementary-school students. CJC entered the fray, and school boards in other jurisdictions, such as Ottawa, Toronto, Windsor, and the Niagara Region, agreed that the book was not appropriate for the intended age group, and placed restrictions on access. But the Kingston and London boards bucked the trend and continued to include the book on their reading lists. Various writers' and librarians' groups also opposed the restrictions.

Jewish organizations were quick to denounce vandalism that occurred at a mosque in the Quebec town of Trois-Rivières in April, when anti-Arab and anti-Muslim messages were affixed to the building. Allan Adel, chair of the League for Human Rights of BBC, said that "hatred knows no boundaries, and when one community is under attack, all our communities are at risk." In September, a fire was started at a Muslim school in Ottawa. Drawing a parallel to the firebombing of a Jewish school in Montreal a few weeks earlier, spokespersons for CJC and the Ottawa Federation condemned the arson attack.

A sensitive intergroup issue arose in Montreal, where a YMCA branch stood across an alley from a Satmar yeshiva. The Satmars, concerned that their children would see women in gym attire exercising through the Y's windows, asked the Y to frost the windows and offered to pay the cost. The Y agreed and the job was done. But some 100 Y members then signed a petition complaining about the action because they lost their view and did not get as much light as before. The underlying issue, whether the Y had to conform to the needs of outsiders while doing nothing illegal on its own private property, attracted media attention because of a larger debate going on in Quebec society about "reasonable accommodation," the extent to which a largely secular society should tolerate minority practices that conflicted with the values of the majority.

In 2005, Ontario decided to depart from the previous parliamentary practice of allowing the premier to determine when to hold an election, and instead to declare the first Thursday of October in every fourth year as election day. For the 2007 election, that would coincide with the Jewish holiday of Shemini Atzeret, and therefore CJC tried to mobilize Jewish organizations to lobby for a change in date.

Culture

The Montreal Israeli Theatre, founded by Milli Raviv, staged its first major production in June. *Rabbi Kameach,* by Shmuel Hasfari, was presented in Hebrew, with simultaneous translation in French and English. Another Hebrew production was *Oil City* by Hillel Mitelpunkt, presented in June with English translation by the Hebrew Theatre Workshop of the Jewish Public Library of Montreal. Sholem Asch's powerful *God of Vengeance* was the main presentation of the Dora Wasserman Yiddish Theatre in Montreal in June. The Yiddish Theatre went on tour to Dresden, Prague, and Vienna in the fall. David Sherman's *Have a Heart,* about a Jewish family with an ailing father trying to cope with the Quebec medical system, premiered at Montreal's Centaur Theatre in June.

Montreal's Saidye Bronfman Centre announced plans in the fall to close its well-known fine-arts school and art gallery after 40 years. Instead, the SBC would now focus on the performing arts, including a new academy. The decision to drop the visual arts, which was quite disappointing to the SBC's clientele, was due to a decision by the YM-YWHA to end its funding for the center's overhead. Under the new system, the SBC would become an agency of Federation CJA, with the Bronfman and Segal families continuing to provide support.

Toronto's Jewish Film Festival, presented in May, screened Israeli films

Summer Story, Something Sweet, The Children's House, and *Until Tomorrow Comes,* and the Dutch films *The Man Who Sold Eichmann and Mengele* and *Goodbye Holland.* Although the Montreal Jewish Film Festival was suspended for a year because of financial difficulties, an Israeli Film Festival there in June screened six films. The Jerusalem Film Festival, held in July, included a Canadian Retrospective program, and directors Robert Lantos and Atom Egoyan were honored with lifetime achievement awards. Simcha Jacobovici presented his new documentary, *The Exodus Decoded.*

The world premiere of the documentary *Chez Schwartz* by Garry Beitel took place at the Calgary International Film Festival in September, telling the story of the famed Montreal delicatessen. *The Making of a Martyr,* Brooke Goldstein's documentary about Palestinian child suicide bombers, won the Best Film Audience Choice Award at the United Nations Documentary Film Festival in April. The first Alex and Ruth Dworkin Prize for the promotion of tolerance through film went to *Steel Toes,* by Arnie Gelbert and Francine Allaire, about a neo-Nazi skinhead accused of murder and his Jewish lawyer. The film had its world premiere and received the prize during Les Rendez-Vous du Cinema Quebecoise in Montreal in February.

Several television documentaries of Jewish interest were broadcast during the year. They included *Encounters with Moses,* the story of media mogul Moses Znaimer, by Mike Sheerin; *Life and Times of Michael Cohl,* the concert promoter, by Barry Avrich; *The Outsider: The Life and Times of Robert Lantos* by Peter Gentile; *Disengaging Democracy* by Igal Hecht, about the pullout from Gaza; and Jonathan Finkelstein's *Braindamadj'd,* the story of television director Paul Nadler's terrible brain injury in a Sinai auto accident and his long struggle to overcome the effects. Documentaries that were screened at various venues included Sydney Pollack's *Sketches of Frank Gehry; Leonard Cohen: I'm Your Man* by Lian Lunson; Ronit Avni's *Encounter Point,* about Israelis and Palestinians who seek peace; and Frederic Bohbot's *Once a Nazi . . . .,* about a Montreal academic who came to terms with his Waffen SS background some 50 years after the war.

The Art Gallery of Ontario, designed by Toronto native Frank Gehry, held an exhibit based on several of his projects beginning in February. Simultaneously, the University of Toronto Art Centre exhibited Gehry's drawings for eight museums that he designed. The Jewish Heritage Centre of Western Canada in Winnipeg held an exhibit in November about the life of Samuel Freedman, Manitoba's first Jewish chief justice.

The Blue Metropolis international literary festival, held in Montreal in April, featured elaborate tributes to two distinguished writers who came from the city, Saul Bellow and Irving Layton. Bellow's widow and Layton's daughter participated in panel discussions about the authors. Both events were later broadcast on CBC radio. Radio Shalom, in Montreal, began broadcasting Jewish programming in Hebrew, English, and French.

Publications

Pierre Elliot Trudeau was the darling of Montreal's Jews and represented the most heavily Jewish constituency in the country in Parliament for nearly 20 years. Yet as a young man he had been unable to distance himself from the ideas of such men as Lionel Groulx and Charles Maurras, both of whom were tainted with anti-Semitic ideology. Max and Monique Nemni dealt with this paradox in *Young Trudeau: Son of Quebec, Father of Canada 1919–1944,* translated from French into English by William Johnson. The book, based on Trudeau's papers, showed the extent to which he was involved in ethnocentric Quebec nationalism in the early 1940s. At the time, Trudeau downplayed the threat of Germany, opposed participation in the war, and idolized right-wing leaders like Marshal Phillipe Pétain.

Hillary Rodham Clinton: Polarizing First Lady by Gil Troy focused on the current presidential candidate's eight years as a president's wife. Insights into the Washington scene from a much different perspective were presented in *The Washington Diaries: 1981–1989* by Allan Gotlieb, who was Canada's ambassador to the U.S. during the Reagan years. The book revealed, among other things, that Prime Minister Trudeau felt "double-crossed" by Israeli prime minister Menachem Begin over the injection of the Jerusalem issue into the 1978 Canadian election campaign, and as a result "refused for a long time to meet with any Canadian Jewish leader."

Several important biographical treatments of Canadian Jews appeared. *Bora Laskin: Bringing Law to Life* by Philip Girard was an admiring biography of Canada's first Jew on the Supreme Court, who then became chief justice and left a lasting imprint on the country's legal system. Former prime minister Jean Chrétien's adviser and confidante Eddie Goldenberg wrote an insider's view of government during a very turbulent period in *The Way It Works: Inside Ottawa.* The opposite side of partisan politics was illuminated by Hugh Segal in *The Long Road Back: The Conservative Journey: 1993–2006,* in which Senator Segal described his attraction to the Conservative option at a time when Jews were overwhelmingly Liberal. Ada Craniford's *Mordecai Richler: A Life in Ten Novels* made the argument that the late writer integrated elements of his own life into his writing, and was also inspired, at some points, by the Bible. Ruth Panofsky's *The Force of Vocation: The Literary Career of Adele Wiseman* examined the complex and troubled life of a writer of great promise who encountered many difficulties later on.

Journalist Noah Richler crisscrossed the country collecting data for *This Is My Country, What's Yours? A Literary Atlas of Canada.* Richler examined the fiction written by leading Canadian writers to try to achieve an understanding of the essence of Canadian identity. A clear love for Montreal was evident in Joe King's *Baron Byng to Bagels: Tales of Jewish Montreal* and in Bill Brownstein's *Schwartz's Hebrew Delicatessen: The Story.*

Several books on the Holocaust were published, including *There Is an Apple in My Freezer: A True Story* by Zanetta Nestel; *At the Mercy of Strangers: Survival in Nazi-Occupied Poland* by Gitel Hopfeld, translated by Simcha Simchovitch; Chava Rosenfarb's *The Cattle Cars Are Waiting, 1942–1944,* translated by Goldie Morgentaler; Peter Simonstein Cullman's *History of the Jewish Community of Schneidemuhl: 1641 to the Holocaust; I Was a Child of Holocaust* Survivors by Bernice Eisenstein; Eric Koch's *I Remember the Location Exactly;* and *Tricks of Fate: Escape, Survival and Rescue* by Morris Gruda, translated by Adam Fuerstenberg.

Other nonfiction works include Sabina Citron's *The Indictment: The Arab-Israeli Conflict in Historical Perspective;* Laura Brandon's *Art or Memorial: The Forgotten History of Canada's War Art;* Yakov Rabkin's attack on Zionism from an ultra-Orthodox perspective, *A Threat from Within: A Century of Jewish Opposition to Zionism; The Bronfmans: The Rise and Fall of the House of Seagram* by Nicholas Faith; and *Brothers of Iron* by Joe and Ben Weider with Mike Steere. An important work of history, *Jews in Poland-Lithuania in the Eighteenth Century* by Gershon David Hundert, covered the rise of Hasidism, the evolving responsibilities of community leadership, interactions with the Church, interest in Kabbalah, and persistent anti-Semitism.

Among the books of fiction were *Suite Française* by Irene Nemirovsky; *Kippour* by Marc-Alain Wolf; *L'Homme qui voulait changer le monde* by Raphael Levy; *The Minyan* by Alvin Abram; *Matters of Hart* by Marianne Ackerman; *The City Man* by Howard Akler; *The House on Lippincott* by Bonnie Burstow; and *Nelcott Is My Darling* by Golda Fried. Volumes of poetry included *September Rain* by Seymour Mayne; *Post-*

modern Light by Paul Hartal; *Drunk From the Bitter Truth* by Anna Margolin, translated by Shirley Kumove; *40 Years of Poetry* by Jack Gelman; and *Surviving the Censor: The Unspoken Words of Osip Mandelstam* by Rafi Aaron.

Among recipients of Canadian Jewish Book Awards in May were Edeet Ravel for *A Wall of Light;* Michael Posner for *The Last Honest Man: Mordecai Richler, an Oral Biography;* Eliezer Segal for *From Sermon to Commentary: Expounding the Bible in Talmudic Babylonia;* Renee Norman for *True Confessions;* Richard Menkis and Norman Ravvin for *The Canadian Jewish Studies Reader;* Sara Ginaite-Rubinson for *Resistance and Survival;* Isabel Vincent for *Bodies and Souls;* Lynne Kositsky for *The Thought of High Windows;* and Mervin Butovsky and Ode Garfinkle for *The Journals of Yaacov Zipper, 1950–1982.*

Personalia

Marshall Rothstein was appointed to the Supreme Court of Canada. Neil Drabkin became chief of staff to the Minister of Public Safety. Sam Katz was reelected mayor of Winnipeg. Richard Levin and Michael Goldbloom were appointed vice principals at McGill University. Charles Ohayon was named president of the Academy of Canadian Cinema and Television.

The following received the Order of Canada: Companion—Bernard Ostry; Officer—Gerald Schwartz; Members—Clayton Ruby and Steven Cummings. Donald Carr and Leon Katz were named to the Order of Ontario and Arnold Frieman to the Order of Manitoba.

Linda Kislowicz was appointed executive vice president of UIA Federations Canada and Barbara Farber was elected president. Moishe Smith was elected president of B'nai Brith International. UJA Federation in Toronto named David Engel to chair its board and Richard Diamond became chair of National Jewish Campus Life. Ted Lyons was elected president of the Jewish Federation of Winnipeg, and Graham Dixon president of the Jewish National Fund for Manitoba and Saskatchewan. Sue Holtzman became president of Na'amat Canada and Talia Klein executive director of Betar-Tagar Canada.

Well-known members of the community who passed away during the year: In January, renowned poet, teacher, and writer Irving Layton, aged 93; prominent philanthropist and cofounder of Birthright Israel Andrea Bronfman, aged 60; Leonard Kitz, former mayor of Halifax, aged 89; former Toronto schoolboard member Mae Waese, aged 74; community worker Lily Barr, aged 81; Sam Ruth, longtime executive director of Toronto's Baycrest Centre, aged 84; and Abe Luxenberg, leader of the Maccabi movement, aged 82. In February, community leader Lester Lazarus, aged 84. In March, Rabbi Sol Tanenzapf, aged 69; and Rudolf Vrba, author, neurologist, and Auschwitz escapee who publicized the truth about the death camp, aged 82. In April, educator Ethel Raicus, aged 86. In May, prominent civil servant Bernard Ostry, aged 78; theater director and playwright Marion Andre, aged 86; and legal scholar and medical ethicist Barney Sneiderman, aged 68. In June, bridge champion Ralph Cohen, aged 79. In July, Thom Farkas, an Israel Air Force pilot killed in action, aged 23; and businessman and writer Edgar Horace Cohen, aged 92. In August, Edwin (Eddie) Goodman, prominent corporation lawyer, Conservative Party activist, and philanthropist, aged 87; Holocaust survivor, educator, and author Ann Kazimirski, aged 84; artist Stanley Lewis, aged 76; celebrated composer John Weinzweig, aged 93; and writer and former alderman Isadore Wolch, aged 98. In September, Bertram Loeb, founder of the IGA supermarket chain, aged 90; and educator Shani Kurtz, aged 77. In October, journalist Sid Adilman, aged 68; Clara Balinsky, distinguished community volunteer, former president of Canadian Hadassah-WIZO, and leader of numerous causes, aged 86; and survivor and Nazi hunter Joseph Riwash, aged 93. In November, former football player Jim Miller, aged 74; businessman and municipal politician Irving Paisley, aged 87; Alexander Grossman, businessman and philanthropist, aged 87; lawyer and community leader Wolfe Goodman, aged 81; community leader Monty Berger, aged 88; Avraham David Niznik, chief rabbi of Montreal, aged 85; and former ORT leader J.A. Lyone Heppner, aged 89. In December, Holocaust survivor and international Jewish lobbyist Philip Katz, aged 82; and Henry (Zvi) Weinberg, scholar of French literature, activist for Soviet Jewry, and retired member of the Knesset, aged 71.

HAROLD M. WALLER

Venezuela

National Affairs

THE CHÁVEZ PHENOMENON

Hugo Chávez was first elected president of Venezuela in December 1998 with 56 percent of the vote, and took office in February 1999, launching what he termed the "Bolivarian Revolution," named after Simón Bolívar, the nineteenth-century liberator of Venezuela. Reelected in 2000 under a new constitution of his own devising, he won a third term in the national election of December 3, 2006, receiving 63 percent of the vote, as against 37 percent for the opposition candidate, Manuel Rosales, governor of Zulia, the richest state in Venezuela and the country's main producer of oil.

The result had been a foregone conclusion, and many Venezuelans opposed to the incumbent stayed home on election day. Although no evidence of outright election fraud surfaced, the president enjoyed the advantages deriving from unlimited political power. His advertising and campaign costs were funded by the government, which also kept the registry of those eligible to vote, and did not share it with the opposition.

The attention that the world press lavished on Chávez almost on a daily basis dwarfed all previous interest that Venezuela had attracted in its 174 years as an independent country. Who really was Hugo Chávez? Since becoming president Chávez had been compared to Argentinean dictator Juan Domingo Perón, a paradigm of fascist populism; with Juan Velasco Alvarado, the military strongman who instituted a leftist dictatorship in Peru that lasted from 1968 until 1975; and with all three of the legendary twentieth-century despots—Mussolini, Hitler, and Stalin. And yet his friends and enemies—even Chávez himself, in fact—tended to agree that the best comparison was with Fidel Castro, who had been not only a political mentor, but also a kind of father figure.

The relationship with Castro began in the late 1960s, when the Cuban dictator send arms and men to help the Partido de la Revolución Venezolana (PRV, Party for the Venezuelan Revolution), led by Douglas Bravo. Adán Chávez, Hugo's oldest brother and the current minister of education, was a leading member of this group, which sought to infiltrate the Venezuelan army and take it over. Hugo Chávez, influenced by his brother, joined the army with the same goal. In 1982, Chávez and four comrades-in-arms made a solemn promise to "break the chains that oppress the people."

They waited ten years before trying, and on February 4, 1992, with Chávez now a lieutenant colonel, he and his friends launched an unsuccessful coup against the democratic government of Carlos Andrés Pérez. For his role in the attempt, Chávez was confined for two years in the military prison of Yare. Soon after his release, Chávez visited Havana, where he was received by Castro with the honors due to a chief of state. Chávez, for his part, gave a passionate speech at Havana University that exuded Marxist ideology.

Another important influence on Chávez was Norberto Ceresole, an otherwise obscure Argentinean sociologist who espoused militarism, fascism, and anti-Semitism. Ceresole's anti-Jewish diatribes and publicly stated Holocaust revisionism led to his deportation from Venezuela in 1999. Ceresole called himself "Chávez's discoverer," and said that his own deportation was not important so long as Chávez was in a position to implement his agenda. Chávez was already president at the time, although his followers did not yet have control of either house of the Venezuelan Congress.

The Western democracies hoped for the best from the new regime despite alarming evidence about its intentions. Soon after Chávez assumed office a letter surfaced that he had written to Ilich Ramírez Sánchez, alias The Jackal, a Venezuelan terrorist serving a life sentence in France. In it Chávez addressed The Jackal as "distinguished compatriot" and told him "there is a time for every purpose, time to gather stones and cast them away, time to ignite the revolution or ignore it, of uniting classes or provoking class struggle." He continued with a quotation from Lenin, and concluded: "With profound faith in the cause and the mission." John Maisto, then serving as U.S. ambassador in Caracas, sought to downplay the letter's significance, saying that "Chávez has to be judged for what he does and not for what he says."

What Chávez would do was weaken all intermediary civic bodies—political parties, Congress, the courts—and, in tight alliance with the military, establish a government that communicated with and appealed directly to the "people." And he would accomplish all this while maintaining the framework of a democratic government, with regular elections and, at least officially, freedom of speech and of the press. What emerged was neither a pure dictatorship nor a true democracy, but a hybrid.

Upon becoming president, Chávez proposed the creation of a Constituent Assembly to draft a new constitution, replacing one that had been in force since 1961. In the elections for the Assembly, Chávez supporters devised a mathematical formula, called *"kino Chávez,"* that allowed him to obtain 94.5 percent of the seats with only 62 percent of the votes. The constitution that emerged, approved overwhelmingly by referendum on April 25, 1999, subjugated all other organs of government to the president's will, replaced the two-house Congress with a unicameral National Assembly, and drastically reduced civilian control over the armed forces, whose leaders were allied with him.

Since December 1998 there were seven elections of different kinds in Venezuela, each of them won by Chávez and his supporters. The breakdown of the vote remained, suspiciously, nearly invariable: 60 percent for Chavists (Chávez's side) and 40 percent for the opposition. The rate of abstention from voting always exceeded 50 percent, with two exceptions: the National Assembly elections in December 2005, in which 83 percent stayed away from the polls, and the presidential election of 2006, when 25 percent were reported as not voting.

Suspicions of voting fraud were expecially widespread after the defeat, under murky circumstances, of a recall referendum in August 2004 that sought the president's ouster. Surveys done after the referendum found that roughly 80 percent of Venezuelans, including a good number of the president's backers, did not think the vote was conducted fairly. If anyone still harbored doubts that the right to secret ballot was violated, Luis Tascón, a Chavist representative in the National Assembly, provided, on his Web site, a list of people who voted for recall. Many of them were subsequently fired from government jobs, and those who worked in the private sector suddenly suffered the termination of their business with public bodies. Later, the government opened a Web page for those who wanted to ask for forgiveness because they had voted for the recall of Chávez.

The persistence of free expression under Chávez was often cited by foreign observers to disprove charges of dictatorship. The government, in fact, heavily influenced the media, most notably through its outright ownership of eight national radio stations and four television stations. Beginning in July 2005 there was also Telesur, a joint TV project with Uruguay, Argentina, and Cuba, financed by and broadcast from Venezuela. Officially designed to offer these and other Latin American countries programming related to their culture, Telesur, like the Venezuelan stations, hewed to the regime's ideological line and promoted a Chávez personality cult.

In addition, government-funded advertising was used to manipulate the privately owned media: in order to ensure their financial survival, some of the print and electronic media avoided criticism of the government and blacklisted journalists known to be hostile to it. Often, sometimes on a daily basis, Chávez himself delivered *cadenas,* political discourses that could last hours, which all radio and TV stations were required to broadcast live. In November 2005 the regime went further, enacting a Law of Social Responsibility for Radio and Television, setting limits on the freedom of the private media. Further legislation in 2006 provided prison terms for those guilty of crimes of "opinion."

In July 2006, Chávez, in the course of one of his *cadenas,* warned that if private radio and TV channels kept "conspiring," he would withdraw their licenses. These words were said as he aimed a Kalashnikov rifle, one of 100,000 recently imported from Russia, at the TV cameras. A few months later, in an address delivered at the Military Academy, Chávez, dressed in his officer's uniform, announced that his government would not renew the license of Radio Caracas Television, which had been on the air for over 50 years, beyond May 2007. He explicitly stated his political motivation: the channel was *"golpista,"* a supporter, he believed, of an attempted coup against him in 2002.

International organizations that monitored freedom of speech, including the Inter-American Press Association and Reporters without Borders, repeatedly condemned actions taken and threats made against the free press in Venezuela. And the Inter-American Commission on Human Rights (IACHR) had received, by the close of 2006, more that a thousand complaints of physical aggression against Venezuelan journalists. During 2006, three journalists and an editor were murdered in the course of attacks on newspaper headquarters and TV stations in the provinces. At the end of 2006, there were, in Venezuela, 76 political prisoners and more than 700 people persecuted for their political activities or opinions, among them many journalists.

SOCIALISM, ANTI-AMERICANISM, OIL

Speaking in January 2005 at the World Social Forum in Porto Alegre, Brazil, President Chávez delivered a manifesto on the "Socialism of the Twenty-First Century." Based, he said, on "solidarity, fraternity, love, freedom, and equality," such socialism opposed capitalism, imperialism, and American hegemony. However Chávez did not explain its positive content, noting only that it remained a work in progress. While "Socialism of the Twenty-First Century" may have been a new phrase, its impulse had been there for a long time. Chávez, like Castro, saw himself as a potential world leader, and to further that goal he exploited anti-American feeling wherever he could.

This was already evident in December 1999, when the state of Vargas was hit with an entire week of rain, and thousands of people were buried under tons of stones and mud. The U.S. offered to send in its army with special equipment to rescue people from the debris, but the Venezuelan government refused the help. Then in August 2000, Chávez paid a solidarity visit to Saddam Hussein, the first president of a Western country to dare visit the Iraqi dictator since the Iraq war ten years earlier. Images of Hussein driving his car around Baghdad in the company of Chávez were broadcast around the world.

On his numerous trips abroad to attend summits and other conferences, Chávez criticized globalization and American imperialism. With the invasion of Iraq by the U.S. and its allies, he stepped up the anti-American rhetoric. In March 2005, Muhammad Hatami, the former president of Iran, visited Caracas, and the two countries entered into an "anti-imperialist alliance." That September 11, the fourth anniversary of the terrorist attacks on the U.S., Chávez declared that the American government itself had orchestrated them. This rhetoric reached a crescendo in Chávez's speech at the U.N. General Assembly in New York on September 22, 2006, when, referring to President Bush's recent speech to that body, he said, "The American people have the Devil at home, it smells like sulfur here . . . ."

Chávez, at the time, was working hard to get Venezuela elected to a nonpermanent seat on the Security Council. With that goal in mind he traveled to the African Union summit in July, in Gambia, and later to Belarus, Russia, Qatar, Mali, Vietnam, and Iran, with the already routine stop in Cuba to keep Fidel Castro, his mentor, posted. In August, Chávez went to Syria, where he expressed solidarity with the Palestinians and with Hezballah, and to China (for the fourth time). Venezuela, however, was not voted onto the Security Council.

Chávez signed agreements of cooperation and commercial deals with many of the nations he visited. Thus after the U.S. canceled the sale of weapons to Venezuela, Russia made the most of the circumstance and sold Venezuela 100,000 Kalashnikov rifles, 40 combat helicopters and 24 fighter-bomber airplanes. Venezuela, in turn, used the arms to foment unrest in neighboring Colombia. In January 2005, the U.S. State Department declared that the Revolutionary Army Forces of Colombia (FARC) had received Russian-made rifles from Venezuela.

Chávez was considered a friend of Colombia's narco-guerrillas. The U.S. often complained about lack of cooperation from the Venezuelan government in the fight against drug trafficking. In Apure, a Venezuelan state near the frontier, where Colombian drug terrorists had camps, they wandered freely and charged a *vacuna,* protection fee, to local ranchers and businessmen. Venezuelans living in the frontier states of Zulia and Táchira were frequent victims of kidnappings by irregular Colombian militias.

The tie with Cuba remained the centerpiece of Venezuelan foreign policy. Since February 1999, when Castro was the star guest at Chávez's first presidential inauguration, the Caracas-Havana connection constantly intensified. Venezuela sent oil to Cuba and, in exchange, Cuba sent Venezuela professionals—doctors (an estimated 18,000 of them), paramedics, sports trainers, teachers, and others. Venezuela sent groups of young people and professionals to Cuba for training, sick people to be treated in Cuban hospitals, and even tourists from low-income neighborhoods who could not afford to pay for their vacations.

Chávez traveled frequently to Havana both on official business and for private meetings. The Cuban ambassador in Caracas was guest of honor at many official events and gave numerous public speeches on Venezuela's internal affairs. Giant portraits of Chávez could be seen all over Havana and other Cuban cities, while photos of Fidel Castro and Che Guevara adorned the walls of many public buildings in Venezuela.

Despite the close relationship, there were big differences between the Cuban revolution, which developed into a classic dictatorship, and the "Bolivarian" one led by Chávez. The distinction was rooted less in any conflict of opinion betwen the two presidents than in the historical circumstances under which each came to power. Castro took over Cuba at the height of the cold war, and received considerable political and material backing—including arms—from the Soviet Union, whereas Chávez came upon the scene in a unipolar world, in which no other nation could provide him with protection from the U.S.

Unlike the situation in Cuba, Venezuela maintained the freedom to leave the country and return, protected the right to private property, and allowed economic and religious freedom. To be sure, as noted above, the Venezuelan government did not necessarily respect the "rules of the game," and the exercise of any right was subject to the president's whim.

When the Venezuelan regime attempted to emulate Cuba and introduce revolutionary ideology into the school system, it largely failed. The government, in 2001, announced plans to alter the elementary-school curriculum. Immediately, middle- and upper-class parents united against the changes. As a result, the government initiative gained traction only in some public schools, which came to be known as "Bolivarian," while the rest of the public schools and all the private institutions maintained their independence. Nevertheless, the threat of possible new moves to harness the educational system for the purposes of the regime remained, not only at the elementary level but in the secondary schools and universities as well. Unlike what happened in Cuba when Castro took power, the middle and upper classes did not leave Venzuela en masse. While some families departed in the early days of the new regime, emigration subsequently moderated. Many families kept two homes, one in Florida or another American city, and one in Venezuela. There were long lines at the Spanish, Italian, and Portuguese consulates, made up of descendants of the immigrants whose families arrived from those countries in the 1950s and 1960s. They want to obtain European Community passports, but only as a safeguard, "in case." Prosperity, the possibility of making fast, easy money, and the hope that Chávez's revolution would remain more rhetorical than real, restrained any massive emigration.

Another way in which Venzuela differed from Cuba—indeed from true dictatorships generally—was the high number of crimes against property and the prevalence of street violence. In Caracas alone, 100 minibuses were robbed, on average, each day during 2006, impelling the drivers' union to organize periodic strikes that stopped traffic on the main thoroughfares. The London-based security company Armor Group considered Venezuela a high-risk country due to its daily average of 530 crimes between 2000 and 2005, a figure that increased over the first few months of 2006.

According to UNESCO, Venezuela was at the top of the list of countries with most deaths by firearms, 22.15 deaths for every 100,000 inhabitants. The mayor of Chacao, a predominantly middle- and upper-class Caracas municipality, announced in October 2006 that of the 7 million firearms in Venezuela's streets, only 50,000 were registered. Over the course of 2006, 1,505 kidnappings took place in Venezuela.

Venezuela was the fifth largest oil exporter in the world, and Chávez took advantage of high oil prices to "buy" friends abroad. Burnishing his populist credentials, the president provided free oil to poor U.S. families in the Bronx, New England, and Milwaukee, as well as to London buses. Caribbean and Central American countries got cheap Venezuelan oil, while other nations, such as Argentina and Uruguay, received financial aid funded by oil revenues. But the biggest beneficiary, naturally, was

Cuba, which, in 2006, got 90,000 barrels of Venezuelan oil daily, of which it resold 50,000 on the international market.

Oil-generated money also paid for the technical advice and military aid that enabled Bolivia's president Evo Morales to nationalize its basic industries, according to opposition groups in that country. Funds also went for the purpose of meddling in the presidential elections of neighboring countries. There were strong indications that Venezuelan help had much to do with the victories of Morales in Bolivia, Daniel Ortega in Nicaragua, and Rafael Correa in Ecuador, and the defeats of Ollanta Humala in Peru and Andrés Manuel López Obrador in Mexico.

Chávez maintained complete control over Venezuela's finances, with no outside controls, and the public had no access to information about the national budget or public expenditures. From 2004 to 2006 the Central Bank of Venezuela transferred 24 billion dollars to governmental accounts, the exact destination of about half of the money remaining unclear. Also, Petróleos de Venezuela (PDVSA), the national oil company, transferred monies to the government with no accountability.

Despite the regime's populist rhetoric, its policies produced a new wealthy class. All across Venezuela new luxury malls were built and still more were under construction. In the streets, meanwhile, one could spot a fair number of expensive cars such as BMWs, Audis, and Mercedes Benz, and consideration was being given to importing Rolls Royce models. The year 2006 saw an astounding 51-percent jump in the sales of new cars, and overall consumption rose by 18 percent. The costs of renting and buying homes rose steeply. Extensive corruption and special privileges given to government supporters led to the emergence of a nouveau riche element often referred to as the "Bolivarian bourgeoisie," whose members often paid for their purchases in cash so as to leave no traces of the expense.

Chávez instituted programs for the poor called "missions," which were accelerated in August 2004, a few months before the scheduled recall referendum, when it appeared that his popularity was decreasing and, according to opinion polls, he might be ousted from the presidency. These "missions" included the construction of many free medical clinics, a program to increase literacy, and subsidies for food and housing. There were also attempts to introduce what was called "citizen- and worker-managed governance" of businesses, and some land was distributed to previously landless people. Four out of every ten Venezuelans received money from the "missions."

Supporters of the government claimed that these policies were bringing substantial benefits to poor Venezuelans, and cited statistics to prove it. Opponents raised doubts about the veracity of this data and countered that the effect of the programs was minimal, noting that 46 percent of the working-age population (some 5,500,000 people) still had neither regular salaries nor any social security. According to the UN, Venezuela was in 72nd place on the international Human Development Index.

Income from oil exports reached $44.875 billion by October 2006, accounting for 80 percent of the national budget. Social expenditure by the government—disbursed via the "missions"—was $5.6 billion. Venezuela's inflation rate of 16.1 percent was Latin America's highest, caused by an excess of liquidity; the growth rate was 9.4 percent; and the balance of payments with the U.S. was $34.9 billion. The government kept control of the foreign exchange. The American dollar remained at 2,150 bolivars in the domestic market and reached 3,500 bolivars in December in the black market.

Venezuela's apparent prosperity, which allowed Chávez both to finance the "missions" and to act as a global philanthropist, was entirely based on the high price of oil. Should oil prices fall, political analysts believed, these programs would have to be cut and Chávez could sustain losses both in his international support and among the domestic poor.

Ironically, despite its anti-American political stance, Venezuela continued to sell between 1,200,000 and 1,500,000 barrels of oil per day to the U.S., for an annual profit of $27–30 billion. The U.S. was also Venezuela's principal trading partner, the amount of trade increasing by 36 percent in 2005.

Anti-Israel or Anti-Semitic?

The increasingly uncertain boundary, in much of the world, between the delegitimization of Israel and the defamation of Jews was especially problematic in Venezuela, a country lacking a strong historical tradition of anti-Semitism.

The various constitutions of the country—including the most recent, promulgated under Chávez in 1999—guaranteed equal rights and obligations for all, and outlawed discrimination on the bais of ethnicity, religion, or culture. Between 1959 and 1993, political power was held by either of the two large parties, Democratic Action (Acción Democrática), which was social democratic, or Social Christian (Social Cristiano, COPEI). Both maintained good relations with the Jewish community. During the 1970s and 1980s, however, there was a great deal of anti-

Zionist agitation emanting from left-wing parties, the Soviet embassy, and the influence of Libyan president Muammar Qaddafi. This ideology made headway in the universities and among some journalists. The Confederation of Jewish Organizations in Venezuela (Confederación de Asociaciones Israelitas, CAIV), the representative body of the Jewish community, worked hard to counter their influence, and Caracas was the site of frequent visits by high-ranking Israeli officials.

Chávez made it clear that a new era in relations with Jews had begun with his presidency. Previously, the leaders of the Jewish community had always paid a courtesy call on the newly inaugurated president to convey good wishes. But Chávez ignored requests by CAIV for such a meeting, and until 2000, the Jewish community had contacts with only one high official, José Vicente Rangel, who served first as foreign minister and then as vice president.

The influence of Norberto Ceresole, the anti-Semitic Argentinean sociologist, on Chávez, as well as the president's letter to Carlos the Jackal (see above, p. 309) gave Venezuelan Jews cause for concern. In fact, neither Chávez nor his ministers—many of whom, in the 1960s, had been communists and were undoubtedly influenced by Soviet propaganda—made any anti-Semitic or anti-Israeli comments during the first years of his government, although the Chavist media published some very offensive articles and cartoons. And when Chávez finally granted an audience to the Jewish leadership in 2000, he was reported to have shown great friendliness, even expressing admiration for some of the achievements of the State of Israel.

The first serious crisis for Jews developed after a short-lived coup against the government on April 11, 2002, that lasted only 48 hours before it was put down. Vice President Rangel and other officials, as well as pro-Chávez journalists, accused Jewish conspirators and the Israeli Mossad of organizing the coup. Their major piece of evidence was a speech delivered by Rabbi Pynchas Brener, senior rabbi of the Israelite Union of Caracas, the capital's main symagogue, supporting the new government that temporarily replaced Chávez. Numerous anti-Semitic statements began to appear in the state-controlled media, and CAIV met many times with Rangel to complain about them.

The issue of Jewish involvement in the coup surfaced again on November 18, 2004, when the state prosecutor, Danilo Anderson, was assassinated by a car bomb in Caracas. Anderson was well known for prosecuting bankers and businessmen suspected of being connected with the failed coup. He was buried as a national hero. As the police began hunting for the guilty parties, some Chavist leaders again accused the Mossad. On November 29, at 6.30 a.m., police raided the site that housed the Hebraica School and the Hebraica Club, on the east side of Caracas, searching, the police later claimed, for the explosives used in Anderson's murder. None were found.

The raid sparked outrage both within the country and abroad, but despite virtually universal condemnation by the international press, the government offered no explanation or apology. Two weeks after the raid, Foreign Minister Alí Rodríguez assured CAIV's president in a private meeting that the Venezuelan government was neither anti-Semitic nor anti-Israel. Some time later a number of the policemen acknowledged, in private conversation, that they made a mistake based on an accusation by an employee Hebraica had fired.

MOUNTING PRESSURE

In the summer of 2005, possibly in preparation for the strengthening of Chávez's relations with Iran and Syria, which would occur in a few months, the Venezuelan media launched an unprecedented anti-Israel and anti-Jewish campaign. Telesur, the Venezuela-based TV station that broadcast through much of Latin America, went on the air in July. During its first four days, Telesur ran, several times a day, a program dedicated to the tragedy of the Palestinian people who were "stripped of their land by Israel," and to Israeli attacks against Palestinians civilians.

Also, Venezolana de Televisión, an official government TV channel, began broadcasting a two-hour program every evening called *La Hojilla* (The Razor Blade), a humor show that President Chávez said he watched regularly. It featured numerous jokes and hostile remarks aimed at Jews— portraying Rabbi Brener as a conspirator and Jewish doctors as guilty of malpractice—and promoted books such as the *Protocols of the Elders of Zion* and *Hitler's War* by David Irving. In 2006, such material became both more offensive and more common on the show.

The National Radio of Venezuela, meanwhile, showcased a historian named Vladimir Acosta who denied that the Holocaust had six million victims and compared Israeli army actions in the Palestinian territories with Nazi crimes against Jews. He said, "Today Gaza is the new Auschwitz," and "Israelis massacre Arabs to do ethnic cleansing."

The print media spouted similar themes. The newspaper *VEA,* an outlet for government propaganda whose editor was an 80-year-old communist, regularly published offensive caricatures and articles. Another official paper, *El Diario de Caracas,* made available for free in hospitals, private clinics, and governmental offices, published two articles in 2006 over Arab-sounding names that called on the Venezuelan people to expel the Jews from the country. There was other evidence that such sentiments were approved by the regime. Venezuela hosted the 2005 World Youth Congress. Every passenger arriving at the Simón Bolívar International Airport in Caracas received a brochure, published by the Ministry of Tourism, containing anti-Zionist messages. The walls of the Sephardi synagogue, located in the center of Caracas, suddenly became frequent targets of graffiti—swastikas and offensive slogans—scrawled by Chavists.

On December 24, 2005, Chávez delivered a Christmas speech in which he referred to the "minority" that, he said, hoarded the world's wealth, and described its members as "the heirs of Christ's murderers." Perhaps not coincidentally, Chávez announced, in early January 2006, an alliance with Iranian president Mahmoud Ahmadinejad, and said he would invite him to visit Venezuela.

Reaction came swiftly. The Simon Wiesenthal Center in Buenos Aires accused Chávez of anti-Semitism. The president, on January 13, denied the charge and denounced the U.S. for organizing a defamation campaign against him. The daily Caracas newspaper *El Nacional,* in its January 21 issue, published a manifesto signed by more than 300 Venezuelan intellectuals rejecting the anti-Semitic innuendoes of Chávez's Christmas speech and denouncing his overture to the president of Iran "who has denied the Holocaust."

On January 31, 2006, President Chávez met with leaders of the five organizations that formed CAIV. Attempting to put the best face possible on the situation, they told Chávez that they did not consider him an anti-Semite, offered him a dossier of the anti-Semitic statements being made in the media, and asked him to take action to bring them to a halt. On February 16, two high-level U.S. officials, Secretary of State Condoleezza Rice and UN ambassador John Bolton, called Chávez an anti-Semite. The government's reply came the same day in an official statement by Vice President José Vicente Rangel, who said American imperialism had lied. Rangel declared: "The State of Venezuela and its government have the best relations with the State of Israel and its government and with the Venezuelan Jewish community. This is an unchanging policy, a state policy, and it is not subject to changes."

But when Israel launched its war against Hezballah in Lebanon in July, Chávez immediately condemned Israel. During the course of the war, both within Venezuela and on his trips abroad, Chávez accused Israel of genocide, and compared its military actions to the Nazi Holocaust.

The government also organized rallies in Caracas and other cities, attended mostly by public employees, against Israel and Zionism. The National Assembly, made up entirely of members loyal to Chávez, approved a resolution on July 6 condemning the State of Israel for "its criminal actions" in Lebanon, one clause reading, "The Israeli war arsenal and all its arms industry could not defeat the Intifada's child-heroes and patriots' hope."

A leader of the Venezuelan Syrian community thanked Chávez for his support of the Palestinian cause and said that the million-and-a-half Arabs living in Venezuela would support him for reelection in December. In fact, no one knew how many Arabs there were in the country, and there was no history of antagonism between Jews and Arabs in Venezuela. In the rallies against Israel organized by the government in July and August, Arabs were not prominent participants.

Nevertheless, some active Arab leaders of the pro-Palestinian and anti-Israel cause held offices in Chávez's government and represented his party in the National Assembly. The best known was Vice Minister of Internal Affairs Tarek El Aissami, whose ministry was responsible for the police and the justice system. He was the son of the leader of the Baath party in Venezuela, and his great-uncle was a close collaborator of Saddam Hussein. El Aissami was the author of numerous anti-Zionist and anti-Semitic articles.

Chávez arrived in Tehran on July 28 for a meeting with President Ahmadinejad. The two men signed several bilateral agreements, and Chávez offered "Venezuela's unconditional support to Iran." On August 2, Chávez announced the recall of the Venezuelan ambassador to Israel with the following words: "It causes indignation to see the State of Israel bombing, running over, murdering and mutilating with the gringo airplanes and the high military power thanks to American support."

In fact, for more than a year there had been no actual Venezuelan ambassador in Israel, the consulate and embassy offices in Tel Aviv had been closed, and it was impossible for any citizen with an Israeli passport to obtain a Venezuelan visa. At the time Chávez announced the recall, his country was represented only by a recently sent business attaché. Israel responded by withdrawing its ambassador from Caracas. But he would return a few weeks later, and, in November, the Venezuelan consulate reopened its doors in Tel Aviv without the Venezuelan press reporting it.

In mid-August a delegation of eight women representatives, among them the president of the National Assembly, traveled to Damascus to offer a solidarity message to the Lebanese people, humanitarian aid, and help for Venezuelan citizens trapped in the war zone. This was followed, on August 29, by a Chávez visit to Syria, where he signed cooperation agreements with President Assad, invited him to visit Venezuela, and once again vilified Israel.

In an effort to mediate between Chávez and world Jewry, Argentinean president Néstor Kirchner had arranged a meeting in Buenos Aires on July 27 for Chávez and Israel Singer, chairman of the World Jewish Congress. Immediately afterward, both men told the press that their talks were productive.

On September 1, however, Singer published an article in the *Jerusalem Post* claiming that the Venezuelan president seemed to believe, erroneously, that opposition to Israel was compatible with good relations with his country's Jews. Singer wrote: "Chávez told us [in Buenos Aires] that he does not have debates with Venezuelan Jews and that he considers them dear citizens . . . . Chávez hates President George W. Bush and vilifies Israel. He meets with Ahmadinejad and courts Syria. Perhaps he really thinks Jews can be separated from Israel, but it is impossible. He cannot be a terrorist's friend and receive support from civilized nations."

Iranian president Ahmadinejad paid an official state visit to Venezuela on September 17. The two presidents called each other "brothers" and signed various agreements. Declaring his support for Iran's nuclear program, Chávez said, "We are the same nation and the same revolution."

Despite the government's clear anti-Israel/anti-Jewish line, it remained doubtful, as 2006 drew to a close, whether these views were shared by much of the population. Probably 90 percent of Venezuelans—the relatively poor and uneducated—had little or no knowledge of the Jewish community or of Middle East issues. And among the economic and social elites that were alienated from the Chávez's government—including what remained of the independent press and the privately owned media—there seemed to be a growing sympathy for Israel and solidarity with the Venezuelan Jews who were under attack from the government.

JEWISH COMMUNITY

About 15,000 Jews lived in Venezuela, the great majority of them in Caracas, the capital. Although there were no exact statistics on the number of Jews who emigrated since Chávez assumed power, the decline in enrollment at the Jewish school in Caracas, which almost all Jewish children attended, suggested that between 10 and 15 percent of the community had left by 2006.

The Jewish community in the country was first organized in 1930, when Spanish-speaking Sephardi Jews from Tetuan and other Moroccan cities founded the Israelite Association of Venezuela (Asociación Israelita de Venezuela). Another wave of Sephardi immigrants arrived in the late 1950s and early 1960s from Spanish Morocco, and easily assimilated into the community. Ashkenazi Jews, mostly natives of Poland, Romania, and Germany, many of them Holocaust survivors, established the Israelite Union of Caracas (Unión Israelita de Caracas) in 1950.

The two communities maintained a certain distance from each other until the Sephardim decided to become involved in the Moral y Luces Herzl-Bialik School, previously established by the Ashkenazim. In 1976 both communities, together with the Zionist Federation of Venezuela (Federación Sionista de Venezuela) and the B'nai B'rith Hebrew Fraternity (Fraternidad Hebrea B'nai B'rith) formed an umbrella body, the Confederation of Jewish Organizations in Venezuela (la Confederación de Asociaciones Israelitas de Venezuela, or CAIV) to represent Jewish interests before the government, in the media, and abroad.

In the late 1970s the Israelite Union and Israelite Association jointly established Hebraica, a social, cultural and sports center in Caracas that also housed the elementary and high schools. Some 90 percent of Jewish children and teenagers attended, about 35 percent of them on scholarship. The fact that both groups patronized these schools had the effect of encouraging marriages between Sephardi and Ashkenazi youngsters and blurring differences between the communities. The two main synagogues remained independent, and other small synagogues were later founded. A separate Orthodox school, Sinai, also functioned

The overwhelming majority of Venezuelan Jews worked in business and industry, or were professionals, such as doctors, engineers, architects, and, to a lesser degree, lawyers. They generally avoided politics. Among younger Jews there were some working in cinema, literature, and the visual arts.

The Jewish community newspaper, El Nuevo Mundo Israelita, appeared every Friday. The Center for Sephardic Studies published a magazine, Maguén-Escudo, four times a year, and the Chabad community had its own magazine, Rumbo a tu Judaísmo (Towards Your Judaism). The Morris E. Curiel Sephardic Museum did not have its own physical site, but curated exhibitions in a number of public places. The Israelite Union presented exhibitions and documentary films about the history of the Ashkenazi community, and published books about the experiences of the immigrants and Shoah survivors.

A number of women's organizations were active, the best known among them being WIZO. These groups cooperated in organized a joint body, the Venezuelan Federation of Jewish Women, in 2001, which became a member of CAIV. The Jewish community operated a health center, Yolanda Katz, which gave free treatment to people of any religion who had no financial resources. Several organizations cared for elderly Jews and the poor.

Jewish life outside the capital was minimal. Thus, so many of the Jews who used to live in Maracaibo, in the state of Zulia, moved to Caracas, that the Maracaibo Jewish school had to accept gentile students in order to survive. There were small Jewish communities in Valencia, in the state of Carabobo — a two-hour ride from Caracas — and on Margarita Island.

Andrés Bello Catholic University, a Jesuit institution, administered the Sigmund and Annie Rotter Institute of Contemporary Judaism and Shoah Studies. The Rotters had been Holocaust survivors, and their children supported the institute. Its director, Prof. Carlos de Armas, developed a program that taught religious and ethnic tolerance to students majoring in education and journalism.

The most heavily attended event in the history of the Jewish community occurred on January 27, 2005, when CAIV commemorated the 60th anniversary of the liberation of Auschwitz. More than 2,000 people were present, about half of them non-Jews. Even though President Chávez and his ministers were invited, only Vice President Rangel attended. A Chavist member of the National Assembly read aloud a statement of solidarity approved unanimously by that body.

In 2006, despite the clear hostility of Chávez's government, Jews were not acting as an intimidated community. They kept up their normal activities, celebrating large weddings and attending synagogue services — the men with *kippot* on their heads. The community continued to maintain its Zionist identity and its close ties to Israel.

Twice during 2006 — in July, when the National Assembly approved a resolution condemning Israel for the war in Lebanon, and in September, when the Iranian president visited — CAIV published statements of protest in some Caracas newspapers. What it would not do, however, was hold public demonstrations for Israel or against Ahmadinejad. Since the government did not shrink from mobilizing groups of rowdies to attack its opponents and break up rallies, taking to the streets was too risky.

The Venezuelan Jewish community, although still functioning more or less normally, was living a reality that was unlike that lived in the past, and certainly far different from the one lived by Jews elsewhere in the West.

PAULINA GAMUS

Brazil

National Affairs

DEMOGRAPHY

According to the Brazilian Institute of Geography and Statistics (IBGE), Brazil had about 185,000,000 inhabitants at the end of 2006. The last official census, completed in 2000, registered a population of approximately 169,000,000. Multiethnic and multicultural, Brazil counted the largest populations of African and Japanese *descent* of any country in the world. According to the 2000 census, which relied on self-identification for racial categorization, Brazil's was 53.7 percent "white," 38.5 percent "mixed-race," 6.2 percent "black," 0.5 percent "Asian," and 0.4 percent "Amerindian." Many of the Brazilians classified as "white" were of European and Middle Eastern background. In recent years the country had attracted significant numbers of Koreans, Chinese, and Palestinians.

Although about 75 percent of the population defined itself as Roman Catholic, the common description of Brazil as the world's largest Catholic country was somewhat misleading, as many self-identified Catholics (more than five million) also practiced syncretistic Afro-Catholic religions, and sometimes other religions as well. The rapidly growing Protestant population had passed the 25-million mark and represented about 15 percent of the population. The overwhelming majority of these were evangelicals, many of them Pentecostal. Some major cities contained more non-Catholic Christians than Catholics. The growing political presence of evangelicals, who strongly supported Israel and Zionism, had the effect of bringing discussions of Jewish-related issues out of the parochial Jewish sphere and into the larger public square. Other religions represented in significant numbers were Islam (the census counted only 28,000, but the actual number was undoubtedly somewhere between one and three million), Spiritism (mainly Kardecists), with two million adherents and representing more than 1 percent of the population, Buddhism, and the so-called New Japanese Religions.

Brazil was one of the most unequal societies in the world, whether measured by income, health, land ownership, or education, and therefore faced difficult policy dilemmas. President Luis Inácio Lula da Silva, elected in 2002, continued the country's now decade-long commitment to open markets, an export/import-based economy, and a relatively free-floating currency. 2006 was a year of modest inflation, slightly over 3 percent, while the economy enjoyed the ninth largest GDP in the world with a growth rate of slightly over 2 percent. Predictions for 2007 were a growth rate of about 3.5 percent and an inflation rate of over 4 percent.

To address the large gap between social classes, President Lula had instituted the Bolsa Família (family grant) plan, which provided funds to poor families on condition that children attend school and undergo vaccination. Even so, about 20 percent of the population—more than 40 million people—still lived below the poverty line, and the Movimento dos Trabalhadores Rurais Sem Terra (Landless Rural Workers' Movement, or MST) continued to challenge the government, charging that Lula and his party had not followed through on their commitment to institute land reform. The 1988 Brazilian constitution had strengthened earlier provisions stating that unutilized lands could be taken over by the government and distributed to landless people, but few of the latter had the financial resources to take advantage of the opportunity and farm the land.

Some MST leaders sought to link their plight to that of the Palestinians. In July 2006 the MST officially declared: "WE DEMAND AN IMMEDIATE HALT TO ISRAEL'S AGRESSION AGAINST THE ARAB PEOPLE," and linked the Israel-Hezballah war to international free-trade agreements and the issue of land reform in Brazil.

The Brazilian constitution allowed the president to serve two four-year terms, and thus President Lula, the candidate of the Workers' Party (PT), ran for a second term in the national elections held in October. The other major candidates were Geraldo Alckmin representing the Brazilian Social Democratic Party (PSDB), and Senator Heloísa Helena, who founded the Socialism and Freedom Party (PSOL) following her expulsion from the Workers' Party for refusing to go along with its neoliberal economic policies. Four minor candidates were also in the race.

The main divide that ran through the campaign might be characterized as scandal vs. poverty reduction. Throughout 2006 Brazilians were transfixed by what came to be known as the *Mensalão* (monthly payment) affair, an apparent votes-for-cash scheme. Accusations first surfaced in 2005, when a member of Congress told reporters that the Workers' Party had paid a number of his colleagues more than US$10,000 per month to vote for certain legislation.

As a result of the scandal many key advisers to President Lula, as well as the head of the Workers' Party, resigned, although the president himself did not appear to be directly involved and no verdicts of guilt were issued by any court. Opposition candidates sought to win votes by criticizing the president for excessive leniency toward the wrongdoers in his party. But the Workers' Party, sure that the masses of voters were more interested in policy than in scandal, spotlighted the benefits of the Bolsa Família plan.

No candidate received a majority in the first round of the voting, a result that most political commentators understood as a slap on the wrist to the Workers' Party for its involvement in the scandals. The second round was held on October 29 between Lula and Alckmin. The president, a charismatic former union leader, maintained the persona he had assumed in the 2002 campaign, that of a well-dressed neo-social democrat à la Tony Blair. Indeed, in spite of the leftist image the U.S. press frequently gave him, along with Presidents Hugo Chávez (Venezuela) and Fidel Castro (Cuba), the Brazilian intellectual left attacked Lula for his liberal policies, especially his commitment to abide by International Monetary Fund agreements, which had led dissatisfied leftists to form the above-mentioned PSOL. Even so, Lula continued in 2006 to be seen as a champion of the poor and dispossessed.

Alckmin, on the other hand, represented a center-right, technocratic approach. He was a physician, a trained anesthesiologist who had worked in a São Paulo public hospital. Alckmin became governor of the state of São Paulo in 2001, and there he instituted state-run health and education programs funded through the privatization of public and state-owned companies.

President Lula won the run-off with over 60 percent of the vote, as Alckmin received fewer votes in the run-off than he had in the first round. While the breakdown of the balloting was largely along class lines, a good number of industrialists and businesspeople supported Lula because of his neoliberal economic policies, particularly the strengthening of the real, Brazil's unit of currency, which rose markedly against the U.S. dollar in 2006. Two of President Lula's most important advisors were Jewish, and he actively courted the support of the Jewish community.

Brazil also held state, gubernatorial, and congressional elections in 2006. The major winners, in terms of percentage of votes, were the Worker's Party, the Brazilian Democratic Movement Party (Partido do Movimento Democrático Brasileiro), the Brazilian Social Democratic Party (Partido da Social-Democracia Brasileira), and the Liberal Front Party (Partido da Frente Liberal).

Israel and the Middle East

Brazil took a middle-of-the-road position on Middle East issues. The Brazilian government continued its strong support of UN Security Council resolutions, including those calling for an end to Israeli occupation of Palestinian territories. Brazil also backed the peaceful creation of a democratic state of Palestine, based on the Beirut Declaration by the League of Arab States and the proposals formulated by the "Quartet" (the U.S., EU, UN, and Russia), including the recognition by all parties of Israel's right to exist. Brazil belonged to the "Rio Group," which had consistently endorsed an immediate cessation of all acts of terrorism, provocation, incitement, and destruction in the Middle East.

Brazil had strong trade relations with Israel, especially in the areas of agriculture, technology, and water usage. A major challenge to Brazil's Middle East policy came in July, during the Israel-Hezballah war, when a Brazilian family of four (including two children) of Lebanese descent was killed in the bombing of Srifa, and another Brazilian child was killed in a strike on Tallousa. Brazilian foreign minister Celso Amorim condemned both incidents. His ministry declared it was "dismayed" at the deaths and opposed to what it termed Israel's "disproportional reaction." It also argued strenuously for dialogue, a cease-fire, and the release of the kidnapped Israeli soldiers.

During the war, Rabbi Henry Sobel, chief rabbi of the Congregação Israelita Paulista and president of the Brazilian Jewish Confederation, helped lead a campaign among Brazilians of Jewish and Lebanese backgrounds to collect clothes, medications, and money for the victims of the conflict. Nevertheless, those of Jewish and Arab descent saw the war quite differently from each other, and the two communities held separate peace rallies in São Paulo in August.

Racism and Anti-Semitism

Despite frequent claims by the Brazilian elite that the country was a "racial democracy," social and economic discrimination against those of African descent was widespread, and the latter often complained about their treatment. There was a high correlation between race and income, with darker-skinned people generally far poorer than others. As Brazilians from the impoverished northeastern part of the country continued to move south into large urban centers like São Paulo and Rio de Janeiro, the number of physical attacks on them grew.

Since the Workers' Party won control of the government in 2002, there had been increasing public acceptance of the fact that racism was a problem in Brazil. Movimento Negro (Black Movement), a broad coalition of Afro-Brazilian groups, was particularly active in consciousness-raising, and many states, cities, and large organizations now had offices that combated racism. A public debate over quotas and affirmative action developed during 2006, and the federal and some state governments began instituting such policies. Some universities, especially those located in areas with large populations of Brazilians of African descent, also instituted affirmative-action programs. The universities had previously been traditional strongholds of "white" Brazilian privilege.

There was virtually no open anti-Semitism. While radical groups occasionally linked Israel to domestic issues (see above, p. 000), even the Anti-Defamation League was able to report only one actual anti-Semitic incident for all of 2006: during the war in Lebanon, rocks were thrown at a synagogue in Campinas (a city of about one million about an hour and a half from São Paulo), and the perpetrators wrote, "Lebanon, the true Holocaust," on the sidewalk.

Several factors kept anti-Semitism to a minimum. First, there was limited contact between the relatively small community of Jews, on the one hand, and the mass of Brazil's impoverished urban and rural people, on the other. Also, Brazil's strong rhetorical commitment to ethnic, cultural, and racial tolerance was backed up by law, making public anti-Semitism a crime. Finally, the wide publicity given to the involvement of some Jewish community leaders in popular movements to combat hunger, poverty, and discrimination gave Brazil's Jews a reputation for social and economic progressivism.

Politicians both at the national level and in major cities considered the Brazilian Jewish vote important enough to warrant politicking in synagogues and Jewish community centers. President Lula was particularly outspoken in condemning anti-Semitism, supporting a World Jewish Congress petition to the UN denouncing anti-Semitism, and repeatedly rejecting all manifestations of Holocaust denial.

Outright anti-Semitic movements in Brazil attracted very few participants. One moribund old group, the Integralists, had its origins in the Ação Integralista Brasileira of the 1930s, which, at its height, had close to one million members. Banned, along with all other political parties, in 1937, it was reconstituted with the return to democracy in 1988, and operated largely in the interior of the state of São Paulo. Two groups, in fact, now competed for the Integralist mantle, the Frente Integralista Brasileira (Brazilian Integralist Front) and the Movimento Integralista e Linearista

Brasileira (Brazilian Integralist and Linearist Movement). Both combined had no more than a few hundred adherents.

There was also a neo-Nazi political party, the Brazilian National Revolutionary Party (PNRB), which had about 200 sympathizers nationwide, plus a number of even smaller groups made up largely of skinheads. While their discourse was at times anti-Semitic, they were committed to generic bigotry and thuggery and did not especially target Jews. Based in the industrial suburbs surrounding Brazil's largest cities, they tended to victimize migrants from the impoverished northeastern states of the country, those of African descent, and homosexuals.

Holocaust-Related Issues

In 2006 President Lula and his cabinet visited the Congregação Israelita Paulista, Latin America's largest synagogue, on Holocaust Memorial Day.

Brazil's best-known Holocaust denier was Siegfied Ellwanger Castan, an elderly, wealthy industrialist who lived in the state of Rio Grande do Sul. Castan's publishing company, Editôra Revisão (Revision Publishing House), had for many years distributed large quantities of books with titles like *Holocaust: Jewish or German?* and *The Lie of the Century.* Distribution of such publications was illegal under Brazil's antiracism laws, and Castan's earlier conviction by the Rio Grande do Sul State Court was confirmed in 2006 by the Supreme Court. He received a prison sentence of 15 months, which could be served through community service. The Supreme Court conviction raised concerns on the part of some advocates of free speech.

A Brazilian of Lebanese descent was awarded second prize by the Iranian Ministry of Culture in its contest for editorial cartoons about the Holocaust. This particular cartoon linked the plight of Palestinians to that of Jews during the Holocaust. Since it did not constitute Holocaust denial and was not, strictly speaking, anti-Semitic, it was not illegal under Brazilian law.

JEWISH COMMUNITY

Demography

The contemporary Brazilian Jewish community, which originated largely after 1920, was ethnically diverse, encompassing Ashkenazim (primarily of Polish and German descent) and Sephardim (a plurality among them of Egyptian descent). Information collected from the 2000 census showed a Jewish population of 86,825, almost all of whom lived in urban areas. Some Brazilian Jewish organizations believed this to be an undercount and placed the number between 120,000 and 140,000.

Probably the most reliable estimate came from Israeli demographer Sergio DellaPergola, who estimated the size of the Jewish population at 96,500 in 2006, a decline from the 1980 figure of 100,000. This made Brazilian Jewry the tenth largest Jewish community in the world. Breakout numbers from the census suggested considerable intermarriage with non-Jews.

The largest Jewish community was in São Paulo, Brazil's most populous city. The Albert Einstein Jewish Hospital sponsored a study of the Jewish community of São Paulo in 2002, which showed a Jewish population of 60,000 out of a total of 10.4 million, significantly higher than the official census figure of 44,000. The findings of this study must be used with caution, however, since DellaPergola, a consultant on the project, publicly cast doubt on the methodologies used. According to the Einstein data, some 60 percent of Jews in São Paulo attended synagogue only on High Holy Days or for social activities, about 14 percent attended weekly, some 13 percent never attended, and 3 percent—representing a small but growing Orthodox community—went every day. The study also showed a low number of students in Jewish day schools.

The second largest Jewish community was in Rio de Janeiro (25,000–30,000 Jews out of a population of 5.85 million), and the third largest in Porto Alegre, Rio Grande do Sul (10,000–12,000 Jews in a population of about 1.36 million). Other significant communities were in Belo Horizonte, Curitiba, Santos, and Recife.

Communal Affairs

The central umbrella body representing all the Jewish federations and communities in Brazil was the Confederação Israelita do Brasil (CONIB), founded in 1951. It included 200 organizations engaged in promoting Jewish and Zionist activities, education, culture, and charity. The Jewish Federation of São Paulo had a standing commission dedicated to fighting racism, and the São Paulo-based Latin American Jewish Committee Section for Interreligious Affairs actively combated racial hatred, with support from the Brazilian National Commission for Catholic-Jewish

Dialogue, an affiliate of the National Conference of Brazilian Bishops. Representatives of local Jewish federations participated on the advisory boards of the special police units that operated in each of the states to investigate racial crimes. All the major international Zionist organizations and youth movements were active in Brazil.

Jewish aid agencies—most notably UNIBES (Jewish Brazilian Social Welfare Association, an umbrella group for a number of agencies) and the Congregação Israelita Paulista Children's Home—served Brazilians of all faiths, and were repeatedly awarded national recognition for their contributions to society. Brazilian Jews published a number of newspapers and journals in Portuguese. The cities with large Jewish populations had luxurious Jewish community centers that hosted a significant number of Jewish cultural and social activities.

Culture

Books about Jews and Jewish issues in Brazil have tended to be hagiographic or memorializing, or to address the varying interpretations of Brazilian immigration policy during World War II. In recent years there was a rise in the number of published religious texts, both Christian and Jewish, in the country, signaling the commensurate growth of Protestant evangelicalism and strictly Orthodox Judaism.

Caio Hamburger's film debut, *O ano em que meus pais saíram em viagem de férias* (The Year My Parents Went on a Holiday Trip), which takes place in a traditional Jewish neighborhood in São Paulo, was a box-office success, and was among the Brazilian films chosen to represent the country at the Berlin Film Festival. A number of major cities held Jewish film festivals that presented a wide range of features and documentaries from around the world on Jewish themes. The Israeli film *Free Zone*, directed by Amos Gitai, did very well in Brazil, going into regular release in São Paulo, Rio de Janeiro, and Porto Alegre.

Brazilian Jewry, like many other Jewish communities in the Americas, continued its fascination with "Sephardism." In Brazil particularly, Ashkenazi and Sephardi Jews, as well as non-Jews, were drawn by the cultural myth that many of the Portuguese explorers of the country in the fifteenth and sixteenth centuries were secret Jews, a belief that had become widespread in elite and middle-class culture.

The growth in the number of M.A. and Ph.D. degrees awarded by major Brazilian universities on topics of Jewish interest signified the emergence of Jewish studies as an important field of research.

Personalia

Perhaps the biggest news story about a "Jewish" personality in 2006 was the death of comedian Cláudio Besserman Vianna (known as Bussunda), who succumbed to a heart attack at the age of 43 while in Germany covering the World Cup. Bussunda was part of a comedy crew known for satirical television shows and films. His humor was not "Jewish" in any traditional sense, and few people knew that Bussunda was a Jew; unlike the case in the U.S., Brazilian Jewish cultural figures rarely identified publicly as Jews. In fact, Bussunda spent his childhood summers in Rio de Janeiro's Kinderland, run by socially and politically progressive Jews, and belonged to a Zionist youth organization. His mother, the psychoanalyst Helena Besserman Vianna, was well-known in Brazil for her denunciation of psychiatrists and psychologists who participated in torture under Brazil's military dictatorship from 1964 to 1984. At the request of his family, Bussunda was buried in a non-Jewish cemetery, and consequently many Brazilians were surprised, and some Jews angry, when Rio de Janeiro's Jewish federation took out memorial advertisements for him.

An equally complicated situation was the reburial of Iara Iavelberg in the Jewish cemetery in Butantã, the ceremony conducted by Rabbi Henry Sobel of Congregação Israelita Paulista. Iavelberg, who had belonged to an antigovernment group that fought against the military dictatorship, was captured by the regime in 1971 at the age of 27 and then mysteriously died. At the time, the government insisted that she had committed suicide, and on that basis she was denied burial in the Jewish cemetery. But since the end of the dictatorship many so-called "suicides in prison" had been shown to be murders. The reburial marked the end of a long legal dispute between Iavelberg's family, which sought the reburial, and the São Paulo *hevrah kadishah,* which was in charge of Jewish burials. Many national leaders as well as the head of the leftist MST (see above, p. 000) attended the ceremony.

The best-known Jews leader in Brazil was probably Rabbi Sobel, in large part because of his activities against discrimination and poverty, and his engagement in interreligious dialogue. Rabbi Nilton Bonder of Rio de Janeiro's Congregação Judaica do Brasil, known as the "green rabbi," wrote extensively, applying Jewish tradition and mysticism to spiritual matters as well as social issues such as the environment. Much of Bonder's work appeared in newspapers that were popular among evangelicals. The Safras, former owners of Banco Safra, constituted one of the most prominent Sephardi families in Brazil. The country's most popular television personality was Silvio Santos (born Senor Abravanel, of Greek Jewish parentage), who was increasingly asserting his Jewish identity. Four Jews were members of the Academia Brasileira de Letras, Brazil's most prominent literary organization. They were Moacyr Scliar, whose works often dealt with Jewish topics; José Mindlin, now retired as director of Metaleve Industries, a large international producer of metal products such as pistons, bearings, and oil pumps, who did much to preserve rare Brazilian books; political scientist and former foreign minister Celso Lafer; and journalist and essayist Arnaldo Niskier.

JEFFREY LESSER

Western Europe

Great Britain

National Affairs

ALTHOUGH BRITAIN had enjoyed a decade without recession, high unemployment, or rampant inflation, the fortunes of Prime Minister Tony Blair and his Labour government were on the downswing. A January poll showed just 36 percent of the public satisfied with Blair's performance as compared to 31 percent who preferred Conservative leader David Cameron. A series of government scandals as well as controversy over foreign policy—particularly the wars in Iraq and Lebanon—took a further toll on the government's standing over the course of the year.

Despite an adequate majority, the government had problems getting legislation through the House of Commons. In March, for example, an education bill that created independent trust schools passed only thanks to Tory support after some 50 Labour MPs defected. The government slid from one crisis to the next. That same month, Tessa Jowell, the culture minister, was investigated on suspicion of breaking the ministerial code of conduct after Milan prosecutors accused her husband, solicitor David Mills, of accepting a £344,000 bribe from Italian prime minister Silvio Berlusconi; she was subsequently cleared.

Then came the disclosure that a number of multimillion-pound loans had secretly been given to the Labour Party before the 2005 election, and that some of the lenders had later been nominated for honors. A police inquiry followed. Not only was Blair himself questioned, but Lord Levy, the prime minister's chief fund-raiser and Middle East envoy, as well as president of Jewish Care, the family and children's service, was arrested, interrogated, and released on bail pending further inquiries. The Loans for Lords (a.k.a. Cash for Honors) affair was still ongoing at the end of the year.

In April, Home Secretary Charles Clarke resigned when it was revealed that foreign nationals had been released from prison without being considered for deportation. Hundreds, including murderers and rapists who should have been deported, had been set free. John Reid, who succeeded Clarke, admitted that the Home Office was "not fit for its purpose."

Disillusionment with the government was reflected in the May elections for local councils, as the Tories recorded their best local election result since 1992. Labour lost more than 300 councillors, its share of the vote dropping to 26 percent. In the wake of this defeat Blair reshuffled his cabinet, replacing Foreign Secretary Jack Straw with Margaret Beckett, and appointing Straw leader of the Commons. John Prescott, deputy prime minister and secretary of state for communities and local government, was relieved of the latter post because of inappropriate behaviour— including a much-publicized affair with his secretary—but retained the office of deputy prime minister.

A dawn raid on a suspected London bomb factory in June—part of the government's antiterror campaign—did nothing to enhance Labour's prestige: no bombs were found and police shot an innocent bystander. A more successful operation was conducted in August, when Scotland Yard claimed to have thwarted a plot to blow up planes flying from the UK to the U.S.

Hostilities between Israel and Hezballah in Lebanon, which erupted during Parliament's summer recess, plunged the government into yet another crisis. In August, Jim Sheridan, a Scottish MP, quit his post as parliamentary private secretary to the Ministry of Defense because of Blair's continuing support for American foreign policy, claiming in particular that American planes carrying arms to Israel were using Scottish airports to refuel. And in September, several ministers, incensed at Blair's failure to call for a ceasefire in Lebanon, pushed for an emergency recall of Parliament from its recess. Then 17 MPs who had formerly been loyal Labour supporters signed a letter calling for Blair's resignation and a change in party leadership as the only way to maintain the government. A junior minister and six government aides resigned when Blair, confirming his intention to stand down by September 2007, refused to name a departure date. Chancellor of the Exchequer Gordon Brown was still assumed to be his successor, and polls in December showed greater satisfaction with the way Brown was doing his job than with the performance of any other Labour politician.

The Conservatives, meanwhile, were given a new lease on life by their young leader David Cameron, and by December the polls showed that

37 percent of those questioned would definitely vote Conservative, 36 percent Labour, and 18 percent Liberal Democrat. Changed leadership did not profit the Liberal Democrats, who elected Sir Menzies Campbell, aged 65, as their leader in March, to replace Charles Kennedy, who had to resign in January after confessing a drinking problem.

Israel and the Middle East

THE GOVERNMENT

At the synagogue service marking the 350th anniversary of the readmission of Jews to the country (see below, pp. 346–47), Prime Minister Blair said, "Britain will always be a true friend of Israel." That proved true during 2006, in defiance, at times, of British public opinion. When Israeli prime minister Ehud Olmert visited London in June, he said that Anglo-Israeli friendship was stronger than ever.

Britain took an unwavering stance against the democratically elected Hamas government in the Palestinian territories, which was committed to Israel's destruction. In February the Foreign Office warned Hamas that there would be no official contact until it recognized Israel and halted terrorism. In a similar vein, Blair told a press conference that British support for the creation of a Palestinian state would cease if Hamas did not abandon violence.

The Palestinian people, however, starved of foreign aid by the West's boycott of Hamas, remained an object of concern. Deploring "the senseless and unjustified" suicide attack on a Tel Aviv falafel bar during Passover (see above, p. 226), Foreign Secretary Straw told a press conference in April that Britain had to be sure that money for Palestinians in need would not filter through Hamas front organizations into funding terrorism. The Department for International Development announced that Britain's £15m aid to Palestinian refugees would be distributed by UNWRA, the UN agency that provided support to the Palestinians, and in May a Foreign Office spokesman said that Israel and the "Quartet" (the U.S., the UN, Russia, and the EU) had accepted this British initiative.

On his June visit to Great Britain, Olmert received qualified support for his "realignment" plan of redrawing Israel's eastern borders unilaterally, although Britain would have preferred Israel to negotiate directly with the Palestinians. Olmert found Blair's "language, attitude and commitment extremely encouraging," but the visit was clouded by reports that IDF bullets had killed Palestinian civilians, including a family picnicking on a Gaza beach. Britain's support for Israel continued even in July, when fighting in Gaza and Lebanon altered the situation. Blair placed the blame on Hezballah, Hamas, and their sponsors in Tehran and Damascus, at the same time stressing that Israel's retaliation must be proportional and minimize civilian casualties. Blair told the House of Commons that the conflict would only end when the kidnapped Israeli soldiers were released and rockets stopped falling on Haifa. Yet in August, International Development Minister Hilary Benn, announcing a doubling of British aid for the reconstruction of Lebanon, bluntly criticized Israeli actions, saying, "It would be very hard to describe the blowing up of power stations and water purification plants as proportionate."

Britain made a bid for a more active role in the peace process. After Lord Levy traveled to Israel and the Palestinian territories for preliminary meetings in August, the prime minister himself arrived in September. "Mr. Blair played a pivotal role in emphasizing the importance of empowering moderates," reported Miri Eisen, the Israeli premier's foreign media advisor, after Blair met Palestinian president Abbas in Ramallah. "His meeting with Olmert," she told the *Jewish Chronicle* of London, "was exceptional in its frankness and openness," and added that Blair, a friend of Israel, also knew how to criticize it in "a very British way."

Back in England, at the Labour Party conference in September, Blair pledged to maintain the search for Middle East peace as a priority, but stressed that no British initiative could succeed without American support. In response to criticism for not urging Israel to accept a cease-fire in Lebanon, Blair said, "The only way the conflict is going to end is when there is a Lebanese government in control of the whole community." Around that time a poll of 625 Israeli adults taken by the British embassy in Tel Aviv found that an overwhelming majority of Israelis saw Blair as a "true friend of Israel," and that about 40 percent viewed British policy as pro-Israel.

The British Foreign Office, in a report issued in October, said it was "deeply concerned" about Syria's support for Hezballah, and condemned once again the abduction of Israeli soldiers and the rocket attacks on Israel. The next month the Foreign Office stated that it continued to press for the return of Cpl. Gilad Shalit, the IDF soldier kidnapped by Hamas in Gaza, and that it was essential "that the Palestinian Authority make every effort to prevent terrorism as set out in the 'road map.'" Israel did not escape criticism either. The Foreign Office expressed concern at its failure to respect Palestinian human rights, its policy of targeted killings, and the firing of shells near populated regions of the Gaza Strip. It urged the IDF to try to avoid civilian casualties and the Israeli government to halt settlement construction and the building of a security barrier on Palestinian land, activity that "was contrary to international law and may threaten the viability of the agreed two-state solution."

The year ended with a flurry of diplomatic activity. Israeli foreign minister Tzipi Livni came to London in November for meetings with Blair and the newly appointed foreign secretary, Margaret Beckett. Livni called for a continuation of the international boycott of the Hamas-led Palestinian Authority as a means of boosting the PA's moderate president, Mahmoud Abbas. Beckett traveled to Lebanon in December to express British support for its elected government. Both the Queen's speech at the opening of Parliament and Blair's address at the Lord Mayor's Banquet at London's Guildhall in November emphasized Britain's commitment to building an alliance of moderate governments in the Middle East, which, Blair said, was at "the core" of the fight against global extremism and terrorism. To this end he urged moderate Arabs and Muslims to work toward creation of a Palestinian government that recognized Israel. Blair toured Turkey, Egypt, Iraq, Dubai, and the Palestinian Authority in December. Prime Minister Olmert, after meeting with him in Jerusalem, said that Blair "brought some excellent ideas."

In April, inquest juries at St. Pancras coroner's court (London) ruled on the deaths of two British peace activists killed by IDF bullets in Gaza in 2003, James Miller and Tom Hurndall (see AJYB 2006, p. 318). They found that Miller had been murdered and Hurndall unlawfully killed. The Israeli embassy declined the coroner's request that the soldier believed responsible for Miller's death attend the inquest, on the grounds that Israeli police had carefully investigated the incident and were unable to establish his guilt. Hurndall's killer had been convicted of manslaughter by an Israeli court and sentenced to eight years imprisonment. The families of Miller and Hurndall pressed Foreign Minister Straw to initiate legal action against the senior Israeli commander they held responsible. In May, Attorney General Lord Goldsmith held talks with officials in Jerusalem about compensation to the families.

In a related matter, Lord Goldsmith said in April that he was considering Israel's request to change legislation whereby a number of IDF officers bound for London had been threatened with arrest for alleged war crimes. In November 2005, for example, General Doron Almog returned from London to Israel without disembarking after being notified that he might be arrested (see AJYB 2006, p. 319).

ANTI-ISRAEL ACTIVITY

By 2006 it was becoming quite difficult to distinguish, in Britain, between criticism of Israeli policies and opposition to Israel's existence, and, even more broadly, between anti-Israel activity and enmity toward Jews. Daniel Shek, chief executive of the British Israel Communications and Research Center (Bicom), noted "a growing feeling that something more fundamental was being challenged by Israel's enemies and detractors in Britain which goes to the heart of Israel's legitimacy." And a spokesman for the Community Security Trust (CST) discerned, in June, "a wave of hostility toward Israel" that "directly affects anti-Semitism."

One manifestation of the prevailing atmosphere was the continuing drive, albeit often unsuccessful, to boycott Israel. In February the Church of England's governing body, its synod, voted to "heed the call" of Palestinian Anglicans and disinvest from companies that profited from the "illegal occupation," such as the American-based multinational Caterpillar company. Chief Rabbi Jonathan Sacks described the decision as "a blow to Christian-Jewish relations," and nine MPs signed a letter to the *London Times* criticizing disinvestment. In March the Church's Ethical Investment Advisory Group upheld its 2005 policy that advised against disinvestment and rejected calls for economic pressure on Israel (see AJYB 2006, p. 320).

In February a newly formed organization, Architects and Planners for Justice in Palestine, announced plans for a campaign of political lobbying against Israel and for disinvestment from Israeli projects in the Palestinian territories. The next month the National Union of Teachers (NUT) decided against proposing a resolution at its annual conference calling on the Britain to impose sanctions and curtail its arms trade with Israel. But in May the Blackpool conference of the National Association of Teachers in Further and Higher Education (Natfhe) passed a motion to boycott those Israeli individuals and organizations that did not publicly declare their opposition to Israel's policy in the territories. NUT and Natfhe merged in June to form the Universities and Colleges Union, and the new body was not bound by the resolution. Anti-Israel activists blockaded the British headquarters of an Israeli fruit-and-vegetable exporter, Agrexco, in August. Seven people had been cleared in January of disturbing public order arising from a similar blockade in November 2004.

Pro- and anti-Israel activity on university campuses continued. In January financial giant Merrill Lynch withdrew from sponsorship of an event at the School of Oriental and African Studies (SOAS) because it featured Hamas supporter Dr. Azzam Tamimi, a leading member of the radical Muslim Association of Britain. In March a motion to twin Manchester University with al-Najah University on the West Bank and a countermotion to twin with the Hebrew University of Jerusalem were both defeated. April's National Union of Students (NUS) conference defeated a proposal by the Federation of Student Islamic Societies and the political group Respect to overturn NUS's ban on the Islamic fundamentalist group Hizb ut-Tahrir. Oxford University's student union decided in June to end its twinning arrangement with Bir Zeit University on the West Bank because supporters of terrorism, including some 23 Hamas members, sat on Bir Zeit's student council.

Events in Gaza and Lebanon during the summer added a new dimension to the debate. Pro- and anti-Israel rallies were held in London and other major cities in July. In Trafalgar Square the Muslim Association of Great Britain, the Stop the War Coalition, and the Palestine Solidarity Campaign (PSC) led a mass meeting to condemn Israel and praise Hizb ut-Tahrir. Speakers included Dr. Tamimi and MP George Galloway. A lower-key, pro-Israel demonstration under the banner "Yes to Peace— No to Terror" was held at the Jewish Free School, Kenton, North London, the following week.

In August the NUS executive passed a motion condemning MP Galloway for publicly supporting Hizb ut-Tahrir, and in November campus groups protested outside the Birmingham University lecture hall where he was speaking. But a survey conducted in September by American pollster Stanley Greenberg for the Israel Project found that public sympathy in Britain for Hizb ut-Tahrir increased as the Middle East conflict dragged on, and that 25 percent of the country's "elite" judged Israel more responsible for the situation than Islamic extremism. Such sentiments were found to be strongly associated with opposition to perceived British and American support for Israel in the Lebanon war, and to anti-Blair feeling generally. In September, too, a Muslim policeman from the Metropolitan Police's special diplomatic protection group asked, on grounds of conscience, to be relieved from guarding the Israeli embassy in London: he objected to Israel's bombing of Lebanon. The PSC held a daylong lobby of Parliament timed to coincide with a debate on the Middle East, with the aim of convincing the government to stop supplying arms to Israel.

Baroness Jenny Tonge, a Liberal-Democratic MP from 1997 to 2005 and now a member of the House of Lords, told a group from the PSC at her party's October conference that "the pro-Israel lobby has got its grips on the Western world." Tonge, who had been removed as party spokesperson on international development in 2004 for declaring sympathy for

Palestinian suicide bombers, was now rebuked by Liberal Democratic leader Sir Menzies Campbell for the "clear anti-Semitic connotations" of her latest remarks. The next month she declared that although "many of us adore the Jewish people," Israel's treatment of the Palestinians was the primary force fueling global Islamic extremism. Tonge apologized in December to British Jews and to her party, even while noting that imputations of anti-Semitism could help shield Israel from justified criticism. She was not anti-Semitic, Tonge said, but was horrified by the international community's decades of inaction in dealing with the "occupation" of Palestine.

War in Lebanon brought increased anti-Israel feeling to the campuses. The Manchester University student union, in November, limited the application of its "no platform for extremism" policy to "fascist" speakers only, thereby opening the door to Hizb ut-Tahrir. In December Leeds University conducted a campus-wide referendum on a motion proposed by PSC students mandating student union authorities to ignore complaints by the campus Jewish Society "as long as Judaism as a faith was not offended." It passed by a vote of 1,421 to 895.

Pro-Israel forces on the campuses enjoyed something of a victory in December, when the national executive committee of the NUS voted to adopt the recommendations and the definitions of anti-Semitism produced in September by the all-party Parliamentary Group against Anti-Semitism (see below, p. 343). Since that group had stated that opposition to the existence of the State of Israel could be a manifestation of anti-Semitism, the NUS action implied acceptance of a connection between anti-Zionism and anti-Semitism.

Jews who openly criticized Israel's actions met considerable reprobation from the communal establishment. But in June, representatives of Jews for Justice for the Palestinians teamed up with the PSC to organize a demonstration outside the House of Commons while Israeli prime minister Olmert was addressing MPs within, and the PSC general secretary delivered a 10,500-signature petition to Downing Street condemning both Olmert's visit and Britain's support for Israel. Representatives of Jews for Justice spoke at the Trafalgar Square meeting in July condemning Israel (see above, p. 340), and the organization placed a £10,000, full-page advertisement in the *London Times* bearing more than 300 signatures, many of Jews prominent in academia and the arts. Under the heading, "What is Israel doing?" it denounced collective punishment of Palestinians in Gaza and the use of Israel's "enormously superior military power to terrorize an entire people."

Poor public relations and biased media coverage were often blamed for anti-Israel sentiment in the country. But an independent review of the BBC's Middle East coverage, commissioned by the BBC governors (see AJYB 2006, p. 322) and published in April, found little indication of deliberate or systematic bias. On the contrary, although the reporting could at times be, in the review's words, "incomplete" and "misleading," there was an evident commitment to be fair, accurate, and impartial.

While this was good news for BBC management, it rejected the review's recommendation to appoint a stronger editorial guiding hand to supervise Middle East news. Instead, management decided to enhance the role of its Middle East editor, currently Jeremy Bowen, in explicating the context of high-profile news programs. Also rejected was a recommendation to be more explicit in the use of language, such as in calling terrorist acts "terrorism." "We should let other people characterize," the BBC explained, "while we report the facts as we know them." Jewish community spokesmen expressed disappointment, noting that the review failed to address the bias implicit in portraying Israel's actions solely in the context of its role as an occupying power, while rationalizing acts of the Palestinians as those of an occupied people.

In June the board of Bicom agreed to launch a three-year, multimillion-pound program to promote Israel's image through the Jewish Leadership Council, CST, and the Friends of Israel groups of the three main political parties. But the impact of Israel's summer war in Lebanon caused recriminations within British Jewry. In September the United Synagogue (US) council attacked the Board of Deputies and the Jewish Leadership Council for their handling of public relations during the conflict, berating what it saw as the community's silence and inertia in the face of anti-Israel propaganda.

The law did its part in restricting anti-Israel activity. In February radical Muslim cleric Abu Hamza was found guilty at the Old Bailey on nine charges, including soliciting others to murder Jews and other non-Muslims; using threatening, abusive or insulting behavior with intent to stir up racial hatred; and possessing a document likely to be useful in committing a terrorist act. He was sentenced to seven years in jail. The CST thought the sentence too light, and also criticized the police for not bringing Abu Hamza to justice sooner. Two radical Islamist groups were banned in July for preaching extreme anti-Israel and anti-Western propaganda. According to the Home Office, Al-Ghurabaa and the Saved Sect had disseminated material that fell within the purview of the 2006 Terrorism Act, which banned the praise, commission, or preparation of terrorism, and made belonging to or encouraging support for a proscribed organization a criminal offense.

Rabbis paid tribute to Sheikh Zaki Badawi, principal of London's Muslim College and cofounder of the Three Faiths Forum, who died in January. The forum, aimed at promoting dialogue between Jews, Christians, and Muslims, received a £50,000 grant from the Home Office in February to employ an education officer who would teach religious tolerance in schools and colleges. Another Home Office grant in May helped young Jews and Arabs set up a joint radio station, Salaam Shalom, in Bristol. That same month saw the launch of the Woolf Institute, a new project for the study of Jewish-Muslim relations that was an extension of the Cambridge Center for the Study of Christian-Jewish Relations.

In December, the Charity Commission launched a formal inquiry into the British charity Interpal on charges of funneling money to Hamas-linked individuals and organizations. A similar investigation into Interpal in 2003 on such charges had not turned up sufficient evidence to ban it (see AJYB 2004, p. 283).

Anti-Semitism

Jews were becoming "more anxious and more vulnerable to abuse and attack than at any other time for a generation or longer," noted the report of the Parliamentary Group against Anti-Semitism, published in September. The group, chaired by former cabinet minister Denis Mac-Shane and consisting of MPs from all parties, had, over the previous year, listened to evidence from public officials, police officers, Jewish leaders, and experts on race relations. There was, the report noted, "a widespread change in mood and tone when Jews are discussed," and evidently anti-Semitism was "becoming respectable among certain sectors of society." The report urged the government, law-enforcement agencies, educators, and the media to take swift action. It also pointed to the financial burden that security measures placed upon the Jewish community: the Board of Deputies' Community Security Trust (CST) cost some £5m annually. MacShane told the *Jewish Chronicle,* "We cannot accept that there should be need for a group of British citizens to spend a large amount of money just to defend themselves."

The CST reported a total of 594 anti-Semitic incidents in 2006, the highest figure since such statistics began to be collected and 12 percent more than the previous high recorded in 2004. The 2006 total included 112 acts of violence, 365 of abusive behaviour, and 70 of property damage. Strangely, a report from the Jerusalem-based Global Forum against Anti-Semitism showed a fall in the number of incidents in Great Britain, from 321 in 2005 to 312 in 2006.

The CST issued a warning to the Jewish community in July, after anti-Semitic mail was received that referred to the Middle East crisis. According to the CST, British Jewry faced "a wave of intimidation" in the wake of Israel's bombing of Lebanon. The war in Lebanon indeed brought an upsurge in anti-Semitic incidents, 168 occurring in July and August 2006, as compared with 73 in the same two months of 2005.

Relations with London's left-wing mayor, Ken Livingstone, seemed to have improved in late 2005, when, at the launch of the London Jewish Forum in December, Livingstone apologized "if I have caused offense to anybody" (see AJYB 2006, p. 327). But he remained at odds with the Jewish community for much of 2006. Early in the year the Adjudication Panel for England suspended him from office for four weeks for likening a Jewish reporter to a concentration-camp guard a year earlier (see AJYB 2006, p. 323), concluding that his comments were "unnecessarily insensitive and offensive." A court decision in March froze the suspension, but Livingstone had to face another official inquiry when, in the course of a press conference, he accused the Reuben brothers, Jewish property developers, of stalling the development of Britain's East London Olympic site, and told them to "go back to Iran and try your luck with the ayatollahs."

Livingstone explained, in the pages of the *Jewish Chronicle,* that his only interest in the Reubens was their effect on the Olympic Games, "not their religion or ethnicity." In June the Greater London Authority's monitoring officer judged that these remarks were not anti-Semitic, as Livingstone had not known at the time that the Reubens were Jewish. The High Court quashed Livingstone's earlier suspension order in October. "We probably won't ever agree on the policies of the Israeli government and the idea that anyone who disagrees with those policies is anti-Semitic," Livingstone told the Board of Deputies at that time. But he nevertheless hoped that it would work with him on matters where they could find common ground.

Controversy at Antony Lerman's appointment as director of the Institute for Jewish Policy Research (see AJYB 2006, p. 326) reignited in March 2006, when journalist Daniel Finkelstein became the fourth trustee in three months to resign from the IJPR board. The resignation was triggered by the board's withdrawal of support from a planned book on anti-Semitism. Finkelstein claimed that the withdrawal was a symptom of a shift in IJPR policy under Lerman, who, in the organization's name, had suggested that the problem of anti-Semitism in Great Britain was exaggerated. IJPR relaunched itself in October: instead of functioning as an organization of the British Jewish community, it would now be a policy think tank for European Jewry.

In April, Board of Deputies director general Jon Benjamin warned that burgeoning support for the extreme right-wing British National Party (BNP) was "of very serious concern," even though Jews were not its main target. The same month, Tory leader David Cameron advised voters to "support any party rather than BNP, which is thriving on hatred." Nonetheless a survey by the Joseph Rowntree Reform Trust found that 25 percent of London's voters would consider voting for the BNP. The party fielded 360 candidates in the May local elections and increased the number of its councillors from 23 to 45, becoming the second largest party in Barking and Dagenham, East London, where it won 11 seats. The local MP, Margaret Hodge, a Labour minister, attributed the rise in BNP fortunes to the unpopularity of the government and to concerns over immigration and public housing in poverty-stricken areas. In November, BNP leader Nick Griffin and publicity director Mark Collett were acquitted of stirring up racial hatred, a charge brought on the basis of speeches they had made at a private meeting in West Yorkshire two years before that were filmed by an undercover reporter for a BBC documentary (see AJYB 2005, p. 325).

JEWISH COMMUNITY

Demography

An unexpectedly healthy demographic profile of the community emerged from *Community Statistics, 2005,* a report by David Graham and Daniel Vulkan released by the community research unit of the Board of Deputies. Whereas the picture had for many years been one of decline, this report showed an increase in the number of circumcisions recorded, from 1,579 in 2004 to 1,640 in 2005. Figures for births, partly derived from the circumcision data and compiled using a new methodology, rose from 3,076 in 2004 to 3,205 in 2005. There were 1,000 marriages under Jewish religious auspices in 2005 as compared to 955 in 2004, much of the increase concentrated in the strictly Orthodox and Reform sectors. The marriages among the strictly Orthodox, indeed, constituting a quarter of the total performed. On the other hand, the number of Jewish religious divorces fell from 274 in 2004 to 249 in 2005. Burials and cremations under Jewish religious auspices fell to 3,221 in 2005 from 3,257 the previous year.

Nevertheless, Rona Hart, head of the community research unit, estimated that a total UK Jewish population of 270,000 in 2005 would shrink to about 260,100 in 2010; 249,000 in 2015; and 229,700 in 2025. She projected that annual Jewish births over those two decades would fall to 2,070.

New analysis of the 2001 national census, published in March, showed that 4,002 Jews immigrated into Britain from April 2000 through April 2001. The largest groups came from the U.S. (1,289) and Israel (972). Rona Hart, in November, said that 9,000 native-born Israelis lived in London in 2006 as compared with 4,000 in 1997. These figures, which excluded illegal and temporary residents, were based on a survey carried out by the Office of National Statistics for the *Evening Standard* newspaper.

The Reform Synagogues of Great Britain announced that its religious court accepted the conversions of 109 adults and 41 children to Judaism in 2006. In 2005 the numbers had been 113 adults and 51 children.

To mark the 350th anniversary of the readmission of Jews to Great Britain (see below) Mayor Livingstone of London commissioned a report on the status of the London Jewish community. Published in December, *The Jewish Population of London* was produced by the data-management and analysis groups of the Greater London Authority, based on 2001 census data. It found that London's 150,000-strong Jewish community was the best-off of ten census groupings, its proportion of self-employed, 27 percent, more than double the overall rate. The average Jewish household consisted of 2.17 persons, though the most common household type (38 percent) consisted of a single person, in most cases an elderly pensioner. Single-parent households made up only 5 percent of the Jewish household total, the lowest rate among all religious groups.

Even so, the economic condition of the strictly Orthodox in Britain gave cause for concern. A report on the Manchester Jewish Community Project published in February pointed to extreme poverty among the city's Haredim.

Communal Affairs

This year marked the 350th anniversary of the readmission of Jews to Great Britain. Although activities were organized nationwide, London was the main focus. Two major events were a commemorative service in June at Britain's oldest synagogue, the seventeenth-century Spanish and

Portuguese Bevis Marks in the City of London, and "Simcha in the Square," a celebration of British Jewish culture and a major rally in Trafalgar Square in September. London's controversial mayor Ken Livingstone (see above, p. 344) was not invited to lead the rally, but he issued a press release expressing his determination that not only would "London remain a city that does not tolerate anti-Semitism," but it would also "positively celebrate the gigantic Jewish contribution to human culture and civilization." He also highlighted his office's funding of the event to the tune of £60,000. The same month, the local council of Barnet, North London, bestowed "freedom of the borough" on Chief Rabbi Jonathan Sacks. Celebrations reached a peak in November, when Queen Elizabeth II hosted a reception for communal leaders and other personalities at St. James's Palace.

In November, the Jewish Leadership Council, an umbrella body with an increased membership of 23 organizations, adopted a new three-pronged program: improving the effectiveness of pro-Israel advocacy; nurturing new communal leadership; and improving welfare and educational services. Task forces were assigned to address each area of concern.

In January, the Jewish National Fund (JNF) announced that David Cameron, leader of the Conservative Party, had agreed to become a patron, and in March, the Duke of Edinburgh hosted a lunch on JNF's behalf. But the dispute with its erstwhile partner, Keren Kayemeth LeIsrael-JNF (KKL), over the right to use the names KKL and JNF to raise funds for Israel in Britain (see AJYB 2006, p. 328) accelerated. In February KKL asked Israeli authorities to investigate Nes Israel, a charity JNF set up in Israel. According to KKL, the £130,000 Nes had received from JNF breached it's commitment to KKL. JNF retorted that it was KKL's failure to say where its money went that had made JNF set up Nes in the first place. In December, JNF threatened legal action if KKL did not agree to mediation before March 2007.

A hotly challenged decision in February allowed every Jew in the country, not just those registered, the right to vote for British delegates to the World Zionist Congress planned for June in Jerusalem. Only 1,296 votes were cast, half of them for Progressive (Reform) and Masorti (Conservative) candidates; more than a third of the ballots were disqualified. The Orthodox Mizrachi group challenged the outcome in an appeal to the Zionist electoral court, and thereby procured an additional seat.

Norwood, Britain's leading Jewish children and family service, announced in March that it was expanding its family center in Stamford Hill, North London, to combat the welfare problems of Hackney's strictly

Orthodox community. These, said Norwood's director of operational services, "involve families with eight, nine, or more children on low or no income, experiencing a high level of poverty." In November, plans to build a 300-home community in Milton Keynes, Buckinghamshire, for strictly Orthodox Stamford Hill Jews were abandoned in favor of expanded development in Stamford Hill itself.

Religion

Trends in British Synagogue Membership, 1990–2005/6, a comprehensive report by Rona Hart and Edward Kafka published by the Board of Deputies, showed that the number of British Jews belonging to synagogues had declined by 18 percent over the previous 15 years, roughly the same rate as the decrease in the overall Jewish population. Some 30 percent of Britain's Jews were not affiliated with a synagogue. Approximately 70 percent of synagogue members lived in Greater London and contiguous areas, while within the London region itself, 41 percent of membership households lived in the three Northwest boroughs of Barnet, Brent, and Harrow.

The mainstream Orthodox sector was particularly hard hit, synagogue membership falling 31 percent, so that its share of the total fell from 66 percent in 1990 to 55 percent. The Union of Orthodox Hebrew Congregations (popularly known as Adath), with a much more Haredi orientation, saw its membership rise by 51 percent, from 5,810 household members in 1990 to 8,800 in 2005/6. The relatively new Masorti grouping grew even faster, increasing by 63 percent to 2,090 membership households in 2005/6, from 1,280 in 1990; Masorti now made up 2.5 percent of households affiliated with synagogues.

The downward trend was quite marked in the provinces. For example, the synagogue in Sunderland closed in March, as only 30 Jews remained in what had once been a thriving Jewish community that supported a yeshiva and a Jewish day school. Only Newcastle and Gateshead remained of what had been 12 viable Jewish communities in the northeast of England.

In April the Union of Orthodox Hebrew Congregations (Adath) was criticized for providing financial support to the anti-Zionist Neturei Karta grouping, and three months later the Adath synagogue in Hendon, North London, threatened to leave the organization unless it dissociated from Neturei Karta. Matters reached a head in December, when a Neturei Karta delegation, including its British leader, Ahron Cohen, attended the Holocaust-denial conference in Tehran. Chief Rabbi Sacks expressed the communal consensus, describing this as "outrageous" and an "unforgivable betrayal of the memory of Holocaust victims."

A report commissioned by the Movement for Reform Judaism, *Getting in Touch — 18 – 35,* found that young adults' absence from the synagogue did not necessarily imply indifference to Judaism. The movement therefore announced plans to raise £500,000 over the next five years to finance an outreach initiative geared to that age group, and hired an American consultant to direct the effort.

Education

The number of Jewish children attending Jewish day schools and nurseries, which stood at 14,660 in 1992, went up to 24,420 by 2004, a rise of 66 percent, according to a report published by the Board of Deputies community research unit. The 2004 total included 12,570 children at primary schools and 8,670 at the secondary level. The numbers of students attending strictly Orthodox schools rose from 5,330 to 10,860; at mainstream Orthodox schools from 9,000 to 12,720; and at Progressive schools from 330 to 910. The number of Jewish schools increased similarly over that time span, from 34 to 69 primary schools and from 22 to 41 secondary schools.

Still more schools were opening and others were in the planning stage. In February the government gave the go-ahead to Anglo-Jewry's first cross-communal secondary school, six months after its first bid for state funding was rejected (see AJYB 2006, p. 330). Scheduled to open in East Barnet in 2009, the school was chosen to pilot a new wave of parent-promoted schools, part of the government's educational reforms. It was expected eventually to take 1,260 students, plus 50 more in a special-education facility run by Norwood child care, with involvement on the part of ORT as well. In April the Huntingdon Foundation opened a new, private Jewish primary school in the Bushey-Watford area.

Statistics prepared for the *Jewish Chronicle* in July by Rona Hart of the Board of Deputies indicated the prospect of a mismatch between planned increases in school places and a shrinking Jewish population in London (see above, p. 000). In July, therefore, the United Synagogue announced plans for the creation of a strategic planning body to oversee Orthodox education in Hertfordshire and in the London area.

Indeed, there was reason to believe that some of the Jewish schools would not fill up. Yavneh College, Britain's newest Jewish secondary school, opened in September in Boreham Wood, Hertfordshire, with 93 students (see AJYB 2006, p. 330). In March, the United Synagogue-sponsored King Solomon High School in Barkingside, East London, found that applications for admission were drastically down—partially due to the opening of Yavneh—and began admitting children who were not Jewish by strict Orthodox definition. Russell Kett, board chairman of the Jewish Free School (JFS), Britain's largest Jewish comprehensive secondary school, in Kenton, North London, warned that it too, for the same reason, might need to admit non-Jewish pupils by 2007. Meanwhile, Jewish demographic decline outside London meant that only about a third of the students at Birmingham's King David, a primary school, were Jewish, and at King David High School, Liverpool, only a quarter.

In October, following a vociferous campaign led by the Board of Deputies, the government dropped a proposed amendment to its Education and Inspections Bill that would have empowered local authorities to force new schools under religious sponsorship to allocate 25 percent of their places to pupils of other faiths or of none. The amendment had been introduced in the House of Lords with the argument that mixing students of different religions would encourage inclusiveness and intergroup understanding.

Foreign Aid

World Jewish Relief (WJR) received a welcome boost in February when Prince Charles hosted a reception at Clarence House, his London home, for about 100 potential supporters. The prince had become interested in WJR activities since he visited Kraków and inspected the WJR community center project there (see below, p. 498).

Under its Gifts in Kind program, WJR had, since June 2005, shipped £3.5m worth of goods to impoverished Jews in Eastern Europe and the former Soviet Union, it was reported in March. Working closely on the ground with the American Jewish Joint Distribution Committee, WJR provided food, household articles, toys, clothing, bedding, and medicine. Even the youngest members of the community rallied to the cause: children at the Bury and Whitefield Jewish primary school produced survival kits as part of the project.

WJR introduced "lifeline cards" in Argentina and the Ukraine so that poor Jews could do their own shopping using these cards instead of receiving food parcels or going to soup kitchens. "This is a way of giving them back their dignity," said Nigel Layton, WJR chairman.

Ukraine was a particular focus of British support. Hampstead Garden Suburb Synagogue, North London, raised over £50,000 at a concert in January to help the Jewish community of Lviv. In February WJR had a fund-raising campaign at South Manchester Synagogue for its Ukrainian projects. Edgware and District Reform Synagogue started a new twinning arrangement with a progressive congregation in Odessa: for 12 years the synagogue had been associated with Kiev's Hatikvah Reform community, and now that it was thriving, Edgware and District wanted to support a newer community that had greater needs.

WJR, which already had a London-Belarus twinning program for young people of bar- and bat-mitzvah age, arranged another twinning arrangement between Jewish Care's Holocaust Survivors' Center, Hendon, North London, and Belarus's Association of Jewish Ghetto and Nazi Camp Prisoners, in Minsk, many of whose members lived in extreme poverty. The Hendon Center started by collecting and sending clothing to Minsk.

The practice of bringing groups of young people from areas affected by the Chernobyl nuclear disaster to Britain for short vacations continued. In June, Radlett United Synagogue, Hertfordshire, joined Radlett and Bushey Reform in hosting children from Grodno, Belarus. November saw the tenth anniversary celebration of the Jewish Chernobyl Children project, which had brought approximately 200 children from Moghilev, Belarus, to London, with support provided by WJR.

West London Synagogue, the Reform movement's flagship congregation, raised £2m, in cooperation with United Jewish Israel Appeal, to equip Shaarei Sholom, a new progressive synagogue in St. Petersburg, Russia.

Publications

For the first time, the 2006 Jewish Quarterly-Wingate literary awards for fiction and nonfiction were combined, the prize going to Imre Kertész, the Hungarian-born 2002 Nobel laureate, for his semiautobiographical novel *Fatelessness*. First published 30 years earlier in Hungarian, it appeared in English translation in 2004.

Books published on religious themes during the year included *Rhythm of the Heart,* a commentary on the Psalms by Rabbi Yitzchok Rubin; *Orthodox Judaism in Britain since 1913: An Ideology Forsaken* by Miri Freud-Kandel; *The Light and Fire of the Ba'al Shem Tov* by Yitzhak Buxbaum; *The Flame of the Heart: Prayers of a Chasidic Mystic,* translated and edited by David Sears with the Breslov Research Institute; *Signposts of the Messianic Age* by John D. Rayner; *Remaking Israeli Judaism: The Challenge of Shas* by David Lehmann and Batia Siebzehner; *The Music of the Hebrew Bible and the Western Ashkenazi Chant Tradi-*

tion by Victor Tunkel; *Out of the Midst of the Fire,* the story of the rescue of the Westminster Synagogue Torah scrolls, by Philippa Bernard; *A Dictionary of Jewish-Christian Relations,* edited by Edward Kessler and Neil Wenborn; *Beyond the Pulpit* by Jeremy Rosen; *The Essence of Kabbalah* by Brian L. Lancaster; *Kabbalah: A Very Short Introduction* by Joseph Dan; *The Christian and the Pharisee: Two Outspoken Religious Leaders Debate the Road to Heaven* by R.T. Kendall and David Rosen; *Siddur Lil'mod v'La'asot,* a new prayer book for young people compiled by LJY-NETZER, the youth arm of the Liberal movement; and, at the other end of the spectrum, a new edition of the venerable Singer *Siddur,* the authorized daily prayer book for Britain's mainstream Orthodox communities, with a new translation and extensive commentary by Chief Rabbi Sacks.

Biographies and autobiographies included two lives of James Parkes, a leading non-Jewish figure in Jewish-Christian studies — *Campaigner Against Anti-Semitism: The Reverend James Parkes, 1896–1981* by Colin Richmond, and *He Also Spoke as a Jew: The Life of the Reverend James Parkes* by Haim Chertok. Also published were *The Bronfmans: The Rise and Fall of the House of Seagram* by Nicholas Faith; *Man in the Shadows,* the autobiography of one-time Mossad chief Efraim Halevy; *Passport to Freedom* by Anthony Laye; *Tea with Einstein and Other Memories* by William Frankel; *Dora B* by Josiane Behmoiras; *The End of Petticoat Lane,* the biography of East End boy Henry Freedman, by Andrew Miller; *Suburban Shaman* by Cecil Helman; *The Rainbow Never Ends* by Aubrey Rose; and Greville Janner's *To Life!*

Books on anti-Semitism included *The Changing Face of Anti-Semitism* by Walter Laqueur; *Anti-Semitism and Modernity: Innovation and Continuity* by Hyam Maccoby; and *The Paradox of Anti-Semitism* by Dan Cohn-Sherbok.

Works of fiction were *Sea Change* by Michael Arditti; *Overexposure* by Hugo Rifkind; *Mandrakes from the Holy Land,* a translation of the Hebrew work by Aharon Megged; *Seeds of Greatness* by Jon Canter; *Made in Heaven* by Adèle Geras; *A Woman in Jerusalem,* a translation of the Hebrew novel by A. B. Yehoshua; *The Righteous Men* by Sam Bourne (nom de plume of journalist Jonathan Freedland); *The People on the Street* by Linda Grant; *Kalooki Nights* by Howard Jacobson; *Our Holocaust* by Amir Gutfreund; and *Disobedience* by Naomi Alderman.

Holocaust literature included *Trust and Deceit* by Gerta Vrbova; *Kristallnacht: Prelude to Disaster* by Martin Gilbert; *Nazism, War and Genocide,* edited by Neil Gregor; *Journey into Freedom* by Peter Hart; *A Thousand Kisses,* edited by Christoph Moss; *Salo's Song* by Barbara

Esser; *A Rose for Reuben: Stories of Hope from the Holocaust* by Robert Rietti; and *Parallel Lines* by Peter Lantos. Historical works varied widely in scope. There were detailed studies such as *Novogrudok: The History of a Shtetl* by Jack Kagan; *A Strange Death* by Hillel Halkin, an investigation of a spy ring that helped the British against the Turks during World War I; *The Triumph of Military Zionism: Nationalism and the Origins of the Israeli Right* by Colin Shindler; *City of Oranges,* Adam LeBor's history of Jaffa; *Expulsion, Britain's Jewish Solution: Edward 1 and the Jews* by Richard Huscroft; *Jews in North Devon during the Second World War* by Helen Fry; and *The Sephardim of Manchester* by Lydia Collins. Others looked at whole communities, such as *Jews in Britain* by Raphael Langhamand; *The Jewish Community of Salonika* by Bea Lewkowicz; and *The Jews of Ethiopia,* edited by Tudor Parfitt and Emanuela Treisan Semi. Taking an even broader view was *The Phases of Jewish History* by Philip Ginsbury and Raphael Cutler.

Books about Jewish art and artists were *Treasures of Jewish Heritage* by David Bindman, Rickie Burman, and others; *Marie-Louise von Motesiczky, 1906–1996,* edited by Jeremy Adler and Birgit Sanders; *Avigdor Arikha from Life* by Duncan Thomson and Stephen Coppel; *Love Revealed: Simeon Solomon and the Pre-Raphaelites* by Colin Cruise; *Once Upon a Time in Lithuania: Sketches and Paintings* by Naomi Alexander; Simon Schama's *Power of Art,* published to accompany Schama's television series of the same name; *Jacob Kramer: Creativity and Loss* by David Manson; and *My Grandparents, My Parents and I: Jewish Art and Culture* by Edward Van Voolen.

Books of poetry were *The Lost Notebook* by Jennie Feldman; *Black Over Red* by Lotte Kramer; *What Is the Purpose of Your Visit?* by Wanda Barford; *What I Never Told Mother* by Joan Gordon; *POT! Anthology,* edited by Michael Horowitz; *The Jewish Pilgrimage* by Geoffrey Hoffman; and *Anglo-Jewish Poetry from Isaac Rosenberg to Elaine Feinstein* by Peter Lawson.

In a class of their own were two books on contemporary affairs, *Londonistan* by Melanie Phillips, and *ADAM: An Anthology of Miron Grindea's ADAM International Review Editorials,* edited by Rachel Lasserson.

Personalia

Honors conferred on British Jews in 2006 included knighthoods for Sir Philip Green for services to the retail industry and Sir David Michels, the former Hilton chief. An honorary knighthood went to Nobel laureate Elie Wiesel in recognition of his contribution to Holocaust studies in Great Britain.

Notable British Jews who died in 2006 included, in January: Rabbi Sholom Krafchik, Leeds *mohel,* aged 44; Victor, Lord Mishcon, major communal personality and lawyer, aged 90; Judith Tankel, prominent Glasgow communal worker, aged 71; Meer Basri, leader of Baghdad Jewry, aged 94; Philip Mishon, who organized the annual Remembrance Day parade, aged 81; in February: Joash Woodrow, artist, aged 78; Sidney Beenstock, key figure in Manchester Jewish education, aged 89; Gerald Fleming, Holocaust historian, aged 84; in March: Marcus Fielding, WIZO UK's executive director, aged 53; Ernest Polack, head of Polack's house, Clifton College, Bristol, aged 75; Muriel Spark, novelist, in Italy, aged 88; in April: Vivian Pereira Mendoza, leading member of the Spanish and Portuguese Congregation and first director of the Polytechnic of the South Bank, London, aged 89; in May: Rabbi Casriel Kaplin, onetime *dayan* of the United Synagogue Beth Din, aged 74; John Simon, national president UK B'nai B'rith, 1975–79, aged 92; in June: Ronald Cass, composer, aged 83; Judd Solo, band leader, aged 88; Louis Glassman, Hebrew scholar and ritual slaughterer, aged 95; in July: Louis Jacobs, the eminently learned and internationally renowned rabbi, scholar, and author, aged 85; Alan Senitt, committed youth leader, aged 27; Theresa Science Russell, Newcastle civic and communal personality, aged 96; in August: Eddie Brown, president of the Jewish National Fund, 1983–95, aged 67; Gerald Bean, national chairman of the Association of Jewish Ex-Servicemen and Women, 1981–83 and 1996–98, aged 72; Sandra Blow, abstract artist, aged 80; Bluma Feld, caterer and hotelier, aged 98; Alfred Sherman, Conservative politician, aged 86; in September: Sir Martin Roth, Cambridge University's first professor of psychiatry, aged 88; Ephraim Gastwirth, religious minister and teacher, aged 85; in October: Reg Freeson, Zionist and former government minister, aged 80; Jonathan Cansino, leading bridge player, aged 67; Hanna Pinner, educator, aged 76; Michael Kester, champion of kosher slaughter, aged 65; in November: Chava Frankel, cofounder of Parnes House school, aged 94; in December: Peter Marsh, journalist and barrister, aged 73; Cyril Blaustein, real-estate developer and Jewish communal official, aged 89.

MIRIAM KOCHAN

France

National Affairs

The most remarkable series of events to occur in France during 2006 was a two-month-long struggle, marked by violence, over a proposed new employment law. The proposal, Contrat première embauche (CPE)—First Employment Contract—was the government's effort to address youth unemployment, a key problem that had led to massive rioting in heavily Arab and black African immigrant ghettos around France in October–November 2005 (see AJYB 2006, pp. 337–39). While the overall French unemployment rate was close to 10 percent, the figure was 23 percent for young people, and possibly double that for those of immigrant origin.

Prime Minister Dominique de Villepin agreed with many economists that a major reason for high unemployment was that social-welfare laws were overly protective of workers' rights. Left-wing governments that ruled France off-and-on since 1936 had instituted legislation that effectively gave much of the French labor force either quasi-ensured continual employment, or the guarantee of major financial compensation in case of dismissal. As a result, employers had become extremely wary of hiring people who had not proven their skills—principally inexperienced youths seeking to enter the workforce—or whom they were not sure they wanted to employ for long periods. While all sorts of temporary work contracts had been introduced in recent years to give employers more flexibility, unemployment remained stubbornly high.

De Villepin's CPE made it easier to dismiss employees under age 26 during their first two years of employment by exempting their employers from the law requiring provable grounds for dismissal. The government reasoned that job prospects for immigrant youths would vastly grow if employers knew they could hire them for trial periods without fear of being "stuck" with them if they were found unsuitable. In addition, a proposed Statute on Equality of Opportunities would have allowed apprenticeships from the age of 14 (replacing compulsory schooling until age 16), night work from the age of 16 (instead of 18), and the withholding of some welfare-benefit payments to families whose children skipped school.

The unexpected result was angry protest emanting from central Paris, just months after the violence that had affected the outer suburbs the year before. Student unions, soon backed by trade unionists, expressed outrage at the proposal, which, they said, violated hard-won labor rights and discriminated against the young. Left-wing parties supported the protesters, saying that the proposed legislation violated the European Union's Social Charter, and that it sought to make youthful employeees as easy to discard as used facial tissue. Indeed, some called it "the Kleenex law."

After de Villepin invoked a little-used parliamentary procedure to have the CPE adopted on March 8–9, the battle—as had happened so often in France—moved to the streets. Students blocked entrances to half the country's universities, and several million people took part in demonstrations in nearly 200 cities and towns around the country. Strikes spread throughout France, including in some public services like the postal system. Serious clashes with police occurred in the Latin Quarter of Paris, a traditional hotbed of youth protest, when anarchists invaded and tried to occupy the main Sorbonne building of Paris University. Police forcibly evacuated and closed down the campus on March 11.

So unpopular had the government's position become that parliamentarians from the prime minister's own ruling UMP party scoffed that the initials CPE really stood for "Comment Perdre une Election" (How to lose an election). Although de Villepin at first dug in his feet, President Jacques Chirac stepped in on March 31 and suggested changes in the proposal that would moderate its effects, but this only encouraged opponents to step up their protests. Finally, on April 10, the government gave in and effectively abandoned the CPE.

An alarming aspect of the affair was that the mostly noisy but peaceful protests by students and trades unionists were regularly marred by the participation, as well, of thousands of violent ethnic French anarchists, as well as black and Arab teenage gangs from the suburbs who had revolted just months before. The anarchists set fire to shops and cars, the teen gangs attacked marchers and passersby to rob them of their possessions (telephones, cash, articles of clothing), stopping only to clash violently with riot police. Jewish organizations warned Jews to stay away from street gatherings for fear of being singled out for abuse, and foreign governments, including the U.S. and Great Britain, advised their citizens to be cautious when traveling in France.

The government was highly embarassed by the turn of events. Opinion polls showed that the popularity of both President Chirac and Prime Minister de Villepin had plunged, not just among their political opponents, but even among their supporters, who faulted them for failing to curb the unrest rapidly.

PRESIDENTIAL POLITICS

Party politics throughout 2006 were dominated by jostling between would-be candidates for the presidential election the next year. The announced date for the first round was April 22, 2007, and, should no candidate get a majority, a run-off between the two top vote-getters would take place on May 6.

Chirac had appointed de Villepin prime minister in May 2005 with the clear intention of blocking the presidential ambitions of Minister of Interior Nicolas Sarkozy, Chirac's one-time protégé who had become his nemesis. Chirac, in fact, elected to his first seven-year term in 1995 and reelected for a five-year term under a new law in 2002, toyed with the idea of running for a third term. But his weak performance during the CPE crisis, coming on the heels of his lack of leadership in the 2005 immigrant riots, dealt a fatal blow to his popularity, which did not go above 25 percent in any of the 2006 opinion polls. De Villepin's poll numbers, following the CPE episode, were equally disastrous.

Sarkozy, in contrast, went from strength to strength, gaining new allies despite Chirac's efforts to stymie his advancement. Sarkozy's only opponent from within his own party, Union for a Popular Movement, was Defense Minister Michèle Alliot-Marie, who saw herself as the conservative answer to the feminine appeal and novelty of the Socialist would-be candidate, Ségolène Royal. But Alliot-Marie, finding very little support from party rank-and-file, dropped out of the contest. Sarkozy officially announced his candidacy on December 28.

Sarkozy was the son of a minor Hungarian aristocrat and political refugee, and of a mother whose own father was born into the once-storied Jewish community of Salonika, then in the Ottoman Empire and now part of Greece. That grandfather, Dr. Benedict ("Benico") Mallah, was the main male role model in Nicolas Sarkozy's life, because his father, Paul Sarkozy de Nagy-Bosca, walked out on his wife and their three sons when Nicolas was four years old, and she moved back with the children to her father's home (her mother had died several years earlier). Dr. Mallah had been sent to boarding school in France in 1904 by his wealthy parents when he was 14 years old. He later graduated from medical school in Paris, where he settled and met his future wife, the former Adèle Bouvier, converting to Roman Catholicism in order to marry her. The conversion was apparently purely formal: Dr. Mallah is not known to have attended church, but neither did he maintain any Jewish links.

Nicolas was baptized and married in church, but as a politician he developed deep and close ties with the French Jewish community. Those ties were perceived as being so strong that leaders of the opposition Socialists unofficially protested that that CRIF (Representative Council of French Jewry), the umbrella body for Jewish organizations in the country, had dropped its traditional political neutrality and was openly backing Sarkozy.

Designation as the Socialist presidential candidate was fiercely contested between Lionel Jospin, Ségolène Royal, Dominique Strauss-Kahn, Laurent Fabius, Jack Lang, François Hollande, and Bernard Kouchner (the latter was not, strictly speaking, a party member, but would have sought the nomination as an outsider.) Interestingly, all except Jospin and Royal were either Jewish or had close Jewish family connections, though only Strauss-Kahn was known as a synagogue member. He had told reporters at the start of the year, "I long thought that being a Jew would be a handicap that would make a negative difference in a presidential race. Today, I still believe it is a handicap, but only with a very marginal minority of anti-Semitic left-wing voters." By October, Jospin, Lang, Hollande, and Kouchner had dropped out. Hollande, the secretary general of the party, still played a major role in the race since he was Royal's longtime partner (they were not married) and the father of their four children.

A formal selection procedure followed, with several three-sided open debates held between Royal, Strauss-Kahn, and Fabius. The party rank-and-file was then asked to choose between them on November 17. Royal won by a wide margin, receiving 60.62 of the vote compared to Strauss-Kahn's 20.69 percent and Fabius's 18.66 percent.

The 54-year-old Royal was the first woman ever to run for president of France as a major-party candidate. She initially wowed the press and public with her charm and the novelty of her personality—a major departure from the classic, mainstream French male political type. Royal had, at different times, held the ministerial portfolios for the environment, family welfare, and education. She had little experience in foreign affairs, as became evident as soon as Royal began to make visits abroad, where she made several verbal gaffes that were immediately highlighted by her opponents.

Royal's most serious mistake, which occurred in Lebanon in December, caused grievous damage to her presidential hopes by projecting an impression of ignorance. While in Beirut, she met with a delegation from the Lebanese National Assembly's Foreign Affairs Committee, which included Ali Ammar, a Hezballah member, who launched into a violent anti-Western diatribe in Arabic, which was translated for Royal. After some particularly scathing comments about U.S. president George Bush, Royal replied that she "shared part of his analysis concerning Bush's policies." This was instantly reported by accompanying French journalists, leading to criticism from opponents in Paris for siding with Hezballah against the U.S. It also apparently contributed to the cancellation of a planned trip to the U.S., after Hilary Clinton indicated—presumably after reading the same reports—that she did not have time to receive Royal.

The situation went from bad to worse the next day, when Royal said, through a spokesman, that she had belatedly learned that Ammar's remarks in Arabic also included a comparison between Israel and Nazi Germany. Royal said that this had not been translated for her, and that she would have walked out of the room had she understood it. No one, in fact, had taken much notice of this comment by the Hezballah man at the time. Journalists suggested that Royal may very well have heard and understood the words spoken, but, like everyone else, ignored them. Her reaction only came after aides decided that night to bring the issue up again, just in case her lack of comment might later be held against her.

Royal also surprised reporters by criticizing, in Beirut, Israeli overflights of Lebanese territory, but justifying them a day later, when she was in Israel. And Royal appeared, when speaking about Iranian nuclear efforts, not to understand the difference between nuclear power for civilian purposes and its use for weapons of mass destruction. Later, touring China, she praised Chinese justice, saying it acted far more rapidly than French justice. Outraged human rights activists quickly noted that China was especially known for swift executions, and that its trials did not recognize the rights of the accused.

Royal's misadventures on her Middle East visit led CRIF to issue a statement, even while Royal was still in the region, deploring that she had "engaged in a dialogue" with a Hezballah representative. Royal's main foreign policy adviser, Julien Dray—a Jew who had sometimes had prickly relations with the organized Jewish community—expressed outrage. He believed the CRIF statement was not only motivated by pro-Sarkozy sentiments, but was also unfair, since Royal had met with a Lebanese parliamentary committee, of which the Hezballah man was only one member.

The quick-tempered Dray was said to have exploded in anger when he met CRIF official Meyer Habib by chance in the lobby of Jerusalem's King David Hotel. According to reports in the French press, Dray shouted: "You've sold your souls to the other camp. Don't expect anything from us. Go back to your friend and master Sarkozy. But you'll pay dearly for this. Ségolène will be elected, and on that day, you'll come crawling on hands and knees to be received by her." Dray's temper got the better of him again the next day, when he heard that Foreign Minister Philippe Douste-Blazy had described Royal's ideas about the Middle East as "simplistic." Dray retorted on national radio, "If Douste-Blazy had any intelligence himself, we'd know about it by now."

When Royal returned from abroad, CRIF president Roger Cukierman hastily arranged a meeting with her to clear the air. Afterwards, CRIF issued a new communiqué insisting it was neutral in the presidential race. But more criticism came from French Jewish publications: Royal had not visited the Western Wall; she declined to make a statement when visiting the Yad Vashem memorial; and she could not find the time to meet with the parents of three Israeli soldiers kidnapped by Hezballah and Hamas. She did meet with Israeli prime minister Ehud Olmert, and had a highly publicized "private" meal with Foreign Minister Tzipi Livni, apparently as part of her campaign of meeting with, and being seen alongside, influential women worldwide.

THE ILAN HALIMI MURDER

The kidnapping and murder of Ilan Halimi was one of the most shocking and traumatic events in the annals of French Jewry since the end of World War II.

Halimi, the 23-year-old son of Moroccan Jewish immigrants, was a salesman in a small Paris telephone shop. He was kidnapped in a Paris suburb on January 21 after being lured to a secluded spot by a teenage girl working for a self-styled "gang of the barbarians," made up of young hoodlums from the Paris suburb of Bagneux. Halimi was tortured while being held for ransom in the basement of a large block of mostly immigrant-inhabited projects. When his family attempted to pay the ransom, the kidnappers failed to appear at designated meeting points, for fear of being caught. Halimi was found by the side of a railway track on February 13, naked and with 80 percent of his body covered with cuts and burns. He died in an ambulance on the way to a hospital.

The gang, except for its leader, was arrested within days. The leader, Youssuf Fofana, fled to the Ivory Coast, where he was arrested on February 22 and extradited to France on March 4. Subsequent police investigation revealed that Fofana was from a Muslim family that came from the Ivory Coast, a former French colony in Africa. His accomplices were mostly of black or Arab origin, but also included a few white Portuguese immigrants and ethnic Frenchmen. Nearly all had police records for small-scale drug trafficking, automobile theft, assault, and similar offences.

Fofana, who had served more than a year in prison for armed robbery, called himself "the brain of the barbarians." After hatching several plans to get money illegally, he had decided on kidnapping, sending young women out to lure potential victims. Before abducting Halimi, the gang had tried, without success, to kidnap six other men, four of them Jews. Fofana told his accomplices that the focus on Jewish victims was "because Jews have money which they suck from the state." In his contacts with Fofana's parents, he realized that they were poor, and suggested, "go ask your rabbi to collect money from the other Jews."

A year after the crime, 18 people were still in prison awaiting trial for the murder-kidnapping. The exact degree to which anti-Semitism was involved in the case was still not entirely clear, except for police statements to the press. Among these was that one of the men told detectives he had stubbed out a cigarette on Halimi's forehead, saying, "This is because you are a Jew."

It was only after the discovery of the dying Halimi that the public became aware of the kidnapping and its possibly anti-Semitic aspect. Interior Minister Sarkozy told the National Assembly on February 21 that while the prime motive for the kidnapping had been to extort money, "the choice of a Jewish victim showed an anti-Semitic background." A memorial service at Paris's main synagogue on February 23 was attended by both President Chirac and Prime Minister de Villepin. (A year after Halimi's death, in February 2007, his body would be disinterred and reburied in Jerusalem.)

Major Jewish and antiracist groups organized a march and demonstration through central Paris on February 26, at whose head walked most of France's major politicians, including Sarkozy and Foreign Minister Douste-Blazy. The crowd of more than 100,000 people, however, was made up overwhelmingly of French Jews, which came as a major disappointment to a Jewish community that had hoped that large sectors of the non-Jewish public would demonstrate solidarity. Roger Cukierman, the CRIF president, said in an interview with the Jewish weekly *Actualités Juives* on March 9 that the failure to make the fight against anti-

Semitism a national priority, particularly on the part of the media, "is very dangerous."

Thousands of newspaper and magazine articles were written about the Halimi affair, and several books were subsequently devoted to the subject. Among them was philosopher Adrian Barrot's *If This Is a Jew,* whose title was modeled on Primo Levi's account of survival at Auschwitz, *If This Is a Man.* Barrot wrote, "This was not just an anti-Semitic crime, this was Nazism in its most basic state; this is the sewer from which Nazism sprang."

Israel and the Middle East

Franco-Israeli relations began the year in a positive fashion, still reflecting the unexpected warmth that marked the visit to Paris in July 2005 of Prime Minister Ariel Sharon (see AJYB 2006, pp. 344–45).

Israeli foreign minister Tzipi Livni visited France in March as part of a tour of West European capitals to update these governments on Israeli policies in the wake of the Hamas victory in the Palestinian Authority elections. Livni gave an interview to the conservative daily newspaper *Le Figaro* in which she said: "If the Islamists are going to use the Palestinian Authority to promote terrorism and hate, that goes completely contrary to the concept which motivated us in supporting the creation of the PA." She discussed with French foreign minister Douste-Blazy the issue of foreign funds donated to the PA, which Israel feared might be used for anti-Israel purposes. Douste-Blazy, however, told Livni that the lack of funds would "lead to chaos in the territories." He said, "A brutal collapse of the Palestinian administration and economy is in no one's interest."

President Chirac telephoned Prime Minister Olmert on March 30, two days after Kadima's strong showing in the Israeli general election, to congratulate him and "to underline the importance which France attaches to its relations of friendship and confidence with Israel." Chirac was also reported to have said that he hoped "the same dynamism which marked ties with former prime minister Sharon would continue." Douste-Blazy also hailed Olmert, saying his party's electoral success was "good news for peace."

Such warm feelings were apparently also felt by the general public. An opinion poll carried out on behalf of CRIF showed that the French had far more positive impressions of Israeli leaders than of Palestinian leaders. Conducted by the Sofres polling group, the survey indicated that 57 percent of the sample were convinced Olmert would improve the living conditions of Israel's population, whereas only 39 percent thought the Palestinian government would do so for its people. The same poll showed that 64 percent of Frenchmen polled and 46 percent of Frenchwomen did not believe the Palestinian government sought peace. Doubts about Palestinian motivations were highest among respondents with the highest levels of education: a full 70 percent of university graduates did not believe that the Palestinians had peaceful intentions, as compared to 55 percent of non-graduates.

The summer crisis over Lebanon, taking place at the same time as Israeli operations in the Gaza Strip, saw France initially adopt a relatively even-handed stance. In the early stages of Israeli military action in response to Hezballah's capture of two Israeli soldiers near the Lebanese border and Hamas's seizure of one soldier near the Gaza Strip demarcation line, President Chirac expressed sympathy with civilians under Israeli bombardment, and also called, in the same statement, for the release of the captured Israeli soldiers and for a halt to rocket fire against Israel. Clearly referring to Syria and Hezballah, Chirac said: "One must stop all forces which endanger the security, stability and sovereignty of Lebanon." Three days later, while blaming Israel for "the destruction of infrastructure and equipment which is indispensable for the running of Lebanon," he was even clearer in placing blame on Hezballah, saying, "there cannot be a politically stable Lebanon . . . if part of its territory is occupied by militias which do not obey the Lebanese government."

France then undertook a major operation to evacuate thousands of French-passport-holders from Lebanon, many of them people born in Lebanon or of Lebanese extraction who held dual citizenship. The part of the evacuation undertaken in south Lebanon close to the Israeli border was closely coordinated with Israeli authorities, ensuring that bus convoys were properly identified so as to avoid their being mistakenly hit by Israeli aircraft.

France played a major role in the see-saw negotiations at the UN in New York and elsewhere that ultimately led to the Security Council's adoption of Resolution 1701, instituting an effective cease-fire and the addition of new contingents to reinforce the UN Interim Force in Lebanon (UNIFIL). Despite the resolution's calls, however, the two kidnapped Israeli soldiers were not released. Lebanese government troops arrived in the area for the first time in decades, but they did not disarm Hezballah, which apparently either pulled out of the area or concealed its weapons.

The summer crisis led to a series of political statements and demonstrations in France. Interior Minister Nicolas Sarkozy said on July 15 that Hezballah was the clear aggressor in the conflict. "Israel must defend itself and has the right to defend itself, but, if one is a friend of Israel as I am, one must advise Israel not to lose control and to overreact." He added, however, that "it is easier to give this advice from Paris than from Haifa," then under bombardment. Two small anti-Israel demonstrations took place in the streets of Paris that same day, one by Hezballah sympathizers, most of them Arabs, and the other by supporters of the Lebanese government who condemned Israel but also asked for Hezballah's disarmament.

French Jewish organizations were very active during the crisis raising funds for Israel, while small groups and individuals went to Israel on self-styled missions to distribute foodstuffs to inhabitants of northern border towns under bombardment. The families of the three kidnapped Israeli soldiers later came to Paris to meet government officials and French Jewish leaders as part of a campaign to secure the release of the three. One of them, Gilad Shalit, captured near Gaza, had dual Franco-Israeli citizenship. One recent immigrant from France who had arrived in Israel shortly before the conflict without his parents was among the Israeli soldiers killed in the conflict.

The Paris suburb of Issy-les-Moulineaux received 30 Israeli teenagers from the town of Nahariya, with which it was twinned, and hosted them at a seaside summer camp for three weeks in August. A group of 13 Israeli youths of Ethiopian origin who lived in northern Israel spent August as guests of the city of Metz, in eastern France, while ten young people from the northern Israeli town of Maalot were received at a Jewish holiday camp on the French Atlantic coast.

The French Foreign Ministry—long suspected by French Jewry of harboring pro-Arab sympathies—issued a public call for funds to aid Lebanese refugees, as it had done often before for refugees in other conflicts. Reminded by French Jewish groups that many Israelis had also been forced from their homes, the ministry donated $200,000 to refurbish a kindergarten for handicapped children in Acre and help build a center for trauma victims in Afula. Paris mayor Bertrand Delanoë, a friend of the Jewish community, visited Israel in November and handed over some $65,000 to aid projects in the north of the country.

In a move clearly connected to French domestic politics, the European Parliament announced in October that a visit to Israel scheduled by a parliamentary delegation from October 28 to November 4 had been "postponed to a further undecided date for technical reasons connected to the delegation's program." The decision was actually due to the presence in the delegation of Marine Le Pen, daughter of, and would-be political heiress to, extreme rightist leader Jean-Marie Le Pen. Marine Le Pen had for several years conducted a discreet campaign to woo Jews and soften the image of her father, whose multiple anti-Semitic outbursts landed him in French courtrooms on several occasions. But according to Jewish community sources, Israeli authorities had said that if Marine Le Pen were in the delegation, there would be no meetings with Israeli officials.

An unexpected mini-crisis broke out between Israel and France on November 8, when French defense minister Alliot-Marie told Parliament that Israeli combat aircraft had carried out what she described as mock attack runs against the headquarters of a French UN battalion at Deir Kifa in south Lebanon on October 31. "We were just seconds away from firing antiaircraft missiles for our defense," she said.

Israeli ambassador Daniel Shek was summoned to the French Foreign Ministry, where he denied any hostile intentions and said the overflights were wrongly interpreted by the French contingent. Shek said Israel had to continue reconnaissance flights over Lebanon since Hezballah was still receiving weaponry from Syria. While Resolution 1701 outlawed such flights, Shek said Israel could not comply until all parts of the resolution, including that calling for the release of the soldiers, were implemented. An IDF officer later visited Paris to draw up procedures to avoid new incidents.

CRIF carried out an opinion poll in November on French attitudes toward Iran. Conducted by the TNS Sofres group among 1,000 respondents, it showed that 80 percent believed Iranian president Mahmoud Ahmadinejad when he said he wanted to wipe Israel from the face of the earth, and 81 percent thought Iran wanted to build nuclear weapons. Although some 79 percent said they favored UN sanctions, only 37 percent wanted Iran expelled from the UN, with 47 percent disagreeing. CRIF president Roger Cukierman commented, "We were rather satisfied because its findings showed that the French are mature and aware of the danger of a nuclear armed Iran."

A Paris court, on October 19, ordered Philippe Karsenty, the (Jewish) director of the Media-Ratings Web site, to pay $1,300 in damages and $4,000 in costs for libeling television journalist Charles Enderlin of the state-owned France 2 network. Enderlin, a French immigrant to Israel and the station's veteran correspondent in the country, was the author of the TV report of the death of a Palestinian child, Muhammad al-Dura, in Gaza in late September 2000 (see AJYB 2001, p. 495). The image had since been used around the world to excoriate Israeli policies.

Enderlin, in fact, had not been present on the scene, but used his Palestinian cameraman's film and authored the text, which blamed Israeli troops for the death. The IDF, however, had since said it was impossible to know who was responsible for the child's death in a cross-fire. Karsenty had claimed on his Web site that the entire scene was faked, and demanded that Enderlin resign. Instead, Enderlin, under fire from French Jewry ever since the affair, sued. The court found that Karsenty brought no proof of his allegations, and cited the Israeli army's own uncertainty about the case.

Philosopher and pro-Israel activist Alain Finkielkraut was acquitted in two separate court cases, on June 27 and July 4, of libel charges. The first had been brought by anti-Zionist Israeli filmmaker Eyal Sivan, and the second by the Movement Against Racism and for Friendship Among Peoples (MRAP). In 2005, Finkielkraut had been the target of a major campaign against him by left-wing groups and publications because of his support of Israel and his remarks about criminal behavior among immigrant communities (see AJYB 2006, p. 341).

The 2006 court cases, however, involved statements Finkielkraut made in 2003. In the first instance, he accused Sivan of "participating in Jewish anti-Semitism" by producing a documentary film comparing the situation of Palestinians to that of Jews in occupied Europe. The Paris court cleared Finkielkraut, saying his statement was fair criticism. In the second case, Finkielkraut had denounced MRAP's support of the UN's World Conference Against Racism, held in Durban, South Africa, in 2001, which had strongly anti-Semitic features. Finkielkraut, in a play on words, insinuated that the self-styled antiracists of MRAP were transforming themselves into anti-Semites. The court dismissed that case as well on the grounds that the accusation of libel had not been clearly proven.

A Paris court, on June 13, ruled that black "comedian" Dieudonné M'bala M'bala had to pay $2,000 in damages and $5,000 in costs to the Jewish television personality Arthur (real name, Jacques Essebag) for libel. Dieudonné, who specialized in goading the French Jewish community and had been virtually excluded from appearing on television due to a string of anti-Semitic outbursts, said Arthur's highly successful production company "actively and financially supports the Israeli army which kills Palestinian children." Another court had already fined him $6,500 on March 10 for incitement to racial hatred against Jews. In that case, Dieudonné had said in a newspaper interview, referring to Jews, "It is all those slaveowners who reconverted themselves into banking and show business who today back Ariel Sharon's policies."

Later in the year, in the wake of the summer war on the Israel-Lebanon border, Dieudonné paid a "solidarity visit" to Lebanon and Syria, accompanied by several ultra-leftist figures, including Thierry Meyssen, author of a book purporting to show that no aircraft crashed into the Pentagon on September 11, 2001. During their visit they met Hezballah leaders, whom they praised for their anti-Israel actions.

Anti-Semitism

After falling by nearly 50 percent between 2004 and 2005, the number of anti-Semitic incidents went up sharply, from 300 in 2005 to 371 in 2006—a 24-percent increase. Incidents involving physical attacks against people rose from 77 to 112. The Service de Protection de la Communauté Juive (SPCJ), the security service maintained by the Jewish community, which worked closely with the police, attributed the worrying trend to tensions surrounding the Halimi affair and Israel's summer conflict in south Lebanon.

When assailants were identified in the most serious incidents, they were overwhelmingly young French nationals of Muslim Arab origin, or—increasingly—blacks of West-Central African origin. Victims of the physical attacks were nearly all young Jews, often minors, set upon haphazardly in the streets of lower-class neighborhoods when they were recognized as Jews. Several non-Jews mistakenly identified as Jews were also attacked.

Aside from the 112 physical attacks, there were 213 incidents involving vandalism or the throwing of objects at Jewish property. This marked a 40-percent rise from the year before, which saw 152 such incidents. Less serious violations, such as threats, false bomb alerts, insults, and hate mail, numbered 158 compared to 148 the year before, a 7-percent increase.

The overwhelming majority of incidents took place in the greater Paris area, particularly in blue-collar neighborhoods where Jewish minorities lived cheek-by-jowl with far more numerous Muslim Arab populations. There were virtually no attacks on Jewish community buildings, such as synagogues or schools, presumably because of the heavy protection afforded them by the state—often, as he himself liked to recall, at the instigation of Interior Minister Sarkozy.

One exception was an attempt to burn down the Mercaz HaTorah boys' school in the rough Paris suburb of Gagny late on the night of November 8, when the building was empty. A window was broken and a firebomb thrown inside, but the blaze was quickly spotted and extinguished by the occupants of a police car on regular night patrol.

Commenting on the 2006 statistics, SPCJ spokesman Ariel Goldman said, "We are no longer in the dramatic period of 2001–02. But neither are we in a zero-incident period like in 1990. What we are going through is a hazy period where there are punctual flare-ups of anti-Semitism. The situation remains worrisome." He expressed concern that after the murder of Ilan Halimi, which should have come as a cautionary warning to French society, the pace of anti-Semitic incidents in fact accelerated.

One incident that drew nationwide attention was the demonstrative presence, on Sunday, May 28, in the Rue des Rosiers—the best known "Jewish street" in Paris—of more than 30 members of "Tribu Ka" (Ka Tribe), a group of black extremists who admired the head of the American black Muslims, Louis Farrakhan. The "Tribu Ka," threatening passersby, said they had come to "settle accounts" with Betar, a militant Jewish nationalist youth group they accused of attacking passing blacks during the February street march in Ilan Halimi's memory. Incidents of Jewish youths attacking innocent Arabs or blacks had indeed marked several large-scale Jewish gatherings in the past. The blacks paraded around the Rue des Rosiers for nearly half an hour before police arrived and searched them for concealed weapons, which Jewish merchants said they had seen. No weapons were found and no arrests made.

The media reported extensively about the story. Politicians flocked to the neighborhood to express sympathy with the Jewish community. Among the first on the scene was Interior Minister Sarkozy, who ordered the "Tribu Ka" disbanded in July. The group held several public meetings since under other names, but stayed away from the Jewish quarter.

Another incident that drew wide attention and stimulated public debate occurred in early November. Jewish shopkeeper René Dahan and his wife were attacked in their home in the quiet Paris suburb of Nogent-sur-Marne by three intruders, two Arabs and one West Indian, who broke in as Mr. Dahan was about to leave for work in the morning. The three were planning to extort money from him, but Dahan leaped on one of them and wrestled his pistol away. A free-for-all ensued, and Dahan fired two shots that caused the men to flee. As the West Indian, a 27-year-old with a long police record, jumped out the window, Dahan fired a third shot that killed him instantly. Police summoned to the crime scene took Dahan away for questioning, and a magistrate ordered him jailed on the charge of manslaughter, since the fatal shot was not fired in self-defense.

There was an immediate uproar from shopkeepers' associations, self-defense groups, and Jewish personalities, who protested the magistrate's decision. Interior Minister Sarkozy intervened publicly and asked Justice Minister Pascal Clement to release Dahan, which he did. Sarkozy's political rival Royal charged that the interior minister was "playing politics" with a case that should have been left in the hands of the judicial system. The two surviving assailants told police they had singled out Dahan because they knew he was Jewish and assumed he was wealthy. By a strange coincidence, Dahan's shop was on the same Boulevard Voltaire in eastern Paris where Ilan Halimi had worked.

On November 23, there was a soccer match between visiting Hapoel Tel Aviv and host Paris St. Germain, a team notorious for the hundreds of Nazi-saluting skinheads who attended its games. Israeli fans who had arrived from Tel Aviv to support their team were placed together in a part of the stadium specially protected by police in anticipation of trouble, but several thousand French Jewish spectators were dispersed throughout the stadium, and they became the target of insults when they hoisted Israeli banners. The likelihood of violence escalated when the Israelis trounced the host team 4-1, and PSG fans, especially the skinhead element, began to harass Jews outside the stadium immediately after the match.

Yaniv Hazout, a young French Jew, was pursued by a gang of such hooligans when he was identified as a Jew after leaving the stadium. Just as he was about to be caught by dozens of potential aggressors, plainclothes policeman Antoine Granomort, a black native of the French West Indian island of Guadeloupe, stepped in to protect him. With dozens of skinheads closing in on them shouting, "Dirty Jew" and "Dirty Arab," Granomort pulled out his service pistol. When knocked to the ground and after losing his glasses, Granomort fired a single bullet which went through the lung of Moroccan-born Mounir Bouchaer and fatally injured Frenchman Julien Quemeneur, who died on the spot from a bullet to the heart. Granomort and Hazout took refuge in a McDonald's restaurant, which was attacked by close to 200 infuriated fans. They broke all the windows before police reinforcements arrived and dispersed the crowd, making several arrests.

Bouchaer was known to police as a soccer hooligan, but Quemeneur was not, and his family and friends insisted he was an ordinary fan. But police footage of the game showed the shaven-headed Quemeneur with a bandana around the lower half of his face, standing and shouting among the most active PSG supporters. Granomort was questioned by police internal disciplinary services, and they accepted his statement that he acted in self-defence. The Jewish community asked that Granomort be treated as a hero and decorated, but it later emerged he was already under investigation within the police department for a criminal act he may have committed several months before.

An opinion poll conducted by the IFOP group on March 2–3 found that 64 percent of the French public believed anti-Semitism was on the rise in the country, as compared to 36 percent who did not think so. The category with the highest percentage of people who did not believe anti-Semitism was increasing was those who had the highest level of education. Commentators explained that this reflected the fact that anti-Semitic incidents rarely occurred in well-to-do neighborhoods.

Holocaust-Related Matters

A French administrative court, on June 7, ordered the SNCF National Railways to pay about $250,000 in damages to Alain Lipietz, a member of the European Parliament representing the French Green Party, as well as to his uncle and his sister, for transporting four members of their family, including Lipietz's father, to the Drancy internment camp in May 1944. Scheduled to be sent from there to Auschwitz, where 76,000 other French Jews were murdered, they were freed that August by advancing allied troops. The court found that the railways "could not have ignored at the time that they were facilitating an operation that was meant to be a prelude to the deportation of the persons involved to death camps."

Lipietz said the ruling demonstrated the responsibility of the Vichy French administration for Nazi policies. But the SNCF appealed the decision on the grounds that it was based on "historically false arguments." Its lawyer, ironically, was Jewish activist Arno Klarsfeld, son of Nazi-hunter Serge Klarsfeld, who was the lawyer for the SNCF in similar cases pending before U.S. courts. Klarsfeld senior, commenting on the Lipietz case in the newspaper Le Monde, wrote, "Could one have demanded that those who drove railways resign and deprive their families of their livelihood? Those who did so were heroes while the others were, and always will be, the majority. Indifference to the sorrows of others is not a crime, it is part of human nature."

The controversy was given considerable space in the Jewish weekly Actualités Juives. Lawyer Corinne Hershkovitch, who represented some 450 families filing legal claims against the SNCF, said many victims felt guilty because Serge Klarsfeld disapproved of their actions. Paul Mingasson, executive director of the SNCF, recalled that the company itself had sponsored the historical research that led to the judicial decision against it, and that the SNCF had not only cooperated with Jewish groups in organizing events to recall the Holocaust, but had gone so far as to affix memorial plaques in railways stations from which Jews had been deported. Serge Klarsfeld told Actualités Juives that "the government has already done what was necessary in paying pensions to survivors and their descendants . . . ."

French Holocaust denier Robert Faurisson was sentenced on October 3 to a suspended three-month prison term and ordered to pay a fine of $10,000. This was the fifth time French courts had found him guilty of such crimes. The charge this time, brought by several human-rights groups, had to do with an interview Faurisson gave in 2005 to Sahar 1, an Iranian television station whose broadcasts could be seen by French dish owners, in which he said, "There never existed a single Nazi gas chamber . . . everything that tourists see at Auschwitz is a lie and a falsehood for tourists."

A Paris court ruled on July 11 that extreme right-wing leader Jean-Marie Le Pen would have to stand trial for new statements he had made minimizing the impact of the Nazi occupation of France. In January 2005 Le Pen told the ultra-rightist weekly *Rivarol* that the occupation had "not been particularly inhumane when you take into account the size of France," and went on to cast the Gestapo in a positive light. In September, the date for the trial was scheduled for June 2007, which led to protests from Serge Klarsfeld, who said that setting the trial after the April–May presidential elections seemed calculated to enable Le Pen to run, as a new condemnation before a French court would immediately bar him from doing so.

L'Est Républicain, a newspaper in Nancy, in the east of France, refused to publish a memorial notice submitted by a local Jew, Joel Volfson, commemorating the 40th anniversary of the death of his father, a merchant deported to Auschwitz in 1944. The paper objected to the notice's reference to "Nazi barbarity," which it found "too violent," and insisted that *L'Est Republicain* retained the right to refuse certain terms in ads. It gave, as another example, the word "murder" when submitted by the families of those killed in car crashes. Local Jewish groups protested, and the French national journalists' union, SNJ, noting that other French newspapers published such ads, called on *L'Est Républicain* to change its policy. The controversy escalated when a spokesman for the newspaper told a Jewish journalist, "What would you say if we were to publish a death notice about a Lebanese civilian killed in the recent war with Israel that would contain the words, "Israeli barbarity?"

Jewish activist Patrick Gaubert, president of the International League against Racism and Anti-Semitism (LICRA), a leading human-rights group created in the 1930s to fight Nazism, denounced ceremonies organized by the Ukrainian community to honor Ukranian national hero

Simon Petliura, who had been a leading pogromist. On May 25, Ukrainian diplomats and expatriates laid a wreath in his honor at the Tomb of France's Unknown Soldier, and Gaubert requested French authorities not to allow this to happen again. Petliura, a key figure in the establishment of Ukraine's short-lived independence in 1917, was responsible for the deaths of hundreds of thousands of Jews there at that time. He went into exile in France when Soviet Russia took over his country, and was assassinated in Paris in 1925 by Samuel Schwarzbard, a Ukrainian-born Jewish veteran of the French army.

On October 16, President Chirac decorated an American, Abraham Foxman, national director of the Anti-Defamation League (ADL), with the insignia of Chevalier (Knight) of the Legion of Honor, in recognition of his efforts to fight anti-Semitism and strengthen ties between France and the American Jewish community. The ceremony took place at the Élysée Palace.

The French government announced on December 21 that a special national tribute would be held in Paris on January 18, 2007, to French nationals who had been designated Righteous Gentiles by Jerusalem's Yad Vashem for saving Jews during World War II. Chirac would preside over the ceremony at the Pantheon building, the resting place of French national heroes. Some 2,740 French nationals were Righteous Gentiles, the third largest national contingent after Poland and the Netherlands.

French Jews of Tunisian origin held a special commemoration on December 10 to mark the 64th anniversary of the arrest of Tunisian Jewish leaders by the German S.S. in 1942, when the country was briefly occupied by the Nazis. Some 5,000 Jews were then interned and placed into forced labor, including the repair of airfields under fire. The Allied victory in Tunisia in May 1943 secured the release of all the Jews but a few, who had been transferred to Europe by plane and sent to concentration camps, the only known cases of such deportations by air.

JEWISH COMMUNITY

Communal Affairs

The governing board of the World Jewish Congress met in Paris on November 16. More than 100 Jewish leaders from 80 countries attended. Prime Minister de Villepin addressed the gathering, pledging that France would continue to fight against anti-Semitism and would reinforce its ties with Israel. Other speakers included Dr. Dalil Boubakeur, president of the Council of French Muslims, and Monsignor André Vingt-Trois, archbishop of Paris. WJC president Edgar Bronfman hailed the presence of these religious leaders and called for a world alliance of religions. Bronfman and others denounced Iranian statements calling for Israel's destruction. WJC leaders were received during their visit by President Chirac.

A group of Jewish female intellectuals successfully challenged, before the nation's courts, one of French Jewry's last all-male bastions, getting the judicial system to declare illegal the exclusion of women from the board of the Jewish Consistory—which managed the religious affairs of the community—in the province of Alsace. When the Consistory system was established by Emperor Napoléon I in the early nineteenth century, only men were allowed to run for election. When religion and state were separated in France in 1905, Alsace was under German rule, and the separation requirement was not applied when it reverted to French control in 1918.

In October 2006, a group of women professors and physicians filed suit to force the Consistory to change its rule banning women, saying that it violated the laws of France and the European Union. The local rabbinate, however, resisted. After the women won their case, a number of Orthodox men resigned from the board, and, after a particularly tense board meeting, Chief Rabbi René Guttman had to be rushed to the hospital. New elections were held in December, and a woman, Sandrine Buchinger, was elected from the city of Mulhouse, winning more votes than any of the men who were competing.

President Chirac presided over a major commemoration on July 12 to mark the 100th anniversary of the rehabilitation of Captain Alfred Dreyfus. It took place on the same spot, on the grounds of L'École Militaire, the French War College, where Dreyfus had been ceremonially stripped of his rank in 1894 while anti-Semites outside shouted for his death. Descendants of Dreyfus and leaders of the French Jewish community were guests at the military ceremony, which received massive media coverage. In his speech Chirac said that the lesson of this episode was that "the rejection of racism and of anti-Semitism, the defense of human rights, and the absolute need to place justice above all are values which are now part of our heritage."

The organized Jewish community gave full support to Robert Redeker, a philosophy professor forced to go underground under police protection after receiving credible death threats in September. Redeker, who taught near Toulouse until forced to suspend his activities, had written an article in the French daily *Le Figaro* on September 19 titled, "What Must the Free World Do in the Face of Muslim Intimidations?" It appeared in the wake of the international controversy earlier in the year over cartoons of Mohammed that led to violent demonstrations in some Muslim countries and a number of deaths (see below, pp. 433–35).

Redeker compared Islam to communism in its heyday, in the manner in which intellectuals feared to criticize it. He noted that passages from the Koran showed Mohammed to have been a "pitiless warlord, looter, killer of Jews, and polygamist," and charged that Muslim holy texts glorified violence and hate. The "death sentences" against Redeker immediately appeared on Islamic Web sites in several languages, containing his photo, home address, and maps showing how to reach his home. CRIF called on the authorities to offer full protection to Redeker and to allow him to teach again, and its president, Roger Cukierman, was onstage when Redeker appeared, with police protection, at a public rally for him in Toulouse, in November.

The remains of Paulina and Hans Herzl, children of Theodor Herzl, founder of the modern Zionist movement, were disinterred from the Jewish cemetery of Bordeaux on September 19, and flown to Israel where they were reburied near their father's on Jerusalem's Mount Herzl the following day. Ceremonies were held at both cemeteries, in the presence of French Jewish leaders and Israeli diplomats. Paulina, who suffered from mental disorders, died in 1930, and Hans committed suicide over her grave the next day. A third child, a younger daughter named Trude, was killed in a Nazi concentration camp in Czechoslovakia and her body was never found.

The French Jewish cable television station TFJ went out of business in November. After an earlier bankruptcy in 2003, it had resumed broadcasting in March 2006 with 16 employees, only to fail once again. Lack of sufficient advertising revenue was blamed in both cases.

Immigration to Israel

Of the 19,624 people worldwide who immigrated to Israel in 2006, approximately 2,900 came from France. Slightly down from the 2005 figure of 3,005, it was still the second largest annual French aliyah in 34 years. The numbers were even more impressive in light of the fact that total aliyah from all countries dropped by 9 percent from 2005, and was the lowest since 1988.

Despite the ongoing Lebanese conflict, the Jewish Agency maintained a scheduled mass arrival of French Jewish immigrants on July 25, when 650 people arrived at Ben Gurion Airport aboard special flights from Paris and Nice. They were personally greeted by Prime Minister Olmert who, referring to bombardments from Lebanon, said that Israel's enemies "may have weapons which can hurt us, but our secret and powerful weapon is the Jewish people who love the State of Israel, who come to live here and to defend it. Our enemies do not understand the special link that ties together Jews around the world wherever they are."

Culture

Many original publications of Jewish interest appeared in France during 2006.

Among the significant books of fiction were Alain Suied's *L'Eveillée* (The Awakened One); Gerald Tenenbaum *Le Geste* (The Gesture); Edeet Ravel's *Trois Mille Amants* (3,000 Lovers); Revisionist Zionist leader Vladimir Jabotinsky's *Les Cinq* (The Five), a French translation from the Russian original, published in Paris in 1934 as a serial in a local Russian-language journal; Nathalie Azoulai's *Les Manifestations* (The Demonstrations); Dominique Laury's *Un Juif par Hasard* (A Jew by Chance); Michael Sabban's *Kotel California;* Gilles Rozier's *La Promesse d'Oslo* (The Oslo Promise); Maurice Attia's *Alger la Noire* (Algiers the Black); Donia Fervante's *Desarrois* (Helplessness); Richard Malka and Paul Gillon's *L'Ordred de Cicéron* (The Order of Cicero); Jonathan Littell's *Les Bienveillantes* (The Kindly Ones), written in French by an American author; and Marc Weitzmann's *Fraternité* (Fraternity).

Books on ideas and current affairs included Alain Finkielkraut and Benny Lévy's *Le Livre et les livres* (The Book and Books); Marie Balmary's *Le Moine et le Psychanalyste* (The Monk and the Psychoanalyst); Henri Meschonnic's *La Pensée et le poème* (Thought and the Poem); Raphael Drai's *L'Etat Purgatoire* (The Purgatory State); Jacqueline Mesnil Amar and André Amar's *Parcours d'Ecriture* (A Journey of Writing); David Saada's *Le Pouvoir de Benir* (The Power to Bless); Rabbi Daniel Farhi's *Profession — Rabbin* (Profession — Rabbi); Shmuel Trigano's *L'Avenir des Juifs de France* (The Future of France's Jews); Liliana Messika and Fabien Ghez's *La Paix Impossible?* (The Impossible Peace?); André Glucksmann's *Une Rage d'Enfant* (A Child's Anger); Elisabeth de Fontenay's *Une Toute Autre Histoire* (A Completely Different History); Catherine Chalier's *La Lettre et L'Esprit* (The Letter and the Spirit);

Fréderic Encel's *Geopolitique du Sionism* (Geopolitics of Zionism); and Rony Brauman and Alain Finkielkraut's *La Discorde* (The Discord).

Some historical works were Brigitte Sion's *Max Ehrlich: Le Théâtre contre la barbarie* (Max Ehrlich: Theater against Barbarism); Gérard Silvain and Joël Kotek's *La Carte Postale Anti-Sémite depuis l'Affaire Dréyfus jusqu'a la Shoah* (Anti-Semitic Postcards from the Dreyfus Affair to the Shoah); Clémence Bouloque and Nicole Sarfaty's *Juives d'Afrique du Nord: Cartes Postales* (North African Jewish Postcards); Pierre Birnbaum's *Prier pour l'Etat: Les Juifs, L'Alliance Royale et la Démocratie* (Praying for the State: Jews, the Royal Alliance, and Democracy); Jo Amiel's *Et si... Un Rève Imaginé* (And If ... An Imagined Dream); Henri Minczeles's *Une Histoire des Juifs de Pologne* (A History of Polish Jewry); Olivier Todd's *Carte d'Identités* (Card of Identities); Albert Lirtzmann's *Bogopol;* Betty Rojtman's *Les début du Bné Akiva en Europe* (The Beginnings of Bnei Akiva in Europe); Gerard Desporte's *Les Dessaisis* (The Dispossessed); and Samuel Blumenfeld's *L'Homme qui Voulait Etre Prince — Les Vies Imaginaires de Michal Waszynski* (The Man Who Wanted to Be a Prince — The Imaginary Lives of Michal Waszynski,

On the subject of Israel there were three works about former prime minister Ariel Sharon: Freddy Eytan's *Sharon, le Bras de Fer* (Sharon, the Iron Arm); Daniel Haik's *Sharon, Un Destin Inachevé* (Sharon, An Unfinished Destiny); and Michel Gurfinkiel's *Le Testament d'Ariel Sharon* (Ariel Sharon's Will), as well as Pierre Razoux's *Tsahal, Nouvelle Histoire de l'Armée Israélienne* (Tsahal, a New History of the Israeli Army).

Holocaust-related books included Laurent Joly's *Vichy Dans La Solution Finale* (Vichy in the Final Solution); Patrick Rotman's *Les Survivants* (The Survivors); Diane Afumado's *Exil Impossible — L'Errance des Juifs du Paquebot St.-Louis* (Impossible Exile — The Wanderings of the Jews of the Passenger Liner St. Louis); Imré Kovac's *Le Vengeur — À la Poursuite des Criminels Nazis* (The Avenger — Hunting the Nazi Criminals); Monique Novodorski-Deniau's *Pithiviers-Auschwitz, 17 juillet 1942* (From Pithiviers to Auschwitz, July 17, 1942); Joseph Minc's *L'Extraordinaire Histoire de ma Vie Ordinaire* (The Extraordinary Story of My Ordinary Life); Laure Adler's *Dans les Pas de Hannah Arendt* (In the Footsteps of Hannah Arendt); Rika Zarai's *L'Esperance a toujours raison* (Hope Is Always Right); and Fréderic Gasquet's *La Lettre de Mon Père* (My Father's Letter).

There were a number of films of Jewish interest. Christophe Malavoy's *Zone Libre* (Free Zone), adapted from a play by Jean-Claude Grumberg, was about the trials and tribulations of a family of Polish Jewish origin hidden in a French farmhouse during the Nazi occupation. Roschdy Zem's *Mauvaise Foi* (Bad Faith) concerned the multiple misunderstandings that can arise when a French Muslim man and an Ashkenazi Frenchwoman, neither of whom are religious, try to inform their respective families of their nuptial intentions. The film was based on the French-Arab director's real-life marriage. Zem, of Moroccan origin, also played an Israeli Jewish father who adopts an Ethiopian Jewish orphan in the film hit *Va, Vis et Deviens* (Live and Become). Élie Chouraqui's *O Jerusalem* was based on the best-selling book of the same name by Dominique Lapierre and Larry Collins; Chantal Akerman's *La-Bas* (Over There) was an impressionistic documentary about the director's recent stay in Israel; Lisa Azuelos's *Comme T'y Es Belle* (How Beautiful You Are) satirized "nouveau riche" Sephardi Jewish women in France; and Joseph Morder's *El Cantor* (The Cantor) focused on a dysfunctional Jewish family.

Deaths

Author and songwriter Jacques Lanzmann died on June 21, aged 79. The son of Polish-Jewish immigrants and the brother of philosopher and film director Claude Lanzmann (*Shoah*), he traveled around the world after World War II, during which he had fought in the *maquis* underground against Nazis and their French collaborators, supporting himself as a welder, cleaner, house painter, and miner (in Chile), before turning to writing. Among his best known works were *Le Rat d'Amérique* (The Rat from America), *Cuir Russe* (Russian Leather), and *Viva Castro*. He wrote some 150 songs for well known French singers.

Social worker and wartime rescuer of Jewish children Vivette Samuel died on July 16, aged 87. The daughter of Nahum Herman, director of the French branch of the Karen Hayesod, who was killed in a Nazi concentration camp, Vivette was the widow of Julien Samuel, the first postwar head of the Fonds Social Juif Unifié—the welfare and educational arm of the organized French Jewish community—and creator of the respected Jewish monthly *L'Arche*. A social worker for Oeuvre de Secours aux Enfants (OSE), a Jewish welfare organization, in Vichy France from 1940 to 1942, she organized the escape from internment camps to Switzerland of about 400 Jewish children. She continued her work underground after the Nazis occupied southern France, and later wrote a book, *Sauver les Enfants* (To Save the Children), recounting her experiences. After the war, she was involved in rehabilitating concentration camp survivors, and later returned to OSE, serving as director general from 1979 through 1985.

Film director Gerard Oury (born Max-Gérard Tannebaum), best known for his blockbuster comedy *The Mad Adventures of Rabbi Jacob,* died on July 20 at the age of 87. A theater and film actor who began his career before World War II, Oury started directing in 1959. The 19 films he directed were seen by an estimated 50 million people, plus another 200 million who saw them on television.

Jewish community activist Kurt Niedermaier died on September 11, aged 83. Born in Germany, he fled to France with his family shortly before World War II, and during the Nazi occupation was hidden together with other youths his age on a farm at Moissac, in central France, run by the UEJF, the French Jewish students' organization. Completing his studies after the war, he was employed by Jewish think tanks and educational organizations, helping create the Israel and Middle East Documentation Center and dealing with the European Parliament.

Writer André Schwarz-Bart, aged 78, died on September 30 on the French West Indian island of Guadeloupe. He was best known for the world-acclaimed *The Last of the Just,* a novel about a Jewish family from the Middle Ages until Auschwitz. Published in 1959, it won the Prix Goncourt, France's top literary award, the same year, and the Jerusalem Prize in 1967. Born in Metz, France, of Polish Jewish immigrant parents, he was deeply marked by the experience of World War II, when he fought for the French Resistance. Both of his parents and two brothers were murdered in Nazi death camps. He also wrote *Pork and Green Bananas* together with his Guadeloupe-born wife Simone, with whom he also wrote the seven-volume encyclopedia *In Praise of Black Women.*

Retired boxer Alphonse Halimi died on November 12, aged 74. The Algerian-born Halimi was world bantamweight champion from 1957 to 1959, and became European champion in 1962 when he won a match in Tel Aviv, the first professional fight ever held in Israel. Halimi always fought with a large Star of David on his shorts.

BERNARD EDINGER

Belgium

National Affairs

Two LANDMARK EVENTS took place in Belgium during February. The Belgian Senate held a solemn ceremony on February 7, with the royal family present, to mark 175 years since the adoption of the nation's constitution, and more than 3,000 elementary-school children were brought there to watch a reenactment of the adoption. Later in the month, the Atomium, the world-famous structure built for the 1958 Brussels World's Fair, was reopened to the public. It had taken more than a year to renovate, at the cost of 27 million euros.

Belgium took a major step toward modernization in 2006 by introducing an electronic identity card the size of a bankcard, with a microchip in it. It was expected to cut down sharply on instances of identity theft.

Local elections, the first since 2000, were scheduled for October 8. These would also be the first such elections to be organized and overseen by the individual Regions rather than the federal government. The contested offices were municipal counselors for 589 cities and towns, representatives on ten provincial councils, and other positions. As election day came out on the second day of Sukkot, a good number of Jews could not vote. But voting was compulsory in Belgium, and so the Jewish Central Consistory issued observant Jews the necessary affidavits enabling them to cast ballots by proxy.

The electoral prospects facing the center-left national governing coalition—made up of Prime Minister Guy Verhofstadt's Dutch-speaking Liberal Democrats, based in Flanders, and the French-speaking Socialists in Wallonia—were marred by a widespread public perception that crime and corruption were out of control.

First, there was the long-running case of serial killer Michel Fourniret (see AJYB 2005, p. 352), who had evaded justice for years and was finally extradited to France in January 2006 to be tried for murdering six girls. Also, a scheme to fix soccer matches, first revealed in the fall of 2005, was corroborated by the VRT broadcast network in 2006, setting off an investigation. Then, Jacques Van Gompel, the Socialist mayor of Charleroi—a city that had been grappling for years with organized crime—was indicted for forgery, use of forged documents, and embezzlement, and was jailed pending trial. According to the crown prosecutor, he and his cronies had been taking public funds for some ten years.

A sensational instance of breakdown of law and order occurred on April 14, when seventeen-year-old Joe Van Holsbeeck was fatally stabbed in Brussels's central train station in the heart of the city, in the middle of rush hour, by a person who was after his MP3 player. The assailants got away but were later identified through evidence preserved on surveillance cameras. They were both minors from Poland, and their trial was expected to take place in 2007. On April 23, about 80,000 people held a silent demonstration in the streets of Brussels in memory of the young victim. And on June 9, two little girls, aged ten and seven, disappeared during a block party. Their bodies were found 20 days later: both had been strangled and one raped. The prime suspect, Abdallah Ait Oud, was arrested shortly afterward but denied any guilt despite strong evidence against him. His trial was also set for 2007.

As widely predicted, the government parties suffered significant losses in the elections. In Wallonia, the major beneficiary was the Christian Democratic Party, and in Flanders it was the right-wing anti-immigrant party Vlaams Belang (Flemish Interest), whose strength in the province rose from 14.9 percent in 2000 to 20.6 percent, second only to the Flemish Christian Democrats. In the city of Antwerp itself, however, Vlaams Belang won only about the same percentage it had in the last election, and garnered just 20 votes on the 55-seat council, two less than the Socialist victors. The Antwerp result came as a relief to Belgians who feared the rise of the extreme right, while Vlaams Belang leader Filip Dewinter, who would have become mayor had his party won in the city, ascribed the result to the immigrant vote.

Prime Minister Verhofstadt expressed disappointment with the results of the elections and noted, "We must acknowledge that the government has had a few bad months and we know that whoever leads faces the most fire." With national elections due in 2007, there was speculation that a weakened Verhofstadt might seek to bolster the coalition by bringing the Christian Democrats into it.

Despite its failure to gain ground in Antwerp, the overall success of Vlaams Belang underscored public concern about integrating Muslims into Belgian life. Muslims living in the country, estimated at about 400,000, constituted close to 4 percent of the total population, making Islam the second largest religion in the country, exceeded only by Roman Catholicism.

A number of controversial incidents involving Muslims occurred during the year. In May, some Catholic churches providing refuge to illegal immigrants found instances of desecration and the de facto transformation of the churches into mosques. Two Muslim teachers in Brussels public schools were fired in July for refusing to remove their headscarves while teaching, a violation of the law requiring religious neutrality in the classroom. And on the night of September 25, not long before the elections, North Africans living the Brussels suburb of La Marolles rioted after hearing that a prisoner had died in his cell. The mayhem—setting cars on fire, rock-throwing, and window-smashing—was repeated the next two nights as well.

Israel and the Middle East

Belgium, whose capital city of Brussels housed the headquarters of the European Union, maintained the EU position on Middle Eastern affairs, supporting the creation of a Palestinian state that would live in peace with Israel. On January 31, after the EU announced it would not recognize the Hamas government that had won the Palestinian elections until Hamas recognized Israel and renounced violence, Belgium's minister of cooperation and development suspended two development projects in the Palestinian Authority. The Foreign Ministry, however, taken by surprise by the move, withheld comment when questioned by reporters.

In March, a Hamas member of the Palestinian parliament applied for a Belgian visa to attend an EU conference in Brussels. Belgium turned down the request, officially for "technical" reasons, but the president of the European Parliament told reporters that the actual reason was the status of Hamas as a terrorist organization. Afterwards, Foreign Minister Karel De Gucht said that Belgium was anticipating that the EU would develop overall guidelines on Hamas visa applications.

The pro-Israel cause in Belgium was seriously undermined on March 25, when Pierre Galand was elected president of the Secular Action Center (*Centre d'Action Laïque*), a highly regarded human-rights nongovernmental organization (NGO). While Galand, then serving as a Socialist senator, was a major humanitarian figure, he was also president of the Belgo-Palestinian Friendship Association and a longtime critic of Israel.

General August Van Daele, Belgium's chief of defense, made an official visit to Israel in late April. He met with the defense minister, the chief of staff, and several other high-ranking military officials, and spent time at Israel Aircraft Industries and at a military base.

With the outbreak of Israel's war with Hezballah in southern Lebanon,

Arab, Lebanese, and Belgian activists protested daily in front of EU headquarters in Brussels, carrying signs with such slogans as "Stop Israeli terrorism" and "Israel today is committing a deliberate crime against Lebanon." A July 20 press conference in the capital featured Bachir Cham, a Belgian-professor born in Lebanon who now ran a Lebanese hospital, charging that Israel was using chemical weapons

In late July, in the midst of the war, a Belgian couple of Lebanese origin filed a lawsuit against Israel's prime minister, defense minister, and chief of staff for war crimes. They said they had been on vacation in Lebanon with their three children when Israeli planes destroyed their apartment, forcing them to flee via Syria. Their suit was filed under Belgium's law of universal jurisdiction, which allowed legal action against intentional crimes committed outside the country.

On August 11, relatives of the Israeli soldiers kidnapped and held captive by Hamas and Hezballah arrived in Brussels for meetings with members of the European Parliament, followed by a press conference. They urged the Europeans to help secure the release of the prisoners, or at least determine their condition. The speaker of the Belgian Chamber of Deputies met separately with the families and promised to contact his counterpart, the speaker of the Lebanese parliament, to obtain information about the men. A pro-Israel rally calling for the release of the prisoners, coordinated with these meetings, took place outside the European Parliament building.

Immediately after the cease-fire came into effect, a Belgian NGO, Medical Aid for the Third World, sent a solidarity mission to southern Lebanon. The group spent a week visiting bombed-out areas, transferred money to local humanitarian agencies, issued statements severely condemning Israel, and urged that Israel be made to pay the costs of rebuilding.

The union representing Belgian military personnel at first expressed some hesitation about contributing troops to the UN international force that would patrol the southern Lebanese border after the war, for fear that the soldiers might be used for the risky job of disarming Hezballah (ten Belgian peacekeepers had been killed in Rwanda). Upon being reassured that they would not have to do this, the union approved, and a 370-person Belgian contingent went to Lebanon. These included 140 combat soldiers, along with medics, engineers, and experts in bomb disposal.

In late December, two of the Belgian members of a UN force clearing mines in southern Lebanon were wounded when they stepped on a cluster bomb.

Racism and Anti-Semitism

Harassment of Jews in Belgium remained a major problem during 2006. There were taunts, assaults, and other anti-Semitic actions, creating a situation in which the Jewish schools in Antwerp had to be protected by high walls and barbed wire, with armed guards manning the entrances. Just as worrisome was the proliferation of anti-Semitic messages and even calls for violence on the Internet.

Orthodox Jews, whose distinctive Jewish appearance made them frequent targets, were sometimes accosted on trains, insulted, and threatened. Outright violence occurred in two cases. Late on the night of October 2, two teenage students of the Wilrijk yeshiva were attacked by a gang of three youths. Although their glasses were broken, neither boy was seriously injured. A complaint was filed at the police station. And on the night of November 30, a group of Hasidic students aged 13–15 arriving for an outing in Beringen were assailed by a group of neighborhood youths of Turkish origin. The latter struck one of the students and then hurled rocks and paving stones that broke the windows of the youth hostel where the students were supposed to say, all the while shouting anti-Semitic insults. As the police could not guarantee the boys' safety, they returned to Antwerp at 2 a.m. The Beringen police took in ten people for questioning, six of whom were minors. Interior Minister Patrick Dewael sent a letter to the Consistory three weeks later expressing dismay over the incident and assuring the Jewish community that the federal government gave high priority to combating racism.

In early February, Jewish storekeepers on Lambert Crickx Street in "The Triangle," a garment-making and wholesaling Brussels neighborhood, were repeatedly harassed and bullied by a man of North African descent, who complained that Jews made too much money.

The crypt of the Memorial to Belgium's Jewish Martyrs, located in Anderlecht, was vandalized on July 24. An urn containing human ashes from Auschwitz-Birkenau was emptied of its contents, a grating was torn off, windows were smashed, documents destroyed, and the ground covered with condoms and excrement. All the doors were intact; the vandals broke in by scaling a wall behind the crypt. Police said that in the absence of anti-Semitic messages or Nazi symbols there was no reason to believe that the perpetrators had anti-Jewish motivations. Three tags were found on a wall, including one with skull and crossbones.

An investigation was launched on August 1 into e-mails that had been sent for more than a year to lawyers and elected officials whose names and e-mail addresses were available on the Internet. The person sending the messages called himself Adel Khedira, and he claimed to be a victim of a mainly French "Jewist" plot that had occult powers and caused "murders, rapes, thefts, disease, hunger, isolation, and slander." In his words, "the Jewists are the basest and most criminal species on Earth."

On December 13, a customer at the Brussels branch of FNAC—a large chain store—found labels affixed to the back covers of books on Judaism. They bore two messages: *"Américains-Israéliens et leurs amis juifs: dominants morbides! Palestine-Irak libres"* (Americans, Israelis, and their Jewish friends: Morbid dominants! Free Palestine and Iraq), and *"Auschwitz: une histoire d'hier pour massacrer les Palestiniens aujourd'hui."* (Auschwitz: A story of the past to massacre Palestinians today.) The scandalized manager took the books off the shelves and notified the authorities.

After many years of legal maneuvering and repeated appeals, the Brussels Appeals Court issued a major decision on April 18 dealing with the dissemination of hate on the Internet. Daniel Féret, chairman of the extreme right-wing *Front National* (National Front), and his right-hand man and Webmaster of the Front's Internet site, Georges-Pierre Tonnelier, were found guilty of inciting racial hatred and discrimination by placing xenophobic tracts and the contents of the party's platform on the site during 1999–2001, at which time Féret was a member of the Federal Chamber of Representatives. Both men were barred from holding public office, Féret for ten years and Tonnelier for seven. Féret was sentenced to 250 hours of community service—to be spent helping integrate foreigners—and Tonnelier was fined 744 euros. Unlike the 2004 court ruling that the Vlaams Blok party was racist and had to dissolve (see AJYB 2005, p. 355), the National Front, in this case, was acquitted and only its leaders convicted as individuals.

Holocaust-Related Matters

On January 27, Holocaust Memorial Day in Belgium—and the anniversary of the liberation of Auschwitz—a commemoration ceremony for the victims was held in Egmont Palace.

The ten-year-old Jewish Museum of Deportation and Resistance (JMDR) in Mechelin was an extremely popular site, receiving about 5,000 adult visitors annually and some 30,000 high-school students, who, with the support and encouragement of the Ministry of Education, were brought to experience the 90-minute guided tour that gave a historical picture of the Holocaust in Belgium and its impact on the Jewish and Gypsy communities. The museum was housed in an actual SS barracks from World War II that had been used to assemble Jews for deportation. Although located in the Flemish part of Belgium, it drew 40 percent of its visitors from the French-speaking area of the country. The JMDR was also a documentation center for information on the persecution of Jews and Gypsies during the Nazi era. In 2006 it scanned, inventoried, and conserved in acid-free boxes five major archival collections: the registry of Jews kept by Belgian municipalities (46,000 names); the lists of Jews maintained by the Jewish communities themselves (34,000 names); the card index created by the Nazi SD of those deported from Drancy to Auschwitz (9,000 names); transport lists of deportees from Mechelen to Auschwitz. (25,000 names); and the files of the Aliens Police. Still ongoing was a project of matching 12,000 surviving photographs to the names of deportees from Mechelen.

In 2005, Prime Minister Verhofstadt asked the JMDR to advise in the planned renovation of the Belgian national exhibition in the Auschwitz State Museum, a project facilitated by the Belgian military authorities and paid for, in part, by the National Lottery and the newly formed Jewish Foundation of Belgium (see below). The new Belgian exhibition was opened on May 7, 2006, in the presence of the prime minister, other government officials, and representatives of the Jewish community.

By 2006, the JMDR, a victim of its own success, could not accommodate all who wished to make use of it. After a Flemish government study suggested that the museum could attract as many as 70,000 people a year if its facilities were enlarged, the government entered into negotiations with the museum about tripling the institution's size. Claude Marinower, a well-known lawyer, MP, and city councilor of Antwerp, headed the negotiating team for the museum.

On June 30, 2005, the Belgian government signed the legal document creating the Fondation du Judaisme de Belgique (Jewish Foundation of Belgium), or FJB, through which compensation would be paid to the Jewish community for property plundered during the Nazi era. This was in fulfillment of a provision of the 2001 law on compensation to individuals stating that the balance of the amounts set aside that were not paid to individual claimants must be made available to the Jewish community.

The JFB, headed by its president, Senator Roger Lallemand, and vice president, Georges Schnek, was mandated to distribute funds to help pay for the Jewish community's social, cultural, and religious activities, and also to combat racism, intolerance, and the violation of human rights. In 2006, under its Solidarity 3000 project, the foundation announced it would pay any Jew who lived in Belgium during all or part of World War II the sum of 3,000 euros, minus amounts already received under the Belgian and German reparations laws. A total of 5,200 applications were received in the course of the year.

JFB money was also allocated to assist needy Jewish victims of the Nazis, discreetly distributed through Jewish social-service agencies; support the Jewish Museum of Deportation and Resistance's "Let's give them faces" program, dedicated to locating and publishing photographs of all 28,902 Jews from Belgium deported via Mechelen and northern France to their deaths; help renovate and update the Belgian pavilion at the Auschwitz-Birkenau State Museum, as noted above; and provide help for children attending Jewish schools whose parents were in serious financial straits.

JEWISH COMMUNITY

Communal Bodies

The Central Jewish Consistory of Belgium—whose history antedated that of Belgium itself—was the official umbrella organization for the country's Jews, representing the community before the government, other official bodies, religious groups, and foreign Jewish communities. Julien Klener, who served as Consistory president, often spoke at government events and at academic convocations. In 2006 he also addressed an ecumenical conference organized by the World Jewish Congress in Brussels and presented the Consistory perspective at public meetings in Sweden, Greece, and Italy.

Beginning in 2005, the Belgian Senate had conducted hearings on whether to require the stunning of animals prior to slaughter so as to minimize pain, a change that would create significant problems for the practice of kosher slaughter (see AJYB 2006, pp. 366–67). The Consistory, as the country's official representative of Judaism, presented the case for the humane nature of kosher slaughter. The issue was settled, at least for the moment, when the High Court of Appeals ruled in 2006 that the matter was a religious one, and separation of religion and state precluded any government action.

Combating anti-Semitism was a major responsibility of the Coordinating Committee of Jewish Organizations in Belgium (CCOJB) in Brussels and the Forum of Jewish Organizations in Antwerp. Thus, for example, the CCOJB sought ways to dialogue with the Muslim Executive of Belgium so as to encourage moderate Muslims to speak out against extremists who spewed anti-Semitism, and the Forum announced it would sue all those who spoke at the Tehran Holocaust-denial conference in December. As Belgian law made denial of the Holocaust a crime, any conference speaker stepping on Belgian soil, it argued, should be liable to prosecution.

Service Social Juif (Jewish Social Service) was the Brussels Jewish community's primary provider of assistance to all those in need, without regard to national, religious or ideological distinctions. On June 22, Jewish Social Service sponsored a multicultural "world meal" during which four different ethnic and cultural communities that regularly made use of its facilities prepared traditional dishes and put on a show. One of the participating groups consisted of Tutsi survivors of the Rwandan genocide, who had been helped by the service since 2002. On August 19, 2006, Viviane Lipsztadt, the service's social assistance coordinator, and Rabbi David Meyer traveled to Rwanda to meet with survivors, visit places of remembrance, and confer with the authorities in charge of preserving the memory of this genocide.

Pro-Israel activities were largely the province of the Belgian Zionist Federation. In 2006, besides speaking out for Israel during the summer war against Hezballah, the federation took steps to help the Israeli community of Kfar Vradim, with which it had maintained a partnership relationship since 2000. After a meeting between a four-member federation delegation and Kfar Vradim leaders on August 8 — held in the center of Israel because the town was too close to the war zone — the Belgian group organized a fund-raising campaign to help the children of Kfar Vradim and offered home hospitality to any of its families who wanted to stay in Antwerp or Brussels until hostilities ended.

Zionist and Israel-oriented cultural activity was carried out by the Ben-Gurion Circle. During 2006 the organization sponsored lectures, film showings, and colloquia on Jewish history, anti-Semitism, Israeli politics, the situation in the Middle East, and the danger of radical Islam. On March 26 it joined with the European Sephardic Institute for a day devoted to the plight of Jewish refugees from Arab countries. The Ben-Gurion Circle also was responsible for the Habonim Dror youth movement, which held educational programs every Saturday afternoon and during school vacations for children age six and up.

The Jewish Secular Community Center (CCLJ) emphasized Jewish cultural and moral values rather than religious practices or Zionism. In 2006 it produced a pamphlet, *Comprendre la Shoah et les génocides du XXE siècle* (Understanding the Holocaust and the Genocides of the Twentieth Century) to be used in Belgian schools, which covered not only the Nazi program to annihilate the Jews, but also attempts to wipe out the Armenians and the Tutsi.

On March 16—as part of a week of action against racism organized by the Movement against Racism, Anti-Semitism, and Xenophobia (MRAX)—the CCLJ hosted a showing of the documentary film *Rwanda, les collines parlent* (Rwanda: the hills speak). Some Hutu deniers of the Tutsi tragedy started heckling, and one issued death threats against the Brussels president of Ibuka, the association of Rwandan victims. The CCLJ issued a statement denouncing this attack on the dignity of the survivors and of the dead.

The CCLJ, in cooperation with other likeminded groups, brought 40 young people aged 15–17 from Belgium, France, Israel, and the Palestinian territories together for ten days in July at Limeil-Brévannes, France, to share their views about human rights, racism, and democracy, and to visit important sites. The organizers later noted that the participants corresponded with each other after the program ended, suggesting that more united them than divided them.

An important communal milestone for Belgian Jews in 2006 was the 70th anniversary of Beth Lechem. Founded in 1936 to provide food to poor Jewish immigrants from Eastern Europe, several of its members were deported and killed during the Holocaust. After World War II it helped those returning from the concentration camps. There were no government subsidies, salaries or operating expenses, as all those involved were volunteers.

Education

Ganenou Athenaeum in Brussels, a Zionist-oriented day school known for providing quality education in both Jewish and secular subjects, encompassed both a primary school and a high school. Starting in the 2006–07 school year, the first four grades were housed in a new building with 13 classrooms. On October 10, to mark the tenth anniversary of the school's twinning arrangement with Collège Saint-Pierre (Saint Peter's Middle School), Princess Mathilde, the wife of Crown Prince Philippe of Belgium, visited Ganenou. The purpose of the twinning was to demonstrate harmony between religions on the basis of shared ethics.

The Jewish Students Union of Belgium (UEJB) celebrated its 60th birthday on December 18. Begun after World War II by a few Jewish students—many of them orphans—who had returned or come out of hiding after the Nazi years, the first meetings were held in private homes or local pubs, and activities were primarily of a social nature. Six decades later, more than 800 people attended its annual ball, and, as one of more than 40 European Jewish student organizations, the UEJB stood as a symbol of the rebirth of Judaism in the Diaspora. Many of its alumni achieved eminence in Belgium and other countries.

The Brussels-based *Institut d'Etudes du Judaïsme* (Institute of Jewish Studies), directed by Prof. Thomas Gergely, was the only university-level establishment in the country to offer degree programs in Jewish studies exclusively. Classes, given in the evening and on Saturday, covered the Jewish experience from Antiquity to the present, as well as Jewish art and Hebrew language and literature. Close to 200 students were enrolled, many of them students at Brussels Free University, which gave credit for these courses. The institute also ran a public lecture series on Jewish topics and participated in a research project, "Jewish Cultures and Medical Tradition in Humanist Europe," which sought to establish a link between medical practices and Jewish identity. A publication series sponsored by the institute, called "la Collection Mosaïque," had been putting out books since 2002.

Interfaith Relations

An exhibition at the ninth-century Saints Michael and Gudule Cathedral in Brussels, held from November 16, 2006, through January 8, 2007, was a unique event in the history of Judeo-Christian relations: the exhibition of the work of a Jewish artist in a church. The artist was Jean-Paul Leon, and the theme of the paintings was the menorah—a key symbol of Judaism—depicted in various ways. Enhancing the impact of the exhibition was the anti-Semitic story told by the church's stained-glass windows. In 1370 the Jewish community of Brussels was accused of stabbing holy wafers, whereupon blood flowed from these "wounds." Several Jews were burnt at the stake for the "crime" and their property confiscated. The fifteenth- and sixteenth-century windows of the cathedral illustrated these scenes, and many of the faithful continued to believe the story into modern times. In 1968, in line with the spirit of Vatican II, the diocesan authorities publicly acknowledged the tendentiousness of the accusations, and some years later a plaque was put up at the site emphasizing the falsity of the legend. The Leon exhibition, encouraged by the local Roman Catholic religious authorities, testified to the excellent relations between Jewish and Christian communities in Brussels. Although their numbers had diminished to three, the Sisters of Zion community in Brussels kept up interfaith activities with Jews. Besides conducted Hebrew classes—steeped in rabbinical sources—for people of all ages and religions, maintaining a library and documentation center, and attending public events of Jewish significance, it participated during 2006 in a conference entitled "Jews, Christians, Muslims, Buddhists, Agnostics, Let's Build Bridges Together—Using My Conviction to Open Up to Others"; played a major role in an interreligious tour of houses of worship in the city, including a synagogue, a Vietnamese pagoda, a Pakistani mosque, and the Orthodox cathedral; and organized two open-house events where it explained to visitors from Belgium and abroad the work it did to narrow the gap between Jews and Christians.

In Flanders, the Forum of Jewish Organizations participated in several meetings called by Minister for Home Affairs Marino Keulen to promote interfaith dialogue. The official policy that Keulen announced as a result of the meetings was to allow construction of new mosques with government support provided that the imams used the Dutch language rather than Arabic.

Culture

The Jewish Museum of Belgium's exhibition on "175 years of Jewish Life in Belgium," which began in 2005, ended on September 3, 2006, European Jewish Culture Day. It was followed, from September 10 through October 20, by an exhibition devoted to the work of photographer Dan Zollman that featured images of Antwerp's Hasidic community. October 18 marked the opening of *Trajectoires et espaces juifs. La schoule de Molenbeek. Facettes d'un judaïsme contemporain,* explaining facets of contemporary Belgian Judaism through an exact replica of a small synagogue in the heart of Brussels. There was also a series of lunchtime lectures offered twice a month on Jewish art and culture. And in partnership with ASF—a group of young volunteers—the museum sponsored some 20 worksites in Europe, with projects ranging from the renovation of apartments for elderly people to support for centers for the handicapped, the building of playgrounds, and, above all, cleaning and refurbishing places of remembrance. Mindful of bolstering its national identity, the museum conducted a number of events and activities in Dutch.

The *Fondation de la Mémoire Contemporaine* (Contemporary Memory Foundation) was created in 1994 to collect information, primarily through interviews, on the recent history of Jews and Judaism in Belgium and their contributions to the nation. The foundation also undertook scientific research into previously obscure aspects of Belgian Jewish history, publishing books on such topics as aid for Jewish war victims after World War II, Jewish education under the German occupation, and illegal immigration to Palestine before the creation of the State of Israel. Its *Cahiers* series published a third set of journals in 2006 focusing mainly on the experiences of German or German-speaking Jews in Belgium.

The Institute of Jewish Audiovisual Memory (IMAJ) screened a number of films of Jewish interest during the year. Often, the showings were followed by talks by the author or producer and discussions with the audience, and on one occasion, after a film on what happened to the Armenians during World War I was shown, a debate was held. Some of the screenings were cosponsored by other Belgian Jewish organizations. IMAJ was responsible for choosing the Israeli films for the Mediterranean Film Festival that was held November 26–December 3.

GEORGES SCHNEK

Netherlands

National Affairs

IMMIGRATION AND DEMOGRAPHY

Always a densely populated country, the Netherlands had a population of over 16 million with a national average of 483 inhabitants per km². Beginning in 2001 calls began to be heard urging limits on immigration. These derived from a perceived threat to Western values from the growing number of Islamic newcomers.

More stringent immigration policies adopted over the next few years began to be felt in 2006, as the country's population grew by less than 2,000 over the course of the year. From April through June it even dropped slightly, the first quarter with a population decline since the government began keeping such statistics. The Netherlands was the only EU country to have more people leave than enter it, and its negative immigration balance—27,000 for 2005 and 19,000 for the first half of 2006—was the largest in Europe.

Tough policies against non-Western immigrants dominated the news. Immigration Minister Rita Verdonk, a.k.a. "Iron Rita," was repeatedly criticized for a string of actions that many deemed inhumane.

In April, left-wing opposition parties demanded Verdonk's resignation for endangering the lives of unsuccessful Syrian asylum seekers by informing the Syrian government about their imminent return, and misinforming the Dutch parliament about this fact. Shortly after the "Syrian incident," Verdonk sought forcibly to return Iranian asylum seekers who risked being persecuted or even killed by the Islamic regime for being homosexuals or converts to Christianity. She reversed this decision only after pressure from all but one of the parties represented in parliament. And on April 28, in the face of a public outcry, an 18-year-old Serbian, Taida Pasic, was deported back to Kosovo just weeks before her Dutch high school exams. Taida had been in the country since 1999. (In May, she passed her exams in the Dutch embassy in Sarajevo.)

In June, the government fell over Verdonk's treatment of Somali-born Ayaan Hirsi Ali, an MP for Verdonk's own party, VVD. Hirsi Ali was a well-known critic of fundamentalist Islam and had been living in safehouses, under constant police surveillance, after receiving death threats (see AJBY 2005, pp. 367–69). Verdonk wrote a letter to Hirsi Ali in May questioning her Dutch citizenship; apparently Hirsi Ali had given a false surname and date of birth on entering the country in 1992. Hirsi Ali responded to the letter by instantly resigning from parliament in a dramatic press conference on May 15, and moving to the U.S. Several nightly debates later, D66, a party in the ruling coalition, quit the cabinet over Verdonk's action, and the government lost its majority.

Verdonk stayed on as minister in the caretaker government, unlike her colleagues Justice Minister Piet Hein Donner and Housing Minister Sybilla Dekker, who resigned on September 21 over fallout from yet another immigration drama, the Schiphol prison fire of 2005 (see AJYB 2006, p. 374). According to an official report issued in 2006, 11 unwanted immigrants awaiting expulsion died and another 15 were severely injured "unnecessarily." The victims, including children imprisoned along with their parents, perished because they were locked up in detention cells when the fire broke out.

Even in December, with the caretaker government including Verdonk still in place, bitter strife over immigration issues continued. Parliament approved a motion to suspend the deportation of 26,000 unsuccessful asylum seekers who had been living in the Netherlands for over five years, pending a general pardon (most other countries, including the U.S., had procedures for legalizing longstanding undocumented immigrants). But the government said it would ignore the motion and proceed with the deportations. During the debate that followed, Verdonk further enraged the majority of MPs by announcing that, whatever points were raised, she would continue deporting these people. Although now forced to relinquish the immigration portfolio, Verdonk stayed on in the cabinet.

POLITICS AND SOCIETY

Elections were held in March for local city councils. PvdA (Labor) and the Socialist Party enhanced their representation. The PvdA won the largest number of combined council seats, 1,988, and the SP garnered 333, more than double its previous number. The Christian Democrats (CDA) and the Liberal VVD, both government parties, were the big losers.

The VVD dominated the news in May, first with the Hirsi Ali incident (see above) and then with an abortive attempt by Rita Verdonk to seize the leadership of the party from its chairman, Mark Rutte, an action described in the media as a "failed coup." The government, as noted above, subsequently fell over the Hirsi Ali issue.

In the November elections, all three government parties lost parliamentary seats to small left-wing and right-wing parties, but the possibilities of forming a coalition different from the old one were slim. The Christian Democrats, whose leader, Jan Pieter Balkenende, headed the previous government, remained the largest party despite its losses. Any combination of CDA with either Labor (PvdA) or the Liberals (VVD) would need a third party to ensure a parliamentary majority, but both of those former government parties excluded cooperation with one or more of the smaller parties. The year ended with the old cabinet still in place.

Interethnic tensions, especially hooliganism at soccer matches, presented an ongoing problem. The followers of Ajax, the popular Amsterdam-based club, continued to be called "the Jews" both by their own fans and those of rival teams: Ajax enthusiasts brandished Israeli flags and decorated themselves with Jewish symbols, while the other side countered with anti-Semitic slogans. In February, a gang of 70 Ajax fans attacked the clubhouse of ADO—a team based in The Hague whose following included rabid neo-Nazis—forced their way in, beat up the eight ADO fans present with bats, stabbed one of them with a sharp instrument, and set fire to the building. Five fans were hospitalized.

A fight broke out on July 29 during a soccer match between Maccabi Tel Aviv and the local team of Den Helder. Four Dutch supporters raised a Palestinian flag and refused to remove it. Maccabi Tel Aviv fans then stormed them, and the match had to be delayed several minutes while order was restored.

On December 10, Ajax spokesman David Endt announced plans to ban Jewish symbols and the fans' favorite war cry, "Jews," from the stadium. Ajax players were to visit schools "to put an end to the Jewish image." Meanwhile, the country's Internet-discrimination watchdog filed a claim against the author of a sports blog who described the only two Jews recently associated with Ajax ("the Jew Jaap van Praag and the Jew Sjaak Swart") using anti-Jewish stereotypes.

In March, nine out of 14 suspected members of the Islamic "Hofstad'" terror group received stiff prison terms, the highest being 15 years. These were the first sentences for belonging to a terror organization since the introduction of new antiterrorist laws. The group's leader, Mohammed Bouyeri, had already been jailed for life in 2005 for murdering filmmaker Theo van Gogh a year earlier (see AJYB 2006, p. 374).

The Dutch economy, which had performed worse than that of any other European country in 2005, improved markedly in 2006, ending a five-year period of weakness. The upturn, part of a general revival of the

European economy, was characterized by a strong expansion of sales to Asian markets.

Israel and the Middle East: The War in Lebanon

Israel, always prominent in the Dutch media, virtually dominated the news during the summer as its troops fought against Hezballah in Lebanon. Initial reports were sympathetic to Israel, focusing on the sufferings of the residents of northern Israel under Hezballah attacks and on the plight of the families of the kidnapped Israeli soldiers. But it did not take long for the words "disproportionate violence" to creep in. As early as July 11, the Christian daily *Trouw,* not known as a particularly anti-Israel paper, carried a cartoon showing an Arab woman with a child being threatened by heavily armed IDF troops claiming, "We only want our corporal back." On July 15, a few dozen demonstrators carrying Palestinian and Lebanese flags chanted slogans such as "Boycott Israel" and "Israel child murderer" in front of the government buildings in The Hague. The next day Foreign Minister Bernard Bot, a Christian Democrat, told his Israeli counterpart Tzipi Livni in a telephone conversation that it was becoming increasingly difficult "to show some understanding as the number of civilian victims grew."

Many Dutch Jews were on holiday or visiting family in Israel when the war broke out. Nevertheless, the Jewish community rallied round the Jewish state, fund-raising for organizations such as Magen David Adom and organizing aid for residents of northern Israel who were under rocket fire. Special prayer meetings were held for Israel and for the kidnapped soldiers, and the rabbinate called on everyone to add two psalms and a special prayer for Israel to their daily prayers.

Eleven members of the Jewish youth group Habonim left for their yearly Israel trip on July 16. Two days later 40 Jewish and Christian organizations held a rally "to show our solidarity with the people of Israel and support Israel's right to defend itself." Some 1,200 people attended, and the speakers included Rabbi Michael Melchior, a member of the Knesset. In November, Dutch Jews joined a demonstration in front of the European Parliament buildings in Brussels, Belgium, in solidarity with the kidnapped Israeli soldiers.

A small but vocal group, Another Jewish Voice, that advocated views at odds with the mainstream Jewish community, received much media attention. Author Hajo Meyer, a prominent member of EAJG, published a book, *The Fall of Judaism,* which claimed that Israeli government policies endangered Jewish survival. Planning a German translation of the book, Meyer sued the German Jewish journalist Henryk Broder for writing a column about it in which he called Meyer a "Judeophobe" and charged that Meyer and his publisher "played Adolf." A German media judge ruled that Broder had to retract the former claim but that the latter was permissible. Meyer went on to outrage most Dutch Jews in October, when he declared that the way Nazis treated Jews at the entrances to the wartime Amsterdam ghetto was "child's play compared to the way Israeli soldiers treat Palestinians in the occupied territories."

On July 18, three parties critical of Israel—Labor, the Socialists, and the Greens—demanded that parliament return from summer recess for an emergency debate on the war in Lebanon, a course seconded by some extra-parliamentary groups, including Another Jewish Voice. In the course of the parliamentary discussion that ensued, on July 20 Foreign Minister Bot declared that "Israel has the right to defend itself" and that both he and the government were "pro-Israel." Hans van Baalen, speaking for the Liberals, "did not see the need for such a debate," and felt that Israel was rightly defending itself against terror attacks from Hamas and Hezballah. On July 23 Van Baalen flew to Israel with two officials of the Dutch Jewish community; he was the only MP to show his solidarity in this way. The delegation was received by Prime Minister Ehud Olmert, Foreign Minister Tzipi Livni, and the Dutch ambassador to Israel.

Meanwhile an anti-Israel demonstration in Amsterdam on July 22 drew about 1,500 people; once again, among the organizing groups was Another Jewish Voice. Achmed Marmouch, a Muslim who was Amsterdam's first Moroccan-born city council chairman, spoke at the rally on behalf of the Labor Party. Protestant and Catholic organizations, however, including one whose spokesman had previously been hostile to Israel, called and wrote officials of the Jewish community expressing solidarity with the people of Israel; some of them included the Dutch Jewish community as well, "with its strong ties to Israel."

As in other European countries, the bombing of Qana on July 30 represented a turning point in public opinion. A poll taken on August 5 showed that only one in three Dutchmen showed some understanding for Israel's actions, and that 39 percent had "come to see Israel in a more negative light" due to the conflict.

In December, Another Jewish Voice chairman Max Wieselmann was invited to address an annual meeting of Christian organizations held at Westerbork, the site where Dutch Jews were interned awaiting deportation to concentration camps. The theme of his talk was "human rights all over the world." Wieselmann compared the Nazi treatment of Jewish Westerbork inmates to Israeli treatment of Palestinians, conceding, however, that the Israelis had "not yet gone that far." A few Dutch Jews praised him for showing "courage," but others, particularly survivors and younger members of the Jewish community, considered it a false comparison, which, made at that particular spot, amounted to "spitting on the graves" of the dead.

Anti-Semitism and Extremism

STATISTICS

In August, CIDI (Center of Information and Documentation on Israel), the nongovernmental organization monitoring racism and anti-Semitism in the Netherlands, published its statistics for 2005 and the first part of 2006. CIDI reported 159 incidents in 2005 as against 327 the year before, a marked decline.

The Lebanon war brought a sharp change: from July through August 9, 2006, CIDI counted 105 incidents — 66 percent of the total number for all of 2005. These included threatening phone calls, anti-Semitic e-mails, graffiti (such as "Juden Raus"), and vandalism of a synagogue. CIDI noted that it did not include in its report any anti-Israel incidents that did not also involve anti-Semitism. And, as always, it counted a series of related incidents as one, and thus a barrage of virulently anti-Semitic and threatening postings on the Jewish Internet forum Joods.nl, forcing the site to close down temporarily, was counted as a single incident. This spike during the war conformed to the previous pattern whereby anti-Semitic incidents tended to proliferate at times of increased violence between Israel and the Palestinians.

Even disregarding the Lebanon-related peak, CIDI warned, the overall decline in the number of incidents was no reason for optimism. The decrease in 2005 was largely due to a decline in the number of anti-Semitic e-mails, from 121 in 2004 to 15 in 2005. But cases involving physical violence actually rose slightly, and the number of personal threats remained roughly the same.

Name-calling, as always, was the largest category of live incidents, and here the author of the CIDI report, Hadassa Hirschfeld, noted another worrying trend: over the 23 years that CIDI had monitored anti-Semitic incidents, Jewish reactions to such name-calling had become much more resigned, so that, in Hirschfeld's words, "This has now reached a point where non-Jewish students call each other "Jew" and others use it to insult policemen. There is even a new word for this: 'being Jewed.'"

Despite the correlation between overt anti-Semitic acts and Israeli-Palestinian violence, the CIDI report cautioned that anti-Semitism existed in the country quite apart from Middle East issues. In a national opinion poll, 10 percent of the Dutch population described themselves as "overt racists" and another 17 percent said they were "racist some of the time." The contribution of Muslim perpetrators towards the total number of anti-Semitic manifestations actually declined, going from 45 percent in 2004 to 38 percent in 2005. An optimistic view would attribute this to several joint Jewish-Muslim educational programs in Amsterdam and to the vigilance of police and other law-enforcement agencies. A more cynical perspective was that the declining percentage of Muslim perpetrators was due to an increase in cases of extreme right-wing anti-Semitism.

INCIDENTS

A number of Jewish cemeteries, buildings, and monuments were vandalized during the year. While some of these actions may have been spontaneous, others must have been planned in advance, since they clearly required an effort — possibly including reconnaissance. Often, swastikas and other Nazi graffiti left at the scene indicated extreme right-wing connections.

On January 27, for instance, two stones were overturned in the Jewish cemetery of Terborg (Gelderland), and others were daubed with Nazi symbols and stickers of the extreme right-wing party Nederlandse Volks Unie. (A mosque in Terborg was similarly targeted.) Near Sliedrecht, a tree from Israel planted near a Holocaust monument was uprooted on three separate occasions in January, and an attempt to burn down the local synagogue was thwarted later in the year. The synagogue and Holocaust monument in Apeldoorn were vandalized.

On February 21 CIDI wrote to the minister of internal affairs expressing severe concern regarding these acts. It complained that "anti-Jewish graffiti are usually removed promptly, but the police do not investigate these incidents," and that the police were treating them not as hate crimes but "just like any other criminal act."

A large number of Holocaust monuments were vandalized on and immediately after May 4, the day the Dutch commemorate their wartime dead. In Klaaswaal a swastika was daubed on the local monument, the one in Renswoude was set on fire, and in Zandvoort three boys wrecked one wreath and stole several others. A plaque in Hoogeveen with Hebrew letters bearing the names of Jewish inhabitants murdered during the war was severely damaged. In Nederlek a wreath placed at the local monument was stolen. In Amsterdam, meanwhile, police were looking for seven young men seen hanging out near a local monument where wreaths had been destroyed. Monuments were also disturbed in Enkhuizen, Zwijndrecht, and Lekkerkerk. In 2005, only one case of May 4 vandalism had been reported, and several organizations expressed concern about the sharp increase this year.

In the Diamantbuurt, an Amsterdam neighborhood where a small group of "Moroccan" boys had terrorized Jewish and other inhabitants in previous years, an elderly Jewish man and a Jewish member of the local council both called the police when stones were thrown through their windows in January. The two had been subjected to spitting and anti-Semitic name-calling before then; the council member had also been targeted for having undergone a sex-change operation.

CIDI launched legal proceedings against several Islamic sources that produced anti-Semitic material. The first suit, in February, was against the Arab European League, which put two anti-Semitic cartoons on its Web site in reaction to the Danish cartoons deemed insulting to the prophet Mohammed. In May, complaints were filed against the publisher and booksellers distributing *A Guide for Islamic Education,* which propagated corporal punishment for women and children; stoning and murdering Jews, homosexuals, and apostates from Islam; and female circumcision. A year earlier the public prosecutor had refused to take action against these passages in the book, saying they were "expressions of religious freedom."

On June 18, reported the *Nieuw Israelitische Weekblad,* the dean of the University of Utrecht ordered retiring professor Piet van der Horst to strike passages about Islamic anti-Semitism from his valediction. This act of academic censorship was reportedly related to the university's plans to open a department of Islamic studies.

One Dutch figure who drew considerable attention to himself for anti-Semitic rhetoric was N.K. (Kees) Mos, pastor of the Messiah Church in Wassenaar. In May, CIDI acquired the text of his virulent sermon, "The Jew in Us," that Mos delivered in 2005. Amid numerous derogatory passages about Jews, it claimed that Hitler's goal, "to definitely expel the Jew from our midst," was "grounded in biblical texts." CIDI demanded his suspension, but the board of his church took no action, although it did concede that the sermon "should not have been delivered like that." On June 4, the words "Nazis Raus!" were sprayed on the church. According to a statement issued to the press by the anonymous perpetrators, the act had been done because "it is unacceptable that the anti-Semite Mos . . . still has not been fired despite his open appreciation for Hitler and the Holocaust."

On June 26, the top official of the nation's Protestant churches declared that he was "not qualified to judge" the sermon but "shared the outrage." Mos, meanwhile, allegedly ill, relinquished his pastoral duties. Then, on August 21, regional church authorities announced that "Mos had withdrawn his sermon and would resume his work." Mos himself did not make any statement until September 4, when he apologized in his own church for what he called "a completely derailed sermon." The year ended without any public apology to the Jewish community.

Gretta Duisenberg, the pro-Palestinian widow of Wim Duisenberg, the former president of the European Central Bank (see AJYB 2003, pp. 428–29), also contributed to Dutch anti-Semitism during 2006. Duisenberg travelled to Lebanon in September. An accompanying journalist from the weekly *Nieuwe Revu* duly took down quotes such as: "Israelis always lie, you can tell by their mugs. Bastards, that's what they are," and, "I approve of those kidnappings. This is their [Hezballah's] only way to set prisoners free. What infuriates me is that the Netherlands will not send troops because they are afraid of hitting a Jew." She also repeated her "joke" of 2002 about wanting "at least six million signatures" in support of a new pro-Hezballah Dutch political party. Despite several criminal complaints from Holocaust survivors against her offensive statements in recent years, Dutch authorities had declined to prosecute.

LAW ENFORCEMENT

The CIDI report noted that the Dutch police and judicial system reacted more aggressively to anti-Semitic incidents in 2005 than before, when few cases were seriously investigated and even fewer prosecuted. The improved pattern of law enforcement continued into 2006.

In January authorities in Deventer criminalized the publication or distribution of the anti-Jewish pamphlet *Stop the Jewish Dictatorship*. The pamphlet had been surfacing, on and off, for several years, usually in big cities. Complaints by CIDI dating back to 2003 had not produced any result until Deventer took action. That same month the creator of a satirical Web site that slurred Jews and homosexuals was fined 1,000 euros. In May, the Dutch maker of the video "Housewitz" was sentenced to 40 hours of community service. The film was a spoof announcement of an electronic music festival supposedly to be held in Auschwitz on May 4 (Dutch Memorial Day). It showed a gate with the inscription *"Tanzen macht frei,"* plus footage of Nazis, concentration camp barracks and inmates, gas chambers, and Jews being deported by train. The Internet antidiscrimination watchdog MDI had filed a complaint in May 2005, but the authorities found "insufficient punishable elements" to prosecute. A second complaint, however, in August 2005, brought a reversal of the decision and, in the end, a conviction on the charge of disseminating discriminatory material.

The police of IJmuiden arrested five youngsters in June for spraying swastikas on buildings during the local Luilak (Lazybones) prank day. Other pranksters caught smearing cars with butter and eggs were made to clean the cars; the police obviously took the swastikas more seriously. In July, a man in Zutphen was sentenced to one year in prison and compulsory psychiatric treatment for hanging a swastika in his window, making threats, and engaging in blackmail. When the police had demanded removal of the swastika, he called out the white power slogan, "Own people first!"

The police apprehended two men, in November, who had overturned nearly all the stones in the Jewish cemetery of Beek the previous month. But the officers "did not find any anti-Semitism" in their motives. Two neo-Nazis who had repeatedly destroyed the trees on a Holocaust memorial near Sliedrecht and attempted to burn down the local synagogue were convicted and sentenced, in November, to 18 months in jail for the arson attempt. On November 25, an attempt by an extreme right-wing group to demonstrate against a Jewish culture festival (or as the group put it, "against the denial of Dutch culture") in Apeldoorn was vetoed by municipal authorities at the request of CIDI and the Central Jewish Organization.

There was progress against anti-Semitism on the legislative front. In June, the Christian Union party sponsored draft legislation to outlaw denial or glorification of the Holocaust. France, Belgium, Switzerland, Germany, Austria, Romania, Slovakia, the Czech Republic, Lithuania, and Poland had already made Holocaust denial illegal. As the law stood in Holland, however, legal proceedings against deniers could only be initiated by survivors or their children, who were presumably personally affected.

Memorializing the Holocaust

Several new Holocaust monuments were erected in 2006 both for Jewish victims and for non-Jews who helped save their Jewish countrymen. Such monuments now existed in most Dutch communities.

A plaque bearing the names of the 29 Jews deported from the small town of Hattem (Gelderland) was erected on the wall of the former synagogue in April, at the initiative of the current owner of the building— an advertising agency. The 56 deported Jewish inhabitants of Zaltbommel were commemorated with a new plaque in May. In November, Mayor Wim Deetman of The Hague unveiled a monument in memory of over 1,700 Jewish children who were deported from the city.

In October, Clémence Ross, the assistant secretary of state, joined with a group of survivors to unveil a plaque in Bergen Belsen commemorating the Dutch victims of the camp; estimates of their number ranged between 1,300 and 3,500. Anne Frank was one of them, and among the initiators of the project was the Anne Frank Foundation.

In February, the Museum of Frisian Resistance put up a panel with the names of all 500 Frisians who had been named Righteous Gentiles by Yad Vashem for risking their lives to save Jews. Of the nearly 20,000 people from all over the world so honored, about 25 percent were Dutch. Maastricht put up a monument for members of the Resistance in May. The town of Hoorn erected a monument to those who hid Jews during the war; it was placed in "het Jeudje" ("the little Jew"), the street where the first Jews settled, possibly as early as 1640. Jews from Hoorn who perished during the war already had their monument, put up in 1970 where the synagogue used to be.

Another planned memorial generated considerable controversy. The predominantly Catholic town of Geleen wanted to put up the statue of a nun, Sister Maria Aloysia, on the spot where her cloister had stood. The Nazis deported her to Auschwitz on August 2, 1942, where she died. But the nun, born Luise Löwenfels, was a convert from Judaism, and was deported, along with six other born-Jewish nuns and the famous born-Jewish philosopher Edith Stein, together with the local Jews, because they were racially Jewish. The projected statue offended many Jews since it appeared to be a Catholic attempt to "appropriate" Holocaust victimhood status, the same complaint that had been voiced several years earlier when the Church declared Edith Stein a saint.

On the Internet, a new Dutch-language Web site, www.anne-in-debuurt.nl, showed where and how Anne Frank lived in Amsterdam before the family was forced to hide in what was now known as the Anne Frank House.

JEWISH COMMUNITY

Demography

The Jewish community in the Netherlands, estimated at approximately 44,000 people in 2001, had undoubtedly declined since that time due to a low birthrate, which itself was the result of prolonged singlehood and late marriage. Despite community efforts, single Jews still found it difficult to find a (Jewish) partner in the Netherlands. Even assuming that it was the same size at it was in 2001, the Jewish community would make up only about 0.275 percent of the total Dutch population of 16.3 million in 2006. Jews, historically "the" minority group in the country, were now almost negligible in comparison to the much more numerous Muslim minority. Almost half of the Jews in the country lived in the Amsterdam area. Communities in the rest of Holland were small, often dwindling, and therefore tended to join with nearby communities for public events.

Communal Affairs

A number of initiatives were made involving synagogues and other community structures. The synagogue in the Jewish hospital in Amstelveen moved to larger premises and celebrated the event with the consecration of a Torah scroll. The Amsterdam Jewish community renovated the cellar of its headquarters to make it available for regular disco parties for Jewish teens. The work started in January. Although it was supposed to be finished in March, the disco had not yet opened as the year ended. The city council of Leiden announced in February that the former Jewish orphanage there, which had been used to house the offices of the local health administration when there were no more Jewish orphans to service, would become a hotel.

Preparations began for the establishment of Immanuel, a new Jewish hospice in Amsterdam, due to open in April 2007. The first Jewish hospice in Europe, it would provide special care in a homelike environment to terminally ill Jewish patients.

Plans were finalized for a Jewish museum in the former synagogue in Elburg, in memory of the town's 21 Jews who were deported during World War II, only one of whom returned afterward. The project had to overcome objections raised by local musical societies that used the building to practice, and claimed they could not find another location.

Several reminders of early Jewish settlement in the country were discovered or refurbished. The old Jewish cemetery in Leek, dating from 1783, was restored: stones that had been removed because they were broken were repaired and put back, and all the Hebrew inscriptions were translated into Dutch for the benefit of the descendants of those buried there. Other cemeteries, such as the one in The Hague dating from 1694, were also restored, usually with restitution monies. In September, archaeologists discovered a forgotten Jewish cemetery in Amersfoort, one of the five oldest in the Netherlands. Its Sephardi section dated from 1670 and the Ashkenazi part from 1727.

The small Jewish community of Leiden spent seven years raising the 140,000 euros necessary to restore its Jewish cemetery, located in Katwijk; the work was completed in 2006. Dating from 1785, the cemetery included the only existing memorial for victims of the "gunpowder disaster" in the city. On January 12, 1807, a ship carrying 37,000 pounds of gunpowder exploded in the harbor, devastating a large part of Leiden, including the Jewish neighborhood, and killing 151. The Jewish victims included 18 children, all pupils of the local Jewish primary school—which was completely destroyed—and their teacher.

There were several communal anniversaries. In March, the Jews of Groningen celebrated the 100th anniversary of their synagogue, two-and-a-half centuries of Jewish life in Groningen, and the rebuilding of the community 25 years ago. Over 1,000 Dutch primary-school children visited an exhibition about "Children during the War" in the synagogue. The Dutch Friends of Magen David Adom celebrated their 25th anniversary in May. Beth Joles, the Dutch old-age home in Haifa, celebrated its 50th anniversary. The umbrella organization of Liberal Judaism, Verbond van Liberaal-Religieuze Joden, celebrated its 75th anniversary; festivities in Amsterdam were attended by Queen Beatrix. The organization renamed itself Verbond voor Progressief Jodendom.

In Holocaust-related news, the digitalization of the wartime archives of the Dutch Red Cross, containing 860,000 records, started on May 4. Jewish Social Work (JMW), the organization that had taken on the activities of the defunct foundations that had handled the affairs of wartime Jewish orphans, held meetings with a number of those orphans who now lived in Israel and were seeking an investigation into the financial management of their inheritance after the war.

A major advance in the restitution of artworks stolen by the Nazis occurred when the Goudstikker collection was finally returned to its heirs. Toward the end of the year an exhibition, "Looted Property," opened in Amsterdam, showing art that was probably stolen from Jewish families during the war. The exhibitors hoped that at least some of the works might be recognized by descendants of the owners and returned.

Culture

Jewish cultural activities in 2006 included several fund-raising events, such as the art exhibition and auction organized by ARZA (Reform Zionists) in January on behalf of the Liberal Jewish community Har El in Jerusalem. There were performances by foreign celebrities, including concerts by pop stars Matisyahu, Eyal Golan, and other Israeli singers, an evening featuring Fran (the "Nanny") Drescher, and a visit from Sacha Baron Cohen as Borat.

The statistics for visitors to Jewish museums during 2005, released in January 2006, showed significant increases from 2004. The Westerbork camp museum drew 120,000 (a rise of 20 percent); 966,000 visited the Anne Frank House (up by 30,000); and 90,345 came to the Jewish Historical Museum in Amsterdam (a 17.5-percent rise).

The Jewish Historical Museum, housed in three old synagogue buildings in the heart of Amsterdam's old Jewish neighborhood, underwent extensive renovations. The date for the official opening of the renovated section was postponed from September 2006 to February 2007, although a new children's museum opened on December 17. In May, workers digging a new cellar beneath one of the buildings uncovered two ritual baths dating from the eighteenth century. It was decided to incorporate them into the building plans and leave them partly visible.

Skijar 2006, the yearly ski trip organized by the Jewish youth organization Ijar, drew 60 participants from ten countries. Limmoed 2006, the annual Jewish study retreat, was held in the new building of the Rosj Pina Jewish primary school, with 120 participants. The biggest yearly event in Jewish Holland, the Jom Havoetbal soccer tournament in Amsterdam attracted some 3,000 players and visitors in June. As usual, there was a waiting list for teams from abroad seeking to participate. The third MaJo football tournament between Jewish and "Moroccan" teams took place in Amsterdam in October, one of many "dialogue" meetings between the two communities.

UEFA, the European soccer league, banned its Israeli teams from playing their home games in Israel, for security reasons. Several of the Israeli teams chose Dutch stadiums as their "at home" venue. However, no spectators were allowed at the first league cup match involving an Israeli team, between Hapoel Tel Aviv and BST Domzale of Slovenia. For later matches, including a match in Nijmegen in which the Israeli national team beat Andorra 4-1 to qualify for the European Championships 2008, members of the Dutch Jewish community were able to secure tickets. The overall ban on spectators was finally lifted in September.

The annual Jewish Film Festival opened in Amsterdam and then toured the country. A symposium on Jewish tradition and modern life was held in the beautifully restored synagogue of Enschede in June. In July, concurrent with the Amsterdam Gay Canal Parade, Jewish gays organized a "Queer Shabbaton" in the Reconstructionist synagogue of Amsterdam. On European Jewish Heritage Day, September 3, six synagogues, the Jewish Cultural Center, and a movie theater with Jewish-themed films held open house in Amsterdam. Other Jewish sites that welcomed visitors for the occasion were in Bourtange, Delft, Enschede, Meerssen, Middelburg, Utrecht, and Winterswijk. Later that month the Israeli embassy organized an Israeli film festival in Amsterdam. November was designated Jewish Culture Month.

Publications of Jewish interest included the first Dutch translation of the *Kitzur Shulhan Arukh* (Concise Code of Jewish Law). *Koosjer Nederlands* (Kosher Dutch) was an over-800-page dictionary of words and expressions that entered the Dutch vocabulary from the Jewish population. *Satelllieten* (Satellites), published by the Jewish Historical Museum, presented Jonas Bendiksen's photos taken in remote parts of the former Soviet Union and the stories behind them. *Synagogen van Nederland* (Synagogues of the Netherlands), with photos by Willy Lindwer, was a compendium of Dutch-Jewish architecture with a detailed description of all existing buildings ever used or still in use as synagogues in the country. *Een duif en een jongen* (A Dove and a Boy) was a Dutch translation of Israeli author Meir Shalev's latest Hebrew novel. In *Nieuwe maan* (New Moon), Renata Kersten described her long and difficult road to conversion to Judaism.

Personalia

In the yearly round of royal honors, Jews who received medals included Hans M. Polak, secretary of the Jewish Communities of Rotterdam and The Hague; Franklin de Liever and Bert Manasse of Amersfoort; Rabbi Jochanan Boosman and Wim Wertheim for their aid to Jewish members of the armed forces; Barry Cohn of Leiden; Jaap Wijnschenk and Uri Coronel of Amsterdam; Irene Berg-Baruch and Bert Woudstra of Enschede; and many others.

Rabbi Raph Evers received an award for his contribution to Jewish adult education from Israel's chief rabbis at the sixth Orthodox General Assembly in Jerusalem in January. Professor Philip Wallage received the biennial Alfred Coini Award from the Maatschappij tot Nut der Israëlieten for his works on accountancy. Silver Carnation Awards (for volunteers working to preserve culture or nature) went to Piet and Ida Sanders and Charles Gomes Casseres. Cassares, who lived on Curaçao, was to receive his award from Queen Beatrix on her visit to the island at the end of the year, but he died, aged 85, before that could happen. Author Harry Mulisch was named "Dutch Personality of the Twentieth Century" by the Dutch Institute in Paris. Photographer Ben Dalsheim, from Leeuwarden, received an Austrian gold medal for his photo, "Order is Order." He refused to travel to Austria to receive the medal, since, he said, "The gala is in Linz, ten kilometers from the concentration camp Mauthausen."

Aaron Betsky, about to leave his post as director of the Dutch Architectural Institute in Rotterdam to become director of the Cincinnati Art Museum, was awarded the Wolfert van Borselen Medal for his contributions to Dutch architecture and the city of Rotterdam. Prof. Bob Pinedo, founder of the Cancer Center Amsterdam, received the IJ Award from the city. The Jewish station Nefesh TV received a Dutch award for the best local TV program. Ruben Stranders was awarded the Bakkenist Young Talent Prize for his thesis on artificial intelligence. Journalist Arthur van Amerongen was a co-winner of the 2006 Journalism Award for his articles on Moroccan immigrants in Amsterdam. Violinist Liza Ferschtman received the prestigious Netherlands Music Award for young classical musicians and was appointed director of the Delft Chamber Music Festival, to be held in 2007.

David Simon, chairman of the Amsterdam Jewish community, resigned for personal reasons on January 18, after 17 years of communal service. Harry Kney-Tal, the new Israeli ambassador, did the rounds of Jewish communities in March. Jochanan Boosman resigned as chief rabbi of the Dutch armed forces and was succeeded by Menachem Sebbach.

Prominent Jews who died during 2006 included Joop Bromet, 58, journalist, author, and art critic; author and Holocaust survivor Ab Caransa, 78; Bill Minco, 84, survivor and wartime Resistance member; Ida Vos, 74, author of novels and children's books; Bea Polak-Biet, 88, former owner of Joachimsthal, Holland's only Jewish bookshop and author of *Recepten uit de Joodse keuken* (Recipes from the Jewish Kitchen), a Dutch-Jewish cooking classic; Lidy Madoc-Van Maarsen, 52, member of the national board of WIZO Netherlands; internationally known Dutch-Jewish pianist Marjo Tal, 91, in Jerusalem; Jaap Blog, 89, who helped rebuild the community after the war; Emanuel (Manes) Wikler, 88, who held many positions in the Dutch Jewish community; Riek Cohen Marcus, 88, supporter of wartime orphans; and Bertje Levisson-Schoonheim, 88, founder and former chair of the women's group of the Liberal community in The Hague.

ELISE FRIEDMANN

Italy and the Vatican

National Affairs

AFTER A BITTERLY FOUGHT election campaign, the center-right coalition headed by Prime Minister Silvio Berlusconi narrowly lost to a center-left bloc headed by Romano Prodi in general elections held April 9–10. Berlusconi refused to concede defeat for several days, but Prodi managed to form a government and was sworn in the following month. While many Italian Jews distrusted some of the leftist parties allied with Prodi because of their pro-Palestinian stance, others countered that Berlusconi's "House of Freedoms" coalition had included small far-right parties directly linked to fascism.

Italian president Carlo D'Azeglio Ciampi completed his seven-year term in May and was replaced by Giorgio Napolitano, a longtime leftist leader.

Israel and the Middle East

ITALY

Middle East issues had a powerful impact on Italian politics and foreign policy throughout the year.

In January, Prime Minister Berlusconi called Israeli prime minister Ariel Sharon's illness and incapacitation "very painful on the human level and absolutely negative on the political level." In February, the government's minister for reforms, Roberto Calderoli, was forced to resign after being seen on television wearing a T-shirt bearing copies of the Danish cartoons of the prophet Mohammed that had triggered bloody riots in several countries. Calderoli, a member of the far-right Northern League, said he wore the shirt to express "solidarity with all those who have been struck by the blind violence of religious fanaticism." His television appearance triggered anti-Italian protests in Libya, where thousands stormed the Italian consulate in Benghazi.

Israel regarded the government of Prime Minister Berlusconi as one of its best friends in Europe, and its fall gave cause for concern. When the new government was announced after the April elections, some Jewish and Israeli observers questioned Prime Minister Prodi's choice for foreign minister, longtime leftist leader and former prime minister Massimo D'Alema. Subsequent events appeared to substantiate their misgivings. D'Alema failed to condemn Hezballah for triggering the war in Lebanon. Then in August, he met in Lebanon with Hezballah leaders, and the Italian media published photos of D'Alema walking arm-in-arm with a Hezballah member of the Lebanese parliament. In November, following an Israeli air strike on Beit Hanoun that killed 19 Palestinians, D'Alema complained that the Jewish world backed Israeli policy indiscriminately. The spokesman for Rome's Jewish community, Riccardo Pacifici, said Jews viewed D'Alema's behavior "not only with apprehension but with indignation . . . ."

Jewish concerns somewhat abated toward the end of the year. D'Alema visited Israel, Jordan, and the Palestinian Authority in December. In a meeting with Palestinian president Mahmoud Abbas and in subsequent televised remarks, D'Alema appealed to "all Palestinian groups" to rally around Abbas, stop launching missiles at Israel, free the Israeli soldier kidnapped in June, and work to put an end to violence.

Israeli leaders sought good relations with the new government. During an official visit to Italy in December, Prime Minister Ehud Olmert praised the ruling coalition and declared Prime Minister Prodi a longstanding friend of Israel, despite certain policy differences. A picture of a beaming Olmert and an equally happy Prodi warmly embracing made the front pages of the national newspapers.

Other leftist politicians, meanwhile, drew sharp criticism for their anti-Israel stance. The one whose activities came under closest scrutiny was Oliviero Diliberto, leader of Italy's small Communist Party, who was avowedly pro-Palestinian. At one point, Diliberto threatened to sue the Milan Jewish community spokesman, Yasha Reibman, for slander, based on an interview Reibman gave in which he accused Diliberto of maintaining ties with Palestinian extremists linked to terrorism and denying Israel's right to exist. In February, Diliberto publicly rejected "every accusation" of anti-Semitism and said that his party "is against the policy of the government of Israel. It is not against the Israeli state." He said he would "continue to demonstrate in favor of the Palestinian state," which actually "means to help in the saving and security of Israel."

In May, before Prodi was sworn in, *Liberazione,* the newspaper of the leftist party Communist Refoundation, a partner in the new coalition, published an anti-Israel cartoon that many critics said crossed the line into anti-Semitism. It showed Israel's separation fence with a gate bearing a sign saying, "Hunger Makes You Free," similar to the sign over the gate to Auschwitz that read, "Work Makes You Free." Jewish leaders, the Israeli embassy, and many political figures condemned the cartoon. Left-wingers made their presence known at a number of demonstrations. In one flagrant case, participants at a pro-Palestinian rally in February chanted anti-Israel slogans and carried banners equating Israel's security wall with apartheid; some went further, burning Israeli and American flags and chanting calls for insurgent attacks against Italian armed forces in Iraq. Authorities launched a criminal investigation. Jewish leaders and politicians from across the political spectrum called for the resignation of the mayor of the small town of Marano, who took part in the demonstration, and who later, in an interview, suggested that the world would be a better place without Israel. Pierfernando Casini, president of the Chamber of Deputies, called the remarks "shameful and irresponsible," and apologized to Israel.

On April 25, a march in Milan marking National Liberation Day was marred by extreme leftist anti-Israel protesters who trampled and burned two Israeli flags and shouted pro-Palestinian slogans. What seemed to have triggered these actions was the carrying of Israeli flags in honor of the Jewish Brigade, an infantry unit that helped liberate Italy during World War II. Romano Prodi, not yet inaugurated as prime minister, and other political leaders condemned the incident, as did the Vatican and Jewish leaders. Israeli ambassador Ehud Gol, noting that the day was also Yom Hashoah, Holocaust Remembrance Day, said that the "barbaric fascist behavior of left-wing extremists" had "profaned" the Liberation Day anniversary. "These people," he went on, "along with those who deny the Holocaust and call for the destruction of the State of Israel are a danger for Western democracy."

A week later, on the evening of May 2, Milan's main synagogue was the site of an impressive pro-Israel rally immediately following the celebration of Israel Independence Day. Hundreds of local citizens attended, and the speakers, including political leaders, strongly condemned anti-Semitism and the delegitimation of the State of Israel.

A group that called itself Left-Wing for Israel was active during the year. Among its leaders were prominent politicians and public intellectuals, including Piero Fassino, leader of the Democratic Party of the Left, the main left-wing party. In the general elections, Emanuele Fiano — son of an Auschwitz survivor, former president of the Milan Jewish community, and high-profile member of Left-Wing for Israel — won a seat in the Chamber of Deputies as part of Prodi's coalition. He told the Milan Jewish monthly *Il Bollettino* that the overwhelming majority of the coalition "was on Israel's side, in a stable way, defending its rights, conscious of the risks to its survival." As for the blatant anti-Zionism of the far-left fringe, it had to be analyzed, he said, condemned, and put into perspective. Fiano called the new president, Napolitano, "a great friend of Israel and the Jews."

Israel's summer war with Hezballah had important repercussions in Italy. The government hosted an international conference in late July in an unsuccessful effort to broker a peace deal, and Italy eventually pledged to send as many as 3,000 troops to serve in the UN peacekeeping force in southern Lebanon.

A delegation of Italian Jews went on a solidarity trip to Israel, August 4–7, and about 150 Israeli youngsters from northern Israeli areas subject to Hezballah attack were brought to Italy for vacation, some of them as part of a program run by the city of Rome to host both Israeli and Palestinian children. At the end of the summer, former Italian president Francesco Cossiga joined Alessandro Ruben, president of the Anti-Defamation League's Italian branch, and businessman Elia Valori, a longtime supporter of Israel, on a solidarity mission to the Jewish state. They met with political figures and also expressed personal condolences to Israeli author David Grossman, whose soldier son was killed during the war.

On the night of July 17, thousands of people, Jews and non-Jews, staged a candlelit rally for Israel in the old Rome ghetto, near the main synagogue. Cultural figures and dozens of senior politicians from across the political spectrum took part, including Mayor Walter Veltroni, right-wing leader Gianfranco Fini, and left-wing leader Piero Fassino. Jewish leaders called the demonstration of bipartisan support for Israel a watershed in Italy's political life.

The rally also constituted something of a send-off for Israeli ambassador Ehud Gol, who was completing his term and would return to Israel not long afterward. In an interview, Gol said that great changes had occurred in how Israel was perceived in Italy since his tenure began. "Today the perception of Israel is positive, maybe better," he told the Rome Jewish monthly *Shalom*. Gol, sometimes criticized for being too close to right-wing elements in Italy, said that even far-left members of the newly elected government had asked to meet with him, "something that would have been impossible even a few years ago." The new ambassador was Gideon Meir, who had previously served as deputy director general of the Israeli Foreign Ministry.

In August, the Union of Italian Islamic Communities (UCOII) ran a virulently anti-Israel paid advertisement in several newspapers. Many considered the ad anti-Semitic. Titled "Nazi Massacres Yesterday, Israeli Massacres Today," it compared Israeli killings of Arab civilians to the Nazi's mass executions of Italians during the German occupation of the country in World War II. Jewish leaders and Italian political leaders condemned the ad, as did some local Muslim organizations.

An Italian cartoonist, Alessandro Gatto, won a prize in the Holocaust cartoon "competition" organized by Iranian president Ahmadinejad. Gatto's drawing showed an Arab looking out of a prison window whose bars were formed from the blue and white stripes on the shirt of a concentration-camp uniform. The stripes recalled the Israeli flag.

Throughout the year there were numerous conferences, lectures, round-tables, and discussions about the Middle East and about the role of Islam in Europe. In March, for example, Left-Wing for Israel sponsored a conference on "The Middle East Seen from Italy." In September, a daylong session on "The Future of Israel—Politics in the Middle East," initiated by a Jewish academic, David Meghnagi, featured leading journalists and political figures. Also in September, a group called the Islamic Anti-Defamation League held a conference in Rome. Advertised as marking the anniversary of the September 11 terror attacks in the U.S., it was actually an anti-Israel event under the title "Peace is an Imperative: Victims of a Victim People."

There were many official visits and cultural exchanges between Italy and Israel both before and after the Italian elections. Francesco Rutelli, president of Italy's Daisy party, visited Israel and the Palestinian territories in March. That same month Israeli foreign minister Tzipi Livni met with Berlusconi, Foreign Minister Gianfanco Fini, and other senior Italian government figures during an official visit to Rome. Berlusconi told her Italy was willing to host a conference aimed at reactivating the "road map" peace process in the Middle East. Livni returned to Rome in August and met with senior government officials and Jewish leaders.

In June, an Italian delegation of more than 100 people, including about 70 high school students, spent three days in Israel on a trip organized and led by Piero Marrazzo, president of Italy's Lazio region (around Rome). Accompanying the students were representatives of the regional government as well as Riccardo Di Segni, chief rabbi of Rome, the president of the Rome Jewish community, and two Italian survivors of Auschwitz. The participating Italian schools had "twinning" arrangements with Israeli high schools. The group visited Jewish and Christian sites and met with Israeli authorities. During the visit, the Lazio officials signed an agreement with Israel for cooperation in medicine and biotechnology. Also in June, a ceremony at the residence of the Italian ambassador to Israel celebrated the 50th anniversary of the Israel-Italy Chamber of Commerce. Some Italian politicians suggested that NATO consider Israel for membership. Defense Minister Antonio Martino raised the issue in a radio interview in February, and was seconded by Undersecretary for Foreign Affairs Gianni Vernetti, who had worked for two months on a kibbutz as a teenager. In November, Marco Panella, head of the Radicals, reiterated an idea he had previously proposed, Israeli membership in the European Union.

THE VATICAN

Starting with his New Year's Day address, which stated that resolving the Israeli-Palestinian conflict was a key to world peace, Pope Benedict XVI issued frequent calls over the course of the year for a Middle East settlement.

In January, the Vatican urged prayers for the health of the stroke-ridden Israeli prime minister, Ariel Sharon. The Vatican foreign minister, Archbishop Giovanni Lajolo, phoned Israel's ambassador to the Holy See to express "deep concern" over Sharon's health and solidarity with the Israeli people. He termed Sharon "a central figure for the peace process."

Speaking before the UN General Assembly in November, the Vatican UN representative said a two-state solution was needed "as the basis for the resolution of the crisis." Benedict made several appeals for an end to bloodshed in Gaza. "I am following with vivid concern the news of the serious deterioration of the situation regarding the Gaza Strip and I wish to express my closeness to the civilian populations that suffer the consequences of acts of violence," he said in November, and prayed that God would "illuminate the Israeli and Palestinian authorities, as well as those of nations that have a particular responsibility in the region, so that they work to end the bloodshed, to multiply the initiatives of humanitarian aid and to favor the immediate resumption of direct, serious and concrete negotiations."

In July, the Vatican issued a statement calling Israeli strikes against Hezballah in southern Lebanon unjustified. The Anti-Defamation League criticized the Vatican's response as "one-sided and short-sighted," adding that "the Vatican continues to be mired in a false paradigm that equates, on the one side, terrorist actions by Islamist extremists who view both Jews and Christians as infidels and seek Israel's destruction, with, on the other side, Israel's right to defend itself and eliminate the ongoing and growing threats to its citizens."

Two outstanding bilateral issues between the Holy See and Israel were the subject of talks during the year—the juridical status of Catholic institutions in Israel and the access of Palestinian Christians to holy sites. During her visit to Italy in March, Foreign Minister Livni discussed these matters in a "very cordial and friendly" meeting with Vatican foreign minister Monsignor Lajolo. Both sides termed bilateral relations "good," but Lajolo said they "could still improve." The same issues were raised again the next month when Shimon Peres, Israel's deputy prime minister, was in Rome, and yet again in December during an audience Prime Minister Olmert had with the pope. At each of these sessions the Israelis expressed great interest in a visit by the pontiff to Israel, and Olmert presented an official invitation. Vatican officials said the pope would go only if there were peace in the region, or at least a stable truce.

It was reported in January that the Vatican had selected an Israeli company, RAD Data Communications, for its Ethernet Internet network. In November, the Vatican sharply criticized the planned gay pride parade in Jerusalem, calling it a "serious affront" to Jews, Muslims, and Christians who believed the city had a "special sacred character."

Anti-Semitism and Racism

Racist hooliganism at soccer matches remained a serious problem. In January, fans of the Roma team displayed neo-Nazi and anti-Semitic banners during a match against Livorno. In July, swastikas were scrawled in Rome's old Jewish ghetto during celebrations marking Italy's victory in soccer's World Cup. And in November, fans of the Livorno team unfurled Palestinian flags and a banner reading "Free Palestine," written in Arabic, during a match with Maccabi Haifa.

Mayor Veltroni organized a meeting at Rome's city hall, in February, between representatives of the Roma and Lazio teams and three Holocaust survivors. One of the Lazio participants was a player, Paolo di Canio, who had been punished in the past for giving the fascist salute during games. Di Canio reiterated his pro-fascist views after the meeting, saying, "I've listened to the stories, but I still have my ideas." And yet he added, "It's important that people are aware of what happened. The race laws [introduced by Mussolini] were terrible. Violence is never a positive thing."

There were several episodes of vandalism against Jewish targets, most of them apparently linked to the situation in the Middle East. About 40 tombstones in Milan's Jewish cemetery were toppled in May. A score of Jewish-owned shops in Rome were defaced in August, the perpetrators also plastering fliers nearby bearing pro-Hezballah slogans. These were signed by a group calling itself "Armed Revolutionary Fascists." In October, swastikas and anti-Semitic slogans were found scrawled on the walls of the synagogue in Naples.

Holocaust-Related Developments

Once again, Holocaust Memorial Day, January 27, had an extremely high profile in Italy. There were scores of educational, cultural, and commemorative events not only on the day itself but also before and after. Among the exhibitions was one in Rome of photographs of Shoah survivors by Adriano Mordenti. Also in Rome, Roma Tre University announced it would initiate a master's-degree course in Holocaust studies, the first in Italy. A cantata on Holocaust themes, *Ricorda cosa ti ha fatto Amalek* (Remember What Amalek Did to You), premiered at Rome's prestigious Auditorium concert hall.

Mayor Veltroni led his annual trip for Rome high-school students to Auschwitz in November. This was an official program of the city's school system. Some 230 teenagers made the trip this year, including a number of Muslims.

The decision taken in 2005 to build a Holocaust museum in Rome caused some tension, since the national government had already, in 2001, decided to construct a national Holocaust museum in Ferrara. The Ferrara project was stalled despite an allocation of funds, but work on the Rome museum — scheduled to open in 2008 on the grounds of Villa Torlonia, the elegant nineteenth-century villa where Benito Mussolini lived from 1925 to 1943 — moved ahead. Nobel laureate Elie Wiesel agreed to be honorary president of the Rome Shoah Museum Foundation, and Marcello Pezzetti, Italy's leading Holocaust scholar, was head of research for the museum. Meanwhile, Villa Torlonia was opened to tour groups in February after a $6-million restoration. Ancient Jewish catacombs were located beneath the grounds.

Pope Benedict traveled to Poland in late May and used the occasion to visit Auschwitz and make brief remarks. He noted that it was difficult for him, as a German, to stand there. Benedict used the Hebrew term "Shoah" to denote the Holocaust, and recalled that the Nazis had wanted to "crush the entire Jewish people [and] cancel them from the register of the peoples of the earth." Some Jewish groups expressed disappointment that the pope did not explicitly condemn the anti-Semitism that led to the Nazi genocide. After returning home, however, speaking to tens of thousands of the faithful in St. Peter's Square, he declared, "Today's humanity must not forget Auschwitz and the other 'factories of death' where the Nazi regime tried to eliminate God in order to take his place. Humanity must not give in to the temptation of racial hatred, which is at the origin of the worst forms of anti-Semitism."

The issue of Pope Pius XII's role during World War II and the Holocaust remained a sore point. In September, some 30,000 files from the 1922–39 pontificate of Pius XI were opened. During that period the future Pius XII (then Cardinal Eugenio Pacelli) served the Vatican as envoy to Nazi Germany and as secretary of state. Scholars said the initial documents from this period showed that Pius XI opposed the fascist regimes that gained strength in Europe in the 1930s. In December, 35 Jewish and Catholic scholars issued a petition urging the Vatican to open all of its Holocaust-era archives.

Also in December, Italian political leaders as well as the Vatican issued statements condemning the Holocaust-denial conference in Tehran.

JEWISH COMMUNITY

Communal Affairs

As many as 35,000 Jews were believed to live in Italy, only about two-thirds of them formally affiliated with Jewish communities. Rome, with about 15,000 Jews (12,000 formally affiliated), and Milan, with about 10,000 (6,500 formally affiliated), were the largest communities. The rest of the country's Jews were scattered in a score of other towns and cities, mostly in the northern and central parts of the country. All established communities were officially Orthodox in orientation and linked under an umbrella organization, the Union of Italian Jewish Communities (UCEI), whose leadership served as the political representative of Italian Jewry.

One newly formed, tiny Jewish community functioned in Trani, in Apulia, from which Jews had been expelled 500 years earlier. The group, aided by a rabbi from Rome, held services in the medieval Scolanova synagogue, long used as a church but returned to Jewish use in 2005.

In Rome, the Young People's Synagogue celebrated 20 years of activity. The congregation was founded in December 1985 by a group of Jews, most of them in their twenties, who reopened a small prayer house in the old Jewish hospital on the Tiber Island, across from the main synagogue. The congregation, which was Modern Orthodox, organized itself on an American model, including study groups, public meetings, and other activities that depended in large part on volunteers.

In Milan, the scholar Haim Baharier played an important role as "master" for a number of well-known Jewish and non-Jewish intellectuals. He gave lectures, classes, and study groups on the Talmud and other subjects. In February, at the initiative of one of his followers, theater director Andrée Ruth Shammah, he led five sessions at Milan's Dal Verme Theater, where he interpreted verses from the book of Genesis, accompanied by music played by several of Italy's top Jewish musicians. Baharier also published a book of his biblical commentaries.

Chabad was very active in several cities, including Rome, Milan and Venice. In Rome, Chabad ran bar mitzvah classes for adults.

Several small Progressive (Reform) groups were active. These included congregations in Milan (Beth Shalom) and Florence (Shir Chadash), an "association" in Rome, and a new *havurah* in Turin. None of these groups was recognized by the UCEI, but the two congregations were affiliated with the World Union for Progressive Judaism. Shir Chadash arranged to get a full-time visiting rabbi in September, Rabbi Robert Rothman, who had served in Rye, N.Y., and in South Africa. He was to work on a volunteer basis at Shir Chadash through June 2007, and also to help Beth Shalom in Milan.

Barbara Aiello, an American Reform rabbi who had served for a time in Milan, started a new congregation in Calabria, Ner Tamid del Sud (Eternal Light of the South), as well as a study center there. On Rosh Hashanah, Aiello officiated at a service in the old synagogue in Ivrea, near Turin, when a Torah scroll given by American donors was dedicated for use by the new Turin *havurah*.

Major changes took place in the established Jewish communal leadership. Seventy-eight-year-old Amos Luzzatto, whose term as president of the UCEI was to have ended at the organization's fifth quadrennial Congress in July, resigned in February, citing health reasons. Lawyer Claudio Morpurgo took over as acting president.

The Congress drew wide media coverage. Prime Minister Prodi and other senior political figures attended the keynote session. Prodi gave a speech that was intently scrutinized as an indicator of his new government's policy toward Jews and Israel. Prodi's remarks drew a mixed response. The audience welcomed his statements condemning anti-Semitism, pledging support for minorities in Europe, and recognizing the strong link between Italian Jews and Israel. But Prodi did not tackle the problem of the perceived double standard used in judging the actions of Israel, on the one hand, and the Palestinians, on the other, nor did he refer to the fate of the kidnapped Israeli soldier in Gaza.

Renzo Gattegna, a lawyer from Rome, was elected president of the UCEI. The newly elected council represented a sharp break with the past: eight of the 15 members had never before served on it. In addition, representatives from the Rome and Milan communities—which accounted for more than two-thirds of Italian Jewry—made up less than half of the council members, with the much smaller provincial communities holding a majority. Representatives of some of the Progressive groups were, for the first time, permitted to attend as observers, and a decision was made to establish a commission to study ways of integrating the Progressives into the established community.

But the meeting also highlighted factionalism within Italian Jewry. Some who attended complained that too much energy was expended in politicking and electioneering, and not enough in discussing the serious challenges facing Italian Jews. Indeed, before the Congress, consultant Roger Abravanel told the Milan Jewish monthly *Il Bollettino* that the administrative structure of organized Jewry in Italy was obsolete and hampered by its imitation of Italian political and administrative models, which themselves were excessively bureaucratic.

In fact, the governing councils of the Jewish communities in Rome and Milan were so split by factionalism that their meetings at times erupted into shouting matches. The president of the Rome community, Leone Paserman, walked out of at least one council meeting to protest the tone of debate. A hotly contested election for the communal leadership in Milan pitted three "parties" against each other—For Israel, a traditionalist group based on a strong defense of Israel; the secular Chai group; and the centrist Kadima, which modeled its positions on the Israeli Kadima party. The election, extensively covered in the local media, ended in a decisive victory for the For Israel group.

Jewish communities were also split along religious and personal lines. In Milan, the case of an American-born woman became a focus of dispute. In a letter to *Il Bollettino,* she described how she tried to enroll her children in a Talmud Torah class organized by a "subcommunity" within the Jewish community, only to have them rejected because their father was not Jewish. Even though, as a Jew, her children were Jewish according to

Jewish law, and the family belonged to the Milan community, she was informed that only children with two Jewish parents could attend the Talmud Torah class.

As many as 10,000 Israelis had dual citizenship with Italy, and Italian Jews followed events in Israel very closely. Communal spokesmen and other leaders, in Rome and Milan in particular, weighed in during media debates and at conferences and meetings on issues of concern to Israel.

Interreligious Relations

Italy's State Council, in February, rejected a petition by a non-Catholic to have a crucifix removed from his son's classroom in a public school. The ruling stated that even in secular settings such as schools, the crucifix—which was displayed in many public places in Italy, including hospitals and courtrooms—had a "highly symbolic, educative function, regardless of the religion professed by pupils."

In January, Rome's chief rabbi, Riccardo Di Segni, headed a small Jewish delegation that met with Pope Benedict XVI at the Vatican. Rome Jewish community president Leone Paserman termed the meeting "a tremendous success, beyond our expectations." He said the pope was "very friendly, reiterating his strong condemnation of anti-Semitism as well as terrorism, and using language such as 'love' and 'the people of Israel,' indicating a positive step in the relationship between Jews and the Catholic Church." The pope expressed concern at recent episodes of anti-Semitism and urged Jews and Christians to work together in a "common mission" against hate. Di Segni thanked Benedict for "denouncing anti-Semitism, past and present, for condemning fundamentalist terrorism, for his attention to the State of Israel, which, for all the Jewish people, is an essential and central reference."

Several other Jewish delegations held high-level meetings at the Vatican. Israel Singer of the World Jewish Congress met with Foreign Minister Lajolo and other officials in January, and discussed, among other matters, the need for Jews and Christians to dialogue with Muslims. In meetings with delegations from the American Jewish Committee in March and the Anti-Defamation League in October, the pope stressed that Jews, Christians, and Muslims must work together for peace and mutual respect.

Pope Benedict offended the Muslim world when, in a speech made during a visit to Germany in September, he cited an obscure text by the fourteenth-century Byzantine emperor Manuel II: "Show me just what

Muhammad brought that was new and there you will find things only evil and inhuman, such as his command to spread by the sword the faith he preached." There were violent demonstrations in some Muslim countries, including the firebombing of two churches in the West Bank. The Vatican asserted that the remarks had been misinterpreted and that the pope wanted to cultivate "respect and dialogue towards other religions and cultures," including Islam. The pope sought to mend fences during a visit to Turkey in November.

A conference was held in Rome to mark two decades since Pope John Paul II's historic visit to the Rome synagogue in April 1986. In the summer, the Vatican published an 80-page compilation of papal speeches and other Vatican material on Catholic-Jewish relations under the title *Awake! Do Not Forget Man, Your Creature.*

There were numerous interfaith meetings throughout the year. The Israeli-Vatican Bilateral Commission on Interreligious Relations convened at the Vatican in March. The three-day gathering of Church officials and representatives of the Israeli Chief Rabbinate dealt with religious perspectives on life and death. The group issued a statement saying that life is a gift from God and thus no person may "decide its value or extent." It affirmed "the principles of our respective traditions that God is the creator and lord of all life and that human life is sacred," and urged Catholics and Jews to "reach out beyond our own bilateral dialogue" in order to "engage and involve the Muslim world and its leaders in respectful dialogue and cooperation."

On September 4, more than 200 representatives of many different religions held a "religious summit" in Assisi under the slogan, "For a world of peace, religions and cultures in dialogue." Italy's president and other senior political figures also took part. The event marked the 20th anniversary of the first such "summit" initiated by the late Pope John Paul II in 1986. In the Jewish delegation were Yonah Metzger, Israel's Ashkenazi chief rabbi, and Rome's chief rabbi, Riccardo Di Segni.

In November, the International Catholic-Jewish Liaison Committee (ILC) met for the 19th time. This year the meeting took place, for the first time, in Cape Town, South Africa. Two topics that drew considerable attention were the care of HIV/AIDS patients and the necessity to reach out so as to strengthen moderate voices within Islam. The ILC was made up of the International Jewish Committee for Interreligious Consultations (IJCIC) and the Vatican's Commission for Religious Relations with the Jews.

There were efforts to foster Jewish-Muslim cooperation. In March,

Chief Rabbi Di Segni made his first official visit to Rome's main mosque to demonstrate support for the Muslim community after the publication of cartoons that satirized Mohammed and touched off violent protests. In May, Di Segni and other Jewish leaders joined Christian and Muslim dignitaries in mourning the death of the mosque's imam, Mahmoud Hammad Shweita. Di Segni said his presence at the memorial service was a gesture of "sympathy and solidarity" that bore witness to the friendly relations between the two faith communities in Rome. A Jewish delegation headed by Milan's chief rabbi, Alfonso Arbib, and the president of the Milan Jewish community, Leone Sued, visited the main Milan mosque during the summer and met with leaders of the Italian Islamic Religious Community organization. Muslim leaders had visited Milan's main synagogue in 2005.

Culture

Numerous Jewish and Jewish-themed cultural events took place in Jewish community centers, museums, theaters, civic spaces, and other venues. In January, the Polish Cultural Institute in Rome hosted a program called Mazel Tov, based on the works of Isaac Bashevis Singer. In February, during a visit to Rome's recently revamped and expanded Jewish Museum in the complex housing the city's main synagogue, President Ciampi called for dialogue and reciprocal respect among "peoples, cultures and religions" for the common benefit of humanity.

In the spring, a monthlong festival of Jewish culture called Oyoyoy took place in the northern Italian town of Casale Monferrato. The Jewish community in Casale, whose ornate synagogue was a Jewish museum, sponsored many cultural events during the year, including an international exhibition of Islamic art that opened at the end of October. The first Festival of Jewish Arts took place in Ferrara in June.

A major exhibit of works by the Italian Jewish painter Amadeo Modigliani was held in Rome during the summer, and it was announced that some 6,000 documents, photographs, and manuscripts relating to Modigliani's life would be moved from France to Italy. In July, the Jewish museum in Trieste held a series of Jewish music concerts called "Erev/Laila." At the end of October, the ninth annual Pitifest festival of Jewish cinema and culture was held in the Tuscan hill town of Pitigliano.

There were many cultural exchanges between Italy and Israel throughout the year, many of them promoted by the culture department of the Israeli embassy. Israeli artists were featured in numerous exhibitions, film presentations, and performances. In the summer, Israeli pop star Ninet Tayeb performed on Italian TV and also gave a benefit concert in Rome. A major exhibition showcasing a century of Israeli art opened in Milan in October. Called "Omanut: 100 Years of Israeli Art," it was sponsored by top political, civic, and Jewish bodies and ran through the end of the year at Milan's most prestigious art venue, the Royal Palace near the Cathedral. In November, a six-day festival of contemporary Israeli film was held in Rome. Reciprocally, the Italian Cultural Institute in Tel Aviv organized exhibitions, concerts, film presentations, and other events in Israel.

Numerous books were published, both fiction and nonfiction, on Jewish themes or by Jewish authors. These included Gabriele Rigano's *Il Caso Zolli* (The Zolli Case), a biography of Rome's wartime chief rabbi, Israel Zolli, who survived the Holocaust and then converted to Catholicism; *The Righteous of Italy: Non-Jews Who Saved Jews, 1943–1945,* detailing the stories of 387 Italian Righteous Gentiles; a travel book, *The Complete Jewish Guide to Italy: Tutto sull' Ebraismo in Italia;* and the novel *Pranzo di Famiglia* (Family Lunch) by Hungarian-born journalist Alessandra Farkas, New York correspondent for the Milan daily *Corriere della Sera,* based on her family's history.

Vincitori e Vinti (Winners and Losers), by television newscaster Bruno Vespa, discussed anti-Semitism and racism in Italian politics. The book sparked considerable debate, some Jews criticizing it for minimizing the importance of traditional Catholic anti-Semitism. The Rome Jewish community's decision to sponsor a book launch for Vespa triggered more complaints. Another important book launch in Rome was for *Café Savoy,* a volume about the Yiddish theater in Europe edited by Paola Bertolone and Laura Quercioli Mincer. Mincer's husband, the actor Olek Mincer, performed scenes from Yiddish plays at the event. Olek Mincer also issued a CD of Yiddish songs.

In February, the Center for American Studies sponsored a roundtable on "Literature Confronting the Challenges of the Contemporary World," whose panel included Israeli author A.B. Yehoshua and Rome Jewish academic David Meghnagi. Deborah Lipstadt, the Emory University professor and author of *Denying the Holocaust,* taught at the Gregorian Pontifical University during the spring semester. In November, the Association of European Jewish Museums held its annual meeting in Venice.

Italy was an enthusiastic participant in the annual European Day of Jewish Culture, held this year on September 3. Although the city of Modena was the national focus of the festivities, events in 55 towns and cities all over Italy attracted 43,000 people, with more than 5,000 lining up in Milan to visit the main synagogue. Among the sites open to the public for the first time on this day were the ruins of a fourth-century synagogue at Bova Marina in Calabria that had been discovered in the 1980s during highway construction. A large mosaic of a menorah and other Jewish symbols that archaeologists had found there and had been kept for 20 years at the National Museum in Reggio Calabria was returned to the Bova Marina site in July. Plans were announced to conserve it in a special building there and to resume excavations. The town of Lugo, near Ravenna, took part in the day's events for the first time this year, and also formed a sister-city relationship with the Israeli town of Yoqneam Illit.

This year the ornate synagogue in Cherasco, near Turin, was opened to the public after restoration.

Personalia

In January, the Vatican named Archbishop Antonio Franco as its new envoy to Israel and Cyprus, and apostolic delegate in Jerusalem and Palestine. Franco, 68, had served in the Philippines since 1999. He replaced Archbishop Pietro Sambi, who was named papal nuncio in Washington.

In the spring, Yossi Bar, the veteran Rome correspondent for the Israeli daily *Yediot Aharonot,* was elected president of the Foreign Press Association, the first time an Israeli journalist had been chosen for this position. In May, the Egyptian-born Italian Muslim journalist Magdi Allam, deputy director of the Milan daily *Corriere della Sera,* received Israel's Dan David award for fostering understanding and tolerance between cultures. He drew a standing ovation at the presentation ceremony in Israel when he declared "We are all Israelis" and "Am Yisrael Chai."

In September, Giacomo Kahn was named the new editor-in-chief of the Rome Jewish monthly magazine *Shalom.* In November, Israeli novelist David Grossman, who wrote occasional columns for the Rome daily *La Repubblica,* was awarded Italy's Premiolino journalism prize for the "extraordinary and exceedingly civil equilibrium with which he has recounted the Israeli-Palestinian conflict to the world." He received another award, the "Roma," given for "peace and humanitarian activities," in December.

Journalist and author Fausto Coen died in Rome in January at the age of 91. Jazz musician Romano Mussolini, the last surviving child of Italy's World War II fascist dictator Benito Mussolini, died in Rome at the age of 78. The youngest of Benito Mussolini's five children, he was the father of right-wing politician Alessandra Mussolini. In April, Massimo Della Pergola, a journalist and sportswriter who created Italy's main soccer pools, died in Milan at the age of 94. In May, Davide Di Veroli, one of Italy's few remaining survivors of Auschwitz, died in Rome at the age of 81, an apparent suicide.

The crusading Italian journalist Oriana Fallaci died at her home in Florence of cancer in September, aged 77. During her controversial career, Fallaci, who was not Jewish, had gone from being a critic of Israel to one of the Jewish state's most vocal supporters. Her most recent work included strongly worded denunciations of anti-Semitism as well as criticism of Islam and of the West's weakness in the face of radical Muslims.

Filmmaker Gillo Pontecorvo died in October at the age of 86. He was most famous for his 1966 film, *The Battle of Algiers*. Born into a wealthy Jewish family in Pisa, he moved to France after Italy's fascist regime imposed anti-Semitic racial laws in 1938, and fought in the resistance during World War II.

RUTH ELLEN GRUBER

Switzerland

National Affairs

SWITZERLAND REMAINED torn between its tradition of isolation, on the one hand, and a new impulse toward openness and engagement, on the other. This ambivalence was illustrated by fierce debates over asylum policies and the rights of minorities.

The country approved, by plebiscite, new asylum legislation that would speed up the expulsion of unwanted asylum seekers, track down all forms of "abuse" of asylum status, and end financial aid to refugees with criminal records. The changes were backed by majorities in each of the Swiss cantons, and passed by a solid overall majority of 67.8 percent. Initiated by the rightist Swiss People's Party, the referendum was supported by other conservative parties but opposed by the political left, churches, and the Jewish community. The Swiss People's Party was buoyed by this success and proceeded to suggest even more far-reaching initiatives, such as making naturalization more difficult and forbidding dual citizenship.

Minister of Justice Christoph Blocher, the best-known leader of the party and one of its two representatives in the government, continued his attacks on Swiss institutions, criticized the government of which he was a part, denounced the country's constitution, and attempted to censor Swiss television.

During a visit to Turkey in October, Blocher said publicly that the Swiss law against racism—passed in 1994 and making it a criminal offense to commit public racist or anti-Semitic acts, or to deny any genocide—gave him a "stomachache," and that it should be "either completely suppressed or revised so that citizens of this country do not fear a lawsuit simply because they express an opinion." Coming as a direct attack by a cabinet minister against a national statute, and pronounced in a foreign country without prior consent from his government, Blocher's statement created a furor in Switzerland. Blocher was also highly critical of Jews who spoke out against the new asylum rules and made a point of mentioning their religion. His party was no friend of Muslims either, gathering signatures for a referendum to "forbid all power symbols of Islam" in Switzerland, including minarets.

Nationalist conservative politicians tied their isolationist policies on the international scene—such as opposition to the European Union and the UN—to xenophobic and racist arguments domestically. Arguing that Switzerland was "a special case," they rejected the guarantee of equal rights for minorities that all other Western democracies espoused. Having lost battles on some of the international issues—plebiscites had secured Switzerland's entry into the UN and special agreements with the EU—these nationalists became increasingly fixated on minority groups within the country.

Switzerland came under criticism for steps it took to cooperate with the U.S. in the war on terror. Swiss banks were charged with breaking national laws by providing banking information to American counterterrorism officials. The banks did not inform customers using the Swift money-transfer service that their data could be passed on to third parties. Swiss senator Dick Marty prepared a report for the Council of Europe that criticized 14 countries for authorizing CIA flights carrying "presumed terrorists" to stop over or to fly across their airspace. According to the report, Switzerland allowed six U.S. noncommercial planes to stop in Switzerland between September 2001 and September 2005, while 76 CIA planes flew over Switzerland.

Israel and the Middle East

On July 5, Minister of Foreign Affairs Micheline Calmy-Rey issued a statement expressing Switzerland's "extreme preoccupation with the current situation in Gaza." It went on to accuse Israel of violating international law by imposing "collective punishment" on the Palestinians, and denied any justification for Israel's destruction of an electric-power plant and the arbitrary arrest of democratically elected Hamas members of the Palestinian parliament. The Swiss Federation of Jewish Communities sharply criticized the foreign minister's position. The International Committee of the Red Cross, based in Geneva, commented on the situation in terms very similar to those of Calmy-Rey.

When Israel launched its invasion of Lebanon in response to the abduction of two Israeli soldiers, Calmy-Rey condemned the move as "disproportionate." The rest of the government, however, maintained silent neutrality and concentrated on the humanitarian aspect, donating the equivalent of about $4 million to the Red Cross for the benefit of civilian victims. Swiss public opinion was certainly against Israeli actions, as demonstrated by a surge of anti-Israel and even anti-Semitic letters sent to newspaper editors (some of which were published) and to well-known

Jewish personalities and organizations. There were also numerous street rallies in support of Hezballah. A pro-Israel rally was organized in Bern, initiated and largely attended by evangelical Christians. About 3,000 gathered at the federal square, where their leader, MP Christian Waber, proclaimed, "Salvation comes from the Jews! This is what says he who gave his life on the cross for us all."

The reconstituted UN Human Rights Council, based in Geneva, convened in emergency session to condemn "gross human-rights violations by Israel in Lebanon." This resolution was approved by the automatic majority created by the African and Asian countries. The new council had now issued three resolutions aimed at a specific country; all of them targeted Israel, to the exclusion of the UN's other 191 member states.

The Swiss government nominated Jean Ziegler, whom it called "one of the best specialists in civil, human, and cultural rights," to serve on the UN Sub-Commission for the Promotion and Protection of Human Rights. The choice drew considerable criticism. For the previous six years Ziegler had served as UN special rapporteur on the right to food, and, instead of dealing with the world's food emergencies, had pursued a blatantly leftist and anti-Israel political agenda. The originator and first recipient of the Muammar Qaddafi Prize for Human Rights, Ziegler had even been critized by UN secretary general Kofi Annan for comparing Israelis to Nazis.

Anti-Semitism and Extremism

Racism, anti-Semitism, and a general hostility toward minorities remained everyday phenomena in Switzerland. While cases of physical violence were rare, people with dark skin, non-Christians, and those who did not lead a conventional lifestyle risked taunts, threats, and discrimination. They were often refused service in restaurants and hotels, charged more for automobile insurance and deposits for apartment rentals, discriminated against in schools and businesses, and subject to stringent police controls. Since the late 1990s, hostility tended to focus on individuals from the former Yugoslavia and Turkey, as well as on Jews, Muslims, and blacks.

The sociology department of the University of Geneva published *Monitoring Misanthropy and Right-Wing Extremist Attitudes in Switzerland: An Exploratory Study*. Directed by Prof. Sandro Cattacin and based on 3,000 oral interviews lasting 40 minutes each, the survey showed that 20 percent of the Swiss population harbored anti-Semitic feelings and 30 percent anti-Muslim feelings, and that 6 percent felt that violence "can solve problems." The study concluded that "right-wing extremism is not a marginal phenomenon."

Right-wing extremist groups remained active, but small and disorganized. Federal police estimated their number at about 1,000, including skinheads, neo-Nazis, and other white supremacists. Their activities were local or regional and consisted of concerts, rallies, and privately printed publications. Some recently founded groups were Helvetica Youth (Helvetische Jugend) and Les Identitaires. Among the veteran anti-Semites and Holocaust deniers were Gaston-Armand Amaudruz, publisher of *Courrier du Continent;* Claude and Mariette Paschoud, publishers of *Le Pamphlet;* and Ernst Indelkofer, publisher of *Recht+Wahrheit.* Internet hate seemed to be on the upswing. Instead of starting their own Web sites, however, which could be shut down, extremists would post their opinions on blogs and other forums located at conventional Web sites.

Erwin Kessler, leader of the Association against Animal Factories (ACUSA) and previously convicted for anti-Semitic articles and incendiary statements about kosher slaughter, got into trouble once more. In his organization's newsletter, which had a circulation of 350,000, he wrote that hens raised in factories were living in "concentration camps." Sued for anti-Semitism, he refused to appear at the first hearing of his case in Geneva.

The most active extreme-right political group was the five-year-old Partei National Orientierter Schweiz, or PNOS (National-Oriented Party of Switzerland). By running candidates in municipal and cantonal elections, the PNOS became the first such party since the end of World War II to take a serious part in Swiss politics. The PNOS aspired to put "an end to multiculturalism," expel most foreigners from Switzerland, and set up internment camps for asylum seekers. Its leader was 28-year-old Sacha Kunz, who also started a record company, "White Revolution," which released music with far-right themes. He was arrested in Germany in 2006 for "diffusion of anticonstitutional propaganda" after police seized 2,000 copies of a German-language skinhead CD that Kunz produced.

The single public event that drew all the extreme-right factions was the annual celebration of August 1, Switzerland's national holiday, officially commemorated on Rütli Mountain in the presence of elected officials. In 2006, for the first time, the traditional event took place under heavy police security; only guests with tickets and identification were allowed to attend. Since 1996, radical right-wingers had tried to hijack, or at least disturb, the commemoration with their loud presence, neo-Nazi dress and banners, and nationalist slogans. The new security measures in 2006 kept away all but a handful of extremists. But about 150 of them, mostly skinheads, tried to disrupt speeches given that day by members of the government in other locations, and marched through small towns carrying torches. Rather than decry the disrupters, the Swiss People's Party criticized the security measures.

Public Holocaust-denial propaganda decreased in Switzerland, two of its most important voices having left the country. Jürgen Graf avoided a 15-month jail sentence by fleeing to Russia. René-Louis Berclaz was forced to disband his organization, Vérité et Justice (Truth and Justice), and, after serving a prison sentence for his Holocaust-denial activities, settled in Romania, where he was arrested in September 2006 after a gun, ammunition, Holocaust-denial publications, and racist CDs were found in his room. He was charged with smuggling weapons and attempting to create a fascist organization.

The only Swiss citizen to attend the Holocaust-denial conference in Tehran in December was Bernhard Schaub. He delivered a speech praising Iranian president Ahmadinejad for endorsing "the fight against the myth of the Holocaust" and called all European Holocaust deniers to join forces with Muslims, since "they have the same enemy . . . which subjugates the whole world to Jewish Capitalism with the help of American fighting elephants, and wants to annihilate independent people, cultures and religions."

Left-wing anti-Semitism was expressed mostly in the guise of anti-Israel or anti-Zionist comments, especially during the war between Israel and Hezballah in Lebanon. Participants at an anti-Israel rally in Bern carried not only Hezballah flags and portraits of Hassan Nasrallah, but also Israeli flags with swastikas, and shouted anti-Semitic slogans. The rally was cosponsored by two mainstream left-of-center parties represented in the parliament, the Green Party and the Socialist Party of Switzerland.

As part of Swiss government efforts to monitor Islamic extremism, the brothers Hani and Tariq Ramadan, grandsons of Muslim Brotherhood founder Hassan al-Bannah, continued to be scrutinized even while they enjoyed many public-speaking opportunities. Tariq Ramadan, denied a U.S. visa by the State Department in 2004 (see AJYB 2006, p. 416), was denied a second time in 2006 because of donations totaling $940 he made to two organizations, the Comité de Bienfaisance et de Secours aux Palestiniens (CBSP) and the Association de Secours Palestinien (ASP), which were considered fund-raising conduits for Hamas. The U.S. consular officer concluded that Ramadan's request was "inadmissible based solely on his actions, which constituted providing material support to a terrorist organization." Ramadan was awarded a two-year research fellowship at Oxford University. While in Great Britain he also served on a task force appointed by Prime Minister Tony Blair to foster British-Muslim understanding.

Holocaust-Related Matters

Eight years after the $1.25-billion global settlement between Swiss banks and plaintiffs on behalf of Holocaust survivors, there were still obstacles that prevented the matter from being closed. A group of U.S. Holocaust survivors complained to Judge Edward Korman, who had crafted the settlement, that it unfairly apportioned more money for survivors living in the former Soviet Union than for those living in the West. In addition, Burt Neuborne, a lawyer representing many of the plaintiffs, asked for a $4.1-million fee, which some survivors charged was a violation of his pledge to work pro bono on this case.

2006 marked ten years since the creation of the Independent Committee of Historians, which was assigned to research Switzerland's policies during World War II, and five years since the publication of its final report. To mark the occasion, Prof. Jean-François Bergier, president of the commission, published a memoir based on interviews he gave to journalists Bertrand Müller and Pietro Boschetti. Assessing his years of work in uncovering the truth about Switzerland's wartime record, he expressed disappointment that the 25-volume historical report had been greeted with silence by the government.

One positive result of the report was the release, in 2006, of a new history text for Zurich high schools, *Hinschauen und Nachfragen* (To Observe and To Question), covering the history of Switzerland "at the time of National Socialism and in relation to present times." Commissioned by the education committee of the Zurich canton, this 150-page book was recommended, not mandatory, reading for students. It differed from previous texts in several respects. The book presented Switzerland not simply as a neutral country, but also as ready to compromise with the Nazis; it emphasized that individual citizens did not live under a totalitarian system and so had the freedom, if they chose to use it, to try to save potential victims; and it stressed that the country had shown insensitivity to human rights and to the postwar need for reparations.

This year brought closure to a nine-year legal wrangle. In 1997, the documentary film *L'Honneur Perdu de la Suisse* (Switzerland's Lost Honor), by journalist Daniel Monnat, was aired, and subsequently shown two more times. The Geneva branch of the Swiss People's Party filed a lawsuit accusing the film of bias. When the case reached the Supreme Court in 2000, the judges ruled for the plaintiff on the grounds that the documentary ridiculed Switzerland's wartime generation and manipulated public opinion. The court banned any further broadcast in any format. The filmmaker appealed to the European Commission for Human Rights in Strasbourg, which finally reached a decision in 2006 that overturned the Swiss Supreme Court and made the documentary available again for public screening.

A law passed in 2004 created a special committee to annul the convictions of Swiss people who had broken the law in order to aid fugitives entering the country illegally during World War II. Eleven individuals had their records cleared during 2006, bringing the total number to over 100.

JEWISH COMMUNITY

The Jews of Switzerland numbered about 17,500 amid a population of some seven million. Like the Swiss people as a whole, Jews were, on the whole, an aging community with a low birthrate.

Michel Halpérin, an active member of the Geneva Jewish community and a leader of the Liberal Party, was named president of Geneva's Grand Conseil, the canton's legislative body, for the year. The position is colloquially referred to as "first citizen of Geneva."

The Department of Judaism at the University of Lausanne—the second to be created in Switzerland after the one at the University of Basel—successfully completed its first academic year. About 100 students attended courses on biblical Judaism, Jewish history and philosophy, and cultural issues in the Jewish experience. An important historical work published in 2006 was Sabine Schreiber's *Hirschfeld, Strauss, Malinsky,* which recounted the story of Jewish life in St. Gallen between 1803, when the first Swiss Jews were emancipated, through 1933, when Jewish refugees began to arrive from other European countries.

The Jewish community of Geneva mourned the death of its chief rabbi, Dr. Alexandre Safran, in July, at the age of 96. Prior to assuming the position in Geneva, Safran had been chief rabbi of Romania from 1940 through 1947. After helping guide that community through the difficult World War II years, he was ousted from office and expelled by the new communist regime in Romania (see below, p. 502).

BRIGITTE SION

Scandinavia

The Danish Cartoon Controversy

Denmark was suddenly thrust into the international spotlight over cartoons of the Islamic prophet Mohammed, commissioned from 12 illustrators, which were published in the right-of-center newspaper *Jyllands-Posten* in September 2005. The following month, Danish prime minister Anders Fogh Rasmussen came under considerable domestic criticism for refusing to meet with ambassadors from 11 Muslim countries who wanted an apology for the cartoons. Rasmussen took the position that the government could not interfere with freedom of the press. Visits by Danish imams to Egypt and Lebanon in December further inflamed sentiment in the Muslim world, and the situation reached crisis level in late January 2006, when Saudi Arabia recalled its ambassador from Copenhagen.

The controversy intensified as a boycott of Danish goods began in Saudi Arabia and quickly spread throughout the Muslim world, followed by mass demonstrations and violence directed against Danish flags, embassies, and, in isolated incidents, Danish citizens. The anger was often also directed against other European and American sites. Islamist organizations and terrorist groups, seeing an opportunity to gain visibility, entered the fray with death threats and violent attacks. The Danish Foreign Ministry issued warnings to Danish citizens to leave certain Muslim areas, including Gaza and Syria, and recommended not visiting a host of Muslim countries.

Adding to worldwide concern, radical Muslim groups rioted in some European capitals, and several Muslim states—Afghanistan, Bahrain, Indonesia, Iran, Syria, and Yemen—as well as the Organization of Islamic States issued statements of indignation against Denmark and demanded apologies. Moderate Islamic voices opposing violence were few and far between, although some Danish Muslims were among the first to speak out in conciliatory terms.

The intense reaction surprised and alarmed not only the people and government of Denmark, but the Western world as a whole. Responses varied. Many media outlets printed, televised, or uploaded all or some of the cartoons as a gesture of solidarity with the cartoonists and in support of freedom of expression. Some leading politicians expressed full backing for the Danish position. But other political and religious figures, including some Roman Catholic and Jewish leaders, condemned the cartoons as insensitive and insulting. Some editors responsible for republishing the cartoons were fired, including one in France and another in Jordan.

Interestingly, the other Scandinavian countries, although victimized by the international violence, were not particularly supportive of Denmark. After the Norwegian newspaper *Magazinet* published all 12 cartoons in January, the country's Foreign Ministry issued a statement expressing regret at the paper's decision. Similarly, when a Swedish political youth movement showed the cartoons on its Web site, Sweden's Foreign Ministry pressured the site to delete the images. Publicity about this government interference, which violated a 1789 Swedish law on the freedom of the press, eventually led to pressure on Foreign Minister Laila Freivalds to resign, which she did. Finland, which was acting president of the European Union during the controversy, issued statements of concern about the offense to Islam and to Muslim sensibilities.

There was hardly unanimity within Denmark itself. For example, quite early on in the controversy, Arla, a large Danish food-production company that did considerable export business with the Muslim world, printed ads in the Arab media apologizing for the cartoons. Nevertheless, Prime Minister Rasmussen stood by his original position backing freedom of the press, and retained the support of most of the country even as the controversy wore on. And while the Muslim economic boycotts took a toll on specific businesses and individuals, they had little effect on the Danish economy as a whole.

Violence appeared to subside somewhat in late February and early March, at which point Rasmussen sought to change the focus of the debate by agreeing to meet with the Arab ambassadors and, after the meeting, seeking to develop a cooperative relationship with local Muslim leaders. In turn, moderate Danish Muslims showed an interest in organizing themselves so as to play a more prominent role, and urged an end to the violence. Notably, there were no reported incidents of counterattacks on Danish Muslims.

A troubling new turn to the story came when an Iranian newspaper issued a call, in February, for cartoons about the Holocaust, claiming that this would serve to expose the alleged hypocrisy of the West on the subject of free speech. The cultural editor of the *Jyllands-Posten* initially embraced the idea and said his paper would run the cartoons concurrently with the Iranian one, but his editor-in-chief vetoed the plan and the Iranian paper ran the Holocaust cartoons on its own, turning them into an international contest.

Some in the West, including Jewish groups, noted that Arab countries had for many years run anti-Semitic cartoons in their largely state-controlled media, but the argument had little impact and there was no substantial new pressure to rein in this form of hatred. The thrust of this Iran-based phase of the cartoon crisis—in effect encouraging the expression of anti-Semitism within Europe—reemerged in December, when Iranian president Ahmadinejad convened an international conference of Holocaust deniers in Tehran.

As the year ended, the legacy of the cartoon controversy was unclear. Many claimed that the strong Muslim response to the cartoons and the West's confused and divided stand marked a clear victory for militant Islam, and that from now on the world media would be careful not to offend Muslims. Others, particularly Danes, believed that the affair strengthened the standing of moderate Muslims within Denmark, who, for the first time, identified themselves as a coherent group. In fact, while the standing of moderate Muslims did rise within the country, radical Danish Muslim leaders saw their prestige rise within international Islam. Saudi Arabia, for example, donated a significant amount of money to build a new mosque in Copenhagen, whose imam was believed to be a radical.

The cartoon controversy also played into a larger national debate within Denmark that had been going on for some time. As early as 2001, Rasmussen's two-party conservative coalition had made overtures to the right-wing nationalist Danish People's Party, which took a strongly anti-immigration stance and highlighted what it considered insurmountable problems in integrating Muslims into Danish society and culture. Indeed, Muslims constituted the largest religious minority in the country (this was the case in Norway as well), with estimates ranging from 2 to 5 percent of the population, and certain Copenhagen neighborhoods were heavily and noticeably Muslim. Capitalizing on the perceived Muslim threat, the Danish People's Party won 13.3 percent of the vote in 2005. Since then, although not part of the formal government coalition, the party was "tolerated," since its support was necessary for the government to sustain a parliamentary majority.

In this way the People's Party's negative views about the Muslim minority gained a much wider hearing, and Denmark passed restrictive immigration and asylum laws. This, in turn, had the effect of polarizing society, as many Danes, particularly on the political left, saw these measures and the rhetoric accompanying them as draconian and racist, and strongly contrary to their own view of the country as a haven of decency and tolerance. Then, when the cartoon controversy hit, each side claimed to be vindicated: the Danes who were already wary of Muslims wanted even harsher measures taken against them, while those on the other side saw the need for reaching out to the Muslim community. What no one would deny was that the affair brought the issue of integrating the Danish Muslim minority, previously somewhat muted, much more into the open.

Israel and the Middle East

Up until the late 1960s, Scandinavians had been generally sympathetic to Israel, visiting the Jewish state by the thousands each year. They were especially impressed with the Israeli kibbutz for its socialist and humanitarian values. Such positive sentiments began to change with the Six-Day War of 1967. Public opinion turned pro-Palestinian, as Scandinavians increasingly saw Israel as a conqueror and colonizer. By the early twenty-first century, the Scandinavian countries' generally left-leaning outlook made them among the leading critics of Israel within Europe, particularly in regard to Israel's handling of the Palestinian conflict and treatment of Palestinians in the territories. The same was true of much of the Scandinavian media. People-to-people contact with Israelis also declined dramatically.

Several Scandinavian countries were leading proponents and funders of Palestinian networks and groups, not all of which were committed to peaceful means of asserting themselves against Israel. Finland, for example, annually contributed about seven million euros toward the publication of Palestinian textbooks, many of which were criticized by Jewish groups for denying Israel's existence.

Sweden presented a particular problem for Israel—in fact Oded Eran who served as Israeli ambassador to the European Union, cited Sweden and Ireland as "the countries that most frequently raise their voices against Israel." In May 2006, when the EU, like the U.S., refused to recognize the newly elected Hamas government of the Palestinian Authority because it espoused violence and did not recognize Israel, Sweden issued a visa to a Hamas delegation, including a cabinet minister, to visit an NGO in southern Sweden. Thus Sweden became the first European country to break the diplomatic boycott of Hamas—a group officially classified as a terrorist entity by the EU.

In the early years of his tenure, Swedish prime minister Göran Persson, who took office in 1996, had presented himself as a friend of Israel, initiating the Living History project to commemorate the Holocaust and teach its lessons to all Swedish citizens, and then in 2000 sponsoring the Stockholm International Conference on the Holocaust. Later, however, he maintained a low profile on issues of Jewish concern and remained silent while the Foreign Ministry leveled strong criticism of Israel. In April 2006, Persson defended a Swedish decision to withdraw from a joint NATO Partnership for Peace exercise in Italy in which Israel was participating.

The outbreak of the summer war between Israel and Hezballah in southern Lebanon brought a loud reaction from all of Europe, including the Scandinavian countries. Finland, in its role as EU president, issued a statement on July 13 saying that the EU was concerned about "disproportionate use of force by Israel," while also acknowledging that Israel's action was a "response to attacks by Hezballah on Israel." The Danish, Norwegian, and Swedish foreign ministers issued similar calls, criticizing both Hezballah and Israel, and calling on the former to return the two soldiers it had kidnapped and the latter to avoid escalation of the conflict.

Suggestions that Israel was violating the requirement of "proportionality" in responding to Hezballah were first raised in regard to strikes on Lebanese infrastructure at the outset of the war, and escalated with the attack on Qana, which resulted in a heavy civilian death toll and negative media images around the world. From that point on, government and media voices in Scandinavia turned increasingly critical of Israel, as was the case elsewhere in Europe. For good measure, Norway also condemned Israel for its actions in Gaza, describing them as "collective punishment."

On August 5, Jostein Gaarder, the well-known Norwegian writer and author of the 1991 international best-seller *Sophie's World,* wrote an article titled "God's Chosen People" that was published in Norway's leading newspaper, *Aftenposten.* Written in a biblical, prophetic style, it declared that post-1967 Israel—that is, the Israel of today—had no right to exist. Gaarder charged that Israeli attacks on Lebanon demonstrated complete disregard for the lives of non-Jews, blamed the Jewish "chosen people" idea for this behavior, and concluded, "We call this racism." The article set off an international controversy, as many felt that the focus on Israel as a state that embodied objectionable Jewish beliefs constituted anti-Semitism. Gaarder responded that he had been misunderstood. In late July, Denmark—whose foreign policy was more aligned with the U.S. than those of its Scandinavian neighbors—issued a statement urging Hezballah and Hamas to disarm and recognize Israel as a necessary step toward ending the larger conflict. Denmark served as a temporary member of the UN Security Council during 2005–06. Its UN ambassador, Ellen Margrethe Løj, fully supported Israel's right to self-defense in speeches to that body, and called repeatedly on Hezballah to release the two Israeli soldiers it was holding.

On August 11, Per Stig Møller, the Danish minister for foreign affairs, cast his country's vote in favor of UN Security Council Resolution 1701, calling for the cessation of hostilities in Lebanon and extending and strengthening the mandate of UNIFIL to monitor the cease-fire. Before the vote he told the Security Council that Hezballah was the main cause of the conflict and that Syria and Iran should be urged to "act responsibly." He also called on Israel to "exercise restraint" and avoid "disproportionate force."

With the passage of the cease-fire resolution, Sweden volunteered to host an international donor conference for Lebanon recovery on August 31. Pledges at the conference from more than 60 countries and from international aid organizations totaled over $940 million. According to reports, leftist groups in Sweden participated in pro-Hezballah demonstrations immediately following the war.

Anti-Semitism

As in other parts of the world, intense criticism of Israel occasionally crossed the line into anti-Semitism in the Scandinavian countries. This was clearly the case with the Gaarder article during the war in Lebanon, mentioned above. Some Jewish groups also criticized Norwegian papers for publishing anti-Israel cartoons during 2006 that employed imagery reminiscent of Nazi propaganda. Some depicted Israeli leaders with classically oversized noses, others suggested that the State of Israel employed allegedly "Old Testament" eye-for-an-eye tactics in combating the Palestinians, or that Israel was engaged in Nazi-style genocide.

A number of attacks on Jews and on synagogues took place in Norway during the year. On February 3, a Molotov cocktail was tossed at the Jewish community center in Trondheim, but no damage resulted.

On July 15—soon after the onset of the Israel-Hezballah war—a Jewish man wearing a *kippah* was assaulted on an Oslo street. The Mosaic Religious Community, the official organization of Norwegian Jews, responded by advising its members not to wear Jewish emblems in public and not to speak Hebrew loudly. On August 2, someone defecated on the steps of the Oslo synagogue, an act captured on video by security cameras. The culprit escaped.

The front of that synagogue was the target of ten gun shots on September 17; luckily, no one was injured. Officials promised to provide tighter security. Nevertheless, Israel's ambassador to Norway, Miryam Shomrat, criticized the Norwegian reaction, noting that neither the royal family nor the prime minister had publicly condemned the latest violence or expressed solidarity with Norwegian Jewry, and claiming that the Jewish community felt very much alone. But the spokeswoman for Oslo's synagogue and the Mosaic Religious Community said that neither body shared the ambassador's view, and that her remarks overstepped her position. Shomrat then apologized for dragging the royal family into politics. The incident demonstrated a real split between Israel's representative in the country and the Norwegian Jewish community.

In Sweden, Chancellor of Justice Gorin Lambertz halted an investigation into the selling of anti-Semitic cassettes at the Grand Mosque of Sweden that called for the killing of Jews, saying that the issue was related to the political situation in the Middle East and therefore not under his jurisdiction. Many critics viewed this as using the Israeli-Palestinian conflict to excuse anti-Semitism.

The Swedish national elections in September 2006 ended the 12-year rule of the Social Democratic Party and brought to power a center-right coalition led by the leader of the Moderate Party, Fredrik Reinfeldt, who would be prime minister. Economic and other domestic issues, rather than foreign policy, decided the election. The new government quickly took steps to ease Jewish fears. In November, it declared that the government would pay for $424,000 of the $707,000 that the Jewish community annually spent for security. The previous Social Democratic government had consistently refused to contribute any funds for that purpose. There was also some hope that relations with Israel would improve under the new coalition.

Reports of anti-Semitic incidents in Denmark picked up at the onset of the cartoon controversy with allegations that Jews were behind the publication of the images. Although there were no acts of violence, threatening comments and letters induced many Jews in Denmark, as in Norway, to avoid publicly identifying themselves as Jews. In the fall, a conference on anti-Semitism under the name "With Our Backs to the Walls" was held in the Danish parliament building in Copenhagen. The leader of Hizb Ut-Tahrir, the most extreme Muslim anti-Israel group in Denmark, was sentenced to two months in prison for distributing fliers urging the killing of Jews. His legal defense was that he had targeted Israeli Jews who were subjugating Palestinians and taking their land, not Danish Jews.

Holocaust-Related Matters

Several Holocaust commemorations in Denmark, Sweden, and Norway—some marking the anniversary of Kristallnacht, some Holocaust Memorial Day, and others noting different events—were hijacked by leftist groups that had anti-Israel agendas. In an ironic twist on the duty of historical remembrance, they used these occasions to focus attention on the "modern-day racism" of Israel. The Jewish organizations in these countries therefore refused to participate, and sometimes staged their own separate ceremonies.

Memory of the Holocaust rescue efforts conducted in Denmark, Sweden, Finland, and Norway during World War II was kept alive by Thanks to Scandinavia, a New York-based institute of the American Jewish Committee. It funded scholarships for Scandinavian teachers, students, and medical professionals to study in the U.S. and Israel (including a special program at Yad Vashem), and sent an annual delegation of Scandinavian journalists and politicians for a weeklong visit to Israel.

JEWISH COMMUNITY

The Scandinavian country with the largest number of Jews was Sweden, whose three communities totaled 10,000 registered members, with another estimated 10,000 Jews living outside the communal structure. Denmark had 2,200 registered Jews and about another 2,500 unregistered. For Finland the numbers were 1,200 official community members and less than 200 nonmembers. The smallest group of Jews lived in Norway, with a total of 850 registered members in the two cities of Oslo and Trondheim, and about 300 more outside these communities.

Scandinavian Jewish communities survived through the taxation of their registered members, but were also eager to receive contributions from other sources. Those who did not join the official communities tended to be of two types: families containing non-Jewish spouses, and Israeli citizens.

The year 2006 marked several milestones for the Jews of Finland. Most important, it was the centennial year of the Helsinki synagogue. The Finnish president and her husband, Scandinavian and Israeli dignitaries, and religious leaders from across the country participated in the celebration. Two important publications were released to mark the event: the first-ever Jewish prayer book containing both the Hebrew text and a Finnish translation, and a book featuring photos of the Helsinki Jewish community from 1850 to 1950. Also, the Maccabi Jewish sports club marked a century of activity in Finland. Finally, Finnish WIZO was alone among the Scandinavian branches of the movement to mark the international women's Zionist organization's 80th anniversary.

Paideia—The European Institute for Jewish Studies in Sweden, based in Stockholm, played a major role in the education and training of Jewish academicians, artists, and communal leaders not only for Scandinavia but for all of Europe. Established in 2000 as a nondenominational academy with financial support from the government, it promoted the study of Jewish texts, hosted short courses and guest lectures by international scholars, and sponsored programs in Israel.

REBECCA NEUWIRTH
STEEN CADAN

Central and Eastern Europe

Germany

National Affairs

GERMANY'S GOVERNMENT, a "grand coalition" of the conservative Christian Democratic Union (CDU) and the center-left Social Democratic Party (SPD), entered its first full year in 2006, headed by Chancellor Angela Merkel (CDU). A poll taken in mid-February gave high ratings to Merkel and her foreign minister, Frank-Walter Steinmeier (SPD). But major domestic challenges loomed: stimulating the economy, revamping the health-care system, and educational reform.

In mid-January, Merkel, committed to mending the damaged U.S.-German relationship, made her inaugural visit as chancellor to Washington, where she discussed a number of controversial issues with American officials: multilateralism, the perceived American preemptive military approach to international conflicts, the Middle East, global warming, and human rights.

While in the U.S., Merkel criticized the detention center at Guantánamo Bay. In doing so she was giving voice to German public opinion about America's war-related policies. Germans reacted sharply to reports that their country might have secretly assisted the U.S. during the Iraq war—even though former chancellor Gerhard Schröder had pledged not to do so—and that it might even have given clandestine help in setting up and running a network of secret prisons in Eastern Europe for terrorism suspects under the so-called "extraordinary rendition program."

As a case in point, a U.S. Federal District Court judge, in May, dismissed a lawsuit by Khaled al-Masri, a German citizen who had been released in 2004 after a year of imprisonment. The judge said that a public trial might compromise national security. At the same time, he ruled that if Masri's allegations of wrongful imprisonment were true he should receive compensation. In June, the BND (Germany's intelligence agency) admitted knowing of al-Masri's seizure much earlier than first acknowledged, and the American Civil Liberties Union said it would appeal the dismissal of his suit.

Germany's antiterror efforts produced several arrests and convictions. In January, Lokman Amin Mohammed became the first person convicted under a new law clamping down on foreign terrorist groups. He received a seven-year prison sentence for assisting Ansar al-Islam, a group allegedly linked to Al Qaeda. In November, it was revealed that terrorists had planned an attack on an El Al passenger jet in Frankfurt. Six suspects were detained and five of them released pending the submission of preliminary findings. Reportedly, one person with access to secure areas of Frankfurt's airport had agreed to smuggle a bag with explosives onto an Israeli airliner, but the plotters wrangled over how much to pay for the job. As some of the post-9/11 antiterror statutes were due to expire in 2007, Interior Minister Wolfgang Schäuble pushed for passage of legislation that would extend them.

Germany and the U.S. continued to share security objectives. Germany maintained the largest contingent under the UN's International Security Assistance Force (ISAF) in Afghanistan/Uzbekistan—about 3,000 soldiers—and the German armed forces continued to contribute to NATO's Kosovo Force (KFOR) and the European Union Force (EUFOR). Though steadfastly opposed to the war in Iraq, Germany renewed its commitment to the training of Iraqi policemen through the end of 2006. However the program was held up when Iraq's government failed to send a new class of recruits.

In September, the Berlin Opera decided not to stage Mozart's *Idomeneo* after receiving a warning from the German equivalent of the FBI that the performance—which included the beheadings of Jesus, Buddha, and Muhammed, and the handing out of the heads to the audience—might draw violent reactions. The program, planned three years earlier, was reinstated after widespread protests, including from Chancellor Merkel.

Relations with Iran remained a problem throughout the year. The Islamic Republic continuously goaded Western leaders, insisting that its nuclear ambitions were purely peaceful, while at the same time issuing threatening statements against Israel. Germany, France, and Great Britain had tried in vain since October 2003 to convince Iran to drop its plans to enrich nuclear fuel. In 2006, Germany—Iran's largest economic partner, with some $4 billion in trade the previous year—played a leading role in condemning the anti-Semitic and anti-Israeli rhetoric of President Mahmoud Ahmadinedjad.

At the Munich Security Conference in February 2006, Merkel compared the West's hesitancy regarding Iran to mistakes made during the Nazi rise to power. She said that "concerns and fears over Iran's nuclear program are legitimate," and refused to rule out military action. Merkel said Iran could avoid potential UN sanctions by accepting enriched uranium from Russia instead of developing its own highly sensitive nuclear technology. And she said that "a president who denies the existence of Israel and the Holocaust cannot expect to receive any tolerance from Germany." Iran's deputy foreign minister for legal and international affairs responded that the threat of UN sanctions would not deter Iran's nuclear program, but did not react to the criticism regarding Israel. According to *Die Welt* newspaper, one-third of Germans said they would back military action against Iran, and four-fifths agreed that Israel was endangered by Iran's nuclear program.

In May, Ahmadinedjad insisted that Holocaust denial was a valid position and should therefore be given a platform. At the same time, he told the German weekly *Der Spiegel* that if Jews were wronged by Europe, Palestinians should not have to pay. "If the Holocaust occurred," he said, "then the Jews have to go back to where they came from." These remarks followed the announcement that the Iranian leader, a big soccer fan, would not come to Germany for the World Cup games as previously expected, and instead would be represented at the opening ceremonies in Munich by Vice President Mohammed Aliabadi. Earlier, critics had urged that Ahmadinedjad not be allowed to enter Germany since he had committed a crime under German law, Holocaust denial.

Former foreign minister Joschka Fischer (Green Party) visited Iran in August as the guest of a Tehran think tank, but rejected calls to renew his political involvement in brokering Middle East peace. Fischer now served as professor of international economic policy at Princeton University's Woodrow Wilson School of Public and International Affairs.

In December, Chancellor Merkel condemned the Iranian president's "Holocaust conference" to which he invited notorious Holocaust deniers. She said it demonstrated clearly the kinds of threats that Israel faced.

THE WORLD CUP

Germany hosted soccer's World Cup in 2006. The monthlong *Weltmeisterschaft,* which began June 9, was deemed a great public-relations success for the country. Germany proved to three million visitors that it not only could host such a major event, but also that the supposedly dour Germans could exude friendliness to strangers. The World Cup motto, "A Time to Make Friends," was meant to boost Germany's public image, according to Franz Beckenbauer, president of the organizing committee. Interior Minister Schäuble set up a National Cooperation and Information Center to take care of security, and the 32 participating nations supplied some 500 liaison officers to help identify and apprehend foreign troublemakers. The European soccer antiracism network FARE joined with FIFA (Fédération Internationale de Football Association) and the German organizing committee to launch a multicultural sports campaign and to set up a multilingual 24-hour hotline for reporting racist incidents during the World Cup.

The games also provided a chance to teach the "Jewish" aspect of soccer history. There were no less than three exhibits on the topic — at the Jewish museums of Frankfurt and Fürth, and at the Centrum Judaicum in Berlin. There was also a conference entitled "Hosted by the Krauts — Updating History in the Soccer Stadium," which documented the exclusion of Jewish athletes from German soccer clubs after 1933 and addressed the problems of anti-Semitism and xenophobia in the postwar culture of soccer fans. It was organized jointly by ASF (Action Reconciliation/Service for Peace), the House of the Wannsee Conference, and the Federal Agency for Civic Education.

Eruptions of extremist activity, in fact, dimmed some of the luster of the World Cup. The German media was full of talk about the bigoted behavior of some soccer fans, and printed dire warnings to visitors to avoid parts of the former East Germany, dubbed "foreigner-free," that were considered hostile to outsiders. In the months leading up to the tournament, right-wing extremists launched racist campaigns against several leading black soccer players. Neo-Nazis came out in force to welcome the Iranian team to Leipzig on June 21, demonstrating their solidarity with the Holocaust-denying President Ahmadinejad.

One incident at the games revealed just how deeply politics could penetrate sports. The government of Ghana apologized to the Arab League after one of its athletes, John Pentsil, waved an Israeli flag to celebrate his team's goals against the Czech Republic in Cologne. When not playing for his national squad, Pentsil was a member of Hapoel Tel Aviv, and two of his Ghananian teammates played for other Israeli soccer teams.

While the World Cup was in progress, two events were held to promote intergroup harmony. About 150 non-Jewish sports fans from Great Britain, Germany, and Poland visited the Dachau memorial outside Munich on June 23, in a program organized by Maccabi of Great Britain and the antiracism initiative of the organization LondonEnglandfans. And in Berlin, Cantor Avitall Gerstetter organized an interfaith soccer tournament for local Turkish-Muslim, Jewish, Christian, and nonreligious amateur athletes; shirts were provided by Adidas and Nike. The Muslims won, beating the Jewish team. Gerstetter applauded the positive impact of the World Cup games on intergroup relations in the country. She said: "When I see Muslim kids running around in Berlin shouting, 'Go, Germany!' and waving the flag, I think it's great that they really feel a part of this society. And that's the way we Jews feel, too—we are at home in Germany."

In September, the German Soccer Association adopted strengthened FIFA regulations providing tough sanctions against clubs whose fans demonstrated xenophobic and anti-Semitic behavior. Also, its referees' committee recommended issuing warnings on the loudspeaker system, or halting and even canceling games, in the event of racist incidents. In October, a task force against xenophobia, racism, and violence in German stadiums was created.

GERMANY AND ISLAM

Concerned about the growing presence of unaculturated Muslims, the State of Baden-Württemberg instituted a "patriotism test" for Muslims already in Germany who applied for citizenship. It included questions about whether a man should beat his wife or marry more than one woman; how one might react to learning that a son was homosexual or that a daughter/sister had been sexually assaulted; and whether the perpetrators of the 9/11 attacks on the U.S. should be considered terrorists or freedom fighters.

The Central Council of Muslims in Germany threatened a lawsuit, saying that the only legitimate question to ask of an applicant for citizenship was whether he or she respected the constitution. Some members of the Turkish Muslim community, however, pointed out that the questionnaire did raise legitimate questions about the treatment of women in some Muslim families. The Jewish community joined civil rights groups in opposition to the test.

Jewish and Muslim leaders also found themselves on the same side in April, when Ursula von der Leyen, the federal family-affairs minister, proposed working with Christian churches to develop guidelines on raising children. Stephan Kramer, secretary general of the Central Council of Jews in Germany (CCJG), said that excluding non-Christian faiths from the project was "quite painful." Von der Leyen said she planned to include other religious groups later, and added that, in her view, Germany's culture was based on "Christian values."

In September, Chancellor Merkel initiated a dialogue with Muslim religious and secular leaders to discuss issues of importance to the community. The plan was to hold two high-level meetings annually over the course of about three years. Meanwhile, Lale Akgün, parliamentary speaker on Islamic affairs for the SPD, said it was high time the government placed Islam on a legal par with other religious groups in the country. Germany had no formal relationship with any one Muslim body. Unlike the Christian churches and the Jewish community, there was no umbrella organization representing all shades of Islam.

Israel and the Middle East

Chancellor Merkel made her first official trip to Israel in January. An earlier plan to travel in December 2005 was postponed after Israeli prime minister Ariel Sharon fell gravely ill. The January trip was also the first visit by an international leader to the Palestinian Territories since the Hamas election victory. But Merkel insisted she would only meet with PA president Mahmoud Abbas, not with Hamas leaders, and made it clear there would be no German financial support for a Hamas-led Palestinian government.

Two days before the trip, Foreign Minister Steinmeier called on the new Palestinian government to renounce violence and recognize Israel. He told *Der Spiegel* magazine that he believed the Palestinian people had voted for Hamas because they wanted social reforms, not because they opposed peace. Israel's ambassador to Germany, Shimon Stein, as well as German Jewish leaders asked Merkel to press Abbas to keep his promise to disarm Palestinian militants.

Steinmeier met in February with Ehud Olmert, then Israel's acting prime minister, and Foreign Minister Tzipi Livni, and reiterated that "there can be no cooperation with a terrorist organization, even if it forms a government." Responding to Olmert's victory in Israel's March elections, Merkel sent her congratulations and said Germany would work with the new government to help bring peace to the region.

In May, Merkel reiterated her support for Israel in a speech at the American Jewish Committee's annual meeting in Washington, D.C. At the gala event, which marked the AJC centennial, Merkel—the first German chancellor ever to address the group's annual meeting—also said that Iran must not be allowed to develop nuclear weapons. She once again demanded that the new Palestinian government "reject violence and acknowledge without ambiguity Israel's right to exist," noting that the decision "lies with Hamas." While in Washington, Merkel met with President Bush. AJC also honored former foreign minister Joschka Fischer at its meeting for his activities on behalf of peace.

In late June, Germany demanded that the Palestinians release the Israeli soldier they had taken hostage on June 25. Also, Foreign Minister Steinmeier spoke with his Israeli counterpart, Livni, reportedly urging Israel to show restraint so as not to exacerbate tensions. Israel's incursion into Lebanon in July, after Hezballah captured two Israeli soldiers and killed eight, drew strong negative reactions in Germany. Despite attempts by some scholars and politicians to explain the context of Israel's reaction, popular sentiment was strongly on the other side.

On July 21, some 2,700 people gathered in Berlin to protest Israeli actions. The protestors—including many Arabs—pointedly distanced themselves from anti-Semites and neo-Nazis. Heike Haensel, an MP for the Party for Democratic Socialism (the reconstituted communists), called for an immediate stop to Israeli military actions and asked the German government to press for a truce. Other smaller demonstrations were held in Bremen, Düsseldorf, and Frankfurt on July 22. In Verden, in Lower Saxony, a protest by some 200 far-rightists led to the arrest of Udo Voigt, head of the neo-Nazi National Democratic Party of Germany, on charges of incitement. Voigt allegedly chanted, "Israel: International Headquarters of Genocide."

Meanwhile, a nonpartisan pro-Israel coalition organized a counter-demonstration on July 28 in Berlin. Its motto was "For Israel—and Its Right to Self-Defense." Some observers expressed disappointment that only about 1,000 people showed up. Speaking at the event, Gideon Joffe, president of the Berlin Jewish community, said that Jews joined with Muslims and Christians in abhorring the suffering of innocent people, and called on Muslims to condemn the terrorist acts of Hezballah.

Several days later, Berlin authorities banned the display of images of Hezballah's leader, Sheik Nasrallah. Berlin's senator of the interior, Ehrhart Körting, said the ban was based on Nasrallah's goal of destroying Israel. He denied that it infringed on freedom of speech or the right to assemble, since promoting Hezballah amounted to disturbing the peace. Actual Hezballah membership in Germany was quite small: according to official reports in 2005, there were about 160 members in Berlin and about 900 nationwide.

On August 10, 70 Jewish and Muslim artists and intellectuals issued an appeal for an immediate ceasefire in Lebanon and for cooperation between their faiths. It appeared in the German daily newspapers *Die Zeit* and *Berlin Tagezeitung.* Among the signatories were Susan Nieman, head of the Berlin-based Einstein Forum, and Navid Kermani, a German expert on Islam.

Also in August, members of Germany's opposition parties—the Greens and the Free Democrats—called for a suspension of arms deliveries to Israel until the conflict was over. Beginning in 1964, former West Germany had delivered patrol boats and missile-defense systems to Israel, and Israel had used German Patriot antimissile systems to defend itself against Saddam Hussein's scud attacks. Most German assistance reportedly came in the form of weapons components and technical support. Now, however, Winfried Nachtwei, the Greens' defense expert, argued that Germany was legally barred from exporting weapons to crisis areas. The Jewish community was taken aback when Rolf Verleger, a CCJG board member, added his voice to the criticism of Israel. The CCJG quickly distanced itself from Verleger, saying his comments did not represent the Jewish community.

Meanwhile, debate began over whether German troops should be included in any potential peacekeeping force in the region. The once-theoretical question of whether Germans in uniforms should help keep Jews and Arabs apart took on a new twist after Olmert directly asked for German troops to participate. Merkel at first hesitated. Foreign Minister Steinmeier called Olmert's request "a remarkable sign of trust," but said no hasty decision would be made. Some worried that Germany would be seen as taking sides in the conflict if it joined a peacekeeping force, and others argued that Germany's military was spread thin through its peacekeeping deployments in Kosovo, Congo, and Afghanistan. Left Party parliamentarian and former communist party leader Gregor Gysi, who was Jewish, said Germany's responsibility for the genocide of European Jewry ruled out any participation.

Stephan Kramer, the CCJG secretary general, said Holocaust survivors in Israel might react negatively to the presence of German troops in the area, but Michel Friedman, head of Keren Hayesod in Germany and a former vice president of the CCJG, said that if Germany sent soldiers it would "show the true colors of its support for Israel, and take responsibility." Solomon Korn, the current CCJG vice president, said he could imagine "coming to a compromise: German soldiers yes, but not directly on the front." On August 16, the government announced it had agreed, in principle, to contribute to a 15,000-member UN peacekeeping force in Lebanon.

Germany also provided two million euros in aid for civilians in southern Lebanon affected by the fighting. In September, Development Minister Heidemarie Wieczorek-Zeul (SDP) visited Lebanon and criticized Israel for bombing civilian targets with cluster bombs. Salomon Korn accused Wieczorek-Zeul of "one-sidedness." She responded that she fully supported Israel's right to exist. Chancellor Merkel said Wieczorek-Zeul's statements were her own personal opinion.

In other Israel-related news, in March, a German broadcaster pulled a documentary on Islamist violence against Christians in Bethlehem, fearing for the safety of his Christian informants there. The film, *Terror against Christians,* by German-Israeli filmmaker Uri Schneider, was to air March 12 on ARD, a Südwestrundfunk affiliate. It was replaced by a documentary about teen mothers. An edited version was shown months later.

A small pro-Israel demonstration was held in October to protest the annual anti-Israel Al Quds Day march by extremist Muslims, which had been established in 1979 by Iran's Islamic revolutionary leader, Ayatollah Khomeini. Some 250 people from the Berlin Association against International Al Quds Day used the occasion to respond to the anti-Israel comments of Iranian president Ahmadinedjad. The anti-Israel demonstration itself attracted only about 300 people this year.

In December, Ehud Olmert made his first official visit as prime minister to Germany. On the agenda in talks between Olmert and Merkel were Iran's nuclear ambitions, the situation in Lebanon, and initiatives to resolve the Israeli-Palestinian conflict. Olmert also visited a Holocaust memorial in Grunewald, the site from which tens of thousands of Berlin Jews were deported to death camps.

Anti-Semitism and Extremism

In 2006, the number of extremist right-wing crimes reported to the police reached a new record, surging from 15,914 in 2005 (the previous high) to at least 18,000, a rise of 14 percent. The number of crimes committed by left-wing extremists went up by 9 percent, to about 5,300. The Interior Ministry released data showing 452 violent anti-Semitic crimes during the first eight months of 2006, up from 363 in the same period the previous year.

According to Germany's domestic intelligence agency, about 10,000 of the roughly 40,000 members of neo-Nazi groups were potentially violent. Most racially motivated incidents took place in former East Germany, a stronghold of the small but vociferous neo-Nazi National Democratic Party of Germany (NPD). Interior Minister Schäuble said that right-wing skinhead music was an important recruitment tool, and announced plans to expand educational efforts to combat the problem.

A survey of 5,000 Germans carried out in November suggested that xenophobia was particularly high in the eastern part of the country, while virulent anti-Semitism was more prevalent in the west. Furthermore, according to the University of Leipzig-Friedrich Ebert Foundation study, while only 9 percent of the national sample was decidedly xenophobic and/or anti-Semitic, about half of those questioned endorsed such thinking to some extent. Researchers Elmar Brähler and Oliver Decker said it was no longer accurate to call the problem only a "fringe" phenomenon. Political scientist Klaus Schröder challenged the findings, saying there was no substantial proof that right-wing extremism had gained a foothold within German society.

Another area of research was the connection between education and anti-Semitism. This was a key theme of the fifth annual study by Wilhelm Heitmeyer, *Deutsche Zustände* (German Situation), put out by the Institute for Interdisciplinary Conflict and Violence Research of the University of Bielefeld. It suggested that while more education generally correlated with reduced prejudice, this did not hold true for Muslims. According to Heitmeyer, Muslim immigrants, not accepted by the mainstream society, tended to defend their faith "at all cost," as their only positive asset. "This creates barriers and hampers self-critical development. We, the majority society, play a significant role in this process," he wrote.

Several anti-Semitic incidents during the year drew particular attention. Perhaps the most shocking was the burning of a copy of Anne Frank's diary by neo-Nazis at a summer solstice festival in the former East German town of Pretzien. The Anne Frank Center in Berlin and local religious and political groups organized emergency programs in response. Thomas Heppener, director of the center, filed suit against three of the alleged perpetrators, and they were arrested. At a town hall meeting following the incident, 1,000 residents of Pretzien showed up to discuss the incident and its repercussions. In another case, teenagers in the town of Parey in the former East German state of Saxony-Anhalt forced a schoolmate to wear a sign bearing the slogan, "I am the biggest pig of all because I hang around with Jews." Police identified three suspects. And in late September, a Maccabi Jewish soccer team left the field after fans of the opposing German team, Altglienicke, threatened them.

The surge in right-wing crimes raised concerns about Germany's public image on the eve of the World Cup Games in June and July (see above). Uwe-Karsten Heye, who had been a spokesperson for former chancellor Gerhard Schröder and later served as consul general in New York, caused an uproar by declaring that xenophobic extremists had made certain areas of Germany de facto off-limits for foreign visitors.

CCJG president Charlotte Knobloch compared the atmosphere in Germany to the situation in 1933, when the National Socialists came to power. But Stephan Kramer, the CCJG general secretary, said that evoking the past in this way was not helpful, as today's Germans were not guilty for the crimes of the past, and that emphasis should be given to education. During meetings with German officials in Berlin, Abraham Foxman, national director of the New York-based Anti-Defamation League, called the incidents and statistics "a wakeup call." The Jewish community had "a right to be concerned," he went on, "but I am not sure it is productive to compare it to the 1930s."

More alarm bells rang in September, when the NPD made gains in the Mecklenburg-Western Pomerania elections. Voters in this former East German state gave the extreme-right party 7.3 percent, more than the 5 percent necessary to win a seat in the state parliament. This was the fourth state in reunified Germany to have such parties represented, joining Lower Saxony in the west, and Saxony and Brandenburg in the east.

Many observers claimed that high unemployment played a role in turning voters to the right: Mecklenburg-Western Pomerania had a jobless rate of 18.2 percent. But shrewd strategy also paid off for the NPD. Gideon Botsch, an expert on right-wing extremism, told Deutsche Welle, Germany's international broadcaster, that the NPD had campaigned vigorously across the state and dressed itself up to look respectable. Members of the party were "in parents' associations in schools and kindergartens, or in sports clubs, and use their position there to relay their ideas to the people," said Botsch. The NPD claimed to have invested $508,000 in the campaign.

This state election had national repercussions. Responding to the result, the federal government announced it would raise the budget for fighting right-wing extremism by $6.3 million. Renewed attention was directed at remaining gaps between how eastern and western Germans embraced democracy. According to the Federal Statistics Office, only 38 percent of eastern Germans said democracy was the best form of government for the country, whereas in western Germany 71 percent approved democracy. And the question of whether the NPD should be banned came up again. A previous attempt to outlaw the party had failed in March 2003 due to a legal loophole (see AJYB 2004, p. 373).

In February, an NPD leader, Thorstein Heise, was convicted of violating laws prohibiting the distribution of anti-Semitic material. He was said to have ordered the production of 6,000 CDs containing "seditious" lyrics, with the intention of selling them in Germany. Heise was ordered to perform 200 hours of community service and to pay a fine of 15,000 euros. In October, the NPD organized a demonstration in Berlin of some 750 extremists in support of Michael Regener, the jailed lead singer of a skinhead musical group. He had been imprisoned in 2003 after judges found that his rock band, "Landser" (Foot Soldiers), was guilty of spreading hate against Jews and foreigners.

There was much debate in Germany over the Danish cartoons depicting the Muslim prophet Muhammed (see above, pp. 433–35). In February, as Jews and non-Jews in Germany reacted with dismay to violent Muslim protests worldwide, Paul Spiegel, president of the CCJG, warned against overreaction on all sides. He said it would make sense "to show more sensitivity to religious sensibilities of Muslim communities" so as to avoid "a clash of cultures." In May, the CCJG and the Turkish Islamic Union held a groundbreaking public discussion in Berlin on "Anti-Semitism, Islamophobia, and Xenophobia." The Israeli and Turkish embassies supported the event.

In July it was announced that former chancellor Schröder would replace the late Johannes Rau, who had been president of Germany, as head of *Gesicht Zeigen!* (Show Your Face!), a group that fought xenophobia and anti-Semitism, cofounded in 2000 by Uwe-Karsten Heye and Paul Spiegel.

Berlin's Center for Research on Anti-Semitism held a three-day "Summer University against Anti-Semitism" in September. Topics included basic definitions and forms of anti-Semitism, its history in Europe, negative stereotypes of Jews in literature, and anti-Israel critique as a form of anti-Semitism.

In November, the Organization for Security and Cooperation in Europe met in Berlin, as a follow-up to the OSCE's 2004 task force on anti-

Semitism. Experts complained that few of the 56 OSCE member states had complied with their 2004 commitments to monitor anti-Semitic crimes. At the same time, European Jewish organizations were reporting an increase in incidents.

Later that month, a conservative legislator apologized for statements insulting to Jews. Henry Nitzche, a CDU Bundestag representative from Saxony, had said in June that Germany needed more patriotism "to finally get out of this cult of guilt" so that the country "will never be run again by multicultural fags in Berlin." It took several months for these comments to surface publicly, and then the Green Party called for the CDU to eject Nitzche. The CCJG, for its part, accused Nitzche of using NPD vocabulary. In fact, the head of the NPD in Saxony had congratulated Nitzche for his statement. He invited Nitzche to become "the first member of the German Parliament to switch to the NPD," and sent him an application for party membership. Nitzche apologized on November 30, saying that "unfortunately, in hindsight, I have to declare that the words I chose were worse than ambiguous."

In December, Berlin was shaken by a report in *Spiegel Online* of increased anti-Semitism in the public schools. Most of the incidents allegedly involved either neo-Nazis or extremist Muslim pupils. The word "Jew" was increasingly used as a curse, the report said. Barbara Witting, director of the Jewish High School in Berlin, was quoted as saying that children had been transferring to her school to avoid discrimination in public schools.

Holocaust-Related Matters

DENIAL

The trial of Ernst Zündel, 66, on charges of incitement to hatred and Holocaust denial recommenced in February, after being postponed in November 2005. Zündel had been deported back to Germany from Canada in 2005, after courts there declared his Internet hate site illegal. According to courtroom observers, sympathizers clapped when the accused appeared in the room. One of Zündel's own attorneys, Jürgen Rieger, had himself once been sentenced for inciting hatred.

In November, extreme right-winger Germar Rudolf denied the Holocaust in front of a court in Mannheim. Rudolf was on trial for incitement to hatred and publishing racist propaganda on the Internet. He had been deported from the U.S. in 2005 after fleeing Germany to avoid a 14-month prison sentence for a 1995 conviction on charges of slander and incitement to hatred. A chemist, Rudolf had published an "expert opinion" in 1991 that the poison gas Zyklon B was never used in the Auschwitz death camp.

In December, a daylong conference on Holocaust denial was held in Berlin, coinciding with the meeting of Holocaust deniers and their sympathizers in Tehran, Iran. The Berlin event was organized by the Technical University of Berlin and the federal Department for Political Education. Speakers, including David Menashri of Israel, emphasized that Holocaust denial was a form of anti-Semitism, and that the Iranian president was using the theme, together with his threats against Israel, to gain international standing among Muslims and Arabs.

MEMORY

One year after it opened, Berlin's Memorial to the Murdered Jews of Europe reported that an estimated 3.5 million people had visited the site, and its underground information center had 490,000 registered visitors. Fears of possible vandalism had proven unfounded, and those who came behaved respectfully, according to memorial officials.

In January, a new permanent exhibit opened at the House of the Wannsee Conference outside Berlin, the villa where 15 top Nazis met in 1942 to organize the "Final Solution." The new exhibit cost about $730,000, funded by the federal government and an educational lottery. Among the items added to the display was a memo, found in a Latvian archive, from SD chief Reinhard Heydrich, written days after he chaired the Wannsee Conference, in which he referred to the "total solution to the Jewish question."

Also in January, an exhibit on Jewish children who hid in wartime Berlin opened at the Anne Frank Center in that city, featuring the stories of several survivors. It was produced jointly by the Center for Research on Anti-Semitism and the Memorial to German Resistance.

Two new Holocaust memorials were given the go-ahead in 2006, after years of debate. In January, the government announced approval of a memorial in central Berlin, near the Jewish memorial, dedicated to the tens of thousands of homosexuals persecuted and murdered under the Nazis. It was expected to cost about $549,000, a sum to be funded by the federal government. The decision came three years after Parliament agreed to the idea in principle. The other new memorial, approved In May, was for the hundreds of thousands of Sinti and Roma murdered by the Nazis. The German government and the Central Council of Sinti and Roma agreed on a design, which would cost the government $2.5 million. Designed by artist Dani Karavan, it, too, was to be located near the large Holocaust memorial.

The Dresdner Bank held a public symposium in February on the results of historical research on its own World War II history. The event, "Dresdner Bank in the Third Reich," was held in the rooms of its foundation, after protests against the original plan to hold it at the Jewish Museum in Berlin. The symposium presented the results of an eight-year research project conducted by an independent commission of historians and led by Klaus-Dietmar Henke. It revealed the institution's close connections with the Nazi terror apparatus, and hence its share of responsibility for the Holocaust

A rather bizarre episode in the history of Holocaust commemoration occurred in mid-March, when the Spanish-born artist Santiago Sierra abruptly canceled a planned installation that involved pumping poison auto exhaust into a former synagogue in Pulheim-Stommeln, near Cologne. It was meant as a memorial to the 750,000 Jews and 5,000 Sinti-Roma asphyxiated with motor-exhaust fumes in 1941 and 1942. Municipal authorities had ruled that only those wearing gas masks could enter, excuding those with beards or larger-than-average heads. Jewish leaders condemned the project from the start, and Sierra finally gave in. He, together with the city of Pulheim and the Cologne Jewish community, announced that they would abandon the exhibit and start from scratch, seeking "an appropriate and fitting remembrance and reminder of the past." Sierra explained that he "did not and does not wish to insult or hurt anyone."

In May, the Moses Mendelssohn Center for European-Jewish Studies in Potsdam announced it was raising funds for a "library of burned books," to contain some 10,000 works by authors whom the Nazis persecuted. Director Julius Schoeps said he wanted the library to send out small collections of such books to German high schools as a living memorial to the victims of Nazi censorship.

Also in May, Germany announced it would support opening the archive of the International Tracing Service (ITS) in Bad Arolsen for use by historians. Since the end of World War II it had been used almost solely to prove the compensation claims of survivors. But the archive could not open its doors until the 11 member countries on the ITS board — Belgium, France, Germany, Greece, Israel, Italy, Luxembourg, the Netherlands, Poland, the UK, and the U.S. — agreed on regulations to protect the privacy of individuals named in the documents. No such agreement was reached before year's end.

The federal government published, in May, a four-volume book naming all 150,000 German Jews known to have died in the Holocaust. The alphabetical listing updated a 1966 edition that did not include victims from former East Germany or areas of Poland that were part of Germany before World War II. The new edition, compiled by the Federal Archive, included information from documents uncovered after German unification in 1990. The government was already preparing a new work which would list all Jews who lived in Germany between 1933 and 1945.

Pope Benedict XVI visited the memorial at the Auschwitz death camp in May (see below, p. 495). While the German-born pope prayed at the site, he drew criticism for failing to mention Germany's responsibility for the Holocaust. Instead, he said the crimes were committed by a "band of criminals," and that the German people had been "used and abused" by the Nazi regime. In June, the Pope authorized the opening of all Vatican archives for the period 1922–39. Historians hoped the files might shed light on how Pope Pius XII reacted to the persecution of the Jews.

June was also the month that the German Federal Intelligence Services admitted it had located Adolf Eichmann—a key architect of the "Final Solution"—in Argentina in the 1950s, but failed to inform Israel. U.S. documents released on June 6 suggested that in 1958 the German agency informed the CIA, but not the Israeli intelligence services, of Eichmann's hiding place and false name. Historian Timothy Naftali said the German government at that time was concerned that Eichmann, if interrogated, would incriminate "rehabilitated" Nazis. The country's state secretary was then Hans Globke, an author of the Nazi Nuremberg Laws that legalized discrimination against Jews.

In July, Charlotte Knobloch, the CCJG president, recommended an overhaul of Holocaust education and teacher training in Germany, particularly in the former East Germany. Teachers groups denied any need for this, pointing out that such education was already mandatory. Teachers union president Josef Kraus said that "no other era of German history [is] studied as intensively in German schools."

Nobel Prize-winning author Günter Grass shocked the country in August, when he publicly admitted his membership in the elite Nazi Waffen-SS toward the end of World War II. The admission came as his new autobiography was about to be released. Ironically, Grass had frequently used his role as one of Germany's great modern writers to preach against society's ills, including its failure to confront the Nazi past.

Grass, 78, now admitted that when he was 17 he was drafted into the

Waffen-SS, where he briefly saw action during the Nazi retreat from the Russian front. Grass was wounded and taken prisoner by American troops. His original statement of membership in the SS, written in a teenage scrawl, had always been available for viewing at the Berlin Wehrmacht documentation center, but, the center's deputy director explained, no one came to look for it, not even Grass's official biographer. Charlotte Knobloch dismissed his confession as a publicity stunt. In the wake of the controversy, the publication date of his autobiography, *Beim Häuten der Zwiebel* (Peeling Onions), was moved up from September to August 16. It was an immediate best-seller.

An exhibit opened in August on the postwar expulsions of ethnic Germans from areas liberated from Nazi rule. It was organized by the conservative German League of Expellees and mounted in the Kronprinzenpalais in Berlin. Critics accused the organizers—who wanted to establish a center dedicated to studying and commemorating this history—of an undifferentiated comparison of the fate of Germans with the fate of victims of Nazi crimes.

The U.S., in September, deported 84-year-old Elfriede Lina Rinkel, a former guard at the Ravensbrück concentration camp, to Germany. A resident of San Francisco, the Leipzig native was found to have concealed her criminal past when coming to the U.S. in 1959.

Also in September, 21 watercolors and drawings attributed to Adolf Hitler were put up for sale through the British auction house Jefferys. The *Guardian* newspaper, which reprinted some of the images, said the media's interest in the sale was an example of "unthinking intoxication with fame and infamy." The works were produced from 1916 to 1918 and had been found in a Belgian attic 60 years later.

In October, the remains of more than 20 people, many of them children, were discovered in a mass grave in the city of Menden, in Sauerland. Experts suspected the dead were victims of the Nazis' so-called euthanasia program, in which an estimated 100,000 mentally or physically handicapped people were murdered between the fall of 1939 and the summer of 1941, when protests by German church leaders brought the program to an end, at least publicly. Soon after the discovery, the German Hygiene Museum in Dresden opened an exhibit about the euthanasia program. It was the work of the U.S. Holocaust Memorial Museum, and this was believed to be the first time that institution had sent an exhibit abroad.

That same month, the Foundation for a German Holocaust Museum, a private body, proposed building a Holocaust museum in the former East

German city of Leipzig, which would memorialize Jewish and other victim groups such as Sinti and Roma, and deserters from the German army. The city administration said it was open to the idea, and negotiations began on the use of the empty former Russian pavilion on the Leipzig fairgrounds. German architect Meinhard von Gerkan was chosen to design the museum, which was still seeking financial backers.

A reunion took place in late October, attended by 46 people, at the former home for Jewish children in Blankenese, near Hamburg. The Warburg banking family had made the site available in 1945 for Jewish children, most of them orphans, and it was administered by the American Jewish Joint Distribution Committee and the UN Relief and Rehabilitation Administration. The event was organized by retired classics scholar Martin Schmidt, a non-Jew who had researched the history of Jews in Blankenese. A book about the home was translated in 2006 from Hebrew into German under the title *Kirschen auf der Elbe, Das Jüdische Kinderheim Blankenese* (Cherries on the Elbe, the Jewish Home for Children in Blankenese).

An agreement was reached in December for German train stations to mount an exhibit on the deportation of Jewish children. At first, railway chief Hartmund Mehdorn had said the the stations were not appropriate sites "for such a serious theme." Critics responded by accusing him of seeking to cover up the complicity of the Nazi-era railroads in the Holocaust. The exhibit, based in part on a project designed by Nazi-hunter Beate Klarsfeld, was expected to open in Berlin on January 27, 2008, Holocaust Remembrance Day. Klarsfeld's exhibit about the 11,000 Jewish children deported from France to death camps had already been shown at 18 French railway stations.

In December, the Shoah Foundation Institute for Visual History granted Berlin's Free University access to its 52,000 survivor testimonies, making it the first non-U.S. institution with access to the archive, created by American film director Steven Spielberg. Most of the video-recorded interviews were with Jewish survivors, but there were also some with homosexuals, Roma, Jehovah's Witnesses, political prisoners, and others.

COMPENSATION

In a breakthrough for Holocaust survivors, the former inmates of three Nazi prison camps in Tunisia became eligible for compensation of about $320 per month from Germany. The development was announced June 13 after meetings between the Conference on Jewish Material Claims

Against Germany and the German Finance Ministry. Claims Conference executive vice president Gideon Taylor estimated that there might only be a few hundred people eligible for the compensation, "but it is still significant," he said.

Germany committed a total of $277 million to this and several related causes, including $26 million for social services through the end of 2007 for Jewish victims of Nazi persecution, up from $11 million in 2005. In addition, Article 2 payments could be applied to 4,000 additional claimants from certain Western European countries whose eligibility was established after negotiations in 2003. The number of recipients in 2006 rose by 8 percent to 49,000. Article 2 had paid more than $1.8 billion to more than 68,000 Holocaust survivors since it began in 1992, following Claims Conference negotiations with the newly unified Germany.

In the fall, Germany's Restitution Authority ruled that the department store chain KarstadtQuelle must return several sites, including the Beisheim Center in central Berlin, to the Claims Conference, representing the Jewish heirs. The Conference had successfully argued that Germany had erred in handing the property over to Karstadt after German unification, based on Karstadt's earlier purchase of businesses that included the former Wertheim properties. The Wertheims had owned a chain of department stores in Germany before fleeing Nazi persecution in 1939. "Karstadt got the land for free from the [then] Berlin government and they then sold it to [German developer Otto] Beisheim for 145 million euros" in 2000, Taylor said. Beisheim built the Ritz Carlton Hotel on the site. The property was worth about $185 million in 2006. KarstadtQuelle, however, said it would appeal the decision.

Two noteworthy looted artworks were returned to their former owners or heirs in 2006. In February, the German Ministry of Finance announced it would return *Fiat Justitia,* an 1857 painting by Carl Spitzweg, to the heirs of Leo Bendel, a German Jewish collector who died in 1940 in Buchenwald. The painting had been on display in the Villa Hammerschmidt, the presidential palace in Bonn, the former West German capital. A government inquiry determined that Bendel had been forced to sell it to a dealer during the Nazi period, and used the proceeds to help his family escape from Germany to Austria. The painting was purchased a few months later on Hitler's orders for a museum he planned. An image of the painting graced the cover of a book translated from German into English in 2006, *Nazi Looted Art: A Handbook to Art Restitution Worldwide,* by Gunnar Schnabel and Monika Tatzkow.

Far more controversial was a decision in June by Thomas Flierl, senator for cultural affairs of the State of Berlin, to return *Strassenszene Berlin,* an iconic Expressionist painting done in 1913 by Ernst Ludwig Kirchner, to the heirs of its former owner. Critics said the decision was based on flimsy evidence and would lead to a hemorrhage of twentieth-century art from German museums. The CCJG, however, defended the move, noting that it could not be established that the original owner had sold the painting voluntarily and for an appropriate sum. Christie's sold it at auction in New York on November 8.

JEWISH COMMUNITY

Demography and Immigration

In 2006, there were approximately 120,000 dues-paying members of Jewish communities in Germany, but the unofficial number was estimated to be as high as 200,000. Most German Jews were post-1989 immigrants from the former Soviet Union; less than 10 percent had roots in prewar Germany. In 1989, there had been only some 28,000 Jews in Germany. Berlin had the largest Jewish community in 2006, with about 11,500 members and perhaps again as many unregistered Jews. Other cities with large communities included Munich, Frankfurt, Düsseldorf, Cologne, and Hamburg.

The rapid growth of Germany's Jewish community slowed due to new immigration policies that had been urged by Israel in 2004, when more ex-Soviet Jews entered Germany than the Jewish state. Only 617 Jewish immigrants came to Germany in the first nine months of 2006, as compared to an average of 15,000 who had arrived each year from 1995 to 2005, according to the German Interior Ministry.

A point system was formally introduced in July, with the announced goal of reducing pressure on existing Jewish communities to integrate newcomers. Under the new system—which reportedly received the approval of the CCJG—points were awarded for education, job experience, knowledge of German, and being under age 45. Exceptions were made for survivors of National Socialist persecution. The federal Ministry for Migration and Refugees would evaluate all requests, and applicants also had to receive confirmation from the CCJG that they would be accepted as members of the Jewish community.

Communal Affairs

The Central Council of Jewish in Germany (CCJG) was the umbrella organization for Germany's 89 local Jewish communities. Founded in 1950, its main task had become the integration of Russian-speaking Jewish immigrants.

In June, two months after the death of CCJG president Paul Spiegel (see below, p. 467), Charlotte Knobloch was nominated to succeed him. The 73-year-old Knobloch—a vice president of the World Jewish Congress and the European Jewish Congress, and head of the Jewish community of Munich and the State of Bavaria—was the first woman to assume this post. She was officially confirmed to a four-year term in November. Knobloch had been born in prewar Germany and survived the Holocaust in hiding. She and her husband, a businessman and concentration-camp survivor, had three children.

Another vital Jewish body was the Frankfurt-based Zentralwohlfahrtstelle, or Jewish Central Welfare Organization. Founded in 1917, it was also primarily concerned with helping the newer members of the community. Other communal institutions included the College of Jewish Studies in Heidelberg; the *Jüdische Allgemeine,* a weekly newspaper published by the CCJG; the *Jüdische Zeitung,* a new, independent monthly; the Jewish Women's Union; and several student organizations.

In November, a new synagogue—Ohel Jakob—and a Jewish community center opened in the center of Munich. For many, this symbolized a new Jewish willingness to demonstrate Jewish identity publicly. The official opening took place on the anniversary of Kristallnacht, November 9, and fulfilled a dream of Knobloch, a longtime leader of the Munich Jewish community. The dedication ceremony took place in the presence of more than 1,000 people, with tens of thousands more watching on TV.

Other new and revived centers for Jewish life appeared in Germany in 2006. In January, a synagogue opened in Pforzheim, 67 years after the destruction of the old one. About 500 Jews lived in the community. Würzburg saw the opening of a new community and cultural center, "Shalom Europa," in October. The complex included a synagogue, classrooms, and a documentation center for Jewish history and culture. The city's 2006 Jewish population was more than 1,100. Also in October, Berlin's Jewish community moved back to its historic headquarters on Oranienburgerstrasse in the city's former eastern section. From the time that Berlin was divided after World War II, the city's Jewish community had had two headquarters.

Two significant Jewish-Catholic dialogues took place during the year. In July, the Israeli embassy and German Bishops Conference held a discussion marking 40 years since Vatican Council II adopted *Nostra Aetate,* the declaration on Church relations with non-Christians. A second meeting took place in October in Berlin, where Vatican and German cardinals met with the Rabbinical Committee of Germany. Karl Cardinal Lehmann, president of the German Bishops Conference, said his group planned to deepen their relationship with both the CCJG and the rabbinical group.

Education

A dramatic, public educational milestone was achieved in September, when Abraham Geiger College, in Potsdam, ordained its first three rabbis in a ceremony cosponsored by the CCJG. Two of the rabbis, Daniel Alter and Tomasz Kucera, headed off to serve German congregations, and the third, Malcolm Mattitiani, took a pulpit in his native South Africa. Thus the Reform movement, which was born in nineteenth-century Germany, ordained the first rabbis in the country since 1942. In May, the German government had announced it would double its support for the college to 150,000 euros ($191,000) a year, a quarter of the school's budget. The CCJG matched that amount and also funded several scholarships. The announcement followed meetings in April between Chancellor Merkel, German Jewish leaders, and international representatives of Reform Jewry.

In the summer, the 30 young men studying in the Orthodox Beis Midrash of Berlin of the Ronald S. Lauder Foundation moved from their location on Rykestrasse to a newly renovated historic synagogue in Brunnenstrasse. The school was also given a new name, Yeshivas Bcis Zion-The Lauder College at the Skoblo Synagogue and Education Center. The CCJG contributed 90,000 euros ($115,000) each year to the Orthodox school, which received no state funding. The program also initiated a Community Kolel for Central Europe, bringing several young rabbis and their families to Berlin to help build an observant community in the former East Berlin neighborhood. In addition, the Lauder Midrasha for women, with 15 students, moved to the Rykestrasse location from Frankfurt, and the Lauder-Nitzan kindergarten opened in August.

Touro College Berlin held its first graduation ceremony in July. The U.S. ambassador to Germany, William R. Tinken, gave the commencement address to the 24 students who had completed the three-year program in business and Jewish studies. The Berlin school was a branch of the New York-based Touro College of Liberal Arts and Sciences. In September, the school launched the Lander Institute for the Communication of the Holocaust and Tolerance, directed by Rabbi Andreas Nachama, former president of Berlin's Jewish community. The institute held its first seminar in October on "War, Genocide and Expulsion: History and the Politics of History in Germany and Poland."

In August, the Limmud Jewish festival of learning—which originated in Nottingham, England—held its first event in Germany. The nondenominational, one-day program of workshops and entertainment on Jewish themes was hosted by Berlin's Centrum Judaicum. And in November, Arzenu, the association of progressive Zionists in Germany, held a seminar in Berlin on the relationship of Rabbi Leo Baeck to Israel.

The CCJG continued its "Jewish Perspectives" educational series with special guest lectures, including British publisher and philanthropist Lord George Weidenfeld on what it meant to be a European Zionist; Hebrew University political scientist Peter Medding on the myth and reality of American Jewish power; and experts Adrea Röpke and Andreas Speit on right-wing extremism.

Culture

Controversy erupted during the 56th annual Berlin International Film Festival in February, where the start-up of the Green House Mediterranean Film Center was announced. Headquartered in Tel Aviv, the project was to include Israeli, Palestinian, Spanish, Czech, and Turkish partners. The European Union would provide funding for the first three years to the tune of 1.9 million euros. Forty Palestinian filmmakers and directors asked the EU to stop Green House, which they called an act of collaboration "with Israeli government-sponsored institutions," and more than 60 Israeli filmmakers, writers, and musicians added their names to the protest. The argument underscored how difficult it was to build even ostensibly nonpolitical programs involving these parties. Both Israelis and Palestinians had been formally accepted as members of the European Film Academy in 2004.

That was not the only film controversy in February; there was another over the Turkish movie *Kurtlar Vadisi—Irak* (Valley of the Wolves—Iraq), a big hit among young Turkish men in Germany. It depicted U.S. soldiers in Iraq trading in human organs surgically removed from Iraqi prisoners by an American Jewish doctor. Reportedly, audiences cheered the film with the cry, "Allah is great!" Jewish leaders and German politicians denounced the film as anti-American and anti-Semitic, and there were calls for it to be banned. CinemaxX, the country's largest chain of movie houses, responded to the complaints by pulling the film from its theaters.

The 12th annual Jewish Film Festival Berlin opened May 17 with a gala screening of *West Bank Story* by U.S. director Ari Sandel, which later also won an Oscar in the category of short films. The festival's prizewinning Israeli submission was *Ushpizin,* a 2004 film by Gidi Dar. The public's top prize went to *The First Time I was Twenty,* also released in 2004, by French director Lorraine Levy. The two-week festival also featured a screening of Charles Lewinksy's *A Completely Ordinary Jew.*

In November, 88-year-old producer Artur Brauner released a new film, *The Last Train,* about the deportation of Jews from Berlin in 1943, which received positive reviews. Brauner, a Holocaust survivor originally from Lodz, Poland, had made more than 20 movies on themes related to the Holocaust.

Berlin-based Jewish filmmaker Dani Levy released a new comedy about Hitler, *Mein Führer: The Truly Truest Truth About Adolf Hitler,* in late December, and it appeared in German theaters after the New Year. The film triggered considerable public debate about the limits of good taste in treating Nazi crimes in a humorous way.

Several new publications focused on the Holocaust. *Dictator, Demon, Demagogue* by Anna Maria Sigmund explored the myths that had developed about Adolf Hitler. Vivian Jeanette Kaplan's *From Vienna to Shanghai* dealt with Jewish refugees in China during World War II. Ayelet Bargur's Hebrew book about a Berlin home for Jewish orphans between the two world wars, *Ahavah Means Love,* was translated into German and published in 2006. Edgar Hilsenrath, an 80-year-old Holocaust survivor who had returned to Germany in 1975, published *Berlin Endstation,* a Holocaust satire.

Verlag Hentrich & Hentrich's Jewish Miniatures series published several new volumes in 2006, including biographies of Heinrich Heine; Sigmund Freud; Berlin surgeon Moritz Katzenstein, a close friend of Albert Einstein; circus strongman Siegmund Breitbart; and actress Helene Weigel.

In the area of religion, a new German translation of the Bible appeared, *The Bible in Fair Language.* One of its goals was to eliminate misogynist and anti-Semitic elements that appeared in previous translations. A new biography of Rabbi Leo Baeck, the renowned German Reform rabbi, was written by Rabbi Walter Homolka.

Awards

On January 25, American Jewish businessman Arthur Obermayer presented the sixth annual Obermayer German Jewish History Awards in Berlin. They honored non-Jewish Germans who contributed toward recording or preserving the Jewish history of their communities. This year's honorees were Robert Kreibig, Johann Fleischmann, Günter Heidt, Rolf Hofmann, Kurt-Willi Julius, and Karl-Heinz Stadtler. All were nominated by Jews from the U.S., Israel, and Europe whose ancestors had fled Nazi Germany. Obermayer himself had roots in Creglingen, Germany.

Also in January, the International Raoul Wallenberg Foundation and the Angelo Roncalli International Committee honored three Berliners for contributions to Jewish-Christian dialogue: Rabbi Nathan Peter Levinson, Michael Mertes, and Pastor Johannes Hildebrandt. The awards were presented in connection with the exhibition "Visas for Life—Diplomats who Saved Jews."

The German Coordinating Council of the Societies for Christian-Jewish Cooperation presented the annual Buber-Rosenzweig medal in March to Dutch Jewish writer and columnist Leon de Winter. The prize, named for the philosophers Martin Buber and Franz Rosenzweig, had been given annually starting in 1968. Also in March, Germany's top Catholic prelate, Karl Cardinal Lehmann, received the annual Abraham Geiger Prize from Germany's Reform movement for his contribution to Catholic-Jewish understanding.

In November, the CCJG presented its annual Leo Baeck Prize to publisher Hubert Burda in recognition of his support for Israel and for the growth of Jewish life in Germany. Burda's father, Franz, profited from the so-called Aryanization, or expropriatation, of Jewish property under the Nazis. Hubert Burda contributed a million euros toward Munich's new Jewish community center.

That same month, the Berlin Jewish community gave its 17th annual Heinz Galinski Prize to Annemarie Renger, and the Jewish Museum in Berlin awarded its Prize of Understanding to conductor Daniel Barenboim, music director of the Berlin State Opera, and Helmut Panke, chairman of the board of BMW. At the ceremony, Barenboim, an outspoken critic of Israeli policies, urged Israel to recognize "the suffering of the Palestinian people."

Deaths

Paul Spiegel, president of the CCJG, died in April at the age of 68. The funeral took place near his home city of Düsseldorf, and a public memorial service was held later. A businessman, Spiegel was elected to head the German Jewish community in January 2000. News of his death drew immediate condolences from a broad spectrum of German political and religious leaders. Chancellor Merkel mourned Spiegel as "a very impressive personality . . . who dedicated himself passionately to building a good future for the Jewish community in Germany."

Spiegel was born on December 31, 1937, in the city of Warendorf near Münster. He and his mother survived the Holocaust in hiding in Belgium; his father survived Buchenwald, Auschwitz, and Dachau. Spiegel's older sister was arrested in 1942 at age 11 while procuring food for the family. She was deported to Auschwitz and murdered. After the war, the three surviving family members returned to Warendorf. Spiegel described the ongoing pain of the Holocaust experience in his 2001 autobiography, *At Home Again? Recollections.* He wrote another book, a guide to basic Judaism, *Was ist Koshcher? Jüdischer Glaube—jüdisches Leben* (What's Kosher? Jewish Belief—Jewish Life), which came out in 2003.

As president of the CCJG he presided over several major developments in the postwar Jewish community. In 2003, he signed the first contract between his organization and the federal government, placing the Jewish community on a legal par with its Catholic and Protestant counterparts. He was also involved in crafting a reparations agreement for surviving Nazi-era slave laborers and in developing legislation on immigration. After a wave of violent xenophobic crimes in Germany in 2000, Spiegel started *Gesicht Zeigen!* (Show Your Face!)—a campaign in which public figures encouraged Germans to stand up against extremism. In his final years, he orchestrated a rapprochement between the CCJG and Reform congregations, paving the way for their official acceptance under its organizational umbrella.

In November, Markus Wolf, son of a Jewish playwright and doctor, died in Berlin at age 83. Known to his family as Misha, he had been the spy chief of communist East Germany. For decades, Western intelligence—which called him "the man without a face"—sought in vain to capture an image of the elusive architect of his country's international intelligence network. At the height of his power he commanded an estimated 4,000 secret agents, and was famous for having infiltrated the highest echelons of the West German government, ultimately perpetrating a security breach that forced Chancellor Willy Brandt to resign. Wolf reexamined his Jewish roots in his later years, though he once told the Swiss Jewish newspaper *Jüdische Rundschau* that he would never identify religiously. He visited Israel once, in 1996, and described it as "a great experience."

In September, the non-Jewish German writer and historian Joachim Fest, author of a highly regarded biography of Adolf Hitler, died at age 79, a week before publication of his autobiography, *Ich Nicht* (Not Me). Fest had been a copublisher and editor at the *Frankfurter Allgemeine Zeitung.* Fest's *Hitler,* published in 1973, was "without a doubt one of the most important books on the subject," said literary critic Marcel Reich-Ranicki upon receiving news of his death. In his own autobiography, Fest described how as a young man he opposed the wishes of his Nazi-hating father and enlisted in the German army in 1944, to avoid conscription into the SS.

TOBY AXELROD

Austria

National Affairs

I N THE OCTOBER national election, the Social Democratic Party of Austria (SPÖ) narrowly defeated the ruling People's Party (ÖVP) by 35.34 percent (68 seats) to 34.33 percent (66 seats), and stood ready to assume power after more than six years in the opposition. Although it was clear that Social Democratic leader Alfred Gusenbauer would be the next chancellor, his options for forming a coalition were severely limited. The SPÖ had ruled out any cooperation with the two far-right parties, the Freedom Party (FPÖ), which received 11.04 percent of the vote (21 seats), and the Alliance for the Future of Austria (BZÖ), which garnered 4.11 percent (7 seats). A coalition with the Green Party, which came in third with 11.05 percent (21 seats), would not provide the Social Democrats with the necessary majority, and so the new government would likely take the form of a grand coalition between the Social Democrats and the People's Party.

Several aspects of the election surprised observers. Although the People's Party had been expected to lose ground, few had thought that it would be defeated. Also, far-right leader Jörg Haider maintained his toehold in national politics: his far-right BZÖ just managed to finish over the 4-percent threshold necessary for parliamentary representation, whereas preelection polls had predicted that it would fall short. The Freedom Party, which Haider had led for two decades before quitting it after a power struggle in 2005, did well enough to ensure that it would play a strong opposition role.

Immigration was a major campaign issue, as many Austrians feared that the proposed entry of Turkey into the European Union would flood the country with cheap labor. Haider had brought the issue of immigration into mainstream politics in the 1990s, pushing the ruling People's Party to toughen citizenship requirements for immigrants. The difference now was the prominence of the religious aspect. According to Peter Paul Hajek, a political analyst at the Austrian Marketing Institute, "it's more about the clash of between Islam and Christianity." In the 2006 election, both the FPÖ and the BZÖ ran blatantly anti-Muslim campaigns. The mainstream conservative People's Party sought anti-immigrant votes by opposing a general amnesty for foreigners who were in the country illegally. Even the Social Democrats ran a campaign promising to crack down on crimes committed by foreigners. Only the Greens stood for a more open attitude towards immigrants.

In the realm of economic policy, the Freedom Party pledged to create 15,000 new research-and-development jobs, achieve full employment by 2010, and lower taxes. But the Social Democrats were apparently more in tune with public sentiment on the economy, making electoral gains on promises to lower the number of unemployed by 100,000 and to reduce salary differences between men and women.

Negotiations between the Social Democrats and the People's Party to form a broad-based coalition dragged on after the election and were not resolved by year's end. As a way out of the impasse, President Heinz Fischer, a former Social Democrat, committed both sides to accept a deadline of January 8, 2007, to reach agreement. Two major stumbling blocks kept the parties apart, both involving programs strongly supported by the Social Democrats and firmly opposed by the People's Party: abolition of university student fees and a reversal of the controversial purchase of 18 Eurofighter jet planes from EADS, the aerospace group. On social issues, the two parties had already agreed to a modest spending increase on social programs and education, and to a rise in individual contributions to the national health system. Both remained outspokenly critical of EU accession talks with Turkey.

A major cultural milestone for Austria during 2006 was the celebration of the 150th birthday of Sigmund Freud, the father of psychoanalysis. To mark the event, the Austrian embassy in Washington, D.C., hosted a symposium on September 15 entitled "A Day of Reflection on Freud's Place in Our Minds." The guests included members of four major American psychoanalytic organizations as well as prominent Freud experts from the academic and cultural worlds. Prof. Eli Zaretsky of the New School for Social Research, author of *Secrets of the Soul: A Social and Cultural History of Psychoanalysis,* delivered the keynote address.

Israel and the Middle East

Diplomatic ties between Israel and Austria were strong, as evidenced by an exchange of official visits by the foreign ministers of the two countries. Israel's Tzipi Livni visited Vienna in March, where she met with Chancellor Wolfgang Schüssel (who was also serving as rotating president of the EU), President Heinz Fischer, and Foreign Minister Ursula

Plassnik. The Austrian foreign minister returned the visit in December, attending a conference celebrating 50 years of diplomatic relations between the two countries. Plassnik met with Prime Minister Ehud Olmert, Deputy Prime Minister Shimon Peres, and Minister of the Interior and Security Avi Dichter.

The Austrian media, with the exception of the far right, presented a balanced picture of Israel's ongoing conflict with Palestinian groups and the larger Arab world. In their coverage of the war between Israel and Hezballah in Lebanon, most newspapers were willing to consider the Israeli side of contentious issues.

In February, when representatives of the European Jewish Congress convened in Vienna, Chancellor Schüssel addressed them and underlined Austria's friendly ties both to Israel and to the Austrian Jewish community. Similar friendly sentiments were expressed by Andreas Khol, president of the Austrian Federal Parliament. He assured the EJC delegates that "the Austrian Parliament is a friend of Israel." Alfred Gusenbauer, head of the Socialist Democratic Party, paid a private visit to Israel in June, before the Austrian election. Gusenbauer met with Olmert, Peres, and Minister of Defense Amir Peretz.

Benjamin Netanyahu, who headed the Likud opposition bloc in the Israeli Knesset, attended the international conference of the Hayek Institute in Vienna in June. The third International Management and Consulting Congress, meeting in Vienna earlier in the year, honored Shimon Peres with a lifetime achievement award for his service in the search for peace in the Middle East. In the cultural arena, there was a lively exchange between Israel and Austria of theatrical, musical, and dance groups.

Anti-Semitism

Austria remained free of physical violence against Jews, and did not experience the kind of public anti-Israel and anti-Jewish manifestations that occurred in other European nations during the Israel's summer war against Hezballah in Lebanon. The war did, however, trigger a surge of anti-Semitic telephone calls, letters, and e-mails to Jewish organizations. On the extreme left, and especially among intellectuals, the Israeli strike into Lebanon brought condemnation. On the extreme right, it was used in the election campaign to win votes.

In the view of Jewish leaders, the FPÖ and the BZÖ attacked Israel during the campaign in a way that verged on anti-Semitism. Haider called

Ariel Muzicant, president of the Israelitische Kultusgemeinde (IKG), the Austrian Jewish community, a "Zionist provocateur." When an Israeli attack in southern Lebanon resulted in the death of an Austrian UN peace-keeper, the two extremist parties launched vitriolic attacks against Muzicant and the Jewish community. The BZÖ leader in the province of Styria demanded that the Jewish communities of Vienna and Graz (capital of the southern region where the UN peace-keeper came from) issue a public condemnation of what he called a "cruel and cowardly murder." A Freedom Party local councilman from Neunkirchen wrote an open letter to the Palestinian community of Austria asserting that the dead man was a victim of "Israeli terrorism" and that "the mass murderers with the Jewish star shall always remain unpunished." In a second letter he attacked Muzicant for criticizing Austrian trade ties with Iran and urged instead a boycott of Israeli goods, saying, "these murderers will not get my money!"

Holocaust-Related Matters

The National Fund (Nationalfund), established in 1995, was responsible for handling payments to Austrian survivors of the National Socialist era. In 2002 the fund was authorized to distribute $150 million, to be paid out as a gesture of compensation for the loss of leased apartments, personal valuables, and household property, with a deadline for applications set for June 2004. Each claimant received $7,000 plus an additional 1,000 euros. The money was distributed in order of the age of the claimant, the oldest first.

Another responsibility of the National Fund was handling payments from the General Settlement Fund (GSF), established by the Austrian government under terms of an agreement signed in Washington, D.C., in 2001. Through voluntary GSF payments, Austria acknowledged its moral responsibility for damages inflicted upon Jews and other victims of Nazism. The money would come from the government and Austrian companies: $210 million was set aside. By the filing deadline, 20,000 claims had been submitted.

However, a condition of the agreement setting up the GSF was that all class-action suits against Austria and/or Austrian companies for Holocaust-related claims had to be dismissed before any payments could be made. Following a protracted and, at times, angry confrontation between the government and the IKG, an agreement was reached whereby the government would provide the IKG 18.2 million euros as final restitution for damages and losses to Austrian communal property during the National Socialist era. In return, the IKG agreed to drop its amicus petition in support of the class-action suit of *Whiteman et al. v. Republic of Austria* and to withdraw from the legal proceedings. This step, in turn, paved the way for a U.S. District Court in New York to dismiss the suit and a second similar one, thereby allowing payments to Holocaust survivors from the GSF (see AJYB 2006, pp. 458–59). During 2006, the National Fund sent out letters to survivors and their heirs whose claims had already been approved, stating that checks would be going out. By the end of the year 9,000 claims had been approved and 5,000 paid.

In October, the National Fund made public its database of artworks held in museums and other collections managed by the Republic of Austria and the city of Vienna, and which, according to the most recent provenance research, may have been expropriated during the Nazi era. The purpose of this initiative was to clarify whether and to whom artworks should be restituted.

The National Fund was also responsible for supporting projects in the field of Holocaust education, providing psychological and medical assistance to survivors, and helping restore Jewish cemeteries and reconstruct synagogues. A synagogue that benefited during 2006 was the one in Baden, which now served both as a house of worship and as a cultural center. In November, the National Fund provided financial support for an exhibit on the *Kindertransport,* the prewar project that removed Jewish children from Germany and some German-occupied lands to Palestine or to neutral countries. Titled *"Für das Kind"* (For the Child), the exhibit was geared to schoolchildren, and included audio and video recordings of people who had been rescued through placement with the *Kindertransport.*

The Holocaust Victims' Information and Support Center (HVISC), or Anlaufstelle, established by the IKG in July 1999, continued its work of promoting and protecting the interests of Jewish Holocaust victims and their heirs in and from Austria. Although the deadline for submitting applications for the restitution of publicly owned real estate was to end on December 31, 2006, Ariel Muzicant, the IKG president, sought to have the federal deadline extended, and also urged the authorities of selected cities and municipalities to take action under terms of the law governing restitution of public property. Only a few heeded the call.

In seeking to identify and quantify real-estate assets owned by the Jewish community prior to 1938, the Anlaufstelle had a team of historians conducting research into properties currently owned by the Austrian government and the city of Vienna (see AJYB 2006, p. 460). The investigation turned up flaws in the initial restitution process. But a three-man arbitration panel charged with the task of deciding specific cases declined to restitute properties in two cases brought to it, leading the IKG to review the procedures used by the panel.

The Commission for Provenance Research, of which the Anlaufstelle was a member, succeeded in having universal standards of provenance research appplied to the holdings of all federal museums and collections. By April 2007 all such repositories would be required to respond to a detailed questionnaire concerning their holdings, the number of artworks acquired since 1938 (when the Nazi government annexed Austria), their research about previous owners of these artworks, and their criteria for determining whether a particular work might be subject to restitution.

In November, the Anlaufstelle requested the Kinsky auction house in Vienna to withdraw a drawing by Egon Schiele from a pending sale since it had been identified by the son of the original owner as stolen property. After Kinsky turned down the request, the IKG obtained a court order prohibiting the drawing from being handed over to the buyer until the completion of a provenance investigation. This was considered a landmark decision since it put auction houses on notice that they would be held accountable. The IKG had more success with the Vienna-based Dorotheum auction house, convincing it to put off two separate auctions involving three artworks, pending the conclusion of an agreement between the consigner and the heirs of the original owners. Following negotiations between the Anlaufstelle and the city of Lienz in eastern Tyrol, the city agreed to restitute a major painting by Albin Egger, *Totendanz,* to the heirs of Melanie Schwartz, the original owner.

In other art news, a three-judge Austrian panel ruled that five of six paintings by Gustav Klimt that were held by the Austrian government should be returned to Mrs. Maria Altmann, who claimed that they were looted from her family by the Nazis. After a long and complicated legal process that went all the way up to the U.S. Supreme Court in 2004 (see AJYB 2005, p. 488), Mrs. Altmann agreed to binding arbitration by the Austrian panel, which ruled unanimously in her favor regarding five of the paintings in January 2006. The next month the Austrian government declined an option to buy the paintings from her. They were then removed from the walls of the Austrian Gallery in the Belvedere Palace and shipped to Los Angeles, where Mrs. Altmann lived, and put on display at the Los Angeles County Museum between April and June. The most famous of the paintings, a portrait of Adele Bloch-Bauer, was purchased in June by Ronald S. Lauder for $135 million, the highest price ever paid for a painting, and placed on permanent display at the five-year-old Neue Galerie in Manhattan. The four other Klimt works were sold at auction in November at Christie's for an estimated $125 million.

Searching for owners of artworks confiscated during the Nazi years, the city of Vienna turned its attention to Israel. In July, the Austrian embassy in Tel Aviv asked Israelis for information that might identify the former owners of 1,545 objects acquired by the Dorotheum, including 550 from art dealers, 12 from public donations, and 212 acquisitions and donations from Julius Fargel, who had been the restorer for the city's collections as well as chief appraiser in the Gestapo Office for the Disposal of the Property of Jewish Emigrants. Under an act passed by the Vienna City Council on April 29, 1999, these were to be restituted, and those whose owners could not be traced would be transferred to the National Fund, which would sell them and use the proceeds for the benefit of the victims of the Nazi regime.

The Anlaufstelle completed the microfilming of 1.5 million images from the Jerusalem holdings of the IKG archives and approximately 500,000 images of its Vienna holdings. The latter included data about births, deaths, and marriages of community members from the end of the eighteenth century until 1938. The microfilming of the Vienna holdings was done in cooperation with the U.S. Holocaust Memorial Museum and the Geneological Society of Utah.

The Austrian Reconciliation Fund, created to resolve issues arising out of the Nazi experience and to address contemporary human rights concerns, concluded its work at the end of 2005, having disbursed payments to 132,000 former slave laborers. Two other bodies that it created, however, continued to function. One was the Future Fund, which supported research on the Holocaust and on threats to peace posed by totalitarian systems, promoted international humanitarian cooperation and respect for human rights, and processed claims filed with the Austrian Reconciliation Fund that had not yet been settled. The other was the Scholarship Fund, which offered scholarships for study at Austrian universities to persons from countries whose citizens were recruited as forced laborers during the Nazi era and to descendants of forced laborers regardless of where they lived. Scholarship recipients were to serve as Austrian "diplomats of reconciliation" in their home countries.

The Austrian Jewish Religious Society joined with the Organization of Jewish Victims of the Nazi Regime to organize a solemn ceremony on May 7 at the site of the Mauthausen concentration camp. The occasion was the 61st anniversary of the liberation of the camp by U.S. troops. Among those addressing the 12,000 people assembled there were

Austrian president Fischer, Cardinal Christoph Schonborn, Ambassador Dan Ashbel of Israel, Chief Rabbi Paul Chaim Eisenberg, and Ariel Muzikant. Hannah Lessing, secretary general of the National Fund, delivered the keynote address, "Gender-Specific Persecution in the Holocaust—The Work of the National Fund."

An Austrian court imposed a three-year sentence in February on British historian David Irving, who pleaded guilty to denying the Holocaust and admitted that he had been wrong in claiming there were no Nazi gas chambers at Auschwitz. He had been arrested in November 2005 on charges stemming from two speeches he made in Austria in 1989 claiming that there was no Nazi policy of annihilating the Jews (see AJYB 2006, pp. 457–58). Irving was convicted under a 1992 Austrian law making Holocaust denial a crime. (A handful of other countries, including Germany, France, Belgium, and Poland, also criminalized denial). Irving's trial and conviction came at a time of intense debate in Europe over the limits of freedom of expression, after a Danish newspaper printed caricatures of the Prophet Mohammed that ignited deadly protests all over the world (see above, pp. 433–35).

In December, an appeals court freed Irving and ruled that he could serve the remainder of his term at home on probation. Noting that Irving had made his remarks about the Holocaust a long time ago, the court declared it unlikely that he would repeat the offense, and said it expected him to leave Austria soon.

Some observers applauded the verdict on free-speech grounds. Deborah Lipstadt, for example, the Emory University historian who won a libel suit that Irving filed against her in England in 1998, said in an interview, "I don't believe that history should be adjudicated in a courtroom," and suggested that Irving's imprisonment risked turning him into a martyr. But the prosecutor, Marie-Luise Nittel, countered that Irving remained a symbol to extremists and thus a danger to society. Hans Raucher, a columnist for the Vienna daily *Der Standard*, agreed, writing: "Denial of the Holocaust is not an opinion, it is a political act which tries to bring Nazi thought into the mainstream." The presiding judge of the appeals court, Ernst Maurer, was known to have close ties to the far-right Freedom Party, and had ruled in favor of party founder Jörg Haider on several occasions when Haider had been accused of trying to whitewash the Nazi record.

In July, the new Vienna Wiesenthal Institute for Holocaust Studies (see AJYB 2006, pp. 461–62) held it first conference. Entitled "The Legacy of Simon Wiesenthal for Holocaust Studies," it was attended by scholars from the U.S., Israel, Poland, Germany, and Austria. Papers were presented by David Bankier, Omer Bartov, Peter Black, Wlodzimierz Borodziej, Christian Gerlach, Anita Grossman, Isabel Heinemann, Raul Hilberg, Bertrand Perz, Tom Segev, and Michael Wildt. The conference was organized in cooperation with the International Research Center for Cultural Studies (IFK) and the Institute for Contemporary History at the University of Vienna. The IKG assisted in funding the event. The institute also launched a Web site and created a board of scholars, with Raul Hilberg as honorary chairman.

A controversy broke out in Salzburg over a documentary film showing the history of the Salzburg festival, the annual summer program dedicated to the performance of great classical music, mainly of Austrian origin. The film, *The Salzburg Festival: A Short History,* raised the hackles of the festival directors, who felt that it overemphasized the event's relationship with the Nazis. The three-and-a quarter-hour film devoted 30 minutes to the Nazi period and included scenes of Hitler and German soldiers sweeping into Salzburg in 1938 as cheering throngs waved flags emblazoned with swastikas. There were also clips showing German officers enjoying the musical performances. The festival was founded in 1920 in the hope that it might help Austria regain a sense of purpose through culture and music after the disaster of World War I. Ironically, two of its prime movers were Jews, the pioneering theater director Max Reinhardt and the poet and librettist Hugo von Hofmannsthal.

Austria held the rotating presidency of the EU during the first six months of 2006, and in that capacity Chancellor Schüssel condemned both the publication of a Holocaust cartoon on the Web site of a Muslim organization in Antwerp and the launch of a Holocaust cartoon "competition" by the Iranian newspaper *Hamshari.* In a statement issued in February, the chancellor declared: "Neither disparaging caricatures of Mohammed nor the denial of the Holocaust or shameful jokes about the Holocaust have any place in a world where cultures and religions should live side by side in a spirit of mutual respect."

Austria joined other Western countries in condemning the government-sponsored Holocaust-denial conference in Tehran. The two-day meeting held in early December, allegedly to air "both sides" of the debate over the historicity of the Holocaust, was attended by deniers and known anti-Semites, and books by David Irving and other revisionists were on conspicuous display. A delegation from "Jews United Against Zionism," organized by the anti-Zionist Neturei Karta, included Moshe Arye Friedman, who claimed to be a rabbi from Austria. He explained: "I am not a denier of the Holocaust, but I think it is legitimate to cast doubt on some statistics."

The Federal Ministry for Foreign Affairs, in cooperation with the Future Fund, published a volume in both German and English, *The Righteous of Austria: Heroes of the Holocaust,* which provided details on the lives of 86 non-Jewish Austrians who risked their lives to save Jews during the war. Publication took place in 2006 to mark 50 years of diplomatic relations between Austria and Israel, and the official release date was May 5, the anniversary of the liberation of the Mauthausen camp by Allied forces in 1945.

JEWISH COMMUNITY

Demography

The number of Jews registered with the IKG stood at 6,934, a net increase of 90 over the previous year. The increase was attributed to the IKG's outreach program directed at unaffiliated Jews and also to the relatively higher birthrate in Sephardi familes than in Ashkenazi families. Knowledgeable observers placed the actual number of Jews in Austria at 12,000–15,000.

Apart from a tiny number of people permitted to enter the country to join their families, immigration from abroad was frozen. Ariel Muzicant, president of the IKG, had been engaged in ongoing discussions with the government to relax the strict immigration laws and allow more Jews into the country, but there was no indication that liberalization would come any time soon.

The overwhelming majority of the country's Jewish population continued to live in Vienna. Only some 300–400 made their homes elsewhere, primarily in the large provincial cities of Graz, Salzburg, Innsbruck, and Linz. An estimated 40 percent of the Vienna Jewish community was now Sephardi, and a majority of the community's population was under 25 years of age. The Sephardi Center, located in the city's second district, now housed two congregations, one of Bukharan Jews and the other of Jews from the former Soviet republic of Georgia. Chabad performed a variety of services for the Sephardi community, for which it received 176,000 euros from the IKG in 2006.

Communal Affairs

Avshalom Hodik, the long-serving secretary general of the IKG, retired in March. The responsibilities of his office were then divided between two successors. Raimund Fastenbauer was named secretary general, but the IKG's financial affairs would be handled by Frederick Herzog.

In April, Jewish Welcome Service (JWS) celebrated its 25th anniversary. Its role was to welcome Jews to Vienna and arrange exchange programs for Austrian, Israeli, and American youth. President Fischer addressed the commemorative event at a ceremony at Vienna's city hall, and thanked Leon Zelman, the head of JWS, for his tireless efforts. Zelman's dedication, Fischer said, had helped bring victims closer to a country that had treated them so badly. In response, Zelman, a survivor of several Nazi camps, said it was a "moral responsibility" that drove him to welcome Jews back to Vienna. Perhaps the best known JWS program was "Welcome to Austria," which had, over the years, brought some 4,000 Jews expelled from Austria during the National Socialist era back to visit Vienna.

It was announced in August that the Center for Jewish Studies at the University of Graz, established in 2000, would be made a permanent university program beginning with the 2007 winter semester. Developed jointly with the Institute of Jewish Studies in Heidelberg, Germany, the program would be called Jewish Studies: History of Jewish Culture, and offer a master's degree.

The Vienna sports club Hakoach ("strength" in Hebrew), considered one of best such clubs before the Nazi takeover of the country, was due to have its own headquarters for the first time since 1938, and would thus no longer have to use the facilities of other gymnasiums and sports clubs. Designed by the architect Thomas Feiger, the new sports center would include three gyms, a fitness room, sauna and wellness areas, tennis courts, weight-lifting rooms, and a 25-meter swimming pool. Construction, scheduled to start in the summer, was to be completed within two years. As part of the plan, the Zvi Peretz Chayes School and an old-age home would be located in the complex. At the request of the IKG, the city council renamed the street on which the center would be built after Simon Wiesenthal. Total costs were estimated at 57 million euros ($74 million); the Austrian government, the city of Vienna, and private sponsors had already pledged 7 million euros.

Culture

Eric R. Kandel, the well-known neuroscientist, published a new book, *In Search of Memory: The Emergence of a New Science of Mind,* a richly detailed autobiography chronicling his life and his research into the human mind. Born in Vienna in 1929, the nine-year-old Kandel fled with his family to the U.S. to escape the Nazis. A professor at the Center for

Neurobiology and Behavior at Columbia University since 1974, he received the Nobel Prize in Physiology or Medicine in 2000 for his work on the cellular basis of learning and memory. In a visit to Vienna in June to present his new book, Kandel was honored at a reception hosted by President Fischer. While expressing admiration for Vienna's cultural life, Kandel — recipient of the Austrian Medal for Science in 2005 — remarked: "I still sense a degree of anti-Semitism in Austria that I don't sense in Germany." He asked his Austrian hosts, "Why do the Viennese not invite more Jews to come in?" In his new book, Kandel wrote, "Vienna's culture was one of extraordinary power, and it had been created and nourished in good part by Jews."

Among the exhibitions mounted by the Vienna Jewish Museum was "On the Analysis of Tyrannies," marking the centenary of the birth of author Manès Sperber, who spent his youth in Vienna and then wandered from place to place until settling in Paris in the 1930s, where he wrote his major works in French: the three-part autobiography *All Our Yesterdays,* the trilogy *Like a Tear in the Ocean,* and *On the Analysis of Tyrannies,* which showed the resemblances between Nazism and Stalinism. In Paris Sperber met André Malraux and Arthur Koestler, and, after the war, joined them in combating totalitarianisms of the right and the left. The exhibition was based on documents as well as audiovisual material, primarily historic radio and TV broadcasts in which Sperber appeared.

Another exhibition at the museum, on view from March 22 to September 17, was "The City of Tolerance: The Aryanized Da Ponte and the Jewish Mozart," a Jewish contribution to Mozart Year 2006. Lorenzo Da Ponte, born Emanuele Conegliano in Vittorio Veneto in 1749 and converted from Judaism to Catholicism when he was 14, received ordination as a priest ten years later. By the time he arrived in Vienna in 1782, he had abandoned the Church, and the next year was appointed librettist to the Imperial Opera, in which capacity he collaborated with Wolfgang Amadeus Mozart on such operatic gems as *The Marriage of Figaro, Don Giovanni,* and *Cosi Fan Tutti.* The exhibition dealt with Da Ponte's Jewish background, explored the significance of Mozart for the people of Vienna and for Austrian Jews, and traced Nazi attempts to "Aryanize" the works of Da Ponte and Mozart.

The museum also mounted an exhibition of the works of three outstanding postwar Austrian artists. Titled "Fantastic—The Jewishness in the Early Masterpieces of Arik Brauer, Ernst Fuchs, and Friedensreich Hundertwasser," it opened on October 11 and ran through January 14, 2007. All three men were born between 1928 and 1930 in Vienna, experienced the Nazi era, and were subsequently persecuted and ostracized because of their Jewish origins.

Another exhibition, "From Josephine Mutzenbacher to Bambi: Felix Salten, Writer—Jouranlist—Emigré," treated the life and times of Felix Salten (1869–1945), the author of *Bambi.* A theater, film, and art critic for the *Neue Freie Presse* as well as a screenwriter, cabaret owner, operetta librettist, travel writer, mentor of young writers, and president of the Austrian PEN Club, he was instrumental in shaping prewar Austrian culture. Salten was forced to flee to Switzerland in 1939, where he died. The exhibition opened on December 6 and was scheduled to run through March 18, 2007.

Personalia

Austrian journalist Huberus Czernin died in Vienna in June 2006. Among his many achievements was helping expose the Nazi past of Kurt Waldheim, the former secretary general of the UN and president of Austria. His investigative reporting about stolen artworks played a major role in the passage of Austria's Art Restitution Law, which, by subjecting museums to provenance searches, immeasurably aided families seeking to locate art confiscated during the Nazi era. Czernin's research was critical in helping Maria Altmann recover the five Klimt paintings looted by the Nazis during World War II (see above, pp. 474–75), as he disproved the government's contention that the widow of Ferdinand Bloch-Bauer, the original owner, had stated that Austria should receive the paintings after her death. Despite illness, Czernin attended the opening of the exhibition when the paintings went on display at the Los Angeles County Museum in April.

Paul G. Fried, professor of European history at Hope College in Michigan, died in July. Fried was the architect of one of the oldest and most highly regarded summer study-abroad programs, the Vienna Summer School, which he inaugurated in 1965.

Jakob Allerhand, a well-known Jewish educator, died in Vienna in December. When World War II broke out, he fled his native Poland and found refuge in Central Asia. He came to Berlin after the war, and began university studies there. In the early 1970s he moved to Vienna, earned a Ph.D. in Jewish studies, and taught the few Viennese—nearly all of them non-Jews—who were interested in Yiddish and Jewish history. Allerhand became the director of the Zvi Peretz Chayes School, the first Jewish day school to open in Vienna since the Holocaust. An ardent Zionist, he imbued the students with a love for Israel and the Hebrew language. His three-volume *History of the Jews* was widely used as a text book in this and other schools. Allerhand was the principal organizer of the Theodor Herzl Symposium that took place in Vienna in June 2004 (see AJYB 2005, p. 445), the fifth and last of a series that began in 1986 to mark the centenary of the publication of Herzl's landmark *Der Judenstaat* (The Jewish State). Allerhand was active in interfaith affairs, and when Cardinal Franz König decided to visit Israel, he had Allerhand accompany him. Allerhand was buried in Haifa.

MURRAY GORDON SILBERMAN

East-Central Europe and the Balkans

Countries in the region were considered some of Israel's best friends in Europe, and, during Israel's summer war with Hezballah in southern Lebanon, both pro-Israel and pro-Hezballah demonstrations took place in several cities. Governments also issued stern denunciations of Holocaust denial in the wake of the denial conference that Iran hosted in December. Still, anti-Semitism, right-wing extremism, and left-wing anti-Zionism continued to plague the region.

Meanwhile, political developments within individual countries— including elections, cabinet reshuffles, and popular protests—also bore potential implications for Jews. Jewish life in most countries in the region continued to develop. Despite the relatively small number of Jews, new religious, social, and cultural possibilities opened up.

Bosnia and Herzegovina

A new law on property restitution, passed in July, aimed at restoring to their rightful owners land and buildings confiscated during the Balkan wars of 1992–95. The Jewish and Christian communities expressed dissatisfaction, arguing that the law discriminated in favor of Muslims.

Before Passover, copies of a full facsimile edition of the famous fourteenth-century Sarajevo Haggadah went on sale for the equivalent of $1,350 each. The idea for the project as well as seed money for it came from James Wolfensohn, a former president of the World Bank. Proceeds from sales would, first, reimburse Wolfensohn and repay a bank loan that had been taken to pay for the publication, and the net profits would then be divided between the publisher and La Benevolencija, the Bosnian Jewish cultural, educational, and humanitarian agency.

During the year, Sarajevo's century-old Ashkenazi synagogue, which also housed the offices of the Jewish community, underwent renovation.

In July, 30 American college students, Jewish and Palestinian, visited the country to study the Bosnian peace accord as a possible model for solutions to the conflict in the Middle East. The trip was organized by Abraham's Vision, a group that encourages dialogue between Jews and Palestinians. In October, Sarajevo was the scene of a three-day conference on the status of Holocaust research in southeastern Europe. The event, organized by the Sarajevo Jewish community and Germany's

Goethe Institute, drew more than 100 academics and other experts from the Balkan states and elsewhere.

Bulgaria

Ceremonies were held in March to mark 63 years since the protests that halted the deportation of Jews from Bulgaria to Nazi death camps. The National Assembly, the nation's parliament, observed a moment of silence, and flowers were laid at a memorial plaque near the parliament building in Sofia that honored Dimitar Peshev, the body's wartime vice president, who led the protests by lawmakers, religious leaders, and ordinary citizens that stopped the deportations. The current speaker, Georgi Pirinski, told the legislators that Peshev's actions "will forever be an honor to the Bulgarian National Assembly," but also reminded them that "another truth should not be forgotten—the fact that 11,343 innocent Jews from Macedonia and Aegean Thrace, which were territories then administered by Bulgarian authorities, were exiled and found their death."

In February, the Israeli defense firm Elbit Systems signed a 57.3-million-euro deal to upgrade 18 Bulgarian military helicopters so as to make them compatible with NATO standards. On a two-day official visit to Bulgaria in June, Israeli president Moshe Katzav laid a wreath at the memorial to Peshev. Katzav and Bulgarian president Georgi Parvanov opened a forum of businessmen representing 15 Israeli and 80 Bulgarian firms that was aimed at boosting economic cooperation. "Bulgaria and Israel have good traditions in cooperating in spheres such as agriculture, food industry, tourism . . . but there are many other opportunities," Parvanov said. During Katzav's visit the two countries signed an agreement for visa-free travel. The Israeli president also met with local Jewish community leaders.

At least 5,000 Jews lived in Bulgaria, about half of them in Sofia. As many as 1,500 lived in Plovdiv and 500 in Varna, with smaller communities scattered in other cities. Bulgarian Jewish communities were linked under the umbrella Shalom organization, and Chabad was also active in the country. The only functioning synagogues were in Sofia and Plovdiv. In April, the Sofia Jewish community opened a second Jewish community center across the street from the synagogue.

In July, some 300–400 demonstrators staged an anti-Israel rally in Sofia, protesting Israel's war on Hezballah in Lebanon. Most of the protesters were believed to be of Lebanese or Palestinian origin.

In October, President Parvanov, a former Socialist running as an independent, won a second five-year term by a landslide over MP Volen Siderov. Siderov, leader of the right-wing party Attack, was known for xenophobic statements and Holocaust denial. In August, a Sofia court ruled that Siderov's public hate speech against Roma, Jews, Turks, homosexuals, and all non-Bulgarians constituted harassment and incitement to discrimination. It ordered him to refrain from any similar statements in the future.

Croatia

The internal squabbles that split the Zagreb Jewish community during 2005 (see AJYB 2006, pp. 473–75) persisted through 2006. Rabbi Kotel Dadon, whose contract was not renewed in 2005, remained in Zagreb, where he and his followers founded a new congregation, Bet Israel, which was accorded government recognition as a separate Jewish community and founded its own school. Winning the backing of the London-based Conference of European Rabbis, it said it would push to receive a share of the established Jewish community's assets. Historian Ivo Goldstein was president of the new group. Beside his rabbinical duties, Dadon also began teaching Judaism and Holocaust studies at Zagreb University, the first time these subjects were taught there.

Mainstream Jewish community leaders, strenuously protesting the official recognition given to Bet Israel on the grounds that it violated Croatian law, hired another Orthodox rabbi, Zvi Eliezer Aloni. In June, Aloni was attacked on a Zagreb street by skinheads who pushed him to the ground while shouting, "Jews out," in German. Around the same time, the Jewish community reported receiving anonymous threatening letters.

The two Zagreb groups held separate celebrations to mark the 200th anniversary of the Jewish community in the city. The Israeli Philharmonic, directed by Zubin Mehta, performed a concert on May 31 to kick off a series of events marking the anniversary. The Croatian government announced it would fund the construction of a new Jewish center on the site of the city's former main synagogue, destroyed in World War II, but work was held up because of the conflict within Zagreb Jewry.

In September, the International Raoul Wallenberg Foundation (IRWF) presented President Stipe Mesic with its Raoul Wallenberg Award 2006. The presentation took place at Croatia's mission to the UN in New York, when Mesic was there to attend the General Assembly session.

In October, a new memorial and museum opened at the site of the infamous World War II Jasenovac death camp, where the Croatian fascist regime killed tens of thousands of Serbs, Jews, and others. President Mesic and Prime Minister Ivo Sanader took part in the ceremony. Even though plans for the new facility had been drawn up with the advice of the U.S. Holocaust Memorial Museum and Yad Vashem, the exhibits drew criticism from the Simon Wiesenthal Center's Efraim Zuroff, who said it did not tell the story of Croatia's wartime Ustasha regime in a clear enough way. Zuroff also pressed for the extradition from Austria of an alleged Croatian war criminal, Milivoj Asner.

Stjepan Steiner, a fighter with the World War II partisans who served as personal physician to the future Yugoslav leader, Marshal Tito, died in January at the age of 90. A cardiologist, he did volunteer work at the Jewish Old Age Home in Zagreb for 25 years. In December, Misha Montiljo, an activist in the Bet Israel Congregation and head of the Croatia-Israel Association, died in Zagreb at the age of 78.

Czech Republic

General elections in June left the Czech Parliament badly split with no clear winner, setting off months of political uncertainty. Mirek Topolanek, finally named prime minister in November at the head of a minority, single-party government, took until the end of December to cobble together a three-party center-right coalition that commanded a majority.

In October, an expert from the Tolerance and Civic Society organization said that neo-Nazism and other extreme right-wing manifestations in the Czech Republic had been relegated to the fringe of public discourse. Nevertheless, activities of neo-Nazi skinhead groups, especially concerts, went on through the year. In August, for example, police detained more than two dozen skinheads who staged a protest outside the Israeli embassy in Prague. There were also episodes of vandalism against Jewish sites. In October, for example, some 49 tombstones in the Jewish cemetery in Zamberk were toppled.

In December, in the wake of the Holocaust-denial conference in Iran, the Czech Senate passed a resolution condemning such denial, which "leads in its consequences to the rule of the lie, to the rejection of people's right to a dignified life, and to the installation of dictatorships and totalitarian regimes."

The Czech Republic enjoyed strong relations with Israel on many levels. In January, the Tivali company, a member of Israel's Osem Group, announced it would set up a $30-million plant near Teplice for the production of vegetarian food products, the company's first in Europe. Also in January, Israel extradited an Israeli citizen, Yakov Moshaylov, to the Czech Republic for trial. He was charged with throwing a grenade at a car owned by an Israeli casino owner in 2004. The attack, outside a casino in downtown Prague, left 18 people injured. In February, the Czech army announced the signing of a $120-million contract for equipment from the Israeli arms manufacturer Rafael.

In the war between Israel and Hezballah, Czech public opinion was generally behind Israel, but there were rallies in favor of both sides. In July, for example, about 200 demonstrators called on the Czech government to speak out against "Israeli aggression" and provide aid to Lebanon and the Palestinians. About 100 supporters of Israel staged a counterdemonstration.

The Czech government tried to help civilians, allocating about $1 million in aid to provide Israel with fire-fighting equipment and the Lebanese government with tents, food, and medicine. "People are suffering on both sides," Foreign Minister Cyril Svoboda told reporters. A number of Czech NGOs raised money to aid Lebanese civilians hit by Israeli strikes.

Czech Jews held a fund-raising campaign for Israeli victims. Some of the money went to help repair Israeli schools and medical facilities struck by Hezballah rockets and for children's recreational programs, and the rest enabled Israelis with disabilities as well as pregnant women and mothers with small children to spend time in the Czech Republic.

About 3,000 Jews were affiliated with Jewish organizations, communities, or institutions in the Czech Republic, though Jewish leaders believed that there were thousands more who were unaffiliated. Prague had the largest community, about 1,500 members. Orthodox, Reform, and Conservative congregations held services, but only a small minority of Prague Jews attended. The factional conflict that had split the Prague community over the previous two years (see AJYB 2006, p. 480) appeared to have settled down following communal elections at the end of 2005.

Brno had the second largest community, with about 600 members. In the fall, a new mikveh was opened in Brno and ground was broken in Prague for a new facility that would house a nursing home, a Jewish community center, and an assisted-living facility. It was expected to cost nearly $7 million.

During the High Holy Days, police put Prague's historic Jewish sites under tight security. The government explained that there had been a terrorist threat. According to news reports, it had involved a plot by Islamic extremists to kidnap Jews and blow up one of the city's synagogues.

In February, Prague hosted a forum on Jewish communal development attended by more than 30 leaders of Jewish organizations from 25 cities across Europe. In April, more than 100 Hasidim converged on the town of Mikulov to mark the 238th anniversary of the death of the Hasidic master Shmuel Shmelke Horowitz, who served as rabbi there and was buried in the historic Jewish cemetery.

This year marked the 100th anniversary of the founding of the Prague Jewish Museum. The occasion was marked by an unprecedented "Year of Jewish Culture" program that included more than 70 events throughout the country. Under the auspices of Parliament, the Ministry of Culture, and the mayor of Prague, the museum partnered with more than 80 other institutions to provide exhibitions, concerts, festivals, and lectures. Among the major exhibits were "The Prague Ghetto in Images" at the Prague City Museum; "Mazel Tov—Good Luck" at the Jewish Museum, focusing on the traditional Jewish wedding ceremony; and an exhibition at the Polish Institute in Prague of works by the artist Bruno Schulz. In August, the Jewish Museum hosted an exhibit, "Defying the Beast," on the museum's activities during the 1906–1940 period. A festival of Jewish culture took place in Mikulov in May.

There were also a number of Holocaust commemorative events. In May, American musicians under the leadership of Murry Sidlin, dean of music at the Catholic University of America, performed *Defiant Requiem,* based on Verdi's famous work, at Terezin, the former concentration camp north of Prague that was now a memorial museum. The performance was in honor of the Terezin prisoners who, in 1943, performed the *Requiem* under the direction of a fellow prisoner, Czech conductor Rafael Schaechter.

Terezin was the scene of a Council of Europe seminar on Holocaust education in April, attended by education ministers from some 30 European countries. Also in April, a Yom Hashoah commemoration was held in downtown Prague, where the names of Czech Jews killed in the Holocaust were read aloud. The ceremony was organized by the Terezin Initiative Institute and the Czech Association of Jewish Youth. In August, a Japanese peace group erected a "peace pole" monument at Terezin.

In October, archaeologists discovered several graves from what appeared to be a long-buried medieval Jewish cemetery outside Pilsen, at a site where an Israeli developer planned to build a shopping mall and parking lot. Lengthy discussions resulted in a compromise whereby the developer agreed to build on stilts so as to protect surviving graves.

There was progress in compensating and restituting Jewish Holocaust losses. In March, the Czech Foundation Fund for Holocaust Victims announced it had completed the process of compensating individual Holocaust victims, having paid out $4.23 million over the previous five years to 516 people. The $8 million remaining in the fund would be used to restore Jewish monuments and support cultural and educational projects. In November, the Czech-German Fund for the Future and the German foundation known as Remembrance, Responsibility and Future launched a project to provide health care and social programs for former prisoners of Nazi concentration camps, ghettos, and other prisons. In November, a new law waived the old deadline of December 31, 2006, for Jews to apply for the return of works of art that had been confiscated from their families during World War II, extending it indefinitely.

In April, Rudolf Slansky, Jr., son of the Jewish Czechoslovak communist leader who was executed after a show trial 1952, died at the age of 71. Slansky served as Czech ambassador to Moscow in the 1990s. In December, the Jewish community held an event in Prague to mark the 80th birthday of the celebrated writer and Auschwitz survivor Arnost Lustig, many of whose books dealt with the Holocaust.

Greece

A delegation from the European Jewish Congress took part in Greece's Holocaust Remembrance Day on January 27. The delegates also met with Prime Minister Kostas Karamanlis and President Karolos Papoulias, the latter telling his visitors that he was determined to combat all forms of historical revisionism and anti-Semitism. In August, Foreign Minister Dora Bakoyannis visited Israel as part of a tour of the Middle East. She met there with her Israeli counterpart, Tzipi Livni, and other senior officials.

In February, Israeli president Moshe Katzav visited Greece. This was the first visit ever by an Israeli head of state; it had taken until 1990 for Greece to grant Israel diplomatic recognition. During his stay, Katzav met with senior Greek officials in Athens and also visited Thessalonika — the historic Salonika, once home to 50,000 Jews and a major center of Jewry in the Balkans. Accompanied by President Papoulias, Katzav laid a wreath at a Holocaust memorial erected in 1997 and visited a museum dedicated to the history of Jews in the city that had opened in 2001. During Katzav's visit, Greek and Israeli representatives signed a cooperation agreement on industrial research and development.

In June, the Greek embassy in Washington organized the presentation, at the U.S. Capitol, of a book on the Holocaust in Greece. Legislators, diplomats, State Department officials, Jewish leaders, and members of the Greek American community attended the event. The book, *Holocaust of Greek Jewry: Monuments and Memories,* was published by the Central Board of Jewish Communities in Greece, with the support of the Greek Ministry of Education and the General Secretariat for Youth.

In May, more than 300 Jews in their twenties and thirties from the Balkans and the Black Sea region of the former Soviet Union met at a beach resort in northern Greece for a three-day gathering called Gesher (Bridge). Organized by the American Jewish Joint Distribution Committee (JDC), it combined social activities—including match-making—with workshops on religious, educational, and cultural issues.

Hungary

In the April general elections, Prime Minister Ferenc Gyurcsany, a socialist, became the first postcommunist Hungarian prime minister to win reelection, and he proceeded to introduce tough measures of economic reform. Violent protests broke out against his government in September after a secret tape surfaced, recorded on the day of the election, on which Gyurcsany was heard telling members of his party's inner circle that his government had "screwed up" and had lied to the country "morning, evening, and night" in order to get reelected.

Demonstrators demanding Gyurcsany's resignation attacked the studios of Hungarian Television. Hundreds were injured in clashes with police, and at least 200 rioters were arrested, many of them right-wing militants and soccer hooligans. They were heard to shout anti-Semitic slogans, and some displayed the red and white flag of Hungary's fascist, Nazi-allied, Arrow Cross movement that ruled during World War II. When the clashes were over as many as 40,000 demonstrators staged a peaceful protest outside the National Assembly, Hungary's parliament, demanding Gyurcsany's ouster. Jews in the capital stepped up security measures during the High Holy Days, but no incidents were reported.

The right-wing party Fidesz won sweeping victories in local elections on October 1. Later in the month another series of violent protests, led by right-wing extremists, disrupted ceremonies in Budapest marking the 50th anniversary of the abortive 1956 Hungarian uprising against the communist regime. As in the September protests, some of the demonstrators carried Nazi-era fascist flags.

Hungarian Jews remained vigilant about anti-Semitism. In November, the synagogue and other Jewish institutions in the town of Vac, north of Budapest, were vandalized and sprayed with anti-Semitic and anti-Israel slogans. That same month an Israeli medical student was assaulted verbally, and then physically, by a police inspector in the Budapest metro.

According to Israeli diplomats, the Hungarian media gave generally balanced coverage to the Israel-Hezballah war, showing the results of rocket attacks on Israel as well as the effects of Israel's attacks. In August, about 120 Israeli children affected by the war, including seven Druze, were brought to Hungary for a holiday. They spent two weeks at the Jewish camp run by the JDC-Lauder Foundation at Szarvas, in southern Hungary. In September, Israeli ambassador Judith Varnai Shorer completed her term and returned to Jerusalem.

At least 100,000 Jews lived in Hungary, the overwhelming majority in Budapest. The main Jewish stream was Neolog, the Hungarian version of Reform, but other congregations, including Orthodox, Conservative, and others, also functioned, and Chabad had a strong presence. Most Hungarian Jews, however, were secular or unaffiliated. Of the smaller Jewish communities in provincial towns, the one in the eastern city of Debrecen was particularly active, hosting an annual conference that drew Hungarian-speaking Jews from neighboring countries, including Romania, Serbia, Slovakia, and Ukraine. These conferences served as a reference point for many Jews in the region.

There were Jewish-themed cultural events and conferences throughout the year. In February, the Jewish monthly *Szombat* organized a two-day conference examining what it called new forms of anti-Semitism, including anti-Zionism and Holocaust denial. The ninth annual Jewish Culture Festival took place in Budapest at the end of August. That same month the fourth annual Conference of European Jewish Women, Activists, Academics, and Rabbis was held at Central European University, whose Jewish studies program also ran a regular lecture series. In November, the Balint Jewish Community Center in Budapest hosted a three-day educational conference called Keset.

Budapest's downtown seventh district, the city's historic Jewish quarter, continued to undergo a steady process of gentrification. Two new kosher eateries opened. Several cafés owned by young Jews functioned in or near the district, and these served as de facto meeting places for young Budapest Jews. The most ambitious of the new cafés, Siraly (meaning "seagull" and, in slang, "fantastic") opened in October, aiming to serve as both a standard café for the general public and as an informal Jewish cultural center. The only avowedly "Jewish" of the new cafés, run by the Masorti youth group Marom, had a mezuzah on the door and featured Jewish cultural and social events such as an eight-day Hanukkah festival that involved all the streams of Jewish life, from Orthodox to secular. It also hosted concerts, had a theater, and maintained a small Jewish library.

There were a number of Holocaust-related commemorations. Hungary marked its first Holocaust Memorial Day on January 27 with a ceremony in the National Assembly and other events. In February, a permanent exhibition was installed in Budapest's Holocaust Memorial Museum, which had opened in 2004.

In the spring, the Hungarian government initiated a Holocaust compensation program that provided survivors up to $1,800 for each immediate family member killed through the involvement of Hungarian collaborators. In September, the Simon Wiesenthal Center identified 92-year-old Sandor Kepiro as a convicted war criminal, found guilty immediately after the war of participating in an action in which thousands of people, including more than 1,200 Jews, were killed in Novi Sad, Serbia. He had fled to Argentina after his trial, however, and then returned to Hungary in 1996.

In September, at a ceremony in Budapest, the Catholic Church beatified Sara Salkahazi, a Hungarian nun killed by Hungarian fascists in 1944 for hiding Jews. In October, Hungarian officials placed a plaque at Pannonhalma Abbey to honor Eduard Benedek Brunschweiler, a Swiss representative of the Red Cross who protected about 3,000 people, including many Jews, at the abbey in 1944–45. On December 3, the Federation of Jewish Communities (MAZSIHISZ) presented its annual "For Jews in Hungary" award to Cardinal Peter Erdo for "strengthening dialogue between the Catholic Church and the Jewish community, and for preserving the memory of the Jews killed during the Holocaust and those who saved them." It was the first time the award had been presented to a representative of the Catholic Church. An award was also presented to Justice Ministry official Erika Planko for her role in aiding the Holocaust compensation process.

Jewish composer and Holocaust survivor Gyorgy Ligeti, who fled Hungary after the abortive 1956 revolution, died in Vienna in June, aged 83. Gyorgy Faludy, an influential poet and translator who fled the fascists in 1938 and later suffered under communist persecution, died at his home in Budapest in September, at the age of 95. In October, philosopher Gyorgy Bence died in Budapest, aged 65.

Macedonia

Only about 200 Jews lived in Macedonia, almost all of them in the capital, Skopje, where they formed a close-knit community that was known for its Mois Hason Choir, which performed a number of times on Macedonian TV, recorded a DVD in its studio, and also released other DVDs of live recordings from concert performances. The choir got excellent reviews from local critics. One of its performances took place on the European Day of Culture in September, at the National Theater in Skopje. Only a minority of the choir's members, however, were Jewish.

Construction of the new Holocaust museum and memorial proceeded throughout the year. The structure was up in December, but the interior and façade still needed work, and a planned exhibition was still in the design stage.

Poland

As the year began, the conservative Law and Justice party was in power, although it controlled only a minority of the parliamentary seats. Law and Justice was headed by Jaroslaw Kaczynski, whose twin brother, Lech, had been elected president in 2005. In July, after Kazimierz Marcinkiewicz resigned as prime minister, Lech Kaczynski named his brother Jaroslaw prime minister.

Both men, conservative Catholics, denounced anti-Semitism several times during the year in speeches and meetings. In May, President Kaczynski met with Poland's chief rabbi, American-born Michael Schudrich, after the latter was attacked on the street on the eve of Pope Benedict's visit to Poland (see below, p. 495). At that meeting Kaczynski pledged "zero tolerance" for anti-Semitism. Ewa Junczyk-Ziomecka, a former deputy director of the planned new Museum of the History of Polish Jews, served as a government minister—undersecretary in charge of social issues and the president's plenipotentiary for interreligious and intercultural dialogue, with an emphasis on Jewish-Polish relations.

In the spring, when it became clear that the minority government could not maintain itself, Law and Justice entered into a coalition with two extreme-right parties. One was the nationalist Catholic League of Polish Families (LPR), whose leader, Roman Giertych, was named education minister, and the other was Self Defense, whose leader, Andrej Lepper, became deputy prime minister.

Giertych and Lepper denied that they or their parties were anti-Semitic.

Giertych especially denounced anti-Semitism repeatedly and described himself in interviews as a friend of Israel and the Jewish people. However, both these parties and/or their leaders had histories of anti-Semitism. The LPR was the ideological heir to the anti-Semitic pre-World-War-II National Democracy (Endecja) party. Giertych's grandfather was a notorious anti-Semitic politician, and his father, Maciej, represented the LPR in the European Parliament. Roman Giertych was honorary chair of the LPR's far-right youth wing, All Polish Youth, whose members included skinheads, some of whom had been filmed giving the Nazi salute and chanting Nazi slogans.

In November, Maciej Giertych fired an assistant after a video of her giving the Nazi salute at an All Polish Youth gathering surfaced on the Internet and in the Polish media. The video also showed participants shouting "Sieg Heil," and gathering around a huge burning swastika. A few days after the video was made public, a leading newspaper ran photographs of the LPR's deputy chairman at a concert of neo-Nazi skinhead music in 2002. In November, the LPR said it was cutting ties with All Polish Youth over the incident.

Another problem was that the LPR was close to Radio Maryja, the Catholic broadcaster notorious for anti-Semitic content. In fact Radio Maryja was also a strong supporter of the Law and Justice party. Observers believed that the radio station's backing was a factor in the party's victory in the 2005 election. Both Kaczynski brothers appeared frequently on its programs.

Radio Maryja had been censured in the past for anti-Semitism, and its activities during 2006 continued to provoke controversy. In April, under strong pressure from the Catholic hierarchy, its founder and director, Father Tadeusz Rydzyk, publicly apologized for anti-Semitic remarks made by a Radio Maryja commentator in March, accusing Jews of using the Holocaust experience for financial gain. Poland, he said, was "being outmaneuvered by Judeans who are trying to force our government to pay extortion money disguised as compensation." Poland's nongovernmental Media Ethics Council condemned the broadcast.

Marek Edelman, the last surviving leader of the World War II Warsaw Ghetto uprising, denounced Radio Maryja and called for a government clampdown on it. The 87-year-old Edelman said, in an open letter published in the media, that "some of these broadcasts are no different from those in the Nazi newspaper, *Der Stürmer*." Later in the year, the commentator guilty of the offensive remark was hired by Polish state radio, a move that also drew protests.

Jewish leaders said that the entry of the two extreme-right parties into the government brought a jump in the number of anonymous threatening letters and cell-phone text messages they were receiving. During the summer, the European Parliament passed a resolution warning of a "general rise in racist, xenophobic, anti-Semitic, and homophobic intolerance" in Poland. The resolution sparked an angry reaction in Poland, as did a report issued by the Anti-Defamation League about rising anti-Semitism in the country. In August, during his first visit to EU headquarters in Brussels, the new prime minister, Jaroslaw Kaczynski, said that claims of growing anti-Semitism were a myth created by the media.

Polish police, collaborating with the FBI, announced in July that they had closed down a Polish-language neo-Nazi Web site that was hosted on a U.S.-based server. In October, customs officials seized a box of about 300 neo-Nazi music CDs sent from the U.S. That same month a bookstore located in a Warsaw church that was notorious for selling anti-Semitic publications closed down.

In November, a group of leading non-Jewish intellectuals, working with the Open Republic Association, an NGO, sued the anti-Semitic publisher Leszek Bubel, head of a right-wing fringe party, saying his anti-Semitic activities offended them as Poles. Some 700 other Poles, including many leading cultural and political figures, signed an open letter supporting the suit.

Pope Benedict XVI made a three-day visit in late May to Poland, homeland of his predecessor, John Paul II. During the trip, the German-born Benedict visited Auschwitz. In a speech at the site, he told how difficult it was for him, as a German, to stand there, and also reflected on how incompatible the evil in Auschwitz seemed to be with the existence of a loving God. "In a place like this, words fail; in the end, there can be only a dread silence," he said, "a silence which itself is a heartfelt cry to God: Why, Lord, did you remain silent?"

During the Auschwitz ceremony, Rabbi Schudrich said kaddish in the pope's presence, and Cantor Simcha Keller, from Lodz, chanted *El Male Rahamim,* the memorial prayer for the dead. Benedict also met with Auschwitz survivors. Afterward, some commentators faulted him for not specifically condemning the anti-Semitism that led to the Holocaust.

Several incidents just before the pope's visit to Poland marred the atmosphere somewhat. The day before Benedict visited Auschwitz, Rabbi Schudrich was assaulted as he came out of synagogue by a man who sprayed pepper spray at him, hit him, and shouted, "Poland for the Poles." Schudrich was unhurt, and the incident was condemned by President

Kaczynski and other officials. A week earlier, youths had shouted anti-Semitic slogans at Schudrich and other Jews. Several months later, a Warsaw court convicted Schudrich's assailant of an act of violence and racially motivated hate speech, but gave him a suspended sentence.

In May, Rev. Michal Czajkowski resigned as cochairman of the Polish Council of Christians and Jews after being accused—and apparently admitting—that he had been a spy for the communist government for more than 20 years. The revelations and resignation came as a heavy blow to Jews and others involved in interfaith dialogue. Czajkowski was one of the most vocal friends of the Jews among the Catholic clergy, and some feared that his downfall and the surrounding scandal could have negative repercussions on Jewish-Catholic relations.

There were a number of Holocaust commemorations during the year, including the annual March of the Living in April, which this year drew about 8,000 participants. In August, a ceremony marked the 62nd anniversary of the liquidation of the Lodz Ghetto. In July, a ceremony in Kielce marked the 60th anniversary of the July 4, 1946 pogrom carried out by a Polish mob on Jewish Holocaust survivors who had returned to the city, leaving 42 Jews dead. A large public monument to the pogrom was dedicated, a sculpture by the American artist Jack Sal. During the year several Poles were awarded the status of Righteous Gentiles by Yad Vashem for saving Jews during the Holocaust.

As usual, Auschwitz was a center of attention. Czech-born Auschwitz survivor Dina Babbitt, now living in California, pressed her claim to be given back seven portraits of Roma (Gypsies) that she had been forced to paint while a prisoner, and which were now part of the Auschwitz Museum. In a similar case, a French man sued to have the suitcase that his father, an Auschwitz victim, had brought with him to the camp. The suitcase had been loaned by the Auschwitz Museum to the Paris-based Foundation for the Remembrance of the Shoah as part of an exhibition, and the man discovered his father's name on it when he went to see the exhibition.

In July, UNESCO's World Heritage Committee agreed with Poland's proposal to change the official name of Auschwitz from "Auschwitz Concentration Camp" to "Former Nazi German Concentration and Death Camp Auschwitz-Birkenau." The formal name change was to be take place in 2007.

The Auschwitz Memorial and Museum got a new director in September, 34-year-old Piotr Cywinski, who announced plans to revamp and modernize the exhibits at the museum part of the former death camp in a way that would facilitate the education of young people about the Shoah. Some of the exhibits dated back more than half a century to the immediate postwar communist period. The International Auschwitz Council, in December, approved Cywinski's plans and also agreed to carry out preservation work.

Israel regarded Poland as one of its closest friends in Europe, and President Kaczynski said he regarded Poland in that role, too. The appointment of Giertych as education minister, however, caused some strain in relations. Israel's ambassador refused to speak with Giertych, whose ministry oversaw Holocaust education in Poland, and asked the president to shift programs for visiting Israeli students from the education ministry to the presidential office, a request that Kaczynski fulfilled. Israeli business investments in Poland amounted to about $2 billion, and the two countries had agreements for military and security cooperation.

President Kaczynski not only paid a three-day official visit to Israel (and the Palestinian Authority) in September, but also met with visiting Jewish groups during the year. While he was in Israel, Kaczynski said Poland was ready to help mediate Middle East peace talks. He also proposed that Irena Sendler, now 96, be nominated for a Nobel Peace Prize. Recognized as a Righteous Gentile in 1965, Sendler, during World War II, worked with Zegota, the Polish underground body that saved Jews. As head of its children's department, she helped smuggle 2,500 Jewish youngsters out of the Warsaw Ghetto.

In July, about 220 people staged a pro-Israel rally organized by the Baptist Church with the backing of several Jewish organizations. In August, the city of Lodz, at the initiative of its mayor, Jerzy Kropiwnicki, paid for 15 Israeli teenagers from the northern Israeli town of Nahariya, which had been hit hard by Hezballah rockets, to have a two-and-a-half-week vacation in Poland. October saw the launch of a Poland-Israel Youth Exchange Program organized by the Museum of Jewish History in Warsaw, which itself was only in the planning stage. In the first phase of the program, eight Polish students received scholarships to study for a semester at the Lowy School for Overseas Students at Tel Aviv University. It was anticipated that in the next phase Israeli students would be brought to Poland to study.

JEWISH COMMUNITY

Although only a few thousand people were formally affiliated with Jewish institutions or organizations, Rabbi Schudrich estimated that at least 20,000 Jews lived in Poland. There were two major Jewish organizations in the country. One was the Union of Jewish Religious Communities in Poland, an umbrella group for eight communities; Warsaw, with 500 members, was the largest. The other was the Cultural and Social Association of Jews in Poland, a secular body that also had a number of local branches. At the beginning of the year, Piotr Kadlcik was reelected president of both the Warsaw Jewish Community and the five-member executive of the Union of Jewish Religious Communities.

The year saw several important milestones in the postcommunist Jewish revival. Several new rabbis took up positions at the High Holy Days. Among them was Mati Pawlak, 29, who was believed to be the first local Jew to become a rabbi and serve in Poland in 40 years. Pawlak also became principal of Warsaw's Lauder-Morasha Jewish school, replacing longtime principal Helise Lieberman. An Israeli, Boaz Pash, became rabbi in Kraków, and Yitzhak Rapoport, a Swede, took up a rabbinical post in Wroclaw, Poland's second largest Jewish community. All three were Orthodox.

On Rosh Hashanah, Warsaw's Progressive (Reform) Jewish congregation, Beit Warszawa, got its first full-time rabbi, 58-year-old New Yorker Burt Schuman, who had previously served a congregation in Altoona, Pennsylvania. Beit Warszawa, which had about 200 members, made other strides during the year, instituting a Sunday school, lectures, Jewish-themed movie nights, informal social gatherings, and an eight-month conversion course. Beit Warszawa was now a reference point for Jews elsewhere in Poland who were seeking a non-Orthodox alternative, or hoping to form a Reform congregation in their city.

A number of new communal institutions were initiated in 20006. A small synagogue opened in Lublin, home to several dozen Jews, early in the year, in the huge building that once housed the prewar Yeshiva Hakhmei Lublin, which was returned to the Jewish community in 2004. In November, ground was broken in Kraków for what would be Poland's first modern Jewish community center, a $1.2-million facility next to the Tempel Synagogue. Funded by the JDC and World Jewish Relief of Great Britain, the center resulted from a visit in 2002 by Britain's Prince Charles. It was expected to provide welfare and medical services as well as cultural, religious, and educational programs.

On several occasions during the year Jewish worship came to long disused synagogues in towns where no Jews now lived. In June, a traditional Shabbat was held in the synagogue in Pinczow, now a Jewish museum. Services were followed by a kosher meal. In October, Shabbat prayers were held in a synagogue in the southeast city of Przemysl that the Nazis had used as a stable. These services opened a weekend dedicated to Polish-Jewish dialogue, and a conference called "Lost Nation: The Jews of Przemysl and the Polish Landscape." For Sukkot, a sukkah was built in Czestochowa, believed to be the first there since the Holocaust. It was put up and decorated by students from an art school, aided by Jewish students from other countries. About 300 people—including visiting Jews who traced their ancestry to Czestochowa—filled the sukkah for lunch.

On Hanukkah, the Warsaw Jewish community, for the first time, lit a public menorah in the square next to the synagogue. The Israeli ambassador and Warsaw's mayor took part in the ceremony, which was organized by five local Jewish organizations. Chabad, which had sponsored public menorah lightings in prior years, held its own lighting ceremony in front of the nearby Palace of Culture. President Kaczynski hosted yet a third candle-lighting ceremony at the presidential palace—another first. Among those present were Rabbi Schudrich and other Jewish leaders, Israeli ambassador David Peleg, and visiting officials from the European Jewish Congress.

There were numerous cultural, educational, and commemorative events throughout the year. The two largest were the annual Festival of Jewish Culture in Kraków and another dedicated to the Yiddish world of Isaac Bashevis Singer that was held in Warsaw in the fall. There were also two Jewish film festivals in Warsaw, as well as a conference on Yiddish language and culture held at Warsaw's Jewish Historical Institute.

Work continued on the planned Museum of the History of Polish Jews, due to open in Warsaw in 2008 or 2009. In September, a tent was erected on the proposed site for a preview of exhibitions and staged educational events. During the year, the Foundation for the Preservation of Jewish Heritage in Poland oversaw the restoration and fencing off of a number of Jewish cemeteries around Poland. Holocaust memorials were erected in some of them.

In March, two teachers—Norman Conard of Fort Scott, Kansas, and Robert Szuchta of Warsaw—received the first annual Irena Sendler Awards, to be given annually to an American and Polish educator who exemplified the teaching of respect for all people, in the spirit of Irena Sendler (see above, p. 000). At the end of December, Brandeis professor Antony Polonsky was awarded the Kraków-based Judaica Foundation's annual Felek Award.

A number of important Polish figures passed away during 2006. Historian Jozef A. Gierowski died in Kraków in February at the age of 83.

He was the founding director of the Research Center on Jewish History and Culture in Poland at Kraków's Jagiellonian University, which, established in 1986, was the first such university Jewish studies institute in postwar Poland. Science-fiction writer Stanislaw Lem, author of *Solaris* and many other works, died in Kraków in March at the age of 84. Born in 1921 in L'viv, which was then part of Poland, Lem survived the Holocaust thanks to forged documents. The Polish poet and essayist Jerzy Ficowski died in Warsaw in May at the age of 82. Not himself Jewish, he composed powerful poems about the Holocaust and its impact on Poland, wrote extensively about Roma (Gypsies), and was a leading expert on the life and work of the Polish Jewish writer and artist Bruno Schulz, who was killed in the Holocaust.

Romania

In April, President Traian Basescu signed into law an emergency ordinance banning organizations and symbols with a fascist, racist, or xenophobic character.

Relations with Israel were strong. Numerous Israeli companies did business in Romania. In March, the two countries signed a military cooperation agreement and pledged to work together to fight terrorism. With Romania slated to join the European Union in January 2007, hundreds of Israelis of Romanian origin applied for citizenship. An estimated 400,000 Romanian Jews came to Israel after World War II.

Between 6,000 and 10,000 Jews lived in Romania, about half them in the capital, Bucharest. Romanian Jewish leaders took part in a variety of international meetings. In May, the executive of the European Jewish Congress met in Bucharest, where the EJC leaders met with Romanian government officials and told them they backed Romania's entry into the European Union. They also urged the government to help make sure that Romania's estimated 800 Jewish cemeteries received proper care.

Also in May, B'nai Brith Romania, in cooperation with B'nai Brith Europe, hosted an international seminar in the Romanian capital. Representatives from 12 countries attended the meeting, whose main theme was how to fight anti-Semitism. That same month, more than 80 young Jews from Romania took part in the Balkan Black Sea Gesher meeting in Greece; several Romanians were on the organizing committee.

At the end of May, Romanian representatives took part in the Eighth International Conference of Regional Jewish Communities, held in Debrecen, Hungary. During the meeting, Aurel Vajner, the president of FE-

DROM, the umbrella organization of the Romanian Jewish communities, worked out a cooperation agreement with the Union of Jewish Communities in Hungary. In August, a 14-member Romanian delegation took part in a solidarity mission to Israel organized by the World Zionist Organization. The group included actress Maya Morgenstern as well as members of the media.

OTER, the Romanian Jewish Youth organization, which maintained a number of chapters around the country, held seminars, conferences, and training sessions for young people throughout the year. In July, more than 40 young people came together in Arad, where they learned about volunteerism and helped clean up a Jewish cemetery.

There were numerous Jewish cultural events. The Jewish State Theater in Bucharest staged a range of performances, including a musical version of the story of Esther. An Israeli film festival took place in Bucharest, March 29–April 2. The Minister of Culture and Religions hosted an all-day conference in April to discuss plans for an "itinerary of Hasidic culture" in Romania. Among the seminars and conferences that took place was "Elie Wiesel's World — Yesterday and Today," which took place during the spring in several Transylvanian cities. In January, after a break of several years, FEDROM reinstituted the awarding of annual prizes to leading Jewish cultural figures. This year it distributed 11 awards.

Many books on Jewish themes and by Jewish authors were published, including some by the Jewish publishing house HaSefer, most notably a Romanian translation of the book *Judaism* by German theologian Hans Küng, which was launched with a lecture delivered by Küng in April. Among other new books was a volume on synagogue history and architecture by Mircea Moldovan. Several Jewish communities held events on the European Day of Jewish Culture, September 3.

There were events commemorating the Holocaust in Romania. In January, a ceremony at Bucharest's main Choral Synagogue marked the 65th anniversary of the violent January 1941 pogrom, carried out by members of the fascist Iron Guard, which left dozens dead and portended the broader Romanian tragedy that was to come. Further ceremonies at the end of June, including an international conference, commemorated the 65th anniversary of the 1941 pogrom in Iasi that left at least 10,000 dead.

Romania marked its third annual Holocaust Memorial Day on October 9 with events around the country. In Bucharest, President Basescu laid the cornerstone for a national Holocaust memorial. In his speech, Basescu expressed concern at the lack of awareness about the Holocaust in Romania despite recent attempts at education. "Finding out the reality did not solve the problem of national conscience regarding the crimes committed by state authorities," he said. "It is a difficult process which requires a change of mentality and the ability to accept reality."

Holocaust education indeed received high priority. Romania, during 2006, was a member of the Task Force for International Cooperation on Holocaust Education, Remembrance, and Research. In the spring, Peninah Zilberman, a former director of the Holocaust Education and Memorial Center of Toronto, held seminars on the subject for teachers in two major cities: in Bucharest she held a session for 58 teachers at the Goren-Goldstein Hebrew Studies Center, and in the Transylvanian city of Cluj she lectured to 30 teachers at Babes-Bolyai University. In December, the Foreign Ministry expressed "deep concern" at the Holocaust-denial conference held in Tehran, and said that attempts to question the Holocaust were "unacceptable."

In July, Alexandre Safran, who became the youngest-ever chief rabbi of Romania in 1940 and served until ousted and expelled by the communist regime in 1947, died in Geneva at the age of 96. He had served as Geneva's chief rabbi from 1948. The author of numerous books on Jewish philosophy and mysticism, Safran also published his memoirs, which described what happened to the Jewish community of Romania during the Holocaust, his rescue efforts during World War II, and his attempts to rebuild the community after the war.

In September, Silviu Brucan, who went from being a communist loyalist to one of the most outspoken critics of dictator Nicolae Ceausescu, died in Bucharest at the age of 90. Brucan's birth name was Saul Bruckner, and he suffered discrimination as a Jew in prewar Romania. In September, Zvi Feine, the JDC country director for Romania for more than a decade, completed his tenure, and was replaced by Jorge Diener, who also headed JDC operations in Hungary and Bulgaria. In November, the Romanian-born Jewish author Norman Manea won France's Medicis Prize for the best non-French book of the year, for his memoir *Hooligan's Run,* which described Manea's return to Romania after the fall of communism.

Serbia

In March, former Serbian and Yugoslav president Slobodan Milosevic died in his cell in The Hague, where he had spent more than four years on trial for war crimes during the Balkan wars of the 1990s. He was 64.

Serbian foreign minister Vuk Draskovic made a three-day official visit to Israel in November. According to knowledgeable observers, one goal of his trip was to win Israeli support for Serbia's drive to maintain control over the strife-torn Kosovo province. In an interview with the *Jerusalem Post,* Draskovic compared Serbia and Israel. "Many newspapers are writing that Israel is terrorist No. 1 in the Middle East [and] that Serbia is terrorist No. 1 in the Balkans. We're not. This is the wrong perception of us—both of us," he said, "We have to support each other." He told the *Post* that the main obstacle to peace in the Middle East was the "stubborn refusal" of certain Arab countries and organizations to recognize Israel's right to exist. Draskovic met with top Israeli officials, and the two countries signed accords easing certain visa restrictions and pledging bilateral cooperation.

Serbian Jewish leaders expressed concern about anti-Semitic and neo-Nazi activities during the year, including the public availability of anti-Jewish publications. In January, 18 alleged neo-Nazis were arrested in Novi Sad and charged with having, in November 2005, disrupted a commemoration of the 1938 Kristallnacht pogroms, and 15 of them were later sentenced to up to a year in prison. The next month anti-Semitic slogans were found scrawled on the fence of a memorial in Nis, near the spot where more than 1,000 were killed during World War II. Skinheads, chanting "Auschwitz, Auschwitz," beat up two Israelis at a rock concert in Belgrade in August; two suspects were arrested.

The Serbian Jewish community issued a statement afterward warning of an increase in such incidents. Serbian president Boris Tadic denounced the attack and called for "the identification of all ultra-right and ultra-nationalist organizations in Serbia." Zarko Korac, a former deputy prime minister, told B92 Radio: "For a long time we lied to ourselves that there is no anti-Semitism in Serbia. Our society will have to sober up and realize that the fact the vast majority of people are not anti-Semitic does not mean there aren't these very aggressive anti-Semitic groups in the society itself."

The state television network broadcast an hour-long program in April called "Serbs and Jews, a Synagogue in the Backyard," which explored the history of Jews in Serbia and relations between Jews and mainstream Serbian society.

Holocaust Memorial Day, January 27, was marked by a number of ceremonies. In Belgrade, Prime Minister Vojislav Kostunica spoke at the dedication of a commemorative plaque and memorial park at Topovske supe, the site of a World War II concentration camp for Jews and Roma. In September, Jelenka and Ljubica Stamenkovic, from a village southeast of Belgrade, were posthumously named Righteous Gentiles; the award was presented to their daughter. This brought the number of Serbian designees to 128.

The Serbian Jewish community, strapped for cash, attempted to cut expenditures and cultivate new sources of income. One potential new source emerged with new government legislation that authorized restitution for property seized from churches and religious communities. But Jewish leaders failed in their efforts to have the law cover property seized as of April 6, 1941, the day the Nazis attacked Yugoslavia (researchers had drawn up a list of some 600 properties owned by Jewish communities and associations at that time), and so only communist-seized property was covered.

In its original form the statute stipulated that restitution claims could be made over the course of two years beginning October 1, 2006, but the starting date was delayed. In June, the JDC organized a seminar on property restitution, attended by representatives of Jewish communities from throughout the former Yugoslavia. It included sessions on how to apply for restitution as well as how to manage properties.

There were squabbles and infighting in some local communities. Early in the year a "Federation of Pancevo Jews" was established in the town of Pancevo, near Belgrade, apparently as a rival to the recognized Pancevo Jewish community, with the aim of obtaining restituted property. In Zemun, a Belgrade suburb with a Jewish community, an investigation was launched into how part of the Jewish cemetery became the private property of a community member, who built a new building on the land and sold it for commercial purposes.

There were numerous cultural, educational, and commemorative events throughout the year. Israel Independence Day was celebrated in Belgrade with a concert featuring the Israeli pop star Rita, accompanied by the Belgrade Philharmonic Orchestra. In May, the Jewish community and city officials in Novi Sad celebrated the 100th anniversary of the groundbreaking for the city's Great Synagogue, which was designed by the prolific Budapest architect Lipot Baumhorn. Numerous dignitaries took part, Cantor Laszlo Fekete from Budapest sang, and there were performances by a choir and an Israeli dance troupe. The 80th anniversary of the synagogue in Belgrade was also marked during 2006.

In June, Jewish young people from all over the former Yugoslavia took part in a program in Nis called Menuha. They worked to clear and make accessible part of the historic Jewish cemetery there and to create a database of information about the graves. All ten Jewish communities in Serbia held events for the European Day of Jewish Culture in September. The community in Zemun, for example, held an exhibition about its revitalization over the past six years.

David Albahari's book *Mamac* won the Most Berlin Award, given in Germany every other year to a "significant contemporary work of literature from Central and Eastern Europe and its translation." Albahari and another Jew, theater director Egon Savin, were among those presented with the City of Belgrade 2005 Award.

Slovakia

The extreme right-wing Slovak National Party (SNS) made big gains in the general elections held in June, winning 11.7 percent of the vote and becoming the third largest party in the country. Led by Jan Slota, the SNS was known for xenophobic and ultra-nationalist stands. The SNS was invited into the ruling coalition by the left-wing SMER party, led by Robert Fico, which won the elections. Also invited was the small right-wing party LS-HZDS, led by former prime minister Vladimir Meciar. In March, before the elections, the Supreme Court banned the neofascist Slovak Community-National Party, which had first registered to participate in elections in 2005.

About 3,000 Jews lived in Slovakia. The two biggest communities were in Bratislava, the capital, and Košice. Jewish communities around the country were linked under the umbrella Central Union of Jewish Religious Communities, based in Bratislava. Events for the European Day of Jewish Culture, held in Bratislava, Košice, and Komarno, attracted several hundred people. In the spring, B'nai Brith Europe launched a two-year program in Bratislava to foster Jewish adult education, particularly for currently unaffiliated Jews. Called Makor, it was sponsored by the German government's Holocaust fund.

More than 170 Slovak Jews competed in the winter Maccabee games that marked the 70th anniversary of the last European winter Maccabee games. This year's competitive events took place in Slovakia, on the very same ski slopes as those of 1936.

In January, the Israeli embassy in Bratislava recognized seven Slovaks as Righteous Gentiles. The only one of the seven who was still alive could not attend due to health reasons.

Slovenia

Israel and Slovenia had extensive and fast-growing economic relations. In February, following a hi-tech forum of Slovenian and Israeli companies held in the Slovene capital, Ljubljana, it was announced that Israel would open a full-scale embassy in the city. Since 1992, when diplomatic relations had been established, they had been handled from the Israeli embassy in Vienna. In March, President Janez Drnovsek made his first visit to Israel, where he met with President Moshe Katzav and other officials. He told Katzav that Slovenians "feel deeply for the people of Israel, whose achievements we have followed with admiration."

Between 200 and 600 Jews were believed to live in Slovenia, of whom 150 were affiliated with the Jewish community. In the fall, Andrej Kozar Beck was reelected to a third term as head of the community.

RUTH ELLEN GRUBER

Former Soviet Union

National Affairs

I N 2006, high energy prices enabled the Russian Federation, with its growing, energy-based economy, to pay off most of its outstanding debt and retain much of its political and economic influence regionally and internationally, further spurring Russia's ambition to dominate the area that had been the Soviet Union.

Russia's position as the leading energy supplier for many of the former Soviet republics and for some European countries, coupled with Moscow's ambition to reestablish itself as the only power center in the area, resulted in a series of conflicts throughout the year with its neighbors and trading partners, from the Russian-Ukrainian gas war in January, to Russia's standoff with Georgia in the fall, to the reevaluations undertaken of the major oil- and gas-production sharing agreements with Western companies. These episodes raised questions about Russia's role in the region and its reliability as a trading partner. The G8 summit in July, hosted by Russia for the first time, focused on energy security, and the topic returned to the forefront of discussion at the Russia-EU summit in November.

Domestically, President Vladimir Putin's "managed democracy" was believed to enjoy the support of most Russians. Indeed, many hoped Putin would stay in power past the end of his second term in 2008, although the president himself repeatedly denied any such ambition. Under Putin, only a decorative role was left for traditional democratic institutions such as political parties, parliament, or elections. Nearly unlimited resources — both political and economic — were concentrated in the hands of a few small and powerful groups within the Kremlin administration. The regime's clear intention was to sideline political dissent, increase the influence of the few large parties — all of which were clearly pro-Kremlin — and negate the protest vote in the parliamentary elections due in December 2007 and the presidential vote scheduled for spring 2008.

Among the most troubling developments of 2006 were the systematic efforts to weaken or eliminate pro-democracy forces by putting pressure on groups that monitored human rights and on media outlets that advocated for the expansion of democratic freedoms. The Kremlin tightene its oversight on nongovernmental organizations (NGOs) by insisting that all NGOs reregister with the authorities in accordance with legislation drafted in 2005 (see AJYB 2006, p. 514).

The tendencies of the current regime appeared even more ominous against the backdrop of pervasive corruption and lack of government transparency, increased activity by extremist fringe groups, and a series of murders that seemed politically motivated. The most shocking of these was the killing of a prominent political investigative journalist, Anna Politkovskaya, whose work had been instrumental in exposing human-rights abuses committed by Russian forces during the conflict with the separatists in Chechnya.

The Russian system served as a model for other authoritarian-minded regimes in the former Soviet Union. Campaigns to stifle civil society and dry up potential sources of democratic activism remained central components of domestic policy in Belarus, Uzbekistan, and Turkmenistan, three countries whose human-rights records were among the worst in the world, and which seemed determined to crush all political opposition and independent media. In Azerbaijan, the regime increased its already tight grip on the media, and Kyrgyzstan too saw a decline in civil and religious freedoms.

Outside the three Baltic states, which were now full-fledged members of the European Union, the only FSU countries that seemed to have progressed on the road toward democratization were Ukraine and Georgia, both of which had seen bloodless regime changes in 2004 (see AJYB 2005, pp. 500–01). But Ukrainian democracy was tarnished by continuing corruption and an economic downturn, creating widespread disillusionment with the results of the Orange Revolution that had propelled President Viktor Yushchenko to power. In the Ukrainian elections, held in March, a record 45 different political parties and blocs competed for parliamentary seats. No clear winner emerged, resulting in a political stalemate and difficulty in forming a governing coalition.

Belarus also conducted a national election in March. President Alexander Lukashenko, a former Soviet collective-farm manager, was reelected for a third term in what most observers described as an undemocratic and obviously rigged vote.

Israel and the Middle East

The first of several points of tension in Russian-Israeli relations during the year occurred after the electoral victory of Hamas in the Palestinian elections, held in January. Although Western nations refused to deal with a Hamas-led government that did not recognize Israel's right to exist, Moscow hosted a top-level Hamas delegation in March for talks with Foreign Minister Sergei Lavrov. They reportedly discussed prospects for Russian economic and political support for the Palestinian Authority. Not only Israel but also a number of Russian Jewish leaders publicly denounced the invitation to a group responsible for multiple attacks against Israeli civilians.

Israel's war against Hezballah during the summer also threatened bilateral relations. The Russian government criticized Israeli military operations in Lebanon as well as in Gaza, and sent humanitarian aid to Lebanese civilians affected by Israeli attacks. Russian Jews believed that such aid should also have been sent to Israelis living near the northern border, especially since many of them had come from Russia. In July, there were two small pro-Israel rallies in Moscow, as well as larger rallies in Kiev and Dneporopetrovsk in Ukraine, both attended by 1,500–2,000 people.

Yet a third bone of diplomatic contention was Russia's assistance to Iran. Moscow, which had significant economic interests in that country, not only continued to supply Tehran with sophisticated conventional weapons, but also provided expertise and technology to help the Iranians develop a nuclear capacity. Russia played a key role in the construction of Iran's first industrial-scale nuclear reactor, in Bushehr.

As Iranian president Ahmadinejad had repeatedly threatened to wipe Israel off the map, the prospect of a nuclear Iran raised serious concern there. This was, indeed, the major item on the agenda when Israeli prime minister Ehud Olmert arrived in Moscow in October for talks with Russian leaders, his first trip abroad after the war in Lebanon. The ostensible occasion for the visit was the 15th anniversary of the reestablishment of diplomatic relations between Russia and Israel following the breakup of the Soviet Union. Putin said that in recent years ties between Israel and Russia had been "completely transformed" and were now based on a greater degree of mutual trust. He sought to assuage Olmert's anxieties about Iran by insisting that its nuclear program did not threaten peace and security in the Middle East.

Indeed, late in the year Russia showed a greater readiness to cooperate with the international community on steps to place Iran's nuclear program under UN supervision. But Russia stopped short of large-scale economic sanctions for fear of hurting Russian companies working in Iran. Most observers agreed, however, that the key factor in Russian policy toward Iran was a desire to counterbalance what it saw as a pro-Israel tilt in U.S. policy in the region.

Ukrainian president Yushchenko canceled a planned visit to Israel in June for reasons that were left unexplained. He had similarly scheduled and then canceled a trip there in 2005. Some speculated that Ukraine feared jeopardizing its relations with Iran and other Muslim countries, which were some of its best trading partners. Israeli president Moshe Katzav visited Kiev in September to participate in commemorative events marking the 65th anniversary of the Babi Yar massacre.

In February, when a delegation of the Conference of Presidents of Major American Jewish Organizations visited Azerbaijan, officials told the Americans that the country would soon upgrade its diplomatic relations with Israel and open a trade mission there. Azerbaijan, a Muslim state in the Caucasus, had begun diplomatic relations with Israel more than ten years before, but had yet to open an embassy in the country; Israel, in contrast, had an embassy in Baku. As 2006 ended, the status quo remained in place. Azerbaijan had long cited its complicated geopolitical situation, particularly its proximity to Iran, as well as its membership in Islamic international organizations as factors making it difficult to upgrade relations with Israel.

Anti-Semitism and Extremism

Since the collapse of the USSR there had been no instances of official governmental anti-Semitism to speak of in any of the former Soviet republics, with the exception of Turkmenistan. Nevertheless, officials in most of the countries occasionally exhibited anti-Jewish attitudes, and anti-Semitic acts by hooligans and extremist groups remained frequent across the FSU.

In 2006, anti-Semitism and xenophobia were still ongoing concerns for Jewish and human-right groups in most countries of the former FSU. The largest number of anti-Semitic incidents occurred in Russia, which witnessed a 20-percent increase over 2005, and Ukraine, where there was a slight decline from the previous year. These two countries also produced many thousands of pieces of anti-Semitic literature, and such ideas were spread even further through multiple Internet sites and blogs.

RUSSIA

According to the Moscow Bureau on Human Rights (MBHR), there were 170 violent attacks on individuals in Russia during 2006 that were motivated by racial, ethnic or religious hatred, in which 51 individuals were killed and 310 injured. Russia's two largest cities, Moscow and St. Petersburg, accounted for more than half these attacks. Most of the victims were people from the Caucasus, Africans, and Asians. Nine Jews were injured. Russian courts found 109 individuals guilty of hate crimes in 2006. According to MBHR, there were some 50,000 neo-Nazi skinheads in Russia, 80 percent of them under the age of 30.

The year's first anti-Semitic incident, and the only one that resulted in injuries, occurred on January 11, when a knife-wielding man stabbed and injured nine men at a Moscow synagogue. The culprit, Alexander Koptsev, 21, said at his trial that he had been inspired by books and Web sites. Koptsev was found guilty in September of attempted murder on racial grounds and of inciting religious hatred. He was given a sentence of 16 years in prison and ordered to undergo psychiatric treatment. Russia's Supreme Court upheld the verdict in December.

Two days later, another young man attempted an attack on synagogue worshipers in the southern Russian city of Rostov-on-Don. In June, the perpetrator, identified as Vadim Domnitsky, 19, was found mentally unfit to stand trial, the court ruling that he must undergo coercive medical treatment in a special hospital.

In February, vandals spray-painted the words "Death to Yids" on the walls of the Hasdei Yerushalayim Jewish charitable center and on the local offices of the Jewish Agency for Israel in Saratov, in central Russia. Ten days later, a swastika was spray-painted on the entrance doors of the same charitable center.

In April, a group of young men, suspected of belonging to a local neo-Nazi skinhead gang, attempted to break into a synagogue in Orenburg, southeast of Moscow. They shattered several windows, shouted anti-Semitic slogans, and painted swastikas on the building, but no one was hurt. Police detained one of the attackers, aged 15.

On the eve of Rosh Hashanah in September, two Russian synagogues were vandalized in separate incidents. Unidentified attackers shattered windows at the synagogue in Astrakhan, southern Russian, and set a door ablaze at the one in Khabarovks, in the far east of the country. No one was hurt in either incident.

In Tver, central Russia, 173 Jewish and Muslim gravestones were desecrated in October. Many were toppled and others spray-painted with swastikas, and leaflets with Nazi symbols were scattered over the graves. This was believed to be the most extensive act of cemetery vandalism in Russia in recent years. A week after the incident, police detained sever members of a banned radical nationalist group suspected of the atta

Also in October, swastikas and anti-Semitic slogans were painted on the walls of the synagogue in Vladivostok.

Two Molotov cocktails were thrown through the windows of a Jewish cultural center in Surgut, Siberia, in November. No one was hurt. Following this incident, the fourth attack on a Jewish facility in Russia in less than two months, the Chabad-led Federation of Jewish Communities, Russia's largest Jewish group, called on the authorities to beef up security at Jewish sites across the country. But not long after, on November 26, unidentified people stormed into Ohr Avner, a Jewish day school in Volgograd, in southern Russia, severely injuring security guards, one of whom lost an eye.

Hanukkah services, in December, were disrupted at a synagogue in Pskov, in northwest Russia, when someone threw a gas canister into the Jewish community center. Worshipers were sickened by the gas and had to leave the service. That same month, a Jewish community center in Ulyanovsk, in the Volga region, was vandalized. Attackers shattered a window and painted a swastika on the wall. A leaflet with threats against the Jewish community was later discovered posted on the building's door. Also in December, a court in the far east of Russia sentenced two teenagers to prison, one for ten years and the other for nine-and-a-half, for the racially-motivated murder of three men of non-Slavic origin, including one Jew.

Human-rights activists and leaders of minority groups had long criticized Russian police and prosecutors for playing down the incidence of hate crimes, and Russian courts for their reluctance to treat crimes motivated by racism and religious hatred in that category. A report by Amnesty International called on the Russian government to establish a plan of action to curtail a rising trend of xenophobic attacks.

There seemed some willingness to take steps in that direction. In February, 12 Russian political parties signed an Anti-Fascist Pact against nationalism, extremism, and xenophobia. It was spearheaded by the pro-Kremlin party United Russia, but among its supporters were also moderate nationalist parties and the leading liberal opposition bloc. The signatories declared nationalism and xenophobia threats to the integrity of the state, and declared: "The activity of all responsible political parties should be aimed at the consolidation of the society and strengthening of the country's unity."

Later in the year there were more signs of progress. In September, the Prosecutor General's Office announced it was setting up a special department to deal with hate crimes. President Putin said, in October, that the "justice system and law enforcement agencies should adequately and promptly respond to manifestations of xenophobia and extremism." And authorities in both Moscow and St. Petersburg banned the so-called Russian March, a street demonstration planned by several ultranationalist groups for November 4, Unity Day, a national holiday in Russia. In 2005, Moscow came under fierce criticism for allowing the march in which thousands of nationalists participated, many sporting Nazi insignia and shouting, "Heil Hitler."

UKRAINE

The major source of anti-Semitism and anti-Zionism in Ukraine remained the Interregional Academy for Personnel Management (MAUP), a private university in Kiev that for years had been publishing periodicals and running academic conferences that defamed Jews and Israel. The Jewish community was particularly alarmed when MAUP, in February, held a commemoration for the Christian boy whose death, 95 years earlier, had led to the infamous Beilis case, in which a Jew was accused of ritual murder. In May, MAUP held a "Dialogue of Civilizations" conference in Kiev, where several speakers delivered anti-Semitic invective; in October, MAUP hosted a book-signing event for David Duke, the American white supremacist who held an honorary doctorate from the university; and at another MAUP conference, in November, "Jewish Bolsheviks" were blamed for organizing the Soviet-era famine in Ukraine.

While President Yushchenko and other government officials condemned MAUP on several occasions and the Ministry of Education revoked the accreditation of several MAUP branches in the provinces on technical grounds, Jewish leaders believed the authorities were not doing enough to combat anti-Semitism, particularly in the MAUP publications.

The Conservative Party of Ukraine, affiliated with MAUP leaders, sought to run candidates in the parliamentary elections, scheduled for March. Despite multiple protests from Jewish and human-rights leaders, the government allowed the ultranationalist party to compete. Headed by MAUP president Georgy Schokin, the party received less than 1 percent of the vote. Nevertheless, an opinion poll conducted in October by the Kiev International Institute of Sociology gave cause for worry. Surveying the attitudes of 2,000 people in 24 regions of the country, it found that 36 percent of Ukrainians did not believe Jews should be citizens, up from 26 percent in 1994. Such sentiments were especially widespread among younger respondents.

In addition to several attacks on individual Jews—most of them directed against people wearing distinctive Orthodox Jewish garb—threats and harassment were common occurrences. In February, Friday evening services at Kiev's Central Brodsky Synagogue were disturbed by an intruder shouting anti-Semitic threats, and in Kerch, in southern Ukraine, a man burst into the Gesher Reform Synagogue and threatened to kill Jews. Also that month, a Holocaust monument in the town of Feodosia was daubed with paint and anti-Semitic graffiti. Another Holocaust memorial, in Sevastopol, was smeared with black paint, swastikas, and graffiti in February, and was vandalized once again in June. Stones were hurled at the Choral Synagogue in downtown Kirovograd in April, a scenario that would recur four more times during the year at the same synagogue, according to local Jewish leaders. And in May, the Ner Tamid Synagogue in Simferopol was the target of stone-throwing.

A yeshiva student, Azariy Menaker, was assaulted in a Kiev subway station in March, but was able to shoot at the three attackers with his pneumatic gun, causing them to flee. They were later detained by the police. Another attack occurred in April, when Vladimir Katzman, the Jewish editor of the popular Kiev weekly *Stolichnye Novosti,* was severely beaten at the entrance to his apartment house in what one Ukrainian Jewish leader said could have been retaliation for the paper's articles against anti-Semitism. That same month, Haim Gorbov, an Orthodox Jew, was stabbed on a street in Dnepropertovsk.

The situation was now so dangerous that the 40 Chabad rabbis working in Ukraine held a conference about the problem on May 15. They issued a call to the authorities to take steps to ensure the safety of Jews in the country and to adopt legislation against anti-Semitism, xenophobia, and intolerance.

But the pattern of disturbing incidents continued. In September, an Orthodox Jewish man wearing traditional garb, Haim Weitzman, was beaten in Odessa, sustaining minor injuries, and unknown vandals threw stones at the synagogue in Chernovtsy, in southwestern Ukraine. In October, 18 tombstones were destroyed in a Jewish cemetery in Gluhov, in the Sumy region of central Ukraine. And in December, three Orthodox Jews were attacked not far from Kiev's main synagogue—an Israeli teacher named Elhanan Shershevsky, another Israeli, and a Ukrainian—all of them wearing traditional Orthodox garb. Shershevsky suffered injuries and a concussion, but the other two were able to escape and call police.

BELARUS

In Belarus, Jewish leaders not only criticized the government for turning a blind eye to anti-Semitism, but also chafed under the country's restrictive law imposing limitations on religious activities by minority faiths, including Judaism.

In January, a line of kosher bread introduced by a local bakery generated a string of anti-Semitic newspaper articles. An editorial in the *Mogilev Register,* a local daily, warned those of the Russian Orthodox faith not to buy kosher bread on the grounds that blood of sacrificed animals was used in baking it. Another daily, the *Evening Mogilev,* cited Orthodox Christian sources to the effect that part of the cost of all kosher products was a tax that benefited local synagogues, and that kosher food, produced in a "sacrilegious and anti-Christian" manner, should not be bought by Christians.

In June, a request from the local education department and a warning from the public prosecutor compelled a Jewish school in Mogilev to remove Jewish symbols, such as menorahs and Stars of David, from classrooms. They were deemed to violate the country's regulations prohibiting the use of public space for religious instruction.

Several acts of anti-Jewish vandalism took place in November. On November 12, a swastika was daubed on the Holocaust memorial in Minsk, known as the Yama (Pit). Found at the site were anti-Semitic leaflets signed by the White Rus Front for Aryan Resistance, a previously unknown group. A nearby sculpture depicting Jews marching to an execution site was smeared with white paint. The same day, swastikas and the words "Beat the Yids!" were discovered on the façade of a building in central Minsk that housed the Israeli Cultural and Information Center, which was affiliated with the Israeli embassy.

Later in the month an explosive device went off at the Holocaust memorial in Brest, in the western part of Belarus, causing minor damage. Local Jews said this was at least the sixth act of vandalism there since the monument was unveiled 14 years earlier. The police, however, described the crime as an act of petty hooliganism and refused to open a criminal investigation. The Jewish community protested the decision.

OTHER REPUBLICS

In Lithuania, 19 Jewish tombstones in a cemetery near the capital of Vilnius were toppled in June. Local Jewish leaders speculated that the des ecration might have been linked to the 65th anniversary of the June 23, 1941, uprising of Lithuanian nationalists against the Soviet Union. President Valdas Adamkus condemned this and other acts of anti-Semitic vandalism.

In the predominantly Muslim Central Asian nations, anti-Semitic incidents were relatively rare, and the governments of Uzbekistan and Kazakhstan—the region's two largest countries that also had Central Asia's biggest Jewish communities—continued to demonstrate friendly attitudes toward Jews.

Jews in Uzbekistan were alarmed after three members of the community in the capital city, Tashkent, were killed in February and in June. But community leaders said they had no reason to believe that Avraham Yagudaev, who died on February 25 of injuries he received two days earlier, and Svetlana Loifer and her daughter, Karina, strangled to death in their home on June 8, were victims of anti-Semitism. A week after the Loifers were killed police arrested a suspect. He later confessed to killing the women in the course of a robbery attempt, and received a lengthy prison sentence.

In October, anti-Semitic graffiti were spray-painted on several buildings in central Baku, the capital of Azerbaijan. Evda Abramov, the only Jewish member of the Azerbaijani parliament, was quoted by the media as saying that the act could have been inspired by agents of the Iranian special services. Iran, Azerbaijan's southern neighbor and most important trading partner, was believed to be irritated by Baku's diplomatic relations with Israel.

Holocaust-Related Developments

Holocaust denial, a widespread phenomenon in Russia, was especially evident on the Internet. At least four Russian Web sites were devoted mostly or exclusively to denial, according to a report released early in the year commissioned jointly by the Moscow-based Holocaust Foundation and the Moscow Bureau on Human Rights. The report noted that one of the sites, Holocaust Revisionism (www.revisio.msk.ru), contained about 400 written items and video clips. Holocaust-denying books were also widely available at Russian bookstores.

In early 2006, Jewish and human-rights activists in Russia called on federal authorities to follow the lead of many other countries in designating January 27 as Holocaust Memorial Day. No official response was forthcoming.

Holocaust-era issues remained extremely sensitive in the Baltic countries. In Latvia, attention focused on the annual parade in Riga commemorating the Latvian SS Legion, scheduled for March. For ultranationalists, wartime collaboration with the Germans signified resistance to Russian domination, and was therefore deemed heroic. President Vaira Vike-Freiberga publicly opposed the event, saying that it brought unnecessary negative attention to Latvia by portraying it as a country of fascists and Nazis. Visiting Israel in February, Vike-Freiberga apologized for Latvia's role in the Holocaust. A special commission of the Estonian parliament announced cancellation of the march just two days before it was to take place. It cited security concerns, as antinationalist and pro-Russian groups had vowed to show up en masse in protest. But the nationalist organizations went ahead with the march anyway, resulting in clashes with police.

In a trial held in March in Vilnius, Lithuania, 85-year-old Algimantas Mykolas Dailide was found guilty of crimes against Jews in Nazi-occupied Lithuania during World War II. From 1941 through 1944 Dailide worked for the Vilnius office of the Nazi-supervised Lithuanian Security Police, and, according to the indictment, participated in the November 1941 arrests of Jews, specifically arresting two Jews who escaped from the ghetto. There was also evidence suggesting that he arrested members of a Polish anti-Nazi underground cell in 1942. Prosecutors requested a five-year jail sentence, the minimum provided under the law, but, in light of the defendant's advanced age and poor health, the court imposed no sentence. This result revived criticism of Lithuania's poor record of prosecuting Nazi wartime criminals: only a few of them had stood trial since Lithuania established its independence from the USSR, and not one had received a prison term.

In September, a bar in Kaunas, Lithuania's second-largest city, hoisted a Nazi flag and greeted customers with an employee dressed as Hitler. This sparked outrage in the Jewish community. The Simon Wiesenthal Center's Israel office blamed this, too, on Lithuania's poor record of prosecuting Nazi-era war criminals, arguing that such laxity on the part of the authorities encouraged an atmosphere tolerant of Nazism in the country.

In Ukraine, state officials and delegations from some 30 countries attended commemorative events marking the 65th anniversary of the Babi Yar massacre near Kiev. The event was jointly organized by the Ukrainian government and Vyacheslav "Moshe" Kantor, a Russian Jewish industrialist who was president of the Russian Jewish Congress and chairman of the board of the European Jewish Congress.

Several Holocaust memorials were dedicated in Ukraine during t' year. In May, a monument was unveiled in Aleksandria, in central Ukraine's Kirovograd region, at the place where 2,500 Jews were killed during the Nazi occupation from 1941 to 1944. In July, a memorial was dedicated in the town of Zolochev in western Ukraine, on the site of the former Jewish cemetery where Nazis and their local collaborators killed 14,000 Jews during those years.

In October, President Yushchenko raised alarm among Jews by signing a decree calling for a law that would extend official recognition to veterans of World War II Ukrainian nationalist brigades, many of whom fought alongside the Nazis. It was estimated that some 10,000 such men were still living in the country. Ever since Ukraine achieved independence in 1991 they had demanded official veteran status similar to that accorded men who had fought in the Red Army. The Organization of Ukrainian Nationalists and the Ukrainian Rebel Army (OUN-URA), the two best known of these organizations, were responsible, according to reputable historians, for killings Jews in western Ukraine during and after World War II while fighting against Soviet rule. In response to complaints, Yushchenko said that disagreements among Ukrainians about the role of these fighters were due to "perverted knowledge of history," which should be resolved as soon as possible. He therefore called for more research to get at the truth.

JEWISH COMMUNITY

Demography

The number of Jews in Russia and other FSU countries continued to decline due to unfavorable demographic processes—an aging Jewish population, high rates of intermarriage, and continuing, although sloweddown, emigration. The largest Jewish communities were in Russia (about 250,000), Ukraine (about 80,000), and Belarus (probably close to 20,000).

Aliyah continued to decline. In calendar year 2006, 7,300 Jewish immigrants from the FSU came to Israel, a 23-percent decrease from the 2005 figure of 9,528. Still, the FSU remained the largest source of aliyah, accounting for roughly 35 percent of new immigrants to Israel in 2006.

At the same time, the number of Russian immigrants to Israel who returned to their native land was reportedly rising at a fast rate. According to Israeli media reports, the number of naturalized Israelis from Russia who went back had increased more than sixfold over the previous three years, drawn by the improved Russian economy. Some maintained homes in both countries. The Israeli Foreign Ministry claimed that these reports were highly exaggerated and suggested that the rate of return was below 5 percent.

Communal Affairs

Jewish communal life in the Russian Federation continued to be dominated by a few umbrella organizations that openly competed with each other. Since 2000 the Kremlin had clearly favored the Federation of Jewish Communities (FJC), led by Rabbi Berel Lazar, the Chabad chief rabbi of Russia. Complementing the political backing it enjoyed from the government was the extensive funding the FJC received from abroad, especially from its primary donor, Israeli diamond merchant Lev Leviev. The Chabad-oriented FJC had expanded its network to some 190 communities across Russia by 2006.

While its budget for the year was not made public, sources within the FJC indicated that there had been a 15-percent increase over the 2005 figure, which had been estimated at $60 million—nearly $36 million of it raised in North America by the group's U.S. arm. Most of the rabbis currently working in the former Soviet Union belonged to the FJC network, 152 rabbinical emissaries (and their families) in Russia and 146 in the rest of the FSU. The group said that about half its rabbis were Russian-born and the rest mostly Israelis and Americans.

A second major national organization was the Congress of Jewish Religious Organizations and Communities (KEROOR), which encompassed non-Hasidic Orthodox congregations and had its own chief rabbi, Adolf Shayevich. KEROOR had about two dozen rabbis in Russia, half of them serving the Moscow community. Its president and major financial supporter was the controversial Russian-Israeli businessman Arkadi Gaydamak. In 2006 Gaydamak donated large sums for the renovation of KEROOR's most prized property, the Moscow Choral Synagogue, which was celebrating its centennial.

The Union of Religious Congregations of Modern Judaism in Russia (OROSIR), the central body of the Reform movement, operated a number of congregations in Russia, Ukraine, and Belarus. Its small size was reflected in its budget, which was only 1–2 percent that of the FJC. OROSIR owned very few synagogue buildings of its own in the FSU renting facilities instead. In 2006, the group purchased space for a ne synagogue in St. Petersburg, Russia's second largest city, which wov when completed, become the first new Reform synagogue to be opened in Russia since the fall of communism.

The Russian Jewish Congress (RJC), founded in 1996, had lost much of its earlier influence with the government and in the community. Vyacheslav "Moshe" Kantor, an industrialist who had good personal relations with the Kremlin, assumed the presidency in 2005. He tried to increase the group's visibility in the international Jewish arena, focusing, in 2006, on Holocaust-related programs (see above, p. 517). The RJC continued to demonstrate little interest in the domestic social and political issues of concern to the Jewish community.

Other Jewish organizations that had some influence in the FSU were not indigenous, but operated from outside the region, with foreign funding. The American Jewish Joint Distribution Committee (JDC) ran significant Jewish welfare programs through its network of Hesed centers. The Jewish Agency for Israel was involved in aliyah as well as Jewish and Zionist education. Hillel, a student group, operated dozens of off-campus student clubs that sought to attract unaffiliated Jewish college youth and young professionals. Some of these groups—particularly the JDC—came under criticism from Russian Jewish leaders for allegedly disregarding the interests and preferences of the local Jewish communities.

In Tajikistan, the country's only synagogue was demolished to make way for the construction of a new presidential complex in Dushanbe, the capital of this predominantly Muslim Central Asian country. The 100-year-old synagogue had served the small community of mainly elderly Jews that remained in the city in the wake of the civil war that followed the collapse of communism in 1991. City officials offered the community a plot of land for a new synagogue, but in the absence of adequate financial compensation there was no money to build it. The FJC entered into negotiations with national and local officials, but no resolution had been reached as the year ended.

Two historic synagogues were rededicated during 2006. President Freiberga of Latvia attended a ceremony at the reopening of the synagogue in Daugavpils, the country's second largest city, which was now home to 400 Jews. The synagogue in Mukachevo, western Ukraine, was dedicated after its restoration was completed. Prior to World War II the town was the seat of the Munkach Hasidic dynasty, now based in the Boro Park section of Brooklyn, New York.

A new Jewish community center, Beit Menachem Tabachnik, opened in Krasnoyarsk, Siberia, in December. It included a synagogue, a kosher soup kitchen, a library, classrooms, and sports and music facilities. The center, believed to be the largest Jewish facility in Siberia, was built and run by the FJC.

Education

There were about 100 Jewish day schools across the FSU, about 70 of them affiliated with the Chabad-run Or Avner network, which also ran some 60 Jewish kindergartens. In December, it opened Maor, a new Jewish educational center in St. Petersburg that included a day school, kindergarten, prayer hall, and kosher kitchen, along with facilities to host communal programs for various age groups.

World ORT sponsored 15 schools in the region that provided training in computers and technology to enable students to compete in the job market. In February, it opened a technology center at Beit Yehudit-Moriah, an Orthodox day school in Moscow.

In May, leaders of the World Jewish Congress, international Jewish scholars, and rabbis participated in a one-day Limmud FSU educational marathon held in Moscow for local Jews. The program was aimed at bringing together Jews from across the communal spectrum and providing a rare opportunity for exchange between proponents of different Jewish ideologies and interests.

The prospect that Russian Orthodox Christianity might be taught in Russian public schools alarmed Jewish leaders. Berel Lazar, the chief rabbi of the FJC, said that the introduction, in four Russian regions, of a new subject, Foundations of Russian Orthodox Culture, would "divide children into different classes" and lead to the ostracism of religious minorities. The new subject was to become an obligatory part of the curriculum in Orel, Belogorod, Kaluga, and Ryazan—all in central Russia. Depending on the region, the subject was to be taught in the primary, middle-school, or high-school years. The move was supported by the Russian Orthodox Church, Russia's largest faith.

A similar development in Ukraine had already met with criticism on the part of some Jewish leaders in 2005 (see AJYB 2006, p. 531). As of September 1, 2006, parents of students in some Ukrainian public schools were required to choose among new elective courses that included Basics of Christian Ethics and Basics of Religious Ethics.

Lev Krichevsky

Australia

National Affairs

AUSTRALIA ENTERED 2006 with the Liberal-National coalition government under Prime Minister John Howard approaching its tenth anniversary, and the economy in good health. The year was marked by rising concern about the impact of climate change. Severe drought and brushfires scorched the south and east of the country, and provincial and local authorities across Australia took measures to preserve the dwindling water supply. Meanwhile, Cyclone Larry laid waste to Innisfail in northern Queensland, Cyclone Glenda stormed across Western Australia, and Cyclone Monica battered remote communities in the Northern Territory.

Australia's military involvement in Iraq and Afghanistan continued amid ongoing debate over the scale and duration of these deployments. Australia recorded its first death in the Iraq conflict when Private Jake Kovco died in an accidental shooting. The government suffered a double embarrassment: the wrong body was initially sent back home for burial, and Kovco's grieving family expressed disbelief and outrage after an inquiry found that he had shot himself.

Closer to home, Australia faced a series of crises in failing states on its doorstep. Violence broke out in East Timor in April, as troops and police fought among themselves in the streets of the capital, Dili. Fiji's military chief staged the country's fourth coup in 20 years, toppling the democratically elected government. Instability and economic deterioration continued in the Solomon Islands and Papua New Guinea as well. These developments highlighted Australia's need to maintain adequate military and security resources for possible local needs.

There was considerable pressure on the federal government to resolve the situation of Australian David Hicks, who had been captured by American forces in Afghanistan in 2001 and held since then in Guantánamo Bay prison on charges of supporting terrorism. In 2006 he accepted a plea bargain. The remainder of his sentence would be served in Australia.

The Australian government was cleared of any wrongdoing in relation to kickbacks that the Australian Wheat Board (AWB) paid to Saddam Hussein's regime in Iraq (see AJYB 2006, p. 535). Terence Cole, head of the commission of inquiry looking into the case, recommended that a task force be established to investigate possible wrongdoing by several former AWB executives. In domestic politics, Prime Minister Howard announced he would stay on to lead the Liberals in the 2007 elections, much to the disappointment of Treasurer Peter Costello, his presumed successor as party leader. In the ranks of the opposition Australian Labor Party (ALP), growing dissatisfaction with party leader Kim Beazley led to his replacement by Kevin Rudd in December, with Julia Gillard as his deputy—a change that triggered high approval ratings. Labor also won four state elections—in South Australia, Tasmania, Queensland, and Victoria.

Israel and the Middle East

The government, led by Prime Minister Howard and Foreign Minister Alexander Downer, continued to offer remarkably consistent support to Israel in 2006. Moreover, despite some differences in approach and emphasis, the opposition ALP leadership made that support bipartisan.

The victory of Hamas in the Palestinian Authority elections in January was greeted with dismay by the Australian government, which indicated it would not deal with Hamas unless three conditions were met: recognition of Israel, renunciation of violence, and a commitment to honor all previous agreements entered into by the PA. In striking contrast, the success of the centrist party Kadima in the Israeli elections in March and the subsequent formation of a government were warmly and enthusiastically welcomed.

Addressing a United Israel Appeal function in Melbourne on April 5, Foreign Minister Downer reiterated Australia's policy toward the Hamas government: "Remember, as a listed entity under the Charter of the United Nations Act 1945, it is illegal for Australians to provide assistance to Hamas. This will constrain any Australian support to the PA as long as Hamas retains its current charter."

Australia's preferences were especially evident when Israel carried out military operations in Gaza and against Hezballah in Lebanon. On July 16, Prime Minister Howard told ABC TV: "As much in all as I deplore the violence and wish it would stop, one has to understand Israel's position. Israel has a right of self-defense. This country has been under constant attack for almost 50 years since it was founded and there's still an unwillingness on the part of many in the region to accept Israel's right to exist." In an interview the next day, Opposition Leader Beazley echoe

Howard, adding that the onus was on Syria and Iran, as supporters of Hezballah, to disarm it. Even as intense media coverage focused on the plight of the 25,000 Australian nationals caught in Lebanon and steps being taken to evacuate them, the federal government maintained its support for Israel.

On July 19, Kevin Rudd, the ALP foreign affairs spokesperson, called for a ceasefire between Israel and both Hezballah and Hamas, and the dismantling of the two terror organizations as called for by UN Security Council Resolution 1559. But Julia Irwin, a federal MP for the ALP, and federal Senator Kerry Nettle of the Green Party marched at an anti-Israel rally in Sydney on July 22, where many banners compared Israel to the Nazis and its actions to the Holocaust. A good number of Hezballah flags were also seen there.

Twenty-six-year-old Asaf Namer, an Israeli-born Australian citizen who was serving in the IDF, was one of nine Israeli soldiers killed in southern Lebanon on July 26 in a blast outside a mosque in the town of Bint J'beil.

Following the passage of UN Security Council Resolution 1701 in August, both Prime Minister Howard and Foreign Minister Downer expressed doubts that it would achieve its desired results. The latter said, "There are a lot of ifs and buts about the resolution," but he nevertheless called on Iran and Syria to support it. Australia declined to contribute troops to an expanded UN Interim Force in Lebanon (UNIFIL). Downer denied this was due to any lack of confidence in UNIFIL's ability to disarm Hezballah.

In an interview with the *Australian Jewish News* in September, Prime Minister Howard explained that his support for Israel was "based on merit" since "the essential justice of the cause of Israel's survival has always been quite manifest." He defended the government's decision to ban the military wings of Hamas and Hezballah but not their political bodies on the grounds that "we have taken the view that you can separate them out."

In September, Iran's nuclear program and its president's call for the destruction of Israel figured prominently in Australian foreign policy. The government supported imposing sanctions on Iran if it failed to adhere to the demands of the UN and the International Atomic Energy Agency.

In New York, at the opening of the UN General Assembly session in September, Foreign Minister Downer, in a meeting with his Iranian opposite number, warned that President Ahmadinejad must stop threatening to wipe Israel off the map. Downer also held talks there, for the first time, with Israeli foreign minister Tzipi Livni, who thanked him for his country's support during the Lebanon war. Downer then met with the wife of kidnapped Israeli soldier Ehud Goldwasser, promising to assist with the release of all three kidnapped soldiers.

On October 16, the ALP shadow defense minister, Robert McClelland, moved a bill in Parliament condemning suicide bombing and proposing the negotiation of an International Convention on Suicide Terrorism that would define terrorism and make it an international crime.

A potential scandal in Israeli-Australian relations was discreetly handled in October. Israel's ambassador in Canberra, Naftali Tamir, was recalled to Jerusalem after his racially tinged comments on promoting closer ties between the two countries were published in an Israeli newspaper. Tamir was quoted as saying: "We are in Asia without the characteristics of Asians. We don't have yellow skin and slanted eyes. Asia is basically the yellow race. Australia and Israel are not. We are basically the white race. We are on the western side of Asia and they are on the southeastern side." A new ambassador was appointed in December, career diplomat Yuval Rotem. Formerly an adviser to several foreign ministers and consul general in Los Angeles, Rotem was expected to arrive in Australia in mid-2007.

In November, the government used its majority to block a resolution proposed in the Senate, Parliament's upper house, by the Australian Democrats—a minor party—and backed by the ALP and the Greens. It called for the government to follow the advice of the International Crisis Group to support an international Middle East peace conference. The government declared the resolution flawed because it did not demand that the Palestinians reject violence, recognize Israel, and accept all previous agreements signed by the PA.

Australia was one of only seven countries to oppose a General Assembly resolution in December calling for an inquiry into the IDF's shelling of a residential area in Gaza's Beit Hanoun the previous month.

Official visits between Israel and Australia mostly flowed from the former to the latter. In March, Israel's Ashkenazi chief rabbi, Yonah Metzger, was the keynote speaker at a dinner celebrating the 50th anniversary of Sydney's ultra-Orthodox Yeshiva Centre. A historic tour of Israel in April by an Australian clergy group that included Catholics, Anglicans, and Uniting Church members was led by Rabbi John Levi, a member of the editorial committee of the Australia/Israel and Jewish Council (AIJAC), under its Rambam program.

Ron Prossor, director general of Israel's Foreign Ministry, arrived in

Australia in June, where he met with the foreign minister and addressed Jewish National Fund functions in Perth, Brisbane, Melbourne, and Sydney. He told an AIJAC luncheon that he hoped Ehud Olmert would be the first sitting Israeli prime minister to visit Australia.

Former Mossad chief Ephraim Halevy visited Australia as a guest of the Australian Friends of the Hebrew University of Jerusalem in October. He declared that Hezballah had been "seriously mauled" by Israel during the Lebanon war. Another visitor that month had a different perspective. Riah Abu al-Assal, the Palestinian Anglican bishop of Jerusalem, blamed Israel for the lack of Middle East peace.

In business news, an agreement was reached in July between Melbourne Water and Mekorot, Israel's national water carrier, to do joint research on methods of water recycling and treatment. The federal communications minister, Senator Helen Coonan, led an Australia-Israel Chamber of Commerce trade delegation to Israel in November. While there she publicly praised the country's entrepreneurial spirit and research-and-development expertise.

The debate over whether Australia should keep its troops in Iraq continued. Prime Minister Howard maintained that his government would not "cut and run," while the opposition ALP proposed varying formulas directed at bringing the troops home. In an ABC TV interview on September 28, Kim Beazley, then the ALP leader, stated that only Australian soldiers guarding the country's diplomats should remain. On December 8, speaking on Australian TV's Channel 7, the party's new leader, Kevin Rudd, asserted that an ALP-led government would withdraw the troops once the current rotation of the Australian detachment ended.

By the end of 2006, 1,450 Australian Defense Force troops were serving in Iraq. This included a 110-person security detachment of infantry and light armored vehicles protecting and escorting government personnel working at the Australian embassy in Baghdad. Approximately 520 soldiers were based in the south, at Tallil Air Base, to provide security for the provinces of Al Muthanna and Dhi Qar. A naval vessel with a crew of 190 was deployed in the Persian Gulf to intercept ships suspected of illegal activity and to protect Iraqi oil platforms.

At a Washington press conference on December 11, Foreign Secretary Downer dismissed the Iraq Study Group recommendation that America should talk to Iran and Syria, saying that such an initiative would not result in major policy changes by those two countries.

Tensions in the Middle East resonated within the Muslim community of Australia. In July, the imam of Sydney's Lakemba Mosque, Sheikh Taj a-Din al-Hilaly, was sacked from the prime minister's Muslim Community Reference Group following publication of his sermons that referred to the Holocaust as a "Zionist lie" and to Israel as a "cancer." In October, al-Hilaly, in a radio interview, promoted violence as a legitimate tactic. He condemned terror attacks in Madrid, London, and New York, but endorsed them in Israel, Iraq, and Afghanistan.

The Syrian minister for expatriates, Dr. Bouthaina Shaaban, visited Australia in September and met with a number of high-ranking government ministers, including Foreign Secretary Downer and Opposition Leader Beazley.

The Media

Not much changed in the Australian media's coverage of the Middle East in 2006. The Melbourne-based broadsheet *The Age* and its Sydney sister paper, the *Sydney Morning Herald,* retained Middle East correspondent Ed O'Loughlin, who tended to view matters from a Palestinian perspective. Indeed, his descriptions of people and events could almost have been written by Palestinian propagandists. Opinion pieces in these papers critical of Israel and the U.S. far outnumbered those that were sympathetic.

The Special Broadcasting Service (SBS) and the Australian Broadcasting Corporation (ABC), the two publicly owned television networks, ran many documentaries on Middle Eastern themes, some interesting and informative but most biased against Israel and/or the U.S. The SBS public-affairs program "Dateline" was particularly anti-Israel, to the extent that its stories about Gaza and Lebanon ignored the Israeli side altogether. These stations' coverage of the Holocaust and anti-Semitism, however, was excellent. In a significant breakthrough, ABC officials, under consistent grilling by Senator Michael Ronaldson of the Liberal Party, finally admitted that Hezballah, Hamas, and Palestinian Islamic Jihad were terrorist organizations, but this did not have a major impact on their coverage.

The media gave considerable prominence to Antony Loewenstein, a Jewish critic of Israel, who became a darling of the anti-Israel Left. Similarly, claims advanced by American professors Stephen Walt and John Mearsheimer that U.S. policy in the Middle East was controlled by a powerful Jewish lobby were covered sympathetically.

As early as the start of the year, when Israeli prime minister Ariel Sharon suffered a debilitating stroke, anti-Israel media voices took opportunity to label him a war criminal. The worst instance was a cartoon in *The Age* suggesting that Sharon was still fit enough to work if he had even minimal movement in his right arm, since that was all he needed "to order a missile strike against an old Palestinian man in a wheelchair." When the newspaper received complaints about the cartoon, it gave space for the cartoonist to write a column that heaped more calumnies on Sharon.

The victory of Hamas in the PA elections and its formation of a government were also exploited by media critics of Israel. Some blamed Israeli policies for bringing about the Hamas accession, while others sought to rebuff criticism of Hamas by drawing parallels between its actions and those of Israeli governments.

The biggest stories of the year were the Israeli incursions into Gaza following the capture of Corp. Gilad Shalit and the subsequent war between Israel and Hezballah in Lebanon. In both cases the media stressed and even exaggerated the destructive impact of Israeli actions on the local populations, while Israel's motivations were often given short shrift, and sometimes not mentioned at all. The *Canberra Times* maintained its reputation as Australia's most anti-Israel mainstream newspaper. Of the 28 opinion pieces it ran between July 14 and August 24 on the situation, 15 were highly critical of Israel, 8 were neutral, and only 5 were favorable. The analysis in its news reporting was equally skewed.

SBS TV's news coverage of Israeli actions not only lacked context, but also, at times, showed blatant bias. For example, it highlighted UN representative Jan Egeland's harsh criticism of Israel, but ignored his equally strong remarks about Hezballah the next day. Also, it prominently featured the deaths of four UN observers killed when an Israeli shell hit their post, but made no mention of UNIFIL reports that Hezballah had been firing at Israel from that location.

As had been the case for years, *The Australian,* a national broadsheet, provided the most objective picture of events. In many editorials, it set out insightfully the true causes of the Middle East conflict, with attention to Israel's reasons for acting as it did, and the opinion pages provided balance. Foreign editor Greg Sheridan presented the fairest and most informative coverage of the Middle East available in the general press.

Iran's nuclear ambitions were a topic of constant media discussion throughout the year. Much of the commentary tended to downplay the threat, arguing that the use of military force against Iran would lead to r greater dangers.

Anti-Semitism

Anti-Semitism had never been a major part of Australian life. While there were incidents of anti-Semitism in the country's history, the phenomenon did not threaten Jewish security, nor did anyone with aspirations to public credibility admit to holding anti-Semitic views or associating with anti-Semitic organizations.

Even so, traditional right-wing notions of Jewish conspiracies had been supplemented in recent years by similar anti-Jewish rhetoric emanating from far-left publications and organizations. The virulence of some public criticism of Israeli actions as well as continued misrepresentation of them (see above) reinforced such tendencies. Public discussion in 2006 also focused on Islamic sources of anti-Semitism. According to reports, the mufti of Australia promoted Holocaust denial in his Sydney mosque, and anti-Jewish books were available in Australian bookshops that served the Muslim community.

There were 442 instances of "racist violence" against Jews reported to the Executive Council of Australian Jewry during 2006. The incidents were categorized under the headings of physical assault, vandalism — including arson attacks — threatening telephone calls, hate mail, graffiti, leaflets, posters, and abusive and intimidating e-mail. Hundreds of Jews and Jewish organizations were targeted, some repeatedly. The number of 2006 incidents, although lower than the record set in 2002, was 47 percent above the average annual figure over the previous 16 years. The categories of assault, face-to-face harassment, and vandalism grew fastest, reaching 56 percent above the average. Incidents of harassment that did not include assault were recorded at a rate 49 percent above the average.

Australia continued to host a plethora of fringe organizations that promoted anti-Semitism, some of which had been involved in extremist political activity for decades. While all opposed the political and economic establishment, Zionism, and Jews — which, they charged, were engaged in a conspiracy against Australia — these groups had a bewildering multiplicity of orientations: far-right, far-left, antiglobalization, anarchist, white supremacist, and militant Muslim.

The Adelaide Institute was a loose conglomeration of the followers of self-proclaimed "Holocaust revisionist" Frederick Toben, who was considered so extreme that David Irving complained that Toben's Web site was a liability to the cause of revisionism. During 2006 Toben not only reiterated the charge of a Jewish conspiracy to run the world, but he als went so far as to publish extracts from a book, *The Hitler We Loved c*

Why. Toben was also a regular poster on neo-Nazi on-line bulletin boards. And he found a platform in Iran: the country's official Mehr news agency issued a long interview with Toben. Geoffrey Muirden, an extreme rightwinger who ran the Adelaide Institute while Toben was incarcerated in a German prison for Holocaust denial, died in 2006.

The Australian League of Rights was described by the Human Rights and Equal Opportunity Commission as "undoubtedly the most influential and effective, as well as the best organized and most substantially financed, racist organization in Australia." Its membership was primarily elderly. Under the leadership of its director, Betty Luks, it held meetings, issued anti-Semitic and anti-Israel publications, and maintained a Web site. Its founder, Eric Butler, died in June 2006. The League received unexpected publicity when the media reported that controversial American actor/director Mel Gibson, who had recently uttered anti-Semitic slurs at a police officer in the U.S. who arrested him for drunk driving, had supported a candidate backed by the League of Rights in the 1987 Australian election.

The Citizens Electoral Councils (CEC), based in a well-staffed office in suburban Melbourne, sent out mass mailings reflecting the views of Lyndon LaRouche, including bizarre and offensive anti-Semitic conspiracy theories involving Jewish and antiracist organizations. The organization spent, over the years, hundreds of thousands of dollars on electoral campaigns, their candidates averaging only around 0.06 percent of the vote.

There were allegations in 2006 that the CEC was seeking to infiltrate the conservative National Civic Council's network of local chapters. Also, it publicized a petition in opposition to Australia's antiterrorism laws that garnered support from far-right and Islamic extremists, and even, for a short time, from a number of prominent Australians who were unaware of the nature of the CEC. Members of the Jewish community in several regions of the country complained about the organization's distribution of propaganda, especially on campuses and outside venues hosting Jewish community functions.

The deceptively named Australian Civil Liberties Union (ACLU) continued to advocate Holocaust denial and the protection of the "rights" of deniers. John Bennett, the group's leader, was on the editorial advisory committee of the *Journal of Historical Review,* published by the Holocaust-denying Institute for Historical Review in California. The 2006 edition of the ACLU's *Your Rights* featured an article by the U.S.-

based denier Mark Weber calling for the repeal of all legislation restricting Holocaust denial.

There were many small groups of racist skinheads. The best known was Australian National Action, which staged rallies in Melbourne and Adelaide, and publishing a newsletter. Its agenda was white-supremacist, anti-immigrant, and anti-Semitic. Another such group, calling itself the White Pride Coalition of Australia, gained notoriety in March 2006 when one of its leaders distributed detailed bomb-making instructions, triggering a police investigation. This individual had previously described Jews as "vile, loathsome bloodsuckers" on the WPCA Web site.

The Australian chapter of the World Church of the Creator—which had no more than three identifiable supporters—established a prominent presence on the Internet and in on-line newsgroups, as well as in the Queensland regional media. Its homepage referred to "the parasitic Jews." "Creators" were urged to "retake" Australia from Jews and non-whites.

JEWISH COMMUNITY

Demography

The latest census, conducted in 2001, showed about 84,000 Jews in Australia, 0.44 percent of the population. This was roughly 4,000 more than in 1996. The actual figure was undoubtedly higher, since religion was an optional question on the census form and was omitted by a quarter of Australians. Jewish community leaders believed that Holocaust survivors were especially likely not to disclose their religion to the government, and that the actual number of Jews in the country was around 120,000.

Melbourne had the largest Jewish population, followed by Sydney. The census showed that most recent Jewish immigrants came from South Africa, and that Hebrew was the preferred language in the homes of 6,000 Australians, presumably former Israelis.

Communal Affairs

There was no change in the leadership of the primary body representing Australia's Jews, as Graeme Leonard continued as president of the Executive Council of Australian Jewry (ECAJ). Philip Chester of Me bourne succeeded Sydney's Ron Weiser as president of the Zionist Federation of Australia. Mark Leibler remained national chairman of the Australia/Israel and Jewish Affairs Council (AIJAC), and Dr. Colin Rubenstein continued as its executive director. AIJAC maintained its close association with the American Jewish Committee. Stanley Roth was succeeded as federal president of the United Israel Appeal by Jack Smorgon in November, while Ron Ferster of Sydney succeeded Melbourne's Michael Naphtali as head of the Jewish National Fund.

Education

More than half of all Jewish children aged 4–18, including almost 70 percent of those aged 4–12, received full-time Jewish education in the 19 Jewish day schools in Australia. Spanning the religious spectrum, these schools continued to rank at the highest level for academic achievement. This reflected the community's major investment in the schools as a means of preserving Jewish continuity. Day-school enrollments continued to grow despite ongoing concerns over high costs and the challenge to the community to find new sources of funding.

There was an increased emphasis on adult education, largely under the influence of the Melton Program, which had nearly 500 students in Sydney and Melbourne. Short-term courses utilizing guest lecturers also proved popular. Top priorities for the future, according to Australian Jewish educators, were expanded Jewish studies on the university level and teacher education to provide quality faculty for the day schools.

At the university level, the Australasian Union of Jewish Students (AUJS) continued to play an active role on campus, particularly in combating anti-Zionist and racist manifestations and in promoting exchange programs with Israel for Jewish students.

Intergroup Relations

Representative bodies of the different religious communities in Australia continued to speak out for religious harmony. The ECAJ, the National Council of Churches in Australia, and the Australian Federation of Islamic Councils repeated their calls for tolerance. A number of Christian groups and leaders of the Baha'i faith condemned anti-Semitic attacks, and Jewish groups joined others in condemning racist vilification of Australian Arabs and Muslims. The Australian Partnership of Religious Organizations (formerly the Australian Partnership of Ethnic and

Religious Organizations) and other multifaith groups, such as the World Conference of Religions for Peace and the Griffith University Multi-Faith Center, provided platforms for contact and cooperation between the Jewish community and other significant religious groups.

There was also direct interfaith activity with the Christian churches. The Uniting Church in Australia in cooperation with the ECAJ convened national dialogues twice each year to discuss joint action to combat prejudice. The Catholic Church had been emphasizing interreligious understanding since the lead-up to its celebration of the year 2000; the Catholic Bishops' Conference and the ECAJ held an "annual conversation" each year. After a number of years of preparation, the Anglican-Jewish Australian Dialogue had its first two formal sessions. These Christian bodies, as a matter of principle, refused to allow racist and anti-Jewish groups to use their premises, and advised their representatives not to share platforms with known extremists.

Australian Jewry's relationships with the local Muslim community were strained not only by the Lebanon war but also by press reports of Muslim religious ideologues blaming Israel and the Jews for the problems of the Islamic world. A potential Arab-Jewish conflict arose in July, when it became known that a Syrian-born Australian citizen, Khalil Eideh, an ALP candidate for the Legislative Council of the state of Victoria, had written to Syrian president Bashar al-Assad in 2002 pledging loyalty to him, describing Israel as a "colonial and Zionist" threat to Syria, and praising Palestinian suicide bombers. Eideh met with the Victoria Jewish Community Council and explained that such rhetoric was simply part of the traditional style of discourse in such letters. He stated that he was not anti-Semitic and that he accepted Israel right to exist. The council accepted Eideh's assurances. He was duly elected in November.

Culture

The Jewish Museum of Australia and the Jewish Holocaust Museum and Research Center, both in Melbourne, and the Sydney Jewish Museum were world-class institutions that maintained extensive permanent collections of Judaica and Holocaust memorabilia. They received visitors in ever increasing numbers, particularly school groups, and hosted numerous cultural events, including literary evenings, book launches, and musical and dramatic presentations. The Adelaide Jewish community maintained a "virtual" museum, the Adelaide Jewish Museum. Another mainstay of Jewish culture was the annual Jewish film festival, which continued to attract large and enthusiastic audiences both in Sydney and Melbourne.

The Australia Israel Cultural Exchange (AICE), founded in 2002, made a significant contribution to the cultural scene in both countries. The third AICE Israeli Film Festival, held in Melbourne in August, was opened by Katriel Schory, director of the Israeli Film Fund. In Israel, AICE mounted exhibitions of Australian Aboriginal art, and conducted an Australian film festival.

Personalia

In January, the government conferred Australia Day Honors on a number of prominent members of the Jewish community. Jack Smorgon, a philanthropist and veteran leader of the United Israel Appeal, was made an Officer of the Order of Australia (AO). Among those appointed Members of the Order of Australia (AM) were Belinda Epstein-Frisch; Dr. Alan Finkel; Ian Lacey; Frank Levy; and Carol Schwartz. The Medal of the Order of Australia (OAM) was presented to Margaret Beadman; Max Lemberg; and Rabbi Benzion Milecki.

The annual round of Queen's Birthday Honors announced in June bestowed awards on a number of other prominent members of the Jewish community. Professor Raymond Lowenthal was named an Officer of the Order of Australia (AO) for services to medicine. This award also went to Leon Hertz, an executive vice president of News Corporation.

Dr. Colin Rubenstein, executive director of AIJAC, was appointed a Member of the Order of Australia (AM). The citation noted "his services to the community through executive roles with a range of Jewish organizations as well as his contribution to the advancement of multiculturalism and to the academic discipline of political science." Others receiving honors in this category were Susan Bures, former editor of the *Australian Jewish Times;* Dr. Herbert Freilich; Joe Gersh; Michael Gudinski; Jill Margo; Prof. Leon Piterman; and Prof. David Weisbrot. Those awarded the Medal of the Order of Australia included Joe Aarons; Peter Bancroft; Reuven Herzog; Rachel Kalman; Gerald Moses; Zipporah Oliver; Dr. Max Shavitsky; Roy Tashi; and Zara Young.

In 2006, the Australian Jewish community mourned the passing of Leslie Caplan (AM), a Sydney-based communal leader who had served as president of both the New South Wales Jewish Board of Deputies and ECAJ; Prof. Rufus Davis, who taught politics at Monash University, Melbourne, and served for many years on AIJAC's editorial board; Lewis

Herman (OAM), the long-time mayor of Ashfield in Sydney; Allan Newell and Arnold Newhouse, both former presidents of the State Zionist Council of New South Wales; Dr. Francis Septimus Owen (OAM), board member and past president of the Newcastle Hebrew Congregation; John Weiner, Holocaust survivor, professional photographer, and educator; and Nathan Zusman, teacher, publisher, and champion of the Yiddish language.

COLIN L. RUBENSTEIN

South Africa

National Affairs

T HE YEAR was dominated by an ongoing leadership struggle within the ruling party, the African National Congress (ANC), in anticipation of President Thabo Mbeki's exit from office in 2009. Jacob Zuma, despite being ousted as deputy president in 2005 amid charges of rape and corruption, remained popular. Following his acquittal on the rape charge in 2006, Zuma continued to draw support, especially in his home province of Kwa-Zulu Natal.

The economy performed at a robust pace, growing by around 5 percent. About a half million new jobs were created during the year, but this hardly made a dent in the unemployment rate, which remained at about 25 percent, or 40 percent if one includes those who had stopped seeking employment. It was anticipated that two government programs, the Accelerated and Shared Growth Initiative (ASGISA) and the Extended Public Works Program, would provide jobs for some of the unemployed.

The gap between rich and poor remained unacceptably high. The Congress of South African Trade Unions (COSATU) blamed the government's policies, which, it claimed, were too friendly to business interests. The Jewish community was well aware of the problem. Speaking at a meeting of the Union of Jewish Women, Arthur Chaskalson, a justice of the Constitutional Court, stressed the need to find solutions to economic inequity within the framework of the South African constitution. "I don't underestimate the difficulty of doing so, but we fail to do so at our peril," he warned.

The shortage of skills among large sectors of the population hindered the delivery of public services at the local level. Many municipalities hardly functioned, while schools, hospitals, and government ministries found it difficult to fill posts. Adding to the disquiet was widespread corruption. The government's affirmative action policies drew widespread criticism, and the Black Economic Empowerment (BEE) program appeared to favor those who were already successful business leaders. Steps were being taken to widen the base of beneficiaries.

HIV/AIDS continued to ravage the country: more than half a million ıth Africans were infected, and the daily death rate from the disease was almost 1,000. The government was now advancing an antiretroviral program, but only after considerable pressure from nongovernmental organizations, most notably the Treatment Action Campaign.

Crime remained another major problem, despite the government's stepped-up allocation of funds to deal with it. Among the most prominent victims in 2006 was Nadine Gordimer, the 82-year-old Jewish novelist and Nobel laureate, whose home was broken into by an intruder. After refusing to surrender her wedding ring, she was assaulted and tied up in a storeroom, but not injured. The brutal killing of two young Jewish men in Cape Town attracted widespread revulsion, as did that of a Jewish woman, Gillian Hurwitz, in Johannesburg. Her murder, noted an editorial in the *SA Jewish Report* (Oct. 13), "will be added by some Jews to the question whether the country has a stable future. Not because they are racists, don't celebrate the new South Africa, or don't want to stay. Rather because the overwhelming feeling—among Jews and most other South Africans—is that they are not safe in their streets, homes, restaurants, shopping malls, and just about every other place."

The Jewish community initiated its own crime-response initiative in Johannesburg, the Glenhazel Active Protection project. Maintaining links with the South African Police Services and the existing neighborhood watches, it monitored suspicious activities through the use of surveillance cameras. "From the Jewish community's point of view," reported Chief Rabbi Warren Goldstein, "crime is a national problem and not a Jewish one, and the nation as a whole is making its voice heard and the government is hearing them and responding." Goldstein was part of the National Religious Leaders Forum that met with President Mbeki about the crime problem in December.

The most prominent Jewish politician on the national scene, Tony Leon, announced in December that he would resign as leader of the Democratic Alliance, the largest opposition party, in May 2007.

Israel and the Middle East

The victory of Hamas in the Palestinian elections at the beginning of the year was greeted with alarm in Jewish circles. In the wake of the voting, the South African Jewish Board of Deputies (SAJBOD), which represented the country's Jews, issued a statement calling on Hamas to recognize unequivocally Israel's right to exist, and to abandon violence in favor of peaceful negotiations. The South African government was on record urging the same course.

Iran was the focus of considerable attention during the year. The issue was first raised in January by Ron Prossor, director general of Israel's Ministry of Foreign Affairs, who was visiting as part of an ongoing political dialogue with South African government departments and their directors general. Prossor, at a press briefing, described an Iranian regime with nuclear weapons as "an existential threat to Israel and a destabilizing force in the entire region." Also commenting was Michael Bagraim, national chairman of the SAJBOD, who expressed concern about the South African government's "worrisome silence on Iran's disgraceful anti-Israel and anti-Jewish remarks."

South Africa was one of only five countries to abstain when the governing body of the International Atomic Energy Agency voted 27-3 to refer Iran's nuclear program to the UN Security Council. Alarmed by the government's position, a delegation from the South African Zionist Federation (SAZF) met with the deputy minister of foreign affairs, Azziz Pahad, to discuss not only Iran's call to "wipe Israel off the map," but also its hosting, in Tehran, of a Holocaust cartoon competition. Pahad affirmed South Africa's concern about the Iranian threat to Israel, and indicated that the absence of a public condemnation was nothing more than an administrative oversight. Pahad reiterated his government's support for a two-state solution to the Israeli-Palestinian conflict.

The *SA Jewish Report,* on February 2, welcomed Pahad's comments as well as the government's view that Hamas should renounce violence and accept the existence of Israel. "South Africa, because of its history and international status, particularly in the Third World, could possibly have some have some influence in achieving this, which would be excellent news for South African Jews," the paper editorialized.

The SAJBOD held a meeting with President Mbeki to discuss several issues, including the Iranian nuclear question and President Ahmadinejad's controversial statements on Israel. Mbeki said his government wanted to help solve the standoff over Iran's nuclear program, and also indicated that it would not meet with Hamas, but would rather work through the Palestinian Authority, headed by President Mahmoud Abbas. Mbeki promised to investigate why the government had not condemned Ahmadinejad's threatening statements and his Holocaust denial.

A delegation of South African Jewish leaders met with PA president Abbas in April, when the latter visited South Africa. In what was described as a cordial session, the delegates reiterated Israel's commitment to work for a lasting peace and endorsed the Israeli government's refusal meet with Hamas until it complied with the Quartet's preconditions.

Afterwards, both the Jewish group and Abbas paid tribute to the South African government for facilitating the meeting. Thus it came as a great disappointment that Abbas uttered particularly vitriolic remarks about Israel when he addressed the South African Parliament.

Whatever goodwill had been built up between the Jewish community and the government was massively damaged by Israel's incursions into Gaza and the new war in Lebanon, events that provoked a storm of criticism. The government condemned Israel's "policy of collective punishment as a direct violation of international law," and called for the immediate cessation of Israel's military offensive.

Shortly after Israel launched "Operation Summer Rain" to retrieve kidnapped Corporal Gilad Shalit, Willie Madisha, president of the powerful Congress of South African Trade Unions (COSATU), called for sanctions against Israel. COSATU was joined at a press conference by the SA Council of Churches; the Palestinian Solidarity Committee; Ali Halimeh, the Palestinian ambassador to South Africa; and Virginia Tilley, an American academic now residing in South Africa and the author of *The One-State Solution*. A professor from Gaza University participated by phone link. One of those present, Blade Nzimande, a leader of the South African Communist Party, said that reports of Israeli activities in Gaza reminded him of an earlier visit he had made to Auschwitz.

A group calling itself Concerned South African Jews also criticized Israel, issuing a statement that claimed: "There is no moral justification for the appalling price [that Lebanese civilians] are being forced to pay by Israel's action." The signatories maintained that "Jewish support for Israel's aggression threatens both the moral and physical survival of the Jewish people."

The overwhelming majority of South Africa's Jews, however, supported Israel's offensive. The SAJBOD and the SAZF issued a joint statement affirming "unswerving solidarity with the people and the State of Israel" and "Israel's right to take appropriate measures to defend its citizens against acts of violence, particularly against terrorism." Special prayer services were held in Johannesburg, Cape Town, and Durban to express support for Israel.

As the war continued and intensified, anti-Israel protests grew louder, culminating in a large demonstration outside the Israeli embassy in Pretoria. The SAJBOD, for its part, issued a statement condemning the government for its one-sided position, calling it "unjust, highly partisan and wholly unreflective of the realities of the current conflict in the M dle East," and arguing that South Africa "seriously undermined its credentials as a credible international player in the quest to achieve a lasting peace in the region." The SAJBOD also denounced media coverage. One specific complaint concerned a cartoon in the *Cape Argus* that depicted missiles instead of candles in a menorah. The newspaper sent the SAJBOD an apology.

While the war was still going on, South African Jews took two major public steps, sending a solidarity mission to Israel and organizing a pro-Israel march in Johannesburg that drew about 5,000 people. The only non-Jewish group that expressed sympathy for Israel were the evangelical Christians. Over 5,000 members of the Shofar Christian Church met for a Feast of Tabernacles rally in support of Israel at Stellenbosch University.

The conflict moved into Parliament in late August, with the introduction of a virulently anti-Israel resolution. The motion, which condemned the Israeli response as disproportionate and accused the Jewish state of contravening international law and the Geneva Conventions, was withdrawn at the last minute to allow for discussions about altering the wording so as to achieve a consensus. But the revised text, which was adopted, contained no changes of any substance. It denounced, and described as international-law violations, "Israel's collective punishment of both the Palestinians and Lebanese peoples"; "the disproportionate response of Israel and the use of military force against civilian targets"; and "the catastrophic humanitarian crisis in Gaza and Lebanon, for which Israel's aggression is responsible." Despite its one-sidedness, the resolution did stop short of calls made by COSATU and others to sever diplomatic relations with Israel.

In its response, the SAJBOD maintained that this "kind of language serves to incite unjustified hatred of Israel that can easily spill over into Jew hatred. We have already seen and heard unfortunate examples of anti-Semitism on our streets in recent years, sometimes not even cloaked in a thin guise of anti-Zionism." The *SA Jewish Report* (Aug. 29) charged that Parliament risked forfeiting its credibility. "If the government still cares how it is perceived by Jews," the paper noted, "it needs to give clear signals that it does understand the different sides' perspectives and that the parliamentary resolution's one-sidedness does not foreshadow an abandonment of the desire to be trusted by both parties."

One of the most vociferous Jewish critics of Israel, Minister of Intelligence Ronnie Kasrils — who had earlier equated Israeli behaviour with that of the Nazis — was scheduled to deliver the keynote address to a seminar on the Israel-Lebanon conflict at the Goethe Institute in Johannesburg. But following an objection from the SAJBOD, the invitation was withdrawn. Kasrils was again denied a platform when the *SA Jewish Report* decided not to publish an article he wrote. The paper explained, "Constructive debate will not be advanced by letting the *SA Jewish Report* be used as a platform to propagate the view that Israel is like the Nazis—a concept utterly offensive to the sensibilities of the vast majority of its readers, including those who are highly critical of Israel, but know what the term 'Nazi' really means."

This was not the end of the matter. The Freedom of Expression Institute (FXI), a nongovernmental organization, lambasted the Jewish newspaper for denying Kasrils his freedom of expression. The paper responded by calling the FXI report biased, as demonstrated by its referring to the *SA Jewish Report* as "a mere extension of Zionism's repressive project."

Adding to the anti-Israel atmosphere was a visit to South Africa by Leila Khalid, the convicted Palestinian hijacker who had been released from a British jail in 1970 as part of a prisoner exchange, and was now an international icon of the Palestinian struggle. The Cape Council of the SAJBOD and the Western Province Zionist Council protested her entry into South Africa. "Romanticizing and lauding the activities and statements of a convicted hijacker in this country serves to fuel the spill-over of the Middle East conflicts to the streets of Cape Town," said Moonyeen Castle, chairman of the Cape Council.

The campuses remained hostile, on the whole, to Israel and its supporters. For example, a mock replica of Israel's "security wall" was displayed on Jameson Plaza at the University of Cape Town, provoking substantial student debate. Nevertheless, most Jewish college students did not shy away from asserting their identity and advocating Israel's cause.

Avrom Krengel, reelected SAZF chairman, Krengel expressed confidence in the future of South African Zionism. Despite budget cuts that limited the scope of programs, he noted, Israel-oriented events were drawing large crowds, and Israel Independence Day was still a central feature of the Jewish communal calendar. Another note of optimism came from the Israeli ambassador, Ilan Baruch, who gave a positive assessment of economic relations between Israel and South Africa, especially in the area of technology.

There was further Israel-related news that was not of a political nature. Twenty-eight nursery and kindergarten teachers from several Jewish day schools participated in a trip to Israel sponsored by the Hebrew Early

Childhood Association. More than 200 students attended the Israel Encounter program in January. Shalom Club SA was a new project launched to train South Africans in Israel through the use of Israel's Mashav training courses. The Jewish National Fund honored two South African Christian Zionists, Dr. Johann Greeff, national director of the Christian Embassy in Israel, and Chris Eden, national director of Bridges for Peace in South Africa.

Anti-Semitism

South Africa, in 2006, recorded its highest annual number of anti-Semitic incidents on record. These incidents were not violent, and generally involved verbal abuse and intimidation. The one exception occurred in Cape Town's West Park Cemetery, where over 70 headstones were vandalized, and even in this case it was not certain whether the perpetrators acted out of anti-Semitic motives or out of sheer hooliganism. Nevertheless, there were alarming press reports that certain sectors of the Muslim population were being indoctrinated to commit violence, and the SAJBOD raised the matter with government officials.

Observers suggested that the growth in the number of incidents mirrored, in large part, rising tensions in the Middle East at a time of hostile media coverage that showed little empathy for Israel's situation. Thus anti-Semitic activity peaked during the summer months, when Israel conducted its incursion into Gaza and fought against Hezballah in Lebanon.

Tony Leon, head of the Democratic Alliance and leader of the opposition in Parliament, was the most visible Jew on the national scene, and he remained an object of anti-Semitic barbs in 2006, especially during a municipal by-election in Cape Town. Invariably, reference was made to his Israeli wife and his Zionist connections.

At an academic seminar in Pretoria sponsored by the Iranian embassy, a South African parliamentarian made a positive reference to the *Protocols of the Elders of Zion*. She was later reported to have explained that when she made the statement she had no idea that the *Protocols* were a forgery.

A special commission looking into the blacklisting of certain political commentators by the public broadcaster, the South African Broadcasting Corporation (SABC), revealed that Paula Slier, a Jewish reporter whose beat was the Middle East, was among those blacklisted. The chief executive for news and current affairs at the SABC, Dr. Snuki Zikalala, justified the decision on the grounds that Slier, "a white Jewish girl," was disqualified because she "supported what's happening in Israel." Michael Bagraim, the SAJBOD chairman, expressed shock, saying, "We have always considered Paula Slier a consummate professional. She writes stories not for the sake of expressing her views but because she wants to tell the truth and bring the true story to the public." The *SA Jewish Report* (Oct. 20) charged that "Zikalala has abused the immense power he wields in numerous directions, not just Israel. Moreover, the complete absence of contrition on his part is startling."

Holocaust-Related Matters

This year, the Cape Town Holocaust Centre's annual Ernest and Renee Sampson Anniversary Lecture was delivered by Dr. John Roth, the Edward J. Sexton Professor of Philosophy and director of the Center for the Study of the Holocaust, Genocide and Human Rights at Claremont-McKenna College in California. Richard Freedman, the Cape Town Centre's newly appointed director, announced several major educational initiatives.

The Council of Kwa-Zulu Natal Jewry and the Kwa-Zulu Natal Zionist Council jointly hosted a function dedicated to the memory of the late Simon Wiesenthal. It took place on January 27, the first international day of commemoration to honor the victims of the Holocaust.

After eight years of legal arguments over technicalities, a case pitting the SAJBOD against Radio 786, owned by the Islamic Unity Convention, was finally heard by the Broadcasting Monitoring and Complaints Committee (BMCC) in March. At issue was an interview broadcast by the station in May 1998 with Dr. Yaqub Zaki, a historian at the Muslim Institute in London, which, billed as an examination of Zionism, was instead a rant about Jewish conspiracies and included Holocaust denial (see AJYB 2001, p. 464).

At the hearing, Radio 786 asked for yet another postponement, and then walked out after its request was denied. The hearing nonetheless went ahead, and the judgement, announced in August, vindicated the SAJBOD. The BMCC found that Zaki's interview constituted hate speech under the terms of the South African constitution, and thus contravened the broadcasting regulations. Radio 786 was ordered to desist from broadcasting hate speech and from "the advocacy of hatred against the Jewish people, including the impairment of their dignity."

JEWISH COMMUNITY

Survey of Communal Attitudes

According to a survey conducted by the Isaac and Jessie Kaplan Centre for Jewish Studies and Research at the University of Cape Town in 2005, South African Jews were more optimistic about their country than they had been seven years earlier, despite concern about rising crime and rampant corruption. This survey was the third in a series, following a 1998 study by the Institute for Jewish Policy Research in London in association with the Kaplan Centre, and an earlier survey in 1991.

Market researcher Shirley Bruk conducted the new survey, which was based on face-to-face interviews with a sample of 1,000 Jewish adults from Cape Town, Durban, Pretoria, and Johannesburg, cities where 90 percent of the approximately 80,000 South African Jews lived. The study, noted Bruk, "shows that South African Jews maintain a strong Jewish identity in its varying forms." She also found that "very few Jews are planning to leave the country. This is a dramatic shift from what emerged in the 1998 survey." Only 8 percent of Jews had emigrated in the 24 years since 1982, and many of them had subsequently returned. However, crime and fears about personal safety were considered serious problems by more than 80 percent of the respondents. While in 1998 Israel and Australia shared first place on the list of countries considered most desirable places to relocate to, Australia was now number one, ahead of Israel.

While anti-Semitism was seen as a major problem "in the world generally" by 73 percent of the sample, most saw it as only a "minor" problem in South Africa, although anti-Zionism was deemed a serious and growing problem there by 85 percent of respondents. Sixty percent felt that, in light of developments in the Middle East, Israel should give up some territory in exchange for credible guarantees of peace. In 1998, 49 percent supported this.

Sabbath observance had risen over the years. The majority of Jewish parents still chose Jewish schools for their children: 70 percent of those with children in middle and high schools, 77 percent with children in primary school, and 96 percent of those with preschool/nursery school children said they patronized Jewish schools.

Summarizing the findings, the director of the Kaplan Centre, Prof. Milton Shain, noted that "the most striking thing about Jews in the new South Africa is the ongoing cohesion within the community, the strength of its communal institutions, its attachment to Israel, and its confidence in South Africa." Shain added that the Jewish community "is also satisfied with their communal institutions, and they appreciate the climate of religious tolerance and diversity within South Africa."

Communal Affairs

The national director of the SAJBOD, Yehuda Kay, was forced to resign in controversial circumstances. In what he believed was a private e-mail to an ANC leader, Kay called certain remarks by Tony Leon, leader of the Democratic Alliance, "toilet reading material." Not only was Kay obliged to step down after the e-mail was publicized, but the SAJBOD issued a formal apology to Leon, which was accepted, and noted that the SAJBOD, as a nonpartisan body, dissociated itself from Kay's views.

In August, the Cape Council of the SAJBOD held its annual conference. Chairman Moonyeen Castle urged members of the community to embrace and respect differences. He said, "We work for good relations between Jews and all other peoples in South Africa, strive to promote the civil liberties of the South African Jewish community and promote the ideals of the new South Africa, where everyone can enjoy freedom from the evils of prejudice, intolerance and discrimination."

An issue of some concern to South African Jews was whether it was constitutionally permissible for faith-based welfare organizations to restrict membership to adherents of that faith, which was the current practice, or whether that constituted a denial of "associational rights." The elimination of such a restriction would make the maintenance of Jewish welfare organizations extremely difficult. It came as a relief, then, that the South African Human Rights Commission ruled that existing practice was constitutional.

The chief rabbi of the British Commonwealth, Dr. Jonathan Sacks, visited South Africa in 2006. He gave fulsome praise to South African Jewish institutions, and stressed the need for strong Jewish education. Also visiting the country was a delegation from the United Israel Appeal (UIA) of Canada, which wanted "to create new bonds with your leadership." Stanley Plotnick, its chairman, said, "We wish to share our vision of supporting Jewish communities all over the world in their efforts to assist Israel and themselves."

In organizational news, the Union of Jewish Women celebrated its 70th anniversary. Also, a new group, a forum for Jewish gays and lesbians, was founded by Dr. David Bilchitz. The 17th Nachum Goldmann Fellowship Program was held outside Cape Town in February, the first time it had ever met on the African continent. In May, a large South African delegation attended the centennial of the American Jewish Committee in Washington, D.C. The Western Cape premier, Ebrahim Rasool, addressed the gathering.

A number of Jewish organizations were heavily engaged in intercommunal work. MaAfrika Tikkun, the Jewish group devoted exclusively to aiding underprivileged South Africans, won three awards during the year for the excellence of its programs. Among its best-known activities were a summer camp for 28 HIV-infected children, a project to provide food for the poor, and the operation of a facility in Alexandra "Township," Johannesburg, that offered medical, education, and old-age services. The Union of Jewish Women continued its outreach activities. Among it many projects was the founding of a crèche for the children of homeless families in Joubert Park, Johannesburg.

The Gauteng Council of the SAJBOD held a commemorative evening marking the 50th anniversary of the Freedom Charter, the document, endorsed by brave South Africans of all races, declaring that the country "belongs to all who live in it," which ultimately led to the end of the apartheid system. A Jewish delegation took part in the 30th anniversary of the 1976 student uprising in Soweto. Michael Bagraim wrote, "This was a very moving experience for all of us, and it brought home to me how imperative it is for us, as Jews, to not only remember our own historical suffering, but also recognize, and display solidarity with, those who have been oppressed."

In November, Rabbi David Rosen, who had served a congregation in South Africa during the 1970s as was now director of international interreligious relations for American Jewish Committee, presided at a meeting in Cape Town of the International Catholic-Jewish Liaison Committee (ICJLC). This was the first time that the ICJLC had met on the African continent. Representatives of all the city's religious groups attended the opening session, which was hosted by Mayor Helen Zille. Four present or former chief rabbis were in attendance: Rabbi Yonah Metzger of Israel, Rabbi Dr. Warren Goldstein of South Africa, Rabbi Michael Schudrich of Poland, and Rabbi Rosen, who had been chief rabbi of Ireland.

In his address, Cardinal Walter Kasper, head of the Vatican Commission for Religious Relations with the Jews, described the transformation of Jewish-Christian relations as the most revolutionary development of the second half of the twentieth century. According to Rabbi Rosen, the mutual respect between Catholics and Jews posed a challenge for both communities—to be a blessing to humanity. The conference provided excellent opportunities for networking, explained Michael Bagraim on behalf of the SAJBOD. "It brought home to us just how much influence the Catholic Church wields in Africa, and how the many senior members of African governments . . . are committed adherents to the Catholic faith . . . . The various Church heads and leadership have indicated that they want to carry the initiative forward to explore the two communities working together for the betterment of South Africa. Through the African Jewish Congress we will explore how we can use this relationship to work with the rest of southern Africa."

Religion

A case involving conversion to Judaism was addressed by the High Court of South Africa in 2006. A bereaved husband who sought to have his wife, a convert, buried according to Orthodox rites was turned down by the bet din (religious court). The head of that tribunal, Rabbi Moshe Kurtsag, expressed compassion on a personal level, but noted that the conversion had not been performed according to traditional Jewish law. "Quickie conversions," he said, solved no problems and only created more difficulties for succeeding generations. The husband turned to the High Court, but it denied his appeal, and the woman was buried by the Progressive congregation. Rabbi Kurtsag maintained that the door was always open to those non-Jews who wanted to enter Judaism through the formal Orthodox route.

A number of celebrations, inductions, and amalgamations took place during the year: Rabbi Gidon Fox was inducted as the new rabbi of the Pretoria Hebrew Congregation; Rabbi Malcolm Mattitiani of Temple Israel in Cape Town was among the first group of rabbis to be ordained in Germany since the 1930s; Chabad celebrated 30 years in the Western Cape Province; Temple Israel, the "mother congregation" of Progressive Judaism in South Africa, celebrated its 70th anniversary and dedicated its new complex in Cape Town; two historic synagogues—Claremont and Wynberg—amalgamated to form the Claremont Wynberg Hebrew Congregation; and the Doornfontein Hebrew Congregation in Johannesburg (known as the Lions Shul) celebrated its centenary.

The Rabbinical Association of the Western Cape and the Union of Orthodox Synagogues (Cape Council) initiated "Shabbat across Cape

Town," modeled on the "Shabbat across America" in the U.S., to provide South African Jews the opportunity "to experience the beauty and warmth of Shabbat."

Education

South Africa's National Department of Education introduced a new school curriculum to take effect in 2008. Under its provisions, all religious study, including Jewish studies, would no longer count for the national matriculation certificate. The SAJBOD entered into dialogue with the government over this initiative.

The financial crisis looming over the Johannesburg Jewish day schools came under discussion at the South African Board of Jewish Education (SAJBE) conference in Johannesburg. Although Fay Lewis, chairman of the SAJBE, reported that the deficit had declined over the past year and that there was now a small surplus, debate focused particularly on one school that was in trouble. A leading businessman, Solly Krok, stressed the need to apply sound commercial principles when considering the plight of the King David Victory Park School. "If the school is not getting by financially, it should be merged with King David Linksfield or Sandton," he told the conference. "It makes no sense in keeping a school open, which is running at a loss, just for a few children." Krok was critical of the SAJBJE's lack of long-term planning and its poor record of investments. But Krok was challenged by others, both parents and educators, who believed that King David Victory Park was viable and should not be closed.

Another issue raised at the conference was the feeling among Progressive Jews that their educational needs were not being met by the day schools. Declared Progressive leader David Lurie, "We should have traditionally based education. The schools belong to the whole community. No one should fall through the cracks and we are about to."

The University of Cape Town announced that beginning in 2007, there would no longer be an independent Department of Hebrew and Jewish Studies. Rather, courses in these fields would be offered by the various disciplinary departments, such as languages, history, and sociology. The Kaplan Centre for Jewish Studies and Research would continue as an autonomous entity within the humanities faculty, enriching the field through teaching and research. The change was part of a broader restructuring of all the small departments within the university.

A number of adult education initiatives were launched. In March, the

Midrasha Adult Education Institute opened, incorporating the Florence Melton Adult Mini-School project of the Hebrew University. October saw the establishment of "Limmud Indaba" in South Africa, modeled on the successful Limmud program that began in Great Britain 26 years earlier. "Indaba" is an African word meaning "a meeting of minds." Dr. Jeremy Wanderer, a lecturer in philosophy at the University of Cape Town who had formerly been involved in Limmud in the UK, expressed the hope that the South African version would "contribute to and change the whole Jewish conversation." He told the *SA Jewish Report* that "South African Jews have gone through an interesting and unique period in history. As an outsider to the community, I think there are lots of people here who have a pretty unique perspective, not only on life in general, but on Jewish life, and I'm hoping that Limmud will create a forum for them to explore and export this particular notion of Jewishness."

Culture

The South African Jewish Museum in Cape Town held two special exhibitions during the year, one on the life and times of world-renowned paleoanthropologist Phillip Tobias, and the other titled "Journeys into the Interior: Unseen Works by Irma Stern 1929–1939."

The exhibition, "Helen Suzman: Fighter for Human Rights," curated by Millie Pimstone and Linda Bester for the Kaplan Centre for Jewish Studies at the University of Cape Town, was mounted at the Cyril Harris Community Centre in Johannesburg. Two other cultural milestones were the Johannesburg Jewish Male Choir's celebration of its 21st birthday, and a special issue of *Jewish Affairs,* the SAJBOD's house journal, on "South African Jews in the Theater."

Publications of Jewish interest included *Defending the Human Spirit: Jewish Law's Vision for a Moral Society* by Chief Rabbi Dr. Warren Goldstein; *Out of Step, Life Story of Politician: Politics and Religion in a World at War* by Jack Bloom; *The Holocaust and Apartheid* by Juliette Peires; and *Prophets and Profits: Managerialism and the Restructuring of Jewish Schools in South Africa* by Chaya Herman.

Personalia

David Goldblatt won the 2006 Hassalblad Award for photography; Tony Leon, leader of the Democratic Alliance, the official opposition party, was elected vice president of the International Council of Jewish

Parliamentarians; Gerald Leissner was awarded an honorary fellowship from the Hebrew University; Marlene Bethlehem became one of five vice presidents of the Memorial Foundation for Jewish Culture; Ronald Bobroff was elected president of the Law Society of the Northern Province, formerly the Transvaal Law Society; and Ronnie Kaplan was honored by the Jaffe Institute for supporting projects in Israel.

Among prominent South African Jews who died in 2006 were Hilda Bernstein, journalist, author, artist, and antiapartheid activist; Prof. Robert Allen Trope, doyen of South African ophthalmology; Reginald Kingsley "Reg" Donner, Jewish communal activist; Lionel Ostrowfsky, prominent leader of the Progressive movement; Dr. Moshe Natas, renowned educator; Joan Goldberg, mainstay of the Jewish Women's Benevolent Society; Dr. Moshe Yagel, teacher and spiritual leader; Solly Yellin, Zionist leader; Rabbi Joseph Fogel, Etz Chayim stalwart; Lozer Karabelnik, Zionist leader; and Phyllis Jowell, a prominent writer about the Jewish heritage.

MILTON SHAIN

World Jewish Population, 2007

T HE WORLD'S JEWISH POPULATION was estimated at 13.155 million at the beginning of 2007 — an increase of about 63,000 over the previous year's revised estimate.[1] While world total population grew by 1.2 percent in 2006,[2] the world Jewish population grew by 0.5 percent. Israel's Jewish population grew by 1.5 percent and the rest of world Jewry diminished on aggregate by –0.2 percent.

Israel's Jewish population (not including more than 300,000 non-Jewish immigrants admitted in the framework of the Law of Return) approached 5.4 million in 2007, or 41 percent of world Jewry. This represented not only a population increase of nearly 80,000 over 2006 but also a watershed in Jewish population history: after critically reviewing all available evidence on Jewish demographic trends, it is plausible to claim that Israel has overtaken the United States in hosting the largest Jewish community worldwide. Dissenting opinions on this issue will be reviewed later in this article.

In the light of available evidence, demography — through daily, imperceptibly slow and multiform changes affecting human birth and death, and the willingness of individuals to identify with a Jewish collective — has thus produced a transition of singular symbolic relevance for Jewish history and destiny. This holds true at least with regard to the *core* Jewish population, not inclusive of non-Jewish members of Jewish households, other non-Jews of Jewish ancestry, and still other non-Jews who may be conversant with or interested in Jewish matters.

Israel's Jewish population growth — even if slower than during the 1990s — reflects the continuing substantial natural increase generated by a combination of relatively high fertility (2.75 children, on average, in 2006) and young age composition (about 25 percent below age 15). Neither of these two factors prevails in any other Jewish community world-

---

[1]The previous estimates, as of January 1, 2006, were published in AJYB 2006, vol. 106, pp. 559–601. See also Sergio DellaPergola, Uzi Rebhun, and Mark Tolts, "Prospecting the Jewish Future: Population Projections 2000–2080," AJYB 2000, vol. 100, pp. 103–46; and previous AJYB volumes for further details on earlier estimates.
[2]Population Reference Bureau, *2007 World Population Data Sheet* (Washington, D.C., 2007).

wide, where instead, leaving aside the possible impact of international migration, Jewish populations tend to decrease at variable paces because of low Jewish birthrates, an increasingly elderly age composition, and a dubious balance between those joining Judaism and those leaving it.

DETERMINANTS OF JEWISH POPULATION CHANGE

Major geopolitical and socioeconomic changes that affected the world scene since the end of the 1980s significantly affected Jewish population trends. Of particularly heavy impact were the political breakup of the Soviet Union; Germany's reunion; the European Union's gradual expansion to 27 states with the addition of ten new members in 2004 and of Romania and Bulgaria in 2007; South Africa's transition to a new regime; political and economic instability in several Latin American countries; and the volatile situation in Israel and the Middle East set off by the Oslo agreements of the 1990s and the second intifada of the 2000s. Large-scale emigration from the former Soviet Union (FSU) and rapid population growth in Israel were the most visible effects, accompanied by other significant Jewish population transfers. Reflecting geographical mobility and increased political fragmentation but also a new consolidation of the global system of nations, over 80 percent of world Jewry live today in two countries, the U.S. and Israel, and 95 percent are concentrated in the ten largest country communities. Six of the G8 countries[3] (the U.S., France, Canada, the United Kingdom, the Russian Republic, and Germany) comprise 87 percent of the total Jewish population outside of Israel. The aggregate of these major Jewish population centers virtually determines the assessment of world Jewry's total size and demographic trends. The continuing realignment of world Jewish population geography toward the major centers of development provides a robust yardstick for explanation and prediction.[4]

A fundamental aspect of population in general and of Jewish population in particular is its perpetual change. Population size and composition reflect a continuous interplay of three major determinants. Two of these are shared by all populations: (a) the balance of vital events (births and deaths); and (b) the balance of international migration (immigration

---

[3]The eight leading world economies, also comprising Japan and Italy.
[4]See Sergio DellaPergola, Uzi Rebhun, and Mark Tolts, "Contemporary Jewish Diaspora in Global Context: Human Development Correlates of Population Trends," *Israel Studies*, 11, 1, 2005, pp. 61–95.

and emigration). Both affect increases or decreases in the physical presence of individuals in a given place. The third determinant consists of identificational changes (accessions and secessions), and applies only to populations — usually referred to as subpopulations — that are defined by some cultural, symbolic or other specific peculiarity, as is the case with Jews.

This last type of change does not affect people's physical presence but rather their willingness or ability to identify with a particular religious, ethnic or otherwise culturally defined group. Some, though not all, of these passages between one identity and another receive formal sanction through ritual ceremonies of one sort or another, and therefore can be measured. The quantitative impact of passages that occur in individual perceptions of and emotional attachments to group identities without any ceremonial event to mark them are much harder to gauge but should not be undervalued.

The country figures presented here for 2007 were updated from those for 2006 in accordance with the known or estimated changes in the interval — vital events, migrations, and identificational changes. In our updating procedure, whether or not exact data on intervening changes were available, we consistently applied empirically ascertained or assumed directions of change, and accordingly added to or subtracted from previous Jewish population estimates. If there was evidence that intervening changes balanced each other off, Jewish population remained unchanged. This procedure proved highly accurate in the past, and when improved Jewish population figures became available in the form of a new census or survey, our annually updated estimates generally proved on target.

Recent research findings basically confirm the estimates we reported in previous AJYB volumes and, perhaps more importantly, our interpretation of the trends now prevailing in the demography of world Jewry.[5] Concisely stated, these involve a positive balance of vital events (Jewish births and deaths) in Israel and a negative one in nearly all other Jewish communities; a positive migration balance for Israel, the U.S., Germany, Canada, Australia, and a few other Western countries, and a negative one

---

[5]For historical background, see Roberto Bachi, *Population Trends of World Jewry* (Jerusalem, 1976); U.O. Schmelz, "Jewish Survival: The Demographic Factors," AJYB 1981, vol. 81, pp. 61–117; U.O. Schmelz, *Aging of World Jewry* (Jerusalem, 1984); Sergio DellaPergola, "Changing Cores and Peripheries: Fifty Years in Socio-demographic Perspective," in Robert S. Wistrich, ed., *Terms of Survival: The Jewish World since 1945* (London, 1995), pp. 13–43; Sergio DellaPergola, *World Jewry beyond 2000: Demographic Prospects* (Oxford, 1999).

in Latin America, South Africa, Eastern Europe, Muslim countries, and some Western European countries as well; a positive balance of accessions and secessions in Israel, and an often negative, or at best uncertain, balance elsewhere.

While allowing for refinements and corrections, the 2007 population estimates highlight the increasing complexity of the sociodemographic and identificational processes underlying the definition of Jewish populations, and hence the estimates of their sizes. This complexity is magnified at a time of pervasive migration between and within countries, often implying bi-local residences and double counts of people on the move or permanently sharing their time between different places. Some of these errors can be corrected at a later stage. Consequently, the analyst has to come to terms with the paradox of the *permanently provisional* nature of Jewish population estimates.

SOURCES OF DATA

Figures on population size, characteristics, and trends are a primary tool in the evaluation of Jewish community needs and prospects at the local level and internationally. The estimates for major regions and individual countries reported in this overview reflect a prolonged and ongoing effort to study scientifically the demography of contemporary world Jewry.[6] Data collection and comparative research have benefited from the collaboration of scholars and institutions in many countries, including replies to direct inquiries regarding current estimates. It should be em-

[6]Many of these activities are carried out by, or in coordination with, the Division of Jewish Demography and Statistics at the A. Harman Institute of Contemporary Jewry (ICJ), the Hebrew University of Jerusalem. Thanks are due to our team members Benjamin Anderman, Judith Even, Uzi Rebhun, Dalia Sagi, and Mark Tolts. We gratefully acknowledge the collaboration of many institutions and individuals in the different countries who supplied information or otherwise helped for this update. We thank in particular Ralph Weill (Basel), Simon Cohn and Claude Kandyoti (Brussels), András Kovács (Budapest), Yaacov Rubel (Buenos Aires), Tally Frankental (Cape Town), Salomon Benzaquen and Tony Beker de Weinraub (Caracas), Frank Mott (Columbus, Ohio), Barry R. Chiswick and Carmel U. Chiswick (Chicago), Ellen Rubinstein (Frankfurt a. M.), Frans van Poppel (The Hague), Lina Filiba (Istanbul), Norma Gurovich, Israel Pupko and Emma Trahtenberg (Jerusalem), David Saks (Johannesburg), Rona Hart and Marlena Schmool (London), Mauricio Lulka (Mexico City), Rafael Porzecanski (Montevideo), Evgueni Andreev and Eugeni Soroko (Moscow), Laurence Kotler-Berkowitz (New York), René Decol (São Paulo), Ira Sheskin (Miami), Allen Glicksman (Philadelphia), Erik H. Cohen (Ramat Gan), Arnold Dashefsky (Storrs, Ct.), Gary Eckstein (Sydney), Leonard Saxe, Charles Kadushin and Benjamin Phillips (Waltham, Mass.), and Hania Zlotnik (the UN).

phasized, however, that the elaboration of a worldwide set of estimates for the Jewish populations of the various countries is beset with difficulties and uncertainties.[7] Therefore users of Jewish population estimates should be aware of the inherent limitations of our estimates. The new figures on Israel, the U.S., and the rest of world Jewry reflect updated information on Jewish population that became available following the major round of national censuses and Jewish population surveys in countries with large Jewish populations over the period 1999–2006. This new evidence generally confirmed our previous estimates, but sometimes suggested upward or downward revisions.

Over the last decades the database available for a critical assessment of the worldwide Jewish demographic picture has significantly expanded. Some of this ongoing research is part of a coordinated effort aimed at updating the profile of world Jewry.[8] However, the amount and quality of documentation on Jewish population size and characteristics is still far from satisfactory.

In recent years important new data and estimates were released for several countries through official population censuses. National censuses yielded results on Jewish populations in Ireland, the Czech Republic and India (1991); Romania and Bulgaria (1992); the Russian Republic and Macedonia (1994); Israel (1995); Canada, South Africa, Australia, and New Zealand (1996 and 2001); Belarus, Azerbaijan, Kazakhstan, and Kyrgyzstan (1999); Brazil, Mexico, Switzerland, Estonia, Latvia, and Tajikistan (2000); the United Kingdom, Hungary, Croatia, Lithuania,

---

[7]For overviews of subject matter and technical issues see Paul Ritterband, Barry A. Kosmin, and Jeffrey Scheckner, "Counting Jewish Populations: Methods and Problems," AJYB 1988, vol. 88, pp. 204–21; and Sergio DellaPergola, "Demography," in Martin Goodman, ed., The Oxford Handbook of Jewish Studies (Oxford, 2002), pp. 797–823.

[8]Following an International Conference on Jewish Population Problems held in Jerusalem in 1987, initiated by the late Roberto Bachi of the Hebrew University and sponsored by major Jewish organizations worldwide, an International Scientific Advisory Committee (ISAC) was established under the chairmanship of Sidney Goldstein. See Sergio DellaPergola and Leah Cohen, eds., World Jewish Population: Trends and Policies (Jerusalem, 1992). An Initiative on Jewish Demography, sponsored by the Jewish Agency during the tenure of Chairman Sallai Meridor, led to an international conference held in Jerusalem in 2002 and to data collection and analysis implemented over the years 2003–2005. Since 2003, the Jewish People Policy Planning Institute (JPPPI), founded by Yehezkel Dror and chaired by Ambassador Dennis Ross, has provided a framework for policy analysis and suggestions on Jewish population issues. See Sergio DellaPergola, Jewish Demography: Facts, Outlook, Challenges, JPPPI Alert Paper 2 (Jerusalem, 2003); The Jewish People Policy Planning Institute Annual Assessment 2004–05, Between Thriving and Decline (Jerusalem, 2005); The Jewish People Policy Planning Institute, The Conference on the Future of the Jewish People 2007, Background Policy Documents (Jerusalem, 2007).

and Ukraine (2001); the Russian Republic, Georgia, and Poland (2002); and Moldova (2004). While population censuses in the U.S. do not provide information on religion, they have furnished relevant data on countries of birth, spoken languages, and ancestry. Permanent national population registers, including information on the Jewish religious, ethnic or national group, exist in several European countries (Switzerland, Norway, Finland, Estonia, Latvia, and Lithuania), and in Israel.

In addition, independent sociodemographic studies have provided valuable information on Jewish demography and socioeconomic stratification, as well as on Jewish identification. Surveys were conducted over the last several years in South Africa (1991 and 1998); Mexico (1991 and 2000); Lithuania (1993); the United Kingdom and Chile (1995); Venezuela (1998–99); Israel, Hungary, the Netherlands, and Guatemala (1999); Moldova and Sweden (2000); France and Turkey (2002); and Argentina (2003 and 2004). In the U.S. important new insights were provided by two large surveys, the National Jewish Population Survey (NJPS, 2000–01) and the American Jewish Identity Survey (AJIS, 2001), as well as a smaller one, the Heritage, Ancestry, and Religious Identity Survey (HARI, 2003). Several other Jewish population studies were separately conducted in major U.S. cities (notably in New York City in 2002 and Boston in 2005—the fifth decennial study in that metropolitan area) and in other countries.

Evidence on Jewish population trends can also be obtained from the systematic monitoring of membership registers, vital statistics, and migration records available from Jewish communities and other Jewish organizations in many countries or cities, notably the United Kingdom, Germany, Italy, Buenos Aires, and São Paulo. Detailed data on Jewish immigration routinely collected in Israel help in the assessment of changing Jewish population sizes in other countries.

Finally, the cross-matching of more than one type of source about the same Jewish population, although not frequently feasible, can provide either mutual reinforcement or important critical insights into the available data.

DEFINITIONS

A major problem with Jewish population estimates periodically circulated by individual scholars or Jewish organizations is a lack of coherence and uniformity in the definitional criteria followed—when the issue of defining the Jewish population is addressed at all. The study of a Jewish population (or of any other group that is part of a broader population) requires solving three main problems: (a) *defining* the target group on the basis of conceptual or normative criteria so as to provide the best possible description of that group—which, in the case of Jewry, is no minor task; (b) *identifying* the group thus defined based on tools that enable, in practical terms, distinguishing and selecting the target group from the rest of the population—through membership lists, types of names, areas of residence, or otherwise; and (c) *covering* the target group through appropriate field work—face to face, by telephone, or otherwise.

Most often in the actual experience of social research the definitional task is performed at the stage of identification, and identification is done at the stage of actual field work. Clearly, the quantitative study of Jewish populations relies only on operational, not normative, definitional criteria, while its conceptual aspects, far from pure theory, heavily depend on practical and logistical feasibility. Moreover, the ultimate technical step—collection of relevant data on the relevant persons—crucially reflects the readiness of people to collaborate in the data-collection effort: the amount, contents, and validity of information gathered depends on the readiness of subjects to participate. But since such readiness reflects the identification outlook of the individuals who are part of the target populations, which in turn is an integral part of what should be investigated, the researcher is caught in a vicious circle. Therefore research findings reflect, with varying degrees of sophistication, only what can be uncovered. Anything beyond that may exist, but only in a virtual world of myths, hopes, and fears, not in reality.

Keeping this in mind, three major definitional concepts provide serious comparative foundations to the study of Jewish demography. They are (a) *core Jewish population;* (b) *enlarged Jewish population;* and (c) *Law of Return Jewish population.*

In most countries out of Israel, the concept of *core Jewish population*[9] includes all persons who, when asked, identify themselves as Jews; or, if the respondent is a different person in the same household, are identified by him/her as Jews. Such a definition of a person as a Jew, reflecting subjective feelings, broadly overlaps but does not necessarily coincide with Halakhah (rabbinic law) or other normatively binding definitions. Inclusion does not depend on any measure of that person's Jewish com-

---

[9]The term was initially suggested in Barry A. Kosmin, Sidney Goldstein, Joseph Waksberg, Nava Lerer, Ariela Keysar, and Jeffrey Scheckner, *Highlights of the CJF 1990 National Jewish Population Survey* (New York, 1991).

mitment or behavior in terms of religiosity, beliefs, knowledge, communal affiliation, or otherwise. The *core* Jewish population includes all converts to Judaism by any procedure, as well as other people who declare they are Jewish. It is also customary to include persons of Jewish parentage who claim no current religious or ethnic identity. Persons of Jewish parentage who adopted another religion are usually excluded, as are other individuals who in censuses or surveys explicitly identify with a non-Jewish group without having converted out.

In the State of Israel, personal status is subject to the rulings of the Ministry of the Interior, which relies on criteria established by rabbinical authorities. In Israel, therefore, *core* Jewish population does not simply express subjective identification but reflects definite legal rules, those of Halakhah, entailing a matrilineal Jewish origin or a conversion to Judaism. Documentation to prove a person's Jewish status may include non-Jewish sources.

The *core* concept offers an intentionally comprehensive and pragmatic approach reflecting the nature of most available sources of data on Jewish population. In countries other than Israel, such data often derive from population censuses or social surveys where interviewees have the option to decide how to answer relevant questions on religious or ethnic preferences.

The question of whether Jewish identification according to this *core* definition can or should exclude association with other religious corporate identities emerged as a major issue in the course of the 2000–01 NJPS. The solution chosen—admittedly after much debate—was to allow for Jews with multiple religious identities to be included under certain circumstances in the standard definition of Jewish population.[10] To accommodate them a category of Persons of Jewish Background (PJBs) was introduced: some of these were included in the Jewish population count and others were not, based on a more thorough evaluation of their

---

[10]In the latter survey, at least in the version initially processed and circulated by UJC, "a Jew is defined as a person whose religion is Judaism, OR whose religion is Jewish and something else, OR who has no religion and has at least one Jewish parent or a Jewish upbringing, OR who has a non-monotheistic religion and has at least one Jewish parent or a Jewish upbringing." See Laurence Kotler-Berkowitz, Steven M. Cohen, Jonathon Ament, Vivian Klaff, Frank Mott, and Danyelle Peckerman-Neuman, with Lorraine Blass, Debbie Bursztyn, and David Marker, *The National Jewish Population Survey 2000–01: Strength, Challenge, and Diversity in the American Jewish Population* (New York, 2003). See also *Contemporary Jewry* (the scholarly journal of the Association for the Scientific Study of Jewry, edited by Samuel Heilman), vol. 25, 2005, which is devoted to critical essays and analyses of NJPS method and findings.

ancestry and childhood. In Canada, by the same token, persons with multiple ethnic identities including a Jewish one were included in the standard Jewish population count. The adoption of such extended criteria by researchers tends to stretch Jewish population definitions beyond usual practices in the past and beyond the abovementioned typical *core* definition. One effect of changing the criteria is to limit the comparability of the same Jewish population over time and of different Jewish populations at the same time.

The *enlarged Jewish population*[11] includes the sum of (a) the *core* Jewish population; (b) all other persons of Jewish parentage who — by *core* Jewish population criteria — are not Jewish currently (or at the date of reference of investigation); and (c) all of the respective further non-Jewish household members (spouses, children, etc.). Non-Jews with Jewish background, as far as they can be ascertained, include: (a) persons who have themselves adopted another religion, even though they may claim to be also Jewish by ethnicity or preference — with the caveat just mentioned for recent U.S. and Canadian data; and (b) other persons with Jewish parentage who disclaim being Jewish. As noted, most PJBs who do not pertain to the *core* Jewish population naturally belong under the *enlarged* definition.[12] It is customary in sociodemographic surveys to consider the religio-ethnic identification of parents. Some censuses, however, also ask about more distant ancestry. For both conceptual and practical reasons, the *enlarged* definition usually does not include other non-Jewish relatives who lack a Jewish background and live in exclusively non-Jewish households.

The *Law of Return,* Israel's distinctive legal framework for the acceptance and absorption of new immigrants, awards Jewish new immigrants immediate citizenship and other civil rights. According to the current, amended version of the *Law of Return,* a Jew is any person born to a Jewish mother or converted to Judaism (regardless of denomination — Orthodox, Conservative, or Reform), who does not have another religious identity. By ruling of Israel's Supreme Court, conversion from Judaism, as in the case of some ethnic Jews who currently identify with another religion, entails loss of eligibility for *Law of Return* purposes. The law as

---

[11]The term *enlarged Jewish population* was initially suggested by Sergio DellaPergola, "The Italian Jewish Population Study: Demographic Characteristics and Trends," in U.O. Schmelz, P. Glikson, and S.J. Gould, eds., *Studies in Jewish Demography: Survey for 1969–1971* (Jerusalem-London, 1975), pp. 60–97.

[12]Kotler-Berkowitz et al., *National Jewish Population Survey 2000–01.*

such does not affect a person's Jewish status—which, as noted, is adjudicated by Israel's Ministry of Interior and rabbinical authorities—but only the specific benefits available under the law, whose provisions extend to all current Jews, their children, and grandchildren, as well as to the respective Jewish or non-Jewish spouses. As a result of its three-generation and lateral extension, the *Law of Return* applies to the large population of all those eligible for aliyah, a category whose scope is significantly wider than the *core* and *enlarged* Jewish populations defined above.[13] It is actually quite difficult to estimate the total size of the *Law of Return* population. Such estimates are not discussed below systematically, but some notion of their possible extent is given for the major countries.

The significant involvement of major Israeli and American Jewish organizations—such as the Jewish Agency for Israel, the American Joint Distribution Committee, or United Jewish Communities (UJC)—in sponsoring data collection tends to complicate research issues. Organizations are motivated by their mission toward their constituencies rather than by unequivocally pure analytic criteria. In turn, the understandable interest of organizations in perpetuating themselves and securing budgetary resources inclines them to address Jewish populations increasingly more similar to the *enlarged* and *Law of Return* definitions than to the *core*.

The following estimates of Jewish population distribution in each continent (Table 1 below), country (Tables 2–9), and major metropolitan areas (Table 10) aim at the concept of *core* Jewish population. The *core* is indeed the necessary starting point for any relevant elaboration about the *enlarged*.

PRESENTATION AND QUALITY OF DATA

Until 1999, Jewish population estimates presented in the *American Jewish Year Book* referred to December 31 of the year preceding by two the date of publication. Since 2000 our estimates refer to January 1 of the current year of publication. Efforts to provide the most recent possible picture entail a short span of time for evaluation and correction of available information, hence a somewhat greater margin of inaccuracy. Indeed,

---

[13]For a concise review of the rules of attribution of Jewish personal status in rabbinic and Israeli law, including reference to Jewish sects, isolated communities, and apostates, see Michael Corinaldi, "Jewish Identity," chap. 2 in his *Jewish Identity: The Case of Ethiopian Jewry* (Jerusalem, 1998).

where appropriate, we revised our previous estimates in the light of newly accrued information on Jewish populations (Tables 1 and 2). Corrections were also applied retrospectively to the 2006 figures for major geographical regions so as to ensure a better base for comparisons with the 2007 estimates. Corrections of the latest estimates, if needed, will be presented in future volumes of the AJYB.

We provide separate figures for each country with approximately 100 or more resident *core* Jews. Residual estimates of Jews living in other smaller communities supplement some of the continental totals. For each of the reported countries in each continent, the four columns in Tables 3–7 provide an estimate of midyear 2006 total population,[14] the estimated 1/1/2007 Jewish population, the proportion of Jews per 1,000 of total population, and a rating of the accuracy of the Jewish population estimate.

There is wide variation in the quality of the Jewish population estimates for different countries. For many Diaspora countries it would be best to indicate a range (minimum–maximum) rather than a definite figure for the number of Jews. It would be confusing, however, for the reader to be confronted with a long list of ranges; this would also complicate the regional and world totals. The figures actually indicated for most of the Diaspora communities should be understood as being the central value of the plausible range of the respective core Jewish populations. The relative magnitude of this range varies inversely to the accuracy of the estimate.

The three main elements that affect the accuracy of each estimate are the nature and quality of the base data, how recent the base data are, and the method of updating. A simple code combining these elements is used to provide a general evaluation of the reliability of the Jewish population figures reported in the detailed tables below. The code indicates different quality levels of the reported estimates: (A) Base figure derived from countrywide census or relatively reliable Jewish population survey; updated on the basis of full or partial information on Jewish population movements in the respective country during the intervening period. (B) Base figure derived from less accurate but recent countrywide Jewish population data; partial information on population movements in the intervening period. (C) Base figure derived from less recent sources, and/or unsatisfactory or partial coverage of a country's Jewish population; up-

---

[14]Data and estimates derived from Population Reference Bureau, *2007 World Population Data Sheet.*

dated according to demographic information illustrative of regional demographic trends. (D) Base figure essentially speculative; no reliable updating procedure. In categories (A), (B), and (C), the year in which the country's base figure or important partial updates were obtained is also stated. For countries whose Jewish population estimate for 2007 was not only updated but also revised in light of improved information, the sign "X" is appended to the accuracy rating.

One additional tool for updating Jewish population estimates is provided by several sets of demographic projections developed at the Institute of Contemporary Jewry of the Hebrew University of Jerusalem.[15] Such projections, based on available data on Jewish population composition by age and sex groups, extrapolate the most likely observed or expected Jewish population trends over the first decades of the twenty-first century. Even where reliable information on the dynamics of Jewish population change is not immediately available, the powerful connection that generally exists between age composition of a population and the respective frequencies of births and deaths and migration movements helps provide plausible scenarios of the developments bound to occur in the short term. Where better data were lacking, we used indications from these projections to refine the 2006 estimates as against previous years. On the other hand, projections are clearly shaped by a comparatively limited set of assumptions, and need to be periodically updated in the light of actual demographic developments.

WORLD JEWISH POPULATION SIZE

The size of world Jewry at the beginning of 2007 was assessed at 13,155,200, constituting 1.99 per 1,000 of the world's total population of 6,625 million. One in about 503 people in the world is a Jew. According to the revised figures, the Jewish people grew between January 1, 2006 and January 1, 2007, by an estimated 65,400 people, or about 0.5 percent. This compares with a total world population growth rate of 1.2 percent (0.1 percent in more developed countries, 1.5 percent in less developed countries). Allowing for imperfections in the estimates, world Jewry continued to be close to zero population growth, with increase in Israel (1.5 percent) overcoming decline in the Diaspora (−0.2 percent).

---

[15]DellaPergola, Rebhun, and Tolts, "Prospecting the Jewish Future" and unpublished tabulations. A new round of population projections currently undertaken in the light of the latest data helped in the current assessment.

TABLE 1. ESTIMATED CORE JEWISH POPULATION, BY CONTINENTS AND MAJOR GEOGRAPHICAL REGIONS, 2006 AND 2007[a]

Region	2006 Original Abs. N.	2006 Revised[b] Abs. N.	2006 Revised[b] Percent[c]	2007 Abs. N.	2007 Percent[c]	Yearly % Change 2006–2007	Jews/1000 Total Population
World	13,089,800	13,092,000	100.0	13,155,200	100.0	0.5	2.0
Diaspora	7,776,000	7,778,200	59.4	7,761,800	59.0	−0.2	1.2
Israel	5,313,800	5,313,800	40.6	5,393,400	41.0	1.5	757.9
America, Total	6,043,200	6,043,200	46.2	6,041,300	45.9	0.0	6.7
North[d]	5,648,500	5,648,500	43.1	5,649,000	42.9	0.0	16.9
Central	51,800	51,800	0.4	51,600	0.4	−0.4	0.3
South	342,900	342,900	2.6	340,700	2.6	−0.6	0.9
Europe, Total	1,505,500	1,507,400	11.5	1,492,700	11.3	−1.0	1.9
European Union[b]	1,121,300	1,133,400[i]	0.0	1,129,800	8.6	−0.3	2.3
Other West	19,700	19,700	0.2	19,500	0.1	−1.0	1.6
Former USSR[e]	330,800	332,700	2.5	322,000	2.4	−3.2	1.6
Other East and Balkans[e]	33,700	21,600[i]	0.0	21,400	0.2	−0.9	0.2
Asia, Total	5,353,300	5,353,600	40.9	5,432,900	41.3	1.5	1.4
Israel	5,313,800	5,313,800	40.6	5,393,400	41.0	1.5	757.9
Former USSR[e]	19,900	20,200	0.2	20,000	0.2	−1.0	0.3
Other	19,600	19,600	0.1	19,500	0.1	−0.5	0.0
Africa, Total	77,700	77,700	0.6	77,200	0.6	−0.6	0.1
North[f]	4,200	4,200	0.0	4,200	0.0	0.0	0.0
South[g]	73,500	73,500	0.6	73,000	0.6	−0.7	0.1
Oceania[h]	110,100	110,100	0.8	111,100	0.8	0.9	3.2

[a]January 1.
[b]Including European Union's ten new entries.
[c]Minor discrepancies due to rounding.
[d]U.S.A. and Canada.
[e]Asian regions of Russia and Turkey included in Europe. Baltic countries included in European Union.
[f]Including Ethiopia.
[g]South Africa, Zimbabwe, and other sub-Saharan countries.
[h]Australia, New Zealand.
[i]After including Bulgaria and Romania in the European Union.

Table 1 gives an overall picture of Jewish population for the beginning of 2007 as compared to 2006. For 2006 the originally published estimates are presented along with somewhat revised figures that take into account, retrospectively, the corrections made in certain country estimates in the light of improved information. These corrections resulted in a net increase of the 2006 estimated size of world Jewry by 2,200. Explanations are given below of the reasons for these minor corrections.

The number of Jews in Israel rose from 5,313,800 in 2006 to 5,393,400 at the beginning of 2007, an increase of 79,600 people, or 1.5 percent. In contrast, the estimated Jewish population in the Diaspora diminished from 7,778,200 (according to the revised figures) to 7,761,800—a decrease of 16,400 people, or –0.2 percent. These changes reflect the continuing Jewish emigration from the FSU and other countries, but also the internal decrease typical of the aggregate of Diaspora Jewry. In 2006, Israel's net migratory balance (immigration minus emigration) amounted to a minor gain of 7,900 core Jews for Israel.[16] This calculation includes Israeli citizens born abroad who entered Israel for the first time. Therefore, internal demographic evolution (including vital events and conversions) produced nearly 90 percent of the recorded growth among the Jewish population in Israel and most of the estimated decline in the Diaspora.

Recently, instances of accession or "return" to Judaism can be observed in connection with the absorption in Israel of immigrants from Eastern Europe, Ethiopia, and, to a minor extent, other countries such as Peru and India, under the comprehensive provisions of the Israeli Law of Return and Law of Entrance.[17] The return or first-time access to Judaism of some of such previously unincluded or unidentified individuals contributed to slowing down the pace of decline of the relevant Diaspora Jewish populations and some gains for the Jewish population in Israel.

As noted, corrections should be introduced in previously published Jewish population estimates in the light of new information that has become available. Table 2 provides a synopsis of the world Jewish population estimates relating to the period 1945–2007, as first published each year in the *American Jewish Year Book* and as corrected retroactively, in-

---

[16]Israel Central Bureau of Statistics, *Statistical Abstract of Israel* (Jerusalem, 2007).

[17]As noted the Law of Return applies to Jews and their extended families. The Law of Entrance applies to all others.

corporating all subsequent revisions. These revised data correct, sometimes significantly, the figures published until 1980 by other authors and since 1981 by ourselves. Thanks to the development over the years of an improved database, these new revisions are not necessarily the same revised estimates that appeared year by year in the AJYB based on the information that was available at each date. It is likely that further retrospective revisions may become necessary reflecting ongoing and future research.

The revised figures in Table 2 clearly portray the slowing down of Jewish population growth globally since World War II. Based on a post-Shoah world Jewish population estimate of 11,000,000, a growth of 1,079,000 occurred between 1945 and 1960, followed by growths of 506,000 in the 1960s, 234,000 in the 1970s, 49,000 in the 1980s, and 32,000 in the 1990s. While it took 13 years to add one million to world Jewry's postwar size, over 46 years were needed to add another million. Since 2000, the slow rhythm of Jewish population growth has slightly recovered,

TABLE 2. WORLD JEWISH POPULATION, ORIGINAL AND CORRECTED ESTIMATES, AND TOTAL POPULATION, 1945–2007

| Year | Jewish Population | | | World Population | | Jews per |
	Original Estimate[a]	Corrected Estimate[b]	Yearly % Change[c]	Total (Millions)[d]	Yearly % Change	1000 of Total Pop.
1945, May 1	11,000,000	11,000,000		2,315		4.75
1950, Jan. 1	11,303,400	11,297,000	0.57	2,524	1.87	4.48
1960, Jan. 1	12,792,800	12,079,000	0.67	3,027	1.83	3.99
1970, Jan. 1	13,950,900	12,585,000	0.41	3,702	2.03	3.40
1980, Jan. 1	14,527,100	12,819,000	0.18	4,447	1.85	2.88
1990, Jan. 1	12,810,300	12,868,000	0.04	5,282	1.74	2.44
2000, Jan. 1	13,191,500	12,900,000	0.02	6,000	1.30	2.15
2005, Jan. 1	13,034,100	13,032,600	0.20	6,396	1.29	2.04
2006, Jan. 1	13,089,800	13,092,100	0.46	6,477	1.27	2.02
2007, Jan. 1	13,155,000		0.48	6,625[e]	1.14	1.99

[a]As published in *American Jewish Year Book,* various years. Some of the estimates reported here as of Jan. 1 were originally published as of Dec. 31 of previous year.
[b]Based on updated, corrected, or otherwise improved information. Original estimates for 1990 and after, and all revised estimates: Division of Jewish Demography and Statistics, The A. Harman Institute of Contemporary Jewry, The Hebrew University of Jerusalem.
[c]Based on revised estimates, besides last year.
[d]Midyear estimate of preceding year. Source: Population Reference Bureau.
[e]Midyear estimate of current year. Source: Population Reference Bureau.

mostly reflecting the growing share of Israel out of the world total. Table 2 also outlines the slower Jewish population growth rate versus global growth, and the declining Jewish share of world population. In 2007 the share of Jews within world population (1.99 per 1,000) was less than half of what it was in 1945 (4.75 per 1,000).

DISTRIBUTION BY MAJOR REGIONS AND COUNTRIES

About 46 percent of the world's Jews reside in the Americas, with over 43 percent in North America. Over 41 percent live in Asia, including the Asian republics of the former USSR (but not the Asian parts of the Russian Republic and Turkey)—most of them in Israel. Europe, including the Asian territories of the Russian Republic and Turkey, accounts for 11 percent of the total. Fewer than 2 percent of the world's Jews live in Africa and Oceania. Among the major geographical regions listed in Table 1, the number of Jews in Israel—and, consequently, in total Asia—increased in 2006. Moderate Jewish population gains were also estimated in Canada and Oceania (Australia and New Zealand). We estimate that Jewish population size diminished to variable extents in Central and South America, in Europe, in the former Soviet republics (both in Europe and Asia), and in Africa. We did not change our estimate of the number of Jews in the U.S. (see below). These regional changes reflect trends apparent in the Jewish population in each of the major countries with some notable exceptions within regions, such as the growth of the German Jewish population within the EU. We now turn to a review of recent trends in the largest Jewish populations.

THE AMERICAS

Jewish population in the Americas (Table 3) is predominantly concentrated in the U.S. (5,275,000, or 87 percent of the continental total), followed by Canada (374,000, 6 percent), South America (341,000, 6 percent), and Central America (52,000, 1 percent).

The United States

Jewish population in the U.S. approached 4.5 million in 1945 and according to available sources it grew by about one million until around

1990.[18] Two competing major surveys independently conducted in 2000-2001—the National Jewish Population Survey (NJPS)[19] and the American Jewish Identity Survey (AJIS)[20]—indicated a *core* Jewish population of 5,200,000 and 5,340,000, respectively, in 2001, as against 5,515,000 in 1990. Population projections had long predicted an eventual decrease in *core* Jewish population in the U.S.[21] reflecting a slowing down of international immigration, postponed Jewish marriages and growing singlehood, rising frequencies of out-marriage (over 50 percent of Jews currently marrying), low Jewish fertility (less than 2 children per woman), attribution to the Jewish side of a minority of the children of intermarriages (up to a third according to the highest projection), and noticeable aging (nearly 20 percent of the Jewish population above 65).

The NJPS was sponsored by United Jewish Communities (UJC), the coordinating body of Jewish federations in the U.S., and advised by a National Technical Advisory Committee (NTAC) chaired by the late Vivian Klaff and by Frank Mott. The NTAC included several leading experts on Jewish population studies and senior Jewish community planners. A national random-digit-dialing (RDD) sample covered the whole U.S. territory subdivided into seven geographical strata based on pre-survey estimates of Jewish population density. Sampling probabilities were proportional to Jewish density in each stratum. Over 175,000 households were screened for possible inclusion based on four questions: (1) What is your religion (or that of other adults in the household), if any? (2) Do you or does any other adult in the household have a Jewish mother or a Jewish father? (3) Were you or any other adult in the household raised Jewish? (4) Do you, or does any other adult in the household, consider your/him/herself Jewish for any reasons? Answers to these questions included options other than yes or no, thus allowing for a nondichotomous

---

[18]Sources and findings are reviewed in Sergio DellaPergola, "Was It the Demography? A Reassessment of U.S. Jewish Population Estimates, 1945–2001," *Contemporary Jewry* 25, 2005, 85–31. See also Ira Rosenwaike, "A Synthetic Estimate of American Jewish Population Movement over the Last Three Decades, in U.O. Schmelz and Sergio Della Pergola, eds., *Papers in Jewish Demography 1977* (Jerusalem, 1980), pp. 83–102;

[19]Kotler-Berkowitz et al., *National Jewish Population Survey 2000–01.*

[20]Egon Mayer, Barry Kosmin, and Ariela Keysar, *American Jewish Identity Survey 2001— AJIS Report—An Exploration in the Demography and Outlook of a People* (New York, 2002). See also Barry A. Kosmin, Egon Mayer, and Ariela Keysar, *American Religious Identification Survey 2001* (New York, 2001).

[21]U.O. Schmelz and Sergio DellaPergola, "The Demographic Consequences of U.S. Jewish Population Trends," AJYB 1983, vol. 83, pp. 141–87; U.O. Schmelz and Sergio DellaPergola, *Basic Trends in American Jewish Demography* (New York, 1988).

resolution of Jewish population definition. Such screening criteria, designed to produce results reflecting UJC planning needs, were not strictly comparable with the 1990 NJPS.

The final unweighted sample included 4,220 Jewish respondents and 303 people of Jewish background (PJB), for a total of 4,523 Jewish households; 625 non-Jews of Jewish background; and 4,027 non-Jews, for a total of 9,175 respondent households. The 4,027 non-Jewish households, interviewed for a National Survey of Religion and Ethnicity (NSRE), supplied data needed to weight and estimate Jewish population size, and to a provide comparative sociodemographic background. The response rate to the screening interview was 28 percent. Weights were directly or indirectly estimated and applied to adjust for the number of telephone lines in the household, and to match sample household and respondent data to the U.S. Census totals for sampling strata, age, gender, and region.[22] Following claims of excessively low respondent rates, selective population undercounts, and other inappropriate procedures during and following fieldwork, the NJPS was submitted to independent professional scrutiny, which concluded that the study—while handicapped by methodological shortcomings such as low response rates, inconsistent survey coverage of relevant subpopulations, and loss of documentation—stood within the range of professionally acceptable research standards and biases.[23]

The total Jewish population was estimated at 5.2 million, including 4.3 million with a clearly Jewish identification, 800,000 persons of Jewish background with no religion and whose Jewish identification was less explicit, and over 100,000 persons either in institutions or who did not report their age. Respondents from the first group, the 4.3 million, were administered a long-form questionnaire, while most respondents from the second group, the 800,000, were administered a short-form questionnaire that covered a limited selection of the survey's variables, containing very little on Jewish identification. The total number of Jews plus non-Jews of Jewish background was estimated at 6.7 million. The 2.9 million households with at least one Jewish member were estimated to include 8.7 million individuals, including a significantly larger non-Jewish component than in 1990.

---

[22]Kotler-Berkowitz et al., *National Jewish Population Survey 2000–01*. See also Charles Kadushin, Leonard Saxe, and Benjamin Phillips, "More Nevuchim (A Guide for the Perplexed) for NJPS 2000-01" (Waltham, Mass., 2004).

[23]Mark Schulman, "National Jewish Population Survey 2000–01: Study Review Memo," prepared for the United Jewish Communities, 2003.

The 2001 AJIS, directed by the late Egon Mayer, and by Barry Kosmin and Ariela Keysar, was privately sponsored, testifying to substantive disagreements within the Jewish community and among its researchers about the relationship between social scientific research and community planning. AJIS was based on a national RDD sample that replicated the methodology of the 1990 NJPS. Out of all successful contacts, a total of 50,238 respondents agreed to be interviewed. Through screening questions, 1,668 respondents qualified for a survey of American Jewish households, a response rate of 18 percent.[24] The estimated core Jewish population, including Jews with no religion and Jews by choice, as well as Jews in institutions, was 5,340,000. Of these, 3,460,000 were born Jews whose religion was Judaism, 170,000 were converts to Judaism/Jews by choice, and 1,710,000 were born Jews with no religion. The total household membership, including Jews and others of Jewish origin, was assessed at 7,690,000. The total of individuals in surveyed households, including those without any current core Jew but excluding persons in institutions, was 9,740,000. The AJIS data conceptually matched the 1990 NJPS figures.

A further national study of American Jews was the Heritage and Religious Identification Survey (HARI), conducted in two phases in 2001–02 for the Institute for Jewish & Community Research.[25] A total of 10,204 individuals were interviewed using random-digit-dialing procedures at a response rate of 29 percent. As this sample was considerably smaller than those in the previously mentioned two surveys, the corresponding statistical errors were much larger. The HARI study yielded an estimate of 6.0 million Jews, defined as those saying that Judaism is their religion or that they had a Jewish background (through a parent or upbringing). Since this definition does not specify the current identificational status of adults and children, it is conceptually closer to an *enlarged* Jewish population than to a *core* Jewish population as defined above. Another 4.2 million individuals were defined as of "Jewish heritage," and 2.5 million more were "connected non-Jewish adults." The grand total of 12,735,000 tends toward and even beyond the extensive criteria of the *Law of Return*.

---

[24]Mayer, Kosmin, and Keysar, *American Jewish Identity Survey;* and Barry A. Kosmin, personal communication.

[25]Gary Tobin and Sid Groenman, *Surveying the Jewish Population in the United States* (San Francisco, 2003). It was published in two parts, *Population Estimate* and *Methodological Issues and Challenges.*

Combined reading of the two major surveys, NJPS and AJIS, suggests a core Jewish population in the range of 5.20–5.35 million in 2001. Even accepting the higher estimate, the revised 2001 estimate was about 300,000–400,000 short of the 5.7 million we had projected for 2002 based on the estimate of 5.515 million in the 1990 NJPS.[26] During the 1990s there was an influx of at least 200,000 Jewish new immigrants from the former Soviet Union, Israel, Latin America, South Africa, Iran, and Western Europe. However, Jewish fertility continued to be low, population composition became significantly more aged, intermarriage rates continued to increase, and propensities to identify with Judaism among younger adults of mixed Jewish and non-Jewish ancestry remained low. These were sufficient reasons for a shrinking core population size. In the historical perspective of Jewish population research in the U.S. over the last 50 years, the new findings were consistent with figures and projections based on earlier sources, such as the 1957 Current Population Survey, the 1970 NJPS, and the 1990 NJPS. The apparent population decline was more likely the product of actual demographic trends than an artifact of insufficient data.[27]

As against these data and interpretations, two different schools of thought have suggested that the number of Jews in the U.S. has been underestimated and in fact may be one million higher than indicated by NJPS and AJIS.

One study, published in the 2006 AJYB, compiled many dozens of local Jewish community studies plus other local estimates to suggest a U.S. Jewish population of possibly 6.0 to 6.4 million.[28] As a first observation, it should be noted that since 1790 the U.S. Census Bureau has conducted a decennial national population count. Not relying on the sum of population statistics from local authorities or on population updates of older databases, every ten years the census assesses anew the current population stock. While costly, the operation is essential to provide fresh and independent information needed for planning. The same rationale should apply to Jewish population studies.

In this specific case, dozens of local Jewish community studies were carried out by different authors with different sponsors, different purposes, different Jewish population definitions, and different data-collection

---

[26]See Kosmin et al., *Highlights of the CJF 1990 National Jewish Population Survey.*
[27]DellaPergola, "Was It the Demography?"
[28]Ira M. Sheskin and Arnold Dashefsky, "Jewish Population in the United States, 2006," AJYB 2006, vol. 106, pp. 133–93.

methods over a span of more than two decades, a lack of consistency that constitutes a fatal flaw. Adding to the problem is the exceptionally high geographical mobility of American Jews[29]—mainly from the Northeast to the South and West—and the inherent diffusion of double residences with the risk of double counts.

Another critical weakness of most local studies is their partial but significant reliance on local community lists that tend to portray the more Jewishly identified portion of the population and to overestimate the total. In the several studies that combine Jewish lists and random sampling, the methodology for merging and weighting returns from the different sampling frameworks and achieve overall population estimates is not uniform. Moreover, several local surveys did not adequately distinguish between the *core* and *enlarged* Jewish populations, and thus provided inflated numbers. On top of this, about 20 percent of the national Jewish population estimate comes from places for which no studies exist but only unverifiable estimates provided by local informants. In no way can the results for the 80 percent of the Jewish population covered by local studies be considered representative of the remaining 20 percent. Without detracting from the importance of local studies, the combined product of summing up and inferring is highly problematic, and cannot seriously match national studies that are based on comprehensive and consistent survey criteria.

A different methodology has been implemented through an ambitious and innovative project undertaken at the Steinhardt Social Research Institute (SSRI) of Brandeis University. A large number of general social surveys were gathered, each including a Jewish subsample. The number of Jewish cases in such national surveys is usually small, but combining many of them together allows for a meta-analysis of a much larger Jewish sample in the context of the U.S. total population.[30]

At first sight, this new effort seemed to confirm existing notions about Jewish population size. Based on an initial review of 74 studies over the period 1990–2005, the median share of Jews among total respondents was 1.94 percent. Allowing for the observed lower share of Jews under

---

[29]Uzi Rebhun and Sidney Goldstein, "Changes in the Geographical Dispersion and Mobility of American Jews, 1990–2001," *Jewish Journal of Sociology* 48, 1, 2006, pp. 5–33.

[30]The project is directed by Leonard Saxe. See Elizabeth Tighe, Leonard Saxe, Darren Brown, Jennifer Dilinger, Aron Klein, and Ashley Hill, *Research Synthesis of National Survey Estimates of the U.S. Jewish Population; Project Summary, Method and Analysis Plan* (Waltham, Mass., 2005).

20, the ratio of Jews to non-Jews aged 20 and above who are the typical respondents to surveys was 0.935. The percentage of Jews among the total U.S. population, including adults and children, should thus be downwardly corrected to 1.814 percent. The 2000 U.S. Census gave a total population of 281,421,906. A median of 1.814 percent Jews would correspond to 5,104,993 individuals. The average survey response rate on religion was 95 percent. Adjusting upwardly the Jewish population for non-response or no reporting of religion, the Jewish population estimate would become 5,373,677. This estimate—nearly identical to the already mentioned AJIS—referred to a period of over 15 years whose midpoint would correspond to a date in the late 1990s. As noted, in 2001 both NJPS and AJIS indicated an ongoing Jewish population reduction. Projecting the SSRI data to 2006, the likely outcome would thus be somewhat lower that the original calculation.

In a later report, the SSRI group suggested a much higher U.S. Jewish population estimate.[31] It did so by relying on 31 surveys selected out of a much broader pool, a comparison for a few cohorts of the estimates from the new merged database with data from the NJPS (the AJIS was ignored), and an evaluation of Jewish school enrollment according to various available sources. This approach has several strengths but also some serious weaknesses:

- The decision to narrow the analysis to a selection of a few surveys deemed by the researchers to be the fittest out of the many more that are available seriously detracts from the randomness of the data. One of the greatest advantages of the whole SSRI project was exactly the unbiased collection of as many sources as possible—each with its own strengths, weaknesses and idiosyncrasies.

- The SSRI review considers only those persons explicitly identified by religion, and then seeks to extrapolate the number of the religiously identified to the total of American Jews. One important SSRI finding is that the more broadly representative the agency conducting a survey (such as the U.S. government, as opposed to the patron of a narrowly defined special constituency), the higher the response rate; and the higher the response rate, the higher the share of Jews in the sample. Since NJPS and AJIS were sponsored by narrowly defined agencies (the Jewish community) and thus, expectedly, had low response rates, their

[31]Leonard Saxe, Elizabeth Tighe, and Benjamin Phillips, with Ariel Libhaber, Daniel Parmer, Jessica Simon, and Graham Wright, *Understanding Contemporary American Jewry* (Waltham, Mass., 2006).

ability to uncover the Jewish population was admittedly on the low side of the range. On the other hand, NJPS and AJIS investigators made special efforts to unveil hidden Jews among the total respondents, which they could do thanks to the very detailed range of questions on personal identity they had at their disposal. Following this effort the total Jewish population turned out to be significantly higher than the number of Jews initially identified by religion. Given this basic difference in survey penetration and administration, it would be quite inappropriate to apply the low NJPS/AJIS ratio of Jews by religion to total Jews in the case of other general surveys that had a much better response rate. But this seems to have been the step followed by the SSRI group to bridge between the original survey figures based on religion and their total Jewish population estimates, resulting in excessively high total estimates.

- Social surveys typically cover adult respondents and do not collect detailed information on each individual in the household, namely children under 18, which NJPS/AJIS did. The assumption that the percent of Jews among total respondents equals the percent of Jews among the total population is gravely fallacious. Indeed, each Jewish respondent brings in not only fewer children because of lower Jewish fertility, but also fewer other adults, because of the group's older age composition and the higher prevalence of smaller households, including many more people living alone. Moreover, while a generic respondent brings in other generic members of the household, determining a certain multiplier, a Jewish respondent brings in other members who are, in many cases, not Jewish, thus determining a lower multiplier. These differences should be weighted into population estimates, something that the SSRI researchers have not done.

- The main thrust of the age cohort comparisons between the meta-analysis and the NJPS is their significant consistency, which supports the basic reliability of NJPS. But two cohorts seem to be exceptions. The inconsistency concerns Jewish adults whose ages in 2001 were 35–44 (born 1957–66) and 45–54 (born 1957–66), hence all part of the so called baby-boomer generation. Indeed, apparent cohort erosion had already been noted in comparing NJPS 2001 with NJPS 1990, and even earlier among the same cohorts in comparisons between NJPS 1970 and NJPS 1990.[32] The crucial question seems to relate to the cultural-ideational patterns of American baby-boomers, and certainly part of

---

[32]DellaPergola, "Was it the Demography?"

the explanation derives from the steady transition among younger adults from a Jewish identification based on religion to one founded on ethnicity, culture, or being "just Jewish." Again, an analysis that relies primarily on the religion category, like the SSRI, is likely to miss the fact that people can feel Jewish through other cultural avenues.

• Whenever a figure provided by NJPS can be matched against a similar figure from another source, the match is usually good. Two such examples are the number of children enrolled in Jewish day schools, compared with school enrollment statistics,[33] and the number of documented immigrants, compared with other institutional data.[34] In the case of day-school education, the comparison of number of pupils with the total number of children gives an enrollment ratio of slightly over 25 percent. While that seems very high, it is absolutely compatible with the empirically demonstrated higher percentage of the Orthodox among younger cohorts of Jews in the U.S., which in turn reflects higher Orthodox birthrates and fewer losses to assimilation.

• General social surveys tend to be based on individual respondents and only a few make available a full roster of the characteristics of all members in a household. Furthermore, religion is seldom the main focus of investigation and is thus usually confined to one background question. Direct knowledge about household size and composition cannot go beyond certain limits, leaving its final determination to inference. The SSRI suggestions that U.S. Jewry might comprise 6.5 and perhaps even 7.5 million individuals, or that the yearly birth cohort might exceed 70,000 newborn become plausible only if the reference category is the *enlarged* concept of total population in households and not the *core* concept of individually identified Jewish population.

All of these considerations militate in favor of the general plausibility of NJPS/AJIS and of the population estimates that can be derived from them. In addition, the approaches that oppose and suggest alternatives to NJPS and AJIS share two critical weaknesses:

• The first is their inability to provide an integrated age composition of the U.S. Jewish population inclusive of Jewish adults and Jewish children. Age composition is a most basic analytic referent, both synthe-

---

[33]Marvin Schick, *A Census of Jewish Day Schools in the United States 2003–2004* (Jerusalem, 2005).

[34]HIAS, *Statistical Report* (New York, annual publication).

sizing past changes and functioning as an agent of future changes. Current age is an intermediary between the demography of two successive generations, in the absence of which discourse about population trends becomes nearly void of content.

• The second, even more crucial, shared weakness of the two critical approaches is their complete lack of historical perspective. If it is true that today there are more than 6 million Jews in the U.S., we expect to be told how many there were in 1990, and at previous dates back to the end of World War II. A population, as we have repeatedly argued, grows or shrinks as a consequence of a limited set of factors whose impact must be assessed along with the overall figure. A much higher figure in 2001 and later implies either that U.S. Jewry recently experienced a fast pace of growth—against all existing evidence—or that all previous estimates should be significantly raised, implying over 50 years of gross mistakes in Jewish population studies. The new higher estimates are suggesting, instead, that the current assessment of U.S. Jewry can be severed from its past. While it is surely legitimate to discuss contemporary U.S. Jewry as a cultural phenomenon not necessarily stemming from its own past or from other strands of Jewish history, this is not appropriate in the realm of population studies.

In the light of this abundant and intriguing evidence, our U.S. Jewish population estimate reflects the well-documented pattern of end of growth and incipient population decrease. As noted, U.S. Jewry is characterized by an aging population composition, and its effectively Jewish fertility levels are significantly below generational replacement due in part to a very incomplete inclusion of the children of out-marriage—admittedly a feature that might change in the future, as suggested by the 2005 Boston study.[35] The number of immigrants has diminished, especially from the FSU. A reading of the current age composition of U.S. Jewry and other current evidence suggests that about 50,000 Jewish births occur annually in the U.S. as compared to nearly 60,000 Jewish deaths, and 5,000 net immigrants. Following these assumptions the 2001 estimate was adjusted to 5,275,000 in 2006, and the same was retained for 2007.

Admittedly, the quality of U.S. Jewish population estimates cannot be compared to the more rigorous sources in Israel and a few other coun-

---

[35]See Leonard Saxe, Charles Kadushin, and Graham Wright, *2005 Boston Jewish Community Study* (Waltham, Mass., 2006).

tries. In the absence of better data, comparisons remain speculative. Even more significantly, Jewish identification tends to reflect the very different constraints and opportunities of the relatively open environment of the U.S., where a multiplicity of overlapping identities can be legitimately held under the general American panoply, as against a closed society still surrounded by a hostile environment, as in Israel. Our estimate of 5,275,000 *core* Jews in the U.S. at the beginning of 2007 is a cautious compromise between the two major 2001 Jewish surveys, the NJPS and the AJIS, also taking into account the findings of many other American social surveys, other institutional data, and population extrapolations produced under different assumptions.

While by the *core* concept the number of Jews in the U.S. today probably falls behind that in Israel, it is beyond dispute that the U.S. has far larger *enlarged* and *Law of Return* populations. The former apparently comprises at least 6.7 million individuals with some recent Jewish ancestry, and 7.7–8.7 million individuals in households with at least one Jew. When the latter's non-Jewish children, grandchildren, and respective spouses are added in—all would be accepted in Israel under the *Law of Return*—we reach a virtual aggregate of 10 to 12 million individuals in the U.S., as against 5.7 million in Israel.

In the U.S., the debate about numbers has been invested with an importance and symbolic meaning that transcends by far the social scientific discipline. In the public debate, Jewish population size has become a proxy for honor, legitimacy, relative visibility in the Jewish world, and probably predominance in its politics and resource allocation. This is, in the end, the gist of the numerical competition between Jewish population figures for the U.S. and Israel. One way to escape from this conundrum would be a continuation of the routine of periodic data collection that UJC established with the 1970, 1990, and 2001 NJPS series. A new study would signal an attitude of respect to R&D in national community planning, and might allow for new comparisons, evaluations of changes in the observed trends, deepened insights, and improved projections for the future.

But in 2007, UJC decided not to sponsor another NJPS in 2010, but at the same time copyrighted the logo NJPS for itself. These momentous decisions raised significant questions about how the organized Jewish community viewed its own mandate, including the role of research as a basis for planning and allocation of resources, and the respective responsibilities of central Jewish institutions and private initiatives. One can only hope that research on U.S. Jewish population and community will

TABLE 3. ESTIMATED CORE JEWISH POPULATION DISTRIBUTION IN THE AMERICAS, 1/1/2007

Country	Total Population	Jewish Population	Jews per 1,000 Population	Accuracy Rating
Canada	32,900,000	374,000	11.4	B 2001
United States	302,200,000	5,275,000	17.5	B 2001
Total North America[a]	335,227,000	5,649,000	16.9	
Bahamas	300,000	300	1.0	D
Costa Rica	4,500,000	2,500	0.6	C 1993
Cuba	11,200,000	500	0.0	C 1990
Dominican Republic	9,400,000	100	0.0	D
El Salvador	6,900,000	100	0.0	C 1993
Guatemala	13,400,000	900	0.1	B 1999
Jamaica	2,700,000	300	0.1	B 1995
Mexico	106,500,000	39,600	0.4	B 2001
Netherlands Antilles	215,000	200	0.9	B 1998
Panama	3,300,000	5,000	1.5	C 1990
Puerto Rico	3,900,000	1,500	0.4	C 1990
Virgin Islands	115,000	300	2.6	C 1986
Other	25,570,000	300	0.0	D
Total Central America	188,000,000	51,600	0.3	
Argentina	39,400,000	184,000	4.7	B 2003
Bolivia	9,800,000	500	0.1	C 1999
Brazil	189,300,000	96,200	0.5	B 2001
Chile	16,600,000	20,600	1.2	C 1991
Colombia	46,200,000	2,900	0.1	C 1996
Ecuador	13,500,000	900	0.1	C 1985
Paraguay	6,100,000	900	0.1	B 1997
Peru	27,900,000	2,100	0.1	C 1993
Suriname	500,000	200	0.4	C 1986
Uruguay	3,300,000	17,900	5.4	B 2006
Venezuela	25,700,000	14,500	0.5	B 1999
Total South America[a]	381,100,000	340,700	0.9	
Total	904,327,000	6,041,300	6.7	

[a]Including countries not listed separately.

continue through other avenues. What is certain is that the dispute about Jewish population estimates in the U.S. is bound to continue.

Canada

The Canadian situation differs significantly both in regard to available databases and substantive population trends. Pending results from the 2006 population census, the 2001 census[36] indicated a decrease in the number of Jews according to ethnicity (including those declaring a religion other than Judaism) from 369,565 in 1991 to 348,605 in 2001 (−20,960, or 5.7 percent). Of the ethnic Jews in 2001, 186,475 indicated a solely Jewish ethnicity, and the other 162,130 mentioned Jewish as one of their several ethnic identities. The percentage with an exclusively Jewish ethnicity thus declined to 53 percent of all those reporting a Jewish ethnicity, down from 66 percent in 1991 and 90 percent in 1981. On the other hand, the number of Canada's Jews according to religion increased from 318,070 in 1991 to 329,995 in 2001 (+11,925, or 3.7 percent). It should be noted that 22,365 Jews entered the country during the decade between the two censuses, and the Jewish population would have decreased by 10,440 (−3.3 percent) were it not for this immigration.

Keeping in mind that some ethnic Jews are not Jewish by religion and that an even greater number of Jews by religion do not declare a Jewish ethnicity, a combined estimate of 370,520 obtained for Canada's Jewish population, up 4 percent from 356,315 in 1991.[37] Assuming continuing immigration to Canada but also some internal attrition, we estimate that the Jewish population grew to 374,000 in 2007, the world's fourth largest. This figure is not strictly comparable with the concept of *core* Jewish population, as it includes some individuals for whom Jewish was only one among multiple ethnic identities, and who may not identify as Jewish if asked. Some of these would probably better be included among the non-Jewish component of the *enlarged* Jewish population. Taking into account all ethnic Jews who profess a non-Jewish religion, and other non-Jewish household members, an enlarged Jewish population of above 450,000 would probably obtain.

---

[36]Detailed information on the 2001 census is available on line from Statistics Canada at . The 2006 census relates to the ethnicity variable only, and the relevant data will be released in 2008.

[37]Charles Shahar, *The Jewish Community of Canada* (Toronto, 2004).

Latin America

In Latin America, the Jewish population was generally in decline, reflecting economic and local security concerns. Nearly 6,000 Jews emigrated from Argentina to Israel in 2002—the highest figure ever in a single year from that country—due to dire economic conditions and special incentives offered on the Israeli side. In 2003 the economic situation eased somewhat and Israel suspended its incentives. About 1,500 Jews emigrated from Argentina to Israel in 2003, declining to 458 in 2004, 397 in 2005, and 293 in 2006.[38] Based on the experience of previous years, approximately 20 percent of these migrants were non-Jewish household members in the *enlarged* population. Partial evidence from different sources indicated that less than half of total Jewish emigration from Argentina went to Israel. Contrary to rumors, permanence rates in Israel of the new immigrants were high, at least during the first year after immigration, with an attrition of about 10 percent leaving within the first three years.[39] Argentina's Jewish population is assessed at 184,000 in 2007, the world's seventh largest.

In 2004 and 2005 two new Jewish population surveys were undertaken in the Buenos Aires metropolitan area (AMBA). Initial claims of a Jewish population of 244,000[40] were founded on significantly inconsistent definitional criteria. Of the 244,000, 64,000 reported being of Christian religion, and another about 20,000 reported some Jewish ancestry but did not consider themselves Jewish. Overall, 161,000 people in the AMBA considered themselves totally or partly Jewish—consistent with our own estimate of 165,000. This figure for the major urban concentration appeared coherent with our countrywide *core* estimate. The 244,000 figure would be a good estimate of the *enlarged* Jewish population in Greater Buenos Aires, while, in the same survey, over 300,000 persons were identified as in some way of Jewish origin or attached to a person of Jewish origin. Another survey limited to the City of Buenos Aires pointed to significant aging of the core Jewish population, reflecting the emigration of younger households over recent years.[41] The current situation implies a

---

[38]See Israel Central Bureau of Statistics at http://www.cbs.gov.il

[39]Shmuel Adler, *Emigration among Immigrants from Argentina that Arrived During the Period 1.1.89–31.12.02* (Jerusalem, 2004).

[40]Adrian Jmelnizky and Ezequiel Erdei, *Estudio de Población Judía en Ciudad de Buenos Aires y Gran Buenos Aires (AMBA)* (Buenos Aires, 2005).

[41]Yaacov Rubel, *La Población Judía de la Ciudad de Buenos Aires, Perfil Socic Demográfico* (Buenos Aires, 2005).

yearly loss of about 500–1,000 through a negative balance of Jewish births and deaths, and emigration.

In Brazil, the 2000 census indicated a rather stable Jewish population of 86,828, up from 86,416 in 1991.[42] Considering the possible omission of individuals who did not answer the census question on religion, we assessed Brazil's Jewish population at 97,000 in 2003 and, allowing for moderate emigration (286 went to Israel in 2005 and 232 in 2006), 96,200 in 2007—the world's tenth largest. The census data were consistent with a systematic documentation effort undertaken by the Jewish Federation of São Paulo that unveiled a total of 47,286 Jews,[43] and an assumption that about one half of Brazil's Jews live in that city. Brazil's enlarged Jewish population (including non-Jewish members of Jewish households) was assessed at 132,191 in 1980 and 117,296 in 1991,[44] and presumably exceeded 120,000 in 2000.

In Mexico, the 2000 census indicated a Jewish population of 45,260 aged five and over.[45] Of these, 32,464 lived in the metropolitan area of the capital, Mexico City, while a most unlikely 12,796 were reported in states other than the Federal District and Mexico State—consistent with erratic figures in past censuses. Allocation of the 0–4 age group based on a 2000 Jewish survey suggested an estimate of about 35,000 Jews in Greater Mexico City and 40,000 nationwide. A Jewish population survey undertaken in 2000 provided a countrywide estimate of 39,870 Jews, of which 37,350 in Mexico City,[46] confirming the results of a previous 1991 survey.[47] In 2007, allowing for some emigration to the U.S. and Israel, we estimated the Jewish population at 39,600, the world's 14th largest.

The fourth largest Jewish community in Latin America is located in

---

[42]See http://ibge.br; René D. Decol, "Brazilian Jews: a Demographic Profile," unpublished paper delivered at the International Conference on Jewish Demography, Jerusalem, 2002.

[43]FISESP (Federação Israelita do Estado de São Paulo), *Recadastramento comunitário 2000–01* (São Paulo, 2002).

[44]René Decol, *Imigraçoes urbanas para o Brasil: o caso dos Judeus,* unpublished Ph.D. dissertation, Universidade Estadual, 1999.

[45]See Instituto Nacional de Estadistica, Geografia e Informatica, *XII Censo General de Poblacion y Vivienda 2000* (Mexico City, 2002).

[46]Comunidad Judía de México, *Estudio socio-demográfico 2000* (Mexico City, unpublished tables, 2000).

[47]Sergio DellaPergola and Susana Lerner, *La población judía de México: Perfil demográfico, social y cultural* (México-Jerusalén, 1995). The project, conducted cooperatively between the Centro de Estudios Urbanos y de Desarrollo Urbano (CEDDU), El Colegio de Mexico, and the Division of Jewish Demography and Statistics of the A. Harman Institute of Contemporary Jewry, The Hebrew University, was sponsored by the Asociación Mexicana de Amigos de la Universidad Hebrea de Jerusalén.

Chile,[48] whose relatively stable Jewish population is now larger than those of Uruguay[49] and Venezuela.[50] Both of the latter countries experienced significant Jewish emigration in recent years. Around 2000, about 20 percent of the former pupils of Jewish schools in Uruguay and over one third of the adult children of Caracas Jews lived in a different country. Based on the recent evidence, the Jewish population estimate for Uruguay was downwardly revised to 17,900 in 2007. The estimate for Venezuela was reduced to 14,500, reflecting ongoing concerns in that community.

EUROPE

Jewish population in Europe tended to be increasingly concentrated in the western part of the continent, and within the European Union (Table 4). The EU, after the addition of Bulgaria and Romania, reached an estimated total of 1,129,800 Jews in 2006 (76 percent of the continent's total Jewish population). The former Soviet republics in Europe outside the EU comprised 322,000 Jews (21 percent). All other European countries comprised 40,900 Jews (3 percent).

The European Union

On May 1, 2004, the EU expanded from 15 to 25 countries, incorporating the three Baltic nations that had been part of the Soviet Union (Estonia, Latvia, and Lithuania), another five that had been part of the Soviet area of influence in Eastern Europe (the Czech Republic, Hungary, Poland, Slovakia, and Slovenia), and two southern European insular countries (Cyprus and Malta). In 2007 two more countries that had been part of the East European Soviet sphere of influence, Romania and Bulgaria, were admitted. The EU's expanded format symbolized an important historical landmark: the virtual boundary between Western and Eastern Europe was erased, with Croatia and Macedonia being the next

---

[48]Gabriel Berger et al., *Estudio Socio-Demográfico de la Comunidad Juí{{igrave}}a de Chile* (Santiago-Buenos Aires, 1995).

[49]Nicole Berenstein and Rafael Porzecanski, *Perfil de los egresados de la Red Formal de Educación Judía Uruguaya* (Montevideo, 2001).

[50]Sergio DellaPergola, Salomon Benzaquen, and Tony Beker de Weinraub, *Perfil sociodemográfico y cultural de la comunidad judía de Caracas* (Caracas, 2000). The survey was sponsored by the Asociación Israelita de Venezuela, the Union Israelita de Caracas, and the Asociación de Amigos de la Universidad Hebrea de Jerusalén.

TABLE 4. ESTIMATED CORE JEWISH POPULATION DISTRIBUTION IN EUROPE, 1/1/2007

Country	Total Population	Jewish Population	Jews per 1,000 Population	Accuracy Rating
Austria	8,300,000	9,000	1.1	B 2001
Belgium	10,600,000	30,500	2.9	C 2002
Bulgaria	7,700,000	2,000	0.3	C 2001
Czech Republic	10,300,000	3,900	0.4	C 2001
Denmark	5,500,000	6,400	1.2	C 2001
Estonia	1,300,000	1,900	1.5	B 2006
Finland	5,300,000	1,100	0.2	B 1999
France[a]	61,700,000	490,000	7.9	B 2002
Germany	82,300,000	120,000	1.5	B 2004
Greece	11,200,000	4,500	0.4	B 1995
Hungary	10,100,000	49,000	4.9	C 2001
Ireland	4,400,000	1,200	0.3	B 2001
Italy	59,300,000	28,500	0.5	B 2002
Latvia	2,300,000	9,700	4.2	B 2005 X
Lithuania	3,400,000	3,100	0.9	B 2001
Luxembourg	500,000	600	1.2	B 2000
Netherlands	16,400,000	30,000	1.8	B 2000
Poland	38,100,000	3,200	0.1	C 2001
Portugal	10,700,000	500	0.0	C 1999
Romania	21,600,000	9,900	0.5	B 2001
Slovakia	5,400,000	2,600	0.5	C 2001
Slovenia	2,000,000	100	0.1	C 1996
Spain	45,300,000	12,000	0.3	D
Sweden	9,100,000	15,000	1.6	C 1999
United Kingdom	61,200,000	295,000	4.8	B 2001
Other[b]	1,400,000	100	0.1	D
Total European Union 27	495,400,000	1,129,800	2.3	
Gibraltar	25,000	600	24.0	B 1991
Norway	4,700,000	1,200	0.3	B 1995
Switzerland	7,500,000	17,700	2.4	B 2000
Total other West Europe[c]	12,695,000	19,500	1.5	

TABLE 4.—*(Continued)*

Country	Total Population	Jewish Population	Jews per 1,000 Population	Accuracy Rating
Belarus	9,700,000	17,500	1.8	B 1999
Moldova	4,000,000	4,500	1.1	B 2004
Russia[d]	141,700,000	221,000	1.6	B 2002
Ukraine	46,500,000	79,000	1.7	B 2001 X
Total FSU Republics	201,900,000	322,000	1.6	
[Total FSU in Europe][e]	208,900,000	336,700	1.6	
Bosnia-Herzegovina	3,800,000	500	0.1	C 2001
Croatia	4,400,000	1,700	0.4	C 2001
Macedonia (FYR)	2,000,000	100	0.1	C 1996
Serbia-Montenegro	10,100,000	1,400	0.1	C 2001
Turkey[d]	74,000,000	17,700	0.2	B 2002
Total other East Europe and Balkans[c]	94,300,000	21,400	0.2	
Total	804,295,000	1,492,700	1.9	

[a]Including Monaco.
[b]Cyprus and Malta.
[c]Including countries not listed separately.
[d]Including Asian regions.
[e]Including Baltic countries.

candidates for EU membership. Ongoing disagreements about the membership of Turkey, an Islamic country, revealed a dilemma in the definition of Europe's own cultural and geopolitical boundaries.

The largest Jewish community in Europe was in France, where a new countrywide survey undertaken at the beginning of 2002 suggested a downward revision to 500,000 *core* Jews plus an additional 75,000 non-Jewish members of Jewish households.[51] Before the survey, our Jewish population estimate stood at 519,000. The difference, cumulated over

---

[51]See Erik H. Cohen with Maurice Ifergan, *Les Juifs de France: Valeurs et identité* (Paris, 2002).

several years, was primarily due to the growing pace of Jewish emigration not only to Israel but also to Canada and other countries. Migration to Israel amounted to 2,545 in 2005 and 2,408 in 2006. Jewish emigration reflected a sense of uneasiness about acts of anti-Jewish intolerance, including physical violence. A 2004 survey of Jewish tourists from France to Israel produced a remarkable estimate of 125,000, or more than 30 percent of all French Jews aged 15 and over.[52] Of these, 23 percent (about 29,000) affirmed their intention to move to Israel in the near future. A distant second candidate for possible emigration was the U.S. While migration intentions are not a proxy for actual migration decisions, the erosion in feelings of security among French Jewry is undisputable. Our 2007 estimate for French Jewry therefore shrinks to 490,000, the third largest in the world.

In the United Kingdom, the 2001 national population census included a voluntary question on religion for the first time since the nineteenth century.[53] The total Jewish population of 266,741 for England, Wales, Scotland, and Northern Ireland closely approximated our 273,500 estimate for 2002. One interesting census finding concerned the spread of Jewish population, which is more diffused over the national territory than was previously believed. This would also indicate a lower degree of Jewish affiliation than previously assumed. At the same time, the community is aging, with 16 percent of Jews below age 15 versus 22 percent above age 65. More detailed data for Scotland (where some of census questions were asked differently than in the rest of the UK) indicated 6,448 people currently reporting Jewish religion as compared to 7,446 who said they were raised as Jews—a net lifetime loss of 13 percent.[54]

About 23 percent of the UK total population indicated that they had no religion while another 7 percent did not answer the question—at a time when much of the organized Jewish community publicly supported participation in the census. In the meantime, detailed census tabulations were obtained by the Institute for Jewish Policy Research and the Board of Deputies of British Jews from the Office for National Statistics. An in-depth profile of the sociodemographic profile of British Jewry thus emerged, along with a better evaluation of the quality of Jewish popu-

---

[52]Erik H. Cohen, *Les touristes de France en Israël 2004* (Jerusalem, 2005).
[53]See Barry Kosmin and Stanley Waterman, *Commentary on Census Religion Question* (London, 2002), a publication of the JPR (Institute for Jewish Policy Research). The census is available at .
[54]Also see *JPR/News,* Spring 2003, p. 6.

lation estimates.[55] Analyses of detailed geographical precincts allowed for estimates of the amount of non-response in areas with higher or lower Jewish densities among the total population. There was a significant correlation between the known Jewish religiosity of a district and non-response to the religion question. On the other hand, post-census surveys of Jews in London and Leeds did not unveil high percentages declaring they had not answered "Jewish" to the question on religion.

Vital statistics routinely collected by the Board of Deputies Community Research Unit on the annual number of Jewish births appeared to be consistent with the census returns. Comparing the uncorrected census returns for the age group 0–9, and the recorded number of Jewish births over the ten years preceding the census, the discrepancy was only 2.5 percent. This confirms that there was an undercount, but one that could not have had a significant impact on Jewish population estimates. The same vital statistics show a continuing excess of Jewish deaths (3,670 in 2002, 3,592 in 2003, and 3,257 in 2004) over Jewish births (2,665 in both 2002 and 2003).[56] The diminishing number of deaths is an obvious symptom of a shrinking population which loses about 1,000 people yearly through a negative vital balance. Shrinking synagogue membership is another indicator. Household membership declined by 17.8 percent between 1990 and 2005, and by 4.5 percent (nearly 1 percent per year) between 2001 and 2005.[57]

We had previously suggested raising the UK Jewish population estimate from the original census count of 266,741 to 300,000 for 2001, or about 12 percent above the original returns, assuming a lower rate of non-response among Jews than in the general population. All in all, this seems a fair resolution. The updating must take into account the negative balance of births and deaths, as well as a moderate increase in emigration

[55]David Graham, Marlena Schmool, and Stanley Waterman, *Jews in Britain: A Snapshot from the 2001 Census,*(London, 2007); David Graham and Stanley Waterman, "Under-enumeration of the Jewish Population in the UK 2001 Census," *Population, Space and Place* 11, 2005, pp. 89–102; David Voas, "Estimating the Jewish Undercount in the 2001 Census: A Comment on Graham and Waterman (2005)," ibid. 13, 2007, pp. 401–07; David J. Graham, Stanley Waterman, "Locating Jews by Ethnicity: A Reply to David Voas (2007)," ibid. pp. 409–14.

[56]The Board of Deputies of British Jews, Community Research Unit, *Report on Community Vital Statistics 2004* (London, 2005). See also Stephen Miller, Marlena Schmool, and Antony Lerman, *Social and Political Attitudes of British Jews: Some Key Findings of the JPR Survey* (London, 1996).

[57]Rona Hart and Edward Kafka, *Trends in British Synagogue Membership, 1990–2005* (London, 2006).

(594 went to Israel in 2006). We estimated the UK's total Jewish population at 295,000 in 2007, the world's fifth largest.

In Germany, Jewish immigration that had brought into the country over 200,000 Jews and non-Jewish family members between 1989 and 2006 significantly diminished. The German government, under pressure because of high unemployment and a crumbling welfare system, limited Jewish immigration from the FSU in 2005. On January 1, 2005 the previous special immigration law (*Kontingentsflüchtlingsgesetz*) was replaced by a new more restrictive law (*Zuwanderungsgesetz*). Jews were to be included in it and thus lose their privileged status as *Kontingentflüchtlinge*. The new law put ability to integrate into German society and good economic prospects before other considerations, and required Jews aspiring to immigrate to Germany to first prove that a Jewish community would accept them as members. Prior knowledge of the German language was necessary, and potential Jewish immigrants also had to prove that they would not be dependent on welfare and that they were willing to integrate into the German labor market.[58]

In 2006, 1,971 immigrants from the former Soviet Union were recorded as new members of German Jewish communities, as compared to 3,124 in 2005, 4,757 in 2004, 6,224 in 2003 and 6,597 in 2002.[59] Admission criteria in the community follow Jewish rabbinical rules. The total number of *core* Jews registered with the central Jewish community grew minimally to 107,794 at the beginning of 2007, versus 107,677 in 2006, 105,733 in 2005 and 102,472 in 2004. Of the current total, only 8,123 were part of the initial pool of 28,081 members that existed at the end of 1990, and the rest were recent immigrants. Between 2002 and 2004, the *enlarged* total of Jews and non-Jewish family members who came to Germany from the FSU was larger than the respective number of FSU migrants to Israel, but this was no longer true in 2005 and 2006.

The age composition of Jewish old-timers—and even more so of newcomers—was extremely skewed toward older ages. In 2006 there were 205 Jewish births and 1,302 Jewish deaths recorded by the Jewish community in Germany. This explains why the growth of the Jewish community was significantly less than the total number of new immigrants. Allowing for delays in joining the organized community and a preference

---

[58] Jewish People Policy Planning Institute Executive Report 3, *Annual Assessment 2006, Deltas Creating Opportunities and Threats* (Jerusalem, 2006).
[59] Zentralwohlfahrtsstelle der Juden in Deutschland (ZWJD), *Mitgliederstatistik; Der ınzelnen Jüdischen Gemeinden und Landesverb{{adieresis}}nde in Deutschland* (Frankfurt Л., 2007).

on the part of some members of a minority not to identify officially with its institutions, we assess Germany's *core* Jewish population at 120,000 in 2007, the world's eighth largest. The *enlarged* Jewish population, inclusive of the non-Jewish relatives of immigrants, is above 206,000, and creates a new framework and new opportunities for Jewish religious, social, and cultural life in Germany, but also raises the degree of dependence on welfare services.[60]

In Hungary, our core estimate of just below 50,000 (the world's 13th largest Jewish community) reflects the unavoidably negative balance of Jewish births and deaths in a country where the total population's vital balance has been negative for several years in a row. Indeed, a survey in 1999 indicated a conspicuously larger *enlarged* Jewish population.[61] However, a demographic extrapolation based on the usually accepted number of post-Holocaust *core* Jewish survivors and accounting for the known or estimated numbers of births, deaths, and emigrants to Israel and other countries since 1945 closely matches our assessment. It should be noted that in the 2001 Hungarian census only 13,000 people reported themselves Jewish by religion.

Belgium's Jewish population was estimated above 30,000, the 15th largest worldwide. Stable numbers reflected the presence of a traditional Orthodox community in Antwerp and the growth of a large European administrative center in Brussels. In 2006, however, 91 went to Israel, reflecting concerns not unlike those experienced in France. Local Jewish population estimates were quite obsolete in comparison with most other EU countries, but the reported order of magnitude was supported by indirect evidence such as the number of votes collected by Jewish candidates at the 2003 legislative elections.

The next two largest Jewish communities in the EU, and globally, were those in the Netherlands and Italy. In the Netherlands, a survey in 2000 estimated a Halakhic Jewish population of 30,072, of which perhaps as many as a third were immigrants from Israel, and an *enlarged* Jewish population of 43,305.[62] In Italy, total Jewish community membership — which

[60]Julius H. Schoeps, Willy Jasper, and Bernard Vogt, eds., *Ein neues Judentum in Deutschland. Fremd und Eigenbilder der russisch-jüdischen Einwanderer* (Potsdam, 1999).
[61]András Kovács, ed., *Jews and Jewry in Contemporary Hungary: Results of a Sociological survey* (London, 2004). The report significantly underestimates emigration over time.
[62]Hanna van Solinge and Marlene de Vries, eds., *De Joden in Nederland Anno 2000: Demografisch profiel en binding aan het joodendom* (Amsterdam, 2001). The survey was undertaken as a collaborative effort between the Stichting Joods Maatschappelijk Werk an NIDI (Netherlands Interdisciplinary Demographic Institute). See also C. Kooyman and Almagor, *Israelis in Holland: A Sociodemographic Study of Israelis and Former Israeli Holland* (Amsterdam, 1996).

historically comprised the overwhelming majority of the country's Jewish population—declined from 26,706 in 1995 to 25,143 in 2001.[63] Our estimate, slightly below 29,000, adequately allocates for non-members.

Former Soviet Union

In the FSU, rapid Jewish population decrease continued, reflecting an overwhelming surplus of Jewish deaths over births, high rates of outmarriage with low rates of Jewish identification of the children, and conspicuous though diminishing emigration. Our 2007 assessment of the total *core* Jewish population in the aggregate of the 15 former Soviet Republics, including the Baltics, was 356,700, of which 345,700 lived in Europe and 20,000 in Asia. At least as many non-Jewish family members were part of the respective households thus creating an *enlarged* Jewish population twice as large as the *core*.[64] The ongoing process of demographic decline was counteracted to some extent by the revival of Jewish cultural and religious activities, including Jewish education.[65]

In the Russian Republic, the October 2002 census indicated 233,600 Jews as against our *core* Jewish population estimate of 252,000 for the beginning of 2003 (derived from the February 1994 Russian Microcensus estimate of 409,000 Jews).[66] Allowing for some census undercounts after the compulsory item on ethnicity *(natsyonalnost)* on identification documents was canceled, the fact that the option not to state an ethnicity was allowed for the first time, and a slight upward revision versus our previous estimate, we evaluate the Jewish population at 221,000 in 2007, the sixth largest in the world.

---

[63]Unione delle Comunità Ebraiche Italiane, *IV Congresso, Relazione del consiglio* (Roma, 2002); Yaakov Andrea Lattes, *Sull'assimilazione in Italia e i metodi per affrontarla* (Ramat Gan, 2005).

[64]Mark Tolts, "Contemporary Trends in Family Formation among the Jews in Russia," *Jews in Russia and Eastern Europe* 2 (57), 2006, pp. 5–23; Tolts, "Major Trends in Post-Soviet Jewish Demography, 1989–2004," forthcoming in Zvi Gitelman and Yaacov Ro'i, eds., *Revolution, Repression, and Revival: The Soviet Jewish Experience* (Lanham, Md., 2007).

[65]Zvi Gitelman, "Becoming Jewish in Russia and Ukraine" in Gitelman, Barry Kosmin, and András Kovács, eds., *New Jewish Identities: Contemporary Europe and Beyond* (Budapest/New York, 2003), pp. 105–37.

[66]Mark Tolts, "Demographic Trends among the Jews of the Former Soviet Union," paper presented at the International Conference in Honor of Professor Mordechai Altshuler on Soviet and Post-Soviet Jewry, Jerusalem, 2003. For a German translation see *Menora: Jahrbuch für deutsch-jüdische Geshichte 2004*, 15 (Berlin/Wien, 2005), pp. 15–44; Tolts, "The Post-Soviet Jewish Population in Russia and the World," *Jews in Russia and Eastern Europe*, 1 (52), 2004, pp. 37–63.

Jewish population size was clearly more stable and resilient in Russia than in the other former Soviet republics. This partly reflected Jewish migration between the various republics and also lower emigration propensities from Moscow and some of the other main urban areas.[67] Nevertheless, the striking imbalance of Jewish births and deaths, and ongoing emigration meant continuing population decline and an elderly age composition. The drop in the number of births to at least one Jewish parent could be estimated at 8,006 in 1988 and 2,177 in 1998. Recorded Jewish deaths were 13,826 in 1988 and 9,103 in 1998. As a result, the estimated negative balance of these vital events was –5,820 in 1988 and –6,926 in 1998.[68] These changes occur in the context of steady net population decrease experienced by the Russian Republic in general, as well as by other European republics of the FSU.

In Ukraine, the population census undertaken on December 5, 2001, yielded 104,300 Jews, whereas we had projected 100,000 on January 1, 2002. Considering that our baseline for the latter estimate were the 487,300 Jews counted in the previous census of January 1989, the fit between expected and actual results was quite remarkable.[69] Taking into account the dramatic pace of emigration since 1989, other major intervening changes among Ukraine's Jews, and continuing emigration at the end of 2001, the census fully confirmed our previous assessment of ongoing demographic trends. Taking into account ongoing emigration, we assess the 2007 *core* Jewish population at 79,000, the 11th largest in the world.

Of the other former Soviet republics in Europe, the largest Jewish population was in Belarus, now downwardly reassessed at 17,700. After the accession to the EU of the three Baltic states of Estonia, Latvia, and Lithuania, Jewish population has been fairly stable and is assessed in 2007 at 14,700. A survey in Moldova found an *enlarged* Jewish population of 9,240 in 2000.[70] According to the results of the Moldova census of October 2004, there were 3,628 Jews, not counting Moldovan territory east

---

[67]Mark Tolts, "Mass *Aliyah* and Jewish Emigration from Russia: Dynamics and Factors," *East European Jewish Affairs* 33, 2003, pp. 71–96.
[68]Tolts, "Demographic Trends"; Tolts, "Demographic Trends among the Jews in the Three Post-Soviet Slavic Republics," paper presented at the 14th World Congress of Jewish Studies, Jerusalem, 2005.
[69]Ukrainian Ministry of Statistics, *Population Census 2001* (Kiyev, 2002); Mark Tolts, *Main Demographic Trends of the Jews in Russia and the FSU* (Jerusalem, 2002).
[70]Malka Korazim and Esther Katz, "Patterns of Jewish Identity in Moldova: The Behavioral Dimension," in Gitelman, Kosmin, and Kovács, eds., *New Jewish Identities*, 159–70.

of the Dniester River. According to the unofficial results of the separate census of November 2004, there were about 1,200 Jews there. We assess the core Jewish population at 4,500 in 2007.

Rest of Europe

After Hungary joined the EU together with Poland (where the 2002 census indicated a Jewish population of 1,100), the Czech Republic, Slovakia, Slovenia, Bulgaria, and Romania, only 40,900 Jews remained in Europe outside the EU and the FSU. Of these, 19,500 lived in Western Europe, primarily in Switzerland (17,700)[71] and 21,400 lived in Eastern Europe and the Balkans, primarily in Turkey. A survey in Istanbul pointed to widespread aging in a community that has experienced significant past emigration. In Istanbul, 14 percent of the Jewish population was under age 18, and 18 percent above age 65.[72]

ASIA

Israel

Jewish population in Asia is mostly affected by the trends in Israel (Table 5). After World War II, Israel (then Palestine) had a Jewish population of over half a million, which grew nearly tenfold over the subsequent 60 years thanks to mass immigration and fairly high and uniquely stable reproduction patterns. Israeli population data are regularly supplied by the Central Bureau of Statistics. Yearly data derive from periodic censuses and a detailed annual account of intervening events (births, deaths, immigrants, and emigrants). The last census was in 1995 and the next one is expected in 2008.

At the beginning of 2007, Israel's *core* Jewish population reached 5,393,400, forming an *enlarged* Jewish population of 5,703,400 when combined with 310,000 non-Jewish members of Jewish households.[73] The number of those who underwent conversion to Judaism remained quite

---

[71]Bundesamt für Statistik, *Wohnbevölkerung nach Religion 2000* (Neuchatel, 2005).
[72]Data provided through the courtesy of the Jewish Community Council.
[73]Israel Central Bureau of Statistics, *Statistical Abstract of Israel* 58 (Jerusalem, 2007). ᴇ also http://www.cbs.gov.il

modest (about 1,900 in 2005, as compared to 1,730 in 2004, 919 in 2003 and 3,533 in 2002). The majority were new immigrants from the FSU.[74] In addition, nearly all new immigrants from Ethiopia underwent conversion before their migration. In 2006, 23,700 new immigrants, including immigrant citizens, arrived in Israel, of whom 15,200 were Jewish.[75] Current emigration reduced this to a net migration balance of 16,600, of whom 7,900 were Jewish.

Israel's Jewish fertility rate rose slightly to 2.75 children per woman, higher than in any other developed country and probably twice or more the effective Jewish fertility level across Diaspora Jewish communities. In 2004, for the first time ever, more than 100,000 Jewish babies were born in Israel. In 2006, 104,500 Jewish births and 33,600 deaths produced a net Jewish natural increase of 70,900. Of the 5,393,400 *core* Jews in 2007, 5,137,800 lived within the pre-1967 borders plus East Jerusalem and the Golan Heights, and about 255,600 lived in the West Bank, where they formed over 10 percent of the total population.

Jews represented 76.0 percent of a total population of 7,116,700 in the State of Israel, including East Jerusalem, the Golan Heights, and the Israeli but not the Palestinian population in the West Bank. Considering the total Jewish and Palestinian legal population of 10,541,700 in the State of Israel and under the Palestinian Authority, Jews represented 51.2 percent, or slightly more than half the total between the Mediterranean Sea and the Jordan River. All of the preceding figures relate to the *core* Jewish population. If the 310,000 non-Jewish members of Jewish households are added to the Jewish side, the *enlarged* Jewish population of 5,703,600 thus obtained represented 80.1 percent of Israel's population (as defined above), and 54.1 percent of the total population of Israel and the Palestinian territories. With the addition of about 180,000 non-Jewish foreign workers residing in Israel, *core* and *enlarged* Jews represented, respectively, 50.3 and 53.2 percent of the total population present in Israel and the Palestinian territories, estimated at 10,721,700 in 2007.

The assessment of the total Palestinian population of the West Bank and Gaza reflected here has been challenged by a group of American and

---

[74]Raly Sa'ar, "Family members of converts not allowed to immigrate with them to Israel," *Ha'aretz*, June 3, 2004.

[75]These data include over 4,000 returning Israelis and immigrant citizens, the foreign-born children of Israelis on their first-time entrance into the country. Not included are foreig[n] workers and illegal residents.

TABLE 5. ESTIMATED CORE JEWISH POPULATION DISTRIBUTION IN ASIA, 1/1/2007

Country	Total Population	Jewish Population	Jews per 1,000 Population	Accuracy Rating
Israel[a]	6,855,200	5,137,800	749.5	A 2007
West Bank and Gaza[b]	3,686,500	255,600	69.3	A 2007
Total Israel and Palestine	10,541,700	5,393,400	511.6	
Azerbaijan	8,400,000	6,800	0.8	C 1999
Georgia	4,500,000	3,500	0.8	B 2002
Kazakhstan	15,100,000	3,700	0.2	B 1999
Kyrgyzstan	5,200,000	800	0.2	B 1999
Turkmenistan	5,400,000	200	0.0	D 1989 X
Uzbekistan	26,500,000	5,000	0.2	D 1989 X
Total former USSR in Asia[c]	75,800,000	20,000	0.3	
China[d]	1,318,000,000	1,500	0.0	D
India	1,131,900,000	5,000	0.0	B 1996
Iran	71,200,000	10,700	0.2	C 1986
Japan	127,700,000	1,000	0.0	C 1993
Korea, South	48,500,000	100	0.0	C 1998
Philippines	88,700,000	100	0.0	D
Singapore	4,600,000	300	0.1	C 1990
Syria	19,900,000	100	0.0	C 1995
Taiwan	22,900,000	100	0.0	D
Thailand	65,700,000	200	0.0	C 1998
Yemen	22,400,000	200	0.0	C 1995
Other	927,158,300	200	0.0	D
Total other Asia	3,848,658,300	19,500	0.0	
Total	3,935,000,000	5,432,900	1.4	

[a]Total population of Israel, including Jews in West Bank and Gaza, 1/1/2006: 7,116,700.
[b]Total Palestinian population in West Bank and Gaza: 1/1/2006: 3,425,000 (our revised estimate).
[c]Including Armenia and Tajikistan. Not including Asian regions of Russian Republic.
[d]Including Hong Kong and Macao.

Israeli investigators who maintained that current population estimates from Palestinian sources were inflated.[76] The Palestinian Central Bureau of Statistics, after a downward revision of over 100,000 to account for expected immigration that did not materialize, estimated the population in the Palestinian territories at 3,762,005 by July 1, 2006.[77] Our own independent assessment, after allocating 240,000 East Jerusalem Arabs to the Israeli side, accounting for a negative migration balance of Palestinians, and further corrections, was 3,330,000 on January 1, 2006, excluding East Jerusalem,[78] and 3,425,000 for 2007 at a 2.85 percent growth rate (versus 2.6 percent among Israeli Arabs). The extant Jewish majority is declining over the whole territory between the Mediterranean Sea and the Jordan River, and within the State of Israel.[79]

Rest of Asia

In the rest of Asia the Jewish population consisted mainly of the rapidly declining communities in the FSU's eight Asian republics, the largest of which was Azerbaijan with 6,800 Jews, followed by Uzbekistan (upwardly corrected to 5,000), Kazakhstan (3,700), and Georgia (3,500).[80] The largest Jewish population in a single country in Asia besides Israel was in Iran. Our estimate there reflects an effort to monitor intensive emigration since the Islamic revolution of the late 1970s. Small Jewish populations, partly of temporary sojourners, exist in various South and East Asian countries. Rapid economic development and growing relations with Israel render these countries receptive to a small but growing Jewish presence.

---

[76]Bennett Zimmerman, Roberta Seid, Michael Wise, Yoram Ettinger, David Shahaf, Ezra Sohar, David Passig, and Avraham Shvout, *Arab Population In the West Bank & Gaza: The Million-and-a-Half Person Gap* (Washington, D.C., 2005); Bennett Zimmerman, Roberta Seid, and Michael L. Wise, *The Million-Persons Gap: The Arab Population in the West Bank and Gaza* (Ramat Gan, 2005).

[77]See www.pcbs.org

[78]Sergio DellaPergola, "Correspondence," in *Azure*, Winter 2007, pp. 3–23.

[79]For an extensive discussion of the background, thrust, and implications of past and current population changes see Sergio DellaPergola, "Demographic Trends in Israel and Palestine: Prospects and Policy Implications," AJYB 2003, vol. 103, pp. 3–68. See also Arnon Sofer and Yevguenia Bistrow, *Israel Demography 2004–2020 in the Light of Disengagement* (Haifa, 2004; in Hebrew).

[80]Tolts, "Demographic Trends."

AFRICA

Jewish population in Africa was mostly concentrated in South Africa (Table 6). According to the 2001 census,[81] the white Jewish population amounted to 61,675. After factoring in the national non-response rate of 14 percent, a corrected estimate of 72,000 obtained. Allowing for a certain proportion of actual Jews reported among South Africa's nonwhites (11,979 blacks, 1,287 coloreds, and 615 Indians, many of whom practice other religions), we assessed the total size of the Jewish community at 75,000 in 2001. Following a moderate continuation of emigration, we estimate South Africa's Jewish population at 71,500 in 2007, the world's 12th largest.

Our revised estimates for North Africa acknowledge the ongoing reduction in the small Jewish populations remaining in Morocco and Tunisia, now assessed at 4,000 overall.

OCEANIA

Continuing immigration produced some increase in the size of Jewish populations in Oceania (Table 7). Australia's 2001 census indicated a Jewish population of 83,500, up about 4,000 from 1996.[82] Taking into account non-response but also the community's rather old age composition, we estimate the core Jewish population at 104,000 in 2007, the ninth largest in the world. The 2001 census also pointed to some Jewish population increase in New Zealand, assessed at 7,000.

DISPERSION AND CONCENTRATION

SIZE AND DENSITY

Reflecting global Jewish population stagnation along with growing concentration in a few countries, 97.5 percent of world Jewry live in the

---

[81]See David Saks, "Community Stable, Ageing—Census," *South African Jewish Report* (Johannesburg, 2003). See also Barry A. Kosmin, Jaqueline Goldberg, Milton Shain, and Shirley Bruk, *Jews of the New South Africa: Highlights of the 1998 National Survey of South African Jews* (London, 1999).

[82]Australian Bureau of Statistics, *Population Census 2001* (Canberra, 2002). See also Gary Eckstein, *Demography of the Sydney Jewish Community 2001* (Sydney, 2003).

TABLE 6. ESTIMATED CORE JEWISH POPULATION DISTRIBUTION IN AFRICA, 1/1/2007

Country	Total Population	Jewish Population	Jews per 1,000 Population	Accuracy Rating
Egypt	73,400,000	100	0.0	C 1998
Ethiopia	77,400,000	100	0.0	C 1998
Morocco	31,700,000	3,000	0.1	C 2006
Tunisia	10,200,000	1,000	0.1	C 2003
Total North Africa[a]	272,100,000	4,200	0.0	
Botswana	1,800,000	100	0.1	C 1993
Congo D.R.	62,600,000	100	0.0	C 1993
Kenya	36,900,000	400	0.0	C 1990
Namibia	2,100,000	100	0.1	C 1993
Nigeria	144,400,000	100	0.0	D
South Africa	47,900,000	71,500	1.5	B 2001
Zimbabwe	13,300,000	400	0.0	B 2001
Other	362,900,000	300	0.0	D
Total other Africa	671,900,000	73,000	0.1	
Total	944,000,000	77,200	0.1	

[a]Including countries not listed separately.

TABLE 7 ESTIMATED CORE JEWISH POPULATION DISTRIBUTION IN OCEANIA, 1/1/2007

Country	Total Population	Jewish Population	Jews per 1,000 Population	Accuracy Rating
Australia	21,000,000	104,000	5.0	B 2001
New Zealand	4,200,000	7,000	1.7	A 2001
Other	9,800,000	100	0.0	D
Total	35,000,000	111,100	3.2	

largest 15 communities, and excluding Israel from the count, 97.2 percent live in the 14 largest communities of the Diaspora, 69.5 percent of them living in the U.S. (Table 8). In 2007, there were at least 100 Jews in 93 different countries (Table 9). Two countries had Jewish populations above 5 million individuals each (Israel and the U.S.), another seven had more than 100,000 Jews, three had 50,000–100,000, five had 25,000–50,000, nine had 10,000–25,000, nine had 5,000–10,000, and 58 countries had less than 5,000. The 67 communities with fewer than 10,000 Jews overall accounted for 1 percent of world Jewry. In only six communities outside of Israel did Jews constitute at least about 5 per 1,000 (0.5 percent) of their country's total population. In descending order by the relative weight (not size) of their Jewish population they were Gibraltar (24.0 Jews per 1,000 inhabitants), the U.S. (17.5), Canada (11.4), France (7.9), Uruguay (5.4), and Australia (5.0).

By combining the two criteria of Jewish population size and density, we obtain the following taxonomy of the 25 Jewish communities with populations over 10,000 (excluding Israel). There are four countries with

TABLE 8. COUNTRIES WITH LARGEST CORE JEWISH POPULATIONS, 1/1/2007

Rank	Country	Jewish Population	%	In the World Cumulative %	%	In the Diaspora Cumulative %
1	Israel	5,393,400	41.0	41.0	=	=
2	United States	5,275,000	40.1	81.1	69.5	69.5
3	France	490,000	3.7	84.8	6.3	75.8
4	Canada	374,000	2.8	87.7	4.8	80.6
5	United Kingdom	295,000	2.2	89.9	3.8	84.4
6	Russia	221,000	1.7	91.6	2.8	87.3
7	Argentina	184,000	1.4	93.0	2.4	89.6
8	Germany	120,000	0.9	93.9	1.5	91.2
9	Australia	104,000	0.8	94.7	1.3	92.5
10	Brazil	96,200	0.7	95.4	1.2	93.8
11	Ukraine	79,000	0.6	96.0	1.0	94.8
12	South Africa	71,500	0.5	96.6	0.9	95.7
13	Hungary	49,000	0.4	96.9	0.6	96.3
14	Mexico	39,600	0.3	97.2	0.5	96.8
15	Belgium	30,500	0.2	97.5	0.4	97.2

The table header spans: % of Total Jewish Population, divided into "In the World" and "In the Diaspora".

over 100,000 Jews and at least 5 Jews per 1,000 of total population: the U.S., France, Canada, and Australia; another four countries with over 100,000 Jews and at least 1 per 1,000 of total population: the UK, Argentina, Russia, and Germany; one country with 10,000–100,000 Jews and at least 5 per 1,000 of total population: Uruguay; nine more countries with 10,000–100,000 Jews and at least 1 per 1,000 of total population: Ukraine, South Africa, Hungary, Belgium, the Netherlands, Chile, Belarus, Switzerland, and Sweden; and seven countries with 10,000–100,000 Jews and less than 1 per 1,000 of total population: Brazil, Mexico, Italy, Turkey, Venezuela, Spain, and Iran.

JEWS IN MAJOR CITIES

The overwhelmingly urban concentration of Jewish populations globally is evinced by the fact that in 2007 more than half (52.1 percent) of world Jewry live in only five metropolitan areas—Tel Aviv, New York, Jerusalem, Los Angeles, and Haifa. Two-thirds of the world's Jews (66.5 percent) live in those five places plus Southeast Florida, Be'er Sheva, Paris, Chicago, Boston, and San Francisco. The largest 20 Jewish population concentrations encompass 77 percent of all Jews worldwide (Table 10).[83] The Jewish population in the Tel Aviv urban conurbation extending from Netanya to Ashdod now exceeds by far that in the New York Standard Metropolitan Area extending from south New York State to parts of Connecticut, New Jersey, and Pennsylvania. Of the 20 largest metropolitan areas of Jewish residence, ten are located in the U.S., four in Israel, two in Canada, and one each in France, the UK, Argentina, and Russia.

OUTLOOK

Beyond the many problems related to Jewish population definitions and data accuracy, it is important to recognize that powerful and consistent trends daily reshape the profile of world Jewry. Reading current data in historical and comparative context, the recent momentum of Jewish de-

---

[83]For Israel estimates see Israel Central Bureau of Statistics, *Statistical Abstract of I rael* 57 (Jerusalem, 2006) Table 2-15. For U.S. estimates see Sheskin and Dashefsky, "Je ish Population in the United States, 2006." Some of the latter figures are somewhat outd and inconsistent with each other regarding definitions and methods.

TABLE 9. DISTRIBUTION OF THE WORLD'S JEWS, BY NUMBER, AND PROPORTION (PER 1,000 POPULATION) IN EACH COUNTRY, 1/1/2007

Number of Jews in Country		Jews per 1,000 Population				
	Total	0.0-0.9	1.0-4.9	5.0-9.9	10.0-24.9	25.0+
Number of Countries						
Total[a]	93	63	23	3	3	1
100–900	35	31	3	-	1	-
1,000–4,900	23	21	2	-	-	-
5,000–9,900	9	4	5	-	-	-
10,000–24,900	9	4	4	1	-	-
25,000–49,900	5	2	3	-	-	-
50,000–99,900	3	1	2	-	-	-
100,000–999,900	7	-	4	2	1	-
1,000,000 or more	2	-	-	-	1	1
Jewish Population Distribution—Absolute Numbers						
Total[a]	13,155,200	303,800	1,195,500	611,900	5,649,600	5,393,400
100–900	11,100	9,300	1,200	-	600	-
1,000–4,900	55,000	48,600	6,400	-	-	-
5,000–9,900	63,800	26,700	37,100	-	-	-
10,000–24,900	143,600	54,900	70,800	17,900	-	-
25,000–49,900	177,600	68,100	109,500	-	-	-
50,000–99,900	246,700	96,200	150,500	-	-	-
100,000–999,900	1,788,000	-	820,000	594,000	374,000	-
1,000,000 or more	10,668,400	-	-	-	5,275,000	5,393,400
Jewish Population Distribution—Percent of World's Jews						
Total[a]	100.0	2.3	9.1	4.7	42.9	41.0
100–900	0.1	0.1	0.0	0.0	0.0	0.0
1,000–4,900	0.4	0.4	0.0	0.0	0.0	0.0
5,000–9,900	0.5	0.2	0.3	0.0	0.0	0.0
10,000–24,900	1.1	0.4	0.5	0.1	0.0	0.0
25,000–49,900	1.4	0.5	0.8	0.0	0.0	0.0
50,000–99,900	1.9	0.7	1.1	0.0	0.0	0.0
100,000–999,900	13.6	0.0	6.2	4.5	2.8	0.0
1,000,000 or more	81.1	0.0	0.0	0.0	40.1	41.0

[a]Grand total includes countries with fewer than 100 Jews, for a total of 1,100 Jews. Minor discrepancies due to rounding. Israel includes West Bank.

TABLE 10.   METROPOLITAN AREAS WITH LARGEST CORE JEWISH POPULATIONS,
1/1/2007

Rank	Metro Area[a]	Country	Jewish Population	Share of World's Jews %	Cumulative %
1	Tel Aviv[b,c]	Israel	2,799,000	21.3	21.3
2	New York[d]	U.S.	2,051,000	15.6	36.9
3	Jerusalem[e]	Israel	675,000	5.1	42.0
4	Los Angeles[d]	U.S.	668,000	5.1	47.1
5	Haifa[b]	Israel	657,500	5.0	52.1
6	Southeast Florida [d, f]	U.S.	527,500	4.0	56.1
7	Be'er Sheva[b]	Israel	350,800	2.7	58.8
8	Paris[g]	France	284,000	2.2	60.9
9	Chicago[d]	U.S.	270,500	2.1	63.0
10	Boston[d]	U.S.	235,000	1.8	64.8
11	San Francisco[d]	U.S.	227,800	1.7	66.5
12	Washington[h]	U.S.	216,300	1.6	68.1
13	Philadelphia[d]	U.S.	206,100	1.6	69.7
14	London[i]	United Kingdom	195,000	1.5	71.2
15	Toronto[j]	Canada	180,000	1.4	72.5
16	Buenos Aires[k]	Argentina	165,000	1.3	73.8
17	Atlanta[h]	U.S.	119,800	0.9	74.7
18	Moscow[l]	Russia	95,000	0.7	75.4
19	Baltimore[h]	U.S.	91,400	0.7	76.1
20	Montreal[i]	Canada	93,000	0.7	76.8

[a]Most metropolitan areas include extended inhabited territory and several municipal authorities around central city. Definitions vary by country. Some of the estimates may include non-core Jews.
[b]As newly defined in the 1995 Israeli Census.
[c]Includes Ramat Gan, Bene Beraq, Petach Tikvah, Bat Yam, Holon, Rishon Lezion, Netanya, and Ashdod, each with a Jewish population above 100,000.
[d]Consolidated Metropolitan Statistical Area (CMSA).
[e]Includes the whole Jerusalem District and parts of Judea and Samaria District.
[f]Miami-Ft. Lauderdale and West Palm Beach-Boca Raton CMSA.
[g]Departments 75, 77, 78, 91, 92, 93, 94, 95.
[h]Metropolitan Statistical Area (MSA).
[i]Greater London and contiguous postcode areas.
[j]Census Metropolitan Area.
[k]Capital Federal and Gran Buenos Aires Partidos (AMBA).
[l]Territory administered by city council.

mographic change in the U.S.—at best tending to zero population growth—contrasts sharply to that of Israel, where there is significant natural increase. This makes the apparent transition of Israel into the largest Jewish population in the world increasingly grounded on empirical foundations. The U.S. is, and will remain, a very large, powerful, and resilient center of Jewish socioeconomic and cultural life. The aggregate of other Diaspora communities is increasingly eroding and their Jewish weight fast diminishing.

Projecting current demographic trends into the future and assuming continuity in the major factors of Jewish population change—admittedly a heavy assumption—the scenario of a growing plurality of world Jewry living in the State of Israel gains plausibility. Whether components of population change related to the family and childbearing, geographical mobility, affiliation, and disaffiliation will remain stable or evolve differently is, of course, a relevant subject for policy planning and interventions in Israel and in Jewish communities around the globe. Such interventions may alter the course of social and demographic developments that carry what are viewed as unwanted implications. Some, related to demographic and cultural behaviors, might impact upon current trends, helping reorient the current Israel-Diaspora demographic balance. The future is not predictable, but important lessons from the past may help formulate plans and expectations.

SERGIO DELLAPERGOLA

Clarifications

The article "Jewish Communal Affairs," published in volume 104 (2004), recounted, on page 97, a physical altercation that took place on October 21, 2003, at UCLA between Rabbi Chaim Seidler-Feller, the Hillel rabbi, and journalist Rachel Neuwirth. On January 19, 2007, as part of a settlement of the case, Seidler-Feller issued a public letter of apology to Neuwirth accepting full responsibility for what occurred.

"Celebrating the 350th," which appeared in volume 106 (2006), mentioned, on page 123, the first women ordained as rabbis by the American Reform and Conservative movements. It omitted Rabbi Sandy Eisenberg Sasso, ordained by the Reconstructionist Rabbinical College in 1974, the second female rabbi in the country.

Directories
Lists
Obituaries

National Jewish Organizations

UNITED STATES

Organizations are listed according to functions as follows:

COMMUNITY RELATIONS

AMERICAN COUNCIL FOR JUDAISM (1943). PO Box 300537, Jamaica Plain Station, Boston, MA 02130. (617)-983-1400. Pres. Stephen L. Naman; Exec. Dir. Rabbi Howard A. Berman. Seeks to advance the universal principles of a Judaism free of nationalism, and the national, civic, cultural, and social integration into American institutions of Americans of Jewish faith. *Issues of the American Council for Judaism; Special Interest Report.* (WWW.A CJNA.ORG)

AMERICAN JEWISH COMMITTEE (1906). The Jacob Blaustein Building, 165 E. 56 St., NYC 10022. (212)751-4000. FAX: (212) 750-0326. Pres. Richard Sideman; Exec. Dir. David A. Harris. Protects the rights and freedoms of Jews the world over; combats bigotry and anti-Semitism and promotes democracy and human rights for all; works for the security of Israel and deepened understanding between Americans and Israelis; advocates public-policy positions rooted in American democratic values and the perspectives of Jewish heritage; and enhances the creative vitality of the Jewish people. Includes Jacob and Hilda Blaustein Center for Human Relations, Project Interchange, William Petschek National Jewish Family Center, Jacob Blaustein Institute for Advancement of Human Rights, Ins on American Jewish-Israeli Relations. *American Jewish Year Book; Commentary; AJC Journal.* (WWW.AJC.ORG)

AMERICAN JEWISH CONGRESS (1918). 825 Third Ave., Ste. 1800, NYC 10022. (212)879-4500. FAX: (212)249-3672. E-mail: pr@ajcongress.org. Pres. Richard Gordon; Exec. Dir. Neil B. Goldstein. Works to foster the creative survival of the Jewish people; to help Israel develop in peace, freedom, and security; to eliminate all forms of racial and religious bigotry; to advance civil rights, protect civil liberties, defend religious freedom, and safeguard the separation of church and state; "The Attorney General for the Jewish Community." *Congress Monthly; Judaism; Inside Israel; Radical Islamic Fundamentalism Update.* (WWW.AJCONGRESS.ORG)

AMERICAN JEWISH PUBLIC RELATIONS SOCIETY (1957). 575 Lexington Ave., Suite 600, NYC 10022. (212)644-2663. FAX: (212)644-3887. Pres. Diane J. Ehrlich; V-Pres., membership, Lauren R. Marcus. Advances professional status of public-relations practitioners employed by Jewish organizations and institutions or who represent Jewish-related clients, services, or products; upholds a professional code of ethics and standards; provides continuing education and networking opportunities at monthly meetings; serves as a clearinghouse for employment opportunities. *AJPRS Reporter; AJPRS Membership Directory.*

ANTI-DEFAMATION LEAGUE OF B'NAI B'RITH (1913). 823 United Nations Plaza, NYC 10017. (212)885-7700. FAX: (212) 867-0779. E-mail: webmaster@adl.org. Natl. Chmn. Glen Lewy; Natl. Dir. Abraham H. Foxman. Seeks to combat anti-Semitism and to secure justice and fair treatment for all citizens through law, education, and community relations. *ADL on the Frontline; Law Enforcement Bulletin; Dimensions: A Journal of Holocaust Studies; Hidden Child Newsletter; International Reports; Civil Rights Reports.* (WWW.ADL.ORG)

ASSOCIATION OF JEWISH COMMUNITY RELATIONS WORKERS (1950). 7800 Northaven Road, Dallas, TX 75230. (214) 615-5229. FAX: (214)373-3186. Pres. Marlene Gorin. Aims to stimulate higher standards of professional practice in Jewish community relations; encourages research and training toward that end; conducts educational programs and seminars; aims to encourage cooperation between community-relations workers and those working in other areas of Jewish communal service.

CANFEI NESHARIM (2002). 111 Eighth Ave., 11th Floor, NYC 10011. (212)284-6745. E-mail: info@canfeinesharim.org. Exec. Dir. Evonne Marzouk. Educates about protecting the environment, from the perspective of Torah and Jewish law; encourages actions to protect the environment. *Compendium of Sources in Torah and Halacha* (biennial); *Newsletter* (monthly e-mail). (WWW.CANFEINESHARIM.ORG)

CENTER FOR JEWISH COMMUNITY STUDIES (1970). Beit Milken, 13 Tel Hai St., Jerusalem 92107, Israel. 972-2-5619281. FAX: 972-25619112. E-mail: jcpa@netvision.net.il or cjcs@worldnet.att.net. Jerusalem office: Jerusalem Center for Public Affairs. Pres. Amb. Dore Gold; Dir. Gen. Zvi Marom; Chmn. Bd. of Overseers Michael Rukin. Worldwide policy-studies institute devoted to the study of Jewish community organization, political thought, and public affairs, past and present, in Israel and throughout the world. Publishes original articles, essays, and monographs; maintains library, archives, and reprint series. *Jerusalem Letter/Viewpoints; Jewish Political Studies Review.* (WWW.JCPA.ORG).

CENTER FOR RUSSIAN JEWRY WITH STUDENT STRUGGLE FOR SOVIET JEWRY/SSSJ (1964). 240 Cabrini Blvd., #5B, NYC 10033. (212)928-7451. FAX: (212)795-8867. Dir./Founder Jacob Birnbaum; Chmn. Dr. Ernest Bloch. Campaigns for the human rights of the Jews of the former USSR, with emphasis on emigration and Jewish identity; supports programs for needy Jews there and for newcomers in Israel and USA, stressing employment and Jewish education. As the originator of the grassroots movement for Soviet Jewry in the early 1960s, possesses unique archives.

COALITION ON THE ENVIRONMENT & JEWISH LIFE (1993). 116 East 27th Street, 10th floor, New York, NY 10016. (212)532-7436. FAX: (212)686-1353. E-mail: info @coejl.org. Exec. Dir. Barbara Lerman-Golomb. Promotes environmental education, advocacy, and action in the American Jewish community. Sponsored by a broad coalition of Jewish organizations; member of the National Religious Partnership for the Environment. *Bi-annual newsletter.* (WWW.COEJL.ORG)

COMMISSION ON SOCIAL ACTION OF REFORM JUDAISM (1953, joint instrumentality of the Union for Reform Judaism and the Central Conference of American Rabbis). 633 Third Ave., 7th fl., NYC 10017. (212)650-4160. FAX: (212)650-4229. E-mail: csarj@urj.org. Wash. Office: 2027 Massachusetts Ave., NW, Washington, DC 20036. Chmn. Robert Heller; Dir. Rabbi Daniel Polish; Dir. Religious Action Center of Reform Judaism, Rabbi David Saperstein. Policy-making body that relates ethical and spiritual principles of Judaism to social-justice issues; implements resolutions through the Religious Action Center in Washington, DC, via advocacy, development of educational materials, and congregational programs. *Tzedek V'Shalom (social action newsletter); Chai Impact (legislative update).*

CONFERENCE OF PRESIDENTS OF MAJOR AMERICAN JEWISH ORGANIZATIONS (1955). 633 Third Ave., NYC 10017. (212)318-6111. FAX: (212)644-4135. E-mail: info@prescon.org. Chmn. June Walker; Exec. V.-Chmn. Malcolm Hoenlein. Seeks to strengthen the U.S.-Israel alliance and to protect and enhance the security and dignity of Jews abroad. Toward this end, the Conference of Presidents speaks and acts on the basis of consensus of its 54 member agencies on issues of national and international Jewish concern.

CONSULTATIVE COUNCIL OF JEWISH ORGANIZATIONS-CCJO (1946). 420 Lexington Ave., Suite 1731, NYC 10170. (212)808-5437. Chmn. Ady Steg & Clemens N. Nathan. A nongovernmental organization in consultative status with the UN, UNESCO, ILO, UNICEF, and the Council of Europe; cooperates and consults with, advises, and renders assistance to the Economic and Social Council of the UN on all problems relating to human rights and economic, social, cultural, educational, and related matters pertaining to Jews.

COORDINATING BOARD OF JEWISH ORGANIZATIONS (1947). 2020 K Street, NW, 7th Floor, Washington, D.C. 20006. (202)857-6540. FAX: (202)857-6689. Exec. V. Pres. Daniel S. Mariaschin. To promote the purposes and principles for which the UN was created.

COUNCIL OF JEWISH ORGANIZATIONS IN CIVIL SERVICE, INC. (1948). 45 E. 33 St., Rm. 601, NYC 10016. (212)689-2015. FAX: (212)447-1633. Pres. Louis Weiser; 1st V.-Pres. Melvyn Birnbaum. Supports merit system; encourages recruitment of Jewish youth to government service; member of Coalition to Free Soviet Jews, NY Jewish Community Relations Council, NY Metropolitan Coordinating Council on Jewish Poverty, Jewish Labor Committee, America-Israel Friendship League. *Council Digest.*

INSTITUTE FOR PUBLIC AFFAIRS (*see* UNION OF ORTHODOX JEWISH CONGREGATIONS OF AMERICA)

INTERNATIONAL LEAGUE FOR THE REPATRIATION OF RUSSIAN JEWS, INC. (1963). 2 Fountain Lane, Suite 2J, Scarsdale, NY 10583. (914)683-3225. FAX: (914)683-3221. Pres. Morris Brafman; Chmn. James H. Rapp. Helped to bring the situation of Soviet Jews to world attention; catalyst for advocacy efforts, educational projects, and programs on behalf of Russian Jews in the former USSR, Israel, and U.S. Provides funds to help Russian Jewry in Israel and the former Soviet Union.

JEWISH COUNCIL FOR PUBLIC AFFAIRS (formerly NATIONAL JEWISH COMMUNITY RELATIONS ADVISORY COUNCIL) (1944). 116 E. 27 St., 10th fl., NYC 10016. (212)684-6950. FAX: (212)686-1353. E-mail: contactus@thejcpa.org. Chair Lois Frank; Exec. Dir. Rabbi Steve Gutow. National coordinating body for the field of Jewish community relations, comprising 13 national and 122 local Jewish community-relations agencies. Promotes understanding of Israel and the Middle East; supports Jewish communities around the world; advocates for equality and pluralism, and against discrimination, in American society. Through the Council's work, its constituent organizations seek agreement on policies, strategies, and programs for effective utilization of their resources for common ends. *Insider (Weekly).* (WWW.JEWISHPUBLICAFFAIRS.ORG)

JEWISH LABOR COMMITTEE (1934). Atran Center for Jewish Culture, 25 E. 21 St.,

NYC 10010. (212)477-0707. FAX: (212)477-1918. Pres. Stuart Appelbaum; Exec. Dir. Avram B. Lyon. Serves as liaison between the Jewish community and the trade union movement; works with the U.S. and international labor movement to combat anti-Semitism, promote intergroup relations, and engender support for the State of Israel and Jews in and from the former Soviet Union; promotes teaching in public schools about the Holocaust and Jewish resistance; strengthens support within the Jewish community for the social goals and programs of the labor movement; supports Yiddish-language and cultural institutions. *Jewish Labor Committee Review; Issues Alert; Alumni Newsletter.*

————, NATIONAL TRADE UNION COUNCIL FOR HUMAN RIGHTS (1956). Atran Center for Jewish Culture, 25 E. 21 St., NYC 10010. (212)477-0707. FAX: (212)477-1918. Exec. Dir. Avram Lyon. Works with the American labor movement in advancing the struggle for social justice and equal opportunity, and assists unions in every issue affecting human rights. Fights discrimination on all levels and helps to promote labor's broad social and economic goals.

JEWISH PEACE FELLOWSHIP (1941). Box 271, Nyack, NY 10960. (914)358-4601. FAX: (914)358-4924. E-mail: jpf@forusa.org. Hon. Pres. Rabbi Philip Bentley; Ch. Murray Polner. Unites those who believe that Jewish ideals and experience provide inspiration for a nonviolent philosophy and way of life; offers draft counseling, especially for conscientious objection based on Jewish "religious training and belief"; encourages Jewish community to become more knowledgeable, concerned, and active in regard to the war/peace problem. *Shalom/Jewish Peace Letter.* (WWW.JEWISHPEACEFELLOWSHIP.ORG)

JEWISH WAR VETERANS OF THE UNITED STATES OF AMERICA (1896). 1811 R St., NW, Washington, DC 20009. (202)265-6280. FAX: (202)234-5662. E-mail: jwv@jwv.org. Natl. Exec. Dir. Herb Rosenbleeth; Natl. Commander Daniel Weiss. Seeks to foster true allegiance to the United States; to combat bigotry and prevent defamation of Jews; to encourage the doctrine of universal liberty, equal rights, and full justice for all; to cooperate with and support existing educational institutions and establish new ones; to foster the education of ex-servicemen, ex-servicewomen, and members in the ideals and principles of Americanism. *Jewish Veteran.*

————, NATIONAL MUSEUM OF AMERICAN JEWISH MILITARY HISTORY (1958). 1811 R St., NW, Washington, DC 20009. E-mail: nmajmh@nmajmh.org. (202)265-6280. FAX: (202)234-5662. Pres. Edwin Goldwasser; Archivist Tom Wildenberg. Documents and preserves the contributions of Jewish Americans to the peace and freedom of the United States; educates the public concerning the courage, heroism, and sacrifices made by Jewish Americans who served in the armed forces; and works to combat anti-Semitism. *The Jewish War Veteran).*

NATIONAL ASSOCIATION OF JEWISH LEGISLATORS (1976). 65 Oakwood St., Albany, NY 12208. (518)527-3353. FAX: (518)458-8512. E-mail: najl01@aol.com. Exec. Dir. Marc Hiller; Pres. Sen. Richard Cohen, Minn. state senator. A nonpartisan Jewish state legislative network focusing on domestic issues and publishing newsletters. Maintains close ties with the Knesset and Israeli leaders.

NCSJ: ADVOCATES ON BEHALF OF JEWS IN RUSSIA, UKRAINE, THE BALTIC STATES AND EURASIA (formerly AMERICAN JEWISH CONFERENCE ON SOVIET JEWRY) (1964; reorg. 1971). 2020 K. Street NW, Suite 7800, Washington, DC 200006. (202)898-2500. FAX: (202)898-0822. E-mail: ncsj@ncsj.org. N.Y. office: 823 United Nations Plaza, NYC 10017. (212)808-0295. Chmn. Edward Robin; Pres. Lesley Israel; Exec. Dir. Mark B. Levin. Coordinating agency for major national Jewish organizations and local community groups in the U.S., acting on behalf of Jews in the former Soviet Union (FSU); provides information about Jews in the FSU through public education and social action; reports and special pamphlets, special programs and projects, public meetings and forums. *Newswatch; annual report; action and program kits; Tekuma.* (WWW.NCSJ.ORG)

————, SOVIET JEWRY RESEARCH BUREAU. Chmn. Denis C. Braham; Pres. Howard E. Sachs. Organized by NCSJ to monitor emigration trends. Primary task is the accumulation, evaluation, and processing of information regarding Jews in the FSU, especially those who apply for emigration.

NATIONAL JEWISH COMMUNITY RELATIONS ADVISORY COUNCIL (*see* JEWISH COUNCIL FOR PUBLIC AFFAIRS)

NATIONAL JEWISH DEMOCRATIC COUNCIL (1990). PO BOX 75308 Washington, DC 20013-5308. (202)216-9060. FAX: (202) 216-9061. E-mail: info@njdc.org. Chmn. Michael Adler; Exec. Dir. Ira N. Forman. An independent organization committed to strengthening Jewish participation in the Democratic party primarily through grassroots activism. The national voice of Jewish Democrats, NJDC is dedicated to fighting the radical right and promoting Jewish values and interests in the Democratic party. (WWW.NJDC.ORG)

REPUBLICAN JEWISH COALITION (1985). 50 F Street, NW Suite 100, Washington, DC 20001. (202) 638-6688. FAX: (202)638-6694. E-mail: rjc@rjchq.org. Natl. Chmn. Sam Fox; Exec. Dir. Matthew Brooks. Promotes involvement in Republican politics among its members; sensitizes Republican leaders to the concerns of the American Jewish community; promotes principles of free enterprise, a strong national defense, and an internationalist foreign policy. *RJC Bulletin.* (WWW.RJCHQ. ORG)

SECURE COMMUNITY NETWORK (2004). (212)284-6940. FAX: (212)284-6949. E-mail: scandesk@scnus.org. Chmn. Mark Broxmeyer; Chmn. Law Enforcement Advisory Comm.: Steven Pomerantz. A national body created by the Conference of Presidents, United Jewish Communities, and American Jewish Committee to inform and educate Jewish organizations so they can adopt and institute intelligent and fiscally prudent security policies, procedures, and tactics in the fight against terrorism. (WWW.SCNUS.ORG)

SHALEM CENTER (1994). 881 High Street, Suite 206. Worthington, OH 43085. (877)298-7300. FAX: (888)766-1506. E-mail: shalem@shalem.org.il. Pres. Yoram Hazony (Israel); Academic Director, Daniel Polisar (Israel). The purposes and activities of the Shalem Center are to increase public understanding and conduct educational and research activities on the improvement of Jewish national public life, and to develop a community of intellectual leaders to shape the state of Israel into a secure, free, and prosperous society. *Azure.* (WWW.SHALEM.ORG.IL/HE-BREW)

SHALOM CENTER (1983). 6711 Lincoln Dr., Philadelphia, PA 19119. (215)844-8494. E-mail: office@shalomctr.org. (Part of Aleph Alliance for Jewish Renewal.) Pres. Rabbi Mordechai Liebling; Exec. Dir. Rabbi Arthur Waskow. National resource and organizing center for Jewish perspectives on dealing with overwork in American society, environmental dangers, unrestrained technology, militarism, and corporate irresponsibility. Initiated A.J. Heschel 25th Yahrzeit observance. Trains next generation of *tikkun olam* activists. Holds colloquia on issues like environmental causes of cancer. *New Menorah.* (WWW.SHALOMCTR.ORG)

STUDENT STRUGGLE FOR SOVIET JEWRY (*see* CENTER FOR RUSSIAN JEWRY)

UN WATCH (1993). 1, rue de Varembé, PO Box 191, 1211 Geneva 20, Switzerland. (41-22)734.14.72. FAX: (41-22)734.16.13. E-mail: unwatch@unwatch.org. Exec. Dir. Hillel Neuer; Chm. Amb. Alfred H. Moses. An affiliate of the AJC, UN Watch measures UN performance by the yardstick of the UN's Charter; advocates the non-discriminatory application of the Charter; opposes the use of UN fora to attack Israel and promote anti-Semitism; and seeks to institutionalize at the UN the fight against worldwide anti-Semitism. *The Wednesday Watch* (English and Spanish). (WWW.UNWATCH.ORG)

UCSJ: UNION OF COUNCILS FOR JEWS IN THE FORMER SOVIET UNION (formerly UNION OF COUNCILS FOR SOVIET JEWS) (1970). 1819 H St., NW, Suite 230, Washington, DC 20005. (202)775-9770. FAX: (202)775-9776. E-mail: ucsj@ucsj.com. Pres. Yosef I. Abramowitz; Natl. Dir. Micah H. Naftalin. Devoted to promoting religious liberty, freedom of emigration, and security for Jews in the FSU (former Soviet Union) through advocacy and monitoring of anti-Semitism, neo-facism, human rights, rule of law, and democracy. Offers educational, cultural, medical, and humanitarian aid through the Yad L'Yad partnership program pairing Jewish communities in the US an the FSU; advocates for refuseniks a political prisoner. (WWW.FSUMONIT COM)

WORLD CONGRESS OF GAY, LESBIAN, BI-
SEXUAL & TRANSGENDER JEWS (1980). 8
Letitia St., Philadelphia, PA 19106-3050.
(609)396-1972. FAX: (215)873-0108. E-
mail: president@wcgljo.org. Pres. David
Gellman (San Francisco, CA); V.-Pres
Luis Perelman (Mexico City, Mexico).
Supports, strengthens, and represents
over 67 Jewish gay and lesbian organiza-
tions across the globe and the needs of
gay and lesbian Jews generally. Chal-
lenges homophobia and sexism within the
Jewish community and responds to anti-
Semitism at large. Sponsors regional and
international conferences. *The Digest.*
(WWW.GLBTJEWS.ORG)

WORLD JEWISH CONGRESS (1936; org. in U.S.
1939). PO Box 90400, Washington DC,
20090. (212) 755-5770. FAX: (212)
755-5883. Pres. Ronald S. Lauder; Bd.
Chmn. Matthew Bronfman. Seeks to in-
tensify bonds of world Jewry with Israel; to
strengthen solidarity among Jews everywhere and secure their rights, status, and interests as individuals and communities; to
encourage Jewish social, religious, and cultural life throughout the world and coordinate efforts by Jewish communities and
organizations to cope with any Jewish
problem; to work for human rights generally. Represents its affiliated organizations-
most representative bodies of Jewish
communities in more than 80 countries and
35 national organizations in American sec-
tion-at UN, OAS, UNESCO, Council of
Europe, ILO, UNICEF, and other governmental, intergovernmental, and international authorities. *WJC Report; Boletin
Informativo OJI; Dialogues; Dateline:
World Jewry; Coloquio; Batfutsot; Gesher.*
(WWW.WORLDJEWISHCONGRESS.ORG)

CULTURAL

American Academy for Jewish Research
(1929). 420 Walnut Street, Philadelphia,
PA 19106. (215)238-1290. FAX: (215)238-
1540. Pres. Robert Chazan. Encourages
Jewish learning and research; holds annual or semiannual meeting; awards
grants for the publication of scholarly
works. *Proceedings of the American Academy for Jewish Research; Texts and Studies; Monograph Series.*

AMERICAN GATHERING OF JEWISH HOLO-
CAUST SURVIVORS. 122 W. 30 St., #205.
NYC 10001. (212)239-4230. FAX: (212)
79-2926. E-mail: mail@americangather-

ing.org. Pres. Benjamin Meed. Dedicated
to documenting the past and passing on
a legacy of remembrance. Compiles the
National Registry of Jewish Holocaust
Survivors-to date, the records of more
than 165,000 survivors and their families-
housed at the U.S. Holocaust Memorial
Museum in Washington, DC; holds an
annual Yom Hashoah commemoration
and occasional international gatherings;
sponsors an intensive summer program
for U.S. teachers in Poland and Israel to
prepare them to teach about the Holocaust. *Together (newspaper).*

AMERICAN GUILD OF JUDAIC ART (1991).
15 Greenspring Valley Rd., Owings Mills,
MD 21117. (410)902-0411. FAX: (410)
581-0108. E-mail: office@jewishart.org.
Pres. David Klass; 1st V.-Pres. Richard
McBee. A not-for-profit membership organization for those with interests in the
Judaic arts, including artists, galleries,
collectors & retailers of Judaica, writers,
educators, appraisers, museum curators,
conservators, lecturers, and others personally or professionally involved in the
field. Helps to promote members' art.
*Hiddur (quarterly); Update (members' net-
working newsletter).* (WWW.JEWISHART.
ORG)

AMERICAN JEWISH HISTORICAL SOCIETY
(1892). 15 W. 16 St., NYC 10011. (212)
294-6160. FAX: (212)294-6161. E-mail:
ajhs@ajhs.cjh.org. Chmn. David Solomon;
Pres./CEO Sidney Lapidus. Collects, catalogues, publishes, and displays material on
the history of the Jews in America; serves
as an information center for inquiries on
American Jewish history; maintains
archives of original source material on
American Jewish history; sponsors lectures
and exhibitions; makes available audiovisual material. *American Jewish History;
Heritage.* (WWW.AJHS.ORG)

AMERICAN JEWISH PRESS ASSOCIATION
(1944). Natl. Admin. Off.: 1828 L St. NW,
Suite 720, Washington, DC 20036.
(202)785-2282. FAX: (202)785-2307. E-
mail: toby@ajpa.org. Pres. Aaron Cohen;
Exec. Dir. Toby Dershowitz. Seeks the advancement of Jewish journalism and the
maintenance of a strong Jewish press in
the U.S. and Canada; encourages the attainment of the highest editorial and
business standards; sponsors workshops,
services for members; sponsors annual
competition for Simon Rockower Awards

for excellence in Jewish journalism. *Membership bulletin newsletter.*

AMERICAN SEPHARDI FEDERATION (1973). 15 W. 16 St., 6ᵗʰ Floor, NYC 10011. (212) 294-8350. FAX: (212)294-8348. E-mail: asf @cjh.org. Pres. David E.R. Dangoor; Exec. Dir. Lynne M. Winters. The central voice of the American Sephardic community, representing a broad spectrum of Sephardic organizations, congregations, and educational institutions. Seeks to strengthen and unify the community through education, communication, advocacy, and leadership development, creating greater awareness and appreciation of its rich and unique history and culture. *Sephardic Today.* (WWW.AMERICANSEFARDI FEDERATION.ORG)

AMERICAN SOCIETY FOR JEWISH MUSIC (1974). c/o The Center for Jewish History, 15 W. 16 St., NYC 10011. (212)294-8328. FAX: (212)294-6161. Pres. Michael Leavitt; V.-Pres. Judith Tischler & Martha Novick; Sec. Fortuna Calvo Roth; Bd. Chmn. Rabbi Henry D. Michelman; Treas. Cantor Nathaniel Benjamin. Promotes the knowledge, appreciation, and development of Jewish music, past and present, for professional and lay audiences; seeks to raise the standards of composition and performance in Jewish music, to encourage research, and to sponsor performances of new and rarely heard works. *Musica Judaica Journal.*

ASSOCIATION OF JEWISH BOOK PUBLISHERS (1962). c/o Jewish Book Council, 15 East 26ᵗʰ Street, 10ᵗʰ Floor, New York, NY 10010. (212)532-4949. FAX: (212)481-4174. Email: arjhill@jewishbooks.com. Pres. Ellen Frankel. As a nonprofit group, provides a forum for discussion of mutual areas of interest among Jewish publishers, and promotes cooperative exhibits and promotional opportunities for members. Membership fee is $85 annually per publishing house.

ASSOCIATION OF JEWISH LIBRARIES (1965). 15 E. 26 St.,10ᵗʰ fl, NYC 10010. (212)725-5359. FAX: (212)481-4174. E-mail: ajl@jewishbooks.org. Pres. Pearl Berger; V.-Pres. Ronda Rose. Seeks to promote and improve services and professional standards in Jewish libraries; disseminates Jewish library information and guidance; promotes publication of literature in the field; encourages the establishment of Jewish libraries and collections of Judaica and the choice of Judaica librarianship as a profession; cocertifies Jewish libraries. *AJL Newsletter; Judaica Librarianship.*

B'NAI B'RITH KLUTZNICK NATIONAL JEWISH MUSEUM (1957). 1640 Rhode Island Ave., NW, Washington, DC 20036. (202) 857-6583. FAX: (202)857-1099. A center of Jewish art and history in the nation's capital, maintains temporary and permanent exhibition galleries, permanent collection of Jewish ceremonial objects, folk art, and contemporary fine art, outdoor sculpture garden and museum shop, as well as the American Jewish Sports Hall of Fame. Provides exhibitions, tours, educational programs, research assistance, and tourist information. *Permanent collection catalogue; temporary exhibit catalogues.*

CENTRAL YIDDISH CULTURE ORGANIZATION (CYCO), INC. (1943 incorporated) (1948-non profit status). 25 E. 21 St., 3rd fl., NYC 10010. (212) 505-8305. FAX: (212) 505-8044. E-mail: cycobooks@earth-link.net. Pres. Dr. Barnett Zumoff; Exec. Officer Hy Wolfe. To promote the Yiddish word that is Cyco's purpose. We do this through the promotion, publication and distribution of Yiddish books, music books, CDs, tapes and albums. All in Yiddish!

CONFERENCE ON JEWISH SOCIAL STUDIES, INC. (formerly CONFERENCE ON JEWISH RELATIONS, INC.) (1939). Bldg. 240, Rm. 103. Program in Jewish Studies, Stanford University, Stanford, CA 94305-2190. (650)725-0829. FAX:(650)725-2920. E-mail: jss@leland.stanford.edu. Pres. Steven J. Zipperstein; V.-Pres. Aron Rodrigue. *Jewish Social Studies.*

CONGREGATION BINA (1981). 600 W. End Ave., Suite 1-C, NYC 10024. (212)873-4261. E-mail: samueldivekar@hotmail. com. Pres. Joseph Moses; Exec. V.-Pres. Moses Samson; Hon. Pres. Samuel M. Daniel; Sec. Gen. Elijah E. Jhirad. Serves the religious, cultural, charitable, and philanthropic needs of the Children of Israel who originated in India and now reside in the U.S. Works to foster and preserve the ancient traditions, customs, liturgy, music, and folklore of Indian Jewry and to maintain needed institutions. *Kol Bina.*

CONGRESS FOR JEWISH CULTURE (1948). 25 E. 21 St., NYC 10010. (212)505-8040. FAX: (212)505-8044. E-mail: kongres @earthlink.net. Exec. Dir. Shane Baker. Congress for Jewish Culture administers the book store CYCO and publishes the world's oldest Yiddish journal, *The Zukunft*. Currently producing a two volume anthology of Yiddish literature in America. Activities include yearly memorials for the Warsaw ghetto uprising and the murdered Soviet Yiddish writers, also readings and literary afternoons. *The Zukunft; Bulletin: In the World of Yiddish.*

ELAINE KAUFMAN CULTURAL CENTER (1952). 129 W. 67 St., NYC 10023. (212) 501-3303. FAX: (212)874-7865. Email: lhard@ekcc.org. Hon. Chmn. Leonard Goodman; Chmn. Phyllis Feder; Pres. Bethany Millard; Exec. Dir. Lydia Kontos. Offers instruction in its Lucy Moses School for Music and Dance in music, dance, art, and theater to children and adults, in Western culture and Jewish traditions. Presents frequent performances of Jewish and general music by leading artists and ensembles in its Merkin Concert Hall and Ann Goodman Recital Hall. The Birnbaum Music Library houses Jewish music scores and reference books. *In Harmony (quarterly newsletter); EKCC Events (bimonthly calendar); Bimonthly concert calendars; catalogues and brochures.* (WWW.EKCC.ORG)

HOLOCAUST CENTER OF THE UNITED JEWISH FEDERATION OF GREATER PITTSBURGH (1980). 5738 Darlington Rd., Pittsburgh, PA 15217. (412)421-1500. FAX: (412)422-1996. E-mail: lhurwitz@ujf.net. Pres. Holocaust Comm. Chair Dr. Barbara Burstin; UJF. Ch. James A. Rudolph; Dir. Linda F. Hurwitz. Develops programs and provides resources to further understanding of the Holocaust and its impact on civilization. Maintains a library, archive; provides speakers, educational materials; organizes community programs. Published collection of survivor and liberator stories. (WWW.UJFHC.NET)

HOLOCAUST MEMORIAL CENTER (1984). 28123 Orchard Lake Rd., Farmington Hills, MI 48334. (248)553-2400. FAX: (248)553-2433. E-mail: info@holocaustcenter.org. Founder & Dir. Rabbi Charles Rosenzveig. America's first free-standing Holocaust center comprising a museum, library-archive, oral history collection, garden of the righteous, research institute and academic advisory committee. Provides tours, lecture series, teacher training, Yom Hashoah commemorations, exhibits, educational outreach programs, speakers' bureau, computer database on 1,200 destroyed Jewish communities, guided travel tours to concentration camps and Israel, and museum shop. Published *World Reacts to the Holocaust; Survey of U.S. Federal, U.S. State and Canadian Provincial Support for Holocaust Education, Newsletter.*

HOLOCAUST MEMORIAL RESOURCE & EDUCATION CENTER OF CENTRAL FLORIDA (1982). 851 N. Maitland Ave., Maitland, FL 32751. (407)628-0555. FAX: (407)628-1079. E-mail: execdir@holocaustedu.org. Pres. Stan Sujka, MD; Bd. Chmn. Tess Wise. An interfaith educational center devoted to teaching the lessons of the Holocaust. Houses permanent multimedia educational exhibit; maintains library of books, videotapes, films, and other visuals to serve the entire educational establishment; offers lectures, teacher training, and other activities. *Newsletter; Bibliography; "Holocaust-Lessons for Tomorrow"; elementary and middle school curriculum.*

HOLOCAUST MUSEUM AND LEARNING CENTER IN MEMORY OF GLORIA GOLDSTEIN (1995) (formerly ST. LOUIS CENTER FOR HOLOCAUST STUDIES) (1977). 12 Millstone Campus Dr., St. Louis, MO 63146. (314)432-0020. FAX: (314)432-1277. E-mail: dreich@jfedstl.org. Chmn. Richard W. Stein; Curator/Dir. Of Ed. Dan A. Reich; Exec. Dir. Barbara Raznick; Dir. Of Admin. & Dev. Brian Bray. Develops programs and provides resources and educational materials to further an understanding of the Holocaust and its impact on civilization; has a 5,000 sq. ft. museum containing photographs, artifacts, and audiovisual displays. *Newsletter.*

INTERNATIONAL ASSOCIATION OF JEWISH GENEALOGICAL SOCIETIES (1988). 4430 Mt. Paran Pkwy NW, Atlanta, GA 30327-3747. (404)261-8662. Fax: (404)228-7125. E-mail: homargol@aol.com. Pres. Anne Feder Lee. Umbrella organization of more than 70 Jewish Genealogical Societies (JGS) worldwide. Represents organized Jewish genealogy, encourages Jews to research their family history, promotes new JGSs, supports existing societies, implements projects of interest to individuals researching their Jewish family histories. Holds annual conference where members learn and exchange ideas. (WWW.IAJGS. ORG)

INTERNATIONAL JEWISH MEDIA ASSOCIATION (1987). U.S.: c/o St. Louis Jewish Light, 12 Millstone Campus Dr., St. Louis, MO 63146. (314)432-3353. FAX: (314)432-0515. E-mail: stlouislgt@aol. com and ajpamr@aol.com. Israel: PO Box 92, Jerusalem 91920. 02-202-222. FAX: 02-513-642. Pres. Robert A. Cohn (c/o St. Louis Jewish Light); Exec. Dir. Toby Dershowitz. 1828 L St. NW, Suite 402, Washington, DC 20036. (202)785-2282. FAX: (202)785-2307. E-mail: toby @dershowitz.com. Israel Liaisons Jacob Gispan & Lifsha Ben-Shach, WZO Dept. of Info. A worldwide network of Jewish journalists, publications and other media in the Jewish and general media, which seeks to provide a forum for the exchange of materials and ideas and to enhance the status of Jewish media and journalists throughout the world. *IJMA Newsletter; Proceedings of the International Conference on Jewish Media.*

INTERNATIONAL NETWORK OF CHILDREN OF JEWISH HOLOCAUST SURVIVORS, INC. (1981). 13899 Biscayne Blvd. Suite 404, N. Miami, FL 33181. (305)919-5690. FAX: (305)919-5691. E-mail: info@hdec.org. Pres. Rositta E. Kenigsberg; Founding Chmn. Menachem Z. Rosensaft. Links Second Generation groups and individuals throughout the world. Represents the shared interests of children of Holocaust survivors; aims to perpetuate the authentic memory of the Holocaust and prevent its recurrence, to strengthen and preserve the Jewish spiritual, ideological, and cultural heritage, to fight anti-Semitism and all forms of discrimination, persecution, and oppression anywhere in the world.

JACOB RADER MARCUS CENTER OF THE AMERICAN JEWISH ARCHIVES (1947). 3101 Clifton Ave., Cincinnati, OH 45220. (513)221-1875 ext. 403. FAX: (513)221-7812. E-mail: aja@cn.huc.edu. Exec. Dir. Dr. Gary P. Zola. Promotes the study and preservation of the Western Hemisphere Jewish experience through research, publications, collection of important source materials, and a vigorous public-outreach program. *American Jewish Archives Journal, Monographs, Pamphlets, booklets, educational materials and posters.*

JEWISH AMERICAN SOCIETY FOR HISTORIC PRESERVATION (1997). 16405 Equestrian Lane, Rockville, MD 20855. (301)977-3637. FAX: (301)977-3888. E-mail: jashp1@msn.com. Pres. Jerry Klinger. Identifies and publicizes sites of American Jewish historical interest; in cooperation with local historical societies and houses of worship, promotes programs to stress the commonality of the American experience. (WWW.JASHP.ORG)

JEWISH BOOK COUNCIL (1946; reorg. 1993). 520 8th Avenue, 4th Floor New York, NY10018. (212)201-2920. E-mail: jbc@ jewishbooks.org. Pres. Lawrence J. Krule; Bd. Chmn. Henry Everett; Exec. Dir. Carolyn Starman Hessel. Serves as literary arm of the American Jewish community and clearinghouse for Jewish-content literature; assists readers, writers, publishers, and those who market and sell products. Provides bibliographies, list of publishers, bookstores, book fairs. Sponsors National Jewish Book Awards, Jewish Book Month, Jewish Book Fair Network. *Jewish Book Annual; Jewish Book World.* (WWW.JEWISHBOOKCOUNCIL. ORG)

JEWISH FEDERATION'S LOS ANGELES MUSEUM OF THE HOLOCAUST (MARTYRS MEMORIAL) (org. mid-1960s; opened 1978). 6006 Wilshire Blvd., Los Angeles, CA 90036. (323)761-8170. FAX: (323)761-8174. E-mail: museumiemp@jewishla.org. Chmn. Gary John Schiller; Director Rachel L. Jayoela. A photo-narrative museum and resource center dedicated to Holocaust history, issues of genocide and prejudice, curriculum development, teacher training, research and exhibitions. *PAGES, a newslettr; Those Who Dared; Rescuers and Rescued; Guide to Schindler's List; Anne Frank: A Teaching.*

JEWISH HERITAGE PROJECT (1981). 150 Franklin St., #1W, NYC 10013. (212)925-9067. E-mail: jhpffh@jps.net. Exec. Dir. Alan Adelson. Strives to bring to the broadest possible audience authentic works of literary and historical value relating to Jewish history and culture. With funding from the National Endowment of the Arts, Jewish Heritage runs the National Initiative in the Literature of the Holocaust. Not a grant giving organization. Distributor of the film *Lodz Ghetto,* which it developed, as well as its companion volume *Lodz Ghetto: Inside*

Community Under Siege; Better Than Gold: An Immigrant Family's First Years in Brooklyn.

JEWISH MUSEUM (1904, under auspices of Jewish Theological Seminary). 1109 Fifth Ave., NYC 10128. (212)423-3200. FAX: (212)423-3232. Dir. Joan H. Rosenbaum; Bd. Chmn. Robert J. Hurst. Expanded museum features permanent exhibition on the Jewish experience. Repository of the largest collection of Jewish related paintings, prints, photographs, sculpture, coins, medals, antiquities, textiles, and other decorative arts-in the Western Hemisphere. Includes the National Jewish Archive of Broadcasting. Tours, lectures, film showings, and concerts; special programs for children; cafe; shop. *Special exhibition catalogues; annual report.* (WWW.THEJEWISHMUSEUM.ORG)

JEWISH PUBLICATION SOCIETY (1888). 2100 Arch St., 2nd fl., Philadelphia, PA 19103. (215)832-0600. FAX: (215)568-2017. E-mail: jewishbook@jewishpub.org. Pres. Allan R. Frank; CEO/Ed.-in-Chief Dr. Ellen Frankel. Publishes and disseminates books of Jewish interest for adults and children; titles include TANAKH, religious studies and practices, life cycle, folklore, classics, art, history. *Booklink JPS Catalogue.* (WWW.JEWISHPUB.ORG)

JUDAH L. MAGNES MUSEUM-JEWISH MUSEUM OF THE WEST (1962). 2911 Russell St., Berkeley, CA 94705. (510)549-6950. FAX: (510)849-3673. E-mail: pfpr@magnesmuseum.org. Pres. Fred Weiss; Dir. Susan Morris. Collects, preserves, and makes available Jewish art, culture, history, and literature from throughout the world. Permanent collections of fine and ceremonial art; rare Judaica library, Western Jewish History Center (archives), Jewish-American Hall of Fame. Changing exhibits, traveling exhibits, docent tours, lectures, numismatics series, poetry and video awards, museum shop. *Magnes News; special exhibition catalogues; scholarly books.*

JUDAICA CAPTIONED FILM CENTER, INC. (1983). PO Box 21439, Baltimore, MD 21282-1439. Voice Relay Service (1-800)735-2258; TDD (410)655-6767. E-mail: lweiner@jhucep.org. Pres. Lois Lilienfeld Weiner. Developing a comprehensive library of captioned and subtitled films and tapes on Jewish subjects; distributes them to organizations serving the hearing-impaired, including mainstream classes and senior adult groups, on a free-loan, handling/shipping-charge-only basis. *Newsletter.*

JUDAICA INSTITUTE OF AMERICA (2007). 3907 Fordham Dr., Baltimore, MD 21215. (443)621-3584. FAX: (925)892-7381. E-mail: info@judin.org. Pres. Ronald J. Schwartz. A nondenominational arts-education initiative that promotes Jewish heritage, literature, identity, and visual culture; supports scholarly research in Judaica. (WWW.JUDIN.ORG)

LEAGUE FOR YIDDISH, INC. (1979). 200 W. 72 St., Suite 40, NYC 10023. (212)787-6675. E-mail: mschaecht@aol.com. Pres. Dr. Zuni Zelitch. Encourages the development and use of Yiddish as a living language; promotes its modernization and standardization; publisher of Yiddish textbooks and English-Yiddish dictionaries; most recent book *The Standardized Yiddish Orthography; Afn Shvel (quarterly).* (WWW.META-LAB.UNC.EDU/YIDDISH/YIDLEAGUE)

LEO BAECK INSTITUTE, INC. (1955). 15 W. 16 St., NYC 10011-6301. (212)744-6400. FAX: (212)988-1305. E-mail: lbaeck@lbi.cjh.org. Pres. Ismar Schorsch; Exec. Dir. Carol Kahn Strauss. A research, study, and lecture center, museum, library, and archive relating to the history of German-speaking Jewry. Offers lectures, exhibits, faculty seminars; publishes a series of monographs, yearbooks, and journals. *LBI News; LBI Yearbook; LBI Memorial Lecture; occasional papers.* (WWW.LBI.ORG)

LIVING TRADITIONS (1994), (c/o WORKMAN'S CIRCLE) 45 East 33rd Street, New York, NY 10016. (212)532-8202. E-mail: info@livingtraditions.org. Pres. Henry Sapoznik; V.-Pres. Sherry Mayrent. Nonprofit membership organization dedicated to the study, preservation, and innovative continuity of traditional folk and popular culture through workshops, concerts, recordings, radio and film documentaries; clearinghouse for research in klezmer and other traditional music; sponsors yearly weeklong international cultural event, "Yiddish Folk Arts Program/'KlezKamp.'" *Living Traditions* (newsletter). (WWW.LIVINGTRADITIONS.ORG)

MARTIN BUBER INSTITUTE (1990), 203 Rocking Stone Ave., Larchmont, NY

10538. (914)833-7731. E-mail: HM64@
columbia.edu. Hon. Chmn. Prof. Maurice Friedman; Pres. Dr. Hune Margulies.
Sponsors seminars, workshops, conferences, and publications to encourage the
exchange of ideas about the life and
thought of Buber. *Martin Buber Review
(annual)*.

MEMORIAL FOUNDATION FOR JEWISH CUL-
TURE, INC. (1964). 50 West Broadway, 34ᵗʰ
Floor, NYC 10004. (212)425-6606. FAX:
(212)425-6602. Pres. Prof. Anita Shapira;
Exec. V.-Pres. Jerry Hochbaum. Through
the grants that it awards, encourages Jewish scholarship, culture, and education;
supports communities that are struggling
to maintain Jewish life; assists professional training for careers in communal
service in Jewishly deprived communities;
and stimulates the documentation, commemoration, and teaching of the Holocaust. (WWW.MFJC.ORG)

MUSEUM OF JEWISH HERITAGE—A LIVING
MEMORIAL TO THE HOLOCAUST (1984). 36
Battery Park Plaza, NYC 10004-1484.
(212)968-1800. FAX: (212)968-1368. Bd.
Chmn. Robert M. Morgenthau; Museum
Pres. Dr. Alfred Gottschalk; Museum
Dir. David Marwell. New York tri-state's
principal institution for educating people
of all ages and backgrounds about 20th-
century Jewish history and the Holocaust.
Repository of Steven Spielberg's Survivors of the Shoah Visual History Foundation videotaped testimonies. Core and
special exhibitions. *18 First Place (newsletter); Holocaust bibliography; educational materials.* (WWW.MJHNYC.ORG)

MUSEUM OF TOLERANCE OF THE SIMON
WIESENTHAL CENTER (1993). 9786 W.
Pico Blvd., Los Angeles, CA 90035-4792.
(310)553-8403. FAX: (310)553-4521. E-
mail: avra@wiesenthal.com. Dean-
Founder Rabbi Marvin Hier; Assoc.
Dean Rabbi Abraham Cooper; Exec. Dir.
Rabbi Meyer May. A unique experiential
museum focusing on personal prejudice,
group intolerance, struggle for civil rights,
and 20th-century genocides, culminating
in a major exhibition on the Holocaust.
Archives, Multimedia Learning Center
designed for individualized research,
6,700-square-foot temporary exhibit
space, 324-seat theater, 150-seat auditorium, and outdoor memorial plaza.
(WWW.WIESENTHAL.COM)

NATIONAL FOUNDATION FOR JEWISH CUL-
TURE (1960). 330 Seventh Ave., 21st fl.,
NYC 10001. (212)629-0500. FAX:
(212)629-0508. E-mail: nfjc@jewishcul-
ture.org. Pres. Carol B. Spinner; Exec.
Dir. Elisa Bernhardt. The leading Jewish
organization devoted to promoting Jewish culture in the U.S. Manages the Jewish Endowment for the Arts and
Humanities; administers the Council of
American Jewish Museums and Council
of Archives and Research Libraries in
Jewish Studies; offers doctoral dissertation fellowships, new play commissions,
and grants for documentary films, recording of Jewish music, contemporary
choreography, fiction and non-fiction writing, and cultural preservation; coordinates community cultural residencies,
local cultural councils, and national cultural consortia; sponsors conferences,
symposia, and festivals in the arts and humanities. *Jewish Culture News;Culture
Currents (electronic)*.

NATIONAL MUSEUM OF AMERICAN JEWISH
HISTORY (1976). Independence Mall E.
55 N. Fifth St. Philadelphia, PA 19106-
2197. (215) 923-3811. FAX: (215) 923-
0763. E-mail: nmajh@nmajh.org. Dir./
CEO Gwen Goodman. The only museum
in the nation to offer education, exhibits,
and programs dedicated to preserving the
history and culture of the Jewish people
in America; located across from the Liberty Bell. (WWW.NMAJH.ORG)

NATIONAL MUSEUM OF AMERICAN JEWISH
MILITARY HISTORY (*see* JEWISH WAR VET-
ERANS OF THE U.S.A.)

NATIONAL YIDDISH BOOK CENTER (1980).
1021 West St., Amherst, MA 01002.
(413)256-4900. FAX: (413)256-4700. E-
mail: yiddish@bikher.org. Pres. Aaron
Lansky; V.-Pres. Nancy Sherman. Since
1980 the center has collected 1.5 million
Yiddish books for distribution to readers
and libraries worldwide; digitized more
than 12,000 Yiddish titles, offered a range
of educational programs in Yiddish and
modern culture, and published *Pakn
Treger,* an award-winning English-language magazine. (WWW.YIDDISHBOOKCEN-
TER.ORG)

ORTHODOX JEWISH ARCHIVES (1978). 42
Broadway, New York, NY 10004.
(212)797-9000, ext. 73. FAX: (212)269-
2843. Exec. V-Pres. Rabbi Shmuel Bloom

& Shlomo Gertzullin; Dir. Rabbi Moshe Kolodny. Founded by Agudath Israel of America; houses historical documents, photographs, periodicals, and other publications relating to the growth of Orthodox Jewry in the U.S. and related communities in Europe, Israel, and elsewhere. Particularly noteworthy are its holdings relating to rescue activities organized during the Holocaust and its traveling exhibits available to schools and other institutions.

RESEARCH FOUNDATION FOR JEWISH IMMIGRATION, INC. (1971). 570 Seventh Ave., NYC 10018. (212)921-3871. FAX: (212)575-1918. Sec./Coord. of Research Herbert A. Strauss; Archivist Dennis E. Rohrbaugh. Studies and records the history of the migration and acculturation of Central European German-speaking Jewish and non-Jewish Nazi persecutees in various resettlement countries worldwide, with special emphasis on the American experience. *International Biographical Dictionary of Central European Emigrés, 1933-1945; Jewish Immigrants of the Nazi Period in the USA.*

SEPHARDIC EDUCATIONAL CENTER (1979). 10808 Santa Monica Blvd., Los Angeles, CA 90025. (310)441-9361. FAX: (310)441-9561. E-mail: newyork@secjerusalem.org. Founder & Chmn. Jose A. Nessim, M.D. Has chapters in the U.S., North, Central, and South America, Europe, and Asia, a spiritual and educational center in the Old City of Jerusalem, and executive office in Los Angeles. Serves as a meeting ground for Sephardim from many nations; sponsors the first worldwide movement for Sephardic youth and young adults. Disseminates information about Sephardic Jewry in the form of motion pictures, pamphlets, and books, which it produces. *Hamerkaz (quarterly bulletin in English).* (WWW.SECJERUSALEM.ORG)

SEPHARDIC HOUSE-THE CULTURAL DIVISION OF ASF (1978). 15 West 16th Street, NYC 10011. (212)294-6170. FAX: (212)294-6149. E-mail: sephardichouse@cjh.org. Pres. Morrie R.Yohai; Dir. Dr. Janice E. Ovadiah. A cultural organization dedicated to fostering Sephardic history and culture; sponsors a wide variety of classes and public programs, film festivals, publication program disseminates materials of Sephardic value; outreach program to communities outside of the New York area; program bureau provides program ideas, speakers, and entertainers; International Sephardic Film Festival every year. *Sephardic House Newsletter; Publication Catalogue.* (WWW. SEPHARDICHOUSE.ORG)

SIMON WIESENTHAL CENTER (1977). 1399 South Roxbury Drive., Los Angeles, CA 90035-4701. (310)553-9036. FAX: (310)553-4521. Email: avra@wiesenthal.com. Dean-Founder Rabbi Marvin Hier; Assoc. Dean Rabbi Abraham Cooper; Exec. Dir. Rabbi Meyer May. Regional offices in New York, Miami, Toronto, Paris, Jerusalem, Buenos Aires. The largest institution of its kind in N. America dedicated to the study of the Holocaust, its contemporary implications, and related human-rights issues through education and awareness. Incorporates 185,000-sq.-ft. Museum of Tolerance, library, media department, archives, "Testimony to the Truth" oral histories, educational outreach, research department, international social action. *Response Magazine.* (WWW.WIESENTHAL.COM)

SKIRBALL CULTURAL CENTER (1996), an affiliate of Hebrew Union College. 2701 N. Sepulveda Blvd., Los Angeles, CA 90049. (310)440-4500. FAX: (310)440-4595. Pres. & CEO Uri D. Herscher; Bd. Chmn. Howard Friedman. Dedicated to exploring the connections between four thousand years of Jewish heritage and the vitality of American democratic ideals. It welcomes and seeks to inspire people of every ethnic and cultural identity. Guided by our respective memories and experiences, together we aspire to build a society in which all of us can feel at home. Skirball Cultural Center achieves its mission through pubic programs that explore literary, visual, and performing arts from around the world; through the display and interpretation of its permanent collections and changing exhibitions; through scholarship in American Jewish history and related publications; and through outreach to the community.. (WWW.SKIRBALL.ORG)

SOCIETY FOR THE HISTORY OF CZECHOSLOVAK JEWS, INC. (1961). 760 Pompton Ave., Cedar Grove, NJ 07009. (973)239-2333. FAX: (973)239-7935. Pres. Rabbi Norman Patz; V.-Pres. Prof. Fred Hahn; Sec. Anita Grosz. Studies the history of Czechoslovak Jews; collects material and disseminates information through the publication of books and pamphlets; conducts annual memorial service for Czech Holocaust victims. *The Jews of Czechoslovakia (3 vols.); Review I-VI.*

THE SOCIETY OF FRIENDS OF TOURO SYNAGOGUE NATIONAL HISTORIC SITE, INC. (1948). 85 Touro St., Newport, RI 02840. (401)847-4794. FAX: (401)845-6790. E-mail: info@tourosynagogue.org. Pres. M. Bernard Aidinoff; Exec. Dir. Michael L. Balaban. Helps maintain Touro Synagogue as a national historic site, opening and interpreting it for visitors; promotes public awareness of its preeminent role in the tradition of American religious liberty; annually commemorates George Washington's letter of 1790 to the Hebrew Congregation of Newport. *Society Update.*

———, TOURO NATIONAL HERITAGE TRUST (1984). 85 Touro St., Newport, RI 02840. (401)847-0810. FAX (401)847-8121. Pres. Bernard Bell; Chmn. Benjamin D. Holloway. Works to establish national education center within Touro compound; sponsors Touro Fellow through John Carter Brown Library; presents seminars and other educational programs; promotes knowledge of the early Jewish experience in this country.

SPERTUS MUSEUM, SPERTUS INSTITUTE OF JEWISH STUDIES (1968). 618 S. Michigan Ave., Chicago, IL 60605. (312)322-1747. FAX: (312)922-6406. Pres. Spertus Institute of Jewish Studies, Dr. Howard A. Sulkin. The largest, most comprehensive Judaic museum in the Midwest with 12,000 square feet of exhibit space and a permanent collection of some 10,000 works reflecting 5,000 years of Jewish history and culture. Also includes the redesigned Zell Holocaust Memorial, permanent collection, changing visual arts and special exhibits, and the children's ARTIFACT Center for a hands-on archaeological adventure. Plus, traveling exhibits for Jewish educators, life-cycle workshops, ADA accessible. *Exhibition catalogues; educational pamphlets.*

———, ASHER LIBRARY, SPERTUS INSTITUTE OF JEWISH STUDIES (approx. 1930), 618 S. Michigan Ave., Chicago, IL 60605. (312) 322-1749, FAX (312) 922-6406. Pres. Spertus Institute of Jewish Studeis, Dr. Howard A. Sulkin; Director, Asher Library, Glenn Ferdman. Asher Library is the largest public Jewish Library in the Midwest, with over 100, 000 books and 550 periodicals; extensive collections of music, art, rare books, maps and electronic resources; nearly 1,000 feature and documentary films available on video cassette. Online catalogue access available. Also, the Chicago Jewish Archives collects historical material of Chicago individuals, families, synagogues and organizations. *ADA accessible.*

SURVIVORS OF THE SHOAH VISUAL HISTORY FOUNDATION (1994). PO Box 3168, Los Angeles, CA 90078-3168. (818)777-7802. FAX: (818)866-0312. Exec. Dir. Ari C. Zev. A nonprofit organization, founded and chaired by Steven Spielberg, dedicated to videotaping and preserving interviews with Holocaust survivors throughout the world. The archive of testimonies will be used as a tool for global education about the Holocaust and to teach racial, ethnic, and cultural tolerance.

UNITED STATES HOLOCAUST MEMORIAL MUSEUM (1980; opened Apr. 1993). 100 Raoul Wallenberg Place, SW, Washington, DC 20024. (202)488-0400. FAX. (202)488-2690. Chmn. Fred S. Zeidman; Dir. Sara J. Bloomfeld. Federally chartered and privately built, its mission is to teach about the Nazi persecution and murder of six million Jews and millions of others from 1933 to 1945 and to inspire visitors to contemplate their moral responsibilities as citizens of a democratic nation. Opened in April 1993 near the national Mall in Washington, DC, the museum's permanent exhibition tells the story of the Holocaust through authentic artifacts, videotaped oral testimonies, documentary film, and historical photographs. Offers educational programs for students and adults, an interactive computerized learning center, and special exhibitions and community programs. *United States Holocaust Memorial Museum Update (bimonthly); Directory of Holocaust Institutions; Journal of Holocaust and Genocide Studies (quarterly).* (WWW.USHMM.ORG)

YESHIVA UNIVERSITY MUSEUM (1973). Center for Jewish History, 15 W. 16 St.., NYC 10011-6301. (212)294-8335. E-mail: dgoldman@yum.cjh.org. Dir. Sylvia A. Herskowitz; Chmn. Erica Jesselson. Collects, preserves, and interprets Jewish life and culture through changing exhibitions of ceremonial objects, paintings, rare books and documents, synagogue architecture, textiles, contemporary art, and photographs. Oral history archive. Special events, holiday workshops, live performances, lectures, etc. for adults and children. Guided tours and workshops are offered. Exhibitions and children's art education programs also at branch galleries on Yeshiva University's Main Campus, 2520 Amsterdam Ave., NYC 10033-3201. *Seasonal calendars; special exhibition catalogues; newsletters.*

YIDDISHER KULTUR FARBAND-YKUF (1937). 1133 Broadway, Rm. 820, NYC 10010. (212)243-1304. FAX: (212)243-1305. E-mail: mahosu@amc.one. Pres./Ed. Itche Goldberg. Publishes a bimonthly magazine and books by contemporary and classical Jewish writers; conducts cultural forums; exhibits works by contemporary Jewish artists and materials of Jewish historical value; organizes reading circles. *Yiddishe Kultur.*

YIVO INSTITUTE FOR JEWISH RESEARCH (1925). 15 W. 16 St., NYC 10011. (212)246-6080. FAX: (212)292-1892. E-mail: yivomail@yivo.cjh.org. Chmn. Bruce Slovin; Exec. Dir. Dr. Carl J. Rheins. Engages in historical research and education pertaining to East European Jewish life; maintains library and archives which provide a major international, national and New York resource used by institutions, individual scholars, and the public; provides graduate fellowships in East European and American Jewish studies; offers Yiddish language classes at all levels, exhibits, conferences, public programs; publishes books. *Yedies-YIVO News; YIVO Bleter.* (WWW.YIVOINSTITUTE.ORG)

——, MAX WEINREICH CENTER FOR ADVANCED JEWISH STUDIES/YIVO INSTITUTE (1968). 15 W. 16 St., NYC 10011. (212) 246-6080. FAX: (212)292-1892. E-mail: mweinreich@yivo.cjh.org. Provides advanced-level training in Yiddish language and literature, ethnography, folklore, linguistics, and history; offers guidance on dissertation or independent research; post-doctoral fellowships available.

YUGNTRUF-YOUTH FOR YIDDISH (1964). 200 W. 72 St., Suite 40, NYC 10023. (212)787-6675. FAX: (212)799-1517. E-mail: ruvn@aol.com. Chmn. Dr. Paul Glasser; V.-Chmn. Marc Caplan; Coord. Brukhe Lang Caplan. A worldwide, non-political organization for young people with a knowledge of, or interest in, Yiddish; fosters Yiddish as a living language and culture. Sponsors all activities in Yiddish: reading, conversation, and creative writing groups; annual weeklong retreat in Berkshires; children's Yiddish play group; sale of shirts. *Yugntruf Journal.*

ISRAEL-RELATED

ABRAHAM FUND (1989). 477 Madison Ave., 4th fl., NYC 10022. (212)303-9421. FAX: (212)935-1834. E-mail: info@AbrahamFund.org. Chmn. Alan B. Slifka, Exec. V.P. Dan Pattir. The Abraham Fund Initiatives (TAFI) seeks to enhance relations between Israel's Jewish and Arab citizens by promoting increased dialogue, understanding, and democracy. Founded in 1989, TAFI has contributed more than $8 million to community-based coexistence projects. TAFI also develops regional and national coexistence programs in partnership with other major institutions in Israel and orchestrates public advocacy campaigns to implement change.

AMEINU (formerly LABOR ZIONIST ALLIANCE, FARBAND LABOR ZIONIST ORDER) (1913). 114 W. 26 St., Suite 1006, NYC 10001. (212)366-1194. FAX: (212) 675-7685. E-mail: executive@ameinu.net. Pres. Kenneth Bob; Exec. Dir. Doni Remba. Seeks to enhance Jewish life, culture, and education in U.S.; aids in building State of Israel as a cooperative commonwealth and its Labor movement organized in the Histadrut; supports efforts toward a more democratic society throughout the world; furthers the democratization of the Jewish community in America and the welfare of Jews everywhere; works with labor and liberal forces in America; sponsors Habonim-Dror labor Zionist youth movement. *Jewish Frontier.* (WWW.JEWISHFRONTIER.ORG)

AMERICA-ISRAEL CULTURAL FOUNDATION, INC. (1939). 51 E. 42nd St., Suite 400, NYC 10017. (212)557-1600. FAX: (212)557-1611. E-mail: info@aicf.org. Chmn. Vera Stern; Pres. William Schwartz. Supports and encourages the growth of cultural excellence in Israel through grants to cultural institutions; scholarships to gifted young artists and musicians. *Newsletter.* (WWW.AICF.ORG)

AMERICA-ISRAEL FRIENDSHIP LEAGUE, INC. (1971). 134 E. 39 St., NYC 10016. (212) 213-8630. FAX: (212)683-3475. E-mail: aifl@aifl.org. Pres. Mortimer B. Zuckerman, Chmn. Bd. Kenneth J. Bialkin, Exec. V. Pres. Ilana Artman. A non-sectarian, non-partisan, not-for-profit organization which seeks to broaden the base of support for Israel among Americans of all faiths and backgrounds. Activities include educational exchanges, missions to Israel for American leadership groups, symposia and public-education activities, and the dissemination of multi media information. *Newsletter.*

AMERICAN ASSOCIATES, BEN-GURION UNIVERSITY OF THE NEGEV (1972). 1430 Broadway, 8th Floor, New York, NY 10018. (212) 687-7721, (800) AABGU. FAX: (212)302-6443. E-mail: info@aabgu.org. Pres. Zvi Alov; Exec. V-Pres. Amos Drory. Since 1972, the American Assoicates, Ben-Gurion University of the Negev has played a vital role in building a world-class center for research and education in the desert. A nonprofit cooperation with ten regional offices throughout the United States, AABGU prides itself on its efficiency and effectiveness in raising funds to help Ben-Gurion University bring knowledge to the Negev and to the world. AABGU plays a vital role in helping BGU fulfill its unique responsisbility to develop the Negev, the focus of the future of Israel.(WWW.AABGU.ORG)

AMERICAN COMMITTEE FOR SHAARE ZEDEK MEDICAL CENTER IN JERUSALEM (1949). 49 W. 45 St., Suite 1100, NYC 10036. (212)354-8801. FAX: (212)391-2674. E-mail: pr@szmc.org.il. Natl. Pres. & Chmn. Intl. Bd. of Gov. Menno Ratzker; Chair Erica Jesselson. Increases awareness and raises funds for the various needs of this 100-year old hospital, including new medical centers of excellence, equipment, medical supplies, school of nursing and research; supports exchange program between Shaare Zedek Jerusalem Medical Center and Albert Einstein College of Medicine, NY. *Heartbeat Magazine.*

AMERICAN COMMITTEE FOR SHENKAR COLLEGE IN ISRAEL, INC. (1971). 855 Ave. of the Americas, #531, NYC 10001. (212) 947-1597. FAX: (212)643-9887. E-mail: acfsc@worldnet.att.net. Pres. Nahum G. (Sonny) Shar; Exec. Dir. Charlotte A. Fainblatt. Raises funds and coordinates projects and research with Shenkar College of Engineering and Design, Israel. A unique government academic institute in Israel dedicated to education and reaseach in areas impacting Israel's industries and its artistic and scientific development. Textile, Fashion, Interior and Product design courses are offered with Scientific courses: Plastics, Chemistry, Software and Industrial Management and Marketing. Certified by Israel's Council of Higher Education, it offers continuing education and complete testing facilities for the textile/apparel industry and plastics engineering. *Shenkar News.*

AMERICAN COMMITTEE FOR THE BEER-SHEVA FOUNDATION (1988). PO Box 179, NYC 10028. (212)534-3715. FAX: (973)992-8651. Pres. Ronald Slevin; Sr. V.-Pres. Joanna Slevin; Bd. Chmn. Sidney Cooperman. U.S. fundraising arm of the Beer-Sheva Foundation, which funds vital projects to improve the quality of life in the city of Beer-Sheva: nursery schools for pre-K toddlers, residential and day centers for needy seniors, educational programs, facilities and scholarships (especially for new olim, the physically and mentally challenged), parks, playgrounds, and other important projects. Also offers special services for immigrants—such as heaters, blankets, clothing, school supplies, etc. *Brochures.*

AMERICAN COMMITTEE FOR THE WEIZMANN INSTITUTE OF SCIENCE (1944). 633 3rd Ave, New York, NY 10017. (212)895-7900. FAX: (212)895-7999. E-mail: info@acwis.org. Chmn. Robert Asher; Pres. Albert Willner, M.D.; Exec. V.-Pres. Martin Kraar. Through 13 regional offices in the U.S. raises funds, disseminates information, and does American purchasing for the Weizmann Institute in Rehovot, Israel, a world-renowned center of scientific research and graduate study. The institute conducts research in disease, energy, the environment, and other areas; runs an international summer science program for gifted high-school students. *Interface; Weizmann Now; annual report.* (WWW.WEIZMANN-USA.ORG)

AMERICAN FRIENDS OF ALYN HOSPITAL (1932). 51 East 42nd Street., Suite 3088, NYC 10017. (212)869-8085. FAX: (212) 768-0979. E-mail: friends@alynus.org. Pres. Minette Halpern Brown; Exec. Dir.

Cathy M. Lanyard. Supports the Alyn Hospital (Woldenberg Family Hospital/Pediatric and Adolescent Rehabilitation Center) in Jerusalem. Treats children suffering from birth defects (such as muscular dystrophy and spina bifida) and traumas (terrorism, car accidents, cancer, and fire), enables patients and their families to achieve independence and a better quality of life. (www.ALYNUS.ORG)

AMERICAN FRIENDS OF ASSAF HAROFEH MEDICAL CENTER (1975). PO Box 21051, NYC 10129. (212)481-5653. FAX: (212)481-5672. Chmn. Kenneth Kronen; Exec. Dir. Rhoda Levental; Treas. Robert Kastin. Support group for Assaf Harofeh, Israel's third-largest government hospital, serving a poor population of over 400,000 in the area between Tel Aviv and Jerusalem. Raises funds for medical equipment, medical training for immigrants, hospital expansion, school of nursing, and school of physiotherapy. *Newsletter.*

AMERICAN FRIENDS OF BAR-ILAN UNIVERSITY (1955). 235 Park Ave. So., NYC 10003. (212)673-3460. FAX: (212)673-4856. Email: nationaladmin@biuny.com, beverlyf@biuny.com. Chancellor Rabbi Emanuel Rackman; Chmn. Global Bd. Aharon Dahan; Pres. Amer. Bd. Melvin Stein; Exec. V.-Pres. Gen. Yehuda Halevy. Supports Bar-Ilan University, an institution that integrates the highest standards of contemporary scholarship in liberal arts and sciences with a Judaic studies program as a requirement. Located in Ramat-Gan, Israel, and chartered by the Board of Regents of the State of NY. *Bar-Ilan News; Bar-Ilan University Scholar; Heritage Newsletter..*

AMERICAN FRIENDS OF BETH HATEFUTSOTH (1976). 633 Third Ave., 21st fl., NYC 10017. (212)339-6034. FAX: (212)318-6176. E-mail: afbhusa@aol.com. Pres. Stephen Greenberg; Chmn. Sam E. Bloch; Exec. Dir. Gloria Golan. Supports the maintenance and development of Beth Hatefutsoth, the Nahum Goldmann Museum of the Jewish Diaspora in Tel Aviv, and its cultural and educational programs for youth and adults. Circulates its traveling exhibitions and provides various cultural programs to local Jewish communities. Includes Jewish genealogy center (DOROT), the center for Jewish music, and photodocumentation center. *Beth Hatefutsoth* (quarterly newsletter).

AMERICAN FRIENDS OF HAIFA UNIVERSITY (*see* AMERICAN SOCIETY OF THE UNIVERSITY OF HAIFA)

AMERICAN FRIENDS OF HERZOG HOSPITAL/EZRATH NASHIM-JERUSALEM (1895). 800 Second Ave., 8th fl., NYC 10017. (212) 499-9092. FAX:(212)499-9085. E-mail: herzogpr@hotmail.com. Co-Pres. Dr. Joy Zagoren , Amir Sternhell; Exec. Dir. Stephen Schwartz. Herzog Hospital is the foremost geriatric and psychiatric health care facility in Israel, and a leading research center in genetics, Alzheimer's and schizophrenia, with expertise in neurogeriatrics, physical rehabilitation, and long-term respiratory care. Its Israel Center for the Treatment of Psychotrauma provides therapy and seminars to help Israelis cope with the ongoing violence. (www.HERZOG HOSPITAL.ORG)

AMERICAN FRIENDS OF LIKUD. P.O.Box 8711, JAF Station, NYC 10116. (212)308-5595. FAX: (212)688-1327. E-mail: Thelikud@aol.com. Natl. Chmn. J. Phillip Rosen, Esq; Pres. Julio Messer,M.D; Natl. V. Pres. Jacques Torczyner; Natl. Treasurer Milton S. Shapiro, Esq.; Exec. Dir. Salomon L. Vaz Dias. promotes public education on the situation in the Middle East, particularly in Israel, as well as advancing a general awareness of Zionism; provides a solid partnership of public support for the State of Israel, its citizens and its democratically-elected governments.

AMERICAN FRIENDS OF MAGEN DAVID ADOM, ARMDI (1940). 888 Seventh Ave., Suite 403, NYC 10106. (212)757-1627. FAX: (212)757-4662. E-mail: info@afmda. org. Pres. Mark D. Lebow; Exec. V.-Pres. Daniel R. Allen. An authorized tax-exempt organization; the sole support arm in the U.S. of Magen David Adom (MDA), Israel's equivalent to a Red Cross Society; raises funds for the MDA emergency medical, ambulance, blood, and disaster services which help Israel's defense forces and civilian population. Helps to supply and equip ambulances, bloodmobiles, and cardiac rescue ambulances as well as 45 pre-hospital MDA Emergency Medical Clinics and the MDA National Blood Service Center and MDA Fractionation Institute in Ramat Gan, Israel. *The Shield.* (www.AFMDA.ORG)

AMERICAN FRIENDS OF NEVE SHALOM/ WAHAT AL-SALAM (1988). 4201 Church Road, Suite 4, NYC 10013. (856) 235-3667. FAX: (856) 235-4674. E-mail: afnswas@oasisofpeace.com. Pres. Deborah First; V.-Pres. Adeeb Fadil; Exec. Dir. Deanna Armbruster. Supports and publicizes the projects of the community of Neve Shalom/Wahat Al-Salam, the "Oasis of Peace." For more than twenty years, Jewish and Palestinian citizens of Israel have lived and worked together as equals. The community teaches tolerance, understanding and mutual respect well beyond its own borders by being a model for peace and reaching out through its educational institutions. A bilingual, bicultural Primary School serves the village and the surrounding communities.

AMERICAN FRIENDS OF RABIN MEDICAL CENTER (1994). 220 Fifth Avenue, Suite 1301, NYC 10001-7708. (212) 279-2522. Fax: (212)279-0179. E-mail: afrmc826@aol.com. Bd. Chmn. Abraham E. "Barry" Cohen; Exec. Dir. Burton Lazarow. Supports the maintenance and development of this medical, research, and teaching institution in central Israel, which unites the Golda and Beilinson hospitals, providing 12% of all hospitalization in Israel. Department of Organ Transplantation performs 80% of all kidney and 60% of all liver transplants in Israel. Affiliated with Tel Aviv University's Sackler School of Medicine. New Directions Quarterly.

AMERICAN FRIENDS OF RAMBAM MEDICAL CENTER (1969). 226 West 26th Street, NYC 10001. (212)644-1049. FAX: (775) 562-5399. E-mail: michaelstoler@princetoncommercial.com. Pres/CEO. Michael R. Stoler. Represents and raises funds for Rambam Medical Center (Haifa), an 887-bed hospital serving approx. one-third of Israel's population, incl. the entire population of northern Israel (and south Lebanon), the U.S. Sixth Fleet, and the UN Peacekeeping Forces in the region. Rambam is the teaching hospital for the Technion's medical school.

AMERICAN FRIENDS OF THE HEBREW UNIVERSITY (1925; inc. 1931). 11 E. 69 St., NYC 10021. (212)472-9800. FAX: (212)744-2324. E-mail: info@afhu.org. Pres. Ira Lee Sorkin; Bd. Chmn. Keith L. Sachs; Exec. Dir. Peter Willner. Fosters the growth, development, and maintenance of the Hebrew University of Jerusalem; collects funds and conducts informational programs throughout the U.S., highlighting the university's achievements and its significance. Wisdom; Scopus Magazine. (WWW.AFHU.ORG)

AMERICAN FRIENDS OF THE ISRAEL MUSEUM (1972). 500 Fifth Ave., Suite 2540, NYC 10110. (212)997-5611. FAX: (212) 997-5536. Pres. Barbara Lane; Exec. Dir. Carolyn Cohen. Raises funds for special projects of the Israel Museum in Jerusalem; solicits works of art for permanent collection, exhibitions, and educational purposes. Newsletter.

AMERICAN FRIENDS OF THE ISRAEL PHILHARMONIC ORCHESTRA (AFIPO) (1972). 122 E. 42 St., Suite 4507, NYC 10168. (212)697-2949. FAX: (212)697-2943. Interim Pres. Lynn Syms; Exec. Dir. Suzanne K. Ponsot. Works to secure the financial future of the orchestra so that it may continue to travel throughout the world bringing its message of peace and cultural understanding through music. Supports the orchestra's international touring program, educational projects, and a wide array of musical activities in Israel. Passport to Music (newsletter).

AMERICAN FRIENDS OF THE OPEN UNIVERSITY OF ISRAEL. 180 W. 80 St., NYC 10024. (212)712-1800. FAX: (212)496-3296. E-mail: afoui@aol.com. Natl. Chmn. Irving M. Rosenbaum; Exec.V.-Pres. Eric G. Heffler. Open Letter. (WWW.OPENU.AC.IL)

AMERICAN FRIENDS OF THE SHALOM HARTMAN INSTITUTE (1976). One Penn Plaza, Suite 1606, New York, NY 10119. (212) 268-0300. FAX: (212)239-4550. E-mail: afshi@afshi.org. Pres. Robert P. Kogod; Exec. Dir. Hana Gilat. Supports the Shalom Hartman Institute in Jerusalem, an international center for pluralist Jewish education and research, serving Israel and world Jewry. Founded in 1976 by David Hartman, the Institute includes: the Institute for Advanced Judaic Studies, with research centers for contemporary halakha, religious pluralism, political thought and peace and reconciliation; the Institute for Teacher and Leadership Training, educating Israeli principals, teachers, graduate students and leaders; and the Institute for Diaspora Education, which offers seminars and sabbaticals to rabbis, educators and lay leaders of diverse ideological commitments. (WWW.HARTMANINSTITUTE.COM)

AMERICAN FRIENDS OF THE TEL AVIV MUSEUM OF ART (1974). 545 Madison Ave., 8th Floor (55 St.), NYC 10022. (212)319-0555. FAX: (212)754-2987. Email: dnaftam@aol.com. Chmn. Steven P. Schwartz; Exec. Dir. Dorey Neilinger. Raises funds for the Tel Aviv Museum of Art for special projects, art acquisitions, and exhibitions; seeks contributions of art to expand the museum's collection; encourages art loans and traveling exhibitions; creates an awareness of the museum in the USA; makes available exhibition catalogues, monthly calendars, and posters published by the museum.

AMERICAN-ISRAEL ENVIRONMENTAL COUNCIL (formerly COUNCIL FOR A BEAUTIFUL ISRAEL ENVIRONMENTAL EDUCATION FOUNDATION) (1973). c/o Perry Davis Assoc., 25 W. 45 St., Suite 1405, NYC 10036. (212)840-1166. Fax: (212)840-1514. Pres. Alan Silberstein. A support group for the Israeli body, whose activities include education, town planning, lobbying for legislation to protect and enhance the environment, preservation of historical sites, the improvement and beautification of industrial and commercial areas, and sponsoring the CBI Center for Environmental Studies located in Yarkon Park, Tel Aviv. *Yearly newsletter; yearly theme oriented calendars in color.*

AMERICAN ISRAEL PUBLIC AFFAIRS COMMITTEE (AIPAC) (1954). 440 First St., NW, Washington, DC 20001. (202)639-5200. FAX: (202)347-4889. Pres. Howard Friedman; Exec. Dir. Howard A. Kohr. Registered to lobby on behalf of legislation affecting U.S.-Israel relations; represents Americans who believe support for a secure Israel is in U.S. interest. Works for a strong U.S.-Israel relationship. *Near East Report.* (WWW.AIPAC.ORG)

AMERICAN-ISRAELI LIGHTHOUSE, INC. (1928; reorg. 1955). 276 Fifth Ave., Suite 713, NYC 10001. (212)686-7110. Pres. Mrs. Leonard F. Dank; Sec. Mrs. Ida Rhein. Provides a vast network for blind and physically handicapped persons throughout Israel, to effect their social and vocational integration into the mainstream of their communities. Center of Services for the blind; built and maintains Rehabilitation Center for blind and handicapped persons (Migdal Or) in Haifa.

AMERICAN JEWISH LEAGUE FOR ISRAEL (1957). 450 7th Avenue, Suite 808, NYC 10123. (212)371-1583. FAX: (646)497-0093. E-mail: ajlims@aol.com. Pres. Dr. Martin L. Kalmanson; Exec. Dir. Jeffrey Scheckner. Seeks to unite all those who, notwithstanding differing philosophies of Jewish life, are committed to the historical ideals of Zionism; works independently of class, party, or religious affiliation for the welfare of Israel as a whole. Not identified with any political parties in Israel. Member of World Jewish Congress, World Zionist Organization. *Newsletter.* (WWW.AMERICAN JEWISHLEAGUE.ORG)

AMERICAN PHYSICIANS FELLOWSHIP FOR MEDICINE IN ISRAEL (1950). 2001 Beacon St., Suite 210, Boston, MA 02135-7771. (617)232-5382. FAX: (617) 739-2616. E-mail: apf@apfmed.org. Pres. Sherwood L. Gorbach, M.D.; Exec. Dir. Ellen-Ann Lacey. Supports projects that advance medical education, research, and care in Israel and builds links between the medical communities of Israel and N. Amer.; provides fellowships for Israeli physicians training in N. Amer. and arranges lectureships in Israel by prominent N. Amer. physicians; sponsors CME seminars in Israel and N. Amer.; coordinates U.S./Canadian medical emergency volunteers for Israel. *APF News.*

AMERICAN SOCIETY FOR TECHNION-ISRAEL INSTITUTE OF TECHNOLOGY (1940). 55 East 59th Street NYC 10022. (212)407-6300. FAX: (212)753-2925 E-mail: info@ats.org. Pres. Evelyn Berger; Chmn. Larry Jackier; Exec. V.-Pres. Melvyn H. Bloom. The American Technion Society (ATS) raises funds for the Technion-Israel Institute of Technology. Based in New York City, it is the leading American organization with more than 20,000 supporters and 197 satellite offices around the country, the ATS is driven by the belief that the economic future of Israel is in high technology and the future of high technology in Israel is at the Technion.. *Technion USA.* (WWW.ATS.ORG)

AMERICAN SOCIETY FOR THE PROTECTION OF NATURE IN ISRAEL, INC. (1986). 28 Arrandale Ave., Great Neck, NY 11024. (212) 398-6750. FAX: (212) 398-1665. E-mail: aspni@aol.com. Co-Chmn. Edward I. Geffner & Russell Rothman. A nonprofit organization supporting the work of SPNI, an Israeli organization devoted to environmental protection and nature education. SPNI runs 26 Field Study Centers and has 45 municipal offices throughout Israel; offers education programs, organized hikes, and other activities; seeks ways to address the needs of an expanding society while preserving precious natural resources. *SPNI News.*

AMERICAN SOCIETY FOR YAD VASHEM (1981). 500 Fifth Ave., 42nd Floor, NYC 10110-4299. (212)220-4304. FAX: (212) 220-4308. E-mail: info@yadvashemusa.org. Chmn. Eli Zborowski; Exec. Dir. Andrew Goldsmith. Development and educational arm of Yad Vashem, Jerusalem, the central international authority created by the Knesset in 1953 for the purposes of commemoration and education in connection with the Holocaust. *Martyrdom and Resistance* (newsletter). (WWW.YADVASHEM.ORG)

AMERICAN SOCIETY OF THE UNIVERSITY OF HAIFA (formerly AMERICAN FRIENDS OF HAIFA UNIVERSITY) (1972). 220 Fifth Ave., Suite 1301, NYC 10001. (212) 685-7880, FAX: (212)685-7883, E-mail: asuhtr@att.net. Pres.Paul Amir; Sec./Treas. Robert Jay Benowitz. Promotes, encourages, and aids higher and secondary education, research, and training in all branches of knowledge in Israel and elsewhere; aids in the maintenance and development of University of Haifa; raises and allocates funds for the above purposes; provides scholarships; promotes exchanges of teachers and students.

AMERICAN ZIONIST MOVEMENT (formerly AMERICAN ZIONIST FEDERATION) (1939; reorg. 1949, 1970, 1993). 633 Third Avenue., NYC 10017. (212)318-6100. FAX: (212)935-3578. E-mail: info@azm.com. Pres. James Schiller; Exec. Dir. Karen J. Rubinstein. Umbrella organization for 20 American Zionist organizations and the voice of unified Zionism in the U.S. Conducts advocacy for Israel; strengthens Jewish identity; promotes the Israel experience; prepares the next generation of Zionist leadership. Regional offices in Chicago and Dallas. Groups in Detroit, Pittsburgh, Washington, DC. *The Zionist Advocate.* (www.azm.org)

Americans for a Safe Israel (AFSI) (1971). 1751 Second Ave, NYC 10128. 1-800-235-3658. FAX: (212)828-1717. E-mail: afsi @rcn.com. Chmn. Herbert Zweibon; Exec. Dir. Barry Freedman. Seeks to educate Americans in Congress, the media, and the public about Israel's role as a strategic asset for the West; through meetings with legislators and the media, in press releases and publications AFSI promotes Jewish rights to Judea and Samaria, the Golan, Gaza, an indivisible Jerusalem, and to all of Israel. AFSI believes in the concept of "peace for peace" and rejects the concept of "territory for peace." *The Outpost* (monthly). (WWW.AFSI.ORG)

AMERICANS FOR PEACE NOW (1984). 1101 14th Street, NW, Sixth Floor, Washington, DC 20005. (202)728-1893. FAX: (202) 728-1895. E-mail: apndc@peacenow.org. Pres. & CEO Debra DeLee; Chmn. Franklin M. Fisher. Conducts educational programs and raises funds to support the Israeli peace movement, Shalom Achshav (Peace Now), and coordinates U.S. advocacy efforts through APN's Washington-based Center for Israeli Peace and Security. *Jerusalem Watch; Peace Now News; Settlement Watch; Fax Facts, Middle East Update (on-line), Benefits of Peace.* (WWW.PEACENOW.ORG)

AMIT (1925). 817 Broadway, NYC 10003. (212)477-4720. FAX: (212)353-2312. E-mail: info@amitchildren.org. Pres. Jan Schechter; Exec. Dir. Arnold Gerson. The State of Israel's official reshet (network) for religious secondary technological education; maintains innovative children's homes and youth villages in Israel in an environment of traditional Judaism; promotes cultural activities for the purpose of disseminating Zionist ideals and strengthening traditional Judaism in America. *AMIT Magazine.*

AMPAL-AMERICAN ISRAEL CORPORATION (1942). 1177 Avenue of the Americas, NYC 10036. (212)782-2100. FAX: (212) 782-2114. E-mail: ampal@aol.com. Bd. Chmn. Daniel Steinmetz; CEO Shuki Gleitman. Acquires interests in businesses located in the State of Israel or that are Israel-related. Interests include leisure-time, real estate, finance, energy distribution, basic industry, high technology, and communications. *Annual report; quarterly reports.*

ARZA/WORLD UNION, NORTH AMERICA (1977). 633 Third Ave., 6th fl., NYC 10017-6778. (212)650-4280. FAX: (212)650-4289.

E-mail: arza/wupjna@urj.org. Pres. Rabbi Stanley M. Davids; Exec. Dir. Rabbi Andrew Davids. Membership organization dedicated to furthering the development of Progressive Judaism in Israel, the FSU, and throughout the world. Encourages Jewish solidarity, promoting religious pluralism and furthering Zionism. Works to strengthen the relationship of N. American Reform Jews with Progressive Jewish communities worldwide and to educate and inform them on relevant issues. *Quarterly newsletter*. (WWW.ARZAWUNA.ORG)

BETAR EDUCATIONAL YOUTH ORGANIZATION (1935). 4 East 34th Street, NYC, 10016. (646)742-9364. FAX: (646)742-9666. E-mail: newyork@betar.org. Pres. Dany Danon; Exec. Officer Itzik Simhon. Betar is a Zionist active college students' movement, which dedicates itself to promoting Israeli issues in the American media. Betar was founded in 1923 by Zeev Jabotinsky, among its' famous alumni are Nenachem Begin and Itzhak Shamir. Betar's goal is the gathering of all Jewish people in their ancient land.

BOYS TOWN JERUSALEM FOUNDATION OF AMERICA INC. (1948). 12 W. 31 St., Suite 300, NYC 10001. (212)244-2766. (800) 469-2697. FAX: (212)244-2052. E-mail: btjny@compuserve.com. Raphael Benaroya, Pres. Michael J. Scharf; Hon. Chmn. Josh S. Weston; Chmn. Raphael Benaroya; Exec. V.-Pres. Rabbi Ronald L. Gray. Raises funds for Boys Town Jerusalem, which was established in 1948 to offer a comprehensive academic, religious, and technological education to disadvantaged Israeli and immigrant boys from over 45 different countries, including Ethiopia, the former Soviet Union, and Iran. Enrollment: over 1,000 students in jr. high school, academic and technical high school, and a college of applied engineering. Boys Town was recently designated as the "CISCO Regional Academy," the first center in Jerusalem for the instruction of the CISCO Networking Management Program. *BTJ Newsbrief*

BRIT TZEDEK V'SHALOM—JEWISH ALLIANCE FOR JUSTICE AND PEACE (2002). 11 E. Adams St., Suite 707, Chicago, IL 60603. (312)341-1205. FAX: (312)341-1206. E-mail: info@btvshalom.org. Pres. Marcia Freedman; Exec. Dir. Elliot Figman. Works for the achievement of a negotiated settlement of the Israeli-Palestinian conflict guided by the traditional Jewish obligation to pursue peace and justice, in the conviction that security for Israel can only be attained through the establishment of an economically and politicvally viable Palestinian state, necessitating an end to Israel's occupation of land acquired in the 1967 war and an end to Palestinian violence; its national office and 30 chapters around the country engage in grassroots political advocacy and public education. *Action Alerts.* (WWW.BTVSHALOM.ORG)

CAMERA-COMMITTEE FOR ACCURACY IN MIDDLE EAST REPORTING IN AMERICA (1983). PO Box 35040, Boston, MA 02135. (617)789-3672. FAX: (617)787-7853. E-mail: media@camera.org. Pres./Exec. Dir. Andrea Levin; Chmn. Joshua Katzen. CAMERA monitors media coverage of Israel, responds to error, omissions, and distortion, promotes factual information and works to educate the media and public about key issues related to conflict in the Middle East. CAMERA encourages members to participate in fostering full and fair coverage through communication with the media. *CAMERA Media Report (quarterly); CAMERA on Campus; CAMERA Media Directory, CAMERA Monographs, Action Alerts, Backgrounders.* (WWW.CAMERA.ORG)

COUNCIL FOR A BEAUTIFUL ISRAEL ENVIRONMENTAL EDUCATION FOUNDATION (*see* AMERICAN-ISRAEL ENVIRONMENTAL COUNCIL)

DEVELOPMENT CORPORATION FOR ISRAEL (formerly STATE OF ISRAEL BONDS) (1951). 575 Lexington Ave., 11th Floor, NYC 10022. (212)644-2663. FAX: (212)644-3887. E-mail: raphael.rothstein@israelbonds.com. Bd. Chmn. Michael Siegal; Pres./CEO Joshua Matza. An international organization offering securities issued by the government of Israel. Since its inception in 1951 has secured $25 billion in investment capital for the development of every aspect of Israel's economic infrastructure, including agriculture, commerce, and industry, and for absorption of immigrants. *Israel Hadashot-News*. (WWW.ISRAELBONDS.COM)

DOR CHADASH (2003). 165 E. 56 St., NYC 10016. (212)696-2151. FAX (212)684-6327. E-mail: info@dorchadashusa.org. Founder/Chmn. David Borowich; Exec. Dir. Scott Richman. A community of more than 10,000 Israeli and American

Jews living in New York brought together by love of Israel; develops educational, social, and cultural programs related to Israeli themes. (WWW.DORCHADASHUSA. ORG)

EMUNAH OF AMERICA (formerly HAPOEL HAMIZRACHI WOMEN'S ORGANIZATION) (1948). 7 Penn Plaza, NYC 10001. (212) 564-9045, (800)368-6440. FAX: (212)643-9731. E-mail: info@emunah.org. Natl. Pres. Heddy Klein; Exec. V.-Pres. Shirley Singer. Maintains and supports 200 educational and social-welfare institutions in Israel within a religious framework, including day-care centers, kindergartens, children's residential homes, vocational schools for the underprivileged, senior-citizen centers, a college complex, and Holocaust study center. Also involved in absorption of Soviet and Ethiopian immigrants (recognized by Israeli government as an official absorption agency). *Emunah Magazine; Lest We Forget.* (WWW.EMUNAH.ORG)

FEDERATED COUNCIL OF ISRAEL INSTITUTIONS—FCII (1940). 4702 15th Ave., Brooklyn, NY 11219. (718)972 5530. Bd. Chmn. Z. Shapiro; Exec. V.-Pres. Rabbi Julius Novack. Central fund-raising organization for over 100 affiliated institutions; handles and executes estates, wills, and bequests for the traditional institutions in Israel; clearinghouse for information on budget, size, functions, etc. of traditional educational, welfare, and philanthropic institutions in Israel, working cooperatively with the Israeli government and the overseas department of the Council of Jewish Federations. *Annual financial reports and statistics on affiliates.*

FRIENDS OF ISRAEL DISABLED VETERANS—BEIT HALOCHEM (1987). 1133 Broadway, Ste. 232, NYC 10010. (212)689-3220. FAX: (212)253-4143. E- mail: info@FID V.org. Bd. Chmn. Richard L. Golden; Exec. Dir. Linda E. Frankel. Raises funds to assist disabled Israeli war victims, including civilian victims of terrorism; maintains four centers in Israel providing physical and emotional rehabilitation for them. (WWW.FIDV.ORG)

FRIENDS OF THE ISRAEL DEFENSE FORCES (1981). 350 5th Avenue, Suite 2011 NYC 10118. (212)244-3118. FAX: (212)244-3119. E-mail: fidf@fidf.com. Chmn. Marvin Josephson; Pres. Jay Zises; Natl. Dir. Brig. Gen. Eliezer Hemeli. Supports the Agudah Lema'an Hahayal, Israel's Assoc. for the Well-Being of Soldiers, founded in the early 1940s, which provides social, recreational, and educational programs for soldiers, special services for the sick and wounded, and summer programs for widows and children of fallen soldiers. (WWW.FIDF.COM)

GESHER FOUNDATION (1969). 25 W. 45 St. Suite 1405, NYC 10036. (212)840-1166. FAX: (212)840-1514. E-mail: gesherfoundation@aol.com. Pres./Founder Daniel Tropper; Chmn. Philip Schatten. Seeks to bridge the gap between Jews of various backgrounds in Israel by stressing the interdependence of all Jews. Runs encounter seminars for Israeli youth; distributes curricular materials in public schools; offers Jewish identity classes for Russian youth, and a video series in Russian and English on famous Jewish personalities.

GIVAT HAVIVA EDUCATIONAL FOUNDATION, INC. (1966). 114 W. 26 St., Suite 1001, NYC 10001. (212)989-9272. FAX: (212) 989-9840. E-mail: mail@givathaviva.org. Chmn. Yvonne Baum Silverman; Exec. Dir. Robert Levy. Supports programs at the Givat Haviva Institute, Israel's leading organization dedicated to promoting coexistence between Arabs and Jews, with 40,000 people participating each year in programs teaching conflict resolution, Middle East studies and languages, and Holocaust studies. Publishes research papers on Arab-Jewish relations, Holocaust studies, kibbutz life. In the U.S., GHEF sponsors public-education programs and lectures by Israeli speakers. *Givat Haviva News; special reports.*(WWW.DIALOGATE. ORG.IL)

HABONIM-DROR NORTH AMERICA (1935). 114 W. 26 St., Suite 1004, NYC 10001-6812. (212)255-1796. FAX: (212)929-3459. E-mail: programs@habonimdror.org. (Mazkir Tnua) Jamie Levin; Shliach Onri Welmer. Fosters identification with progressive, cooperative living in Israel; stimulates study of Jewish and Zionist culture, history, and contemporary society. Sponsors summer and year programs in Israel and on kibbutz, 7 summer camps in N. America modeled after kibbutzim, and *aliyah* frameworks. *B'Tnua (on-line and print newsletter).* (WWW.HABONIMDROR. ORG)

HADASSAH, THE WOMEN'S ZIONIST ORGA-NIZATION OF AMERICA, INC. (1912). 50 W. 58 St., NYC 10019. (212)355-7900. FAX: (212)303-8282. Pres. Nancy Falchuk; Exec. Dir. Morlie Hammer Levin. Largest women's, largest Jewish, and largest Zionist membership organization in U.S. In Israel: Founded and funds Hadassah Medical Organization, Hadassah College of Jerusalem, Hadassah Career Counseling Institute, Young Judaea summer and year-course programs, as well as providing support for Youth Aliyah and JNF. U.S. programs: Jewish and women's health education; advocacy on Israel, Zionism and women's issues; Young Judaea youth movement, including six camps; Hadassah Leadership Academy; Hadassah-Brandeis Institute for International Research on Jewish Women; Hadassah Foundation. *Hadassah Magazine; Update; Hadassah International Newsletter; Medical Update; American Scene.* (WWW.HADASSAH.ORG)

———, YOUNG JUDAEA (1909; reorg. 1967). 50 W. 58 St., NYC 10019. (212)303-8014. FAX: (212)303-4572. E-mail: info@youngjudaea.org. Natl. Dir. Seth Finkelstein. Religiously pluralistic, politically nonpartisan Zionist youth movement sponsored by Hadassah; seeks to educate Jewish youth aged 8-25 toward Jewish and Zionist values, active commitment to and participation in the American and Israeli Jewish communities; maintains six summer camps in the U.S.; runs both summer and year programs in Israel, and a jr. year program in connection with both Hebrew University in Jerusalem and Ben Gurion University of the Negev. College-age arm, Hamagshimim, supports Zionist activity on campuses. *Kol Hat'nua; The Young Judaean; Ad Kahn.* (WWW.YOUNGJUDAEA. ORG)

HASHOMER HATZAIR, SOCIALIST ZIONIST YOUTH MOVEMENT (1923). 114 W. 26 St., Suite 1001, NYC 10001. (212)627-2830. FAX: (212)989-9840. E-mail: mail@hashomerhatzair.org. Dir. Guy Tsfoni; Natl. Sec. Moran Banai. Seeks to educate Jewish youth to an understanding of Zionism as the national liberation movement of the Jewish people. Promotes aliyah to kibbutzim. Affiliated with Kibbutz Artzi Federation. Espouses social-ist-Zionist ideals of peace, justice, democracy, and intergroup harmony. *Young Guard.* (WWW.HASHOMERHATZAIR. ORG)

INTERNS FOR PEACE INTERNATIONAL (1976). 475 Riverside Dr., Room 240., NYC 10115. (212)870-2226. FAX: (914)686-8896. E-mail: ifpus@mindspring.com. Intl. Dir. Rabbi Bruce M. Cohen; Intl. Coord. Karen Wald Cohen. An independent, nonprofit, nonpolitical educational program training professional community peace workers. In Israel, initiated and operated jointly by Jews and Arabs; over 250 interns trained in 35 cities; over 80,000 Israeli citizens participating in joint programs in education, sports, culture, business, women's affairs, and community development; since the peace accord, Palestinians from West Bank and Gaza training as interns. Martin Luther King Project for Black/Jewish relations. *IFP Reports Quarterly; Guidebooks for Ethnic Conflict Resolution.* (WWW.INTERNSFOR-PEACE.ORG)

ISRAEL CANCER RESEARCH FUND (1975). 1290 Avenue of the Americas, NYC 10104. (212)969-9800. FAX: (212)969-9822. E-mail: mail@icrfny.org. Pres. Yashar Hirshaut, M.D.; Chmn. Leah Susskind; Exec. V.P. Donald Adelman. The largest single source of private funds for cancer research in Israel. Has a threefold mission: To encourage innovative cancer research by Israeli scientists; to harness Israel's vast intellectual and creative resources to establish a world-class center for cancer study; to broaden research opportunities within Israel to stop the exodus of talented Israeli cancer researchers. *Annual Report; Research Awards; ICRF Brochure; Newsletter.*

ISRAEL HISTADRUT FOUNDATION (*see* ISRAEL HUMANITARIAN FOUNDATION)

ISRAEL HUMANITARIAN FOUNDATION (IHF) (1960). 276 Fifth Ave., Suite 901, NYC 10001. (212)683-5676, (800)434-5IHF. FAX: (212)213-9233. E-mail: info@ihf .net. Pres. Marvin M. Sirota; Exec.V.-Pres. Stanley J. Abrams. Since 1960, Israel Humanitarian Foundation (IHF) has funded more than 130 social service projects in Israel that provide funds and programs in a diverse range of areas. IHF strives to improve the standard of living of the Israeli population through its support for education, youth in need, elder care, the disables, and medical care & research projects that directly benefit thousands of people in need.

ISRAEL POLICY FORUM (1993). 165 East 56th Street, 2nd Floor, NYC 10022. (212)245-4227. FAX: (212)245-0517. E-mail: ipf@ipforum.org. 1030 15 St., NW, Suite 850, Washington, DC 20005. (202)842-1700. FAX:(202)842-1722. E-mail: ipf@ipforum.org. Pres. Seymour Reich; Exec. Dir. David Elcott. An independent leadership institution whose mission is to encourage an active U.S. role in resolving the Arab-Israeli conflict. IPF generates this support by involving leaders from the business, political, entertainment, academic, and philanthropic communitites in the peace effort, and by fostering a deeper understanding of the peace process among the American public. *Forum Fax, Washington Bulletin, Security Watch.* (WWW.IPFORUM.ORG)

THE JERUSALEM FOUNDATION, INC. (1966). 60 E. 42 St., Suite 1936, NYC 10165. (212) 697-4188. FAX: (212) 697-4022. E-mail: info@jfoundation.com. Chmn. Kenneth J. Bialkin; Exec. Dir. Dorothy Kauffman. A nonprofit organization devoted to improving the quality of life for all Jerusalemites, regardless of ethnic, religious, or socioeconomic background; has initiated and implemented more than 1,500 projects that span education, culture, community services, beautification, and preservation of the city's historic heritage and religious sites.

JEWISH INSTITUTE FOR NATIONAL SECURITY AFFAIRS (JINSA) (1976). (202)667-3900. E-mail: info@jinsa.org. Pres. Norman Hascoe; Exec. Dir. Mark Broxmeyer. A nonprofit, nonpartisan educational organization working within the American Jewish community to explain the link between American defense policy and the security of the State of Israel; and within the national security establishment to explain the key role Israel plays in bolstering American interests. (WWW.JINSA.ORG)

JEWISH INSTITUTE FOR THE BLIND-JERUSALEM, INC. (1902, Jerusalem). 15 E. 26 St., NYC 10010. (212) 532-4155. FAX: (212) 447-7683. Pres. Rabbi David E. Lapp; Admin. Eric L. Loeb. Supports a dormitory and school for the Israeli blind and handicapped in Jerusalem. *INsight.*

JEWISH NATIONAL FUND OF AMERICA (1901). 42 E. 69 St., NYC 10021. (212)

879-9300. (1-800-542-TREE). FAX: (212) 570-1673. E-mail: communications@jnf. org. Pres. Ronald S. Lauder; Exec. V.-Pres. Leonard L. Kleinman. Jewish National Fund is the American fund-raising arm of Keren Kayemeth LeIsrael, the official land agency in Israel and is celebrating its 100th Anniversary this year. JNF works in the following areas: water resource development, afforestation and ecology, eduction, tourism and recreation, community development and research. (WWW.JNF.ORG)

JEWISH PEACE LOBBY (1989). 8604 Second Avnue, PMB 317, Silver Spring, MD 20910. (301)589-8764. FAX: (301)589-2722. Email: peacelobby@msn.com. Pres. Jerome M. Segal. A legally registered lobby promoting changes in U.S. policy vis-a-vis the Israeli-Palestinian conflict. Supports Israel's right to peace within se cure borders; a political settlement based on mutual recognition of the right of self-determination of both peoples; a two-state solution as the most likely means to a stable peace. *Annual Report.*

KEREN OR, INC. JERUSALEM CENTER FOR MULTI-HANDICAPPED BLIND CHILDREN (1956). 350 Seventh Ave., Suite 200, NYC 10001. (212)279-4070. FAX: (212)279-4043. E-mail: kerenorinc@aol.com. Chmn. Dr. Edward L. Steinberg; Pres. Dr. Albert Hornblass; Exec. Dir. Rochelle B. Silberman. Funds the Keren-Or Center for Multi-Handicapped Blind Children at 3 Abba Hillel Silver St., Ramot, Jerusalem, housing and caring for over 70 resident and day students who in addition to blindness or very low vision suffer from other severe physical and/or mental disabilities. Students range in age from 1 1/2 through young adulthood. Provides training in daily living skills, as well as therapy, rehabilitation, and education to the optimum level of the individual. *Insights Newsletter.*

MACCABI USA/SPORTS FOR ISRAEL (formerly UNITED STATES COMMITTEE SPORTS FOR ISRAEL) (1948). 1926 Arch St., 4R, Philadelphia, PA 19103. (215)561-6900. Fax: (215)561-5470. E-mail: maccabi@maccabiusa.com. Pres. Toni Worhman. Sponsors U.S. team for World Maccabiah Games in Israel every four years; seeks to enrich the lives of Jewish youth in the U.S., Israel, and the Diaspora through athletic, cultural, and educational programs; develops, promotes, and supports international, national, and regional athletic-based activities and facilities. *Sportscene Newsletter; Commemorative Maccabiah Games Journal; financial report.* (WWW.MACCABIUSA.COM)

MERCAZ USA (1979). 155 Fifth Ave., NYC 10010. (212)533-7800, ext. 2016. FAX: (212)533-2601. E-mail: info@mercazusa.org. Pres. Rabbi Steven S. Wolnek; Exec. Dir. Rabbi Robert R. Golub. The U.S. Zionist organization for Conservative/Masorti Judaism; works for religious pluralism in Israel, defending and promoting Conservative/Masorti institutions and individuals; fosters Zionist education and *aliyah* and develops young leadership. *Mercaz USA Quarterly Newsletter.* (WWW.MERCAZUSA.ORG)

MERETZ USA FOR ISRAELI CIVIL RIGHTS AND PEACE (1991). 114 W. 26 St., Suite 1002, NYC 10001. (212)242-4500. FAX: (212)242-5718. E-mail: mail@meretzusa.org. Pres. Lawrence I. Lerner; Exec. Dir. Charney V. Bromberg. A forum for addressing the issues of social justice and peace in Israel. Educates about issues related to democracy, human and civil rights, religious pluralism, and equality for women and ethnic minorities; promotes the resolution of Israel's conflict with the Palestinians on the basis of mutual recognition, self-determination, and peaceful coexistence. *Israel Horizons.* (WWW.MERETZUSA.ORG)

NA'AMAT USA, THE WOMEN'S LABOR ZIONIST ORGANIZATION OF AMERICA, INC. (1925). 350 Fifth Ave., Suite 4700, NYC 10118-4799. (212)563-5222. FAX: (212) 563-5710. E-mail: naamat@naamat.org. Natl. Pres. Alice Howard. Part of the World Movement of Na'amat (Movement of Working Women and Volunteers), the largest Jewish women's organization in the world, it helps provide social, educational, and legal services for women, teenagers, and children in Israel. It also advocates legislation for women's rights and child welfare in Israel and the U.S., furthers Jewish education, and supports Habonim Dror, the Labor Zionist youth movement. *Na'amat Woman magazine.* (WWW.NAAMAT.ORG)

NATIONAL COMMITTEE FOR LABOR ISRAEL (1923). 275 Seventh Ave., NYC 10001. (212)647-0300. FAX: (212)647-0308. E-mail: ncli@laborisrael.org. Pres. Jay Mazur; Exec. Dir. Jerry Goodman; Chmn. Trade Union Council Morton Bahr. Serves as a bridge among Israel's labor sector, including its General Federation of Labor, Histadrut, the American labor movement, the Jewish community and the general public. Brings together Jews and non-Jews to build support for Israel and advance closer Israel-Arab ties. Cooperates with Israels labor sector. National in scope, it conducts education in the Jewish community and among labor groups to promote better relations with labor Israel. Raises funds for youth, educational, health, social and cultural projects in Israel from a constituency which includes labor unions, foundations, government agencies and individual donors and supporters. *Occasional background papers* (WWW.LABORISRAEL.ORG)

NEW ISRAEL FUND (1979). 1101 14th St., NW, 6th fl., Washington, DC 20005-5639. (202) 842-0900. FAX: (202)842-0991. E-mail: info@nif.org. New York office: 165 E. 56 St., NYC 10022. (212)750-2333. FAX: (212)750-8043. Pres. Larry Garber; Exec. Dir. Norman S. Rosenberg. A partnership of Israelis and North Americans dedicated to promoting social justice, coexistence, and pluralism in Israel, the New Israel Fund helps strengthen Israeli democracy by providing grants and technical assistance to the public-interest sector, cultivating a new generation of social activists, and educating citizens in Israel and the Diaspora about the challenges to Israeli democracy. *Quarterly newsletter; annual report; other reports..* (WWW.NIF.ORG)

PEF ISRAEL ENDOWMENT FUNDS, INC. (1922). 317 Madison Ave., Suite 607, NYC 10017. (212)599-1260. Chmn. Sidney A. Luria; Pres. B. Harrison Frankel; Sec. Mark Bane. A totally volunteer organization that makes grants to educational, scientific, social, religious, health, and other philanthropic institutions in Israel. *Annual report.*

POALE AGUDATH ISRAEL OF AMERICA, INC. (1948). 2920 Avenue J, Brooklyn, NY 11210. (718)258-2228. FAX: (718)258-2288. Pres. Rabbi Fabian Schonfeld. Aims to educate American Jews to the values of Orthodoxy and aliyah; supports kibbutzim, trade schools, yeshivot, moshavim, kollelim, research centers, and children's homes in Israel. *PAI News; She'arim; Hamayan.*

———, WOMEN'S DIVISION OF (1948). Pres. Miriam Lubling; Presidium: Sarah Ivanisky, Tili Stark, Peppi Petzenbaum. Assists Poale Agudath Israel to build and support children's homes, kindergartens, and trade schools in Israel. *Yediot PAI.*

PRO ISRAEL (1990). 1328 Broadway, Suite 435, NYC. (212)594-8996. FAX: (212) 594-8986. E-mail: proisrael@aol. com. Pres. Dr. Ernest Bloch; Exec. Dir. Rabbi Julian M. White. Educates the public about Israel and the Middle East; provides support for community development throughout the Land of Israel, particularly in Judea, Samaria, Gaza, and the Golan Heights. Projects include the Ariel Center for Policy Research and Professors for a Strong Israel.

RELIGIOUS ZIONISTS OF AMERICA (1909). 7 Penn Plaza, Suite 205, NYC 10001. (212)465-9234. FAX: (212)465-9246. Email: mizrachi@rza.org. Pres. Rabbi Yosef Blau, Exec. Dir. Alan Mond. Disseminates ideals of religious Zionism; conducts cultural work, educational program, public relations; raises funds for religious educational institutions in Israel, including yeshivot hesder and Bnei Akiva. *Voice of Religious Zionism.* (WWW.RZA. ORG)

———, BNEI AKIVA OF THE U.S. & CANADA (1934). 7 Penn Plaza, Suite 205, NYC 10001. (212)465-9536. FAX: (212)465-2155. Shaliah, Rabbi Shaul Feldman; Natl. Dir. Steve Frankel. The only religious Zionist Youth movement in North America, Educating thousands of youths from grade school throughout the US and Canada. We have five summer camps in North America and a summer program in Israel. We educate towards the values of the Religious Zionist Movement which sees the place of all Jews, in Israel, involved in social action, and committed to Orthodox Torah values. *Akivon; Pinkas Lamadrich; Daf Rayonot; Me'Ohalai Torah; Zraim.*(WWW.BNEIAKIVA.ORG)

———, NATIONAL COUNCIL FOR TORAH EDUCATION (1939). 7 Penn Plaza, Suite 205, NYC 10001. (212)465-9234. FAX: (212)465-9246. E-mail: mizrachi@rza. org. Pres. Aaron S. Tirschwell; Chmn. Rabbi Mark Dratch. Organizes and supervises yeshivot and Talmud Torahs; prepares and trains teachers; publishes textbooks and educational materials; organizes summer seminars for Hebrew educators in cooperation with Torah Department of Jewish Agency; conducts ulpan. *Ohr HaMizrach, Torat Yisrael (weekly).* (WWW.RZA.ORG)

SCHNEIDER CHILDREN'S MEDICAL CENTER OF ISRAEL (1982). 130 E. 59 St., Suite 1203, NYC 10022. (212)759-3370. FAX: (212)759-0120. E-mail: mdiscmci@aol. com. Bd. Chmn. H. Irwin Levy; Exec. Dir. Shlomit Manson. Its primary goal is to provide the best medical care to children in the Middle East. *UPDATE Newsletter*

SOCIETY OF ISRAEL PHILATELISTS (1949). 24355 Tunbridge Lane, Beachwood, OH 44122. (216)292-3843. Pres. Robert B. Pildes. MD; Exec. Secry. Howard S. Chapman; Journal Ed. Dr. Oscar Stadtler. Promotes interest in, and knowledge of, all phases of Israel philately through sponsorship of chapters and research groups, maintenance of a philatelic library, and support of public and private exhibitions. *The Israel Philatelist; monographs; books.*

TEL AVIV UNIVERSITY: AMERICAN COUNCIL (FORMERLY AMERICAN FRIENDS OF TEL AVIV UNIVERSITY, INC.) (1955). 39 Broadway, 15th Floor., NYC 10006. (212)742-9070. FAX: (212)742-9071. E-mail: info @tauac.org. Pres. Sam Witkin; Natl. Chmn. Joel Tauber. Promotes higher education at Tel Aviv University, Israel's largest and most comprehensive institution of higher learning. Included in its nine faculties are the Sackler School of Medicine with its fully accredited NY State English-language program, the Rubin Academy of Music, and 70 research institutes, including the Moshe Dayan Center for Middle East & African Studies and the Jaffe Center for Strategic Studies. *Tel Aviv University News; FAX Flash, Connections Newsletter (quarterly).*

THEODOR HERZL FOUNDATION (1954). 633 Third Ave., 21st fl., NYC 10017. (212)339-6040. FAX: (212)318-6176. E-mail: info@midstream.org. Chmn. Kalman Sultanik; Sec. Sam E. Bloch. Offers cultural activities, lectures, conferences, courses in modern Hebrew and Jewish subjects, Israel, Zionism, and Jewish history..

———, HERZL PRESS. Chmn. Kalman Sultanik; Dir. of Pub. Sam E. Bloch. Serves as "the Zionist Press of record," publishing books that are important for the light they shed on Zionist philosophy, Israeli history, contemporary Israel and the Diaspora and the relationship between them. They are important as contributions to Zionist letters and history. *Midstream.*

TO SAVE A LIFE (2003). 16405 Equestrian Lane, Rockville, MD 20855. (301)977-3637. FAX: (301)977-3888. E-mail: tosavealife@hotmail.com. Pres. Jerry Klinger. Provides an opportunity to give directly, efficiently, and personally to help needy Israelis; identifies small charities that are below the radar screen. (WWW.TSAL.ORG)

TSOMET-TECHIYA USA (1978). 185 Montague St., 3rd fl., Brooklyn, NY 11201. (718)596-2119. FAX: (718)858-4074. E-mail: eliahu@aol.com. Chmn. Howard B. Weber. Supports the activities of the Israeli Tsomet party, which advocates Israeli control over the entire Land of Israel.

UNITED CHARITY INSTITUTIONS OF JERUSALEM, INC. (1903). 1467 48 St., Brooklyn, NY 11219. (718)633-8469. FAX: (718)633-8478. Chmn. Rabbi Charlop; Exec. Dir. Rabbi Pollak. Raises funds for the maintenance of schools, kitchens, clinics, and dispensaries in Israel; free loan foundations in Israel.

UNITED STATES COMMITTEE SPORTS FOR ISRAEL (*see* MACCABI USA/SPORTS FOR ISRAEL)

US/ISRAEL WOMEN TO WOMEN (1979). 45 West 36th Street, 10th Floor, NYC 10018. (917) 351-0920. FAX: (917) 351-0921. E-mail: info@usisraelwomen.org. Ch. Nina Kaufman, esq.; Exec. Dir. Joan Gordon. Provides critical seed money for grassroots efforts advocating equal status and fair treatment for women in all spheres of Israeli life; targets small, innovative, Israeli-run programs that seek to bring about social change in health, education, civil rights, domestic violence, family planning, and other spheres of Israeli life. *Newsletters.*(WWW.USISRAELWOMEN.ORG)

VOLUNTEERS FOR ISRAEL (1982). 330 W. 42 St., Suite 1618, NYC 10036-6902. (212)643-4848. FAX: (212)643-4855. E-mail: vol4israel@aol.com. Pres. Jeanne S. Schachter; Vice Pres. Carol Stein. Provides aid to Israel through volunteer work, building lasting relationships between Israelis and Americans. Affords persons-aged 18 and over the opportunity to participate in various duties currently performed by overburdened Israelis on IDF bases and in other settings, enabling them to meet and work closely with Israelis and to gain an inside view of Israeli life and culture.

WOMEN'S LEAGUE FOR ISRAEL, INC. (1928). 160 E. 56 St., NYC 10022. (212)838-1997. FAX: (212)888-5972. E-mail: wliny@aol.com. Pres. Harriet Lainer; Exec. Dir. Dorothy Leffler. Maintains centers in Haifa, Tel Aviv, Jerusalem, Natanya. Projects include Family Therapy and Training, Centers for the Prevention of Domestic Violence, Meeting Places (supervised centers for noncustodial parents and their children), DROR (supporting families at risk), Yachdav-"Together" (long-term therapy for parents and children), the National Library for Social Work, and the Hebrew University Blind Students' Unit.

WORLD CONFEDERATION OF UNITED ZIONISTS (1946; reorg.1958). 130 E. 59 St., NYC 10022. (212)371-1452. FAX: (212)371-3265. Co-Pres. Marlene Post & Kalman Sultanik. Promotes Zionist education, sponsors nonparty youth movements in the Diaspora, and strives for an Israel-oriented creative Jewish survival in the Diaspora. *Zionist Information Views* (in English and Spanish).

WORLD ZIONIST ORGANIZATION-AMERICAN SECTION (1971). 633 Third Ave., 21st fl., NYC 10017. (212)688-3197. Chmn. Kalman Sultanik. As the American section of the overall Zionist body throughout the world, it operates primarily in the field of aliyah from the free countries, education in the Diaspora, youth and Hechalutz, organization and information, cultural institutions, publications; conducts a worldwide Hebrew cultural program including special seminars and pedagogic manuals; disperses information and assists in research projects concerning Israel; promotes, publishes, and distributes books, periodicals, and pamphlets concerning developments in Israel, Zionism, and Jewish history. *Midstream.*

———, DEPARTMENT OF EDUCATION AND CULTURE (1948). 633 Third Ave., 21st fl.,

NYC 10017. (212)339-6001. FAX: (212)826-8959. Renders educational services to boards and schools: study programs, books, AV aids, instruction, teacher-in-training service. Judaic and Hebrew subjects. Annual National Bible Contest; Israel summer and winter programs for teachers and students.

———, ISRAEL ALIYAH CENTER (1993). 633 Third Ave., 21st fl., NYC 10017. (212)339-6060. FAX: (212)832-2597. Exec. Dir. N. Amer. Aliyah Delegation, Kalman Grossman. Through 26 offices throughout N. Amer., staffed by *shlichim* (emissaries), works with potential immigrants to plan their future in Israel and processes immigration documents. Through Israel Aliyah Program Center provides support, information, and programming for olim and their families; promotes long-term programs and fact-finding trips to Israel. Cooperates with Tnuat Aliyah in Jerusalem and serves as American contact with Association of Americans and Canadians in Israel.

YOUTH RENEWAL FUND. 250 W. 57th Street, Suite 632., NYC 10107. (212)207-3195. FAX: (212)207-8379. E-mail: info@youthrenewalfund.org. Pres. Samuel L. Katz; Exec. Dir. Karen L. Berman. The Youth Renewal Fund was established in 1989 to provide supplemental education to disadvantaged youth in Israel. Since inception, YRF has implemented over $10 million in programs that have benefited over 19,500 Israeli children. (WWW.YOUTHRENEWAL FUND.ORG)

ZIONIST ORGANIZATION OF AMERICA (1897). ZOA House, 4 E. 34 St., NYC 10016. (212)481-1500. FAX: (212)481-1515. E-mail: info@zoa.org. Natl. Pres. Morton A. Klein. Strengthens the relationship between Israel and the U.S. through Zionist educational activities that explain Israel's importance to the U.S. and the dangers that Israel faces. Works on behalf of pro-Israel legislation; combats anti-Israel bias in the media, textbooks, travel guides, and on campuses; promotes *aliyah*. Maintains the ZOA House in Tel Aviv, a cultural center, and the Kfar Silver Agricultural and Technical High School in Ashkelon, which provides vocational training for new immigrants. *ZOA Report; Israel and the Middle East: Behind the Headlines.*(WWW.ZOA.ORG)

OVERSEAS AID

AMERICAN FRIENDS OF THE ALLIANCE ISRAÉLITE UNIVERSELLE, INC. (1946). 420 Lexington Ave., Suite 1731, NYC 10170. (212)808-5437. FAX: (212)983-0094. E-mail: afaiu@onsiteaccess.com. Pres. Albert Sibony; Asst. Batya Minkowitz. Participates in educational and human-rights activities of the AIU and supports the Alliance system of Jewish schools, teachers' colleges, and remedial programs in Israel, North Africa, the Middle East, Europe, and Canada. *Alliance Review.*

AMERICAN JEWISH JOINT DISTRIBUTION COMMITTEE, INC.—JDC (1914). 711 Third Ave., NYC 10017-4014. (212)687-6200. FAX (212)370-5467. E-mail: newyork@jdcny.org. Pres. Ellen Heller; Exec. V.-Pres. Steven Schwager. Provides assistance to Jewish communities in Europe, Asia, Africa, and the Mideast, including welfare programs for Jews in need. Current concerns include: Rescuing Jews from areas of distress, facilitating community development in the former Soviet Union; helping to meet Israel's social service needs by developing innovative programs that create new opportunities for the country's most vulnerable populations; youth activities in Eastern Europe and nonsectarian development and disaster assistance. *Annual Report; Snapshots. JDC's Activities in the Former Soviet Union; JDC: One People, One Heart.* (WWW.JDC.ORG).

AMERICAN JEWISH PHILANTHROPIC FUND (1955). 122 E. 42 St., 12th fl., NYC 10168-1289. (212)755-5640. FAX: (212)644-0979. Pres. Charles J. Tanenbaum. Provides college scholarship assistance to Jewish refugees through pilot programs being administered by the Jewish Family Service in Los Angeles and NYANA in New York.

AMERICAN JEWISH WORLD SERVICE (1985). 45 West 36th Street., NYC 10018. (212)736-2597. FAX: (212)736-3463. E-mail:jws@ajws.org. Chmn. Marty Friedman; Pres. Ruth W. Messinger. Provides nonsectarian, humanitarian assistance and emergency relief to people in need in Africa, Asia, Latin America, Russia, Ukraine, and the Middle East; works in partnership with local nongovernmental organizations to support and implement self-sustaining grassroots development projects; serves as a vehicle through which the Jewish community can act as global citizens. *AJWS Reports (newsletter)*. (WWW.AJWS.ORG)

ORT AMERICA (1922, reorg. 2006). 75 Maiden Lane, 10th fl.. NYC 10038. (212) 505-7700. FAX: (212)674-3057. E-mail: www.americanort.org; www.waort.org. Pres. Doreen Hermelin; Exec. Dir. Hope Kessler. Consolidation of American ORT and Women's American ORT that coordinates all ORT operations in the U.S., promotes and raises funds for ORT, a nonpolitical organization and the largest nongovernmental global education and training organization in the world. With past and present activities in over 100 countries, ORT has educated nearly 4 million people in a global network of high schools, colleges, apprenticeship programs and teacher training institutes. ORT's global network enables its 300,000 students in more than 60 countries to pursue fruitful careers and live lives of hope. Students at ORT schools everywhere around the world rely on funds raised by American ORT to help them meet tuition costs, build the most up-to-date learning facilities and furnish them with cutting-edge learning tools, computers, laboratories and other equipment. In Israel, 100,000 students attend 145 schools and training centers; there are 47 ORT schools and centers in the CIS (the former Soviet Union) and in the Baltic States; and in the U.S., over 15,000 students are served by ORT's Technical Institutes in Chicago, Los Angeles, and New York, and in Jewish day school programs in Atlanta, Chicago, Cleveland, Detroit, Florida, Los Angeles, and the National Capital Area (Washington, D.C.). Jewish day school students are served by ORT compute technology programs in Atlanta, Cleveland and Miami. (WWW.AORT.ORG, WWW.WAORT.ORG)

CONFERENCE ON JEWISH MATERIAL CLAIMS AGAINST GERMANY, INC. (1951). 15 E. 26 St., Rm. 906, NYC 10010. (212)696-4944. FAX: (212)679-2126. E-mail: info@claimscon.org. Exec. V.-Pres. Gideon Taylor. Represents Jewish survivors in negotiations for compensation from the German government and other entities once controlled by the Nazis. Also an operating agency that administers compensation funds, recovers Jewish property and allocates funds to institutions that serve Holocaust survivors. The Claims Conference—made up of the conference on Jewish Material Claims Against Germany and the Committee for Jewish Claims on Austria—is one of the founders of the World Jewish Restitution Organization, Memorial Foundation for Jewish Culture and the United Restitution Organization. *Newsletter; Annual Report; Guide to Restitution and Compensation; Special Update*. (WWW.CLAIMSCON.ORG)

HIAS, INC. (HEBREW IMMIGRANT AID SOCIETY) (1880; reorg. 1954). 333 Seventh Ave., NYC 10001-5004. (212)967-4100. FAX: (212)967-4483. E-mail:public@hias.org. Chair Jerome S. Teller; Pres. & CEO Gideon Aranoff. The oldest international migration and refugee resettlement agency in the United States, dedicated to assisting persecuted and oppressed people worldwide and delivering them to countries of safe haven. As the migration arm of the American Jewish community, it also advocates for fair and just policies affecting refugees and immigrants. Since its founding in 1881, the agency has rescued more than four and a half million people. *Bi-Annual report.*

JEWISH FOUNDATION FOR THE RIGHTEOUS (1986). 305 Seventh Ave., 19th fl., NYC 10001. (212)727-9955. FAX: (212)727-9956. E-mail: jfr@jfr.org. Pres. Melvin L. Merians; Exec. V.P. Stanlee J. Stahl. Provides monthly support to 1,700 aged and needy Righteous Gentiles living in 30 countries who risked their lives to save Jews during the Holocaust. The Foundation's education program focuses on educating teachers and their students about the history of the Holocaust and the significance of altruistic behavior for our society. *Newsletter* (3 times a year). (WWW.JFR.ORG)

NORTH AMERICAN CONFERENCE ON ETHIOPIAN JEWRY (NACOEJ) (1982). 132 Nassau St., Suite 412, NYC 10038. (212)233-5200. FAX: (212)233-5243. E-mail: nacoej@aol.com. Pres. Judith L. Wolf; Exec. Dir. Barbara Ribakove Gordon. Provides programming for Ethiopian Jews in Israel in the areas of education (elementary school, high school and college) and cultural preservation. Assists Ethiopian Jews remaining in Ethiopia. National speakers bureau offers programs to synagogues, schools, and Jewish and non-Jewish organizations. Exhibits of Ethiopian Jewish artifacts, photos, handicrafts, etc. available. *Lifeline (newsletter)*. (WWW.NACOEJ.ORG)

RE'UTH WOMEN'S SOCIAL SERVICE, INC. (1937). 130 E. 59 St., Suite 1200, NYC 10022. (212)836-1570. FAX: (212)836-1114. Chmn. Ursula Merkin; Pres. Rosa Strygler. Maintains, in Israel, subsidized housing for self-reliant elderly; old-age homes for more dependent elderly; Lichtenstadter Hospital for chronically ill and young accident victims not accepted by other hospitals; subsidized meals; Golden Age clubs. Recently opened a wing for chronically ill children. *Annual dinner journal.*

THANKS TO SCANDINAVIA, INC. (1963). The American Jewish Committee, 165 East 56th Street, 8th Fl., NYC 10022. (212)891-1403. FAX: (212)838-2120. Email: tts@ajc.org. Pres. Richard Netter; Exec. Dir. Rebecca Neuwirth. Provides scholarships and fellowships at U.S. universities and medical centers and Israeli educational institutions to students/teachers/medical professionals from Bulgaria, Denmark, Finland, Norway, and Sweden in lasting appreciation of the rescue of Jews during World War II and to build friendships based on those examples of courage and humanity in history. (WWW.THANKSTO SCANDINAVIA.ORG)

UJA FEDERATION OF NORTH AMERICA. (1939). (*see* UNITED JEWISH COMMUNITIES)

UNITED JEWISH COMMUNITIES (1999). 111 Eighth Ave., 11th fl , NYC 10011-5201. (212)284-6500. FAX: (212)284-6822. Chmn. Joseph Kanfer; Pres./CEO Howard Rieger. Formed from the merger of the United Jewish Appeal, the Council of Jewish Federations and United Israel Appeal, is the dominant fundraising arm for North American Jewry, and represents 189 Jewish Federations and 400 independent communities across the continent. It reflects the values and traditions of education, leadership, advocacy and social justice, and continuity of community that define the Jewish people.

RELIGIOUS AND EDUCATIONAL ORGANIZATIONS

AGUDATH ISRAEL OF AMERICA (1922). 42 Broadway, NYC, 10004. (212)797-9000. FAX: (646)254-1600. E-mail: shafran@

agudathisrael.org. Exec. V.-Pres. Rabbi Shmuel Bloom; Exec. Dir. Rabbi Boruch B. Borchardt. Mobilizes Orthodox Jews to cope with Jewish problems in the spirit of the Torah; speaks out on contemporary issues from an Orthodox viewpoint; sponsors a broad range of projects aimed at enhancing religious living, education, children's welfare, protection of Jewish religious rights, outreach to the assimilated and to arrivals from the former Soviet Union, and social services. *Jewish Observer; Dos Yiddishe Vort; Coalition.*

———, AGUDAH WOMEN OF AMERICA-N'SHEI AGUDATH ISRAEL (1940). 42 Broadway, NYC 10004. (212)363-8940. FAX: (212)747-8763. Presidium Aliza Grund & Rose Isbee; Dir. Hannah Kalish, Esq. Organizes Jewish women for philanthropic work in the U.S. and Israel and for intensive Torah education. Its new division, N'shei C.A.R.E.S., (Community, Awareness, Responsibility, Education, & Support), conducts seminars and support groups promoting the health and well-being of Jewish women and their families.

——— -, BOYS' DIVISION-PIRCHEI AGUDATH ISRAEL (1925) 42 Broadway, NYC 10004 (212)797-9000. Natl. Coord. Rabbi Shimon Grama. Educates Orthodox Jewish children in Torah; encourages sense of communal responsibility. Branches sponsor weekly youth groups and Jewish welfare projects. National Mishnah contests, rallies, and conventions foster unity on a national level. *Leaders Guides.*

———, GIRLS' DIVISION—BNOS AGUDATH ISRAEL (1921). 42 Broadway, NYC 10004. (646)254-1600. Natl. Dir. Leah Zagelbaum. Sponsors regular weekly programs on the local level and unites girls from throughout the Torah world with extensive regional and national activities. *Kol Bnos.*

———, YOUNG MEN'S DIVISION—ZEIREI AGUDATH ISRAEL (1921). 42 Broadway, NYC 10004. (212)797-9000, ext. 57. Dir. Rabbi Labish Becker. Educates youth to see Torah as source of guidance for all issues facing Jews as individuals and as a people. Inculcates a spirit of activism through projects in religious, Torah-educational, and community-welfare fields. *Am Hatorah; Daf Chizuk.*

AGUDATH ISRAEL WORLD ORGANIZATION (1912) 42 Broadway, 14th Floor, NYC

10004. (212)797-9000. FAX: (212)254-1650. UN Rep. Prof. Harry Reicher, Esq. Represents the interests of Orthodox Jewry on the national and international scenes. Sponsors projects to strengthen Torah life worldwide.

ALEPH: ALLIANCE FOR JEWISH RENEWAL (1963; reorg. 1993). 7000 Lincoln Drive, #B2, Philadelphia, PA 19119-3046. (215)247-9700. FAX: (215)247-9703. E-mail: alephajr@aol.com. Bd. Chmn. Linda Jo Doctor; Exec. Dir. Debra Kolodny. Serving the worldwide grassroots movement for Jewish spiritual renewal, ALEPH organizes and nurtures communities, trains lay and rabbinic leaders, creates new liturgy and adult learning resources, sponsors conferences, retreats and seminars and works for social and environmental justice. New Menorah online journal and KolAleph/Or Hador combined quarterly newsletter of the Aleph and the Network of Jewish Renewal Communities (NJRC). (WWW.ALEPH.ORG)

AM KOLEL JUDAIC RESOURCE CENTER (1990). 15 W. Montgomery Ave., Rockville, MD 20850. (301)309-2310. FAX: (301)309-2328. E-mail: amkolel @aol.com. Pres. David Shneyer. An independent Jewish resource center, providing a progressive Jewish voice in the community. Activities include: religion, educational and cultural programs; classes, workshops and seminars; interfaith workshops and programs; tikkun olam (social action) opportunities. The staff provides training and resources to emerging and independent communities throughout N. America. Am Kolel sponsors Jews United for Justice, the Center for Inclusiveness in Jewish Life (CIJL) and Yedid DC. Directory of Independent Jewish Communities and Havurot in Maryland, DC and Virginia; Rock Creek Haggadah.

AMERICAN ASSOCIATION OF RABBIS (1978). 350 Fifth Ave., Suite 3304, NYC 10118. (212)244-3350, (516)244-7113. FAX: (516)344-0779. E-mail: tefu@aol.com. Pres. Rabbi Jeffrey Wartenberg; Exec. Dir. Rabbi David L. Dunn. An organization of rabbis serving in pulpits, in areas of education, and in social work. Quarterly bulletin; monthly newsletter.

AMERICAN STUDENTS TO ACTIVATE PRIDE (ASAP/OU College Affairs) (1993). 11 Broadway, 14th fl., NYC 10004. (212)563-4000. FAX: (212)564-9058. E-mail: davidfel @ix.netcom.com. Pres. Zelda Goldsmith; Natl. Dir. Rabbi David Felsenthal; Chmn. Bernard Falk. A spiritual fitness movement of Jewish college students promoting Torah learning and discussion. Supports 100 learning groups at over 65 campuses as well as regional and national seminars and shabbatonim. Good Shabbos (weekly); Rimon Discussion Guide (monthly); Jewish Student College Survival Guide (yearly).

ASSOCIATION FOR JEWISH STUDIES (1969). Center for Jewish History, 15 W. 16 St., NYC 10011. (917)606-8249. FAX: (917)606-8222. E-mail: ajs@ajs.cjh.org. Pres. Sara Horowitz; Exec. Dir. Rona Sheramy. Seeks to promote, maintain, and improve the teaching of Jewish studies in colleges and universities by sponsoring meetings and conferences, publishing a newsletter and other scholarly materials, aiding in the placement of teachers, coordinating research, and cooperating with other scholarly organizations. AJS Review; AJS Perspectives. (WWW.BRANDEIS.EDU/AJS)

ASSOCIATION FOR THE SOCIAL SCIENTIFIC STUDY OF JEWRY (1971). c/o Prof. Carmel U. Chiswick, Department of Economics (m/c 144), University of Illinois at Chicago, 601 S. Morgan Street, Chicago, Il 60607-7121. (312)996-2683. FAX: (312)996-3344. E-mail: exec@assj.org. Pres. Sherry Israel; V.-Pres. Riv-Ellen Prell; Sec.-Treas. Carmel Chiswick. Journal Ed. Samuel Heilman; Mng. Ed. Uriel Heilman. Arranges academic sessions and facilitates communication among social scientists studying Jewry through meetings, journal, newsletter and related materials and activities. Contemporary Jewry; Newsletter (electronic).

ASSOCIATION OF HILLEL/JEWISH CAMPUS PROFESSIONALS (see TEKIAH: ASSOCIATION OF HILLEL/JEWISH CAMPUS PROFESSIONALS)

ASSOCIATION OF ORTHODOX JEWISH SCIENTISTS (1948). 25 W. 45st. Suite 1405, NYC 10036. (212)840-1166. FAX: (212) 840-1514. E-mail: aojs@jerusalemail. com. Pres. Allen J. Bennett, M.D.; Bd. Chmn. Rabbi Nachman Cohen. Seeks to contribute to the development of science within the framework of Orthodox

Jewish tradition; to obtain and disseminate information relating to the interaction between the Jewish traditional way of life and scientific developments—on both an ideological and practical level; to assist in the solution of problems pertaining to Orthodox Jews engaged in scientific teaching or research. Two main conventions are held each year. *Intercom; Proceedings; Halacha Bulletin; newsletter.*

B'NAI B'RITH HILLEL FOUNDATIONS (*see* HILLEL)

B'NAI B'RITH YOUTH ORGANIZATION (1924, became independent in 2002). 2020 K Street, NW, 7ᵗʰ Floor, Washington, DC 20006. (202)857-6633. FAX: (212)857-6568. Chmn. Howard Wohl; Exec. Dir. Matthew Grossman. Organized in local chapters, BBYO is a youth led international organization offering leadership opportunities and Jewish programming, which helps Jewish teenagers achieve self-fulfillment and contribute to the community. Assists members acquire a greater knowledge and appreciation for the Jewish religion, culture and the State of Israel. (WWW.BBYO.ORG)

CANTORS ASSEMBLY (1947). 3080 Broadway, Suite 613, NYC 10027. (212)678-8834. FAX: (212)662-8989. E-mail: caoffice @aol.com. Pres. Joseph Gole; Exec. V.-Pres. David Propis. Seeks to unite all cantors who adhere to traditional Judaism and who serve as full-time cantors in bona fide congregations to conserve and promote the musical traditions of the Jews and to elevate the status of the cantorial profession. *Annual Proceedings; Journal of Synagogue Music.* (WWW.CANTORS.ORG)

CENTER FOR CHRISTIAN-JEWISH UNDERSTANDING OF SACRED HEART UNIVERSITY (1992). 5151 Park Ave., Fairfield, CT 06825. (203)365-7592. FAX: (203)365-4815. E-mail: jhe@sacredheart.edu. Pres. Dr. Anthony J. Cernera; Exec. Dir. Rabbi Joseph H. Ehrenkranz. An educational and research division of Sacred Heart University; brings together clergy, laity, scholars, theologians, and educators with the purpose of promoting interreligious research, education, and dialogue, with particular focus on current religious thinking within Christianity and Judaism. *CCJU Perspective.*

CENTRAL CONFERENCE OF AMERICAN RABBIS (1889). 355 Lexington Ave., NYC 10017. (212)972-3636. FAX: (212)692-0819. E-mail: info@ccarnet.org. Pres. Peter S. Knobel; Exec. V.-Pres. Rabbi Steven Fox. Seeks to conserve and promote Judaism and to disseminate its teachings in a liberal spirit. The CCAR Press provides liturgy and prayerbooks to the worldwide Reform Jewish community. *CCAR Journal: A Reform Jewish Quarterly; CCAR Yearbook.* (WWW.CCARNET. ORG)

CLAL—NATIONAL JEWISH CENTER FOR LEARNING AND LEADERSHIP (1974). 440 Park Ave. S., 4th fl., NYC 10016-8012. (212)779-3300. FAX: (212)779-1009. E-mail: info@clal.org. Pres. Rabbi Irwin Kula; Chmn. Fern K. Hurst; Exec. V.-Chmn. Donna M. Rosenthal. Provides leadership training for lay leaders, rabbis, educators, and communal professionals. A faculty of rabbis and scholars representing all the denominations of Judaism make Judaism come alive, applying the wisdom of the Jewish heritage to help shape tomorrow's Jewish communities. Offers seminars and courses, retreats, symposia and conferences, lecture bureau and the latest on-line information through CLAL web site. *Sacred Days calendar; monographs; holiday brochures; CLAL Update.* (WWW.CLAL.ORG)

COALITION FOR THE ADVANCEMENT OF JEWISH EDUCATION (CAJE) (1977). 261 W. 35 St., #12A, NYC 10001. (212)268-4210. FAX: (212)268-4214. E-mail: cajeny@caje. org. Pres. Iris Petroff; Exec. Dir. Jeffrey Lasday. The Coalition for the Advancement of Jewish Education (CAJE), the largest membership organization of Jewish educators in North America, hosts annual conferences and offers outreach programming, teacher recruitment and mentoring, a Job Bank, and a Curriculum Response Service. CAJE has established an Early Childhood Department. Though its Hanukat CAJE Committee, CAJE advocates on behalf of Jewish educators. *Jewish Education News; CAJE Page; timely curricular publications; Hanukat CAJE series.* (WWW.CAJE.ORG)

CONGRESS OF SECULAR JEWISH ORGANIZATIONS (1970). 19657 Villa Dr. N., Southfield, MI 48076. (248)569-8127. FAX: (248)569-5222. E-mail: csjd@csjd.org.. An umbrella organization of schools and adult clubs; facilitates exchange of curricula and educational programs for children and adults stressing the Jewish historical and cultural heritage and the continuity of the Jewish people. *New Yorkish (Yiddish literature translations); Haggadah; The Hanuka Festival; Mame-Loshn.*

CONVERSION TO JUDAISM RESOURCE CENTER (1997). 74 Hauppauge Rd., Rm. 53, Commack, NY 11725. (631) 462-5826. E-mail: inform@convert.org. Pres. Dr. Lawrence J. Epstein; Exec. Dir. Susan Lustig. Provides information and advice for people who wish to convert to Judaism or who have converted. Puts potential converts in touch with rabbis from all branches of Judaism.

COUNCIL FOR JEWISH EDUCATION (1926) 11 Olympia Lane, Monsey, NY 10952-2829. (845)368-8657, Fax (845)369-6583. E-mail: mjscje@aol.com. Pres. Dr. Morton J. Summer; Editor Rabbi Irwin E. Witty. Fellowship of Jewish education professionals-administrators, supervisors, and teachers in Hebrew high schools and Jewish teachers colleges-of all ideological groupings; conducts national and regional conferences; represents the Jewish education profession before the Jewish community; cooperates with Jewish Agency Department of Education in promoting Hebrew culture and studies. *Journal of Jewish Education.*

FEDERATION OF JEWISH MEN'S CLUBS (1929). 475 Riverside Dr., Suite 832, NYC 10115. (212)749-8100; (800)288-FJMC. FAX: (212)316-4271. E-mail: international@fjmc.org. Intl. Pres. Dr. Robert Braitman; Exec. Dir. Rabbi Charles E. Simon. Promotes principles of Conservative Judaism; develops family education and leadership training programs; offers the Art of Jewish Living series and Yom HaShoah Home Commemoration; sponsors Hebrew literacy adult-education program; presents awards for service to American Jewry. Latest innovation-"The Ties that Bind," a motivational and instructional video about Tefillin. *Torchlight; Hearing Men's Voices.* (WWW.FJMC.ORG)

FEDERATION OF RECONSTRUCTIONIST CONGREGATIONS AND HAVUROT (*see* JEWISH RECONSTRUCTIONIST FEDERATION)

HILLEL: THE FOUNDATION FOR JEWISH CAMPUS LIFE (formerly B'NAI B'RITH HILLEL FOUNDATIONS) (1923). Charles and Lynn Schusterman International Center, Arthur and Rochelle Belfer Building, 800 Eight Street, NW, Washington, DC 20001-3724. (202)449-6500. FAX: (202)449-6600. E-mail: info@hillel.org. Chmn. Edgar M. Bronfman; Pres. Wayne Firestone. The largest Jewish campus organization in the world, Hillel: The Foundation for Jewish Campus Life, is committed to creatively empowering and engaging Jewish students through its network of over 500 regional centers, campus-based foundations, program centers and affiliates. *The Hillel Annual Report; Shavua Tov. Israel Update.* (WWW.HILLEL.ORG)

INSTITUTE FOR COMPUTERS IN JEWISH LIFE (1978). 7074 N. Western Ave., Chicago, IL 60645. (773)262-9200. FAX: (773)262-9298. E-mail: rosirv@aol.com. Pres. Thomas Klutznick; Exec. V.-Pres. Dr. Irving J. Rosenbaum. Explores, develops, and disseminates applications of computer technology to appropriate areas of Jewish life, with special emphasis on Jewish education; creates educational software for use in Jewish schools; provides consulting service and assistance for national Jewish organizations, seminaries, and synagogues.

INTERNATIONAL FEDERATION OF SECULAR HUMANISTIC JEWS (1983). 224 West 35th Street, Suite 410, NYC 10024. (212)564-6711. FAX: (212)564-6721. E-mail: info@ifshj.org. Co-Ch. Felix Posen (Europe), Yair Tzaban (Israel). The International Federation of Secular Humanistic Jews provides a voice for secular Jews worldwide in their common goal to foster Secular Humanistic Judaism as an option for modern Jewish identity. The IFSHJ develops awareness of Secular and Humanistic Judaism by serving as a resource and for general information, and developing literature, conferences, and communications that promote philosophy of Secular and Humanistic Judaism in the world community. *Newsletter (Hofesh); Contemplate: International Journal of Secular Jewish Thought.*

INTERNATIONAL INSTITUTE FOR SECULAR HUMANISTIC JUDAISM (1985). 28611 West Twelve Mile Rd., Farmington Hills, MI 48334. (248)476-9532. FAX: (248)476-8509. E-mail: iishj@iishj.org. Established in 1985 in Jerusalem to serve the needs of a growing movement, its two primary purposes are to commission and publish educational materials and to train rabbis, leaders, teachers, and spokespersons for the movement. The Institute has two offices-one in Israel (Jerusalem) and one in N. America and offers educational and training programs in Israel, N. America, and the countries of the former Soviet Union. The N. American office, located in a suburb of Detroit, offers the Rabbinic Program, the Leadership Program, and the Adult Education Program. *Brochure, educational papers, and projects.*

JEWISH CHAUTAUQUA SOCIETY, INC. (sponsored by NORTH AMERICAN FEDERATION OF TEMPLE BROTHERHOODS) (1893). 633 Third Ave., NYC 10017. (212)650-4100/(800)765-6200. FAX: (212)650-4189. E-mail: jcs@urj.org. Pres. Irving B. Shnaider; Chancellor Stuart J. Aaronson; Exec. Dir. Doug Barden. Works to promote interfaith understanding by sponsoring accredited college courses and one-day lectures on Judaic topics, providing book grants to educational institutions, producing educational videotapes on interfaith topics, and convening interfaith institutes. A founding sponsor of the National Black/Jewish Relations Center at Dillard University. *ACHIM Magazine.*

JEWISH EDUCATION IN MEDIA (1978). PO Box 180, Riverdale Sta., NYC 10471. (212)362-7633. FAX: (203)359-1381. Pres. Ken Asher; Exec. Dir. Rabbi Mark S. Golub. Devoted to producing television, film, and video-cassettes for a popular Jewish audience, in order to inform, entertain, and inspire a greater sense of Jewish identity and Jewish commitment. "L'Chayim," JEM's weekly half-hour program, which is seen nationally on NJT/National Jewish Television, features outstanding figures in the Jewish world addressing issues and events of importance to the Jewish community. (www.LCHAYIM.COM)

JEWISH EDUCATION SERVICE OF NORTH AMERICA (JESNA) (1981). 111 Eighth Ave., 11th fl., NYC 10011. (212)284-6950. FAX: (212)284-6951. E-mail: info@jesna.org. Pres. Donald Sylvan, Ph.D.; Bd. Ch. Diane Troderman. The Jewish Federation system's educational coordinating, planning, and development agency. Promotes excellence in Jewish education by initiating exchange of ideas, programs, and ma-

terials; providing information, consultation, educational resources, and policy guidance; and collaborating with partners in N. America and Israel to develop educational programs. *Agenda: Jewish Education; planning guides on Jewish Renaissance; research reports; Jewish Educators Electronic Toolkit.* (WWW.JESNA. ORG)

JEWISH ORTHODOX FEMINIST ALLIANCE (JOFA) (1997). 520 Eighth Ave., 4th fl.., NYC 10018. (212)679-8500. FAX: (212)679-7428. E-mail: jofa@jofa.org. Pres. Carol Kauffman Newman; Exec. Dir. Robin Bodner. Dedicated to expand the spiritual, ritual, intellectual, and political opportunities for women within the framework of *Halakhah* through meangful participation and equality in family life, synagogues, houses of learning, and Jewish communial organizations. *JOFA Journal, Quarterly Newsletter.* (WWW.JOFA. ORG)

JEWISH OUTREACH INSTITUTE (1987). 1270 Broadway, Ste. 609, NYC 10001. (212) 760-1440. FAX: (212)760-1569. E-mail: info@joi.org. Pres. Terrence A. Elkes; Exec. Dir. Rabbi Kerry Olitzky. An independent national organization that conducts programs and services to empower and assist the Jewish community in welcoming and fully embracing all members of interfaith families—and anyone else looking to explore connections to the Jewish heritage—into Jewish life. *The Inclusive, The Inclusive Professional.* (www .JOI.ORG)

JEWISH RECONSTRUCTIONIST FEDERATION (formerly FEDERATION OF RECONSTRUCTIONIST CONGREGATIONS AND HAVUROT) (1954). 7804 Montgomery Ave., Suite 9, Elkins Park, PA 19027-2649. (215)782-8500. Fax: (215)782-8805. E-mail: info@jrf.org. Pres. Daniel Cedarbaum; Exec. V.-Pres. Carl Sheingold. Provides educational and consulting services to affiliated congregations and havurot; fosters the establishment of new Reconstructionist communities. Publishes *Kol Haneshamah,* an innovative series of prayer books, including a new mahzor and haggadah; provides programmatic materials. Regional offices in New York, Los Angeles, Chicago, Philadelphia, and Washington DC. *Reconstructionism Today.* (WWW.JRF.ORG)

———, RECONSTRUCTIONIST RABBINICAL ASSOCIATION (1974). 1299 Church Rd., Wyncote, PA 19095. (215)576-5210. FAX: (215)576-8051. E-mail: info@therra.org. Pres. Rabbi Brant Rosen; Exec. Dir. Rabbi Richard Hirsh. Professional organization for graduates of the Reconstructionist Rabbinical College and other rabbis who identify with Reconstructionist Judaism; cooperates with Jewish Reconstructionist Federation in furthering Reconstructionism in the world. *Newsletters; position papers.* (WWW.THERRA.ORG)

———, RECONSTRUCTIONIST RABBINICAL COLLEGE (*see* p. 652)

JEWISH TEACHERS ASSOCIATION—MORIM (1931). 45 E. 33 St., NYC 10016-5336. (212)684-0556. Pres. Phyllis L. Pullman; V.-Pres. Ronni David; Sec. Helen Parnes; Treas. Mildred Safar. Protects teachers from abuse of seniority rights; fights the encroachment of anti-Semitism in education; offers scholarships to qualified students; encourages teachers to assume active roles in Jewish communal and religious affairs. *Morim JTA Newsletter.*

KULANU, INC. (formerly AMISHAV USA) (1993). 11603 Gilsan St., Silver Spring, MD 20902. (301)681-5679. FAX: (301) 681-1587. Email: jdzeller@umich.edu. Pres. Jack Zeller; Sec. Karen Primack. Engages in outreach to dispersed Jewish communities around the world who wish to return to their Jewish roots. Current projects include the formal conversion of Shinlung-Menashe tribesmen in India currently practicing Judaism, and supplying materials and rabbis for conversos/marranos in Mexico and Brazil. *Newsletter.*

NATIONAL COMMITTEE FOR FURTHERANCE OF JEWISH EDUCATION (1941). 824 Eastern Pkwy., Brooklyn, NY 11213. (718) 735-0200; (800)33-NCFJE. FAX: (718) 735-4455. Pres. Dr. Steven Rubel; Bd. Chmn. Rabbi Shea Hecht; Chmn. Exec. Com. Rabbi Sholem Ber Hecht. Seeks to disseminate the ideals of Torah-true education among the youth of America; provides education and compassionate care for the poor, sick, and needy in U.S. and Israel; provides aid to Iranian Jewish youth; sponsors camps and educational functions, family and vocational counseling services, family and early intervention, after-school and preschool programs, drug and alcohol education and prevention; maintains schools in Brooklyn and Queens. Every year distributes 25,000 toys/gifts through Toys for Hospitalized children; runs the Release-time program of Greater NY, offers classes FT/PT through Hadar Hatorah Rabbinal Seminary. *Panorama; Cultbusters; Intermarriage; Brimstone & Fire; Focus; A Life Full of Giving.*

NATIONAL COUNCIL OF YOUNG ISRAEL (1912). 3 W. 16 St., NYC 10011. (212)929-1525. FAX: (212)727-9526. E-mail: ncyi @youngisrael.org. Pres. Shlomo Mostofsky; Exec. V.-Pres. Rabbi Pesach Lerner. Through its network of member synagogues in N. America and Israel maintains a program of spiritual, cultural, social, and communal activity aimed at the advancement and perpetuation of traditional, Torah-true Judaism; seeks to instill in American youth an understanding and appreciation of the ethical and spiritual values of Judaism. Sponsors rabbinic and lay leadership conferences, synagogue services, rabbinic services, rabbinic and lay leader training, rabbinic placement, women's division, kosher dining clubs, and youth programs. *Viewpoint Magazine; Divrei Torah Bulletin; NCYI Suggestion Box; The Rabbi's Letter.* (WWW.YOUNGISRAEL.ORG)

———, AMERICAN FRIENDS OF YOUNG ISRAEL IN ISRAEL—YISRAEL HATZA'IR (1926). 3 W. 16 St., NYC 10011. (212)929-1525. FAX: (212)727-9526. E-mail: ncyi@ youngisrael.org. Pres. Meir Mishkoff. Promotes Young Israel synagogues and youth work in Israel; works to help absorb Russian and Ethiopian immigrants.

———, YOUNG ISRAEL DEPARTMENT OF YOUTH AND YOUNG ADULTS ACTIVITIES (reorg. 1981). 111 John Street, Suite 450., NYC 10038. (212)929-1525; (800)617-NCYI. FAX: (212)243-1222. Email: youth@yiyouth.org. Pres. Shlomo Z. Mostofsky. Fosters varied program of activities for the advancement and perpetuation of traditional Torah-true Judaism; instills ethical and spiritual values and appreciation for compatibility of ancient faith of Israel with good Americanism. Runs leadership training programs and youth shabbatonim; support programs for synagogue youth programs; annual national conference of youth directors;

ACHVA summer programs for teens IN Israel and U.S.; Nachala summer program in Israel for Yeshiva H.S. girls and Natzach summer program for Yeshiva H.S. boys. *Torah Kidbits; Shabbat Youth Manual; Y.I. Can Assist You; Synagogue Youth Director Handbook.* (WWW.YIY-OUTH.ORG)

NATIONAL HAVURAH COMMITTEE (1979). 7135 Germantown Ave., Philadelphia, PA 19119-1720. (215)248-1335. FAX: (215) 248-9760. E-mail: institute@havurah.org. Ch. Sherry Israel. A center for Jewish renewal devoted to spreading Jewish ideas, ethics, and religious practices through havurot, participatory and inclusive religious mini-communities. Maintains a directory of N. American havurot and sponsors a weeklong summer institute, regional weekend retreats. *Havurah! (newsletter).* (WWW.HAVURAH.ORG)

NATIONAL JEWISH CENTER FOR LEARNING AND LEADERSHIP (*see* CLAL)

NATIONAL JEWISH COMMITTEE ON SCOUTING (Boy Scouts of America) (1926). 1325 West Walnut Hill Lane, PO Box 152079, Irving, TX 75015-2079. (972)580-2000. FAX: (972)580-7870. Chmn. Rabbi Peter Hyman. Assists Jewish institutions in meeting their needs and concerns through use of the resources of scouting. Works through local Jewish committees on scouting to establish Tiger Cub groups (1st grade), Cub Scout packs, Boy Scout troops, and coed venturer crews in synagogues, Jewish community centers, day schools, and other Jewish organizations wishing to draw Jewish youth. Support materials and resources on request.

NATIONAL JEWISH GIRL SCOUT COMMITTEE (1972). 33 Central Dr., Bronxville, NY 10708. (914)738-3986, (718)252-6072. FAX: (914)738-6752. E-mail: njgsc@aol.com. Chmn. Rabbi Herbert W. Bomzer; Field Chmn. Adele Wasko. Serves to further Jewish education by promoting Jewish award programs, encouraging religious services, promoting cultural exchanges with the Israel Boy and Girl Scouts Federation, and extending membership in the Jewish community by assisting councils in organizing Girl Scout troops and local Jewish Girl Scout committees. *Newsletter.*

NATIONAL JEWISH HOSPITALITY COMMITTEE (1973; reorg. 1993). PO Box 53691, Philadelphia, PA 19105. (800)745-0301.

Pres. Rabbi Allen S. Maller; Exec. Dir. Steven S. Jacobs. Assists persons interested in Judaism-for intermarriage, conversion, general information, or to respond to missionaries. *Special reports.*

NORTH AMERICAN ALLIANCE FOR JEWISH YOUTH (199650 West 58th Street, NYC, NY, 10019 (212)494-1023. FAX: (212) 906-9371. E-mail: info@naajewishyouth. org. Chmn. Joseph E. Brenan; Dir. Heather Kibel. Serves the cause of informal Jewish and Zionist education in America; provides a forum for the professional leaders of the major N. American youth movements, camps, Israel programs, and university programs to address common issues and concerns, and to represent those issues with a single voice to the wider Jewish and Zionist community. Sponsors annual Conference on Informal Jewish Education for Jewish youth professionals from across the continent.

OZAR HATORAH, INC. (1946). 625 Broadway, 11th Fl. NYC, 10012. (212)253-7245. FAX: (212) 437-4773. Email: agutman@ ozarhatorah.org. Pres. Henry Shalom; Sec. Sam Sutton; Exec. Dir. Rabbi Jean Paul Amoyelle. An international educational network which builds Sephardic communities worldwide through Jewish education.

PANIM: THE INSTITUTE FOR JEWISH LEADERSHIP AND VALUES (FORMERLY WASHINGTON INSTITUTE FOR JEWISH LEADERSHIP & VALUES) (1988). 6101 Montrose Road, Suite 200, Rockville, MD 20852. (301) 770-5070. FAX: (301) 770-6365. E-mail: info@panim.org. Founder/Pres. Rabbi Sidney Schwarz; Bd. Chmn. Mark Levitt. Institute for Jewish Leadership and Values is a non-profit educational organization dedicated to the renewal of American Jewish life through the integration of Jewish learning, values and social responsibility. Our flagship program, *Panim el Panim*: High School in Washington, each year brings over 1,000 Jewish teens from across the country to Washington, D.C. to learn about political and social activism in the context of Jewish learning and values. We also sponsor the Jewish Civics Initiative, the largest national Jewish service/learning program for teens. The Institute also sponsors a Synagogue Transformation Project, and conducts leadership training. *Jewish Civics: A*

Tikkun Olam/World Repair Manual; Jews, Judaism and Civic Responsibility.

PARDES PROGRESSIVE ASSOCIATION OF RE-FORM DAY SCHOOLS (1990). 633 Third Ave., NYC 10017-6778. (212)650-4000. FAX: (480)951-0829. E-mail: educate@urj.org. Pres. Zita Gardner; Chmn. Carol Nemo. An affiliate of the Union for Reform Judaism; brings together day schools and professional and lay leaders committed to advancing the cause of full-time Reform Jewish education; advocates for the continuing development of day schools within the Reform movement as a means to foster Jewish identity, literacy, and continuity; promotes cooperation among our member schools and with other Jewish organizations that share similar goals. *Visions of Excellence (manual).*

P'EYLIM-LEV L'ACHIM (1951). 1034 E. 12 St. Brooklyn, NY 11230. (718)258-7760. FAX: (718)258-4672. E-mail: joskarmel @aol.com. Natl. Dir. Rabbi Joseph C. Karmel; Exec. V.-Pres. Rabbi Nachum Barnetsky. Seeks to bring irreligious Jews in Israel back to their heritage. Conducts outreach through 12 major divisions consisting of thousands of volunteers and hundreds of professionals across the country; conducts anti-missionary and assimilation programs; operates shelters for abused women and children; recruits children for Torah schools.

RABBINICAL ALLIANCE OF AMERICA (Igud Harabonim) (1942). 3 W. 16 St., 4th fl., NYC 10011. (212)242-6420. FAX: (212)255-8313. Pres. Rabbi Abraham B. Hecht. Seeks to promulgate the cause of Torah-true Judaism through an organized rabbinate that is consistently Orthodox; seeks to elevate the position of Orthodox rabbis nationally and to defend the welfare of Jews the world over. Also has Beth Din Rabbinical Court for Jewish divorces, litigation, marriage counseling, and family problems. *Perspective; Nahalim; Torah Message of the Week; Registry.*

RABBINICAL ASSEMBLY (1901). 3080 Broadway, NYC 10027. (212)280-6000. FAX: (212)749-9166. Pres. Rabbi Perry Rank; Exec. V.-Pres. Rabbi Joel H. Meyers. The international association of Conservative rabbis; actively promotes the cause of Conservative Judaism and works to benefit *klal yisrael*; publishes learned texts, prayer books, and works of Jewish inter-est; administers the work of the Committee on Jewish Law and Standards for the Conservative movement; serves the professional and personal needs of its members through publications, conferences, and benefit programs and administers the movement's Joint Placement Commission. *Conservative Judaism; Proceedings of the Rabbinical Assembly; Rabbinical Assembly Newsletter.*

RABBINICAL COUNCIL OF AMERICA, INC. (1923; reorg. 1935). 305 Seventh Ave., Suite 1200, NYC 10001. (212)807-7888. FAX: (212)727-8452. Pres. Rabbi Shlomo Hochberg; Exec. V.-Pres. Rabbi Basil Herring. Promotes Orthodox Judaism in the community; supports institutions for study of Torah; stimulates creation of new traditional agencies. *Hadorom; Tradition.* (WWW.RABBIS.ORG)

SOCIETY FOR HUMANISTIC JUDAISM (1969). 28611 W. Twelve Mile Rd., Farmington Hills, MI 48334. (248)478-7610. FAX: (248) 478-3159. E-mail: info@shj.org. Pres. Miriam Jerris; Exec. Dir. M. Bonnie Cousens. Serves as a voice for Jews who value their Jewish identity and who seek an alternative to conventional Judaism, who reject supernatural authority and affirm the right of individuals to be the masters of their own lives. Publishes educational and ceremonial materials; organizes congregations and groups. *Humanistic Judaism (quarterly journal); Humanorah (quarterly newsletter).* (WWW.SHJ.ORG)

TEKIAH: ASSOCIATION OF HILLEL/JEWISH CAMPUS PROFESSIONALS (1949). c/o Hillel Foundation of New Orleans, 912 Broadway, New Orleans, LA 70118. (504)866-7060. FAX: (504)861-8909. E-mail: president@tekiah.org. Pres. Rabbi Jeffrey Kurtz-Lendner. Seeks to promote professional relationships and exchanges of experience, develop personnel standards and qualifications, safeguard integrity of Hillel profession; represents and advocates before the Foundation for Jewish Campus Life, Council of Jewish Federations. *Handbook for Hillel Professionals; Guide to Hillel Personnel Practices.* (WWW.TEKIAH.ORG)

TEVA LEARNING CENTER/SHOMREI ADAMAH (1988). 307 Seventh Ave., #900, NYC 10001. (212)807-6376. FAX: (212)924-5112. E-mail: teva@tevacenter.org. Co-Dir. Nili Simhai; Asst. Dir., Noam Dolgin Exists to renew the ecological wisdom inherent in Judaism. Runs Jewish environmental education programs for Jewish day schools, synagogues, community centers, camps, university groups and other organized groups. *Let the Earth Teach You Torah, Ecology and the Jewish Spirit.* (WWW.TEVA CENTER.ORG)

TORAH SCHOOLS FOR ISRAEL–CHINUCH ATZMAI (1953). 40 Exchange Pl., NYC 10005. (212)248-6200. FAX: (212)248-6202. Exec. Dir. Rabbi Henach Cohen. Conducts information programs for the American Jewish community on activities of the independent Torah schools educational network in Israel; coordinates role of American members of international board of governors; funds special programs of Mercaz Hachinuch Ha-Atzmai B'Eretz Yisroel; funds religous education programs in America and abroad.

TORAH UMESORAH–NATIONAL SOCIETY FOR HEBREW DAY SCHOOLS (1944). 160 Broadway, NYC 10038. (212)227-1000. FAX: (212)406-6934. E-mail: umesorah@aol. com. Exec. V.-Pres. Rabbi Joshua Fishman. Establishes Hebrew day schools and Yeshivas in U.S. and Canada and provides a full gamut of services, including placement, curriculum guidance, and teacher training. Parent Enrichment Program provides enhanced educational experience for students from less Jewishly educated and marginally affiliated homes through parent-education programs and Partners in Torah, a one-on-one learning program. Publishes textbooks; runs shabbatonim, extracurricular activities; national PTA groups; national and regional teacher conventions. *Olomeinu-Our World.*

———, NATIONAL ASSOCIATION OF HEBREW DAY SCHOOL PARENT-TEACHER ASSOCIATIONS (1948). 160 Broadway, NYC 10038. (212)227-1000. FAX: (212)406-6934. Natl. PTA Coord. Bernice Brand. Acts as a clearinghouse and service agency to PTAs of Hebrew day schools; organizes parent education courses and sets up programs for individual PTAs. *Fundraising with a Flair; PTA with a Purpose for the Hebrew Day School.*

———, NATIONAL CONFERENCE OF YESHIVA PRINCIPALS (1956). 160 Broadway, NYC 10038. (212)227-1000. FAX: (212)406-6934. E-mail: umesorah@aol.com. Pres. Rabbi Rabbi Schneur Aisenstark; Exec. V.-

Pres. Rabbi Joshua Fishman. Professional organization of elementary and secondary yeshivah/day school principals providing yeshivah/day schools with school evaluation and guidance, teacher and principal conferences-including a Mid-Winter Conference and a National Educators Convention; offers placement service for principals and teachers in yeshivah/day schools. *Directory of Elementary Schools and High Schools.*

———, NATIONAL YESHIVA TEACHERS BOARD OF LICENSE (1953). 160 Broadway, NYC 10038. (212)227-1000. Exec. V.-Pres. Rabbi Joshua Fishman; Dir. Rabbi Yitzchock Merkin. Issues licenses to qualified instructors for all grades of the Hebrew day school and the general field of Torah education.

UNION OF AMERICAN HEBREW CONGREGATIONS (see UNION FOR REFORM JUDAISM)

UNION FOR REFORM JUDAISM (formerly UNION OF AMERICAN HEBREW CONGREGATIONS) (1873). 633 Third Ave., NYC 10017-6778. (212)650-4000. FAX: (212) 650-4169. E-mail: urj@urj.org. Pres. Rabbi Eric H. Yoffie; V.-Pres. Rabbi Lennard R. Thal; Bd. Chmn. Russell Silverman. Serves as the central congregational body of Reform Judaism in the Western Hemisphere; serves its approximately 900 affiliated temples and membership with religious, educational, cultural, and administrative programs. *Reform Judaism.* (WWW.URJ.ORG)

———, AMERICAN CONFERENCE OF CANTORS (1953). 5591 Chamblee Dunwoody Rd. Bldg. 1360, Ste. 200, Atlanta, GA 30338. (770)390-0006. FAX: (770)390-0020. E-mail: accantors@aol.com. Pres. Richard Cohen, Exec. V.-Pres. Scott E. Colbert Exec. VP; Dir. of Placement Barbara Ostfeld; Admin. Asst. Deborah Barber. Members are invested or certified by accredited seminaries, i.e., Hebrew Union College-Jewish Insitute of Religion School of Sacred Music. Through the Joint Cantorial Placement Commission, the ACC serves Reform congregations seeking cantors. Dedicated to creative Judaism, preserving the past, and encouraging new and vital approaches to religious ritual, liturgical music and ceremony. *Koleinu* (monthly).

———, COMMISSION ON SOCIAL ACTION OF REFORM JUDAISM (see p. 607)

———, COMMISSION ON SYNAGOGUE MAN-AGEMENT (URJ-CCAR) (1962). 633 Third Ave., NYC 10017-6778. (212)650-4040. FAX: (212)650-4239. Chmn. Marshall Krolick; Dir. Dale A. Glasser. Assists congregations in management, finance, building maintenance, design, construction, and art aspects of synagogues; maintains the Synagogue Architectural Library.

———, NATA (NATIONAL ASSOCIATION OF TEMPLE ADMINISTRATORS) (1941). 6114 La Salle Ave., Box 731, Oakland, CA 94611. (800)966-6282. FAX: (925)283-7713. E-mail: nataorg@hotmail.com. FTA Elizabeth L. Hirsh. Professional organization for URJ synagogue administrators. Sponsors graduate training in synagogue management with Hebrew Union College; offers in-service training, workshops, and conferences leading to certification; provides NATA Consulting Service, NATA Placement Service for synagogues seeking advice or professional administrators; establishes professional standards. *NATA Journal.*

———, NATE (NATIONAL ASSOCIATION OF TEMPLE EDUCATORS) (1955). 633 Third Ave., 7th fl., NYC 10017-6778. (212)452-6510. FAX: (212)452-6512. E-mail: nate-off@aol.com. Pres. Lori Sagarin; Exec. Dir. Rabbi Stanley T. Schickler. Represents educators within the general body of Reform Judaism; fosters the full-time profession of the Jewish educator; encourages the growth and development of Jewish religious education consistent with the aims of Reform Judaism; stimulates communal interest in and responsibility for Jewish religious education. *NATE NEWS.* (WWW.RJ.ORG/NATE)

———, NORTH AMERICAN FEDERATION OF TEMPLE BROTHERHOODS (1923). 633 Third Ave., NYC 10017. (212)650-4100. FAX: (212)650-4189. E-mail contact@ nftb.org Pres. Aaron Bloom; JCS Chancellor Stuart J. Aaronson; Exec. Dir. Douglas Barden. Dedicated to enhancing the world through the ideal of brotherhood, NFTB and its 300 affiliated clubs are actively involved in education, social action, youth activities, and other programs that contribute to temple and community life. Supports the Jewish Chautauqua Society, an interfaith educational project. *ACHIM (formerly Brotherhood magazine)* (WWW.RJ.ORG/NFTB)

———, URJ DEPARTMENT OF JEWISH EDUCATION (1923). 633 Third Ave., 7th fl., NYC 10017. (212)650-4112. FAX: (212) 650-4229. E-mail: jkatzew@urj.org. Chmn. Dr. Rabbi Jan Katzew, Robert Heller; Dir. Dr. Rabbi Jan Katzew. Long-range planning and policy development for congregational programs of lifelong education; materials concerning Reform Jewish Outreach, Teacher Development and Reform Day Schools; activities administered by the URJ Department of Education. *V'Shinantam; Torah at the Center, Family Shabbat Table Talk, Galilee Diary, Jewish Parent Page.*

———, WOMEN OF REFORM JUDAISM—THE FEDERATION OF TEMPLE SISTERHOODS (1913). 633 Third Ave., NYC 10017. (212)650-4050. FAX: (212)650-4059. E-mail: wrj@urj.org. Pres. Rosanne Selfon; Exec. Dir. Shelley Lindauer. Serves more than 600 sisterhoods of Reform Judaism; promotes interreligious understanding and social justice; provides funding for scholarships for rabbinic students; founded the Jewish Braille Institute, which provides braille and large-type Judaic materials for Jewish blind; supports projects for Israel; is the women's agency of Reform Judaism, an affiliate of the URJ; works in behalf of the Hebrew Union College-Jewish Institute of Religion and the World Union for Progressive Judaism. *Notes for Now; Art Calendar; Windows on WRJ.* (WWW.RJ.ORG/WRJ)

———, YOUTH DIVISION AND NORTH AMERICAN FEDERATION OF TEMPLE YOUTH (1939). 633 Third Ave, NYC 10017-6778. (212)650-4070. FAX: (212) 650-4199. E-mail: youthdivision@urj.org. Dir. Rabbi Michael Mellen. Dedicated to Jewishly enhancing the lives of the young people of North America's Reform congregations through a program of informal education carried out in URJ Camp-Institutes (11 camps for grades 2 and up), URJ/NFTY Israel Programs (summer and semester), European and domestic teen travel, NFTY/Junior & Senior High School Programs (youth groups), and Kesher/College Education Department (Reform havurot on campuses).

UNION FOR TRADITIONAL JUDAISM (1984). 241 Cedar Lane, Teaneck, NJ 07666. (201)801-0707. FAX: (201)801-0449. Pres. Burton G. Greenblatt; Exec. V.-Pres.

Rabbi Ronald D. Price. Through innovative outreach programs, seeks to bring the greatest possible number of Jews closer to an open-minded observant Jewish lifestyle. Activities include Kashrut Initiative, Operation Pesah, the Panel of Halakhic Inquiry, Speakers Bureau, adult and youth conferences, and congregational services. Includes, since 1992, the Morashah rabbinic fellowship. *Hagahelet* (quarterly newsletter);*Cornerstone* (journal); *Tomeikh Kahalakhah* (Jewish legal responsa).

UNION OF ORTHODOX JEWISH CONGREGATIONS OF AMERICA (1898). 11 Broadway, 14th fl., NYC 10004. (212)563-4000. FAX: (212)564-9058. E-mail: ou@ou.org. Pres. Stephen J. Savitsky; Exec. V.-Pres. Rabbi Dr. Tzvi Hersh Weinreb. Serves as the national central body of Orthodox synagogues; national OU kashrut supervision and certification service; sponsors Institute for Public Affairs; National Conference of Synagogue Youth; National Jewish Council for the Disabled; Israel Center in Jerusalem; Torah Center in the Ukraine; New Young Leadership Division; Pardes; provides educational, religious, and organization programs, events, and guidance to synagogues and groups; represents the Orthodox Jewish community to governmental and civic bodies and the general Jewish community. *Jewish Action magazine; OU Kosher Directory; OU Guide to Kosher for Passover Foods; Keeping Posted (NCSY); Synagogue Trends; Our Way magazine; Yachad magazine; Luach & Limud Personal Torah Study, Leadership Briefing, Behind the Union Symbol* .(WWW.OU.ORG)

———, INSTITUTE FOR PUBLIC AFFAIRS (1989). 11 Broadway, 14th fl., NYC 10004. (212)613-8124. FAX: (212)613-0724. E-mail: ipa@ou.org. Pres. Stephen J. Savitsky; Chmn. Mark Bane; Dir. Nathan Diament. Serves as the policy analysis, advocacy, mobilization, and programming department responsible for representing Orthodox/traditional American Jewry. *IPA Currents (quarterly newsletter).*

———, NATIONAL CONFERENCE OF SYNAGOGUE YOUTH (1954). 11 Broadway, 14th fl., NYC 10004. (212)563-4000. E-mail: ncsy@ou.org. Dir. Rabbi Steven Burg. Central body for youth groups of Orthodox congregations; provides educational guidance, Torah study groups, community service, program consultation, Torah library, Torah fund scholarships, Ben Zakkai Honor Society, Friends of NCSY, weeklong seminars, Israel Summer Experience for teens and Camp NCSY East Summer Kollel & Michlelet, Teen Torah Center. Divisions include Senior NCSY, Junior NCSY for preteens, Our Way for the Jewish deaf, Yachad for the developmentally disabled, Israel Center in Jerusalem, and NCSY in Israel. *Keeping Posted with NCSY; Darchei Da'at.*

———, WOMEN'S BRANCH (1923). 156 Fifth Ave., NYC 10010. (212)929-8857. Pres. Sophie Ebert. Umbrella organization of Orthodox sisterhoods in U.S. and Canada, educating women in Jewish learning and observance; provides programming, leadership, and organizational guidance, conferences, conventions, Marriage Committee and projects concerning mikvah, Shalom Task Force, and Welcoming Guests. Works with Orthodox Union Commissions and outreach; supports Stern and Touro College scholarships and Jewish braille publications; supplies Shabbat candelabra for hospital patients; NGO representative at UN. *Hachodesh; Hakol.*

UNION OF ORTHODOX RABBIS OF THE UNITED STATES AND CANADA (1902). 235 E. Broadway, NYC 10002. (212)964-6337(8). Dir. Rabbi Hersh M. Ginsberg. Seeks to foster and promote Torah-true Judaism in the U.S. and Canada; assists in the establishment and maintenance of yeshivot in the U.S.; maintains committee on marriage and divorce and aids individuals with marital difficulties; disseminates knowledge of traditional Jewish rites and practices and publishes regulations on synagogal structure; maintains rabbinical court for resolving individual and communal conflicts. *HaPardes.*

UNION OF SEPHARDIC CONGREGATIONS, INC. (1929). 8 W. 70 St., NYC 10023. (212)873-0300. FAX: (212)724-6165. Pres. Rabbi Marc D. Angel; Bd. Chmn. Edward Misrahi. Promotes the religious interests of Sephardic Jews; prints and distributes Sephardic prayer books. *Annual International Directory of Sephardic Congregations.*

UNITED LUBAVITCHER YESHIVOTH (1940). 841-853 Ocean Pkwy., Brooklyn, NY

11230. (718)859-7600. FAX: (718)434-1519. Supports and organizes Jewish day schools and rabbinical seminaries in the U.S. and abroad.

UNITED SYNAGOGUE OF CONSERVATIVE JUDAISM (1913). 155 Fifth Ave., NYC 10010-6802. (212)533-7800. FAX: (212) 353-9439. E-mail: info@uscj.org. Pres. Judy Yudof; Exec. V.-Pres. Rabbi Jerome M. Epstein. International organization of 760 Conservative congregations. Maintains 17 departments and 15 regional offices to assist its affiliates with religious, educational, youth, community, and administrative programming and guidance; aims to enhance the cause of Conservative Judaism, further religious observance, encourage establishment of Jewish religious schools, draw youth closer to Jewish tradition. Extensive Israel programs. *United Synagogue Review; Art/Engagement Calendar; Program Suggestions; Directory & Resource Guide; Book Service Catalogue of Publications.* (WWW.USCJ.ORG)

———, COMMISSION ON JEWISH EDUCATION (1930). 155 Fifth Ave., NYC 10010. (212)533-7800. FAX: (212)353-9439. E-mail: education@uscj.org. Chmn. Temma Kingsley; Dir. Rabbi Robert Abramson. Develops educational policy for the United Synagogue of Conservative Judaism and sets the educational direction for Conservative congregations, their schools, and the Solomon Schechter Day Schools. Seeks to enhance the educational effectiveness of congregations through the publication of materials and in-service programs. *Tov L'Horot; Your Child; Shiboley Schechter; Advisories.*

———, COMMISSION ON SOCIAL ACTION AND PUBLIC POLICY (1958). 155 Fifth Ave., NYC 10010. (212)533-7800. FAX: (212)353-9439. Chmn. Hon. Jerry Wagner; Dir. Sarrae G. Crane. Develops and implements positions and programs on issues of social action and public policy for the United Synagogue of Conservative Judaism; represents these positions to other Jewish and civic organizations, the media, and government; and provides guidance, both informational and programmatic, to its affiliated congregations in these areas. *HaMa'aseh.*

———, JEWISH EDUCATORS ASSEMBLY (1951). 426 W. 58 St., NYC 10019.

(212)765-3303. FAX: (212)765-3310. Pres. Dr. Mark S. Silk; Exec. Dir. Susan Mitrani Knapp. The Jewish Educators Assembly is the professional organization for the Jewish educators within the Conservative movement. The JEA provides a forum to discuss the trends and challenges within Conservative Jewish education as well as provides professional development and a sense of community for educational directors. Services offered: annual conference, placement service, career services, research grants, personal benefits and *V'Aleh Ha-Chadashot* newsletter.

———, KADIMA (reorg. 1968). 155 Fifth Ave., NYC 10010-6802. (212)533-7800. FAX: (212)353-9439. E-mail: kadima@uscj.org. Dir. Karen L. Stein; Dir. of Youth Activities Jules A Gutin. Involves Jewish preteens in a meaningful religious, educational, and social environment; fosters a sense of identity and commitment to the Jewish community and the Conservative movement; conducts synagogue-based chapter programs and regional Kadima days and weekends. *Mitzvah of the Month; Kadima Kesher; Chagim; Advisors Aid; Games;* quarterly *Kol Kadima* magazine.

———, NORTH AMERICAN ASSOCIATION OF SYNAGOGUE EXECUTIVES (1948). 155 Fifth Ave., NYC 10010. (212)533-7800, ext 2609. FAX: (631)732-9461. E-mail: office@naase.org. Pres. Judith Kranz, FSA, ATz; Hon. Pres. Amir Pilch, FSA; Exec. Dir. Harry Hauser. Aids congregations affiliated with the United Synagogue of Conservative Judaism to further the aims of Conservative Judaism through more effective administration (Program for Assistance by Liaisons to Synagogues—PALS); advances professional standards and promotes new methods in administration; cooperates in United Synagogue placement services and administrative surveys. *NAASE Connections Newsletter; NAASE Journal.*.

———, UNITED SYNAGOGUE YOUTH (1951). 155 Fifth Ave., NYC 10010. (212)533-7800. FAX: (212)353-9439. E-mail: youth@uscj.org. Pres. Jesse Olitzky; Exec. Dir. Jules A. Gutin. Seeks to strengthen identification with Conservative Judaism, based on the personality, development, needs, and interests of the adolescent, in a mitzvah framework.

Achshav; Tikun Olam; A.J. Heschel Honor Society Newsletter; SATO Newsletter; USY Program Bank; Hakesher Newsletter for Advisors.

VAAD MISHMERETH STAM (1976). 4907 16th Ave., Brooklyn, NYC 11204. (718)438-4980. FAX: (718)438-9343. Pres. Rabbi David L. Greenfield. A nonprofit consumer-protection agency dedicated to preserving and protecting the halakhic integrity of Torah scrolls, tefillin, phylacteries, and mezuzoth. Publishes material for laymen and scholars in the field of scribal arts; makes presentations and conducts examination campaigns in schools and synagogues; created an optical software system to detect possible textual errors in stam. Teaching and certifying sofrim worldwide. Offices in Israel, Strasbourg, Chicago, London, Manchester, Montreal, and Zurich. Publishes *Guide to Mezuzah* and *Encyclopedia of the Secret Aleph Beth. The Jewish Quill; and many other publications.*

WOMEN'S LEAGUE FOR CONSERVATIVE JUDAISM (1918). 475 Riverside Dr., NYC 10115. (212)870-1260. FAX: (212)772-3507. Email: womensleague@wlcj.org Pres. Gloria Cohen; Exec. Dir. Bernice Balter. Parent body of Conservative (Masorti) women's synagogue groups in U.S., Canada, Puerto Rico, Mexico, and Israel; provides programs and resources in Jewish education, social action, Israel affairs, American and Canadian public affairs, leadership training, community service programs for persons with disabilities, conferences on world affairs, study institutes, publicity techniques; publishes books of Jewish interest; contributes to support of Jewish Theological Seminary of America. *Women's League Outlook* magazine; *Ba'Olam world affairs newsletter.*

WORLD COUNCIL OF CONSERVATIVE/MASORTI SYNAGOGUES (1957). 155 Fifth Ave., NYC 10010. (212)533-7800, ext. 2014, 2018. FAX: (212)533 9439. E-mail: worldcouncil@compuserve.com. Pres. Rabbi Alan Silverstein; Rabbi of Council, Rabbi Benjamin Z. Kreitman. Organize and support Conservative/Masorti congregations in Latin America, Europe, Australia and South Africa. *World Spectrum.*

WORLD UNION FOR PROGRESSIVE JUDAISM (1926). 633 Third Ave. NYC 10017. (212)650-4280. FAX: (212)650-4289. E-mail: arzawupjna@urj.org. Chair Steven M. Bauman; Exec. Dir. Rabbi Uri Regev. International umbrella organization of Liberal Judaism; promotes and coordinates efforts of Liberal congregations throughout the world; starts new congregations, recruits rabbis and rabbinical students for all countries; organizes international conferences of Liberal Jews. *World News.* (WWW.WUPJ.ORG)

SCHOOLS, INSTITUTIONS

ACADEMY FOR JEWISH RELIGION (1956). 6301 Riverdale Avenue, Riverdale, NY 10471. (718)543-9360. FAX: (718)543-1038. E-mail: admin@ajrsem.org. Acting Pres. Rabbi David Greenstein; Dean Rabbi Dr. Ora Horn Prouser. The pluralistic rabbinic and cantorial seminary uniting teachers and students from all streams of Judaism, passionately committed to their own paths, yet respectful and supportive of the paths of others. Emphasis on integrating learning, practice, and spirit through traditional and contemporary approaches. Training for congregations, chaplaincy, education, community work. (WWW.AJRSEM.ORG)

ANNENBERG RESEARCH INSTITUTE (*see* CENTER FOR JUDAIC STUDIES)

BALTIMORE HEBREW UNIVERSITY (1919). 5800 Park Heights Ave., Baltimore, MD 21215. (410)578-6900; (888)248-7420. FAX: (410)578-6940. E-mail: bhu@bhu.edu. Bd. Chmn. Erika Schon. Offers BA and MA degrees in Jewish studies (MAJS); MA in Jewish education (MAJE), and Jewish communal service (MAJCS). Concentrations in biblical and ancient Near Eastern civilization, contemporary Jewish studies, Jewish thought and mysticism, literature, history, and rabbinics. Dual master's degree opportunities available as well as certificate programs in nonprofit management and education. Lifelong learning programs; Joseph Meyerhoff Library; distinguished lecture series. (WWW.BHU.EDU)

———, BERNARD MANEKIN SCHOOL OF UNDERGRADUATE STUDIES. Dean Dr. Barbara G. Zirkin. BA upper division Jewish studies; *LaDa'at* program for high school juniors and seniors.

———, PEGGY MEYERHOFF PEARLSTONE SCHOOL OF GRADUATE STUDIES. Dean Dr. Barbara G. Zirkin. PhD and MA programs: MA in Jewish studies; MAJE in Jewish education; PhD in Jewish studies; dual master's degrees, some jointly with the University of Maryland.

———, LEONARD AND HELEN R. STULMAN SCHOOL OF CONTINUING EDUCATION. Director of lifelong learning Elaine Eckstein. Noncredit programs open to the community, including Jewish studies and Hebrew language courses, trips, retreats, and seminars; *Me'ah,* an intensive group study program..

BRAMSON ORT COLLEGE (1977). 69-30 Austin St., Forest Hills, NY 11375. (718) 261-5800. Dean of Academic Services Barry Glotzer. A two-year Jewish technical college offering certificates and associate degrees in technology and business fields, including accounting, computer programming, electronics technology, business management, office technology. Additional locations in Brooklyn.

BRANDEIS-BARDIN INSTITUTE (1941). 1101 Peppertree Lane, Brandeis, CA 93064. (805)582-4450. FAX: (805)526-1398. E-mail: info@thebbi.org. Pres. Dr. Lee T. Bycel; Chair, Bd. Of Dir. Helen Zukin. A Jewish pluralistic, nondenominational educational institution providing programs for people of all ages: BCI (Brandeis Collegiate Institute), a summer leadership program for college-age adults from around the world; Camp Alonim, a summer Jewish experience for children 8-16; Gan Alonim Day Camp for children in kindergarten to 6th grade; weekend retreats for adults with leading contemporary Jewish scholars-in-residence; Jewish music concerts; Family Days and Weekends, Grandparents Weekends, Elderhostel, Young Adult programs, dance weekends, institute for newly marrieds. *Monthly Updates; BBI Newsletter.*

BRANDEIS UNIVERSITY (1948). 415 South St., Waltham, MA 02454. (781)736-2000. Pres. Jehuda Reinharz; Provost Irving Epstein; Exec. V.-Pres./CEO Peter B. French; Sr. V.-Pres. of Devel. Nancy Winship. Founded in 1948 by the American Jewish community, Brandeis University is a private, coeducational, and nonsectarian institution of higher learning and research located in Waltham, Massachusetts, enrolling approximately 3,100 undergraduate students and 1,200 graduate students. While Brandeis maintains a special rela-

tionship with the Jewish community, it welcomes students and faculty of all backgrounds and beliefs. The University's principal components are the undergraduate College of Arts and Sciences, the Graduate School of Arts and Sciences, The Heller School for Social Policy and Management, the Graduate School of International Economics and Finance, and the Rabb School of Summer and Continuing Studies. *Various newsletters, scholarly publications.*

———, NATIONAL WOMEN'S COMMITTEE (1948). MS 132, Waltham, MA 02454-9110. (781) 736-4160. FAX: (781)736-4183. E-mail: bunwc@brandeis.edu. Pres. Marcia F. Levy; Exec. Dir. Joan C. Bowen. Provides support for Brandeis University and its Libraries. It connects Brandeis, a non-sectarian university founded by the American Jewish community, to its members and their communities through programs that reflect the ideals of social justice and academic excellence. In addition to its fundraising activities, NWC offers its members opportunity for intellectual pursuit, continuing education, community service, social interaction, personal enrichment and leadership development. Open to all, regardless of race, religion, nationality or gender. *Connecting.*

CENTER FOR JUDAIC STUDIES, School of Arts and Sciences, University of Pennsylvania. 420 Walnut St., Philadelphia, PA 19106. (215)238-1290. FAX: (215) 238-1540. Dir. David B. Ruderman. *Jewish Quarterly Review.*

CLEVELAND COLLEGE OF JEWISH STUDIES (1964). 26500 Shaker Blvd., Beachwood, OH 44122. (216)464-4050. FAX: (216) 464-5827. Pres. David S. Ariel; Dir. of Student Services Diane M. Kleinman. Provides courses in all areas of Judaic and Hebrew studies to adults and college-age students; offers continuing education for Jewish educators and administrators; serves as a center for Jewish life and culture; expands the availability of courses in Judaic studies by exchanging faculty, students, and credits with neighboring academic institutions; grants bachelor's and master's degrees.

DROPSIE COLLEGE FOR HEBREW AND COGNATE LEARNING (*see* CENTER FOR JUDAIC STUDIES)

GRATZ COLLEGE (1895). 7605 Old York Rd., Melrose Park, PA 19027. (215)635-7300. FAX: (215)635-7320. Bd. Chmn. Dr. Matti K. Gershenfeld.; Pres. Dr. Jonathan Rosenbaum. Offers a wide variety of undergraduate and graduate degrees and continuing education programs in Judaic, Hebraic, and Middle Eastern studies. Grants BA and MA in Jewish studies, MA in Jewish education (joint program in special needs education with La Salle U.), MA in Jewish music, MA in Jewish liberal studies, MA in Jewish communal studies, certificates in Jewish communal studies (joint program with U. of Penna. School of Social Work and Temple U), Jewish education, Israel studies, Judaica librarianship (joint program with Drexel U.), and Jewish music. Joint graduate program with Reconstructionist Rabbinical College in Jewish education and Jewish music. Netzky Division of Continuing Education and Jewish Community High School. *Various newsletters, annual academic bulletin, scholarly publications, centennial volume, Gratz newsletter and occasional papers.*

HEBREW COLLEGE (1921). 160 Herrick Road, Newton Centre, MA 02459. (617)559-8600. FAX: (617)559-8601. Pres. Dr. David M. Gordis; Ch. Bd. Dir. Mickey Cail; Hon. Ch. Bd. Trustees Ted Benard-Cutler. Through training in Jewish texts, history, literature, ethics, and Hebrew language, prepares students to become literate participants in the global Jewish community. Offers graduate and undergraduate degrees and certificates in all aspects of Jewish education, Jewish studies, and Jewish music; serves students of all ages through its Prozdor High School, Camp Yavneh, Ulpan Center for Adult Jewish Learning, and Me'ah–One Hundred Hours of Adult Jewish Learning. *Hebrew College Today; Likut.* (WWW.HEBREWCOLLEGE.EDU)

————, NATIONAL CENTER FOR JEWISH POLICY STUDIES (1998). 160 Herrick Road, Newton Centre, MA 02459. (617)559-8790. FAX: (617)559-8791. E-mail: jewishpolicy@hebrewcollege.edu. Dir. Dr. David M. Gordis; Assoc. Dir. Rabbi Zachary I. Heller; Chmn. Howard I. Friedman. An international research and development resource for American Jewry that bridges the gap between academics, community leaders, professionals, and the organizations and institutions of Jewish life. *Bulletins, various newsletters, monographs, research reports, and books.*

HEBREW SEMINARY OF THE DEAF (1992). 4435 W. Oakton, Skokie, IL 60076. (847) 677-3330. FAX: (847)677-7945. E-mail: hebrewsemdeaf@juno.com. Pres. Rabbi Douglas Goldhamer; Bd. Chmn. Alan Crane. Trains deaf and hearing men and women to become rabbis and teachers for Jewish deaf communities across America. All classes in the 5-year program are interpreted in Sign Language. Rabbis teaching in the seminary are Reform, Conservative, and Reconstructionist.

HEBREW THEOLOGICAL COLLEGE (1922). 7135 N. Carpenter Rd., Skokie, IL 60077. (847)982-2500. FAX: (847)674-6381. E-mail: htc@htcnet.edu. Chancellor Rabbi Dr. Jerold Isenberg; Rosh Hayeshiva Rabbi Shlomo Morgenstern. Hebrew Theological College, a fully accredited insitution, includes the Bet Midrash for Men, Blitstein Institute for Women, Kanter School of Liberal Arts and Sciences, Fasman Yeshiva High School, Community Service Devision, Silber Memorial Library, Bellows Kollel, Israel Experience Program and Yeshivas HaKayitz summer camp. *Likutei Pshatim, Or Shmuel, Academic Journal.* (WWW.HTCNET.EDU)

HEBREW UNION COLLEGE–JEWISH INSTITUTE OF RELIGION (1875). 3101 Clifton Ave., Cincinnati, OH 45220. (513)221-1875. FAX: (513)221-1847. Pres. Rabbi David Ellenson; Chancellor Emer. Dr. Alfred Gottschalk; V.-Pres. Devel. Erica S. Frederick; Chmn. Bd. Govs. Barbara Friedman; Provost Dr. Norman J. Cohen. Academic centers: 3101 Clifton Ave., Cincinnati, OH 45220 (1875), Dean Rabbi Kenneth Ehrlich. 1 W. 4 St., NYC 10012 (1922), Dean Rabbi Shirley Idelson. FAX: (212) 388-1720. 3077 University Ave., Los Angeles, CA 90007 (1954), Dean Rabbi Lewis Barth; FAX: (213)747-6128. 13 King David St., Jerusalem, Israel 94101 (1963), Dean Rabbi Michael Marmur; FAX: (972-2)6251478. Prepares students for Reform rabbinate, cantorate, Jewish education and educational administration, communal service, academic careers; promotes Jewish studies; maintains libraries, archives, and museums; offers master's and doctoral degrees; engages in archaeological excavations; publishes scholarly works through Hebrew Union

College Press. *American Jewish Archives; Bibliographica Judaica; HUC-JIR Catalogue; Hebrew Union College Annual; Studies in Bibliography and Booklore; The Chronicle; Kesher.* (WWW.HUC.EDU)

——, AMERICAN JEWISH PERIODICAL CENTER (1957). 3101 Clifton Ave., Cincinnati, OH 45220. (513)221-1875, ext. 396. FAX: (513)221-0519. Dir. Herbert C. Zafren. Maintains microfilms of all American Jewish periodicals 1823-1925, selected periodicals since 1925. *Jewish Periodicals and Newspapers on Microfilm (1957); First Supplement (1960); Augmented Edition (1984).*

——, BLAUSTEIN CENTER FOR PASTORAL COUNSELING. 1 West 4th Street, NYC, 10012. (212)824-2238. FAX: (212)388-1720. Email: nwiener@huc.edu. Dir. Nancy Wiener. In partnership with CCAR, prepares spiritual leaderss to sensitively and capably help congregants to deal with the critical issues they face throughout their lives; enables rabbinical students to complete a variety of supervised clinical experiences, including a year of congregational workd as well as pastoral counseling internships, and an academic grounding in psychodynamics and pastoral counseling; and develops new approaches to teaching counseling skills, grounding reflections on practical field work experiences in the teachings of Jewish texts.

——, CENTER FOR HOLOCAUST AND HUMANITY EDUCATION. 3101 Clifton Ave., Cincinnati, OH 45220. (513)221-1875, ext. 355. FAX: (513)221-1842. Email: holocaustandhumanity@huc.edu. Dir. Dr. Racelle R. Weiman. Co-sponsored by Hebrew Union College-Jewish Institute of Religion and Combined Generations of the Holocaust of Greater Cincinnati; offers graduate level courses for educational professionals and clergy; surveys and assesses Holocaust education needs in public and private sectors; innovates curriculum development and evaluation; provides teacher training, pedgogic resources, and programming for general public of all ages and faiths; convenes conferences and symposia; cooperates with university consortium on outreach initiatives; creates traveling exhibits; fosters tolerance education and prejudice reduction in the school system.

——, EDGAR F. MAGNIN SCHOOL OF GRADUATE STUDIES (1956). 3077 University Ave., Los Angeles, CA 90007. (213)749-3424. FAX: (213)747-6128. E-mail: magnin@huc.edu. Dir. Dr. Reuven Firestone. Supervises programs leading to DHS, DHL, and MA degrees; participates in cooperative PhD programs with U. of S. Calif.

——, GRADUATE STUDIES PROGRAM. 1 W. 4 St. NYC 10012. (212)824-2252. FAX: (212)388-1720. E-mail: nysgrad@huc.edu. Dir. Dr. Carol Ochs. Offers the DHL (doctor of Hebrew letters) degree in a variety of fields; the MAJS (master of arts in Judaic studies), a multidisciplinary degree; and is the only Jewish seminary to offer the DMin (doctor of ministry) degree in pastoral care and counseling.

——, HUC-UC CENTER FOR THE STUDY OF ETHICS AND CONTEMPORARY MORAL PROBLEMS (1986). 3101 Clifton Ave., Cincinnati, OH 45220. (513)221-1875, EXT. 367. FAX: (5130221-1842. Email: ethics@huc.edu. Dir. Dr. Jonathan Cohen. Co-sponsored by Hebrew Unon College-Jewish Institute of Religion and the University of Cincinnati; dedicated to the study of contemporary moral problems on the basis of valuews that are at the heart of Judeo-Christian and secular ethical traditions; provides forum for open discussion and reflection on important moral dilemmas that arise in modern life; promotes the incorporation of ethical values in personal life, professional practice, and community development; lauching MA and PhD programs in Jewish and Comparative Law and Applied Ethics; offering development programs for legal, medical, and social work professionals; promoting cooperative research among academic institutions, social service, and not-for-profit organizations in Greater Cincinnati.

——, IRWIN DANIELS SCHOOL OF JEWISH COMMUNAL SERVICE (1968). 3077 University Ave., Los Angeles, CA 90007. (800)899-0925. FAX: (213)747-6128. E-mail: swindmueller@huc.edu. Dir. Dr. Steven F. Windmueller. Offers certificate and master's degree to those employed in Jewish communal services, or preparing for such work; offers joint MA in Jewish education and communal service with Rhea Hirsch School; offers dual degrees with the School of Social Work, the

School of Public Administration, the Annenberg School for Communication, Marshall School of Business and the School of Gerontology of the U. of S. Calif. and with other institutions. Single master's degrees can be completed in 15 months and certificates are awarded for the completion of two full-time summer sessions. (WWW.HUC.EDU)

———, JACOB RADER MARCUS CENTER OF THE AMERICAN JEWISH ARCHIVES (*see* p. 613)

———, JEROME H. LOUCHHEIM SCHOOL OF JUDAIC STUDIES (1969). 3077 University Ave., Los Angeles, CA 90007. (213)749-3424. FAX: (213)747-6128. Dir. Dr. Reuven Firestone. Offers programs leading to MA, BS, BA, and AA degrees; offers courses as part of the undergraduate program of the U. of S. Calif.

———, NELSON GLUECK SCHOOL OF BIBLICAL ARCHAEOLOGY (1963). 13 King David St., Jerusalem, Israel 94101. (972)2-6203333. FAX: (972)2-6251478. Dir. Avraham Biran. Offers graduate-level research programs in Bible and archaeology. Summer excavations are carried out by scholars and students. University credit may be earned by participants in excavations. Consortium of colleges, universities, and seminaries is affiliated with the school. Skirball Museum of Biblical Archaeology (artifacts from Tel Dan, Tel Gezer, and Aroer).

———, RHEA HIRSCH SCHOOL OF EDUCATION (1967). 3077 University Ave., Los Angeles, CA 90007. (213)749-3424. FAX: (213)747-6128. Dir. Sara Lee. Offers PhD and MA programs in Jewish and Hebrew education; conducts joint degree programs with U. of S. Calif.; offers courses for Jewish teachers, librarians, and early educators on a nonmatriculating basis; conducts summer institutes for professional Jewish educators.

———, SCHOOL OF EDUCATION (1947). 1 W. 4 St., NYC 10012. (212)824-2213. FAX: (212)388-1720. E-mail: nysed@huc.edu. Dir. Jo Kay. Trains teachers and principals for Reform religious schools; offers MA degree with specialization in religious education.

———, SCHOOL OF GRADUATE STUDIES (1949). 3101 Clifton Ave., Cincinnati, OH 45220. (513)221-1875, ext. 230. FAX: (513)

221-0321. E-mail: gradschool@huc.edu. Dir. Dr. Adam Kamesar. Offers programs leading to MA and PhD degrees; offers program leading to DHL degree for rabbinic graduates of the college.

———, SCHOOL OF JEWISH STUDIES (1963). 13 King David St., Jerusalem, Israel 94101. (972)2-6203333. FAX: (972)2-6251478. E-mail: jerusalem@huc.edu. Acting Pres. Dr. Norman J. Cohen; Dean Rabbi Michael Marmur; Assoc. Dean Rabbi Shaul R. Feinberg. Offers first year of graduate rabbinic, cantorial, and Jewish education studies (required) for North American students; graduate program leading to ordination for Israeli rabbinic students; non-degree Beit Midrash/Liberal Yeshivah program of Jewish studies (English language); in-service educational programming for teachers and educators (Hebrew language); Hebrew Ulpan for immigrants and visitors; Abramov Library of Judaica, Hebraica, Ancient Near East and American Jewish Experience; Skirball Museum of Biblical Archaeology; public outreach programs (lectures, courses, concerts, exhibits).

———, SCHOOL OF SACRED MUSIC (1947). 1 W. 4 St., NYC 10012. (212)824-2225. FAX: (212)388-1720. Dir. Cantor Israel Goldstein. Trains cantors for congregations; offers MSM degree. *Sacred Music Press.*

———, SKIRBALL CULTURAL CENTER (*see* p. 616)

INSTITUTE OF TRADITIONAL JUDAISM (1990). 811 Palisade Ave., Teaneck, NJ 07666. (201)801-0707. FAX: (201)801-0449. Rector (Reish Metivta) Rabbi David Weiss Halivni; Dean Rabbi Ronald D. Price. A nondenominational halakhic rabbinical school dedicated to genuine faith combined with intellectual honesty and the love of Israel. Graduates receive "yoreh yoreh" smikhah.

JEWISH THEOLOGICAL SEMINARY (1886; reorg. 1902). 3080 Broadway, NYC 10027-4649. (212)678-8000. FAX: (212) 678-8947. Chancellor Dr. Arnold Eisen; Bd. Chmn. Gershon Kekst. Operates undergraduate and graduate programs in Judaic studies; professional schools for training Conservative rabbis, educators and cantors; the JTS Library; the Ratner Center for the Study of Conservative Judaism; Melton Research Center for Jewish Education; the Jewish Museum; Ramah Camps and the Ivry Prozdor high-school honors program. Other outreach activities include the Distance Learning Project, the Finkelstein Institute for Religious and Social Studies, and the Wagner Institute lay leadership program. *Academic Bulletin; JTS Magazine; Gleanings; JTS News.* (WWW.JTSA.EDU)

———, ALBERT A. LIST COLLEGE OF JEWISH STUDIES (formerly SEMINARY COLLEGE OF JEWISH STUDIES—TEACHERS INSTITUTE) (1909). 3080 Broadway, NYC 10027. (212)678-8826. Dean Dr. Shuly Rubin Schwartz. Offers complete undergraduate program in Judaica leading to BA degree; conducts joint programs with Columbia University and Barnard College enabling students to receive two BA degrees.

———, GRADUATE SCHOOL OF JTS (formerly INSTITUTE FOR ADVANCED STUDY IN THE HUMANITIES) (1968). 3080 Broadway, NYC 10027-4649. (212)678-8024. FAX: (212)678-8947. E-mail: gradschool@jtsa.edu. Dean Dr. Stephen P. Garfinkel; Asst. Dean Dr. Bruce E. Nielsen. Programs leading to MA, DHL, and PhD degrees in Judaic studies; specializations include Ancient Judaism, Bible and Ancient Semitic Languages, Interdepartmental Studies, Jewish Art and Material Culture, Jewish Education, Jewish History, Jewish Literature, Jewish Philosophy, Jewish Women's Studies, Liturgy, Medieval Jewish Studies, Midrash, Modern Jewish Studies, Talmud and Rabbinics, and Dual Degree Program with Columbia University School of Social Work.

———, H.L. MILLER CANTORIAL SCHOOL AND COLLEGE OF JEWISH MUSIC (1952). 3080 Broadway, NYC 10027. (212)678-8036. FAX: (212)678-8947. Dean Cantor Henry Rosenblum. Trains cantors, music teachers, and choral directors for congregations. Offers full-time programs in sacred music leading to degree of MSM, and diploma of *Hazzan.*

———, JEWISH MUSEUM (*see* p. 614)

———, LIBRARY OF THE JEWISH THEOLOGICAL SEMINARY. 3080 Broadway, NYC 10027. (212)678-8075. FAX: (212)678-8998. E-mail: library@jtsa.edu. Librarian Dr. Mayer E. Rabinowitz. Contains one of the largest collections of Hebraica and Judaica in the world, including manuscripts, incunabula, rare books, and Cairo Geniza material. The 320,000-item collection includes books, manuscripts, periodicals, sound recordings, prints, broadsides, photographs, postcards, microform, videos and CD-ROM. Exhibition of items from the collection are ongoing. Exhibition catalogs are available for sale. The Library is open to the public for on-site use (photo identification required). *Between the Lines.* (WWW.JTSA.EDU/LIBRARY)

———, LOUIS FINKELSTEIN INSTITUTE FOR RELIGIOUS AND SOCIAL STUDIES (1938). 3080 Broadway, NYC 10027. (212)870-3180. FAX: (212)678-8947. E-mail: finkelstein@jtsa.edu. Dir. Dr. Alan Mittleman. Since 1938 has maintained an innovative interfaith and intergroup relations program, pioneering new approaches to dialogue across religious lines. Through scholarly and practical fellowship, highlights the relevance of Judaism and other contemporary religions to current theological, ethical, and scientific issues, including the emerging challenge of bioethics.

———, MELTON RESEARCH CENTER FOR JEWISH EDUCATION (1960). 3080 Broadway, NYC 10027. (212)678-8031. E-mail: stbrown@jtsa.edu. Dir. Dr. Steven M. Brown; Admin. Lisa Siberstein-Weber. Develops new curricula and materials for Jewish education; prepares educators through seminars and in-service programs; maintains consultant and supervisory relationships with a limited number of pilot schools; develops and implements research initiatives; sponsors "renewal" retreats. *Gleanings; Courtyard: A Journal of Research and Reflection on Jewish Education.*

———, NATIONAL RAMAH COMMISSION (1947). 3080 Broadway, NYC 10027. (212)678-8881. FAX: (212)749-8251. Pres. Alan H. Silberman; Natl. Dir. Mitchell Cohen. Sponsors an international network of 16 summer camps located in the US, Canada, S. America, Russia, and Israel, emphasizing Jewish education, living, and culture; offers opportunities for qualified college students and older to serve as counselors, administrators, specialists, etc., and programs for children with special needs (Tikvah program); offers special programs in U.S. and Israel, including National Ramah Staff Training

Institute, Ramah Israel Seminar, Ulpan Ramah Plus, and Tichon Ramah Yerushalayim. Family and synagogue tours to Israel and summer day camp in Israel for Americans.

———, PROJECT JUDAICA (1992). 3080 Broadway, NYC 10027. (212)678-8983. Dir. Dr. David Fishman. Students in this intensive, five year program sponsored with YIVO and the Russian State University for the Humanities in Moscow pursue the university's general curriculum while majoring in Jewish history and culture taught by JTS faculty and advanced students. Graduates receive a diploma (the equivalent of an MA) or a candidate of sciences degree (the equivalent of a PhD) from RSUH.

———, RABBINICAL SCHOOL (1886). 3080 Broadway, NYC 10027. (212)678-8817. Dean Allan Kensky. Offers a program of graduate and professional studies leading to the degree of Master of Arts and ordination; includes one year of study in Jerusalem and an extensive field-work program.

———, RADIO AND TELEVISION (1944). 3080 Broadway, NYC 10027. (212)678-8020. Produces radio and TV programs expressing the Jewish tradition in its broadest sense, including hour-long documentaries on NBC and ABC. Distributes cassettes of programs at minimum charge.

———, REBECCA AND ISRAEL IVRY PROZDOR (1951). 3080 Broadway, NYC 10027. (212)678-8824. E-mail: prozdor@jtsa. edu. Principal Rhonda Rosenheck; Community Advisory Board Chmn. Michael Katz. The Hebrew high school of JTS, offers a program of Jewish studies for day school and congregational school graduates in classical texts, Hebrew, interdisciplinary seminars, training in educational leadership, and classes for college credit. Classes meet one evening a week and on Sundays in Manhattan and at affiliated programs. *High School Curricula.*

———, SAUL LIEBERMAN INSTITUTE FOR TALMUDIC RESEARCH (1985). 3080 Broadway, NYC 10027. (212)678-8994. FAX: (212)678D8947. E-mail: liebinst@jtsa.edu. Dir. Shamma Friedman; Coord. Jonathan Milgram. Engaged in preparing for publication a series of scholarly editions of selected chapters of the Talmud. The following projects support and help disseminate the research: Talmud Text Database; Bibliography of Talmudic Literature; Catalogue of Geniza Fragments.

———, SCHOCKEN INSTITUTE FOR JEWISH RESEARCH (1961). 6 Balfour St., Jerusalem, Israel 92102. (972)2-5631288. FAX: (972)2-5636857. E-mail: sjssg@vms.huji. ac.il. Dir. Dr. Shmuel Glick. Comprises the Schocken collection of rare books and manuscripts and a research institute dedicated to the exploration of Hebrew religious poetry (*piyyut*). *Schocken Institute Yearbook (P'raqim).*

———, WILLIAM DAVIDSON GRADUATE SCHOOL OF JEWISH EDUCATION (1996). 3080 Broadway, NYC 10027. (212) 678-8030. E-mail: edschool@jtsa.edu. Dean Dr. Aryeh Davidson. Offers master's and doctoral degrees in Jewish education; continuing education courses for Jewish educators and Jewish communal professionals; and programs that take advantage of the latest technology, including distance learning and interactive video classrooms.

MAALOT–A SEMINARY FOR CANTORS AND JUDAISTS (1987). 15 W. Montgomery Ave., Suite 204, Rockville, MD 20850. (301)309-2310. FAX: (301)309-2328. Pres./Exec. Off. David Shneyer. An educational program established to train individuals in Jewish music, the liturgical arts, and the use, design, and application of Jewish customs and ceremonies. Offers classes, seminars, and an independent study program.

MESIVTA YESHIVA RABBI CHAIM BERLIN RABBINICAL ACADEMY (1905). 1605 Coney Island Ave., Brooklyn, NY 11230. (718)377-0777. Exec. Dir. Y. Mayer Lasker. Maintains fully accredited elementary and high schools; collegiate and postgraduate school for advanced Jewish studies, both in America and Israel; Camp Morris, a summer study retreat; Prof. Nathan Isaacs Memorial Library; Gur Aryeh Publications.

NER ISRAEL RABBINICAL COLLEGE (1933). 400 Mt. Wilson Lane, Baltimore, MD 21208. (410)484-7200. FAX: (410)484-3060. Rosh Hayeshiva, Rabbi Aharon Feldman; Pres. Rabbi Sheftel Neuberger. Trains rabbis and educators for Jewish communities in America and worldwide. Offers bachelor's, master's, and doctoral degrees in talmudic law, as well as teacher's diploma. College has four divisions: Israel Henry Beren High School, Rabbinical College, Teachers Training Institute, Graduate School. Maintains an active community-service division. Operates special programs for Iranian and Russian Jewish students. *Ner Israel Update; Alumni Bulletin; Ohr Hanair Talmudic Journal; Iranian B'nei Torah Bulletin.*

RABBINICAL COLLEGE OF TELSHE, INC. (1941). 28400 Euclid Ave., Wickliffe, OH 44092. (216)943-5300. Roshei Hayeshiva and Pres. Rabbi Zalman Gifter and Rabbi Yitzchok Sorotzkin ; V.-Pres. Rabbi Abba Zalka Gewirtz. College for higher Jewish learning specializing in talmudic studies and rabbinics; maintains a preparatory academy including a secular high school, postgraduate department, teacher-training school, and teachers' seminary for women. *Pri Etz Chaim; Peer Mordechai; Alumni Bulletin.*

RECONSTRUCTIONIST RABBINICAL COLLEGE (1968). 1299 Church Rd., Wyncote, PA 19095. (215)576-0800. FAX: (215)576-6143. E-mail: rrcinfo@rrc.edu. Pres. Dan Ehrenkranz; Bd. Chmn. Donald L. Shapiro; Genl. Chmn. Aaron Ziegelman. Coeducational. Trains rabbis and cantors for all areas of Jewish communal life: synagogues, academic and educational positions, Hillel centers, federation agencies, and chaplaincy for hospitals, hospices, and geriatric centers; confers title of rabbi and cantor and grants degrees of Master and Doctor of Hebrew Letters and Master of Arts in Jewish Studies. *RRC Report; Reconstructionist.*(WWW.RRC.EDU)

SPERTUS INSTITUTE OF JEWISH STUDIES (1924). 618 S. Michigan Ave., Chicago, IL 60605. (312)922-9012. FAX: (312)922-6406. Pres. Howard A. Sulkin; Dean Dr. Dean Bell; Museum Dir. Rhoda Rosen; Lib. Dir. Glenn Ferdman. An accredited institution of higher learning offering one doctor of Jewish studies degree; master's degree programs in Jewish studies, Jewish education, Jewish communal service, and human-services administration; plus an extensive program of continuing education. Major resources of the college encompass Spertus Museum, Asher Library, Chicago Jewish Archives, and Spertus College of Judaica Press.

———, SPERTUS MUSEUM (*see* p. 617)

TOURO COLLEGE (1970). Executive Offices: 27 West 23rd Street., NYC 10010. (212)4630400. FAX: (212)627-9049. Pres. Dr. Bernard Lander; Bd. Chmn. Mark Hasten. Non-profit comprehensive college with Judaic Studies, Liberal Arts and professional programs leading to BA, BS, MA, MS and JD degrees at campuses in NYC and Long Island; emphasizes relevance of Jewish heritage to Western civilization. Undergraduate and graduate degree programs in Moscow and Jerusalem. California campuses offer DO degree and distance learning BS, MS, MBA and PhD degrees.

———, COLLEGE OF LIBERAL ARTS AND SCIENCES. 27-33 W. 23 St., NYC 10010. (212)463-0400. FAX: (212)627-9144. Exec. Dean Stanley Boylan. Offers comprehensive Jewish studies along with studies in the arts, sciences, humanities, and preprofessional studies in health sciences, law, accounting, business, computer science, education, and finance. Women's Division, 160 Lexington Ave., NYC 10016. (212)213-2230. FAX: (212)683-3281. Dean Sara E. Freifeld.

———, INSTITUTE OF JEWISH LAW. (631) 421-2244, ext. 335. A constituent of Touro College Jacob D. Fuchsberg Law Center, the Institute of Jewish Law provides an intellectual framework for the study and teaching of Jewish law. Coedits *Dinei Israel* (Jewish Law Journal) with Tel Aviv University Law School.

———, JACOB D. FUCHSBERG LAW CENTER (1980). Long Island Campus, 300 Nassau Rd., Huntington, NY 11743. (516) 421-2244. Dean Howard A. Glickstein. Offers studies leading to JD degree.

———, MOSCOW BRANCH. Oztozhenka #38, Moscow, Russia 119837. Offers BS program in business and BA program in Jewish studies.

———, SCHOOL OF GENERAL STUDIES. Midtown Main Campus, 27 W. 23 St., NYC 10010. (212)463-0400; Harlem Main Campus, 240 E. 123 St., NYC 10035; Sunset Park extension, 475 53rd St., Brooklyn, NY 11220; Flushing Extension, 133-35 Roosevelt Ave., Queens, NY 11374. Dean Stephen Adolphus. Associate and bachelor degree programs in human services, education N-6, computing, business and liberal arts; special emphasis on service to non-traditional students.

———, TOURO COLLEGE FLATBUSH CENTER (1979). 1602 Ave. J, Brooklyn, NY 11230. (718)252-7800. Dean Robert Goldschmidt. A division of the College of Liberal Arts and Sciences; options offered in accounting and business, education, mathematics, political science, psychology, special education and speech. Classes are given on weeknights and during the day on Sunday.

——— —, TOURO COLLEGE ISRAEL. 20 Pierre Koenig St., Jerusalem, Israel. (02)6796666. FAX: (02)6796688. V-Pres., Israel, Matityahu Adler; Dean of Faculty, Israel, Prof. Moshe Lieberman. Touro College Israel offers both undergraduate and graduate degrees in management, marketing, economics, finance, and accounting. Touro College also offers a graduate degree in Jewish Studies. Courses in both these programs are given in Hebrew. In addition undergraduate courses in our one year program are offered in English. (www. TOURO.EDU)

——— —, TOURO COLLEGE SCHOOL OF HEALTH SCIENCES (1986). 1700 Union Blvd, Bay Shore, NY 11706. (516)665-1600. FAX: (516)665-6902. E-mail: edwarda@touro.edu. Pres. Dr. Bernard Lander; Dean Dr. Joseph Weisberg. Offers the following programs: MS/MD with Faculty of Medicine, Technion Institute, Israel; BS/MS Occupational Therapy; BS/MS Physical Therapy; MS Public Health; Advanced MS Orthopedic Physical Therapy; MS Forensic Examination; MS Clinical Engineering; MS Early Intervention; MS Gerontology; BS Physician Assistant; AAS Occupational Therapy Assistant; AAS Physical Therapists Assistant.

———, TOURO GRADUATE SCHOOL OF JEWISH STUDIES (1981). 160 Lexington Ave., NYC 10016. (212)213-2230. FAX: (212) 683-3281. E-mail: moshesh@touro.edu. Pres. Bernard Lander; Dean Michael A. Shmidman. Offers courses leading to an MA in Jewish studies, with concentrations in Jewish history or Jewish education. Students may complete part of their program in Israel through MA courses offered by Touro faculty at Touro's Jerusalem center.

UNIVERSITY OF JUDAISM (1947). 15600 Mulholland Dr., Los Angeles, CA 90077. (310)476-9777. FAX: (310)476-0347. E-mail: gleuenthal@uj.edu. Pres. Dr. Robert D. Wexler. The College of Arts and Sciences is an accredited liberal arts college for undergraduates offering a core curriculum of Jewish, Western, and non-Western studies, with majors including bioethics (a premedical track in partnership with Cedars-Sinai Medical Center), business, English, Jewish studies, journalism, literature & politics, political science, psychology, and U.S. public policy. Accredited graduate programs in nonprofit business administration (MBA), and Jewish education. The Ziegler School of Rabbinic Studies provides an intensive four-year program with Conservative ordination. Home of the Whizin Center for the Jewish Future, a research and programming institute. Offers the largest adult Jewish education program in the U.S., cultural-arts programs, and a variety of outreach services for West Coast Jewish communities. *Vision.* (WWW.UJ.EDU)

WEST COAST TALMUDICAL SEMINARY (Yeshiva Ohr Elchonon Chabad) (1953). 7215 Waring Ave., Los Angeles, CA 90046. (323)937-3763. FAX: (323)937-9456. Dean Rabbi Ezra Schochet. Provides facilities for intensive Torah education as well as Orthodox rabbinical training on the West Coast; conducts an accredited college preparatory high school combined with a full program of Torah-talmudic training and a graduate talmudic division on the college level. *Torah Quiz; Kovetz Migdal Ohr; Kovetz Ohr HaMigdal.*

YESHIVA TORAH VODAATH AND MESIVTA TORAH VODAATH RABBINICAL SEMINARY (1918). 425 E. 9 St., Brooklyn, NY 11218. (718)941-8000. Bd. Chmn. Chaim Leshkowitz. Offers Hebrew and secular education from elementary level through rabbinical ordination and postgraduate work; maintains a teachers institute and community-service bureau; maintains a dormitory and a nonprofit camp program for boys. *Chronicle; Mesivta Vanguard; Thought of the Week; Torah Vodaath News; Ha'Mesifta.*

———, YESHIVA TORAH VODAATH ALUMNI ASSOCIATION (1941). 425 E. 9 St., Brooklyn, NY 11218. (718)941-8000. Pres.

George Weinberger. Promotes social and cultural ties between the alumni and the schools through classes and lectures and fund-raising; offers vocational guidance to students; operates Camp Ohr Shraga; sponsors research fellowship program for boys. *Annual Journal; Hamesivta Torah periodical.*

YESHIVA UNIVERSITY (1886). Wilf Campus, 500 W. 185 St., NYC 10033-3201. (212)960-5400. FAX: (212)960-0055. Chancellor Dr. Norman Lamm; Pres. Richard Joel; Chmn. Bd. of Trustees Ronald P. Stanton. The nation's oldest and most comprehensive independent university founded under Jewish auspices, with 18 undergraduate and graduate schools, divisions, and affiliates; widespread programs of research and community outreach; publications; and a museum. A broad range of curricula lead to bachelor's, master's, doctoral, and professional degrees. Undergraduate schools provide general studies curricula supplemented by courses in Jewish learning; graduate schools prepare for careers in medicine, law, social work, Jewish education, psychology, Jewish studies, and other fields. It has seven undergraduate schools, seven graduate and professional schools, and four affiliates. *Yeshiva University Review; Yeshiva University Today.* (www.YU.EDU)

Yeshiva University has four campuses in Manhattan and the Bronx: Wilf Campus, 500 W. 185 St., NYC 10033-3201; Midtown Campus, 245 Lexington Ave., NYC 10016-4699; Brookdale Center, 55 Fifth Ave., NYC 10003-4391; Jack and Pearl Resnick Campus, Eastchester Rd. & Morris Pk. Ave., Bronx, NY 10461-1602.

Undergraduate schools for men at Wilf Campus (212)960-5400: Yeshiva College (Bd. Chmn. Joshua L. Muss; Dean Dr. Norman T. Adler) provides liberal arts and sciences curricula; grants BA degree. Isaac Breuer College of Hebraic Studies (Dean Dr. Michael D. Shmidman) awards Hebrew teacher's diploma, AA, BA, and BS. James Striar School of General Jewish Studies (Dean Dr. Michael D. Shmidman) grants AA degree. Yeshiva Program/Mazer School of Talmudic Studies (Max and Marion Grill Dean Rabbi Zevulun Charlop) offers advanced course of study in Talmudic texts and commentaries. Irving I. Stone Beit Midrash Program (Dean Dr. Michael D.

Shmidman) offers diversified curriculum combining Talmud with Jewish studies.

Undergraduate school for women at Midtown Campus (212)340-7700: Stern College for Women (Bd. Chmn. Marjorie Diener Blenden; Dr. Monique C. Katz; Dean Dr. Karen Bacon) offers liberal arts and sciences curricula supplemented by Jewish studies programs; awards BA, AA, and Hebrew teacher's diploma.

Sy Syms School of Business at Wilf Campus and Midtown Campus offers undergraduate business curricula in conjunction with study at Yeshiva College or Stern College; grants BS degree.

———, ALBERT EINSTEIN COLLEGE OF MEDICINE (1955). Eastchester Rd. & Morris Pk. Ave., Bronx, NY 10461-1602. (718)430-2000. Pres. Richard Joel; Chmn. Bd. Robert A. Belfer; Marilyn and Stanley M. Katz Dean Dr. Allen M. Siegel. Prepares physicians and conducts research in the health sciences; awards MD degree; includes Sue Golding Graduate Division of Medical Sciences (Dir. Dr. Anne M. Etgen), which grants PhD degree. Einstein's clinical facilities and affiliates encompass Jack D. Weiler Hospital of Albert Einstein College of Medicine, Jacobi Medical Center, Montefiore Medical Center, Long Island Jewish Medical Center, Beth Israel Medical Center, Bronx-Lebanon Hospital Center, and Rose F. Kennedy Center for Research in Mental Retardation and Developmental Disabilities. *Einstein; Einstein Today; Einstein Quarterly Journal of Biology and Medicine.*

———, AZRIELI GRADUATE SCHOOL OF JEWISH EDUCATION AND ADMINISTRATION (1945). 245 Lexington Ave., NYC 10016-4699. (212)340-7705. FAX: (212)340-7787. Pres. Richard Joel; Chmn. Bd. Moshael J. Straus; Dir. Dr. Yitzchak S. Handel. Offers MS degree in Jewish elementary and secondary education; specialist's certificate and EdD in administration and supervision of Jewish education. Block Education Program, subsidized by a grant from the Jewish Agency's Joint Program for Jewish Education, provides summer course work to complement year-round field instruction in local communities.

———, BELFER INSTITUTE FOR ADVANCED BIOMEDICAL STUDIES (1978). Eastchester Rd. & Morris Pk. Ave., Bronx, NY 10461-

1602. (718)430-2801. Dir. Dr. Dennis Shields. Integrates and coordinates the Albert Einstein College of Medicine's postdoctoral research and training-grant programs in the basic and clinical biomedical sciences. Awards certificate as research fellow or research associate on completion of training.

————, BENJAMIN N. CARDOZO SCHOOL OF LAW (1976). 55 Fifth Ave., NYC 10003-4391. (212)790-0200. E-mail:lawinfo@ymail.yu.edu. Pres. Richard Joel; Chmn. Bd. Of Directors Earle I. Mack; Dean Paul R. Verkuil. Offers a rigorous and enriched legal education leading to juris doctor (JD) degree and two LLM programs—in intellectual property and in general law. Programs and services include Jacob Burns Institute for Advanced Legal Studies; Jacob Burns Center for Ethics in the Practice of Law; Bet Tzedek Legal Services Clinic, including the Herman J. Stich Program for the Aged and Disabled; Cardozo International Institute/Uri and Caroline Bauer Israel Program; Leonard and Bea Diener Institute of Jewish Law; Floersheimer Center for Constitutional Democracy; Ford Foundation Program in International Law and Human Rights; Samuel and Ronnie Heyman Center on Corporate Governance; Kukin Program for Conflict Resolution; Romie Shapiro Program in International Law and Human Rights; Stephen B. Siegel Program in Real Estate Law; Sol S. Singer Research Program in Real Property Law; Howard M. Squadron Program in Law, Media, and Society; Center for Professional Development. *Cardozo Life; Cardozo Law Review; Cardozo Arts and Entertainment Law Journal; Cardozo Women's Law Journal; Cardozo Journal of International and Comparative Law; Cardozo Studies in Law and Literature; Post-Soviet Media Law and Policy Newsletter; New York Real Estate Reporter.*

————, BERNARD REVEL GRADUATE SCHOOL OF JEWISH STUDIES (1935). 500 W. 185 St., NYC 10033-3201. (212)960-5253. Pres. Richard Joel; Chmn. Bd. Mordecai D. Katz; Dean Dr. David Berger. Offers graduate programs in Bible, Talmudic studies, Jewish history, and Jewish philosophy; confers MA and PhD degrees. Harry Fischel Summer Program offers the Revel program during the summer.

————, FERKAUF GRADUATE SCHOOL OF PSYCHOLOGY (1957). Eastchester Rd. & Morris Pk. Ave., Bronx, NY 10461-1602. (718)430-3941. FAX: (718)430-3960. E-mail: gill@aecom.yu.edu. Pres. Richard Joel; Chair Bd. Dr. Jayne G. Beker; Dean Dr. Lawrence J. Siegel. Offers MA in applied psychology; PsyD in clinical and school-clinical child psychology; and PhD in developmental and clinical health psychology. Programs and services include the Leonard and Muriel Marcus Family Project for the Study of the Disturbed Adolescent; Max and Celia Parnes Family Psychological and Psychoeducational Services Clinic.

————, (affiliate) PHILIP AND SARAH BELZ SCHOOL OF JEWISH MUSIC (1954). 560 W. 185 St., NYC 10033-3201. (212)960-5353. FAX: (212)960-5359. Dir Cantor Bernard Beer. Provides professional training of cantors and courses in Jewish liturgical music; conducts outreach; publishes *Journal of Jewish Music and Literature,* awards associate cantor's certificate and cantorial diploma.

————, (affiliate) RABBI ISAAC ELCHANAN THEOLOGICAL SEMINARY (1896). 2540 Amsterdam Ave., NYC 10033-9986. (212) 960-5344. FAX: (212)960-0061. Chmn. Bd. Julius Berman. Leading center in the Western Hemisphere for Torah study and rabbinic training. RIETS complex encompasses 15 educational entities and a major service and outreach center with some 20 programs. Grants semikhah (ordination) and the degrees of master of religious education, master of Hebrew literature, doctor of religious education, and doctor of Hebrew literature. Includes Rabbi Joseph B. Soloveitchik Center of Rabbinic Studies; Gabriel Levine Post-Graduate School for Rabbinic Studies; Morris and Nellie L. Kawaler Rabbinic Training Program; Irving I. Stone Rabbinic Internship Program; Aaron, Martha, Isidore N., and Blanche Rosansky Foundation Contemporary Halakhah Program.

Kollelim include Marcos and Adina Katz Kollel (Institute for Advanced Research in Rabbinics); Kollel l'Horaah (Yadin Yadin) and External Yadin Yadin; Israel Henry Beren Institute for Higher Talmudic Studies (HaMachon HaGavohah L'-Talmud); Bella and Harry Wexner Kollel Elyon and Semikhah Honors Program; Ludwig Jesselson Kollel Chaverim; Caroline and Joseph S. Gruss Institute in Jerusalem.

RIETS sponsors one high school for boys (Manhattan) and one for girls (Queens). The Center for the Jewish Future (Dir. Rabbi Kenneth Brander) provides personal and professional service to the rabbinate and related fields, as well as educational, consultative, organizational, and placement services to congregations, schools, and communal organizations around the world; coordinates a broad spectrum of outreach programs, including Association of Modern Orthodox Day Schools and Yeshiva High Schools, Stone-Sapirstein Center for Jewish Education, Gertrude and Morris Bienenfeld Department of Rabbinic Services, Gindi Program for the Enhancement of Professional Rabbinics, Continuing Rabbinic Education Initiatives, Leadership Education and Development Program (LEAD), Kiruv College Outreach Program, Community Kollel and Beit Midrash and Boardroom Learning Programs, Project Kehillah, Myer and Pauline Senders Off-Campus Lecture Series, Jewish Medical Ethics Consultation Service, National Commission on Torah Education.The Torah U-Madda Project, supported by the Joseph J. and Bertha K. Green Memorial Fund, includes the Orthodox Forum and publishes the *The Torah U-Madda Journal* and *Ten Da'at*.

Sephardic components are Jacob E. Safra Institute of Sephardic Studies and the Institute of Yemenite Studies; Sephardic Community Program; Dr. Joseph and Rachel Ades Sephardic Outreach Program; Maybaum Sephardic Fellowship Program.

———, WOMEN'S ORGANIZATION (1928). 500 W. 185 St., NYC 10033-3201. (212) 960-0855. Chmn. Natl. Bd. Dinah Pinczower. Supports Yeshiva University's national scholarship program for students training in education, community service, law, medicine, and other professions. Its Torah Chesed Fund provides monthly stipends to needy undergraduate students.

———, WURZWEILER SCHOOL OF SOCIAL WORK (1957). 500 W. 185 St., NYC 10033-3201. (212)960-0800. FAX: (212)960-0822. Pres. Richard Joel; Chair Bd. David I. Schachne; Dorothy and David I. Schachne Dean Dr. Sheldon R.

Gelman. Offers graduate programs in social work and Jewish communal service; grants MSW and PhD degrees and certificate in Jewish communal service. MSW programs are: Concurrent Plan, 2-year, full-time track, combining classroom study and supervised field instruction; Plan for Employed Persons (PEP), for people working in social agencies; Block Education Plan (Dir. Dr. Adele Weiner), which combines summer course work with regular-year field placement in local agencies; Clergy Plan, training in counseling for clergy of all denominations; Silvia and Irwin Leiferman Center for Professional Training in the Care of the Elderly. *Jewish Social Work Forum.*

———, (affiliate) YESHIVA OF LOS ANGELES (1977). 9760 W. Pico Blvd., Los Angeles, CA 90035-4701. (310)772-2424. FAX: (310)772-7661. E-mail: mhmay@ wiesenthal.com. Dean Rabbi Marvin Hier; Bd. Chmn. Samuel Belzberg; Dir. Academic Programs Rabbi Sholom Tendler. Affiliates are Yeshiva University High Schools of Los Angeles, Jewish Studies Institute and Kollel Torah MiTzion.

———, YESHIVA UNIVERSITY MUSEUM (see p. 617)

YESHIVAT CHOVEVEI TORAH (1999). 475 Riverside Drive, Suite 244., NYC 10015. (212)666-0036. FAX: (212) 666-5633. Dean Rabbi Avi Weiss. Dedicated to the training of open Orthodox rabbis who will lead the Jewish community and shape its spiritual and intellectual character in consonance with modern and open Orthodox values and commitments, emphasizing the encounter with classical Jewish texts not just as an intellectual exercise but as a form of divine service. (WWW.YC-TORAH.ORG)

SOCIAL, MUTUAL BENEFIT

ALPHA EPSILON PI FRATERNITY (1913). 8815 Wesleyan Rd., Indianapolis, IN 46268-1171. (317)876-1913. FAX: (317) 876-1057. E-mail: office@aepi.org. Internatl. Pres. Dr. Jay Levine; Exec. V.-Pres. Sidney N. Dunn. International Jewish fraternity active on over 100 campuses in the U.S. and Canada; encourages Jewish students to remain loyal to their heritage and to assume leadership roles in the community; active in behalf of the State of Israel and Magen David Adom among other causes. *The Lion of Alpha Epsilon Pi (quarterly magazine)*.

AMERICAN ASSOCIATION OF JEWS FROM THE FORMER USSR, INC. (AAJFSU) (1989). 100 Church Street, Suite 1608, NYC 10007. (212) 964-1946. FAX: (212)964-1946. E-mail: GeorgeZilberman@yahoo.com. Pres. Yury Zilberman; Bd. Chmn. Mark Gurevich. National not-for-profit, grassroots mutual assistance and refugee advocacy organization, which unites and represents interests of over 600,000 Russian speaking Jewish refugees and legal immigrants from the former Soviet Union. It has chapters and independent associations in seven states, including New York, Ohio, Colorado, New Jersey, Massachusetts, Wisconsin and Maryland. The national organization is a member of the National Immigration Forum and it is affiliated with the United Jewish Communities, Washington Action Office. It has become a founding member of the Jewish Community Relations Council of New York and the New York Immigration Coalition. Local Chapters work in cooperation with Jewish Federation and New York Chapter works in cooperation with JCRC, NYANA, HIAS and UJA-Federation of New York. The AAJFSU assists newcomers in their resettlement and vocational and cultural adjustment, fosters their Jewish identity and involvement in American civic and social affairs, fights anti-Semitism and violation of human rights in the FSU and the U.S. through cooperation with other human rights organizations and advocacy organizations, supports struggle of Israeli Jews for sustainable peace, collects money for Israeli victims of terror, provides assistance in social safety net and naturalization of the elderly and disabled, provides advocacy in cases of political asylum for victims of anti-Semitism in the FSU. *Chronicles of Anti-Semitism and Nationalism in Republics of the Former USSR (in English, annually); Information Bulletin (in Russian, quarterly)*.

AMERICAN FEDERATION OF JEWS FROM CENTRAL EUROPE, INC. (1938). 570 Seventh Ave., NYC 10018. (212)921-3871. FAX: (212) 575-1918. Pres. Fritz Weinschenk; Exec. Asst. Dennis E. Rohrbaugh. Seeks to safeguard the rights and interests of American Jews of German-speaking Central European descent, es-pecially in reference to restitution and indemnification; through its affiliate Research Foundation for Jewish Immigration sponsors research and publications on the history, immigration, and acculturation of Central European émigrés in the U.S. and worldwide; through its affiliate Jewish Philanthropic Fund of 1933 supports social programs for needy Nazi victims in the U.S.; undertakes cultural activities, publications; member, Council of Jews from Germany, London.

AMERICAN VETERANS OF ISRAEL (1951). 136 E. 39 St., NYC 10016. E-mail: spielgelsi@aol.com. Pres. Samuel Z. Klausner; V-Pres. David Kaplan. Maintains contact with American and Canadian volunteers who served in Aliyah Bet and/or Israel's War of Independence; promotes Israel's welfare; holds memorial services at grave of Col. David Marcus; is affiliated with World Mahal. *Newsletter*.

ASSOCIATION OF YUGOSLAV JEWS IN THE UNITED STATES, INC. (1941). 130 E. 59 St., Suite 1202, NYC 10022. (212)371-6891. V.-Pres. & Chmn. Emanuel Salom; Sec. Dr. Joseph Stock. Assistance to all Jews originally from Yugoslavia—Bosnia, Serbia, Croatia—and new settlers in Israel. *Bulletins*.

BNAI ZION—THE AMERICAN FRATERNAL ZIONIST ORGANIZATION (1908). 136 E. 39 St., NYC 10016. (212)725-1211. FAX: (212) 684-6327. Pres. Michael J. Lazar; Exec. V.-Pres. Mel Parness. Fosters principles of Americanism, fraternalism, and Zionism. The Bnai Zion Foundation supports various humanitarian projects in Israel and the USA, chiefly the Bnai Zion Medical Center in Haifa and homes for retarded children-Maon Bnai Zion in Rosh Ha'ayin and the Herman Z. Quittman Center in Jerusalem Ahava Project. Also supports building of new central library in Ma'aleh Adumim. In U.S. sponsors program of awards for excellence in Hebrew for high school and college students. Chapters all over U.S. *Bnai Zion Voice* (quarterly).(WWW.BNAIZION.COM)

BRITH ABRAHAM (1859; reorg. 1887). 136 E. 39 St., NYC 10016. (212)725-1211. FAX: (212)684-6327. Grand Master Robert Freeman. Protects Jewish rights and combats anti-Semitism; supports Soviet and Ethiopian emigration and the safety and dignity of Jews worldwide;

helps to support Bnai Zion Medical Center in Haifa and other Israeli institutions; aids and supports various programs and projects in the U.S.: Hebrew Excellence Program-Gold Medal presentation in high schools and colleges; Camp Loyaltown; Brith Abraham and Bnai Zion Foundations. *Voice.*

BRITH SHOLOM (1905). 3939 Conshohocken Ave., Philadelphia, PA 19131. (215)878-5696. FAX: (215) 878-5699. Pres. Seymour Rose; Exec. Dir. Roy Shenberg; Exec. V. P., Jerome Verlin. Fraternal organization devoted to community welfare, protection of rights of Jewish people, and activities that foster Jewish identity and provide support for Israel. Through its philanthropic arm, the Brith Sholom Foundation (1962), sponsors Brith Sholom House in Philadelphia, nonprofit senior-citizen apartments; and Brith Sholom Beit Halochem in Haifa, Israel, rehabilitation, social, and sports center for disabled Israeli veterans, operated by Zahal. Chmn. Martin Winit; Exec. Dir. Saundra Laub. *Brith Sholom Digest; monthly news bulletin.*

FREE SONS OF ISRAEL (1849). 250 Fifth Ave., Suite 201, NYC 10001. (212)725-3690. FAX: (212)725-5874. Grand Master Arlene Hoberman Kyler; Grand Sec. Ronald J. Laszlo. Oldest Jewish fraternal-benefit society in U.S. Affordable membership men & women (18+). Supports Israel, UJA projects, non-sectarian toy drives/philanthropies. Social Action fights anti-Semitism, supports human rights. Member benefits-IBM Metro Credit Union, scholarships, cemetery, discounted Long Term Care Insurance, educational and social functions, Free Model Seder. *Free Sons Reporter.* (WWW.FREESONS.ORG)

JEWISH LABOR BUND (Directed by WORLD COORDINATING COMMITTEE OF THE BUND) (1897; reorg. 1947). 25 E. 21 St., NYC 10010. (212)475-0059. FAX: (212) 473-5102. Acting Pres. Motl Zelmanowics; Sec. Gen. Benjamin Nade. Coordinates activities of Bund organizations throughout the world and represents them in the Socialist International; spreads the ideas of socialism as formulated by the Jewish Labor Bund; publishes books and periodicals on world problems, Jewish life, socialist theory and policy, and on the history, activities, and ideology of the Jewish Labor Bund. *Unser*

Tsait (U.S.); *Lebns-Fragn* (Israel); *Unser Gedank* (Australia).

SEPHARDIC JEWISH BROTHERHOOD OF AMERICA, INC. (1915). 97-45 Queens Blvd., Rm. 610, Rego Park, NY 11374. (718)459-1600. Pres. Bernard Ouziel; Sec. Irving Barocas. A benevolent fraternal organization seeking to promote the industrial, social, educational, and religious welfare of its members. *Sephardic Brother.*

SIGMA ALPHA MU FRATERNITY *(1909).* 9245 No. Meridian St., Ste. 105, Indianapolis, IN 46260. (317)846-0600. FAX: (317)846-9462. E-mail: samhq@sam.org. Sup. Prior Leland P.Manders; Exec. Dir. Aaron M. Girson. Founded at the City College of NY as a fraternity of Jewish men, currently active on 70 campuses across North America. Encourages students to take an active role on campus, offers leadership opportunities and financial aid to members and scholarships to leaders of Jewish youth groups. *Octogonian of Sigma Alpha Mu (quarterly).*

WORKMEN'S CIRCLE/ARBETER RING (1900). 45 E. 33 St., NYC 10016. (212)889-6800. FAX: (212)532-7518. E-mail: member@circle.org. Pres. Martin Krupnick; Exec. Dir. Robert Kestenbaum. Fosters Jewish identity and participation in Jewish life through Jewish, especially Yiddish, culture and education, friendship, mutual aid, and the pursuit of social and economic justice. Offices are located throughout the U.S. and Canada. Member services include: Jewish cultural seminars, concerts, theater, Jewish schools, children's camp and adult resort, fraternal and singles activities, a Jewish Book Center, public affairs/social action, health insurance plans, medical/dental/legal services, life insurance plans, cemetery/funeral benefits, social services, geriatric homes and centers, and travel services. *The Call.* (WWW.CIRCLE.ORG)

ZETA BETA TAU FRATERNITY (1898). 3905 Vincennes Rd., Suite 300, Indianapolis, IN 46268. (317)334-1898. FAX: (317)334-1899. E-mail: zbt@zbtnational.org. Pres. Kenneth L. Simon, M.D.; Exec. Dir. Jonathan I. Yulish. Oldest historically Jewish fraternity; promotes intellectual awareness, social responsibility, integrity, and brotherhood among over 5,000 undergrads and 110,000 alumni in the U.S. and Canada. Encourages leadership and diversity through mutual respect of all heritages; nonsectarian since 1954. A brotherhood of Kappa Nu, Phi Alpha, Phi Epsilon Pi, Phi Sigma Delta, Zeta Beta Tau. *The Deltan (quarterly).* (WWW.ZBT.ORG)

SOCIAL WELFARE

AMC CANCER RESEARCH CENTER (formerly JEWISH CONSUMPTIVES' RELIEF SOCIETY, 1904; incorporated as American Medical Center at Denver, 1954). 1600 Pierce St., Denver, CO 80214. (303)233-6501. FAX: (303)239-3400. E-mail: edelmanj@amc.org. Pres./CEO Bob R. Baker; Exec. V-Pres. Research Dr. Tom Slaga. A nationally recognized leader in the fight against cancer; employs a three-pronged, interdisciplinary approach that combines laboratory, clinical, and community cancer-control research to advance the prevention, early detection, diagnosis, and treatment of the disease. The exclusive scientific focus of our work is the prevention and control of cancer and other major diseases. *The Quest for Answers; Annual Report.* (WWW.AMC.ORG)

AMCHA FOR TSEDAKAH (1990). 9800 Cherry Hill Rd., College Park, MD 20740. (301)937-2600. Pres. Rabbi Bruce E. Kahn. Solicits and distributes contributions to Jewish charitable organizations in the U.S. and Israel; accredits organizations which serve an important tsedakah purpose, demonstrate efficiency and fiscal integrity, and also support pluralism. Contributors are encouraged to earmark contributions for specific organizations; all contributions to General Fund are forwarded to the charitable institutions, as operating expenses are covered by a separate fund. *Newspaper supplement.*

AMERICAN JEWISH CORRECTIONAL CHAPLAINS ASSOCIATION, INC. (formerly NATIONAL COUNCIL OF JEWISH PRISON CHAPLAINS) (1937). 10 E. 73 St., NYC 10021-4194. (212)879-8415. FAX: (212) 772-3977. (Cooperates with the New York Board of Rabbis.) Supports spiritual, moral, and social services for Jewish men and women in corrections; stimulates support of correctional chaplaincy; provides spiritual and professional fellowship for Jewish correctional chaplains; promotes sound standards for correctional chaplaincy; schedules workshops and research to aid chaplains in counseling and with

religious services for Jewish inmates. Constituent, American Correctional Chaplains Association. *Chaplains Manual.*

AMERICAN JEWISH SOCIETY FOR SERVICE, INC. (1950). 15 E. 26 St., Rm. 1029, NYC 10010. (212)683-6178. Email: aud1750@aol.com. Founder/Chmn. Henry Kohn; Pres. Lawrence G. Green; Exec. Dirs. Carl & Audrey Brenner. Conducts voluntary work-service camps each summer to enable high school juniors and seniors to perform humanitarian service.

ASSOCIATION OF JEWISH AGING SERVICES (formerly NORTH AMERICAN ASSOCIATION OF JEWISH HOMES AND HOUSING FOR THE AGING) (1960). 316 Pennsylvania Ave., SE, Suite 402, Washington, DC 20003. (202) 543-7500. FAX: (202)543-4090. E-mail: ajas@ajas.org. Pres. Jodi L. Lyons; Chmn. Michael Ellentuck. Represents nearly all the not-for-profit charitable homes and housing for the Jewish aging; promotes excellence in performance and quality of service through fostering communication and education and encouraging advocacy for the aging; conducts annual conferences and institutes. *Directory; The Scribe (quarterly newsletter).*

ASSOCIATION OF JEWISH CENTER PROFESSIONALS (1918). 15 E. 26 St., NYC 10010-1579. (212)532-4949. FAX: (212) 481-4174. E-mail: ajcp@jcca.org. Pres. Susan Bender; Exec. Dir. Harvey Rosenzweig. Seeks to enhance the standards, techniques, practices, scope, and public understanding of Jewish community center professionals and kindred agency work. *Kesher.*

ASSOCIATION OF JEWISH COMMUNITY ORGANIZATION PERSONNEL (AJCOP) (1969). 14619 Horseshoe Trace, Wellington, FL 33414. (561)795-4853. FAX: (561)798-0358. E-mail: marlene@ajcop.org. Pres. Rabbi Daniel Allen; Exec. Dir. Louis B. Solomon. An organization of professionals engaged in areas of fund-raising, endowments, budgeting, social planning, financing, administration, and coordination of services. Objectives are to develop and enhance professional practices in Jewish communal work; to maintain and improve standards, practices, scope, and public understanding of the field of community organization, as practiced through local federations, national agencies, other organizations, settings, and private practitioners. *Prolog (quarterly newspaper); Proceedings (annual record of papers and speeches).* (WWW.AJCOP.ORG)

ASSOCIATION OF JEWISH FAMILY AND CHILDREN'S AGENCIES (1972). 620 Cranbury Rd., Suite 102, E. Brunswick, NJ 08816-5419. (800) 634-7346. FAX: (732)432-7127. E-mail: ajfca@ajfca.org. Pres. Bert J. Goldberg; Bd. Chair. Lawrence Abramson. The national service organization for Jewish family and children's agencies in the U.S. and Canada. Reinforces member agencies in their efforts to sustain and enhance the quality of Jewish family and communal life. Operates the Elder Support Network for the national Jewish community. *Tachlis (quarterly); Professional Opportunities Bulletin; Executive Digest (monthly).* (WWW.AJFCA.ORG)

AVODAH: THE JEWISH SERVICE CORPS (1996). 116 East 27th Street,. 10th Floor, NYC 10016. (212)545-7759. FAX: (212)686-1353. E-mail: info@avodah.net. Exec. Dir. Rabbi David Rosenn. Combines direct antipoverty work in NYC and Washington D.C. with Jewish study and community-building; corps members live together and work full-time for a year on housing, welfare, and education, and other matters. (WWW.AVODAH.NET)

BARON DE HIRSCH FUND (1891). 130 E. 59 St., 12th fl., NYC 10022. (212)836-1358. FAX: (212)453-6512. Pres. Jenny Morgenthal; Mng. Dir. Lauren Katzowitz. Aids Jewish immigrants in the U.S. and Israel by giving grants to agencies active in resettlement, focusing on educational, community development, and vocational training.

B'NAI B'RITH (1843). 2020 K St., NW, Washington, DC 20006. (202)857-6600. FAX: (202)857-2700. Pres. Moishe Smith; Exec. V.-Pres. Daniel S. Mariaschin. International Jewish organization, with affiliates in 58 countries. Offers programs designed to ensure the preservation of Jewry and Judaism: Jewish education, community volunteer service, expansion of human rights, assistance to Israel, housing for the elderly, leadership training, rights of Jews in all countries to study their heritage. *International Jewish Monthly; B'nai B'rith Today.* (WWW.BNAIBRITH.ORG)

———, ANTI-DEFAMATION LEAGUE OF (see p. 606)

———, HILLEL (see p. 636)

———, KLUTZNICK MUSEUM (see p. 611)

———, YOUTH ORGANIZATION (see p. 635)

CITY OF HOPE NATIONAL MEDICAL CENTER AND BECKMAN RESEARCH INSTITUTE (1913). 1500 E. Duarte Rd., Duarte, CA 91010. (626)359-8111. FAX: (626) 301-8115. E-mail: dhalper@coh.org. Exec. V. P. Krontiris; Medical and Scientific Affairs Theodore. City of Hope is one of the world's leading research and treatment centers for cancer and other life-threatening diseases, including diabetes and HIV/AIDS. A pioneer in the fields of bone marrow transplantation and genetics, City of Hope is a Comprehensive Cancer Center, the highest designation bestowed by the National Cancer Institute, and a founding member of the National Comprehensive Cancer Network. *City of Hope Cancer Research Center Report.*

CONFERENCE OF JEWISH COMMUNAL SERVICE (*see* JEWISH COMMUNAL SERVICE ASSOCIATION OF N. AMERICA)

COUNCIL OF JEWISH FEDERATIONS (*see* UNITED JEWISH COMMUNITIES)

INTERNATIONAL ASSOCIATION OF JEWISH VOCATIONAL SERVICES (formerly JEWISH OCCUPATIONAL COUNCIL) (1939). 1845 Walnut St., Suite 640, Philadelphia, PA 19103. (215) 854-0233. FAX: (215)854-0212. E-mail: coheng@iajvs.org. Exec. Dir. Genie Cohen; Vivian Seigel, President. Not-for-profit membership association of Jewish-sponsored social service agencies in the U.S., Canada, and Israel. Provides member agencies with technical, informational, and communications support; researches funding opportunities, develops collaborative program models, and represents Jewish vocational network nationally and internationally. Sponsors annual conference for members. Member agencies provide a wide range of educational, vocational, and rehabilitation services to both the Jewish and non-Jewish communities. *Executive quarterly newsletter.* (WWW.IAJVS.ORG)

INTERNATIONAL COUNCIL ON JEWISH SOCIAL AND WELFARE SERVICES (1961). c/o American Jewish Joint Distribution Committee, 711 Third Ave., NYC 10017. (NY liaison office with UN headquarters.) (212)687-6200. FAX: (212)370-5467. E-mail: newyork@jdcny.org. Pres. Eugene J. Ribokoff; Exec. V. P. Steven Schwager. Provides assistance to Jewish communities in Europe, Asia, Africa, and the Mideast, including welfare programs for Jews in need. Current concerns include: Rescuing Jews from areas of distress, facilitating community development in the former Soviet Union; helping to meet Israel's social service needs by developing innovative programs that create new opportunities for the country's most vulnerable populations; youth activities in Eastern Europe and nonsectariean development and disaster assistance. *Annual Report, JDC's Activities in the Former Soviet Union; JDC: One People One Heart, Crisis in Argentina Monthly Update.*

JBI INTERNATIONAL (FOUNDED IN 1931 AS THE JEWISH BRAILLE INSTITUTE OF AMERICA, INC.) (1931). 110 E. 30 St., NYC 10016. (212)889-2525. FAX: (212)689-3692. E-mail: sradinsky@jbilibrary.org. Pres. Dr. Ellen Isler; Exec. V.-Pres. Israel A. Taub. Provides Jewish books for the visually impaired, blind and reading-disabled on tape, in large print, and in Braille. International program serves clients in more than 50 countries; sponsors special programs in Israel and Eastern Europe. Periodical and journals available to our subscribers include *Moment, Tikkun, the Jerusalem Reporter and Commentary.* (WWW.JBILIBRARY.ORG)

JEWISH CHILDREN'S ADOPTION NETWORK (1990). PO Box 147016, Denver, CO 80214-7016. (303)573-8113. FAX: (303)893-1447. E-mail: jcan@qwest.net. Pres. Stephen Krausz; Exec. Dir. Vicki Krausz. An adoption exchange founded for the primary purpose of locating adoptive families for Jewish infants and children. Works with some 200 children a year, throughout N. Amer., 85-90% of whom have special needs. No fees charged for services, which include birth-parent and adoptive-parent counseling. *Quarterly newsletter.* (WWW.USERS.QWEST.NET/JCAN)

JEWISH COMMUNAL SERVICE ASSOCIATION OF N. AMERICA (1899; formerly CONFERENCE OF JEWISH COMMUNAL SERVICE). 15 E. 26 St., Suite 917, NYC 10010-1579. (212)532-0167. FAX: (212)532-1461. E-mail: info@jcsana.org. Pres. Dr. Audrey S. Weiner; Exec. Dir. Brenda Gevertz. Serves as forum for all professional philosophies in community service, for testing new experiences, proposing new ideas, and questioning or reaffirming old concepts; umbrella organization for 7 major Jewish communal service groups. Concerned with advancement of professional personnel practices and standards. *Journal of Jewish Communal Service; Concurrents.*

JEWISH COMMUNITY CENTERS ASSOCIATION OF NORTH AMERICA (formerly JWB) (1917). 520 Eighth Avenue., NYC 10018. (212)532-4949. FAX: (212)481-4174. E-mail: info@jcca.org. Chair Edward H. Kaplan; Pres. Allan Finkelstein. The leadership network of, and central agency for, the Jewish Community Center movement, comprising more than 275 JCCs, YM-YWHAs, and camps in the U.S. and Canada, which annually serve more than one million members and an additional million non-member users. JCC Association offers a wide range of services and resources to strengthen the capacity of its affiliates to provide educational, cultural, social, Jewish identity-building, and recreational programs to enhance the lives of North American Jews of all ages and backgrounds. Additionally, the movement fosters and strengthens connections between North American Jews and Israel as well as with world Jewry. JCC Association is also the only U.S. government-accredited agency for serving the religious and social needs of Jewish military personnel, their families, and patients in VA hospitals through JWB Chaplains Council. *JCC Circle; Chaplines; other newsletters for JCC professiona*ls. (www.JCCA.ORG)

———, JEWISH WELFARE BOARD JEWISH CHAPLAINS COUNCIL (formerly COMMISSION ON JEWISH CHAPLAINCY) (1940). 15 E. 26 St., NYC 10010-1579. (212)532-4949. FAX: (212)481-4174. E-mail: nathanlandman@jcca.com. Chmn. Rabbi David S. Goldstein; Dir. Rabbi David Lapp; Dep. Dir. Rabbi Nathan M. Landman. Recruits, endorses, and serves Jewish military and Veterans Administration chaplains on behalf of the American Jewish community and the major rabbinic bodies; trains and assists Jewish lay leaders where there are no chaplains, for service to Jewish military personnel, their families, and hospitalized veterans. *CHAPLINES newsletter.*

JEWISH FAMILY AND CHILDREN'S PROFESSIONALS ASSOCIATION (*see* Jewish Social Services Professionals Association)

JEWISH FUND FOR JUSTICE (1984). 330 7th Avenue, Suite 1902, NYC 10001. (212) 213-2113. FAX: (212)213-2233. E-mail: jfjustice@jfjustice.org. Bd. Chmn. John Levy; Exec. Dir. Marlene Provizer. The Jewish Fund for Justice is the only national Jewish organization solely committed to fighting the injustice of poverty in America. By assisting on a non-denominational basis grassroots organizations struggling for decent housing, schools and jobs, and by helping Jews develop community-based, social justice partnerships, the Jewish Fund for Justice brings to life the core Jewish values of *tikkun olam* (repair of the world) and *tzedakah* (righteous giving). Giving opportunities include general support, family, wedding, and youth endowment funds and planned giving. *Annual report, newsletter.* (WWW.JEWISHJUSTICE. ORG)

JEWISH FUNDERS NETWORK (1990). 15 E. 26 St., Suite 1038, NYC 10010. (212) 726-0177. FAX: (212) 726-0195. E-mail: jfn@jfunders.org. Pres. Mark Charendoff. International agency providing leadership, programs and services to help Jewish grantmakers be more effective and strategic in their philanthropy. JFN members collaborate and plan so that their money can be used to effectively change the world. Key initiatives: International Conference, regional programs, publications, strategic partnerships, web site, consultation, resources and referral. *Quarterly Newsletter, Reports on Philanthropy.*

JEWISH SOCIAL SERVICES PROFESSIONALS ASSOCIATION (JSSPA) (1965). c/o AJFCA, 620 Cranbury Rd., Suite 102, E. Brunswick, NJ 08816-0549. (800) 634-7346. FAX: (732)432-7127. E-mail: ajfca@ajfca. org. Chmn. Jaclynn Faffer; Chair Elect Norman Keane. Brings together executives, supervisors, managers, caseworkers, and related professionals in Jewish Family Service and related agencies. Seeks to enhance professional skills, improve personnel standards, further Jewish continuity and identity, and strengthen Jewish family life. Provides a national and regional forum for professional discussion and learning; functions under the auspices of the Association

of Jewish Family and Children's Agencies. *Newsletter.* (WWW.AJFCA.ORG)

JEWISH WOMEN INTERNATIONAL (1897). 2000 M. Street, NW Suite 207, Washington, DC 20036. (202)857-1300. FAX: (202)857-1380. E-mail: jwi@jwi.org. Pres. Barbara Rabkin; Exec. Dir. Gail Rubinson. Jewish Women International breaks the cycle of violence by developing emotionally healthy adults, empowering women and strengthening families. Jewish Women International accomplishes its goals through direct service programs, education, advocacy and the promotion of "best practice" models. Offers programs in the United States, Canada, and Israel. *Jewish Woman Magazine (quarterly).* (WWW.JEWISHWOMEN.ORG)

JWB (*SEE* JEWISH COMMUNITY CENTERS ASSOCIATION OF NORTH AMERICA)

LEVI HOSPITAL (1914). 300 Prospect Ave., Hot Springs, AR 71901. (501)624-1281. FAX: (501) 622-3500. E-mail: levihospital @hsnp.com. Pres. Philip M. Clay; Admin. Patrick G. McCabe. Offers outpatient rehab, including therapy sessions in large thermal heated pool. Other programs: adult/geriatric inpatient and outpatient psychiatric program, child/adolescent psychiatric clinic, hospice care, home health care, osteoporosis clinic, Levi Rehabilitation Unit, a cooperative effort of Levi and St. Joseph's hospitals (inpatient rehab). *The Progress Chart; The Legacy.*

MAZON: A JEWISH RESPONSE TO HUNGER (1985). 1990 S. Bondy Drive, Suite 260, Los Angeles, CA 90025. (310)442-0020. FAX: (310)442-0030. E-mail: mazonmail@mazon.org. Exec. Dir. Eric Schockman, PhD. A grant-making and fund-raising organization that raises funds in the Jewish community and provides grants to nonprofit 501(c)(3) organizations which aim to prevent and alleviate hunger in the United States and abroad. Grantees include food pantries, food banks, multi-service organizations, advocacy, education and research projects, and international relief and development organizations. *Annual Report, 2 newsletters each year.*

NATIONAL ASSOCIATION OF JEWISH CHAPLAINS (1988). 901 Route 10, Whippany, NJ 07981. (973)929-3168. FAX: (973) 736-9193. E-mail: cecille3@juno.com.

Pres. Rabbi Stephen Roberts; Natl. Coord. Cecille Allman Asekoff. A professional organization for people functioning as Jewish chaplains in hospitals, nursing homes, geriatric, psychiatric, correctional, and military facilities. Provides collegial support, continuing education, professional certification, and resources for the Jewish community on issues of pastoral and spiritual care. *The Jewish Chaplain.*

NATIONAL COUNCIL OF JEWISH PRISON CHAPLAINS, INC. (*see* AMERICAN JEWISH CORRECTIONAL CHAPLAINS ASSOCIATION, INC.)

NATIONAL COUNCIL OF JEWISH WOMEN (1893). 53 W. 23 St., NYC 10010. (212) 645-4048. FAX: (212)645-7466. E-mail: actionline@ncjw.org. Pres. Phyllis Snyder; Exec. Dir. Stacy Kass. Works to improve the lives of women, children, and families in the United States and Israel; strives to insure individual rights and freedoms for all. NCJW volunteers deliver vital services in 500 U.S. communities and carry out NCJW's advocacy agenda through a powerful grassroots network. *NCJW Journal; Washington Newsletter.*(www. NCJW.ORG)

NATIONAL INSTITUTE FOR JEWISH HOSPICE (1985). PO Box 48025, Los Angeles, CA 90048. (800)446-4448. 330 Broad Ave., Englewood, NJ 07631. (201)816-7324. FAX: (201)816-7321. Pres. Rabbi Maurice Lamm; Exec. Dir. Shirley Lamm. Serves as a national Jewish hospice resource center. Through conferences, research, publications, referrals, and counseling services offers guidance, training, and information to patients, family members, clergy of all faiths, professional caregivers, and volunteers who work with the Jewish terminally ill. *Jewish Hospice Times.*

NATIONAL JEWISH CHILDREN'S LEUKEMIA FOUNDATION (1990). 7316 Avenue U, Brooklyn NY 11234. (718)-251-1222. FAX: (718)-251-1444. E-mail: info@leukemiafoundatin.org. Pres./Founder Zvi Shor. Dedicated to saving the lives of children. Programs: Bone Marrow Donor Search, Stem Cell Banking-freezing cells from babies' umbilical cords for long-term storage, in case of need for bone marrow; Make-A-Dream-Come True-granting wishes for terminally ill children; Referral Service;

Patient Advocacy. (WWW.LEUKEMIAFOUNDATION.ORG)

NATIONAL JEWISH MEDICAL AND RESEARCH CENTER (formerly NATIONAL JEWISH HOSPITAL/NATIONAL ASTHMA CENTER) (1899). 1400 Jackson St., Denver, CO 80206. (800)222-LUNG. E-mail: lungline@njc.org. Pres./CEO Michael Salem, MD; Bd. Chmn. Steve Arent. The only medical and research center in the United States devoted entirely to respiratory, allergic, and immune system diseases, including asthma, tuberculosis, emphysema, severe allergies, AIDS, and cancer, and autoimmune diseases such as lupus. Dedicated to enhancing prevention, treatment, and cures through research, and to developing and providing innovative clinical programs for treating patients regardless of age, religion, race, or ability to pay. *New Directions; Medical Scientific Update.*(WWW.NATIONALJEWISH. ORG)

NORTH AMERICAN ASSOCIATION OF JEWISH HOMES AND HOUSING FOR THE AGING (*see* ASSOCIATION OF JEWISH AGING SERVICES)

UNITED JEWISH COMMUNITIES (*see* p. 633)

UNITED ORDER TRUE SISTERS, INC. (UOTS) (1846) Linton International Plaza, 660 Linton Blvd.-Ste. 6, Delray Beach, FL 33444 (561)-265-1557. Pres. Marion Polonsky; Fin. Sec. Betty Peyser; Treas. Rose Goldberg. Charitable, community service, especially home supplies, etc., for indigent cancer victims; supports camps for children with cancer. *Inside UotS.* (WWW.UOTS.ORG)

WORLD COUNCIL OF JEWISH COMMUNAL SERVICE (1966; reorg. 1994). 711 Third Ave., 10th fl., NYC 10017. (212)687-6200. FAX: (212)370-5467. Pres. Howard Charish; Assoc. Pres. Dr. Jack Habib; Exec. V.-Pres. Theodore Comet. Seeks to build Jewish community worldwide by enhancing professional-to-professional connections, improving professional practice through interchange of experience and sharing of expertise, fostering professional training programs, and stimulating research. Conducts quadrennial conferences in Jerusalem and periodic regional meetings. *Proceedings of international conferences; newsletters.*

PROFESSIONAL ASSOCIATIONS*

AMERICAN ASSOCIATION OF RABBIS (Religious, Educational)

AMERICAN CONFERENCE OF CANTORS, UNION FOR REFORM JUDAISM (Religious, Educational)

AMERICAN JEWISH CORRECTIONAL CHAPLAINS ASSOCIATION, INC. (Social Welfare)

AMERICAN JEWISH PRESS ASSOCIATION (Cultural)

AMERICAN JEWISH PUBLIC RELATIONS SOCIETY (Community Relations)

ASSOCIATION OF HILLEL/JEWISH CAMPUS PROFESSIONALS (Religious, Educational)

ASSOCIATION OF JEWISH CENTER PROFESSIONALS (Social Welfare)

ASSOCIATION OF JEWISH COMMUNITY ORGANIZATION PERSONNEL (Social Welfare)

ASSOCIATION OF JEWISH COMMUNITY RELATIONS WORKERS (Community Relations)

CANTORS ASSEMBLY (Religious, Educational)

CENTRAL CONFERENCE OF AMERICAN RABBIS (Religious, Educational)

COUNCIL OF JEWISH ORGANIZATIONS IN CIVIL SERVICE (Community Relations)

INTERNATIONAL JEWISH MEDIA ASSOCIATION (Cultural)

JEWISH CHAPLAINS COUNCIL, JWB (Social Welfare)

JEWISH COMMUNAL SERVICE ASSOCIATION OF N. AMERICA (Social Welfare)

JEWISH EDUCATORS ASSEMBLY, UNITED SYNAGOGUE OF CONSERVATIVE JUDAISM (Religious, Educational)

JEWISH SOCIAL SERVICES PROFESSIONALS ASSOCIATION (Social Welfare)

JEWISH TEACHERS ASSOCIATION–MORIM (Religious, Educational)

NATIONAL ASSOCIATION OF HEBREW DAY SCHOOL ADMINISTRATORS, TORAH UMESORAH (Religious, Educational)

NATIONAL ASSOCIATION OF JEWISH CHAPLAINS (Social Welfare)

NATIONAL ASSOCIATION OF TEMPLE ADMINISTRATORS, UNION FOR REFORM JUDAISM (Religious, Educational)

NATIONAL ASSOCIATION OF TEMPLE EDUCATORS, UNION FOR REFORM JUDAISM (Religious, Educational)

NATIONAL CONFERENCE OF YESHIVA PRINCIPALS, TORAH UMESORAH (Religious, Educational)

NORTH AMERICAN ASSOCIATION OF SYNAGOGUE EXECUTIVES, UNITED SYNAGOGUE OF CONSERVATIVE JUDAISM (Religious, Educational)

RABBINICAL ALLIANCE OF AMERICA (Religious, Educational)

RABBINICAL ASSEMBLY (Religious, Educational)

RABBINICAL COUNCIL OF AMERICA (Religious, Educational)

RECONSTRUCTIONIST RABBINICAL ASSOCIATION (Religious, Educational)

UNION OF ORTHODOX RABBIS OF THE U.S. AND CANADA (Religious, Educational)

WORLD CONFERENCE OF JEWISH COMMUNAL SERVICE (Community Relations)

WOMEN'S ORGANIZATIONS*

AMIT WOMEN (Israel-Related)

BRANDEIS UNIVERSITY NATIONAL WOMEN'S COMMITTEE (Educational)

EMUNAH WOMEN OF AMERICA (Israel-Related)

HADASSAH, THE WOMEN'S ZIONIST ORGANIZATION OF AMERICA (Israel-Related)

JEWISH WOMEN INTERNATIONAL (Social Welfare)

JEWISH ORTHODOX FEMINIST ALLIANCE (Reliigous, Educational)

NA'AMAT USA, THE WOMEN'S LABOR ZIONIST ORGANIZATION OF AMERICA (Israel-Related)

NATIONAL COUNCIL OF JEWISH WOMEN (Social Welfare)

UOTS (Social Welfare)

Women of Reform Judaism—Federation of Temple Sisterhoods, Union for Reform Judaism (Religious, Educational)

---

*For fuller listings see under category in parentheses

WOMEN'S AMERICAN ORT, ORT AMERICA (Overseas Aid)

WOMEN'S BRANCH OF THE UNION OF ORTHODOX JEWISH CONGREGATIONS OF AMERICA (Religious, Educational)

WOMEN'S DIVISION OF POALE AGUDATH ISRAEL OF AMERICA (Israel-Related)

WOMEN'S LEAGUE FOR CONSERVATIVE JUDAISM (Religious, Educational)

WOMEN'S LEAGUE FOR ISRAEL, INC. (Israel-Related)

WOMEN'S ORGANIZATION, YESHIVA UNIVERSITY (Religious, Educational)

YOUTH AND STUDENT ORGANIZATIONS*

AGUDATH ISRAEL OF AMERICA (Religious, Educational)

B'NAI B'RITH YOUTH ORGANIZATION (Religious, Educational)

BNEI AKIVA OF NORTH AMERICA, RELIGIOUS ZIONISTS OF AMERICA (Israel-Related)

HABONIM—DROR NORTH AMERICA (Israel-Related)

HASHOMER HATZAIR, SOCIALIST ZIONIST YOUTH MOVEMENT (Israel-Related)

HILLEL (Religious, Educational)

KADIMA, UNITED SYNAGOGUE OF CONSERVATIVE JUDAISM (Religious, Educational)

NATIONAL CONFERENCE OF SYNAGOGUE YOUTH, UNION OF ORTHODOX JEWISH CONGREGATIONS OF AMERICA (Religious, Educational)

NATIONAL JEWISH COMMITTEE ON SCOUTING (Religious, Educational)

NATIONAL JEWISH GIRL SCOUT COMMITTEE (Religious, Educational)

NORTH AMERICAN ALLIANCE FOR JEWISH YOUTH (Religious, Educational)

NORTH AMERICAN FEDERATION OF TEMPLE YOUTH, UNION FOR REFORM JUDAISM (Religious, Educational)

STUDENT STRUGGLE FOR SOVIET JEWRY— see CENTER FOR RUSSIAN JEWRY (Community Relations)

YOUNG JUDAEA/HASHACHAR, HADASSAH (Israel-Related)

YUGNTRUF–YOUTH FOR YIDDISH (Cultural)

CANADA

AISH HATORAH (1981). 949 Clark Ave., W., Thornhill, ONT L4J8G6. (905)764-1818. FAX: (905)764-1606. E-mail: www. Aish.com. Edu. Dir. Rabbi Ahron Hoch; Dr. Allan Seidenfeld. An educational center, a community center, and a network of synagogues throughout Toronto; seeks to reawaken Jewish values, ignite Jewish pride and promote Jewish unity through education; reaches out to Jews from all backgrounds in a friendly, warm and nonjudgmental environment. *Shabbat Shalom Fax, Monthly newsletter-Village Shul, Winter, Spring, Summer, Fall Calendars.* (www. AISH.EDU)

B'NAI BRITH CANADA (1875). 15 Hove St., Downsview, ONT M3H 4Y8. (416) 633-6224. FAX: (416)630-2159. E-mail: fdimant@bnaibrith.ca. Pres. Rochelle Wilner; Exec. V.-Pres. Frank Dimant. Canadian Jewry's major advocacy and service organization; maintains an office of Government Relations in Ottawa and co-sponsors the Canada Israel Committee; makes representations to all levels of government on matters of Jewish concern; promotes humanitarian causes and educational programs, community projects, adult Jewish education, and leadership development; dedicated to the preservation and unity of the Jewish community in Canada and to human rights. *The Jewish Tribune.*

———, INSTITUTE FOR INTERNATIONAL AFFAIRS (1987). E-mail: institute@bnaibrith.ca. Ch. Rochelle Wilner; Natl. Dir. Ruth Klein. Identifies and protests the abuse of human rights worldwide. Advocates on behalf of Israel and Jewish communities in distress. Monitors national and international legislation dealing with war crimes. Activities include briefs and consultations with governmental and non-governmental organizations, research and public education, advocacy and community mobilization, media monitoring, and international conferences and fact-finding missions. *Ad hoc publications on human rights issues.*

*For fuller listings see under category in parentheses

———, LEAGUE FOR HUMAN RIGHTS (1964). Co-Chmn. Marvin Kurz & Dr Harriet Morris. National volunteer association dedicated to combating racism, bigotry, and anti-Semitism. Educational programs include multicultural antiracist workshops, public speakers, Holocaust education, Media Human Rights Awards; legal and legislative activity includes government submissions, court interventions, monitoring hate-group activity, responding to incidents of racism and anti-Semitism; community liaison includes intergroup dialogue and support for aggrieved vulnerable communities and groups. Canadian distributor of ADL material. *Heritage Front Report: 1994; Anti-Semitism on Campus; Skinheads in Canada; Annual Audit of Anti-Semitic Incidents; Holocaust and Hope Educators' Newsletter; Combatting Hate: Guidelines for Community Action.*

———, NATIONAL FIELD SERVICES DEPARTMENT. Natl. Dir. Pearl Gladman. Services community affordable housing projects, sports leagues, food baskets for the needy; coordinates hands-on national volunteer programming, Tel-Aide Distress Line; responsible for lodge membership; direct-mail campaigns, annual convention and foundation dinners.

CANADIAN FRIENDS OF CALI & AMAL (1944). 7005 Kildare Rd., Suite 14, Côte St. Luc, Quebec, H4W 1C1. (514)484-9430. FAX: (514)484-0968. Pres. Harry J.F. Bloomfield, QC; Exec. Dir. Fran Kula. Incorporates Canadian Association for Labour Israel (Histadrut) and Canadian Friends of Amal; supports comprehensive health care and education in Israel. Helps to provide modern medical and surgical facilities and the finest vocational, technical education to the Israeli people of all ages.

CANADIAN FRIENDS OF THE HEBREW UNIVERSITY OF JERUSALEM (1944). 3080 Yonge St., Suite 5024, Toronto, ONT M4N 3N1. (416) 485-8000. FAX: (416) 485-8565. E-mail: inquiry@cfhu.org. Pres. Ronald Appleby; Natl. Dir. Charles S. Diamond. Represents the Hebrew University of Jerusalem in Canada; serves as fund-raising arm for the university in Canada; recruits Canadian students and promotes study programs for foreign students at the university; sponsors social and educational events across Canada.

CANADIAN JEWISH CONGRESS (1919; reorg. 1934). 100 Sparks Street, Suite 650, Ottawa, Ontario K1P 5B7. (613)233-8703. FAX: (613)233-8748. E-mail: canadianjewishcongress@cjc.ca. Co-pres. Sylvain Abitbol & Rabbi Reuven Bulka. The community's national voice on public affairs, Canadian Jewish Congress works with governments, community organizations and other partners to fight antisemitism and racism, to promote positive links to Israel and to other Jewish communities, and to support humanitarian and human rights efforts. *DAIS; National Archives Newsletter; regional newsletters.*

CANADIAN YOUNG JUDAEA (1917). 788 Marlee Ave., Suite 205, Toronto, ONT M6B 3K1. (416)781-5156. FAX: (416) 787-3100. E-mail: cyj@idirect.com. Natl. Exec. Dir. Risa Epstein. Strives to attract Jewish youth to Zionism, with goal of aliyah; educates youth about Jewish history and Zionism; prepares them to provide leadership in Young Judaea camps in Canada and Israel and to be concerned Jews. *Judaean L'Madrich; Young Judaean.*

CANADIAN ZIONIST FEDERATION (1967). 5151 Côte St. Catherine Rd., #206, Montreal, PQ H3W 1M6. (514)739-7300. FAX: (514)739-9412. Pres. Kurt Rothschild; Natl. Sec. Florence Simon. Umbrella organization of distinct constituent member Zionist organizations in Canada; carries on major activities in all areas of Jewish life through its departments of education and culture, aliyah, youth and students, public affairs, and small Jewish communities, for the purpose of strengthening the State of Israel and the Canadian Jewish community. *Canadian Zionist.*

———, BUREAU OF EDUCATION AND CULTURE (1972). Pres. Kurt Rothschild. Provides counseling by pedagogic experts, in-service teacher-training courses and seminars in Canada and Israel; national pedagogic council and research center; distributes educational material and teaching aids; supports annual Bible contest and Hebrew-language courses for adults; awards scholarships to Canadian high-school graduates studying for one year in Israel.

HADASSAH–WIZO ORGANIZATION OF CANADA (1917). 1310 Greene Ave., Suite 900,

Montreal, PQ H3Z 2B8. (514)937-9431. FAX: (514)933-6483. E-mail: natoff @canadian-hadassah-wizo.org. Natl. Pres. Rochelle Levinson; Natl. Exec. V.-Pres. Lily Frank. Largest women's volunteer Zionist organization in Canada, located in 43 Canadian cities; dedicated to advancing the quality of life of the women and children in Israel through financial assistance and support of its many projects, day-care centers, schools, institutions, and hospitals. In Canada, the organization promotes Canadian ideals of democracy and is a stalwart advocate of women's issues. *Orah Magazine.*

HASHOMER HATZAIR (1913). 1111 Finch Ave. W., #456, Downsview, ONT M3J 2E5. (416)736-1339. FAX: (416)736-1405. E-mail: mail@givathaviva.ca. Shlicha-Ora Merin; Pres. Sheryl Neshel; Sec. Lipa Roth. A Zionist youth movement established over 80 years ago with centers all over the world. In Toronto, there are weekly meetings during the school year where children get a strong sense of their Jewish identity and connection to Israel, celebrate Jewish holidays together and learn to be contributing members of the community. Hashomer Hatzair runs a 6-day residential winter camp and a 6-week summer camp for youth ranging from 7-16 on Otty Lake.

INTERNATIONAL JEWISH CORRESPONDENCE (IJC) (1978). c/o Canadian Jewish Congress, 1590 Dr. Penfield Ave., Montreal, PQ H3G 1C5.9 (514)931-7531. FAX: (514)931-0548. E-mail: barrys@cjc.ca. Founder/Dir. Barry Simon. Aims to encourage contact between Jews of all ages and backgrounds, in all countries, through pen-pal correspondence. Send autobiographical data and stamped self-addressed envelope or its equivalent (to cover cost of Canadian postage) to receive addresses.

JEWISH IMMIGRANT AID SERVICES OF MONTREAL (JIAS) (1922). 5500 Westbury, 2nd Floor, Montreal, Quebec H3W-2W8. (514)342-9351. FAX: (514)342-0287. E-mail: jiasmail@aol.com. Pres. Joe Kislowicz; Exec. Dir. Shellie Ettinger. JIAS is a national organization assisting the lawful entry of Jews into Canada, as well as their settlement and integration. *JIAS News for Clients.*

JEWISH NATIONAL FUND OF CANADA (Keren Kayemeth Le'Israel, Inc.) (1901). 1980 Sherbrooke St. W., Suite 500, Montreal, PQ H3H 1E8. (514)934-0313. FAX: (514) 934-0382. E-mail: mtl@jnf.canada.org. Natl. Pres. Sandra Posluns; Exec. V.-Pres. Joe Rabinovitch. Fund-raising organization affiliated with the World Zionist Organization; involved in afforestation, soil reclamation, and development of the land of Israel, including the construction of roads and preparation of sites for new settlements; provides educational materials and programs to Jewish schools across Canada.

LABOUR ZIONIST ALLIANCE OF CANADA (1909). 272 Codsell Ave., Downsview, ONT M3H 3X2. (416)630-9444. FAX: (416)630-9451. Pres. Josef Krystal; City Committee Chmn. Montreal-Harry Froimovitch. Associated with the World Labor Zionist movement and allied with the Israel Labor party. Provides recreational and cultural programs, mutual aid, and fraternal care to enhance the social welfare of its membership; actively promotes Zionist education, cultural projects, and forums on aspects of Jewish and Canadian concern.

MERETZ CANADA (1950s). 1111 Finch Ave. W., Suite 456, Downsview, ONT M3J 2E5. (416)736-1339. FAX: (416)736-1405. Pres. Joseph Podemski., Vice Pres. Lipa Roth. Acts as a voice of Socialist-Democratic and Zionist points of view within the Jewish community and a focal point for progressive Zionist elements in Canada; affiliated with Hashomer Hatzair and the Givat Haviva Educational Center.

MIZRACHI ORGANIZATION OF CANADA (1941). 296 Wilson Ave., North York, ONT M3H 1S8. (416)630-9266. FAX: (416)630-2305. Pres. Jack Kahn. Promotes religious Zionism, aimed at making Israel a state based on Torah; maintains Bnei Akiva, a summer camp, adult education program, and touring department; supports Mizrachi-Hapoel Hamizrachi and other religious Zionist institutions in Israel which strengthen traditional Judaism. *Mizrachi Newsletter.*

NATIONAL COMMUNITY RELATIONS COMMITTEE OF CANADIAN JEWISH CONGRESS (1936). 4600 Bathurst St., Toronto, ONT M2R 3V2. (416)631-5673. FAX: (416)

635-1408. E-mail: mprutschi@ujafed.org. Chmn. Ellen T. Cole; Pres. Keith M. Landy; Dir. Manuel Prutschi. Seeks to safeguard the status, rights, and welfare of Jews in Canada; to combat anti-semitism, and promote understanding and goodwill among all ethnic and religious groups.

NATIONAL COUNCIL OF JEWISH WOMEN OF CANADA (1897). 118-1588 Main St., Winnipeg, MAN R2V 1Y3. (204)339-9700. FAX: (204)334-3779. E-mail: info@ncjwc. org. Chmn. Carol Slater; Natl. V.-Pres. Roz Fine & Brenlee Gurvey Gales. Dedicated to furthering human welfare in the Jewish and general communities, locally, nationally, and internationally; through an integrated program of education, service, and social action seeks to fulfill unmet needs and to serve the individual and the community. *National ByLines.*

ORT CANADA (1948). 3101 Bathurst St., Suite 604, Toronto, ONT M6A 2A6. (416)787-0339. FAX: (416) 787-9420. E-mail: info@ort-toronto.org. Pres. Arthur Silber; Exec. Dir. Joel Shapiro. Chapters in 11 Canadian cities raise funds for ORT's nonprofit global network of schools where Jewish students learn a wide range of marketable skills, including the most advanced high-tech professions. *Focus Magazine.*

STATE OF ISRAEL BONDS (CANADA-ISRAEL SECURITIES, LTD.) (1953). 970 Lawrence Ave. W., Suite 502, Toronto, ONT M6A 3B6. (416)789-3351. FAX: (416)789-9436. Pres. Norman Spector; Bd. Chmn. George A. Cohon. An international securities organization offering interest-bearing instruments issued by the government of Israel. Invests in every aspect of Israel's economy, including agriculture, commerce, and industry. Israel Bonds are RRSP-approved.

UIA FEDERATIONS OF CANADA (1998). 4600 Bathurst St., Suite 315, Toronto, ONT M2R 3V3. (416)636-7655. FAX: (416) 636-9897. E-mail: info@uiafed.org. Pres. Barbara Farber; Exec. V-Pres. Linda Kislowicz. The national Jewish fund-raising organization and community-planning body for Canada.

Jewish Federations, Welfare Funds, Community Councils

UNITED STATES

ALABAMA

BIRMINGHAM

BIRMINGHAM JEWISH FEDERATION (1936; reorg. 1971); Box 130219 (35213-0219); (205)879-0416. FAX: (205)803-1526. E-mail: federation@bjf.org. Pres. Brenda Weinstein; Exec. Dir. Richard Friedman. (WWW.BJF.ORG)

MOBILE

MOBILE JEWISH WELFARE FUND, INC. (inc. 1966); One Office Park, Suite 219 (36609); (334)343-7197. FAX: (334)343-7197. E-mail: mjwfl23@aol.com. Pres. Eileen Susman.

MONTGOMERY

JEWISH FEDERATION OF MONTGOMERY, INC. (1930); 2820 Fairlane Dr. (36120-0058); (334)277-5820. FAX: (334)277-8383. E-mail: jfedmgm@aol.com. Pres. Alan Weil; Admin. Dir. Susan Mayer Bruchis.

ARIZONA

PHOENIX

JEWISH FEDERATION OF GREATER PHOENIX (1940); 12701 N. Scottsdale Rd., Suite 201 (85254); (480)634-4900. FAX: (480)634-4588. E-mail: info@jewishphoenix.org. Pres. Neil Hiller; Exec. Dir. Arthur Paikowsky. (WWW.JEWISHPHOENIX.ORG)

TUCSON

JEWISH FEDERATION OF SOUTHERN ARIZONA (1946); 3822 East River Rd., Suite 100 (85718); (520)577-9393. FAX: (520)577-0734. E-mail: cbaldwin@jfsa.org. Pres.& CEO Stuart Mellan. (WWW.JEWISHTUCSON.ORG)

ARKANSAS

LITTLE ROCK

JEWISH FEDERATION OF ARKANSAS (1911); 425 N. University (72205); (501)663-3571. FAX: (501)663-7286. E-mail: jflar@aristotle.net. Pres. Doris Krain; Exec. Dir. Ziva Starr. (WWW.JEWISHARKANSAS.COM)

CALIFORNIA

EAST BAY

JEWISH FEDERATION OF THE GREATER EAST BAY (INCLUDING ALAMEDA & CONTRA COSTA COUNTIES) (1917); 401 Grand Ave., Oakland (94610-5022); (510)839-2900. FAX: (510)839-3996. E-mail: admin@jfed.org. Pres. Rob Ruby (WWW.JFED.ORG)

FRESNO

JEWISH FEDERATION OF FRESNO; 295 W. Cromwell Ave., Suite 111 (93711-6161); (559)432-2162. FAX: (559)432-0425.

LONG BEACH

JEWISH FEDERATION OF GREATER LONG BEACH AND W. ORANGE COUNTY (1937; inc. 1946); 3801 E. Willow St. (90815); (562) 426-7601. FAX: (562)424-3915. E-mail: webmaster@jewishlongbeach.org. Pres. Richard Lipeles; Exec. Dir. Deborah Goldfarb. (WWW.JEWISHLONGBEACH.ORG)

LOS ANGELES

JEWISH FEDERATION COUNCIL OF GREATER LOS ANGELES (1912; reorg. 1959); 6505 Wilshire Blvd., 8th fl. (90048); (323)761-8000. FAX: (323)761-8235. E-mail: webcoordinator@jewishla.org. Pres. John R. Fishel. (WWW.JEWISHLA.ORG)

ORANGE COUNTY

JEWISH FEDERATION OF ORANGE COUNTY (1964; inc. 1965); 1 Federation Way, Irvine (92603-0174); (949)435-3484. FAX: (949) 435-3485. E-mail: info@jfoc.org. Pres. Charles Karp; Exec. Dir. Bunnie Mauldin. (WWW.JFOC.ORG)

PALM SPRINGS

JEWISH FEDERATION OF PALM SPRINGS AND DESERT AREA (1971); 255 N. El Cielo, Suite 430 (92262-6990); (760)325-7281. FAX: (760)325-2188. E-mail: msjfedps@gte.net. Pres. Howard Levy; Exec. Dir. Jim Levitas. (WWW.JEWISHPALMSPRINGS.ORG)

SACRAMENTO

JEWISH FEDERATION OF THE SACRAMENTO REGION (1948); 2351 Wyda Way (95825); (916)486-0906. FAX: (916)486-0816. E-mail: federation@jewishsac.org. Pres. Dana Edelstein; Exec. Dir. Michal Kohane. (WWW.JEWISHSAC.ORG)

SAN DIEGO

UNITED JEWISH FEDERATION OF SAN DIEGO COUNTY (1936); 4950 Murphy Canyon Rd. (92123); (858)571-3444. FAX: (858)571-0701. E-mail: fedujf@ujfsd.org. Pres. Gary Jacobs; Exec. V-Pres. Stephen M. Abramson. (WWW.JEWISHINSANDIEGO.ORG)

SAN FRANCISCO

JEWISH COMMUNITY FEDERATION OF SAN FRANCISCO, THE PENINSULA, MARIN, AND SONOMA COUNTIES (1910; reorg. 1955); 121 Steuart St. (94105); (415)777-0411. FAX: (415)495-6635. E-mail: info@sfjcf.org. Pres. John Pritzker; Exec. V-Pres. Phyllis Cook. (WWW.SFJCF.ORG)

SAN GABRIEL AND POMONA VALLEY

JEWISH FEDERATION OF THE GREATER SAN GABRIEL AND POMONA VALLEYS; 258 W. Badillo St. (91723-1906); (626)967-3656. FAX: (626)967-5135. E-mail: sgpvfed@aol. com. (WWW.SGPV.ORG)

SAN JOSE

JEWISH FEDERATION OF GREATER SAN JOSE (incl. Santa Clara County except Palo Alto and Los Altos) (1930; reorg. 1950); 14855 Oka Rd., Suite 2, Los Gatos (95030); (408)358-3033. FAX: (408)356-0733. E-mail: info@jvalley.org. Pres. Steve Greenberg; Exec. Dir. Jyl Jurman. (WWW.JEWISH SILICONVALLEY.ORG)

SANTA BARBARA

SANTA BARBARA JEWISH FEDERATION (1974); 524 Chapala St. (93190); (805)957-1115. FAX: (805)957-9230. E-mail: sbjfed@silcom.com. Exec. Dir. Shelly Katz. (WWW.JEWISHSANTABARBARA.ORG)

VENTURA COUNTY

JEWISH FEDERATION OF VENTURA COUNTY; 7620 Foothill Rd. (93004); (805)647-7800. FAX: (805)647-0482. E-mail: ujavtacty@worldnet.att.net

COLORADO

DENVER/BOULDER

ALLIED JEWISH FEDERATION OF COLORADO (1936); 300 S. Dahlia St., Denver (80222); (303)321-3399. FAX: (303)322-8328. E-mail: information@ajfcolorado.org. Chmn. Noel Ginsburg; Pres. & CEO:Doug Seserman. (WWW.JEWISHCOLORADO.ORG)

CONNECTICUT

BRIDGEPORT

JEWISH FEDERATION OF EASTERN FAIRFIELD COUNTY. (1936; reorg. 1981); 4200 Park Ave. (06604-1092); (203)372-6567. FAX: (203)374-0770. E-mail: comments@jccs.org. Pres. & CEO Eli Kornreich. (WWW.JCCS.ORG)

DANBURY

THE JEWISH FEDERATION OF GREATER DANBURY, INC. (1945); 69 Kenosia Ave. (06810); (203)792-6353. FAX: (203)748-5099. E-mail: info@thejf.org. Pres. Daniel Wolinsky; Exec. Dir. Norman Greenstein. (WWW.THEJF.ORG)

EASTERN CONNECTICUT

JEWISH FEDERATION OF EASTERN CONNECTICUT, INC. (1950; inc. 1970); 28 Channing St., New London (06320); (860) 442-8062. FAX: (860)443-4175. E-mail: jfec@worldnet.att.net. Pres. Myron Hendel; Exec. Dir. Jerome E. Fischer.

GREENWICH

GREENWICH JEWISH FEDERATION (1956); One Holly Hill Lane (06830-6080); (203)622-1434. FAX: (203)622-1237. E-mail: pezmom3@aol.com. Pres. Martin J. Flashner; Exec. Dir. Pamela Ehrenkranz.

HARTFORD

JEWISH FEDERATION OF GREATER HARTFORD (1945); 333 Bloomfield Ave., W. Hartford (06117); (860)232-4483. FAX: (860) 232-5221. E-mail: info@jewishhartford.org. Pres. Robert Nabolchek; Exec. Dir. Catherine Fischer Schwartz. (WWW.JEWISHHARTFORD.ORG)

NEW HAVEN

JEWISH FEDERATION OF GREATER NEW HAVEN (1928); 360 Amity Rd., Woodbridge (06525); (203)387-2424. FAX: (203)387-1818. E-mail: marinak@megahits.com Pres. David Schaefer; Exec. Dir. Neil Berro. (WWW.JEWISHNEWHAVEN.ORG)

NORWALK
(See Westport)

STAMFORD

UNITED JEWISH FEDERATION (inc. 1973); 1035 Newfield Ave., PO Box 3038 (06905); (203)321-1373. FAX: (203)322-3277. E-mail: office@ujf.org. Pres. Martin Greenberg; Dir. of Dev. Gary Geller. (WWW.UJF.ORG)

WESTERN CONNECTICUT

JEWISH FEDERATION OF WESTERN CONNECTICUT (1938); 444 Maine St. N., Southbury (06488); (203)267-5121. FAX: (203) 267-3392. E-mail: jfedwtby@aol.com. Pres. Dan Goodman; Exec. Dir Rob Zwang. (WWW.JFED.NET)

WESTPORT-WESTON-WILTON-NORWALK

UJA/FEDERATION OF WESTPORT—WESTON—WILTON—NORWALK (inc. 1980); 431 Post Road E., Suite 22, Westport (06880); (203)226-8197. FAX: (203)226-5051. E-mail: rkessler@optonline.net. Pres. Ed Goldstein; Exec. Dir. Robert Kessler. (WWW.UJAFEDERATION.ORG)

DELAWARE

WILMINGTON

JEWISH FEDERATION OF DELAWARE, INC. (1934); 100 W. 10th St., Suite 301 (19801-1628); (302)427-2100. FAX: (302)427-2438. E-mail: jfdinfo@shalomdel.org; Pres. Barry Kayne; Exec. V. Pres. Samuel H. Asher. (WWW.SHALOMDELAWARE.ORG)

DISTRICT OF COLUMBIA

WASHINGTON

THE JEWISH FEDERATION OF GREATER WASHINGTON, INC. (1935); 6101 Montrose Rd., Rockville, MD (20852); (301)230-7200. FAX: (301)230-7265. E-mail: info@jewishfedwash. org. Pres. David Butler; Exec. V.-Pres. Misha Galperin. (WWW.SHALOMDC.ORG)

FLORIDA

BREVARD COUNTY

JEWISH FEDERATION OF BREVARD (1974); 108-A Barton Ave., Rockledge (32955); (407)636-1824. FAX: (407)636-0614. E-mail: jfbrevard@aol.com. Pres. Gary Singer; Exec. Dir. Joanne Bishins.

BROWARD COUNTY

JEWISH FEDERATION OF BROWARD COUNTY (1943; 1968); 5890 S. Pine Island Rd., Davie (33351-7319); (954)252-6900. FAX: (954) 252-6892. E-mail: info@jewishfedbroward. org. Pres. Eric Stillman. (WWW.JEWISH BROWARD.ORG)

COLLIER COUNTY

JEWISH FEDERATION OF COLLIER COUNTY (1974); 1250 Tamiami Trail N., Suite 202, Naples (33940); (941) 263-4205. FAX: (941)263-3813. E-mail: jfccfl@aol.com. Pres. David Willens. (WWW.JEWISHNAPLES.ORG)

DAYTONA BEACH
(See Volusia & Flagler Counties)

FT. LAUDERDALE
(See Broward County)

GAINESVILLE

JEWISH COUNCIL OF NORTH CENTRAL FLORIDA; 1861 NW 21 St. (32604); (352) 371-3846. E-mail: oberger@gnv.fdt.net.

JACKSONVILLE

JACKSONVILLE JEWISH FEDERATION, INC. (1935); 8505 San Jose Blvd. (32217); (904)448-5000. FAX: (904)448-5715. E-mail: jaxjewishfed@jon.jfny.org. Pres. Guy Benrubi; Exec. V.-Pres. Alan Margolies. (WWW.JEWISHJACKSONVILLE.ORG)

LEE COUNTY

JEWISH FEDERATION OF LEE AND CHARLOTTE COUNTIES (1974); 6237-E Presidential Court, Ft. Myers (33919-3568); (941)481-4449. FAX: (941)481-0139. E-mail: jfedswfl@aol.com. Pres. Herb Freed; Exec. Dir. Annette Goodman. (WWW.JEWISHFEDERATIONSWFL.ORG)

MIAMI

GREATER MIAMI JEWISH FEDERATION, INC. (1938); 4200 Biscayne Blvd. (33137); (305)576-4000. FAX: (305)573-4584. E-mail: info@gmjf.or. Pres. Michael M. Adler; Exec. V.-Pres. Jacob Solomon. (WWW.JEWISHMIAMI.ORG)

ORLANDO

JEWISH FEDERATION OF GREATER ORLANDO (1949); 851 N. Maitland Ave.; PO Box

941508, Maitland (32794-1508); (407)645-5933. FAX: (407)645-1172. E-mail: slandes@jfgo.org. Pres. James S. Grodin; Exec. Dir. Susan Bodner. (WWW.ORLANDOJEW-ISHFED.ORG)

PALM BEACH COUNTY

JEWISH FEDERATION OF PALM BEACH COUNTY, INC. (1962); 4601 Community Dr., W. Palm Beach (33417-2760); (561)478-0700. FAX: (561)478-9696. E-mail: info@jfedpbco.org. Pres. Norman P. Goldblum; Exec. V.-Pres. Jeffrey L. Klein. (WWW.JEWISH PALMBEACH.ORG)

JEWISH FEDERATION OF SOUTH PALM BEACH COUNTY, INC. (1979); 9901 Donna Klein Blvd. Boca Raton (33428-1788); (561)852-3100. FAX: (561)852-3136. E-mail: dstern @jewishboca.org. (WWW.JEWISHBOCA.ORG)

PENSACOLA

PENSACOLA JEWISH FEDERATION; 800 No. Palafox (32501); (850)434-7992.

PINELLAS COUNTY

JEWISH FEDERATION OF PINELLAS COUNTY, INC. (incl. Clearwater and St. Petersburg) (1950; reincorp. 1974); 13191 Starkey Rd., #8, Largo (33773-1438); (727) 530-3223. FAX: (727)531-0221. E-mail: pinellas@jfed-pinellas.org. Pres. David Abelson; Interim Exec. Dir. Bonnie Friedman. (WWW.JFED-PINELLAS.ORG)

SARASOTA-MANATEE

SARASOTA-MANATEE JEWISH FEDERATION (1959); 580 S. McIntosh Rd. (34232-1959); (941)371-4546. FAX: (941)378-2947. E-mail: info@smjf@org. Pres. Scott Gordon; Exec. Dir. Howard Tevlowitz. (WWW.SMJF. ORG)

TALLAHASSEE

APALACHEE FEDERATION OF JEWISH CHAR-ITIES; PO Box 14825 (32317-4825); (850)877-3989; FAX: (850)877-7989. E-mail: mdlevy@pol.net.

TAMPA

TAMPA JEWISH FEDERATION (1941); 13009 Community Campus Dr. (33625-4000); (813)264-9000. FAX: (813)265-8450. E-mail: info@jewishtampa.com. Pres. Lili Kaufman; Exec. V.-Pres. Gary Gould. (WWW.JEWISHTAMPA.COM)

VOLUSIA & FLAGLER COUNTIES

JEWISH FEDERATION OF VOLUSIA & FLA-GLER COUNTIES, INC. (1980); 733 S. Nova Rd., Ormond Beach (32174); (904)672-0294. FAX: (904)673-1316. Pres. Steven I. Unatin; Exec. Dir. Gloria Max.

GEORGIA

ATLANTA

JEWISH FEDERATION OF GREATER ATLANTA, INC. (1905; reorg. 1967); 1440 Spring St., NW (30309-2837); (404)873-1661. FAX: (404)874-7043. E-mail: webmaster@jfga. org. Pres. Martin Kogon; Exec. Dir. Steven A. Rakitt. (WWW. SHALOMATLANTA.ORG)

AUGUSTA

AUGUSTA JEWISH FEDERATION (1937); 898 Weinberger Way, Evans (30809-3636); (706)228-3636. FAX: (706)868-1660/823-3960. E-mail: augustafed1@knology.net. Exec. Dir. Leah Ronen.

COLUMBUS

JEWISH FEDERATION OF COLUMBUS, INC. (1944); PO Box 6313 (31906); (706)568-6668. Pres. Murray Solomon; Sec. Irene Rainbow.

SAVANNAH

SAVANNAH JEWISH FEDERATION (1943); 5111 Abercorn St. (31403); (912)355-8111. FAX: (912)355-8116. E-mail: jeafederationhot-line@savj.org. Pres. Merry Bodziner; Exec. Dir. Sharon Paz. (WWW.SAVJ.ORG)

ILLINOIS

CHAMPAIGN-URBANA

CHAMPAIGN-URBANA JEWISH FEDERATION (1929); 503 E. John St., Champaign (61820); (217)367-9872. FAX: (217)344-1540. E-mail: cujf@shalomcu.org. Pres. Anthony E. Novak; Exec. Dir. Lee Melhado. (www. SHALOMCU.ORG)

CHICAGO

JEWISH FEDERATION OF METROPOLITAN CHICAGO/JEWISH UNITED FUND OF METRO-POLITAN CHICAGO (1900); Ben Gurion Way, 1 S. Franklin St. (60606-4694); (312)346-6700. FAX: (312)444-2086. E-mail: we-binfo@juf.org. Pres. Steven B. Nasatir. (WWW.JUF.ORG)

JOLIET

JOLIET JEWISH WELFARE CHEST (1938); 250 N. Midland Ave. at Campbell St. (60435); (815)741-4600.

PEORIA

JEWISH FEDERATION OF PEORIA (1933; inc. 1947); 2000 W. Pioneer Pwky., Suite 10B (61615-1835); (309)689-0063. FAX: (309)

689-0575. Pres. Larry Seitzman; Exec. Dir. Susan Katz.

QUAD CITIES

JEWISH FEDERATION OF QUAD CITIES (1938; comb. 1973); 1705 2nd Ave., Suite 405, Rock Island (61201); (309)793-1300. FAX: (309)793-1345. E-mail: qcfederation@juno.com. Pres. Paul Light; Exec. Dir. Ida Kramer.

ROCKFORD

JEWISH FEDERATION OF GREATER ROCKFORD (1937); 1500 Parkview Ave. (61107); (815)399-5497. FAX: (815)399-9835. E-mail: rockfordfederation@juno.com. Pres. Sterne Roufa; Exec. Dir. Marilyn Youman.

SOUTHERN ILLINOIS

JEWISH FEDERATION OF SOUTHERN ILLINOIS, SOUTHEASTERN MISSOURI, AND WESTERN KENTUCKY (1941); 3419 W. Main, Belleville (62223); (618)398-6100. FAX: (618)398-0539. E-mail: silfed@simokyfed.com. Co-Pres. Harvey Cohen & Carol Rudman; Exec. Dir. Steven C. Low. (WWW.SIMOKYFED.COM)

SPRINGFIELD

SPRINGFIELD JEWISH FEDERATION (1941); 2815 Old Jacksonville Rd., Ste 103A (62704); (217)787-7223. FAX: (217)787-7470. E-mail: sjf@springnet1.com. Pres. Rita Victor; Exec. Dir. Gloria Schwartz

INDIANA

FORT WAYNE

FORT WAYNE JEWISH FEDERATION (1921); 227 E. Washington Blvd. (46802-3121); (219)422-8566. FAX: (219)422-8567. E-mail: fwjewfed@aol.com. Pres. Larry Adelman. (WWW.JEWISHFORTWAYNE.ORG)

INDIANAPOLIS

JEWISH FEDERATION OF GREATER INDIANAPOLIS, INC. (1905); 6705 Hoover Rd. (46260-4120); (317)726-5450. FAX: (317) 205-0307. E-mail: info@jfgi.org. Pres. Richard Leventhal; Exec. V.-Pres. Harry Nadler. (WWW.JFGI.ORG)

LAFAYETTE

JEWISH FEDERATION OF GREATER LAFAYETTE (1924); PO Box 3802, W. Lafayette (47906); (765)426-4724. E-mail: jfgl1@aol.com. Pres. Earl Prohofsky; Admin. Judy Upton.

NORTHWEST INDIANA

JEWISH FEDERATION OF NORTHWEST INDIANA (1941; reorg. 1959); 2939 Jewett St., Highland (46322); (219)972-2250. FAX: (219)972-4779. E-mail: defwej@aol.com. Pres. Carol Karol; Exec. Dir. Michael Steinberg. (WWW.JFEDOFNWI.COM)

ST. JOSEPH VALLEY

JEWISH FEDERATION OF ST. JOSEPH VALLEY (1946); 3202 Shalom Way, South Bend (46615); (219)233-1164. FAX: (219)288-4103. E-mail: receptionist@jewishfed.org. Pres. Alan Brown; Exec. V.-Pres. Deborah Barton Grant. (WWW.JFEDSJV.ORG)

IOWA

DES MOINES

JEWISH FEDERATION OF GREATER DES MOINES (1914); 910 Polk Blvd. (50312); (515)277-6321. FAX: (515)277-4069. E-mail: jcrc@dmjfed.org. Pres. Toni Urban; Exec. Dir. Elaine Steinger. (WWW.DMJFED.ORG)

SIOUX CITY

JEWISH FEDERATION OF SIOUX CITY (1921); 815 38th St. (51104-1417); (712)258-0618. FAX: (712)258-0619. Pres. Michele Ivener; Admin. Dir. Doris Rosenthal.

KANSAS

KANSAS CITY

See Listing Under Missouri

WICHITA

MID-KANSAS JEWISH FEDERATION, INC. (serving South Central Kansas) (1935); 400 N. Woodlawn, Suite 8 (67208); (316)686-4741. FAX: (316)686-6008. E-mail: jpress@mkjf.org. Pres. Jill S. Docking; Exec. Dir. Sandy Diel. (WWW.MKJF.ORG)

KENTUCKY

CENTRAL KENTUCKY

CENTRAL KENTUCKY JEWISH FEDERATION (1976); 340 Romany Rd., Lexington (40502-2400); (606)268-0672. FAX: (606)268-0775. E-mail: ckjf@jewishlexington.org. Pres. Martin Barr; Exec. Dir. Daniel Chejfec. (WWW.JEWISHLEXINGTON.ORG)

LOUISVILLE

JEWISH COMMUNITY FEDERATION OF LOUISVILLE, INC. (1934); 3630 Dutchmans Lane (40205); (502)451-8840. FAX: (502)458-0702. E-mail: jfed@iglou.com. Pres. Steven Shapiro; Exec. Dir. Alan S. Engel. (WWW.JEWISHLOUISVILLE.ORG)

LOUISIANA

BATON ROUGE

JEWISH FEDERATION OF GREATER BATON ROUGE (1971); 3354 Kleinert Ave. (70806); (504) 387-9744. FAX: (504)387-9487. E-mail: jfedofbr@postoffice.att.net. Pres. Harvey Hoffman.

NEW ORLEANS

JEWISH FEDERATION OF GREATER NEW ORLEANS (1913; reorg. 1977); 3747 W. Esplanade Ave., Metairie (70002-3524); (504)780-5600. FAX: (504)780-5601. E-mail: shalom@jewishnola.com. Pres. Allan Bissinger; Exec. Dir. Michael Weil. (www.JEWISHNOLA.ORG)

SHREVEPORT

NORTHERN LOUISIANA JEWISH FEDERATION (1941; inc. 1967); 4700 Line Ave., Suite 117 (71106-1533); (318)868-1200. FAX: (318) 868-1272. E-mail: nljfed@bellsouth.net. Pres. Rick Murov; Exec. Dir. Howard L. Ross. (www.NLJFED.ORG)

MAINE

LEWISTON-AUBURN

LEWISTON-AUBURN JEWISH FEDERATION (1947); 74 Bradman St., Auburn (04210); (207)786-4201. FAX: (207)783-1000. Pres. Scott Nussinow.

PORTLAND

JEWISH COMMUNITY ALLIANCE OF SOUTHERN MAINE (1942); 57 Ashmont St. (04103); (207)773-7254. FAX: (207)772-2234. E-mail: info@mainejewish,org. Pres. Emily Sandberg. (www.MAINEJEWISH.ORG)

MARYLAND

BALTIMORE

THE ASSOCIATED: JEWISH COMMUNITY FEDERATION OF BALTIMORE (1920; reorg. 1969); 101 W. Mt. Royal Ave. (21201-5728); (410) 727-4828. FAX: (410)752-1327. E-mail: information@jewishhowardcounty.org. Chmn. Barbara L. Himmelrich; Pres. Darrell D. Friedman. (www.ASSOCIATED.ORG)

COLUMBIA

JEWISH FEDERATION OF HOWARD COUNTY; 8950 Rte. 108, Suite 115, Columbia (21045); (410)730-4976; FAX: (410)730-9393. E-mail: info@jewishhowardcounty.org. Pres. Kenneth Goodman; Exec. Dir. Roberta Greenstein. (www.JEWISHHOWARDCOUNTY.ORG)

MASSACHUSETTS

BERKSHIRE COUNTY

JEWISH FEDERATION OF THE BERKSHIRES (1940); 235 East St., Pittsfield (01201); (413) 442-4360. FAX: (413)443-6070. E-mail: jreichbaum@berkshire.net. Pres. Stephen Rudin; Exec. Dir. Jaquelynne Reichbaum. (www.JEWISHBERKSHIRES.ORG)

BOSTON

COMBINED JEWISH PHILANTHROPIES OF GREATER BOSTON, INC. (1895; inc. 1961); 126 High St. (02110-2700); (617)457-8500. FAX: (617)988-6262. E-mail: info@cjp.org. Chmn. Robert Beal; Pres. Barry Shrage. (www.CJP.ORG)

MERRIMACK VALLEY

MERRIMACK VALLEY JEWISH FEDERATION (Serves Andover, Haverhill, Lawrence, Lowell, Newburyport, and 22 surrounding communities) (1988); PO Box 937, Andover (01810-0016); (978)688-0466. FAX: (978) 688-1097. E-mail: jan@mvjf.org. Pres. James H. Shainker; Exec. Dir. Jan Steven Brodie. (www.MVJF.ORG)

NEW BEDFORD

JEWISH FEDERATION OF GREATER NEW BEDFORD, INC. (1938; inc. 1954); 467 Hawthorn St., N. Dartmouth (02747); (508)997-7471. FAX: (508)997-7730. Co-Pres. Harriet Philips, Patricia Rosenfield; Exec. Dir. Wil Herrup.

NORTH SHORE

JEWISH FEDERATION OF THE NORTH SHORE, INC. (1938); 2 E. India Square, Suite 200 (01970-3707); (978)745-4222. FAX: (978) 741-7507. E-mail: mail@jfns.org. Pres. Robert Salter; Exec. Dir. Neil A. Cooper. (www.JFNS.ORG)

SPRINGFIELD

JEWISH FEDERATION OF GREATER SPRINGFIELD, INC. (1925); 1160 Dickinson St. (01108); (413)737-4313. FAX: (413)737-4348. E-mail: cfschwartz@jewishspring field.org. Pres. Harold Berman. (www.JEWISH SPRINGFIELD.ORG)

WORCESTER

JEWISH FEDERATION OF CENTRAL MASSACHUSETTS (1947; inc. 1957); 633 Salisbury St. (01609); (508)756-1543. FAX: (508)798-0962. E-mail: bluks@jfcm.org. Pres. Bruce Hertzberg; Exec. Dir. Howard Borer. (www.JFCM.ORG)

MICHIGAN

ANN ARBOR

JEWISH FEDERATION OF WASHTENAW COUNTY/UJA (1986); 2939 Birch Hollow Dr. (48108); (734)677-0100. FAX: (734)677-0109. E-mail: info@jewishannarbor.org. Pres. Morley Witus; Exec. Dir. Jess Levin. (WWW.JEWISHANNARBOR.ORG)

DETROIT

JEWISH FEDERATION OF METROPOLITAN DETROIT (1899); 6735 Telegraph Rd., Suite 30, PO Box 2030, Bloomfield Hills (48301-2030); (248)642-4260. FAX: (248)642-4985. E-mail: jfmd@jfmd.org. Pres. Larry Jackier; Exec. V.-Pres. Robert Aronson. (WWW.THISISFEDERATION.ORG)

FLINT

FLINT JEWISH FEDERATION (1936); 619 Wallenberg St. (48502); (810)767-5922. FAX: (810)767-9024. E-mail: fjf@tm.net. Pres. Dr. Steve Burton; Exec. Dir. Joel B. Kaplan. (HTTP://USERS.TM.NET/FLINT)

GRAND RAPIDS

JEWISH COMMUNITY FUND OF GRAND RAPIDS (1930); 4127 Embassy Dr. SE (49546-2418); (616)942-5553. FAX: (616)942-5780. E-mail: jcfgr@iserv.net. Pres. Richard Stevens; Admin. Dir. Rosalie Stein; V.P. Maxine Shapiro. (WWW.JEWISHGRANDRAPIDS.ORG)

MINNESOTA

MINNEAPOLIS

MINNEAPOLIS JEWISH FEDERATION (1929; inc. 1930); 13100 Wayzata Blvd., Suite 200, Minnetonka (55305); (612)593-2600. FAX: (612)593-2544. E-mail: webmaster@jewishkc.org. Pres. Michael Horovitz; Exec. Dir. Joshua Fogelson. (WWW.JEWISHMINNESOTA.ORG)

ST. PAUL

UNITED JEWISH FUND AND COUNCIL (1935); 790 S. Cleveland, Suite 227 (55116); (651)690-1707. FAX: (651)690-0228. E-mail: webmaster@ujfc.org. Pres. James Stein; Exec. Dir. Eli Skora. (WWW.JEWISHMINNESOTA.ORG)

MISSOURI

KANSAS CITY

JEWISH FEDERATION OF GREATER KANSAS CITY MO/KS (1933); 5801 W. 115 St., Overland Park, KS (66211-1824); (913)327-8100. FAX: (913)327-8110. E-mail: webmaster@jewishkc.org. Pres. Howard Jacobson; Exec. Dir. Todd Stettner. (WWW.JEWISHKANSASCITY.ORG)

ST. JOSEPH

UNITED JEWISH FUND OF ST. JOSEPH (1915); 1816 Walnut (64503); (816)233-1186. FAX: (816)233-9399. Elliot Zidell; Exec. Sec. Sherri Ott.

ST. LOUIS

JEWISH FEDERATION OF ST. LOUIS (incl. St. Louis County) (1901); 12 Millstone Campus Dr. (63146-9812); (314)432-0020. FAX: (314)432-1277. E-mail: submit@jfedstl.org. Pres. Heschel Raskass; Exec. V.-Pres. Barry Rosenberg. (WWW.JEWISHSTLOUIS.ORG)

NEBRASKA

LINCOLN

JEWISH FEDERATION OF LINCOLN, INC. (1931; inc. 1961); PO Box 67218 (68506); (402)489-1015. FAX: (402)476-8364. Pres. Herb Friedman; Exec. Dir. Karen Sommer.

OMAHA

JEWISH FEDERATION OF OMAHA (1903); 333 S. 132nd St. (68154-2198); (402)334-8200. FAX: (402)334-1330. E-mail: pmonsk@top.net. Pres. Steven Pitlor; Exec. Dir. Jan Goldstein. (WWW.JEWISHOMAHA.ORG)

NEVADA

LAS VEGAS

JEWISH FEDERATION OF LAS VEGAS (1973); 2317 Renaissance Dr. (89119-7520); (702)732-0556. FAX: (702)732-3228. Bd. Chr. Michael Unger; Exec. Dir. Meyer Bodoff. (WWW.JEWISHLASVEGAS.COM)

NEW HAMPSHIRE

MANCHESTER

JEWISH FEDERATION OF GREATER MANCHESTER (1974); 698 Beech St. (03104-3626); (603)627-7679. FAX: (603) 627-7963. E-mail: office@jewishnh.com. Exec. Dir. Adam M. Solender. (WWW.JEWISHNH.ORG)

NEW JERSEY

ATLANTIC AND CAPE MAY COUNTIES

JEWISH FEDERATION OF ATLANTIC AND CAPE MAY COUNTIES (1924); 501 N. Jerome Ave., Margate (08402); (609)822-4404. FAX: (609)822-4426. E-mail: karen@jewishbytheshore.com. Pres. Marc Lowenstein; Exec. V.-Pres. Bernard Cohen. (WWW.JFEDACM.COM)

BERGEN COUNTY

UJA FEDERATION OF NORTHERN NEW JERSEY (merged 2004); 111 Kinderkamack Rd., River Edge (07661); (201)488-6800. FAX: (201)488-1507. E-mail: contact@jewishbergen.org. Pres. Dr. Leonard Cole; Exec. V.-Pres. Howard E. Charish. (WWW.JEWISH BERGEN.ORG)

CENTRAL NEW JERSEY

JEWISH FEDERATION OF CENTRAL NEW JERSEY (1940; merged 1973); 1391 Martine Ave., Scotch Plains (07076); (908)889-5335. FAX: (908)889-5370. E-mail: azjhai@jfedcnj.org. Pres. Robert Kuchner; Exec. V.-Pres. Stanley Stone. (WWW.JFEDCNJ.ORG)

CLIFTON-PASSAIC

JEWISH FEDERATION OF GREATER CLIFTON-PASSAIC (1933); 199 Scoles Ave., Clifton (07012-1125). (973)777-7031. FAX: (973) 777-6701. E-mail: yymushkni@jfedcliftonpassaic.com. Pres. Mark Levenson; Exec. V.-Pres. Yosef Y. Muskin.

CUMBERLAND COUNTY

JEWISH FEDERATION OF CUMBERLAND COUNTY (inc. 1971); 1063 E. Landis Ave. Suite B, Vineland (08360-3752); (856)696-4445. FAX: (856)696-3428. E-mail: questions@jfedcc.org. Pres. Edward Roth; Exec. Dir. Kirk Wisemayer. (WWW.JFEDCC.ORG)

METROWEST NEW JERSEY

UNITED JEWISH FEDERATION OF METRO-WEST (1923); 901 Route 10, Whippany (07981-1156); (973)929-3000. FAX: (973)884-7361. E-mail: webmaster. Pres. Kenneth R. Heyman; Exec. V.-Pres. Max L. Kleinman. (WWW.UJFMETROWEST.ORG)

MIDDLESEX COUNTY

JEWISH FEDERATION OF GREATER MIDDLESEX COUNTY (org. 1948; reorg. 1985); 230 Old Bridge Tpk., S. River (08882-2000); (732)432-7711. FAX: (732)432-0292. E-mail: info@jf-gmc.org. Pres. Roy Tanzman; Exec. Dir. Gerrie Bamira. (WWW.JEWISH-MIDDLESEX.ORG)

MONMOUTH COUNTY

JEWISH FEDERATION OF GREATER MONMOUTH COUNTY (1971); 100 Grant Ave., PO Box 210, Deal (07723-0210); (732)531-6200-1. FAX: (732)531-9518. E-mail: info@jewishmonmouth.org. Exec. Dir. Howard Gases. (WWW.JEWISHMONMOUTH.ORG)

OCEAN COUNTY

OCEAN COUNTY JEWISH FEDERATION (1977); 301 Madison Ave., Lakewood (08701); (732)363-0530. FAX: (732)363-2097. Pres. Dr. Bernie Grabelle; Exec. Dir. Danny Goldberg.

PRINCETON MERCER BUCKS

UNITED JEWISH FEDERATION OF PRINCETON MERCER BUCKS (merged 1996); 4 Princess Rd., Suite 206, Lawrenceville (08648-2207); (609)530-0400. FAX: (609)219-9040. E-mail: mailbox@ujfpmb.org. Pres. Carol Pollard; Exec. Dir. Andrew Frank. (www. UJFPMB.ORG)

SOMERSET COUNTY

JEWISH FEDERATION OF SOMERSET, HUNTERDON & WARREN COUNTIES (1960); 775 Talamini Rd., Bridgewater (08807); (908)725-6994. FAX: (908)725-9753. E-mail: info@jfedshaw.org. Pres. Jo Ann Chase; Exec. Dir. Diane S. Naar. (WWW.JFEDSHAW.ORG)

SOUTHERN NEW JERSEY

JEWISH FEDERATION OF SOUTHERN NEW JERSEY (incl. Camden, Burlington, and Gloucester counties) (1922); 1301 Springdale Rd., Suite 200, Cherry Hill (08003-2769); (856)751-9500. FAX: (856)751-1697. E-mail: imorrow@jfedsnj.org. Pres. Dr. Robert Belafsky; Exec. V.-Pres. Jeff Klein. (WWW.JFEDSNJ.ORG)

NEW MEXICO

ALBUQUERQUE

JEWISH FEDERATION OF GREATER ALBUQUERQUE (1938); 5520 Wyoming Blvd., NE (87109-3167); (505)821-3214. FAX: (505) 821-3351. E-mail: infor@jewishnewmexico.org. Pres. Janice Posters; Exec. Dir. Sam Sokolove. (WWW.JEWISHNEWMEXICO.ORG)

NEW YORK

ALBANY

(See Northeastern New York)

BROOME COUNTY

JEWISH FEDERATION OF BROOME COUNTY; 500 Clubhouse Rd., Vestal (13850); (607) 724-2332; FAX: (607)724-2311. (WWW.TOER.NET/JFEDERATION)

BUFFALO (INCL. NIAGARA FALLS)

JEWISH FEDERATION OF GREATER BUFFALO, INC. (1903); 787 Delaware Ave. (14209); (716)886-7750. FAX: (716)886-1367. E-mail: info@jfedbflo.com. Exec. Dir. Daniel G. Kantor. (WWW.JFEDBFLO.COM)

DUTCHESS COUNTY

JEWISH FEDERATION OF DUTCHESS COUNTY; 110 Grand Ave., Poughkeepsie (12603); (845)471-9811. FAX: (845) 471-3233. E-mail: director@jewishdutchess.org. Exec. Dir. Bonnie Meadow. (WWW.JEWISH-DUTCHESS.ORG)

ELMIRA-CORNING

JEWISH CENTER AND FEDERATION OF THE TWIN TIERS (1942); Grandview Ave. Extension, Elmira (14905-0087); (607)734-8122. FAX: (607)734-8123. Pres. John Spiegler; Admin. Diane Huglies.

NEW YORK

UJA-FEDERATION OF JEWISH PHILAN-THROPIES OF NEW YORK, INC. (incl. Greater NY, Westchester, Nassau, and Suffolk counties) (Fed. org. 1917; UJA 1939; merged 1986); 130 E. 59 St. (10022-1302); (212)980-1000. FAX: (212)888-7538. E-mail: contact@ujafedny.org. Pres. John M. Shapiro; Exec. V.-Pres. & CEO John Ruskay. (WWW.UJAFEDNY.ORG)

NORTHEASTERN NEW YORK

UNITED JEWISH FEDERATION OF NORTH-EASTERN NEW YORK (1986); The Golub Center, 184 Washington Ave. Ext., Albany (12203); (518)783-7800. FAX: (518)783-1557. E-mail: info@jewishfedny.org. Pres. Dr. Lewis Morrison; Exec. Dir. Rodney Margolis. (WWW.JEWISHFEDNY.ORG)

ORANGE COUNTY

JEWISH FEDERATION OF GREATER ORANGE COUNTY (1977); 68 Stewart Ave., Newburgh (12550); (845)562-7860. FAX: (914)562-5114. E-mail: . Pres. Mona Rieger; Admin. Dir. Joyce Waschitz.

ROCHESTER

JEWISH COMMUNITY FEDERATION OF GREATER ROCHESTER, NY, INC. (1939); 441 East Ave. (14607-1932); (716)461-0490. FAX: (716)461-0912. E-mail: info@jewishrochester.org. Pres. Eli N. Futerman; Exec. Dir. Lawrence W. Fine. (WWW.JEW-ISHROCHESTER.ORG)

ROCKLAND COUNTY

JEWISH FEDERATION OF ROCKLAND COUNTY (1985); 900 Route 45, Suite 1, New City (10956-1140); (914)362-4200. FAX: (914)362-4282.

SCHENECTADY

(See Northeastern New York)

SYRACUSE

SYRACUSE JEWISH FEDERATION, INC. (1918); 5655 Thompson Rd. So., DeWitt (13214-0511); (315)445-2040. FAX: (315)445-1559. Pres. Gershon Vincow; Exec. V.-Pres. Richard Friedman. (WWW.SJFED.ORG)

TROY

(See Northeastern New York)

ULSTER COUNTY

JEWISH FEDERATION OF ULSTER COUNTY (1951); 159 Green St., Kingston (12401); (845)338-8131. FAX: (845)338-8131. E-mail: infor@ucjf.org. Pres. Michelle Tuchman; Exec. Dir. Joan Plotsky. (WWW.UCJF.ORG)

UTICA

JEWISH COMMUNITY FEDERATION AND CENTER OF UTICA (1950; reorg. 1994); 2310 Oneida St. (13501-6009); (315)733-2343. FAX: (315)733-2346. E-mail: jccl@borg.com. Pres. Ann Siegel; Exec. Dir. Barbara Ratner-Gantshar.

NORTH CAROLINA

ASHEVILLE

WESTERN NORTH CAROLINA JEWISH FEDERATION (1935); 236 Charlotte St. (28801-1434); (828)253-0701. FAX: (828)254-7666. Pres. Stan Greenberg; Exec. Dir. Marlene Berger-Joyce.

CHARLOTTE

THE JEWISH FEDERATION OF GREATER CHARLOTTE (1938); 5007 Providence Rd. (28226-5849); (704)366-5007. FAX: (704)944-6766. E-mail: jfgc@shalomcharlotte.org. Pres. Bob Abel; Exec. Dir. Sue Worrel. (WWW.JEWISHCHARLOTTE.ORG)

DURHAM-CHAPEL HILL

DURHAM-CHAPEL HILL JEWISH FEDERA-TION & COMMUNITY COUNCIL (1979); 3700 Lyckan Pkwy., Suite B, Durham (27707-2541); (919)489-5335. FAX: (919)489-5788. E-mail: federation@shalomdch.org. Pres. Lew Margolis; Exec. Dir. Orit Ramler Szulik. (HTTP://SHALOMDCH.ORG)

GREENSBORO

GREENSBORO JEWISH FEDERATION (1940); 5509C W. Friendly Ave. (27410-4211); (336)852-5433. FAX: (336)852-4346. E-mail: info@shalomgreensboro.org. Pres. Nancy Brenner; Exec. Dir. Marilyn Chandler. (WWW.SHALOMGREENSBORO.ORG)

RALEIGH

RALEIGH-CARY JEWISH FEDERATION (1987); 8210 Creedmoor Rd., Suite 104 (27613); (919)676-2200. FAX: (919)676-2122. E-mail: info@rcjf.org. Pres. Jim Maass; Exec. Dir. Judah Segal. (WWW.RCJF.ORG)

OHIO

AKRON

AKRON JEWISH COMMUNITY FEDERATION (1935); 750 White Pond Dr. (44320-1128); (330)869-CHAI (2424). FAX: (330)867-8498. Pres. David Kock; Exec. Dir. Michael Wise. (WWW.JEWISHAKRON.ORG)

CANTON

CANTON JEWISH COMMUNITY FEDERATION (1935; reorg. 1955); 2631 Harvard Ave., NW (44709-3147); (330)452-6444. FAX: (330) 452-4487. E-mail: cantonjcf@aol.com. (JEWISHCANTON.ORG)

CINCINNATI

JEWISH FEDERATION OF CINCINNATI (1896; reorg. 1967); 4050 Executive Park Dr. (45241); (513) 985-1500. FAX: (513)985-1503. E-mail: info@jfedcin.org. Pres. Marc Fisher; CEO Shepard Englander. (WWW.JEW ISHCINCINNATI.ORG)

CLEVELAND

JEWISH COMMUNITY FEDERATION OF CLEVELAND (1903); 1750 Euclid Ave. (44115-2106); (216)566-9200. FAX: (216) 861-1230. E-mail: info@jcfcleve.org. Exec. V.-Pres. & CEO Stephen Hoffman. (www. JEWISHCLEVELAND.ORG)

COLUMBUS

COLUMBUS JEWISH FEDERATION (1926); 1175 College Ave. (43209); (614)237-7686. FAX: (614)237-2221. E-mail: webmaster@tcjf.org. Pres. & CEO Marsha Hurwitz. (WWW.JEWISHCOLUMBUS.ORG)

DAYTON

JEWISH FEDERATION OF GREATER DAYTON (1910); 4501 Denlinger Rd. (45426-2395); (937)854-4150. FAX: (937)854-2850. Pres. Joseph Bettman; Exec. V.-Pres. Peter H. Wells. (WWW.JEWISHDAYTON.ORG)

STEUBENVILLE

JEWISH COMMUNITY COUNCIL (1938); 300 Lovers Lane (43952); (614)264-5514. FAX: (740)264-7190. Pres. Curtis L. Greenberg; Exec. Sec. Jennie Bernstein.

TOLEDO

JEWISH FEDERATION OF GREATER TOLEDO

(1907; reorg. 1960); 6505 Sylvania Ave., Sylvania (43560-3918); (419)885-4461. FAX: (419)885-3207. E-mail: jftoledo@cjfny.org. CEO Joel S. Beren. (WWW.JEWISHTOLEDO. ORG)

YOUNGSTOWN

YOUNGSTOWN AREA JEWISH FEDERATION (1935); 505 Gypsy Lane (44504-1314); (330)746-3251. FAX: (330)746-7926. E-mail: samkoopl@juno.com. Pres. Dr. Ronald Roth; Dir. Bonnie Deutsch-Burdman.

OKLAHOMA

OKLAHOMA CITY

JEWISH FEDERATION OF GREATER OKLAHOMA CITY (1941); 710 W. Wilshire, Suite C (73116-7736). (405)848-3132. FAX: (405) 848-3180. E-mail: office@jfedokc.org. Pres. Harriet Carson; Exec. Dir. Edie S. Roodman. (WWW.JFEDOKC.ORG)

TULSA

JEWISH FEDERATION OF TULSA (1938); 2021 E. 71 St. (74136); (918)495-1100. FAX: (918)495-1220. E-mail: federation@jewishtulsa.org. Pres. Andrew M. Wolov; Exec. Dir. Barry Abels. (WWW.JEWISHTULSA.ORG)

OREGON

PORTLAND

JEWISH FEDERATION OF PORTLAND (incl. Northwest Oregon and Southwest Washington communities) (1920; reorg. 1956); 6651 SW Capitol Hwy. (97219); (503)245-6219. FAX: (503)245-6603. E-mail: federation@jewishportland.org. Pres. Rob Shlachter; Exec. Dir. Charles Schiffman. (WWW.JEWISHPORTLAND.ORG)

PENNSYLVANIA

BUCKS COUNTY

(See JEWISH FEDERATION OF GREATER PHILADELPHIA)

ERIE

JEWISH COMMUNITY COUNCIL OF ERIE (1946); 1611 Peach St., Suite 405 (16501-2123); (814)455-4474. FAX: (814)455-4475. E-mail: jcceri@erie.net. Pres. Robert Cohen; Admin. Dir. Cynthia Penman; Dir. Barbara Singer. (WWW.JCCERI.ORG)

HARRISBURG

UNITED JEWISH COMMUNITY OF GREATER HARRISBURG (1941); 3301 N. Front St. (17110-1436); (717)236-9555. FAX: (717)

236-8104. E-mail: communityreview@desu-pernet.net. Pres. Raphael Aronson; Exec. Dir. David Weisberg. (WWW.JEWISHHARRIS BURG.COM)

LEHIGH VALLEY

JEWISH FEDERATION OF THE LEHIGH VAL-LEY (1948); 702 N. 22nd St., Allentown (18104); (610)821-5500. FAX: (610)821-8946. E-mail: ivfed@enter.net. Exec. Dir. Mark Goldstein.

PHILADELPHIA

JEWISH FEDERATION OF GREATER PHILA-DELPHIA (incl. Bucks, Chester, Delaware, Montgomery, and Philadelphia counties) (1901; reorg. 1956); 2100 Arch St. (19103); (215)832-0500. FAX: (215)832-1510. E-mail: webmaster@philafederation.org. Pres. & CEO Ira M. Schwartz. (WWW.JEWISH PHILLY.ORG)

PITTSBURGH

UNITED JEWISH FEDERATION OF GREATER PITTSBURGH (1912; reorg. 1955); 234 McKee Pl. (15213 3916); (412)681-8000. FAX: (412) 681-3980. E-mail: ujfinformation@ujfpitts-burgh.org. Pres. & CEO Jeff Finkelstein; Chmn. Daniel H. Shapira. (WWW.UJF.NET)

READING

JEWISH FEDERATION OF READING, PA., INC. (1935; reorg. 1972); 1700 City Line St. (19604); (610)921-2766. FAX: (610)929-0886. E-mail: stanr@epix.net. Pres. Sheila Lattin; Exec. Dir. Jay Steinberg. (WWW.READ INGJEWISHCOMMUNITY.ORG)

SCRANTON

JEWISH FEDERATION OF NORTHEASTERN PENNSYLVANIA (1945); 601 Jefferson Ave. (18510); (570)961-2300. FAX: (570)346-6147. E-mail: jfednepa@epix.net. Pres. Louis Nivert; Exec. Dir. Mark Silverberg. (WWW.JFEDNEPA.ORG)

WILKES-BARRE

JEWISH FEDERATION OF GREATER WILKES-BARRE (1950); 60 S. River St. (18702-2493); (570)822-4146. FAX: (570)824-5966. E-mail: wbreport@aol.com. Pres. Murray Ufberg; Exec. Dir. Don Cooper.

RHODE ISLAND

PROVIDENCE

JEWISH FEDERATION OF RHODE ISLAND (1945); 130 Sessions St. (02906); (401)421-4111. FAX: (401)331-7961. E-mail: shalom @jfri.org. Pres. Edward D. Feldstein; Exec. Dir. Steven R. Silverfarb. (WWW.JFRI.ORG)

SOUTH CAROLINA

CHARLESTON

CHARLESTON JEWISH FEDERATION (1949); 1645 Raoul Wallenberg Blvd., PO Box 31298 (29407); (843)571-6565. FAX: (843)852-3547. E-mail: webmaster@jew-ishcharleston.org. Co-Pres. Wendy Goer and Paul Saltzman; Exec. Dir. Ellen J. Katzman. (WWW.JEWISHCHARLESTON.ORG)

COLUMBIA

COLUMBIA JEWISH FEDERATION (1960); 4540 Trenholm Rd., PO Box 6968 (29206-4462); (803)787-2023. FAX: (803)787-0475. E-Mail: Ternercjf@hotmail.com. Pres. Stephen Serbin; Exec. Dir. Steven Terner.

SOUTH DAKOTA

SIOUX FALLS

JEWISH WELFARE FUND (1938); 510 S. First Ave. (57102-1003); (605)332-3335. FAX: (605)334-2298. E-mail: asnh94@prodigy. com. Pres. Laurence Bierman; Exec. Sec. Stephen Rosenthal.

TENNESSEE

CHATTANOOGA

JEWISH COMMUNITY FEDERATION OF GREATER CHATTANOOGA (1931); 3601 Ring-gold Rd. (37412); PO Box 8947 (37412); (423)493-0270. FAX: (423)493-9997. E-mail: mdzik@jcfgc.com. Pres. Susan Diste fano; Exec. Dir. Michael Dzik. (WWW.JCFGC. COM)

KNOXVILLE

KNOXVILLE JEWISH FEDERATION, INC. (1939); 7800 Deane Hill Dr. (37919); (865)693-5837. FAX: (865)694-4861. E-mail: ajcckjf@aol.com. Pres. Scott B. Hahn; Exec. Dir. Dr. Jeff Gubitz. (WWW.JEWISH-KNOXVILLE.ORG)

MEMPHIS

MEMPHIS JEWISH FEDERATION (incl. Shelby County) (1935); 6560 Poplar Ave. (38138-3614); (901)767-7100. FAX: (901)767-7128. E-mail: jfeld@memjfed.org. Pres. Louise Sklar; Exec. Dir. Jeffrey Feld. (WWW.MEM JFED.ORG/MJF)

NASHVILLE

NASHVILLE JEWISH FEDERATION (1936); 801 Percy Warner Blvd. (37205-4009); (615)356-3242. FAX: (615)352-0056. E-mail: jnashjfed @aol.com. Pres. Fred Zimmerman; Exec. Dir. Steven J. Edelstein. (WWW.NASHVILLE JCC.ORG)

TEXAS

AUSTIN

JEWISH COMMUNTY ASSOCIATION OF AUSTIN (1939; reorg. 1956); 7300 Hart Lane (78731); (512)735-8000. FAX: (512)735-8001. E-mail: austinjfed@jfaustin.org. Pres. Linda Millstone; Exec. Dir. Sandy Sack. (WWW.SHALOMAUSTIN.ORG)

BEAUMONT

BEAUMONT JEWISH FEDERATION; PO Box 1891 (77704-1981); (409)832-2881.

CORPUS CHRISTI

COMBINED JEWISH APPEAL OF CORPUS CHRISTI; 750 Everhart Rd. (78411-1906); (512)855-6239. FAX: (512)853-9040.

DALLAS

JEWISH FEDERATION OF GREATER DALLAS (1911); 7800 Northaven Rd. (75230-3226); (214)369-3313. FAX: (214)369-8943. E-mail: contact@jfgd.org. Pres. Donald Schaffer; Exec. Dir. Gary Weinstein. (WWW.JEWISHDALLAS.ORG)

EL PASO

JEWISH FEDERATION OF EL PASO, INC. (1937); 405 Wallenberg Dr. (79912-5605); (915)584-4437. FAX: (915)584-0243. Pres. Richard Krasne; Exec. Dir. Larry Harris. (WWW.JEWISHELPASO.ORG)

FORT WORTH

JEWISH FEDERATION OF FORT WORTH AND TARRANT COUNTY (1936); 4255 Bryant Irvin Rd. #209 (76008); (817)569-0892. FAX: (817)569-0895. E-mail: jfed@tarrantfederation.org. Pres. Harold Gernsbacher; Exec. Dir. Naomi Rosenfield.

HOUSTON

JEWISH FEDERATION OF GREATER HOUSTON (1936); 5603 S. Braeswood Blvd. (77096-3907); (713)729-7000. FAX: (713)721-6232. E-mail: lwunsch@houstonjewish.org. Pres. Joe Williams; Exec. V.-Pres. Lee Wunsch. (WWW.HOUSTONJEWISH.ORG)

SAN ANTONIO

JEWISH FEDERATION OF SAN ANTONIO (incl. Bexar County) (1922); 12500 NW Military Hwy., Suite 200 (78231); (210)302-6960. FAX: (210)408-2332. E-mail: markfreedman@jfsatx.org. Pres. Alan Petlin; Exec. Dir. Mark Freedman. (WWW.JFSATX.ORG)

WACO

JEWISH FEDERATION OF WACO & CENTRAL TEXAS (1949); PO Box 8031 (76714-8031);

(817)776-3740. FAX: (817)776-4424. E-mail: debhersh@aol.com. Pres. Harry Smith; Exec. Sec. Deborah Hersh. (WWW.AGUDATH-JACOB.ORG/FED.HTM)

UTAH

SALT LAKE CITY

UNITED JEWISH FEDERATION OF UTAH (1936); 2 North Medical Drive (84113); (801)581-0102. FAX: (801) 581-1334. Pres. Robert Wolff; Exec. Dir. Donald Gartman.

VIRGINIA

RICHMOND

JEWISH COMMUNITY FEDERATION OF RICHMOND (1935); 5403 Monument Ave., PO Box 17128 (23226-7128); (804)288-0045. FAX: (804)282-7507. E-mail: webmaster@jewishrichmond.org. Pres. Stewart Kasen; Exec. Dir. Ellen Chernack. (WWW.JEWISHRICHMOND.ORG)

TIDEWATER

UNITED JEWISH FEDERATION OF TIDEWATER (incl. Norfolk, Portsmouth, and Virginia Beach) (1937); 5000 Corporate Woods Dr., Suite 200, Virginia Beach (23462-4370); (757)965-6100. FAX: (757)965-6102. E-mail: ujft@ujft.org. Pres. David Brand; Exec. V.-Pres. Harry Graber. (WWW.JEWISHVA.ORG)

VIRGINIA PENINSULA

UNITED JEWISH COMMUNITY OF THE VIRGINIA PENINSULA, INC. (1942); 2700 Spring Rd., Newport News (23606); (757)930-1422. FAX: (757)930-3762. E-mail: unitedjc@ujvp.org. Pres. Roy H. Lasris; Exec. Dir. Robert Kessler. (WWW.UJCVP.ORG)

WASHINGTON

SEATTLE

JEWISH FEDERATION OF GREATER SEATTLE (incl. King County, Everett, and Bremerton) (1926); 2031 Third Ave. (98121); (206)443-5400. FAX: (206)443-0306. E-mail: info@jeishinseattle.org. Pres. & CEO Barry M. Goren. (WWW.JEWISHINSEATTLE.ORG)

WEST VIRGINIA

CHARLESTON

FEDERATED JEWISH CHARITIES OF CHARLESTON, INC. (1937); PO Box 1613 (25326); (304)345-2320. FAX: (304)345-2325. E-mail: mzltov@aol.com. Pres. Stuart May; Exec. Sec. Lee Diznoff.

WISCONSIN

MADISON

MADISON JEWISH COMMUNITY COUNCIL, INC. (1940); 6434 Enterprise Lane (53719-1117); (608)278-1808. FAX:(608)278-7814. E-mail: mjcc@mjcc.net. Pres. Diane Seder; Exec. Dir. Steven H. Morrison. (WWW.JEW-ISHMADISON.ORG)

MILWAUKEE

MILWAUKEE JEWISH FEDERATION, INC. (1902); 1360 N. Prospect Ave. (53202); (414)390-5700. FAX: (414)390-5782. E-mail: info@milwaukeejewish.org. Pres. Stephen L. Chernof; Exec. V.-Pres. Richard H. Meyer. (WWW.MILWAUKEEJEWISH.ORG)

CANADA

ALBERTA

CALGARY

CALGARY JEWISH COMMUNITY COUNCIL (1962); 1607 90th Ave. SW (T2V 4V7); (403)253-8600. FAX: (403)253-7915. E-mail: dpowers@cjcc.ca. Pres. Nate Feldman; Exec. Dir. Myrna Linder. (WWW.CJCC.CA)

EDMONTON

JEWISH FEDERATION OF EDMONTON (1954; reorg. 1982); 7200 156th St. (T5R 1X3); (780)487-5120. FAX: (780)481-1854. E-mail: edjfed@net.com. Pres. Stephen Mandel; Exec. Dir. Lesley A. Jacobson.

BRITISH COLUMBIA

VANCOUVER

JEWISH FEDERATION OF GREATER VANCOUVER (1932; reorg. 1987); 950 W. 41st Ave., Suite 200 (V5Z 2N7); (604)257-5100. FAX: (604)257-5110. E-mail: jfed@jfgv.com. Pres. Sondra Green; Exec. Dir. Mark Gurvis. (WWW.JFGV.COM)

MANITOBA

WINNIPEG

JEWISH FEDERATION OF WINNIPEG/COMBINED JEWISH APPEAL (1938; Reorg. 1973); 123 Doncaster St., Suite C300 (R3N 2B2); (204)477-7400. FAX: (204)477-7405. E-mail: bfreedman@aspercampus.mb.ca. Pres. Edward Lyons; Exec. V.-Pres. Jonathan Kroft. (WWW.JEWISHWINNIPEG.ORG)

ONTARIO

HAMILTON

UJA/JEWISH FEDERATION OF HAMILTON/WENTWORTH & AREA (1932; merged 1971); PO Box 7258, 1030 Lower Lions Club Rd., Ancaster (L9G 3N6); (905)648-0605 #305. FAX: (905)648-8350. E-mail: cnuscauja@on.aibn.com. Pres. Bonnie Loewith; Exec. Dir. Gerald Fisher. (WWW.JEWISHHAMILTON.ORG)

LONDON

LONDON JEWISH FEDERATION (1932); 536 Huron St. (N5Y 4J5); (519)673-3310. FAX: (519)673-1161. Pres. Ron Wolf; Off. Mgr. Debra Chatterley. (WWW.JEWISHLONDON.CA)

OTTAWA

UNITED JEWISH APPEAL OF OTTAWA (1934); 21 Nadolny Sachs Private (K2A 1R9); (613) 798-4696. FAX: (613)798-4695. E-mail: uja@jccottawa.com. Pres. Mitchell Bellman; Exec. Dir. Jack Silverstein. (WWW.JEWISHOTTAWA.ORG)

TORONTO

UJA FEDERATION OF GREATER TORONTO (1917); 4600 Bathurst St. (M2R 3V2); (416)635-2883. FAX: (416)631-5715. E-mail: info@oujafed.org. Pres. Joseph Steiner; Exec. V.-Pres. Allan Reitzes. ()

WINDSOR

JEWISH COMMUNITY FEDERATION (1938); 1641 Ouellette Ave. (N8X 1K9); (519)973-1772. FAX: (519)973-1774. Pres. Jay Armeland; Exec. Dir. Harvey Kessler. (WWW.JEWISHWINDSOR.ORG)

QUEBEC

MONTREAL

FEDERATION CJA (formerly ALLIED JEWISH COMMUNITY SERVICES) (1965); 1 Carrie Cummings Square (H3W 1M6); (514)735-3541. FAX: (514)735-8972. E-mail: fcja@federationcja.org. Pres. Steven Cummings; Exec. V.-Pres. Danyael Cantor. (WWW.FEDERATIONCJA.ORG)

Jewish Periodicals

UNITED STATES

ALABAMA

DEEP SOUTH JEWISH VOICE (1990). PO Box 130052, Birmingham, 35213. (205)322-9002. E-mail: informationr@dsjv.com. Lawrence M. Brook. Monthly. (WWW.DEEP SOUTHJEWISHVOICE.COM)

ARIZONA

ARIZONA JEWISH POST (1946). 2601 N. Campbell Ave., #205, Tucson, 85719. (520)319-1112. FAX: (520) 319-1118. E-mail: pbraun@azjewishpost.com. Phyllis Braun. Fortnightly. Jewish Federation of Southern Arizona.

JEWISH NEWS OF GREATER PHOENIX (1948). 1625 E. Northern Ave., Suite 106, Phoenix, 85020. (602)870-9470. FAX: (602)870-0426. E-mail: editor@jewishaz.com. Deborah Susser. Weekly. (WWW. JEWISHAZ.COM)

CALIFORNIA

AMERICAN RABBI (1968). 22711 Cass Ave., Woodland Hills, 91364. (818)225-9631. E-mail: amrabbi@pacbell.net. Ed.-in-Ch./ Pub. David Epstein; Ed. Harry Essrig. Quarterly.

JEWISH NEWS WEEKLY OF NORTHERN CALIFORNIA (1946). 225 Bush St., Suite 1480, San Francisco, 94104-4281. (415)263-7200. FAX: (415)263-7223. E-mail: edit@jweekly.com. Woody Weingarten. Weekly. San Francisco Jewish Community Publications, Inc.

JEWISH COMMUNITY CHRONICLE (1947). 3801 E. Willow St., Long Beach, 90815. (562)426-7601, ext. 1021. FAX: (562)595-5543. E-mail: jchron@surfside.net. Marian Leb Martin. Fortnightly except January, July & August/ once per month 21 issues a year. Jewish Federation of Greater Long Beach & West Orange County.

JEWISH COMMUNITY NEWS (1976). 14855 Oka Rd., Suite 2, Los Gatos, 95030. (408)358-3033. FAX: (408)356-0733. E-mail: jcn@jfgsj.org. Cecily Ruttenberg. Monthly. Jewish Federation of Greater San Jose.

JEWISH JOURNAL OF GREATER LOS ANGELES (1986). 3660 Wilshire Blvd., Suite 204, Los Angeles, 90010. (213)368-1661. FAX: (213) 368-1684. E-mail:editor@jewishjournal. com. Susan Freudenheim. Weekly. (WWW. JEWISHJOURNAL.COM)

JEWISH NEWS (1973). 15060 Ventura Blvd., Suite 210, Sherman Oaks, CA 91403. (818)786-4000. FAX: (818)380-9232. Phil Blazer. Monthly. (Also weekly Sunday TV and radio broadcasts in LA, NY, and Miami.)

JEWISH SPORTS REVIEW. 1800 S. Robertson Blvd., #174, Los Angeles, 90035. (800) 510-9003. E-mail: shel@jewishsportsreview.com. Shel Wallman/Ephraim Moxson. Bimonthly. (WWW.JEWISHSPORTSREVIEW. COM)

LOS ANGELES JEWISH TIMES (1897). 5455 Wilshire Blvd., Suite 903, Los Angeles, 90036. (323)933-0131. FAX: (323)933-7928. E-mail: lajtart@aol.com. Ed.-in-Chief Joe Bobker; Mng. Ed. Jane Fried. Weekly.

SAN DIEGO JEWISH TIMES (1979). 4731 Palm Ave., La Mesa, 91941. (619)463-5515. FAX: (619) 463-1309. E-mail: msirota @sdjewishtimes.com. Michael Sirota. Fortnightly. (WWW.SDJEWISHTIMES.COM)

SHALOM L.A. (1988). 16027 Ventura Blvd., #400, Encino, 91436. (818)783-3090. FAX: (818)783-1104. E-mail: news@

sholomla.net. Gal Shor. Weekly. Hebrew. (WWW.SHALOMLA.COM)

TIKKUN MAGAZINE (1986). 2342 Shattuck Ave., Suite 1200, Berkeley, 94704. (510)644-1200. FAX: (510)644-1255. E-mail: magazine@tikkun.org. Michael Lerner. Bimonthly. Institute for Labor & Mental Health. (WWW.TIKKUN.ORG)

WESTERN STATES JEWISH HISTORY (1968). 22711 Cass Ave., Woodland Hills, 91364. (818)225-9631. E-mail: amrabbi@pacbell.net. Gladys Sturman. Quarterly. Western States Jewish History Association.

COLORADO

INTERMOUNTAIN JEWISH NEWS (1913). 1275 Sherman St., Suite 214, Denver, 80203-2299. (303)861-2234. FAX: (303)832-6942. E-mail: miriam@ijn.com. Miriam Goldberg. Weekly. (WWW.IJN.COM)

CONNECTICUT

CONNECTICUT JEWISH LEDGER (1929). 740 N. Main St., W. Hartford, 06117. (860)231-2424. Fax: (860)231-2428. E-mail: editorial@jewishledger.com. Lisa Lenkiewicz. Weekly. (WWW.JEWISHLEDGER.COM)

JEWISH LEADER (1974). 28 Channing St., PO Box 1468, New London, 06320. (860)442-7395. FAX: (860)443-4175. E-mail: jfecmim@aol.com. Mimi Perl. Biweekly. Jewish Federation of Eastern Connecticut.

DELAWARE

JEWISH VOICE. 100 W. 10th St., Suite 301, Wilmington, 19801. (302) 427-2100. FAX: (302) 427-2438. E-mail: lynn.edelmam@shalomdel.org. Lynn Edelman. 22 times per year. Jewish Federation of Delaware.

DISTRICT OF COLUMBIA

AZURE (1996). 5505 Connecticut Ave., NW, Suite 1140, Washington, 20015. (877)298-7300. FAX: (888)766-1506. E-mail: patrick@shalemcenter.org. Dan Polisar. Quarterly. Hebrew/English. The Shalem Center. (WWW.AZURE.ORG.IL)

B'NAI B'RITH INTERNATIONAL JEWISH MONTHLY (1886, under the name Menovah). 2020 K Street, NW, 7th Floor, Washington, DC 20006. (202)857-2708. FAX: (202)857-2781. E-mail: ijm@bnaibrith.org. Editor Elana Harris. Quarterly. B'nai B'rith International.

CAPITAL COMMUNIQUÉ (1991). 777 N. Capital St., NE, Suite 305, Washington, 20002. (202)216-9060. FAX: (202)216-9061. Jason Silberberg. Biannually. National Jewish Democratic Council.

THE JEWISH VETERAN (1896). 1811 R St., NW, Washington, 20009-1659. (202)265-6280. FAX: (202)234-5662. E-mail: jwv@jwv.org. Seymour "Sy" Brody. 5 times per year. Jewish War Veterans of the U.S.A. Quarterly

MOMENT (1975). 4710 41 St., NW, Washington, 20016. (202)364-3300. FAX: (202)364-2636. E-mail: editor@momentmag.com. Hershel Shanks. Bimonthly. Jewish Educational Ventures, Inc.

FSU MONITOR (1990). 1819 H Street, NW, Suite 230, Washington, 20006. (202)775-9770. FAX: (202)775-9776. E mail: ucsj@ucsj.com. Nickolai Butkevich. Quarterly. Union of Councils for Soviet Jews.

NEAR EAST REPORT (1957). 440 First St., NW, Suite 607, Washington, 20001. (202)639-5254. FAX: (202) 347-4916. Dr. Raphael Danziger. Fortnightly. Near East Research, Inc.

SECURITY AFFAIRS (1976). 1717 K St., NW, Suite 800, Washington, 20006. (202)833-0020. FAX: (202)296-6452. E-mail: info@jinsa.org. Jim Colbert. Quarterly. Jewish Institute for National Security Affairs.

WASHINGTON JEWISH WEEK. See under MARYLAND

FLORIDA

CHRONICLE (1971). 580 S. McIntosh Rd., Sarasota, 34232. (941)371-4546. FAX: (941)378-2947. Barry Millman. Biweekly. Sarasota-Manatee Jewish Federation.

FEDERATION STAR (2001). 1250 Taimai Trail, No. Ste. 202, Naples 34102. (941)263-4205. E-mail: jfccfk@aol.com. Susan Frank. Biweekly. Jewish Federation of Collier County.

HERITAGE FLORIDA JEWISH NEWS (1976) 207 O'Brien Road, Ste. 101, Fern Park 32730. (407)834-8787. FAX: (407)834-8277. E-mail: news@orlandoheritage.com. Lyn Payne. Weekly. (WWW.HERITAGE.COM)

JACKSONVILLE JEWISH NEWS (1988). 8505 San Jose Blvd., Jacksonville, 32217. (904)448-5000. Fax: (904)448-5715. E-

mail: srgnews@aol.com. Susan R. Goetz.
Monthly. Jacksonville Jewish Federation.
(WWW.JEWISHJACKSONVILLE.COM)

JEWISH JOURNAL (1977). 1701 Green Rd.,
Deerfield Beach, 33064. (954)574-5328.
FAX: (954)698-6719. E-mail: speskoff
@tribune.com. Stan Peskoff. Weekly.
South Florida Newspaper Network.

JEWISH PRESS OF PINELLAS COUNTY
(Clearwater-St.Petersburg) (1985). PO
Box 6970, Clearwater, 33758-6970; 1101
S. Belcher Road, Suite H, Largo, FL
33771. (727)535-4400. FAX:(727)530-
3039. E-mail: jewishpress@aol.com.
Karen Wolfson Dawkins. Biweekly. Jewish Press Group of Tampa Bay (FL), Inc.
in cooperation with the Jewish Federation of Pinellas County. (WWW.JEWISH-
PINELLAS.ORG)

JEWISH PRESS OF TAMPA (1987). PO
Box 6970, Clearwater 33758-6970. (813)
871-2332. FAX: (727)535-4400. E-mail:
jewishpress@aol.com. Karen Wolfson
Dawkins. Biweekly. Jewish Press Group
of Tampa Bay (FL), Inc.

L'CHAYIM (2003). 6237-E Presidential
Court, Ft. Myers 33919. (941)481-4449.
FAX: (941)481-0139. Deborah Robbins
Millman. Biweekly. Jewish Federation of
Lee & Charlotte Counties.

THE NEWS (2002). 108-A Barton Ave., Rockledge 32955. (407)636-1824. FAX: (407)
636-0614. Ann C. Samuels. Biweekly. Jewish Federation of Brevard County.

SARASOTA-MANATEE JEWISH NEWS (2000).
580 S. McIntosh Rd., Sarasota 34232.
(941)371-4546. Howard Trevlowitz. Weekly. Sarasota/Manatee Jewish Federation.
(WWW.SMJF.ORG)

SHALOM TODAY-BROWARD (1994). 200 E.
Las Olas Blvd., 10th Floor, Ft. Lauderdale
33301. (954)356-4000. FAX: (954) 429-
1207. E-mail: shalom@sun-sentinel.com.
Bob Gremillion. Weekly. Jewish Federation of Broward County.

SHALOM TODAY-PALM BEACH (1994). 3333
S. Congress Ave., Delray Beach 33445.
(561)243-6600. FAX: (561)243-6546. E-
mail: shalom@sun-sentinel.com. Michelle
Simon & Bruce Warshal. Weekly. Jewish
Federation of Palm Beach County.

GEORGIA

ATLANTA JEWISH TIMES (1925).1117 Perimeter Center West, Suite N311, Atlanta,

GA 30338. (404)564-4550. FAX:
(404)252-1172. E-mail: mjacobs. Michael
Jacobs. Weekly. (WWW.ATLJEWISHTIMES.
COM)

ILLINOIS

CHICAGO JEWISH NEWS (1994). 5301 W.
Dempster, Skokie, Ill 60077. (847)966-
0606. FAX: (847)966-1656. E-mail:
paulinecjn@attglobal.net. Pauline Year-
wood. Weekly. (WWW.CHICAGOJEWISH-
NEWS.COM)

CHICAGO JEWISH STAR (1991). PO Box 268,
Skokie, 60076-0268. (847)674-7827. FAX:
(847)674-0014. E-mail: chicagojewish-
star@comcast.net. Douglas Wertheimer.
Fortnightly.

JEWISH COMMUNITY NEWS (1941). 6464 W.
Main, Suite 7A, Belleville, 62223. (618)398-
6100. FAX: (618)398-0539. E-mail: Steve
Low. Quarterly. Jewish Federation of
Southern Illinois. (WWW.SIMOKYFED.COM)

JUF NEWS & GUIDE TO JEWISH LIVING IN
CHICAGO (1972). One S. Franklin St., Rm.
701G, Chicago, 60606. (312)357-4848.
FAX: (312)855-2470. E-mail: sondra-
fargo@juf.org. Sondra Fargo. Monthly
(Guide, annually). Jewish United Fund/
Jewish Federation of Metropolitan Chi-
cago.

INDIANA

ALEPH: HISTORICAL STUDIES IN SCIENCE
AND JUDAISM (2001). Indiana University
Press, 601 N. Morton St., Bloomington,
47404. (812)855-3830. FAX: (812)855-
8507. E-mail: kcaras@indiana.edu. Edi-
torial address: Sidney Edelstein Center,
Hebrew University of Jerusalem, Givat
Ram, Jerusalem 91904, Israel. Gad
Freudenthal. Annual.

BRIDGES: A JOURNAL OF JEWISH FEMINISM
(1996).4860 Washtenaw Ave, Ann Arbor,
MI 48108. (734)395-4438. FAX:
(812)855-8507. E-mail: clare@bridges
journal.org. Editorial address: P.O. Box
1206, Ann Arbor, MI 48106. Clare Kin-
berg. Semiannual. (WWW.BRIDGESJOUR-
NAL.COM)

HISTORY AND MEMORY (1995). Indiana
University Press, 601 N. Morton St.,
Bloomington 47404. (812)855-3830.
FAX: (812)855-8507. E-mail: kcaras@in-
diana.edu. Editorial address: School of
History, Tel Aviv University, Ramat Aviv,
Tel Aviv 69978 Israel. Gadi Algazi. Semi-
annual.

INDIANA JEWISH POST AND OPINION (1935). 238 S. Meridian St., #502, Indianapolis, 46225. (317)972-7800. FAX: (317)972-7807. E-mail: ads@indy.rr.com. Gabriel Cohen. Weekly.

ISRAEL STUDIES (1996). Indiana University Press, 601 Morton St., Bloomington 47404. (812)855-3830. FAX: (812)855-8507. E-mail: kcaras@indiana.edu. Editorial address: Ben-Gurion Research Center, Sede-Boker Campus, Israel 84990. Three times a year.

JEWISH SOCIAL STUDIES: HISTORY, CULTURE, AND SOCIETY (1939, new series 1995). Indiana University Press, 601 N. Morton St., Bloomington 47404. (812) 855-3830. FAX: (812)855-8507. E-mail: kcaras@indiana.edu. Editorial address: Taube Center for Jewish Studies, Bldg. 240, Rm. 203, Stanford University, Stanford, CA 94305-2190. Steven J Zipperstein, Aron Rodrigue. Three times a year.

NASHIM (2001). Indiana University Press, 601 N. Morton St., Bloomington 47404. (812)855-3830. FAX: (812)855-8507. E-mail: kcaras@indiana.edu. Editorial address: P.O. Box 16080, Jerusalem 91160, Israel. Renée Levine Melammed. Semiannual.

NATIONAL JEWISH POST AND OPINION (1932). 238 S. Meridian St., Indianapolis, 46225. (317)972-7800. FAX: (317)972-7807. E-mail: jpost@surf.ici.com. Gabriel Cohen. Weekly. (WWW.JEWISHPOSTOPINION.COM)

PROOFTEXTS: A JOURNAL OF JEWISH LITERARY HISTORY (1980). Indiana University Press, 601 N. Morton St., Bloomington, 47404. (812)855-8507. FAX: (812)855-8507. E-mail: kcaras@indiana.edu. Editorial address: Dept. of Hebrew Language, Box 46, Jewish Theological Seminary, 3080 Broadway, NY, NY 10027-4649. Jeremy Dauber, Barbara Mann. Three times a year.

KANSAS

KANSAS CITY JEWISH CHRONICLE (1920).4370 W. 109th Street, Suite 300. Overland Park, KS, 66211. (913)381-1010. FAX: (913)381-9889. E-mail: chronicle@sunpublications.com. Rick Hellman. Weekly. Sun Publications. (WWW.KCJC.COM)

KENTUCKY

COMMUNITY (1975). 3630 Dutchmans Lane, Louisville, 40205-3200. (502) 451-8840.

FAX: (502) 458-0702. E-mail: jfed @iglou.com. Sheila Steinman Wallace. Biweekly. Jewish Community Federation of Louisville.

LOUISIANA

JEWISH CIVIC PRESS (1965). 924 Valmont St., New Orleans 70115. (504)875-8784. E-mail: jewishcivicpress.com. Claire & Abner Tritt. Monthly.

JEWISH NEWS (1995). 3747 W. Esplanade Avenue, Suite 307, Metairie, LA 70002. (504)780-5614. FAX: (504)780-5601. E-mail: jewishnews@jewishnola.com. Julie Schwartz. Fortnightly. Jewish Federation of Greater New Orleans.

MARYLAND

BALTIMORE JEWISH TIMES (1919). 1040 Park Ave, Suite 200., Baltimore, 21201. (410) 752-3504. FAX: (410)752-2375. E-mail: editor@jewishtimes.com. Neil Rubin. Weekly. (WWW.JEWISHTIMES.COM)

WASHINGTON JEWISH WEEK (1930, as the National Jewish Ledger). 11426 Rockville Pike, Suite 236, Rockville 20852. (301) 230-2222. FAX: (301)881-6362. E-mail: wjweek@aol.com. Debra Rubin. Weekly. (WWW.WASHINGTONJEWISHWEEK.COM)

MASSACHUSETTS

AMERICAN JEWISH HISTORY (1892). 160 Herrick Road, Newton Centre, MA 02459. (671)559-8880. FAX: (671)559 8881. E-mail: ajhs@ajhs.org. Eli Faber. Quarterly. American Jewish Historical Society.

THE JEWISH ADVOCATE (1902). 15 School St., Boston, 02108. (617)367-9100. FAX: (617) 367-9310. E-mail: kristine@thejewishadvocate.com. Y.A. Korff. Weekly. (WWW.THEJEWISHADVOCATE.COM)

THE JEWISH CHRONICLE (1927). 131 Lincoln St., Worcester, 01605. (508)752-3400. E-mail: chronicle.editor@verizon.net. Ellen Weingart. Fortnightly.

JEWISH GUIDE TO BOSTON & NEW ENGLAND (1972). 15 School St., Boston, 02108. (617)367-9100. FAX: (617)367-9310. Rosie Rosenzweig. Irregularly. The Jewish Advocate.

THE JEWISH JOURNAL/NORTH OF BOSTON (1976). 201 Washington St., PO Box 555, Salem, 01970. (978)745-4111 .FAX: (978)745-5333. E-mail: editorial@jewishjournal.org. Bette Keva. Biweekly.

Russian section. North Shore Jewish Press Ltd. (WWW.JEWISHJOURNAL.ORG)

THE JEWISH NEWS OF WESTERN MASSACHUSETTS (*see* Jewish Advocate)

METROWEST JEWISH REPORTER (1970). 76 Salem End Rd., Framingham, 01702. (508)872-4808. FAX: (508)879-5856. Marcia T. Rivin. Monthly. Combined Jewish Philanthropies of Greater Boston.

PAKN-TREGER (1980). 1021 West St., Amherst, 01002. (413)256-4900. FAX: (413)256-4700. E-mail: pt@bikher.org. Nancy Sherman. Three times a year. National Yiddish Book Center.

SH'MA (1970). 90 Oak Street, 4th Floor, Newton MA 02459. (781)449-9894. FAX: (781)449-9825. E-mail: susanb@jflmedia.com. Susan Berrin. Monthly. Jewish Family & Life.

MICHIGAN

DETROIT JEWISH NEWS (1942). 29200 Northwestern Highway, Ste. 110, Southfield, 48034. (248)354-6060. Fax: (248) 304-8885. E-mail: rsklar@jnonline.com. Arhur Hurwitz. Weekly. (WWW.JNON LINE.US)

HUMANISTIC JUDAISM (1968). 28611 W. Twelve Mile Rd., Farmington Hills, 48334. (248)478-7610. FAX: (248)478-3159. E-mail: info@shj.org. M. Bonnie Cousens, Ruth D. Feldman. Quarterly. Society for Humanistic Judaism. (www. SHJ.ORG)

WASHTENAW JEWISH NEWS (1978). 2935 Birch Hollow Dr., Ann Arbor, 48108. (734)971-1800. FAX: (734)971-1801. E-mail: wjna2@aol.com. Susan Kravitz Ayer. Monthly. (WWW.HVCN.ORG)

MINNESOTA

AMERICAN JEWISH WORLD (1912). 4509 Minnetonka Blvd., Minneapolis, MN 55416. (952)259-5280. FAX: (952)920-6205. E-mail: ajw@bcmn.com. Mordecai Specktor. Weekly.

MISSISSIPPI

DEEP SOUTH JEWISH VOICE (*see* Alabama)

MISSOURI

JEWISH CURRENT EVENTS (1958). P.O. Box 16683, St. Louis, 63105. (314-482-3869. E-mail: lraileanu@jewishcurrentevents. com. Michael S. Raileanu. Semi-monthly,

Oct.–May. (WWW.JEWISHCURRENTEVENTS. COM)

KANSAS CITY JEWISH CHRONICLE. *See under* KANSAS

ST. LOUIS JEWISH LIGHT (1947; reorg. 1963). 12 Millstone Campus Dr., St. Louis, 63146. (314)743-3600. FAX: (314)432-0515. E-mail: dbaugher@thejewishlight. com. David Baugher. Weekly. (www.STL JEWISHLIGHT.COM)

NEBRASKA

JEWISH PRESS (1920). 333 S. 132 St., Omaha, 68154. (402)334-6450. FAX: (402)334-5422. E-mail: ckatzman@jewishomaha.org. Carol Katzman. Weekly. Jewish Federation of Omaha.

NEVADA

JEWISH REPORTER (1976). 3909 S. Maryland Pkwy., Suite 400, Las Vegas, 89119-7520. (702)948-5129. FAX: (702)967-1082. E-mail: editor@jewushlasvegas.com. Leah Brown. Bimonthly. Jewish Federation of Las Vegas.

LAS VEGAS ISRAELITE (1965). PO Box 14096, Las Vegas, 89114. (702)876-1255. FAX: (702)364-1009. Michael Tell. Bimonthly.

NEW JERSEY

AVOTAYNU (1985). 155 N. Washington Ave., Bergenfield, 07621. (201)387-7200. FAX: (201)387-2855. E-mail: info@avotaynu. com. Sallyann Amdur Sack. Quarterly.

JEWISH CHRONICLE (1982). 1063 East Landis Ave.,Suite B, Vineland, 08360. (856)696-4445. FAX: (856)696-3428. E-mail: kirkw@jfedcc.com. Kirk Weissmeyer. Bimonthly. The Jewish Federation of Cumberland County.

JEWISH COMMUNITY NEWS & JEWISH STANDARD (1931). 1086 Teaneck Rd., Teaneck, 07666. (201) 837-8818. FAX: (201) 833-4959. E-mail: pr@jewishmediagroup. com. Rebecca Kaplan Boroson. Weekly. Jewish Federation of North Jersey and Jewish Federation of Greater Clifton-Passaic.

JEWISH COMMUNITY VOICE (1941). 1301 Springdale Rd., Suite 250, Cherry Hill, 08003-2762. (856)751-9500, ext. 248. FAX: (856)489-8253. E-mail: bkessler@ jfedsnj.org. Harriet Kessler. Biweekly. Jewish Federation of Southern NJ.

THE JEWISH JOURNAL (OCEAN COUNTY) (1999). 320 Raritan Ave., Suite 203, Highland Park, 08904. (732)393-0023. FAX: (732)393-0026. E-mail: jewish@castle.net. Ron Ostroff. Monthly. Published in cooperation with the Jewish Federation of Ocean County.

JEWISH STAR (1985). 230 Old Bridge Turnpike, South River, 08882-2000. (732)432-7711. FAX: (732)432-0292. E-mail: mfertig@thejewishstar.com. Mayer Fertig. Fortnightly. Jewish Federation of Greater Middlesex County.

JEWISH VOICE & OPINION (1987). 73 Dana Place, Englewood, 07631. (201) 569-2845. FAX: (201)569-1739. Susan L. Rosenbluth. Monthly.

JOURNAL OF JEWISH COMMUNAL SERVICE (1899). 3084 State Hwy. 27, Suite 9, Kendall Pk., 08824-1657. (732)821-1871. FAX: (732)821-5335. E-mail: jcsana@aol.com. Gail Naron Chalew. Quarterly. Jewish Communal Service Association of North America.

NEW JERSEY JEWISH NEWS (1947). 901 Route 10, Whippany, 07981-1157. (973) 929-3137. FAX: (973)887-5999. E-mail: mleitzes@njjewishnews.com. Andrew Silow-Carroll. Weekly. United Jewish Federation of MetroWest. (WWW.NJJEWISHNEWS.COM)

THE SPEAKER (1999). 320 Raritan Ave., Suite 203, Highland Park, 08904. (732)393-0023. FAX: (732)393-0026. E-mail: jewish@castle.net. Ron Ostroff. Monthly. Published in cooperation with the Jewish Federation of Somerset, Hunterdon & Warren Counties.

NEW MEXICO

NEW MEXICO JEWISH LINK (1971). 5520 Wyoming NE, Albuquerque, 87109. (502)821-3214. FAX: (505)821-3351. E-mail: susan@jewishnewmexico.org. Susan Abonyi. Monthly. Jewish Federation of Greater Albuquerque.

NEW YORK

AFN SHVEL (1941). 200 W. 72 St., Suite 40, NYC, 10023. (212)787-6675. E-mail: yidleague@aol.com. Quarterly. Yiddish. League for Yiddish, Inc. (WWW.LEAGUEFORYIDDISH.COM)

AGENDA: JEWISH EDUCATION (1949). JESNA, 111 Eighth Ave., Suite 11E, NYC, 10011-5201. (212)284-6950. FAX:

(212)284-6951. E-mail: info@jesna.org. Amy Stein. Twice a year. Jewish Education Service of North America, Inc.

ALGEMEINER JOURNAL (1972). 225 E. Broadway, NYC, 10002. (212)267-5561. FAX: (212)267-5624. E-mail: Algemeiner@aol.com. Yosef Y. Jacobson. Weekly. Yiddish-English. (WWW.ALGEMEINER.COM)

AMERICAN JEWISH YEAR BOOK (1899). 165 E. 56 St., NYC, 10022. (212)751-4000. FAX: (212)751-4017. E-mail: research@ajc.org. David Singer, Lawrence Grossman. Annually. American Jewish Committee.

AMIT (1925). 817 Broadway, NYC, 10003. (212)477-4720. FAX: (212)477-5213. E-mail: amitmag@amitchildren.org. Charlotte Schneierson. Quarterly. AMIT (formerly American Mizrachi Women). (WWW.AMITCHILDREN.ORG)

AUFBAU (1934). 2121 Broadway, NYC, 10023. (212)873-7400. Voice mail: (212) 579-6578. FAX: (212)496-5736. E-mail: aufbau2000@aol.com. Monika Ziegler/Andreas Mink/Irene Armbruster. Fortnightly. German-English. New World Club, Inc.

BUFFALO JEWISH REVIEW (1918). 15 E. Mohawk St., Buffalo, 14203. (716)854-2192. FAX: (716)854-2198. E-mail: buffjewrev@aol.com. Rita Weiss. Weekly. Kahaal Nahalot Israel. (WWW.BUFFALOJEWISHREVIEW.ORG)

THE CALL (1933). 45 E. 33 St., NYC, 10016. (212)889-6800, ext. 225. FAX: (212)532-7518. E-mail: socolove@circle.org. Emily Socolov. Three times a year. The Workmen's Circle/Arbeter Ring.

CCAR JOURNAL: A REFORM JEWISH QUARTERLY (formerly JOURNAL OF REFORM JUDAISM) (1953). 355 Lexington Ave., NYC, 10017. (212)972-3636. FAX: (212)692-0819. Ed. Stephen Pearce. Mng. Ed. Elliot Stevens. Quarterly. Central Conference of American Rabbis. (WWW.CCARNET.ORG)

CIRCLE (1943). 15 E. 26 St., NYC, 10010-1579. (212)532-4949. FAX: (212)481-4174. E-mail: info@jcca.org. Miriam Rinn. JCC Circle Quarterly. Jewish Community Centers Association of North America (formerly JWB).

COMMENTARY (1945). 165 E. 56 St., NYC, 10022. (212)751-4000. FAX: (212)891-6700. E-mail: mail@commentarymagazine.com. Ed. Neal Kozodoy; Ed.-at-Large

Norman Podhoretz. Monthly. American Jewish Committee.

CONGRESS MONTHLY (1933). 825 Third Ave., Ste. 1800, NYC, 10022. (212)879-4500. Rochelle Mancini. Six times a year. American Jewish Congress.

CONSERVATIVE JUDAISM (1945). 3080 Broadway, NYC, 10027. (212)280-6065. FAX: (212)749-9166. E-mail: rapubs@jtsa.edu. Rabbi Martin S. Cohen. Quarterly. Rabbinical Assembly and Jewish Theological Seminary of America.

FORVERTS (Yiddish Forward) (1897). 45 E. 33 St., NYC, 10016. (212)889-8200. FAX: (212)684-3949. Boris Sandler. Weekly. Yiddish. Forward Association, Inc. (www.YIDDISH.FOWARD.COM)

FORWARD (1897). 45 E. 33 St., NYC, 10016. (212)889-8200. FAX: (212)447-6406. E-mail: newsdesk@forward.com. J. J. Goldberg. Weekly. Forward Newspaper, L.L.C.

HADAROM (1957). 305 Seventh Ave., NYC, 10001. (212)807-7888. FAX: (212)727-8452. Rabbi Gedalia Dov Schwartz. Annual. Hebrew. Rabbinical Council of America

HADASSAH MAGAZINE (1914). 50 W. 58 St., NYC, 10019. (212)688-0227. FAX: (212)446-9521. Alan M. Tigay. Monthly (except for combined issues of June-July and Aug.-Sept.). Hadassah, the Women's Zionist Organization of America.

HEEB MAGAZINE (2002). P.O. Box 687, NYC, 10012. E-mail: info@heebmagazine.com. Joshua Neuman. Quarterly. (WWW.HEEBMAGAZINE.COM)

I.A.J.E. NEWSLETTER (1999). (718)339-0337. E-mail: sanuav@stjohns.edu. Victor D. Sanua. International Association of Jews from Egypt.

JBI VOICE (1978). 110 E. 30 St., NYC, 10016. (212)889-2525, (800)433-1531, FAX (212) 689-3692. Email: dbarbara@jblibrary.org. Dena Barbara. Ten times a year in U.S. (Audiocassettes). English. Jewish Braille Institute Of America. (WWW.JEWISHBRAILE.ORG)

JEWISH ACTION (1950). 11 Broadway, NYC, 10004. (212)613-8146. FAX: (212)613-0646. E-mail: ja@ou.org. Nechama Carmel. Quarterly. Orthodox Union. (OU.ORG/JEWISH__ACTION)

JEWISH BOOK ANNUAL (1942). 15 E. 26 St., 10th fl., New York, NY 10010. (212)532-4949, ext. 297. E-mail: jbc@jewishbooks.org. Dr. Stephen H. Garrin. Hebrew & English with bibliography in Yiddish. Jewish Book Council, Jewish Book Annual published by Jewish Book Council.

JEWISH BOOK WORLD (1945). 15 E. 26 St., NYC, 10010. (212)532-4949, ext. 297. FAX: (212)481-4174. E-mail: jbc@jewishbooks.org. Esther Nussbaum. Three times annually. Jewish Book Council.

JEWISH BRAILLE REVIEW (1931). 110 E. 30 St., NYC, 10016. E-mail:dbarbara@jbilibrary.org. (212)889-2525, (800)433-1531. Dena Barbara. 10 times a year in U.S. (braille). English. Jewish Braille Institute of America.

JEWISH CURRENTS (1946) 45 East 33rd Street, 4th floor, NYC, 10016. (212)924-5740. FAX: (212)414-2227. Bimonthly. Association for Promotion of Jewish Secularism, Inc. (WWW.JEWISHCURRENTS.ORG)

JEWISH EDUCATION NEWS (1980). 261 W. 35 St., Fl. 12A, NYC 10001. (212) 268-4210. FAX: (212)268-4214. E-mail: publications@caje.org. Mng. Ed. Judi Resnick. Triannually. Coalition for the Advancement of Jewish Education.

JEWISH FRONTIER (1934). P.O. Box 4013, Amity Station, New Haven, CT 06525. (203)397-4903. FAX: (212)675-7685. E-mail: jewishfrontier@yahoo.com. Nahum Guttman-Graff. Bimonthly. Labor Zionist Letters, Inc. Managing Editor Bennett Lovett-Graff

JEWISH HERALD (1984). 1689 46 St., Brooklyn, NY 11204. (718)972-4000. E-mail: jewishherald@aol. Com. Leon J. Sternheim. Weekly.

JEWISH JOURNAL (1969). 11 Sunrise Plaza, Valley Stream, 11580. (516)561-6900. FAX: (516)561-6971. Paul Rubens. Weekly.

JEWISH OBSERVER (1963). 42 Broadway, NYC, 10004. (212)797-9000. FAX: (646) 254-1600. E-mail: nwolpin@aol.com. Rabbi Nisson Wolpin. Monthly (except July and Aug.). Agudath Israel of America. (WWW.SHEMAYISRAEL.COM/JEWISHOBSERVER)

JEWISH OBSERVER OF CENTRAL NEW YORK (1978). 5655 Thompson Road, DeWitt, NY 13214. (315)445-2040 ext. 116. FAX: (315)445-1559. E-mail: jocny@aol.com.

Bette Siegel. Biweekly. Syracuse Jewish Federation, Inc.

JEWISH POST OF NY (1993). 262 West 38th St., NYC, 10018. (212)398-1313. FAX: (212)398-3933. E-mail: jpost@nais.com. Ed. Gad Nahshon. Monthly. Link Marketing & Promotion, Inc.

JEWISH PRESS (1950). 338 Third Ave., Brooklyn, 11215. (718)330-1100. FAX: (718)935-1215. E-mail: editor@jewishpress.com. Jerry Greenwald. Weekly. (WWW.THEJEWISHPRESS.COM)

JEWISH TELEGRAPHIC AGENCY COMMUNITY NEWS REPORTER (1962). 330 Seventh Ave., 11th fl., NYC, 10001-5010. (212) 643-1890. Fax: (212)643-8498. Email: . Lisa Hostein. Monthly.

JEWISH TELEGRAPHIC AGENCY DAILY NEWS BULLETIN (1917). 330 Seventh Ave., 11th fl., NYC, 10001-5010. (212)643-1890. FAX: (212)643-8498. Exec. Ed. Mark Joffe; Ed. Lisa Hostein. Daily.

JEWISH TELEGRAPHIC AGENCY WEEKLY NEWS DIGEST (1933). 330 Seventh Ave., 11th fl., NYC, 10001-5010. (212)643-1890. FAX: (212)643-8498. E-mail: www.jta.org/info@jta.org. Exec. Ed. Mark Joffe; Ed. Lisa Hostein. Weekly.

JEWISH TRIBUNE. PMB #372, 169 South Main St., New City, 10956; Exec. off. (mailing address): 115 Middle Neck Rd., Great Neck, 11021. (845)352-5151. FAX: (516)829-4776. E-mail: lijeworld@aol. com. Jerome W. Lippman. Weekly. Jewish Tribune; Long Island Jewish World; Manhattan Jewish Sentinel.

JEWISH WEEK (1876; reorg. 1970). 1501 Broadway, NYC, 10036-5503. (212)921-7822. FAX: (212)921-8420. E-mail: editor@jewishweek.org. Gary Rosenblatt. Weekly. (WWW.THEJEWISHWEEK.COM)

JEWISH WORLD (1965). 3 Vatrano Road, Albany, 12205. (518)459-8455. FAX: (518) 459-5289. E-Mail: News@jewishworldnews.org. Sam S. Clevenson. Weekly.

JOURNAL OF JEWISH EDUCATION-CJE (formerly Jewish Education) (1929). 11 Olympia Lane, Monsey, NY 10952. (845)368-8657. FAX: (845)369-6538. E-mail: mjscje@aol.com. Rabbi Irwin E. Witty. Three times a year. Council for Jewish Education.

JOURNAL OF REFORM JUDAISM. See CCAR Journal

JTS PUBLICATIONS (1991). 3080 Broadway, NYC 10027. (212)678-8950. FAX: (212) 864-0109. E-mail: jowerner@jtsa.edu. Three times a year. The Jewish Theological Seminary. Asst. Dir. of Pub. Jodi Werner.

JUDAISM (1952). 825 Third Ave., Ste. 1800, NYC, 10022. (212)360-1500. FAX: (212)249-3672. Editor's address: Kresge Col., U. of California, Santa Cruz, CA, 95064. (831)459-2566. FAX: (831)459-4872. E-mail: judaism@cats.Ucsc.edu. Prof. Murray Baumgarten. Quarterly. American Jewish Congress.

KASHRUS MONTHLY-YOUR UPDATE ON KOSHER (1990). PO Box 204, Brooklyn, 11204. (718)336-8544. Rabbi Yosef Wikler. Monthly. Kashrus Institute. (EDITORIAL@KASHRUSMAGAZIN.COM)

KASHRUS MAGAZINE-THE PERIODICAL FOR THE KOSHER CONSUMER (1980). PO Box 204, Brooklyn, 11204. (718)336-8544. E-mail: editorial@kashrusmagazine.com. Rabbi Yosef Wikler. Five times per year (January, March, May, July, October). Kashrus Institute. (WWW.KASHRUSMAGAZINE.COM)

KOL HAT'NUA (Voice of the Movement) (1975). c/o Young Judaea, 50 W. 58 St., NYC, 10019. (212)303-4576. FAX: (212)303-4572. E-mail: info@youngjudaea.org. Dov Wilker. Quarterly. Hadassah Zionist Youth Commission-Young Judaea.

KULTUR UN LEBN-CULTURE AND LIFE (1960). 45 E. 33 St., NYC, 10016. (212) 889-6800. Fax: (212)532-7518. E-mail: wcfriends@aol.com. Joseph Mlotek. Quarterly. Yiddish. The Workmen's Circle.

LIKUTIM (1981). 110 E. 30 St., NYC, 10016. (212)889-2525. Joanne Jahr. Two times a year in Israel (print and audiocassettes). Hebrew. Jewish Braille Institute of America.

LILITH-THE INDEPENDENT JEWISH WOMEN'S MAGAZINE (1976). 250 W. 57 St., #2432, NYC, 10107. (212)757-0818. FAX: (212) 757-5705. E-mail: lilithmag@aol.com. Susan Weidman Schneider. Quarterly. (WWW.LILITHMAG.COM)

LONG ISLAND JEWISH WORLD (1971). 115 Middle Neck Rd., Great Neck, 11021. (516)829-4000. FAX: (516)829-4776. E-mail: lijeworld@aol.com. Jerome W. Lippman. Weekly.

MANHATTAN JEWISH SENTINEL (1993). 115 Middle Neck Rd., Great Neck, 11021. (212)244-4949. FAX: (212)244-2257. E-mail: lijeworld@aol.com. Jerome W. Lippman. Weekly.

MARTYRDOM AND RESISTANCE (1974). 500 Fifth Ave., 42nd Floor, NYC, 10110-4299. (212)220-4304. FAX:(212)220-4308. E-mail: yadvashem@aol.com. Ed. Dr. Harvey Rosenfeld; Ed.-in-Chief Eli Zborowski. Bimonthly. International Society for Yad Vashem.

MEOROT (2007, formerly EDAH JOURNAL). 475 Riverside Dr., Ste. 244, NYC, 10115. (212)666-0036. FAX: (212)666-5633. E-mail: meorotjournal@yctorah.org. Dr. Eugene Korn. Semiannual. Yeshivat Chovevei Torah.

MIDSTREAM (1954). 633 Third Ave., 21st fl., NYC, 10017. (212)339-6020. FAX: (212)318-6176. E-mail: midstreamthf@aol.com. Leo Haber. Eight times a year. Theodor Herzl Foundation, Inc. (WWW.MIDSTREAMTHF.COM)

NA'AMAT WOMAN (1925). 350 Fifth Ave., Suite 4700, NYC, 10118-4799. (212)563-5222. FAX: (212)563-5710. Judith A. Sokoloff. Quarterly. English-Yiddish-Hebrew. NA'AMAT USA, the Women's Labor Zionist Organization of America.

NEW VOICES MAGAZINE (1991). 114 W. 26 St., #1004, NYC 10001. (212)674-1168. FAX: (212)929-33459. E-mail: editor @newvoices.org. Ilana Sichel. Five times per academic year. Jewish Student Press Service. (WWW.NEWVOICES.ORG)

OLOMEINU-OUR WORLD (1945). 5723 18th Ave., Brooklyn, 11204. (718)259-1223. Fax: (718)259-1795. Email: mail@tupublications.com. Rabbi Yaakov Fruchter. Monthly. English-Hebrew. Torah Umesorah-National Society for Hebrew Day Schools.

PASSOVER DIRECTORY (1923). 11 Broadway, NYC, 10004. (212)613-8135. FAX: (212) 613-0772. Email: lieberd@ou.org Deborah Lieber. Annually. Union of Orthodox Jewish Congregations of America.

PRESENTENSE MAGAZINE (2006). 214 Sullivan St., Ste. 2A, NYC, 10012. E-mail: editor @presentensemagazine.org. Ariel Beery. Semiannual. Independently published by volunteer-based grassroots network.

PROCEEDINGS OF THE AMERICAN ACADEMY FOR JEWISH RESEARCH (1920). 51 Washington Sq. South, NYC, 10012-1075. (212)998-3550. FAX: (212)995-4178. Dr. Nahum Sarna. Annually. English-Hebrew-French-Arabic-Persian-Greek. American Academy for Jewish Research.

RCA RECORD (1953). 305 Seventh Ave. NYC, 10001. (212)807-7888. FAX: (212)727-8452. Rabbi Mark Dratch. Quarterly. Rabbinical Council of America.

REFORM JUDAISM (1972; formerly DIMENSIONS IN AMERICAN JUDAISM). 633 Third Ave., 6th fl., NYC, 10017. (212)650-4240. Aron Hirt-Manheimer. Quarterly. Union for Reform Judaism. (URJ.ORG/RJMAG)

THE REPORTER (1971). 500 Clubhouse Rd., Vestal, 13850. (607)724-2360. FAX: (607) 724-2311. E-mail: TReporter@aol.com. Judith S. Huober. Weekly. Jewish Federation of Broome County, Inc.

THE REPORTER (1966). 315 Park Ave. S., NYC 10010. (212)505-7700. FAX: (212) 674-3057. E-Mail: editor@waort.org. Marlene A. Heller. Semi-Annual. Women's American Ort, Inc.

RESPONSE: A CONTEMPORARY JEWISH REVIEW (1967). Columbia University Post Office, PO Box 250892, NYC, 10025. E-mail: response@panix.com. Chanita Baumhaft. Annual.

RUSSIAN FORWARD (1995). 45 E. 33 St., NYC, 10016. (212)889-8200. FAX: (212) 448-9124. E-mail: rforward99@yahoo.com. Leonid Shkolnik. Weekly. Russian.

SOJOURN: THE JEWISH AMERICAN SAGA (2006). 80 Broad St., NYC 10004. (800)325-8152. E-mail: rkaplan@SojournSaga.com. Robert Kaplan. Bimonthly.

SYNAGOGUE LIGHT AND KOSHER LIFE (1933). 47 Beekman St., NYC, 10038. (212)227-7800. Rabbi Meyer Hager. Quarterly. The Kosher Food Institute.

TORAH U-MADDAH JOURNAL (1989). Att. Dr. David Shatz, 245 Lexington Ave., NYC 10016. (917)326-4856. FAX: (212)340-7788. E-mail: shatz@yu.edu. Dr. David Shatz. Annual. Center for the Jewish Future, Yeshiva University.

TRADITION (1958). 305 Seventh Ave., NYC, 10001. (212)807-7888. FAX: (212)727-8452. Rabbi Shalom Carmy. Quarterly. Rabbinical Council of America.

UNITED SYNAGOGUE REVIEW (1943). 155 Fifth Ave., NYC, 10010. (212)533-7800. FAX: (212)353-9439. E-mail: info@uscj. org. Lois Goldrich. Semiannually. United Synagogue of Conservative Judaism.

UNSER TSAIT (1941). 25 E. 21 St., 3rd fl., NYC, 10010. (212)475-0059. Bimonthly. Yiddish. Jewish Labor Bund.

VIEWPOINT MAGAZINE (1952). 3 W. 16 St., NYC, 10011. (212)929-1525, ext. 131. E-mail: Ncyi@youngisrael.org. Esther Altman. Quarterly. National Council of Young Israel.

VOICE OF THE DUTCHESS JEWISH COMMUNITY (1989). 110 Grand Ave., Poughkeepsie, 12603. (845)471-9811. FAX: (845)471-3233. E-mail: director@jewishdutchess.org. Business off.:500 Clubhouse Rd., Vestal, 13850. (607)724-2360. FAX: (607)724-2311. Sandy Gardner and Judith Huober. Monthly. Jewish Federation of Dutchess County, Inc.

WOMEN'S LEAGUE OUTLOOK MAGAZINE (1930-4/5 4/5 Riverside Drive, Suite 820, New York, 10115. (212)870-1260. FAX: (212)870-1261. E-mail: rkahn@wlcj.org. Janet Arnowitz. Quarterly. Women's League for Conservative Judaism. (WWW.WLCJ.ORG)

WYOMING VALLEY JEWISH REPORTER (formerly WE ARE ONE) (1995). 500 Clubhouse Rd., Vestal, 13850. (607)724-2360. FAX: (607)724-2311. E-mail: wbreport@aol.com. Gail Wachtel. Every other week. Wilkes-Barre Jewish Community Board.

YEARBOOK OF THE CENTRAL CONFERENCE OF AMERICAN RABBIS (1890). 355 Lexington Ave., NYC, 10017. (212)972-3636. FAX: (212)692-0819. Rabbi Elliot L. Stevens. Annually. Central Conference of American Rabbis.

YIDDISH (1973). Queens College, NSF 350, 65-30 Kissena Blvd., Flushing, 11367. (718)997-3622. Joseph C. Landis. Quarterly. Queens College Press.

DI YIDDISHE HEIM (1958). 770 Eastern Pkwy., Brooklyn, 11213. (718)735-0458. Rachel Altein, Tema Gurary. Twice a year. English-Yiddish. Neshei Ub'nos Chabad-Lubavitch Women's Organization.

DOS YIDDISHE VORT (1953). 84 William St., NYC, 10038. (212)797-9000. Joseph Friedenson. Bimonthly, (November-December monthly). Yiddish. Agudath Israel of America.

YIDISHE SHPRAKH (1941). 15 W. 16 St., NYC, 10011. (212)246-6080, ext. 6139. FAX: (212) 292-1892. Irregularly. Yiddish. YIVO Institute for Jewish Research.

YIVO BLETER (1931). 15 W. 16 St., NYC, 10011. (212)246-6080. FAX: (212)292-1892.E-mail: yivomail@yivo.cjh.org. Dr. David E. Fishman. Biannually. Yiddish. YIVO Institute for Jewish Research.

THE YOUNG JUDAEAN (1909). 50 W. 58 St., NYC, 10019. (212)303-4588. FAX: (212) 303-4572. Email: ugoldflam@young judaea.org. Uri Goldflam. Quarterly. Young Judaea Zionist Youth Movement/ Hadassah.

YUGNTRUF: YIDDISH YOUTH MAGAZINE (1964). 200 W. 72 St., Suite 40, NYC, 10023. (212)787-6675. FAX: (212)799-1517. E-mail: yugntruf@yugntruf.org. Elinor Robinson. Two to four times a year. Yiddish. Yugntruf Youth for Yiddish.

ZUKUNFT (THE FUTURE) (1892). 25 E. 21 St., NYC, 10010. (212)505-8040. FAX: (212)505-8044. Chaim Beider & Yonia Fain. Quarterly. Yiddish. Congress for Jewish Culture.

NORTH CAROLINA

CHARLOTTE JEWISH NEWS (1978). 5007 Providence Rd., Charlotte, 28226. (704)944-6765. FAX: (704) 365-4507. E-mail: amontoni@shalomcharlotte.org. Amy Montoni. Monthly (except July). Jewish Federation of Greater Charlotte.

JEWISH FEDERATION NEWS (1986). 8210 Creedmoor Rd., Suite 104, Raleigh, 27613. (919)676-2200. FAX: (919)676-2122. E-mail: beth.nathison@rcjf.org. Beth Nathison. Monthly. Wake County Jewish Federation.

MODERN JUDAISM (1980). Oxford University Press, 2001 Evans Rd., Cary, 27513. (919)677-0977. FAX: (919)677-1714. E-mail: jnlorders@oup-usa.org. (Editorial address: Center for Judaic Studies, Boston University, 745 Commonwealth Ave., Boston, 02215. (617)353-8096. FAX: (617)353-5441.) Steven T. Katz. Three times a year.

OHIO

AKRON JEWISH NEWS (1929). 750 White Pond Drive, Akron, 44320. (330)835-

0013, Ext. 313. FAX: (330)867-8498. E-mail: lisahoffman@jewishakron.org. Lisa Hoffman. Fortnightly. Fifteen times a year. Jewish Community Board of Akron. (WWW.AKRONJEWISHNEWS.COM)

AMERICAN ISRAELITE (1854). 18 W. 9th St., Ste. 2, Cincinnati, 45202-1371. (513)621-3145. FAX: (513)621-3744. E-mail: aiarticles@fuse.net. Netanel Deutsch. Weekly. (WWW.AMERICANISRAELITE.COM)

AMERICAN JEWISH ARCHIVES JOURNAL (1948). 3101 Clifton Ave., Cincinnati, 45220-2488. (513)221-1875. FAX: (513) 221-7812. E-mail: aja@cn.huc.edu. Ed. Dr. Gary P. Zola; Mng. Ed. Dr. Frederic Krome. Twice a year. Jacob Rader Marcus Center, American Jewish Archives, HUC-JIR. (www. AMERICANJEWISHARCHIVES.ORG)

CLEVELAND JEWISH NEWS (1964). 23880 Commerce Park, Ste. 1, Cleveland, 44122. (216)991-8300. FAX: (216)991-8200. E-mail: editorial@cjn.org. Cynthia Dettelbach. Weekly. Cleveland Jewish News Publication Co. (WWW.CLEVELANDJEWISH-NEWS.COM)

INDEX TO JEWISH PERIODICALS (1963). PO Box 18525, Cleveland Hts., 44118. (216) 381-4846. FAX: (216)381-4321. E-mail: index@jewishperiodicals.com. Lenore Pfeffer Koppel. Annually. Available in book and CD-ROM form. (WWW.JEWISH PERIODICALS.COM)

JEWISH JOURNAL (1987). 505 Gypsy Lane, Youngstown, 44504-1314. (330)744-7902. FAX: (330)746-7926. Email: yojjournal@aol.com Sherry Weinblatt. Biweekly (except July/Aug.). Youngstown Area Jewish Federation. (WWW.JEWISHJOUR-NALPLUS.COM)

OHIO JEWISH CHRONICLE (1922). 2862 Johnstown Rd., Columbus, 43219. (614)337-2055. Fax: (614)337-2059. E-mail: ojc@insight.rr.com. Kris Galloway. Weekly.

STARK JEWISH NEWS (1920). 2631 Harvard Ave. NW, Canton, 44709. (330)452-6444. FAX: (330)452-4487. E-mail: starkjewishnews@aol.com. Karen Phillippi. Monthly. Canton Jewish Community Federation. (WWW.JEWISHCANTON.ORG)

STUDIES IN BIBLIOGRAPHY AND BOOKLORE (1953). 3101 Clifton Ave., Cincinnati, 45220. (513)221-1875. FAX: (513)221-0519. E-mail: lwolfson@huc.edu. Editor David J. Gilner; Managing Editor Laurel S. Wolfson. Irregularly. English-Hebrew-

etc. Library of Hebrew Union College-Jewish Institute of Religion.

TOLEDO JEWISH NEWS (1951). 6505 Sylvania Ave., Sylvania, 43560. (419)724-0363. FAX: (419)724-0423. E-mail: sharon@jewishtoledo.org. Laurie Cohen. Monthly. United Jewish Council of Greater Toledo.

OKLAHOMA

TULSA JEWISH REVIEW (1930). 2021 E. 71 St., Tulsa, 74136. (918)495-1100. FAX: (918)495-1220. Ed Ulrich. Monthly. Jewish Federation of Tulsa. (WWW.JEWISH-TULSA.ORG)

OREGON

JEWISH REVIEW (1959). 6680 SW Capitol Highway, Portland, OR 97219. Edit.: (503) 245-4340. FAX: (503) 245-4342. Adv.: (503) 546-9883. FAX: (503) 620-3433. E-mail: news@jewishreview.org. Paul Haist. Regular column in Russian. Fortnightly. Jewish Federation of Portland. (WWW.JEWISHREVIEW.ORG)

PENNSYLVANIA

COMMUNITY REVIEW (1925). 3301 N. Front St. Annex, Harrisburg, 17110. (717)236-9555, ext.3402. FAX:(717)236-2552. E-mail: localnews@jewishfedhbg.org. Carol L. Cohen. Fortnightly. United Jewish Community of Greater Harrisburg.

CONTEMPORARY JEWRY (1974), under the name JEWISH SOCIOLOGY AND SOCIAL RESEARCH). Graduate Center CUNY, Room 6112-13, 365 Fifth Avenue, New York, NY 10016. (212) 817-8772. FAX: (914) 235-6717. E-mail: heilman@qc.edu. Samuel C. Heilman. Annually. Association for the Social Scientific Study of Jewry.

JERUSALEM LETTER/VIEWPOINTS (1978). 1515 Locust St., Suite 703, Philadelphia, 19102. (215)772-0564. FAX: (215)772-0566. Zvi R. Marom. Fortnightly. Jerusalem Center for Public Affairs.

JEWISH CHRONICLE OF PITTSBURGH (1962). 5600 Baum Blvd., Pittsburgh, 15206. (412)687-1000. FAX:(412)687-5119. E-mail: lchottiner@pittchron.com. Lee Chottiner. Weekly. Pittsburgh Jewish Publication and Education Foundation.

JEWISH EXPONENT (1887). 2100 Arch St., Philadelphia, 19103. (215)832-0740. FAX: (215)569-3389. E-mail: csmilk@jewish exponent.com. Jonathan Tobin. Weekly.

JEWISH PERIODICALS / 693

Jewish Federation of Greater Philadelphia. (WWW.JEWISHEXPONENT.COM)

JEWISH POLITICAL STUDIES REVIEW (1989). 1515 Locust St., Suite 703, Philadelphia, 19102. (215)772-0564. FAX: (215)772-0566. Mark Ami-El. Twice a year. Jerusalem Center for Public Affairs.

JEWISH QUARTERLY REVIEW (1910). 420 Walnut St., Philadelphia, 19106. (215)238-1290. FAX: (215)238-1540. E-mail: jqroffice@sas.upenn.edu. Ed. David M. Goldenberg; Mng. Ed. Bonnie L. Blankenship. Quarterly. Center for Advanced Jewish Studies, University of Pennsylvania.

NEW MENORAH (1978). 7318 Germantown Ave., Philadelphia, 19119-1793. (215)247-9700. FAX: (215)247-9703. Rabbi Arthur Waskow, PhD. Quarterly. Aleph: Alliance for Jewish Renewal.

RECONSTRUCTIONISM TODAY (1993). Beit Devora, 7804 Montgomery Ave., Suite 9, Elkins Park, 19027-2649. (215)782-8500. FAX. (215)782-8805. E-mail: jrfnatl@aol. com. Lisa Kelvin Tuttle. Quarterly. Jewish Reconstructionist Federation.

THE RECONSTRUCTIONIST (1935). 1299 Church Rd., Wyncote, 19095-1898. (215) 576-5210. Fax: (215)576-8051. E-mail: rhirsh@therra.org. Rabbi Richard Hirsh. Semiannually. Reconstructionist Rabbinical College.

RHODE ISLAND

JEWISH VOICE AND HERALD (FORMERLY JEWISH VOICE OF RHODE ISLAND) (1973). 130 Sessions St., Providence, 02906. (401)421-4111. FAX: (401)331-7961. E-mail: jrubin@jfri.org. Jonathan Rubin. Bi-weekly. Jewish Federation of Rhode Island. (WWW.JFRI.ORG)

RHODE ISLAND JEWISH HERALD (1930). 99 Webster St., Pawtucket, 02860. (401)724-0200. FAX: (401)726-5820. Luke O'Neill. Weekly. Herald Press Publishing Company.

RHODE ISLAND JEWISH HISTORICAL NOTES (1951). 130 Sessions St., Providence, 02906. (401)331-1360. FAX: (401)272-6729. E-mail: rjhist@aol.com. Leonard Moss. Annually. Rhode Island Jewish Historical Association.

SOUTH CAROLINA

CHARLESTON JEWISH VOICE (2001). 1645 Wallenberg Blvd., Charleston, 29407.

(843)571-6565. Fax: (843)556-6206. E-mail: robyncohen@comcast.net. Robyn Cohen. Monthly. Charleston Jewish Federation.

TENNESSEE

HEBREW WATCHMAN (1925). 4646 Poplar Ave., Suite 232, Memphis, 38117. (901)763-2215. FAX: (901)763-2216. E-mail: hebwat@bellsouth.net. Herman I. Goldberger. Weekly.

OBSERVER (1934). 801 Percy Warner Blvd., Suite 102, Nashville, 37205. (615)354-1637. FAX: (615)352-0056. E-mail: judy@jewishnashville.org. Judith A. Saks. Biweekly (except July). Jewish Federation of Nashville. (WWW.NASHVILLE.UJCFED-WEB.ORG)

SHOFAR. PO Box 8947, Chattanooga, 37414. (423)493-0270, Ext. 12. FAX: (423) 493-9997. E-mail: shofar@jcfgc.com. Rachel Schulson. Ten times a year. Jewish Federation of Greater Chattanooga.

TEXAS

JEWISH HERALD-VOICE (1908). P.O. Box 153, Houston, 77001-0153. (713)630-0391. FAX: (713)630-0404. E-mail: editor@jhvonline.net. Jeanne Samuels. Weekly. Four special issues:Rosh Hashanah; Passover; Wedding Planner; Bar/Bat Mitzvah Planner. (WWW.JHVONLINE.COM)

JEWISH JOURNAL OF SAN ANTONIO (1973). 8434 Ahern, San Antonio, 78213. (210) 828-9511. FAX: (210)342-8098. Barbara Richmond. Monthly (11 issues). Jewish Federation of San Antonio.

VIRGINIA

RENEWAL MAGAZINE (1984). 5041 Corporate Woods Drive, Suite 150, Virginia Beach, 23462. (757)671-1600. FAX: (757)671-7613. E-mail: news@ujft.org. Reba Karp. Quarterly. United Jewish Federation of Tidewater.

SOUTHEASTERN VIRGINIA JEWISH NEWS (1959). 5000 Corporate Woods Drive, Suite 200, Virginia Beach, 23462. (757)671-1600. FAX: (757)671-7613. E-mail: news@ujft.org. Terri Denison. 22 issues yearly. United Jewish Federation of Tidewater. (WWW.JEWISHVA.ORG)

WASHINGTON

JEWISH TRANSCRIPT (1924). 2041 Third Ave., Seattle, 98121. (206)441-4553. FAX: (206)441-2736. E-Mail: Editor@jtnews.

net. Joel Magalnick. Fortnightly. Jewish Federation of Greater Seattle. (www.JT-NEWS.NET)

WISCONSIN

WISCONSIN JEWISH CHRONICLE (1921). 1360 N. Prospect Ave., Milwaukee, 53202. (414)390-5888. FAX: (414)271-0487. E-mail: elana@milwaukeejewish.org. Elana Kahn-Oren. Weekly. Milwaukee Jewish Federation. (WWW.JEWISHCHRONICLE.ORG)

INDEXES

INDEX TO JEWISH PERIODICALS (1963). PO Box 22780, Beachwood, OH 44122. (216) 921-5566. FAX: (603)806-0575. E-mail: index@jewishperiodicals.com. Lenore Pfeffer Koppel. Annually. Available in book and CD-ROM form. (WWW.JEWISHPERIODICALS.COM)

NEWS SYNDICATES

JEWISH TELEGRAPHIC AGENCY, INC. (1917). 330 Seventh Ave., 17th fl., NYC., 10001-5010. (212)643-1890. FAX: (212)643-8498. Mark J. Joffe, Lisa Hostein. Daily.

CANADA

CANADIAN JEWISH HERALD (1977). 17 Anselme Lavigne, Dollard des Ormeaux, PQ H9A 1N3. (514)684-7667. FAX: (514) 684-7667. Ed./Pub. Dan Nimrod. Irregularly. Dawn Publishing Co., Ltd.

CANADIAN JEWISH NEWS (1971). 1500 Don Mills Rd., Suite 205, North York, ONT M3B 3K4. (416)391-1836. FAX: (416) 391-0829 (Adv.); (416)391-1836. FAX: (416)391-0829. E-mail: jrosen@cjnews.com. Jeff Rosen. 50 issues a year. Some French. (WWW.CJNEWS.COM)

CANADIAN JEWISH OUTLOOK (1963). #3-6184 Ash St., Vancouver, BC V5Z 3G9. (604)324-5101. FAX:(604)325-2470. E-mail: cjoutlook@telus.net. Carl Rosenberg. Six times per year. Canadian Jewish Outlook Society. (WWW.VCN.BC.CA/OUT-LOOK)

DAIS (1985) (formerly INTERCOM). 100 Sparks St., #650, Ottawa, ONT KIP 5B7. (613)233-8703. FAX: (613)233-8748. E-mail: canadianjewishcongress@cjc.ca. Jack Silverstone. Three times a year. Canadian Jewish Congress.

DIRECTIONS (1998) (formerly DIALOGUE (1988)). 1 Carré Cummings, Suite 202, Montreal, Quebec H3W 1M6. (514)345-64111. FAX: (514)345-6412. E-mail: etay@cjc.ca. Eta Yudin. Quarterly. French-English. Canadian Jewish Congress, Quebec Region.

JEWISH FREE PRESS (1990). 8411 Elbow Dr., SW Calgary, AB. T2V 1K8. (403)252-9423. Fax: (403)255-5640. Judy Shapiro. Fortnightly.

JEWISH POST & NEWS (1987). 113 Hutchings St., Winnipeg, MAN R2X 2V4. (204) 694-3332. FAX: (204)694-3916. E-mail: jewishp@mts.net. Matt Bellan. Weekly. (WWW.JEWISHPOSTANDNEWS.COM)

JEWISH STANDARD (1928). 1912A Avenue Road, Suite E5, Toronto, ONT M5M 4A1. (416)537-2696. FAX: (416)789-3872. E-mail: thejewishstandardasympatico.ca. Ed./Pub. Michael Hayman. Monthly.

JEWISH STANDARD (1928). 5184, Chemin de la Cote-des-Neiges, Suite 407, Montreal, Quebec H3T 1X8. Email: thejewishstandardasympatico.ca. Ed./Pub. Michael Hayman. Monthly

JEWISH TRIBUNE (1950). 15 Hove St., Toronto, ONT M3H 4Y8. (416)633-6224. FAX: (416)633-6299. E-mail: editor@jewishtribune.ca. Norm Gordner. B'nai Brith Canada, Bimonthly. (WWW.JEWISH TRIBUNE.CA)

JEWISH INDEPENDENT (formerly WESTERN BULLETIN) (1930). 291 E. Second Ave., Vancouver, BC V5T 1B8. (604)689-1520. FAX: (604)689-1525. E-mail: editor@jewishindependent.ca. Cynthia Ramsay. Weekly. Western Sky Communications Ltd. (WWW.JEWISHINDEPENDENT.CA)

JOURNAL OF PSYCHOLOGY AND JUDAISM (1976). 1747 Featherston Dr., Ottawa, ONT K1H 6P4. (613)731-9119. Reuven P. Bulka. Quarterly. Center for the Study of Psychology and Judaism.

OTTAWA JEWISH BULLETIN (1954). 21 Nadolny Sachs Private., Ottawa, ONT K2A 1R9. (613)798-4696. FAX: (613) 798-4730. E-mail: bulletin@ottawajewish bulletin.com. Barry Fishman. Nineteen times a year. Ottawa Jewish Bulletin Publishing Co. Ltd. (WWW.OTTAWAJEWISH BULLETIN.COM)

SHALOM (1975). 5670 Spring Garden Rd., Suite 508, Halifax, NS, B3J 1H1. (902)422-7491. FAX: (902)425-3722. E-mail: jgoldberg@theajc.ns.ca. Jon M. Goldberg. Quarterly. Atlantic Jewish Council.

LA VOIX SÉPHARADE (1975). 5151 Chemin de la Cote, St. Catherine, Montreal, PQ H3W 1M6. (514)733-4998, FAX: (514) 733-3158. E-mail: elieb@fedcjamtl.org. Ed. James Dahan; Pub. Elie Benchitrit. Bimonthly (five times a year). French and occasional Spanish and English. Communauté Sépharade du Québec.

NEWS AND VIEWS (1942) (formerly WINDSOR JEWISH FEDERATION). 1641 Ouellette Ave., Windsor, ONT N8X 1K9. (519)973-1772. FAX: (519)973-1774. Exec. Dir. Harvey Kessler. Quarterly. Windsor Jewish Federation.

WORLD OF LUBAVITCH (1980). 770 Chabad Gate, Thornhill, ONT L4J 3V9. (905)731-7000. FAX: (905)731-7005. Rabbi Moshe Spalter. Quarterly. English. Chabad Lubavitch of Southern Ont.

Obituaries: United States*

AUERBACH, ARNOLD ("RED"), professional basketball coach; b. Brooklyn, N.Y., Sept. 20, 1917; d. Washington, D.C., Oct. 28, 2006. Educ.: George Washington U. (BS, MA). Served U.S. Navy, 1943–46. Coach, Washington Capitals, 1946–49; Tri-cities Blackhawks, 1949–50; Boston Celtics, 1950–66, genl. mgr., 1966–84, pres., 1984–97, 2001–. Won 12 Natl. Basketball Assn. Eastern Div. titles, nine NBA championships as coach and another seven as genl. mgr. and pres.; coached 11 consecutive NBA all-star games; 14 of players he coached are in NBA Hall of Fame, 30 became pro coaches, three won coach-of-the-year award; lowered racial barriers by drafting first black player in NBA (1950), starting an all-black team (1964), and hiring first black head coach in pro sports (1966); conducted numerous basketball clinics and demonstrations in U.S. and abroad, including USSR and Israel. Rec.: NBA Coach of the Year Award, 1965 (the award was named in his honor in 1967); Natl. Basketball Hall of Fame, 1969; chosen all-time NBA coach, 1980. Au.: *Basketball for the Player, Fan and Coach* (1953); *Red Auerbach: Winning the Hard Way* (1966); *Red Auerbach: An Autobiography* (1977); *On and Off the Court* (1986); *MBA: Management by Auerbach* (1994); *Let Me Tell You a Story: A Lifetime in the Game* (2005).

AVRICH, PAUL, historian, educator; b. Brooklyn, N.Y., Aug. 4, 1931; d. NYC, Feb. 16, 2006. Educ.: Cornell U. (BA); Columbia U. (MA, PhD). Served U.S. Air Force, Korean War. After being in first group of American exchange students in USSR, 1961, taught history at Queens Coll. and City U. of N.Y. Graduate Center, rising from instr. to prof., 1962–99, distinguished prof., 1982–99. His collection of over 20,000 manuscripts and publications on the history of anarchism was donated to the Library of Cong.; named his cats after anarchist thinkers Kropotkin and Bakunin. Au.: *The Russian Anarchists* (1967); *Kronstadt 1921* (1970); *Russian Rebels, 1600–1800* (1972); *An American Anarchist: The Life of Voltairine de Cleyre* (1978); *The Modern School Movement: Anarchism and Education in the U.S.* (1980); *The Haymarket Tragedy* (1984); *Bakunin and Nechaev* (1987); *Anarchist Portraits* (1988); *Sacco and Vanzetti: The Anarchist Background* (1991); *Anarchist Voices: An Oral History of Anarchism in America* (1996). Rec.: Guggenheim Fellowship, 1967–68; Natl. Endowment for the Humanities Fellowship, 1972–73; Philip Taft Labor Hist. Award, 1984.

BRONFMAN, ANDREA, philanthropist; b. London, England, May 30, 1945; d. NYC, Jan. 23, 2006, after being hit by a car; in

---

*Including American Jews who dies between January 1 and December 31, 2006.

U.S. since 1998. Active in Jewish and Zionist affairs in Great Britain, Canada, and U.S.; founder, Montreal women's Group of 35 for Soviet Jews; creator and dir., "A Coat of Many Colours: Two Centuries of Jewish Life in Canada" traveling exhibition; cochair, together with husband Charles Bronfman, of Andrea and Charles Bronfman Philanthropies, which helped initiate Taglit-Birthright Israel program to send young Jews for free ten-day trips to Israel, Assn. of Israel's Decorative Arts (AIDA), which brought the work of Israeli artists to U.S. galleries, Gift of N.Y. to help families of 9/11 victims, Jewlicious Web site, J-Dub record co., *Heeb* magazine, many other causes. Bd. mem., Amer. Jewish Joint Distribution Com., Amer. Friends of the Israel Philharmonic Orchestra, Breast Cancer Research Found.; trustee, Jewish Museum, NYC. She and her husband became first North Americans to be named honorary citizens of Jerusalem, 2003.

BUTTONS, RED (AARON CHWATT), comedian, actor; b. NYC, Feb. 5, 1919; d. Los Angeles, Calif., July 13, 2006. Served U.S. Army in entertainment unit, 1943–46. Began singing for pennies on street corners as a child; first appeared on stage at age 12 as "Little Skippy," winning amateur contest at Fox Corona Theater; while attending high school worked as bellhop and singer at a bar; first Catskills performance, 1935; performed as comedian in burlesque houses beginning 1939 (was onstage the night police raided Minsky's); first Broadway appearance in *Vicki*, 1942; while in army appeared on stage in *Winged Victory* and its film version, 1944; after entertaining troops in Europe returned to U.S. where he worked in night clubs and made occasional guest appearances on TV shows; became an instant success in "Red Buttons Show" on CBS TV, 1952–55; award-winning dramatic performance in film *Sayonara*, 1957; also appeared on screen in *Imitation General* (1958), *Hatari!* (1962), *The Longest Day* (1962), *A Ticklish Affair* (1963), *They Shoot Horses, Don't They?* (1969), *The Poseidon Adventure* (1972), *Gable and Lombard* (1976), and *It Could Happen to You* (1994); appeared on TV as a regular on "The Dean Martin Celebrity Roast" in 1970s and other shows; Broadway one-man show, *Buttons on Broadway*, 1995. Rec.: Acad. of Radio and Television Best Comedian Award, 1954; Acad. Award for Best Supporting Actor, 1957; Friars Club Lifetime Achievement Award, 1982.

CHITRIK, YEHUDA, rabbi, educator; b. Krasnolok, Russia, Aug. 28, 1899; d. Brooklyn, N.Y., Feb. 14, 2006; in U.S. since 1983. Educ.: Yeshiva Tomchei Temimim, Lubavitch, Russia (ordination). Chabad teacher and ritual slaughterer, while earning a living as a factory worker, Kharkov, Ukraine, 1926–1941; Chabad emissary, teacher of Holocaust survivors, Belgium and the Netherlands, 1946–49; teacher, Chabad Yeshiva, Montreal, Canada, and mgr. of a free-loan fund, 1949–1970s. A close disciple of fifth Lubavitcher rebbe and associate of the sixth, was recognized as the preeminent source of the movement's folklore and oral traditions. Au.: *Reshumot Devorim*, four volumes of stories, some translated into English and published as *From My Father's Shabbos Table: A Treasury of Chabad Chassidic Stories* (1991).

COMDEN, BETTY (ELIZABETH COHEN), playwright; b. Brooklyn, N.Y., May 3, 1917, d. NYC, Nov. 23, 2006. Educ.: NYU (BS). Writer, performer, Revuers, at Village Vanguard and other night clubs, 1939–44; wrote Broadway musicals with collaborator Adolph Green: *On the Town* (1944–45), *Billion Dollar Baby* (1945), *Bonanza Bound* (1947), *Two on the Aisle* (1951), *Wonderful Town* (1953), *Peter Pan* (1954), *Bells Are Ringing* (1956), *Say, Darling* (1958), *Do, Re, Mi* (1960), *Subways Are for Sleeping* (1961–62), *Fade Out–Fade In* (1964), *Hallelujah, Baby* (1967), *Applause* (1970–72), *On the Twentieth Century* (1978), *The Madwoman of Central Park* (1979), *A Doll's Life* (1982), *Singin' in the Rain* (1985–86), *The Will Rogers Follies* (1991). Comden-Green movie screenplays: *Good News* (1947), *The Barkleys of Broadway* (1949), *Take Me Out to the Ball Game* (1949), *On the Town* (1949), *The Bandwagon* (1953). Au.: *Off Stage* (1995). Rec.: Tony Award, 1968, 1970, 1982, 1983, 1991; Grammy Award, 1992; named to Songwriters Hall of Fame, 1980; Kennedy Center Lifetime Achievement Award, 1991.

DRAPER, THEODORE, historian; b. Brooklyn, N.Y., Sept. 11, 1912; d. Princeton, N.J., Feb. 21, 2006. Educ.: Brooklyn Coll. (BS), Columbia U. Served U.S. Army, World War II. Reporter, *Daily Worker* 1935–37; foreign editor, *New Masses*, 1937–40; editor, Tass News Agcy., 1940;

fellow, Hoover Institution, 1960–68; fellow, Inst. for Advanced Study, Princeton U., 1968–73. Au.: *The Six-Weeks War: France, May 10–June 25, 1940* (1944); *The Roots of American Communism* (1957); *American Communism and Soviet Russia* (1960); *Castro's Revolution: Myths and Realities* (1962); *Castroism, Theory and Practice* (1965); *Abuse of Power* (1967); *Israel and World Politics* (1968); *The Dominican Revolt* (1968); *The Rediscovery of Black Nationalism* (1970); *Present History* (1983); *A Present of Things Past* (1990); *A Very Thin Line* (1991); *A Struggle for Power: The American Revolution* (1996). Prolific contributor to *Reporter, Commentary, New Leader, Encounter, N.Y. Review of Books.* Rec.: Amer. Hist. Assn. Herbert Feis Award for Non-Academically Affiliated Historians, 1990.

EPSTEIN, BARBARA, editor; b. Boston, Mass., Aug. 30, 1929; d. NYC, June 16, 2006. Educ.: Radcliffe Coll. (BA). Editor, Doubleday and Co., 1949–54; editor, Dutton, McGraw-Hill, *Partisan Review,* late 1950s; founder, coeditor, *N.Y. Review of Books,* 1963–. While at Doubleday edited English translation of Anne Frank's *Diary of a Young Girl.* Together with her then husband and two friends, conceived the idea for the *N.Y. Review of Books* at her dinner table during the 1962–63 N.Y. newspaper strike, and the biweekly quickly became a major organ of literary and political expression, expertly edited and expressing the left-of-center sensibility of N.Y. intellectuals. Coeditor: *A Middle East Reader* (1991); *First Anthology: Thirty Years of the New York Review of Books* (1994); *Striking Terror: America's New War* (2002); *The Company They Kept: Writers on Unforgettable Friendships* (2006).

FEUER, CY (SEYMOUR), producer; b. Brooklyn, N.Y., Jan. 15, 1911; d. NYC, May 17, 2006. Educ.: Juilliard School of Music. Served U.S. Army Air Corps, 1942–45. Played trumpet for political campaigns, in theaters, Radio City Music Hall, traveling orchestras, 1927–38; West Coast rep., Brunswick Records, 1938–39; head, music dept., Republic Pictures, 1939–42, 1945–47; partner, Feuer and Martin Prods., NYC, 1947–; pres., League of Amer. Theaters and Producers, 1989–. Together with Ernest Martin, produced on Broadway *Where's Charley?* (1948);

Guys and Dolls (1950); *Can-Can* (1953); *The Boy Friend* (1954); *Silk Stockings* (1955); *Whoop-Up* (1958); *How to Succeed in Business Without Really Trying* (1961, Pulitzer Prize for Drama, Tony Award for Best Musical); *Little Me* (1962); *Skyscraper* (1965); *Walking Happy* (1966); *The Goodbye People* (1968); *The Act* (1977). Produced films *Cabaret* (1972, winner of eight Acad. Awards); *Piaf* (1975); *A Chorus Line* (1985). Au.: *I Got the Show Right Here* (2003).

FRANK, REUVEN, TV producer; b. Montreal, Canada, Dec. 7, 1920; d. Englewood, N.J., Feb. 5, 2006; in U.S. since 1940. Educ.: U. Toronto; CCNY (BS); Columbia U. School of Journalism (MSc). Served U.S. Army, 1943–46. Reporter, editor, Newark *Evening News,* 1947–50; writer, NBC TV News, 1950–51, chief writer and editor, "Camel News Caravan," 1951–54, "Background," "Outlook," "Time Present," "Chet Huntley Reporting," 1954–56, "Huntley-Brinkley Report," 1956–62, supervised five NBC documentaries, 1962–63; exec. producer; "Huntley-Brinkley Report," 1963–66; NBC TV exec. v.-pres., 1967–68, pres., 1968–73, 1982–84, sr. exec. producer, 1973–82. Widely considered the "founding father" of TV evening news; pioneered network coverage of political conventions. Au.: *Out of Thin Air: The Brief Wonderful Life of Nightly News* (1991). Rec.: Sigma Delta Chi Award for TV news writing, 1954; Robert E. Sherwood Award (1958, 1959); four Emmy and two Peabody Awards over the years for "Huntley-Brinkley Report"; George Polk Award (1961); three Emmys for documentary "The Tunnel" (1962); special Emmy for defending "public's right to know" from government interference (1970).

FREEDMAN, JAMES, college president; b. Manchester, N.H., Sept. 21, 1935; d. Cambridge, Mass., Mar. 21, 2006. Educ.: Harvard U. (AB); Yale U. (LLB). Reporter, Manchester *Union Leader,* 1959–60; law clerk for Judge Thurgood Marshall, Federal Court of Appeals, 1962–63; assoc., Paul, Weiss, Rifkind, Wharton & Garrison, NYC, 1963–64; asst. prof., assoc. prof., prof., U. Pa. Law School, 1964–82, university ombudsman, 1973–76, assoc. provost, 1978, dean, 1979–82; pres., distinguished prof. law and political science, U. Iowa, 1982–87;

pres., Dartmouth Coll., 1987–98. At Dartmouth led overhauling of the curriculum, ending of racial and gender disparities, eliminating vestiges of anti-Semitism, but also angered political conservatives on campus. Au.: *Crisis and Legitimacy: The Administrative Process and American Government* (1978); *Idealism and Liberal Education* (1996); *Liberal Education and the Public Interest* (2003). Pres., Amer. Acad. of Arts and Sciences, 2000–01; mem., Amer. Law Inst.; mem., Amer. Jewish Com. bd. of govs., chr., Domestic Policy Comm., 2001–04; bd. trustees, Brandeis U. Rec.: Anti-Defamation League William O. Douglas Award, 1992, Civil Rights Award, 2000; Amer. Jewish Com. Natl. Distinguished Leadership Award, 2003; many others.

FRIEDAN, BETTY, author, feminist activist; b. Peoria, Ill., Feb. 4, 1921; d. Washington, D.C., Feb. 4, 2006. Educ.: Smith Coll. (AB); U. Calif. at Berkeley. Research fellow, U. Calif. at Berkeley, 1943; editor, Federated Press, 1944–46, reporter, U.E. News, 1946–47; writer, lect. on women's issues, 1957–; founding pres., NOW (Natl. Org. for Women), 1966–70, chair, adv. com., 1970–72; organizer, Women's Strike for Equality, 1970, Natl. Women's Political Caucus, 1971, Internat'l Feminist Conf., 1973, First Women's Bank, 1973, Economic Think Tank for Women, 1974; v.-pres., Natl. Assn. for Repeal of Abortion Laws, 1970–73; visiting prof., Temple U., 1972, Queens Coll., 1975, Yale U., 1985; sr. research assoc. Columbia U. 1979–82; distinguished visiting prof., U. Southern Calif., 1987; dir., New Paradigm Program, Cornell U. Inst. for Women and Work, 1998– . Au.: *The Feminist Mystique* (1963); *It Changed My Life: Writings on the Women's Movement* (1976); *The Second Stage* (1981); *The Fountain of Age* (1992); *Beyond Gender: The New Politics of Family and Work* (1998); *Life So Far* (2000); many magazine articles. Mem., natl. bd., Girl Scouts USA, 1976–82; exec. com., Amer. Jewish Cong., cochair, natl. comm. on women's equality, 1984–85. Rec.: Humanist of the Year Award, 1974; Mort Weisinger Award for outstanding magazine journalism, 1979; Eleanor Roosevelt Leadership Award, 1989.

FRIEDMAN, MILTON, economist, educator; b. Brooklyn, N.Y., July 31, 1912; d. San Francisco, Calif., Nov. 16, 2006. Educ.:

Rutgers U. (AB); U. Chicago (AM); Columbia U. (PhD). Assoc. economist, Natl. Resources Com., 1935–37; mem., research staff, Natl. Bureau of Economic Research, 1937–45, 1948–81; prin. economist, tax research div., U.S. Treasury Dept., 1941–43; assoc. dir. research, statistical research group, War Research Div., Columbia U., 1943–45; assoc. prof. economics and statistics, U. Minn., 1945–46, assoc. prof. economics, U. Chicago, 1946–48, prof., 1948–62, Paul Snowden Russell distinguished service prof., 1962–82, emer., 1983–; fellow, Hoover Institution, Stanford U., 1983–; columnist, *Newsweek,* 1966–83; created and starred in "Free to Choose" ten-part PBS TV series, 1980. Au.: *Taxing to Prevent Inflation* (1943); *Essays in Positive Economics* (1953); *A Theory of the Consumption Function* (1957); *A Program for Monetary Stability* (1960); *Price Theory. A Provisional Text* (with Rose Friedman, 1962); *Capitalism and Freedom* (1962); *A Monetary History of the United States, 1867–1960* (with Anna Schwartz, 1963); *Inflation: Causes and Consequences* (with Robert Roosa, 1963); *The Balance of Payments* (1967); *An Economist's Protest* (1972); *There's No Such Thing as a Free Lunch* (1975); *Price Theory* (with Robert Gordon and others, 1976); *Free to Choose* (with Rose Friedman, 1980); *Tyranny of the Status Quo* (with Rose Friedman, 1984); *Two Lucky People* (with Rose Friedman, 1998); many others. Rec.: Nobel Prize for Economics, 1976; Presidential Medal of Freedom, 1988; Natl. Medal of Science, 1988.

GILMAN, RICHARD, critic; b. NYC, Apr. 30, 1923; d. Kusatsu, Japan, Oct. 28, 2006. Educ.: U. Wis. (BA). Served U.S. Marine Corps, 1943–46. Freelance writer, 1950–54; assoc. editor, *Jubilee* magazine, 1954–57; drama critic, literary editor, *Commonweal,* 1961–64; assoc. editor, drama critic, *Newsweek,* 1964–67; literary editor, *New Republic,* 1968–70; prof. drama, Yale U., 1967–98. Pres., PEN Amer. Center, 1981–83. Au.: *The Confusion of Realms* (1970); *Common and Uncommon Masks* (1971); *The Making of Modern Drama* (1974); *Decadence: The Strange Life of an Epithet* (1979); *Faith, Sex, Mystery: A Memoir* (1987); *Chekhov's Plays* (1996); *The Drama Is Coming Now* (2005). Rec.: George Jean Nathan Award for Literary Criticism, 1971.

GINZBURG, RALPH, editor, publisher; b. Brooklyn, N.Y., Oct. 28, 1929; d. NYC, July 6, 2006. Educ.: CCNY (BBA); Henry George School of Economics (diploma). Served U.S. Army, 1950–51. Copyboy, N.Y Daily Compass, 1949–50; rewrite editor, Washington Times-Herald, 1950–51; freelance writer, photographer, 1951–53; staff writer, NBC, 1954–55; managing bd., Look magazine, 1955–56; articles editor, Esquire, 1956–58, Eros, 1962–63 (in which capacity he was convicted for obscenity and served eight months in federal prison in 1972, but also helped set off the "sexual revolution"), Fact, 1964–68 (sued by Barry Goldwater for publishing an article claiming he was psychologically unfit to be president), Avant Garde, 1968–71, Moneysworth, 1971–84; freelance photojournalist, 1984–. Au.: An Unhurried View of Erotica (1956); 100 Years of Lynching (1961); Eros on Trial (1964); Castrated: My Eight Months in Prison (1973); I Shot New York (1999).

GOLDBERG, ITCHE (YITZHAK), Yiddish scholar, left-wing activist; b. Apt, Poland, Mar. 22, 1904; d. NYC, Dec. 27, 2006; in U.S. since 1932. Educ.: Poznanski Teachers Sem., Warsaw, Poland; McMaster U., Toronto, Canada. Yiddish teacher, Workmen's Circle schools, Toronto, N.Y., Philadelphia, 1920s; when the Jewish socialists split over the Russian revolution he took the pro-Communist side and managed its Yiddish school system, Arbeter Ordn Shuln, expanding it to 140 schools nationwide; dir., Camp Kinderland (known as the "red-diaper camp), 1930s and 1940s; dir., natl. school and culture, Jewish People's Fraternal Order (part of Internat'l Workers Order, the pro-Communist labor federation), 1937–51; editor, Yungvarg children's magazine, 1937–51; editor, Yiddishe Kultur, 1964–2004; prof. Yiddish, Queens Coll., NYC, 1970–85; turned against Stalinism after the execution of Russian Yiddish writers, 1952; asked to don tefillin and put muzuzot on doors six months before his death. Au.: Essayen (1981); Essayen Tsvey (2004); Yiddish textbooks; Yiddish translations of Western classics; more than 20 librettos for Yiddish operas.

HERTZBERG, ARTHUR, rabbi, historian; b. Lubaczow, Poland, June 9, 1921; d. Englewood, N.J., Apr. 17, 2006; in U.S. since 1926. Served as chaplain, U.S. Air Force,

1951–53. Educ.: Johns Hopkins U. (AB); Jewish Theol. Sem. (ordination, MHL); Columbia U. (PhD). Hillel dir., Mass. State Coll., Smith Coll., 1943–44; rabbi, Cong. Ahavath Israel of Oak Lane, Philadelphia, Pa., 1944–47, West End Synagogue, Nashville, Tenn., 1947–56, Temple Emanu El, Englewood, N.J., 1956–85 (emer., 1985–); lect. hist., Columbia U., 1961–68, adj. prof., 1968–90, visiting scholar, Mideast Inst., 1991–; prof. religion, Dartmouth Coll., 1985–91, emer., 1991–; Bronfman visiting prof. humanities, NYU, 1991–. Pres., Conf. on Jewish Social Studies, 1967–72; mem., exec. com., World Zionist Org., 1969–78, Jewish Agcy. for Israel, 1969–71, bd. of govs., 1971–78; pres., Amer. Jewish Cong., 1972–78, Amer. Jewish Policy Found., 1978–; v.-pres., World Jewish Cong., 1975–91. Au.: The Zionist Idea (1959); The French Enlightenment and the Jews (1968); Being Jewish in America (1979); The Jews in America: Four Centuries of an Uneasy Encounter (1989); Jewish Polemics (1992); A Jew in America: My Life and a People's Struggle for Identity (2003); hundreds of articles.

HIMMELFARB, MILTON, writer, communal worker; b. NYC, Oct. 21, 1918; d. NYC, Jan. 4, 2006. Educ.: CCNY (BA, MS); Jewish Theol. Sem. Coll. (BHL); U. Paris; Columbia U. Staff mem., Amer. Jewish Com., 1942–55, dir., Info. and Research Services, 1955–86; editor, AJYB, 1959–86; contrib. editor, Commentary, 1960–86; visiting prof., Jewish Theol. Sem., 1967–68, 1971–72, Yale Coll., 1971; Reconstructionist Rabbinical Coll., 1972–73; mem., U.S. Holocaust Memorial Council, 1986–89. Au.: The Jews of Modernity (1973); Jews and Gentiles (2007). Ed.: Zero Population Growth— For Whom? (1975). See David Singer, "Remembering Milton Himmelfarb," AJYB 2006, pp. 695–710, for a fuller treatment.

HIRSCHHORN, DAVID, businessman, philanthropist; b. Prague, Czechoslovakia, Apr. 16, 1918; d. Baltimore, Md., Sept. 6, 2006; in U.S. since 1922. Educ.: Rutgers U.; NYU (BA, MBA). Served U.S. Army Air Force, WWII. Worked at Ronson Corp., Newark, N.J., rising from office boy to asst. to the pres., then establishing his own consulting firm, 1945–58; Amer. Trading and Prod. Corp., rising to pres. and bd. chmn., 1958–92, bd. mem., 1992–06.

Pres., David and Barbara B. Hirschhorn Found., 1986–, Jacob and Hilda Blaustein Found., 1990–2000. Pres., Baltimore chapter, Amer. Jewish Com., mem., natl. bd. of govs., comms. on internat'l affairs, interreligious affairs, contemporary Jewish life, hon. v.-pres., founder, Hilda K. Blaustein Inst. for leadership training, founder and mem., admin. council and exec. com., Jacob Blaustein Inst. for the Advancement of Human Rights; bd. mem., The Associated: Jewish Community Fed. of Baltimore, Baltimore Inst. for Christian and Jewish Studies, Jacob Blaustein Inst. for Desert Research of Ben-Gurion U. Rec.: Hon. doctorate, Ben-Gurion U., 1994; Amer. Jewish Com. Natl. Distinguished Leadership Award, 2005.

JACOBS, JANE, urban planner; b. Scranton, Pa., May 4, 1916; d. Toronto, Canada, Apr. 25, 2006. Educ.: Columbia U. extension school. Asst. women's page editor, Scranton *Tribune,* 1933–34; sec., stenographer, freelance writer, NYC, late 1930s; feature writer, Office of War Info., WWII; assoc. editor, *Architectural Forum,* 1952–61; chair, Joint Com. to Stop the Lower Manhattan Expressway, 1962, and again in 1968 (when she was arrested), succeeding in stopping the project championed by Robert Moses that would have gutted Greenwich Village; after moving to Toronto in 1968 was active in opposing construction of Canadian expressways through existing neighborhoods, getting arrested twice. Au.: *The Death and Life of Great American Cities* (1961); *The Economy of Cities* (1969); *The Question of Separatism: Quebec and the Struggle for Sovereignty* (1980); *Cities and the Wealth of Nations* (1984); *Systems of Survival* (1994); *The Nature of Economies* (2000); *Dark Age Ahead* (2004). Rec.: Rockefeller Found. grants, 1950s; Officer of Order of Canada, 1996; Amer. Sociological Assn. Lifetime Achievement Award, 2002; Shaughnessy Cohen Prize for Political Writing, 2005.

KUNITZ, STANLEY, poet; b. Worcester, Mass., July 29, 1905; d. NYC, May 14, 2006. Educ.: Harvard U. (AB, MA). Served U.S. Army as writer and editor, 1943–45. Editor, Wilson Library Bulletin, 1928–43; taught literature, Bennington Coll., 1946–49; prof. English, Potsdam State Teachers Coll., 1949–50; dir., Potsdam Summer Workshop in Creative Arts, 1949–53; lect., New School, 1950–57; dir., poetry workshop, NYC YMHA, 1958–62; lect., Columbia U., 1963–66; visiting prof. at many universities around the country; poetry consultant, U.S. Library of Cong., 1974–76. Au.: *Intellectual Things* (1930); *Living Authors* (1931); *Passport to the War* (1944); *Selected Poems, 1928–58* (1958); *The Testing-Tree* (1971); *The Terrible Threshold* (1974); *The Coat Without a Seam* (1974); *A Kind of Order, A Kind of Folly* (1975); *The Poems of Stanley Kunitz, 1928–78* (1979); *The Wellfleet Whale and Companion Poems* (1983); *Next-to-Last Things* (1985); *Interviews and Encounters* (1993); *Passing Through: The Later Poems, New and Selected* (1995); *The Collected Poems* (2000); *The Wild Braid: A Poet Reflects on a Century in the Garden* (2005). Rec.: Guggenheim Fellowship, 1945–46; Ford Found. grant, 1957–58; Pulitzer Prize for Poetry, 1959; Bollingen Prize, 1987; designated N.Y. State Poet, 1987–89; Natl. Medal of the Arts, 1993; Natl. Book Award, 1995; Jewish Achievement Award, Natl. Found. for Jewish Culture, 2000; U.S. Poet Laureate, 2000–01.

LEVINE, LAWRENCE., historian, educator; b. NYC, Feb. 27, 1933; d. Berkeley, Calif., Oct. 23, 2006. Educ.: CCNY (BA); Columbia U. (MA, PhD). Lect. hist., CCNY, 1959–61; instr., Princeton U., 1961–62; asst. prof., U. Calif., Berkeley, 1962–67; assoc. prof., 1967–70, prof., 1970–84, Margaret Byrne prof., 1984–94; visiting prof., George Mason U., 1994–. Au.: *Defender of the Faith* (1965); *Black Culture and Black Consciousness* (1977); *High Brow/Low Brow* (1988); *The Unpredictable Past* (1993); *The Opening of the American Mind* (1996); *The People and the President* (with Cornelia Roettcher, 2002). Ed.: *The Shaping of 20th-Century America* (1964); *The National Temper* (1968). Pres., Org. of Amer. Historians, 1992–93; pres., Cong. Beth El, Berkeley, 1979–82. Rec.: Woodrow Wilson Fellowship, 1982–83; MacArthur Fellowship, 1983; Center for Advanced Studies in the Behavioral Sciences Fellowship, 1991–92; Guggenheim Fellowship, 1994.

LIPSET, SEYMOUR MARTIN, political sociologist, educator; b. NYC, Mar. 18, 1922; d. Arlington, Va., Dec. 31, 2006. Educ.: CCNY (BS); Columbia U. (PhD). Lect. sociology, U. Toronto, 1946–48; asst. prof., U. Calif., Berkeley, 1948–50; asst., assoc. prof, Columbia U. graduate school, 1950–56; asst. dir., Bureau of Applied Social Research, 1954–56; prof. sociology, U. Calif., Berkeley, 1956–66, dir., Inst. of Internat'l Studies, 1962–66; visiting prof., Harvard U., 1965–75, George Markham prof., 1974–75; prof., Stanford U., 1975–92, Caroline S.G. Munro prof., 1981–92, sr. fellow, Hoover Institution, 1975–; Hazel prof., George Mason U., 1990–. Au.: *Agrarian Socialism* (1950); *Union Democracy* (with others, 1956); *Social Mobility in Industrial Society* (with R. Bendix, 1959); *Political Man* (1960, exp. edition 1981, translated into 20 languages); *The First New Nation* (1963, exp. edition 1979); *Revolution and Counter Revolution* (1968, exp. edition, 1988); *The Politics of Unreason* (with Earl Raab, 1970, exp. edition 1978); "Jewish Academics in the United States" (with E.C. Ladd, AJYB 1971); *Rebellion in the University* (1972); *Group Life in America* (AJC, 1972); *Professors, Unions, and American Higher Education* (1973); *The Divided Academy* (with David Riesman, 1975); *The Confidence Gap* (1983); *Consensus and Conflict* (1987); *Continental Divide: The Institutions and Values of the United States and Canada* (1990); *American Exceptionalism* (1996); *Jews and the New American Scene* (with Earl Raab, 1996); *It Didn't Happen Here* (2000). Edited many books, including *American Pluralism and the Jewish Community* (1990). Pres., Amer. Political Science Assn., 1981–82, Amer. Sociological Assn., 1992–93; natl. chmn., B'nai B'rith Hillel Found., 1975–79; pres., Amer. Profs. for Peace in the Middle East, 1977–81; chmn., natl. faculty cabinet, United Jewish Appeal, 1981–84. Rec.: MacIver Award, 1962: Gunnar Myrdal Prize, 1970; Guggenheim Found. Fellowship, 1971–72; Marshall Sklare Award, 1993.

MEED, BENJAMIN (BENJAMIN MIEDZYRECKI), advocate for Holocaust survivors; b. Warsaw, Poland, Feb. 19, 1918; d. NYC, Oct. 24, 2006; in U.S. since 1946. Educ.: yeshiva, public high school, business school, Warsaw. Confined with family in Warsaw Ghetto by Nazis, 1940, and used for forced labor; escaped and smuggled some of his family out, passing as a gentile and working for the underground, and during Warsaw Ghetto revolt, 1943, helping several Jews escape through the sewers; in U.S. after the war worked as furrier and then in import-export; with his wife, Vladka, helped found Warsaw Ghetto Resistance Org., 1966, World Gathering of Jewish Holocaust Survivors, 1981, Amer. Gathering of Jewish Holocaust Survivors, first conference 1983 (which sought to prevent Pres. Reagan from visiting Bitburg cemetery, 1985), and Benjamin and Vladka Meed Registry of Jewish Holocaust Survivors, which collects names of survivors in U.S. to facilitate locating relatives; mem., adv. bd., President's Comm. on the Holocaust, which recommended creation of a natl. Holocaust museum; mem., governing council, U.S. Holocaust Memorial Museum, 1980–2004, chairing its com. on permanent exhibits; a founder of Museum of Jewish Heritage—A Living Memorial to the Holocaust, NYC, 1997; mem., negotiating com., Conf. on Jewish Material Claims against Germany; established Summer Seminar on Holocaust and Jewish Resistance to enable schoolteachers to incorporate material about Holocaust in the curriculum.

MINCER, JACOB, economist, educator; b. Tomaszow, Poland, July 15, 1922; d. NYC, Aug. 20, 2006; in U.S. since 1948. Educ.: Emory U. (BA); Columbia U. (PhD). Asst. prof. economics, CUNY, 1954–59; postdoctoral fellow, U. Chicago, 1958–59; assoc. prof., Columbia U., 1960–62, prof., 1962–91, Joseph L. Buttenweiser prof., 1979–91, emer., 1991–; mem., research staff, Natl. Bureau of Economic Research, 1960–. Au.: *Economic Forecasts and Expectations* (1969); *Schooling, Experience and Earnings* (1974); *Studies in Human Capital* (1982); *Studies in Labor Supply* (1993). Rec.: Hillel Found. scholarship enabling him to attend college, 1948; Guggenheim Fellowship, 1971; Inst. for the Study of Labor lifetime achievement award, 2002; Soc. of Labor Economists career achievement award, 2004 (this award now named after him).

MITOFSKY, WARREN, pollster; b. Jersey City, N.J., Sept. 17, 1934; d. NYC, Sept. 1, 2006. Educ.: Guilford Coll. (BA); U.N.C.; U. Minn. Designed surveys for U.S. Census Bureau, 1960s, where, together with Joseph Waksberg, he developed the technique of random digit dialing; pollster, CBS News, 1967–90, pioneering use of the exit poll in the 1967 Kentucky gubernatorial election and using it for the first time nationally in

1972; initiated collaborative CBS News/N.Y. Times polling consortium, 1976; created and directed Voter Research Service (later Voter News Service), 1990–, which supplied polling data to all the networks and aroused controversy in 2004 by predicting a victory for John Kerry in the presidential election; created and directed Mitofsky Internat'l, 1993–, which conducted exit polls in Russia, Mexico, and elsewhere around the world. Pres., Amer. Assn. for Public Opinion Research, Natl. Council of Public Polls; fellow, Amer. Statistical Assn.

MURRAY, JAN (MURRAY JANOFSKY), entertainer; b. NYC, Oct. 4, 1916; d. Beverly Hills, Calif., July 2, 2006. Worked in vaudeville beginning 1934, then in Catskills resort hotels as "tummler"; performed in Las Vegas beginning in 1940s; became first comic TV host on "Songs for Sale" (1950–51), followed by "Dollar a Second" (1953–57), "Treasure Hunt" (1956–59), "Charge Account" (1960–62), frequent panelist, "Hollywood Squares," frequent guest host, "The Tonight Show," and appeared on many other TV shows; acted in over 20 films, including *A Man Called Dagger* (1967), *Tarzan and the Great River* (1967), *Which Way to the Front?* (1970), *The History of the World, Part I* (1981), *Fear City* (1984). Tireless performer for Jewish causes ("anything Jewish I never turn down"), including hosting Chabad West Coast Telethon for 18 years; hosted legendary annual Passover seder for fellow comedians.

NEWMAN, ARNOLD, photographer; b. NYC, Mar. 3, 1918; d. NYC, June 6, 2006. Educ.: U. Miami. Photographer, Philadelphia, 1938; portrait studio, West Palm Beach, Fla., 1939–42, Newman Portrait Studio, Miami Beach, 1942–46, Arnold Newman Studios, NYC, 1946–; adj. prof. photography, Cooper Union, NYC, 1968–75; visitor/lect., Inst. for Advanced Study, Princeton, N.J., 1991. Pioneered "environmental portraiture," his portraits of world leaders and other celebrities often appearing in books and magazines such as *Life, Look, Fortune, Esquire, Vanity Fair*. His work is exhibited at Museum of Modern Art, Metropolitan Museum of Art, Chicago Art Inst., Smithsonian Institution, Philadelphia Museum of Art, London Photography Gallery, Israel Museum, and elsewhere; retrospective exhibitions held at Natl. Portrait Gallery, Washington, 1992, and at other museums. Au.: *Bravo Stravinsky* (1967); *One Mind's Eye* (1974); *Faces USA* (1978); *The Great British* (1979); *Artists: Portraits from Four Decades* (1980); *Arnold Newman—Five Decades* (1986); *Arnold Newman in Florida* (1987). Rec.: Photokina Award, 1951; Amer. Soc. of Magazine Photographers Lifetime Achievement Award, 1975; hon. fellow, Israel Museum of Jerusalem, 1986.

OSTOW, MORTIMER, psychiatrist, neuroscientist; b. Brooklyn, N.Y., Jan. 8, 1918; d. NYC, Sept. 23, 2006. Served U.S. Public Health Service, 1942–46. Educ.: Columbia U. (BA, MA); NYU (MD); N.Y. Psychoanalytic Inst. Private practice of psychiatry and psychoanalysis, NYC, 1948–; attending neurologist, Mt. Sinai Hosp., 1949–60; attending physician, Montefiore Hosp., 1960–66; visiting prof. pastoral psychology, Jewish Theol. Sem., 1953–66, dir., Bernstein Pastoral Psychiatry Center, 1966–89, emer., 1990–. Championed a psychoanalytic understanding of anti-Semitism and other forms of intolerance, tracing such feelings to childhood experiences. Au.: *Drugs in Psychoanalysis and Psychotherapy* (1962); *The Psychology of Melancholy* (1970); *Myth and Madness: The Psychodynamics of Anti-Semitism* (1996). Ed.: *Sexual Deviation: Psychoanalytic Insights* (1974); *Judaism and Psychoanalysis* (1981). Rec.: Sigmund Freud Award, Amer. Soc. of Psychoanalytic Physicians, 1995.

OSTROFF, HOWARD, communal worker; b. NYC, Sept. 22, 1923; d. NYC, Mar. 2, 2006. Educ.: CCNY. Served U.S. Army, 1942–45. Worked for Amalgamated Housing Cooperative, 1947–53; v.-pres., United Housing Found., 1953–66, exec, v.-pres., 1966–74; pres., 1974–85, building more than 30,000 units of affordable cooperative housing; chmn., Co-op League, 1972–74; genl. mgr., Forward Assn., 1976–98, launching English edition, 1990, and Russian edition, 1995. Pres., Workmen's Circle; bd. mem., UJA-Fed. Greater N.Y., YIVO Inst. for Jewish Research, Folksbiene Yiddish Theater, Atran Found., Tamiment Inst., HIAS, ORT, Jewish Labor Com., Natl. Com for Labor Israel.

ROSENTHAL, A.M. (ABRAHAM MICHAEL), newspaper editor; b. Sault Ste. Marie, Ontario, May 2, 1922; d. NYC, May 10, 2006; in U.S. since 1926. Educ.: CCNY (BS). CCNY campus correspondent, *N.Y. Times,* 1943–44, staff reporter, 1944-46, UN correspondent, 1946–54, assigned to New Delhi, 1954–58, Warsaw, 1958–59 (when he wrote the classic article "There Is No News from Auschwitz"), Geneva, 1960–61, Tokyo, 1961–63, metropolitan editor, 1963–66, asst. managing editor, 1967–68, assoc. managing editor, 1968–69, managing editor, 1969–77, exec. editor, 1977–86, columnist, 1987–99; columnist, N.Y. *Daily News,* 2000–04. Among the innovations he brought to the *Times* were expansion of news coverage, development of new sections of the paper, reporting trends in popular culture, publ. of a natl. edition; under his direction both circulation and ad revenue rose dramatically; made the decision to publish "Pentagon Papers," 1971, which led to landmark Supreme Court decision; as he got older became increasingly concerned about the security of Israel and human rights around the world. Au.: *One More Victim: The Life and Death of a Jewish Nazi* (with Arthur Gelb, 1967); *Thirty-Eight Witnesses: The Kitty Genovese Case* (1999). Rec.: Pulitzer Prize for internat'l reporting, 1960; Guardian of Zion Award, Bar-Ilan U., 1999; Presidential Medal of Freedom, 2002; numerous other awards and citations.

RUBIN, WILLIAM, art curator; b. NYC, Aug. 11, 1927; d. Pound Ridge, N.Y., Jan. 22, 2006. Educ.: Columbia U. (AB, MA, PhD); U. Paris. Served U.S. Army, late 1940s. Prof. art hist., Sarah Lawrence Coll., 1952–67; prof., CUNY graduate div., 1960–68; adj. prof., NYU Inst. of Fine Arts, 1968–; Amer. editor, *Art International* magazine, 1959–64; chief curator painting and sculpture, Museum of Modern Art, NYC, 1968–73, dir. painting and sculpture, 1973–88, emer., 1988–. Acquired major works for the museum by twentieth-century artists and expanded its holdings in the area of abstract expressionism. Among the major exhibitions he arranged were "Dada, Surrealism and their Heritage," 1968; "New American Painting and Sculpture," 1969; "Stella," 1970; "Miro," 1973; "Picasso: A Retrospective," 1980; "Giorgio DeChirico," 1982; "Primitivism in Twentieth-Century Art," 1984; "Picasso and Braque," 1989. Au.: *Modern Sacred Art and the Church of Assy* (1961); *Dada*

and Surrealist Art (1969); *Frank Stella* (1970); *Picasso in the Collection of the Museum of Modern Art* (1972); also edited numerous art books. Rec.: Chevalier, French Legion of Honor, 1979, officer, 1991.

SCHWARTZ, MELVIN, physicist, educator; b. NYC, Nov. 2, 1932; d. Ketchum, Idaho, Aug. 28, 2006. Educ.: Columbia U. (AB, PhD). Assoc. physicist, Brookhaven Natl. Laboratory, 1956–58; asst., assoc. prof. physics, Columbia U., 1958–63, prof., 1963–66, 1991–97; Stanford U., 1966–83, consulting prof., 1983–91; chmn., Digital Pathways, Inc., Mountain View, Calif., a computer-security co., 1970–91; assoc. dir. high energy and nuclear physics, Brookhaven Natl. Laboratory, 1991–97, where he was in charge of the construction of four detectors at the Relativistic Heavy Iron Collider. Mem., bd. of govs., Weizmann Inst. of Science. Rec.: Guggenheim Fellowship, 1968; Nobel Prize in Physics, 1988, for generating neutrinos.

SPELLING, AARON, TV producer; b. Dallas, Tex., Apr. 22, 1923; d. Los Angeles, Calif., June 23, 2006. Educ.: Sorbonne; Southern Methodist U. (BA). Served U.S. Army Air Corps, 1942–45. Acted and directed on stage, TV, wrote scripts, 1950s; produced TV shows beginning 1959 that proved immensely popular; co-pres., Thomas-Spelling Prods., 1972–76; pres., Aaron Spelling Prods., 1977–86, chmn., CEO, 1986–. Among the more than 40 TV shows he produced were "Burke's Law" (1963–65); "Daniel Boone" (1964–70); "Honey West" (1965–66); "The Mod Squad" (1968–73); "Starsky and Hutch" (1975–79); "Family" (1976–80); "Charlie's Angels" (1976–81); "The Love Boat" (1966–86); "Fantasy Island" (1978–84); "Hart to Hart" (1979–84); "Dynasty" (1981–89); "T.J. Hooker" (1982–87); "Hotel" (1983–88); "Beverly Hills 90210" (1990–2000); "Melrose Place" (1992–99); "Charmed" (1998–2006); "Seventh Heaven" (1996–). Produced 13 feature films and many TV movies, including Emmy Award winners *Day One* (1989) and *And the Band Played On* (1993). Rec.: Eugene O'Neil Awards, 1947, 1948; NAACP Image Awards, 1970, 1971, 1973, 1975; Beverly Hills B'nai B'rith Man of the Year, 1972, 1985.

SPERTUS, HERMAN, businessman, philanthropist; b. Lubach, Russia, Mar. 10,

1901; d. Chicago, Ill., Apr. 5, 2006; in U.S. since 1923. Upon arrival in U.S. worked in a factory, opened a business in wrought-iron products, and then manufactured lamps until he went bankrupt in 1929; with the new popularity of inexpensive cameras started, together with his brother, Metalcraft (later Intercraft) for the production of brass picture frames, 1933, which, by the time it was sold in 1992, was the largest in the world; during WWII diverted production entirely to navigational instruments for U.S. Navy. Became major supporter of Chicago Coll. of Jewish Studies, 1968, renamed Spertus Coll., 1970, and founded Spertus Museum; both institutions, plus Asher Library, were renamed Spertus Inst. of Jewish Studies, 1993. A founder of Council for Jewish Elderly, ORT Training School, North Shore Cong. Israel, Bernard Horwich Jewish Community Center, Amer. Israel Cultural Found., Amer. Friends of the Israel Museum; other major philanthropic gifts went to Chicago United Way, Art Museum of Chicago, many others; oldest person to chair annual campaign of Chicago Jewish United Fund, 1980, raising record sum of $36 million. Rec.: Chicago Sr. Citizen Hall of Fame, 1981; Rosenwald Award, Metropolitan Jewish Fed., 1993.

STROCHLITZ, SIGMUND, advocate for Holocaust survivors; b. Bedzin, Poland, Feb. 1, 1917; d. New London, Conn., Oct. 16, 2006; in U.S. since 1951. Educ.: Jagiellonian U., Kraków. Arriving in U.S. after surviving Birkenau and Bergen-Belsen, established Whaling City Ford, a successful car dealership in New London, Conn.; a close associate of Elie Wiesel, he was named to President's Comm. on the Holocaust, 1978, chairing its remembrance com. in charge of recommending plans for the projected museum; appointed to U.S. Holocaust Memorial Council, serving until 1986; largely responsible for natl. commemoration of Holocaust Memorial Day in Capitol Rotunda and by each U.S. state government; played a key role securing Nobel Peace Prize for Wiesel, 1986. Pres., Amer. Friends of Haifa U., Temple Beth El, New London; bd. mem., Bar-Ilan U.; trustee, Amer. Jewish Cong. Endowed Strochlitz Inst. of Holocaust Studies, Haifa U.; Strochlitz Judaic Teaching Fellowship, Bar-Ilan U.; Strochlitz Holocaust Resource Center, Jewish Fed.

Eastern Conn. Rec.: Elie Wiesel Remembrance Award, 1986; Ellis Island Medal of Honor, 1997.

STUART, LYLE (LIONEL SIMON), publisher, author; b. NYC, Aug. 11, 1922; d. Englewood, N.J., June 24, 2006. Served U.S. Merchant Marine, 1938–42, U.S. Army, 1942–44. Reporter, Internat'l News Service, 1945, Variety, 1945–46; script writer, Voice of America, 1946; editor, Music Business magazine, 1946–48; founder and publisher, Exposé, 1951, The Independent, 1951–75; business mgr., MAD magazine, 1952–54; pres., Citadel Press, 1954, Lyle Stuart Inc., 1954–89, University Books, Hot News, 1983, Barricade Books, 1990–97. Published many controversial but highly successful books, such as Fidel Castro's History Will Absolve Me (1961), The Rich and the Super-Rich (1968); The Sensuous Woman (1969); Naked Came the Stranger (1969); The Anarchist Cookbook (1970); Jackie Oh! (1978); and The Turner Diaries (1996). Au.: The Secret Life of Walter Winchell (1953); Casino Gambling for the Winner (1978); Lyle Stuart on Baccarat (1983); Map of Life (1993).

TEITELBAUM, MOSHE, rabbi; b. Ujfeherto, Hungary, Nov. 17, 1914; d. NYC, Apr. 24, 2006; in U.S. since 1946. Educ.: Hungarian yeshivot. Head of yeshiva in Karecska, 1936–39; rabbi, Zenta, Yugoslavia, 1939–44; deported to Auschwitz, 1944, where his first wife and children were killed; rabbi of Sighet, Romania, 1945–48, fled the communist regime and came to U.S., living in Brooklyn, N.Y., and functioning as the Sigheter rebbe; succeeded his childless uncle as Satmar rebbe, 1980, and under his leadership the sect grew to over 100,000 people worldwide, with assets estimated in the hundreds of millions of dollars. Au.: Berach Moshe, a five-volume Torah commentary.

WASSERSTEIN, WENDY, playwright; b. Brooklyn, N.Y., Oct. 18, 1950; d. NYC, Jan. 30, 2006. Educ.: Mt. Holyoke Coll. (BA); CCNY (MA); Yale Drama School (MFA). First play, Any Woman Can't, staged by Playwrights Horizons, NYC, 1973; followed by Happy Birthday (1974); Montpellier Pizz-zazz (1974); When Dinah Shore Ruled the Earth (1975); Uncommon Women and Others (1977, filmed for TV); Isn't It Romantic (1981); Tender Offer (1983); The Man in the Case (1986); Miami (1986); The Heidi Chronicles (1989, filmed for TV); The Sisters

Rosensweig (1993); *An American Daughter* (1997); *Old Money* (2000); *Third* (2005). Au.: *Bachelor Girls* (1990); *Shiksa Goddess* (2001); *Sloth* (2005); *Elements of Style* (2006). Initiated "Open Doors" program to expose underprivileged NYC high-school students to theater, 1998. Rec.: Joseph Jefferson Award, Dramalogue Award, 1975; Guggenheim Fellowship, 1983; Pulitzer Prize for Drama, N.Y. Drama Critics Circle Award, Tony Award for Best Play, 1989;

WELLES, ELLIOT (KURT SAUERQUELL), Nazi hunter; b. Vienna, Austria, Sept. 18, 1927; d. NYC, Nov. 28, 2006; in U.S. since 1949. Deported with his mother to Riga ghetto, 1940, where she was killed, transferred to Stutthof concentration camp, escaped to Vienna, 1945; after arrival in N.Y. worked at several menial jobs; employed as waiter at Lorelei restaurant and became part owner; dir. European affairs, dir. task force on Nazi war criminals, Anti-Defamation League, late 1970s–2003; with help of U.S. Office of Special Investigations traveled to Germany and located the former SS officer who murdered his mother, who was tried by a German court, convicted, and given a short jail sentence; known especially for persistence in tracking down and bringing to justice Latvian collaborator Boleslav Maikovskis, whose trial was suspended because of the defendant's ill health in 1994, and labor camp commander Josef Schwammberger, extradited from Argentina to Germany and sentenced to life in prison in 1992.

WILLIS, ELLEN, journalist, cultural critic; b. NYC, Dec. 14, 1941; d. NYC, Nov. 9, 2006. Educ.: Barnard Coll. (BA); U. Calif., Berkeley. Columnist and editor, *Ms, Village Voice, Rolling Stone,* first pop-music critic, *New Yorker,* 1960s–1980s; prof. journalism, NYU, 1990–, founder and dir., cultural reporting and criticism program (the only such program in the U.S.), 1995–. A founder of Redstockings consciousness-raising feminist group, 1969; No More Nice Girls street theater pro-choice group; Feminist Anti-Censorship Task Force, 1980s; History in Action on-line radical feminist discussion group; Take Back the Future anti-Bush org., 2000s. Au.: *Beginning to See the Light: Pieces of a Decade* (1981); *No More Nice Girls: Countercultural Essays* (1992); *Don't Think, Smile! Notes on a Decade of Denial* (1999); numerous essays in *Nation, Dissent, New Yorker, Rolling Stone, Village Voice, N.Y. Times,* and elsewhere on politics, women's issues, popular music, films, and religion.

YOSKOWITZ, JAY, communal worker; b. Brooklyn, N.Y. June 9, 1946; d. Scarsdale, N.Y., May 2, 2006. Educ.: CCNY (BA, MA); Hebrew Union Coll. School of Jewish Communal Service (certificate). Texas and Oklahoma regional dir., B'nai B'rith Youth Org., 1970–72; asst. exec. dir., Jewish Fed. Greater Houston, 1972–75, assoc. exec. dir., 1975–77; exec. dir., Jewish Fed. Greater Des Moines, 1977–81; dir., personnel services, Council of Jewish Federations, 1982-85; exec. dir., Jewish Fed. Greenwich, Conn., 1986–87; natl. field dir., Jewish Natl. Fund, 1987–90; assoc. exec. v.-chmn., United Israel Appeal, 1990–93, exec. v.-chmn., 1993–98; exec. v.-pres., Council of Jewish Federations, 1998–99; sr. v.-pres., campaign, Amer. Technion Soc., 1999–. Rec.: Mandelkern Distinguished Service Award, Assn. of Jewish Community Org. Personnel, 2004.

Calendars

SUMMARY JEWISH CALENDAR, 5767–5771 (Sept. 2006–Aug. 2011)

HOLIDAY	5767 (2006)			5768 (2007)			5769 (2008)			5770 (2009)			5771 (2010)		
Rosh Ha-shanah, 1st day	Sa	Sept.	23	Th	Sept.	13	T	Sept.	30	Sa	Sept.	19	Th	Sept.	9
Rosh Ha-shanah, 2nd day	S	Sept.	24	F	Sept.	14	W	Oct.	1	S	Sept.	20	F	Sept.	10
Fast of Gedaliah	M	Sept.	25	S	Sept.	16	Th	Oct.	2	M	Sept.	21	S	Sept.	12
Yom Kippur	M	Oct.	2	Sa	Sept.	22	Th	Oct.	9	M	Sept.	28	Sa	Sept.	18
Sukkot, 1st day	Sa	Oct.	7	Th	Sept.	27	T	Oct.	14	Sa	Oct.	3	Th	Sept.	23
Sukkot, 2nd day	S	Oct.	8	F	Sept.	28	W	Oct.	15	S	Oct.	4	F	Sept.	24
Hosha'na' Rabbah	F	Oct.	13	W	Oct.	3	M	Oct.	20	F	Oct.	9	W	Sept.	29
Shemini 'Azeret	Sa	Oct.	14	Th	Oct.	4	T	Oct.	21	Sa	Oct.	10	Th	Sept.	30
Simhat Torah	S	Oct.	15	F	Oct.	5	W	Oct.	22	S	Oct.	11	F	Oct.	1
New Moon, Heshwan, 1st day	S	Oct.	22	F	Oct.	12	W	Oct.	29	S	Oct.	18	F	Oct.	8
New Moon, Heshwan, 2nd day	M	Oct.	23	Sa	Oct.	13	Th	Oct.	30	M	Oct.	19	Sa	Oct.	9
New Moon, Kislew, 1st day	T	Nov.	21	S	Nov.	11	F	Nov.	28	T	Nov.	17	S	Nov.	7
New Moon, Kislew, 2nd day	W	Nov.	22							W	Nov.	18	M	Nov.	8
Hanukkah, 1st day	Sa	Dec.	16	W	Dec.	5	M	Dec.	22	Sa	Dec.	12	Th	Dec.	2
New Moon, Tevet, 1st day	Th	Dec.	21	M	Dec.	10	Sa	Dec.	27	Th	Dec.	17	T	Dec.	7
New Moon, Tevet, 2nd day	F	Dec.	22				S	Dec.	28	F	Dec.	18	W	Dec.	8
Fast of 10th of Tevet	S	Dec.	31	W	Dec.	19	T	2009 Jan.	6	S	Dec.	27	F	Dec.	17

	2007	2008	2009	2010	2011
New Moon, Shevat	Sa Jan. 20	T Jan. 8	M Jan. 26	Sa Jan. 16	Th Jan. 6
Hamishshah-'asar bi-Shevat	Sa Feb. 3	T Jan. 22	M Feb. 9	Sa Jan. 30	Th Jan. 20
New Moon, Adar I, 1st day	S Feb. 18	W Feb. 6	T Feb. 24	S Feb. 14	F Feb. 4
New Moon, Adar I, 2nd day	M Feb. 19	Th Feb. 7	W Feb. 25	M Feb. 15	Sa Feb. 5
New Moon, Adar II, 1st day		F Mar. 7			S Mar. 6
New Moon, Adar II, 2nd day		Sa Mar. 8			M Mar. 7
Fast of Esther	Th Mar. 1	Th Mar. 20	M Mar. 13	Th Feb. 25	Th Mar. 17
Purim	S Mar. 4	F Mar. 21	T Mar. 14	S Feb. 28	S Mar. 20
Shushan Purim	M Mar. 5	Sa Mar. 22	W Mar. 15	M Mar. 1	M Mar. 21
New Moon, Nisan	T Mar. 20	S Apr. 6	Th Mar. 26	T Mar. 16	T Apr. 5
Passover, 1st day	T Apr. 3	S Apr. 20	Th Apr. 9	T Mar. 30	T Apr. 19
Passover, 2nd day	W Apr. 4	M Apr. 21	F Apr. 10	W Mar. 31	W Apr. 20
Passover, 7th day	M Apr. 9	Sa Apr. 26	W Apr. 15	M Apr. 5	M Apr. 25
Passover, 8th day	T Apr. 10	S Apr. 27	Th Apr. 16	T Apr. 6	T Apr. 26
Holocaust Memorial Day	S Apr. 15	F May 2*	T Apr. 21	S Apr. 11	S May 1
New Moon, Iyar, 1st day	W Apr. 18	M May 5	F Apr. 24	W Apr. 14	W May 4
New Moon, Iyar, 2nd day	Th Apr. 19	T May 6	Sa Apr. 25	Th Apr. 15	Th May 5
Israel Independence Day	M Apr. 23	Th May 8	W Apr. 29	M Apr. 19	M May 9
Lag Ba-'omer	S May 6	F May 23	T May 12	S May 2	S May 22
Jerusalem Day	W May 16	M June 2	F May 22*	W May 12	W June 1
New Moon, Siwan	F May 18	W June 4	S May 24	F May 14	F June 3
Shavu'ot, 1st day	W May 23	M June 9	F May 29	W May 19	W June 8
Shavu'ot, 2nd day	Th May 24	T June 10	Sa May 30	Th May 20	Th June 9
New Moon, Tammuz, 1st day	Sa June 16	Th July 3	M June 22	Sa June 12	Sa July 2
New Moon, Tammuz, 2nd day	S June 17	F July 4	T June 23	S June 13	S July 3
Fast of 17th of Tammuz	T July 3	S July 20	Th July 9	T June 29	T July 19
New Moon, Av	M July 15	Sa Aug. 2	W July 22	M July 12	M Aug. 1
Fast of 9th of Av	T July 24	S Aug. 10	Th July 30	T July 20	T Aug. 9
New Moon, Elul, 1st day	T Aug. 14	S Aug. 31	Th Aug. 20	T Aug. 10	T Aug. 30
New Moon, Elul, 2nd day	W Aug. 15	M Sept. 1	F Aug. 21	W Aug. 11	W Aug. 31

*Observed Thursday, a day earlier, to avoid conflict with the Sabbath.

CONDENSED MONTHLY CALENDAR
(2006–2009)

2006, Jan. 1–29]   ṬEVET (29 DAYS)   [5766

Civil Date	Day of the Week	Jewish Date	SABBATHS, FESTIVALS, FASTS	PENTATEUCHAL READING	PROPHETICAL READING
Jan. 1	S	Ṭevet 1	New Moon, second day; Ḥanukkah, seventh day	Num. 28:1–15 Num. 7:48–53	
2	M	2	Ḥanukkah, eighth day	Num. 7:54–8:4	
7	Sa	7	Wa-yiggash	Gen. 44:18–47:27	Ezekiel 37:15–28
10	T	10	Fast of 10th of Ṭevet	Exod. 32:11–14 Exod. 34:1–10 (morning and afternoon)	Isaiah 55:6–56:8 (afternoon only)
14	Sa	14	Wa-yeḥi	Gen. 47:28–50:26	I Kings 2:1–12
21	Sa	21	Shemot	Exod. 1:1–6:1	Isaiah 27:6–28:13 Isaiah 29:22–23 *Jeremiah 1:1–2:3*
28	Sa	28	Wa-'era'	Exod. 6:2–9:35	Ezekiel 28:25–29:21

Italics are for Sephardi Minhag.

2006, Jan. 30–Feb. 28] SHEVAṬ (30 DAYS) [5766

Civil Date	Day of the Week	Jewish Date	SABBATHS, FESTIVALS, FASTS	PENTATEUCHAL READING	PROPHETICAL READING
Jan. 30	M	Shevaṭ 1	New Moon	Num. 28:1–15	
Feb. 5	Sa	6	Bo'	Exod. 10:1–13:16	Jeremiah 46:13–28
11	Sa	13	Be-shallaḥ (Shabbat Shirah)	Exod. 13:17–17:16	Judges 4:4–5:31 *Judges 5:1–31*
13	M	15	Ḥamisha 'asar bi-Shevaṭ		
18	Sa	20	Yitro	Exod. 18:1–20:23	Isaiah 6:1–7:6; 9.5–6 *Isaiah 6: 1–13*
25	Sa	27	Mishpaṭim (Shabbat Sheḳalim)	Exod. 21:1–24:18 30:11–16	II Kings 12:1–17 *II Kings 11:17–12:17*
28	T	30	New Moon, first day	Num. 28: 1–15	

Italics are for Sephardi Minhag.

2006, Mar. 1–29]   ADAR (29 DAYS)   [5766

Civil Date	Day of the Week	Jewish Date	SABBATHS, FESTIVALS, FASTS	PENTATEUCHAL READING	PROPHETICAL READING
Mar. 1	W	Adar 1	New Moon, second day	Num. 28:1–15	
4	Sa	4	Terumah	Exod. 25:1–27:19	I Kings 5:26–6:13
11	Sa	11	Teẓawweh (Shabbat Zakhor)	Exod. 27:20–30:10 Deut. 25:17–19	I Samuel 15:2–34 *I Samuel 15:1–34*
13	M	13	Fast of Esther	Exod. 32:11–14 Exod. 34:1–10 (morning and afternoon)	Isaiah 55:6–56:8 (morning and) afternoon)
14	T	14	Purim	Exod. 17:8–16	Book of Esther (night before and morning)
15	W	15	Shushan Purim		
18	Sa	18	Ki tissa' (Shabbat Parah)	Exod. 30:11–34:35 Num. 19: 1–22	Ezekiel 36:16–38 *Ezekiel 36:16–36*
25	Sa	25	Wa-yaḵhel, Peḵude (Shabbat Ha-ḥodesh)	Exod. 35:1–40:38 Exod. 12:1–20	Ezekiel 45:16–46:1 *Ezekiel 45:18–46:15*

Italics are for Sephardi Minhag.

2006, Mar. 30–Apr. 28]   NISAN (30 DAYS)   [5766

Civil Date	Day of the Week	Jewish Date	SABBATHS, FESTIVALS, FASTS	PENTATEUCHAL READING	PROPHETICAL READING
Mar. 30	Th	Nisan 1	New Moon	Num. 28:1–15	
Apr. 1	Sa	3	Wa-yiḵra'	Levit. 1:1–5:26	Isaiah 43:21–23
8	Sa	10	Ẓaw (Shabbat Ha-gadol)	Levit. 6:1–8:36	*Malachi 3:4–24*
12	W	14	Fast of Firstborn		
13	Th	15	Passover, first day	Exod. 12.21–51 Num. 28:16–25	Joshua 5:2–6:1, 27
14	F	16	Passover, second day	Levit. 22:26–23:44 Num. 28:16–25	II Kings 23:1–9, 21–25
15	Sa	17	Ḥol Ha-mo‘ed, first day	Exod. 33:12–34:26 Num. 28:19–25	Ezekiel 37:1–14
16	S	18	Ḥol Ha-mo‘ed, second day	Exod. 13:1–16 Num. 28:19–25	
17	M	19	Ḥol Ha-mo‘ed, third day	Exod. 22:24–23:19 Num. 28:19–25	
18	T	20	Ḥol Ha-mo‘ed, fourth day	Num. 9: 1–14 Num. 28:19–25	
19	W	21	Passover, seventh day	Exod. 13:17–15:26 Num. 28:19–25	II Samuel 22:1—51
20	Th	22	Passover, eighth day	Deut. 15:19–16:17 Num. 28:19–25	Isaiah 10:32–12:6
22	Sa	24	Shemini	Levit. 9:1–11:47	Isaiah 10:32–12:6
25	T	27	Holocaust Memorial Day		
28	F	30	New Moon, first day	Num. 28:1–15	

Italics are for Sephardi Minhag.

2006, Apr. 29–May 27]   IYAR (29 DAYS)   [5766

Civil Date	Day of the Week	Jewish Date	SABBATHS, FESTIVALS, FASTS	PENTATEUCHAL READING	PROPHETICAL READING
Apr. 29	Sa	Iyar 1	Tazria', Meẓora' New Moon, second day	Levit. 12:1–15:33 Num. 28:1–15	Isaiah 66:1–24
May 3	W	5	Israel Independence Day		
6	Sa	8	Aḥare Mot, Ḳedoshim	Levit. 16:1–20:27	Amos 9:7–15 *Ezekiel 20:2–20*
13	Sa	15	Emor	Levit. 21:1–24:23	Ezekiel 44:15–31
16	T	18	Lag Ba-'omer		
20	Sa	22	Be-har, Be-ḥukkotai	Levit. 25:1–27:34	Jeremiah 16:19–17:14
26	F	28	Jerusalem Day*		
27	Sa	29	Be-midbar	Num. 1:1–4:20	Hosea 2:1–22

*Jerusalem Day celebrated May 25, to avoid conflict with the Sabbath.

Italics are for Sephardi Minhag.

2006, May 28–June 26]   SIWAN (30 DAYS)   [5766

Civil Date	Day of the Week	Jewish Date	SABBATHS, FESTIVALS, FASTS	PENTATEUCHAL READING	PROPHETICAL READING
May 28	S	Siwan 1	New Moon	Num. 28:1 15	
June 2	F	6	Shavu'ot, first day	Exod. 19:1–20:23 Num. 28:26–31	Ezekiel 1:1–28, 3:12
3	Sa	7	Shavu'ot, second day	Deut. 15:19–16:17 Num. 28:26–31	Habbakuk 3:1–19 *Habbakuk 2:20–3:19*
10	Sa	14	Naso'	Num. 4:21–7:89	Judges 13:2–25
17	Sa	21	Be-ha'alotekha	Num. 8:1–12:16	Zechariah 2:14–4:7
24	Sa	28	Shelaḥ lekha	Num. 13:1–15:41	Joshua 2:1–24
26	M	30	New Moon, first day	Num. 28·1–15	

Italics are for Sephardi Minhag.

2006, June 27–July 25]   TAMMUZ (29 DAYS)   [5766

Civil Date	Day of the Week	Jewish Date	SABBATHS, FESTIVALS, FASTS	PENTATEUCHAL READING	PROPHETICAL READING
June 27	T	Tammuz 1	New Moon, second day	Num. 28:1–15	
July 1	Sa	5	Ḳoraḥ	Num. 16:1–18:32	I Samuel 11:14–12:23
8	Sa	12	Ḥuḳḳat, Balaḳ	Num. 19:1–25:9	Micah 5:6–6:8
13	Th	17	Fast of 17th of Tammuz	Exod. 32:11–14 Exod. 34: 1–10 (morning and afternoon)	Isaiah 55:6–56:8 (afternoon only)
15	Sa	19	Pineḥas	Num. 25:10–30:1	Jeremiah 1:1–2:3
22	Sa	26	Maṭṭot Masʻe	Num. 30:2–36:13	Jeremiah 2:4–28; 3:4 *Jeremiah 2:4–28; 4:1–2*

Italics are for Sephardi Minhag.

2006, July 26–Aug. 24]   AV (30 DAYS)   [5766

Civil Date	Day of the Week	Jewish Date	SABBATHS, FESTIVALS, FASTS	PENTATEUCHAL READING	PROPHETICAL READING
July 26	W	Av 1	New Moon	Num. 28:1–15	
29	Sa	4	Devarim (Shabbat Ḥazon)	Deut. 1:1 3:22	Isaiah 1:1–27
Aug. 3	Th	9	Fast of 9th of Av	Morning: Deut. 4:25 40 Afternoon: Exod. 32:11–14 Exod. 34:1–10	(Lamentations is read the night before) Jeremiah 8:13–9:23 (morning) Isaiah 55:6–56:8 (afternoon)
5	Sa	11	Wa-etḥannan (Shabbat Naḥamu)	Deut. 3:23–7:11	Isaiah 40:1–26
12	Sa	18	'Eḳev	Deut. 7:12–11:25	Isaiah 49:14–51:3
19	Sa	25	Re'eh	Deut. 11:26–16:17	Isaiah 54:11–55:5
24	Th	30	New Moon, first day	Numbers 28:1–15	

Italics are for
Sephardi Minhag.

2006, Aug. 25–Sept. 22]   ELUL (29 DAYS)   [5766

Civil Date	Day of the Week	Jewish Date	SABBATHS, FESTIVALS, FASTS	PENTATEUCHAL READING	PROPHETICAL READING
Aug. 25	F	Elul 1	New Moon, second day	Num. 28:1–15	
26	Sa	2	Shofeṭim	Deut. 16:18–21:9	Isaiah 51:12–52:12
Sept. 2	Sa	9	Ki teẓe'	Deut. 21:10–25:19	Isaiah 54:1–10
9	Sa	16	Ki tavo'	Deut. 26: 1–29:8	Isaiah 60:1–22
16	Sa	23	Niẓẓavim, Wa-yelekh	Deut. 29:9–31:30	Isaiah 61:10–63:9

Italics are for
Sephardi Minhag.

2006, Sept. 23–Oct. 22]   TISHRI (30 DAYS)   [5767

Civil Date	Day of the Week	Jewish Date	SABBATHS, FESTIVALS, FASTS	PENTATEUCHAL READING	PROPHETICAL READING
Sept. 23	Sa	Tishri 1	Rosh Ha-shanah, first day	Gen. 21:1–34 Num. 29:1–6	I Samuel 1:1–2:10
24	S	2	Rosh Ha-shana, second day	Gen. 22:1–24 Num. 29:1–6	Jeremiah 31:2–20
25	M	3	Fast of Gedaliah	Exod. 32:11–14 Exod. 34:1–10 (morning and afternoon)	Isaiah 55:6–56:8 (afternoon only)
30	Sa	8	Ha'azinu (Shabbat Shuvah)	Deut. 32:1–52	Hosea 14:2–10 Micah 7:18–20 Joel 2:15–27 *Hosea 14:2–10* *Micah 7:18–20*
Oct. 2	M	10	Yom Kippur	Morning: Levit. 16:1–34 Num. 29:7–11 Afternoon: Levit. 18:1–30	Isaiah 57:14–58:14 Afternoon: Jonah 1:1–4:11 Micah 7:18–20
7	Sa	15	Sukkot, first day	Levit. 22:26–23:44 Num. 29:12–16	Zechariah 14:1–21
8	S	16	Sukkot, second day	Levit. 22:26–23:44 Num. 29:12–16	I Kings 8:2–21
9–12	M–Th	17–20	Hol Ha-mo'ed, first through fourth days	M: Num. 29:17–25 T: Num. 29:20–28 W: Num. 29:23–28 Th: Num. 29:26–34	
13	F	21	Hosha'na' Rabbah	Num. 29:26–34	
14	Sa	22	Shemini 'Azeret	Deut. 14:22–16:17 Num. 29:35–30:1	I Kings 8:54–66
15	S	23	Simhat Torah	Deut. 33:1–34:12 Gen. 1:1–2:3 Num. 29:35–30:1	Joshua 1:1–18 *Joshua 1:1–9*
21	Sa	29	Be-re'shit	Gen. 1:1–6:8	1 Samuel 20:18–42
22	S	30	New Moon, first day	Num. 28:1–15	

Italics are for Sephardi Minhag.

2006, Oct. 23–Nov. 21]   ḤESHWAN (29 DAYS)   [5767

Civil Date	Day of the Week	Jewish Date	SABBATHS, FESTIVALS, FASTS	PENTATEUCHAL READING	PROPHETICAL READING
Oct. 23	M	Ḥeshwan 1	New Moon, second day	Num. 28:1–15	
28	Sa	6	Noaḥ	Gen. 6:9–11:32	Isaiah 54:1–55:5 *Isaiah 54:1–10*
Nov. 4	Sa	13	Lekh lekha	Gen. 12:1–17:27	Isaiah 40:27–41:16
11	Sa	20	Wa-yera'	Gen. 18:1–22:24	II Kings 4:1–37 *II Kings 4:1–23*
18	Sa	27	Ḥayye Sarah	Gen. 23:1–25:18	I Kings 1:1–31
21	T	30	New Moon, first day	Num. 28:1–15	

Italics are for Sephardi Minhag.

2006, Nov. 22–Dec. 21]   KISLEW (29 DAYS)   [5767

Civil Date	Day of the Week	Jewish Date	SABBATHS, FESTIVALS, FASTS	PENTATEUCHAL READING	PROPHETICAL READING
Nov. 22	W	Kislew 1	New Moon, second day	Num. 28:1 15	
25	Sa	4	Toledot	Gen. 25:19–28:9	Malachi 1:1–2:7
Dec. 2	Sa	11	Wa-yeẓe'	Gen. 28:10–32:3	Hosea 12:13–14:10
9	Sa	18	Wa-yishlaḥ	Gen. 32:4–36:43	Hosea 11:7–12:12 *Obadiah 1:1–21*
16	Sa	25	Wa-yeshev; Hanukkah, first day	Gen. 37:1–40:23 Num. 7:1–17	Zechariah 2:14–4:7
17– 20	S W	26 29	Hanukkah, second to fifth days	S: Num. 7:18 29 M: Num. 7:24–35 T: Num. 7:30–41 W: Num. 7:36 47	
21	Th	30	New Moon, first day; Hanukkah, sixth day	Num. 28:1–15 Num. 7:42–47	

Italics are for Sephardi Minhag.

2006, Dec. 22–Jan. 19, 2007] ṬEVET (29 DAYS) [5767

Civil Date	Day of the Week	Jewish Date	SABBATHS, FESTIVALS, FASTS	PENTATEUCHAL READING	PROPHETICAL READING
Dec. 22	F	Ṭevet 1	New Moon, second day; Ḥanukkah, seventh day	Num. 28:1–15 Num. 7:48–53	
23	Sa	2	Mi-ḳeẓ; Ḥanukkah, eighth day	Gen. 41:1–44:17 Num. 7:54–8:4	Zechariah 2:14–4:7
30	Sa	9	Wa-yiggash	Gen. 44:18–47:27	Ezekiel 37:15–28
31	S	10	Fast of 10th of Ṭevet	Exod. 32:11–14 Exod. 34:1–10 (morning and afternoon)	Isaiah 55:6–56:8 (afternoon only)
Jan. 6	Sa	16	Wa-yeḥi	Gen. 47:28–50:26	I Kings 2:1–12
13	Sa	23	Shemot	Exod. 1:1–6:1	Isaiah 27:6–28:13 Isaiah 29:22–23 *Jeremiah 1:1–2:3*

Italics are for
Sephardi Minhag.

2007, Jan. 20–Feb. 18]   SHEVAṬ (30 DAYS)   [5767

Civil Date	Day of the Week	Jewish Date	SABBATHS, FESTIVALS, FASTS	PENTATEUCHAL READING	PROPHETICAL READING
Jan. 20	Sa	Shevaṭ 1	Wa-'era'; New Moon	Exod. 6:2–9:35 Num. 28:9–15	Isaiah 66: 1 24
27	Sa	8	Bo'	Exod. 10:1–13:16	Jeremiah 46:13–28
Feb. 3	Sa	15	Be-shallaḥ (Shabbat Shirah) Ḥamishar 'Asar bi-Shevaṭ	Exod. 13:17–17:16	Judges 4:4–5:31 *Judges 5:1–31*
10	Sa	22	Yitro	Exod. 18:1–20:23	Isaiah 6:1–7:6; 9:5–6 *Isaiah 6: 1–13*
17	Sa	29	Mishpaṭim (Shabbat Shekalim)	Exod. 21:1–24:18 Exod. 30:11–16	II Kings 12: 1–17 *II Kings 11:17–12:17*
18	S	30	New Moon, first day	Num. 28: 1–15	

Italics are for Sephardi Minhag.

2007, Feb. 19–Mar. 19]   ADAR (29 DAYS)   [5767

Civil Date	Day of the Week	Jewish Date	SABBATHS, FESTIVALS, FASTS	PENTATEUCHAL READING	PROPHETICAL READING
Feb. 19	M	Adar 1	New Moon, second day	Num. 28:1–15	
24	Sa	6	Terumah	Exod. 25:1–27:19	I Kings 5:26–6:13
Mar. 1	Th	11	Fast of Esther	Exod. 32:11–14 Exod. 34:1–10 (morning and afternoon)	Isaiah 55:6–56:8 (afternoon only)
3	Sa	13	Teẓawweh (Shabbat Zakhor)	Exod. 27:20–30:10 Deut. 25:17–19	I Samuel 15:2–34 *I Samuel 15:1–34*
4	S	14	Purim	Exod. 17:8–16	Book of Esther (night before and morning)
5	M	15	Shushan Purim		
10	Sa	20	Ki tissa' (Shabbat Parah)	Exod. 30:11–34:35 Num. 19: 1–20	Ezekiel 36:16–38 *Ezekiel 36:16–36*
17	Sa	27	Wa-yaḳhel, Peḳude (Shabbat Ha-ḥodesh)	Exod. 35:1–40:38 Exod. 12:1–20	Ezekiel 45:16–46:18 *Ezekiel 45:18–46:15*

Italics are for
Sephardi Minhag.

2007, Mar. 20–Apr. 18]   NISAN (30 DAYS)   [5767

Civil Date	Day of the Week	Jewish Date	SABBATHS, FESTIVALS, FASTS	PENTATEUCHAL READING	PROPHETICAL READING
Mar. 20	T	Nisan 1	New Moon	Num. 28:1–15	
24	Sa	5	Wa-yiḳra'	Levit. 1:1–5:26	Isaiah 43:21–44:23
31	Sa	12	Ẓaw (Shabbat Ha-gadol)	Levit. 6:1–8:36	Malachi 3:4–24
Apr. 2	M	14	Fast of Firstborn		
3	T	15	Passover, first day	Exod. 12:21–51 Num. 28:16–25	Joshua 5:2–6:1, 27
4	W	16	Passover, second day	Levit. 22:26–23:44 Num. 28:16–25	II Kings 23:1–9, 21–25
5	Th	17	Ḥol Ha-mo'ed, first day	Exod. 13:1–16 Num. 28:19–25	
6	F	18	Ḥol Ha-mo'ed, second day	Exod. 22:24–23:19 Num. 28:19–25	
7	Sa	19	Shabbat Ḥol Ha-mo'ed, third day	Exod. 33:12–34:26 Num. 28:19–25	Ezekiel 37:1–14
8	S	20	Ḥol Ha-mo'ed, fourth day	Num. 9: 1–14 Num. 28:19–25	
9	M	21	Passover, seventh day	Exod. 13:17–15:26 Num. 28:19–25	II Samuel 22:1—51
10	T	22	Passover, eighth day	Deut. 15:19–16:17 Num. 28:19–25	Isaiah 10:32–12:6
14	Sa	26	Shemini	Levit. 9:1–11:47	II Samuel 6:1–7:17 *II Samuel 6:1–19*
15	S	27	Holocaust Memorial Day		
18	W	30	New Moon, first day	Num. 28:1–15	

Italics are for Sephardi Minhag.

2007, Apr. 19–May 17]　　　IYAR (29 DAYS)　　　[5767

Civil Date	Day of the Week	Jewish Date	SABBATHS, FESTIVALS, FASTS	PENTATEUCHAL READING	PROPHETICAL READING
Apr. 19	Th	Iyar 1	New Moon, second day	Num. 28:9–15	
21	Sa	3	Tazria', Meẓora'	Levit. 12:1–15:33	II Kings 7:3–20
23	M	5	Israel Independence Day		
28	Sa	10	Aḥarei Mot, Ḳedoshim	Levit. 16:1–20:27	Amos 9:7–15 *Ezekiel 20:2–20*
May 5	Sa	17	Emor	Levit. 21:1–24:23	Ezekiel 44:15–31
6	S	18	Lag Ba-'omer		
12	Sa	24	Be-har, Be-ḥuḳḳotai	Levit. 25:1–27:34	Jeremiah 16:19–17:14
16	W	28	Jerusalem Day		

Italics are for Sephardi Minhag.

2007, May 18–June 16]   SIWAN (30 DAYS)   [5767

Civil Date	Day of the Week	Jewish Date	SABBATHS, FESTIVALS, FASTS	PENTATEUCHAL READING	PROPHETICAL READING
May 18	F	Siwan 1	New Moon	Num. 28:1–15	
19	Sa	2	Be-midbar	Num. 1:1–4:20	Hosea 2:1–22
23	W	6	Shavu'ot, first day	Exod. 19:1–20:23 Num. 28:26–31	Ezekiel 1:1–28, 3:12
24	Th	7	Shavu'ot, second day	Deut. 15:19–16:17 Num. 28:26–31	Habbakuk 3:1–19 *Habbakuk 2:20–3:19*
26	Sa	9	Naso'	Num. 4:21–7:89	Judges 13:2–25
June 2	Sa	16	Be-ha'alotekha	Num. 8:1–12:16	Zechariah 2:14–4:7
9	Sa	23	Shelaḥ lekha	Num. 13:1–15:41	Joshua 2:1–24
16	Sa	30	Koraḥ; New Moon, first day	Num. 16:1–18:32 Num. 28:9–15	Isaiah 66:1–24 *Isaiah 66:1–24* *I Samuel 20:18, 42*

Italics are for Sephardi Minhag.

2007, June 17–July 15]   TAMMUZ (29 DAYS)   [5767

Civil Date	Day of the Week	Jewish Date	SABBATHS, FESTIVALS, FASTS	PENTATEUCHAL READING	PROPHETICAL READING
June 17	S	Tammuz 1	New Moon, second day	Num. 28:1–15	
23	Sa	7	Ḥukkat	Num. 19:1–22:1	Judges 11:1–33
30	Sa	14	Balak	Num. 22:2–25:9	Micah 5:6–6:8
July 3	T	17	Fast of 17th of Tammuz	Exod. 32:11–14 Exod. 34: 1–10 (morning and afternoon)	Isaiah 55:6–56:8 (afternoon only)
7	Sa	21	Pineḥas	Num. 25:10–30:1	Jeremiah 1:1–2:3
14	Sa	28	Maṭṭot Masʻe	Num. 30:2–36:13	Jeremiah 2:4–28; 3:4 *Jeremiah 2:4–28 4:1–2*

*Italics are for
Sephardi Minhag.*

2007, July 16–Aug. 14]   AV (30 DAYS)   [5767

Civil Date	Day of the Week	Jewish Date	SABBATHS, FESTIVALS, FASTS	PENTATEUCHAL READING	PROPHETICAL READING
July 16	M	Av 1	New Moon	Num. 28:1–15	
21	Sa	6	Devarim (Shabbat Ḥazon)	Deut. 1:1–3:22	Isaiah 1:1–27
24	T	9	Fast of 9th of Av	Morning: Deut. 4:25–40 Afternoon: Exod. 32:11–14 Exod. 34:1–10	(Lamentations is read the night before) Jeremiah 8:13–9:23 (morning) Isaiah 55:6–56:8 (afternoon)
28	Sa	13	Wa-etḥannan (Shabbat Naḥamu)	Deut. 3:23–7:11	Isaiah 40:1–26
Aug. 4	Sa	20	'Eḳev	Deut. 7:12–11:25	Isaiah 49:14–51:3
11	Sa	27	Re'eh	Deut. 11:26–16:17	Isaiah 54:11–55:5
14	T	30	New Moon, first day	Numbers 28:1–15	

Italics are for Sephardi Minhag.

2007, Aug. 15–Sept. 12]   ELUL (29 DAYS)   [5767

Civil Date	Day of the Week	Jewish Date	SABBATHS, FESTIVALS, FASTS	PENTATEUCHAL READING	PROPHETICAL READING
Aug. 15	W	Elul 1	New Moon, second day	Num. 28:1–15	
18	Sa	4	Shofeṭim	Deut. 16:18–21:9	Isaiah 51:12–52:12
25	Sa	11	Ki teẓe'	Deut. 21:10–25:19	Isaiah 54:1–10
Sept. 1	Sa	18	Ki tavo'	Deut. 26:1–29:8	Isaiah 60:1–22
8	Sa	25	Niẓẓavim, Wa-yelekh	Deut. 29:9–31:30	Isaiah 61:10–63:9

Italics are for
Sephardi Minhag.

2007, Sept. 13–Oct. 12]   TISHRI (30 DAYS)   [5768

Civil Date	Day of the Week	Jewish Date	SABBATHS, FESTIVALS, FASTS	PENTATEUCHAL READING	PROPHETICAL READING
Sept. 13	Th	Tishri 1	Rosh Ha-shanah, first day	Gen. 21:1–34 Num. 29:1–6	I Samuel 1:1–2:10
14	F	2	Rosh Ha-shana, second day	Gen. 22:1–24 Num. 29:1–6	Jeremiah 31:2–20
15	Sa	3	Ha'azinu (Shabbat Shuvah)	Deut. 32:1–52	Hosea 14:2–10 Micah 7:18–20 Joel 2:15–27 *Hosea 14:2–10* *Micah 7:18–20*
16	S	4	Fast of Gedaliah	Exod. 32:11–14 Exod. 34:1–10 (morning and afternoon)	Isaiah 55:6–56:8 (afternoon only)
22	Sa	10	Yom Kippur	Morning: Levit. 16:1–34 Num. 29:7–11 Afternoon: Levit. 18:1–30	Isaiah 57:14–58:14 Afternoon: Jonah 1:1–4:11 Micah 7:18–20
27	Th	15	Sukkot, first day	Levit. 22:26–23:44 Num. 29:12–16	Zechariah 14:1–21
28	F	16	Sukkot, second day	Levit. 22:26–23:44 Num. 29:12–16	I Kings 8:2–21
29	Sa	17	Shabbat Ḥol Ha-mo'ed, first day	Exod. 33:12–34:26 Num. 29:17–22	Ezekiel 38:18–39:16
30–Oct. 2	S-T	18-20	Ḥol Ha-mo'ed, second through fourth days	S: Num. 29:20–28 M: Num. 29:23–31 T: Num. 29:26–34	
3	W	21	Hosha'na' Rabbah	Num. 29:26–34	
4	Th	22	Shemini 'Aẓeret	Deut. 14:22–16:17 Num. 29:35–30:1	I Kings 8:54–66
5	F	23	Simḥat Torah	Deut. 33:1–34:12 Gen. 1:1–2:3 Num. 29:35–30:1	Joshua 1:1–18 *Joshua 1:1–9*
6	Sa	24	Be-re'shit	Gen. 1:1–6:8	Isaiah 42:5–43:10 *Isaiah 42:5–21*
12	F	30	New Moon, first day	Num. 28: 1–15	

Italics are for Sephardi Minhag

2007, Oct. 13–Nov. 10 ḤESHWAN (29 DAYS) [5768

Civil Date	Day of the Week	Jewish Date	SABBATHS, FESTIVALS, FASTS	PENTATEUCHAL READING	PROPHETICAL READING
Oct. 13	Sa	Ḥeshwan 1	Noah; New Moon, second day	Gen. 6:9–11:32 Num. 28:1–15	Isaiah 66:1–24
20	Sa	8	Lekh lekha	Gen. 12:1–17:27	Isaiah 40:27–41:16
27	Sa	15	Wa-yera'	Gen. 18:1–22:24	II Kings 4:1–37 *II Kings 4:1–23*
Nov. 3	Sa	22	Ḥayye Sarah	Gen. 23:1–25:18	I Kings 1:1–31
10	Sa	29	Toledot	Gen. 25:19–28:9	I Samuel 20:18–42

Italics are for Sephardi Minhag.

2007, Nov. 11–Dec. 9   KISLEW (29 DAYS)   [5768

Civil Date	Day of the Week	Jewish Date	SABBATHS, FESTIVALS, FASTS	PENTATEUCHAL READING	PROPHETICAL READING
Nov. 11	S	Kislew 1	New Moon, second day	Num. 28:1–15	
17	Sa	7	Wa-yeẓe'	Gen. 28:10–32:3	Hosea 12:13–14:10
24	Sa	14	Wa-yishlaḥ	Gen. 32:4–36:43	Hosea 11:7–12:12 *Obadiah 1:1–21*
Dec. 1	Sa	21	Wa-yeshev	Gen. 37:1–40:23	Amos 2:6–3:8
5	W	25	Hanukkah, first day	Num. 7:1–17	
6–7	Th–F	26–27	Hanukkah, second and third days	Th. Num. 7.18–29 F: Num. 7:24–35	
8	Sa	28	Mi-ḳeẓ Hanukkah, fourth day	Gen. 41:1–44:17 Num. 7:30–35	Zechariah 2:14–4:7
9	S	29	Hanukkah, fifth day	Num. 7:36–47	

Italics are for Sephardi Minhag.

2007, Dec. 10–Jan. 7, 2008]   ṬEVET (29 DAYS)   [5768

Civil Date	Day of the Week	Jewish Date	SABBATHS, FESTIVALS, FASTS	PENTATEUCHAL READING	PROPHETICAL READING
Dec. 10	M	Ṭevet 1	New Moon; Ḥanukkah, sixth day	Num. 28:1–15 Num. 7:42–47	
11	T	2	Ḥanukkah, seventh day	Num. 7:48–59	
12	W	3	Ḥanukkah, eighth day	Num. 7:54–8:4	
15	Sa	6	Wa-yiggash	Gen. 44:18–47:27	Ezekiel 37:15–28
19	W	10	Fast of 10th of Ṭevet	Exod. 32:11–14 Exod. 34:1–10 (morning and afternoon)	Isaiah 55:6–56:8 (afternoon only)
22	Sa	13	Wa-yeḥi	Gen. 47:28–50:26	I Kings 2:1–12
29	Sa	20	Shemot	Exod. 1:1–6:1	Isaiah 27:6–28:13 Isaiah 29:22–23 *Jeremiah 1:1–2:3*
Jan. 5	Sa	27	Wa-'era'	Exod. 6:2–9:35	Ezekiel 28:25–29:21

Italics are for Sephardi Minhag.

2008, Jan. 8 – Feb. 6] SHEVAṬ (30 DAYS) [5768

Civil Date	Day of the Week	Jewish Date	SABBATHS, FESTIVALS, FASTS	PENTATEUCHAL READING	PROPHETICAL READING
Jan. 8	T	Shevaṭ 1	New Moon	Num. 28: 1–15	
12	Sa	5	Bo'	Exod. 10:1–13:16	Jeremiah 46:13–28
19	Sa	12	Be-shallaḥ (Shabbat Shirah)	Exod. 13:17–17:16	Judges 4:4–5:31 *Judges 5:1–31*
22	T	15	Ḥamisha 'Asar bi-Shevaṭ		
26	Sa	19	Yitro	Exod. 18:1–20:23	Isaiah 6:1–7:6; 9:5–6 *Isaiah 6:1–13*
Feb. 2	Sa	26	Mishpaṭim	Exod. 21:1–24:18	Jeremiah 34:8–22 33:25–26
6	W	30	New Moon, first day	Num. 28:1–15	

Italics are for Sephardi Minhag.

2008, Feb. 7–Mar. 7   ADAR I (30 DAYS)   [5768

Civil Date	Day of the Week	Jewish Date	SABBATHS, FESTIVALS, FASTS	PENTATEUCHAL READING	PROPHETICAL READING
Feb. 7	Th	Adar I 1	New Moon, second day	Num. 28:1–15	
9	Sa	3	Terumah	Exod. 25:1–27:19	I Kings 5:26–6:13
16	Sa	10	Teẓawweh	Exod. 27:20–30:10	Ezekiel 43:10–27
23	Sa	17	Ki tissa'	Exod. 30:11–34:35	I Kings 18:1–39 *I Kings 18:20–39*
Mar. 1	Sa	24	Wa-yaḳhel	Exod. 35:1–38:20	I Kings 7:40–50
7	F	30	New Moon, first day	Num. 28:1–15	

Italics are for Sephardi Minhag.

2008, Mar. 8–Apr. 5   ADAR II (29 DAYS)   [5768

Civil Date	Day of the Week	Jewish Date	SABBATHS, FESTIVALS, FASTS	PENTATEUCHAL READING	PROPHETICAL READING
Mar. 8	Sa	Adar II 1	Pekude, New Moon, second day (Shabbat Shekalim)	Exod. 38:21–40:38 Num. 28:9–15 Exod. 30:11 16	II Kings 12:1–17 *II Kings 11:17–12:17* Isaiah 66:1, 24
15	Sa	8	Wa-yikra' (Shabbat Zakhor)	Deut. 25: 17–19	I Samuel 15:2–34 *I Samuel 15:1–34*
20	Th	13	Fast of Esther	Exod. 32:11–14 Exod. 34: 1–10 (morning and afternoon)	Isaiah 55:6–56:8 (afternoon only)
21	F	14	Purim	Exod. 17:8–16	Book of Esther (night before and morning)
22	Sa	15	Ẓaw	Levit. 6:1–8:36	Jeremiah 7:21–8:3 9:22–23
29	Sa	22	Shemini (Shabbat Parah)	Levit. 9:1–11:47 Num. 19:1–20	Ezekiel 36:16–38 *Ezekiel 36:16–36*
Apr. 5	Sa	29	Tazria' (Shabbat Ha-hodesh)	Levit. 12: 1–13:59 Exod. 12:1–20	Ezekiel 45:16–46:1 *Ezekiel 45:18–46:15* I Sam. 20:18, 42

*Italics are for
Sephardi Minhag.*

2008 Apr. 6–May 5]   NISAN (30 DAYS)   [5768

Civil Date	Day of the Week	Jewish Date	SABBATHS, FESTIVALS, FASTS	PENTATEUCHAL READING	PROPHETICAL READING
Apr. 6	S	Nisan 1	New Moon	Num. 28:1–15	
12	Sa	7	Mezora'	Lev. 14:1–15:33	II Kings 7:3–20
17	Th	12	Fast of Firstborn		
19	Sa	14	Aḥarei Mot (Shabbat Ha-gadol)	Lev. 16:1–18:30	Malachi 3:4–24
20	S	15	Passover, first day	Exod. 12:21–51 Num. 28:16–25	Joshua 5:2–6:1, 27
21	M	16	Passover, second day	Levit. 22:26–23:44 Num. 28:16–25	II Kings 23:1–9, 21–25
22	T	17	Ḥol Ha-mo'ed, first day	Exod. 13:1–16 Num. 28:19–25	
23	W	18	Ḥol Ha-mo'ed, second day	Exod. 22:24–23:19 Num. 28:19–25	
24	Th	19	Ḥol Ha-mo'ed, third day	Exod. 34:1–26 Num. 28:19–25	
25	F	20	Ḥol Ha-mo'ed, fourth day	Num. 9:1–14 Num. 28:19–25	Ezekiel 37:1–14
26	Sa	21	Passover, seventh day	Exod. 13:17–15:26 Num. 28:19–25	II Samuel 22:1–51
27	S	22	Passover, eighth day	Deut. 15:19–16:17 Num. 28:19–25	Isaiah 10:32–12:6
May 1	Th	26	Holocaust Memorial Day		
3	Sa	28	Ḳedoshim	Levit. 16:1–20:27	Amos 9:7–15 *Ezekiel 20:2–20*
5	M	30	New Moon, first day	Num. 28: 1–15	

Italics are for Sephardi Minhag.

2008, May 6–June 3]   IYAR (29 DAYS)   [5768

Civil Date	Day of the Week	Jewish Date	SABBATHS, FESTIVALS, FASTS	PENTATEUCHAL READING	PROPHETICAL READING
May 6	T	Iyar 1	New Moon, second day	Num. 28: 9–15	
8	Th	3	Israel Independence Day		II Kings 7:3–20
10	Sa	5	Emor	Levit. 21:1–24:23	Ezekiel 44:15–31
17	Sa	12	Be-har	Levit. 25:1–26:2	Jeremiah 32:6–27
23	F	18	Lag Ba-'omer		
24	Sa	19	Beḥuḳḳotai	Levit 26:3–27:34	Jeremiah 16:19–17:14
31	Sa	26	Be-midbar	Num. 1:1–4:20	Hosea 2:1–22
June 2	M	28	Jerusalem Day		

Italics are for
Sephardi Minhag.

2008, June 4–June 16]   SIWAN (30 DAYS)   [5768

Civil Date	Day of the Week	Jewish Date	SABBATHS, FESTIVALS, FASTS	PENTATEUCHAL READING	PROPHETICAL READING
June 4	W	Siwan 1	New Moon	Num. 28:1–15	
7	Sa	4	Naso'	Num. 4:21–7:89	Judges 13:2–25
9	M	6	Shavu'ot, first day	Exod. 19:1–20:23 Num. 28:26–31	Ezekiel 1:1–28; 3:12
10	T	7	Shavu'ot, second day	Deut. 15:19–16:17 Num. 28:26–31	Habbakuk 3:1–19 *Habbakuk 2:20–3:19*
14	Sa	11	Be-ha'alotekha	Num. 8:1–12:16	Zechariah 2:14–4:7
21	Sa	18	Shelaḥ lekha	Num. 13:1–15:41	Joshua 2:1–24
28	Sa	25	Ḳoraḥ	Num. 16:1–18:32	I Samuel 11:14–12:22
July 3	Th	30	New Moon, first day	Num. 28:1–15	

Italics are for
Sephardi Minhag.

2008, July 4–Aug. 1]   TAMMUZ (29 DAYS)   [5768

Civil Date	Day of the Week	Jewish Date	SABBATHS, FESTIVALS, FASTS	PENTATEUCHAL READING	PROPHETICAL READING
July 4	F	Tammuz 1	New Moon, second day	Num. 28:1–15	
5	Sa	2	Ḥukkat	Num. 19:1–22:1	Judges 11:1–33
12	Sa	9	Balak	Num. 22:2–25:9	Micah 5:6–6:8
19	Sa	16	Pineḥas	Num. 25:10–30:1	I Kings 18:46–19:21
20	S	17	Fast of 17th of Tammuz	Exod. 32:11–14 Exod. 34:1–10 (morning and afternoon)	Isaiah 55:6–56:8 (afternoon only)
26	Sa	23	Maṭṭot	Num. 30:2–32:42	Jeremiah 1:1–2:3

Italics are for
Sephardi Minhag.

2008, Aug. 2–Aug. 31]   AV (30 DAYS)   [5768

Civil Date	Day of the Week	Jewish Date	SABBATHS, FESTIVALS, FASTS	PENTATEUCHAL READING	PROPHETICAL READING
Aug. 2	Sa	Av 1	Mas'e, New Moon	Num. 33:1–36:13 Num. 28:9–15	Jeremiah 2:4–28; 3:4 *Jeremiah 2:4–28; 4:1–2* Isaiah 66:1, 23
9	Sa	8	Devarim (Shabbat Ḥazon)	Deut. 1:1–3:22	Isaiah 1:1–27
10	S	9	Fast of 9th of Av	Morning: Deut. 4:25–40 Afternoon: Exod. 32:11–14 Exod. 34:1–10	(Lamentations is read the night before) Jeremiah 8:13–9:23 (morning) Isaiah 55:6–56:8 (afternoon)
16	Sa	15	Wa-etḥannan (Shabbat Naḥamu)	Deut. 3:23–7:11	Isaiah 40:1–26
23	Sa	22	'Eḳev	Deut. 7:12–11:25	Isaiah 49:14–51:3
30	Sa	29	Re'eh	Deut. 11:26–16:17	Isaiah 54:11–55:5 *Isaiah 54:11–55:5 I Samuel 20:18, 42*
31	S	30	New Moon, first day	Numbers 28:1–15	

Italics are for Sephardi Minhag.

2008, Sept. 1 – Sept. 29   ELUL (29 DAYS)   [5768

Civil Date	Day of the Week	Jewish Date	SABBATHS, FESTIVALS, FASTS	PENTATEUCHAL READING	PROPHETICAL READING
Sept. 1	M	Elul 1	New Moon, second day	Num. 28:1–15	
6	Sa	6	Shofeṭim	Deut. 16:18–21:9	Isaiah 51:12–52:12
13	Sa	13	Ki teẓe'	Deut. 21:10–25:19	Isaiah 54:1–10
20	Sa	20	Ki tavo'	Deut. 26:1–29:8	Isaiah 60:1–22
27	Sa	27	Niẓẓavim	Deut. 29:9–30:20	Isaiah 61:10–63:9

Italics are for
Sephardi Minhag.

Civil Date	Day of the Week	Jewish Date	SABBATHS, FESTIVALS, FASTS	PENTATEUCHAL READING	PROPHETICAL READING
Sept. 30	T	Tishri 1	Rosh Ha-shanah, first day	Gen. 21:1–34 Num. 29:1–6	I Samuel 1:1–2:10
Oct. 1	W	2	Rosh Ha-shanah, second day	Gen. 22:1–24 Num. 29:1–6	Jeremiah 31:2–20
2	Th	3	Fast of Gedaliah	Exod. 32:11–14 Exod. 34:1–10 (morning and afternoon)	Isaiah 55:6–56:8 (afternoon only)
4	Sa	5	Wa-yelekh (Shabbat Shuvah)	Deut. 31:1–30	Hosea 14:2–10 Micah 7:18–20 Joel 2:15–27 *Hosea 14:2–10* *Micah 7:18–20*
9	Th	10	Yom Kippur	Morning: Levit. 16:1–34 Num. 29:7–11 Afternoon: Levit. 18:1–30	Isaiah 57:14–58:14 Afternoon: Jonah 1:1–4:11 Micah 7:18–20
11	Sa	12	Ha'azinu	Deut. 32:1–52	II Samuel 22:1–51
14	T	15	Sukkot, first day	Levit. 22:26–23:44 Num. 29:12–16	Zechariah 14:1–21
15	W	16	Sukkot, second day	Levit. 22:26–23:44 Num. 29:12–16	I Kings 8:2–21
16–17	Th–F	17–18	Ḥol Ha-mo'ed, first and second days	Th: Num. 29:17–25 F: Num. 29:20–28	
18	Sa	19	Shabbat Ḥol Ha-mo'ed, third day	Exod. 33:12–34:26 Num. 29:23–28	Ezekiel 38:18–39:16
19	S	20	Ḥol Ha-mo'ed, fourth day	Num. 29:26–31	
20	M	21	Hosha'na' Rabbah	Num. 29:26–34	
21	T	22	Shemini 'Aẓeret	Deut. 14:22–16:17 Num. 29:35–30:1	I Kings 8:54–66
22	W	23	Simḥat Torah	Deut. 33:1–34:12 Gen. 1:1–2:3 Num. 29:35–30:1	Joshua 1:1–18 *Joshua 1:1–9*
25	Sa	26	Be-re'shit	Gen. 1:1–6:8	Isaiah 42:5–43:10 *Isaiah 42:5–21*
29	W	30	New Moon, first day	Num. 28: 1–15	*Italics are for Sephardi Minhag.*

2008, Oct. 30–Nov. 27]   ḤESHWAN (29 DAYS)   [5769

Civil Date	Day of the Week	Jewish Date	SABBATHS, FESTIVALS, FASTS	PENTATEUCHAL READING	PROPHETICAL READING
Oct. 30	Th 1	Ḥeshwan 1	New Moon, second day	Num. 28:1–15	
Nov. 1	Sa	3	Noaḥ	Gen. 6:9–11:32	Isaiah 54:1–55:5 *Isaiah 54:1–10*
8	Sa	10	Lekh lekha	Gen. 12:1–17:27	Isaiah 40:27–41:16
15	Sa	17	Wa-yera'	Gen. 18:1–22:24	II Kings 4:1–37 *II Kings 4:1–23*
22	Sa	24	Ḥayye Sarah	Gen. 23:1–25:18	I Kings 1:1–31

Italics are for Sephardi Minhag.

2008 Nov. 28–Dec. 27]   KISLEW (30 DAYS)   [5769

Civil Date	Day of the Week	Jewish Date	SABBATHS, FESTIVALS, FASTS	PENTATEUCHAL READING	PROPHETICAL READING
Nov. 28	F	Kislew 1	New Moon, second day	Num. 28:1–15	
29	Sa	2	Toledot	Gen. 25:19–28:9	Malachi 1:1–2:7
Dec. 6	Sa	9	Wa-yeze	Gen. 28:10–32:3	Hosea 12:13–14:10
13	Sa	16	Wa-yishlah	Gen. 32:4–36:43	Hosea 11:7–12:12 *Obadiah 1:1–21*
20	Sa	23	Wa-yeshev	Gen. 37:1–40:23	Amos 2:6–3:8
22	M	25	Hanukkah, first day	Num. 7:1–17	
23–26	T–F	26–29	Hanukkah, second to fifth days	T: Num. 7:18–29 W: Num 7:24–35 Th: Num. 7:30–41 F: Num. 7:36–47	
27	Sa	30	Mi-kez, Hanukkah, sixth day, New Moon, first day	Gen. 41:1–44:17 Num. 28:9–15 Num. 7:48–53	Zechariah 2:14–4:7

Italics are for Sephardi Minhag.

2008, Dec. 28–Jan. 25, 2009] ṬEVET (29 DAYS) [5769

Civil Date	Day of the Week	Jewish Date	SABBATHS, FESTIVALS, FASTS	PENTATEUCHAL READING	PROPHETICAL READING
Dec. 28	S	Ṭevet 1	New Moon, second day, Ḥanukkah, seventh day	Num. 28:1–15 Num. 7:48–53	
29	M	2	Ḥanukkah, eighth day	Num. 7:54–8:4	
Jan. 3	Sa	7	Wa-yiggash	Gen. 44:18–47:27	Ezekiel 37:15–28
6	T	10	Fast of 10th of Ṭevet	Exod. 32:11–14 Exod. 34:1–10 (morning and afternoon)	Isaiah 55:6–56:8 (afternoon only)
10	Sa	14	Wa-yeḥi	Gen. 47:28–50:26	I Kings 2:1–12
17	Sa	21	Shemot	Exod. 1:1–6:1	Isaiah 27:6–28:13 Isaiah 29:22 23 *Jeremiah 1:1–2:3*
24	Sa	28	Wa-'era'	Exod. 6:2–9:35	Ezekiel 28:25–29:21

Italics are for Sephardi Minhag.

Index